Internet Law and Regulation

AUSTRALIA
Law Book Co.
Sydney

CANADA and USA
Carswell
Toronto

HONG KONG
Sweet & Maxwell Asia

NEW ZEALAND
Brookers
Wellington

SINGAPORE and MALAYSIA
Sweet & Maxwell Asia
Singapore and Kuala Lumpur

Internet Law and Regulation

THIRD EDITION

by

Graham J H Smith

Partner, Bird & Bird

and contributors from Bird & Bird

Simon Chalton, Consultant

Morag Macdonald, Partner

Hilary Pearson, Partner

Trystan Tether, Partner

Simon Topping, Partner

Sally Trebble, Barrister

Richard Ward, Partner

Sweet & Maxwell
London

First edition 1996
Second edition 1997
Third edition 2002

Published by
Sweet & Maxwell
100 Avenue Road
London NW3 3PF
(http://www.sweetandmaxwell.co.uk)

Typeset by YHT Ltd, London
Printed in Great Britain by Bookcraft (Bath) Ltd

No natural forests were destroyed to make this product: only farmed timber was used
and replanted

A CIP catalogue record for this book is available from the British Library

ISBN 0421 705906

The authors have asserted their rights under the Copyright, Designs and Patents Act
1988 to be identified as the authors of this work.

Overseas Contributors

Australia
Corrs Chambers Westgarth
Melbourne

Stephen Stern
Matthew Swinn

Belgium
Bird & Bird
Bruxelles

Raphaël Bailly
Agnès Maqua

Canada
Aird & Berlis LLP
Toronto

Donald M Cameron

Finland
Roschier Holmberg
Helsinki

Rainer Hilli

France
Bird & Bird
Paris

Stéphane Lemarchand

Germany
Wessing
München

Thomas Raab

Hong Kong
Bird & Bird
Hong Kong

Edward Alder
Richard Fawcett

Israel
Eitan, Pearl, Latzer & Cohen-Zedek
Herzlia

Tally Eitan
Sally Gillis
Iris Pappo
Avihai Schieber

Japan
The Chambers of Mr Ikuo Takahashi
Fukushima

Ikuo Takahashi

The Netherlands
Ekelmans Den Hollander
Amsterdam

Bert Oosting

New Zealand
Bell Gully
Auckland

Malcolm Webb

Singapore
Rodyk & Davidson
Singapore

Gilbert Leong
Lee Ai Ming

Sweden
Bird & Bird
Stockholm

Jim Runsten
Hampus Vallien

Switzerland
Dr. Widmer & Partners
Berne

Dr. Ursula Widmer
Konrad Bähler

USA
Brown Raysman Millstein Felder
   & Steiner LLP
New York City

Dov H Scherzer

Contents

Preface to the Third Edition   xxi
Preface to the First Edition   xxiii
Table of Cases   xxv
Table of Statutes   xxxv
Table of Statutory Instruments   xxxix
Table of European Legislation and International Conventions   xli
Table of Foreign Legislation   xlv

1   Overview of the Internet   1
       1.1   The Internet: what is it?   1
       1.2   The Internet: who's who and what do they do?   3
              1.2.1   Infrastructure and network providers   3
              1.2.2   Content providers   5
              1.2.3   Hosts   7
              1.2.4   Administrators   8
              1.2.5   Access providers   9
              1.2.6   Navigation providers   11
              1.2.7   Transaction facilitators   11
       1.3   Broadband networks—goodbye to the information superhighway   12

2   Copyright, Patents and Confidential Information   13
       2.1   Introduction   13
       2.2   Copyright—general   13
              2.2.1   Digitisation and dematerialisation of information   13
              2.2.2   The WIPO Treaties   15
              2.23   Europe—the Copyright in the Information Society Directive   16
              2.2.4   USA—the Digital Millennium Copyright Act 1998   21
       2.3   What is copyright?   22
              2.3.1   The development of copyright   22
              2.3.2   What is protected?   22
              2.3.3   Authorship and ownership   23
              2.3.4   Period of copyright   23
       2.4   Moral rights   24
       2.5   Database right   24
       2.6   Copyright and database right infringement   27
              2.6.1   Introduction   27

	2.6.2	Applying copyright to the Internet	29
	2.6.3	Web linking and related activities	32
2.7	Liability of hosts and access providers for third party material		42
	2.7.1	The Electronic Commerce Directive	42
	2.7.2	U.S. and other cases	42
	2.7.3	U.S. Digital Millennium Copyright Act	44
	2.7.4	United Kingdom analysis	45
	2.7.5	Linking liability	45
	2.7.6	Caches and mirrors	47
	2.7.7	Remedies for infringement	48
2.8	Electronic publishing on the Internet—copyright issues		49
2.9	Protection of confidential information		50
	2.9.1	What is protectable confidential information?	51
	2.9.2	What is an obligation of confidence?	51
	2.9.3	How does an obligation of confidence arise?	51
	2.9.3	How long does an obligation of confidence last?	53
	2.9.4	How is confidential information protected?	54
	2.9.6	Theft and industrial espionage	54
	2.9.7	Transmitting confidential information by the Internet	55
	2.9.8	Misuse of confidential information on the Internet	55
2.10	Patents		57
	2.10.1	Patents and protecting ideas	57
	2.10.2	Patenting the Internet	58
	2.10.3	Business method patents—U.S.	58
	2.10.4	Internet Publications as Prior Art under the EPC	60
	2.10.5	Patentability of software—Europe	62
	2.10.6	Patentability of software—United Kingdom	65
	2.10.7	Business method patents—Europe	66
	2.10.8	Patent Infringement and the Internet	68
3	**Trade Marks and Domain Names**		**73**
3.1	Trade marks and branding		73
	3.1.1	Trade marks	73
	3.1.2	Branding—choice and use	75
	3.1.3	Proper use	75
3.2	Trade mark clashes on the Internet		76
	3.2.1	Genuine disputes	76
	3.2.2	Cybersquatting	78
3.3	Domain names		78
	3.3.1	What are domain names and how do they work?	78
	3.2.2	Who controls the domain name system?	79
	3.3.3	How does substantive law apply to domain names?	83
	3.3.4	Scrutiny of domain name applications	88
	3.3.5	Trade marks and domain names—the future	91
	3.3.6	The rise of the domain name dispute	91
	3.3.7	Domain name registry dispute policies	100
	3.3.8	Corporate trade mark and domain name protection policies	102
3.4	Metatags, wordstuffing and keyword sales		104
	3.4.1	Metatags	104

	3.4.2	Wordstuffing	106
	3.4.3	Search engine keyword sales	106
3.5	Non-United Kingdom domain names—Australia		107
	3.5.1	The .au domain	107
	3.5.2	Registration Process	107
	3.5.3	Dispute Resolution Policy	108
	3.5.4	Other means of resolving "cybersquatting" disputes	109
3.6	Non-United Kingdom domain names—Belgium		110
	3.6.1	Domain Name Registration Authority	110
	3.6.2	Registration System	110
	3.6.3	Dispute Settlement Procedure	111
	3.6.4	Court Decisions	112
	3.6.5	Protection of Domain Names under Belgian Law	112
3.7	Non-United Kingdom Domain Names—Canada		113
	3.7.1	Domain name registration	113
	3.7.2	Domain name disputes	116
3.8	Non-United Kingdom domain names—Finland		121
	3.8.1	Registration	121
	3.8.2	Disputes	122
	3.8.3	Comments	123
3.9	Non-United Kingdom domain names—France		123
	3.9.1	Registration	124
	3.9.2	Disputes	124
3.10	Non-United Kingdom domain names—Germany		126
	3.10.1	Status of Germany's domain name registry	126
	3.10.2	General description of Germany's domain name system	126
	3.10.3	Disputes policy	126
	3.10.4	Legal cases in Germany	127
	3.10.5	Relevant laws	128
3.11	Non-United Kingdom domain names—Hong Kong		129
	3.11.1	Registration	129
	3.11.2	Disputes	130
3.12	Non-United Kingdom domain names—Israel		132
	3.12.1	Registration	132
	3.12.2	Resolving question of rights to domain names at the registration stage	132
	3.12.3	Domain name disputes	133
3.13	Non-United Kingdom domain names—Japan		135
	3.13.1	Registration	135
	3.13.2	Disputes Resolution Policy	136
	3.13.3	Legal cases	138
	3.13.4	Legislation	139
3.14	Non-United Kingdom domain names—The Netherlands		140
	3.14.1	Registration	140
	3.14.2	Disputes	141
3.15	Non-United Kingdom domain names—New Zealand		142
	3.15.1	Registration of domain names	142
	3.15.2	Domain name disputes	144

3.16   Non-United Kingdom domain names—Singapore   144
        3.16.1   Registration   144
        3.16.2   Disputes   145
3.17   Non-United Kingdom domain names—Sweden   146
        3.17.1   Introduction   146
        3.17.2   The domain name regulations   146
        3.17.3   Applicable legislation and disputes under the ".se" TLD   148
3.18   Non-United Kingdom domain names—Switzerland   148
        3.18.1   Status of Switzerland's domain name registry   148
        3.18.2   General description of Switzerland's domain name system   148
        3.18.3   Disputes   149
        3.18.4   Legal cases in Switzerland   149
        3.18.5   Relevant Laws   151
3.19   Non-United Kingdom domain names—USA   152
        3.19.1   Domain names   152
        3.19.2   Registration   153
        3.19.3   ICANN domain name dispute resolution policy   153
        3.19.4   Relationship between UDRP proceedings and remedies
                  under other U.S. law   154
        3.19.5   The Anticybersquatting Consumer Protection Act   155
        3.19.6   Disputes under the ACPA   156
        3.19.7   Damage awards   158
        3.19.8   Domain names used for criticism or as parody   158
        3.19.9   State anticybersquatting statutes   159
        3.19.10   Meta tags and other forms of Internet trademark infringement   159

4   Defamation   171
    4.1   Introduction   171
    4.2   Defamation—general   172
    4.3   Liability for defamatory statements over networks   172
           4.3.1   Nature of problem posed by dissemination over networks   172
           4.3.2   Defamation Act 1996—the Section 1 defence for
                    secondary disseminators   175
           4.3.3   Judicial analysis of the Section 1 defence   177
           4.3.4   Publication at common law and the 1996 Act   178
           4.3.5   Authors, editors and publishers under the 1996 Act 179
           4.3.6   Which Internet players can claim subordinate disseminator
                    status?   181
           4.3.7   Defamation Act 1996—standard of care   184
    4.4   What constitutes publication?   186
           4.4.1   E-mail   187
           4.4.2   Liability for linked content   187
    4.5   Some U.S. comparisons   188

5   Content Liability and Protection   193
    5.1   Introduction   193
    5.2   Incorrect information—negligence liability   193
           5.2.1   General principles of negligence liability   193
           5.2.2   Liability for incorrect information   194

5.3	Incorrect information—strict liability		197
5.4	Viruses		197
	5.4.1	Negligence liability for virus dissemination	197
	5.4.2	*Rylands v. Fletcher* and virus dissemination	198
	5.4.3	Liability in trespass for virus dissemination	199
5.5	Restricting liability		199
	5.5.1	Unilateral notices and contractual terms	199
	5.5.2	Preventing liability arising	201
	5.5.3	Territory statements	202
	5.5.4	Consumer protection legislation	202
5.6	Protecting content		204
5.7	Liability of on-line intermediaries		204
	5.7.1	Electronic Commerce Directive	204
	5.7.2	Beyond the Electronic Commerce Directive	209
5.8	Employer liability, e-mail and Internet access policies		212
	5.8.1	Electronic communication risks	212
	5.8.2	Liability for acts of employees	213
	5.8.3	Employment Tribunal decisions	217
	5.8.4	Electronic communication policies	218
5.9	Employer access to workplace communications		219
	5.9.1	Regulation of Investigatory Powers Act 2000	219
	5.9.2	The RIP Act Lawful Business Practice Regulations	227
	5.9.3	The Data Protection Act 1998	231
	5.9.4	The Human Rights Act 1998	234
6	**Enforcement and Jurisdiction**		**241**
6.1	Enforcement in England		241
	6.1.1	Identifying the defendant	242
	6.1.2	Identifying the wrongdoer—*Norwich Pharmacal* orders	242
	6.1.3	Transient nature of Internet evidence	245
	6.1.4	Transportability of sites	245
	6.1.5	Mirror sites	247
6.2	Jurisdiction—when can the claimant bring proceedings in England?		247
	6.2.1	Background	247
	6.2.2	Jurisdiction—Defendant domiciled within a Brussels Convention Contracting State	249
	6.2.3	Jurisdiction—Defendant not domiciled within a Brussels Convention Contracting State	263
	6.2.4	Extra-territorial injunctions	265
6.3	"Country of origin" rules		266
	6.3.1	Background	266
	6.3.2	The Electronic Commerce Directive	266
6.4	Australia		278
	6.4.1	Misuse of Registered and Unregistered Trade Marks	278
	6.4.2	Copyright	280
	6.4.3	Defamation	281
	6.4.4	Misleading information/False representations—Trade Practices Act 1974/State Fair Trading Acts	282

	6.4.5	Liability of Internet Service Providers for infringing content	283
	6.4.6	Cybercrimes	284
6.5	Belgium		285
	6.5.1	Jurisdiction applicable to foreign web sites	285
	6.5.2	Which law will a Belgian court apply?	286
	6.5.3	Criminal responsibility: defamation and slander	288
	6.5.4	Content liability	289
	6.5.5	Copyright infringement	290
	6.5.6	Trademark law	290
6.6	Canada		291
	6.6.1	Jurisdiction	291
	6.6.2	Defamation	291
	6.6.3	Inaccurate information	293
	6.6.4	Copyright	293
	6.6.5	Trade marks	294
6.7	Finland		294
	6.7.1	Defamation	294
	6.7.2	Content liability	295
	6.7.3	Copyright infringement	296
	6.7.4	Trade mark infringement	297
6.8	France		298
	6.8.1	Introduction	298
	6.8.2	Governing law and jurisdiction for foreign websites	298
	6.8.3	Defamation	299
	6.8.4	Copyright	300
	6.8.5	Trademarks	300
	6.8.6	Content liability	300
6.9	Germany		301
	6.9.1	Jurisdiction	301
	6.9.2	Defamation	302
	6.9.3	Incorrect information	302
	6.9.4	Copyright	302
	6.9.5	Trade marks	303
6.10	Hong Kong		303
	6.10.1	Jurisdiction	303
	6.10.2	Defamation	308
	6.10.3	Liability for Erroneous or Misleading Content	309
	6.10.4	Copyright	309
	6.10.5	Trade marks	310
	6.10.6	Online gambling	310
	6.10.7	Reunification	312
	6.10.8	Conclusions	313
6.11	Israel		313
	6.11.1	Jurisdictional issues relating to foreign Web site proprietors	313
	6.11.2	Forum non conveniens	314
	6.11.3	Defamation	315
	6.11.4	Content liability	316
	6.11.5	Copyright	316

	6.11.6	Trade marks	318
	6.11.7	Web site notices	319
6.12	Japan		319
	6.12.1	General	319
	6.12.2	Judicial jurisdiction	319
	6.12.3	Choice of law	321
	6.12.4	Cases	322
	6.12.5	Territory notices	323
6.13	The Netherlands		323
	6.13.1	Jurisdiction	323
	6.13.2	Applicable law	325
	6.13.3	Copyright	326
	6.13.4	Trade mark/trade name in a web site	327
6.14	New Zealand		328
	6.14.1	Defamation	328
	6.14.2	Content Liability	329
	6.14.3	Copyright Infringement	330
	6.14.4	Trade Mark Infringement	332
6.15	Singapore		333
	6.15.1	Jurisdiction	333
	6.15.2	Defamation	333
	6.15.3	Inaccurate Information	334
	6.15.4	Copyright	334
	6.15.5	Trade marks	336
	6.15.6	Territory disclaimers	336
	6.15.7	General	336
6.16	Sweden		337
	6.16.1	General Principles of Penal Jurisdiction	337
	6.16.2	General Principles of Civil Jurisdiction	338
	6.16.3	Server Location	339
	6.16.4	Defamation	339
	6.16.5	Content liability	339
	6.16.6	Copyright Law generally	340
	6.16.7	Copyright infringement	340
	6.16.8	Trade Mark Infringement	341
6.17	Switzerland		341
	6.17.1	International jurisdiction of Swiss courts—general comments	341
	6.17.2	Defamation	342
	6.17.3	Content liability	343
	6.17.4	Copyright infringement	344
	6.17.5	Trademark infringement	345
6.18	USA		345
	6.18.1	U.S. jurisdictional analysis	345
	6.18.2	Internet jurisdiction analysis	347
	6.18.3	Some additional practitioner notes	350
	6.18.4	Disclaimer defence?	353

7   **Data Protection**   367
     7.1   Why data protection is relevant to the internet   367
           7.1.1   Publishing personal data   367
           7.1.2   Holding material on an internal database or computer system
                    with Internet connectivity   368
           7.1.3   Sending information by Internet e-mail   368
           7.1.4   Acquisition of data from a person visiting an Internet resource
                    such as a Web site   369
     7.2   EU Directive on Data Protection   371
           7.2.1   General   371
           7.2.2   Applicable national law   371
           7.2.3   Cross-border data transfers to non-EEA countries   372
           7.2.4   Application of the Directive to the Internet   372
     7.3   The 1998 Act's definitions   374
           7.3.1   "Data"   374
           7.3.2   "Personal data"   374
           7.3.3   "Processing"   375
           7.3.4   "Data controller"   376
           7.3.5   "Data processor"   376
           7.3.6   "Obtaining", "recording", "using" and "disclosing"   376
     7.4   The 1998 Act's data protection principles   377
           7.4.1   First principle (fair and lawful obtaining and processing)   377
           7.4.2   Second principle (specified and lawful purposes)   381
           7.4.3   Third, fourth and fifth principles (adequacy, relevance,
                    up-to-dateness and period of retention)   381
           7.4.4   Sixth principle (rights of data subjects)   382
           7.4.5   Seventh principle (security)   382
           7.4.6   Eight principle (transborder data flows)   383
     7.5   The 1998 Act's exemptions   385
           7.5.1   Primary exemptions   386
           7.5.2   Miscellaneous exemptions   388
     7.6   Offences under the 1998 Act   390
     7.7   Enforcement and remedies under the 1998 Act   390
           7.7.1   Enforcement notices (sections 40 and 41)   390
           7.7.2   Request for assessment (section 42)   391
           7.7.3   Information notices (sections 43 and 44)   391
           7.7.4   Powers of entry and inspection (section 50 and Schedule 9)   393
           7.7.5   Civil Remedies   393
     7.8   Transitional provisions (Schedule 8)   398
     7.9   Conclusions   399

8   **Telecommunications and Broadcast Regulation**   401
     8.1   Introduction   401
           8.1.1   Regulatory background   402
     8.2   Telecommunications licensing and regulation   403
           8.2.1   Licensing systems   403
           8.2.2   Interconnection and access   404
           8.2.3   Competition rules   405
           8.2.4   Regulation of the Internet and ISPs   405

	8.3	Licensing Internet Service Providers	405
	8.3.1	Licensing Internet systems and services	406
	8.3.2	Voice and data	406
	8.3.3	Internet voice telephony services	407
	8.3.4	Voice over IP	408
	8.4	Access rights and network services	409
	8.4.1	Interconnection and peering	409
	8.4.2	Access to end-users	411
	8.5	Broadcasting regulation	412
	8.5.1	Background	412
	8.5.2	Broadcasting licensing in the United Kingdom	412
	8.6	Future regulation	417
	8.7	Conclusion	418

9   Contracts between Internet Service Providers, Content Owners and Others   421

	9.1	Introduction	421
	9.2	Contracts for the provision of a Web site	421
	9.2.1	The contract with the Web site designer	421
	9.2.2	The contract for building the Web site	422
	9.2.3	The contract for Web site hosting	427
	9.3	Sponsorship and advertising agreements	429
	9.3.1	The rights being granted in respect of the Web site	430
	9.3.2	Positioning and size	430
	9.3.3	Obligations in relation to promotion of Web site	430
	9.3.4	Hypertext links	430
	9.3.5	Intellectual property	431
	9.3.6	Use of information about visitors to the site	431
	9.4	Internet access agreements	431
	9.5	Peering agreements	433

10   Electronic Contracts and Transactions   435

	10.1	Introduction	435
	10.1.1	Comparison with the law relating to electronic data interchange	435
	10.1.2	Current means of forming contracts in relation to the Internet	436
	10.1.3	The typical subject matter of contracts currently formed over the Internet	437
	10.1.4	Content of contracts	437
	10.2	Exclusions, limitations and consumer protection measures	438
	10.2.1	The Distance Selling Directive	439
	10.2.2	The Electronic Commerce Directive	444
	10.3	International contracts	448
	10.4	Forming electronic contracts	449
	10.4.1	Introduction: the formation of a contract	449
	10.4.2	Pre-contractual information	450
	10.4.3	Offer/invitation to treat	451
	10.4.4	Acceptance and communication of acceptance	452
	10.4.5	Revocation and lapsing of offer	455
	10.4.6	Consideration and intention to create legal relations	456

	10.4.7	Incorporation of terms	456
	10.4.8	Certainty of identity of parties	457
10.5	Formalities of contracting		458
10.6	Electronic signatures		459
	10.6.1	General law on signatures	459
	10.6.2	E.U. Electronic Signatures Directive	464
10.7	Electronic transactions legislation—a discussion		470
	10.7.1	Background	470
	10.7.2	Removing obstacles to electronic transactions	470
	10.7.3	Achieving certainty	471
	10.7.4	Traps to be avoided when legislating for electronic commerce	472
	10.7.5	Facilitation versus prescription	472
	10.7.6	The evolution of electronic transactions legislation	474
	10.7.7	Efficient and inefficient rules	476
	10.7.8	Facilitating without requiring the use of electronic transactions	477
10.8	Evidence—proving the transaction		478
	10.8.1	Which law of evidence?	478
	10.8.2	Proving the transaction	479
	10.8.3	Factors affecting weight of evidence	484
	10.8.4	Electronic records procedures	485

11 Payment Mechanisms for Internet Commerce   **491**
11.1	The ideal Internet payment mechanism		491
11.2	The reward for successful mechanisms		492
11.3	Adaptation of conventional payment mechanisms for Internet commerce		492
	11.3.1	Cash	492
	11.3.2	Cheque	493
	11.3.3	EFTPOS	493
	11.3.4	Credit, charge or debit card	494
11.4	The present reality		494
	11.4.1	Card issuer's joint liability with supplier	495
	11.4.2	International acceptance	495
	11.4.3	Immediate settlement and credit period	496
11.5	Weaknesses in current card payment mechanism		496
	11.5.1	Security	496
	11.5.2	Transaction costs	497
	11.5.3	Limitation of buyers and sellers who can use it	498
	11.5.4	Privacy	498
11.6	Conclusion on present reality		498
11.7	Electronic cash: similar names, different concepts		499
	11.7.1	Electronic cash systems operating on EFTPOS principles	499
	11.7.2	"True" electronic cash	501
	11.7.3	Advantages and disadvantages of true electronic cash as an Internet payment mechanism	502
11.8	Acceptance of true electronic cash systems		503
	11.8.1	Convertibility	503
	11.8.2	Good credit backing	504
	11.8.3	Low vulnerability to fraud	504

11.9   Systems in the middle of the spectrum   504
11.10   Fraud involving abuse of credit/charge/debit cards and analogous
         systems   504
         11.10.1   The basic principle   505
         11.10.2   Exceptions to the basic principle   505
         11.10.3   Alteration of the basic principle by express contract terms   505
         11.10.4   Retailer risk where fraudulent payment innocently received   505
         11.10.5   Transmission of card numbers through the Internet   506
11.11   Fraud involving true electronic cash   506
         11.11.1   Stolen electronic cash   506
         11.11.2   Counterfeit money   507
11.12   Who can issue electronic cash? The FSMA 2000 and the EMI Directive   508
         11.12.1   Account-based and cash-based systems   508
         11.12.2   The deposit taking restriction   508
         11.12.3   Deposit taking and account-based systems   509
         11.12.4   Deposit taking and cash-based systems   509
         11.12.5   The Electronic Money Institutions Directive   510
         11.12.6   What is an EMI and what is "electronic money"   510
         11.12.7   Waivers   511
         11.12.8   Supervision of EMIs and requirements for authorisation   511
         11.12.9   Unauthorised schemes after the EMI Directive   512
11.14   Should true electronic money offer payment anonymity?   512
11.15   Conclusion   514

12   Prohibited and Regulated Activities   517
     12.1   Introduction   517
     12.2   Cross-border content   517
            12.2.1   Why international action?   518
            12.2.2   National action—the urge to regulate   523
            12.2.3   National action—illegality, language, culture, political and
                     religious expression   525
            12.2.4   Responses to national action   529
            12.2.5   Differing approaches to an international convention   531
     12.3   Gambling   536
     12.4   Pornography and sexual offences   538
            12.4.1   Obscenity   539
            12.4.2   Child pornography   542
            12.4.3   On-line harassment and offensive electronic communications   546
            12.4.4   Public display of indecent matter   547
            12.4.5   Sex tourism   548
            12.4.6   Cross-border content standards   548
            12.4.7   Chat rooms   548
     12.5   Contempt of court   549
            12.5.1   Criminal contempt   549
            12.5.2   International aspects of contempt   551
            12.5.3   Third parties and injunctions   551
     12.6   Financial services   552
            12.6.1   Regulated activities and financial promotion   552
            12.6.2   Two key areas of concern   552

	12.6.3	The Financial Services and Markets Act 2000	553
	12.6.4	The General Prohibition	553
	12.6.5	Regulated Activities	554
	12.6.6	Exclusions	555
	12.6.7	Financial Information Web Sites	555
	12.6.8	Overseas Financial Service Providers	556
	12.6.9	Financial Promotions Restriction	557
	12.6.10	The Financial Promotion Restriction and Overseas Financial Service Providers	558
	12.6.11	Exclusion from Financial Promotion Restriction for hosts and access providers	559
12.7	Pharmaceuticals		559
12.8	Advertising on the Internet		560
12.9	Encryption		562
	12.9.1	Introduction	562
	12.9.2	Technical background	563
	12.9.3	The Legal Environment	566
	12.9.4	Dealings in encryption products	566
	12.9.5	Cryptography services/service providers	569
12.10	Computer misuse		570
	12.10.1	The Computer Misuse Act 1990	570
	12.10.2	E-mail viruses and the 1990 Act	572
	12.10.3	Access to websites and the 1990 Act	573
13	**Tax**		579
13.1	Introduction		579
13.2	Emerging tax policy—an overview		580
13.3	VAT		581
	13.3.1	Summary of United Kingdom VAT law	582
	13.3.2	Basic elements of VAT	582
	13.3.3	Exports	585
	13.3.4	"Input" and "Output" Vat	586
	13.3.5	VAT implications of e-commerce	586
13.4	Customs duties		598
	13.4.1	Computer software	599
	13.4.2	Goods ordered electronically but delivered by traditional means	599
13.5	Direct Taxes		599
13.6	Characterisation of income and withholding taxes		600
	13.6.1	U.K. law	600
	13.6.2	The problem	600
	13.6.3	Current position	601
13.7	Taxable presence issues		601
	13.7.1	U.K. law	602
	13.7.2	Applying the rules to e-commerce	602
13.8	Quantifying business profits and transfer pricings		603
13.9	Other points		604

14   Competition Law and the Internet   607
  14.1   Relevant markets   608
         14.1.1   Access markets   608
         14.1.2   Internet/E-commerce—specific markets   611
         14.1.3   B2C Products and Services Sold over the Internet   612
         14.1.4   B2B Markets   616
         14.1.5   Geographic market   618
         14.1.6   Characteristics of Internet and E-commerce markets   619
  14.2   The E.C. Merger Regulation   620
         14.2.1   The Thresholds   621
         14.2.2   Control and Joint Control   622
         14.2.3   Full Function   623
  14.3   Notification Requirement Under the Merger Regulation   623
         14.3.1   Assessment by the E.C. Commission   624
         14.3.2   Decisions in Merger Cases Relating to E-Commerce and
                   the Internet   624
  14.4   Application of Article 81 of the E.C. Treaty   627
         14.4.1   The Scope of Article 81   627
         14.4.2   The Effect of Falling Within Article 81(1)   631
         14.4.3   Exemption from Article 81(1)   631
         14.4.4   Individual exemption   631
         14.4.5   Block exemption regulations   632
         14.4.6   The Technology Transfer Block Exemption   632
         14.4.7   Technology Transfer Block Exemption—Other Specific Clauses 637
         14.4.8   The Vertical Agreement Block Exemption   641
         14.4.9   The implications of Article 81 for the distribution of goods
                   and services through the Internet   651
         14.4.10   Application of Article 81 to IPR licences other than patent and
                   know-how licences   652
         14.4.11   Particular cases which have been considered under Article 81 655
         14.4.12   Concerns in B2B Marketplaces   657
         14.4.13   Standardisation Agreements   662
  14.5   Abuse of dominance and Article 82 of the E.C. Treaty   670
         14.5.1   Dominance   670
         14.5.2   Abuse   673
         14.5.3   Cases Specifically Related to E-commerce   679
  14.6   U.K. Competition Law   681
         14.6.1   U.K. Merger Law   681
         14.6.2   The U.K. Competition Act 1998   682
         14.6.3   The 1998 Act—The Chapter I Prohibition   682
         14.6.4   The 1998 Act—the Effect of Falling Within the Chapter I
                   Prohibition   684
         14.6.5   The 1998 Act—Exclusions From The Chapter I Prohibition 684
         14.6.6   The 1998 Act—Exemption From the Chapter I Prohibition 685
         14.6.7   The Chapter II prohibition   686
         14.6.8   Enforcement Agencies And Responsibilities   690
         14.6.9   Small agreements and conduct of minor importance   692
         14.6.10   Enforcement by private parties   692

14.6.11   Transitional Provisions   692
14.6.12   Cases related to E-commerce under the 1998 Competition Act   693

Technical Glossary   701
Index
                                                                                   709

Preface to the Third Edition

This, the third edition of this work, comes at the tail end of a feverish bout of legislative activity. A glut of new legislation, mostly emanating from Brussels, now affects the Internet and e-commerce. The Electronic Signatures Directive, the Electronic Commerce Directive, the Copyright in the Information Society Directive and directives relating to credit institutions and electronic money have all specifically addressed the electronic environment. The Distance Selling Directive, the Database Directive and the Brussels Regulation on jurisdiction also have significant implications for the Internet. The Electronic Communications Act 2000 and the Regulation of Investigatory Powers Act 2000, both almost entirely home-grown United Kingdom legislation, are also important. The Human Rights Act 1998 now underlies everything.

Since the second edition the dotcom boom has come and gone. The potential of e-commerce is now viewed with greater realism than during those heady days when everyone in town seemed to be armed with a business plan, a concocted name and a non-disclosure agreement. What has not changed is that the Internet continues to be blamed for everything from child abuse to terrorism.

In the preface to the second edition I expressed the hope that the Internet would survive the attentions being lavished on it by governments around the globe. The Internet has indeed survived the dotcom era, the headlines and the attentions of governments with characteristic resilience.

For this edition the international coverage has expanded with the addition of Belgium, New Zealand and Switzerland. We have added a substantial new chapter on competition law. The existing work has been updated and expanded, both to accommodate new subject matter and to treat some areas in greater depth.

This edition is well over double the length of the last. Despite the increase in size the structure, sequence and organisation of the book has changed little since the writing of the first edition in autumn 1995. Paradoxically, in an area so reputedly fast-moving as the Internet, the least change in content has been to Chapter 1 (Overview of the Internet). The typical description of the Internet in 1995 was technical, revolving around protocols such as http, www, telnet, ftp and gopher. Our approach was instead to create a functional taxonomy of Internet actors thrown up by the technology: network providers, access providers, hosts and so on. That scheme has proved robust, accommodating technological changes within a structure that still holds good. A similar functional approach now underpins the liability of electronic intermediaries provisions of the Electronic Commerce Directive.

With each new edition it becomes more difficult to attribute particular sections of the book to individual authors. Doing the best I can, the authorship is as follows:

Chapter 1   Graham Smith
Chapter 2   Hilary Pearson, Graham Smith, Morag Macdonald; updated for this edition
            by Hilary Pearson and Graham Smith
Chapter 3   Morag Macdonald, updated and expanded for this edition by Graham
            Smith; and non-UK contributors
Chapter 4   Graham Smith
Chapter 5   Graham Smith
Chapter 6   Graham Smith and non-UK contributors
Chapter 7   Simon Chalton
Chapter 8   Graham Defries, updated for this edition by Sally Trebble
Chapter 9   Rory Graham, updated for this edition by Graham Smith and Felicity Reeve
Chapter 10 Rory Graham, updated and expanded for this edition by Graham Smith
Chapter 11 Trystan Tether
Chapter 12 Cross-border content, Computer misuse: Graham Smith
            Gambling, Pornography, Contempt, Advertising: Hilary Pearson, updated
            and expanded for this edition by Graham Smith
            Financial services: Trystan Tether
            Encryption: Lorna Brazell
            Pharmaceuticals: Jane Mutimear
Chapter 13 Richard Ward
Chapter 14 Simon Topping

Thanks also to Jane Mutimear for commenting on the domain names material; and to Cecilia Cheung who checked citations with her customary cheerfulness and efficiency. However, all errors remain the authors'.

Sofia Lopez earned my gratitude for spending several weeks of her stay at Bird & Bird organising my heaps of research materials into usable form.

Thanks are due to the States of Guernsey for permission to adapt, as part of Chapter 10, extracts from a report prepared by Bird & Bird in connection with their electronic transactions legislation.

The domestic law is that of England and Wales. The law is stated as at July 31, 2001, although it has been possible to incorporate some more recent developments.

At the time of writing the Electronic Signatures Directive ought to have, but has not, been implemented in the United Kingdom. A second round of consultation is awaited. The Electronic Commerce Directive is due to be implemented in January 2002. Important as these two measures are, to have deferred publication until after their domestic implementation would have stretched the period since the last edition beyond acceptability. We hope to issue a supplement dealing with the implementation of these two measures. We also hope to publish some updates to accommodate other significant developments. These will be available at the publisher's website, www.sweetandmaxwell.co.uk.

My thanks go to Sweet & Maxwell, for their patience and for ensuring that this edition finally became a reality.

Graham J H Smith
Hammersmith
October 2001

Preface to the First Edition

In 1973 an enterprising American publisher released a book entitled *Essential Government Economic Controls, Regulations and Guidelines*, consisting entirely of blank pages. The reader's first reaction to a book on Internet Law and Regulation might be that the content would be equally insubstantial. However, the suggestion that the Internet has no law is born of wishful thinking more than of cogitation. Local laws of each jurisdiction do apply to activities conducted using the Internet. While enforcing such laws presents new challenges, the pan-political nature of the Internet may in fact render it vulnerable rather than immune to the laws of jurisdictions around the world.

The purpose of this book is to draw together the most relevant law and legislation in England and Wales and analyse how it applies to activities carried on by means of the Internet. This exercise is unavoidably selective. We have tried to include issues that have arisen in practice, have caused concern or should be giving pause for thought. Although some international aspects are discussed, the focus is primarily English law. We have not set out to write a textbook of comparative law.

The Internet and the uses to which it is put change by the day. The law is stated as at 31 December 1995, although it has been possible to take account of some more recent developments. Until case law develops, the task of applying the law to the Internet is to some extent speculative. We hope that readers will bear that in mind when using the book.

The individual authorship of the chapters is as follows: Graham J H Smith: 'What is the Internet?', 'Defamation' and 'Content Liability and Protection'; Rory Graham: 'Contracts between Hosts, Content Providers and Others' and 'Making Contracts over the Internet'; Hilary Pearson: 'Intellectual Property' (co-author) and 'Prohibited and Regulated Activities'; Morag Macdonald: 'Intellectual Property' (co-author); Simon Chalton: 'Data Protection'; David Kerr and Graham Defries: 'Telecommunications and Broadcast Regulation'; Trystan Tether: 'Payment Mechanisms over the Internet'; and Richard Ward: 'Tax'.

The seeds of this book were sown during a series of seminars given by some of the authors during the summer of 1995. Out of those seminars grew the idea of a book. To convert the idea into text was a daunting prospect, and thanks are due to all those who made it happen: to my fellow authors who produced their contributions with only light touches of the whip (administered in part by Jane Gunter); to those who assisted with some of the chapters, Mark O'Conor, Gaynor Clements, Ravinder Chahil, Nicholas Perry and Dominic Cook; and to John Lambert, who reviewed a draft of Chapter 1 for technical accuracy. Joanna Hicks of FT Law & Tax fostered the idea and remained enthusiastic and firm in equal measure. Any errors remain those of the authors.

It is sometimes suggested that the Internet should be regulated. I hope this book shows that the Internet does not exist in a legal vacuum. Unless and until the existing law is found wanting there should be a presumption against further legislation. As to the form of any legislation that may be required, let there be a presumption against regulation of a discretionary nature, in favour of known, certain laws capable of general application.

Graham J.H. Smith
Hammersmith
February 1996

Table of Cases

3DO Co. v. Poptop Software Inc., 1998 U.S. Dist. LEXIS 21281 (ND Cal October 27, 1998) 6-340
A&M Records v. Napster Inc., 239 F. 3d 1004 (9th Cir 2001) 6-345
A-G v. Punch Ltd [2001] 2 All E.R. 655 5-051
ACLU v. Reno, 929 F. Supp. 824 (DC Epa 1996). 6-349, 12-010, 12-056
AKZO v. Commission, Case C-62/86 [1991] E.C.R. 461 . . . . 14-197, 14-204
ALS Scan Inc. v. RemarQ Communities Inc., 239 F. 3d 619 (4th Cir 2001) 6-345
AOL/Time Warner, Case COMP/M.1845, October 11, 2000 . . . . 14-019, 14-024, 14-025
AT&T Corp. v. Excel Communications, 172 F. 3d 1352 (Fed. Crr. 1999) 2-141
Abovepeer Inc. v. RIAA, 1:01CV632 (NDNY, filed April 30, 2001) 6-345
Abu Attiah v. Arbitisi, Supreme Court Reports, Vol. 39(1), p. 365 (1985) 6-231
Abu Jihalah v. East Jerusalem Electric Company Ltd, Supreme Court Reports, Vol. 44(1), p. 554
  (1993) 6-230, 6-232
Advanced Software Inc. v. Datapharm Inc., 1998 U.S. Dist. LEXIS 22091 6-340
Air India v. Wiggins [1980] 1 W.L.R. 815; [1980] 2 All E.R. 593; (1980) 71 Cr. App. R. 213; 124 S.J. 478 . . 6-187
Airey v. Ireland (1979-80) 2 E.H.R.R. 305 5-111
Algemeen Dagblad B.V. v. Eureka Internetdiensten. See PCM v. Krante.com
Alitalia-Linee Aeree Italiane SpA v. Casinoalitalia.com, 128 F. Supp. 2d 340 (ED Va 2001). 6-335, 6-339
Alphacell Ltd v. Woodward [1972] A.C. 824; [1972] 2 W.L.R. 1320; [1972] 2 All E.R. 475; 70 L.G.R.
  455; [1972] Crim. L.R. 41; 116 S.J. 431 5-061
American Civil Liberties Union v. Reno, 929 F. Supp. 824 (ED Pa 1996); aff'd 521 U.S. 844 (1997) 6-349
American Information Corp v. American Infometrics Inc., 139 F. Supp. 2d 696 (D Md 2001) 6-342
Amway Corp v. P&G, 2000 U.S. Dist. LEXIS 372 (WD Mich January 6, 2000). 6-338
Anderson v. New York Telephone Co., 1974 35 N.Y. 2d 746 . . . . 4-007, 4-057
Anton Piller KG v. Manufacturing Processes Ltd [1976] Ch. 55; [1976] 2 W.L.R. 162; [1976] 1
  All E.R. 779; [1976] F.S.R. 129; [1976] R.P.C. 719; (1975) 120 S.J. 63 2-115
Arsenal Football Club plc v. Reed [2001] I.P.D. 24037. . . . . 3-028, 3-033, 3-080
Asahi Metal Industry Co. Ltd v. Superior Court, 480 U.S. 102 (1984) 6-335
Ashdown v. Telegraph Group Ltd [2001] EWCA Civ 1142. 2-080
Atkins v. DPP; *sub nom.* DPP v. Atkins [2000] 1 W.L.R. 1427; [2000] 2 All E.R. 425; [2000] 2 Cr.
  App. R. 248; (2000) 97(13) L.S.G. 42; (2000) 144 S.J.L.B. 148 . . . . 12-076, 12-077, 12-078,
                                                                                          12-079, 12-080, 12-081
Att.-Gen. v. Punch Ltd [2001] All.E.R. 655 12-098
 - v. Times Newspapers [1991] 2 All. E.R. 12-098
Avnet Incorporated v. Isoact Ltd [1998] F.S.R. 16 . . . . 3-037, 3-076, 3-079, 3-081
BMB Compuscience Canada Ltd v. Bramalea Ltd (1989) 22 C.P.R. (3d) 561 (F.C.T.D.) 3-109
BP v. Commission [1978] E.C.R. 1513 14-196
BT v. Rodrigues [1998] Masons C.L.R. Rep. 93 5-067
Bailey v. Turbine Design Inc., 86 F. Supp. 2d 790 (WD Tenn 2000). 6-349
Bally Total Fitness Holding Corp. v. Faber, C.D. Calif., No. CV 98-1278 (MANx), 21.12.98 . . . . 3-030, 3-058
 - v. -, 29 F. Supp. 2d 1161 (C.D. Cal. 1998) 3-232
Bancroft & Masters Inc. v. augusta Nat'l Inc. 223 F. 3d 1082 (9th Cir 2000) 6-342
Baron v. Crown Prosecution Service, June 13, 2000, unreported 12-087
Barrett v. Catacombs Press, 44 F. Supp. 2d 717 (ED Pa 1999) 6-337, 6-342, 6-349
Batzel v. Smith, 2001 U.S. Dist. LEXIS 8929 (CD Cal June 5, 2001) 6-337, 6-342
Bell Actimedia Inc. v. Puzo (Communications Globe Tete) (1999) 2 C.P.R. (4th) 289 (F.C.T.D.). 3-113
Bell Express Vu Limited Partnership v. Tedmonds & Co. Inc. [2001] O.J. No. 1558 (Ont. S.C.J.) 3-116
Bensusan Restaurant Corp. v. King, 126 F. 3d 25; 1997 U.S. App. LEXIS 23742. . . . . 3-012, 6-337
Berezobsky v. Forbes Inc. [1999] E.M.L.R. 287 6-209

Berkshire C.C. v. Olympic Holidays (1994) 158 J.P. 421; (1994) 13 Tr. L.R. 251; [1994] Crim.
    L.R. 277; (1994) 158 J.P.N. 337 10-029
Bier v. Mines de Potasse d'Alsace, Case 21/76 [1978] Q.B. 708; [1977] 3 W.L.R. 479; [1976]
    E.C.R. 1735; [1977] 1 C.M.L.R. 284; 121 S.J. 677; (1977) 121 S.J. 677 6-263
Bihari v. Gross, 119 F. Supp. 2d 309 (S.D.N.Y. 2000). 3-238
Bochan v. La Fontaine, 68 F. Supp. 2d 692 (ED Va 1999) 6-349
Bookmakers' Afternoon Greyhound Services Ltd v. Wilf Gilbert (Staffordshire) Ltd [1994]
    F.S.R. 723. . . . . 2-064, 2-067, 12-078
Bridgestone Firestone Inc. v. Myers, WIPO D2000-0190 . . . . 3-028, 3-030, 3-049
Brinkibon v. Stahag Stahl [1983] 2 A.C. 34; [1982] 2 W.L.R. 264; [1982] 1 All E.R. 293; [1982] 1
    Lloyd's Rep. 217; [1982] Com. L.R. 72; [1982] E.C.C. 322; 126 S.J. 116 6-198
British Columbia Automobile Association v. Office and Professional Employees' International
    Union, Local 378 (2001) 10 C.P.R. (4th) 423 (B.C.S.C.) 3-114
British Horseracing Board Ltd v. William Hill Organisation Ltd [2001] R.P.C. 612 2-050
British Leyland v. Commission, Case 226/84 [1986] E.C.R. 3263 14-203
British Sugar plc v. James Robertson & Sons Ltd [1997] E.T.M.R. 118; [1996] R.P.C. 281; (1996) 19(3)
    I.P.D. 19023 3-059
British Telecommunications plc v. One in a Million Ltd (1998) I.P.R. 289; [1999]
    F.S.R. 1, CA. 3-035, 3-036, 3-038, 3-039, 3-048, 3-049,
                                                            3-056, 3-057, 3-058, 3-059, 3-060, 3-081, 3-090, 3-149
Britannia Building Society v. Prangley, June 12, 2000, unreported 3-030, 3-060
BroadBridge Media LLC v. Hypercd.com, 106 F. Supp. 2d 505 (S.D.N.Y. 2000) 3-224
Brookfield Communications Inc. v. West Coast Entertainment Corporation, 174 F. 3d 1036
    (9th Cir. 1999) 3-079, 3-238
Brydges v. Dix (1891) 7 T.L.R. 215 10-073
Buddyusa Inc. v. RIAA, 1:01CV631 (NDNY filed April 30, 2001) 6-345
Burger King Corp v. Rudzewicz, 471 U.S. 462 (1985) 6-333, 6-335, 6-336
C.B.S. Songs v. Amstrad Consumer Electronics [1988] A.C. 1013; [1988] 2 W.L.R. 1191;
    [1988] 2 All E.R. 484; [1988] 2 F.T.L.R. 168; [1988] R.P.C. 567; (1988) 132 S.J. 789 . . . . 2-059, 2-095
CCN v. Data Protection Registrar [2001] 1 All E.R. 788 7-037
Cadbury Confectionery Ltd v. The Domain Name Company Ltd, September 27, 1996, HC,
    Auckland, unreported 3-192, 3-194
Calder v. Jones, 465 U.S. 783 (1984) 6-341, 6-342
Cambridge Water Co. v. Eastern Counties Leather plc [1994] 2 A.C. 264; [1994] 2 W.L.R. 53;
    [1994] 1 All E.R. 53; [1994] 1 Lloyd's Rep. 261; [1994] Env. L.R. 105; [1993] E.G.C.S. 211; (1994)
    144 N.L.J. 15; (1994) 138 S.J.L.B. 24 . . . . 5-016, 5-019
Canada Post v. Sunview Management Group, unreported 3-118
Canadian Kennel Club v. Continental Kennel Club (1997) 77 C.P.R. (3d) 470 (F.C.T.D.) 3-117
Candler v. Crane, Christmas & Co. [1951] 2 K.B. 164; [1951] 1 All E.R. 426; [1951] 1 T.L.R. 371;
    95 S.J. 171 5-007
Canon Kabushiki Kaisha v. Metro Goldwyn Mayer Inc. [1998] All E.R. (EC) 934; [1998] E.C.R. I-5507;
    [1999] 1 C.M.L.R. 77; [1998] C.E.C. 920; [1999] E.T.M.R. 1; [1999] F.S.R. 332; [1999] R.P.C. 117 3-032
Caparo Industries plc v. Dickman [1990] 2 A.C. 605; [1990] 2 W.L.R. 358; [1990] 1 All E.R. 568;
    [1990] B.C.L.C. 273; [1990] B.C.C. 164; [1990] E.C.C. 313; [1955-95] P.N.L.R. 523; (1990) 87(12)
    L.S.G. 42; (1990) 140 N.L.J. 248; (1990) 134 S.J. 494; (1990) 5-006, 5-008
Carpenter v. United States, 484 U.S. 19 (1997) 2-134
Cattle v. Stockton Waterworks (1875) 10 L.R. 453, QB 5-016
Cellcom Israel Ltd v. T.M. Aquanet Computer Communications Ltd, Tel Aviv District Court
    Civil File 649/96, unreported 3-153, 3-158, 3-160
Cementhandelaren v. Commission, Case 8/72 [1972] E.C.R. 977; [1973] C.M.L.R. 7 14-067
Christian Book Distributors Inc. v. Great Christian Books Inc., 137 Md App 367 (CT App 2001) 6-351
City of Tel Aviv (Rates Division) v. Zarfat, Tel Aviv District Court Civil file 002527/99, July 11, 2000. . . 6-229
City Central Ltd v. Chanel (French Societe Anonyme) Dinim v'od (District Court), Vol. 26(5)
    p. 351 (1995) 6-245
Clipper Maritime Ltd v. Shirlstar Container Transport Ltd (The "Anemone") [1987] Lloyd's Rep.
    546 . . . . 10-075, 10-084
Coditel SA v. Cine Vog Films SA [1982] E.C.R. 338 14-148
Cody v. Ward, 954 F. Supp. 43 (D Conn 1997) 6-351
Commercial Solvents v. Commission, Cases 6 & 7/73 [1974] E.C.R. 223; [1974] 1 C.M.L.R. 309 14-208
CompuServe Inc. v. Cyber Promotions Inc., 962 F. Supp. (S.D. Ohio 1997) 2-090
Cooper v. Independent News Auckland Ltd, April 21, 1997 unreported 6-279
Corinne Bodson v. Pompes Funebres des Regions Liberees SA, Case 30/87 [1998] E.C.R. 2479 14-203
Cubby Inc. v. Compuserve Inc., 776 F. Supp. 135 (S.D.N.Y. 1991). 4-001, 4-054
Cuccioli v. Jekyll & Hyde Neue Metropol Bremen Theater Production GMBH & Co., 2001 U. S Dist.
    LEXIS 8699 (S.D.N.Y. June 28, 2001) 6-350

Cybersell Inc. v. Cybersell Inc, 130 F3d 414 (9th Cir 1997) 6-341
DB Breweries Ltd v. The Domain Name Company Ltd, unreported, HC, Auckland, March 15, 2001 3-192
DPP v. Atkins. See Atkins v. DPP
DPP v. Bignall (1998) Crim. L.R. 53 12-157
DVD Copy Control Assoc. v. McLaughlin, CV-786804 (Super Ct Cal, Santa Clara Cty, January 21,
    2000) 6-346, 6-347
Dawson v. Pepin, 2001 U.S. Dist. LEXIS 10074 (WD Mich March 29, 2001). 6-339
De La Bere v. Pearson Ltd [1908] 1 K.B. 280. 5-005
Debtor, Re a [1996] 2 All E.R. 345. 10-074
DeCCS case; Universal City Studios Inc. v. Corley, SD Cal. August 17, 2000 2-107
Denco v. Joinson [1991] 1 W.L.R. 330; [1992] 1 All E.R. 463; [1991] I.C.R. 172; [1991] I.R.L.R. 63 5-067
Derby v. Weldon (No. 9) [1991] 1 W.L.R. 652; [1991] 2 All E.R. 901 10-069
Diageo plc v. John Zuccarini, WIPO Case D2000-0996 3-030
Direct Line Group Ltd v. Direct Line Estate Agency [1997] F.S.R. 374 3-014
- v. Purge I.T. Ltd, WIPO D2000-0583. 3-030
Donoghue v. Stevenson; *sub nom.* McAlister v. Stevenson [1932] A.C. 562; 1932 S.C.
    (H.L.) 31; 1932 S.L.T. 317; [1932] W.N. 139; 101 L.J. P.C. 119; 37 Com. Cas. 350; 48 T.L.R.
    494; 147 L.T. 281 . . . . 5-002, 5-006, 5-009
Douglas v. Hello! [2001] 2 All E.R. 289. . . . . 2-119, 5-112, 5-110, 5-116
Dunn v. IBM United Kingdom Ltd (Case no. 2305 87/97), September 4, 1968 5-069
Dunnes Stores Ltd v. Mandate [1996] 2 C.M.L.R. 120 12-124
EDIAS Software Int'l LLC v. Basis Int'l Ltd, 947 (D Ariz 1996). 6-342, 6-349
ESAB Group Inc. v. Centricut LLC, D.S.C., No. 4:98-1654-22, 1/15/99 . . . . 2-163, 6-337
Eastern Power Ltd v. Azienda Communate Energia and Ambiente [1999] O.J. 3275, Ontario CA. 6-198
EasyJet Airline Co. Ltd v. Dainty, February 19, 2001, unreported. 3-030, 3-060
eBay Inc. v. Bidder's Edge, NDCA 2000 100 F. Supp. 2d 1058 . . . . 2-089, 2-090, 6-348
E-Cards v. King, No. 99-CV-3726 (N.D. Cal. May 10, 2000) 3-234
eFax.com Inc. v. Oglesby [2000] 23(4) I.P.D. 29031 3-066
Eisenman, Shanks v. Kimron, Supreme Court Reports, Vol. 54(3), p. 817 (2000) 6-226, 6-238, 6-239
Electronics Boutique Holdings Corp. v. Zuccarini, 2000 U.S. Dist. LEXIS 15719 (E.D. Pa. October 30,
    2000) 3-230
Eli Lilly & Co. v. Natural Answers Inc., 233 F. 3d 456 (7th Cir. 1999). 3-239
Emphasis Ltd [1995] V.A.T.D.R. 419 (13759). 13-025
Ephraim Mizrachi v. Nobel's Explosives Co Ltd, Supreme Court Reports, Vol. 32(2), p. 115 (1977) 6-226
Ernest Bloomers v. The Israeli Chapter of the International Federation of Record Industry,
    District Court Reports, Vol. 1982(2) p. 156. 6-237
Euromarket Designs Inc. v. Crate & Barrell Ltd, 96 F. Supp. 2d 824 (ND Ill May 16, 2000) . 3-004, 3-039, 6-352
- v. Peters [2001] F.S.R. 288. . . . . 3-001, 6-203, 6-214
Exxon Corporation v. Exxon Insurance Consultants International Ltd [1982] Ch. 119;
    [1981] 3 All E.R. 241; [1982] R.P.C. 69; 125 S.J. 527. . . . . 2-055, 3-029
Eyre v. Nationwide News Pty Ltd [1967] N.Z.L.R. 851. 6-279
FCC v. Pacifica Foundation, 438 U.S. 726 (1978). 12-010
FSS Travel and Leisure Systems Ltd v. Johnson [1998] I.R.L.R. 382; [1999] I.T.C.L.R. 218; [1999] F.S.R.
    505 2-125
Faccenda Chicken Ltd v. Fowler [1987] Ch. 117; [1986] 3 W.L.R. 288; [1986] 1 All E.R. 617; [1986]
    I.C.R. 297; [1986] I.R.L.R. 69; [1986] F.S.R. 291; (1986) 83 L.S.G. 288; (1986) 136 N.L.J. 71; (1986) 130
    S.J. 573 2-124
Fiona Shevill v. Presse Alliance SA, Case C-68/93 . . . . 6-263, 6-264, 6-265
First National Bank plc v. Loxleys (a firm) [1997] P.N.L.R. 211; [1996] E.G.C.S. 174; (1996) 93(43)
    L.S.G. 26; (1997) 141 S.J.L.B. 6; [1996] N.P.C. 158 . . . . 5-003, 5-031
First Sport Ltd v. Barclays Bank plc [1993] 1 W.L.R. 1229; [1993] 3 All E.R. 789; (1993) 12 Tr. L.R.
    69 . . . . 10-081, 11-044
Firstpost Homes v. Johnson [1995] 1 W.L.R. 1567; [1995] 4 All E.R. 355; [1996] 1 E.G.L.R. 175; [1996]
    13 E.G. 125; (1995) 92(28) L.S.G. 30; (1995) 139 S.J.L.B. 187; [1995] N.P.C. 135 10-071
Fowler v. Broussard, 2001 U.S. Dist. LEXIS 573 (ND Tex January 22, 2001) 6-351
France v. Dutton [1891] 2 Q.B. 208 10-071
French Connection Ltd v. Sutton [2000] E.T.M.R. 341; [2000] I.T.C.L.R. 509; (2000) 23(2) I.P.D. 23013 3-066
Frou Frou Biscuits (Kfar Saba) Ltd v. Froumine & Sons Ltd & Frou-Bisc Ltd, Supreme Court Reports,
    Vol. 23(2), p. 43 (1969). 6-241
GTE New Media Services Inc. v. Bellsouth Corp., 199 F3d 1343 (DC Cir 2000). 6-337
Gale's Application [1991] R.P.C. 463. . . . . 2-156, 2-157
General Motors Corp. v. Yplon S.A. [1999] All E.R. (EC) 865; [1999] E.C.R. I-5421; [1999] 3 C.M.L.R. 427;
    [1999] C.E.C. 528; [1999] E.T.M.R. 950; [2000] R.P.C. 572; (1999) 22(11) I.P.D. 22112. 3-032
Gillette Co. v. Adi ZS Import Marketing & Distribution Ltd, Tel Aviv District Court, Civil File 649/96,
    unreported 3-157

Glaxo plc v. Glaxowellcome Ltd [1996] F.S.R. 388. . . . . 3-014, 3-042
Godfrey v. Demon Internet Ltd [2000] 3 W.L.R. 1020; [1999] 4 All E.R. 342; [1999] E.M.L.R. 542;
    [1998-99] Info. T.L.R. 252; [1999] I.T.C.L.R. 282; [1999] Masons C.L.R. 267; (1999)
    149 N.L.J. 609 . . . . 4-005, 4-016, 4-023, 4-029, 4-032,
                                                                               4-034, 4-041, 4-042, 4-054
Goldsmith v. Sperrings Ltd [1977] 1 W.L.R. 478; [1977] 2 All E.R. 566; 121 S.J. 304. 4-043
Goodman v. J. Eban Ltd [1954] 1 Q.B. 550; [1954] 2 W.L.R. 581; [1954] 1 All E.R. 763;
    98 S.J. 214 . . . . 10-073, 10-074
Green v. BCNZ [1998] 2 N.Z.L.R. 490. 6-285
Gridiron.com Inc. v. National Football League, 106 f. Supp. 2d 1309 (SD Fla July 11, 2000) 6-350
Gutnick v. Dow Jones & Co. Inc. [2001] V.S.C. 305. . . . . 6-209, 12-053
HKSAR v. Cheung Kam Keung [1988] 2 H.K.C. 156. . . . . 6-188, 6-189
HKSAR v. H Takeda [1998] 1 H.K.L.R.D. 931. 6-188
HKSAR v. Tam Hei Lun [2000] H.K.E.C. 6-189
HKSAR v. Wong Tat Man [2000] H.K.E.C. 6-188
Halford v. United Kingdom [1997] I.R.L.R. 471; (1997) 24 E.H.R.R. 523; 3 B.H.R.C. 31; [1998]
    Crim. L.R. 753; (1997) 94(27) L.S.G. 24. . . . . 5-112, 5-114
Hard Rock Café Int'l Inc. v. Morton, 1999 U.S. Dist. LEXIS 13760 (S.D.N.Y. September 9, 1999) 6-347
Harrods Ltd v. Harrodian School Ltd [1996] R.P.C. 697; (1996) 19(10) I.P.D. 19090. . . . . 3-048, 3-061
Harrow LB v. WH Smith Trading Ltd [2001] E.W.H.C. Admin. 469, June 19, 2001. . . . . 4-048, 5-054
Hasbro Inc. v. Internet Entertainment Group, 1996 U.S. Dist. LEXIS 11626 (W.D. Wash. February 9,
    1996) 3-230
Harbuck v. Aramco Inc., 1999 U.S. Dist. LEXIS 16892 (ED Pa October 22, 1999). 6-339
Havas Numerique, SNC and Cadres On Line S.A. v. Keljob, E-commerce Law reports, Vol. 1,
    Issue 2, p. 16. 2-081
Hearst Corp v. Goldberger, 1997 U.S. Dist. LEXIS 2065, 55 (S.D.N.Y. Feb 26, 1997) 6-337, 6-349
Hedley Byrne & Co. Ltd v. Heller & Partners Ltd [1964] A.C. 465; [1963] 3 W.L.R. 101; [1963]
    2 All E.R. 575; [1963] 1 Lloyd's Rep. 485; 107 S.J. 454; (1963) 107 S.J. 454. . . . . 5-003, 5-024, 6-210
Helicopteros Nacionales de Colombia, SA v. Hall, 466 U.S. 408 (1984) 6-334
Henderson v. Merrett Syndicates Ltd [1994] 3 All E.R. 506, HL 5-003
Hilti v. Commission, Case C-53/92 P [1994] E.C.R. I-667; [1994] 4 C.M.L.R. 614; [1994] F.S.R. 760 14-206
Hird v. Wood [1894] 38 S.J. 234 4-052
Hirepool Auckland Ltd v. Uren, 2000, unreported 6-291, 6-292
Hoffman-La Roche v. Commission, Case 85/76 E.C.R. 461. 14-197
Hoida v. Hindi & The Israel Technion, Supreme Court Reports, Vol. 44(4), p. 545 (1990). 6-226
Hotel Security Checking Co. v. Lorraine Co., 160 F. 467. 2-141
Huth v. Huth [1915] 3 K.B. 32 4-051
ICI Ltd v. Commission, Case 48/69 [1972] E.C.R. 619. 14-065
ITV Technologies Inc. v. WIC Television Ltd (1997) 77 C.P.R. (3d) 486 (F.C.T.D.). 3-111
Innersense International Inc. v. Manegre (2000) 47 C.P.C. (4th) 149 (Alta Q.B.) 3-112
Innovations (Mail Order) Ltd v. Data Protection Registrar, Case DA/92 31/49/1 7-030
Inset Systems Inc. v. Instruction Set Inc., 937 F. Supp. 161 (D Conn 1996) 6-339
Intellectual Reserve Inc. v. Utah Lighthouse Ministry Inc., 75 F. Supp. 2d 1290 (CD Utah 1999). 6-347
Intercon Inc. v. Bell Atlantic Internet Solutions Inc., 205 F3d 1244 (10th Cir 2000) 6-342
Intermatic Inc. v. Toeppen, 947 F. Supp. 1227 (N.D. III, 1996). 3-230
International Shoe Co. v. Washington, 326 U.S. 310, 316 (1945). 6-335
International Telephone Link Pty Ltd v. IDG Communications Ltd, February 20, 1998, unreported 6-277
Investasia Ltd v. Kodansha Co. Ltd [1999] 3 H.K.C. 515. . . . . 6-207, 6-209
Irish Continental Group v. CCI Morlaix [1995] 5 C.M.L.R. 177 14-199
Itravel2000.com Inc. (c.o.b. Itravel) v. Fagan [2001] O.J. No. 943 (Ont. S.C.J.) 3-112
Iveson v. Harris (1802) 7 Ves. 251, 32 E.R. 102 12-099
Jeanette Winterson v. Hogarth, WIPO D2000-0235 3-065
Jenkins v. Gaisford (1863) 3 Sw. & Tr. 93 10-072
Jeri-Jo Knitwear v. Club Italia, 94 F. Supp. 2d 457 (S.D.N.Y. 2000) 6-337, 6-347
Jews for Jesus v. Brodsky, 993 F. Supp. 282, 307 (D.N.J. 1998) aff'd, 159 F. 3d 1351 (3d Cir. 1998) 3-230
Jif Lemon Case. See Reckitt and Colman Products Ltd v. Borden Inc.
Job Edwards Ltd v. Birmingham Navigations [1924] 1 K.B. 341 5-018
Johnston v. Ireland (1987) 9 E.H.R.R. 203 5-111
Jones v. Tower Boot Co Ltd. See Tower Boot Co. Ltd v. Jones
Kalman v. PCL Packaging (U.K.) [1982] F.S.R. 406 2-166
Kelly v. Arriba Soft Corp [2000] Ent. L.R. 11(3), N-38. 2-093
Khan v. United Kingdom, May 20, 2000, E Ct HR 5-059
Kitechnology BV v. Unicor GmbH Plastmachinen [1994] I.L.Pr. 568; [1995] F.S.R. 765 2-121
Klinghoffer v. SNC Achille Lauro, 937 F2d 44 (2d Cir 1991). 6-333
Koch & Sterzel/X-ray Apparatus, Case T26/86 [1988] E.P.O.R. 72 . . . . 2-152, 2-161

Kollmorgen Corp v. Yaskawa Electric Corp, 1999 U.S. Dist. LEXIS 20572 (WD Va December 13, 1999) . . . 6-339
Koninklijke Philips Electronics v. Kurapa C. Kang, WIPO D2001-0163 3-030
Kremen v. Cohen, No. C 98-20718 JW (N.D. Cal. April 3, 2001) 3-234
LB Cambden v. Hobson, *The Independent*, January 28, 1992. 10-132
Labouchere v. IMG Holland, 1997 I.E.R. 44 . . . . 3-185, 6-276
LaSalle National Bank v. Vitro Sociedad Anonima, 85 F. Supp. 2d 857 (ND Il1 2000) 6-340b
Lawyers Online Ltd v. Lawyeronline Ltd , July 7, 2000, unreported. 3-066
Levin (Application for a Writ of Habeas Corpus), Re. See R v. Governor of Brixton Prison, ex p. Levin
Ligue Contre le Racisme et L'Antisemitisme v. Yahoo! Inc. No RG:00/05308 (TGI Paris,
    November 20, 2000). 6-342, 6-352, 12-028
Lister v. Hesley Hall Ltd [2001] 2 All E.R. 769 5-060
Lobay v. Workers and Farmers Publishing Co. [1939] 2 D.L.R. 272. 5-064
Lockheed Martin Corp v. Network Solutions Inc., 985 F. Supp. 949, 957 (C.D. Cal. 1997) aff'd 194 F. 3d
    980 (9th Cir. 1999). 3-230
London Joint Stock Bank v. Macmillan [1918] A.C. 777. 11-042
Lofton v. Turbine Design Inc., 100 F. Supp. 2d 404 (ND Miss 2000). 6-342, 6-349
Lucent Technologies Inc. v. Lucentsucks.com, 95 F. Supp. 2d 528 (E.D. Va. 2000) 3-232
Lunney v. Prodigy Services Company, 250 A.D. 2d 230; 94 N.Y. 2d 242. . . . . 4-007, 4-057
MBNA America Bank NA v. Freeman, July 17, 2000, unreported. 3-062
McAlister v. Stevenson. See Donoghue v. Stevenson
Macconnell v. Schwamm, 2000 U.S. Dist. LEXIS 13850 (SD Cal July 25, 2000). 6-341
McCullagh v. Lane Fox and Partners Ltd 49 Con. L.R. 124; [1996] P.N.L.R. 205; [1996] 1 E.G.L.R. 35;
    [1996] 18 E.G. 104; [1995] E.G.C.S. 195; [1995] N.P.C. 203 5-031
McDonough v. Fallon McElligot Inc., 1996 U.S. Dist. LEXIS 15139, 7 (SD Cal August 6, 1996) 6-337
Magnetic Audiotape Antitrust Litigation, 2001 U.S. Dist. LEXIS 5160 (S.D.N.Y. Apr 25, 2001) 6-337
Magnetics Ltd v. Discopy (Israel) Ltd, Tel Aviv District Court Civil File 001627/01, unreported 3-161
Malaysia Air Lines, Supreme Court, Showa 56 (1981) October 16 Minshu 35, Vol. 7, p.1224. 6-248
Masquerade Music Ltd and Others v. Springsteen [2001] 4 E.M.L.R. 654 10-133
Marc Rich & Co. v. Bishop Rock Marine [1996] A.C. 211; [1995] 3 W.L.R. 227; [1995] 3 All E.R. 307;
    [1995] 2 Lloyd's Rep. 299; [1996] E.C.C. 120; (1995) 145 N.L.J. 1033; (1995) 139 S.J.L.B. 165 5-004
Marchant v. Ford [1936] 2 All E.R. 1510 4-005
Marckx v. Belgium (1979-80) 2 E.H.R.R. 330 5-111
Market Opinion and Research International Ltd v. BBC , June 17, 1999 . . . . 4-017, 4-018, 4-026
Marks & Spencer plc v. Cottrell, February 26, 2001, unreported 3-014, 3-042, 3-063
Merrill Lynch Inc's Application [1989] R.P.C. 561. . . . . 2-156, 2-157
Metal Industry Co. Ltd v. Superior Court, 480 U.S. 102 (1987) 6-333
Michelin v. Commission, Case 322/81 [1983] E.C.R. 3461; [1985] 1 C.M.L.R. 282; [1985] F.S.R. 250 14-193
Micro Leader Business v. Commission, Case T-198/98, December 16, 1999 14-212
Millennium Entertainment v. Millennium Music LP, 33 F. Supp. 2d 907 (D Or 1999) 6-337, 6-339, 6-340
Minge v. Cohen, 2000 U.S. Dist. LEXIS 403 (ED La January 19, 2000). 6-337
Mink v. AAAA Dev LLC, 190 F3d 333, 336 (5th Cir 1999) 6-339
Molson Breweries v. Kuettner (1999) 3 C.R. (4th) 479 (F.C.T.D.) 3-112
Morse v. Future Reality Ltd (Case no. 54571/95), October 25, 1996 5-070
Mothercare UK Ltd v. Penguin Books Ltd [1988] R.P.C. 113. 3-033
Mullen v. Barr, 1929 S.C. 461 5-009
Myers v. DPP [1965] A.C. 1001; [1964] 3 W.L.R. 145; [1964] 2 All E.R. 881; (1964) 48 Cr. App. R.
    348; 128 J.P. 481; 108 S.J. 519 10-137
NMTV v. Jobserve (2001) 24(6) I.P.D. 24038, *Times*, January 25, 2001 14-014
Napster 2-102
National Rivers Authority v. Alfred McAlpine Homes East Ltd [1994] 4 All E.R. 286; [1994] Env.
    L.R. 198; (1994) 158 J.P.N. 390; [1994] E.G.C.S. 10; [1994] N.P.C. 6. 5-061
National Westminster Bank Ltd v. Barclays Bank International Ltd [1975] Q.B. 654; [1975] 2 W.L.R.
    12; [1974] 3 All E.R. 834; [1974] 2 Lloyd's Rep. 506; 118 S.J. 627. 10-078
Network Multimedia Television Ltd. v. Jobserve Ltd, Chancery Division Judgment HC
    0005478 of April 5, 2001 14-262
New Zealand Post Ltd v. Lend (1998) 8 T.C.L.R. 502 . . . . 3-192, 3-193, 6-290, 6-291, 6-292
Niemitz v. Germany (1992) 16 E.H.R.R. 97 6-117
Northland Insurance Cos v. Blaylock, 115 F. Supp. 2d 1108 (D. Minn. 2000) 3-235
Oceano Grup Editorial SA v. Rocio Murciano Quintero, June 27, 2000 10-040
Oggi Advertising Ltd v. McKenzie (1998) 6 N.Z.L.B.C. 102, 567; (1998) 8 T.C.L.R. 363; [1999]
    1 N.Z.L.R. 631; (1998) 44 I.P.R. 661 . . . . 3-192, 3-193, 3-194
Orr v. Union Bank of Scotland [1854] Macq H.L. Cas. 512 . . . . 11-041, 11-043
Oscar Bronner GmbH & Co. KG v. Mediaprint Zeitungs-und Zeitschriftenverlag GmbH & C. KG,
    Mediaprint Zeitungsvertriebsgesellschaft mbH & Co. KG, Mediaprint Anzeigengesellschaft mbH &
    Co. KG Case C-7/97 14-211

Ouders van Nu/Ouders Online, I.E.R. 1996 44. . . . . 3-184, 6-275
Oxford v. Moss (1979) 68 Cr. App. R. 183; [1979] Crim. L.R. 119 . . . . 2-131, 2-135
PCM v. Krante.com; *sub nom.* Algemeen Dagblad B.V. v. Eureka Internetdiensten, District Court of
    Rotterdam, August 22, 2000; E-commerce Law Reports, Vol. 1, Issue 2, p. 12 2-087
PEINET Inc. v. O'Brien (1995) 61 C.P.R. (3d) 334 (P.E.I.S.C.). 3-111
Panavision Int'l L.P. v. Toeppen, 945 F. Supp. 1296 (C.D. Cal. 19960; aff'd 141 F. 3d 1316 (9th Cir.
    1998) 3-20, 6-341
Paradise Mombasa Tours (1997) Ltd v. New Soil Technologies Ltd, Tel Aviv District Court Civil
    File 001509/01. . . . . 3-161, 6-236
Parisi v. Netlearning Inc., 139 F. Supp. 2d 745 (E.D. Va. 2001) 3-226
Parr v. Derwentside D.C. (Case No. 2501507/98), September 23, 1998 5-068
Passies/Gaos, I.E.R. 2000 41; I.E.R. 2001 10. . . . . 3-185, 6-276
Fujitsu Ltd, Re [1996] R.P.C. 511. 2-157
People v. World Interactive Gaming Corp, 185 Misc 2d 852 (NY Sup Ct 1999) 6-339
People for the Ethical Treatment of Animals v. Doughy, 113 F. Supp. 2d 915 (E.D. Va. 2000). 3-236
Petterson's Application (T1002/92). 2-154
Pfizer Ltd v. Eurofood Link (UK) Ltd [2000] E.T.M.R. 896; [2001] F.S.R. 17 3-032
Philips v. Eyre (1870–71) L.R. 6 Q.B. 1 6-295
Philips Electronics v. Remington Consumer Products [1998] R.P.C. 283 . . . . 3-033, 3-034
Pitman Training Ltd v. Nominet UK and Pearson Professional Ltd [1997-98] Info. T.L.R. 177;
    [1998] I.T.C.L.R. 17; [1997] F.S.R. 797; (1998) 17 Tr. L.R. 173; [1998] Masons C.L.R. 125; (1997)
    20(8) I.P.D. 20080. 3-064
Playboy Enterprises Inc. v. Chuckleberry Publishing Inc., 939 F. Supp. 1032
    (S.D.N.Y. 1996) 3-012, 6-269, 6-337
- v. Frena, 839 F. Supp. 1552 (MD Fla. 1993). 2-099, 6-345
- v. Netscape Communications, 2000 U.S. Dist. LEXIS 13418 (C.D. Cal. Septemner 12, 2000) 3-241
- v. Terri Welles, 78 F. Supp. 2d 1066 (S.D. Cal. 1999). 3-079, 3-240
- v. Webbworld Inc. 991 F. Supp. 543 (ND Tex 1997) 6-345
Plessey v. Siemens [1988] E.C.R. 384. 14-073
Porsche Cars North America Inc. v. Spencer, 2000 U.S. Dist. LEXIS 7060 (May 18, 2000 E.D.
    Cal. 2000) 3-230
Port of Genoa, Case 179/90 [1991] I E.C.R. 5889. 14-196
Premier Brands UK Ltd v. Typhoon Europe Ltd [2000] E.T.M.R. 1071; [2000] F.S.R. 767; (2000) 23(5)
    I.P.D. 23038; (2000) 97(5) L.S.G. 35. . . . . 3-032, 3-059
Price Meats Ltd v. Barclays Bank PLC [2000] 2 All E.R. (Comm.) 346. 11-041
Prince plc v. Prince Sports Group Inc. [1997-98] Info. T.L.R. 329; [1998] F.S.R. 21; [1998] Masons
    C.L.R. 139 . . . . 3-065, 3-013
Prince Blucher, ex p. Debtor [1931] 2 Ch. D. 70 10-071
Procter & Gamble/Magenta, District Court of Amsterdam, February 24, 2000 3-186
Qimron v. Shanks, District Court Reports, vol. 1993(3), p. 10, at 21 6-239
Quokka Sports Inc. v. Cup Int'l Ltd, 99 F. Supp. 2d 1105 (ND Cal 1999) 6-339
R v. Bow Street Metropolitan Stipendiary Magistrate, ex p. Government of the United States
    of America [1990] 4 All E.R. 1 2-132
- v. Bow Street Stipendiary Magistrate, ex p. Government of the United States of America
    [1999] 4 All E.R. 2 . . . . 12-158, 12-161, 12-162
- v. - [2000] 2 A.C. 216 5-067
- v. Bowden [2001] Q.B. 88; [2000] 2 W.L.R. 1083; [2000] 2 All E.R. 418; [2000] 1 Cr. App.
    R. 438; [2000] 2 Cr. App. R. (S.) 26; [2000] Crim. L.R. 381; (1999) 96(47) L.S.G. 29; (2000)
    144 S.J.L.B. 5 . . . . 12-075, 12-076,
                                                                                                        12-077, 12-079
- v. Broadcasting Standards Commission, ex p. British Broadcasting Corporation [2000] 3
    W.L.R. 1327; [2000] 3 All E.R. 989; [2000] E.M.L.R. 587; [2000] H.R.L.R. 374; [2000] U.K.H.R.R.
    624; [2000] C.O.D. 322; (2000) 97(17) L.S.G. 32; (2000) 144 S.J.L.B. 204 5-117
- v. Cochrane [1993] Crim.L.R. 48, CA 10-132
- v. Cowper [1890] 24 Q.B.D. 533 10-071
- v. Department of Health, ex p. Source Informatics Ltd [2001] 1 All E.R. 788 7-027
- v. Fellows, R v. Arnold [1997] 2 All E.R. 548; [1997] 1 Cr. App. R. 244; [1998] Masons C.L.R. Rep.
    121; [1997] Crim. L.R. 524 . . . . 2-065, 10-070,
                                                                                                        12-065, 12-084
- v. Foxley [1995] 2 Cr. App. R. 523; (1995) 16 Cr. App. R. (S.) 879; [1995] Crim. L.R. 636. 10-141
- v. Governor of Brixton Prison, ex p. Levin; *sub nom.* Levin (Application for a Writ of Habeas
    Corpus), Re [1997] A.C. 741; [1997] 3 W.L.R. 117; [1997] 3 All E.R. 289; [1998] 1 Cr. App. R. 22;
    [1997] Crim. L.R. 891; (1997)
    94(30) L.S.G. 28; (1997) 147 N.L.J. 990; (1997) 141 S.J.L.B. 148. 10-135
- v. Kahn [1997] A.C. 558 5-059

R v. P [2001] 2 W.L.R. 463 5-059
- v. Pettigrew (1980) 71 Cr. App. R. 39; [1980] Crim. L.R. 239 . . . . 10-135, 10-136
- v. Radio Authority, ex p Bull [1998] Q.B. 294; [1997] 3 W.L.R. 1094; [1997] 2 All E.R. 561;
    [1997] E.M.L.R. 201; [1997] C.O.D. 382; (1997) 147 N.L.J. 489 12-008
- v. Shephard [1993] A.C. 380; [1993] 2 W.L.R. 102; [1993] 1 All E.R. 225; (1993) 96 Cr. App. R.
    345; (1993) 157 J.P. 145; [1993] Crim. L.R. 295; (1993) 143 N.L.J. 127; (1993) 137 S.J.L.B. 12 10-132
- v. Waddon [1999] I.T.C.L.R. 422; [1999] Masons C.L.R. 396 . . . . 12-067, 12-084
- v. Whiteley (1991) 93 Cr. App. R. 25; (1991) 155 J.P. 917; [1992] E.C.C. 485; [1993]
    F.S.R. 168; [1991] Crim. L.R. 436; (1991) 155 J.P.N. 378; (1991) 135 S.J. 249 . . . . . . 5-011, 5-013, 5-020, 12-150
- v. Wright, June 4, 2001, CA 5-059
RTE and ITP v. Commission, Cases C-241/91 P and C-242/91 [1995] E.C.R. I-743 14-209
Rad v. Chai, Supreme Court Reports, Vol. 40(2), p. 141 (1986) 6-229, 6-230
Rannoch Inc. v. Rannoch Corp., 52 F. Supp. 2d 681 (ED Va1999) 6-337
Raytheon's Application [1993] R.P.C. 427 2-157
Real Networks Inc. v. Streambox Inc. 2000 U.S. Dist. LEXIS 1889 (WD Wash January 18, 2000) 6-346
Reckitt and Colman Products Ltd v. Borden Inc.; *sub nom.* Jif Lemon Case [1990] 1 W.L.R. 491;
    [1990] 1 All E.R. 873; [1990] R.P.C. 341; (1990) 134 S.J. 784; [1990] 1 W.L.R. 491[1990] 1 All E.R. 873 . . 3-037
Referee Enterprises v. Planet Ref Inc., 2001 U.S. Dist. LEXIS 9303 (E.D. Wisc. January 24, 2001) 3-225
Register.com v. Verio Inc., 126 F. Suypp. 2d 239 (S.D.N.Y.) 2000) 6-348
Religious Technology Centre v. Lerma, 1996 U.S. Dist. LEXIS 15454 (ED Va October 4, 1996) 6-345
Religious Technology Centre v. Netcom On-line Communication Services Inc., 907 F. Supp. 1361
    (ND Cal. 1995) 1-024, 2-100, 2-105, 4-046,
                                                                                                                    5-057, 6-35
Remia v. Commission, Case 42/84 [1985] E.C.R. 2545; [1987] 1 C.M.L.R. 1; [1987] F.S.R. 190 14-067
Remick v. Manfredy, 238 F3d 248, 259 (3d Cir 2110) 6-337
Revell v. Lidoy, 2001 U.S. Dist. LEXIS 3133 (ND Tex March 20, 2001) 6-342, 6-349
Riches, McKenzie & Herbert v. Source Telecomputing Corp. (1992) 46 C.P.R. (3d) 563 (TMBd) 3-109
Rickards v. Lothian [1913] A.C. 263 5-019
Roadtech Computer Systems Ltd v. Mandata (Management and Data Services) Ltd [2000]
    E.T.M.R. 970, Ch.D 3-080
Roberts-Gordon LLC v. Superior Radiant Products LTD, 85 F. Supp. 2d 202 (WD NY 2000) 6-342
Rylands v. Fletcher (1868) L.R. 3 H.L. 330 . . . . 5-012, 5-016, 5-019
Sabel v. Puma [1997] E.C.R. I-6191; [1998] 1 C.M.L.R. 445; [1998] C.E.C. 315; [1998]
    E.T.M.R. 1; [1998] R.P.C. 199 3-032
Sacchi, Case 155/73 [1974] E.C.R. 409; [1974] 2 C.M.L.R. 177 14-066
Saltman Engineering v. Campbell [1963] 3 All E.R. 413 (Note); (1948) 65 R.P.C. 203 2-110
Sarl Stepstone France v. Sarl Ofir France, Commercial Court of Nanterre, November 8, 2000 2-086
Saskatoon Star Phoenix Group Inc. v. Norton (2001) 12 C.P.C. (4th) 4 (Sask. Q.B.) 3-112
Schelde Delta Shipping BV v. Astarte Shiping Ltd (The Pamela) [1995] 2 Lloyd's Rep. 249 . . . . 10-051, 10-056
Scientology v. XS 4ALL cs, March 12, 1996 [Mediaforum 1996/4] 2-103
Sea Containers v. Stena Sealink [1994] O.J.L 15/8 14-199
Sealink/B & I [1992] 5 C.M.L.R. 225 14-196
Sega Enterprises v. MAPHIA, 948 F. Supp. 923 (ND Cal 1996) 6-345
Sega Enterprises v. Maphia, EIPLR, January 10, 1997 2-101
Sega Enterprises v. Sabella, 1996 U.S. Dist. LEXIS 20470 (ND Cal December 18, 1996) 6-345
Shaha v. Serderian, Supreme Court Reports, Vol. 29(4), p. 734 (1985) 6-233
Shechem Arabic Insurance Company v. Abed Zerikat, Supreme Court Reports, Vol.
    48(3), p. 265 (1994) 6-231
Shetland Times Ltd v. Wills 1997 S.C. 316; 1997 S.L.T. 669; 1997 S.C.L.R. 160; [1997] E.M.L.R.
    277; [1997-98] Info. T.L.R. 1; [1998] I.T.C.L.R. 49; [1997] F.S.R. 604; (1997) 16 Tr. L.R. 158;
    [1998] Masons C.L.R. 159; [1998] Masons C.L.R. Rep. 159 . . . . 2-070, 2-078, 2-095, 6-347
Shields v. Zuccarini, 2001 U.S. App. LEXIS 13288 (3d Cir. 2001) 3-233
Singer Manufacturing Co. v. Loog [1882] 8 App. Cas. 15 . . . . .3-050, 3-055, 3-056,
                                                                                                                    3-057, 3-058
Smith v. Eric S Bush [1990] 1 A.C. 831; [1989] 2 W.L.R. 790; [1989] 2 All E.R. 514; (1989)
    21 H.L.R. 424; 87 L.G.R. 685; [1955-95] P.N.L.R. 467; [1989] 18 E.G. 99; [1989] 17 E.G. 68; (1990)
    9 Tr. L.R. 1; (1989) 153 L.G. Rev. 984; (1989) 139 N.L.J. 576; (1989) 133 S.J. 597 5-031
Smith v. Hobby Lobby Stores Inc., 968 F. Supp. 1356, 1364-65 (WD Ark 1997) 6-339
Smythe v. Bayleys Real Estate Ltd (1993) 5 T.C.L.R. 454, 472; [1994] A.N.Z. Conv.R. 424, 428-429 6-282
Sohei/Yamamoto's Application, Case T769/92 [1996] E.P.O.R. 253 . . . . 2-153, 2-155
Spiliada Maritime Corp v. Cansulex Ltd [1987] A.C. 460; [1986] 3 W.L.R. 972; [1986] 3 All E.R.
    843; [1987] 1 Lloyd's Rep. 1; [1987] E.C.C. 168; [1987] 1 F.T.L.R. 103; (1987) 84 L.S.G. 113;
    (1986) 136 N.L.J. 1137; (1986) 130 S.J. 925 6-231
Sporty's Farm L.L.C. v. Spotsman's Market Inc., 202 F. 3d 489 (2d Cir. 2000) 3-230
Standard Bank London Ltd v. Bank of Tokyo Ltd [1996] 1 C.T.L.R. T-17 . . . . 10-079, 10-081

State Street Bank & Trust Co. v. Signature Financial Group Inc., 47 U.S.P.Q. 2d 1596. 2-141
Statue of Liberty Case [1968] 1 W.L.R. 739; [1968] 2 All E.R. 195; [1968] 1 Lloyd's Rep.
     429; (1968) 112 S.J. 380. 10-135
Stepstone v. Ofir [2000] EBLR 87; E-commerce Law Reports Vol. 1, issue 2, p. 14 2-086
Stratton Oakmont v. Prodigy, 995 NY Misc LEXIS 229 . . . . 4-001, 4-027, 4-054, 4-056, 4-058
Sun Life Assurance Company of Canada v. W H Smith and Son Ltd (1934) 150 L.T.R. 211, CA. 4-010
Sun Microsystems Inc. v. Lai Sun Hotels International Ltd [2000] 2 H.K.L.R.D. 616 3-150
Sunday Times v. United Kingdom (1992) 14 E.H.R.R. 229 (Spycatcher Case) 2-120, 2-130, 12-097
Suze Randall Photography v. Reactor Inc., 2000 U. S. Dist. LEXIS 6576 (ND Ill May 12, 2000) 6-350
Tai Hing Cotton Mills [1985] 3 W.L.R. 317, PC. 11-041, 11-042
Taiwan Ento Air Lines, Tokyo District court, Showa 61 (1986) June 20 Hanrei Jiho Vol. 1196,87 6-249
Takenaka (UK) Ltd v. Frankl [2001] EWCA Civ. 348 . . . . 10-078, 10-150
Tasini v. New York Times, Electronic Commerce and Law Report, Vol. 6, No. 7, July 7, 2001, p. 700 . . . 2-116
Tech Heads Inc. v. Desktop Service Center Inc., 105 F. Supp. 2d 1142 (D Ore July 11, 2000) 6-352
Tele-Direct (Publications) Inc. v. Klimchuk (1997) 77 C.P.R. (3d) 23 (F.C.T.D.) 3-117
Tele-Event Ltd v. Aruzey Zahav & Co. District Court Reports, Vol. 1994(2), p. 328 6-237
Tesco Supermarkets Ltd v. Nattrass [1972] A.C. 153; [1971] 2 W.L.R. 1166; [1971] 2 All E.R.
     127; 69 L.G.R. 403; 115 S.J. 285. 5-061
Thomas v. News Group Newspapers Ltd, TLR, July 25, 2001. 12-087
Thornton v. Shoe Lane Parking Ltd [1971] 2 Q.B. 163; [1971] 2 W.L.R. 585; [1971] 1 All E.R. 686;
     [1971] 1 Lloyd's Rep. 289; [1971] R.T.R. 79; (1970) 115 S.J. 75. 10-060
Ticketmaster Corp. v. Tickets.com Inc., U.S. Dist. Ct., C.D. Cal, March 27, 2000 . . . . . 2-081, 2-089, 2-090, 6-347
- v. – 2001 U.S. App. LEXIS 1454 (9th Cir January 22, 2001) 6-347
Tiercé Ladbroke v. Commission, Case T-504/93, judgment of June 12, 1997. 14-210
Toronto.com v. Sinclair (c.o.b. Friendship Enterprises) (2000) 6 C.P.R. (4th) 487 (F.C.T.D.) 3-111
Torrac Investments Pty Ltd v. Australian National Airline Commission (1985) ANZ Conv. R. 82 10-075
Totalise plc v. The Motley Fool, February 19, 2001, unreported 4-032, 7-062
Tower Boot Co. Ltd v. Jones; sub nom. Jones v. Tower Boot Co Ltd [1997] 2 All E.R. 406; [1997]
     I.C.R. 254; [1997] I.R.L.R. 168; (1997) 147 N.L.J. 60. 5-064
Trebor Bassett Ltd v. The Football Association [1997] F.S.R. 211; (1996) 19(12) I.P.D. 19116 3-041
Turberville v. Stampe (1697) 1 Ld.Raym 264. 5-018
Turner Broadcasting System Inc. v. FCC, 114 S. Ct 2445 (1994). 12-010
Ty Inc. v. Clark, 2000 U.S. Dist. LEXIS 383 (ND I11 January 14, 2000) 6-340
Ty Inc. v. Parvin, WIPO D2000-0688. 3-072
UMG Recordings Inc. v. MP3.com Inc., 92 F. Supp. 2d 349 (S.D.N.Y. 2000) 6-345
U.S. v. Cohen, No 00-1574 (2d Cir July 31, 2001) 6-339
- v. Sklyarov, No 5-01-257 (ND Cal filed July 7, 2001) 6-346
Unger v. Paris Israel Movies Ltd, Supreme Court Reports, Vol. 20(5), p. 6 (1966). 6-226
United Brands v. Commission, Case 27/76 [1978] E.C.R. 207; [1978] 1
     C.M.L.R. 429 . . . . .14-196, 14-203, 14-205, 14-208
United Greeks Inc. v. Klein, 2000 U.S. Dist. LEXIS 5670 (N.D.N.Y. May 2, 2000) 3-230
United States v. Cherif, 943 F. 2d 692 (7th Circuit) 2-134
- v. Girard, 601 F. 2d 69 (2nd Circuit 1979). 2-134
- v. LaMaccia, 871 F. Supp. 535 (D Mass. 1994). 2-103
- v. Morrison, 859 F. 2d 151(4h Circuit 1988) 2-134
- v. Riggs and Neidorf, 741 F. Supp. 556 (ND I1 1990) 2-134
Universal City Studios Inc. v. Reimerdes, 82 F. Supp. 2d 211 (S.D.N.Y. 2000). 6-346, 6-347
VNU Business Publications BV v. Monster Board BV [2000] E.T.M.R. 111 3-083
Vacwell Engineering Co. Ltd v. BDH Chemicals Ltd [1971] 1 Q.B. 111; [1970] 3 W.L.R. 67; [1970] 3 All
     E.R. 553 (Note); 114 S.J. 472. 5-002
Van Landewyck v. Commission, Cases 209/78 [1980] E.C.R. 3125; [1981] 3 C.M.L.R. 134 14-065
Venables v. News Group Newspapers Ltd [2001] 1 All E.R. 908; [2001] E.M.L.R. 10; (2001)
     151 N.L.J. 57 . . . . 5-050, 5-111, 12-099
Vicom/ Viacom, Re, Case T208/84 [1987] E.P.O.R. 74 . . . . 2-152, 2-155, 2-157
Victor Chandler International Ltd v. Customs & Excise Commissioners [2000] 1 W.L.R. 1296;
     [2000] 2 All E.R. 315; (2000) 97(11) L.S.G. 36; (2000) 150 N.L.J. 341; (2000) 144 S.J.L.B. 127. . . 10-069, 12-061
Video Cassette Recorders [1978] O.J.L 47 . . . . 14-182, 14-183, 14-186
Viho Europe v. Commission, Case C-73/95 [1997] All E.R. (E.C.) 163; [1996] E.C.R. I-5457;
     [1997] 4 C.M.L.R. 419; [1997] I.C.R. 130; (1997) 16 Tr. L.R. 59. 14-066
Virtual Works Inc. v. Volkswagen of America Inc., 238 F. 3d 264 (4th Cir. 2001) 3-231
Virtuality LLC v. Bata Ltd, 138 F. Supp. 2d 677 (D Md 2001). 6-339
Vizetelly v. Mudie's Select Library Ltd [1900] 2 Q.B. 170 . . . . 4-047, 4-048
Völk v. Vervaecke, Cases 19 & 20/74 [1975] E.C.R. 499 14-069
Vulcan Northwest Inc. v. Vulcan Ventures Corp. (2001) 12 C.P.R. (4th) 95 (F.C.T.D) 3-112
Wal-Mart Stores Inc. v. wallmartcanadasucks.com and Kenneth J. Harvey, WIPO D2000-1104. 3-030

Wal-Mart Stores Inc. v. Walsucks and Walmart Puerto Rico, WIPO D2000-0477. 3-030
Wang's Application [1991] R.P.C. 463. 2-156
Washington v. Townsend, Washington Court of Appeals, April 5, 2001-10-07   5-085
Washington Speakers Bureau Inc. v. Lading Authorities Inc., 33 F. Supp. 2d 488
    (E.D. Va. 1999); aff'd, 217 F. 3d 843 (4th Cir. 2000) 3-230
Weber-Stephen Products Co. v. Armitage Hardware, 2000 U.S. Dist. LEXIS 6335
    (N.D. III, May 3, 2000). 3-225
Weldon v. "The Times" Book Co. Ltd (1912) 28 T.L.R. 143 4-010
Weller v. Foot & Mouth Disease Research Institute [1966] 1 Q.B. 569; [1965] 3 W.L.R. 1082;
    [1965] 3 All E.R. 560; [1965] 2 Lloyd's Rep. 414; 109 S.J. 702 5-013
Westminster C.C. v. Croyalgrange Ltd [1986] 1 W.L.R. 674; [1986] 2 All E.R. 353; (1986) 83 Cr.
    App. R. 155; (1986) 150 J.P. 449; 84 L.G.R. 801; [1986] Crim. L.R. 693; (1986) 83 L.S.G.
    2089; (1986) 136 N.L.J. 491; (1986) 130 S.J. 409 5-053
Williams v. America Online Inc., Mass. Super. Ct., No 00-0962, February 8, 2001 (ECLR Vol. 6) 9-037
World-Wide Voklswagen Corp v. Woodson, 444 U.S. 286, 294 (1980). 6-335
X and Y v. Netherlands (1986) 8 E.H.R.R. 235 5-111
X County Council v. A [1984] 1 W.L.R. 1422; [1985] 1 All E.R. 53; [1985] Fam. Law 59; (1984)
    81 L.S.G. 3259 12-099
X/Open Group [1987] O.J.L 35. . . . . .14-176, 14-178, 14-179, 14-181
Yahoo! Inc. v. La Ligue Contre Le Racisme, 2001 U.S. Dist. LEXIS 7565 (ND Cal June 7, 2001) 6-342
Zeran v. America Online Inc., 1997 129 F. 3d 327. 4-058
Zippo Manufacturing Co. v. Zippo Dot Com Inc. 952 F. Supp. 1119 (WD Pa 1997) 6-338, 6-339, 6-341
Zomba Recording Corp v. Deep, 01-CV-4452 (S.D.N.Y., filed May 24, 2001). 6-345

Table of Statutes

1677 Statute of Frauds (c. 3)
 s. 4 . . . . 10-075, 10-110
1709 Copyright Act 2-041, 6-185
1882 Bills of Exchange Act (45 & 46
 Vict. c. 61) 11-047
1893 Sale of Goods Act (56 & 57 Vict. c. 71)
 s.4 10-110
1925 Law of Property Act (15 & 16 Geo.
 5, c. 20) 10-071
1938 Evidence Act (1 & 2 Geo.
 6, c. 28) 10-131, 10-132
1949 Wireless Telegraphy Act (12, 13 & 14 Geo. 6,
 c. 54) 2-132
1952 Finance Act (15 & 16 Geo. 6 & 1 Eliz. 2, c.
 33) 12-061
1956 Copyright Act (5 Eliz. 2, c.
 74) 2-059, 2-067, 12-078
1959 Obscene Publications Act (8 Eliz. 2, c. 66) . . .
 12-064, 12-065, 12-068, 12-075, 12-082
 s. 1(2) 12-064
 s. 1(3)(a) 12-065
 (b) 12-065, 12-084
 (4) 12-065, 12-068, 12-085
 s. 2 12-069
 s. 2(1) 12-066
 s. 2(5) 5-053
1963 Betting, Gaming and Lotteries Act
 (c. 2) 12-058
1965 Criminal Evidence Act (c. 20) 10-136
1967 Misrepresentation Act (c. 7) 10-045
1968 Gaming Act (c. 65) 12-058
1971 Criminal Damage Act (c. 48) 5-011,
 5-013, 12-150
 Unsolicited Goods and Services Act
 (c. 30) 10-070
1973 Fair Trading Act (41) . . .14-220, 14-223, 14-234
1974 Consumer Credit Act (c.
 39) 10-008, 10-070, 11-043
 s. 56 11-012
 s. 75 11-012
1976 Lotteries and Amusements Act (c. 32) . 12-058
 s. 1 12-059
 s. 2 12-060
 s. 14 12-059
 Restrictive Trade Practices Act (c. 34) . . 14-223
 Adoption Act (c. 36) 5-047
 s. 58(1) 5-047
 Resale Prices Act (c. 53) 14-223
 s. 14 14-261
1977 Restrictive Trade Practices Act (c. 19) . . 14-223

1977 Patents Act (c. 37)
 s. 60 2-162
 (1) 2-162
 (2) 2-162
 (3) 2-162
 Unfair Contract Terms Act (c. 50) 5-024,
 5-029, 10-009, 11-043
 s. 2 10-009
 (1) 5-030
 s. 3 10-009
 s. 6 10-009
 s. 11 10-009
 (3) 5-030
 s. 13(1) 5-031
1978 Interpretation Act (c. 30) 9-020, 10-069
 Sched. 1 10-069
 Protection of Children Act (c. 37) 12-065,
 12-073, 12-074, 12-075, 12-077,
 12-079, 12-082
 s. 1(1)(a) 12-073, 12-074, 12-075, 12-081
 (b) 12-073, 12-074, 12-081
 (c) 12-073, 12-074, 12-081
 (d) 12-073, 12-074, 12-085
 (2) 12-083
 s. 7 . . . . 12-073, 12-075
1979 Sale of Goods Act (1979 c. 54)
 s. 8(2) 10-047
1980 Competition Act (1980 c. 21) 14-223
1981 Indecent Displays (Control) Act (c. 42)
 s. 1(1) 12-088
 (2) 12-088
 (3) 12-088
 Contempt of Court Act (c. 49) . . 4-032, 12-092
 Betting and Gaming Duties Act (c. 63) . 12-058
 s. 9(1)(b) 12-061
1984 Telecommunications Act (c. 12) . .5-085, 8-004,
 8-006, 8-050, 12-086
 s. 3 12-009
 s. 4(1) 8-006
 s. 7 . . . . 8-006, 8-014
 Data Protection Act (c. 35) 7-007, 7-010,
 7-012, 7-019, 7-021, 7-025, 7-028, 7-037,
 7-041, 7-043, 7-045, 7-048, 7-077, 7-078
 s. 36 7-091
 Video Recordings Act (c. 39) 5-054
1985 Companies Act (c. 6)
 s. 26(1)(c) 3-044
 s. 28 3-044
 Interception of Communications Act
 (c. 56) 2-132, 5-074, 5-078

1986 Insolvency Act (c. 45)
        s. 257 10-074
      Financial Services Act (c. 60) . . 12-103, 12-113
1987 Banking Act (c. 22). 11-054
      Consumer Protection Act (c. 43). 10-010
        Pt I 5-011
        s. 7 5-011
        s. 39 10-029
1988 Malicious Communications Act (c. 27) . 12-086
        s. 1(1) 12-086
      Criminal Justice Act (c. 33). . . . 10-140, 12-075,
                                      12-077, 12-078
        s. 7 12-078
        s. 23 10-140
        s. 24 . . . . 10-136, 10-140
        s. 27 . . . . 10-133, 10-144
        s. 160 12-074
        Sched. 2 10-147
      Copyright, Designs and Patents Act
        (c. 48) 2-041, 2-042, 2-043,
              2-047, 2-049, 2-057, 2-059, 2-061, 2-062,
              2-105, 2-113, 6-211, 9-003, 10-069, 12-085,
                                                  13-052
        s. 3(2) 2.43
        s. 3A. 2-043
        s. 6(1) 2-068
        s. 7(1) 2-069
            (2)(a) 2-069
            (5) 2-070, 2-079
        s. 9(3) 9-013
        s. 17 . . . . 2-064, 2-078
            (2) 2-004
            (6) 2-004, 6-272
        s. 18 2-065
        s. 19 2-067
        s. 20 . . . . 2-068, 2-078
        s. 21 2-071
        ss. 22-26 2-072
        s. 23 5-053
        s. 24(2) 2-080
        s. 50A-C 2-071, 2-112
        s. 70 . . . . 2-095, 2-096
        s. 90 9-003
        s. 171(3) 2-080
        s. 175 2-065
        s. 178 . . . . 2-043, 9-003, 10-117
        s. 296 2-057
1989 Law of Property (Miscellaneous Provisions)
        Act (c. 34) 10-068
        s. 2 10-071
1990 Computer Misuse Act (c. 18) 2-132, 2-136,
                                      5-012, 5-011, 12-150
        s. 1 . . . . .12-151, 12-153, 12-156, 12-157
        s. 2 . . . . 12-153, 12-155
        s. 3 . . . . 12-154, 12-155, 12-159
            (6) 5-013, 12-150
        s. 17(5) 12-161
            (7) 12-150, 12-155
            (8) 12-155
      Timeshare Act (c. 35) 10-015
      Contracts (Applicable Law) Act (c. 36) . 10-038,
                                      10-040, 10-126
        Sched. 1 10-038
        art. 5. 10-038
        art. 9(5) 10-127

1990 Broadcasting Act (c. 42) . . .8-033, 8-034, 8-046,
                          12-009, 12-068, 12-086, 12-088
        s. 2(6) 8-035
        s. 6(1) 8-039
        s. 13 8-034
        s. 46 . . . . . . 8-036, 8-038, 8-039, 8-044, 8-051
            (1) 8-034, 8-035
            (2)(c) 8-037
        s. 47 8-044
        s. 72 . . . . 8-045, 8-046, 8-047
            (1) 8-046
            (2) 8-047
        s. 92(2)(a) 12-008
        s. 97 . . . . 8-043, 8-044
        s. 112 . . . . 8-043, 8-044
            (2) 8-045
        s. 113 8-045
        s. 166 4-004
        Sched. 15, para. 3. 12-070
        para. 4. 12-068
1994 Value Added Tax Act (c. 23) 13-008
        Sched. 5 . . . . 13-012, 13-029
      Trade Marks Act (c. 26) 3-001,
                                      3-007, 3-029, 3-049
        s. 9(1) 3-031
        s. 10 . . . . 3-031, 3-033, 3-080
            (1)-(3) 3-031, 3-032
            (1) 3-076
            (2) 3-034, 3-081
            (3) 3-013, 3-034, 3-035,
                          3-045, 3-059, 3-060, 3-062
            (4)-(6) 3-031
        s. 11 3-031
        s. 12 3-031
        s. 16 3-042
      Criminal Justice and Public Order Act
        (c. 33) 12-064, 12-065
1995 Civil Evidence Act (c. 38). 10-129,
                                      10-139, 10-147
        s. 8 . . . . 10-133, 10-143
1996 Arbitration Act (c. 23) 10-069
      Sexual Offences (Conspiracy and Incitement)
        Act
        (c. 29) 12-089
        s. 2(3) 12-089
      Defamation Act (c. 31) 4-001, 4-002, 4-005,
              4-008, 4-044, 4-047, 5-055, 5-064, 9-025
        s. 1 . . 4-005, 4-013, 4-017, 4-021, 4-043, 5-064
            (1) 4-014
            (a) 4-023, 4-027
            (b) 4-019, 4-040
            (c) 4-040
            (2) 4-016, 4-023, 4-030, 4-035, 4-038, 4-041
            (3) 4-005, 4-007, 4-014, 4-016,
                          4-022, 4-023, 4-032, 4-041, 4-053
            (a) 4-016, 4-037
            (c) 4-016, 4-022, 4-032, 4-034,
                                      4-036, 4-039
            (d) 4-017, 4-019
            (e) 4-016, 4-020, 4-034, 4-036
        s. 17(1) 4-021
      Broadcasting Act (c. 55) 8-033
1997 Protection from Harassment Act
        (c. 40) 12-087
        s. 7(3) 12-087

1998   Data Protection Act
           (c. 29) 2-132, 5-073, 5-101,
                        7-007, 7-012, 7-019, 7-022, 7-025,
                   7-028, 7-033, 7-040, 7-041, 7-043, 7-046,
                   7-048, 7-050, 7-076, 7-077, 7-078, 7-084,
                              9-023, 10-032, 10-097, 12-128
       s. 1(1) 7-026
           (2) 7-026
       s. 2 7-033
       s. 3 7-058
       s. 7 . . . . 7-051, 7-058, 7-060, 7-089, 7-090
           (1)(b)(iii) .7-044
           (c)(i). 7-044
       s. 8 . . . . 7-051, 7-058, 7-089
       s. 10 . . . . 7-044, 7-051, 7-058, 7-092
       s. 11 7-094
       s. 12 .7-058, 7-095
       s. 13 . . . . 7-043, 7-050, 7-098
       s. 14 .7-044, 7-099
           (1) 7-051, 7-058
           (2) 7-051, 7-058
           (3) 7-051, 7-058
       s. 24 7-100
       s. 27 7-051
       s. 28 .7-054, 7-087
       s. 29 7-055
       s. 30 7-056
       s. 31 7-057
       s. 32 7-058
           (4)(b) 7-059
       s. 33 7-060
       s. 34 7-061
       s. 35 7-062
           (1) 7-062
           (2) 7-062
       s. 36 7-063
       s. 42 . . . . .7-050, 7-090
       s. 43 . . . . 7-080, 7-090, 7-091
       s. 44 7-080
       s. 47(1) 7-082
       s. 50 7-086
       s. 51(3)(b) 5-104
       Sched. 1 7-008
       Pt II 7-034
       para. 2. 7-051
       para. 5. 7-040
       para. 11. . . . . .7-046, 9-020
       para. 12. . . . . .7-046, 9-020
       para. 13. 7-048
       Sched 2 . . . . 7-003, 7-008, 7-009, 7-051
       Sched 3 . . . . .7-033, 7-051
       Sched 7 . . . . .7-052, 7-064
       para. 1. 7-064
       para. 2. 7-066
       para. 3. 7-067
       para. 4. 7-068
       para. 5. 7-069
       para. 6. 7-070
       para. 7. 7-071
       para. 8. 7-072
       para. 9. 7-073
       para. 10. 7-074
       para. 11. 7-075
       Sched. 8 7-102

       Sched. 9 7-086
       Pt IV 7-052
       Competition Act (c. 41) 14-001, 14-223,
                                                       14-260
       s. 2 . . . . 14-223, 14-231
           (1) 14-225
           (3) 14-229
           (4) 14-231
       s. 6 14-237
       s.10 14-236
       s. 18 . . . . 14-223, 14-264
           (1) 14-240
       s. 60 . . . . 14-224, 14-241, 14-260
       Sched. 1, para. 1(1) 14-234
       para. 6. 14-234
       Human Rights Act (c. 42). 2-119, 4-044,
                                    5-057, 5-059, 5-073, 5-110,
                                                   5-112, 7-106
       s. 3(1) 4-044
       s. 4(2) 4-044
       s. 6(1) 4-044, 5-110
           (3) 4-044
               (b) 5-110
           (5) 5-110
       s. 12 7-059
           (4) 12-008
1999   Finance Act (c. 16) 13-066
2000   Regulation of Investigatory Powers Act
           (c. 23) . . 2-132, 5-057, 5-073, 7-041, 12-136
       s. 1 5-097
           (1) 5-074
           (2) 5-074
           (3) 5-074, 5-078, 5-092, 5-093, 5-095, 5-097
           (6) 5-074
           (7) 5-079
       s. 2(1) 5-075
           (2) 5-078, 5-081
           (6) 5-078
           (7) 5-079, 5-082, 5-083
           (8) 5-080, 5-082
       s. 3(3) 5-096
       s. 4 5-097
           (2) 5-096, 5-097
       s. 49(9) 12-149
       s. 50 12-149
       s. 51 12-149
       s. 78(5) 5-097
       Electronic Communications Act (c. 7). .10-113,
                                                       12-149
       s. 7 . . . . 10-076, 10-085, 10-088,
                                    10-115, 10-124, 10-136
       s. 8 . . . . 10-122, 10-124
           (4) 10-099
       s. 14 12-133
       Pt I 12-134
       Financial Services and Markets Act
           (c. 8) 11-054, 12-100, 12-108, 12-110
       s. 19 . . . . 11-054, 12-104
       s. 21 12-113
       s. 25 12-104
       s. 26 12-102
       s. 30 12-115
2001   Criminal Justice and Police Act (c. 16)
       s. 43 12-086

Table of Statutory Instruments

1986 Insolvency Rules (S.I. 1986 No. 1925)
r. 8.2(3) 10-074
1988 Control of Misleading Advertisements Regulations (S.I. 1988 No. 915). 12-124
1994 Unfair Terms in Consumer Contracts Regulations (S.I. 1994 No. 3159) . . . 5-029, 10-011,
10-040, 10-096
1996 Copyright and Related Rights Regulations (S.I.
1996 No. 2967). 2-065
Advanced Television Services Regulations (S.I.
No. 3197). 8-006
1997 Telecommunications (Interconnection) Regulations (S.I. 1997 No. 2931) 8-009
Copyright and Rights in Databases Regulations
(S.I. 1997 No. 3032) 2-049, 2-082
reg. 6 2-083
reg. 16(2). 2-085
reg. 19. 2-083
reg. 23. 9-003
Telecommunications (Open Network Provi-
sion) Voice Telephony Regulations (S.I.
1998 No. 1580). 8-021
1999 Unfair Terms in Consumer Contracts Regulations (S.I. 1999 No. 2083) . . . 5-029, 11-043
2000 Competition Act 1998 (Small Agreements and
Conduct of Minor Significance) Regulations (S.I. 2000 No. 262). 14-259
Competition Act 1998 (Land and Vertical
Agreements) Exclusion Order (S.I. 2000
No. 310) 14-233
Consumer Protection (Distance Selling) Regulations (S.I. 2000 No. 2334) 10-012,
10-013, 10-040
reg. 5(1) 10-014
regs 7-20 10-015
reg. 7 10-018
(1) 10-017
(a). 10-020
(2) 10-017
(3) 10-018
reg. 8 . . . . . . .10-019, 10-023, 10-024, 10-025
(2) 10-019, 10-020, 10-025
(3) 10-020
reg. 9 10-023
reg. 10. . . . . 10-020, 10-024, 10-120

(3) 10-025
(4) 10-025
(d) 10-023
reg. 11. 10-025
reg. 12. 10-025
reg. 13. 10-024
reg. 19(2)-(8) 10-015
(7) 10-018
reg. 20. 10-015
reg. 25. 10-018
(5) 10-025
reg. 26. 10-018
reg. 27. 10-018
Dual-Use Items (Export Control) Regulations
(S.I. 2000 No. 2620) 12-143
Telecommunications (Lawful Busines Practice)
(Interception of Communications) Regulations (S.I. 2000 No. 2699) 5-059
para. 2. 5-098
para. 3(1). 5-097, 5-098, 5-102
(2) 5-098
(a). 5-098
(b). 5-099
Companies Act 1985 (Electronic Communications) Order (S.I. 2000 No. 3373) . . 10-122
2001 Financial Services and Markets Act 2000
(Regulated Activites) Order (S.I. 2001 No.
544). 11-054, 12-106, 12-112
art. 3 12-110
art. 5 . . . . 11-054, 11-056
(2) 11-055
art. 9 11-055
Unfair Terms in Consumer Contracts (Amend-
ment) Regulations (S.I. 2001 No.
1186) 5-029
Financial Services and Markets Act 2000
(Financial Promotion) Order (S.I. 2001 No.
1335) 12-113, 12-116
art. 12 12-115
(1)(b) 12-115
(2) 12-115
(4) 12-116
art. 18 12-117
Stop Now Orders (E.C. Directive) Regulations
(S.I. 2001 No. 1422) 10-018

Table of European Legislation and International Conventions

Directives

1977 Dir 77/388 (Sixth Council Directive) [1977] O.J.
       L 145/1 13-008
       Art. 1 13-036
       Art. 9(3) 13-034, 13-036
       Art. 9.2(e) 13-012, 13-036
1985 Dir 85/374 (Directive on Product Liability)
       [1985] O.J. L210/29 5-011
1989 Dir 89/522 (Television without Frontiers
       Directive) 12-045
1990 Dir 90/388 (Services Directive) [1990] O.J.
       L192/10. 8-021
1991 Dir 91/250 (European Software Directive)
       [1991]
       O.J. L122/42 . . . . 2-044, 2-077
       Art. 4(A) 6-271, 6-272
       Art. 4(c) 14-212
1992 Dir 92/28 [1992] O.J. L 113/13 12-119,
                                                 12-120
1993 Dir 93/13 (Unfair Contract Terms Directive)
       [1993] O.J. L95/29 . . 5-029, 10-011, 10-096
       Art. 3 10-040
1995 Dir 95/46 (Data Protection Directive) [1995]
       O.J. L281/31 . . . . . . .5-037, 5-094, 7-007,
                        7-009, 7-012, 7-013, 7-015, 7-050
       Art. 2(c) .7-013
             (h) 7-050
       Art. 4 7-014
       Art. 25. .7-015
       Art. 26(1). 7-018
             (2). 7-018
       Art. 29. . . . . 7-018, 7-037
       Art. 32(2). 7-102
       Sched. 4, para. 8 7-050
       para. 9. 7-050
1996 Dir 96/9 (Database Directive) [1996] O.J.
       L 77/20. . . . . 2-050, 2-082
       Art. 4(A) .6-271
       Art. 7(1) .2-052
             (5) 2-052, 2-053
1997 Dir 97/7 (Protection of Consumers in Respect
       of Distance Contracts) [1997] O.J.
       L 144. 10-013
       Dir 97/33 (E.U. Interconnection Directive)
       [1997] O.J. L 199/32. 8-009
       Art. 1 8-009

1997 Dir 97/66 (Telecommunications Data Protec-
       tion Directive) [1998] O.J. L24/1 . . .5-037,
                                              5-081, 5-088,
                                     5-094, 10-032, 12-127
       Art. 2 5-091
       Art. 5 . . . . .5-088, 5-092, 5-093
             (1) 5-091, 5-092
             (2) 5-089, 5-092
       Art. 12. 12-127
1998 Dir 98/34 (Transparency Directive) [1998] O.J.
       L 37/35Art. 1(2) 5-035
       Dir 98/10 (Revised Voice Telephony Directive)
       [1998] O.J. L 101/24. 8-021
       Dir 98/48 . . . . .5-035, 10-026
1999 Dir 99/59 [1999] O.J. L162/64
       Art. 2 13-037
       Dir 99/93 (E.U. Electronic Signatures Directive)
       [2000] O.J. L13/12 . . . . 10-082, 10-113
       Art. 1 . . . . 10-04, 10-100
       Art. 2.1 10-084
       Art. 3.3 10-093
       Art. 3.7 10-099
       Art. 4 10-099
       Art. 5.1 . . . . 10-085, 10-090
       Art. 5.2 . . . . 10-085, 10-088
       Art. 6 10-096
       Art. 6.1 10-094
       Art. 6.2 10-095
       Art. 6.3 10-095
       Art. 6.4 10-096
       Art. 7 10-098
       Art. 8.2 10-097
       Art. 9 10-126
             (2) 10-126
       Art. 11.1(a) 10-099
       Art. 14(1). 10-126
             (2) 10-126
2000 Dir 2000/28 [2000] O.J. L 275/37 11-058
       Dir 2000/31 (Electronic Commerce Directive)
       [2000] O.J. L178/1 . . . .1-018, 2-010, 2-013,
                      2-106, 2-113, 4-002, 5-022, 5-034,
                          5-047, 10-012, 10-026, 12-045,
                                     12-048, 12-127
       Art. 1 5-035
             (1) 5-035
             (2) 5-035
             (4) 5-036
             (5) 5-037

2000 Art. 1.6. 12-027
      Art. 2 10-033
          (a) 5-035
      Art. 2(f). 10-031
      Art. 3.6 12-046
      Art. 5 10-028
      Art. 5.2 10-029
      Art. 6 10-030
      Art. 7 10-032
      Art. 8 10-033
      Art. 10. . . . . 5-022, 10-035
      Art. 11. . . . . 10-034, 10-036
          (3). 5-039
      Arts 12-15 . . . . 2-098, 5-034
      Art. 12. 5-038
      Art. 13. . . . . 2-014, 5-039, 5-043
      Art. 14. . . . . 5-038, 5-041, 5-053
      Art. 15. . . . . 5-045, 12-052
      Art. 18.2 10-036
      Art. 21. . . . . 4-038, 4-053
      Recital 17 10-026
      Dir 2000/46 11-058
2001 Dir 2001/29 (Copyright Directive) [2001] O.J.
          L167/10. . . . . 2-012, 2-113
      Art. 2 . . . . 2-014, 2-017
      Art. 3 . . . . 2-015, 2-017
      Art. 4 2-017
          (2) 2-016
      Art. 5 2-017
          (1) 2-013, 2-014
          (2) 2-017
              (a) 2-017
              (b) 2-018
              (c) 2-019
              (d) 2-021
              (e) 2-022
          (3) 2-017
              (a) 2-023
              (b) 2-024
              (c) 2-025
              (d) 2-026
              (e) 2-027
              (f). 2-028
              (g) 2-029
              (h) 2-030
              (i) 2-031
              (j) 2-032
              (k) 2-033
              (l) 2-034
              (m) 2-035
              (n) 2-036
              (o) 2-037
          (4) 2-017
          (5) 2-017
      Art. 6 2-038
      Art. 7 2-038

Regulations

1996 Technology Transfer Block Exemption Regula-
          tion 240/96 [1996] O.J. L 21/2 14-121,
                                          14-077, 14-078
      Art. 1 14-080

          (a) 14-199
          (b) 14-139
          (c) 14-125
          (1) 14-083
          (1)(1) 14-092
          (1)(2) 14-092
          (1)(3)-(1)(6) 14-093
          (1)(7) 14-095
          (1)(8) 14-096
          (2) 14-093
          (3) 14-093
          (4) 14-093
      Art. 2 14-080
          (1) 14-116
          (1)(1) 14-100
          (1)(2) 14-101
          (1)(3) 14-102
          (1)(4) 14-099
          (1)(5) 14-098
          (1)(7) 14-111
          (1)(8) 14-106
          (1)(9) 14-104, 14-108, 14-111
          (1)(10). 14-103
          (1)(11). 14-113
          (1)(12). 14-109
          (1)(13). 14-106
          (1)(15). 14-112
          (1)(16). 14-112
          (1)(17). 14-104
          (1)(18). 14-104
          (3) 14-120
          (5) 14-122
      Art. 3 14-081
          (1) 14-110, 14-125
          (2) 14-104
          (3) 14-105
          (4) 14-106
          (5) 14-108
          (6) 14-099
          (7) 14-092
      Art. 4 14-128
          (a) 14-129
          (b) 14-129, 14-130, 14-134
          (c) 14-135
          (d) 14-136
          (e) 14-137
          (2)(a) 14-098
          (b) 14-112
      Art. 5 14-138
          (a) 14-139
          (b) 14-140
          (c) 14-141
          (1)(1) 14-089
          (1)(2) 14-090
          (1)(3) 14-091
          (1)(4) 14-088
          (1)(5) 14-078, 14-087
      Art. 6(1) 14-085
          (2) 14-085
          (3) 14-085
      Art. 8(1) 14-084
      Art. 9(2)(a) 14-125
          (2)(c) 14-125
          (2)(d) 14-125
      Art. 10(1). 14-078, 14-084

(2) 14-078, 14-084
(3) 14-078
(4) 14-084
(12). 14-093
(14). 14-083
(15). 14-085

Treaties & Conventions

Berne Convention 1886. . . . . 2-044, 6-314
  Art. 5 6-255
  Art. 5.2 6-267
  Art. 9 2-009
European Convention on Human Rights
  1950 12-013
  Art. 8 . . . . 5-111, 5-112, 5-115, 5-117
    (1) 5-113
    (2) 5-111, 5-113, 5-115
  Art. 10. . . . . 2-038, 2-080, 5-117
Treaty of Paris 1951 3-099
  Art. 8 3-100
World Convention 1952 6-314
Universal Copyright Convention 1952 . . 2-044
E.C. Treaty/Treaty of Rome 1957 12-045
  Art. 81. . . . . 14-001, 14-002, 14-026,
               14-082, 14-083, 14-107, 14-142,
    14-148, 14-149, 14-150, 14-152,14-155,
            14-157, 14-158, 14-161, 14-167,
            14-168, 14-171, 14-189, 14-199,
            14-204, 14-209, 14-210, 14-224,
               14-229, 14-233, 14-260

    (1). 14-064, 14-066, 14-068,
  14-069, 14-070, 14-073, 14-074, 14-075,
  14-074, 14-075, 14-080, 14-092, 14-153,
       14-157, 14-176, 14-177, 14-183,
       14-184, 14-185, 14-186, 14-187
    (2). 14-073
    (3). 14-073, 14-074, 14-074,
  14-075, 14-115, 14-148, 14-149, 14-180,
     14-183, 14-184, 14-185, 14-186,
              14-190, 14-236
  Art. 82. . . . . 14-002, 14-068, 14-155,
  14-192, 14-203, 14-204, 14-205, 14-207, 14-224,
         14-241, 14-246, 14-248, 14-260
  Art. 85(1). 14-069, 14-070
  Art. 86(c). 14-205
Brussels Convention 1968 (or Lugano Conven-
  tion 1988) 6-261, 10-039
  Art. 2 6-261
  Art. 5(3) 6-263, 6-264
  Art. 6(1) 6-261
Patent Cooperation Treaty 1970 2-139
European Patent Convention 1973 2-139
  Art. 52. 2-149
    (1) 2-160, 2-162
    (2) 2-159, 2-160, 2-161
    (c). 2-153, 2-155
    (3) 2-150, 2-153, 2-155
  Art. 54(2). 2-146
    (3) 2-146
  Art. 55. 2-148
  Art. 89. 2-146
Rome Convention 1980 . . . . . . 10-038, 10-126

Table of Foreign Legislation

Australia

Trade Practices Act 1974 3-090
Trade Marks Act 1995 3-091
Electronic Transactions Act 1999
    s.14 10-119
Broadcasting Services Amendment (Online
    Services) Act 1999 12-016

Canada

Trade-marks Act
    s. 4 3-108
    s. 9(1) 3-104
    s. 19 3-108
    s. 20 3-108
    s. 22 . . . . 3-108, 3-114, 3-116

Finland

Act on Unfair Business Practices 3-121
    art. 2 3-124
Trade Marks Act 3-121
Trade Names Act 3-121, 3-123

France

French Civil Code
    art. 1382 6-179
    art. 1383 6-179
Intellectual Property Code
    arts 122-4 2-081

Germany

Multimedia Act 1997 12-020

Holland

Benelux Trade Mark Act . .3-101, 6-270, 6-274
    s. 13A, para. 1(a) 3-083
Code of Civil Procedure
    art. 126 6-261
        (1) 6-261
        (3) 6-261

        (7) 6-261
Copyrights Act 1912 . . . . 2-087, 6-267,
                       6-271, 6-272
    art. 45(I) 6-272
    art. 47 6-267

Hong Kong

Bill of Rights Ordinance
    Chapter 383 6-205
Computer Crimes Ordinance 6-191
Control of Obscene and Indecent Articles
    Ordinance
    s. 2 6-188
Copyright Ordinance
    Chapter 528 6-211
    s. 26 6-212
    s. 118 6-189
Crimes Ordinance
    s. 24 6-188
    s. 161 6-189
Criminal Jurisdiction Ordinance 6-190
    6-191
    6-205
Defamation Ordinance
    Chapter 21 6-206
    s. 8 6-206
Electronic Transactions Ordinance
    s. 17 6-194
        (c) 6-197
    s. 19 . . . . 6-194, 6-197
        (4) 6-200
        (5)(b) 6-200
Gambling Ordinance
    Chapter 148 6-215
High Court Ordinance (Rules)
    Order 11 .6-193
        Rule 1(I)(d)(i) 6-200
Organised and Serious Crimes Ordinance
    s. 25 6-189
Reunification Ordinance
    Chapter 2601 6-223
Sexual Discrimination Ordinance
    Chapter 480 6-188
Theft Ordinance
    s. 23 6-188
Trade Descriptions Ordinance 3-149
Trade Marks Ordinance
    Chapter 43 6-214

Ireland

Electronic Commerce Act
  s. 31 3-027

Israel

Standard Terms Contracts Law
  s. 3 6-244
  s. 4(1) 6-244
Copyright Act 1911 6-237
  s. 1(2) 6-237, 6-238
  s. 2(2) 6-238
  s. 2(3) 6-239
  s. 8 6-239
  s. 35(1) 6-237
Copyright Ordinance 1934 6-237
Defamation Law 1965
  s. 2(b)(1) 6-233
      (2) 6-233
  s. 7 6-233
  s. 11 6-234
  s. 12 6-234
Contracts (General Parts) Law 1967
  s. 30 6-244
Civil Wrongs Ordinance (New Version) 1968
  s. 3 6-233
  s. 59 3-159
Property Law 1969 . . . . .3-156, 3-160
  s. 17 . . . . 3-160, 6-243
Chattels Law 1971 . . . . .3-156, 3-160
  s. 8 . . . . 3-160, 6-243
Trademarks Ordinance (New Version)
      1972 . . . . .3-156, 6-241, 6-243
  s. 1 3-157
      (3) 6-242
      (4) 6-242
  s. 46 6-241
  s. 46(A)
      (a) 6-242
      (b) 6-242
  s. 47 6-241
Contracts (General Parts) Law 1973 3-156
  s. 59 3-155
  s. 61(b) 3-155
Unjust Enrichment Law 1979 . . . .3-156, 3-163
  s. 1 3-163
Consumer Protection Law 1981 . .3-156, 3-164
  s. 7 . . . . 3-164, 6-235
      (a) 6-235
Unjust Enrichment Law 1981
  s. 1 6-243
Civil Law Procedure Regulations 1984
  r. 477. 6-226
  r. 500. . . . . 6-226, 6-230
      (6) 6-226, 6-227
      (7) 6-226, 6-227, 6-235
      (10) 6-226
Computer Law 1995
  s. 7 6-236
Copyright Ordinance (1996 amendment)
  s. 3
      b 6-238

f. 6-238
Commercial Torts Law 1999. . . . .3-156, 3-164
  s. 1 . . . . 3-159, 6-243
  s. 2 . . . . 3-164, 6-236
      (a) 6-235
      (b) 6-235
  s. 3 3-162
  s. 4 6-236

Japan

Civil Procedure Law
  art. 2. 6-248
  art. 5. 6-248
  art. 8. 6-248
  art. 15 6-248
Copyright Law. 6-255
  art. 23 6-256
Horei Law
  art. 11 6-253
      s. 1 6-252
      s. 2 6-252
      s. 3 6-252
Trade Mark Law
  art. 30 3-178
Unfair Competition Law 3-179

New Zealand

Trade Marks Act 1953 3-193
Fair Trading Act 1986 3-193
Fair Trading Act 1996 6-280
  s. 3 6-281
Defamation Act 1992 6-278
Consumer Guarantees Act 1993 6-282
Copyright Act 1994 6-284

Singapore

Copyright Act 3-197, 6-298
  s. 139 6-301
Trade Marks Act 3-197, 6-302

Sweden

Marketing Practices Act 3-204, 3-205
Penal Code. 6-307, 6-312
Trade Mark Act 3-204, 3-205
Trade Names Act. 3-204, 3-205

United States

Copyright Act 2-039, 2-103
Electronic Signatures in Global and National
      Commerce Act 10-115
Federal Arbitration Act 3-226
Federal Trademark Dilution Act. 3-230
Uniform Electronic Transactions Act . .10-115
Communications Act 1934 6-345
Trade Mark Act 1946 (Lanham Act). . . .3-225

s. 43 3-227
Computer Fraud and Abuse Act 1986 . . 2-103
Utah Digital Signature Act 1995 10-113
Communications Decency Act 1996 . . 12-010,
                                   12-012, 12-090
Digital Millennium Copyright Act
    1998 . . . . 2-038, 2-040, 2-057,
                        2-107, 2-110, 6-346
    Title I 2-040
    Title II 2-104, 6-345
Anticycybersquatting Consumer Protection
    Act 1999 . . . . .3-224, 3-227
Uniform Computer Information Transactions
    Act 1999

s. 203(4) 6-198
Online Copyright Infringement Liability Lim-
    itation Act 2001
§ 202 6-345
§ 512 6-345
    (a) 6-345
    (b) 6-345
    (c) 6-345
    (d) 6-345
    (k)(1) 6-345
        (A) 6-345
        (1). 6-345
        (i) 6-345

1

Overview of the Internet

1.1 The Internet: what is it?

The Internet is often described as a network of networks. That is true but incomplete. A   **1–001**
full description has to encompass the Internet's physical parts, its functions and the
players who create and use it.

Physically, the Internet is a collection of packet computer networks, glued together by a
set of software protocols called TCP/IP (Transmission Control Protocol/Internet
Protocol) (see Figure 1.1 below). These protocols allow the networks and the computers
attached to them to communicate and (using a common address system) to find other
computers attached to the Internet. The core of the Internet was originally a set of high
capacity backbone networks in the USA. Over the years many thousands of other
networks around the world have adopted Internet protocols and linked into the Internet,
so that today it is virtually impossible to identify the physical boundaries of the Internet.[1]
These boundaries are further blurred by private internets ("intranets"): internal company
networks connected to the Internet which make use of Internet protocols and Internet-
compliant software such as Web browsers. Intranets are hidden from the public Internet
by a protective "firewall", configured so that the intranet cannot (or should not) be
accessed from outside. An "extranet" denotes an intranet that selected outsiders, such as
suppliers and customers, may access.

Links to the Internet are also being made from personal organisers, telephones, pagers,
television sets and other devices beyond the bounds of the traditional business and
personal computer markets. The Internet now can really be described only in terms of the
features that bind its components together—common software protocols and addressing
systems—and its public accessibility.

From the point of view of the domestic end-user the unique feature of the Internet is   **1-002**
the ability, during one telephone connection to a local Internet access provider, to hop
around the world from one Internet site to another using one piece of Internet-compliant
software. The precursors of the Internet—traditional bulletin boards and on-line
services—often required dedicated user software; and the user had to terminate the
telephone connection and redial to access a new service. On the Internet, instead of
having to dial separate telephone numbers for each on-line service, the user needs only
one telephone number for the Internet access provider. The user then types or clicks a
relatively simple address to access each Internet site. The corporate user, accessing the

Figure 1.1 The Internet—a typical arrangement

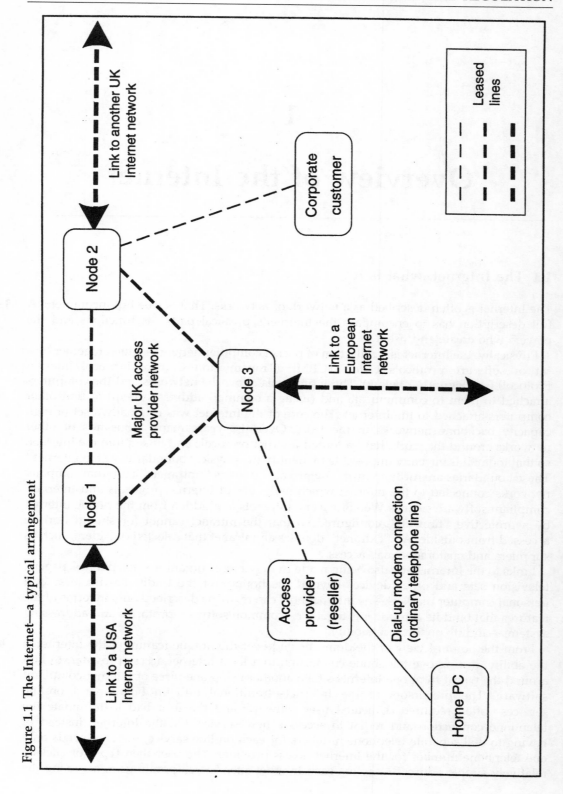

Internet from the company network behind a firewall, can browse a site on the Internet as if it were part of the company network.

While an underlying collection of networks makes up the Internet, various applications designed to work with Internet protocols provide facilities to users of the Internet. The more significant applications are the World Wide Web, electronic mail, file downloading (using file transfer protocol (ftp)) and Usenet newsgroups.

Internet e-mail is the oldest and still probably the most widespread application of the Internet. The Internet form of e-mail address has become universally popular, with Internet e-mail addresses now common on company letterheads and business cards. On the Internet, mail is addressed using the form "joebloggs@yourco.com", where "joebloggs" is the name of the individual and "yourco.com" is the domain name of the host at which Joe Bloggs has his Internet account. The host (a computer accessible from the Internet which stores data) might be a commercial Internet access provider, or the company or institution for which Joe Bloggs works. The domain name is the plain language address of a computer or network on the Internet. **1–003**

Ftp is the protocol used to download a software program or other file from an Internet site to the user's own computer. Ftp is normally invoked automatically when a user selects a file to download from, say, a Web site to his computer.

Usenet newsgroups are public discussion forums, to which users can post "articles" (*i.e.* public messages) and contribute to a continuing thread of messages on a particular topic. Newsgroups are organised into thousands of separate subject areas, ranging from the serious and the frivolous to the dubious. **1-004**

The World Wide Web is a system of joining documents to each other across the Internet by hypertext links. The Web, on which the rapid growth of the Internet since 1994 has been built, is described in more detail in paragraph 1.2.2 below.

We should also mention Internet Relay Chat (IRC) and similar real time messaging technologies. These allow participants to converse in real time on their screens, the conversation scrolling up the screen as the discussion continues. This is a much more ephemeral medium than newsgroups, where users can read and reply to posted messages days or weeks later.

1.2 The Internet: who's who and what do they do?

We now look at the building-blocks of the Internet and how they fit together conceptually, physically and commercially. **1–005**

Imagine the Internet as a play. The key to the plot is to identify the players and understand their roles. A player on the Internet often performs more than one role. When determining the legal consequences of activities on the Internet, it is important to identify which roles the person is performing. For instance, what is generically known as an Internet service provider may perform some or all of the roles of network provider, host and access provider. It is necessary to look behind the outward description of the player, identify each of its actual roles and apply the relevant law to that activity.

1.2.1 Infrastructure and network providers

The core infrastructure of the Internet consists largely of routers or switches (computers designed to receive and forward packets of data), hosts (which store programs and data) **1–006** and pipes (telecommunications connections which link the hosts and routers together). Hosts, routers and switches are owned by various government and private organisations whose computers are fully connected into the Internet. Many of the pipes tend to be owned by telecommunications companies, who typically either provide Internet-compliant routing and switching facilities themselves or lease capacity to network providers who add those facilities to create sections of the Internet. The telecommunications companies are of great importance to the Internet and are intimately involved in it. Many telecommunications companies have expanded from infrastructure into network and Internet service provision. Originally, the American telecommunications companies such as Sprint and MCI were the most important to the Internet. Now, with the increasing international take-up of the Internet, non-U.S. companies such as BT are also heavily involved.

1–007   Network providers have both physical links to and contractual relations with other networks and their providers. The physical connection (which may be a bilateral link to the other network, or at a special purpose multilateral traffic exchange centre such as MAE-East in Washington DC, or LINX in London) enables traffic to flow direct from one network to the next. The contractual arrangement (often known as a "peering agreement") governs the exchange of traffic between the networks. Considerable problems were originally posed by Appropriate Use Policies, whereby certain networks (typically government-funded ones) prohibited commercial traffic. These problems are now a thing of the past as the Internet infrastructure has become privately funded.

1–008   The pricing aspects of peering arrangements are noteworthy. The Internet model has been mutual exchange or a flat-rate charge for connection to a network, irrespective of the amount of traffic passed across the connection. This model extends to the typical flat rate end-user charge. Concerns have been expressed that if access providers were asked to pay for their connections on a per-packet basis, they would have to abandon the flat rate for the end-user. In any event, access providers are increasingly adopting differing charging structures in order to differentiate themselves. Concerns have also been expressed at suggestions that the international settlements system applicable to traditional voice telecommunications traffic might be applied to Internet traffic in place of a free market.

If there is no direct physical connection and peering agreement in place between two networks, the traffic has to find another route. Messages use the Internet protocols to route around gaps or blockages. So a user in London accessing a site down the road could find that the message is routed via America.

1–009   This can happen if the user's Internet access provider is, say, a U.S. company with an international network but no peering arrangement with another English network. The user dials in to an English node of the access provider's network, but the network's gateway to the rest of the Internet is in the USA. The message has to go from the user to the London node, across the access provider's network to America, transfer to another Internet-compliant U.S. network, travel back across the Atlantic to another English network and thence to the target English site. The route, however, is unpredictable. So not only is responsibility for ensuring safe delivery of a message diffused among various networks, but the identity of those networks cannot necessarily be predicted in advance. This poses obvious problems if the sender wishes to have one person take legal responsibility for end-to-end delivery of the message. This has led some global corporations or alliances to build international networks offering, at a premium price, end-to-end transport of Internet traffic within their networks.

1–010   The capacity, or "bandwidth", of the pipes which carry Internet traffic affects the amount of data which can be carried and the speed at which it is delivered to the user. While the backbones of the Internet are typically high bandwidth, the last link to the home user is typically a low bandwidth connection. The home user often accesses the Internet via a modem and an ordinary telephone line. Although these are increasingly fast, they are still at the bottom end of the capacity scale. A commercial user may have a higher capacity leased line or ISDN (Integrated Services Digital Network) connection. Academic institutions are often connected directly into high bandwidth elements of the Internet such as JANET (the United Kingdom academic network). Some commercial users also have high capacity connections to the Internet. ADSL (Asymmetric Digital Subscriber Line), a new technology which allows fast transmission over ordinary copper telephone lines, is now being made available to the domestic market.

1.2.2 Content providers

Content providers are among the most important people on the Internet. They range from multinational companies to individuals. The Internet may have approximated more closely than anything to Marshall McLuhan's adage that the medium is the message, but even on the Internet content is king.   **1–011**

Content comes in many forms. It divides generally into real-time and downloadable content. Real-time content is that which can be viewed or heard as the user accesses it, either delivered in batches or by maintaining a continuous stream of data. A page of text on the World Wide Web is, in a sense, an example of real-time content. It appears on screen as the data, sent in batches, reaches the PC from the Internet site. Graphics also appear in real time, but more slowly because of higher bandwidth requirements.

Many developments in Internet applications are aimed at expanding the range of real-time applications and overcoming constraints imposed by lack of bandwidth. Audio (speech and music), video, animation, video-conferencing and voice telephony are examples of real-time applications in which great progress has been made. However, the paucity of bandwidth in the last connection to the home is a real hindrance to such applications, especially video (streaming video is receivable through a domestic modem, although to nowhere near the quality of television). They also tend to make greater demands on Internet capacity generally, because of the need to maintain a more or less continuous flow of data across the networks. This may also create a need for more sophisticated protocols than current TCP/IP. This is not a problem with downloadable content, which can be transmitted in bursts with no effect other than on the speed of download.   **1–012**

Downloadable content takes the form of a file which can be copied from the Internet site to the user's own computer. The user, once off-line from the Internet, uses his own applications to read, view or play the file. The Internet protocol ftp (file transfer protocol) is typically used to download files from the Internet. Content can range from simple text files, graphics and video to computer programs, updates and patches. Content may be free or paid for.

The Internet application that has made content accessible and interesting to the average user is the World Wide Web. The Web is a hypertext Internet application which allows the user, during the course of one telephone connection and using familiar graphical software interfaces, to point click and jump across the Internet, leaping from one seductively designed Web site to the next. Before the Web, reading and downloading files from the Internet required expert ability with arcane software.   **1–013**

The Web creates a mesh of software links between documents. Clicking on a hypertext link in a Web document can take the user to another part of the same document, to another document on the same computer, or to a document on another computer on the other side of the world. This is made possible by the addressing scheme of the Internet (which enables each computer to be uniquely identified) and the HTTP (HyperText Transmission Protocol), HTML (HyperText Mark-up Language) and other protocols and document formats which underlie the Web. By means of these a unique Uniform Resource Locator (URL) is created for each document on the Web. Creating a link is simply a matter of coding selected text in the document so that it points at the target URL. The user sees the text as highlighted and clicking on it takes the user to the document represented by the target URL. A link may be created to the home page of the target site, or to a page within it (a practice known as deep-linking which, while not always controversial, has sometimes led to litigation).

An innovation called frames has added further sophistication to the Web. A site using frames can be designed so that when the user clicks on a link to an external site, he sees the contents of the external site within a border generated by the original site. So frames provide an opportunity to encase someone else's site in advertising generated by the linking site. This use of frames is controversial and has led to litigation in the USA.

The Web achieves a Holy Grail of computing: the ability to browse through documents. It allows the user to browse not just one document, but a world-wide collection of documents. Hence programs that access the Web are known as Web browsers.

1–014   The growth in commercial activity on the Internet is built around the Web. Any self–respecting company has a Web site. Many of these are essentially still promotional. But a rapidly increasing number of sites offer electronic commerce facilities, in the retail (business to consumer "B2C") sector using payment by credit card. There are many news services, both on-line versions of existing publications and entirely new titles, and on-line banking services. Any "soft" product seems to be a good candidate for selling or supporting via the Web: music, computer software, news, books and almost any sort of service. Perhaps surprisingly, some high-value "hard" products have also proven successful, PCs being an obvious example. Sites enabling users to shop around car dealers have proven popular. In the wake of the dot-com boom, a few "pure-play" B2C Internet companies have survived to face a challenging future. In the business to business (B2B) sector, one of the first serious uses of the Web was by a global corporation that moved its purchasing activities to a Web site through which its suppliers could bid for contracts. Currently, B2B exchanges are exciting considerable interest.

1–015   The legal consequences of the Web can be subtle. Boundaries of ownership and responsibility are blurred. The traditional paper document or book exists as a self-contained unit, easily distinguishable from the next one on the shelf. The Web takes the covers off the books and stitches the pages together. So new boundary markers have to be put in place if the user is not to be confused about whose document he is looking at. Strong branding of sites, entry pages, exit pages and ownership notices are becoming common on the Web. Questions also arise as to whether linking to other sites can generate legal liabilities in respect of content on the target site, such as for defamation or copyright infringement. These questions have to be considered separately in the context of each right and liability.

Lawyers also need to appreciate that the site proprietor has limited control over the appearance of the Web site to the user. Browsers may interpret the HTML tags in numerous different ways, so that for instance point sizes of text may differ. These may also be affected by, for instance, the screen resolution at which the user is accessing the site. At the extreme, the user may not "see" the text at all. Some software translates the text of a Web site into audio, for the benefit of blind users. All these issues can assume especial importance where laws or regulations require matters to be brought to the notice of the user in a particular way, or specify the appearance of forms which the user has to complete. While the latest versions of HTML are tending to afford the site designer greater control over the appearance of the site on the user's screen, these matters will remain important.

1.2.3 Hosts

A host is a digital storage place accessible via the Internet. The type of data stored on the host can vary from computer programs to text documents to graphics or any other kind of data. The way in which the files are stored can also vary, the Internet protocol used to store them dictating the software needed to access it, such as ftp or the World Wide Web. A host may also act as a storage place for Usenet newsgroups, or for holding Internet e-mail in subscribers' mailboxes. Hosts are often also referred to as servers, thus mail server or news server.   **1–016**

   The owner of a host has a spectrum of possible relationships to the data stored on the host. It may own and actively control all of the data, as in the case of a company that self-hosts an ftp resource. At the other end of the range the host owner may have only the most tenuous connection with the stored content. A Usenet news server is a good example. Usenet is a system of thousands of discussion groups on a huge variety of topics, to which anyone can post a public message. The Usenet host receives automatic updating newsgroup feeds from other Usenet hosts. It receives postings direct from its own subscribers, sending out its own updates to other Usenet hosts.

   The Usenet host in practice has only two main potential areas of control: selecting the newsgroups for which it takes feeds and monitoring postings from its own subscribers. The other main choice it has is over how long to retain postings on the server. Some servers "scroll off" postings after a few days. Until the advent of domain name disputes (see Chapter 3) Usenet discussion groups and traditional proprietary on-line discussion groups gave rise to more litigation activity, mostly concerned with defamation, than any other area of the Internet.   **1–017**

   Between the ends of the spectrum are numerous variations. A host may store its own material or material held on behalf of other parties, for free or for reward as a commercial service. The material may be ephemeral or it may be permanent. The host owner may be actively involved in the process of placing the material on the host, for instance if it provides Web design and HTML coding services; or it may do nothing more than provide a storage area, bandwidth and a URL, taking no part in the selection and design of the materials. The host may promote itself as a desirable area to visit such as an interactive shopping mall, an on-line magazine, or some other form of umbrella site with a unifying identity; or promotion may be left entirely up to individual content providers, so that each collection of resources on the host appears to the world at large entirely separate and unconnected with any other.

   The legal responsibilities of the host will vary according to the exact nature of the role that it has assumed. It has, to date, been impossible to generalise about those responsibilities. They have had to be analysed separately for each type of right and liability, in the light of the actual role that the host owner plays. Liability for defamation has had its own set of rules, liability for copyright infringement another set, trade mark   **1–018** infringement another and so on. The determining factors for one species of liability do not necessarily map on to another species. However, this is starting to change. The Electronic Commerce Directive, which has to be implemented before January 17, 2002, will create uniform liability thresholds for hosts and conduits (*i.e.* network and access providers) across a wide range of liabilities, at least for damages.

One specialised variety of host plays an important role in the functioning of the Internet: the domain name server. The domain name is the plain language address of an entity on the Internet. The domain name has the form "yourinc.com", "yourltd.co.uk", "youruni.ac.uk", etc. Computers accessing the Internet have to have a way of finding which computer corresponds to which domain name. So there is a distributed system of domain name servers, or simply name servers, which hold frequently updated databases of domain names. There are many thousands of name servers, ultimately taking their cue from "source of authority" name servers which hold, or can identify, authoritative lists of domain names. Domain names are allocated by various organisations connected with the Internet Society.

1–019   As well as the list of domain names, a name server holds the IP (Internet Protocol) addresses that correspond to the domain names. The IP address has the form 194.72.244.100. This is the address understood by Internet-compliant computers. So when a computer is asked to access "yourco.com", it looks up the domain name in its local name server, finds out the IP address and uses that to send its query out over the Internet.

IP addresses are understood by routers and switches, the computer way-stations around the Internet that receive and forward messages. Each router contains routing tables which store the locations of the networks connected to the Internet and thus enable the router to know where to send the message. For instance, if a router receives a message and discerns from the destination IP address that the destination network is directly connected to the router's local network, it will send the message to that network. If there is no direct connection it will forward the message on to a network closer to the destination network. Routers may contain instructions to bar traffic to or from particular networks, or to carry only traffic received from certain networks.

Inclusion on databases of domain names and on routing tables is vital to maintaining a presence on the Internet. These addressing systems are of particular interest to those seeking to enforce intellectual property rights, who may want to explore ways of trying to isolate or close down a pirate site. National authorities bent on compelling access providers to block access to objectionable sites also take a keen interest in Internet addressing systems.

1.2.4 Administrators

1–020   The glue that holds the Internet together, and ultimately the only feature common to all its disparate parts, is the set of Internet protocols. These evolved and developed over time under the guidance of various bodies associated with the Internet Society, who promulgated Internet protocols and guided other aspects of Internet evolution. The effectiveness of these protocols depended on the accepted legitimacy of these bodies, and the people associated with them, within the Internet community. In new and fast-developing fields such as the World Wide Web the committee method of promulgating protocols came under strain as software vendors, especially in the "browser wars" between Netscape and Microsoft, adopted extensions to existing standards before they were promulgated. The increasing pace of commercialisation of the Internet has continued to cause *de facto* standards to evolve continuously out of competitive activity, in tandem with the standards activities of bodies such as the World Wide Web Consortium (W3C).

Until late 1998 or early 1999 one influential body, IANA (the Internet Assigned Numbers Authority, largely synonymous with the late Dr Jon Postel) performed two especially important co-ordinating functions. These related to identifying computers connected to the Internet and giving them unique names and addresses. The domain name system and IP address system, for the co-ordination of which IANA was mainly responsible until the transition to ICANN (the Internet Corporation for Assigned Names and Numbers) are described in Chapter 3. These systems are both crucial to the operation of the Internet. There have been concerns that in the foreseeable future the Internet will run out of domain names and numerical addresses. New domain spaces have been introduced in 2001. Schemes such as a new version of IP addressing which will provide many more IP addresses and more facilities than the current system are under consideration.

1–021

The actual allocation of blocks of IP addresses to individual organisations is carried out by the American Registry for Internet Numbers (ARIN) for the Americas (North and South), sub-Saharan Africa and the Caribbean; by Réseaux IP Européens Network Coordination Centre (RIPE) for Europe and surrounding areas and by Asia-Pacific Network Information Center (APNIC) for the Asia Pacific region.

1.2.5 Access providers

The first access providers were academic institutions and government bodies, with high capacity Internet-compliant links to other such bodies. They provided Internet access to staff, faculty and students who had access to the institution's own network.

1–022

The typical access provider is now a commercial organisation selling Internet access to home and commercial users. Commercial access providers are commonly known as Internet service providers, or ISPs. ISPs range from large organisations (sometimes telephone companies) with their own geographically dispersed networks, local dial-up numbers (POPs, or Points of Presence) around the country and numerous connections to other Internet-compliant networks, to small providers who provide one or two local telephone numbers and a single connection into someone else's network. These small providers are often in effect local re-sellers of capacity on a large ISP's network. It is increasingly common for ISPs to strike deals whereby a telephone company provides local telephone numbers for the ISP around the country. The calls are then routed through the telephone company's network to the ISP, the caller paying only for a local rate call. This type of arrangement is known as providing "virtual POPs".

ISPs will provide a variety of services, ranging from a cheap dial-up account suitable for the home user, to a permanent leased-line connection aimed at commercial use. The typical dial-up account-holder will pay a fixed monthly access fee and will pay the local call charges on top. The leased-line account-holder has no usage-based charges at all, as the leased line provides capacity at a fixed rental. Leased lines are expensive, so are attractive only to high-volume users such as businesses. Other variations such as ISDN connections are also possible.

1-023

ISPs often provide additional services, such as Web site hosting and design. This is an example of someone on the Internet playing more than one role. The access provider role is to provide facilities to communicate with the Internet. The access provider who stores Web pages for its customers, or maintains a collection of Usenet newsgroups, is adding the role of host to that of access provider. Similarly, an access provider generally maintains its own domain name server (DNS). This is in theory not a necessary part of providing Internet access, as a customer can configure its Internet client software to access a domain name server elsewhere if the access provider does not maintain its own DNS. In practice, an access provider will provide client software to its customer, pre-set to use the access provider's domain name servers.

The multi-role Internet Service Provider

Access provider

ReadyNet Ltd is an Internet Service Provider. As an access provider (or conduit), it leases from a network provider a telecommunications link providing 2Mb per second of bandwidth (capacity). This connects to a larger backbone provider, which in turn has a transatlantic link to the U.S. Internet and links to other European networks. ReadyNet offers a service whereby for a flat monthly fee, users can dial up its computers, access the Internet and send and receive e-mail.

Software distributor

ReadyNet provides software for its users to install on their PCs to enable them to dial up the service, browse the Web and send and receive e-mail.

Host

ReadyNet provides free Web space for its dial-up customers and offers to design, host and maintain Web sites for its business customers. It also stores e-mail sent and received by its customers. It acts as a domain name system server for its customers and hosts a selection of Usenet newgroups. It also hosts discussion forums on its own Web site.

Cache

ReadyNet eases the load on its bandwidth by storing on its own servers temporary copies of frequently accessed pages from third party Web sites. User requests are diverted to those pages instead of being routed across further telecommunications links to the third party Web site.

Content Provider

ReadyNet has created its own content-rich Web site for its users, offering news, opinions and many other content items. Most of these are bought in from third parties.

1–024   The Californian case of *Religious Technology Center v. Netcom On-line Communication Services Inc.*[2] provides a good example of the multiple roles often performed by Internet service providers. Netcom is introduced in the judgment as a large Internet access provider. But the question of its liability for alleged copyright infringement in fact turned around a detailed analysis of its role as a Usenet host. This case is discussed in more detail in Chapter 2.

Although the terms Internet service provider and ISP are in universal usage, they are potentially confusing because they do not distinguish between the underlying roles of access provider, host and others. In this book we will therefore, where appropriate, eschew the use of "Internet service provider" and "ISP" in favour of the terminology introduced in this chapter. Where those terms are used, the reader should be alert to understand which role or roles are under discussion.

1.2.6 Navigation providers

A common complaint about the Internet is that the content is distinguished by quantity rather than quality; or if there is quality content out there, there is no easy way either of finding it or of knowing the quality of what you have found when you get there.

1–025

Navigation providers, close relations of content providers and hosts, act as signposts to quality information. They may take many forms. Umbrella sites such as online shopping malls are effectively navigation providers, attracting customers to their collection of selected retailers who pay for space on the mall. So are content collators and customisers. These range from relatively conventional on-line newspapers, to the now common sites which allow the user to select categories of news or other content, or which watch the user's reading habits and display selected content based on that. Such sites may produce some of their own content, but are more likely to have done deals with content providers enabling them to select from a pool of quality-assured information.

Currently, some of the most important navigation providers are search engines and directories. These catalogue resources across the Internet, so that the user can either perform a keyword search for relevant sites, or consult a structured directory for sites of interest. Many of these have become "portals", designed to be the user's permanent gateway to the Web.

1–026

As navigation providers compete and gain reputations for effective sifting of wheat from chaff, so they have become some of the strongest brands on the Internet. As such they can command higher prices for third party advertising and sponsorship on their sites. Search engines and directories are probably the best known sites on the Internet at present, and among the most successful in attracting banner advertising. Content sifted by navigation providers may be stored on hosts owned and operated by someone else. Thus navigation providers will tend to be at the centre of some of the more complex sets of contractual relationships to be found on the Internet.

1.2.7 Transaction facilitators

The advent of commerce on the Internet has stimulated investment in ways and means of overcoming perceived shortcomings: mainly lack of security and inability to identify with certainty whom you are communicating with. As these problems are addressed, so vendors are proposing and licensing various security and digital signature products. Trusted intermediaries who would verify identities and credit standing are beginning to emerge. As these systems develop, so there is likely to emerge a role of transaction facilitator who, whether by licensing software or active involvement at the time of the transaction, reduces the transaction risk to an acceptable level.

1-027

1.3 Broadband networks—goodbye to the information superhighway

1–028   The information superhighway (also known as the Global Information Infrastructure, the infobahn and others) never did exist. It was a political artefact. When a broadband network providing the features of the promised information superhighway does come into existence it will most likely be an extension of the Internet.

The main features that will distinguish a broadband network from the Internet are capacity, especially in the last link to the home, the ability to sustain continuous data streams and the ability to plan the provision of bandwidth. Parts of the Internet have very high capacity, but only in the way that the trunk routes in voice telephone networks have high capacity. Some end-users themselves have high capacity links to the Internet. But while the typical home user still accesses the Internet via a modem and a copper wire connection, the ability to provide high-bandwidth content such as graphics, audio and (especially) video will remain limited. Various schemes to solve this problem have been mooted or are under development: optical fibre into the home by telephone companies, co-axial or optical fibre from cable companies, and wireless and satellite reception. Technologies such as ADSL, which squeeze compressed video down existing copper wire, are coming on stream. The next promised land is third generation (3G) mobile telephone networks, which will provide broadband mobile data connectivity. Whatever the method, broadband technologies all have the object of allowing instant, real-time, interactive audio, graphics and video to be provided to the consumer.

1–029   While the Internet grew up, until the mid-1990s, almost unnoticed by regulatory authorities, broadband is in their sights even before it exists. Once real-time video is contemplated, interactive networks start to resemble and impinge upon the highly regulated mass-market of television to the living room. That being of more interest to the regulators than the hobbyist in the back room, the scene is set for regulatory confusion as the two worlds collide and merge. That confusion is epitomised by the continuing struggle of policy-makers to understand that content on the Internet is most akin to personal speech, and should be subject only to the laws applicable to personal speech rather than the more restrictive content rules and discretionary regulation historically applied to broadcast content.

1–030   Two other worlds are also in collision: the computer industry and the consumer electronics industry. The consumer electronics industry has tended to produce dumb but reliable equipment: televisions, video recorders and so on. The computer industry produces dumb but reliable hardware, intelligent but relatively unreliable software, and has tended to sell it to customers who regard trying to get it all to work as a stimulating and satisfying challenge. If the information superhighway moves the focus of interactive applications from the back room to the living room, the living room consumer will demand the simplicity and reliability of consumer electronics equipment. In advance of the broadband network attempts are already under way to bring the Internet into the living room. Set-top boxes are adding Internet connectivity to television sets. Whether these ventures will be successful in opening up a new market remains to be seen.

---

1. For a stunning collection of visualisations of the structure of the Internet, see www.cybergeography.org (especially the topology and geography sections).
2. November 21, 1995, ND Cal.

2

Copyright, Patents and Confidential Information

2.1 Introduction

Intellectual property laws govern the subsistence and scope of property rights in the intangible fruits of human creativity and labour: writing, drama, music and art; craft, inventions and knowledge. Appropriately defined property rights help to transform those fruits into money, another intangible. Digitisation enables both the raw fruits and their monetary products to be reduced to bits of information stored electronically and routed around networks.

2–001

The laws of intangibles have to adapt to cope with this new digital form of subject matter. Chapter 11 describes the interaction of the Internet and the laws of money. This and the next chapter address the areas of intellectual property law of most relevance to the Internet. Copyright and its neighbouring rights are probably the first intellectual property rights which spring to mind. Copyright is the nearest thing to a "bit right". However, patent law cannot be ignored in the increasingly technical environment of the Internet. Confidential information has also to be considered. Trade marks and branding, considered in Chapter 3, are a vital aspect of trading on the Internet and are key to resolving disputes over domain names.

2.2 Copyright—general

2.2.1 Digitisation and dematerialisation of information

Perhaps the most far-reaching aspect of the computer revolution has been the digitisation of information. Traditionally, most information has been transmitted by graphic means, such as letters or drawings, or by waves, such as sound waves or electro-magnetic signals. Computers can only operate on binary numbers, so information must be reduced to such digital form if it is to be manipulated by a computer.

2–002

The development of inexpensive computing power and bandwidth has made it advantageous to transform many kinds of information from analogue to digital form for transmission. We have already seen the digital CD replace the vinyl record, and telephone conversations are increasingly transmitted digitally. As more information is converted to bits, so previously distinct forms of transmitted content—radio, TV, telephone—become varieties of digital data, capable of being carried over the same networks.

There are two main advantages of digitisation: copying and transmission can be made to take place without degradation, so that every copy is perfect; and copies can be made very quickly and cheaply. So a document can be sent via the Internet to potentially millions of people for only the relatively low transmission costs. While this has obvious benefits for humankind, it also makes possible copyright infringement on a scale previously unknown.

Convergence of primary and secondary infringement

2–003   The application of traditional copyright law to open public global networks such as the Internet is bedevilled by copyright's roots being in the protection of information contained in tangible media such as books. Distribution of the information contained in those media required two separate, slow and costly steps: copying from one tangible medium to another, followed by transport of the new copy to a distant location. Thus the acts of copying and distribution were clearly distinguishable and formed the basis of the distinction made in copyright law between acts of primary infringement (such as copying), for which the defendant is strictly liable irrespective of knowledge, and acts of secondary infringement (such as distribution) for which the defendant is liable only if he is fixed with some degree of guilty knowledge.

The advent of digital technology has overturned the underlying assumptions of the original law. Digitisation has caused the cost of copying to fall to virtually zero. With the advent of digital communications networks such as the Internet the cost of distribution has also become zero and the speed of distribution instantaneous.

2–004   What is more, the distinction originally drawn between copying and distribution has blurred. In the attempt to apply copyright law to the age of computers, and in particular to infringement of copyright in computer programs, the idea was born that infringement could occur through the creation of a transient copy in the RAM (random access memory) of a computer. In the United Kingdom this is at present reflected in section 17(2) and (6) of the Copyright, Designs and Patents Act 1988. However, any distribution of a copyright work over an electronic network inevitably results in the creation of at least a transient copy at the receiving end, and possibly further transient copies at points in between. In this context the distinction between primary and secondary infringement starts to break down. Every act of electronic distribution is also an act of copying if a transient copy counts as infringement.

Extending the control of the copyright owner

2–005   A further consequence of categorising the making of a transient copy as a restricted act is to make reading the copyright work an act potentially controllable by the copyright owner. The person who reads a book does not commit any restricted act. A person who reads an electronic work necessarily creates a transient copy in the course of doing so and therefore potentially falls under the control of the original copyright owner.

The copyright legislators have had in the past to develop copyright laws to take account of yesterday's new media: the film, broadcast television, radio and cable television industries. These were in some respects precursors to networks such as the Internet. But they lacked both interactivity and the plummeting costs of electronic document creation which render every individual user of the Internet potentially both a reader and a publisher.

Digitisation

The older aspects of copyright law based on tangible media are difficult to apply to the   **2–006**
Internet because of dematerialisation. The newer provisions relating to broadcast and
cable transmission may potentially apply to the Internet in unforeseen ways, because the
provisions tended to be formulated with particular communication technologies and
distribution models in mind.

Lack of material objects is not the only problem for intellectual property rights owners
posed by the digitisation of information. Information in digital form is much more easily
manipulated and adapted than traditional forms of information, and the changes are
much harder to detect. In the days of typewriters if the typist made a mistake it could
only be corrected by painting over the incorrect characters with correcting fluid or
something similar and then typing in the correct characters. As this correction was easily
detected with the naked eye, the only way to produce a "clean" copy was to retype the
whole page. Now, with word processing software, mistakes are banished for ever with a
few keystrokes. Hollywood provides much more sophisticated examples of manipulation
of digital information. The dinosaurs in *Jurassic Park* were images created in a computer
and combined with film images of human actors in such a way that the viewer is unable
to detect the difference. Indeed, the technology has reached such a level that even human
actors can be recreated by computer. When the star was accidentally killed half way
through shooting the film *The Crow*, the film was completed using images of the actor
created by digital manipulation of existing footage.

Such digital manipulation can make it very difficult to detect, or to prove, infringement   **2–007**
of the copyright in the work which has been used as the starting point. Would we
recognise the Mona Lisa if all the colours were altered and the face changed by
"morphing" to that of the sitter as a child, albeit still with that mysterious smile? If the
use of the original work is detected, the mere fact that the original has been changed does
not prevent copyright infringement, as one of the rights given to the author is the right to
distribute modified copies of the work.

These issues make uncertain the intellectual property protection of information
distributed via the Internet and similar information highways. If there is no real
protection, and owners of works which have required a great deal of effort and expense
to create find that electronic distribution means that they are unable to obtain a
reasonable return for their works, perhaps because of widespread unpaid copying, they
will be reluctant to use this method of distribution. The Internet and other information
highways will not develop as hoped if commercially important information is withheld
from them.

2.2.2 The WIPO Treaties

It is no surprise, in the light of these developments, that the challenge of seeking to apply   **2–008**
traditional copyright laws to the Internet has provoked considerable international
activity. This culminated in a diplomatic conference held under the auspices of the World
Intellectual Property Organisation in December 1996, out of which came agreed texts for
two treaties (on copyright and on performances and phonograms) intended to adapt
copyright law to the challenges of the digital age. A third treaty on establishing a *sui
generis* database right failed to achieve consensus.

Some of the main features of the treaty on copyright are: **2–009**

- The establishment of a digital transmission right, described in the treaty as the exclusive right of the authors of literary and artistic works to authorise any communication to the public of their works, by wire or wireless means, including the making available to the public of their works in such a way that members of the public may access these works from a place and at a time individually chosen by them.

- Contracting Parties are at liberty to provide for limitations of, or exceptions to, rights in certain special cases that do not conflict with a normal exploitation of the work and do not unreasonably prejudice the legitimate interests of the author.

- Contracting Parties shall provide adequate legal protection and effective legal remedies against circumvention of copy-protection technology.

No consensus was reached on an article concerning whether temporary and incidental reproduction should be included in the reproduction right. No such article was therefore included in the treaty. After debate a substantial majority agreed the following statement to be included in the records of the conference: "...that it is understood that the storage of a protected work in digital form in an electronic medium constitutes a reproduction within the meaning of Article 9 of the Berne Convention." It was recorded that the question of what constitutes storage was left open.

2.2.3 Europe—the Copyright in the Information Society Directive

History

2–010　In July 1995 the European Commission published a Green Paper entitled "Copyright and Related Rights in the Information Society". In the introduction the Commission stated that full development of the information society in Europe would require harmonisation of laws, including intellectual property, to ensure that right holders would make material available while balancing the interests of users. The "information society" is a dreadful piece of Commission jargon which has not only polluted the copyright field, but also underlies the E.U. Electronic Commerce Directive.

2–011　The Green Paper identified certain issues key to the application of copyright to the new technology. These were the new services, in particular the effects of digitisation and the interactive nature of such services, the new market structures and the importance of cross-border services. These raised a number of legal issues, including the identification of the "author", the applicability of the traditional concept of "originality" as a condition for protection, the concept of "first publication" when a work can be simultaneously disseminated world-wide, the concept of "fair use", and the scope of exclusive rights giving the right to prohibit exploitation of the work. The paper then went on to examine the existing law in certain key areas and to pose a series of questions relating to each of those areas.

2–012　A Communication from the European Commission in November 1996 following the consultation process on the Green Paper concluded that rights in "on-demand" services should be protected by a further harmonised right of "communication to the public". The Commission noted that the question of "private use" exceptions to such a right was controversial, with right holders suggesting that such an exception would put new services at risk and user groups taking an opposite view. Limitations and exceptions would have to be harmonised across Europe, along the lines also proposed for further harmonisation of the reproduction right. In this case the Commission proposed widening the right holder's exclusive right of reproduction in cases where certain acts of reproduction would risk unreasonably prejudicing the right holder's interests or would conflict with normal exploitation of his intellectual property. In some cases a licence combined with a right to remuneration might suffice, and in others closely defined fair use exceptions would be appropriate. The Commission also proposed that the harmonised right should make clear that digitisation, scanning, uploading and downloading of protected material were covered by the right, as would be transient and other ephemeral acts of reproduction. Lastly, the distribution right should be harmonised so that only the first sale within the Community by or with the consent of the right holder exhausts the right; and exhaustion should not apply to services, including on-line services.

The Commission then published a draft "Directive on the harmonisation of certain aspects of copyright and related rights in the Information Society" in November 1997. After much further debate and lobbying a Parliament and Council Directive[1] was adopted on May 22, 2001. This has to be implemented by Member States before December 22, 2002.

General

The Directive is intended to harmonise, to a degree, rules on reproduction right, a right of communication to the public by wire or wireless means (including on-demand services), the distribution right and legal protection of anti-copying systems and information for managing rights. It includes implementation of some aspects of the WIPO treaties of 1996. The Directive does not, however, directly address the question of who is liable for copyright infringement in a network environment. This is dealt with, at least as far as the activities of on-line intermediaries are concerned, in the liability provisions of the Electronic Commerce Directive[2], to which the Copyright Directive is stated to be without prejudice. Those provisions are discussed in Chapter 5. However, the exception to the right of reproduction in Article 5(1) for temporary acts of reproduction (discussed below) is relevant to certain acts by users and service providers. **2–013**

The main provisions of the directive deal with definitions of the rights of reproduction, communication with the public and distribution, as well as protection of the use of technical measures to prevent unauthorised copying. These main provisions, in their original and amended form, are discussed in detail below.

Right of reproduction

The reproduction right provided in Article 2 includes permanent and temporary, direct and indirect reproductions of the whole or part of the copyright work by any means and in any form. This must be taken to include non-visible temporary copies of a work in the working memory of a computer. However, there is an exception to this right under Article 5(1). This exception covers "temporary acts of reproduction" "which are transient or incidental and an integral and essential part of a technological process and whose sole purpose is to enable: (a) a transmission in a network between third parties by an intermediary, or (b) a lawful use of a work or other subject matter to be made, and which have no independent economic significance". Recital (33) states that to the extent that they meet these conditions, this exception should include acts which enable browsing as well as acts of caching to take place, including those which enable transmission systems to function efficiently, provided that the intermediary "does not modify the information and does not interfere with the lawful use of technology, widely recognised and used by **2–014** industry, to obtain data on the use of the information". This wording echoes, but does not fully replicate, that of Article 13 of the Electronic Commerce Directive concerning caching. Recital (33) goes on to say that a use should be considered lawful where it is authorised by the rightholder or not restricted by law. The wording of the Article 5(1) represents a compromise between providing protection for technology designed to ensure the efficient operation of networks, yet at the same time to ensure that networks do not operate as vectors for the transmission of pirated content.

It is to be observed that this Article is broader than the WIPO treaties, because there was no agreement at the diplomatic conference on temporary reproductions.

Right of communication to the public

2–015 The "communication to the public" right for authors provided in Article 3 covers electronic communication of a work to the public "by wire or wireless means, including ... in such a way that members of the public may access them from a place and at a time individually chosen by them". Recital (23) makes clear that this is intended to include broadcasting. A narrower right is granted to performers, phonogram producers, film producers and broadcasters, applying only to "making available to the public, by wire or wireless means, in such a way that members of the public may access them from a place and at a time individually chosen by them". Neither right is exhausted by communication or making available to the public. Recital (27) states that the mere provision of physical communications facilities does not of itself amount to communication.

Distribution right

2–016 The distribution right, which relates to the original work and physical copies, is limited to authors. Article 4(2) provides that this right will only be exhausted by a first sale by or with the consent of the right holder in the Community.

Exceptions to copyright

2–017 The stated aim of the Directive is harmonisation of the law of copyright and related rights (Recital (1) *et sec.*). The exceptions to copyright infringement currently differ significantly between Member States and therefore would seem to be an area where harmonisation is required. However, apart from the exception for incidental technological copying referred to above, all the exceptions dealt with in Article 5 are made optional; so there is no guarantee that there will be harmonisation of copyright law even after this Directive becomes law. Exceptions to copyright is the area which has attracted the most debate and criticism, and Article 5 was extensively amended by the Parliament. All exceptions in Article 5 are to be applied "only in certain special cases which do not conflict with a normal exploitation of the work or other subject-matter and do not unreasonably prejudice the legitimate interests of the rightholder" (Article 5(5)).

The optional exceptions are contained in Article 5(2) (limitations to the exclusive right of reproduction provided in Article 2) and Article 5(3) (limitations to both the Article 2 right of reproduction and the Article 3 right of communication to the public); Article 5(4) provides that where Member States may provide for an exception to the reproduction right pursuant to these exceptions, they may also apply these exceptions to the Article 4 right of distribution, "to the extent justified by the purpose of the authorised act of reproduction".

Article 5(2)(a)—photocopying
This is subject to fair compensation to the right holder.   **2–018**

Article 5(2)(b)—copying for private use
This allows copying on any medium for private and non-commercial use. This is subject   **2–019**
to a requirement that the rightholders should receive fair compensation, which takes
account of the application (or not) of technological copy protection measures.

Article 5(2)(c)—libraries
This is an exception for organisations such as libraries and archives to make copies for   **2–020**
non-commercial purposes. However, the exception must be for specific acts of
reproduction which must not be for direct or indirect economic or commercial advantage.
Recital (40) states that the exception should not cover on-line delivery.

Article 5(2)(d)—ephemeral fixations made by broadcasters
This allows ephemeral recordings by broadcasters for their own broadcasts, and extends   **2–021**
to official archival preservation of these recordings on grounds of exceptional
documentary character.

Article 5(2)(e)—hospitals, prisons, etc.
This exception relates to reproduction of broadcasts made by social institutions pursuing   **2–022**
non-commercial purposes, subject to the rightholder receiving fair compensation.

Article 5(3)(a)—teaching and scientific research
This relates to use for the sole purpose of illustration for teaching or scientific research.   **2–023**
The source, including the author's name, must be indicated unless this is impossible. The
exception applies to the extent justified by the non-commercial purpose to be achieved.

Article 5(3)(b)—disability
This covers non-commercial use for disabled people, where the use is directly related to   **2–024**
the disability and of a non-commercial nature. Talking books for the blind would be an
example.

Article 5(3)(c)—reporting of current events, etc.
This relates to published articles on current economic, political or religious topics, in   **2–025**
cases where such use is not expressly reserved, subject to indicating the source including
the author's name, and to reporting of current events to the extent justified by the
informatory purpose and as long as the source (including the author's name) is indicated,
unless that is impossible.

Article 5(3)(d)—criticism and review
This has to relate to a work already lawfully made available to the public. It is subject to   **2–026**
conditions including naming the source, including the author, unless that it impossible.

Article 5(3)(e)—public interest
This covers use for public security, or the reporting of an administrative, parliamentary   **2–027**
or judicial procedure.

Article 5(3)(f)—political speeches

2–028   Use of political speeches, extracts of public lectures or similar to the extent justified by the informatory purpose and provided that the source, including the author's name, is indicated, except where this turns out to be impossible;

Article 5(3)(g)—official and religious celebrations

2–029   Use during religious celebrations or official celebrations organised by a public authority;

Article 5(3)(h)—sculptures in public places

2–030   Use of works, such as works of architecture or sculpture, made to be located permanently in public places;

Article 5(3)(i)—incidental inclusion

2–031   Incidental inclusion of a work or other subject-matter in other material;

Article 5(3)(j)—art exhibitions and sales

2–032   Use for the purpose of advertising the public exhibition or sale of artistic works, to the extent necessary to promote the event, excluding any other commercial use;

Article 5(3)(k)—caricature, etc.

2–033   Use for the purpose of caricature, parody or pastiche;

Article 5(3)(l)—equipment

2–034   Use in connection with the demonstration or repair of equipment;

Article 5(3)(m)—reconstruction of buildings

2–035   Use of an artistic work in the form of a building or a drawing or plan of a building for the purposes of reconstructing the building;

Article 5(3)(n)—on-line research and private study in public libraries

2–036   Use (by communication or making available) for the purpose of research or private study, to individual members of the public by dedicated terminals on the premises of establishments referred to in Article 5(2)(c) of works not subject to purchase or licensing terms which are contained in their collections;

Article 5(3)(o)—Miscellaneous

2–037   Use in certain other cases of minor importance where exceptions or limitations already exist under national law, provided that they only concern analogue uses and do not affect the free circulation of goods and services within the Community, without prejudice to the other exceptions and limitations contained in Article 5.

Prevention of circumvention of technical protection measures

2–038   Article 6 requires Member States to prohibit the circumvention of technical protection measures designed to protect copyright works, which the person concerned carries out in the knowledge, or with reasonable grounds to know, that he or she is pursuing that objective. The knowledge test has particular relevance in the case of dual use technology, which can be used to crack copy protection but which also has other uses.[3] Such technology is within the Article, but subject to the knowledge requirement.

Any legislation based on this Article which purported to prohibit the publication of information about technical protection measures would need to bear in mind Article 10 of the European Convention on Human Rights, protecting freedom of expression. First Amendment issues have already arisen in the USA in connection with the U.S. legislation (the Digital Millennium Copyright Act (DMCA)).

Article 7 of the Directive prohibits the removal or alteration of electronic rights management information and makes ancillary provisions.

2.2.4 USA – the Digital Millennium Copyright Act 1998

The U.S. administration in 1994 set up an Information Infrastructure Task Force to plan for and implement the National Information Infrastructure (NII). The task force included the Information Policy Committee, dealing with issues relating to the use of information on the NII. As part of the Information Policy Committee's work, a working group on Intellectual Property Rights was set up, chaired by the U.S. Commissioner of Patents and Trademarks. After issuing a preliminary draft report in July 1994 and taking both oral and written evidence from a large number of interested organisations and individuals, the working group issued its final report in September 1995.

2–039

After examining the existing state of the U.S. law, and the arguments for and against intellectual property protection for various kinds of information on the NII, the working group proposed to deal with the main problems that it perceived arising from dealings with works in cyberspace by amending the U.S. Copyright Act.

At least some of these amendments were made by the Digital Millennium Copyright Act 1998 ("DMCA"). Title I of the DMCA implements the WIPO treaties by prohibiting the circumvention of copyright protection systems and protecting the integrity of copyright management information. The former provisions caused a great deal of controversy while the legislation was going through Congress, as they provide a sweeping prohibition on the circumvention of "technological protection measures", regardless of whether infringement occurs as a result. Also prohibited is the manufacture, importation and distribution of devices primarily intended for such circumvention. Groups which had benefited from the fair use exemption from copyright infringement, such as librarians, teachers and software developers pointed out that such a broad prohibition would effectively remove the fair use provisions and leave them at the mercy of the copyright owners, thus tilting the current balance heavily in favour of the content provider against the users. As a result, Congress added a long list of exemptions for non-profit libraries, archives and educational establishments, for law enforcement and intelligence activities and reverse engineering provisions for software developers which adopt the language of the European Software Protection Directive.

2–040

The enforcement of the DMCA copyright protection circumvention provisions is proving controversial. The threat of action under the Digital Millennium Copyright Act (DMCA) has been used to prevent an academic from presenting a paper about weaknesses in music access-control technologies. This has resulted in a First Amendment lawsuit aimed at establishing the right of the academic to present the paper.[4] In July 2001 a Russian programmer, Dmitry Sklyarov, the author of a program that disables restrictions on Adobe eBooks, who had presented at the Las Vegas Defcon-9 hacker conference, was arrested and charged with an offence under the DMCA of trafficking in a product designed to circumvent copyright protection for electronic books (Adobe eBooks).[5] Adobe subsequently recommended his release and withdrew support for the criminal complaint.[6] At the time of writing the charges remain pending.

2.3 What is copyright?

2.3.1 The development of copyright

2–041   Copyright developed to deal with the analogue world. Historically, our present system of copyright grew out of attempts by the government to control the information revolution brought about by the development of printing. The right to print books was given exclusively to members of the guild of stationers, which was a recognised body with privileges that made it susceptible to government influence. When unlicensed publishing began to flourish, the guild members sought a law to prevent this. The Copyright Act 1709 gave the author and his assigns the exclusive right to print a book. The exclusive rights and the types of work protected gradually increased through a series of statutes, culminating in the present legislation, the Copyright, Designs and Patents Act 1988 (the 1988 Act).

2.3.2 What is protected?

2–042   Because of the historical development, the 1988 Act contains a list of the types of work protected, in three categories. These are:

- literary works, dramatic, musical or artistic works;

- sound recordings, films, broadcasts or cable programmes; and

- the typographical arrangement of a published edition.

    Compilations (defined to exclude databases), computer programs and databases are included as literary works, while films include video recordings and any moving image. Some publicly accessible on-line databases and web sites will come within the definition of cable programmes.

2–043   In order to be protected, the work must be original. There is no definition of "originality" in the 1988 Act. Case law in the United Kingdom has required only that the work is not copied and has a minimal amount of creativity, reflecting the approach of the United Kingdom courts to copyright as an economic, rather than a personal, right. The position regarding originality of databases is now modified as a consequence of the introduction of database right (discussed below). Section 3A of the 1988 Act provides that a literary work consisting of a database is original if, and only if, by reason of the selection or arrangement of the contents of the database the database constitutes the author's own intellectual creation. Generally, mere facts are regarded as non-copyright.

    Copyright only comes into existence when the work is recorded, in writing or otherwise.[7] The 1988 Act[8] defines a "writing" to include "any form of notation or code, whether by hand or otherwise and regardless of the method by which, or medium in or on which, it is recorded". So the contents of a screen will be copyrightable (subject to its meeting the other criteria, such as originality). This is not because the display on the screen constitutes a recordal—it may not,[9] but because the screen contents are stored, even if only transiently, in the memory of the computer.[10] On the Internet, material and information is accessed and (temporarily at least) resides in the computer's RAM (random access memory). In order for the user to see that information, it must be copied into the computer's memory. This chapter will show that such activity can constitute infringement of the rights of a copyright owner.

It is generally accepted that copyright protects the expression of ideas but not ideas themselves. The European Software Directive[11] provides that "Ideas and principles which underlie any element of the computer program, including those which underlie its interfaces, are not protected by copyright under this Directive". This provision was not expressly incorporated in the United Kingdom Software Regulations on the ground that it was already part of judge-made copyright law in the United Kingdom.   **2–044**

Copyright does not subsist in a work unless the author is a qualifying person or the work was first published in a qualifying country. A qualifying person includes a British citizen, an individual domiciled or resident in the United Kingdom or another country to which the Act has been extended (including the member states of the Berne Convention and the Universal Copyright Convention), or a body incorporated under the law of the United Kingdom or another country to which the Act has been extended. A qualifying country includes the United Kingdom or another country to which the Act has been extended (including the member states of the Berne Convention and the Universal Copyright Convention).

2.3.3 Authorship and ownership

The author of a work is the person who creates it. A work of joint authorship is produced by the collaboration of two or more authors in which the contribution of each author is not distinct from that of the other author or authors. In the case of a literary work which is computer-generated, the author is by statute the person by whom the arrangements necessary for the creation of the work are undertaken. The term "computer-generated" means that "the work is generated by computer in circumstances such that there is no human author of the work".   **2–045**

In general, the author of a work is the first owner of any copyright in it. However, where the work is made by an employee in the course of his employment, his employer is the first owner of any copyright in the work subject to any agreement to the contrary. This only applies to employees, not to contractors, so the mere fact that a work has been commissioned and paid for does not give the ownership of the copyright to the commissioning party. It is important therefore to ensure that appropriate mechanisms are in place to deal with the ownership of the rights in content. For example, an organisation may wish to put up information onto a Web site. That information may have come from a number of sources, external developers and consultants, internal employees, etc. The organisation in question will therefore need to be certain that it secures assignments of rights from any third parties, and be sure that any employees created the content during the course of their employment.

2.3.4 Period of copyright

Copyright in original literary, dramatic, musical or artistic works of European origin now lasts for 70 years beyond the year in which the author died. If there are joint authors then copyright duration is linked to the last death of any identifiable author. Computer generated works are protected for 50 years from the end of the year of creation. Copyright in sound recordings, broadcasts or cable programmes lasts for 50 years from the end of the year in which the work was first made or released or broadcast. Copyright in films   **2–046** expires 70 years from the end of the year in which the last of the director, screenplay author, dialogue author or composer of music written specially for the film dies. Copyright in the typographical arrangement of a published edition lasts for 25 years from the year of first publication. Works originating outside the European Economic Area are given the same period of protection as in their native country.

This different treatment of types of works will cause problems with digital products containing a variety of content, *e.g.* a multimedia product containing film, photographs, text and sound. The copyright in the individual elements of the product will expire at different times.

2.4 Moral rights

2–047   The rights pertaining to copyright discussed above are economic rights. The Continental systems of copyright have long recognised another set of rights, which belong to the creator of the work even if he or she does not own the economic rights. These are known as the moral rights. A system of moral rights was introduced into English law for the first time by the 1988 Act. There are four elements to moral rights which subsist alongside copyright:

- The paternity right: which is the right to be identified as author (or director of a film). This right does not exist unless it is asserted by the author or film maker.

- The integrity right: the right to object to the derogatory treatment of a work.

- False attribution: the right not to suffer false attribution of a work. This lasts for life plus 20 years only.

- Privacy of photographs: this is the right of a person commissioning photographs not to have copies issued to the public.

Moral rights cannot be assigned, but they may be waived. Infringement of the above rights is actionable as a breach of a statutory duty. The moral rights of paternity and integrity do not apply to computer programs or computer-generated works.

2.5 Database right

2–048   In 1992 the European Commission issued a draft Directive to harmonise the protection of databases in the E.U. Comments from interested parties revealed many deficiencies, and the draft was extensively amended by the European Parliament. Extensive negotiations between the member states resulted in a directive being adopted on March 11, 1996, to be implemented by January 1, 1998.

"Database" is defined as: "a collection of works, data or other independent materials arranged in a systematic or methodical way and capable of being individually accessed by electronic or other means". This will include non-computer databases, on-line databases, CD-ROMs and CD-I (but not music CDs). The content materials may be protected by their own individual copyrights, which are not affected by the Directive. A database as a whole will qualify for copyright protection if there is creativity in the selection or arrangement of its contents. This test is wider than the test currently applied by most European countries, but narrower than the test used by the United Kingdom and the Republic of Ireland. However, under transitional provisions, existing databases currently protected by copyright will retain that protection for the full copyright term.

A new *sui generis* right is given to database proprietors for any database whether or not it and/or its contents are protected by copyright. This is the right to prevent the unauthorised extraction and/or re-utilisation of all or a substantial part of the database. This right will last for 15 years from the first public availability of the database, and can be renewed if there has been a substantial change which would result in the database being considered a "substantial new investment". This means that databases which are subject to regular significant updating could in theory be protected forever. This right, however, is only given to proprietors who are E.U. nationals or residents, although it may be extended to nationals of third countries who give equivalent protection to databases of E.U. origin—which currently would probably exclude the USA, although there is currently legislation in Congress to provide a similar form of database protection under U.S. law.   **2–049**

This directive was implemented in the United Kingdom by the Copyright and Rights in Databases Regulations 1997, which came into force on January 1, 1998. These regulations amend the Copyright, Designs and Patents Act 1988 so as to bring the standard of originality for subsistence of copyright in databases into line with that required by the directive, to specify what constitutes adaptation and fair dealing in relation to a database, and to specify the permitted acts by a person who has a right to use a database. The Regulations further create the new database right, giving the maker of a database in which there has been a substantial investment in obtaining, verifying or presenting the contents the right to prevent extraction or re-utilisation of all or a substantial part of the contents.

The William Hill *case*

The first case on the scope of database right to reach the English courts has resulted in a reference to the European Court of Justice. In *British Horseracing Board Ltd and others v. William Hill Organisation Ltd*[12] the Court of Appeal, while inclined to uphold the judge's findings in favour of the claimants, decided to refer a number of questions concerning the interpretation of the Database Directive to the ECJ. The facts were that the main claimant (BHB) is the governing authority for the British horseracing industry. In 1985 the claimant Weatherbys, on behalf of the claimant the Jockey Club, started to compile an electronic database of (among other things) registered horses, their owners and trainers, their handicap ratings, details of jockeys, and fixture list information (venues, dates, times, race conditions and entries and runners). After June 1993 Weatherbys maintained and developed the database on behalf of BHB.   **2–050**

The database was constantly updated. The cost of continuing to obtain, verify and present the contents of the database was approximately £4,000,000 per annum, involving about 80 staff and extensive computer software and hardware. The database contained details of over one million horses. An estimated total of 800,000 new records or changes to existing records were made each year.

Information from the database, in particular information about forthcoming races, was made available in various ways. This included circulation of essential extracts to the racing industry, including publication in BHB's journal the Racing Calendar. There were also electronic feeds, the Declaration Feed and Raw Data Feed (RDF). The Declaration Feed contained a list of races, declared runners and jockeys, distances and names of races, race times and numbers of runners in each race and other information. It was made   **2–051** available to subscribers by Racing Pages Ltd, a joint venture between Weatherbys and the Press Association. Satellite Information Services (SIS) was allowed to use information from the database to provide services to its own subscribers. One such service was the RDF, consisting of details of meetings, races and the list of runners and other related information. SIS also supplied FACTS, comprising television coverage, audio and captions for race meetings.

2–052   William Hill, a large bookmaker, provided Internet betting on horseracing from a web site. It had formal licences for the Declarations Feed and for the FACTS service. It also received the RDF from SIS. This was supplied with no formal contract. However SIS had no right, and had not purported to, sublicense William Hill to use the RDF on its web site.

William Hill made use of certain information from the RDF on its web site: the identity of the horses in a race, the date and time of the race and the identity of the racecourse. BHB objected to this use. It claimed that the use made each day was an extraction or reutilisation of a substantial part of the database (contrary to Article 7(1) of the Directive); or that, if each day's use was an insubstantial part, the use amounted to a repeated and systematic extraction and reutilisation of insubstantial parts of the database (contrary to Article 7(5)).

On Article 7(1) William Hill argued (1) that it had not used a part, in a relevant sense, of BHB's database; (2) even if it had used a part, it was not a substantial part; (3) the use did not amount to an extraction from the database; (4) it was not a reutilisation of the database.

2–053   Laddie J. at first instance found in favour of BHB on all points. On (1) William Hill had argued that what was protected by the database right was not the mere contents of the database, but its "database-ness", *i.e.* the systematic or methodical arrangement and individual accessibility of the materials, so that acts which do not take any aspect of that do not infringe the right. The judge rejected this, holding that once the preconditions to subsistence of the right were satisfied, the specified modes of use of the contents would infringe. On (2), the judge found that William Hill were making use of the most recent and core information and taking advantage of the completeness and accuracy of the information, which were the product of the investment in obtaining and verifying the data. This was, both qualitatively and quantitatively, a substantial part of the contents. On (3), the judge found that there was extraction even though the use was indirect, in the sense that the use made was of data that had already been removed from the database by SIS. On (4), the judge rejected the argument that the right to restrain use of a substantial part of the database was lost once it had been made available to the public.

On Article 7(5) the judge rejected William Hill's argument that each day's use was a single extraction from a new database. The judge held that it was a single database in a constant state of refinement, the term of protection for which was constantly being renewed. The judge also held that the use unreasonably prejudiced the legitimate interests of BHB and found infringement under Article 7(5).

2–054   On appeal William Hill contended that the judge had given a wide meaning to the database right and that the effect was that information that might have been thought to have entered the public domain and to be freely usable might prove to be derived from a database, the right in which was protected, even though the user was unaware of that ultimate source and right.

The Court of Appeal stated that it would be quite likely to support the conclusions of the judge. However, given the room for reasonable doubt it concluded that there should be a reference to the ECJ, essentially covering the points argued by William Hill.

2.6 Copyright and database right infringement

2.6.1 Introduction

Copyright is infringed by doing any of the prohibited acts (as to which, see below) in relation to the whole or a substantial part of the work. It can be very difficult to determine whether a "substantial part of the work" has been copied. A single word or a single note of music cannot be the subject of copyright, even when the word is an invented word such as "Exxon".[13] The courts have held that copyright in a work is infringed by taking a "substantial" part of it, and the test of substantiality is quality rather than quantity. Thus, were Beethoven's 5th Symphony still in copyright, few would doubt that the copying of those instantly recognisable first four notes would be actionable infringement. Similarly, "Reader, I married him" would likely be held to be a substantial part of *Jane Eyre*. The test seems to be whether the part taken has itself some originality and merit; or, put another way, whether a substantial part of the author's skill and labour has been taken. **2–055**

There are a number of statutory limitations on the scope of the exclusive rights, which provide a defence to a charge of copyright infringement. Fair dealing with some classes of copyright work for research or private study, or for criticism or review, or reporting of current events; or the incidental inclusion in another work (*e.g.* a statue in the background of a photograph of a city square) is not infringement. There are detailed provisions dealing with those educational uses and those activities of libraries which are exempt from infringement liability. The time-shifting exceptions, although primarily aimed at recording from television, may be of some relevance. **2–056**

Copyright infringement may also be a criminal offence, although there must be either a commercial motive or distribution to such an extent as to seriously affect the copyright owner before there is criminal liability for copyright infringement.

Copy-protection
The 1988 Act introduced protection for copies of a work issued to the public in an electronic form which is copy-protected. References to copy-protection include "any device or means intended to prevent or restrict copying of a work or to impair the quality of copies made". Under section 296 it is copyright infringement to make or distribute a device specifically designed or adapted to circumvent the form of copy-protection employed, knowing or having reason to believe that it will be used to make infringing copies, or to publish information intended to enable or assist persons to circumvent the copy-protection. These provisions will clearly catch devices sold deliberately to de-encrypt encrypted messages or information. These provisions may be compared with those of the U.S. Digital Millennium Copyright Act, discussed below, which creates criminal offences. **2–057**

Exclusive rights of copyright owners
The copyright owner's exclusive rights are the rights to copy, issue copies of the work to the public, perform, show or play in public, to broadcast or include it in a cable programme service and to make adaptations. Copyright is infringed by doing any of those acts without the consent of the copyright owner. These acts constitute primary infringement. **2–058**

Authorisation
It is also a primary infringement of copyright, for which the person authorising is strictly **2–059**

liable, to authorise another to do an act of primary infringement. "Authorise" is not defined in the Act. Its meaning was considered by the House of Lords in *C.B.S. Songs v. Amstrad Consumer Electronics*,[14] which concerned the marketing by the defendant of a high speed twin-headed cassette recorder. The House of Lords held that authorisation means the grant or purported grant, which may be express or implied, of the right to do the act complained of, whether the intention is that the grantee should do the act on his own account or only on account of the grantor. Merely enabling someone else to infringe copyright does not suffice. Although this case was decided under the Copyright Act 1956, the principles hold good for the Copyright Designs and Patents Act 1988. The House of Lords considered both the sale of the machines themselves and the manner of advertising them. In relation to the sale of the machines, their Lordships stated:

> "No manufacturer and no machine confers on the purchaser authority to copy unlawfully. The purchaser or other operator of the recorder determines whether he shall copy and what he shall copy. By selling the recorder Amstrad may facilitate copying in breach of copyright, but do not authorise it."

This finding was against the factual background that, notwithstanding that it was statistically certain that most, but not all consoles were used for the purpose of home copying in breach of copyright, the machine was capable of being used for lawful purposes and the decision whether to use it for lawful or unlawful purposes was entirely that of the purchaser.

2–060 A lawful purpose could arise either because the material being copied was not the subject of copyright protection at all, or because the user had permission to copy copyright content, or because the user fell within limited rights to copy granted by the Copyright Act.

The separate allegation was made that by their advertisement Amstrad had authorised the infringement. Amstrad had advertised the advantages of its high-speed twin-head tape recorder with an asterisked footnote to the effect that the recording and the playback of certain material might only be possible by permission.

Although commenting somewhat negatively on the advertising, the House of Lords stated that: "the advertisement did not authorise the unlawful copying of records; on the contrary, the footnote warned that some copying required permission and made it clear that Amstrad had not authority to grant that permission".

Therefore, neither the sale of the machine, nor the particular advertising was found to constitute authorisation.

Secondary infringement

2–061 The importation, sale, distribution, possession in the course of business or public distribution of an infringing article is also infringement, as is permitting a place of public entertainment to be used to perform an infringing work in public. This is called "secondary infringement". Acts of secondary infringement require an element of knowledge or reason to believe that the article was an infringing copy. There is also a special secondary infringement provision for remote copying by means of networks. A person who transmits the work over a telecommunications system (which does not include broadcasting or cable) knowing or having reason to believe that infringing copies of the work will be made by means of the reception of the transmission in the United Kingdom or elsewhere is himself an infringer. A "telecommunications system" is broadly defined by the 1988 Act as "a system for conveying visual images, sounds or other information by electronic means''.

Electronic media
The 1988 Act made provision for electronic media. Copying includes storing the work in   **2–062**
any medium by electronic means, and translation of a computer program includes
conversion from source to object code or translation into a different source code. The term
''electronic'' means ''actuated by electric, magnetic, electro-magnetic, electro-chemical or
electro-mechanical energy''. The 1988 Act provides that copying includes the making of a
copy which is transient or incidental to some other use of the work, so that an
unauthorised copy made temporarily in RAM while accessing a copyright work on the
Internet would prima facie render the person viewing the work an infringer.

2.6.2 Applying copyright to the Internet

Activities on the Internet potentially fall within a variety of infringement provisions.   **2–063**
Some activities throw into clear relief the problems of classification caused by the historic
roots of copyright in tangible media. Some examples of these will be considered
individually. First, we will examine the potentially relevant acts of primary infringement
in turn.

Infringement by copying—section 17 of the 1988 Act
It is a restricted act to copy a work. Copying includes storing the work in any medium by   **2–064**
electronic means. Copying in relation to any description of work includes the making of
copies which are transient or are incidental to some other use of the work. The
proliferation of transient, temporary and permanent copies which arises on a network
means that there will almost certainly be a copy somewhere on the basis of which a
wronged copyright owner can base his complaint. It may also be arguable that the user's
screen display itself amounts to a copy.[15] Usually the target defendant will have created a
copy of the work on his own computer system. However, on a public network that is not
always the case. The copies may be created on some other person's system. Further,
persons on whose equipment the copies are created as a result of the target defendant's
activities may be relatively innocent intermediaries or end-users, who may (depending
on the circumstances) seek to invoke the protection of fair use, fair dealing, implied
licence or other defences. The copyright owner who wishes to rely on copying may
sometimes have to argue that the defendant has in some way copied remotely (*e.g.* by
causing the copy to be stored on someone else's computer), or resort to alleging
authorisation of primary infringement by someone else. These difficulties are
compounded if the activities are carried on cross-border.

Infringement by issue of copies to the public—section 18 of the 1988 Act
It is a restricted act to issue to the public copies of a work. These provisions were   **2–065**
amended by the Copyright and Related Rights Regulations 1996, which came into force
on December 1, 1996. The amended provisions create a regime of exhaustion of rights
within the EEA, but not internationally. The section, as amended, gives the copyright
owner the right to control the act of putting into circulation copies not previously put into
circulation in the EEA, but not any subsequent distribution, sale, hiring or loan of those
copies or any subsequent importation of those copies into the EEA.
   This section is aimed at what can loosely be described as publishing. Its obvious

application is to permanent copies issued on tangible media such as books or disks. However, on the face of it the section may apply equally to copies issued in intangible and even transient form, such as when a person makes a work available for viewing and/ or download from a Web site. There may be contrary arguments to the effect that the stream of bits from the Web site to the viewer's computer does not constitute a copy at any one time, so that no new copy comes into existence until the bits are assembled at the recipient computer; and if that is so, how can the Web site proprietor have issued the copy? Another related argument could be that the Web site proprietor has not actively issued copies. He has only passively made the site available and it is the act of a third party visiting the site which causes the copy to be made. Such arguments may be unconvincing to a court seeking to ensure that the legislation retains its effectiveness in a digital context,[16] although perhaps stronger in the case of copies for downloading at the viewer's option rather than for viewing. It is also noteworthy that "publication" (which is now relevant only to subsistence of copyright) in relation to a work is defined in section 175 of the 1998 Act, which states that it "means the issue of copies to the public" and "includes ... making it available to the public by means of an electronic retrieval system". Whether this reinforces, detracts from or has no effect on the argument that "issue of copies to the public" in section 18 effectively includes making available by means of an electronic retrieval system is perhaps debatable.

2–066   The section applies in an amended form to computer programs, for instance preserving a rental right for the copyright owner. The Act does not define "computer program". It should be noted that even in its simplest (HTML) form, a Web page could be regarded as a computer program. An HTML page consists of text, marked up with instructions upon which the browsing computer will act to format the page on the screen, fetch components from other computers and so on in order to assemble the page at the viewer's computer. The raw HTML text is commonly known as "source code" (a term used in connection with computer programs). More complex pages making use of Java applets (mini-programs delivered to the user's computer when the Web site is accessed), or with sections written in languages such as JavaScript, are effectively indistinguishable from traditional program source code.

Infringement by performance—section 19 of the 1988 Act

2–067   It is a restricted act to perform in public a literary, dramatic or musical work, or to play or show in public a sound recording, film, broadcast or cable programme. Performance includes any mode of visual or acoustic presentation, including presentation by means of a sound recording, film, broadcast or cable programme. Where copyright in a work is infringed by its being performed, played or shown in public by means of apparatus for receiving visual images or sounds conveyed by electronic means, the person by whom the visual images or sounds are sent, and in the case of a performance the performers, are not to be regarded as responsible for the infringement.

It is not clear whether public performance is restricted to what happens at the receiving screen, or whether making material available on a Web site for public consumption could in itself constitute public performance. The former probably fits better with the scheme of the Act, given that there are separate categories of infringement by broadcasting and inclusion in a cable programme service. Infringement by performance does not appear to be restricted to a performance of a theatrical or declamatory nature. It has been held in a case under the 1956 Act[17] that a greyhound racecard was performed when it was transmitted by satellite to a television monitor in a bookmaker's shop.

Infringement by broadcasting or inclusion in a cable programme service—section 20 of the 1988 Act

It is a restricted act to broadcast a work or to include it in a cable programme service. This **2–068** applies to literary, dramatic, musical or artistic works and also to sound recordings and films or a broadcast or cable programme. A "broadcast" means a transmission by wireless telegraphy of visual images, sounds or other information which is capable of being lawfully received by members of the public, or is transmitted for presentation to members of the public (section 6(1)). It is unlikely that the broadcast provisions will apply to the Internet, which is essentially a telecommunications network. However, network and infrastructure providers are using a wider variety of delivery mechanisms. For instance, there are now mixed path systems whereby the user receives data by high bandwidth satellite link, but sends requests and other data back to the access provider by ordinary low bandwidth telephone connection (which could be fixed link or mobile). The distinction between broadcast and cable programme service based on technical means of delivery will become increasingly difficult to maintain. It should also be noted that the person setting up the Web site has no means of knowing by what route or means his content will be conveyed to the end-user beyond the Web site's own connection to the Internet.

A cable programme service is a service which consists wholly or mainly in sending **2–069** visual images, sounds or other information by means of a telecommunications system, otherwise than by wireless telegraphy, for reception: (a) at two or more places (whether for simultaneous reception or at different times in response to requests by different users), or (b) for presentation to members of the public and which are not subject to an exception (section 7(1)). The main relevant exception is in section 7(2)(a), which provides that a service or part of a service is excepted of which it is an essential feature that while visual images, sounds or other information are being conveyed by the person providing the service there will or may be sent from each place of reception, by means of the same system or (as the case may be) the same part of it, information (other than signals sent for the operation or control of the service) for reception by the person providing the service or other persons receiving it.

It seems tolerably clear that much information provided on Web sites will constitute part of a cable programme service unless the service falls within the exception. The exception would clearly exclude video-conferencing and services such as Internet Relay Chat, so long as "while" is given a pragmatic meaning. Insistence on strict technical simultaneity could result in some such services not being excluded. From a pragmatic point of view, however, mutual exchange of information in real time is of the essence of such services.

Whether a Web site would fall within the exception could depend on its nature. It **2–070** could be of the essence of a Web shopping site that the visitor provides information which could go beyond "signals for the operation or control" of the service, such as name, address and credit card information. But it would be highly debatable whether the information was provided "while" the information from the site was being conveyed. Other Web sites could more clearly fall outside the exception. In the Scottish case of *Shetland Times Ltd v. Wills*,[18] Lord Hamilton found that a newspaper Web site was prima facie a cable programme service. It was argued against that, that the site encouraged callers to contact the site proprietor and submit comments and suggestions. Lord Hamilton found that it was plainly arguable that the exception did not apply. The facility to make comments or suggestions did not appear to him to be an essential element in the service, the primary function of which was to distribute news and other items. It was in any event arguable that that facility was a severable part of the service.

A person infringes if he includes a work in a cable programme service. Inclusion of a work in a cable programme service means its transmission as part of the service (section 7(5)). References to the person including it are to the person providing the service (section 7(5)). This presumably means the person who sends the images, sounds or other information. Translated to a Web site, if the site is self-hosted the proprietor of the site would appear to be the infringer. If the hosting is outsourced to a third party host the host would appear to be the infringer, although the content provider would presumably be liable for authorising the infringement.

Infringement by making adaptation or act done in relation to adaptation—section 21 of the 1988 Act

2–071   It is a restricted act to make an adaptation of a literary, dramatic or musical work. Adaptation includes translation. In relation to computer programs (which may have wide ranging effect on the Web—see above) an adaptation means an arrangement or altered version of the program or a translation of it. A translation of a computer program includes a version of the program in which it is converted into or out of a computer language or code or into a different computer language or code. It should be noted that under section 50C of the 1988 Act, it is not an infringement of copyright for a lawful user of a copy of a computer program to copy or adapt it, provided that the copying or adapting (a) is necessary for his lawful use; and (b) is not prohibited under any term or condition of an agreement regulating the circumstances in which his use is lawful. There are also separate provisions relating to back-up copies and reverse engineering under sections 50A and 50B of the 1988 Act.

2–072   *Secondary infringement*

Sections 22–26 of the 1988 Act set out various categories of secondary infringement: importing an infringing copy, possessing or dealing with an infringing copy, providing means for making infringing copies, permitting the use of premises for an infringing performance and provision of apparatus for an infringing performance. The common factor in all of these categories is a requirement of knowledge: for instance, in the case of importation, possession or dealing, that the person knew or had reason to believe that the article was an infringing copy of the work. In general, given the convergence of copying and distribution in the on-line environment and the consequent likelihood of primary infringement, secondary infringement will be of lesser importance.

We now turn to some examples of scenarios peculiar to the Internet which have posed particular problems for analysis of the copyright position.

2.6.3 Web linking and related activities

2–073   The Web, we have observed, is a system of hypertext links which enables the browser to skip from one document to another by clicking on a highlighted part of the document. The Web is no respecter of boundaries or ownership. The Web has flourished precisely because a Web page author can create links which point to documents on any other site, whether or not he has any connection with it. In the light of this the question is sometimes asked whether the proprietor of a site has any right to control who links to his site. This is not necessarily just a question of copyright. Database right is also important. There could be trade mark or passing off questions, or in some countries moral rights or unfair competition aspects. Here we will review some aspects of the copyright and database right position.

How an ordinary hypertext link works

The technical aspects of Web linking are important to the copyright analysis. An HTML link is a pointer to the address of a page, or perhaps to a place within a page, stored on a host. The author of a Web page can create a link to another part of the same page, to another document on his own site, or to a document on any other Internet host whose address he knows or can find out. So if a Web page author wanted to create a link to Bird & Bird's Web site he would use the following text: <A HREF="http://www.twobirds.-com"> Bird & Bird</A>. When read by a Web browser using a typical configuration that code would appear as <u>Bird & Bird</u> on the user's screen. "http://www.twobirds.com" is the address (or 'URL'—Uniform Resource Locator) of the target Web site, in this case that of Bird & Bird. The <A HREF ... > code instructs the computer to fetch the home page directly from the target site when the user clicks on the <u>Bird & Bird</u> link. The author can target a particular page inside the site by noting the URL of that page and using that in the link.

2–074

It should be stressed that using the link does not cause any copy of the target page to be created, at any stage, on the author's Web server. Nothing happens on the target site until the link is clicked by the user. When the link is clicked the user's browser establishes a connection direct to the target site and fetches the target page directly from it, just as if the user had typed in the URL on his browser to go to the site. The use receives the target page directly from the target site, not via the author's site. This form of link is the defining feature of the Web.

Deep linking

Where a link is created not to the home page of the target site, but to a subsidiary page, this is known as "deep linking". The Web is full of deep links which provoke no objection. Some deep links, however, threaten the business model and revenues of the target site. For instance, if the target site depends on advertising revenues those may be reduced if users are directed straight to a subsidiary page, bypassing pages with advertising.

2–075

Inline linking – the virtual document

Another form of HTML link, the "inline" link, may also be relevant. A Web page is built up of text and images. But the images are stored separately on the server. This enables the user to disable images and read the pages in "text-only" mode if he so desires. So the HTML text document has to include a code which not only tells the user's browser the URL of the image, but also instructs the browser to load the image automatically as part of the document if the user has not disabled images. The code to achieve that is <IMG SRC ... >. Using this code to instruct the user's browser to assemble documents from the Web host's own collection of data is unexceptional. However, the <IMG SRC ... > code can be used to target images on other sites, in the same way as an ordinary link except that the target images load automatically at the user's computer. In the same way as the ordinary link, no copy of the image is made on the host's server. The <IMG SRC ... > link could be used to build up a complete "virtual document" consisting of images sourced from other hosts—but which on the home host consists of nothing but a few lines of text with pointers to the URLs of the target images. The version of the document including the images is automatically assembled only when the user fetches the page from the home host, and comes into existence only on the user's screen and in his computer. The effect for the user is almost the same as if the home host had copied the images on to his own host.[19] But by using pointers to the genuine works the home host avoids the clearly

2–076

infringing activity of storing copies on his own system.

These HTML examples are relatively simple and illustrate the principle. Using more sophisticated programming techniques (*e.g.* using Java and JavaScript) it would be possible to create sophisticated virtual documents drawing on other hosts' content, but which in the same way as the examples do not involve the home host in creating, or causing to be created, any copies other than those in the user's computer which would also come into existence if the user were to access the target host direct.

Linking and copyright infringement

2–077 Do either of these examples constitute copyright infringement and if so why? Whichever route to infringement is examined, the answer seems to boil down (at least for the virtual document created by in-line linking) either to a question of fair use or fair dealing, or to a question of the scope of the implied licence granted by the target host to the public to access its site. There is a further twist in the possible effect of the E.U. Software Directive and its United Kingdom equivalent legislation if the Web pages in question are regarded as computer programs (as to which see above).

Inclusion in a cable programme service

2–078 The issue has been touched on in the Scottish case of *Shetland Times Ltd v. Wills* (see above). The case, in which the pursuer (plaintiff) was granted an interim interdict (*i.e.* injunction) against the defender (defendant) over aspects of its "Shetland News" Web site, has attracted considerable publicity, being interpreted as holding that linking to another Web site can infringe copyright. However, the judgment was given at an interim interdict stage before a full trial. Further, any linking issues were somewhat over-shadowed by the allegation that the defender had included actual copies of headlines from the plaintiff's site on its Web site. The judgment was notable for holding that the pursuer had a prima facie case that its Web site constituted a cable programme service under the 1988 Act and that the defender was infringing under both section 17 (copying) and section 20 (inclusion in a cable programme service). Although the question of links from the defender's allegedly copied headlines to the equivalent news stories within the pursuer's site featured in the judgment, and the judge found in considering the balance of convenience that "it was fundamental to the setting up by the pursuers of their Web site that access to their material should be gained only by accessing their Web directly" (as opposed to bypassing the front page by links from the defender's site directly to the pursuer's news stories), it is certainly not clear that the judge held there was a prima facie case that the links (as opposed to the headlines) constituted infringement. The case was settled before full trial, on terms permitting the Shetland News to link to *Shetland Times* stories under certain conditions. These require the Shetland News to acknowledge, using a specified legend, the *Shetland Times* as the source of the linked story and to provide links and adjacent logo button links to the *Shetland Times* online headline page.

2–079 If, by way of example, the discussion of linking and infringement centres around the ground of inclusion in a cable programme service, the analysis may be along the following lines. We have seen that a person infringes if he includes a work in a cable programme service; and that inclusion of a work in a cable programme service means its transmission as part of the service (section 7(5)). Assuming that the defendant's Web site is a cable programme service, does he include the claimant's work in that service by linking to it? Were it not for the definition of "inclusion" in section 7(5), the answer would probably be "yes". But inclusion means transmission as part of a cable programme service. We have seen that the user's browser establishes a direct connection to the target site, so that the defendant's Web site does not transmit the linked material. Whether the link is user-activated or automatic, the target Web site transmits the work. With an automatic link, it is true that the defendant's Web site directly causes the target Web site to transmit the material. With a user-activated link it may be argued that the causal link is broken (*quaere* whether including a user-activated link on the page would amount to authorisation).

Even if the defendant's Web site causes the target Web site to transmit the work, there is still the question whether that is done without the consent of the owner of the target Web site. That is a question of the scope of express or implied licence granted by the target Web site owner to persons to access the site. It is quite possible that a court would regard the assembly of a virtual document by automatic links to selected content on a target Web site as outside the scope of the implied licence and therefore infringing. It is perhaps more difficult to see how a claimant alleging infringement by inclusion in a cable programme service could succeed on user-activated links, even if he could establish that inclusion of the links on the defendant's Web site was an act of authorisation. The claimant would have to show authorisation of an infringing act by the user, and while the user would be causing the work to be transmitted by clicking on the link, he would not be doing so *as part of a cable programme service*—other than any operated by the claimant itself. The claimant would have to argue that its own Web site was a cable programme service and that the particular act of transmission as part of its own cable programme service was without express or implied consent and therefore an infringing act by the user. However, there is a problem with section 7(5), which provides that references to the person including a work in a cable programme service are to the person providing the service (which would appear to absolve from infringement the user, who while he may by clicking on the unauthorised link cause the transmission to occur as part of the service on the claimant's Web site, is difficult to characterise as the person providing the service).

Copying

A similar analysis based on the copying route to infringement produces a similar result for automatic links, based on the scope of the implied licence to copy and the inevitability of the user creating at least a transient copy in the course of assembling the virtual document as directed by the defendant's Web site. For user-activated links the result is slightly different from inclusion in a cable programme service, because the user will always create a copy in the RAM of his computer. This is always potentially a restricted act, so in this case instead of the argument falling on the point of the user not providing a cable programme service, it advances to the question of whether the defendant has authorised the – user's acts by including the links on his page and the scope of the implied licence to copy attaching to the claimant's Web site. Given the fact that the *raison d'etre* of the Web is linking, one might think that the implied licence would be bound to cover user-activated links. However, it does raise two possibilities: first, that a court in the factual circumstances of a particular case may be persuaded to find that what the defendant has done is so beyond the pale as to be outside the scope of any implied licence; and second, it raises the question whether a claimant could gain the right to control (and charge for) linking to his site by seeking to assert an express prohibition on unauthorised linking to the site. These considerations may lead on to questions of whether there is a minimum use of material on its Web site from which a claimant may not derogate, either by virtue of fair use or fair dealing considerations, or by invocation of the doctrine of derogation from grant, or on some other public interest ground.[20]

A claimant could possibly seek to invoke the secondary infringement provision of

2–080

section 24(2) of the 1988 Act (transmitting a work over a telecommunications system (which does not include broadcasting or cable) knowing or having reason to believe that infringing copies of the work will be made by means of the reception of the transmission in the United Kingdom or elsewhere). This could be appropriate if it was thought that the Web site was not a cable programme service. However, its potential application to the situations discussed is debatable.

2–081   In a U.S. case, *Ticketmaster Corp., et al v. Tickets.com, Inc.*[21] The plaintiff alleged copyright infringement based (among other things) on deep linking to pages of the plaintiff's web site. The judge, on a motion to dismiss, observed "Hyperlinking does not itself involve a violation of the Copyright Act ... since no copying is involved. The customer is automatically transferred to the particular genuine web page of the original author. There is no deception in what is happening. This is analogous to using a library's card index to get a reference to particular items, albeit faster and more efficiently." Some contrasting European decisions based on database right are discussed below.

Linking and database right

2–082   The advent of a database right, created in United Kingdom law by the implementation of the E.U. Database Directive (discussed above), may provide a further basis on which a qualifying Web site owner may seek to assert control over those linking to its site. The Directive is implemented by the Copyright and Rights in Databases Regulations 1997.

Web sites as databases

2–083   The definition of "database"—a collection of independent works, data or other materials which are arranged in a systematic or methodical way and are individually accessible by electronic or other means (Regulation 6)—is sufficiently wide to include a collection of materials on a Web site. The owner of the database right has, under Regulation 16, the right to prevent the extraction or re-utilisation of all or a substantial part of the contents of his database without his consent. "Extraction" means the permanent or temporary transfer of contents to another medium by any means and in any form. "Re-utilisation" means making the contents available to the public by any means. "Substantial" means substantial in terms or quality or quantity or a combination of both. Under Regulation 19, the lawful user of a database which has been made available to the public in any manner is entitled to extract or re-use insubstantial parts of the contents of the database for any purpose.

It is likely that the contents of at least some Web sites would constitute a database for the purpose of the Regulations and that, if the database has been made by a qualified person, database right would subsist in the Web site. We will assume in this discussion for simplicity that one Web site may constitute one database. However, especially given the seamlessly linked nature of the Web, it is quite likely that one database may not be coterminous with one Web site. The question whether any particular Web site would qualify as a database depends on how widely "systematic or methodical" is to be interpreted. A simple Web site typically consists of a number of static pages of text and graphics, linked by hypertext links. The result has a structure of a sort, and typically considerable thought goes into the arrangement of the contents. However, the structure is essentially free-form rather than comprised of information organised into pre-defined records and fields in the manner of a traditional structured database. In short, in a simple Web site the systematic and methodical aspects are more in the means of access to the information (the links) than in the data itself.

2–084   Many Web sites show more systematic and methodical characteristics in the underlying data. At the simplest level the text and graphics files are organised in hierarchical directory structures—not necessary for the operation of a site, but useful for ease of maintenance. Often the Web page seen by the user contains selected data, perhaps in the form of a table, generated dynamically from a traditional database engine driving the Web site. In considering this issue, the terms of the Directive itself need to be borne in mind. Recital (21) states that, although the materials have to be arranged systematically or methodically, it is not necessary for those materials to have been physically stored in an organised manner. Recital (40) stresses that the object of the database right is to ensure protection of any investment in obtaining, verifying or presenting the contents of a database for the limited duration of the right. These recitals suggest that a wide interpretation of "systematic or methodical" arrangement may be appropriate.

Linking as infringement of database right

Turning to infringement, it appears that the person who accesses a Web site may extract **2–085** content from the site to his own computer, within the definition in the Regulations, at least if temporary transfer includes transfer to the relatively transient medium of RAM. That is the equivalent for copyright purposes of making a copy. The person who creates a link provides a pointer to the target site, thereby assisting the user to extract from the target site, but does not himself extract data from that site. It is arguable that the person creating the link makes the target content available to the public, and thereby re-utilises the target content within the meaning of the Regulations. Whether that would constitute re-utilising a substantial part of the database would depend on the circumstances, but where the link brings up the contents of an entire page that could very well be a substantial part, particularly when the quality test is applied. Under Regulation 16(2), repeated and systematic extraction or re-utilisation of insubstantial parts of the contents of a database any amount to extraction or re-utilisation of a substantial part of those contents. That suggests that creating a collection of links to content on the same Web site may constitute re-utilisation of a substantial part, even if each individual link re-utilises only an insubstantial part. Arguably, even repeated use of the link by different users amounts to repeated re-utilisation for the purposes of Regulation 16(2). A real life example to which this could apply occurred in the US, where a fan of the *Dilbert* comic strip created a series of links to comic strips on the *Dilbert* Web page of the owner of the copyright in the strips, United Media Services. In this way he created a new (and, he asserted, improved) *Dilbert* Web site, in which the comic strips were displayed in a new and different context and manner. While each individual drawing and strip is the subject of copyright, and it was with copyright infringement that United Media Services threatened the fan, in the E.U. the assertion of database right would have been an alternative to deal with the re-utilisation of substantially all of the comic strips on the official *Dilbert* site.

A number of decisions on database right and deep linking have issued in different **2–086** European countries.

In *Stepstone v. Ofir*[22], a German decision, the plaintiff and defendant were both on-line job agencies, competing with each other. The defendant created deep links to a substantial number of vacancies on the plaintiff's site. The plaintiff claimed that defendant automatically searched its database and copied and disseminated substantial parts of the it. It claimed that this, as well as the deep links, infringed its database right. The defendant claimed that copying only took place when the user accessed the database, and that there was an implied licence to create the links. The court granted an injunction against the defendant. The court held (1) that Stepstone's collection of job advertisements was a database; (2) that enabling users to have direct access to Stepstone's job vacancies, by-passing the main pages, infringed the exclusive right of copying, distribution and representation, in particular distribution which included making parts of the database available; and that the defendant had made repeated and systematic use of insubstantial parts; (3) That what the defendant had done was prejudicial to Stepstone, since it undermined its business concept and deprived it of advertising revenue; (4) that the question of implied consent did not arise where such prejudice existed.

Stepstone also sued Ofir in France. In a decision of the Nanterre Tribunal of Commerce,[23] the court held that the deep links to Stepstone's job vacancies did not infringe any intellectual property right.

2–087   In *PCM v. Kranten.com*,[24] the plaintiffs were newspapers who operated Web sites containing selections of news reports and articles from their newspapers. The home pages contained indexes to the contents. The defendants placed equivalent indexes on a page of their web site entitled "National Newspapers", with deep links to the relevant articles and news items. The plaintiffs alleged copyright and database right infringement and sought an interim injunction. The court held (1) that the argument that the home page was bypassed, causing loss of advertising revenue, was of little importance because there was nothing preventing the user from going to the home page; (2) the links were likely to have a promotional effect and it was unlikely that the plaintiffs were suffering real damage; (3) deep linking was not a reproduction of the linked work, so there was no copyright infringement; (4) while there had been a reproduction of the list of articles and news items, this was saved from copyright infringement by specific provisions of the Dutch Copyright Act 1912 permitting reproduction of work by a press medium provided the source is indicated; (5) it could not be said that the plaintiffs had invested substantially in the contents of the lists of titles of news items and articles. These were therefore not protected by database right. An interim injunction was refused.

2–088   In *NVM v. De Telegraaf*[25] the plaintiff was the Dutch Association of Real Estate Agents. It operated a database of properties for sale. The defendant, a national newspaper, operated a search engine called "El Cheapo". It searched other sites, including that of the plaintiff, for properties and presented the results to the user. The first instance judge ruled in favour of the claimants on database right, also holding that there was no copyright infringement. On appeal, the Court of Appeals of the Hague overturned the finding on database right. The defendant argued that the plaintiff's database was not protectable, since it was only a fusion of the individual databases of NVM agents. The appeals court held that there was no protection where the database could be regarded as a "spin-off" of the main activity of the database owner.

In *Havas Numerique, SNC and Cadres On Line S.A. v. Keljob*,[26] the plaintiff was a leading French jobs website. The defendant operated a jobs search engine which had established deep links to specific jobs advertised on the plaintiff's site. The plaintiff sued under articles of the Intellectual Property Code implementing the database right and prohibiting the act of representing a work without the consent of its author. The Paris Commercial Court, in an interim ruling at first instance, distinguished between the implicit authorisation for simple hypertext links and deep links, for which there was no such authorisation and which had a variety of damaging consequences, including amounting to an appropriation of the work and financial efforts of others. This was so, even though the defendant stated that it was not in competition with the plaintiff. On appeal, the Paris Court of Appeal found that Keljob operated a search engine which presented the results of the search to users and openly redirected them the target site. Keljob merely queried the database from time to time and did not download it. The court, reversing the decision at first instance, found that this did not infringe the database right, nor was there passing off. A decision on the full merits is yet to be given.

Spidering
An issue that arises in connection with deep linking is "spidering". This is the automated   **2–089**
searching of a target site with a view to creating links to elements of the site. Some of the activities in issue in the deep linking cases discussed above amount to spidering, particularly in the search engine cases where the site makes automated searches of the target site in order to create the deep links to the target site. In the *U.S. Ticketmaster v. Tickets.com* case discussed above one of the allegations made by the plaintiffs was that in the course of searching the target site to extract (unprotectable) factual information for use on the defendant's site, the defendants made temporary copies of copyright material from the target site. The plaintiffs argued that this was copyright infringement, even if only factual information and not the copies themselves were used on the defendant's site. The court held[27] that it was arguable, in the context of an application for an interim injunction, that this would be protected by the U.S. fair use doctrine (as applied to copying for the purpose of reverse engineering a computer program to obtain non-protectable information).

The plaintiffs in *Ticketmaster v. Tickets.com* also sought to rely on the doctrine of trespass to chattels, following the decision in *eBay Inc. v. Bidder's Edge*.[28] The *eBay* case was another spidering case. In this case the defendants had created an auction consolidation site, which used spiders to aggregate auction items from other sites. The parties had tried, but failed, to come to a licensing arrangement permitting Bidder's Edge to spider the eBay site. eBay made available on its servers a "robots.txt" file in accordance with the Robot Exclusion Standard.[29] When the defendants continued to spider the eBay site, the plaintiffs attempted to prevent access from Bidder's Edge by blocking IP addresses that the defendants were believed to be using. The defendants countered by using proxy servers to rotate IP addresses.

The evidence was that the defendant's spider would make about 100,000 accesses per   **2–090**
day to the plaintiff's site, which eBay assessed at between 1.11 per cent and 1.53 per cent of the total load on its listing servers. An average 10 million searches per day were made by users on the eBay site. Trespass arguments had already successfully been invoked by ISPs against bulk e-mailers,[30] where there was clear evidence that the volume of e-mail was affecting the operation of the plaintiff's system. In the *eBay* case, the court relied upon the potential harm that would ensue should aggregators generally be allowed free rein to spider the plaintiff's site and granted a preliminary injunction against the defendant. The court found that eBay was likely to be able to demonstrate at trial that the defendant's activities diminished the quality or value of eBay's computer systems, in that it was depriving eBay of the ability to use the portion of its personal property for its own purposes that was occupied in processing the defendant's searches. If the preliminary injunction were denied, and other aggregators began to crawl the eBay site, there would be little doubt that the load on eBay's computer system would qualify as a substantial impairment of condition or value.

In *Ticketmaster*, the court found that there was no evidence of either physical harm to the chattel or obstruction to its basic function and declined to grant a preliminary injunction.

The U.S. cases invoking trespass can be viewed as an attempt to fill a gap resulting from the lack of a database right in the USA. There may at first sight, therefore, be less need for the development of a similar doctrine in Europe where database protection exists. However, it should not be forgotten that there are so far very few countries outside the European Economic Area to which database right protection has been extended. In cases where that protection is not available, it may be possible to resort to trespass theories in the United Kingdom. Trespass is discussed in more detail in Chapter 5, in connection with liability for the dissemination of viruses.

Framing

2–091   An issue related to Web linking is the use of frames on a Web site. Frames are an HTML enhancement which enable the Web site designer to split the screen into a number of separate areas, or frames. Each frame can be made to act independently, so that while one frame access new pages the others (which will typically contain menu buttons and advertising banners) remain in place. The use of frames as a way of navigating content on one site is uncontroversial. However, frames can be used to access other sites. So when the user clicks on a link to another site from within a frame, instead of the target site's content completely replacing the pointing site's content, it appears surrounded by the material in the frames remaining from the pointing site. This arrangement has potential to undermine the assumptions on which advertising and sponsorship deals are done. For example, if RedBurger agree to sponsor a site, they are unlikely to be amused when the site contents appear to the user surrounded by frames of advertising from YellowBurger.

2–092   However, the question whether the practice is unlawful is far from clear. As far as copyright is concerned, the arguments will be similar to those applicable to ordinary linking. Other intellectual property rights may also be relevant. In the USA a group of on-line news providers commenced litigation against Total News Inc, complaining of its framing practices at its Total News Web site. The Total News site consisted of lists of links to on-line news sites, identified by the names of the plaintiffs. The plaintiffs complained that when their sites appear in the Total News frame their content is partially obscured to fit the frame, reduced in size and placed alongside the Total News logo, menus, URL and advertisements. The plaintiffs particularly complained that advertisers may buy space on a Web site based on the expectation that their advertisement will appear in a certain location or slot, be of a certain size or duration, or be free of the "clutter" of competing advertisements, particularly advertisements for competing products; and that the framing activities of the defendants may defeat any of those expectations. This claim, based on misappropriation, trade mark dilution, trade mark infringement, false designations of origin, false representations and false advertising, deceptive acts and practices, copyright infringement and tortious interference with advertising contracts, was settled before trial. Under the settlement, Total News can continue linking, but may not display the target content within a frame or (in effect), purposefully using an intermediate site as a conduit to frame one of the plaintiffs' pages.

Search engines

2–093   Other activities can give rise to similarly difficult questions, and to the sometimes novel application of existing laws to new situations. For instance, while the position of general search engines is well established on the Internet, it can already be seen from the discussion above that when a search engine enters into competitive activity, operations that are acceptable in a wider context are likely to come under close legal scrutiny. Similarly, when a general search engine extends its activities into new types of content it may find that it is challenged. This occurred in the U.S. case of *Kelly v. Arriba Soft Corp*,[31] which concerned a "visual" search engine. This operated in the same way as a traditional text search engine, save that it indexed images found on the Web by its spider or crawler software. The captured images were copied onto Arriba's server and briefly retained in order to reduce them to a thumbnail form. The full size images were then deleted from Arriba's server and the thumbnails indexed. Clicking on the thumbnail would load the full-size image from the target web site, together with the URL for the web site where it originated. In a later version, clicking on the thumbnail opened two windows: one containing the full-size image, the other containing the full target web page. The Plaintiff was a photographer who complained about the use of images obtained from his web site in this way. The court found that the reproduction and display of the images were protected by the U.S. fair use provisions. Although the display of the full-size image in a window out of context from the target web page was a factor that told against fair use, on the whole the purpose and character of the defendant's use was transformative rather than expoitative and was a fair use. The fact that the thumbnail deep-linked to the image on the plaintiff's site did not produce harm or adverse impact that would detract from that.

Search engines are vulnerable to a particular form of linking, whereby a third party web page includes a query box that transmits the user's search query back to the search engine. The third party site then displays the results page generated by the search engine. The question can arise whether this "front-end" can be created without permission. Again, and depending on exactly how the unauthorised "front-end" has been built and presented, the various forms of intellectual property right that we have discussed, and perhaps trespass, may be relevant. In this type of case attention may need to be paid to whether the unauthorised front-end incorporates any source code derived from the search engine site in order to construct and transmit the search query to the target search engine. **2–094**

Peer to peer

We mention below the US Napster case, involving peer to peer technology. The U.S. approach to authorisation may be compare with that set out in the *Amstrad* case, above. **2–095**

The time-shifting provisions of the 1988 Act may also be noted. Section 70 of the 1988 Act provides: "the making for private and domestic use of a recording of a broadcast or cable programme solely for the purpose of enabling it to be viewed or listened to at a more convenient time, does not infringe any copyright in the broadcast or cable programme or any work included in it."

We discuss below the definition of "cable programme". It appears to be capable of reading on to some content provided over the Internet. Thus, some content downloaded from the Internet could be regarded as part of a "cable programme" within the meaning of section 70. As discussed below, there is some support for this in the decision of the Scottish court in *Shetland Times v. Wills*.[32]

The result of this could be that some content downloaded from the Internet might benefit from the protection of section 70, so long as the making was for private and domestic use and the purpose of "making the recording" (if this can read on to downloading) was for time shifting. **2–096**

However, it should be noted that the US Napster court rejected a fair use argument based on "space-shifting". This was an argument that users who already owned an audio CD were simply downloading files to listen to music they already owned. The argument was rejected, largely on the grounds that the users were simultaneously distributing the copyright material to the general public. Similar objections would most likely disapply section 70 of the 1988 Act.

2.7 Liability of hosts and access providers for third party material

2–097 The person who sends infringing material over the Internet may not be traceable, so that the copyright owner has to look elsewhere for suitable defendants. Can the Internet host or access provider be liable for copyright infringement?

2.7.1 The Electronic Commerce Directive

2–098 The following discussion addresses the position under the current legislation. When the Electronic Commerce Directive is implemented, as it must be before January 17, 2002, "information society service providers" who act as conduits or hosts, or engage in caching, will be able to invoke the protection of Articles 12 to 15 of the Directive, at least in relation to damages. These liability provisions are described in Chapter 5. Internet service providers and telecommunications companies will be among those who will be able to invoke these provisions for some of these activities. However, the provisions are without prejudice to the ability of a court or administrative authority, in accordance with a Member State's legal system, to require the service provider to terminate or prevent an infringement. So even for those within the scope of the Directive, it seems likely (depending on exactly how the Directive is implemented) that exposure to risk of an injunction will still have to be assessed according to the underlying rules of liability. Again depending on how the Directive is implemented, it may be that if the protection of the Directive is lost (*e.g.* because the service provider has become aware of the unlawful material), the claimant may still have to show that the service provider is a person who is liable in accordance with the underlying law. This will depend on whether the Directive is implemented as an overlay on the existing legislation, merely providing an additional defence for service providers, or whether it is more intimately woven into it.

2.7.2 U.S. and other cases

2–099 It is clear from the scope of the exclusive rights of the copyright owner that any Internet host or access provider who uses or knowingly permits others to use his Internet service to disseminate unauthorised copies of copyright works is in danger of a civil action for infringement. There is also a risk of infringement even if the host or access provider does this unknowingly.

There have already been a number of cases in the U.S. which have involved bulletin boards containing copyright material which could be downloaded by those accessing the board. In *Playboy Enterprises Inc v. Frena*,[33] the defendant's bulletin board had distributed unauthorised copies of photographs from the *Playboy* magazine. The defendant was held to have infringed *Playboy*'s copyright, even though he claimed that he did not himself put such material on his board and was unaware that some of his subscribers were doing so. The mere fact that he was making copies available was an infringement. Also, the fact that subscribers were able to view the photographs on their computer screen constituted an infringement of the public display right.

2–100 An early decision from California, *Religious Technology Center v. Netcom Online Communications Services*,[34] dealt with the liability of a Usenet host. Although overtaken by subsequent U.S. legislation, the case is still interesting for the analysis of who causes an infringement to occur. The case involved postings to a Usenet newsgroup on a bulletin board (BBS) connected to the Internet by Netcom, a large Internet service provider. A former scientologist posted portions of scientology works to the alt.religion.scientology newsgroup, resulting in an action for copyright infringement. The suit was brought against the former scientologist, the BBS and Netcom.

Usenet newsgroups are automatically copied from one computer to the next across the Internet. The plaintiffs argued that copies of the newsgroup postings were made and held on Netcom's computers for up to 11 days after they were posted, and that Netcom were thus direct infringers and strictly liable irrespective of their knowledge of the contents of the posting.

The court had to consider whether "possessors of computers are liable for incidental copies automatically made on their computers using their software as part of a process initiated by a third party". Neither Netcom nor the BBS initiated the copying, which resulted from the former scientologist posting the articles to the alt.religion.scientology newsgroup. The copying then followed from the automatic process of replicating newsgroups across the Usenet system.

Netcom was held not to be a direct infringer. Any copies on its machines were made automatically and the court did not find workable "a theory of infringement that would hold the entire Internet liable for activities that cannot reasonably be deterred". The court said that although copyright is a strict liability statute, there should still be some element of volition or causation which is lacking where a system is merely used to create a copy by a third party. The court made a similar finding in respect of alleged infringement of the plaintiff's right of public distribution and display.

The plaintiff also argued that distribution of these postings after Netcom had been given notice of infringement constituted contributory infringement (which requires knowledge of the infringing activity). That question was left to go to trial.

In *Sega Enterprises v. Maphia*[35] the Northern District Court of California followed **2–101** *Netcom* and declined to hold a BBS operator liable for direct copyright infringement, notwithstanding that the activities of the BBS operator was more participatory than were those of the *Netcom* defendants. The plaintiff had not shown that the defendant personally uploaded or downloaded files or caused that to occur. The most it had shown was that the defendant operated his BBS, he knew infringing activity was occurring and solicited others to upload games. However, the court went on to hold the defendant liable for contributory infringement.

The U.S. *Napster* case involved a web site that was not, strictly speaking, a host at all. **2–102** Napster distributed from its web site "peer-to-peer" software, which enabled its users to make MP3 compressed music files stored on individual user hard drives available to other Napster users, to search for MP3 music files stored on other users' computers and to transfer copies of MP3 files between individual users. Napster's servers provided facilities for the indexing and searching of MP3 files available from users logged on to the Napster system and other functions such as a chat room. The plaintiffs, seeking a preliminary injunction, claimed that the Napster users were engaged in the wholesale reproduction of copyright works, all constituting direct infringement. The court found that this was likely and that the plaintiffs would likely succeed at trial in establishing that Napster users did not have a fair use defence. The court went on to find Napster liable for contributory infringement. This did not follow merely because peer-to-peer file sharing technology may be used for infringing purposes. However, the evidence was sufficient to show that the plaintiffs would likely establish at trial that Napster knew or had reason to know of its users' infringements of their copyrights. The evidence was also sufficient to show that the plaintiffs would likely succeed at trial in holding Napster vicariously liable for their users infringements. This arose from a combination of Napster's failure to police the system and the financial benefit that accrued to it from the continuing presence of infringing files on the system. A preliminary injunction was granted.

2–103 In a Dutch case on liability of hosts, *Scientology v. XS 4ALL cs*,[36] the President of the District Court of The Hague held that Internet providers are not liable for possible copyright infringement on their servers, unless it was clear and evident that the information contained on their servers would infringe copyrighted works of third parties.

A well-publicised U.S. criminal case involved a student at MIT who operated a bulletin board which invited the free exchange of commercial software. He made no personal gain from these activities, which allegedly cost software publishers over $1 million in lost sales, so the criminal provisions of the U.S. Copyright Act did not apply. Instead he was prosecuted under the U.S. Computer Fraud and Abuse Act 1986. Although the court characterised his behaviour as "heedlessly irresponsible, and at worst as nihilistic, self-indulgent and lacking in any fundamental sense of values", it dismissed the indictment on the grounds the Copyright Act provided exclusively for criminal copyright infringement, so a "back-door" prosecution under the 1986 Act was not permitted (see *United States v. LaMaccia*[37]).

2.7.3 US Digital Millennium Copyright Act

2–104 There are now statutory provisions in the U.S. dealing with copyright liability of Internet service providers, Title II of the DMCA (see Section 2.2.4). This provides a number of "safe harbours"; if the service provider's activities come within one of these safe harbours it will not be liable for any monetary relief (including damages, court costs and attorney's fees) for any claims of infringement based on these activities, and also the types of injunctions that can be issued are limited.

The wording of the legislation is very complicated, but basically there are four safe harbours. The first is "conduit" activities, transmission, routing or providing connections; provided the ISP is a mere conduit and does not modify the content, it qualifies for protection. The same is true for automatic caching. The other two safe harbours, hosting content provided by users and linking, will only apply if the ISP does not have actual knowledge of the infringement and is not aware of facts or circumstances from which infringing activity would be apparent, and the ISP must not receive a direct financial benefit from the infringing activity. In order to qualify for any of the safe harbours the ISP must have a termination policy for repeat offenders, and must comply with certain technical measures. The first of these is that the ISP must accommodate and not interfere with "standard technical measures", which are those that have been developed pursuant to a broad consensus of copyright owners and service providers in an open standards process, available to anyone to use on non-discriminatory terms and which do not place an undue burden on the ISP. Individual safe harbours have their own additional requirements. For caching, hosting and linking, the ISP must be able to expeditiously remove or disable access to material claimed to be infringing upon notification of a claim of infringement and must provide a method for communicating such notifications, such as designated agent listed in a directory compiled by the Copyright Office.

2.7.4 United Kingdom analysis

So far there has been no United Kingdom civil copyright infringement decision relating to an Internet host's liability for third party activities. As United Kingdom law, unlike U.S. law, has specific provisions discussed above dealing with electronic copying, there seems to be no reason why United Kingdom courts would not hold that an Internet host could be liable for copyright infringement by either issuing unauthorised copies of the work to the public or by, in effect, showing or playing the work in public in cases of works such as photographs and video games.

2–105

The English courts could perhaps go further than did the U.S. courts. Under the 1988 Act, copying includes storing the work in any medium by electronic means. The storage is undoubtedly on the Internet host's computer, even though a third party may have put it there. It remains to be seen whether an English court would take a similar public policy approach to that adopted by the court in *Netcom* and refuse to find direct infringement for automatic copying occurring during storage and onward transmission of infringing material resulting from a third party's actions, such as with Usenet newsgroups or with transmission and storage of e-mail messages. The policy aspects may also take on a different hue once the Electronic Commerce Directive is implemented.

It should also be borne in mind that under English law a person who authorises copyright infringement is strictly liable for the infringement. A host who makes material available for downloading may be vulnerable to a complaint of authorising infringement even if he did not know or had no reason to believe that the material infringed.

2–106

Similar questions regarding responsibility may arise where infringing material is placed on a Web site. Arrangements for control of content may diverge widely from the simple example of the site where the host owner is responsible for the content. The host may rent space on the site to an intermediary who themes and promotes the space as an attractive site on which content providers can place their wares. If a content provider places infringing material on the site, the question of the liability of the host and of the intermediary may have to be considered.

2.7.5 Linking liability

Liability for authorising infringement may also arise when a Web site owner provides visitors to the site with access to copyright material on another site, for example by hypertext links. There is unlikely to be liability on the Web site owner where the link is to a legitimate site but the visitor acts in an unauthorised way, *e.g.* by copying material onto his hard disk despite having notice that this is not authorised. Liability is more likely when the link is to a site which is known or believed to carry pirate software or other unauthorised material.

2–107

There has been an increasing number of cases in which linking to unlawful material has been enjoined, although none (other than possibly the Nottinghamshire County Council JET Report case discussed in Chapter 6) in the United Kingdom. In the U.S. *DeCSS* case[38], concerning the publication on a website of software alleged to allow users to decode DVD discs, part of the judgment concerned the defendant's links to other sites carrying the software. The judge had to decide whether creating such links amounted to "offering DeCSS to the public" or "providing or otherwise trafficking in it", within the DMCA.

2–108   The defendants' links were of three types: (1) links to a web page on an outside site that does not itself contain a link to DeCCS, but links either directly or indirectly via a series of other pages to another page on the same site that posts the software; (2) links to a web page on an outside site that does contain a link to DeCCS, with our without other text and links; (3) links to a DeCSS file on an outside site that automatically starts to download without further user intervention.

As to the third type, the judge held that there was no serious question that this fell within the anti-trafficking provisions of DeCCS. The defendants were engaged in the functional equivalent of transferring the DeCSS code to the user themselves.

As to the second type, substantially the same was held to be true of the defendants' hyperlinks to web pages that displayed nothing more than the DeCSS code or presented the user only with the choice of commencing a download of DeCSS and no other content. The only distinction was that the entity extending to the user the option of downloading the program was the transferee site rather than defendants, which the court held to be "a distinction without a difference".

2–109   The judge also considered links to pages that offered "a good deal of content other than DeCSS but that offer a hyperlink for downloading, or transferring to a page for downloading, DeCSS". He regarded these as potentially more troublesome. He said: "If one assumed, for the purposes of argument, that the *Los Angeles Times* Web site somewhere contained the DeCSS code, it would be wrong to say that anyone who linked to the *Los Angeles Times* Web site, regardless of purpose or the manner in which the link was described, thereby offered, provided or otherwise trafficked in DeCSS merely because DeCSS happened to be available on a site to which one linked.' However, he went on to distinguish that situation from the one under consideration, in which "Defendants urged others to post DeCSS in an effort to disseminate DeCSS and to inform defendants that they were doing so. Defendants then linked their site to those 'mirror' sites, after first checking to ensure that the mirror sites in fact were posting DeCSS or something that looked like it, and proclaimed on their own site that DeCSS could be had by clicking on the hyperlinks on defendants' site. By doing so, they offered, provided or otherwise trafficked in DeCSS, and they continue to do so to this day".

2–110   The court observed that anything that would impose strict liability on a web site operator for the entire contents of any web site to which the operator linked would raise grave constitutional concerns, as web site operators would be inhibited from linking for fear of exposure to liability. The judge for this and other constitutional reasons held that there should be 'no injunction against, nor liability for, linking to a site containing circumvention technology, the offering of which is unlawful under the DMCA, absent clear and convincing evidence that those responsible for the link (a) know at the relevant time that the offending material is on the linked-to site, (b) know that it is circumvention technology that may not lawfully be offered, and (c) create or maintain the link for the purpose of disseminating that technology'. He enjoined the defendants Eric Corley and 2600 Enterprises, Inc. (other defendants having previously settled with the plaintiffs) from (*inter alia*): "knowingly linking any Internet Web site operated by them to any other web site containing DeCSS, or knowingly maintaining any such link, for the purpose of disseminating DeCSS".

After this judgment (which is under appeal) the defendants removed the links to other DeCCS sites, but continued to publish the Web addresses and URLs of those sites.

In another case the Mormon Church obtained a preliminary injunction restraining the publication of web addresses of sites containing material alleged to infringe copyright. The court found that it was likely that the defendants knew, or should have known, that the websites contained the copies and so were likely to be liable for contributory infringement.[39]

2.7.6 Caches and mirrors

Another thorny issue on the Internet is caching and mirroring. A cache is an electronic store of material, usually in the context of the Internet Web pages or their components, copied from somewhere else. Different types of cache have varying characteristics, but they all have the common purpose of enabling the Internet to function more efficiently by reducing the load on communications link. The idea of a cache is to store content locally, so that if the content has not changed since the last access the browser will load up the locally stored copy instead of accessing the original remote site. The most familiar type of cache to end users of the Internet is that created by popular Web browsers. These create caches on the hard disk of the user's computer. Like most caches the contents are temporary, in the sense that they change dynamically as the user accesses further Web sites and the browser decides what to add to and delete from the cache. However, they are certainly not transient and are stored on the disk between browser sessions like any other electronic file. Other caches may be created by companies with intranets. Some firewalls create an intermediate cache of pages between the internal and external network. Or a company may wish to reduce traffic on its external communications links by creating a cache of commonly accessed pages for internal access. Internet service providers often create caches for the use of their subscribers. Lastly, it has been known for bodies to create special local cache sites containing collections of Web sites, which people can access in preference to the original, remote sites. This type of cache is closer to a mirror site (see below) than a normal cache. What is common to all these varieties of cache is that they involve storing electronic copies of copyright works, which is clearly a restricted act and therefore potentially infringing. **2–111**

Although caches are generally understood to be beneficial to the efficient working of the Internet, there are parties who can be prejudiced by their use and who could have reason to object. Many Web sites are free to access, generating revenue from advertising based on the number of visitors to the site. Such a site needs to have accurate visitor statistics to support its advertising rates. If the visitor accesses a cached version of the page bearing the advertisement, then unless some technical means can be found to transmit the "hit" to the original site, the visitor will be lost to the statistics. Many sites have real-time elements: stock prices perhaps, or advertisements that change every few seconds. The timely operation of such features may be prejudiced if the visitor is accessing through a cache. Caching may prejudice charging systems based on recording visits to the original site. **2–112**

Although caching is prima facie an infringing act, it does not follow that all types of caching are necessarily so. There may be an implied licence to cache, if the practice is widespread and generally accepted, or possibly if the person creating the cache can demonstrate that the Internet could not function effectively without it so that the person putting the material on the public Internet must be taken to have consented to it. That would be a matter for expert technical evidence if the issue were litigated. Browser caches are so common that there is likely to be an implied licence for that.

To the extent that Web pages are computer programs (see above), the provisions of sections 50A and 50C of the 1988 Act may be relevant—at least to browser caching. Section 50A legitimises the making of a back-up copy of a program by a lawful user, which it is necessary for him to have for the purposes of his lawful use. It might be arguable that a browser cache is the equivalent of a back-up copy of a traditional program. However, there are at least two problems with this. First, it will be difficult to argue necessity. The user can turn off his browser cache and the browser will continue to function, albeit more slowly. Second, the browser will often cache discrete elements of the Web site (especially graphic elements), which do not constitute a computer program. Similar problems would be encountered in seeking to apply section 50C, which legitimises (subject to contrary agreement) the copying or adapting by a lawful user of a computer program if it is necessary for his lawful use.

2–113   It is difficult to see how caching could be brought within any of the fair dealing provisions of the 1988 Act. What is really required to enable copyright law to adapt to changing technology and practices is a more flexible fair use provision, the advantage of fair use compared with implied licence being that the copyright owner cannot reverse its effect by express prohibition. Even then, the problem with a fair use doctrine in relation to an activity such as caching is that it is not possible to assess fairness only as a function of the activity of caching. What may be fair in relation to one type of Web site may be unfair in relation to another, so that a person creating a dynamic, changing, cache for efficiency purposes would still need some means of distinguishing between individual Web sites. Some Web sites have in fact included anti-caching clauses in their copyright licences or site use agreements.

A mirror site, while created like a cache to lessen the load on communications links, is a more permanent collection of data, typically containing files (such as software programs) for the user to download to disk. So a software company may create a number of mirror sites around the world from which local users can download programs, upgrades, patches and so on. Someone who created an unauthorised mirror site would not be able to argue for the existence of an implied licence, unless he could demonstrate a custom permitting it. Some kinds of caching will be covered by the Copyright Directive (discussed above) and by the Electronic Commerce Directive (discussed in Chapter 5), when implemented.

2.7.7 Remedies for infringement

2–114   In a civil action for infringement of copyright the successful claimant may be awarded an injunction to prevent further infringement, damages or an account of profits, an order for delivery up or destruction of infringing copies in the defendant's possession or control, and costs. There is also a right to seize infringing copies found on sale, but this remedy is subject to a number of conditions.

The owner of copyright in published literary works (including computer programs) may in certain circumstances be able to prevent importation of infringing copies by giving notice to HM Customs & Excise requesting them to treat infringing copies of the work as prohibited goods, in which case importation of such copies will be prohibited for up to five years and any found by Customs will be liable to forfeiture.

2–115   The claimant may be able to seize infringing goods and evidence relating to the infringement by a seizure order, previously known as an *Anton Piller* order. This originated in *Anton Piller KG v. Manufacturing Processes Ltd*,[40] where the Court of Appeal approved the grant of an *ex parte* order authorising the claimant's solicitor to enter the defendant's premises and remove evidence of copyright infringement. The claimant must show that:

(a)   the claimant has a strong prima facie case;

(b)   the actual or potential damage to the claimant's interest is very serious;

(c)   the defendant is likely to have infringing copies of the work in his possession; and

(d)   there is a real possibility that if the defendant is forewarned he might destroy the evidence.

Conviction for criminal copyright infringement carries a maximum of two years imprisonment and/or a fine.

2.8 Electronic publishing on the Internet – copyright issues

Distributing copyright material electronically via the Internet is becoming increasingly common. At first it was mainly software that was distributed this way, but now most newspapers publish an on-line version, technical book publishers find it a convenient way to provide updates (as is the case with this book), and with improvement in compression technologies it is becoming viable to distribute music and videos over the Internet.   **2–116**

The first copyright question that arises is whether the publisher has the right to distribute the work in this way. There have been two reported cases, one in the U.S. and one in France, where journalists objected to having their copy, originally submitted for print, reproduced in an on-line publication. In the U.S. case, *Tasini v. New York Times*, a number of freelance journalists sued a number of publishers to whom they had submitted articles for print and who had then reused the articles in various electronic publications. Their contracts with the publishers had not assigned copyright, so the issue was whether what the publishers had done came within the scope of rights given to the owner of the copyright in a collective work, which is how the original print publications are classed for U.S. copyright purposes. The owner of the collective work can use a contribution owned by another for the purpose of reproducing the collective work, any revision of that collective work and any later collective work in the same series.[41] The US Supreme Court held that the revision right did not include rights to republish individually copyrighted articles from the collective work in electronic media. The databases on which the articles are stored reproduce articles separately, not as part of the collective work. Unlike conversion of newsprint to microfilm, the transfer to a database is not a mere transfer of the collective work from one medium to another, because it allows users to access individual articles.[42]

The French case, *Union Syndicale des Journalistes Français CFDT v. Societé Plurimédia* also found in favour of the authors. The court in a summary determination decided that publication on-line was not the same as print publications, and, as it was a form of exploitation unforeseen at the time the Union had negotiated the collective contract for its members with the publishers, it was not covered by the contract, so that the publishers had not acquired the right to reproduce the articles in this new medium. It is interesting that the defendant Plurimedia was not a publisher but an ISP which carried certain on-line news services. The court held that it should have verified with the publishers whether they had the right to publish these materials on the Internet, and it was enjoined from making these news services available so long as the newspapers and the journalists   **2–117** did not have a contract permitting on-line publication. If this decision is followed, it will have the unfortunate result of making the ISP responsible for determining for itself its customers' right to publish on-line whatever they put on their Web page.

2–118   Distribution of works electronically via the Internet has commercial attractions for publishers. The considerable costs of printing books or making CDs (in both cases from material which is already in digital form) and of storing and distributing the resulting physical objects are almost completely avoided. Innovative ways of buying works are possible. For example, the number of times or the length of time for which you could play a piece of music could be limited, so you would pay less for access to a pop song that you only wanted to listen to a few times than with physical recordings for which you pay the same however few or many times you listen to them. However, the ease with which digital works can be copied provides the publishers with the nightmare of widespread copying with no financial return. Although all unauthorised copies would be infringing, it would be completely unrealistic to catch and sue the thousands of individuals world wide who end up with these copies. The best that the law can provide in the way of protection is through contract (see the discussion in Chapter 10 for formation of contracts over the Internet). Such contracts do have the merit of bringing to the user's attention to what she can or cannot do with the materials she is purchasing. Instead, technological methods of protection are increasingly relied upon. The first of these is "digital watermarking", the inclusion in the work of digital signals which identify, *inter alia*, whether the copy is authorised or not. The U.S. recording industry has set up an anti-piracy consortium (Secure Digital Music Initiative, "SDMI"), which recently announced that it had selected a system of watermarking which will enable music players fitted with the system to refuse to play unauthorised copies. In Europe, the Commission has been funding the IMPRIMATUR programme to establish standard copyright management systems for the whole range of industries that produce works in electronic format. As discussed above, the 1996 WIPO treaties include protection for anti-copying and rights management systems.

2.9 Protection of confidential information

2–119   United Kingdom law provides legal protection for various types of confidential information. In general, this is a body of law which has developed through case law, although there is some legislation, mainly dealing with personal information (data protection) and things such as telephone tapping. Most recently, following the introduction of the Human Rights Act 1998, the courts have developed the law of confidential information to embrace the concept of privacy.[43] However, we are here concerned with the confidential information of commercial entities, which is mainly protected through case law development. This case law has developed over the last two hundred years, and has shown itself capable of adapting to new circumstances and technologies. While there as yet few cases dealing with modern information technology, there is no reason why the case law should not continue to develop to cover it. This flexibility makes the law of confidential information useful in the fast changing world of IT.

2.9.1 What is protectable confidential information?

The primary requirement for protection is that the person seeking protection has kept the **2–120** information secret. The definition frequently quoted is that of Lord Greene M.R. in *Saltman Engineering v. Campbell*,[44] that confidential information is something which is not "public property or public knowledge". This secrecy need not be absolute in that it may be known by more than one person, provided that that person is not free to make the information public. It is a less stringent test than the test for novelty under patent law.

There are no defined limits on the type of confidential information that will be protected. The main categories involved in decided cases are technical information (sometimes referred to as "trade secrets" or "know how"), commercial information such as customer lists, personal information such as confidences between spouses or private photographs, ideas for plays, TV shows and the like and government information (*e.g.* the *Spycatcher* case). It may very well be that the confidential information is comprised of public information and the confidentiality attaches to the selection; for example, the names and addresses on a customer list may be published in directories but the protectable information is the fact that those particular names and addresses represent this company's customer base. Such information is clearly of value, both to the company and potentially to its competitors, and will be kept secret.

There is no specific requirement that confidential information must be of value in order to be protected, but in practice most of the remedies which could be granted by a court which has found that there has been a breach of confidence require that this breach has in some way damaged the person whose information it is.

2.9.2 What is an obligation of confidence?

Although cases discuss confidentiality in terms of being a property right, like the other **2–121** forms of intellectual property, the preferred view is that confidential information law is an exercise of the court's equitable jurisdiction,[45] a law of obligations rather than of property rights. Therefore, once confidentiality of the information is established, the next requirement for protection is that the confidential information was disclosed in circumstances which imposed an obligation on the confidant to respect the confidentiality of the information.[46]

2.9.3 How does an obligation of confidence arise?

There are a number of "circumstances which impose an obligation to respect the **2–122** confidentiality of the information" recognised in the case law. The most common are legally enforceable contractual obligations and the obligations imposed by the law on employees. However, the courts have also developed an equitable jurisdiction to restrain breaches of confidence where there is no legal relationship between the parties. As it is important to understand the basis on which an obligation of confidence may be imposed, each of these is considered in more detail below.

Contract
Contractual obligations of confidentiality may be either express or implied.

The best way of ensuring that a recipient of confidential information is bound by an **2–123** obligation of confidence is to impose it by an express, written agreement. Such agreements may be very short, dealing only with the obligation of confidence, or the obligation may form part of a much longer agreement, for example a know-how licence or development agreement. It is also a good idea to provide expressly that the contract may be terminated immediately if there is a breach of the obligation of confidence.

An obligation of confidentiality will be implied in a contract under the same rules as other implied terms, namely to give the transaction the effect the parties clearly intended. However, there are obvious dangers in having to rely upon an implied term, as it will only be enforced if a court believes that there was such need for the term and that both parties would have agreed to its inclusion at the time the contract was entered into if they had thought about the matter. The best practice is always to include an express obligation of confidentiality.

Employees and contractors

2–124   A well drafted employment contract will contain express obligations of confidence, as well as dealing with post-employment issues such as a non-compete provision. Similarly, when an independent contractor is hired, that contract should contain an express obligation of confidence whenever there is any chance that the contractor will learn company confidential information. When the contractor is likely to help to develop confidential information or any other intellectual property, there should be an obligation to protect the confidentiality and to assign all rights to the employer.

Even in the absence of an employment contract, certain obligations of confidentiality are imposed by law on employees. A distinction must be drawn between the situation where the employment is continuing and that where is has ended. However, there are general principles which apply to both, and these were discussed fully in the leading case *Faccenda Chicken Ltd v. Fowler*,[47] which involved an ex-employee starting a competing business selling chickens by home delivery. These principles are as follows:

(1)   The obligations of confidence of the employee are governed by his contract of employment.

(2)   Where there is no express obligation, there are obligations implied by law into this contract.

(3)   While the employee remains employed, there is an implied term imposing a duty of good faith and fidelity, which encompasses an obligation of confidence. The extent of this duty depends upon the nature of the employment—a senior manager is held to a higher standard than the caretaker.

(4)   To determine whether any particular item is covered by the obligation, all circumstances must be considered, particularly the nature of the employment, the nature of the information, whether the employee was made aware by the employer of the confidentiality of the information and whether the relevant information can be isolated from the general knowledge that the employee is free to use in another employment or disclose.

2–125   Once the employment ends, the implied duty of good faith continues but becomes narrower in scope. There is now a potential conflict between an obligation of confidentiality and the rule against restraint of trade. Anyone must be free to use their general stock of knowledge and skill in a subsequent employment, even if that knowledge and skill has been gained during the previous employment. The problem is distinguishing between what the employee must be free to use and what is information belonging to his former employer which is the subject of a continuing obligation of confidence. The courts tend to find in favour of mobility of labour unless the former employer has taken express steps to indicate what information he considers to be proprietary and confidential. For the application of these principles to computer programmers see *FSS Travel and Leisure Systems Ltd v. Johnson and another.*[48]

Obligations arising from specific relationships

Certain professions are obliged to maintain the confidentiality of disclosures made by their clients, in particular doctors, lawyers, bankers and priests. These obligations are in general imposed by professional rules, and are enforced both by the governing body of the relevant profession and by the courts. Certain private relationships carry implied obligations of confidentiality, in particular marriage. Fiduciary relationships, such as between a company and its directors, a partnership and its individual partners, trustee and beneficiary and principal and agent, carry within the general duty of loyalty and good faith implied by such relationships an obligation of confidentiality.

2–126

Equity

There are cases where there is no contractual relationship of any kind between the parties, but it would be shocking if the recipient of clearly confidential information were therefore under no obligation to keep it secret and not to use it other than for the purpose for which it was disclosed. The courts have used their general equitable jurisdiction to deal with such circumstances. Indeed, the equitable concepts of good faith and fair dealing may be applied even when the parties have an express contractual confidentiality agreement. The advantage of the equitable jurisdiction is that it is flexible, and can be adapted to the particular circumstances of the case. The main requirement for the imposition of an equitable obligation of confidence on the recipient of information is that the recipient knew or, from the circumstances should have known, that the information was confidential and was being imparted for a limited purpose.

2–127

The equitable jurisdiction is particularly useful in the case where there has been a disclosure in breach of an obligation of confidence to a third party. Provided that the circumstances were such that the third party knew or should have known that the disclosure should not have been made, he can be restrained from further disclosing or misusing the information.

2.9.4 How long does an obligation of confidence last?

The general rule is that, unless the parties agree to the contrary, the obligation of confidence lasts as long as the information remains confidential.

2–128

Where there is an express contractual obligation of confidence, then the contract may specify the term of this obligation. This can be for a specified period or may be expressed to last as long as the information retains its confidential nature. Where no period is specified, the obligation is in effect of perpetual duration, although once the information becomes fully disclosed to the public other through a breach of the obligation of confidence there would be no damage to the confider if the confidant itself disclosed the information.

Where the person under the obligation of confidence has in breach of that obligation made the information public, or has continued to use the information after termination of an agreement permitting him to do so and the information has become public in some other way, the courts acknowledge that making that person subject to a continuing obligation when the rest of the world is free to use the information can be a somewhat draconian remedy. In such cases they may apply what is called the "springboard" doctrine. Inherently, this "special disability" must be of limited duration; it is usually an injunction for the period which it would take a competitor without the special knowledge to get up and running, or it may take the form of royalties for such period.

2.9.5 How is confidential information protected?

2–129   The main way of protecting confidential information is through a civil action for breach of an obligation of confidentiality. Provisional remedies, particularly an interim injunction, can be of great value in cases of breach of confidentiality where the full disclosure of the secret lets the "cat out of the bag" and where damages either cannot be readily calculated or are an inadequate remedy. Many breach of confidentiality cases are in fact decided by the outcome of the hearing for an interim injunction. Cases where the person under an obligation has acted in an underhand way, which particularly occurs in cases where a departing employee makes secret preparations by smuggling out confidential documents (increasingly these days by e-mail) before giving in his notice and departing to his own or another's competing business, are particularly suitable for a search order).

An injunction may also be granted as a final remedy. In light of the springboard doctrine, this may be limited in duration. In suitable cases the defendant may also be ordered to destroy or deliver up the items which contain the confidential material; for example, customer lists or drawings in the case of a departing employee. The claimant in a case involving a breach of a contractual obligation of confidence will be awarded damages on the normal compensatory basis that applies to any breach of contract. In theory, a court of equity cannot grant damages (a legal remedy) but only an account of profits. An account of profits is difficult to carry out, and in many cases the wrongdoer has made no, or only very small profits compared to the loss to the wronged person. By statute the court can grant damages in lieu of an injunction, but in some cases where the breach was of an equitable injunction the court has nevertheless awarded both an injunction and damages without further explanation.

2–130   A special defence is that the disclosure was in the public interest. This most often applies either to government information (*e.g.* the *Spycatcher* case) or to information about people in public life, but it could apply to commercial information. For example, the defendant may have been given information in confidence that shows that a product is dangerous. The cases show the courts trying to balance the general public interest in maintaining confidentiality with specific public interests which may be considered to override this general public interest, but it is very hard to derive any black and white rules from the case law. In general, the more egregious the information that is disclosed, and the purer the motives of the defendant in making the disclosure, the more likely it is that a court will find that this defence has been made out.

2.9.6 Theft and industrial espionage

2–131   Under English law, pure information is not subject matter capable of being stolen under the Theft Act. This was decided in *Oxford v. Moss*,[49] in which a student "borrowed" the papers for the exam he was about to sit, copied and returned them. As the university had not been "permanently deprived" of the papers, this did not come within the statutory definition of theft. In 1997 the Law Commission issued a consultation paper examining the issues and recommending the creation of an offence of the unauthorised disclosure or misuse of confidential information. The Government has so far shown no interest in adopting this suggestion into its legislative programme.

Other criminal statutes which may provide some assistance in the case of espionage are the Wireless Telegraphy Act 1949 and the Regulation of Investigatory Powers Act 2000, which deal with unauthorised interception of communications. The 1949 Act covers use of wireless telegraphy to obtain the contents of a message, however sent, while the RIP Act 2000 covers interception by any means of communications made by post or on telecommunications networks. Unlike its predecessor, the Interception of Communications Act 1985, the RIP Act 2000 applies to both private and public networks. The Computer Misuse Act 1990, introduced to deal with hacking which the previous criminal law could not cope with, requires unauthorised access to a computer. Although this does not cover employees making an authorised access for an unauthorised purpose, the lack of authority relates to the actual data involved. So, an employee with password access to the system, but who was authorised to access only certain accounts, would commit an offence in accessing other accounts[50]; whereas an employee who was authorised to access and copy confidential information but who copied that information for his own use would appear not to commit an offence. The specific offences cover unauthorised modification of the contents, so covers introduction of viruses and the like, or access in order to commit another serious offence. As we have seen, copying information is not theft, so this provision does not help in most espionage situations. Government information is generally covered by the Official Secrets Act. At present the only viable approaches are often to use the civil law of confidentiality or, where personal data is involved, to invoke the provisions of the Data Protection Act 1998 (see Chapter 7).   **2–132**

2.9.7 Transmitting confidential information by the Internet

The nature of the Internet means that transmissions on it are not in general secure. Therefore, use of the Internet to transmit confidential information could endanger the secrecy needed for legal protection. Ideally, such information should be sent encrypted. Where encryption is impossible or impracticable and the Internet must be used, clear notices that the information is confidential, should not be disclosed or copied and is only intended for the named recipient should be attached to each item of data. This will help to establish a basis for an equitable obligation of confidence in the event of deliberate or accidental interception of the data by a third party.   **2–133**

2.9.8 Misuse of confidential information on the Internet

Some Internet users are the same kind of people who tend to carry out computer hacking, "phone phreaking" or similar activities. This group of people tend to believe that any kind of property right in information is basically wrong, particularly if that information is owned by the government or big business, and take great pride in discovering and making available such confidential information.   **2–134**

It is, therefore, not surprising that there have been a number of cases in the U.S. which involve the publication of stolen proprietary information. For example, in *United States v. Riggs and Neidorf*,[51] the defendants had between them hacked into a Bell Telephone Company computer, obtained highly confidential information about that computer company's emergency telephone number system, and had published it in a magazine. This was the first case which addressed whether electronic transfer of confidential information from one computer to another across state lines constituted interstate transfer of stolen property. The court held that there should be no distinction between transferring electronic information on a floppy disk and actually transferring it by electronic impulses from one computer's magnetic storage to another's.

2–135   The position in the United Kingdom is somewhat different, as there is no legislation specifically directed to dishonest appropriation of pure information. The current law is that information is not property capable of being stolen; this was the holding in *Oxford v. Moss*,[52] in which a university student broke into the examination committee's premises, studied and made a copy of the exam paper and departed, leaving the original exam paper behind. These activities were held not to be theft.

As regards civil remedies, the Internet service provider is unlikely to be under an express contractual obligation of secrecy with the owner of the confidential information. It is possible that the equitable obligation will apply. However, it is obvious that there would be considerable difficulties for the claimant in proving that such an obligation existed, particularly in the case of a defendant service provider who claimed ignorance of what was on its service. It may be that specific legislation covering misappropriation of confidential information will be required as electronic networks grow in importance in this country.

2–136   However, there may very well be criminal liability in some of the more serious cases. For example, where an Internet service is used to publish passwords to allow unauthorised entry into a computer system, the service provider may be liable for any offence under the Computer Misuse Act 1990 that is then committed. The exact liability will depend on the circumstances. If it is actually advertised to a community of people who are likely to carry out computer hacking that passwords are available from this host, this would amount to incitement to commit an offence under the Computer Misuse Act. In a case involving police radar detectors, it was held that advertising an article for sale, representing its virtue to be that it may be used to do an act which is an offence, is an incitement to commit that offence—even if the advertisement is accompanied by a warning that the act is an offence. To establish incitement, it must be proved that the defendant knew or believed that the person incited has the necessary *mens rea* to commit the offence, but as the *mens rea* for an offence under section 1 of the Computer Misuse Act is merely that the defendant intends to secure access to a program and knows that such access is unauthorised, this will probably not be too difficult to establish.

An alternative approach is to charge the Internet host with aiding, abetting, counselling or procuring commission of an offence. In each case, the defendant must have the intention to do the acts which he knows to be capable of assisting or encouraging the commission of a crime, but does not actually need to have the intent that such crime be committed. Which type of participation is most applicable will depend on circumstances: the distinction given by a leading textbook on criminal law is that there must be a causal link for it to be procurement; aiding requires assistance but not consensus nor causation; while abetting and counselling require consensus but not causation.

There is also the possibility of a charge of conspiracy, if the necessary agreement between the service provider and subscriber could be demonstrated.

There have also been cases where improperly obtained credit card numbers have been   **2–137**
placed on computer bulletin boards, thus facilitating the making of fraudulent purchases
using that card number. Here again, if the host knew or ought to have known this was
going on, he may have liability as a secondary participant in the crime that is then
committed.

In the case of defence information, it should be noted that, in a case in California, a
hacker who obtained information from a Defence computer was charged with espionage,
even though there was no evidence that he ever passed the information on or intended to
supply it to an enemy of the U.S. In the United Kingdom, placing stolen government
confidential information onto the Internet is likely to fall foul of the Official Secrets Acts.

2.10 Patents

2.10.1 Patents and protecting ideas

While copyright protects the expression of ideas, the patent system is intended to protect   **2–138**
the ideas themselves.

Patents are "available for any inventions, whether products or processes, in all fields of
technology, provided that they are new, involve an inventive step, and are capable of
industrial application",[53] subject to some possible exceptions (exceptions relevant to the
Internet are discussed below). The basis for the patent system is that, in exchange for the
inventor publishing details of an invention and how to put it into effect he will obtain
from the state a limited monopoly over his invention, but that after the expiry of the
patent the invention will be available for the public to use freely. Patents thus contrast
with confidential information, and a choice must be made between these methods of
protection. Most countries publish patent applications 18 months after filing, unless the
application is previously withdrawn (which will maintain trade secret protection if the
applicant believes that a patent will not be granted).

A patent is essentially national in nature and is granted by the individual patent offices
of various countries in the world. A patent gives its owner a monopoly for a fixed period
of time (generally 20 years from filing) in the use of the inventive idea described in the
section of the patent known as the "claims". To be patentable an invention must be
"new", *i.e.* not have been made available to the public before the "priority date"—the
date of the earliest patent application for the invention in any country of the world. The
applicant for a patent can only rely on a priority date where either the subsequent
national filings in those countries where protection is sought or an international Patent
Cooperation Treaty application (discussed below) are made within one year of the
priority date and the priority is claimed. There must also be an inventive advance over
what was previously known, also expressed by saying that the invention must not be
"obvious".

Although patent protection is currently national, there are international conventions   **2–139**
which can reduce the number of patent applications that have to be prosecuted to grant.
The Patent Cooperation Treaty (PCT), to which most countries belong, permits a single
application to be filed and to undergo a single prior art search, and provides an option of
a single initial examination, before the national phase in which the remainder of the
prosecution process must be carried out in each of the selected countries. Making a PCT
application has the advantage of delaying the time at which a decision must be made as
to whether filings in other countries, with the associated expense, should be made. The

European Patent Convention (EPC), which covers the European Community, Switzerland, Monaco and Liechtenstein, goes further in providing a single route to the grant of a European Patent, which then operates in each of the countries designated by the patentee as a bundle of national patent rights, governed by the domestic laws of each of the designated countries, except for the availability for nine months after grant of a central challenge to validity by means of the opposition procedure. The European Patent Convention also effected a significant harmonisation of substantive patent law throughout Europe.

2.10.2 Patenting the Internet

2–140
As far as the Internet is concerned, the patent system applies particularly to those unseen but vital technical aspects which make the Internet and the traffic on it possible. These "unseen" aspects include such things as the hardware, software and communications interfaces and protocols used not only to interface across equipment but to allow improved and more user-friendly access for humans to the Internet. They also include the ingenious compression and encryption algorithms used to improve speed of transfer of information and the amount of information which can be transmitted.

An interesting recent example of a patent for just such an "unseen" component is the compression technique at the centre of the controversy surrounding Unisys and CompuServe. An aspect of the public domain graphics compression software produced by CompuServe incorporates a compression technique which Unisys claimed it owned, namely the. GIF graphics file format. When CompuServe started to charge for this software in order to pay a royalty to Unisys, not unsurprisingly, there was an outcry largely, one suspects, because Unisys had been so late in coming forward with its rights claim. The basis for the claim was a patent owned by Unisys claiming the compression algorithm in question.

Such patents cover technical inventions, which are indisputably the kind of thing the patent system is designed to protect. A much more controversial type of patent originating from the U.S., that covering business methods, has potentially a similarly wide effect on Internet applications.

2.10.3 Business method patents—U.S.

2–141
For most of the twentieth century it was accepted that there was a judicially created so-called "business methods exception" to statutory subject matter, relying on the *Hotel Security* case decided by the 2nd Circuit in 1908.[54]

Almost as soon as it became accepted that software could be a patentable invention, patents for achieving various methods of doing business using software were applied for. Merrill Lynch were pioneers in filing patents on computerised methods of doing financial transactions. Many people questioned whether the patent system should ever be used to protect business methods which were only "technical" in that a computer was being used to carry them out, and the USPTO were rejecting many such applications on the basis of the "business methods exception". However, in 1998 the US appeal court for patent matters, the Court of Appeals for the Federal Circuit (CAFC), reversed a lower court's ruling in the *State Street Bank* case that a method of managing mutual funds was not patentable subject matter.[55] The CAFC ruled that the so-called "business methods exception" was in fact a myth, and that the same tests for patentability (new and non-obvious, useful) applied to business methods as had always applied to industrial methods. This same court confirmed this approach in *AT&T Corp v. Excel Communications Inc.*,[56] going even further to make it clear that the fact that the claims in issue were pure method claims with no recital of use of a computer was irrelevant to the question of their patentability. The Court strictly limited the mathematical algorithms exception to algorithms in the abstract, any process applying the algorithm to a new and useful purpose is potentially patentable, and also said that there was no invariable rule that this useful end must involve a "physical transformation" to be patentable. This seems to confirm that non-statutory exclusions from patentability, however venerable, would no longer automatically be applied.

For many new Internet and e-commerce companies, the ownership of a patent or at least patent applications is a vital part of their assets in persuading investors to pour large sums of money into the company. It is not surprising, therefore, to find that there are already a large number of U.S. patents relating to Internet business methods, and that litigation has already started. For example Priceline.com, which has obtained U.S. Patent No 5,794,207 on its method of "buyer-driven pricing", has sued Microsoft alleging that its "Expedia" Web site is infringing this patent. In a case which has caused a lot of controversy, Amazon.com, the on-line bookstore, sued its main competitor, Barnes & Noble, for infringement of its "one-click purchasing" patent, U.S. No 5,960,411. Although Amazon won the first round by obtaining a preliminary injunction just before the Christmas season forcing its rival to change the way customers on its site transact purchases, this has now been reversed on appeal, with the CAFC casting doubt on the validity of the patent. Two MIT professors have sued the "Ask Jeeves" site for using their patents on natural language searching. Other patents which could cover a lot of e-commerce activities are Cybergold's patent on a method of paying Web surfers for paying attention to on-line adverts, DoubleClick's patent on a method of keeping track of Internet advertisements and who is looking at them and Sightsound.com's patent on downloading music online.

2–142

The Internet business bonanza led to a number of lawsuits by companies that had older patents which did not refer to the Internet but which they alleged had claims broad enough to cover Internet activities. Trying to enforce such patents can be hazardous; when Compton's newMedia, the owners of *Encyclopedia Britannica*, announced that they had been granted a patent covering a computer-based multimedia searching system and that it would be seeking royalties from the multimedia industry, there was an outcry. As a result, the U.S. Patent Office initiated a re-examination of the validity of the patent on the basis of the prior art turned up by the protestors, and rejected all the claims. Undeterred, E-Data has launched extensive litigation over its patent covering down-loading music or books to special terminals in shops against companies delivering music and other information on-line to users' computers; although the claims were narrowly construed by a District court so as not to cover on-line delivery, the Federal Circuit reversed this in November 2000, holding that the claims could cover real time delivery to a home personal computer. However, most attempts to assert pre-Internet patents against Internet businesses seem to be failing, unless the both the claims and the description were very widely worded – thus making them more vulnerable to being found invalid. This has not prevented British Telecom from recently dusting off an old teletext patent and asserting that it covers hypertext linking.

2–143

This activity has led to a great deal of very vocal criticism of some of the business method patents issuing from the USPTO, which in turn has led to attempts by that Office to improve both the quality of the examination process and the examiners carrying it out. The databases searched for applications in Class 705, into which most business method applications fall, have been considerably expanded to include numerous non-patent literature databases. A number of examiners with business qualifications and experience have been recruited for this group. All applications in this class have to have a second review before a notice of grant is issued.

2–144   The U.S. Congress has also acted. A new "prior user" defence to patent infringement was added to the patent statute in 1999. This applies only to patents for a "a method of doing or conducting business". The defendant must prove that, acting in good faith, he "actually reduced the subject matter to practice at least one year before the effective filing date of such patent, and commercially used the subject matter before the effective filing date of such patent". It remains to be seen if this defence will be much used in practice; there are uncertainties as to how broadly a court would interpret the definition of a "business method" and, in proving his case the defendant will be admitting literal infringement—fatal if his prior use defence fails unless he can successfully challenge the patent's validity. A more extensive bill dealing with business method patents was introduced into the House on April 3, 2001. This proposes that all business method applications should be published at 18 months, there would be a presumption of obviousness if the patent merely disclosed the computer implementation of a known business method, there would be the ability for members of the public to submit prior art to the USPTO in respect of published, pending patents and there would be a post-grant opposition procedure. In litigation the issue of validity would be decided on the normal civil burden of proof, rather than the heavier burden currently borne by the challenger, and the patentee would have to disclose whether a validity search had been carried out.

2–145   While some argue that these type of patents go far beyond what the patent system is meant to protect, a great deal of investment is today being poured into these areas. Unless that investment is given some reward, opportunities will be missed and pioneers can find themselves pushed by those with more financial muscle out of markets their innovation has established. It is often the case that innovation, far from being stifled by the patent system as is sometimes thought to be the case, is actually a direct result of an attempt to "design around" a patent which is particularly dominant in a field.

One of the real problems with patent protection in this area is that many people do not realise that it is available. There is a wide-spread belief that software is not patentable in Europe. Stated this broadly, the belief is not correct, as is discussed below. However, there is still considerable uncertainty as to what kinds of innovations in this field are patentable. In particular, as between the European-wide patenting system operating through the European Patent Office and the United Kingdom national system (which run in parallel to each other), there has recently been considerable divergence over what is and is not patentable *vis-à-vis* what are generically termed "software" patents. This is discussed below.

2.10.4 Internet Publications as Prior Art under the EPC

2–146   Prior art, for which the EPC uses the term "state of the art", is defined in Article 54(2):

> "The state of the art shall be held to comprise everything made available to the public by means of a written or oral description, by use, or in any other way, before the date of filing of the European patent application."

The "date of filing" in the case of an application entitled to priority under an international convention is that priority date (Article 89). U.S. entities should note, however, that there is no grace period equivalent to the one year period of 35 U.S.C. §102(b).

In addition, Article 54(3) provides that the state of the art (for novelty but not for obviousness) also includes "the content of European patent applications as filed", which were filed before the priority date of the patent in issue but which were published after that filing date.

The EPC itself does not provide any definition of what is encompassed by "made available to the public". For the purposes of examination the EPO Guidelines apply, which define the term as follows:

> "A written description ... should be regarded as made available to the public if, at the relevant date, it was possible for members of the public to gain knowledge of the content of the document and there was no bar of confidentiality restricting the use or dissemination of such knowledge."[57]

The validity of a granted patent is decided by the courts of the country where that particular patent is registered. This means that the question of what is meant by "made available to the public" will be decided under national law in most cases where the issue arises, although the national court may give some weight to the EPO Guidelines.

In theory, anything placed in plain text on the World Wide Web is available to any   **2–147**
member of the public anywhere in the world who manages to find it through luck or a suitable search. This may not be true of material which is in encrypted form, or which is only available by use of a password. However, a number of questions are raised; the first, and least troublesome, is whether this information in electronic form is a "written" description, even if it is never downloaded and printed out. Unlike the equivalent U.S. provision[58] which refers to "a printed publication", the EPC wording is sufficiently broad that Web pages and other electronic documents clearly will come within it. A second, and more difficult question, is the status as prior art of a disclosure made on an obscure Web site, perhaps only appearing for a short time. Previous case law dealing with traditional paper publications have indicated that the presence of only a single copy, anywhere in the world, will constitute prior art provided that copy is available to any member of the public who chose to read it. The issue is probably the practical one of proof of the public availability of the information, rather than the legal status as prior art of such information. Another question which relates to proof results from the ease with which electronic information can be altered. Typically, such prior art is put forward several years after it became available by an accused infringer seeking to invalidate the patent. He must prove that the information was publicly available before the patent's priority date. In the case of printed publications with a publication date on the cover page this is not usually a problem (unless the publication date is very close to the priority date, when it is also necessary to prove when the document became available), because forging such a date would be very difficult. Forging the date of an electronic document would be easy; it will be necessary to provide an audit trail of the document to ensure that has not happened. Finally, information posted to a corporate intranet could be held to be publicly available if enough people are able to read it, particularly those outside the group of those who need to know about the invention.

This shows that companies must take care that they do not lose patent rights by   **2–148**
publishing information about new products or developments on the Internet (or even

their intranet) before they have filed a patent application to obtain a priority date. Even a confidential publication has risks. Although a hacker breaking into the confidential file would probably be under an equitable obligation of confidence, if that hacker then posted the information openly on the Internet those accessing that information without knowledge of the way it was obtained would be free to use it, and so there would have been a public disclosure. In Europe there would still be a six month period from the first date of such unauthorised public disclosure in which a patent application could be filed,[59] but that may not be true in other countries.

2.10.5 Patentability of software—Europe

2–149   The European Patent Convention provides that certain types of things will not be regarded as patents and will consequently not be patentable.

Article 52 of the European Patent Convention (implemented now by 17 European countries) states that:

> '(1)   European patents shall be granted for any inventions which are susceptible of industrial application, which are new, and which involve an inventive step.
> (2)   The following in particular shall not be regarded as inventions within the meaning of paragraph 1:
>   (a)   discoveries, scientific theories and mathematical methods;
>   (b)   aesthetic creations;
>   (c)   schemes, rules and methods for performing mental acts, playing games or doing business, and programs for computers;
>   (d)   presentations of information.
> (3)   The provisions of paragraph 2 shall exclude patentability of the subject-matter or activities referred to in that provision only to the extent to which a European patent relates to such subject-matter or activities as such.
> (4)   ...'

2–150   Possibly, because it saw how many software patents were being granted by the U.S. Patent Office or possibly due to pressure from the computer industry, the European Patent Office (EPO) has, in its decisions concerning patentability of this type of patent, tried to circumscribe as closely as possible the above exclusion as it relates to programs for computers. To do this, it has relied upon the limitation placed on the exclusions to patentability by Article 52(3) and has pinned its colours to the mast of the final two words, "as such". In essence, it has said that the exclusion from patentability for programs for computers will only apply where the invention claimed consists solely of a computer program running on a "known" computer. The EPO Guidelines say:

> "A computer program claimed by itself or as a record on a carrier, is not patentable irrespective of its content. The situation is not normally changed when the computer program is loaded onto a known computer. If, however, the subject-matter as claimed makes a technical contribution to the known art, patentability should not be denied merely on the ground that a computer program is involved in its implementation. This means, for example, that program-controlled machines and program-controlled manufacturing and control processes should normally be regarded as patentable subject-matter."

The EPO has then developed from this the doctrine of "technical effect". When this doctrine is described in the EPO Guidelines in the following fashion this doctrine appears to have a logical and understandable basis: **2–151**

"It follows also that, where the claimed subject-matter is concerned only with the program-controlled internal working of a known computer, the subject-matter could be patentable if it provides a technical effect. As an example, consider the case of a known data-processing system with a small fast working memory and a larger but slower further memory. Suppose that the two memories are organised under program control, in such a way that a process which needs more address space than the capacity of the fast working memory can be executed at substantially the same speed as if the process data were loaded entirely in that fast memory. The effect of the program in virtually extending the working memory is of a technical character and might therefore support patentability."

However, when looked at in terms of some of the decisions that have been made by the EPO Board of Appeal on the subject of "technical effect", the sense of the doctrine and a clear distinguishing line between the patentable and unpatentable seems to be lacking.

The doctrine was first developed in the case of *Re Vicom* (T208/84) which essentially concerned a new method of handling the images for a CAD (computer aided design) system. In this case, the Board of Appeal decided that: **2–152**

"the method described in the patent was susceptible of industrial application since it could be used (for example) in investigating the properties of a real or simulated object or in designing an industrial article."

The Board also decided that:

"...a mathematical method as such is an abstract concept prescribing how to operate on numbers, without producing any direct technical result. By contrast, where a mathematical method is used in a technical process, the process is carried out on a physical entity (for example, an image stored as an electrical signal) by some technical means which produces a change in that entity."

To a computer programmer, the distinction made in this latter paragraph may appear baffling but this has been the basis for all subsequent decisions of the EPO in this area.

Following the *Re Vicom* decision, the technical effect doctrine was developed by the EPO Board of Appeal in *Koch & Sterzel/X-ray Apparatus* (T26/86). This involved a patent for a data processing device which was used to adjust certain parameters of X-ray apparatus where the prior art used the same apparatus and the same known computer but a different computer program. It was held that the patent was valid as the invention has to be assessed as a whole and the use of non-technical means did not detract from the overall technical teaching. The Board commented that the rule followed by the original German court dealing with this matter, ie that since the only new element for the invention was excluded from patentability the whole apparatus was not patentable, was "impractical".

Since these two decisions, there have been several cases decided by the EPO Board of Appeal in this area although none of these matters have gone to the extended Board of Appeal. Six of the cases concerned IBM text handling patents which were all held to be **2–153** invalid. These decisions all seem to have been based on the idea that text processing is not a 'technical' activity and, therefore, the effect of the program on the displayed text was not a technical one. Interestingly, the same six IBM text processing patents have been granted in the U.S. by the U.S. Patent Office.

1994 seemed to be the turning point in the EPO's approach to software patents, with two important cases. In the first, *Sohei/Yamamoto's Application* (T 769/92), the applicant claimed a computer system for plural types of independent management including at least financial and inventory management and a method for operating said system. Data for the various types of management which could be performed independently from each other with this system could be inputted using a single "transfer slip", in the form of an image displayed on the screen of the display unit of the computer system, for example. This would seem to be a "method of doing business", and thus excluded from patentability under Article 52 (2)(c) even if it did not fall at the first hurdle because it involved software.

The Technical Board of Appeal held that an invention comprising functional features implemented by software is not excluded from patentability under Article 52(2)(c) and (3), if technical considerations concerning particulars of the solution of the problem the invention solves are required in order to carry out that same invention. Such technical considerations lend a technical nature to the invention in that they imply a technical problem to be solved by implicit technical features. An invention of this kind does not pertain to a computer program as such under Article 52(3). They also found that non-exclusion from patentability cannot be destroyed by an additional feature which as such would itself be excluded, as in the present case features referring to management systems and methods which may fall under the "methods for doing business" exclusion from patentability (Article 52(2)(c)).

2–154   The second decision, *Petterson's Application* (T 1002/92), related to a system for determining the queue sequence for serving customers at a plurality of service points. The system gave the customer the possibility of selecting one particular service point; it comprised, in particular, a turn-allocating unit, terminals for each service point, an information unit which indicated the particular turn-number and the particular free service point to the customer. The corresponding Swedish application had been rejected by the Swedish patent office and the rejection upheld through the Swedish courts. The EPO Board of Appeal took the view that the claim was directed to an apparatus which comprised, inter alia, computer hardware operated by a particular computer program. The program determined output signal of the hardware was used for an automatic control of the operation of another system component (the information unit) and thus solved a problem which was of a technical nature. Further, the fact that one of the practical applications of the system concerned the service of customers of "a business" did not mean that the claimed subject matter must be equated with a method for doing business. Other 1994 decisions which show this more liberal approach of the Board of Appeals include two IBM cases, T 59/93 relating to a method for the interactive rotation of displayed graphic objects (overturning rejections that this was a mathematical method, a method of doing business, a computer program and presentation of information on the basis that the entirety of the claimed method was not excluded under any of these heads) and T 453/91, a method for VLSI-chip design and manufacture (rejection of design method claims upheld as having no tangible result, manufacturing claims allowed as having a technical effect).

2–155   A startling demonstration of how far the Board of Appeal is prepared to go in giving Article 52(2)(c) a liberal interpretation was given in the recent IBM cases, T 0935/97 and T

1173/97. In both cases IBM had included claims for a computer program product which had the effect of making a computer carry out certain actions, as well as the more conventional claims to a programmed computer capable of carrying out these actions and to the method. T 0935/97 relates to a technique of displaying information in the obscured portion of an overlapped window in another part of the screen. T 1173/97 relates to a method of resource recovery in a computer system. The Examining Division had allowed the method and apparatus claims, but unsurprisingly (in view of existing case law) had rejected claims to the program product as software "as such" and therefore not saved from the exclusion of Article 52(2)(c) by Article 52(3).

The Board considered that the exclusion only related to software with no technical character. Technical character would be found when the execution of the software instructions resulted in some "further technical effect", such as the solution of a technical problem (*e.g. Viacom*) or where technical considerations are required to arrive at the invention (*e.g. Sohei*). The Board stated that it would be illogical to grant a patent for a method and for a programmed computer carrying out the method, but nor for the software that in fact produces the technical effect. This approach is in line with the current U.S. approach to patentability of the programs themselves.

2.10.6 Patentability of software—United Kingdom

The United Kingdom court has only considered the issue of patentability of software patents on five occasions (although the United Kingdom Patent Office has obviously opined on the matter a number of times now) and only then in relation to the grant of patents rather than in full blown infringement actions. On the first such occasion, *Merrill Lynch Inc's Application*[60] which reached the Court of Appeal, the court found that the trading system claimed in the patent application was not patentable as it was a means of performing a business method. The interesting thing to note in this instance is that the claims for this application were subsequently amended essentially to link the method claimed to the relevant apparatus and communications means and the patent was then granted.   **2–156**

The next case after this, *Gale's Application*,[61] involved an application for a patent for a read-only memory (ROM) chip on which was stored a novel method for calculating a square root. This was found not to be a patentable invention as not having a technical effect. Then there was *Wang's Application*[62] which involved a computer system operable as an expert system and which was also found not to be patentable.

Then the United Kingdom High Court considered the matter in *Raytheon's Application*[63] which involved a pattern recognition system. Both the Patent Office and the Patents High Court on appeal agreed in this instance that this patent application related to no more than a conventional computer processing information. Bearing in mind the nature of this invention and the nature of the invention in the case of *Re Vicom*, it is difficult to see how one can reconcile these two decisions, as they would both appear to achieve what the EPO thinks of as a technical effect. Possibly the judge in this instance did not appreciate the incredibly complex procedure that the human brain must go through in order to achieve the pattern recognition which it does.   **2–157**

More recently, in *Re Patent Application No 9204959.2 by Fujitsu Ltd*,[64] Laddie J. made a detailed review of the cases. He referred in particular to the leading cases in the European Patent Office of *Re Vicom* and IBM/Text Processing and the two cases of this type which had been looked at by the United Kingdom Court of Appeal, *Merrill Lynch* and *Gale's*

Application. Having done so his conclusion on the issue of patentability for software is best summarised by saying that the United Kingdom court considers that the issue of patentability is an issue of substance and not form. Thus, where it is clear that a computer program printed out on paper will not be patentable, similarly a computer program sitting on the hard disk of a computer will not be patentable. The issue is whether when the computer program is actually run on that computer it causes the computer to operate in a novel way and/or produce a novel result which in itself is not excluded from patentability under section 1(2) of the Act. Although he decided that the claims were not to a computer program "as such", they were still excluded form patentability as being a method of performing a mental act.

On appeal,[65] Aldous L.J., after referring to the need to construe the United Kingdom Patents Act in the light of EPO decisions, decided that this invention was not analogous to that in *Viacom*, and disagreed with Laddie J. in holding that the claims were to a computer program as such, but stating that it was "doubtful" that this was a method of performing a mental act.

2–158   On April 19, 1999, following the EPO IBM case decisions allowing claims directed to the software itself discussed above, the United Kingdom Patent Office issued a practice note stating that it would follow the EPO lead and change its practice with respect to claims to computer programs. In future, it will accept claims to programs themselves or on a carrier when the program running on a computer would produce a technical effect more than would necessarily follow merely from the running of any program on the computer.

Thus, it can be seen that even those who are of the school of thought that this sort of idea should not be patentable should be aware that patents are being obtained in this field and be wary of infringing them. Even if something is considered not to be patentable in Europe it may well nevertheless be given patent protection in the U.S. where a similar battle over what is and is not patentable in this area has been raging for some time now. Whatever the outcome of that battle, it can be said that more of this type of patent is granted by the U.S. Patent Office and since anyone trading on the Internet cannot fail at least to offer access in the U.S. this is something worth bearing in mind from both sides of the fence. On the one hand, a potential patentee should consider obtaining patent protection in the U.S. even if it is not available elsewhere; and on the other hand, in considering copying the techniques of others on the Internet, the existence of patent protection, if nowhere else than in the U.S., should be considered.

2.10.7 Business method patents – Europe

2–159   On the face of it, business method patents do not appear to be available in Europe, as Article 52(2), discussed above, also excludes methods of doing business from patentability. However, as we have seen in the case of software, this is not an absolute bar. Indeed, the key 1995 *Sohei* case involved a business method, a financial trading system. The technical effect test applied equally to this as to a purely technological system.

Other patents for computer systems which carry out business methods have been granted; for example, in 1997 Citibank obtained EP 0 762 304 for a computer system for an automated warrant trading system. However, the claims tend to concentrate on the system itself, rather than the method it carries out. For example, claim 1 reads: Computer system for data management including at least the management of data relating to the trading of warrants, comprising a data processing system, and input unit, a display unit and a data input unit receiving at least warrant rates, wherein

- the display unit displays a first mask having a format allowing the input of a request for specific data including at least warrant rates by the input unit

- the data input is read if the request is input by the input unit

- the display unit displays a second mask including the requested data, and

- the data processing system holds the requested data for a predetermined time period T_{set} and performs a transaction relating to the specific data, if a transaction request is input by the input unit during a predetermined time period T_{set}.

This patent is currently in opposition proceedings, brought by several competitors to the patentee. The grounds of opposition include "lack of technical character" and that these claims are for "a method of doing business as such", as well as novelty and inventiveness attacks. The patentee has added some limitations to distinguish over prior art. A preliminary opinion of the Opposition Division seems to indicate that they are not inclined to accept the Article 52(2) challenges to patentability, but doubtless there will be more lengthy procedures, including appeals, before this patent's validity is settled.

However, a recent decision of the Appeal Board of the EPO seems to go against the tide   **2–160** of decisions discussed above. An application for an "Improved Pension Benefits System" EP-A 0 332 770 was rejected in September 2000 (Decision T0931/95). Claim 1 of this application reads:

"A method of controlling a pension benefits program by administering at least one subscriber employee account on behalf of each of subscriber employer's enrolled employees, each of whom is to receive periodic benefits payments, said method comprising:

providing to a data processing means information from each said subscriber employee defining the number, earnings and ages of all enrolled employees of the said subscriber employer;

determining the average age of all enrolled employees by average age computing means;

determining the periodic cost of life insurance for all enrolled employees of said subscriber employer by life insurance cost computing means; and

estimating all administrative, legal, trustee and government premium yearly expenses for said subscriber employer by administrative cost computing means;

the method producing, in use, information defining each subscriber employer's periodic monetary contribution to a master trust, the face amount of a life insurance policy on each enrolled employee's life to be purchased from a life insurer and assigned to the master trust and to be maintained in full force and effect until the death of the said employee, and the periodic benefits to be received by each enrolled employee upon death, disability or retirement."

There were also claims to apparatus to carry out the method.

The Examining Division rejected the application on the grounds that the invention was excluded under Article 52(2) as a method for doing business and lacking any technical character. One of the grounds on which the applicant challenged this decision was that there was no requirement of "technical character" in the EPC. This ground was rejected on the basis of the consistent case law of the EPO Appeals Board, concluding that there is an implicit requirement in Article 52(1) EPC that an invention must have "technical character" in order to be patentable.

2–161   The Board also considered the issue as to whether the invention here had "technical character". They considered that the method claims were claims only to a method of doing business, the fact that it used 'technical means' for a "purely non-technical purpose and/or for processing purely non-technical information" "does not necessarily confer a technical character to such a method." However, they did consider that "a computer system suitably programmed for use in a particular field, even if that is the field of business and economy, has the character of a concrete apparatus in the sense of a physical entity, man-made for a utilitarian purpose and is thus an invention within the meaning of Article 52(1) EPC." They justified this rather artificial distinction by reference to the wording of Article 52(2), which does not refer to "apparatus" but only to "schemes, rules and methods".

However, the applicant's victory was short-lived, as the Board then, at its own initiative (this was not an issue on appeal), considered whether the apparatus claims were patentable over the prior art identified in the application itself and held that they were not, for lack of inventive step. Unfortunately, in doing so they ignored the case law that requires that the claimed invention must be looked at as a whole when considering whether there is an inventive step (*e.g. Koch & Sterzel*), stating "… the improvement envisaged by the invention according to the application is an essentially economic one … which, therefore, cannot contribute to inventive step." On this basis they had no difficulty in finding there was no inventive step so the application should be rejected. If this approach is followed in other cases, turning the clock back 20 years, then there seems little chance that even apparatus claims for business methods will be granted unless there is clearly something clever technically involved in the implementation of the method.

2.10.8 Patent Infringement and the Internet

Infringing acts

2–162   Under United Kingdom law infringement is defined by section 60 of the 1977 Patents Act. Section 60(1) deals with direct infringement. For a product, the infringing acts are making, disposing of, offering to dispose of, use, importation and keeping the product for any reason. Process patents are infringed by a person who uses or offers for use in the United Kingdom when he knows or it is obvious to a reasonable person in the circumstances that its unauthorised use would be an infringement. It is also an infringement of a process patent to dispose of , offer to dispose of, use, import or keep any product "obtained directly by means of that process".

Indirect infringement is covered by section 60(2), which makes it an infringement to supply or offer to supply someone not entitled to work the invention "with any of the means, relating to an essential element of the invention, for putting the invention into effect", provided that there is actual or deemed knowledge that "those means are suitable for putting, and are intended to put, the invention into effect in the United Kingdom." However, under section 60(3), this provision does not apply to staple commercial products unless the supply or offer of supply is made for the purpose of inducing the person to whom the supply is made or is offered to infringe the patent.

Except for use of a patented process relating to the Internet itself (such as the Lycos search engine patent), or the electronic transfer (disposal or import) of software which forms an essential part of a patented invention, the only possible infringing act that could be carried out over the Internet is an offer to dispose. While an offer for sale is clearly covered, it is doubtful whether a mere advertisement, which is normally classed as an invitation to treat rather than an offer, is an "offer to dispose". In the U.S. it has been held that merely listing products on a Web site did not qualify as an "offer to sell" under U.S. patent law.[66] However, it may be possible to persuade a court that such an advertisement is a threat to dispose and that it should give injunctive relief on a *quia timet* basis. Obviously, where the Web site is set up to actually accept orders then there is no problem in finding an offer to dispose.

2–163

Liability for infringement

The Patents Act sets out the acts that constitute infringement, but does not expressly deal with who is liable for such acts. The United Kingdom courts apply the tort rules, in particular in determining the liability for acts by servants and agents and whether persons are joint tortfeasors.

2–164

The latter is relevant when determining whether a parent company can be liable for the infringing acts of a subsidiary. The case law is clear that ownership by the parent of an infringing subsidiary is not enough on its own to make the parent also liable. There must be some evidence of "common design" (also referred to as "concerted action" or "agreed on common action" in some cases) to carry out the infringing acts. A finding that there has been such a common design will in each case depend upon the facts, but examples of parent company activities that could lead to a finding of common design are manufacture and supply to the subsidiary of the infringing article, control of worldwide marketing by its subsidiaries, acting in such a way as to lead customers for the infringement to believe that they are dealing with the parent (*e.g.*, calling the subsidiary a "sales office" in its marketing literature).

Corporate Web sites may provide ammunition for a patentee seeking to join the parent of an infringing subsidiary in an infringement action, particularly where that parent is located in a different jurisdiction. Very often the parent's Web site will have a generic rather than country specific domain name (*e.g.* 'Bigco.com', rather than Bigco.co.uk), and potential customers are likely to look for generic domain names first. The parent company's Web site will usually provide information about world-wide operations, and may tend to give a picture of a single global organisation, with the national subsidiaries integrated rather than independent. For example, national subsidiaries may not have independent Web sites but merely their own pages within the parent site. Similarly, listing of national subsidiaries as "sales offices", particularly when combined with some kind of offer of the infringing goods, is evidence of a common design to dispose of the goods in the United Kingdom between foreign parent and United Kingdom subsidiary.

2–165

Jurisdiction

The issue of jurisdiction is a tricky one in relation to the Internet. The United Kingdom case law is that the offer to dispose must be an offer *within the jurisdiction* to dispose of infringing products *in* the jurisdiction: *Kalman v. PCL Packaging (U.K.).*[67] In that case the offer involved transfer of title in the U.S. to a United Kingdom company, so the court held that the U.S. defendant had not made an offer which involved disposal in the United

2–166

Kingdom of infringing products. It did not make any finding on whether the offer itself, made in the U.S. but communicated by telex to the United Kingdom, was an offer "within the jurisdiction". There has not yet been any United Kingdom case law on whether an offer made on a foreign based Web site accessible in the United Kingdom is an offer within the jurisdiction.

1. Directive 2001/29 [2001] O.J. L167/10
2. Directive 2001/31 [2000] O.J. L178/1
3. See, for instance, "Jail Time in the Digital Age", Lawrence Lessig, *The New York Times* July 30, 2001.
4. This is the subject of a a lawsuit by the academic concerned, Dr Edward Felten, seeking to establish that he and his team have a First Amendment right to present their research (Electronic Frontier Foundation, www.eff.org/Legal/Cases/Felten_v_RIAA/20010606_eff_felten_pr.html).
5. Directive 91/250 [1991] 0.J. L122/42
6. See Lessig, n. 3 above; also E.C.L.R. July 25, 2001 p 776.
7. www.adobe.com/aboutadobe/pressroom/pressreleases/200107/20010723dcma.html.
8. 1988 Act, s. 3(2).
9. S. 178.
10. See n. 15 below.
11. A separate copyright would subsist in earlier copywriting or design work on which the contents or appearance of the screen was based.
12. [2001] R.P.C. 612, Laddie J.; July 31 2001 (unreported) Court of Appeal.
13. *Exxon Corporation v. Exxon Insurance Consultants International Ltd* [1982] Ch. 119.
14. [1988] A.C. 1013.
15. In *Bookmakers' Afternoon Greyhound Services Ltd v. Wilf Gilbert (Staffordshire) Ltd* [1994] FSR 723, a case under the 1956 Act, Aldous J (as he then was) held that a race card transmitted by satellite link to a bookmaker's shop was reproduced in a material form when the bookmaker turned on the monitor and the race card materialised on the screen. However, it is arguable that such an interpretation does not conform with the scheme of the 1988 Act.
16. In the different context of a prosecution under the Obscene Publications Act 1959, the Court of Appeal, while conceding for the sake of argument that active steps were necessary, was unimpressed with an argument that a defendant's giving certain others passwords access did not amount to "showing" the pictures as contended by the prosecution. Although the defendant in that case did more than merely make the archive available because he had taken steps to issue passwords and so on, it would be surprising if a defendant who had to take fewer active steps because he gave unrestricted access would thereby have escaped liability. See *R v. Fellows, R v. Arnold* [1997] 2 All ER 548 (also discussed in Chapter 6).
17. *Bookmakers' Afternoon Greyhound Services Ltd v. Wilf Gilbert (Staffordshire) Ltd* [1994] FSR 723.
18. [1997] FSR 604.
19. The observant user might notice the browser status bar indicating that elements of the page were being fetched from the target site. However, that is nothing unusual in an environment where, for instance, banner advertisements are often supplied by servers other than the website's own servers.
20. The Court of Appeal has now confirmed, in *Ashdown v. Telegraph Group Ltd* [2001] EWCA Civ 1142, that rare cases could arise where the right of freedom of expression under Article 10 of the European Convention of Human Rights comes into conflict with the protection afforded by the 1988 Act. This could give rise the a public interest defence under s. 171(3) of the 1988 Act. Further, the circumstances in which the public interest might override copyright are not capable of precise categorisation or definition. They are not limited to cases in which enforcement of copyright would offend against the policy of the law. Nor need the circumstances derive from the work in question, as opposed to the ownership of the copyright.
21. US Dist. Ct., C.D. Cal March 27, 2000 (www.gigalaw.com/library/ticketmaster-tickets-2000-03-27.html).
22. Landgericht Köln, February 28 2001, Electronic Business Law June 2001 p. 13; [2000] EBLR 87; E-Commerce Law Reports Vol 1 Issue 2, p.14. See also "The Database Right Revolution Begins", G. Taylor, *Managing Intellectual Property* May 2001 p. 18.
23. *Sarl Stepstone France v. Sarl Ofir France*, Commercial court of Nanterre, November 8, 2000 (www.legalis.net/cgi-iddn/french/affiche-jnet.cgi?droite=decisions/dt_auteur/ord_tcomm-nanterre_081100.htm).
24. Sub. nom. *Algemeen Dagblad B.V. and Others v. Eureka Internetdiensten* District Court of Rotterdam August 22 2000, E-Commerce Law Reports Vol 1 Issue 2 p. 12. See also "Applying the Database Act to On Line Information Services" S.J.H. Gijrath and B.J.E. Gorissen *Copyright World* Dec 2000/Jan 2001 p. 14.
25. See "El Cheapo comes out on top" D. Oosterbaan, World eBusiness Law Report July 17, 2001; also G. Taylor, *op. cit.* And S.J.H. Gijrath/B.J.E. Gorissen *op. cit.*
26. E-commerce Law Reports Vol. 1 Issue 2 p. 16 (first instance); on appeal, World Internet Law Report August 2001 p. 15.
27. Hearing August 10, 2000 (www.gigalaw.com/library/ticketmaster-tickets-2000-08-10-p1.html).
28. NDCA 2000 100 F Supp 2d 1058. See "Protecting Web Site Databases through Intentional Tort or Contract:

eBay meets UCITA" K.M. McDermott, *Journal of Internet Law* Sept. 2000, 15; and "Virtual Trespass in Cyberspace?" D A Guberman, *World Internet Law Report* 12/00, 27.

29. The Robot Exclusion Standard can be found at www.robotstxt.org/wc/norobots.html. It enables websites to promulgate, in the robots.txt file, its policies for visiting robots (i.e. webcrawlers and spiders). Search engine programmers and other robot users can program their robots to respect the guidelines that they encounter.
30. *e.g. CompuServe, Inc. v. Cyber Promotions*, Inc., 962 F. Supp. 1015 (S.D. Ohio 1997).
31. [2000] Ent. L.R. 11(3), N-38.
32. [1997] FSR 604.
33. 839 F Supp 1552 (MD Fla 1993).
34. 907 F. Supp. 1361 (ND Cal. 1995).
35. EIPLR Jan. 10 1997, p 63.
36. March 12, 1996 [Mediaforum 1996/4].
37. 871 F Supp 535 (D Mass 1994).
38. *Universal City Studios, Inc and others v. Corley and Others* SD Cal August 17, 2000.
39. *New York Times CyberLaw Journal* "Copyright Decision Threatens Freedom to Link" C.S. Kaplan December 10, 1999.
40. [1976] Ch 55.
41. 17 U.S.C. section 201(c)
42. Electronic Commerce and Law Report, Vol 6 No. 7, July 4, 2001, p. 700.
43. *Douglas v. Hello!* [2001] 2 All E.R. 289.
44. [1948] 65 R.P.C. 203
45. *Kitechnology BV v. Unicor GmbH Plastmachinen* C.A. [1995] F.S.R. 765, at 777-8.
46. The requirement of receipt in circumstances importing an obligation of confidence has now been removed for privacy cases (*Douglas v. Hello!*, above).
47. C.A. [1987] Ch. 117.
48. C.A. [1998] I.R.L.R. 382.
49. [1979] 68 Cr.Law Rep.119
50. *R v. Bow Street Metropolitan Stipendiary Magistrate and Another, ex p. Government of the United States of America* [1999] 4 All ER 1.
51. 741 F Supp 556 (ND Il 1990). Other US cases involve Defence Department information (*United States v. Morrison*, 859 F 2d 151 (4th Circuit 1988)), law enforcement records (*United States v. Girard*, 601 F 2d 69 (2nd Circuit 1979)), banking information (*United States v. Cherif*, 943 F 2d 692 (7th Circuit 1991)) and stock market information (*Carpenter v. United States*, 484 US 19 (1987)).
52. (1978) 68 Cr App R. 183.
53. TRIPs Article 27(1)
54. *Hotel Security Checking Co. v. Lorraine Co.*, 160 F. 467.
55. *State Street Bank & Trust Co. v. Signature Financial Group. Inc.*, 47 U.S.P.Q.2d 1596.
56. 172 F.3d 1352 (Fed. Cir. 1999).
57. Guidelines C IV 5.2
58. (35 USC § 102)
59. (EPC Art 55)
60. [1989] R.P.C. 561 (first instance reported at [1988] R.P.C. 1).
61. [1991] R.P.C. 305.
62. [1991] R.P.C. 463.
63. [1993] R.P.C. 427.
64. [1996] R.P.C. 511.
65. [1997] R.P.C. 608.
66. *ESAB Group Inc. v. Centricut LLC*, D.S.C., No. 4:98-1654-22, 1/15/99
67. [1982] F.S.R. 406.

3

Trade Marks and Domain Names

3.1 Trade marks and branding

3.1.1 Trade marks

The Internet, in particular the World Wide Web, is from a commercial point of view a **3–001** combination of a shop window and an advertising hoarding. Branding and, therefore, trade marks are consequently vital aspects of trading on the Internet. However, unlike a traditional advertising campaigns an "advertisement" placed on the Internet will by default be a global campaign, in the sense that it is available worldwide. This makes the legal position more than usually troublesome. We discuss in detail in Chapter 6 whether the mere availability in the United Kingdom of a non-United Kingdom web site, without more directed targeting, amounts to use of a trade mark in the United Kingdom under the Trade Marks Act 1994.[1]

First and foremost, trade marks are national by nature. They can be registered or unregistered. The protection offered to unregistered trade marks varies considerably from country to country, both as to extent (ranging from none to strong) and as to the legal basis on which they are protected (such as unfair competition in some countries, or passing off in the United Kingdom). The laws relating to registered trade marks are far more uniform across the globe. Therefore it is such registered rights which should be of most interest to those who wish to entrench their ability to use their brands on the Internet.[2]

When a trade mark is registered, it is designated as covering certain goods or services **3–002** only. A registered trade mark gives the owner the exclusive right to use that mark on the goods or services for which it is registered in the countries in which it is registered. Anyone else who then uses that mark without the authority or licence of the trade mark owner in any of those countries on the relevant goods or services will be infringing the registered trade mark. They may then be subject to injunctions preventing them from continuing to use the mark and awards of damages to compensate the trade mark owner.

Although registered trade mark regimes are relatively uniform from country to country, there still exist significant differences. For example, in some countries it is the first person to use the trade mark in relation to the relevant goods or services who has the priority right over others to claim ownership of the mark. However, in other countries it is the first person to register the mark who obtains such priority ownership rights, regardless of what use others have previously made of the mark. This is one major reason why ownership of registered trade marks tends to be so fragmented around the world.

3–003   Indeed, it is not unusual for a trade mark to be owned by different, unrelated companies in different countries. Very few companies will have any trade marks which they have registered in all countries of the world. So an advertisement put on the Internet in one country by the owner of that mark in that country may infringe the registered trade mark of another company which has it registered in a country in which the advertisement in question is accessed and read.

This is not an entirely new problem. It has already been encountered with, for example, the cross-border nature of satellite broadcasting—particularly when, as is so often still the case in Europe, trade mark ownership is split between countries. The direct sales advertising on such satellite broadcasts necessarily reaches the whole footprint of the satellite (or, for encrypted broadcasts, at least those countries in which transmission decoders are legitimately supplied). Such advertising, although legal in the country at which it is directed, may infringe a trade mark in another country into which the satellite footprint spills over. Spillover problems can also occur in the physical world of print media, where the advertiser does not control the ultimate destination of copies of the newspaper or magazine in which he advertises.[3]

3–004   Nevertheless, advertising on the Internet raises spillover concerns to a vastly different degree than does advertising in print media such as newspapers and magazines. These have to be physically distributed, while the World Wide Web is constantly available in any country in the world to anyone who has the equipment capable of accessing it. Advertising on the Web does not depend on any form of physical distribution which might limit its availability in certain countries. The issue of spillover advertising has thus become especially vexed with information flowing all around the globe on the Internet.

However, as discussed in detail in Chapter 6, mere availability in the United Kingdom may not be sufficient to amount to infringement. Even in the physical world the mere availability of an advertisement in a magazine circulating in the United Kingdom (even primarily in the United Kingdom) has been held not necessarily to amount to an infringement of a United Kingdom registered trade mark.[4] All the more may this be true of the mere availability of a web site.[5]

While registered trade marks are national in nature, there are some international trade mark registration systems either in place or currently being created which may help to give trade mark owners an easier means of broadening their ownership. But even these by no means give global coverage and certainly do not deal with existing clashing registered rights. For example, the Community Trade Mark is a unitary right effective for the whole of the E.U.

3–005   There are also two systems called the Madrid Arrangement and the Madrid Protocol which make it easier to extend trade mark registrations in certain countries to any of the other countries who are part of this system. A U.S. federal trade mark registration will cover a very large and commercially worthwhile market even though, strictly speaking, it is only a registration in one country.

It is likely that only large companies will be financially able to register their brands as trade marks throughout the world. It will only be the well-established brands or those relating to new types of goods which will not experience some sort of clash somewhere in the world. Therefore, a brand owner will have to be realistic as to what sort of coverage it requires and what level of risk in terms of infringement is acceptable. One way to look at this is to draw up a list of major markets for the goods in question together with those countries where infringement is most likely to occur and ensure that trade mark registration has been secured at least in those.

3.1.2 Branding—choice and use

One interesting aspect of using brands on the Internet is the difference, compared with   **3–006**
print media, of the interface with the viewer or prospective purchaser. The on-line
interface will generally be very limited. There may be little opportunity to give a large
amount of information about the product, or the information may have to be split up into
numerous small, separately accessible, chunks. In this context the brand itself may
convey a comparatively large amount of information.

Brands are often thought of as badges of origin and quality. Skilful advertising
campaigns can augment this with more inchoate values such as service, innovation, value
or market leadership. Products may be sold in a catalogue type fashion where the
purchaser never sees the item until after it has been purchased. The nature of the Web
means that not only is it interactive, but also visual. Usually distinctive brands are now
scattered all over Web pages cheek by jowl with each other, reinforcing the need to have a
strong visual identity—one, incidentally, capable of achieving impact at the low graphic
resolutions typical of the Web.

The interactive and visual nature of the World Wide Web has also meant that a wider   **3–007**
variety of types of trade marks have been and will in the future be used. Word and logo
marks are the most popular and widely used, but as audio becomes more prevalent on
the Web, tunes and distinctive jingles could well become popular.[6] Under the Trade
Marks Act 1994 registration of sounds became possible, enabling registration of marks
such as the Direct Line jingle. Other examples of sound marks could include the Intel
note-series or the Windows startup chimes. Animated trade marks may also become
popular and are registrable.

In Europe any distinctive non-descriptive sign is registrable as a trade mark. This is
also the case in the majority of countries in the world. Trade marks simply consisting of a
word are the most common, followed closely by logos. But even single colours can be
registered as trade marks provided they have become distinctive of the particular goods
or services sold or offered by the company claiming exclusive rights to the colour.

The range and number of disputes which have arisen over domain names also
demonstrates how important Internet branding has become. This specific area is
discussed in more detail below.

3.1.3 Proper use

The traditional need to ensure proper use of trade marks so as to maintain their strength   **3–008**
and value still applies to the Internet. If a company does find itself enjoying the benefit of
that extraordinarily valuable asset (particularly for the Internet), a global trade mark, it
should pay more attention than ever to ensuring that it is not put in jeopardy by misuse.

It is important for example that a mark is not used in such a way as to allow it to lose its
distinctiveness and become generic. The mark should always be depicted as registered
and in consistent colours and styles. Trade mark notices and the like are as appropriate, if
not more so, for trade marks used on a Web site as for those used on paper. They should
state who the trade mark owner is.

Since there is a widely, but mistakenly, held belief that any material (including a trade mark or distinctive logo) on a Web page can freely be copied on to other Web pages, it is advisable (although strictly speaking not legally necessary) to make clear in any trade mark notice that copying and use of the mark may only be done under licence from the proprietor.

Some companies for a variety of different reasons are only too happy to promote such use of their trade marks since, amongst other things, it is a useful form of advertising. However, if this is the case they would still want such use to be subject to an appropriate licence so that the mark is not put in jeopardy by misuse. A trade mark notice can easily point to a place on the Web page giving details of the relevant licence. The licence should extend to any other relevant rights, such as copyright.

3–009   Most companies with valuable brands will have proper use handbooks and these should be updated to refer to use of their marks on the Web. In appropriate circumstances, sections of such a proper use handbook can be put on the company's Web page if it is prepared to license others to use its marks in certain circumstances. A company might also want to consider making this proper use information available through their Web pages for reference by, for example, journalists.

One major use to which trade marks are put on the Internet is in sponsorship arrangements, often where Web pages are sponsored by a particular brand owner and a branded link to the brand owner's Web site is placed on the sponsored page. In such circumstances, the way in which the brand is used is entirely in the hands of the sponsored Web site proprietor. Therefore the sponsor will want to ensure by way of appropriate contract that such use is, for example, proper as well as dealing with issues of liability dealt with elsewhere in this book. Similar considerations will also apply to contracts with publishers and advertisers on the Internet.

3.2 Trade mark clashes on the Internet

3–010   Inevitably, clashes between competing trade mark owners, and between trade mark owners and infringers, have occurred on the Internet. These can generally be divided into genuine disputes and cybersquatting (or domain name piracy).

3.2.1 Genuine disputes

3–011   "Genuine" disputes include:

- the same mark owned and used by different persons (whether in the same country or different countries) in respect of different goods or services;

- the same mark owned and used by different persons in different countries in relation to the same goods or services (the "split mark").

Both of these types of disputes may be regarded as genuine disputes, since both parties have a legitimate claim to some rights in the mark. The advent with the Internet of cheap cross-border on-line commerce has exposed such latent clashes between the owners of the same marks in different countries, or even in different regions of the same country.[7] These owners may have traded in ignorance of each other for years, the Internet providing the first marketplace in which they have been brought into conflict. Or they may have clashed previously, but the Internet has provided a new commercial context in which the old dispute is re-opened.[8]

The first type of genuine dispute (same mark, different goods or services) is often only a problem in relation to domain names, since only the desire to register the identical domain name brings the parties into conflict at all.[9] This, of course, assumes that it is clear that the trade mark is being used by the different individuals in relation to different goods or services. However, where, for some reason this is not clear, it should be possible to clarify this by way of notice or disclaimer on the relevant Web page. Domain names are dealt with in detail below.

As to the second type of genuine dispute, the "split mark" where the same mark in respect of the same goods and services is owned by different companies in different countries, it has been argued that it might be acceptable simply to state in a notice that the goods in question are not available for sale to that country. Arguably, this would mean that the mark was not being used as a trade mark in that country since the company is not engaging in trade there. It may also be advisable to identify the other owner of the mark and the territory in which it owns the mark.[10]

In the United Kingdom some support for this approach—at least where the notice is a true reflection of the facts—can be gained from *Euromarket Designs Inc. v. Peters and another*[11] (The *"Crate & Barrel"* case). However, the efficacy of this approach will depend very much on the laws of the individual countries involved and the facts of any particular case, since what use of a trade mark in one country may amount to trade mark infringement may be different in another country. It is also unlikely that a notice would be considered in isolation, without considering other evidence of the practice of the web site owner.

Hopefully in most such instances it will be possible for the relevant companies to come to mutually beneficial trade mark co-operation agreements allowing them to continue to use the trade mark with suitable disclaimers or in a certain fashion on their Web pages even though those Web pages will inevitably be accessible in each other's territories.[12] Whatever the solution, the key will be pragmatism since as the global marketplace gets even smaller, the potential for trade mark clashes is bound to increase.

As to the future, common sense suggests that if the objective is to encourage peaceful co-existence of potentially clashing web sites across national borders, then there should be a threshold requirement that a claimant trade mark owner establish that the defendant has targeted or directed his web site at the jurisdiction in question. That would tend to restrict disputes to those where there is real prospect of damage through competition under a similar mark.

The WIPO Standing Committee on the Law of Trade Marks has published a discussion paper[13] addressing this question. It suggests that only use of a sign on the Internet which has a "commercial effect" in a Member State shall constitute use of a sign for the purposes of determining infringement of industrial property rights in a mark or other sign. As to commercial effect, the Committee suggests a non-cumulative, non-exhaustive list of factors to be taken into account. Generally these go to the question whether the user of the sign is doing business with customers and others in the Member State, or directing the Internet activity towards it, taking into account factors such as language, currency, territory disclaimers, degree of interactivity, provision of contact details and use of a ccTLD (country code Top Level Domain—see discussion of domain names below).

3–012

3–013

3.2.2 Cybersquatting

3–014   A rather different type of clash is the phenomenon of cybersquatting. This is a new incarnation of the old practice of registering company names in advance of their registration by the "true" owner of the name (for instance where a company has announced an intention to expand its activities to other countries) with the intention of exacting a substantial price from the company to transfer the new company to it. Such practices were looked upon with disfavour by the English courts.[14] Cybersquatters, similarly, register domain names before the trade mark owners have done so, with a view to exacting a price for transferring the domain name to the trade mark owner. Cybersquatters have also been known as domain name pirates and domain name hijackers. The terms are interchangeable. Occasionally cybersquatters go further and create fake web sites, sometimes for the purpose of perpetrating frauds upon the public.[15] Domain names and cybersquatting are discussed in detail below.

3.3 Domain names

3–015   The major new trade mark issue that has arisen with the Internet relates to domain names. Thanks to the proliferation of "cybersquatting", domain names have acted as a lightning rod, stimulating heated debate and polarising opinions over the appropriate relationship of intellectual property rights to domain names, the ease of registration of domain names, how to prevent abusive domain name registrations and many other related topics. The debate has also become entangled with disputes about appropriate institutional structures for managing the technical features of the Internet, so that questions such as whether new classes of domain name should be made available have been discussed in parallel with the question of who should be empowered to make that decision.

3.3.1 What are domain names and how do they work?

3–016   What is a domain name? A word of technical explanation is appropriate. Computers on the Internet recognise each other by IP addresses. Each computer attached to the Internet has a unique IP address, which may be allocated to it permanently or temporarily.[16] An IP address has a form such as 194.72.244.100.[17] While fine for computers, this is not user-friendly for human beings. So in 1984/85[18] the domain name system (DNS) was introduced. This overlays the IP address system, allowing alphanumeric identifiers to be used such as "twobirds.co.uk". When the user types in to a browser, for instance, "www.twobirds.co.uk", the browser sends a request to look up a database table in its local DNS name server,[19] receives the corresponding IP address (either from the local server or through a series of queries to locate an authoritative name server[20]) and uses that IP address to contact the target Internet computer (*e.g.* a web site host).[21] The process of finding out the IP address that corresponds to a domain name is known as "resolving" the domain name.

The DNS database is, like most aspects of the Internet, distributed across many computers. They co-ordinate with each other, and utilise technical methods to determine which of the many thousands of DNS servers holds authoritative information about which groups of domain names. There is, however, a hierarchical element to the DNS.

Certain "root" servers are ultimately authoritative in that they hold (in the "root zone file") the definitive information about which other name servers are authoritative for which domains.[22] Among the 13 root servers[23] the "A" root server is first among equals, the other 12 servers taking their cue from it. The "A" root server is currently located in Herndon, Virginia, USA and is operated by Verisign, Inc (formerly Network Solutions Inc.), although subject to oversight by the U.S. Department of Commerce who must approve any changes to the root zone file.[24/25]

The domain name system is organised into various classes of domain types, known as domain spaces or just domains. Until mid-2001 there were seven non-localised, or generic domains: .com, .org, .net, .gov, .edu, .mil, .int. These (or at least the three available for general use, .com, .org and .net and the new generic domains being introduced from 2001) are now known as gTLDs (generic top level domains). Additionally there are nearly 250 country-specific domains, now known as ccTLDs (country code top level domains).[26] The ccTLD for the United Kingdom is '.uk'.   **3–017**

3.3.2 Who controls the domain name system?

Historical overview

Until the late 1990s overall responsibility for deciding what top level domains could be created and who should manage the country code top level domains was vested, in a somewhat informal fashion,[27] in a loosely formed group or project called IANA (the Internet Assigned Numbers Authority). IANA, which was the central coordinator for the assignment of unique parameter values for Internet protocols generally,[28] was run by and synonymous with[29] the late Dr Jon Postel,[30] one of the original founders of the Internet, based in the University of Southern California's Information Sciences Institute. IANA's legitimacy to discharge this responsibility derived partly from the respect in which Jon Postel was held within the Internet community.[31] However, the U.S. Internet was funded to a degree by U.S. government contracts (*e.g.* from the National Science Foundation which ran NSFNet, which became the Internet backbone, and from the Defence Advanced Projects Research Agency (DARPA)), so that an element of legitimacy of the early Internet institutions such as IANA also derived from the sanction of the U.S. funding bodies. Indeed the U.S. government, when it came to consider these matters closely in 1997/98, made clear that it regarded IANA's functions as being carried out on behalf of the U.S. government, and the transfer of functions to a private sector body as representing the privatisation of domain name management functions.[32] The 1999 contract between the University of Southern California and the Internet Corporation for Assigned Names and Numbers (ICANN), providing for the transition (subject to U.S. government approval) of IANA's functions from USC to ICANN, recites that USC had been operating IANA as a research project pursuant to a Teranode Network Technology contract awarded by DARPA to USC.[33]   **3–018**

Identifying a conventional legal source of authority over, and responsibility for, the domain system during the period before the introduction of ICANN was a somewhat elusive quest, especially since in practice the degree of involvement of the US government was less obvious to outside observers than it became subsequently.[34] The pursuit of an "authority trail" was, rather like seeking the source of a great river, liable to leave the explorer stranded in a muddy field.[35] However, although the authority of IANA may have been largely derived from consensus and legitimacy within the Internet community, it was none the less valid or real for that. The tradition of "bottom-up"   **3–019** processes for validating decisions about the Internet was so strong that it was recognised in the 1998 U.S. Government Green and White Papers on management of the domain name system, and has been translated into an elaborate, formalised consensus structure for ICANN.[36]

As funding of the Internet and ownership of the U.S. Internet backbone was moved into private hands in the mid-1990s, as government contracts expired and as the Internet came to be used by commerce and the public at large, so wider communities and interest groups came to have an interest in the future of the Internet. This created immense tensions, academia, commerce, the Internet community, intellectual property proponents, the U.S. government, the European Commission, existing domain name registration managers, country code domain space managers and others all promoting their own perceptions of how the Internet should be run.

3–020   The resulting, extraordinarily painful, worldwide consensus-building process culminated in the acceptance in November 1998 of an application from ICANN, a not-for-profit body incorporated in California, as the body to take responsibility for future policy for the technical operation of the Internet—effectively to be the "new IANA". ICANN is a consensus-based body intended to represent a broad church of constituencies with interests in the effective operation of the Internet. Jon Postel would almost certainly, but for his untimely death on October 16, 1998, have been the first head of ICANN. Provision has been made for the transfer of most of the functions of IANA to ICANN.[37] Indeed the IANA name lives on under the ICANN umbrella, and within the context of ICANN, IANA continues to make decisions on matters such as delegation of ccTLDs.[38] ICANN has direct policy control over the gTLDs. It does not exercise operational control over the ccTLDs, although one of its tasks is to pursue contractual arrangements with the operators of ccTLDs.

ccTLDs

3–021   A wide variety of organisations, some state, some private, have responsibility delegated by IANA for managing country code domains.[39] The reasons for this variety are mainly historical, reflecting differing political perspectives around the world as to whether such control should be in state or private hands. Each ccTLD is able to organise and sub-divide its own domain space as it wishes within general policy laid down by IANA.[40] This leads to local differences in domain structures. So for instance, the most commonly used commercial sub-domain in the United Kingdom name space is named "co.uk", whereas in Hong Kong it is named ".com.hk".

Each ccTLD tends to have its own local requirements for registration, which vary widely. Some are extremely restrictive, for instance permitting registrations only by locally registered companies.

gTLDs

3–022   IANA had originally provided for three generally available gTLDs: .com, .org and .net. .com was intended for use by companies and commercial enterprises, .org by non-commercial organisations and .net by network providers. In recent years, however, these restrictions have broken down so that all three have effectively become available for general use.

Registration of .com, .org and .net domain names was for a long time contracted out by the National Science Foundation under the auspices of the U.S. Department of Commerce exclusively to a private company, Network Solutions Inc., (NSI) for a period which was initially due to expire in March 1998. It was common at that time to refer to NSI as

InterNIC, and to InterNIC as providing the registration of .com domain names, since that was the name under which NSI provided its registration services.[41] However, the U.S. Department of Commerce has now reclaimed control of InterNIC as a neutral network information centre, stating that NSI was only one of several companies involved in the development of InterNIC as an integrated network information centre.[42]

Increasing the number of gTLDs

The lengthy process of debating the transfer of IANA's responsibilities and the migration away from NSI's exclusive registration rights was accompanied by vigorous debate over proposals to expand the number of gTLDs beyond the existing three available for general use (.com, .org and .net).[43]   **3–023**

Jon Postel had originally proposed in May 1996 a great expansion, allowing 150 new gTLDs to be established by up to 50 new competing registries, for a wide variety of business areas.[44] The Internet Society then promoted the formation of the Internet International Ad Hoc Committee[45] to consider this and other issues. The IAHC included representatives from the World Intellectual Property Organisation (WIPO), the International Telecommunications Union (ITU) and the International Trade Mark Association (INTA). The IAHC process culminated in the signature of a gTLD Memorandum of Understanding (gTLD-MoU)[46] on May 1, 1997, upon the signature of which the IAHC dissolved. This recommended the establishment of seven new gTLDs: .firm, .store, .web, .arts, .rec, .nom and .info. It also recommended a worldwide system of competing registrars, to replace the exclusive right held by NSI, after the expiry of NSI's contract with the U.S. government National Science Foundation. The competing registrars were to be members of a Council of Registrars, which would be incorporated in Switzerland. There would also be a Policy Oversight Committee. WIPO would organise a dispute resolution procedure. The IAHC was succeeded on its dissolution by an interim Policy Oversight Committee.

The U.S. government at this point became more actively involved in debating the appropriate mechanism for moving Internet governance (including decisions about new gTLDS and competing registrars)[47] to the private sector. This intervention started with a White House report[48] "A Framework for Global Electronic Commerce" dated July 1, 1997, accompanied by a Presidential directive[49] tasking the U.S. Department of Commerce to "support efforts to make the governance of the domain name system private and competitive and to create a contractually based self-regulatory regime that deals with potential conflicts between domain name usage and trademark laws on a global basis". The Department of Commerce issued a Green Paper on January 30, 1998,[50] followed by a White Paper on June 5, 1998.[51] By this time, especially since the U.S. Government papers were proposing that a not-for-profit body based in the USA should take on the major co-ordinating, policy and oversight role, the debate had evolved into a geo-political controversy conducted at the highest levels in the U.S. Government and the European Commission over whether the domain system and Internet should be run from the USA. This was resolved in July 1998, when the European Commission issued a communication[52] accepting the U.S. government White Paper proposals as a basis for the way forward. The process resulted in the acceptance of an application by ICANN to be the not-for-profit body. ICANN, was to be tasked with (among other things) deciding on the appropriate expansion of the gTLD name space, and on devising uniform domain name disputes procedures.   **3–024**

ICANN started its formal work in 1999. The uniform disputes resolution policy (UDRP) introduced by ICANN in December 1999[53] is discussed below. Competing registrars were introduced, starting with testbed registrars in April 1999. After further long drawn out debate and the solicitation of applications from putative operators of new gTLD registries, a final decision was taken in November 2000 to select seven new gTLDs and to open negotiations with their proposed operators.[54] The seven selected new gTLDs were .biz, .info, .name, .pro, .aero, .coop and .museum. Of these, the first four are unsponsored (*i.e.* will be operated by a neutral registry operator), and three are sponsored (*i.e.* will be run by industry or sector representative bodies). The only unsponsored gTLD intended for unrestricted use is .info. .biz is intended for businesses, .coop for cooperatives, .name for individuals and .pro for professions such as accountants, lawyers and physicians.

3–025   The first new gTLDs to come into operation are .biz[55] and .info.[56] .info became operational in October 2001, and .biz is anticipated to become operational in November 2001. Both have put in place complex pre-launch procedures designed to reduce the initial potential for cybersquatting.[57] Thereafter each will register domain names on a first-come first-served basis and will operate the ICANN UDRP procedures (.biz will also operate a Restrictions Dispute-Resolution Policy for complaints that domain names have been registered in violation of the .biz name registration restrictions, such as that the domain name is not being, or will not be, used primarily for a bona fide business or commercial purpose).

Mention should also be made of the proposed .eu domain space, promoted by the European Commission for use by European companies. A proposed Regulation[58] to govern the operation of a .eu domain space is currently awaiting a Council common position. Any such proposal would have to be accepted by ICANN. Being neither a ccTLD (which are based on the ISO 3166 list of country codes)[59] nor a gTLD, the .eu domain would be anomalous in terms of the current TLD structure.

The '.uk' domain space

3–026   For a long time responsibility for the ".uk" name space was delegated by IANA to Dr Willie Black, a United Kingdom academic, working in conjunction with a collection of industry representatives called the United Kingdom Naming Committee. In August 1996 responsibility was transferred to Nominet United Kingdom, a company limited by guarantee,[60] whose managing director is Dr Black. The members of Nominet are drawn from those persons with an interest in the Internet. Those providing domain name registration services can become Tag Holder members, who alone are entitled to use Nominet's automatic domain name registration system.

The .uk domain space is divided into a number of second level domains (SLDs): .co.uk, .org.uk, .ltd.uk, .plc.uk, .ac.uk, .gov.uk and some others. Most of these are operated by Nominet and are open for registration of third level domain names (3LDs), such as twobirds.co.uk. Some of the SLDs are restricted and some of those (such as .ac.uk and .gov.uk) are not operated by Nominet. One SLD (parliament.uk) has been allocated to a single organisation for use as its domain name.

Mention should also be made of certain types of domain name which, although they may appear at first glance to be a branch of the official domain space structure described above, are in fact rather different. An example is ".uk.com". It is possible to apply to the proprietor of this domain name for allocation of a sub-domain, such as "twobirds.uk.-com". This looks very much like a ccTLD. However, it is not a ccTLD.

3–027   ".uk.com" is an ordinary domain name registered under the ".com" gTLD. The arrangements to allocate sub-domains within it have been made autonomously by the owner of the 'uk.com' domain name. So, if the owner of the 'uk.com' domain name were to lose the rights to that domain name (*e.g.* by failing to renew the subscription[61]), then all sub-domain registrants beneath it would lose their sub-domains. This is a different situation from registering directly under ".com", since the continuing existence of the ".com" TLD depends directly on ICANN which is a consensus-based body. It is also different from registering directly under a ccTLD such as ".co.uk", since although the continuing existence of the ".uk" TLD (and of the second level domains within it such as .co.uk) depends to some extent on Nominet, that is also a consensus-based body whose delegation of the .uk domain space could only be changed by a decision of IANA.[62] IANA (now operated under the auspices of ICANN—see discussion above), has a recognised place within the structure of Internet governance, has designated ".uk" as the appropriate name space for the United Kingdom in accordance with ISO 3166 and co-ordinates the operation of the root servers which recognise the relevant domain name spaces.

The contracts between ICANN and the seven new gTLDs will prohibit the operators of the new gTLDs from permitting the registration of two letter second level domains such as ISO country codes.

3.3.3 How does substantive law apply to domain names?

The function of a domain name

We have already alluded to the potential for increased trade mark clashes on the Internet. Most of the clashes that have occurred have been sparked by disputes over the use of domain names.   **3–028**

As we have described, a domain name is an unique alphanumeric address which resolves to the unique numerical (IP) address of a server on the Internet. For the Web, a domain name is the basis of an address for any given Web site.[63] So, for example, Bird & Bird has the domain name "twobirds.com". This means that Bird & Bird's Web site has the unique address http://www.twobirds.com. However, in addition to its function as an address a domain name often also has a second role which is of great legal significance. Since it is generally an alphanumeric address, a URL incorporating the domain name can also act as a memorable way for people to access any given Web site. It can, therefore, be not only an address but also a specific identifier. One analogy is with the freephone 800 numbers used for voice telephony which spell a word using the letters associated with a telephone keypad (*e.g.* (1)-800-AIRWAYS). The significance of the role as an identifier may vary from one domain name to the next. A domain name may correspond to a company's trading name or one of its brand names, represent the name of a non-profit organisation, represent a generic class of goods, services or interests, identify a topic of debate or controversy, represent an allegiance of the web site owner[64] or be used in numerous other ways.[65]

Given its potential role as an identifier, the immediately obvious methods of restraining misuse of a domain name are by asserting infringement of a United Kingdom or Community registered trade mark under the Trade Marks Act 1994, or by alleging that the use of the domain name amounts to passing off.[66] In a blatant case it may also be possible to establish that the domain name amounts to an instrument of fraud, whose owner can be subjected to legal remedies even if trade mark infringement or passing off has not been established. However, domain names and registered trade marks are not coterminous. They differ from each other in at least four significant ways. These are summarised in the following table: **3–029**

Trade mark	Domain name
Trade mark registrations are national or regional.	Domain names (whether gTLDs or ccTLDs) are visible in all countries, especially when pointed to live web sites.[67]
Trade mark registrations protect use of the mark in the course of trade.	The purpose of the domain name registrant may be commercial or non-commercial.
A trade marks is registered for specified categories of goods or services.	The registration of a domain name (at least in open TLDs) is not linked to any specific class of goods or services.
The same trade mark can be registered for different goods and services by numerous different applicants.	Only one instance of a domain name can be registered.[68]

We draw attention to these differences not to criticise them, but to illuminate some of the underlying distinctions between registered trade marks and domain names (see also the later discussion on scrutiny of domain name registrations, in which we elaborate on the reasons why these distinctions exist). The lack of congruence between registered trade marks and domain names means that a trade mark registration cannot be (or ought not to be capable of being) brought to bear on the registration of a domain name without some consideration of the use to which the domain name registration is likely to be, or is being, put.

3–030   When considering the likely use of a domain name, it would be naïve to think of domain names only as technical addresses, with no potential for wider characteristics as identifiers. It is equally inappropriate to assume that every domain name is registered for a commercial purpose and therefore potentially falls within the scope of someone's registered trade mark. The proper application of trade mark law should require evidence of actual or intended use, or grounds on which relevant use can properly be inferred. Not every potential use of a domain name, even as an identifier, necessarily falls within the ambit of trade mark protection (*e.g.* identifying a topic of controversy, or exercising rights to criticise a company or its products[69]). So it should not be assumed that the mere registration of a domain name which includes someone's trade mark will automatically result in a finding of trade mark infringement or passing off.

However, especially in the case of domain names incorporating very well known trade marks, a court would almost certainly require convincing evidence to displace the natural suspicion that the domain name has been registered for nefarious purposes. Protestations of innocent purposes are likely to be disbelieved, even on an application for summary judgment, if they are inconsistent with surrounding evidence.[70] As we shall see from the caselaw discussed below, English courts have generally been ready to draw an inference of a nefarious purpose from appropriate evidence of surrounding conduct.

The Trade Marks Act 1994

3–031   Section 9(1) of the Trade Marks Act 1994 provides that the proprietor of a registered trade mark has exclusive rights in the trade mark which are infringed by use of the trade mark in the United Kingdom without his consent; and that the acts amounting to infringement are specified in section 10. Section 10 (1) to (3) provides as follows:

"(1) A person infringes a registered trade mark if he uses in the course of trade a sign which is identical with the trade mark in relation to goods or services which are identical with those for which it is registered.

(2) A person infringes a registered trade mark if he uses in the course of trade a sign where because—

    (a)   the sign is identical with the trade mark and is used in relation to goods or services similar to those for which the trade mark is registered, or

    (b)   the sign is similar to the trade mark and is used in relation to goods or services identical with or similar to those for which the trade mark is registered,

there exists a likelihood of confusion on the part of the public, which includes the likelihood of association with the trade mark.

(3) A person infringes a registered trade mark if he uses in the course of trade a sign which—

    (a)   is identical with or similar to the trade mark, and

    (b)   is used in relation to goods or services which are not similar to those for which the trade mark is registered,

where a trade mark has a reputation in the United Kingdom and the use of the sign, being without due cause, takes unfair advantage of, or is detrimental to, the distinctive character or the repute of the trade mark. . . ."

Certain definitions and qualifications to these provisions are set out in sections 10(4) to (6) and in sections 11 and 12. While these are of general importance, we do not propose to address them in this short introduction to the rights granted under the Act.

A claimant has to overcome a lower hurdle under section 10(1), where the defendant's **3–032** sign is *identical* with the trade mark and is used in relation to goods or services which are *identical* to those for which the mark is registered, since there is no requirement to establish a likelihood of confusion. Where either one or the other is not identical but similar, then under section 10(2) the claimant has to show a likelihood of confusion. For this purpose a mere association between the two marks as a result of their analogous semantic context is insufficient. While the greater the distinctiveness of the mark, the greater the likelihood of confusion, the assessment of confusion is a matter of global appreciation of a number of factors.[71] Marks with a highly distinctive character, either *per se* or because of the reputation they possess on the market, enjoy broader protection in practice under section 10(2) than marks with a less distinctive character. A greater degree of similarity between the marks may offset a lesser degree of similarity between the goods and services, and vice versa. The likelihood of confusion includes the risk that the public might believe that the goods or services in question come from the same undertaking (or economically linked undertakings).[72] Under section 10(2), therefore, there may be substantial dissimilarity between the goods and services in question, yet confusion may still be proved. However, confusion must still be as to the origin of the goods or services.[73]

Where the sign used is either identical or similar to the registered mark, but the goods or services are not similar, then infringement is possible only under section 10(3). For section 10(3) the trade mark must be shown to have a reputation in the United Kingdom, and while there is no requirement to prove likelihood of confusion[74] the use of the sign must be without due cause, take unfair advantage of, or be detrimental to, the distinctive character or the repute of the trade mark. It may be that a mere likelihood of association between the marks would be sufficient to establish unfair advantage/detriment.[75]

3–033　　An issue potentially of great significance to infringement by use of domain names is whether it is a requirement of section 10 of the Act that the allegedly infringing sign be used "as a trade mark" (*i.e.* in a way that indicates trade origin). If there is no such requirement, then (subject to the defences set out above), trade mark registrations may be used to restrain a variety of types of use in the course of trade that would not have amounted to infringement under the pre-1994 United Kingdom trade mark law. For instance, under the old law it was held to be unarguable that the use of the words "Mother Care" in the title of a book about the problems facing working mothers was use in a trade mark sense.[76]

This issue was considered by the Court of Appeal in *Philips Electronics v. Remington Consumer Products*.[77] The Court of Appeal set out its view that use in a trade mark sense was not required, but referred the issue to the European Court of Justice. The point was most recently considered by Laddie J. in *Arsenal Football Club plc v. Reed*.[78] He stated:

"If registration of a sign as a trade mark in respect of a particular class of goods gives a right to restrain any use of that sign in relation to those goods, whether that use is in a trade mark sense or not, the Act, and the Trade Mark Directive (89/104/EEC) on which it was based, will have created a new and very wide monopoly."

After considering the Court of Appeal decision in *Philips v. Remington*, and the possibility that the European Court of Justice would determine the reference in that case on another ground, he also referred the issue to the European Court of Justice.

3–034　　Even if use in a trade mark sense is not required, it is still necessary to show "use" (or threatened use) of the sign "in the course of trade" and "in relation to" goods or services. In the case of domain names these are real hurdles. It is not immediately obvious how, for instance, the mere registration of a domain name with no surrounding evidence as to its proposed use by the registrant is to be held to constitute use (or threatened use) in the course of trade. In the absence of evidence, the court has to fall back on inference. However, especially given the fact that it is no longer (if it ever was) realistic to infer intended commercial use from registration in .com or in .co.uk, in the absence of evidence such inference may be hard to draw.

The requirement to show that the threatened use is "in relation to" goods or services may be difficult to satisfy in the case of mere registration if there is no evidence of the intended use of the domain name. For instance, the mere facts that the registration of the domain name will be visible via the Internet (via a WHOIS search), and that if pointed to a web site the web site will be accessible over the Internet, do not of themselves mean that the domain name will be used in relation to the provision of Internet-related services. In the case of trade marks sufficiently well known to satisfy the requirements of section 10(3), there is no requirement to show that the sign is to be used in relation to similar goods or services. Indeed, section 10(3) only applies where the goods and services are not similar. Where they are similar, section 10(2) must be relied upon since the sections are mutually exclusive.

3–035　　However in practice, in domain name cases, the requirements of section 10(3) appear to have amounted only to a requirement to show a threat to use it in relation to some service of any description. In appropriate circumstances a court may require little persuasion to reach this conclusion. Thus, in *British Telecommunications plc and others v. One in a Million Ltd and Others*,[79] the Court of Appeal held that even assuming that there was a requirement for the purposes of section 10(3) that the use be trade mark use, that requirement was satisfied in that case:

> "Upon that basis I am of the view that threats to infringe have been established. The appellants seek to sell the domain names. ... The domain names indicate origin. That is the purpose for which they were registered. Further, they will be used in relation to the services provided by the registrant who trades in domain names".

In most cases the claimant trade mark owner will have some evidence of the registrant's intended use of the domain name. Although not strictly relevant to the question of infringement, intention is relevant to ascertaining any threatened use and to consideration of appropriate remedies. Further, the court may readily infer that intended passing off is likely to occur, even if there is a possibility that it would not occur.[80] Common scenarios are that the domain name may be pointed ("delegated") to a web site, or the registrant may have communicated with the trade mark owner and, typically in the case of cybersquatters, have offered to sell the domain name to the trade mark owner or threatened to sell it to a third party. Or the claimant may be able to gather evidence of a pattern of conduct on the part of the registrant in relation to other domain names registered by him. Such evidence may enable the court to make findings or to draw inferences as to the intended conduct of the registrant.[81]

Often, the evidence will reveal an attempt or threat to sell the domain name. Since that may be the only evidence of commercial activity on the part of the registrant, it will be important to consider whether an attempt to trade in the domain name itself is sufficient to constitute use of the relevant sign "in the course of trade". If so, then in many cases of mere registration, the attempt or threat to sell the domain name will be sufficient to satisfy the requirement. In *One in a Million* the deputy judge at first instance found that trading in domain names was sufficient to constitute use in the course of trade for the purposes of section 10(3):   **3–036**

> "The use of a trade mark in the course of the business of a professional dealer for the purpose of making domain names more valuable and extracting money from the trade mark owner is a use in the course of trade."[82]

On appeal, the Court of Appeal did not explicitly address the point. However, it explicitly affirmed the reasoning of the court below on the question of registered trade mark infringement.

Passing off
To avoid the risk of failing to satisfy the statutory requirements of the Trade Marks Act, claimants in domain name cases typically also assert a case of passing off. Passing off, being a common law tort, is flexible and can be adapted to the needs of the moment.   **3–037**

The traditional requirements of passing off are threefold: that the claimant has established goodwill among the public in relation to its goods or services, such that its mark is distinctive of the goods or services; a misrepresentation by the defendant likely to lead persons wishing to buy the goods or services to be misled into buying the goods or services of the defendant; and that the claimant is likely to suffer damage.[83]

3–038   As with registered trade mark infringement, in the case of a mere domain name registration with no surrounding evidence it is difficult to see how all the requirements of the tort of passing off can be satisfied. However, it will be seen from the discussion below that in the *One in a Million* case the Court of Appeal overcame such difficulties in a number of ways. First, in that case there was surrounding evidence of the intentions of the defendants. Second, the court held (perhaps surprisingly, in the light of the second element of the tort), that the availability of the domain name registration details on a WHOIS search were sufficient to constitute passing off.[84] Third, the court applied an old doctrine of equipping oneself with an instrument of fraud, holding that the domain names in question were instruments of fraud in the hands of the defendants. For the purpose of the "instrument of fraud" doctrine it is unnecessary to show a threat to pass off by the possessor of the instrument. The court was even prepared to hold that some of the domain names in the case were "inherently deceptive", enabling remedies to be applied with no evidence of intended use.

It should be emphasised that the evidence in *One in Million* was severely prejudicial to the defendants, establishing a blatant case of cybersquatting. How the reasoning of the case will be applied to less blatant cases remains to be seen.

Overseas domain name registrations

3–039   The potential interaction between the Court of Appeal's approach in *One in a Million* and the treatment of cross-border trade mark issues in *Crate & Barrel* has yet to be explored. In *Crate & Barrel* (discussed fully in Chapter 6), Jacob J. suggested that for a trade mark to be held to be used within the jurisdiction, there had to be more than mere visibility. Some element of directing towards or targeting the United Kingdom was necessary. In that case, he regarded a .ie domain name as either indicating that the local Dublin shop advertised on the web site was in Ireland, or as neutral.

So what is the approach if a cybersquatter registers a domain name in a non-United Kingdom ccTLD? If (apart from the suffix) it is identical to a well-known United Kingdom trade mark consisting of an unique word, does it follow from *One in a Million* that it is inherently deceptive and that passing off is occurring because of the availability of proprietorship details in a WHOIS search? Or does the court, following *Crate & Barrel*, have to consider whether there is evidence of directing or targeting to the United Kingdom? How would this be proved in the case of a mere registration? If the registrant has approached the United Kingdom trade mark owner with an offer to sell, then that is likely to be persuasive if the usual implicit threat to misuse or dispose of the domain name elsewhere can be inferred so as to threaten damage to the trade mark owner's United Kingdom goodwill. If not, then there must be a real doubt whether mere registration of a non-United Kingdom ccTLD domain name is sufficient to constitute use or threatened use within the United Kingdom.

One exception to this doubt may be those ccTLDs that are marketed for the non-territorial connotations of their suffixes. For instance, .tv is the ccTLD for Tuvalu. It is of particular interest to the media sector. As such, it is in practice more like a gTLD than a ccTLD.

3.3.4 Scrutiny of domain name applications

3–040   Each national or regional registry has its own rules for handling domain name applications and disputes. The rules for much of the .uk domain space were substantially loosened when Nominet assumed responsibility in August 1996. However the under-lying rule for allocating domain names, at least in open domain spaces available for general use, has always tended to be "first come, first served".

Domain name registries generally do not behave like a trade marks or patents registry. There is little or no detailed examination procedure such as would be appropriate for an application for a registered trade mark or other registered intellectual property right.[85] The primary concern of a domain name registry is to ensure that domain names registered are unique, as this is a fundamental technical requirement of the Internet. This is similar to the basic checks made by the United Kingdom Companies Registry when registering the names for companies, which are largely restricted to eliminating identical or closely similar applications. The commercial imperatives with company names and domain names are identical: they need to be available for use immediately and at minimal cost, rather than after the months and with the significant cost typically required to register a trade mark.

Over time, various domain name registries have developed rules which they enforce by **3–041** way of contract with anyone registering a domain name with them. These may provide, for example, that the applicant will not register a domain name where it is clearly not commercially entitled to use such a name, or that the applicant can only register a domain under that particular country designation if it has an established place of business in that country. There has been considerable pressure from some trade mark owners, as the incidence of cybersquatting has increased, to introduce closer scrutiny of domain name applications. The main result of this has been the introduction of the post-registration ICANN Uniform Disputes Resolution Procedure. Most recently the new .biz and .info gTLD operators have implemented pre-launch procedures designed to reduce the incidence of cybersquatting in the start-up phase of these new gTLDs. After launch, however, there will be no examination of applications. Domain names will be available for use within minutes of being applied for.

Some may think that a domain name simply should not be accepted for registration if it is the same as or similar to an existing registered trade mark, or at least a well-known mark. However, this is an over-simplistic view. This argument partly stems from an assumption that a name can be inherently deceptive, simply by reason of its similarity to a trade mark,[86] so that a domain name similar to a registered trade mark would be bound to infringe. But if that were correct, then (for instance) a journalist mentioning a product name (or domain name) in a newspaper article would infringe by mere mention of the name.[87] That would lead to monopolisation of the language, which is not the function of trade mark law. It is the context within which, and the purposes for which, a name is used, as well as the degree of similarity to the mark, that determines whether it is confusingly similar or deceptive. That context does, of course, include the fact that domain names generally fulfil an identifying function, and other factors inherent in the domain name and Internet system: the ubiquity of search engines, and the existence of WHOIS searches to ascertain the registrants of domain names. However, care needs to be taken to ensure that, in the enthusiasm to punish bad actors, the essential step of determining whether the accused domain name is in fact confusingly similar or deceptive is not overlooked or reduced to a vestigial test.[88]

It may be thought that domain names are a species of intellectual property, and so (like **3–042** some registered intellectual property rights) should be subjected to close scrutiny and examination before the domain name is issued. But as a matter of principle the analogy is false.

Domain names are not intellectual property rights. Domain names can be the object against which intellectual property rights are asserted, but they are not the subject of intellectual property rights. So a trading name may be the subject of registered trade mark. The trade mark registration may be infringed by someone who (broadly) uses a mark, or a confusingly similar mark, in the course of trade in relation to the goods or services for which it is registered. The mode of use of the mark is the object against which the registered mark is brought to bear. The mode of use may be in manifold different ways: by advertising, shop front hoarding, business circular, packaging, letterhead, company name or, indeed, domain name. Whichever the vehicle, it is the use (actual, threatened or inferred) of the trade mark in a prohibited way that triggers the infringement, not the mere existence in some form in the hands of the defendant of the word or other sign corresponding to the trade mark.

The registered mark may be a means by which the defendant can be forced to deliver up infringing materials,[89] or to change the name of a company[90] or transfer a domain name, or (in extreme circumstances) have the domain name transferred on his behalf by a court official.[91] None of that, however, renders a domain name the subject of intellectual property rights. It makes as little sense to speak of a domain name being intellectual property as it does a letterhead.[92] Possession of a letterhead *per se* confers no rights on its possessor other than possessory title to the physical letterhead. Registration of a domain name *per se* confers no rights, other than those limited quasi-possessory rights granted contractually by the registrar who issues the domain name.[93]

3–043   Registration of a domain name does achieve a practical blocking effect against anyone else seeking to register the identical domain name, but that confers no legal right. Its efficacy (or otherwise) depends on whether the registration and use of the domain name infringes the intellectual property rights of some third party. Indeed the blocking effect may constitute a ground for finding that the registration does infringe the intellectual property rights of others.[94] The use of letterhead and domain name alike may be protected or restrained by intellectual property rights, but they themselves are not the subject of intellectual property rights.

It is appropriate to scrutinise applications for registered intellectual property rights which, if granted, confer powerful and wide ranging exclusionary legal rights which can be used as the basis for litigation against third parties. But as we have seen, a domain name confers no such legal rights. The appropriate analogy is with registration of company names, which in the United Kingdom are granted with minimum scrutiny and maximum speed. Like domain names company names confer on the registrant no rights against third parties, but have a practical blocking effect against registration of identical company names. Like domain names, they confer no legal right to use the registered company name.

3–044   Like domain names company names are the object, not the subject of intellectual property rights. Whether they infringe third party rights depends on how they are used. Since (apart from any inference as to likely use that a court may be prepared to draw in the circumstances of a particular case) the proposed use cannot be ascertained from the mere fact of registration, company names are subject to minimal scrutiny.[95] The starting point in principle for domain names has to be that it is similarly inappropriate to subject applications to anything other than scrutiny for compliance with formal requirements and that, given the commercial undesirability of introducing cost and delay into the domain name application process, any proposed departure from that has to be strongly justified.

This is not to ignore the magnitude of the problem of cybersquatting. However, the remedies for that ill should not be founded on a misconception that domain names are a variety of registered intellectual property right.

3.3.5 Trade marks and domain names—the future

Quite apart from the difficult cross-border trade mark issues thrown up by the Internet,   **3–045**
domain names have acted as a lightning rod for a wider debate about the proper scope,
function and limits of trade marks and related rights. Should the proprietor of a well
known mark have rights to prevent use of the mark in areas beyond those for which he
uses the mark himself (such as provided in section 10(3) of the 1994 Act)? If so, how much
far should that protection extend? Should such rights extend to use which, while not use
as a trade mark, could arguably harm the reputation of the trade mark owner? Should
well-known (or even less well-known) people, such as politicians, be granted protection
for the use of their mere names, even if they do not exploit their names commercially? For
instance, the USA has granted a specific right against registration of a living person's
name as a domain name with intent to profit from the name by selling it—probably a
broader right than any in the offline world. This was introduced in the U.S.
Anticybersquatting Consumer Protection Act. An inkling of some of the activities that
may have been of particular concern to the US Congress can perhaps be discerned from
the fact that ACPA mandated the Secretary of Commerce to prepare a report
recommending guidelines and procedures in connection with the registration of personal
names, including (specifically) domain names that included the personal names of
government officials, official candidates and potential candidates for political office.[96]

The controversy that has surrounded the introduction of new gTLDs has been fuelled   **3–046**
by concern over the potential for aggravating the problem of cybersquatting. There was
concern that trade mark owners would be put to further expense in policing the new
gTLDs. Some parties favoured limited expansion of domains and closer scrutiny of
domain name applications. On the other hand, the existing domain space was nearing
capacity. The debate has also been fuelled by disagreement about the extent of bad faith,
abusive registration (cybersquatting properly so-called), as opposed to registrations that
have given rise to disputes for other reasons, such as between pre-existing good faith
competing trade mark owners in different countries or different market sectors. There has
been an unfortunate tendency to blame the domain name system for both types of
dispute, when the latter type in reality derives from the need for trade mark registration
systems generally to evolve to cope with low cost cross-border e-commerce.

Even with cybersquatting properly so-called, care has to be taken if measures to
combat it are not to put into the hands of trade mark owners rights of broader scope than
they possess by virtue of their trade mark registrations, leading to problems such as
"reverse domain name hijacking" (when domain name registrants are wrongly deprived
of their domain names by a third party's invocation of, say, a disputes procedure).

The debate over this and other aspects of Internet governance will continue.[97]

3.3.6 The rise of the domain name dispute

The immediate availability of domain names, together with the slowness in the early days   **3–047**
of the Web of many companies to wake up to the significance of the Internet as a
significant commercial medium, provided an environment in which the first serious
domain name disputes could arise. The first incident to receive public attention occurred

in 1994 when journalist Josh Quittner registered the domain "mcdonalds.com" and wrote about it in *Wired* magazine.[98] McDonalds, the hamburger chain, did not see the amusing side of this and instructed their lawyers to take action on the basis of their trade mark registration. This dispute was settled on payment by McDonalds of a sum of money to charity. Other companies regretted their tardiness in embracing the Internet when they discovered that their rivals had already taken what, in their view, should have been their domain name. The same October 1994 article in *Wired* revealed that 14 per cent of the U.S. Fortune 500 companies had their names registered by others.[99] Since those early days the need to nurture and protect a company's brands on the Internet has become well appreciated. From something that started as an obscure preserve of the company IT department, domain names have risen to a topic high on the agenda of corporate intellectual property strategists.

Domain name disputes—United Kingdom caselaw

3–048   There has been a lengthening series of United Kingdom court cases concerning domain names. One has reached the Court of Appeal: the *One in a Million* case in which the Court of Appeal stamped firmly on blatant domain name piracy. The possible application of the Court of Appeal's reasoning to less blatant cases has yet to be worked out. The bulk of the reasoned judgment concerns passing off and instruments of fraud, rather than registered trade mark infringement. Although findings of registered trade mark infringement were made, they were not as fully reasoned as the remainder of the judgment.

The first cybersquatting case to come before the English courts was the *Harrods* case. This was heard by the High Court in December 1996. In this instance, the department store Harrods sued not only the domain name owner (Mr Lawrie), but also NSI and the various computer/Internet companies that allegedly "conspired" with the domain name owner in his registration of the "harrods.com" domain name. NSI provided a statement to the effect that it would abide by the decision of the English court.

3–049   Harrods claimed infringement of registered trade marks, passing off and conspiracy. The conspiracy claim was based on the allegation that the purpose of the defendants could only be to demand money from Harrods or to prevent Harrods' own use of the name. Although the defendants served a defence, most of them did not appear at the hearing of Harrods' application for summary judgment. In this instance, the relief sought was an injunction against the defendants using the Harrods mark and an order that the defendants "take all steps as lie within their respective powers to release or facilitate the release of the domain harrods.com". Lightman J., found no difficulty with the suggestion that there was registered trade mark infringement and passing off and granted the order sought. In the absence of the defendants no reasons were given.

In July 1998 the Court of Appeal handed down its decision in *British Telecommunications plc and Others v. One in a Million Ltd and Others*.[100] The plaintiffs were Marks & Spencer plc, Ladbroke Group plc, J Sainsbury plc. Virgin Enterprises Ltd and British Telecommunications plc—all well-known business enterprises. The defendants were dealers in Internet domain names who, over an extended period, specialised in registering the names and marks of well known commercial or other enterprises without their consent. In this case domain names registered by one or other of the defendants included "sainsburys.com", "j-sainsbury.com", "ladbrokes.com", "marksandspencer.-com", "marksandspencer.co.uk", "virgin.org", "bt.org" and others. Except in one case (which was said to have arisen as a result of an administrative mistake) none of the domain names was in use as the name of an active Internet site. They had simply been registered by the defendants and were available for such use.

The plaintiffs alleged passing off and infringement of their registered trade marks under the Trade Marks Act 1994. They sought summary judgment and succeeded at first instance. The defendants appealed to the Court of Appeal. Aldous L.J. delivered the judgment of the court. The defendants' appeal was dismissed.

The Court of Appeal found four different grounds on which to hold against the defendants: two varieties of passing off and two varieties of creating instruments of fraud. It also found that the defendants had infringed the plaintiffs' registered trade marks. However, the judgment contained comparatively little analysis of that finding. **3–050**

In the case of both passing off and creating an instrument of fraud the Court distinguished between unique or inherently deceptive names and non-unique names. The significance of finding the defendants liable for creating instruments of fraud is that a defendant may be restrained from possessing or disposing of an instrument of fraud even if the defendant is itself not guilty of passing off or threatened passing off. For instance, in the old case of *Singer Manufacturing Co. v. Loog*,[101] the defendant was an importer of sewing machines who wrote a leaflet describing the machines as using the Singer mechanism, which he supplied to retailers with the machines. The importer was not himself passing off as there was no deception in relation to the retailers. The question was whether the importer had created an instrument of fraud (namely the leaflet) which would enable to retailer to pass off to ultimate customers. In that particular case it was held that the leaflet was not an instrument of fraud, the context in which the Singer name was used being such that the possibility of passing off by the retailer was too remote.

The four main grounds on which the Court of Appeal held the defendants liable can be categorised as follows.

Passing Off—Unique Name   The Court of Appeal held that in the case of unique names, *i.e.* names which denoted only the plaintiff (such as marks&spencer.com and burgerking.co.uk) the registration of the name constituted passing off. This created a false suggestion of association or connection with the name. Aldous L.J. illustrated this by means of the example of a WHOIS search, whereby a person looking up a domain name by means of a WHOIS search would be misled into believing that the indicated proprietor of the domain name was connected or associated with, for instance, Marks & Spencer plc. This also constituted an erosion of the exclusive goodwill of Marks & Spencer plc. **3–051**

The Court also considered separately the evidence of intended or threatened use and held that there was an express or implied threat to trade using the domain name or to equip another to do so and that this amounted to a threat to pass off.

Passing Off—Name not Unique   In this category, for instance virgin.co.uk, the defendants argued that the domain name did not necessarily denote the plaintiffs. In this case the Court held that there was sufficient evidence of intended or threatened use of the domain name to constitute passing off. **3–052**

Instrument of Fraud—Name inherently Deceptive   The Court of Appeal held that in the case of unique names (such as marks&spencer.com or burgerking.co.uk) the name was inherently deceptive so that any realistic use would result in passing off. That of itself constituted the name an instrument of fraud and could be restrained by the Court. The Court described an inherently deceptive name as one which "will, by reason of its similarity to the name of another, inherently lead to passing off". **3–053**

3–054   Instrument of fraud—Name not inherently deceptive   In the case of other names, which would not inherently lead to passing off, the Court would assess whether the name was registered with a view to fraud. The Court should consider the similarity of the names, the intention of the defendant, the type of trade and all the surrounding circumstances.

This classification suggests that if a name is inherently deceptive the Court should ignore any evidence put forward by the defendant regarding the purpose for which the name was registered. However, it is difficult to understand the characterisation of an inherently deceptive name as being a name which "will by reason of its similarity to the name of another, inherently lead to passing off". It cannot be the case that similarity to the name of another is the only criterion to determine whether a domain name is inherently deceptive. For instance, it must be necessary to consider at least the uniqueness or fame of the trade mark. If similarity were the only criterion then, for instance, virgin.co.uk would be inherently deceptive.

3–055   It should also, we suggest, be necessary to consider the context of the domain name registration. The case of *Singer v. Loog* (see above) was the first case in which the distinction was drawn between documents which were inherently deceptive and those in which it was relevant to consider the surrounding circumstances. Lord Selborne in that case said that "...unless the documents were fabricated with a view to such a fraudulent use of them, or unless they were in themselves of such a nature to suggest, or readily and easily led themselves to, such a fraud (which in my opinion they were not), the supposed consequences too remote, speculative and improbable to be imputed to the defendant, or to be a ground for the interference of a court of justice with the course of the defendant's business. There is no evidence that, in point of fact, any such use was ever made of them. The "directions for use" spoke unmistakeably of "Frister and Rossmann's shuttle sewing machine"; and no one, however, careless, could read in that document, the words "on Singer's improved system" without seeing and understanding their context."

It is apparent from that quotation that the context within which the use of the Singer name was made was crucial to the Court's finding that neither were the documents fabricated with a view to a fraudulent use, nor were they inherently deceptive.

3–056   It is, therefore, a little surprising to find that the Court of Appeal, describing that passage, said: "the Lord Chancellor contemplated that even where a party is not himself passing off an injunction would be granted in two circumstances; first, when fraudulent use was intended; secondly, when the name was inherently deceptive, and the name readily and easily lent itself to such a fraud". It can be seen from the passage quoted that the court in *Singer v. Loog* was discussing not the name alone, but the document which provided the context for the use of the name. The court's finding was as to whether the document was inherently deceptive, not whether the name was inherently deceptive.

We suggest, therefore, that it is wrong to look at a domain name purely as a "naked name"; and that just as the document in *Singer v. Loog* provided context for the use of the name, so in some circumstances the nature of the particular domain name may provide context which can affect whether the name is to be regarded as inherently deceptive. Although that qualification is not apparent on the face the broad statement made by the Court of Appeal, we suggest that it should be applied to it.

The significance of this qualification can be illustrated as follows. Some of the domain names in question in the *One in a Million* case were ".org" domain names. The Court of Appeal stated that "there is an argument, which does not matter, about whether [.org] is confined to non-profit making organisations". Clearly, given the overwhelming evidence against the defendants in the *One in a Million* case about their intentions regarding the domain name, in this case that argument did not matter. And perhaps, in the case of .com registrations, the practice of companies registering their own names and brands as .com domain names is so well established that it is reasonable to conclude that a .com domain name can be inherently deceptive.

However, one can envisage situations in which the nature of the top level domain might be significant.[102] As Aldous L.J. pointed out early in his judgment, "Web sites are used for many activities such as advertising, selling, requesting information, criticism, and the promotion of hobbies". What if, for instance, ICANN decided to create a ".discuss" top level domain, with the intention that this be used for Web sites discussing, among other things, the products and activities of commercial organisations? Such discussion would almost certainly extend to criticism, as mentioned by Aldous L.J.

3–057

What would be the position if a person registered "wellknownname.discuss" as a domain name? This could be regarded as analogous to creating a Usenet newsgroup incorporating a well-known brand name. Such newsgroups do exist (see, for instance, the sub-groups of rec.autos) and appear not to have been the subject of trade mark litigation. Is such a domain name to be regarded as inherently deceptive because of its similarity to a famous trade mark and therefore to be injuncted with no further consideration? Or does the nature of that particular top level domain provide context (as the surrounding document contents in *Singer v. Loog* provided context) from which it could be concluded that the domain name is not inherently deceptive, allowing the defendant to adduce evidence of the purpose for which the domain name was registered? It is suggested that the holdings of the Court of Appeal in the *One in a Million* case ought not to provide the basis for automatic restraint of such a registration and that the context provided by the particular TLD in question should be taken into account in determining whether the domain name is or is not inherently deceptive.

A parallel can be drawn with "sucks" sites. These are web sites set up by disgruntled consumers, often using the domain name "wellknownnamesucks.com". In the US case of *Bally Total Fitness Holding Corp v. Faber*[103] the defendant created a web site called Bally Sucks, criticising the plaintiff. The court held that this did not constitute infringement of the BALLY trade mark and did not tarnish the mark under federal dilution law. Although the defendant did not own or use the "ballysucks.com" domain name, the court commented that if he had done so that would not necessarily be a trade mark violation. ICANN UDRP decisions on "sucks" and similar domain names have shown little consistency, especially on the question whether a "sucks" domain name is confusingly similar to the trade mark concerned.[104]

3–058

One in a Million is a case in which the understandable enthusiasm of the Court of Appeal to provide a firm platform on which to find against domain name abuse and restrain mere registrations has resulted in some over-broad wording in the judgment. If taken literally, that wording could result in over-wide protection for trade mark owners. However, it is suggested that when one has regard to the main source of the distinction between inherently deceptive and other instruments of fraud, namely *Singer v. Loog*, the importance of context as a basis on which to ameliorate those undesirable potential consequences becomes apparent.

Registered trade mark infringement

As to registered trade mark infringement, the Court of Appeal decision in *One in a Million* contained relatively little reasoning in support of the finding of infringement under section 10(3) of the 1994 Trade Marks Act. At first instance[105] Deputy Judge Mr Jonathan Sumption Q.C. stated that the plaintiffs' argument was that "Marks & Spencer" was registered for a variety of goods and services; that the word "marksandspencer" as part

3–059

of a domain name was clearly similar; that the trade mark "Marks & Spencer" clearly had a reputation in the United Kingdom; and that it was clear that the defendants' use of the mark was detrimental to the trade mark, if only by damaging the plaintiff's exclusivity.

The defendants resisted summary judgment for trade mark infringement on two grounds: first that there was no use "in the course of trade" as required by the Act, and secondly that section 10(3) implicitly required confusion and there had been none. (The question of whether confusion is a requirement of section 10(3) now appears to have been resolved against any such requirement—see *Premier Brands United Kingdom Ltd v. Typhoon Europe Ltd and Another*.[106])

On the first issue, the judge held that trading in domain names is sufficient to constitute "use in the course of trade". He followed the then authority of *British Sugar plc v. James Robertson & Sons Ltd*[107] in finding that there was no requirement that the use be "as a trade mark". The judge did not decide whether likelihood of confusion was a requirement of section 10(3), but found in the Marks & Spencer case that if there was such a requirement it was satisfied by the inherent propensity of the domain name to confuse. In the other cases he found that the likelihood of confusion was made out beyond argument on the evidence of the history of the defendants' activities. As mentioned above, the Court of Appeal explicitly approved the judge's reasoning on this part of the case.

3–060   *One in a Million* has been applied in two further cases, both involving blatant cybersquatting. In *Britannia Building Society v. Prangley & Others*,[108] the claimant was a substantial and well-known building society. It applied for summary judgment for passing off against the defendant, who had registered britanniabuildingsociety.com. The defendant had not yet delegated the domain name to a web site, but claimed that he intended to use the domain name to advertise a business that he was in the process of establishing to provide British builders to Iranians. The court found the defendant's evidence to be "wholly incredible" and relied on certain statements in the defence to support the finding that the defendant regarded the domain name as a commercially usable instrument (there was a dispute on the evidence as to whether the defendant had or had not offered to sell the domain name to the claimant). The judge also found the domain name in question to be inherently deceptive and an instrument of fraud. He indicate that there might be rather more doubt about the cause of action in trade mark infringement, but found it unnecessary to reach a conclusion on that. He granted injunctions ordering the transfer of the domain name to the claimant and restraining further misuse of the claimant's name.

In *EasyJet Airline Co. Limited and Others v. Dainty*,[109] the claimants were a well known airline (easyJet) and various associated companies including easyEverything and easyRentacar. EasyEverything promoted Internet cafes, and easyRentacar rented vehicles. Both the airline and the car rental company took bookings largely over the Internet. The defendant was an individual who registered the domain name easy-realestate.co.uk,[110] which he wanted to use for a cut-price estate agency that he wished to establish. The claimants sued for passing off and applied for summary judgment.

3–061   It was noteworthy that the claimants did not have a business in the property field. The question therefore arose whether the claimants could establish the likelihood of damage, an essential element of passing off. The deputy judge held, relying on *Harrods Ltd v. Harrodian School Ltd*[111] that although the claimants would not lose any prospective customers, it was legitimate to consider possible damage to the claimant's goodwill and to their own reputation in the conduct of their various business enterprises.

As to deception, the deputy judge (while agreeing that the claimants were not entitled to appropriate the word "easy" and prevent any businessman from using any name which includes the name "easy"), relied upon the close resemblance of the defendant's web site to the claimants' get-up. He also relied on surrounding factual circumstances, including a previous approach to easyJet and certain misrepresentations made by the defendant to easyJet designed (so the judge held) to increase the price at which easyJet might be prepared to pay for the domain name. For both reasons he concluded that the likelihood of deception was made out.

As to remedies, the judge in addition to restraining injunctions ordered the transfer of the domain name to the claimants. While the domain name itself was not inherently deceptive, the get-up of the web site in total was adapted to be used for passing off and, if used in any of a variety of manners indicated by the defendant probably would lead to passing off. The deputy judge was also concerned that the defendant might sell the domain name to a third party who might be a malefactor. Since the judge was satisfied on the evidence that the domain was a vehicle of fraud, he concluded that notwithstanding that the domain name was not inherently deceptive, an order for transfer should be made.

In *MBNA America Bank NA and Another v. Freeman*[112] the application was for an interlocutory injunction pending trial against the defendant who had registered www.mbna.co.uk. The claimants, the world's largest independent credit card issuer, claimed infringement of a Community Trade Mark for a stylised representation of "mbna", and passing off. The interlocutory injunction claimed was to restrain the defendant firstly from operating or using any web site with the domain name or any domain name including "mbna" and secondly from selling or offering for sale or otherwise dealing with the domain name www.mbna.co.uk. The defendant's evidence was that he chose the domain name for a future "banner exchange" business, and that mbna stood for Marketing Banners for Net Advertising. He also produced evidence of an existing web site that he had operated for the previous 18 months. The claimants suggested that the acronym was not properly descriptive of a banner exchange business, and that it the absence of a credible explanation for the use of the domain name it should be inferred that the defendant had deliberately chosen to use it in order to take advantage of the claimants' goodwill to increase the number of visitors to his web site. They also claimed infringement in respect of a dissimilar business under section 10(3) of the Trade Marks Act 1994.

3–062

The judge found that the claimants had an arguable case, but that he was in no position to decide whether it was more likely to succeed or to fail at trial. As to remedies, having considered the balance of convenience he granted an interlocutory injunction pending trial restraining the sale or other dealings with the domain name, but declined to restrain the defendant from activating his web site. In this he was at least partially influenced by the "impression of business competence" that the Defendant, who represented himself, made at the hearing. This impression was reinforced by positive publicity in a national newspaper.

It can be seen from the above cases that credibility is crucial. For a defendant to stand any chance of succeeding in these cases, it is imperative that his evidence of why he chose the domain name and his intentions for it be credible and consistent with the surrounding circumstances.

3–063

In the case of a wholly recalcitrant defendant who wilfully disobeys court orders for transfer of a domain name, the court may invoke its power to order that a court official execute the transfer.[113]

With the advent of the ICANN UDRP, discussed below, there are likely to be relatively few further cases involving bad faith gTLD registrations. However, litigation over genuine disputes is still likely, as is litigation involving ccTLDs. For .uk registrations the introduction in September 2001 of Nominet's new Dispute Resolution Service[114] may reduce the need to resort to the courts.

Other U.K. cases involving Internet and domain name issues

3–064   For cases on the question whether the mere availability of a foreign web site constitutes use of a trade mark within the United Kingdom, see the discussion in Chapter 6.

As we have discussed above, the lack of congruence between the scope of registered trade marks and the use of domain names mean that two persons who might quite legitimately wish to use the same domain name in areas of trade which do not clash cannot do so, since only the first one of these will actually obtain the domain name it wants. So a Scottish car repairer and a worldwide hamburger chain cannot both use "mcdonalds.com".

This situation arose in the United Kingdom and came to the attention of the United Kingdom courts in *Pitman Training Ltd v. Nominet United Kingdom and Pearson Professional Ltd.*[115] In this case a dispute arose between two companies, both entitled to use the Pitman name in different fields of business. One of the companies, Pearson Professional, had registered "pitman.co.uk" in February 1996 for the use of its Pitman Publishing division. It was the intention of Pitman Publishing in due course to set up a Web site, but it did not immediately intend to use the domain name. In March 1996 Pitman Training, through its ISP, checked whether "pitman.co.uk" was available and was informed that it was. "pitman.co.uk" became delegated to Pitman Training, who started to use it in July 1996 (no one was able to offer any clear explanation to the court as to how this was possible). In December 1996 Pitman Publishing discovered that it no longer had the domain name. Its solicitors wrote to Nominet, relying on the fact that it had been first in time to register. Nominet in due course wrote to Pitman Training informing them that the domain name was being transferred back to Pitman Publishing. Pitman Training sued, alleging against Pitman Publishing passing off, interference with contract and abuse of process. At the full hearing of Pitman Training's application for an interlocutory injunction, the judge held that none of the causes of action were reasonably arguable and thereby gave practical effect to Nominet's "first come, first served" rule.

3–065   An interesting dispute over the domain name "prince.com" arose in *Prince plc v. Prince Sports Group Inc.*[116] The English High Court considered whether the defendant Prince Sports Group Inc issued unjustified threats of trade mark infringement proceedings against Prince plc, arising out of its use of the domain name "prince.com". Prince plc, which is in fact a computer company, had registered "prince.com" in 1995. On January 16, 1997 attorneys for Prince Sports Group, a sports equipment company, wrote to Prince plc stating that the registration had come to their clients' attention, informing it of various U.S. trade mark registrations owned by them and also stating that their client had registered the PRINCE mark in many other countries throughout the world including the United Kingdom. The letter demanded immediate agreement to assign 'prince.com' to avoid litigation. On January 29, 1997 Prince Sports' attorneys wrote to NSI, copied to Prince plc, setting out its U.S. trade mark registrations and asking for the domain name to be put on hold. NSI wrote to Prince plc on February 25, 1997 and on April 28, 1997 Prince plc commenced proceedings against Prince Sports Group Inc alleging unjustified threats of trade mark proceedings and applied for summary judgment. Prince Sports Group did not contend at the hearing that there was infringement of any United Kingdom trade mark, and the arguments mainly concerned whether the letter in fact amounted to an unjustified threat and whether Prince plc should be granted any relief. The judge held that the letter was an unjustified threat and granted a declaration to that effect and an injunction restraining the issuance of further threats.

The "prince.com" dispute, when it was first reported in the media, was widely thought to show that the then NSI disputes policy favoured US-based companies. This was because Prince plc, having used the domain name for well over a year (and their trading name in the United Kingdom previous to that), were suddenly faced with the prospect of losing the use of it if NSI put it 'on hold' as a result of the U.S. company's citation of its U.S. registered trade marks. The ICANN UDRP (which succeeded the NSI procedures) does take account of rights in unregistered marks.[117]

eFax.com Inc v. Oglesby[118] is a straightforward application to Internet facts of established **3–066** principles governing passing off and the grant of interim injunctions. Perhaps the main lesson to be drawn from this case is that, just as in the off-line world, the choice of a descriptive name for an internet or e-commerce service is likely to render the protection of that name difficult, at least until sufficient advertising, marketing and trading has taken place to render the name distinctive of the services offered. (For contrasting cases see *Lawyers Online Ltd v. Lawyeronline Ltd*[119] and *French Connection Ltd v. Sutton*[120]).

The case involved an application by the Claimant eFax.com Inc for an interim injunction restraining the Defendant Mr Mark Oglesby pending trial of the action from passing off his services as and for those of the Claimant by use of the name "efax". The Defendant had registered and was using the domain name efax.co.uk.

The Judge found that on the evidence presently available (and to put it at its lowest) the Claimant might well have a difficult task at trial in establishing a distinctive goodwill in the word "efax" sufficient to support a case in passing off. However, that did not lead to the conclusion that the claim was bound to fail or that there was no serious issue to be tried. He therefore refused to strike out the claim. However, in assessing the likelihood of confusion if no interlocutory injunction was granted, since the only confusion relevant is that which results from a misrepresentation by the Defendant it was necessary for the Judge to revisit the arguments and the evidence as to the allegedly descriptive and generic nature of the word efax. This was because since, to the extent that the word was descriptive of and generic in relation to the Defendant's business, the use of it by the Defendant in relation to his business could not amount to a misrepresentation or deception and any resulting confusion from mere description could not be relied upon in support of the claim in passing off.

The Judge concluded that any confusion which might hereafter result from the fact that **3–067** both Claimant and Defendant were offering similar services in the United Kingdom under the name "efax" would in all likelihood be attributable to the descriptive nature at the name rather than to any "misrepresentation" by the Defendant to the effect that he was carrying on the Claimant's business. The Judge also took into account other differences such as the fact that the Defendant charged for his service while the Claimant did not and that the two web sites were different in appearance.

Taking into account the status quo as at November 12, 1999 when the action was commenced, and also the fact that the Defendant acquired the efax.co.uk domain name a full year before the Claimant first launched its service worldwide in February 1999, the Judge declined to grant an interim injunction.

3.3.7 Domain name registry dispute policies

History

3–068 As domain name disputes became more of a problem the domain name registries introduced registration fees, rules about how they would act when disputes arise and, to a certain extent, rules on when they might refuse to register a domain name.

Typically, applicants seeking to register a domain name with the relevant domain name registry were required to enter into a contract incorporating the terms of these dispute policies so that the registry in question could enforce those policies by way of the law of contract. Applicants were often also required to give warranties to the registry, for instance that the use of the domain name would not contravene any third party's rights.

Before the creation of ICANN and the subsequent introduction of competing gTLD registrars there was only one registrar (NSI) issuing .com, .net and .org domain names. NSI had its own disputes policy which went through a number of iterations. That was discontinued when NSI adopted the ICANN Uniform Dispute Resolution Policy (UDRP), to which all ICANN-accredited registrars issuing gTLD domain names have to adhere.

Country code domain name registries generally continue to have their own disputes policies and rules relating to what can and cannot be registered, although a small number have voluntarily adopted the ICANN UDRP.

ICANN Uniform Dispute Resolution Policy

3–069 The Uniform Dispute Resolution Policy was adopted by ICANN in August 1999. It was implemented by registrars in the gTLDs (global top level domains) .com, .org and .net during December 1999 and January 2000. It provides third parties who would otherwise have to prove in court that registration of a domain name infringes their trade mark rights with an alternative to litigation in the case of abusive registration of domain names, *i.e.* those registered in bad faith. It is not intended for disputes between parties each of whom may have legitimate claims to the domain name.

A domain name registrant is bound to the UDRP by his contract with the issuing registrar. The contract requires the registrant to submit to a mandatory administrative proceeding in the event that a third party asserts to the registrar that

(i)   the registrant's domain name is identical or confusingly similar to a trademark or service mark in which the complainant has rights; and

(ii) the registrant has no rights or legitimate interests in respect of the domain name; and

(iii) the registrant's domain name has been registered and is being used in bad faith.

3–070 In the administrative proceeding, the complainant must prove that each of these three elements are present. The UDRP goes on the provide that the following circumstances, in particular but without limitation, if found by the Panel to be present, shall be evidence of the registration and use of a domain name in bad faith:

(i)   circumstances indicating that the registrant has registered or has acquired the domain name primarily for the purpose of selling, renting, or otherwise transferring the domain name registration to the complainant who is the owner of the trademark or service mark or to a competitor of that complainant, for valuable consideration in excess of the registrant's documented out-of-pocket costs directly related to the domain name; or

(ii)   the registrant has registered the domain name in order to prevent the owner of the trademark or service mark from reflecting the mark in a corresponding domain name, provided that the registrant has engaged in a pattern of such conduct; or

(iii)   the registrant has registered the domain name primarily for the purpose of disrupting the business of a competitor; or

(iv)   by using the domain name, the registrant has intentionally attempted to attract, for commercial gain, Internet users to the registrant's web site or other on-line location, by creating a likelihood of confusion with the complainant's mark as to the source, sponsorship, affiliation, or endorsement of the registrant's web site or location or of a product or service on the registrant's web site or location.

The UDRP then goes on to set out a number of circumstances, in particular but without   **3–071**
limitation, any of which if found by the Panel to be proved based on its evaluation of all evidence presented, shall demonstrate the registrant's rights or legitimate interests to the domain name:

(i)   before any notice to the registrant of the dispute, the registrant's use of, or demonstrable preparations to use, the domain name or a name corresponding to the domain name in connection with a bona fide offering of goods or services; or

(ii)   the registrant (as an individual, business, or other organization) has been commonly known by the domain name, even if the registrant has acquired no trademark or service mark rights; or

(iii)   the registrant is making a legitimate noncommercial or fair use of the domain name, without intent for commercial gain to misleadingly divert consumers or to tarnish the trademark or service mark at issue.

Up to July 30, 2001, 4111 proceedings had been commenced under the UDRP involving 7,219 domain names. Of those proceedings, 3,750 had been resolved (3,316 by decision, 434 otherwise).

A complainant may select the dispute-resolution service provider to which to submit   **3–072**
his complaint from among those approved by ICANN. At the time of writing four providers have been approved: WIPO, eResolution, The National Arbitration Forum and CPR Institute for Dispute Resolution. Proceedings generally take place in writing (including on-line), with no in-person hearings unless exceptionally ordered by the panel. ICANN maintains a complete database, accessible on its web site,[121] of all UDRP panel decisions.

The panel is given discretion under UDRP Rules of Procedure paragraph 15(a) to apply any rules and principles of law that it deems applicable.[122]

A UDRP panel decision to transfer or cancel a domain name will be implemented by the domain name registrar unless, within 10 business days, the domain name registrant files with the registrar official documentation evidencing the commencement of legal proceedings against the complainant in one of the jurisdictions to which the complainant has submitted under the UDRP Rules of Procedure.[123] The complainant is required to submit to the jurisdiction of at least one of a court jurisdiction at the location of either:

- the principal office of the domain name registrar with which the registrant registered a domain name the subject of the complaint (so long as the registrant submitted in its registration agreement to that jurisdiction for court adjudication of disputes concerning or arising from the domain name); or

- the registrant's address as shown in the domain name registrar's WHOIS database at the time the UDRP complaint is submitted to the UDRP dispute resolution provider.

The decisions record of the various UDRP dispute-resolution service providers is attracting unprecedented academic and professional scrutiny, addressing issues such as the consistency and quality of decision-making, forum-shopping between providers and so on[124].

Nominet

3–073 In the United Kingdom, Nominet until September 2001 operated a policy whereby any disputes which arose were first addressed by an expert chosen from a panel put together by Nominet. If the opinion of that expert did not satisfy the parties then Nominet proposed some form of mediation.

In September 2001 Nominet introduced a new disputes procedure.[125] Rather than adopt the ICANN UDRP, Nominet has adopted an independent procedure, the Dispute Resolution Service ("DRS"). The DRS contains significant differences, both in substance and procedure, from the ICANN UDRP. The most obvious procedural differences are a mediation phase before referral to an independent expert, and the provision of a right of appeal to a three person panel of independent experts. The substantive differences include the lack of an explicit requirement on the Complainant to prove bad faith, in favour of a requirement to show that registration, acquisition or use of the domain name "took unfair advantage of or was unfairly detrimental to the Complainant's rights".

3.3.8 Corporate trade mark and domain name protection policies

3–074 Corporate policies concerning registrations of domain names differ quite substantially. Some companies may have registered only one or two domain names for their main trade mark or trading name, while others have created large domain name portfolios. For example, by late 1995 Proctor & Gamble had registered a whole series of domain names referring to certain common complaints such as badbreath.com, headache.com and diarrhoea.com. Meanwhile Kraft had also registered over 150 of its product names as domain names.[126]

Clearly, it would be a mammoth task to register every trade mark which a company has in each top level domain, *i.e.* "twobirds.co.uk", "twobirds.fr", "twobirds.de" etc, even if this were permitted by each country's local registration rules. At present there are over 250 such top level domains. With the new gTLDs this growth in domains will continue. This leads to the conclusion that a company must largely rely on its registered trade mark rights for domain name protection.

However, one should also look at this in the light of the way in which domain names are used. If a user is seeking to find a particular Web site, he may go about it in a number of different ways. He may type in the correct URL to his browser, he may jump from a link on another Web site to the site in question, or he may carry out a search using one of the search engines such as AltaVista. Quite often, if there is a particular company whose Web site a user wishes to find, he might first simply try typing in the company's name with either the ".com" extension or the commercial extension for the country in which that company normally resides. This is possibly the major reason why domain names are so seriously fought over, since this ad hoc access is specifically facilitated by an appropriate domain name. However, with the advent of enhanced keyword services such as RealNames, which are increasingly incorporated into browsers, the importance of domain names as identifiers may decline in the long term.

A good rule of thumb when trying to formulate a domain name registration policy is to   **3–075**
identify the "crown jewel" trade marks of the company and then to register these at least in the commercial designation for the country where the company normally trades and, if the company is an international one, to register them as a ".com" domain name as well. This will not stop others registering similar marks with, for example, simply an addition of an "s" or a hyphen but it will guard against the most blatant domain name grabbing and blackmail activities. Then one needs to review the company's trade mark registrations to ensure that they adequately back up the trading activity of the company on the Internet. In view of the speed of change presently being seen on the Internet, for the immediate future it would also be wise to repeat this review on at least an annual if not, six monthly basis.

Clearly, trade mark registrations in relevant territories for the main stem of the domain name will afford considerable protection. However, in some, but not all, countries it is also possible to register the full domain name (including the extension) as a trade mark provided that it will itself be used in a trade mark sense. An example would be using the full domain name in advertising the relevant Web site, so that the domain name is clearly used as branding for the Web site. Certainly, in the United Kingdom Trade Marks Registry full domain names will be accepted for registration as a trade mark. Thus "twobirds.com" could be registered as a United Kingdom trade mark in relation to legal services. However, the Trade Mark Registry makes clear that the extension (in this case ".com") cannot be regarded as a distinctive element of the mark.

Avnet Incorporated v. Isoact Ltd[127] gives a useful indication of the appropriate classes in   **3–076**
which to register trade marks for Internet-related services. The plaintiffs unsuccessfully applied for summary judgment for trade mark infringement under section 10(1) of the Trade Marks Act 1994. The requirement for infringement under section 10(1) is that the defendant's use be of a mark and services identical to those for which the plaintiff's mark is registered.

The plaintiff had the mark AVNET registered in Class 35 for "advertising and promotional services . . . all included in Class 35". Its business was selling technical goods through a physical catalogue. The defendant's business as an Internet Service Provider was quite different from that of the plaintiff and was not commercially in conflict with it. The defendant specialised in aviation, using the names Aviation Network and Avnet. The defendant had a Web site address "www.avnet.co.uk". They provided a service to their customers which included giving customers an e-mail address and their own Web page.

Jacob J. had to consider whether what the defendant was doing constituted providing advertising and promotional services. He decided that it did not do so. The defendant did no more than provide a place where their customers could put up whatever they liked. They did not assist their customers to write their copy. They did not require or expect their customers to put up advertisements.

The judge went on to consider whether, if he were wrong on this, the services were   **3–077**
"included in Class 35". The informal view of a Trade Mark Registry officer provided over

the telephone was that if an ISP were renting out advertising space on a Web site to customers, then it might possibly fall within Class 35. However, if it were providing only the usual services of an ISP by providing users with access to the Internet then it would fall within Class 42. The judge commented that whilst this could not be the last word on the subject, he did not think that the defendant's activities did fell within Class 35 as explained by the Registrar's officer—certainly not to the standard required for summary judgment.

The case therefore gives some guidance on the appropriate class for registration of trade marks for some Internet-related services, particularly those provided by an Internet Service Provider. It also illustrates that the fact that a company is described as an "Internet Service Provider" is not determinative of its potential liability for its activities. The court in this case looked at what the defendant actually did—in this case, whether or not it provided advisory services to its customers as well as providing e-mail and hosting services—in determining whether it infringed the trade mark. If, for instance, the Defendant had provided copy-writing services and advice on how to advertise most effectively on the Web, the result might well have been different.

3.4 Metatags, wordstuffing and keyword sales

3.4.1 Metatags

3–078   Two practices against which trade mark laws may be invoked are the misuse of metatags and the related practice of "wordstuffing". Both involve the use of text that is hidden from the casual user of the web site, but is visible to search engines and to anyone who peruses the HTML or similar source code[128] of the site.

Metatags are contained in the "Meta" section of the a web page. This section contains metadata, i.e. information about the web page. The web browser understands that this data is not to be presented to the user and keeps it hidden in normal browsing. The "Meta" section is itself divided into a number of sub-sections, including "Description" and "Keywords". "Description" is used to provide a short abstract describing the site or page. That abstract will appear on the results page of a search engine that lists the site or page as a hit. "Keywords" is used by search engines to assess the relevance of the page or site to the search term that the user has entered into the search engine. Intelligent use of keywords can result in a higher relevance ranking on a search engine listing. The term "metatags" is generally used to indicate the "Keywords" sub-section of the "Meta" section.

3–079   Keywords in particular are open to abuse. Some businesses have been tempted to attempt to divert business to their sites by including their competitors' names and brands in their own keywords. The result of this is that when a user types the competitor's name into a search engine, the resulting list of hits will include both companies. The user will not know why the company has appeared in the list of hits, since the metatag keywords remain hidden (although of course the search term entered by the user will most likely appear at the top of the list as a reminder of the search term that he has entered). And it is likely to be clear to the user (unless the perpetrator has also adopted a confusingly similar company name) that the company is not the competitor, especially since as judicially noted by Jacob J. in *Avnet Incorporated v. Isoact Ltd*)[129]: "someone searching using a word may find Web pages or data in a wholly different context from that which he was seeking. Users of the Internet know that that is a feature of the Internet and that their search may produce an altogether wrong Web page or the like. That might be an important matter for the courts to take into account when considering trade mark and like problems."

As with domain names, there is in principle a broad range of uses to which metatags may be put, and the question of trade mark infringement or passing off should be considered in the light of the particular use. The cases of a dealer who lists the brand names of goods that he supplies, or of a specialist magazine that lists the brands and manufacturers that it writes about, have to be considered differently from the company who lists its competitors' names. In the USA, for instance, use of a competitor's trade mark as a metatag has been held to violate the Lanham Act.[130] However, a former Playmate of the Year 1981 who included the words Playboy and Playmate in the metatags of her personal web site was held entitled to do so.[131]

In the only English case so far on metatags, *Roadtech Computer Systems Ltd v. Mandata (Management and Data Services) Ltd*,[132] the claimant complained about the defendant's inclusion of the words "Roadrunner" and "Roadtech" in the metatags of its web site. The claimant was the proprietor of a registered trade mark for ROADRUNNER for computer software, programs and support services and used both its own name and the trade mark in the course of its business. Both the claimant and the defendant supplied computer software to the road haulage industry and both had web sites. The Master found trade mark infringement on the basis of admissions made by the defendant, and passing off in the absence of a positive defence and there being no serious challenge to the presence of the necessary ingredients for passing off. On the evidence he found that it was established that a misrepresentation had been made by Mandata in that it falsely indicated to Internet users that its web site was in some way connected with Roadtech. **3–080**

For trade mark infringement, the questions regarding infringement by metatags are to some extent simpler than those concerning domain names, since *ex hypothesi* the defendant is operating a live web site which provides evidence as to the nature of his activities. It should be relatively easy, for instance, to determine whether the defendant is using the sign "in the course of trade". The problems associated with the mere registration of domain names do not arise. However, the invisibility of metatags may raise a different problem as to whether the sign is being used in relation to goods or services within the meaning of section 10 of the Act. That is particularly so since the cases to date stress that, at least when considering whether the use of the sign is use in a trade mark sense (if that be required), it is the likely impact of the use on the customer, or the customer's perception, that counts.[133] However, since there is nothing in the Act that explicitly requires the sign to be visible to the customer a broad view of these provisions of the Act could result in a finding of infringement.

The requirement to show likelihood of confusion for the purposes of section 10(2) may cause problems. As Jacob J. pointed out in *Avnet*, Internet users are used to obtaining search results that 'contain hits of varying degrees of irrelevance. Whether the courts would be prepared to find confusion on the basis that the user is taken to the web site as a result of the search engine hit, even if it is clear when the user reaches the site that it is not connected with that of the trade mark owner ("initial interest confusion"), remains to be seen. The problem with such a doctrine is in showing that the use of the metatag has caused any confusion when the user does not expect only to receive hits for sites connected with the company whose name he has entered into the search engine. Indeed, the typical user is likely to expect to receive hits for sites containing references to the company, and would be most disappointed to receive hits only for sites emanating from or commercially connected with the company. The user cannot know whether the site is listed as a "hit" on the results page because of misuse of a metatag, some idiosyncrasy of **3–081** the search algorithm, or because the word is included in the site for some innocent reason (such as quoting a newspaper article that mentions the word). Since the user is most unlikely to assume that every 'hit' on the list emanates from the trade mark owner, why should the user make that assumption in the case of the particular "hit" that appears as a result of the misused metatag? The claimant's argument would, perhaps, be that if from the abstract accompanying the hit it is clear that the site is a commercial company, especially one in the same or similar field as the trade mark owner, then the user might draw the conclusion that the company was connected to the brand name that he had entered to the search engine where he would not do so on the basis of other abstracts. In cases of difficulty resort may perhaps be had to the principle expressed in *One in a Million*, that where confusion is intended by the defendant then the court may readily infer that it is likely to occur, even if there is a possibility that it would not occur.[134]

For passing off, it is not immediately easy to see exactly where or when the deception or misrepresentation arises in metatag and similar cases. The argument would be similar to that concerning the likelihood of confusion under section 10(2) of the Trade Marks Act 1994.

Lastly, as with domain names, if it can be established that the defendant is in possession of an instrument of fraud, then the court will be prepared to grant appropriate remedies notwithstanding that the strict requirements of passing off or trade mark infringement are not satisfied.

3.4.2 Wordstuffing

3–082 "Wordstuffing" is a simple way of hiding text in a web page. It takes the simple form of formatting text so that it appears in the same colour as the page background—or rather does not appear, since the text merges invisibly into the background. The text is still present on the page, so that it will be indexed by search engines, but is invisible on the page itself.

3.4.3 Search engine keyword sales

3–083 A related issue is raised by the practice of some search engine companies of selling keywords. The practice consists of agreeing, for a fee, to tie banner advertisements to the keyword entered by the user, so that particular advertisements appear on the results page for a particular keyword. A problem arises if the search engine sells a keyword consisting of a trade mark to a competitor, so that the competitor's advertisement appears on the results page when the keyword has been entered.

This issue has been considered by the Dutch courts in *VNU Business Publications BV v. The Monster Board BV*.[135] The claimants were the proprietors of Benelux registered trade marks INTERMEDIAIR and INTERMEDIAIR ONLINE, for magazines and online services relating to the advertisement of employment vacancies. The claimants operated a web site under the INTERMEDIAIR ONLINE trade mark. The defendants, who operated a Dutch career site in competition with the claimants, concluded an agreement with a search engine, Vindex, whereby when (among others) the word Intermediair was entered into the search engine, a large click-through colour advertisement for the defendant's career site appeared on the upper part of the screen. The claimants sued for trade mark infringement in summary proceedings. The court provisionally held that, contrary to section 13A, paragraph 1(a) of the Benelux Trade Mark Act, the use of the trade mark constituted 'economic trafficking' of the trade mark. The defendants' argument that any infringement was by the user of the search engine failed.

In Germany the cosmetics manufacturer Estée Lauder sued the search engine Excite Inc over its sale of the keywords "Estee Lauder", "Clinique" and "Origins" to a discount outlet, Fragrance Counter, whose banner advertisements would appear in response to entry of the keywords. The banner advertisements in this case included Estée Lauder trade marks, in a form such as "Clinique@fragrancecounter". The court found trade mark infringement by the use of the marks in the banner advertisements. As to the keywords, the court declined to hold that there was trade mark infringement, basing its decision instead on unfair competition. The court expressed doubts regarding trade mark infringement where the mark was not used visibly.[136] Estée Lauder commenced similar proceedings against the same parties in the USA. The dispute has now settled, with iBeauty (as Fragrance Counter is now called) voluntarily agreeing not to use Estée Lauder trade marks as Internet keywords.[137]   **3–084**

3.5 Non-United Kingdom domain names—Australia

3.5.1 The .au domain

Administrator
The administrator of the .au domain is currently Robert Elz, an employee of the University of Melbourne. However, the formal process of redelegation of the management of the .au ccTLD from Mr Elz to auDA (.au Domain Administration Limited) is almost complete. auDA is an industry self-regulatory body.   **3–085**

3.5.2 Registration Process

The registration process for the .au ccTLD differs from those generally applied by the various ICANN endorsed registrars for the .com and other gTLDs. There are a number of different registrars for the different second level domains (2LDs). For example, in 1996 Robert Elz granted Melbourne IT Pty Ltd ("Melbourne IT") a licence for the administration of the com.au 2LD. Internet Names Worldwide, a division of Melbourne IT, is the current registrar for the com.au 2LD.   **3–086**

Certain eligibility requirements apply depending on which second level domain (2LD) is chosen. For example, in order to register under the com.au 2LD, the applicant must be an "eligible commercial entity", that is, a commercial entity registered and trading in Australia, such as a company incorporated in Australia or a business registered with the relevant State government. The domain name must either be identical to or an abbreviation of the name of the commercial entity. Accordingly, individuals are not able to register a domain name under the com.au 2LD unless they have a business name registration. However, individuals are able to register personal names under the id.au 2LD, although this 2LD does not appear to be used very often given the unique policy of having third level domains named after native Australian flora and fauna.

Some of the other more common 2LDs are net.au which is available to organisations providing network services, edu.au for educational institutions, gov.au for government bodies and asn.au for unincorporated bodies, political parties, trade unions and clubs. The 2LD org.au can be used by registered organisations that do not fall within the other   **3–087**

2LDs. Some of these 2LDs, such as com.au, are "open" domains, that are generally open to the general public, provided the other eligibility requirements are met. On the other hand, 2LDs such as gov.au, are "closed", so that registrations of domain names will only be granted to those within a defined community with a common interest.

At present, generic words that represent commercial categories or sectors such as "cars" or "winery" or "mining" cannot be registered as a domain name in the com.au 2LD but they can be in all the other 2LDs. Australian place names cannot be registered as a com.au or net.au domain name either. Proposals have been made to remove this restriction, but no agreement has yet been reached on how the names are to be allocated. It is the current policy of Melbourne IT Ltd to reject registrations of names that are offensive or obscene.

3–088   Changes to the domain name eligibility and allocation policies for the .au ccTLD have recently been accepted and are expected to take effect in late 2001. In terms of allocation, the present limit of one domain name licence per entity has been removed. It will shortly be possible to obtain a com.au registration provided the entity has an Australian trade mark registration or application.

The domain name must have a "substantial and close connection" with the entity, which means that it must either be the name of the entity, a name by which it is widely known, or a trade mark of the entity.

An applicant will also need to demonstrate a "good faith" intention to use the domain name licence for the purpose envisaged by the 2LD. Licensing a domain name for the sole purpose of selling it, for the purpose of diverting trade from another business or web site, deliberate licensing of misspellings of another entity's company or brand name, or licensing then passively holding a domain name to prevent another from licensing it have all been expressly listed as not being in "good faith".

3.5.3 Dispute Resolution Policy

3–089   The domain name dispute resolution policy is also in the process of reform. At present, there is no effective dispute resolution policy.

The soon to be introduced .au dispute resolution policy is based heavily on the UDRP (Uniform Dispute Resolution Policy). However, there are some important differences which should be noted:

(a)   there is an expansion of the grounds on which a complaint can be made to include 'names', not just trade marks and service marks (auDA commentary on the policy defines name as "business name (or other) name");

(b)   there is a relaxation of the requirements for establishing bad faith, for example, either bad faith at the time of registration or at the time of use need be shown, not necessarily both; a "pattern of conduct" in registering domain names in order to prevent the owner of a name or mark from obtaining the name need not be shown; and the conduct in bad faith need not be directed toward the complainant;

(c)   there is a clarification of the defence of bona fide offering of goods and services by the specific exclusion of "offering of domain names"; and

(d)   there is a limitation of transfer on the domain name to successful complainants only if the complainant is otherwise eligible to obtain a licence for the domain name, in keeping with the strict eligibility requirements applying to the .au namespace.

The policy is intended to apply more broadly than domain name disputes. It is intended to provide a single arbitration framework for all disputes that may arise in relation to policies regulating domain names and services provided in relation to the administration of the domain name system. This may involve disputes between registrants, parties with competing legal interests, registrars, registries and auDA.

3.5.4 Other means of resolving "cybersquatting" disputes

The consumer protection provisions of the Trade Practices Act 1974 and passing off
There have not been any court judgments in Australia to date concerning domain name   **3–090** disputes. The common law tort of passing off and the consumer protection provisions of the *Trade Practices Act* 1974 and equivalent State Fair Trading Acts which prohibit misleading and deceptive conduct and the making of false and misleading statements can provide some protection against cybersquatting. It is likely that the English decision in *British Telecommunications plc v. One in a Million Ltd*[138] will be given some (albeit, not binding) weight by any Australian court which addresses this issue.

Trade Marks Act 1995
Proceedings would rarely be brought in Australia under the *Trade Marks Act* 1995 in a   **3–091** domain name dispute as misleading and deceptive conduct would more easily be made out.

If proceedings were brought under the *Trade Marks Act* 1995, it may be quite difficult in Australia to successfully argue that the act of the registration of a domain name incorporating a trade mark constitutes trade mark infringement.

Mere registration of a domain name incorporating the trade mark without actual use of it will not constitute trade mark infringement, as the threshold requirement of "use as a trade mark" under the *Trade Marks Act* 1995 will not have been made out. In other words, the name must have been used in relation to goods or services.

Where the domain name is being used in respect of a site that offers goods and/or services, it may be possible to argue that the domain name is use as a trade mark. In addition, to establish infringement, it needs to be shown that the trade mark has been used for goods or services in respect of which the trade mark has been registered.[139] The only exception may be for "well known" marks which may be infringed by the use of the mark as a trade mark for unrelated goods or services, ie goods or services that are not of the same description or closely related to the registered goods or services. This is quite likely to be so in a cybersquatting case where the fame of the mark provides the incentive for the cybersquatter to register the domain name in the first place. However, a cybersquatter is probably less likely to actually be offering goods and services on any web site associated with the domain name.

3.6 Non-United Kingdom domain names—Belgium

3.6.1 Domain Name Registration Authority

3–092   Until recently the top-level domain ".be" was managed by an academic institution, the Catholic University of Louvain (KUL). The Belgian DNS Registration office [140]was part of the computer department of the Catholic University of Louvain (KUL) from the end of the 1980s until the end of 1999.

However, following the exponential increase in the number of requests for registration of Belgian domain names during the 1990s,[141] the management of the domain ".be" was transferred to a non profit organisation, DNS Belgique (or DNS.be), established at the beginning of 1999.[142] Its founding members are:

(1)   The Belgian Association of Internet Access Providers[143] (a.s.b.l. ISPA Belgium)

(2)   The Belgian organisation for inter-professional studies of telecommunications services (Organisation belge des études interprofessionnelles des services de télécommunications, a.s.b.l. Beltug);

(3)   The Federation of Belgian Companies (Fédération des enteprises belges a.s.b.l. Fabrimetal-Fabit), which includes, in particular, telecommunication and electronic components companies.

The telecommunications regulatory authority, the Belgian Institute for Postal Services and Telecommunications (BIPT—Institut belge des services postaux et des télécommutions), only has an advisory role in this organisation.[144]

3.6.2 Registration System

3–093   Major changes were effectuated as to the role of DNS Belgium and to the conditions of registration of the ".be" domain names. Those changes entered into force on December 11, 2000 and have led to a significant increase in registrations.[145]

Indeed, before that date, applications for ".be" domain names were reserved for legal commercial entities, corporations, public institutions, and public or private organisations. Consequently, applications for ".be" domain names by private individuals for non-commercial matters or by informal groups were not accepted. Besides, prior to any registration, the applicant had to evidence his right to the domain name. Common nouns and generic names were not accepted unless they referred to a registered trademark. Moreover, applications were only accepted if the applicant was established in Belgium. In addition, applications for domain names based on a trademark were only accepted if the trademark was registered in Belgium.

3–094   From December 11, 2000, the system was liberalised. As to the role of DNS Belgium, it has been reduced only to the management of the ".be" domain. DNS Belgium does not take registrations anymore: the registration procedure was transferred to registrars. As to the conditions of registration, they have been removed. Only the "first come, first serve" principle applies. In order to deal with disputes arising from the liberalisation, DNS Belgium has developed a fast dispute settlement procedure, which follows the rules of the Belgian Arbitrage Centre, the CEPANI.

3.6.3 Dispute Settlement Procedure

Article 10 of the *Terms and conditions of domain name registrations under the ".be" domain operated by DNS*, Version 1.1, of December 7, 2000[146] provides for the rules applying to dispute settlement. **3–095**

Article 10.a provides that the rules for this procedure are to be applied in a mandatory way.

Following the WIPO recommendations regarding dispute resolution, "the complainant must prove, before one of the administrative-dispute-resolution service providers listed at the web site of DNS Belgium, that:

(i)   the licensee's domain name is identical or confusingly similar to a trademark or service mark filed in the Benelux or the Community in which the complainant has rights;

(ii) the licensee has no rights or legitimate interests in the domain name;

(iii) the licensee's domain name has been registered or is being used in bad faith".[147]

The three elements are cumulative.

According to Article 10.b.2, "the following circumstances will be considered as evidence of the registration or use of a domain name in bad faith: **3–096**

(i)   circumstances indicating that the domain name was registered or acquired primarily for the purpose of selling, renting, or otherwise transferring the domain name registration to the Complainant who is the owner of the trademark or service mark or to a competitor of that Complainant, for valuable consideration in excess of the costs directly related to the domain name;

(ii) the domain name was registered in order to prevent the owner of a trademark or service mark from reflecting the mark in a corresponding domain name, provided that the licensee has engaged in a pattern of such conduct;

(iii) the domain name was registered primarily for the purpose of disrupting the business of a competitor;

(iv) the domain name was intentionally used to attract, for commercial gain, Internet users to the licensee's web site or other on-line location, by creating a likelihood of confusion with the Complainant's mark as to the source, sponsorship, affiliation, or endorsement of the licensee's web site or location or of a product or service on his web site or location".[148]

Moreover, "any of the following circumstances will demonstrate the rights or legitimate interests of the licensee to the domain name if a complaint is filed: **3–097**

(i)   before any notice to the licensee of the dispute, his use of, or demonstrable preparations to use, the domain name or a name corresponding to the domain name in connection with a bona fide offering of goods or services;

(ii) the licensee (as an individual, business, or other organisation) has been commonly known by the domain name, even if he has acquired no trademark or service mark rights;

(iii) the licensee is making a legitimate non-commercial or fair use of the domain name, without intent for commercial gain to misleadingly divert consumers or to tarnish the trademark or service mark at issue".[149]

Article 10.g provides that these rules for dispute settlement do not prevent either the licensee or the complainant from submitting the dispute to the courts.

3.6.4 Court Decisions

3–098   Because of the strict conditions of registration that applied before December 11, 2000, and because cases were often settled during proceedings, not many decisions have been rendered by Belgian courts regarding ".be" domain names.

The *Roland* case is one of the rare cases in this respect. The President of the commercial court of Oudenaarde ordered the cessation of use of domain names containing the name "roland", considered as an act contrary to fair trade practices since "Roland" is a trademark and the court considered that at least a special mention should be made to refer to the distributor.

Several disputes concerning ".com" domain names have been decided upon by the Belgian courts.[150] In this respect, the decision of April 1, 1998 of the Brussels Court of Appeal constitutes a major precedent as regards domain name grabbing (Tractebel case[151]). The principles developed by the Brussels Court of Appeal in this decision would also seem to be applicable to ".be" domain names.

3–099   In this typical case of domain name grabbing, the domain name tractebel.com, had been registered by Capricom, a company established in Delaware, represented by a Belgian citizen, who reserved the name with Network Solution Inc. In fact, Capricom had also reserved the names of more than ten famous Belgian companies. Capricom intended to reach a settlement with these companies for the transfer of the domain names, by having them pay a higher price than the usual registration fee. Tractebel brought an action against Capricom before the Brussels Commercial Court. The action was rejected on the basis that Capricom's operations were simply "business opportunity". However, the Court of Appeal overturned the decision. It held that by registering the "tractebel.com" domain name, and thus, prohibiting Tractebel from accessing the Internet using this domain name, Capricom had violated Article 8 of the Treaty of Paris[152] protecting commercial names[153] and this constituted an act contrary to fair trade practices.[154]

3.6.5 Protection of Domain Names under Belgian Law

3–100   The registration of a domain name does not give any right to that name. Nevertheless, several provisions of Belgian Law can be invoked to settle a dispute regarding domain names.

In cases where a domain name is identical to the name of a business or institution, Article 8 of the Treaty of Paris is applicable. Case law provides that this provision may only be invoked if there is a possibility of confusion,[155] but also specifies that this possibility of confusion has to be associated with a possibility of deception.[156] Consequently, if a domain name would deceive third parties as to the identity of the domain name holder, ownership of this domain name could be contested.

In addition, the Act of July 14, 1991 on trade practices and information to and protection of the consumer[157] protects commercial names against unfair trade practices,[158] independently of any risk of confusion.

As regards trademarks registered with the Benelux Trademark office, the Benelux Trademark law[159] offers adequate protection from trademark infringement.

Finally, a draft law adopted on November 12, 1999 aims to introduce a provision prohibiting all persons apart from the owner of the trademark or the commercial name to register this name as a domain name.[160] This law has not been adopted so far.

3–101

3.7 Non-United Kingdom domain names—Canada

3.7.1 Domain name registration

Since December 1, 2000, the Canadian .ca domain name registry has been operated by the Canadian Internet Registry Authority ("CIRA"). CIRA is a not-for-profit registry. CIRA's mandate is to provide professional registry services and to preserve the .ca domain as a Canadian resource that is operated for and managed by Canadians for Canadians. CIRA operates the .ca domain name registry, maintains the .ca database, handles complaints by Registrants about Registrars and is charged with implementing and administering a domain name dispute resolution service.

3–102

History

Before 2000, the .ca domain was administered by the CA Domain Committee, established at the University of British Columbia by John Demco, CA Registrar. The CA Domain Committee was comprised of 30 members representing various Internet organisations, service providers, universities and defence establishments.[161] The .ca domain was registered with InterNIC by CDNnet in May, 1987.[162] It was based on a combination of the Domain Name System (DNS) framework and the CCITT X.500 directory service standard.

3–103

Previously, .ca domains were distributed pursuant to a policy which attempted to structure Canada's domain name space according to Canadian federal and provincial political jurisdictions. Canadian subdomain names frequently read as follows: "entity.-city.province.ca."[163] Applications for subdomain names at the national level ("entity.ca") were required to include documentation showing that the entity was federally incorporated or maintained business offices in more than one province or territory (international offices were not considered). A business could also avoid being restricted to use of a provincial sub-domain if it owned a federally registered trade mark.[164] This restrictive policy requiring the use of sub-domains is no longer mandatory.

Formerly, it was CA Domain's policy to limit individuals and organisations to a single domain name, regardless of the number of trade marks that the organisation owned or the number of business divisions the organisation may have had.

Entitlement

CIRA has implemented rules and procedures for new domain name registrations. Now, in order to be eligible to obtain a .ca domain name, the applicant must comply with CIRA's "Canadian Presence Requirements".

3–104

CIRA's Canadian Presence Requirements provide that the applicant must be any of:

(a)   a Canadian citizen;

(b)   a permanent resident of Canada;

(c)   a legal representative of (a) or (b);

(d)   a corporation under the laws of Canada or any province or territory of Canada;

(e)   a trust established and subsisting under the laws of a province or territory of Canada, more than 66 per cent of whose trustees meet one of the conditions set out in paragraphs (a) to (d) above;

(f)   a partnership, more than 66 per cent of whose partners meet one of the conditions set out in paragraphs (a) to (e) above, which is registered as a partnership under the laws of any province or territory of Canada;

(g)   an association (an unincorporated organisation, association or club):

      (i)   at least 80 per cent of whose members:

            (1)   are ordinarily resident in Canada (if such members are individuals); or
            (2)   meet one of the conditions set out in paragraphs (a) to (f) above (if such members are not individuals);

and   (ii)   at least 80% of whose directors, officers, employees, managers, administrators or other representatives are ordinarily resident in Canada;

(h)   a trade union which is recognised by a labour board under the laws of Canada or any province or territory of Canada and which has its head office in Canada;

(i)   a political party registered under a relevant electoral law of Canada or any province or territory of Canada;

(j)   an educational institution (a university or college which is located in Canada and which is authorized or recognised as a university or college under an Act of the legislature of a province or territory of Canada; or a college, post-secondary school, vocational school, secondary school, pre-school or other school or educational institution which is located in Canada and which is recognised by the educational authorities of a province or territory of Canada or licensed under or maintained by an Act of Parliament of Canada or of the legislature of a province or territory of Canada;

(k)   a Library, Archive or Museum that:

      (i)   is located in Canada; and
      (ii)   is not established or conducted for profit or does not form part of, or is not administered or directly or indirectly controlled by, a body that is established or conducted for profit, in which is held and maintained a collection of documents and other materials that is open to the public or to researchers;

(l)   a Hospital which is located in Canada and which is licensed, authorised or approved to operate as a hospital under an Act of the legislature of a province or territory of Canada;

(m)   Her Majesty the Queen Elizabeth the Second and her successors;

(n)   an Indian band and any group of Indian bands;

(o)   Aboriginal Peoples (Any Inuit, First Nation, Metis or other people indigenous to Canada, any individual belonging to any Inuit, First Nation, Metis or other people indigenous to Canada and any collectivity of such Aboriginal peoples;

(p)   Her Majesty the Queen in right of Canada, a province or a territory; an agent of Her Majesty the Queen in right of Canada, of a province or of a territory; a federal, provincial or territorial Crown corporation, government agency or government entity; or a regional, municipal or local area government;

(q)   a person which does not meet any of the foregoing conditions, but which is the owner of a trade-mark which is the subject of a registration under the *Trade-marks Act (Canada)* R.S.C. 1985, c.T-13 as amended from time to time, but in this case such permission is limited to an application to register a .ca domain name consisting of or including the exact word component of that registered trade-mark; or

(r)   a person which does not meet any of the foregoing conditions, but which is a Person intended to be protected by subsection 9(1) of the *Trade-Marks Act (Canada)* [the owners of certain official marks] at whose request the Registrar of Trade-marks has published notice of adoption of any badge, crest, emblem, official mark or other mark pursuant to subsection 9(1), but in this case such permission is limited to an application to register a .ca domain name consisting of or including the exact word component of such badge, crest, emblem, official mark or other mark in respect of which such Person requested publications.

Registration Procedure

Registration requests are dealt with on a first-come first-served basis. CIRA offers **3–105** registration services through approved Registrars. The Applicant must select a CIRA Certified Registrar who will act on its behalf in submitting a Registration Request for the registration of a domain name to CIRA. A domain name may be registered for a period of one (1) to ten (10) years.

Domain names are not case sensitive. The domain name must be between two and 50 characters long. CIRA maintains a registry of reserved domain names that are not available for registration (including country code TLDs, and gTLDs, to prevent registration of Asomething.com.ca@, etc.), names that might indicate an association with a municipality (such as city.ca, ville.ca), and major Canadian municipalities and landmarks.

A domain name will not be registered if the domain name is an exact match in all respects to a previously registered .ca domain name which is registered in the name of another person at any level, whether second, third or fourth, unless such other person consents in writing to the registration. For example, if abc.on.ca (third level) is registered, another person cannot obtain a Registration for abc.on.ca, abc.ca (second level) or abc.ottawa.on.ca (fourth level) without the written consent of the registrant of abc.on.ca. Third or fourth level domain names may be "upgraded" to second level names only with the consent of others who own domain names having the same prefix.

The obligation is on the Applicant to ensure that it has the right to use the domain **3–106** name which is the subject of the Registration Request and that the registration or use of the domain name does not violate any third party intellectual property rights or other rights, does not defame any person and does not contravene any applicable laws including Canadian federal, provincial and territorial human rights legislation and the Criminal Code.

The Canadian Intellectual Property Office is now accepting registration of domain names as trade marks. To date, all applicants have been forced to disclaim the top level domain name suffix.

3.7.2 Domain name disputes

CIRA's Dispute Resolution Policy

3–107   Although CIRA does not yet have a dispute resolution policy in place, a draft policy was posted on September 26, 2000 and the final policy is expected sometime in 2001. CIRA's draft policy is not intended to apply to disputes between parties who have registered domain names in good faith and based on legitimate interests. Specifically, under the draft policy a complainant must show that: (a) the registrant's .ca domain name is "confusing" with a "mark" owned by the complainant; (2) the registrant has no "rights" in Canada or other legitimate interest to the domain name; and (3) the registrant registered the domain name in "bad faith". Each of the terms "confusion", "mark", "rights" and "bad faith" are more particularly explained in the draft policy. Basically, the indicia of bad faith are: (1) registering a domain name without any intention of using it; (2) registering a domain name primarily for the purpose of selling it; (3) having offered to sell, rent, license or otherwise transfer the registration to the complainant; (4) registering a domain name solely to prevent the rightful owner from using it; (5) trying to disrupt the business of the complainant; (6) registering multiple domain names to intentionally create confusion; and (7) providing false or misleading information to the registrar. There are also a list of factors which mitigate against bad faith. Once a complaint is filed, no changes can be made to the registration of the domain name. The remedies that the draft policy proposes to make available are cancellation, suspension or transfer of the registration. The draft policy does not exclude other legal remedies—either party can bring the matter before a court at any time during or after the arbitration. If a lawsuit is commenced within 15 days of an arbiter's decision, the remedy awarded will be stayed pending the outcome of the legal action.

Traditional Legal Remedies

3–108   While a body of Canadian case law on domain name disputes is slowly developing, the law of trade marks and unfair competition remains generally applicable and of particular relevance in these matters. In Canada, a trade mark is used in association with services when the trade mark is used in advertising the service or displayed during the performance of the service. It is used in association with wares if it is marked on the wares or otherwise associated with the ware at the time of transfer in the property or possession of the ware, in the normal course of trade.[165] If the trade mark is not registered, then a common law action of passing off would apply and a determination would be made as to whether customers or consumers would be confused by a defendant's use of its trade mark.

The owner of a registered trade mark has the exclusive right to use the mark in relation to the goods and services for which the mark is registered.[166] Use of a confusingly similar trade mark constitutes an infringement of the trade mark owner's exclusive right.[167] The owner of a registered trade mark can also prevent use of the trade mark which results in the depreciation of the value of the goodwill associated with the registered mark.[168]

In order to establish infringement, or depreciation of the goodwill in a registered mark, a plaintiff must show that the offending mark was used in relation to the provision of goods or services in Canada. Services are often provided on the Internet in conjunction with the display of trade marks and trade names. If the site provides services to, and is regularly accessed by, customers in Canada, in the normal course of trade, then the mark would be considered to be in use in Canada.[169] A mark would be used in respect of a transaction on the Internet in respect of wares if the mark is displayed at the time of transfer of the property or possession of the goods (such as an electronic text). Software, documents, videos, music and other such products transferred over the Internet in association with a trade mark would likely constitute use of the trade mark.[170]

In order for a trade mark to be registered in Canada, it must either be in actual use in Canada, or the registrant must intend to use the trade mark in Canada or it must be used and registered abroad, in a country of origin of the applicant.

If the trade mark is not registered, rights can be asserted under the common law tort of passing-off. In order to sustain an action, the plaintiff has to demonstrate the existence of a requisite level of goodwill in the minds of the public, and that a misrepresentation was made by the defendant to the public resulting in actual or potential damage to the plaintiff.[171]

Canadian courts have resolved claims to domain names in both the gTDLs as well as the .ca domain. Significant Canadian cases on domain name disputes are set out below.

3–109

3–110

Interlocutory Relief

Typically, domain name claimants will seek an interlocutory injunction preventing the domain name registrant from using the domain name pending trial. Interlocutory relief has, generally, been difficult to obtain in Canadian domain name disputes.

3–111

No infringement established:

- In *PEINET Inc. v. O'Brien*[172] the plaintiff, the owner of the peinet.pe.ca domain name, sued a former employee who had obtained the domain name pei.net and applied for an interlocutory injunction to prevent the use of the domain name. The application was dismissed, the plaintiff having failed to establish infringement or passing off. In passing, the court remarked that the plaintiff had not explained the Internet very well.

No irreparable harm proven:

- In *ITV Technologies Inc. v. WIC Television Ltd.*[173] the Federal Court of Canada first granted an interim injunction and then dismissed an interlocutory injunction against ITV Technologies.[174] ITV Technologies was trying to expunge WIC's trade mark registrations for the mark "ITV" in order to undermine WIC's case before NSI against ITV Technologies over the domain name itv.net. WIC had used ITV as a trade mark since 1974 for television broadcasting and program production. WIC has also registered itv.ca as a domain name. ITV Technologies was "net-casting" from its web site since late 1995. ITV Technologies posted a disclaimer on its web site stating "ITV.net has no affiliation with CITV" and provided a link to the WIC site. In dismissing WIC's application for an interlocutory injunction, the court was not satisfied that irreparable harm would be caused.

- Irreparable harm was not made out in *Toronto.com v. Sinclair (c.o.b.*

Friendship Enterprises)[175] and toronto2.com was not prevent from using its domain name pending trial.

3–112 The ease with which domain names can be transferred to parties beyond the jurisdiction of the Canadian courts has been a factor taken into consideration when injunctions have been granted:

- In *Innersense International Inc. v. Manegre*[176] an Alberta Court granted an *ex parte* interim injunction restraining the defendants from directly or indirectly selling or transferring registration of the domain name innersense.com. Apparently, one of the defendants, a former employee, was responsible for registering the domain name with NSI. The domain name registration expired and the domain name was registered by the second defendant, the brother of the former employee. The defendants then offered the domain name for sale in the press. Applying the traditional test of (1) serious issue, (2) irreparable harm, and (3) balance of convenience, in determining whether or not to grant the injunction, the Court found that "problems with the possibly simple and quick transferability and marketability of this Internet Domain Site and with respect to Internet Domain Sites generally literally to any point in the world, lead me to believe that the balance of convenience or inconvenience is best served by granting the Application."

- In *Itravel2000.com Inc. (c.o.b. Itravel) v. Fagan*[177] the Court granted an interlocutory injunction which prevented the defendant from transferring the domain name itravel.ca pending trial (an order analogous to a *Mareva* injunction where assets are ordered not to be removed from the jurisdiction pending the trial). Although the defendant was an admitted cybersquatter, of particular interest in this case was the fact that there were numerous potential legitimate claimants to the domain name. Presumably, the plaintiff could not recover the domain name from one of these third parties and so used the interlocutory injunction to make sure that it was first in line for the domain name.

  However, in *Molson Breweries v. Kuettner*[178] the Court would not accept deposit of the domain name into Court to ensure its "safekeeping" pending trial.

  If these *Mareva*-like orders become commonplace, then it will be imperative to file suit as early as possible to prevent other legitimate claimants to the domain name in question from gaining an advantage.

- In *Saskatoon Star Phoenix Group Inc. v. Norton*[179] the plaintiff was the publisher of "The StarPhoenix", a daily newspaper, in Saskatchewan. The plaintiff also operated a web site at thestarphoenix.com which displayed news stories and banner ads. The defendant registered the domain name saskatoonstarphoenix.-com and displayed the same material as found on the plaintiff's site except that the defendant replaced the plaintiff's banner ads with its own. The Court found that the defendant was in the business of registering domain names. One of the defendant's other web sites had a "courtesy link" to "The StarPhoenix" which took a browser to the defendant's web site. The plaintiff commenced an action in passing off. The plaintiff had evidence, in the form of emails, of browsers actually being confused by the defendant's site. The plaintiff was granted an interlocutory injunction. The defendant did not defend the passing off action, was noted in default, and the court ordered $5000.00 in damages (despite no actual loss being shown), a permanent injunction, transfer of the domain name registrations and costs against the defendant. The Court considered, but refused to award punitive damages because domain name actions were relatively new. The Court did find that, in the future, punitive damages could be awarded on the facts of this case.

- In *Vulcan Northwest Inc. et al. v. Vulcan Ventures Corp.*[180] the plaintiffs, two venture capital firms affiliated with Paul Allen, billionaire and former partner of Bill Gates, brought a passing off action against a penny stock mining exploration company that traded on the CDNX. The plaintiffs applied for an interlocutory injunction restraining the defendant from identifying itself as Vulcan Ventures. The plaintiff had applied for, but not yet registered the trade-mark VULCAN VENTURES. In granting the interlocutory injunction, the Court found that: "[t]he potential for confusion is obvious and much of it may never come to the plaintiffs' attention thus making the damages unknown and irreparable." (at 100) The Court specifically found that the defendant "has an investor Internet site, Stockhouse.com" that contained links to news about the plaintiffs. The affiliation between Stockhouse.com and the defendant was unclear. This case seems to have lowered the threshold for an interlocutory injunction.

"Use" of a trade-mark by Internet access in Canada

The situation is relatively straightforward where the trade-mark user's web site is based in Canada.[181] An interlocutory injunction was granted in *Bell Actimedia Inc. v. Puzo (Communications Globe Tête)* prohibiting the use of lespagesjaunes.com or any other domain name confusingly similar with it. The plaintiff, Bell Actimedia, is the company that produces and distributes trade and telephone directories in Canada. Bell Actimedia also provides business listings on the Internet through the domain names yellowpages.ca, pagesjaunes.ca, canadayellowpages.com and pagesjaunescanada.com. Bell has owned registered trade marks for YELLOW PAGES and PAGES JAUNES for over 50 years. The defendant, Communications Globe Tête registered the domain name lespagesjaunes.com and used its site to market a business directory of the French-speaking world. Communications Globe Tête claimed that Bell's trade marks only protected against use of a confusingly similar name in Canada and that Communications Globe Tête was entitled to use their domain name in any country other than Canada despite the fact that the impugned web site was hosted in Montreal, Canada. Unfortunately, the court did not take the opportunity to address the territorial argument in granting the injunction. Presumably, the issue will have to be answered if the matter ever goes to trial.

3–113

British Columbia Automobile Association v. Office and Professional Employees' International Union, Local 378[182] was an action for passing off, trade mark infringement and copyright infringement in relation to Internet web sites. The plaintiff, British Columbia Automobile Association ("BCAA") claimed that the defendant, Office and Professional Employees' International Union, Local 378 (the "Union"), a union representing 170 office employees of BCAA, copied design elements and trade marks from BCAA's web site and posted those copies on the Union's own web site. BCAA also complained that the Union was guilty of passing off and had depreciated the goodwill of BCAA's trade marks by using them in domain names and meta-tags. In March of 1999, the Union registered the domain names bcaaonstrike.com and picketline.com and later bcaabacktowork.com. All three of the Union's domain names took a browser to the Union's web site. BCAA alleged that the Union copied fundamental design elements from the BCAA web site. BCAA sent the

3–114

Union a cease and desist letter. In response, the Union modified certain portions of their web site and the meta-tags coded into their web site, however, the Union continued to reproduce a substantial part of the BCAA web site meta-tags. Although BCAA alleged that the Union's unamended site infringed BCAA's copyright in its own web site, BCAA did not advance that claim in respect of the amended site. The causes of action advanced against the amended site were passing off and depreciation of goodwill under section 22 of the Trade marks Act. BCAA alleged that use of the domain names bcaaonstrike.com and Bcaabacktowork.com and the use of BCAA and other BCAA trade marks in meta-tags constituted passing off because the Union was intercepting people looking for the BCAA web site. It is important to note that by October of 1999, and well in advance of trial, the Union had removed the meta-tags which included BCAA trade marks from its web site and had also inserted commas between the words "British Columbia Automobile Association".

The Court considered the law of passing off as well as the developing body of British, American and Canadian law on passing off through the use of domain names and meta-tags.

3–115   The Court took notice of the fact that the Union was not making a commercial use of the web site and was using BCAA's trade marks in connection with a labour relations dispute. The Court found that the Union's current web site was not passing itself off for the BCAA web site because there was no confusion or possibility of confusion in the mind of an Internet user that the Union's web site was associated with or belonged to BCAA. The Court based this conclusion on the following facts: (1) the Union's domain name was not identical to BCAA's trade marks; (2) the Union is not using meta-tags identical to BCAA's trade marks; (3) the Union's web site is not competing commercially with BCAA; (4) the use of similar meta-tags or domain names is of less significance in a labour relations or consumer criticism situation, partly because there is less likelihood of confusion; and (5) even though the incorporation of the acronym BCAA into the Union's domain name was intentional, it is not a misrepresentation as long as the Union doesn't represent that its web site belongs to, or is associated with, BCAA.

The Court found that in the context of a labour dispute, there was a reasonable balance to be struck between intellectual property rights and freedom of expression. The Court also found that an earlier version of the Union's web site was inherently confusing and that Union was guilty of passing off based on the earlier version of the web site. The Court refused to grant an injunction or to order the Union to deliver up the domain names which incorporated the BCAA trade mark.

The Court also found that the Union was not making a commercial use of BCAA's marks, they were only providing information and, therefore, the Union was not "using" BCAA's marks as required for the purposes of section 22 of the *Trade Marks Act* (which defines "use" as "use in the normal course of trade").

3–116   A similar finding was made of "non-commercial use" in *Bell ExpressVu Limited Partnership v. Tedmonds & Co. Inc.*[183] where the Court refused to grant summary judgment enjoining the defendant from using the domain name expressvu.org on the basis that there was no evidence that the defendant was making a "commercial use" of the plaintiff's trade mark. The defendant was allegedly selling U.S. satellite decoding technology in Canada. The plaintiff held the registered trade mark EXPRESSVU and had registered the domain name expressvu.com. The defendant was using expressvu.org to post information relating to the legal action. Of significant interest for future disputes, the Court found authority for its reasons in an administrative decision issued under the UDRP implicitly recognising the value of these decisions as precedent.

Foreign Web Sites ''Using'' Trade-marks in Canada

Where a foreign web site ''purposely targets'' Canadian customers, Canadian courts may **3–117** consider the Canadian web site to be using trade-marks in Canada. The *Tele-Direct (Publications) Inc. v. Klimchuk*[184] case suggests that the Canadian Federal Court considers trade mark rights to be infringed in Canada (and therefore a trade mark to have been used in Canada) when an American web site purposely targets Canada with the use of trade marks registered in Canada. In *Tele-Direct*, the court found that the American defendants had knowingly used Tele-Direct's registered Canadian trade marks YELLOW PAGES and/or Walking Fingers design trade marks on their Internet site located in the United States and were purposely attempting to find customers in Canada. While use of the trade marks in the United States was permissible (the marks had become generic there), the court found that the American companies were attempting to circumvent Canadian trade mark law by using the plaintiff's registered trade marks in Canada.

On the other hand, where a foreign web site is passive, it appears the court will not assert jurisdiction over its operators. In *Canadian Kennel Club v. Continental Kennel Club*[185] the Federal Court indicated that it would not assert jurisdiction over a U.S. web site that was not actively soliciting customers from Canada.

An apparent ''trans-national border order'' was granted by the Federal Court of **3–118** Canada in *Canada Post v. Sunview Management Group*[186] Sunview, an American corporation with registered offices in New York registered the domain name mailposte.com with NSI in the United States. Canada Post is the owner of several Canadian registered trade marks and official marks, including MAIL POSTE & Design and POSTE MAIL & Design. On October 19, 1998, Canada Post obtained an interim and interlocutory injunction against Sunview's use of the mark. This injunction was made permanent on January 11, 1999. The order prohibited Sunview from using the words MAIL POSTE or any other words likely to be confusing therewith in connection with its web site or domain name. Two aspects of the judgment are interesting. First, the court ordered that the original domain name declaration be deposited with the Canadian court. Second, the court directed that the domain name be transferred, conveyed or assigned to Canada Post. It is somewhat surprising to see the Federal Court of Canada granting an order such as this, particularly where the Federal Court does not have the means to ensure compliance with NSI, the American based registry. Nevertheless, the order was enforced and Canada Post now owns the domain name.

3.8 Non-United Kingdom domain names—Finland

3.8.1 Registration

The registration of domain names in Finland is currently administrated by EUnet Finland **3–119** Oy, a private limited liability Internet operator. During 1997 the administration of registration of domain names is planned to be transferred to the Telecommunications Administration Centre, which is not an Internet service provider. The current registration practice is based upon the rules of the Finnish Commercial Internet Exchange (FICIX).

The main principle for registration of commercial domain names is currently that the applicant must have registered such name with the Finnish Trade Register kept by the National Board on Patents and Registration. The domain name shall comprise of a registered trade name, supplementary trade name or the distinctive part thereof in order to be registered with EUnet Finland Oy.

The change of registration authority also encompasses proposed new rules for registration of commercial domain names. In the proposed system not only registered but also established trade names, secondary identifiers and trade marks are accepted as domain names. The new rules also include the possibility to appeal against the decision of the registration authority.

3–120   The applicant for a domain name registration shall inform the registration authority of the relevant authority based upon which the applicant claims registration. The registration authority has direct access to official registers in Finland and consequently evidence on a Finnish trade name or trade mark registration is not required to be filed attached to the application.

The tradition for registration of domain names in Finland has been rather strict compared with several other countries. For example, Finnish companies have previously not been able to register their trade marks to the same extent as companies in other countries. The change of registration authority and new regulations regarding registration of domain names will certainly improve this situation. However, the final outcome of the reform will have to be evaluated later when the new registration practice has been in force for a while.

3.8.2 Disputes

3–121   At the time of writing there is no explicit legislation regulating domain names and thereto related disputes. Therefore, in order to protect intellectual property rights and business interests the business community has to rely upon prevailing trade mark, trade name and unfair competition legislation mainly comprised in the Trade Marks Act, the Trade Names Act and the Act on Unfair Business Practices.

As a general comment, the strict registration practice in Finland has resulted in a situation where conflicts concerning domain names registered in Finland are relatively rare and no court practice to rely upon has therefore developed. The domain name piratism is consequently to a large extent an international problem for those Finnish corporations who operate on an international level.

National laws, nevertheless, provide protection against domain name piratism, even if the definitions, for example, of trade mark and trade name infringement with regard to domain names may be somewhat different from the traditional concept of infringement.

Trade Marks Act

3–122   The Trade Marks Act gives an exclusive right to the owner of a trade mark to use such mark in order to identify his products or services. If the trade mark or a confusingly similar mark is used commercially in order to identify the products or services of another person or company without proper consent, that will be regarded as trade mark infringement. As a rule, the use of another's trade mark as a domain name, for example, on a World Wide Web home page of a commercial entity, would constitute trade mark infringement. The situation becomes more complicated with regard to domain names for non-commercial entities as non-commercial use would not constitute trade mark infringement. The activities of an individual or a non-commercial entity may, however, be regarded as commercial. Another complication may be that the trade mark protection for other than famous trade marks is restricted to the class of goods or services of registration.

Trade Names Act

The provisions of the Finnish Trade Names Act give an exclusive right to the holder of **3–123** the trade name. A domain name constitutes an infringement of such exclusive right in case it, without proper authorisation, may indicate an untrue commercial relationship. Consequently, unauthorised use of another's trade name as a domain name for a commercial entity's World Wide Web home page would in most cases constitute trade name infringement.

Unfair competition

The Act on Unfair Business Practices comprises a general provision that prohibits acts **3–124** that are contrary to good business practice or otherwise unfair from the point of view of another business entity. In the preparatory works for the Act, the legislator has stated that the general provision is formulated in such manner that it also shall be applicable regardless of changes in the business environment. The general provision of the Act on Unfair Business Practices has been regarded as a complement in certain situations where commercial identifiers are not subject to statutory protection under intellectual property legislation. The general clause could, theoretically, be applicable for the protection of domain names that are not subject to trade mark or trade name protection in Finland, but nevertheless, are distinctive and valuable for the owner of the domain name. It should, however, be observed that the general principle of free competition is prevailing and copying, for example, of product names and product packagings traditionally has been accepted, unless there exists a risk for confusion among the public of the relevant commercial origin of the products or services.

Article 2 of the Act on Unfair Business Practices prohibits commercial activities that may be regarded as misleading. The use of another's trade mark, trade name or other commercial identifier may also be misleading and prohibited by the Market Court.

3.8.3 Comments

The unregulated situation, both with regard to international conventions and national **3–125** legislation, leaves several questions concerning the protection and use of domain names unanswered and subject to court practice. As such court practice in Finland has not yet been developed, it is difficult to give guidelines for situations where, for example, employees have registered domain names comprising of unregistered trade marks of their employer or registrations of trade marks as domain names made by distributors or other contractual partners. Some of the uncertainties might be avoided through legislative measures, which, however, are not foreseeable in the near future.

3.9 Non-United Kingdom domain names—France

Over the last few years, the domain name seems to have become an important aspect of **3–126** international trade, which is fully understood by French companies. As communication via Internet is perceived as an open door to the entire world of corporate activities and the domain name as the sole means of identifying such communication for the user, it is not surprising that domain names have become objects of trade and have acquired a real economic value to the benefit of their holders.

3.9.1 Registration

3–127 In France, the Institut National de Recherche en Informatique et en Automatique (INRIA), which, by delegation from the RIPE NCC (authorised by the Internet Assigned Number Authority, IANA) was the first organisation responsible for the attribution and management of domain names. Since January 1, 1998, the power of this organisation has been transferred to an association controlled by the state, the Association Française pour le Nommage Internet en Corporation (AFNIC). AFNIC France may only issue domain names for the ".fr" zone.

In practice, any company that wishes to obtain a domain name must contact an Internet service provider, which is authorised to create domain names via a contract entered into with AFNIC for the .fr zone or ICANN for top level domain names (".com", ".net", ".org"). This service provider then handles relations with AFNIC or ICANN.

Although, as in most countries, the rule of "first come, first served" is applied by AFNIC, AFNIC insists on compliance with the "Charte de Nommage" which it has drafted. This charter describes the process of allocating a *.fr* domain name. According to the charter, any name concerning public order, morals, Internet functions, as well as any party to the Convention of Paris cannot be registered as a domain name. Initially, generic domain names were also prohibited, however, since March 24, 2001, they have been made available.

3–128 The allowed domain names are divided into three categories: the public domain, the sectorial domain and the conventional domain.

The public domain corresponds to names ending in ".fr", ".asso.fr", ".nom.fr", ".presse.fr", ".prd.fr", ".tm.fr" and ".com.fr". The ".fr" domain is reserved exclusively for companies. In order to obtain a domain name ending in ".fr", the applicant company must provide AFNIC France with proof of the registration of its name with the Registry of Trade and Companies. The domains ".asso.fr", ".nom.fr", ".presse.fr", ".prd.fr" and ".tm.fr" also require certain registration formalities. For example, to register a ".tm.fr", which is reserved for trademarks, the applicant must provide AFNIC France with proof of its certificate of registration with the INPI (Institut National de la Propriété Industrielle). In addition, only the holder of the trademark rights (not a licensee) will be granted a domain name. Subject to these conditions, the domain name may be registered with the ".tm.fr". Furthermore, if the applicant is an association, it must provide AFNIC France with a copy of the declaration to the prefecture or the notice that appeared in the *Official Journal*.

The ".com.fr" domain is the sole domain which can be registered without carrying out registration formalities. Nevertheless, the applicant must be a French citizen or residing in France and be major.

The sectorial domain concerns regulated professional activities such as lawyers (.avocat.fr), doctors (medecin.fr), pharmacists (.pharmacien.fr), etc.

The conventional domain was created by AFNIC for specific authorities such as academies (ac-nom.fr), embassies (amb-nom.fr), etc. For both the sectorial and the conventional, the applicant must carry out certain registration formalities.

Although strict, the rules set out by AFNIC France do not eliminate all risks of conflicts.

3.9.2 Disputes

3–129 The only task of AFNIC France is to verify the availability of the domain name requested with regard to names already registered on the Internet. This means that the domain name is granted without ensuring that there is no conflict between the domain name and the rights of any prior trademark, known trademark, corporate name or copyright. Moreover, the principle of speciality is not taken into account either. Thus, a holder of rights to a trademark for a determined class of products or services may, if it is the first to be granted a related domain name, prevent any other holder of the same trademark for another class of products or services from benefiting from the domain name relating to such trademark.

Disputes between holders of domain names legally obtained from AFNIC France and holders of prior rights can only increase.

There are several different legal grounds on which such conflicts may be resolved under French law.

A distinction must be made, depending on whether the name in conflict with the domain name is or is not a trademark.

In the case of a trademarks, the resolution of the conflict depends on whether the domain name was registered before or after the trademark.   **3–130**

If the domain name is registered after the trademark, the trademark law is applicable. The registrant of the trademark could file an action against the registrant of the domain name (*Atlantel* case[187]). However, the protection of the mark is not "automatic". The domain name and the trademark in question must designate the same product or service. Insofar as a web site can be considered a communication service, the trademark must be registered beforehand for telecommunication products or services (class 38) (*Célio* case[188]). Furthermore, the preliminary action, based on article L. 716-6 Intellectual Property Code, must be completed by an action on the merits in a brief time (*Ebay* case[189]). If the conditions of protection are not fulfilled with respect to the trademark law, the registrant could also act for unfair competition or parasitism, especially if the trademark is famous (*L'Oréal*,[190] *Lancôme*,[191] *Altavista*[192] cases).

When the trademark is registered after the registration of the domain name, the trademark law is not applicable and the registration of the domain name is thus lawful (*Oceanet* case[193]).

In the case of a conflict between a commercial name or another distinctive sign registered with the Registry of Trade and Companies, the mechanisms of civil liability most often allow for compensation of the loss suffered. Thus, for example, the fact that a company exploited a domain name identifying the corporate name of a competitor may be considered as an act of unfair competition. Consequently, the domain name is condemned when it has been registered after the company name (*Lumiservice* case[194]). Again, without there necessarily being any competition between the two companies in dispute, the act of taking advantage of the reputation of the other to attract clientele for example, may be sanctioned as a parasitic action. Case law has generally held that undue profit from the work and reputation of others is unlawful (*Altavista* case[195]). Nevertheless, the holder of the domain name can win the conflict if the activities are different and there is no risk of confusion (*Alice* case[196]).   **3–131**

In spite of the creation of the Uniform Resolution Domain Policy and the "administrative regulation of conflict", the French system for allocating domain names does not provide for any mechanism of dispute settlement. Consequently, serious disputes will probably continue to arise surrounding domain names.

3.10 Non-United Kingdom domain names—Germany

3.10.1 Status of Germany's domain name registry

3–132   In Germany domain names are approved and centrally registered under the national top level domain, ".de" by DeNIC (Deutscher Network Informations Center, www.denic.de) in Frankfurt. DeNIC is a registered cooperative whose members are Internet service providers providing their customers with local Internet access. Applications for domain name registrations can be directly filed with DeNIC's service, "DeNICdirect". All necessary information can be obtained by logging on DeNIC's homepage. However, DeNIC advises registration through service providers who are members of DeNIC as it is generally less complicated and also more cost–effective for the user. The list of the DeNIC members can also be downloaded from the Internet by logging on the above mentioned domain name. Most of the supraregional service providers are members of DeNIC. Other service providers normally also offer applications for registration of domain names (through DeNIC members) as a service. Since February 1997 domain names can no longer be reserved and only applications dealing with the grant of domain names for immediate use are processed. Information on registered domain names can be obtained from the DeNIC homepage.

3.10.2 General description of Germany's domain name system

3–133   At present DeNIC only awards domain names with the suffix ".de'. No distinction is made between private and commercial domain names (when granted by DeNIC); however, many service providers charge different fees depending on whether the application is filed for private or commercial use of the domain name. In 2000 DeNIC changed its conditions for registration and also relaxed the requirements for domain name owners. This means that the domain name owner needs no longer be domiciled or resident in Germany. It is, on the contrary, sufficient if the applicant names an administrative representative domiciled or resident in Germany, who acts as person authorised to accept service in the case of lawsuits. This permits foreign companies to have domain names registered in Germany in their name.

3.10.3 Disputes policy

3–134   DeNIC awards domain names on the basis of the principle "first come, first served" without any verification of possible conflicts. Applicants are not required to declare that they are owners of equivalent trade mark rights, etc. However, the applicant has to assure that he is entitled to use the domain name and that the domain name neither infringes any rights of third parties nor violates any laws. On signing the registration contract the customer also undertakes to indemnify DeNIC in respect of any damage sustained by DeNIC because of claims asserted by third parties due to a non-authorised use of the domain name.

Disputes cannot be brought before DeNIC for a solution. However, the owners of prior trade mark rights can file a so-called wait application with DeNIC if they consider their rights infringed by the registration or use of a domain name. The applicant filing a wait application needs first of all to provide prima facie evidence to DeNIC of his being the owner of trademark rights, name rights or any other rights infringed by the domain name. Prima facie evidence can be provided by presenting trademark certificates, extracts from the Commercial Register, court decisions or the like. Furthermore the applicant has to declare that he will try to solve the dispute with the domain name owner and to obtain the release of the domain name. In this case the applicant has to release DeNIC from all possible claims of the domain name owner.

The effect of a wait application is that DeNIC registers the dispute in its records for the domain name in question with the consequence that the domain name owner can continue to use the domain name but not assign it any more. The registration of the dispute is valid for one year and can be renewed if the applicant proves that the dispute has not yet been terminated. Thereafter it is up to the applicant to come to terms with the domain name owner or to settle the dispute by recourse to the civil courts.   **3–135**

3.10.4 Legal cases in Germany

A great number of court judgments have been rendered in connection with domain names in the past years in Germany. Most of them deal with a conflict between trademark rights or name rights and domain names. This subject is dealt with in detail below. Moreover the courts have dealt with the issue of how far DeNIC can be made responsible as registration authority for such trademark or name right infringements. The German Federal Court of Justice decided in 2000 that DeNIC need not verify whether the registration of a domain name infringes trade mark rights of third parties. It is only in rare and exceptional cases in which the infringement of a right is obvious that DeNIC has to interfere and refuse registration.   **3–136**

In some of the lawsuits the question at issue was whether generic terms can be registered as domain names. Lower courts partly held the opinion that such generic terms must not be monopolised as domain names for one single company. The grounds for these decisions were that Internet users frequently enter on the off-chance generic terms together with the national top-level domain ".de" as address to then be routed to the homepage of a specific provider who had this generic term registered as domain name. The argument put forward was that this behaviour involves a competitive disadvantage for all other companies of the same branch. However, the German Federal Court of Justice has decided that generic terms can be registered as domain names in Germany. German courts have meanwhile confirmed in several decisions that the registration and use of a domain name can constitute a right in the form of a trade designation according to § 5 MarkenG. If a domain name is distinctive within the meaning of the Trademark Act and is used in trade and business for specific goods or services, the domain name owner can assert rights in this domain name and is vested with the rights resulting from the pertinent provisions of the Trademark Act. This means that the owner of a domain name can also take action against the registration and use of trademarks and company names of later priority in the case of a likelihood of confusion within the meaning of the trademark law.

The registration and use of a domain name identical or confusingly similar to a registered mark can be a trademark infringement under certain circumstances. In any event a trademark is infringed if the goods or services offered on the domain name homepage are identical or similar within the meaning of trademark law to those for which the trademark is protected. In such a case the trademark owner can not only claim a cease and desist and the cancellation of the domain name but can also claim damages   **3–137** from the domain name owner. Whether the trademark owner can also claim a surrender of the domain name is a moot issue. Until now most courts sustained claims for a surrender or assigment. However, there are decisions in which it was correctly held that a claim for assignment can hardly be justified under the law and that the trademark owner can merely claim a cancellation of the domain name.

If a domain name is only registered without being used, the question at issue under trademark law is whether the mere registration represents an infringement. The problem which arises in this respect is that it is not foreseeable whether the domain name will ever be used in trade and business and for which goods and services it will be used. A domain name which is only registered does strictly spoken not provide the similarity of goods and services required for a trademark infringement. Nevertheless some courts confirmed an infringement of prior trade mark rights of by the mere registration of a domain name on the grounds that the registration of the domain name involves the risk that the domain name will be used for the goods and services covered by the trade mark. This risk alone was said to justify the trade mark owner's claim for cancellation. But many objections have been opposed to these decisions and it is not yet predictable which line of authorities will in the end serve as case law.

No trade mark rights are infringed if a domain name is used exclusively for private purposes and not for trade and business since the requirement of acting in trade and business is not met.

3–138   If a registered or used domain name is identical to a company name or the name of a widely known person, the owner of the company name or the name can enforce his name rights against the domain name owner under § 12 BGB (German Civil Code) and claim a cease and desist and cancellation of the domain name unless the domain name owner can substantiate his being entitled to use this name because it is e.g. his name.

In cases of domain name grabbing as well as in cases in which advantage is obviously taken of a well-known trademark or a famous name by the registration or use of a domain name, the domain name owner can be sued for unfair competition or on basis of the legal provisions on the protection of well-known trademarks and signs even in the absence of a likelihood of confusion within the meaning of the trademark law.

3.10.5 Relevant laws

3–139   If the registration or use of a domain name infringes trademark or company name rights, the provisions of the Trademark Act come into play, namely § 14 and § 15 MarkenG which grant the owner of a trademark or the owner of a company name or a title the right to claim a cease and desist and damages.

3–140-3–141   ∋ 12 BGB protecting the general rights to a name comes primarily into play in cases of domain name disputes. This legal provision does not exclusively protect the name of natural persons but also of companies and even self-governing legal entities under public law such as a community (as in the case of Heidelberg). This legal provision permits the legitimate bearer of a name to forbid anyone else use of the name. If someone else is using the same name without authorisation, the bearer of the name can ask him to refrain from doing so.

3.11 Non-United Kingdom domain names—Hong Kong

3.11.1 Registration

Hong Kong's domain name registry is known as the Hong Kong Domain Name **3–142**
Registration Company Limited ("HKDNR"). Since June 1, 2001, it has replaced the Joint
Universities Computer Centre ("JUCC") to administer the Hong Kong Network
Information Centre ("HKNIC") and has taken over the responsibility of administering
".hk" domain names. Its role is to oversee the registration and assignment of Internet
domain names ending with ".com.hk", ".org.hk", ".gov.hk", ".edu.hk" and ".net.hk"
and any other second level domains to be introduced from time to time in Hong Kong.

The Hong Kong system for domain name registration is essentially on a "first come,
first served" basis. HKDNR does not check domain names applied for against registered
trade marks, neither does it pre-vet applications for domain names. HKDNR is not
obliged to enquire at the registration stage whether an applicant is entitled to register the
domain name for which it has applied in Hong Kong. Furthermore, HKDNR's domain
name registration agreement expressly states that the domain name applicant shall be
responsible for use of the domain name once registered.

In order to apply for a ".hk" domain name the applicant must prove that it is a **3–143**
commercial entity, a not for profit organisation, an entity managing network
infrastructure machines and services, a bureau or department of the Government of
HKSAR or a school or educational institution in HKSAR. For example, an applicant who
wants to register a ".com.hk" domain name must submit its Business Registration
Certificate issued by the Inland Revenue Department as documentary proof. HKDNR's
domain name registration rules allow an applicant to register multiple domain names.
However, HKDNR does not at present accept applications for registration of domain
names for individuals.

Under HKDNR's domain name registration agreement each applicant is required to
warrant and represent that all statements in its application are true, that it has the right to
use the domain name, that it intends to use the domain name (which use shall be bona
fide for its own benefit), that the use or registration does not interfere with or infringe the
rights of any third party in any jurisdiction and that it is not seeking to use the domain
name for any unlawful purpose.

At the time of the request for the domain name or within one month after the **3–144**
application, the applicant must have operational a name service from at least two
independent Internet servers for that domain name. HKDNR levies a nominal non-
refundable fee (currently HK$200) for registration of a new domain name or modification
of an existing domain name. Domain names are registered initially for a period of one
year. Thereafter, the domain name can be renewed annually subject to the current terms
and conditions and payment of a fee.

An applicant may transfer the registration of its domain name to another party.
However, both parties (*i.e.* the transferor and transferee) must mutually consent to the
transfer and sign HKDNR's Transfer Form. Furthermore, the transferee must provide the
same documentary proof which an applicant for a domain name would be required to
produce when applying for a fresh domain name, for example, proof of incorporation
and registration and evidence of mutual consent. It must also agree to be bound by the
terms and conditions of the domain name registration agreement. A fee (currently
HK$700) will be charged for the transfer. This fee includes the initial registration fee for
the new domain name.

HKDNR has adopted a Domain Name Dispute Resolution Policy ("Dispute Resolution Policy"). The Dispute Resolution Policy sets forth the terms and conditions in connection with a dispute between the applicant and any party other than the HKDNR with regard to the registration and use of the applicant's ".hk" domain name. The Hong Kong International Arbitration Centre has been appointed to be the first ".hk" domain name dispute resolution service provider. All domain name disputes will be resolved by mandatory arbitration proceedings.

3–145 In addition, under HKDNR's domain name registration agreement, the domain name applicant is required to defend, indemnify and hold harmless HKDNR, its directors, officers, committee members, employees and agents from all liabilities, losses, damages, costs legal, professional and other expenses of any nature resulting from any claim, action or demand arising out of, or related to, the registration or use of the domain name. Such claims shall include, without limitation, those based upon trade or service mark infringement, dilution, tortious interference with contract or prospective business advantage, passing off, defamation or injury to business reputation.

Finally, as a result of the handover from JUCC to HKDNR, all ".hk" domain name holders who registered prior to June 1, 2001 have (at no extra cost) to re-register and update their registered information with HKDNR before May 31, 2002. Furthermore, domain name holders who registered with HKNIC prior to February 19, 2001 can choose to be bound by the domain name registration agreement in use when they registered their domain name ("Old Agreement") or HKDNR's new domain name registration agreement ("New Agreement"). The key difference between the Old Agreement and the New Agreement is that, for the cost of an annual renewal fee, those who choose the New Agreement will be allowed to register additional names or transfer domain names. This is not permitted under the Old Agreement. All registrants, regardless of whether they are subject to the Old Agreement or the New Agreement, must abide by the Dispute Resolution Policy.

3.11.2 Disputes

Arbitration

3–146 As part of the reform of Hong Kong's domain name registration system, HKDNR has also introduced a new domain name dispute resolution policy that seeks to expedite and reduce the costs of resolving cybersquatting disputes.

Under the new dispute resolution policy, the owner of a ".hk" domain name will be subject to a mandatory arbitration proceeding if HKDNR receives a complaint from a third party asserting that:

(i)   the domain name is identical or confusingly similar to a trade mark or service mark in Hong Kong in which the complainant has rights; and

(ii) the owner of the domain name has no rights or legitimate interests in respect of the domain name; and

(iii) the domain name has been registered and is being used in bad faith.

It is expressly stated under the new policy that the acquisition of a domain name primarily for the purpose of selling the domain name to the complainant or a competitor of the complainant for consideration exceeding the actual out-of-pocket expenses directly related to registration of the domain name shall be considered as evidence of bad faith.

The complainant shall be responsible for paying the fees of the arbitration. The **3–147** exception is where the complainant elects to have the dispute heard by a single arbitrator, but the respondent exercises its right to have the dispute heard by a panel of three arbitrators. In this case, the arbitration fees will be payable in equal shares by the complainant and the respondent. Under the current policy, the fees for resolving a dispute will be HK$8,000 by one arbitrator or HK$16,000 by three arbitrators. The arbitrators will be provided by the Hong Kong International Arbitration Centre ("HKIAC").

The complainant must prove all of the three requirements as stated above in order to succeed in an arbitration. As this new dispute resolution policy aims to expedite the resolution of cybersquatting disputes and to allow the rightful owner to re-claim a domain name with minimal costs, the only remedies to which a complainant is entitled under such policy will be either an order to cancel the registration of the domain name or an order to transfer the domain name to the complainant. A complainant who wishes to seek remedies beyond this scope must go through the Court unless both parties agree to submit the whole of the dispute to arbitration.

Court Proceedings

Use of a domain name is liable to give rise to a cause of action in Hong Kong in one of **3–148** three ways: as infringement of a registered trade mark, as passing off or as a criminal offence under the Trade Descriptions Ordinance.

Infringement of a registered trade mark may arise on the basis that the use of the domain name by its holder is use of such name as a trade mark, or that it imports a reference to the proprietor of the registered mark, in circumstances where the use is made in relation to goods or services which are the same as, or of the same description as, those specified in the trade mark registration. Such use of the domain name will only be actionable if it results in a likelihood of confusion. Likelihood of confusion does not have to be shown, however, if the domain name is used for the goods or services actually specified in the trade mark registration and the domain name is identical to the registered mark.

Passing off may arise where the trade mark (whether or not it is registered) has a **3–149** protectable goodwill in Hong Kong which will be damaged by confusion arising from use of the domain name.

It is also an offence under the Trade Descriptions Ordinance in Hong Kong falsely to apply a trade mark to goods. This includes using such a mark in any manner which is likely to be taken as referring to those goods. Use of a domain name to advertise goods, for which the same name is registered as a trade mark by another party, would arguably fall within the scope of this offence. The criminal penalty is a fine of up to HK$500,000 and up to five years imprisonment on conviction on indictment, and a fine of up to HK$100,000 and up to two years imprisonment on summary conviction.

In addition to the above causes of action, any persons attempting to register potentially desirable domain names, with a view to selling them on at a profit, may also be susceptible to a *quia timet* action on the basis that there is a serious and immediate risk of wrongdoing, even though there may yet have been no infringing act within Hong Kong. It is likely that the decision of the English Courts in the *One in a Million case* (see section 3.3.6 above) would also be followed in Hong Kong.

There have been several domain name disputes in Hong Kong which the parties in **3–150** dispute have attempted to resolve the matter through legal proceedings since the MTR case, Hong Kong's first passing off action arising from the registration of a domain name.

In the MTR case, the Mass Transit Railway Company (commonly abbreviated to MTRC) sued a local company, Beezweb Productions Ltd, for registering the domain name "mtrc.com" with InterNIC. In *Sun Microsystems Inc v Lai Sun Hotels International Ltd.*,[197] Sun Microsystems, a renowned information technology company which conducts its Internet business using the domain name www.sun.com, claimed against Lai Sun, a public listed company in Hong Kong, for passing off. One of the factors Sun Microsystems relied on was the fact that Lai Sun had registered and used a domain name esun.com. Sun Microsystems applied unsuccessfully for an interim injunction against Lai Sun. It is believed that both of the above cases have been settled out of court. To date, there is yet to be a reported case in Hong Kong on cybersquatting. With the introduction of the new dispute resolution policy, any decision made by the panel of arbitrators will be published on the HKIAC's Web site at www.hkiac.org.

3.12 Non-United Kingdom domain names—Israel

3.12.1 Registration

Israel domain name registry

3–151 The organisation responsible for administering Internet domain names under the top-level domain name for Israel is the Israel Internet Association ("ISOC-IL"), which is a member of the international Internet Society.[198] ISOC-IL is a registered non-profit organisation, which derives its authority to operate the Israel domain name registry from IANA. There is no governmental regulation of the registry's operations.

Domain name registration policy

3–152 The current rules governing the registration of domain names (the "Rules") came into effect on January 1, 1999.[199] The registry allocates third level domain names under the top .il level, and has already allocated tens of thousands of domain names. The domain names are divided into eight second level domain name categories; .k12.il. [200], .org.il, .ac.il, .gov.il, .muni.il,[201] .net.il,[202] .co.il, and .idf.il[203]. Commercial entities are allocated domain names in .co.il. The registry accepts generic domain names for registration, but not (i) names which contain obscene or foul language, which would injure public order or sensibilities, or which do not comply with the laws of Israel, (ii) the name "www", (iii) names containing less than three characters, and (iv) names which are identical to top level domain names.

Domain name registrations must be renewed every two years. Registrations are transferable, and domain names are portable from one Internet service provider to another.

3.12.2 Resolving questions of rights to domain names at the registration stage

3–153 A maximum of ten domain names are allocated to each applicant. The Rules do not provide for examination of the availability of a domain name prior to its allocation.[204] However, the applicant must state in the application form that to the best of his or her knowledge the domain name sought is available and does not infringe the rights of any other party. Each applicant must also consent to be bound by the Rules, which inter alia, grant authority to ISOC-IL to refuse or to cancel domain name allocations on the ground of misrepresentation. ISOC-IL may exercise this authority against applicants who knowingly request allocation of a domain name to which a third party has better rights.

3.12.3 Domain name disputes

ISOC-IL Advisory Committee
An external Advisory Committee established under the Rules offers resolution of **3–154** disputes relating to domain name allocations within four to five months from the date of submission of a petition. Standing is given to applicants and domain name holders who wish to overturn allocation decisions made by ISOC-IL, to third parties who are challenging domain name allocations, and to ISOC-IL, in cases where it wishes to obtain an advisory opinion regarding a domain name allocation. Petitioners and respondents retain their rights to institute court proceedings relating to the dispute.

The Advisory Committee must determine domain name disputes in accordance with the Rules, giving due regard to previous Advisory Committee rulings. ISOC-IL is bound to implement Advisory Committee decisions pending any court decision regarding the disputed domain name.

The Advisory Committee has made three determinations to date. The three domain **3–155** names in dispute were "waltdisney.co.il" (decision dated January 28, 2000), "habitat.-co.il" (decision dated August 18, 2000), and "snapple.co.il" (decision dated February 25, 2001). In each case, on petition by the registered trademark owner, a domain name that was identical to the registered trademark was transferred from the individual who had been allocated the domain name and who in each case was held to have acted in bad faith, to the registered owner of the trademark.[205] The Advisory Committee has decided that since the allocation and use of domain names have global implications, it is appropriate to apply international standards that outlaw cybersquatting[206] when judging whether a domain name holder has complied with good faith obligations imposed by Israeli law.[207] In ordering transfer of domain names, the Advisory Committee has also relied on the existence of the torts of passing off, unfair intervention with access to a business, and unjust enrichment (these causes of action are described in the next section), as well as on section 9.2.1(b) of the Rules, which requires an active domain name server to be established within one year of the allocation date.

Legislation and Case Law
A wide variety of laws are applicable to domain name disputes. The Trademarks **3–156** Ordinance (New Version) 1972 regulates domain names that operate as trademarks. The Commercial Torts Law 1999 and the Unjust Enrichment Law 1979 proscribe certain kinds of unfair behaviour, and use of a domain name that creates a likelihood of confusion. In some circumstances, laws that focus on property rights (the Property Law 1969 and the Chattels Law 1971), or on the public interest (the Consumer Protection Law 1981, and the Contracts (General Parts) Law 1973), apply.

Based on existing judicial standards, the following doctrines may influence the resolution of domain name disputes.

Trademark infringement
Use of a domain name which is the same as or similar to a trademark registered in Israel, **3–157** in relation to the goods and services for which the trademark is registered, may constitute trademark infringement.[208] Evidence regarding confusion of the public or of damage

suffered by the registered owner is not required in order to establish infringement.[209]

Use of a domain name which is the same as or similar to a "famous mark", may also constitute trademark infringement.[210] Where the famous mark is registered in Israel, use of the same or a similar domain name in relation to any goods and services will be prohibited, if such use is likely to indicate an association between the web site and the proprietor of the famous mark and will probably result in injury to the proprietor of the famous mark. Where the "famous mark" is not registered in Israel, protection will be afforded against third party use of a domain name in relation to the same or similar, goods or services, as those for which the mark is famous.

3–158   In *Cellcom Israel Ltd v T.M. Aquanet Computer Communications Ltd.,*[211] the owner of the trademark "Cellcom", which was registered in respect of telecommunication services, applied for an interlocutory injunction of use of its trademark in an action for trademark infringement. The respondent was an Internet service provider that operated a web site using the domain name "cellcom.co.il". The service provided by the respondent enabled customers to receive emails messages on cellular phones. The court held that the services provided by the applicant and the respondent were in fact the same, and that the registered trademark was a "famous mark". Despite this, the judge did not consider the trademark infringement claim, having decided that there were sufficient grounds to grant an injunction on the basis of other causes of action, namely passing off, and theft of goodwill.

Passing off

3–159   A dealer that causes its assets or services to be mistaken for those belonging to, or connected to, another dealer, is liable for the tort of passing off.[212] This law may allow registered and unregistered trademark owners to prevent third parties used their trademarks as domain names.

In the *Cellcom* case, the respondent was enjoined from using the domain name "cellcom.co.il" because the applicant established a prima facie likelihood of winning its passing off action. The law applied in the *Cellcom* case was based on the previous definition of the tort of passing off.[213] The decision would almost certainly have gone the same way under the new, broader, definition.

In the case of a "famous mark", anti-dilution protection is afforded even where the domain name is used in relation to goods or services dissimilar to those sold by the proprietor of the famous mark.[214]

Misappropriation of Goodwill

3–160   The Property Law 1969 and the Chattels Law 1971, when read together, proscribe the act of trespass on an incorporeal property right such as goodwill.[215] The courts have frequently resorted to these property laws in order to prevent damage to trademark owners, particularly in cases involving misappropriation of famous marks. In the *Cellcom* case, these laws were used for the first time in order to grant a remedy in a domain name dispute. The judge held that the respondent's use of the domain name "cellcom.co.il" caused damage to Cellcom Israel Limited's proprietary rights.[216]

Unfair intervention

3–161   In 1999, the legislature created a new tort of unfair intervention. Pursuant to section 3 of the Commercial Torts Law 1999, a dealer may not unfairly impede the access of customers, employees or agents to the business, asset, or service, of another dealer.

A recent district court decision, *Magnetics Limited v. Discopy (Israel) Limited,*[217] established two rules regarding application of the tort to domain name disputes. First, "access" includes electronic access. Secondly, no company or individual engaged in business may register a domain name that is identical to a competitor's trademark if this prevents the competitor from using its trademark for the purposes of Internet activity. The parties to this case were competitors, but it is likely that the rules will extend to dealers who are not competitors.[218]

It is feasible that the courts will use the unfair intervention law in order to prohibit cyber squatting. There is no case law on the question of whether a cyber squatter is a "dealer". However, The Advisory Committee of ISOC-IL has decided that holding a domain name without making use of it may constitute unfair intervention. In the Habitat decision, the Committee used section 3 to justify transferring a domain name from the holder to the registered trademark owner. It determined that domain names are intended to be used, and therefore continued non-use of the domain name by the respondent was unfairly preventing the petitioner from making legitimate business use of its business name and registered trademark in order to attract customers via the internet.[219]

3–162

Unjust Enrichment

The Unjust Enrichment Law 1979 provides that a person from whom a benefit is unlawfully obtained can claim restitution.[220] The courts have frequently resorted to this law in order to prevent damage to trademark owners, particularly in cases involving misappropriation of famous marks.

The courts may interpret this Law as granting a right of redress in a domain name dispute.[221] Outside the court system, the ISOC-IL Advisory Committee has already applied the unjust enrichment law to a domain name dispute. In ordering the transfer of the domain name to the registered trademark owner in the *Snapple* decision, the Committee noted that in addition to committing the tort of passing off, the respondent had also infringed the provisions of section 1 of the Unjust Enrichment Law.

3–163

Consumer protection legislation

The Commercial Torts Law and the Consumer Protection Law both outlaw misleading advertising.[222] This may cover use of a domain name by anyone other than the company with which Israeli consumers associate the name. The Commercial Torts Law grants "dealers" who suffer damage as a result of the publication of a false description standing to sue another "dealer" who is responsible for the publication. There have been no Internet cases regarding this legislation.

3–164

3.13 Non-United Kingdom domain names—Japan

3.13.1 Registration

Most of the computers connected to the Internet which are located in Japan are administered under the JP domain. The two letter code JP represents Japan in accordance with ISO 3166. JP is a hierarchical domain where JP is on the top most level.

In order to contribute to the development of computer networks, the organisation JPNIC allocates and maintains internationally unique JP domain names to organisations that possess or administer computer networks. JPNIC allocates domain names down to the third level. These domain names represent the name of the organisations. Organisations which have a third level domain name maintain the domain names that

3–165

are below the fourth level. Geographic domain names are excluded.

JPNIC is the country Network Information Centre (NIC) of Japan. All information concerning JP domain names, IP network numbers, name servers, contact persons, and network providers in Japan are collected into the JPNIC database. The JPNIC Web server may be accessed at http://www.nic.ad.jp/index.html. JPNIC was formerly an organisation without juridical personality. It has now become a body incorporated for a public purpose.

3–166   A domain name consists of several levels. For example the service provider's domain name "infosphere.or.jp" consists of three parts. ".JP" is the top level domain. ".or" is a generic term for an organisation. "Infosphere" is the third level domain.

The eight types of generic domain are as follows:

AC = university, college or other academic organisation

ED = high school, junior high school, elementary school and educational organisation

CO = a corporation

GO = an organisation in the Japanese government

OR = an organisation which does not belong to AC, ED; CO or GO

GR = organisation without legal personality

NE = a network service, e.g. service provider

AD = a member of JPNIC.

As mentioned above, the domain used for commercial purposes is the "co.jp" domain. Domain names are allocated in the order of arrival at JPNIC.

3–167   A corporation wanting to be allocated a domain name should apply to JPNIC. The contents of the application form involve information such as name and addresses of the organisation, technical administrator, persons in charge of technical matters and persons in charge of financial matters.

JPNIC checks the application form and informs the applicant whether the domain name is allocable or not within ten days from the date of the application. According to the public documents of JPNIC, JPNIC allocates the requested domain name if the generic name of the domain name conforms to the JPNIC structure and the requested domain name does not conflict with registered domain names.

The registration of the company must be submitted in the case of the ".co" domain. But it does not follow that applicants must have the same company name as the domain name.

In addition, a General-Use JP domain (*e.g.* http://www.comit.jp) has been available since May 21, 2001. Allocation of General-Use JP domains has been managed by Japan Registry Services Co. Ltd (JPRS). JPRS was incorporated on December 26, 2000, to administer JP domain name registration and management, and to carry out operation of the domain name system.

3.13.2 Disputes Resolution Policy

3–169   Rules for the JP Domain Name Dispute Resolution Policy[223] ("DRP") were made public on July 19, 2000, revised on October 10, 2000 and implemented on November 10, 2000.

Structure

An applicant in the JP domain should agree on this DRP (article 2 of DRP rule) and when **3–170**
an administrative panel makes a decision about the disputes (article 3), the parties should
obey the decision.

According to article 3 of the DRP rule:

> "The Center will transfer or cancel the domain name registration under the
> following circumstances:
>
> (1) Subject to the provisions of Art. 8, the receipt by the Center of written
> instructions from the Registrant or its authorised agent to take such action;
> (2) The receipt by the Center of the original (a copy of the original may be
> acceptable if circumstances require) of an order from a court or arbitration
> tribunal, in each case of competent jurisdiction, requiring such action; and/or
> (3) The receipt by the Center of a decision of an Administrative Panel requiring
> such action in JP Domain Name Dispute Resolution Proceedings to which the
> Registrant was a party and which was conducted under this Policy or a later
> version of this Policy adopted by the Center (See Art. 4 (i) and (k) of the Policy
> below.)"

Cause of action

The complainant should prove the three following elements; **3–171**

> "(1) the domain name of the Registrant is identical or confusingly similar to any
> mark such as trademark or service mark in which the Complainant has rights
> or legitimate interests; and
> (2) the Registrant has no rights or legitimate interests in respect of the domain
> name registration; and
> (3) the domain name of the Registrant has been registered or is being used in bad
> faith (unfair purpose)."

As to "bad faith", the rule says that "To determine whether or not there are factual **3–172**
elements provided by this Article (a) (iii), the panel of the dispute-resolution service
provider shall consider that the registration or use of a domain name is in bad faith
(unfair purpose) if the Panel found especially the following circumstances, in particular
but without limitation.

(1) circumstances indicating that the Registrant has registered or has acquired the
domain name primarily for the purpose of selling, renting, or otherwise
transferring the domain name to the Complainant or to a competitor of that
Complainant, for valuable consideration in excess of the out-of-pocket costs
(amount to be confirmed by documentation) directly related to the domain name;
or

(2) the Registrant has registered the domain name in order to prevent the
Complainant from reflecting any trademarks or other indication in a corresponding domain name, provided that the Registrant has engaged in plural numbers of
such interference; or the Registrant has registered the domain name primarily for
the purpose of disrupting the business of a competitor; or

(3)   by using the domain name, the Registrant has intentionally attempted to attract, for commercial gain, Internet users to the web site or other on-line location of the Registrant, by intending to make confusion as to the source, sponsorship, affiliation, or endorsement of the web site or location or of a product or service thereon.''

Defence

3–173   The defence of the domain name holder is described in subsection c of article 4

''(1)   before the Registrant receives any notice of the dispute related to the subject domain name by any third party or the dispute-resolution service provider, the Registrant uses, or apparently demonstrate preparations to use, the domain name or a name corresponding thereto, in order to offer goods or services without any bad faith (unfair purpose); or

(2)   the Registrant has been commonly known by any name under the domain name, regardless of registration or others by the Registrant of any trademark and other indications.

(3)   The Registrant is using the domain name for a noncommercial purpose or is making fair use of the domain name, without intent for commercial gain to misleadingly divert consumers by utilizing the trademark and other indications of the Complainant or to tarnish any trademark and other indications of the Complainant.''

3.13.3 Legal cases

3–174   Although many examples of domain name problems are reported in Japan, only one legal case, in the Toyama district court, has so far been reported in Japan.

Facts

3–175   Plaintiff (Japan Consumer Credit Service) is a company whose main business is consumer credit services and uses ''jaccs'' as their trade mark. Defendant (Nippon Kaisyo, Inc.) is a company which sells portable toilets and is the holder of the domain name ''jaccs.co.jp''. The defendant has a home page under the domain name which has link text which links to a web page which shows their selling goods, mobile phone and company name.

The Plaintiff filed a suit that request injunction of use of ''http://www.jaccs.co.jp'' as the domain name and prohibition of indication of the ''jaccs'' on the home page based on the Unfair Competition Prevention law.

Judgment

3–176   Toyama District Court granted the Plaintiff's request on December 6, 2000.

Three issues are disputed in this proceeding;

(a)   Is the domain name use ''use of the indication of goods and so on.''?

The Unfair Competition Prevention Law prohibits the use of the mark as the ''indication of the goods''. The court said that whether the domain name use is regarded as the ''indication of the goods'' or not is decided by the total consideration of the meaning of the characters of the domain names and the contents showed in the web pages reached by the domain name. The court said that the domain name use is considered as the indication of goods in this case.

(b) abuse of right defence

The defendant made an abuse of right defence saying that the domain name is registered only on the first-come, first-serve theory. The court didn't admit this defence because JPNIC can cancel the registration of the domain name and the defendant had bad faith.

(c) Is it appropriate for the injunction of the use of the "jaccs" on the home page?

The court prohibit the defendant to use the "jaccs" on his web page saying it is obvious the use of "jaccs" on his web page is use for "indication of goods".

3.13.4 Legislation

Generally speaking, the Trade Mark Law and the Unfair Competition Law are relevant to a domain name dispute. **3–177**

Trade Mark Law

As mentioned above, a "pirate" can register the famous trade mark of another as his own **3–178** domain name in Japan. Whether such pirate would infringe the trade mark or not depends on the actual usage of the domain name. According to art 30 of the Trade Mark Law of Japan, "A trade mark owner may establish an exclusive use right with respect to the trade mark concerned". Prohibited "use" includes: "Acts of displaying or distribution of advertisements, priced catalogues or transaction papers relating to goods, to which mark is applied." When a domain name is used on a Web page in such a way that, for instance, the domain name is used as the advertisement of goods of a similar kind to the goods of the registered mark, that will be an infringement of the registered trade mark. However, the Trade Mark Law does not apply when the domain name is shown only in the window of the browser. Nor does it apply when the domain name is used in a way which is not related to goods or services.

Unfair Competition Law

Trade Mark Law is of no assistance in some cases. One situation is the case in which the **3–179** pirate uses the domain name in an advertisement of goods which are not of a similar kind. Another is the case in which the pirate uses the domain name just to catch the eye. The Unfair Competition Law provides some heads of protection. "Well-known badge of recognition" protection and "Distinguishing badge of recognition" protection are relevant to domain name disputes.

"Well-known badge of recognition" protection needs three requirements:

(a) well-known badge of recognition;

(b) similar badge of recognition;

(c) confusion.

"Distinguishing badge of recognition" protection needs three requirements:

(a)   distinguishing badge of recognition;

(b)   similar badge of recognition;

(c)   use as own badge of recognition.

"Distinguishing badge of recognition" protection is thought to be effective against the dilution of famous brands.

In order to prevent cybersquatting the Unfair Competition Prevention Law is being amended. The Unfair Competition Law passed the Parliament on June 22, 2001 and it will be enacted (probably) next year.

According to the amendment, activity consisting of obtaining the right to use, hold and/or use the same or similar domain name to the indication of the goods of another other person for the purpose of unfair profit or harm to the other should be prohibited as unfair competition.

3.14 Non-United Kingdom domain names—The Netherlands

3.14.1 Registration

3–180   In The Netherlands the "naming authority" authorised to register domain names is the Foundation Internet Domain Registration Netherlands (Stichting Internet Domein Registratie Nederland SIDN), established in 1996, and exclusively authorised to register domain names with the top-level domain ".nl" The Stichting Internet Domein Registratie Nederland has its own Web site (http://www. sidn.nl) and was established in 1996 as an independent foundation and professional organisation to ensure efficient and fair registration of domain names. Before 1996, domain names where registered by volunteer organisations within the University of Amsterdam (ie Centrum voor Wiskunde en Informatica).

The Stichting Internet Domein Registratie Nederland has established and published a Regulation for the Registration of Domain Names (Reglement voor Registratie van Domeinnamen), which sets out the rules with regard to the registration of domain names with the top-level domain ".nl"

Applications for the registration of a domain name can only be submitted through e-mail by a service provider registered with and participating in the Stichting Internet Domein Registratie Nederland. A domain name with the top-level domain ".nl" can be registered by or on behalf of a company domiciled in The Netherlands as well as by a private person with residence in The Netherlands.

Applications
3–181   An application to register a domain name with the top level domain ".nl" must be lodged with SIDN. However, registration can only be obtained through those Internet service providers (ISPs) who are members of SIDN and a standard application form can be downloaded from their web sites. SIDN examines whether the requested domain name is available. It does not examine whether the domain name is registered as a trademark with the Benelux Trademark Office or as a trade name with the Chamber of Commerce Trade Registry. The SIDN registration regulations provide for some grounds of refusal, for example in case the domain name applied for is excluded from registration.

Information on the applicant must be provided together with the application. The applicant can be either a legal or a natural person. In case a legal person is concerned, it should in principle have its seat or an effective commercial establishment in the Netherlands. Furthermore, it should remit an excerpt from the Chamber of Commerce Trade Registry or from any other official registry. In case a natural person is concerned, he or she should be a resident of the Netherlands. Together with the application, a copy of his/her passport or other official means of identification should be remitted. Furthermore, the choice of domain names by natural persons is submitted to some restrictions. Finally, applicants are obliged to provide SIDN with a written indemnity including that the domain name applied for does not infringe any right of third parties, since SIDN does not check whether any older IP rights exist.

Fees

The fee for registration will usually be around EUR 50, and about the same amount again **3–182** for each domain name on a yearly basis.

Time consumed for registration

The average registration period of a domain name amounts to approximately two weeks. **3–183**

Article 6 of the Regulation for the Registration of domain names with the top-level domain ".nl" (Reglement voor Registratie van Domeinnamen) explicitly provides that the applicant must declare that the domain name does not infringe any rights of third parties.

Applicants are obliged to sign a written indemnification concerning damages, costs and expenses incurred by the Stichting Internet Domein Registratie Nederland with regard to any claim for infringement of (proprietary) rights of third parties.

3.14.2 Disputes

No Dispute Resolution Policy

Contrary to other Benelux countries, for example Belgium, SIDN does *not* provide for a **3–184** dispute resolution policy or a policy to place domain names on hold in case rights in domain names have been infringed by third parties. In such a case, an action should be brought before the competent District Court., either in the form of regular or summary relief proceedings. Many decisions have already been rendered on this subject. Some of those are discussed below.

In *Ouders van Nu/Ouders Online*[224] it was held that the Benelux trademark OUDERS ONLINE (Parents Online) registered for an electronic magazine published on the Internet and the domain name Ouders.nl (Parents.nl) did not infringe the Benelux trademark OUDERS VAN NU (Parents of Today) registered for a "traditional" magazine. The reason therefore was that the distinctive character of OUDERS VAN NU was considered to be limited, since it was basically the same as its target group, whereas the additions "online" and ".nl" sufficiently stressed that the defendants trademark and domain name related to another media. No likelihood of association was therefore established. Decision affirmed on appeal.

In *Labouchere v. IMG Holland*[225] it was held that IMG Holland's registration and use of **3–185** the domain names Labouchere.com, SNS Bank.com, Delta Lloyd.com and so on infringed the trademarks and trade names of the corresponding financial institutions. IMG Holland was prevented from using these domain names and ordered to immediately "re-route" the infringing domain names to the .nl domain names of the financial institutions. In the mean time, IMG Holland was ordered to arrange for assignment of its .com domain names to the relevant financial institutions.

In first instance of *Passies/Gaos*[226] it was held that the mere registration of the domain name www.passies.com did not amount to the use of an identical or corresponding trademark. On appeal however[227], the Court reversed this aspect of the first instance decision, by stipulating that the mere possibility of use or the possibility to sell the domain name concerned did constitute such use. Since the Court, just like the President, considered that Gaos did have far less interest in the domain name concerned than Passies, the transfer thereof to Passies was ordered.

3–186   In *Procter & Gamble/Magenta*[228], the foundation Magenta had registered on behalf of one of his employees the domain name www.ariel.nl. ARIEL being one of the trademarks owned by Procter & Gamble, this company had requested for its transfer. The ground invoked was trademark infringement, for the trademark was used without valid reason in the course of trade. However, Magenta replied that the web site was used for private purposes of its employee, who had chosen this name as the Hebrew equivalent of "lion", being his favorite animal. The President esteemed that Procter & Gamble had not successfully established that the trademark ARIEL was used in the course of trade, which was detrimental to the repute of this mark and therefore dismissed Procter's claim.

In *Unilever/Name Space*[229] the cybersquatter Name Space, who had registered over 45,000 domain names of third parties, was ordered to transfer various domain names with extension .nl to Unilever and other companies. The required use in the course of trade without valid reason had been established, so that the President had no mercy on the cybersquatter.

3–187   As may follow from the above, many trademark infringement cases relating to domain names have been litigated within the framework of a preliminary relief action (*kort geding*) before the Presidents of the District Courts of The Netherlands. One of the reasons therefor is that the transfer of an infringing domain name can be readily obtained, whereas it would take much longer to obtain the same in regular proceedings. An aspect which should not be disregarded however is that the plaintiff in summary relief proceedings may be ordered to institute regular proceedings within a limited period of time after the summary relief decision. This is because it cannot be excluded that these summary relief proceedings qualify as "provisional measures", as specified in the Article 50 (6) of the TRIPS treaty, which loose their effect if not followed by regular proceedings. A final decision on this issue still has to be taken by the European Court of Justice.

All sorts of new questions have arisen in connection with the all-encompassing nature of the Internet, not only within the field of copyright infringement and trade mark infringement, but also on the issues of jurisdiction and applicable law. These issues are discussed in Chapter 6.

3.15   Non-United Kingdom domain names—New Zealand

3.15.1   Registration of domain names

3–188   New Zealand has one domain name registry, managed and operated by InternetNZ Limited ("InternetNZ") (formerly the Internet Society of New Zealand Inc). Established in 1996 to manage the domain name system, they established a subsidiary company called The New Zealand Internet Registry Limited (trading as "Domainz") to operate the registration system. At the time of writing, InternetNZ has indicated its intention to replace the registry system with a shared registry system where all parties interested in registering domain names would be able to do so directly, thereby removing Domainz's monopoly on the registry.

The domain name system in New Zealand is similar in structure to systems adopted in other countries. The New Zealand domain name space has three elements:

- the country code top-level domain ("ccTLD") ".nz";

- a second level domain (denoting a "community of interest", such as ".co"), and

- a third level domain (selected by the domain holder and usually a word or words, such as "bellgully").

Each element is separated by a full stop. Each complete name (for example "bellgully.co.nz") may only consist of alpha-numeric characters (but may include a hyphen) and must be unique.

InternetNZ adopts the Internet Corporation for Assigned Names and Numbers **3–189** ("ICANN") policy and develops local policy for the .nz domain space. Domainz follows InternetNZ policy in registering domain names, and requires that all name holders agree to be bound by published policies and Terms of Service.

InternetNZ has established a set of principles for the use of second level domains. These principles are based on the concept of "communities of interest". InternetNZ manages second level domains, and has a procedure for creation of new second level domains, as they are needed. At present there are ten existing second level domains—.ac, .co, .cri, .gen, .govt, .iwi, .mil, .net, .org, .school. However, InternetNZ has granted authority to other organisations to moderate membership of the .cri, .govt, .iwi, and .mil second level domains.

When selecting a third level name, it must be unique within the selected second level **3–190** domain. In other words, it cannot be identical to the second and third levels of a domain name that has already been registered.

Domainz does not pre-vet applications for domain names; nor do they require applicants to declare they are the owners of the equivalent trade marks. However they do require applicants to warrant they are "entitled to register the name". Domainz will also refuse to register names which it considers offensive.

The registration of domain names is carried out on a "first come, first served" basis. That is, the registration of a name within any second level domain in the ".nz" domain space is simply a case of being first to apply.

It is InternetNZ policy that neither InternetNZ nor Domainz will play a part in **3–191** deciding whether the name holder has a right to the registration of the name. If a domain name conflicts with another domain name or a trade mark, it is up to the name holders to resolve the conflict. InternetNZ states that any applicant or name holder will be liable for costs incurred by InternetNZ or Domainz in the event of a dispute.

Domainz acknowledges that registration does not give the name holder a property right in the name. They state that it is a delegation of the unique name to a name holder enabling it to connect to the Internet using the domain name. Registration does not confer on the name holder any other rights in the name.

Domainz will cancel a registration if a name holder does not comply with the published policies or Terms of Service, or fails to pay the required fees.

3.15.2 Domain Name Disputes

3–192   There have been a number of disputes over the ownership of domain names and several cases have been heard in the High Court of New Zealand, mainly at interlocutory level. Most of these cases have been decided in favour of a trade mark owner (whether a registered trade mark or not) seeking to prevent use and ongoing registration of domain names by cyber-squatters, or parties who the plaintiff believes has no right to hold or use the domain name.

The most notable cases are *Cadbury Confectionery Ltd v. The Domain Name Company Ltd.*,[230] *Oggi Advertising Ltd v. McKenzie*,[231] *New Zealand Post Ltd v. Leng*[232] and *DB Breweries Ltd v. The Domain Name Company Ltd.*[233] These cases have all settled or defendants have consented to orders sought by the plaintiffs, including injunctions.

3–193   The laws relevant to these disputes are trade mark infringement under the Trade Marks Act 1953, the tort of passing off, contravention of the Fair Trading Act 1986 (which prohibits misleading or deceptive conduct and false representations in trade) and other torts such as unlawful interference in trade.

Generally, plaintiffs have applied these laws to a domain name dispute in much the same way as any conventional dispute concerning alleged unauthorised use of a name or other "sign" by a trader.

Where the defendant is using the domain name, such as use of "nzpost.com" by the defendant in the *New Zealand Post* case, the plaintiff can readily argue misrepresentation, confusion or deception, and damage to its reputation. Even when the defendant has made no use of the domain name, and has merely registered the name with a view to selling it for a fee, plaintiffs have nevertheless argued misrepresentation, likelihood of confusion or deception, misleading conduct, and damage to their reputation and goodwill, *e.g.* in the *Oggi* case.

3–194   In the *DB* case, the High Court awarded DB Breweries Ltd the domain name "db.co.nz" after the plaintiff successfully argued that the letters "DB" were part of the company's intellectual property and that the company was commonly known by these letters.

ISOCNZ (the previous name for InternetNZ) and Domainz have also been involved in the dispute process. In the *Cadbury* case, the High Court ordered ISOCNZ to transfer to the trade mark owners certain domain names that incorporated their well-known trade marks and were held by the defendant. The plaintiff in the *Oggi* case joined ISOCNZ as a party to the proceeding, due to it accepting the domain name in question for registration by the defendants. ISOCNZ were ultimately found not to be liable.

Both InternetNZ and the Electronic Commerce Subcommittee of the New Zealand Law Society are currently considering whether there should be an alternative to the courts for resolving domain name disputes in New Zealand. Many see a localised version of ICANN's Uniform Domain Name Dispute Resolution Policy (UDRP) (as used to settle ".com" disputes) as being a viable arbitration alternative to expensive litigation. A working group green paper on the topic is expected to be issued in July or August 2001.

3.16 Non-United Kingdom domain names—Singapore

3.16.1 Registration

3–195   At present, the Singapore domain name registry is administered by the Singapore

Network Information Centre Pte Ltd, or SgNIC. This is a private limited company which is wholly owned by the Infocomm Development Authority of Singapore (iDA). The iDA is a statutory board created by the merger of the former National Computer Board (NCB) and Telecommunication Authority of Singapore (TAS). to build upon the synergies derived from the respective converging industries. One of its objectives is to promote the use of information technology in Singapore.

SgNIC took over Technet's domain name registry function when it decided to sell and thereafter transform Technet into Singapore's second commercial Internet Access Service Provider (IASP).

Besides the IDA, three current IASPs (CyberWay Pte Ltd, Pacific Internet Pte Ltd and Singapore Telecommunications Ltd) in Singapore set the policies and directions of SgNIC.

Applications to register a domain name must be made electronically. At present, there are six types of second level domain names under the ".sg" top level. The following three second level names would be most relevant to commercial organisations: **3–196**

> .com.sg Applicants for this domain must be commercial entities registered with the Singapore Registry of Companies and Businesses. A foreign company which is not so registered under Singapore law may only apply for such a domain name if it has a representative in Singapore, *e.g.* a distributor. This local representative must be authorised by the foreign company to apply for the domain name.
> .net.sg This domain is for network providers in Singapore. Essentially, all applicants under this category must have been licensed with the iDA.
> .org.sg Non-profit organisations would apply under this category. However, such organisations should also be registered with the Singapore Registry of Societies.

It is clear from the above that SgNIC's policy is not to allow the registration of a domain name in Singapore if the applicant/registrant has no presence in Singapore.

An applicant would also have to warrant that the use of the domain name requested would not infringe the trade mark of others.

3.16.2 Disputes

At the time of writing there does not appear to be any reported dispute or legal cases in Singapore concerning the ownership of domain names.   **3–197**

In the event that a dispute arises regarding the use and/or ownership of a domain name, the case would probably have to be dealt with under the existing Trade Marks Act, Copyright Act (if the domain name qualifies for copyright protection) and the common law (the tort of passing off).

The Singapore Trade Marks Act adopts the Nice classification for goods and services. That being the case, each trade mark would have to be registered for particular goods or services. It should be noted that, in general, the Trade Marks Act itself does not foreclose the possibility of two different persons owning the same or similar trade marks but for different and completely unrelated goods or services. In order to succeed in an infringement action against the domain name owner under the Trade Marks Act 1998, the trade marks owner would either have to show that (1) the domain name is *identical to* the registered mark in relation to goods or services which are *identical* with those for which it is registered, or (2) that the domain name is *confusingly* identical or similar to the registered trade mark in question, that the domain name (the allegedly infringing mark) has been used in the course of trade and that such use has been on identical or similar goods or services as those included in the specification of the registered trade mark. In the case of well known marks, the protection would extend to goods or services which are dissimilar to those which are covered by the registration, if confusion to the public is likely to exist.

3–198   If the cause of action is the tort of passing off, then the plaintiff would have to show that it has the requisite goodwill, that the domain name owner has misrepresented himself and/or his goods or services as the plaintiff or those of the plaintiff and that the plaintiff has suffered or will suffer damage. Whether use of a name *per se* will constitute an actionable misrepresentation is by no means a settled issue; there is, in general, no ownership of a name. Unless the plaintiff is of such high repute and he enjoys goodwill in connection with a business associated with his name, similarities between a domain name and the trading name of another may not necessarily mean that the trader would win a passing off suit.

3.17 Non-United Kingdom domain names—Sweden

3.17.1 Introduction

3–199   NIC-SE Network Information Centre Sweden AB ("NIC-SE") is the registry and co-ordinator of the Swedish national top level domain ("TLD") ".se". NIC-SE only registers domain names for organisations with a permanent business or operation within Sweden. The domain name has to reflect the name of the organisation as stated on the registration certificate issued by the Swedish authorities.

    Stiftelsen InternetInfrastruktur (the "II-Foundation") was formed in 1997 by the Swedish part of the Internet Society. The II-Foundation has in turn formed NIC-SE, which co-ordinates and runs the national register. An English translation of the current Swedish domain name regulations are available at www.iis.se/index_en.shtml. The regulations are set by the II-Foundation. The official regulations are in Swedish but there is an English translation.

    The II-Foundation has also founded Nämnden för Domännamnsregler (the "NDR") which has been given the task by the II-Foundation of maintaining and developing the regulations. Nämnden för Överklagande av Domännamn (the "NÖD") was also founded by the II-Foundation and is the final instance of appeal.

3.17.2 The domain name regulations

3–200   The II-Foundation's vision for the allocation of domain names under the ".se" top level domain is that

> *"The national top domain ".se" shall be the natural home address for all users who have a connection to Sweden. This shall be effected without any risk to or deterioration of future technical developments or the emergence of new services. The domain shall be distinguished by stability and security, at the same time as the administration shall be quick, flexible, predictable and unbureaucratic."*

The second version of the regulations is the one currently in force and the regulations came into force on April 3, 2000. According to the regulations all applications for domain names must be filed through one of NIC-SE's certified agents. There are currently around 240 certified agents and the complete list can be found at www.nic-se.se/registrering.shtml.

A domain name can only consist of the letters a-z, the numbers 0-9 and the hyphen. It   **3–201** must be started and ended by a letter or a digit, and cannot consist of just digits. The domain name should contain at least three characters, and have a maximum of 63. There is however a possibility to get acceptance for a shorter domain name if the applicant can make evident that the applicant is known to the general public under such shorter name. The domain name shall refer to an enterprise with a connection to Sweden, and reflect the name of the enterprise as this is stated on the registration certificate issued by the Swedish authorities.

Only one domain name can be registered per enterprise name. Since Sweden has a possibility for limited liability companies to register so called "secondary names" it is possible for an enterprise to have more than just one domain name.

An application will be turned down if the domain name (i) is identical to a previously   **3–202** registered domain name, (ii) if the domain name is evidently designed to cause offence or is in breach of good custom, (iii) if the domain name is designed to mislead the general public, or (iv) if the domain name consists solely of a geographical word.

NIC-SE will apply a "first come, first served" principle for the allocation of domain names, *i.e.* applications will be dealt with in the order they are received by NIC-SE.

Trademarks can only be registered under a sub-domain (www."trademark".tm.se). In order for a trademark to be registered it must be protected as (i) a national distinctive mark for goods or services, which is registered with the Swedish Patent and Registration Office (the "PRV") and has acquired legal force in Sweden, (ii) an international distinctive mark, which is protected in accordance with the so-called Madrid protocol and after designation have been registered *and* the registration has acquired legal force in Sweden, or (iii) a distinctive mark, which by means of registration, such as the European Community trade mark (the "EC mark") with the OHIM registration authority in Alicante, Spain, have legal force in Sweden.

There are also a number of other sub-domains, such as ".org.se" for non-profit organisations, ".parti.se" for political parties, ".press.se" for periodical publications (magazines) and ".pp.se" for private individuals.

NIC-SE is entitled to cancel a registration if the registered domain name should conflict   **3–203** with applicable laws or a final judgment or decision on infringement.

According to the II-Foundation the regulations for the registration of domain names under the ".se" TLD have been designed to provide "*stability and security*" by means, among other things, of the requirement that an applicant shall be able to demonstrate a registered right to a name in Sweden. The regulations have often been criticised for being too strict. However, according to a poll made during spring 2001 more than half (52 per cent) of the certified agents, participating in the poll, did not want to have more liberal regulations.

NDR, whose task is to develop the regulations, has proposed two different sets of new regulations, one whereby periodical publications and political parties should be entitled to register directly under the ".se" TLD and another one whereby the whole system is changed and the applicant himself is responsible for ensuring that the domain name is not infringing any third party right. In both proposals there is also a set of rules for dispute resolutions, which are similar to the ICANN's Uniform Domain-Name Dispute-Resolution Policy (the "UDRP").

3.17.3 Applicable legislation and disputes under the ".se" TLD

3–204   There is no specific domain name legislation in Sweden. However, the Swedish Trade Mark Act, the Swedish Trade Names Act and the Swedish Marketing Practices Act for example, all apply to the use of domain names.

Because of the strict regulations, the ".se" TLD has proven not to be interesting for so called "cybersquatters". There has not been any domain name disputes under the ".se" TLD. There are however some Swedish court decisions on domain names under the ".net" and ".com" TLDs. Recently a Swedish district court found that a company that had registered "volvo-tuning.com" and informed the public that it was in the business of tuning Volvo cars was infringing the rights of the car manufacturer Volvo.

Both the Swedish Trade Mark Act and the Swedish Trade Names Act prohibits unauthorised use of a protected name in the course of business. The mere registration of a domain name, without adding any content to the relevant domain, would probably not constitute an infringement according to the abovementioned acts. In the "volvo-tuning" case mentioned above the registrant had added some content trying to market its services and it was found that the registrant was infringing another party's right. The registrant was ordered by the court either to de-register or change the domain name under a penalty.

3–205   Furthermore, the Swedish Marketing Practices Act could be used in some cases since it states that all marketing practices must be consistent with generally accepted marketing practices and otherwise fair in relation to consumers and undertakings. For example if someone uses a trademark belonging to someone else and such use causes confusion as to the origin of a product in its marketing, it can be seen as a violation of the requirement referred to above.

3.18 Non-United Kingdom domain names—Switzerland

3.18.1 Status of Switzerland's domain name registry

3–206   In Switzerland the registration of domain names is carried out by SWITCH, a foundation constituted under private law. The main function of SWITCH is to operate high–performance telecommunications networks for Switzerland's universities. However, since 1987 SWITCH has also been responsible for the registration of second-level domain names in Switzerland (the ".ch" domain) and since 1993 has also had responsibility for the Principality of Liechtenstein (the ".li" domain). Domain name registration is managed by a department within SWITCH, which is partly autonomous.

3.18.2 General description of Switzerland's domain name system

3–207   Domain names can be registered both by private individuals and by companies subject to the same conditions. Individuals and companies resident outside Switzerland may also register.

A one-off registration fee and annual maintenance charges are payable in return for registration. In the event of late payment, SWITCH reserves the right to delete the domain name in question if the overdue payment is not received despite repeated reminders.

3–208   Unlike the ".uk" or ".fr" domains in the United Kingdom and France, the ".ch" domain is not subdivided into special sub-domains for companies, public bodies, universities or private individuals, for example. The domain name may be constituted as desired, provided that it consists of a minimum of three and a maximum of 24 characters and abides by the general rules which apply for technical reasons in relation to domain names (*e.g.* no special characters other than hyphens may be used). There is no limitation on the number of domain names which may be registered for a particular owner. However, in its policy, SWITCH reserves the right to refuse applications for registration which are clearly improper.

SWITCH can register both active and inactive domain names. "Inactive" means that a domain name is registered for an individual or a company and thus cannot be registered by any third party even though the domain name concerned is not yet being effectively used.

The conditions which have to be observed and the charges payable have been set out by SWITCH in two policies which are published on the SWITCH web site.[234]

Discussions are currently in progress in Switzerland on the revision of the Ordinance on address elements, the so-called Verordnung über Adressierungselemente (AEFV) issued by BAKOM, the Federal Office for Communications. One of the main aims of the revision is to amend the regulations governing the TLD ".ch". There will be a Registry operating a central database containing the registered domain names together with several accredited Registrars, who will handle registration of domain names and conclude contracts with holders of domain names.   **3–209**

During the course of the consultation procedure it has become clear that the main Internet Service Providers in Switzerland have only minimal interest in acting as Registrars in Switzerland. Therefore, it is uncertain whether there will be more than one Registrar in Switzerland.

3.18.3 Disputes

SWITCH registers domain names on a "first come—first served" basis. In so doing it does not carry out any check on the entitlement of the applicant to the domain name in question, eg. to establish whether the applicant is the owner of an identical or similar trademark or trade name. The applicant himself/itself is solely responsible for ensuring that the rights of third parties are not infringed.   **3–210**

SWITCH will only check in the case of names of villages, towns, districts and cantons whether the relevant local authority has given its consent to registration. However, although it is not obliged to do so, SWITCH reserves the right to issue a warning in the case of registration applications of which the legality is doubtful. But if the applicant insists on registering after receiving such a warning, the registration will proceed.

Disputes arising in relation to domain names must be argued exclusively in court directly between the registered domain name owner and the third party, which believes its rights have been infringed. SWITCH will only delete a domain name after the dispute has been settled by means of a corresponding, legally valid judgment.

3.18.4 Legal cases in Switzerland

The number of judgments in Switzerland on cases involving domain names is, compared with Germany, somewhat low. In most cases, disputes are settled out of court.   **3–211**

Mention can be made of two Supreme Court judgements by the Swiss Federal Court. In a decision on February 11, 1999 in the case of *"rytz.ch"* the Federal Court ruled that a company called Rytz Industriebau AG, which had been registered under this name in the Commercial Register since 1983, might continue to use the domain name "rytz.ch" although another company, Rytz et Cie SA, had registered the trademark "Rytz" in 1995. The Court came to this decision on the grounds of a balance of interests: It took the view that it would be unacceptable, if a company who had openly used the same family name for the last twenty years were unable to use this name as a domain name solely because of the existence of a more recent trademark.

3–212   The second case involving a comment by the Swiss Federal Court on the issue of domain names was its decision of May 2, 2000 in the case of *"berneroberland.ch"*. This domain name had been registered in 1996 by an IT company who had already registered other domain names with geographic designations from the well-known tourist region of Berner Oberland. "Berner Oberland Tourismus", the association representing tourist bodies in the Berner Oberland, successfully applied for a deletion of the registration. In this particular case the Swiss Federal Court upheld a judgment by a lower court, the commercial court for the canton of Berne. The Swiss Federal Court concluded that the use of the domain name created a risk of confusion—as defined by law of unfair competition—with the applicant, "Berner Oberland Tourismus". This was because users searching for tourist products would assume that behind the domain name "berner-oberland.ch" was an official tourism provider representing the entire region of the Berner Oberland. Moreover, this was a reasonable assumption, because official tourist bodies in many other regions and locations operate web sites both inside and outside Switzerland under domain names that are the same as their geographic designation.

There have also been cases in the canton courts, which sought the legal protection afforded by temporary injunctions.

3–213   In the case of *"artprotect.ch"* the Court upheld an application for a temporary injunction. In this instance the current holder of the domain name "artprotect.ch" was required to desist from using a domain name and assign it to the applicant. The applicant had entered into an agreement with the defendant regarding the creation of a database and web site for lost and stolen works of art. On the basis of this agreement the defendant registered the domain name "artprotect.ch". For its part the applicant filed the trademark "Artprotect". Following a difference of opinion between the parties the domain name was deactivated by the defendant (in whose name it had originally been registered) with the result that customers of the applicant were no longer able to access the database. In its decision on March 15, 1999 the Court of first instance dismissed a claim on the basis of trademark law, as it did not regard the mere registration of a domain name as a use that represented a breach of trademark law. However, it upheld a claim under competition law. The refusal of the defendant to release the domain name represented a major obstacle to the applicant's ability to operate on the market. By deactivating the domain name the defendant created a situation in which existing customers of the applicant were no longer able to access the database from the Internet address that they had previously been using. In addition, by retaining the domain name the defendant was preventing access to the applicant in the future. The applicant's claim was also protected under contract law. Under the terms of the contract on the planning and creation of the web site the defendant, in addition to setting up the web site, was also obliged to lodge the necessary applications with the registration body. In other words the court upheld the claim by the applicant that the defendant was required to register the applicant as the holder of the domain name "artprotect.ch". In its ruling of May 7, 1999 the court of second instance in Berne upheld the decision of the lower court and ordered the defendant to re-register "artprotect.ch" in the name of the applicant.

In the case of *"hotmail.ch"*, which was the subject of a legally binding ruling by the **3–214** Court of first instance on May 2, 2000, Microsoft brought an action against an IT firm located in the canton of Basel-Landschaft. The latter had registered in its name the domain name "hotmail.ch". Microsoft operated a free email service on the Internet called Hotmail. Microsoft was able to demonstrate that it had a trademark for such services with priority dating from April 10, 1997, whereas the domain name had not been registered until August 13, 1997. Not surprisingly the Court agreed that the plaintiff's trademark had been infringed and made it clear that the use of a third party's trademark represented at least an infringement of trademark law, provided that the use was for the purpose of selling goods or services. Contrary to the argument put forward by the defendant in its defence the Court did not regard the term "hotmail" as public property and so it upheld the protectability of the trademark. Finally, in terms of the position under competition law it ruled that the use of a third-party's trading name as a domain was likely to result in confusion, because users, who entered the name "hotmail" into a search engine or typed it in direct, would not be directed to the plaintiff's web site, as they might have expected.

In a case of "luzern.ch", which is still pending, the issue is again that of the protection **3–215** of a geographic designation as a domain name. On one side is the city of Lucerne, who would like to use their name as a domain name and on the other side a private company, who has been using the name "luzern.ch" for years and operates a portal with that name on the subject of Lucerne. The Higher Regional Court for the canton of Lucerne has already published its response to an application for a temporary injunction and ordered the private company—citing *inter alia* the law of unfair competition and the law on names—to refrain from offering email addresses at "@luzern.ch" to third parties and operating the associated mail server.

3.18.5 Relevant Laws

The laws which are relevant to domain name disputes are trademark law, trade name **3–216** law, the law of names and the law relating to unfair competition.

The owner of a trademark is protected against the use of a domain name which is identical or similar to its trademark for designating a web site which displays advertising or offers for goods or services which are identical or similar to the goods or services for which the trademark is registered. However, trademark law does not offer any protection if the domain name was registered and used before the trademark was registered. Trademark protection is not enforceable against brands, which have been used prior to trademark registration to the extent of this prior use. There has not yet been a judicial decision as to whether trademark law offers protection against the simple registration of a similar domain name (without using it in the context of advertising or offering goods or services) and thus specifically against domain name grabbing.

Protection for the trade names entered in the Commercial Register exists only in **3–217** relation to identical or similar brands which are also used as the name of companies. The extent to which a domain name can be understood to be the name of a company due to the circumstances of its use, and thus the extent to which trade name law can be applied at all, has to be considered in each individual case.

The law of names protects private individuals and companies against the use of their names or substantial parts of their names by third parties, which use the names or parts of names as domain names. There has not yet been a judicial decision under the law of names as to whether the simple registration of a name as a domain name, without its active use, constitutes an infringement of the law of names. However, as the rightful bearer of a name has a claim to the use of its name, and as the law of names provides for a special complaint if the use of a name is contested, actions against domain name grabbing can be brought on the basis of the law of names.

3–218　　In addition to the possibility of protection for trademarks, tradenames and names mentioned above, there is protection under the Federal Law against Unfair Competition. Specifically, generating the risk of potential confusion through the use of brands which are identical or similar to those used by others, is deemed to be unfair.

This protection is very important for all brands which are not registered as trademarks and for trademarks which are only registered abroad but not in Switzerland, but are at least familiar here.

Under the terms of the Law against Unfair Competition, it is not only the generation of confusion which is unfair. Any conduct which results in the influencing of competition through unfair means is prohibited. It can therefore be assumed that domain name grabbing is unfair. This is because it makes it impossible for the rightful owner of a certain brand to register this as its domain name, a situation which may be detrimental to its market position.

3.19 Non-U.K. domain names—USA

3–219　　The conflict between the current system of domain name registration and the rights of trademark holders is the subject of much discussion. This issue has given rise to a growing number of disputes between trademark holders and registrants of domain names. In 1999, the domain name management system and the domain name dispute resolution process were significantly modified and a new United States cybersquatting law was enacted. Disputes continue to arise.[235]

3.19.1 Domain names

3–220　　A domain name serves a dual purpose. It marks the location of a Web site within cyberspace, much like a postal address in the real world, but it may also indicate to users some information as to the content of the site, and, in instances of well-known trade names or trademarks, may provide information as to the source of the contents of the site.

Unlike the traditional trademark environment, however, where identical trademarks can co-exist in different markets, in the current domain name system a unique trademark can only be used by one entity within a particular top-level domain (*e.g.*, ".com"). For example, there can only be one "www.apple.com" in cyberspace, but there could be trademarks used by Apple Computers, the Apple Grocery Store, Apple Clothing and Apple Records for their separate products without creating consumer confusion as to source.

Internet users often rely on domain names to search for particular home pages on the World Wide Web and other resources on the Internet. Thus, the use of a well–known trademark in a domain name can be an important source of visitors to a given Web site. The number of disputes over the registration of known trademarks as domain names has escalated in the past several years.

3.19.2 Registration

While most of the controversy in the United States is focused on the generic top-level   **3–221**
domains (gTLDs),[236] such as ".com", the U.S., like most other countries, has its own
country-code top-level domain (ccTLD), designated by ".us".[237] As of June 2001, the U.S.
top-level domain is administered by VeriSign, Inc., which is also the registry for the
".com," ".net," and ".org" gTLDs. With few exceptions, the naming hierarchy under the
".us" TLD is based on geography: the second-level domain corresponds to a state, the
third-level domain to a locality, such as a city or county, and the fourth-level domain to
an organization or individual. For example, under this system, the domain name of New
York City's Metropolitan Transportation Authority is "mta.nyc.ny.us." Although any
computer in the U.S. may be registered under the ".us" TLD, it has been unpopular with
businesses. Instead, state and local government entities, libraries and local public schools
have been the predominate users.

In the future, the ".us" TLD may become more widely used. On June 12, 2001 the U.S.
Department of Commerce issued a Request for Quotations (RFQ) for management and
coordination of the ".us" TLD. One of its stated objectives in doing so is to "promote
increased use of the '.us' TLD by the Internet community of the United States." This RFQ
includes new functions that will facilitate the registration of second-level domains
directly under the ".us" TLD. Thus, rather than registering a domain name of
"company.city.state.us," one may someday be able to register simply as "company.us."

3.19.3 ICANN domain name dispute resolution policy

On October 24, 1999, the Internet Corporation for Assigned Names and Numbers   **3–222**
(ICANN) adopted the Uniform Domain Name Dispute Resolution Policy (UDRP), which
incorporates by reference the Rules for Uniform Domain Name Dispute Resolution
Policy.[238] The policy and rules provide mechanisms to contest the propriety of domain
name registrations in the ".com," ".net," and ".org" generic TLDs and certain country-
code TLDs.[239]

The policy adopted by ICANN sets forth an arbitration-like procedure for resolving
domain name disputes. To invoke the policy, a complainant must describe the grounds
on which the complaint is made including in particular: "(1) the manner in which the
domain name(s) is/are identical or confusingly similar to a trademark or services mark in
which the [c]omplainant has rights; and (2) why the Respondent (domain name holder)
should be considered as having no rights or legitimate interests in respect of the domain
name(s) that is/are the subject of the complaint; and (3) why the domain name(s) should
be considered as having been registered in bad faith."[240] In order to prevail, a
complainant must prove each of these three elements. When a complainant asserts the
presence of these three elements, the registrant is required to submit to the mandatory
administrative proceeding. A trademark holder is not required to have a trademark
registration in order to initiate the dispute resolution process, *i.e.* even common law
trademark right-holders may invoke ICANN's dispute resolution policy against alleged
infringers who adopt confusingly similar variations of a common law mark.

The Policy sets forth a number of factors to be considered as evidence of registration   **3–223**
and use in bad faith. Such factors include: (1) facts indicating that the registrant has
registered the domain name "primarily for the purpose of selling, renting, or otherwise
transferring the domain name registration to the complainant who is the owner of the

trademark or service mark or to a competitor of that complainant, for valuable consideration in excess of [the registrant's] documented out-of-pocket costs directly related to the domain name;" (2) facts indicating that the registrant has "registered the domain name in order to prevent the owner of the trademark or service mark from reflecting the mark in a corresponding domain name" provided that the registrant has "engaged in a pattern of such conduct;" (3) facts indicating the registrant has registered the domain name "primarily for the purpose of disrupting the business of a competitor;" or (4) facts indicating that the registrant, by using the domain name, intentionally attempted to attract, for commercial gain, Internet users to its web site or other on-line location, "by creating a likelihood of confusion with the complainant's mark as to the source, sponsorship, affiliation, or endorsement" of the registrant's web site or location, or of a product or service on its web site or location.[241] Remedies under the ICANN policy are limited to the cancellation or transfer of an infringing domain name.

3.19.4 Relationship between UDRP proceedings and remedies under other U.S. law

3–224　　Domain name dispute remedies for trademark owners in the U.S. are not limited to UDRP proceedings. In fact, even during the pendency of a UDRP proceeding, a mark owner may be able to utilise judicial remedies. For example, in *BroadBridge Media LLC v. Hypercd.com*,[242] the plaintiff had registered the "hypercd.com" domain name and then mistakenly allowed it to lapse, whereupon an individual in Canada registered the name and refused during subsequent negotiations to relinquish it back to plaintiff. The plaintiff instituted a UDRP proceeding contesting the registration and simultaneously filed an *in rem* proceeding under the Anticybersquatting Consumer Protection Act (ACPA)[243] seeking immediate return of the domain name.

In addressing plaintiff's motion for preliminary relief, the court in *BroadBridge* cited UDRP 4(k) and UDRP Rule 18 in concluding that the plaintiff had not waived its right to proceed in federal court by filing the UDRP proceeding. In fact, the court noted that by the time of the judicial hearing, the arbitration panel had exercised its discretion to suspend the administrative proceeding pending the outcome of the litigation. Under the unique circumstances of the case, including the fact that the plaintiff had already expended substantial funds in reliance on its use of the domain name and that plaintiff's ability to provide customer support through its "hypercd.com" e-mail address was impaired, the court ordered the immediate transfer of the domain name back to plaintiff.[244]

3–225　　*Weber-Stephen Products Co. v. Armitage Hardware*,[245] was the first federal case to touch on the question of what weight should be given to the decisions of UDRP arbitrators. In that case, the defendant sought to stay plaintiff's UDRP proceeding, arguing that it would be irreparably harmed if the decision of the arbitrators foreclosed its ability to litigate its defenses in the federal court proceeding. The district court refused to stay the UDRP proceeding, concluding that the proceeding would not harm the interests of the defendant because the court was not bound by the decision of the UDRP arbitrators. The court left open the issue, however, of what weight, "if any," it would give to the arbitration decision once it was rendered.[246]

One U.S. court that was presented squarely with the deference issue, *Referee Enterprises v. Planet Ref Inc.*,[247] appears to have accorded no deference at all to the UDRP proceeding. The plaintiff Referee Enterprises, owner of the mark "Referee" for a magazine, was the unsuccessful complainant in a UDRP proceeding against the assignee of the "eReferee.com," "eReferee.net" and "eReferee.org" domain name registrations. The UDRP arbitrator ruled that Planet Ref had a legitimate interest in the domain names and was not using them in bad faith.[248] Referee Enterprises then filed an action in federal court under the Lanham Act claiming trademark infringement, dilution, unfair competition and false designation of origin in the defendant's use of the eReferee domain names. In January 2001, the federal district court reversed the outcome of the UDRP proceeding and preliminarily enjoined Planet Ref from any use of the eReferee domain names, as well as any other domain name including the term "referee" in any form. The court's summary order contains no reference to the UDRP proceeding, suggesting both by the contrary result and the absence of discussion that it was given no deference whatsoever.

Parisi v. Netlearning Inc.[249] confirmed the development that had been apparent in these earlier decisions: US courts will not consider themselves bound by the decisions of UDRP arbitrators. In *Parisi*, the plaintiff, holder of the "netlearning.com" domain name, sought a declaration of lawful use under the ACPA and a declaration of non-infringement under the Lanham Act. The defendant, Netlearning, Inc., argued that it was entitled to the disputed domain name pursuant to the prior decision of a UDRP panel[250] and that the plaintiff's complaint constituted an improper motion to vacate an arbitration award in violation of the Federal Arbitration Act (FAA).[251] The U.S. District Court for the Eastern District of Virginia ruled that, among other things, ICANN's UDRP was intended to permit "comprehensive, de novo" court review of arbitration decisions, and that the FAA did not bar the relief sought by the plaintiff. The court therefore refused to dismiss the plaintiff's complaint.

3–226

3.19.5 The Anticybersquatting Consumer Protection Act

In 1999, the U.S. Congress passed the Anticybersquatting Consumer Protection Act (ACPA),[252] amending §43 of the Trademark Act of 1946 (also known as the Lanham Act). The ACPA establishes that a person who registers, traffics in or uses a domain name that is identical or confusingly similar to a protected mark, or that is dilutive of a famous mark, will be subject to civil liability if he has a bad faith intent to profit from that mark.[253]

3–227

The Act outlines nine factors that may lead to a finding of bad faith. A court may consider, but is not limited to consideration of, any of the following factors[254]:

- any rights to the domain name the registrant may have;

- whether the domain name consists of the registrant's legal name or a name by which the registrant is known;

- any prior use of the domain name by the registrant in connection with the bona fide offering of goods or services;

- the registrant's bona fide non-commercial or fair use of the mark in a site accessible under the domain name;

- any intent on the part of the registrant to divert consumers from the mark owner's site to a location that will harm the goodwill of the mark owner;

- any offer made by the registrant to sell the domain name, without having used the domain name, as well as any pattern of this behaviour;

- the registrant's provision of false contact information when applying for the registration of the domain name, the registrant's intentional failure to maintain accurate contact information, or the registrant's prior conduct indicating a pattern of such conduct;

- whether the registrant has registered multiple domain names that are identical or confusingly similar to protected marks, or which dilute famous marks; and

- the extent to which the mark incorporated in the person's domain name registration is or is not distinctive and famous.

The Act provides that there shall be no finding of bad faith if the court determines that the registrant reasonably believed the use of the domain name was fair or was otherwise lawful.[255]

3–228   A finding of liability may lead to forfeiture or cancellation of the domain name, or transfer of the domain name to the owner of the mark.[256] Moreover, plaintiffs are entitled to actual damages and profits, or if they so elect at any time prior to a final judgement, statutory damages in the amount of not less than $1000 and not greater than $100,000 per domain name.[257]

The Act specifically affords protection to personal names.[258] A person who (1) registers a domain name consisting of, or similar to, the name of another living person, (2) without that person's consent, and (3) with the specific intent to profit from that person's name by selling the domain name to that person or to any third party, will be subject to civil liability.[259] However, an exception exists for a person who registers such a domain name in good faith if: (1) the name is used with, affiliated with, or related to a copyrighted work, (2) the person registering the name is the copyright owner or licensee of the work, (3) the person intends to sell the domain name in conjunction with the lawful exploitation of the work, and (4) such registration is not prohibited by contract between the registrant and the named person.[260] Successful plaintiffs are entitled to injunctive relief and, at the court's discretion, costs and attorney fees.[261]

3–229   An additional right created by the Act is the right of a mark owner to file an *in rem* action against the domain name itself (as opposed to the registrant of the domain).[262] An *in rem* action can be brought only if *in personam* (i.e., personal) jurisdiction cannot be obtained or if the appropriate defendant can not be found after notice is sent and published by means directed by the court.[263] Remedies in an *in rem* action are limited to forfeiture, cancellation or transfer of the domain name.[264]

Under the Act, a domain name registrar, domain name registry, or other domain name registration authority is not liable for damages for the registration or maintenance of a domain name for another absent a showing of bad faith intent to profit from such registration or maintenance of the domain name.[265]

3.19.6 Disputes under the ACPA

3–230   Prior to enactment of the ACPA, the central legal tools for resolving domain name disputes were federal trademark infringement and anti-dilution statutes.[266] However, this legal framework was often considered to be inadequate and to provide unsatisfying results.[267] The ACPA has removed what some had considered to be burdensome hurdles, such as proving that the alleged Internet infringer made "commercial use" of the registered mark. The Act has been invoked regularly to deal with domain name disputes.[268]

In one of the first appellate court rulings under the ACPA, a panel of the United States Court of Appeals for the Second Circuit in *Sporty's Farm L.L.C. v. Sportsman's Market Inc.*[269] ruled unanimously that a Christmas tree company's domain name, "sportys.com," was registered with a bad faith intent to profit from a distinctive mark. "Sporty's" was a trademark registered by a mail order company, Sportsman's Farm, in conjunction with its aviation products. "Sportys.com" was registered by another aviation catalog company, then sold to a wholly-owned subsidiary called Sporty's Farm, which sold Christmas trees.

After a bench trial to resolve the ensuing domain name dispute, the district court ordered Sporty's Farm to relinquish the domain name, but limited the judgement on Sportsman's Market's trademark dilution claims to such injunctive relief. On appeal by both parties, the Second Circuit panel applied the then-new anticybersquatting law, finding it "clear that the new law was adopted specifically to provide courts with a preferable alternative to stretching federal dilution law when dealing with cybersquatting cases." The panel affirmed the judgement below, holding that "sporty's" was a distinctive mark, and that the domain name was "confusingly similar" to the mark. On the issue of bad faith, the court found overwhelming evidence that "sportys.com" was registered in the first place to keep Sportsman's from using that domain name, and that the Christmas tree subsidiary was created so that the domain name could then be used in a commercial fashion to protect against infringement claims. The Second Circuit panel also found the injunction issued by the district court to be proper under the ACPA, but that damages under the Act were unavailable because "sportys.com" was registered and used by Sporty's Farm prior to the passage of the Act.

3–231

In another case, the court in *Virtual Works, Inc. v. Volkswagen of America, Inc.*[270] found that plaintiff had violated the ACPA by registering a domain name with a bad-faith intent to profit from a previously registered trademark. The court found the following to be direct evidence of bad faith: (1) Virtual Works' statement at deposition that, when registering "vw.net," two of its principals acknowledged that "vw.net" might be confused with Volkswagen and left open the possibility of someday selling the domain for "a lot of money"; and (2) the terms of Virtual Works' offer to sell the domain to Volkswagen, where it threatened to sell the domain at auction to the highest bidder unless Volkswagen made Virtual Works an offer within 24 hours. In addition, the court found the following facts to be circumstantial evidence of bad faith: (1) the famousness of the VW mark; (2) the similarity of "vw.net" to the VW mark; (3) the admission that Virtual Works never once did business as VW nor identified itself as such; and (4) the availability of "vwi.org" and "vwi.net" at the time Virtual Works registered "vw.net," either of which name would have satisfied Virtual Works' own stated criterion of registering a domain name that used only two or three letters, but would have eliminated any risk of confusion with respect to the VW mark.

3–232

Another way in which cybersquatters have attempted to profit from famous marks is by "typosquatting", *i.e.* registering likely misspellings of those marks. In *Shields v. Zuccarini*,[271] the United States Court of Appeals for the Third Circuit upheld a lower court's grant of summary judgement, a permanent injunction, and award of statutory damages and attorneys' fees to plaintiff under the ACPA. The defendant had registered five variations of plaintiff's web site "joecartoon.com": "joescartoon.com," "joecarton.-com," "joescartons.com," "joescartoons.com" and "cartoonjoe.com." Once a user entered one of these sites, he was unable to exit without clicking through a series of

3–233

advertisements, each of which paid between ten and twenty-five cents to defendant. The court found the defendant's behaviour to be a "classic example of a specific practice the ACPA was designed to prohibit."

3.19.7 Damage awards

3–234 Domain name disputes have occasionally resulted in substantial damage awards.[272] For example, in *Kremen v. Cohen*,[273] the court awarded $65 million for damages resulting from fraud and forgery in connection with the appropriation of the "sex.com" domain name. In that case, the defendant fraudulently obtained the registration of the domain name by sending a forged letter to Network Solutions, Inc., the domain name registrar. The court found that defendant had reaped profits exceeding $40 million in the five years he operated the "sex.com" web site. The damage award included $25 million in punitive damages.

  In *E-Cards v. King*[274] E-Cards, a San Francisco-based electronic greeting card company, was awarded $4 million by a jury in the Northern District of California, which found that a Canadian competitor, Ecards.com, had engaged in unfair competition. According to the companies' web sites, E-Cards was founded in 1995, and Ecards.com was started in 1996. The jury apparently agreed with E-Cards' charge that the similarity of the names was causing confusion in the marketplace, although the verdict may be viewed as granting the plaintiff exclusive rights to a generic term.[275]

3.19.8 Domain names used for criticism or as parody

3–235 Companies have attempted to use the ACPA, traditional trademark law and the UDRP to stop web sites that are critical of their products or services, but with mixed results. The developing trend appears to be that courts will permit domain names to be used for sites that are used exclusively to criticize or parody the trademark owner, but will afford less protection to sites that directly or indirectly engage in some type of commercial activity.

  For example, in *Northland Insurance Cos. v. Blaylock*,[276] a federal district court declined to grant preliminary relief to Northland Insurance Companies, the owner of the mark "Northland Insurance" in a suit brought against an individual who maintained a web site critical of the company at "www.northlandinsurance.com." The plaintiff, which maintained its own web site at "www.northlandins.com," sought relief under the ACPA, common law of trademark infringement, and federal and state trademark anti-dilution statutes. The domain name in question linked to a second web site containing an account of the defendant's ongoing insurance claim disputes with the company. The defendant admitted that he had chosen the domain name deliberately to attract the attention of Internet users who were searching for the plaintiff's web site. The site offered no competitive products, nor did it solicit any commercial activity. The district court rejected plaintiff's argument that the use of the domain name created "initial interest" confusion based upon its close proximity to the domain name of the plaintiff's actual web site because, the court found, the defendant did not appear situated to benefit financially or commercially from his web site. The court also rejected the plaintiff's ACPA claim on the ground that there was insufficient evidence in the record that the defendant intended to profit from the sale of the domain name or to use it for any purpose other than commentary.[277]

In contrast, the court in *People for the Ethical Treatment of Animals v. Doughy*[278] ordered   **3–236**
the owner of the domain name "peta.org" to relinquish the registration to the non-profit
organisation People for the Ethical Treatment of Animals (PETA), even though he
claimed his web site was a parody. The defendant's web site contained information
captioned "People Eating Tasty Animals" and included a statement that the purpose of
the web site was to be a "resource for those who enjoy eating meat, wearing fur and
leather, hunting, and the fruits of scientific research." The site also contained numerous
links to commercial web sites advertising leather goods and meats. The court found that
the inclusion of even one link to another commercial site was sufficient to constitute a
commercial use of the plaintiff's registered mark, even though the defendant himself did
not actually place goods and services in the stream of commerce. The defendant was
found to have both diluted and blurred the PETA mark, and to have caused actual
economic harm to the PETA mark by lessening its selling power as an advertising agent
for PETA's goods and services.

3.19.9 State anticybersquatting statutes

State anticybersquatting statutes need to be considered as well. For example, in August   **3–237**
2000, California enacted an anticybersquatting law that makes it unlawful for a person
acting in bad faith to register, use or traffic in an Internet domain name that is identical or
confusingly similar to the personal name of another living person or "deceased
personality."[279] The legislation is intended to apply to personal names that are not
necessarily famous or registered as trademarks and thus may not fall under the federal
ACPA. The statute includes a list of factors to be used in evaluating "bad faith" which is
nearly identical to the list of factors in the federal ACPA. The remedies for violation of the
law include injunctive relief, restitution and civil penalties of up to $2,500 per violation.[280]

3.19.10 Meta tags and other forms of Internet trademark infringement

Meta tags are text embedded in the hypertext markup language (HTML) used to create   **3–238**
web sites. The tags, which are not visible to viewers of a web page but can be seen by
viewing the source of the HTML, contain data such as keywords that are used by search
engines to locate web sites.
      Courts have ruled that a defendant who uses someone else's trademark in meta tags or
in some other unauthorised way in conjunction with e-commerce may be infringing the
trademark.[281] For example, in *Brookfield Communications v. West Coast Entertainment*,[282] the
U.S. Court of Appeals for the Ninth Circuit held that the defendant's use of the plaintiff's
registered service mark "moviebuff" in its meta tags caused "initial interest" confusion
under the Lanham Act. The defendant owned the trademark "The Movie Buff's Movie
Store," registered the domain name "moviebuff.com," and used "moviebuff" in its web
site meta tags. Brookfield owned the trademark "Moviebuff" and sued for trademark
infringement and unfair competition. The court held that "by using 'moviebuff.com' or
'MovieBuff' to divert people looking for 'MovieBuff' to its web site, West Coast
improperly benefits from the goodwill that Brookfield developed in its mark." The court
compared the use of another's trademarks in one's meta tags to Company A posting a
sign on the highway indicating that Company B's store is at Exit 7 (while Company B is
really at Exit 8), hoping that consumers who get off at Exit 7 looking for Company B will

see Company A's store and shop there.

3–239   In another case involving meta tags, *Eli Lilly & Co. v. Natural Answers Inc.*,[283] the United States Court of Appeals for the Seventh Circuit upheld the district court's grant of a preliminary injunction sought by Eli Lilly & Co., manufacturer of Prozac, a prescription drug used to treat clinical depression. The district court enjoined the defendant Natural Answers' use of the name "Herbrozac" on a non-prescription, herbal "mood elevator" marketed on the defendant's web site. The web site contained source code that included the term "Prozac" as a meta tag, and described Herbrozac as "a powerful, and effective all-natural and herbal formula alternative to the prescription drug Prozac." Citing the phonetic similarity of Herbrozac to Prozac, as well as the defendant's references to Prozac in the web site meta tags, the district court found a risk of initial interest confusion under the Lanham Act. On appeal, the circuit court found that the use of Prozac in the meta tags, while not evidence of actual confusion, was nevertheless "significant evidence" of the defendant's intent to confuse and mislead: "The fact that one actively pursues an objective greatly increases the chances that the objective will be achieved."[284] In so ruling, the court cited the *Brookfield Communications* opinion for its comparison of defendant's use of meta tags to "posting a sign with another's trademark in front of one's store."

3–240   The use of another's trademark in meta tags does not always constitute infringement. In *Playboy Enterprises Inc. v. Terri Welles Inc.*,[285] the defendant was a model who had appeared in *Playboy* magazine several times, had been awarded the title of "Playmate of the Year 1981," and had identified herself as a "playmate" and a "playmate of the year" since 1980 with plaintiff's knowledge. The code for defendant's web site at http:// www.terriwelles.com included the words "Playboy," "Playmate" and "Playboy Playmate of the Year 1981" in the meta tags. Playboy, which owned federally registered trademarks for the terms "Playboy," "Playmate" and "Playmate of the Year" alleged, among other things, that defendant's use of Playboy's registered trademarks in its meta tags infringed Playboy's trademarks by causing "initial interest confusion." The court disagreed, finding "fair use" in defendant's use of the words in a descriptive sense, with no intent to deceive. The court noted that if someone was attempting to find Welles's web site, but didn't remember her name, they might enter key words such as "Playboy," "Playmate" or "Playboy Playmate of the Year 1981" because such terms "identify her source of recognition to the public." While crafting its analysis, the court cautioned that it must "be careful to give consumers the freedom to locate desired sites while protecting the integrity of trademarks and trade names."[286]

3–241   *Playboy Enterprises Inc. v. Netscape Communications*[287] involves a different use of plaintiff's trademarks on the Internet. In this case, which Playboy is currently appealing, the court granted defendants' motions for summary judgement on Playboy's trademark infringement, trademark dilution and unfair competition claims against Excite, Inc. and Netscape Communications. Playboy alleged that Excite and Netscape sold Playboy's trademarks to hard-core pornography advertisers and then targeted their banner ads to appear whenever a user searched for "Playboy" or "Playmate" on defendants' search engines. The court denied Playboy's claim of trademark dilution, ruling that the defendants did not make a trademark use of Playboy's marks. In addition, while the court admitted Playboy's survey evidence showing that consumers were confused by the banner ads, it nonetheless ruled that defendants' use of Playboy's trademarks created no likelihood that consumers would be confused as to the source of defendant's search services.

1. The most recent considered judicial discussion of these issues is in *Euromarket Designs Inc. v. Peters and another* [2001] F.S.R. 288, also known as the *Crate & Barrel* case.
2. This is not to downplay the usefulness of rights other than registered trade marks in pursuing Internet infringers. In the United Kingdom, passing off has proved to be a particularly flexible and potent weapon against infringers such as domain name pirates (see the discussion of domain name disputes in the main text).
3. See discussion in Chapter 6, contrasting the effect of U.K. spillover circulation in defamation (liability) and trade mark infringement (no liability) respectively.
4. *Crate & Barrel* (above).
5. *ibid.*
6. It is increasingly common, for instance, to associate a tune with the home page of a web site. This plays through the user's computer loudspeakers as the page is loaded. While it may be debatable whether such practices attract or deter users, such tunes would certainly be candidates for registration as trade marks.
7. See, for example *Bensusan Restaurant Corporation v. King* (126 F. 3d 25, 1997 U.S. App. LEXIS 23742).
8. See *e.g. Playboy Enterprises Inc. v. Chuckleberry Publishing, Inc* 939 F. Supp. 1032 (SDNY 1996), a cross-border US/Italian dispute in which the court had to interpret a previous settlement agreement between the protagonists.
9. See *e.g. Prince plc v. Prince Sports Group, Inc* [1998] F.S.R. 21, discussed in the main text below. In the case of a well-known trade mark, the trade mark owner may be in a position to assert rights in respect of goods or services different from those for which the mark is registered. See the discussion of s. 10(3) of the Trade Marks Act 1994 in the main text below.
10. See www.scrabble.com for an example of a split mark web entry page.
11. Above.
12. Any such agreement, and indeed, notices concerning the non-availability of goods and services in particular countries, would need to be prepared with due to regard to any constraints imposed by competition law.
13. *Protection of Industrial Property Rights in Relation to the Use of Signs on the Internet* SCT/5/2, WIPO Standing Committee on the Law of Trademarks, Industrial Designs and Geographical Indications, June 21 2000.
14. *Glaxo plc v. Glaxowellcome Ltd* [1996] F.S.R. 388. The defendant company Glaxowellcome Ltd was registered at the time of the merger of Glaxo and Wellcome. The court found that the defendants were engaged in a "dishonest scheme to appropriate the plaintiffs' goodwill in the names Glaxo and Wellcome, and to extort a substantial sum for not damaging it". The court ordered the defendants to change the name of their company from Glaxowellcome Ltd to enable the merged company to take the name. In *Direct Line Group Ltd v. Direct Line Estate Agency* [1997] F.S.R. 374, Laddie J. also granted an interlocutory injunction restraining passing off against defendants with a track record of incorporating companies with famous names, stating that the court would "view with extreme displeasure any attempt by traders to embark upon a scam designed to make illegitimate use of other companies' trade marks".
15. See *e.g. Marks & Spencer plc v. Cottrell and others* Ch.D., Lightman J., 26 February 2001 (unreported).
16. As with most technical explanations of the Internet, this is a simplification. For instance, a company with many individual computers on its network may appear to the outside world to have one IP address (that of its firewall). The individual computers behind the firewall may have a set of private IP addresses allocated internally, which are invisible to computers on the outside of the firewall. The effect, therefore, as seen from the public Internet, is that the whole of the company's network has only one IP address.
17. This is the form of IP version 4. This will change if and when IP version 6 is introduced.
18. See *e.g.* RFC 921 www.rfc-editor.org/rfc/rfc921.txt.
19. The identity of the name server, or DNS server, is set in the browser preferences. Usually, the name server will be provided by the ISP from whom the user obtains his Internet access services.
20. If the local name server is authoritative for the requested domain name, or has cached a recent request for the name, then that server will return the corresponding IP address. If not, the browser will send a query out to the most general server (*e.g.* that responsible for ".uk". If that server does not have the corresponding IP address it will return the name of the authoritative name server for the next level down (*e.g.* ".co"). The process repeats until the browser finds the authoritative name server for the requested domain name, which will return the corresponding IP address.
21. A practical way of demonstrating that the domain name system sits on top of the IP address system is to find out the IP address of a web site and to type that into the browser instead of the normal URL. The browser will connect to the site in the normal way, if anything a little more quickly since it does not have to translate the URL into the IP address before making the connection.
22. There are occasional attempts to create "alternative roots", which would recognise a different or larger set of domains than those recognised by the root servers operated by Verisign. However an alternative root will not succeed unless it gains wide acceptance among ISPs, who have to configure their domain name servers to recognise the alternative root if their users are to be able to see domain names registered with it. An early attempt to do this can be seen at www.alternic.org. A more recent attempt (see www.new.net) involves two strategies: creation of an alternative root and provision of a browser plug-in that offers users the appearance of extra gTLDs . Such attempts excite great controversy in the Internet community. See, for instance, www.icann.org/icp/icp-3-background/lynn-statement-09jul01.htm for views on this topic.

23. See www.wia.org/pub/rootserv.html for a map of the 13 Internet root servers as at Feb. 1, 1998. The organisation of the root server system is under review by ICANN (see Memorandum of Understanding dated 25 November 1998 between US Department of Commerce and ICANN and Amendment 2 thereto dated August 30, 2000; also see ICANN Status Reports to USDoC dated June 15, 1999 and June 30, 2000. All documents referred to are available at www.ntia.doc.gov, other than 15 June 1999 ICANN Status Report at www.icann.org/general/statusreport-15june99.htm.)

24. See Amendments 11 and 19 to the Cooperative Agreement between NSI and the US Department of Commerce dated October 7, 1998 and November 10, 1999 respectively. Both amendments are accessible via www.ntia.doc.gov/ntiahome/domainname/domainhome.htm. The practical operation of the root server system is discussed in Section D2 of the ICANN "Proposal to the US Government to perform the IANA Function" dated February 2, 2000 (www.icann.org/general/iana-proposal-02feb00.htm).

25. The importance of the "A" root server was illustrated by the controversy that erupted in February 1998 when the late Jon Postel conducted what was afterwards described as a "test", in which he asked the operators of the subsidiary root servers to redirect them to point to the "B" root server at his university, the University of Southern California, instead of to the "A" root server on the NSI computer in Herndon, Virginia. For an account of the incident see "US Government Counters Claims that DNS Root-Servers were "Hijacked" *E.C.L.R.* February 11, 1998 p. 179. In a separate incident Eugene Kashpureff, proprietor of the 'alternative root' AlterNIC, pleaded guilty in March 1998 to computer fraud charges after diverting traffic from NSI to AlterNIC (see www.infowar.com/hacker/hack_032998i_j.html-ssi).

26. For a full list of ccTLDs and the persons responsible for managing them see www.iana.org/cctld/cctld-whois.htm.

27. "IANA has functioned as a government contractor, albeit with considerable latitude, for some time now. Moreover IANA is not formally organised or constituted. It describes a function more than an entity..." (U.S. Department of Commerce White Paper, Management of Internet Names and Addresses, June 5, 1998.) See also, especially regarding IANA's process of delegation of responsibility for country code domains, interview with Dr. Willie Black, *Computers and Law* 1999, 10(3), 25–29.

28. Thus IANA was also responsible for allocating blocks of IP addresses. IANA delegated this to three regional registries: for Europe, RIPE NCC (Réseaux IP Européens Network Coordination Centre), for USA until December 1997 InterNIC (*i.e.* Network Solutions Inc) and for the Far East APNIC (Asia Pacific Network Information Centre). In December 1997 the responsibility for the Americas (North and South), sub-Saharan Africa and the Caribbean was transferred, with the support of the National Science Foundation (to whom NSI were contracted) and IANA, to ARIN (American Registry for Internet Numbers). For details of these registries and their functions see www.ripe.net/ripencc/about/regional/index.html.

29. See Vint Cerf's remembrance of Jon Postel, RFC-2468 'I remember IANA', October 17, 1998, at http://ftp.isi.edu/in-notes/rfc2468.txt.

30. www.postel.org/jonpostel.html

31. IANA was, for instance, "chartered" by the Internet Society to act as "the clearinghouse to assign and coordinate the use of numerous Internet protocol parameters" (www.ietf.org/overview.html).

32. See www.ntia.doc.gov/ntiahome/domainname/domainhome.htm for a collection of US government press releases and papers on the management of the Internet numbering and domain name systems from 1997 onwards. As early as November 1995 a claim had been made that the Federal Networking Council (comprising representatives of 18 US Federal administrative agencies) owned the domain name number space and held policy control over the .com, .org and .net name spaces—see M. St. Johns, "FNC's Role in the DNS Issue" Harvard University DNS Workshop November 20, 1995 (ksgwww.harvard.edu/iip/GIIconf/fnc.html).

33. See www.icann.org/general/usc-icann-transition-agreement.htm.

34. See *e.g.* David W. Maher "Trademarks on the Internet: Who's in Charge?" (1996) (www.aldea.com/cix/maher.html) A comprehensive, although sceptical, account of Internet governance at this time is contained in a paper by Robert Shaw of the International Telecommunications Union, "Internet Domain Names: Whose Domain is This?" (people.itu.int/~shaw/docs/dns.html). In addition to IANA, a number of other bodies, many associated with the Internet Society (ISOC), had (and still have) roles in the technical management and evolution of the Internet. These include the Internet Engineering Task Force (IETF), the Internet Architecture Board (IAB), InterNIC (run by Network Solutions Inc on behalf of the US Department of Commerce) and the Internet Engineering Steering Group (IESG).

35. See the section "Climbing the Domain Space Authority Trail" in Shaw, *op. cit.*

36. For an ironic but comprehensive depiction of the pre-ICANN and post-ICANN consensus structures, see www.wia.org/icann/before_icann.htm and www.wia.org/icann/after_icann-gac.htm. For a review of ICANN's progress in seeking to achieve consensus and legitimacy, see "The consensus machine", *The Economist* June 10, 2000.

37. ICANN/USC transition agreement (n. 33 above).

38. See, for instance, the various IANA decisions on the delegation and re-delegation of ccTLDs listed at www.iana.org/domain-names.htm. It would seem, however, that the necessary changes to the "A" root server root zone file to implement such a decision require the approval of the US Department of Commerce (see main text above).

39. The full root zone WHOIS database, listing all the ccTLD operators, is at www.iana.org/cctld/cctld-whois.htm.
40. See RFC 1591 and IANA ccTLD Delegation Practices Document (ICP-1) (May 21, 1999), both available at www.iana.org/domain-names.htm.
41. See *e.g* the 2nd edition of this book, at p. 48.
42. See www.internic.net/faqs/domain-names.html and Amendment 19 dated November 10, 1999 to the Cooperative Agreement between NSI and the US Government (n. 24 above).
43. The convoluted history of the process is well documented. www.wia.org includes in its reference materials a number of detailed graphical timelines. The 1998 U.S. government Green Paper and White Paper referred to in the text both contain useful technical descriptions and detailed histories from a US government perspective, as does the more recent US General Accounting Office report "Department of Commerce: Relationship with the Internet Corporation for Assigned Names and Numbers" (www.gao.gov/new.items/og00033r.pdf). Comprehensive collections of contemporaneous documents are available at the old IAHC site (www.iahc.org) and at www.gltd-mou.org.
44. The original Postel proposal was revised, and in June 1996 the Internet Society's board of trustees endorsed a version in principle.
45. The IAHC was dissolved on May 1, 1997. See www.iahc.org.
46. www.gtld-mou.org.
47. See, for instance, the August 12, 1999 news item on the www.gtld-mou.org web site.
48. www.ecommerce.gov/framewrk.htm.
49. www.ecommerce.gov/presiden.htm.
50. Published in the Federal Register on February 20, 1998: www.ntia.doc.gov/ntiahome/domainname/022098fedreg.htm.
51. www.ntia.doc.gov/ntiahome/domainname/6_5_98dns.htm.
52. COM(1998) 476 Final, July 29, 1998.
53. For a detailed timetable of the introduction of the UDRP see www.icann.org/udrp/udrp-schedule.htm.
54. www.icann.org/tlds/.
55. Operated by Neulevel Inc (www.neulevel.biz).
56. Operated by Afilias, LLC (www.afilias.info).
57. For a summary of the pre-launch procedures see www.icann.org/announcements/icann-pr15may01.htm.
58. COD/2000/0328 'Proposal for a European Parliament and Council regulation on the implementation of the Internet Top Level Domain ".EU".
59. http://www.din.de/gremien/nas/nabd/iso3166ma/index.html.
60. Nominet's web site is at www.nominet.org.uk.
61. Forgetting to renew an important domain name is not necessarily a fantastic notion. In a famous incident in 1999, Microsoft forgot to pay the renewal fee for hotmail.com, with the result that the Hotmail service went down. A public-spirited computer consultant paid the $35 renewal fee by his credit card, and service was restored. J.P. Morgan & Co suffered a similar lapse in June 2000.
62. However, if the U.K. were to legislate for a different body to operate the .uk domain space, then under its promulgated delegation policy IANA would respect that and re-delegate to the new body. No such steps have been proposed in the U.K. However, in its Electronic Commerce Act 2000 (s. 31) the Irish government has taken powers to authorise, prohibit or regulate the registration and use of the .ie domain name in Ireland. The Governmental Advisory Committee of ICANN has adopted as a principle that "governments or public authorities maintain ultimate policy authority over their respective ccTLDs and should ensure that they are operated in conformity with domestic public policy objectives, laws and regulations, and international law and applicable international conventions" and is seeking to ensure that ICANN contracts with ccTLD operators are tripartite contracts between ICANN, the ccTLD operator and the respective country's government (www.icann.org/committees/gac/communique-10mar01.htm). However, this policy stance elides the unexceptional position that a ccTLD operator should be subject to the laws of the country in which it is established with the controversial stance that the local government should be directly involved at a policy level in the operation of a ccTLD.
63. Domain names are also, of course, used for Internet purposes other than the Web. They form the second part (after the @ symbol) of Internet e-mail addresses, and also serve as addresses for other Internet sites, such as those for downloading files using the ftp protocol.
64. *E.g.* pop group or film star fan sites; c.f *Arsenal Football Club plc v. Matthew Reed* [2001] I.P.D. 24037, in which Laddie J. held that the name "Arsenal" and certain designs applied to souvenirs and memorabilia (particularly scarves) for sale to Arsenal supporters would be perceived by those to whom they were directed as a badge of loyalty, support or affiliation, not as an indication of origin.
65. In *One in a Million*, Aldous L.J. in the Court of Appeal made the bald statement, when considering registered trade mark infringement, that "The domain names indicate origin. That is the purpose for which they were registered." That could be taken as suggesting that all registered domain names (in whatever domain space) always and inevitably indicate origin. That, we suggest, overstates the position. It should always necessary to consider in each case whether the domain name in question in fact acts as an indicator of origin. See, for references to US cases emphasising the need for a factual inquiry in each case rather than a *per se* rule, the ICANN UPRD decision in *Bridgestone Firestone Inc, and others v. Myers* (WIPO D2000-0190).

And note the contrasting comments made by Aldous L.J. in the *One in a Million* case concerning the use of web sites for criticism and the promotion of hobbies (see discussion in the main text).

66.   It is most unlikely that the use of a domain name would amount to copyright infringement, given the difficulties of proving that the name of a company constitutes an original literary work *Exxon Corp v. Exxon Insurance Consultants International Ltd.* [1982] Ch. 119 CA.

67.   Even when not pointed to a live web site, the domain name has limited visibility through a WHOIS search. This was relied upon by the Court of Appeal in the *One in a Million* case (see discussion in main text).

68.   While each domain name is unique, so that only one instance of the domain can be registered, there are often possibilities for avoiding the blocking effect of an existing domain name registration by registering a minor variation, such as with a hyphen, or with an additional word incorporated in the domain name, or by registering under a different TLD. When the domain names in question correspond to a trade mark, especially a well-known trade mark, and are registered for nefarious purposes by someone with no legitimate interest in the mark, this would most likely be regarded as cybersquatting and be restrainable. Where the registration is done for legitimate purposes, by someone who either has a legitimate interest in the mark or who credibly does not intend to use the domain name in a way that would infringe the trade mark or amount to passing off or as an instrument of fraud, then the practice is (or at least ought to be) unexceptionable (see the following discussion in the main text).

69.   The practice of establishing "grudge" or "lemon" sites for the purpose of airing grievances about a company or its products has become widespread (see, for instance, "Wide Open to the Web Warriors", *Marketing* February 4, 1999; "Surfers seek vengeance on corporate enemies", *The Times* May 10, 1999). These are often established under a domain name incorporating the epithet "sucks" to indicate the nature of the site. So-called "sucks" sites have been the subject of litigation in the USA (see *e.g. Bally Total Fitness Holding Corp v. Faber* C.D. Calif. No. CV 98-1278 DDP (MANx), 21.12.98) and have also given rise to some of the most controversial decisions to emanate from the ICANN UDRP process (see, for instance, the undefended case of *Diageo plc v. John Zuccarini* (WIPO Case D2000-0996) and the decisions referred to therein). For examples of contrasting decisions on "sucks" domain names involving the same company see *Wal-Mart Stores, Inc. v. wallmartcanadasucks.com and Kenneth J. Harvey* (WIPO D2000-1104) and *Wal-Mart Stores, Inc. v. Walsucks and Walmart Puerto Rico* (WIPO D2000-0477). See also, in a decision in favour of the domain name registrant concerning the use of the domain name "bridgestone-firestone.net" for purposes of criticism, *Bridgestone Firestone Inc, and others v. Myers* (WIPO D2000-0190). Another recent decision in favour of a complainant is *Koninklijke Philips Electronics v. Kurapa C. Kang* (WIPO D2001-0163). The panelist held that the domain name "antiphilips.com" was confusingly similar to the trade mark Philips, mainly on the grounds that although English speakers might not be confused, non-English speakers could be—a line of reasoning first used in *Direct Line Group Ltd & Others v. Purge I.T. Ltd.* (WIPO D2000-0583).

70.   See, for instance, *Britannia Building Society v. Prangley and others* Ch.D, June 12, 2000 (unreported) and *easyJet Airline Co. Ltd and others v. Dainty* Ch.D, 19 February 2001 (unreported).

71.   *Sabel v. Puma* [1998] 1 C.M.L.R. 445.

72.   *Canon Kabushiki Kaisha v. Metro Goldwyn Mayer Inc* [1999] 1 C.M.L.R. 77.

73.   *Pfizer Ltd and another v. Eurofood Link (United Kingdom) Ltd* [2001] F.S.R. 17.

74.   *Premier Brands United Kingdom Ltd v. Typhoon Europe Ltd and Another;* [2000] F.S.R. 767 *Sabel v. Puma* (above).

75.   *Pfizer* (above) para. 35, *General Motors Corp v. Yplon S.A.* [1999] 3 C.M.L.R. 427.

76.   *Mothercare United Kingdom Ltd v. Penguin Books Ltd* [1988] R.P.C. 113.

77.   [1998] R.P.C. 283.

78.   [2001] I.P.D. 24037.

79.   Above.

80.   See *e.g.* Aldous L.J. in *One in a Million* "If it be the intention of the defendant to appropriate the goodwill of another, or to enable others to do so, I can see no reason why the court should not infer that will happen, even if there is a possibility that such an appropriation would not take place."

81.   Note for instance the remarks of Deputy Judge Jonathan Sumption Q.C. in *British Telecommunications plc and Others v. One in a Million Ltd amd Others* [1998] F.S.R. 265 at first instance, commenting on the Defendants' argument that a .org suffix differentiated the domain name from the trade mark: "The defendants make much of this point, but I am not impressed by it for the simple reason that although the words are probably capable of an innocent use, that is not the use that these Defendants intend."

82.   Above.

83.   *Reckitt and Colman Products Ltd v. Borden, Inc* [1990] R.P.C. 341 HL.

84.   Contrast this finding with the comments of Jacob J. in *Avnet Incorporated v. Isoact Ltd* [1998] F.S.R. 16, also quoted in the main text. He stated that it is a general problem on the Internet that it works on words (alone) and not on words in relation to goods and services, so that someone searching using a word may find Web pages or data in a wholly different context from that which he was seeking. He said that users of the Internet know that that is a feature of the Internet and that their search may produce an altogether wrong Web page or the like. He went on to say said that that might be an important matter for the courts to take into account when considering trade mark and like problems. Clearly the Court of Appeal in *One in a Million* made no such allowance when considering WHOIS searches.

85.   For domain spaces which are restricted in their use, or in who can apply for them, there may be some examination of the applications. For instance some of the new gTLDs are restricted, and ccTLDs may

operate restriction policies for part or all of their domain spaces.

86. Indeed, the Court of Appeal apparently fell into this trap in the *One in a Million* case.
87. See *e.g. Trebor Bassett Ltd v. The Football Association* [1997] F.S.R. 211.
88. See, for instance, the Panelist's finding in UDRP decision WIPO D2000-0996 22 October 2000 that the domain name "guinness-beer-really-sucks.com" was confusingly similar to the trade mark GUINNESS. See also the other UDRP panel decisions and U.S. cases referred to in that decision, including WIPO case D2000-0636 July 4, 2000 which concerned exclusively English parties. Other "sucks" cases are mentioned in n. 69 above.
89. Trade Marks Act 1994, s. 16.
90. *Glaxo plc v. Glaxowellcome Ltd* [1996] F.S.R. 388 (n. 14 above).
91. *Marks & Spencer plc v. Cottrell and others* (above).
92. It is sometimes loosely said that, for instance, computer software forms part of the intellectual property of a computer company. As an economic statement that is true. As a legal statement it is not. It would be legally correct to say that the exclusive right to copy (etc.) the computer software forms part of the intellectual property of the company.
93. To the extent that a registrar might be regarded as exercising a public law function the registrant could also assert such public law rights against the registrar as might be available to him.
94. See Aldous L.J. in *One in a Million*: "The purpose of the so-called blocking registration was to extract money from the owners of the goodwill in the name chosen. Its ability to do so was in the main dependent upon the threat, express or implied, that the appellants would exploit the goodwill by either trading under the name or equipping another with the name so he could do so."
95. The prohibition on registering a company name the same as one already registered (not, it should be noted, the same as a registered trade mark) is contained in s. 26(1)(c) of the Companies Act 1985. He Act also provides a post-registration procedure whereby if a company name has been registered under a name which is the same as an existing one or, in the opinion of the Secretary of State, too like an existing name, then the Secretary of State can, within 12 months, direct the company to change the name (s. 28). Companies House does not undertake any investigation of trade mark rights when registering company names.
96. The report to Congress, dated January 18, 2001, is available at www.uspto.gov/web/offices/dcom/olia/tmcybpiracy/repcongress.pdf. It recommends no new guidelines and procedures and counselled "legislative restraint at this time". This is perhaps unsurprising, given that the public consultation prior to the report generated a total of 14 responses.
97. Most recently, for areas said to be of concern to intellectual property rights owners and others, see the Interim Report of the Second WIPO Internet Domain Name Process, April 12, 2001. For material critical of ICANN and its policies, a good starting point is www.icannwatch.org.
98. "Billions registered", *Wired* October 1994 (www.wired.com/wired/archive/2.10/mcdonalds.html).
99. Of course, especially given the lack of uniqueness of some of the names, not all of these were necessarily instances of cybersquatting.
100. [1999] F.S.R. 1, CA
101. [1882] 8 App. Cas. 15
102. Note the commentary on potential differences between ".com" and ".net" in the ICANN UDRP decision in *Bridgestone Firestone, Inc. and others v. Myers* (WIPO D2000-0190).
103. C.D. Calif., No. CV 98-1278 DDP (MANx), 21.12.98
104. See n. 69 and 88 above.
105. Above.
106. [2000] F.S.R. 767.
107. [1996] R.P.C. 281. See discussion above as regards the current position on the question whether use as a trade mark is required for infringement.
108. Ch.D Rattee J., June 12, 2000 (unreported).
109. Ch.D Mr Bernard Livesey Q.C., 19 February 2001 (unreported).
110. The judgment refers to the defendant having registered easyRealestate.co.uk as a domain name. However, the use of the capitalised "R" in a domain name is meaningless, since domain names are case insensitive. Nothing in the conclusions appears to turn on the use of the capitalised R, although the judge does refer to it as one of the distinctive features of the get-up used by the claimants.
111. [1996] R.P.C. 697.
112. Ch.D Mr Nicholas Strauss Q.C., July 17, 2000 (unreported).
113. As occurred in *Marks & Spencer plc v. Cottrell and Others* Ch.D Lightman J., 26 February 2001 (unreported). The defendant was found to have committed thirteen breaches of various court orders, including an order to assign various domain names to the claimant.
114. See n. 125, below, for a description of Nominet's disputes procedures.
115. [1997] F.S.R. 797.
116. [1998] F.S.R. 21.
117. See for instance *Jeanette Winterson v. Hogarth* (WIPO D2000-0235).
118. [2000] 23(4) I.P.D. 29031.
119. Ch.D. HH Judge Boggis Q.C., July 7, 2000 (unreported).

120. [2000] E.T.M.R. 341.
121. www.icann.org.
122. The question of what law the panel should apply is one that has excited surprisingly little controversy so far, given that the applicable law and the territoriality of the complainant's rights tend to go hand in hand. However, it is potentially of considerable importance in cases where a complainant has secured a trade mark registration in only one or two countries and deploys those against a respondent in a country where the complainant has, and could obtain, no registration. See the concerns about this expressed by the dissenting panelist in *Ty Inc. v. Parvin* (WIPO D2000-0688).
123. UDRP, Rule 4(k).
124. For a somewhat critical appraisal of the UDRP record, see *Rough Justice—An Analysis of ICANN's Uniform Dispute Resolution Policy* by Dr Milton Mueller (http://dcc.syr.edu/roughjustice.htm). See also Prof. Michael Geist, *Fair.com?: An Examination of the Allegations of Systematic Unfairness in the ICANN UDRP.* (http://aix1.vottawa.ca/~geist/geistudrp.pdf); and M. Scott Donahey, "The UDRP: Fundamentally Fair, But Far From Perfect" (2001) Electronic Commerce and Law Report Vol. 6 No. 34 p. 937.
125. http://www.nominet.org.uk/ref/drs.html.
126. "Welcome to paranoia.com", *The Economist*, September 16, 1995.
127. [1998] F.S.R. 16.
128. The source code of a web site page differs from that of an ordinary computer program in that it is easily accessible to the user. Web site pages consist of text incorporating various codes which are interpreted, as the page is loaded, by the user's web browser. The web browser formats and presents the text in accordance with the codes and hides the codes from the user. It is trivial task in any browser or web page authoring program to view the codes. (In Netscape the command is "View ǀ Page Source". In Internet Explorer it is View ǀ Source.) The source code of a computer program, on the other hand, is normally 'compiled' into object code (*i.e.* a series of 1s and 0s that can be understood only by a computer). The object code version is released to purchasers, but the source code is normally retained by the software developer and treated as highly confidential.
129. [1998] F.S.R. 16.
130. *Brookfield Communications, Inc. v. West Coast Entertainment Corporation*, 174 F.3d 1036 (9th Cir. 1999).
131. *Playboy Enterprises, Inc. v. Terri Welles* 78 F. Supp. 2d 1066 (S.D. Cal. 1999).
132. [2000] E.T.M.R, 970, Ch.D, Master Bowman.
133. See *Arsenal v. Reed* (above), citing *Euromarket*.
134. See *e.g.* Aldous L.J. in *One in a Million* "If it be the intention of the defendant to appropriate the goodwill of another, or to enable others to do so, I can see no reason why the court should not infer that will happen, even if there is a possibility that such an appropriation would not take place."
135. [2000] E.T.M.R, 111, District Court of the Hague (Civil Law Division).
136. "Sale of Keywords: Trademark violation, Unfair Competition or Proper E-Advertising?", R. Mann, [2000] E.I.P.R. 378
137. Estée Lauder press release, August 8, 2000.

Australia
138. (1998) 42 I.P.R. 289.
139. The wider infringement test also covers goods of the same description as the registered goods, services that are closely related to the registered goods, services of the same description as the registered services and goods that are closely related to the registered services. However, in relation to this wider infringement test, there is a defence if the use will not deceive or cause confusion.

Belgium
140. See the site of the Belgian Association of Internet Providers, hereafter called "ISPA Belgium", http://www.ispa.be.
141. In January 1994, only 129 domain names ".be" were registered against 25,000 six years later; cfr. the site http://www.dns.be.
142. The non profit association DNS Belgium started its activities at the beginning of the year 2000.
143. *cf.* http://www.dns.be.
144. BIPT wished to avoid a new legislation in the regard creating new problems; see ISPA Belgium web site, "Constitution of DNS BELGIQUE ASBL", loc. cit.
145. Between November 2000 and July 2001, the total number of ".be" domain names went from 40.000 to almost 150.000, due to the changes of the conditions for registration.
146. See the web site http://www.dns.be for the text of these Terms and conditions.
147. Article 10.b.1.
148. Article 10.b.2.
149. Article 10.b.3.
150. Comm. Brussels, January 3, 1997, Indacom Case, *D.I.T.*, 1997/4, p. 37; Comm. Brussels, October 23, 1997, Cockerill Sambre Case, *D.A.O.R.*, 98, liv. 45, p. 101 (the president declared the re-opening of the debates); Comm. Brussels, November 24, 1997, Cockerill Sambre Case, *D.A.O.R.*, 98, book 46, p.51; Brussels, April 1, 1998, Tractebel Case, *J.L.M.B.*, 1998, p. 1588–1608, note E. WERY, delivered in appeal at Comm. Brussels, June 11, 1997, *R.D.C.*, 97, p. 726.
151. See reference in n. 150

152. Treaty of Paris, March 20, 1883 for the industrial protection, revised in Brussels on December 14, 1900, in Washington on June 2, 1911, in the Hague on November 6, 1925, in London on June 2, 1934, in Lisbon on October 31, 1958 (approved by the Belgian Law of April 27, 1965), and in Stockholm on July 14, 1967 (approved by the Belgian Law of September 26, 1974).

153. Article 8 stipulates that "the commercial name is protected in every country of the Union, without obligation of registration or subscription, be it part of a commercial or manufacturing trademark".

154. Article 93 of the Act of July 14, 1991 on trade practices and information to and protection of the consumer, published in the *Moniteur Belge* on August 29, 1991.

155. Cass. June 21, 1993, *Arr. Cass.*, 1993, p. 606.

156. See Tractebel case, reference in n. 150.

157. See reference of publication in n. 154.

158. See Tractebel case, reference in n. 150.

159. Article 13.A.1.d.

160. See "communiqué" on site http://www.fgov.be.

Canada

161. CA Domain Committee, ftp.cdnnet.ca/ca-domain/committee-members, April 4, 1997.

162. The CA Domain: An Introduction, ftp.cdnnet.ca/ca-domain/introduction, July 1, 1994.InterNIC, Network Solutions, Inc is a US corporation which functions as a central domain name registry under contract with the National Science Foundation (NSF).

163. *ibid.* CCITT is an international standards organisation similar to ISO.

164. *ibid.*

165. Canadian Trade Marks Act, RSC c. T.13, s. 4

166. Trade Marks Act, s. 19.

167. Trade Marks Act, s. 20

168. *ibid.*, s. 22.

169. *Riches, McKenzie & Herbert v Source Telecomputing Corp.* (1992) 46 C.P.R. (3d) 563 (TMBd). Discussed by Andrea Rush in "Internet Domain Name Protection: A Canadian Perspective" (1996) 11 I.P.J. 1.

170. *BMB Compuscience Canada Ltd v Bramalea Ltd* (1989) 22 C.P.R. (3d) 561 (FCTD). See discussion in *Internet Study*, pp. 112, 113.

171. *ibid.* at p. 9.

172. (1995) 61 C.P.R. (3d) 334 (P.E.I.S.C.)

173. (1997) 77 C.P.R. (3d) 486 (F.C.T.D.)

174. (1997) 77 C.P.R. (3d) 495 (F.C.T.D.)

175. (2000) 6 C.P.R. (4th) 487 (F.C.T.D.)

176. (2000) 47 C.P.C. (4th) 149 (Alta Q.B.)

177. [2001] O.J. No. 943 (Ont. S.C.J.)

178. (1999) 3 C.P.R. (4th) 479 (F.C.T.D.)

179. (2001) 12 C.P.C. (4th) 4 (Sask. Q.B.)

180. (2001) 12 C.P.R. (4th) 95 (F.C.T.D.)

181. (1999) 2 C.P.R. (4th) 289 (F.C.T.D.)

182. (2001) 10 C.P.R. (4th) 423 (B.C.S.C.)

183. [2001] O.J. No. 1558 (Ont. S.C.J.)

184. (1997) 77 C.P.R. (3d) 23 (F.C.T.D.)

185. (1997) 77 C.P.R. (3d) 470 (F.C.T.D.)

186. (unreported)(Court No. T-1800-98)(F.C.T.D.)(*per* Dube J., January 11, 1999)

France

187. *TGI Bordeaux*, Référé, juillet 22, 1996, no. 1366/96–1543/96, Revue Droit de l'Informatique et des télécoms 1997, p.2.

188. *Célio (SA Laurent)* c/M. Eric J., TGI Paris, 3ème ch.,19/10/1999.

189. *EBay Inc. c/ Forum on the Net et iBazard Group CA Paris*, Référé, 01/12/2000

190. *L'Oréal, Parfums Guy Laroche, The Polo Lauren Company, Cacharel et Ralph Lauren* c/ PLD Enterprises, TGI Paris, 27/03/1998.

191. *La S.N.C Lanc#153;me Parfums et beauté c/ La S.A Grandtotal Finances Ltd*, TGI Nanterre, Référé, 16/09/1999

192. *AV Internet Solutions Limited c/ Monsieur R. P., Sarl Adar Web*, Tribunal de commerce de Paris, 28/01/2000.

193. *Microcaz c/ Océanet et S.F.D.I.*, TGI Mans, 1ère ch., 29/06/1999

194. *Société Lumiservice c/ Monsieur Thierry P* TGI Marseille, Référé, 18/12/1998

195. *AV Internet Solutions Limited c/ Monsieur R. P.*, Sarl Adar Web, Tribunal de commerce de Paris, 28/01/2000.

196. *Alice c/ Alice* Cour d'appel de Paris, 04/12/1998.

Hong Kong

197. [2000] 2 HKLRD 616

Israel

198. Further information regarding ISOC-IL is available on its web site at http://www.isoc.org.il.

199. The previous ISOC-IL rules governed domain names registered between April 1996 and December 1998. Both sets of rules are posted on the ISOC-IL web site.

200. Restricted to use by kindergartens and schools.

201. Restricted to use by municipal and local government authorities.
202. Restricted to use by Internet service providers possessing a valid Internet operating license from the Ministry of Communications.
203. Restricted to use by Israeli military entities.
204. ISOC-IL allocates domain names on a "first come, first served" basis. This rule is purely technical, and registration per se does not establish rights to a domain name. See Rule 3.3c of the Rules, which was applied in *Cellcom Israel Limited v.T.M. Aquanet Computer Communications Limited*, Tel Aviv District Court Civil File 10909/99, decision dated September 8, 1999 (unreported).
205. Advisory Committee decisions are published on the ISOC-IL web site at www.isoc.org.il/fr_reload.html?-domains/acp.3 An earlier decision regarding the domain name "toysrus.co.il" was made by consent of the parties on October 18, 1999. The Committee ordered the transfer of the domain name from the holder to the trademark owner.
206. The Advisory Committee applied a test of bad faith that it derived from ICANN rules, WIPO policy, and provisions of the United States Anti Cyber Squatting Consumer Protection Act 1999.
207. In each case, the Advisory Committee determined that the domain name holder was subject to sections 59 and 61(b) of the Contracts (General Part) Law, 1973. Section 59 provides that "In carrying out an obligation pursuant to a contract, one must act in an acceptable manner and in good faith; such is also the case in using a right derived from a contract". Section 61(b) extends the Law, where deemed appropriate and with relevant changes, to non-contractual acts and obligations. The Committee cites Supreme Court authority that allows quasi-judicial bodies to revoke legal actions performed in bad faith.
208. Trademarks Ordinance (New Version) 1972, s. 1.
209. *Gillette Co. v. Adi ZS Import Marketing & Distribution Ltd*, Tel Aviv District Court Civil File 649/96 (unreported).
210. Trademarks Ordinance (New Version) 1972, s. 1.
211. *Cellcom Israel Limited v.T.M. Aquanet Computer Communications Limited*, Tel Aviv District Court Civil File 10909/99, decision dated September 8, 1999 (unreported)
212. Commercial Torts Law 1999, s. 1.
213. Civil Wrongs Ordinance (New Version) 1968, s. 59.
214. This principle is well established in Israeli law for non-Internet related use. In relation to domain names, to date only the Advisory Committee of ISOC-IL has applied the rule to dissimilar services (in the *Snapple* decision). In the *Cellcom* case, the district court held that the trademark "*Cellcom*" had a reputation for Internet related services even though the trademark owner was not engaged in an Internet related business. However, as the court noted, the applicant's telecommunication services and the respondent's email delivery services to cellular telephones are similar. (*Cellcom Israel Limited v. T.M. Aquanet Computer Communications Limited*, Tel Aviv District Court Civil File 10909/99, decision dated September 8, 1999 (unreported)).
215. Property Law 1969, s. 17 and Chattels Law 1971, s. 8.
216. *Cellcom Israel Limited v. T.M. Aquanet Computer Communications Limited* Tel Aviv District Court Civil File 10909/99, decision dated June September 8, 1999 (unreported)
217. *Magnetics Limited v. Discopy (Israel) Limited* Tel Aviv District Court Civil File 001627/01, decision dated June 3, 2001 (unreported).
218. In the Tel Aviv District Court case of *Paradise Mombasa Tours (1997) Limited v. New Soil Technologies Limited* the court held that the respondent was unfairly impeding customer access to the applicant's business, and granted an interlocutory injunction to halt the operation of a web site. The respondent had operated an Internet site on which it conducted marketing activities for the applicant. The applicant's name was used as the domain name for the site. Despite the termination of the relationship, the respondent continued to make the web site, which contained outdated information, available to the public. The judge held that the respondent had contravened section 4 (entitled "Perpetrator and Injured Party") of the Commercial Torts Law 1999. However, section 4 simply adds conditions to the requirements of sections 1 to 3 of the Law, and the judge in fact used the language of section 3 when describing the tort committed by the respondent. (*Paradise Mombasa Tours (1997) Limited v. New Soil Technologies Limited*, Tel Aviv District Court Civil File 001509/01, decision dated May 8, 2001).
219. Habitat decision, ISOC-IL Advisory Committee decision dated August 18, 2000)
220. Unjust Enrichment Law 1979, s. 1.
221. *Snapple* decision, ISOC-IL Advisory Committee Decision dated February 25, 2001.
222. Commercial Torts Law 1999, s. 2, and Consumer Protection Law 1981, s. 7.

Japan
223. www.nic.ad.jp/en/regist/dom/doc/jp-drp-rule-e.html.

The Netherlands
224. (President of the District Court of Amsterdam September 20, 1996, I.E.R. 1996, 44)
225. (President of the District Court of Amsterdam May 15, 1997, I.E.R. 1997, 44)
226. (President of the Distict Court of Utrecht February 24, 2000, I.E.R. 2000, 41)
227. (Amsterdam Appeal Court December 7, 2000, I.E.R. 2001, 10)
228. (President of the District Court of Amsterdam February 24, 2000)
229. (President of the District Court of Amsterdam April 7, 2000, IER 2000, 28)

New Zealand

230. Unreported, HC, Auckland, September 27, 1996, Morris J.
231. (1998) 6 N.Z.B.L.C. 102,567; (1998) 8 T.C.L.R. 363; [1999] 1 N.Z.L.R. 631; (1998) 44 I.P.R. 661.
232. (1998) 8 T.C.L.R. 502.
233. Unreported, HC, Auckland, March 15, 2001, Randerson J.

Switzerland

234. www.nic.ch/terms/policy.html and www.nic.ch/-terms/fees.html.

USA

235. For a more complete discussion of trademark issues related to Internet domain names, see Julian S. Millstein, Jeffrey D. Neuburger, Jeffrey P. Weingart, *Doing Business on the Internet: Forms & Analysis* (Law Journal Press, 1997–2001).
236. Please see section 3.3 for further information on registration of gTLDs.
237. There are three other TLDs reserved for the exclusive use of certain U.S. entities: ".gov" is reserved for U.S. federal government agencies, ".mil" is reserved for the U.S. military, and ".edu" is reserved for educational institutions in the U.S. granting four year degrees. For further information, see the gTLD page of the Internet Assigned Numbers Authority's web site available at http://www.iana.org/gtld/gtld.htm.
238. The policy and rules are available at http://www.icann.org/udrp/udrp.htm.
239. Country-code TLD dispute resolution policies vary. For more information, contact the manager of the ccTLD of interest. Contact information for each ccTLD is available at http://www.iana.org/cctld/cctld-whois.htm.
240. UDRP Rule 3(b)(ix)(1) to (3).
241. UDRP 4(b).
242. *BroadBridge Media LLC v. Hypercd.com* 106 F. Supp. 2d 505 (S.D.N.Y. 2000).
243. For information regarding the ACPA, see *infra* section 3.19.5.
244. BroadBridge Media LLC, 106 F. Supp. 2d at 509–512.
245. *Weber-Stephen Products Co. v. Armitage Hardware* 2000 U.S. Dist. LEXIS 6335 (N.D. Ill. May 3, 2000).
246. *Weber-Stephen Products Co. v. Armitage Hardware* 2000 U.S. Dist. LEXIS 6335 at 7
247. *Referee Enterprises v. Planet Ref, Inc.* 2001 U.S. Dist. LEXIS 9303 (E.D. Wisc. January 24, 2001).
248. *Referee Enterprises, Inc. v. Planet Ref, Inc.* No. FA0004000094707 (N.A.F. June 26, 2000).
249. *Parisi v. Netlearning, Inc.* 139 F. Supp. 2d 745 (E.D. Va. 2001).
250. *Netlearning, Inc. v. Parisi*, No. FA0008000095471 (N.A.F. October 16, 2000).
251. 9 U.S.C. § 1, *et seq.*
252. Anticybersquatting Consumer Protection Act of 1999, Pub. L. 106–113, div. B, Sec. 1000(a)(9) (title III), November 29, 1999, 113 Stat. 1536, 1501A-545 (enacted by reference in the District of Columbia Appropriations Act, which incorporated by reference S. 1948, 106th Cong. §§ 3001–3010 (1999) (see Title III Trademark Cyberpiracy Prevention)), codified at 15 U.S.C. §§ 114, 116, 117, 1125, 1127, 1129 (1999).
253. 15 U.S.C. § 1125(d)(1)(A). The Act also specifically provides protection for trademarks, words, or names associated with the American Red Cross and the United States Olympic Committee. 15 U.S.C. § 1125(d)(1)(A)(ii)(III).
254. 15 U.S.C. § 1125(d)(1)(B)(i).
255. 15 U.S.C. § 1125(d)(1)(B)(ii).
256. 15 U.S.C. § 1125(d)(1)(C).
257. 15 U.S.C. § 1117(d).
258. 15 U.S.C. § 1129.
259. 15 U.S.C. § 1129(1)(A).
260. 15 U.S.C. § 1129(1)(B).
261. 15 U.S.C. § 1129(2).
262. 15 U.S.C. § 1125(d)(2).
263. 15 U.S.C. § 1125(d)(2)(A).
264. 15 U.S.C. § 1125(d)(2)(D)(i).
265. 15 U.S.C. § 1114(2)(D)(iii).
266. In a claim for trademark infringement under the Lanham Act, the trademark owner must show that the defendant is using a mark confusingly similar to a valid, protectible mark. 15 U.S.C. § 1114, 1125(a). A trademark owner can also file a claim for trademark dilution under the Federal Trademark Dilution Act. Under that Act, a trademark owner must establish that its mark is famous, that the defendant used the mark in commerce after the mark became famous, and that the defendant's use dilutes the distinctiveness of the mark. 15 U.S.C. § 1125(c). Unlike a claim for trademark infringement, in a dilution case a plaintiff need not show competition between the parties or a likelihood of confusion resulting from the defendant's use of the mark. The Dilution Act has been applied to a number of domain name disputes. In several cases, courts have held that defendants who registered plaintiffs' trademarks as domain names had diluted the plaintiffs' trademarks. *See, e.g., Panavision Int'l, L.P. v. Toeppen*, 945 F. Supp. 1296 (C.D. Cal. 1996), *aff'd* 141 F. 3d 1316 (9th Cir. 1998) (registration of "panavision.com" and "panaflex.com" domain names diluted Panavision's trademarks); *Intermatic, Inc. v. Toeppen*, 947 F. Supp. 1227 (N.D. Ill. 1996) (registration of "intermatic.com" diluted Intermatic's trademark); *Hasbro, Inc. v. Internet Entertainment Group*, 1996 U.S. Dist. LEXIS 11626 (W.D. Wash. Feb. 9, 1996) (registration of "candyland.com" domain name probably

diluted Hasbro's trademark in the famous board game).

267. In general, courts have held that the mere registration of a domain name that incorporates someone else's trademark is not a "use in commerce." See, *e.g., Lockheed Martin Corp. v. Network Solutions, Inc.*, 985 F. Supp. 949, 957 (C.D. Cal. 1997), *aff'd*, 194 F.3d 980 (9th Cir. 1999); *Jews for Jesus v. Brodsky*, 993 F. Supp. 282, 307 (D.N.J. 1998), aff'd, 159 F.3d 1351 (3d Cir. 1998). However, when a domain name registrant has registered a domain name incorporating a trademark with the intent to sell the name to the trademark owner, courts have held that registration is a use in commerce for Lanham Act purposes. See *Panavision*, 141 F. 3d at 1324. Courts have also found trademark infringement when a party registers a domain name containing the trademark of a competitor. See *Washington Speakers Bureau, Inc. v. Leading Authorities, Inc.*, 33 F. Supp. 2d 488 (E.D. Va. 1999), *aff'd*, 217 F.3d 843 (4th Cir. 2000).

268. *See, e.g., Porsche Cars North America, Inc. v. Spencer*, 2000 U.S. Dist. LEXIS 7060 (May 18, 2000 E.D. Cal. 2000) (novel pre-ACPA *in rem* action was dismissed; on appeal, court held ACPA applies retroactively and remanded, effectively resurrecting Porsche's claims); *Electronics Boutique Holdings Corp. v. Zuccarini*, 2000 U.S. Dist. LEXIS 15719 (E.D. Pa. October 30, 2000) (imposing ACPA statutory damages in a cybersquatting case where defendant had registered five domain names that were slight misspellings of plaintiff's trademarks); *United Greeks, Inc. v. Klein*, 2000 U.S. Dist. LEXIS 5670 (N.D.N.Y. May 2, 2000) (awarding ACPA statutory damages and attorneys' fees in a cybersquatting case where defendant had registered five domain names containing plaintiff's trademarks).

269. *Sporty's Farm L.L.C. v. Sportsman's Market, Inc.*, 202 F.3d 489 (2d Cir. 2000).

270. *Virtual Works, Inc. v. Volkswagen of America, Inc.*, 238 F.3d 264 (4th Cir. 2001).

271. *Shields v. Zuccarini*, 2001 U.S. App. LEXIS 13288 (3d Cir. 2001).

272. In addition to cases awarding compensatory damages, see *Shields v. Zuccarini*, 2001 U.S. App. LEXIS 13288 (3d Cir. 2001) (awarding $50,000 in statutory damages plus $40,000 in attorney fees in a cybersquatting case).

273. *Kremen v. Cohen*, No. C 98-20718 JW (N.D. Cal. April 3, 2001).

274. *E-Cards v. King*, No. 99-CV-3726 (N.D. Cal. May 10, 2000).

275. The defendant Ecards.com filed an appeal to the Ninth Circuit, but the matter was settled in September 2000.

276. *Northland Insurance Cos. v. Blaylock*, 115 F. Supp. 2d 1108 (D. Minn. 2000).

277. *See also Lucent Technologies, Inc. v. Lucentsucks.com*, 95 F. Supp. 2d 528 (E.D. Va. 2000) (noting in dicta that domain names signalling parody or criticism of a company "seriously undermine" the necessary claims under the ACPA of bad faith and likelihood of confusion). In *Bally Total Fitness Holding Corp. v. Faber*, 29 F. Supp. 2d 1161 (C.D. Cal. 1998), the defendant created a web site called Bally Sucks (at http://www.compupix.com/ballysucks/) that criticized the health club company. Bally sued, alleging trademark infringement and dilution and unfair competition. The court granted defendant Faber's motion for summary judgment on the trademark infringement claim, explaining that there was no likelihood of confusion because "no reasonable consumer comparing Bally's official site to Faber's site would assume Faber's site [came] from the same source" or was affiliated with or sponsored by Bally. The judge also granted defendant's motion for summary judgment on the trademark dilution claim because Bally failed to show Faber's use of the Bally mark was a commercial use.

278. *People for the Ethical Treatment of Animals v. Doughy*, 113 F. Supp. 2d 915 (E.D. Va. 2000).

279. Cal. Bus. & Prof. Code §17525–17528 (Deering 2001).

280. As of mid-2001, there were no reported cases arising under the California statute and, although no other state legislatures had passed similar laws, an anticybersquatting bill was introduced in Hawaii's House of Representatives. H.B. 1221, 21st Leg. (Haw. 2001). As of mid-2001, the Hawaii bill had passed in the House and had been referred to the Senate's Judiciary Committee. In addition, California and New Jersey state legislatures had bills pending that would outlaw the registration of certain domain names in connection with elections, such as those consisting of or similar to the names of candidates, without permission of the candidates. S.B. 412, 2001–02 Reg. Sess. (Ca. 2001) and A.B. 2997 & S.B. 2010, 209th Leg. (N.J. 2001).

281. Note, however, that one court has held that the ACPA does not apply to meta tags. *Bihari v. Gross*, 119 F. Supp. 2d 309 (S.D.N.Y. 2000).

282. *Brookfield Communications v. West Coast Entertainment*, 174 F.3d 1036 (9th Cir. 1999).

283. *Eli Lilly & Co. v. Natural Answers, Inc.*, 233 F.3d 456 (7th Cir. 2000).

284. *ibid.* at 465.

285. *Playboy Enterprises Inc. v. Terri Welles Inc.*, 78 F. Supp. 2d 1066 (S.D. Cal. 1999), *appeals docketed*, Nos. 00-55009, 00-55229, 00-55537 & 00-55538 (9th Cir. Jan. 11, 2000) (granting defendants' motion for summary judgment).

286. *ibid.* at 1095.

287. *Playboy Enterprises Inc. v. Netscape Communications* 2000 U.S. Dist. LEXIS 13418 (C.D. Cal. Sept. 12, 2000), *appeals docketed*, Nos. 00-56648 & 00-56662 (9th Cir. Oct. 6, 2000) (granting defendants' motion for summary judgment).

4

Defamation

4.1 Introduction

Defamation liability was one of the first areas of law to come before the courts in the field of on-line services. It continues to be a lively source of activity. Two decisions in 1991 and 1995[1] set the pace in the USA. The first reported United Kingdom Internet defamation litigation occurred in 1994. The plaintiff Dr Laurence Godfrey sued another academic, Dr Phillip Hallam-Baker, alleging that he had caused defamatory Usenet postings to be published. That litigation was subsequently settled. Dr Godfrey was more recently the plaintiff in the first reported judgment under the Defamation Act 1996.[2] In 1996 a judge in an English defamation case was reported to have allowed a plaintiff to serve notice of a writ and an *ex parte* injunction out of the jurisdiction on a defendant via Internet e-mail, when only the defendant's e-mail address was known.[3] Significant damages have been paid out in defamation actions concerning internal company e-mails.[4]

4–001

The Defamation Act 1996 came into force on September 4, 1996. The Act includes provisions designed to address the question of who is liable, and to what standard, for defamatory statements disseminated over computer and telecommunications networks such as the Internet.

The relative abundance of decisions and legislative activity in this area reflects a combination of factors: the endemic informality of e-mail and similar communications, a tradition of robust and uninhibited discussions on Usenet newsgroups and a wide selection of defendants (in addition to the author) for a prospective claimant to consider suing. Publication and dissemination of any information on the Internet requires the involvement of many different entities including hosts, network providers and access providers. As these will often have deeper pockets than the author, the extent of their liability for defamatory content handled by them is of great significance.

4–002

The Defamation Act 1996 was one of the first attempts in the world to legislate for what has now become known as liability of on-line intermediaries. However, the Act will require amendment before January 17, 2002 as a result of the adoption of the Electronic Commerce Directive. This creates common European threshold liability standards in respect of on-line intermediaries for most types of civil and criminal activity including defamation.[5]

The cross-border nature of the Internet raises the liability stakes in two ways: since publication is potentially to the whole world, that could increase the level of damages;

and the claimant could have a wide choice of jurisdictions in which to pursue a defendant.[6]

4.2 Defamation—general[7]

4–003   A defamatory statement is one which would tend to lower the claimant in the estimation of right-thinking members of society generally or cause him to be shunned or avoided. A defamatory statement may constitute either slander or libel. A slanderous statement is one which is issued verbally, or not committed to permanent form. If the statement is in permanent form it will amount to libel. The importance of the distinction lies in the fact that a claimant alleging slander must prove special damage, in other words some actual financial loss. A claimant alleging libel need not do so.

While there is no definitive ruling on whether electronically disseminated communications amount to libel, in general they are likely to do so. A person who posts a Usenet article, sends an e-mail or creates a Web page, is committing content to a database on a host computer. The electronic data resides on that database until deleted. That is true whether the data is text, graphics, audio or video. This, it is submitted, is more than a transient form and is likely to be held to be libel, not slander. The position may perhaps be more doubtful in the case of Internet Relay Chat or video-conferencing, which are more transient forms of communication over the Internet.

4–004   Section 166 of the Broadcasting Act 1990 provides that the publication of words in the course of any programme included in a programme service shall be treated as publication in a permanent form. It is possible that certain services containing sounds or visual images provided over the Internet could constitute programme services and therefore would fall within this provision. (See Chapter 8 for a discussion of what services may be covered by this.)

When considering this area it should always be remembered that defamation cases have generally been tried before a judge and jury, and that the jury has been the arbiter of questions of fact.[8] In a jury trial the judge directs the jury on what the law is and should leave to the jury questions of fact, including facts that must be decided in order that the judge may determine a question of law (such as whether the facts amount to publication). References in this chapter to "the court" should be read with this is mind.

4.3 Liability for defamatory statements over networks

4.3.1 Nature of the problem posed by dissemination over networks

Publication at common law

4–005   Before the Defamation Act 1996,[9] English law cast a wide net of liability for publication of a defamatory statement. Anyone who participated in or authorised the publication was liable. So in hard copy publishing the author, the editor, the publisher, the printer, the distributor and the vendor were all potentially liable, albeit (as explained below) subject to different standards of liability. But someone who merely facilitated, as opposed to participated in, publication did not publish the statement at all and would escape any liability. So the supplier of newsprint would not have been held to have published the statement, whereas the printer would have been.[10] The first issue to consider in the context of networks such as the Internet is where the line is to be drawn between authorising or participating in publication on the one hand, and mere facilitation on the other.

We discuss here the position at common law. The enactment of section 1(3) of the Defamation Act 1996 may, however, possibly have had the practical effect of bringing within the scope of potential liability some persons who at common law were only facilitators. This is discussed below.

Godfrey v. Demon Internet Ltd[11] provides the first judicial guidance as to who **4–006** participates in or authorises publication on the Internet. The case establishes that an Internet service provider who hosts and makes newsgroups available publishes the contents of those newsgroups at common law. The judge found that the defendant, because it had chosen to store the newsgroup in question on its servers, and was able to obliterate postings to the newsgroup, was a publisher at common law.

After reviewing the authorities the judge concluded:

"in my judgment the Defendants, whenever they transmit and whenever there is transmitted from the storage of their news server a defamatory posting, publish that posting to any subscriber to their ISP who accesses the newsgroup containing that posting. Thus every time one of the Defendant's customers accesses 'soc.culture.thai' and sees that posting defamatory of the Plaintiff there is a publication to that customer. …. I do not accept Mr Barca's argument that the Defendants were merely owners of an electronic device through which postings were transmitted. The Defendants chose to store 'soc.culture.thai' postings within their computers. Such postings could be accessed on that newsgroup. The Defendants could obliterate and indeed did so about a fortnight after receipt."

The judgment does beg the question whether if a defendant (such as a telephone **4–007** company who had done nothing other than passively transmit data through its system) were able to establish that it was "merely [the owner] of an electronic device through which postings were transmitted" it could successfully argue that it did not publish the offending statement.[12] However, commenting on the U.S. *Lunney v. Prodigy*[13] case, Morland J. stated that (unlike in the *Lunney* case) in English law Prodigy would clearly have been the publisher of an e-mail message sent over its system. If that is the case it is difficult to see why the same should not apply to a telephone company transmitting voice traffic. The transmissions of the two are both passive and to all intents and purposes indistinguishable. Indeed in the era of digital networks voice and data may form part of the same digital bitstream. Yet it had been thought that at common law a telephone company could argue that it merely facilitated, and did not participate in, publication of voice traffic.[14]

Primary and subordinate disseminators at common law
We have mentioned that although a wide variety of actors were held to be publishers at **4–008** common law, they were subject to different standards of liability. The common law distinguished between the "first or main" publisher and subordinate disseminators. The first or main publisher was strictly liable, whether or not it knew of the defamatory statement. Thus the proprietors of a newspaper would be liable for a libel contained in a classified advertisement, even if there were thousands of such advertisements in the publication. The fact that it might be very difficult to check each and every advertisement did not relieve the newspaper of strict liability.

Subordinate disseminators could take advantage of a defence of innocence. This common law "distributors' defence" was available to a defendant who could show that it did not know that the publication contained the libel; that it was not by reason of any negligence that it did not know that there was a libel in it; and that it did not know, nor ought to have known, that the publication was of a character likely to contain libellous matter.

The Defamation Act 1996 reforms the common law distributors' defence by introducing a statutory scheme covering all types of media including electronic dissemination. However, the Act does not expressly abolish the common law subordinate disseminator's defence and it may have survived the introduction of the Act.[15]

Primary and subordinate dissemination over networks

4–009   Before the Internet there were already difficulties in applying the common law distributors' defence to print media.[16] The distinction between primary publisher and subordinate disseminator then had to be revisited with the advent of electronic dissemination over networks.

Applying the traditional distinction to electronic dissemination is not easy. In hard copy publishing the content tends to be selected, collated and conveniently wrapped inside discrete covers. The first or main publishers can be identified as those who participate in creating the wrapped product, and subordinate disseminators or distributors as those who receive the wrapped product and pass it down the chain to the ultimate purchaser.

4–010   Much (but by no means all) electronically disseminated content is created and distributed in unwrapped form, just as the author provides it. So in many cases it is no longer easy or even possible to distinguish between publication and distribution. A typical example of this is an on-line discussion forum or a Usenet newsgroup, where members of the public can place messages directly onto a database accessible by anyone else equipped with the appropriate software. The collation and wrapping function of the traditional publisher has disappeared, or at least has been reduced to the routine task of maintaining the organisation of the messages by topic, date order or author. The discussion forum proprietor may choose whether or not to exercise the remaining function of selecting content.[17]

The proprietors of on-line discussion forums emphasise the practical impossibility of vetting messages placed on their services[18]—which under the old common law begged the question: are they akin to distributors for whom this is a relevant matter,[19] or to primary publishers for whom it is not? The practical impossibility of vetting messages did not of itself determine the legal status of an on-line provider. Only if it could claim subordinate disseminator status in the first place would that become a relevant factor in determining negligence.

Variety of relationships between Internet actors and content

4–011   It should be emphasised, however, that the illustration of the Usenet newsgroup, with its individual messages made instantly available by their authors, is only one aspect of publication on the Internet. Many variations are possible, ranging from permanent to ephemeral, with differing relationships between the parties involved. Some publishing on the Internet, when carefully crafted and vetted copy is placed on permanent Web sites or where electronic versions of well-known journals and magazines are created, is more like hard copy publishing and advertising.

Some examples of the variety of relationships between disseminator and content are:

- An Internet service provider hosts and makes available Usenet newsgroups, receiving automatic updating feeds from other Usenet hosts and disseminating postings made by its own customers.

- The proprietor of a Web journal includes a "letters to the editor" feature on the journal's Web site. Unlike the print version of the journal, in which letters to the editor are selected and edited for periodic publication, on-line readers are free to post "letters" directly to a forum on the Web site. Other readers can reply in like manner.

- An academic collates interesting postings from a Usenet newsgroup and periodically e-mails them to subscribers to an electronic mailing list.

- An Internet service provider provides both Internet access and free Web hosting facilities to its customers.

- A telecommunications operator agrees to provide and manage a virtual network to enable a group of companies to operate an intranet. All the group's e-mail traffic and requests for documents flow over the network.

- A Web design company receives text from its customer, codes the text using HTML and Java, and passes the finished product by e-mail to another company which will host the Web site.

- A search engine indexes Web sites and displays a customised list of links to relevant Web pages in response to search terms entered by the user.

These examples raise issues both of whether the person has participated in the publication (as opposed to merely facilitating it) and also whether they have done so as a primary or secondary publisher.

In some of these examples the collation and wrapping functions of the original **4–012** publisher (content provider) remain, although the person disseminating the material may be more or less removed from the content provider. In other examples no collation takes place at all, for instance in the case of e-mail traffic. In all cases distribution from the originating site or person to the end-user is an even more mechanical procedure than in the case of hard copy works, the electronic material simply becoming part of the general packet data traffic transmitted through the Internet.

Interesting questions could also arise as to the status of mirror sites—sites which agree to act as a local duplicate host for a foreign site, to enable local users to obtain faster access—or sites which, say, hold duplicates of a number of different third party electronic magazines and newspapers. Such sites have features both of distributors and primary publishers in the traditional analysis. They are distributors in the sense that they receive a third party's publication. But in another sense they are doing nothing different from the original host who agrees to hold a publication.

4.3.2 Defamation Act 1996—the Section 1 defence for secondary disseminators

The Defamation Act 1996 introduced a codified scheme of responsibility for publication **4–013** of defamatory statements. The Act not only addresses liability for electronic dissemination, but also reforms the law relating to liability for print publications, for instance by moving printers into the category of secondary publishers. Although the scheme of the

Act is clearly inspired by the common law distinction between primary and subordinate disseminator, the Act creates such a new and complex statutory structure that old cases on distributors' liability may be of little assistance, other than in broad terms, in determining the boundaries of liability. The Act was subject to various amendments to the responsibility for publication provisions during its passage through Parliament.

The Section 1 defence under the 1996 Act

4–014   Under section 1(1) of the Act a person has a defence in defamation proceedings if he can show that:

(a)   he was not the author, editor or publisher of the statement complained of,

(b)   he took reasonable care in relation to its publication, and

(c)   he did not know, and had no reason to believe, that what he did caused or contributed to the publication of a defamatory statement.

In determining whether a person took reasonable care, or had reason to believe that what he did caused or contributed to the publication of a defamatory statement, regard is to be had to:

(a)   the extent of his responsibility for the content of the statement or the decision to publish it;

(b)   the nature or circumstances of the publication; and

(c)   the previous conduct or character or the author, editor or publisher.

Section 1(2) of the Act defines "author", "editor" and "publisher". It provides that:

An "author" is the originator of the statement (but does not include someone who did not intend that his statement be published at all).

An "editor" is a person having editorial or equivalent responsibility for the content of the statement or the decision to publish it.

A "publisher" is a commercial publisher, that is, a person whose business is issuing material to the public, or a section of the public, who issues material containing the statement in the course of that business.

These definitions are "further explained" in section 1(3), which sets out five categories of persons who are not to be considered the author, editor or publisher of a statement. In a case not within these categories the court may have regard to them by way of analogy in deciding whether a person is to be considered the author, editor or publisher of a statement. These categories are therefore the equivalent of the common law subordinate disseminators.

4–015   The five categories are persons who are "only" involved:

"(a)   in printing, producing, distributing or selling printed material containing the statement;

(b)   in processing, making copies of, distributing, exhibiting or selling a film or sound recording (as defined in Part 1 of the Copyright, Designs and Patents Act 1988) containing the statement;

(c)   in processing, making copies of, distributing or selling any electronic medium in or on which the statement is recorded, or in operating or providing any equipment, system or service by means of which the statement is retrieved, copied, distributed or made available in electronic form;

(d)   as the broadcaster of a live programme containing the statement in circumstances in which he has no effective control over the maker of the statement;

(e)   as the operator or provider of access to a communication system by means of which the statement is transmitted, or made available, by a person over whom he has no effective control.''

For transmission across networks the most relevant categories of subordinate disseminators are likely to be (b), (c), (d) and (e), although (a) may possibly be relevant if resort is to be had to the analogy provision.

4.3.3 Judicial analysis of the Section 1 defence

The Demon Internet *case*
The courts have so far rendered two decisions that address the scope of these categories   **4–016**
of subordinate disseminator. In *Godfrey v. Demon Internet Ltd* (see paragraph 4–006), Morland J. had no hesitation in finding that Demon, when hosting Usenet newsgroups, was not a publisher within the meaning of sections 1(2) and (3) of the Act. He found that Demon was "clearly" not a publisher within the meaning of sections 1(2) and 1(3) and could "incontrovertibly" avail itself of section 1(1)(a). However, the judge undertook no analysis of the explanatory categories. Presumably he considered that Demon's activities came within either or both of sections 1(3)(c) or (e). It is implicit in the decision that some degree of selection of content does not preclude a person from "only" being involved in those categories. This follows from the judge's reliance, in finding that Demon published the contents of the newsgroups within the common law meaning, on the fact that Demon's activities were more than passive in that they chose to host the particular newsgroup to which the offending article was posted.

The live broadcast exception—section 1(3)(d)
The scope of the live broadcast exception has also been judicially considered. In *Market*   **4–017**
Opinion and Research International Limited and another v. BBC[20] Gray J. ruled that the use of a time delay device whereby a broadcast could be delayed by 7–10 seconds would not mean that the broadcast ceased to be live, notwithstanding that the use of the delay device entailed recording the programme and broadcasting the recording. The judge held that the contrary conclusion would run counter to the ordinary understanding of what is meant by a live broadcast. He went on to say that it would also run counter to the legislative purpose underlying the Act and in particular section 1, because whenever such a mechanism was used the broadcaster would lose the protection of section 1. The legislative purpose of section 1 of the Act was to narrow the scope of the liability of publishers in certain defined circumstances.

In considering the potential wider implications of the rulings, it should be noted that ''broadcaster'' and ''programme'' are not defined in the Act. These may therefore bear different, possibly wider, meanings from in the Broadcasting Act 1990, especially given the statutory encouragement to argue by analogy from the explanatory sub-sections.

'Effective control' in the live broadcast exception

4–018 The meaning of "effective control" in the live broadcast exception was also considered in the *MORI v. BBC* case. The case concerned defamatory comments made by an interviewee during the course of a live television interview. The BBC relied upon section 1 for its defence.

The claimant argued that the BBC could rely on sub-section (d) only in the absence of any ability to prevent the maker from making the statement and that if a degree of effective control were possible, then the BBC could not rely on the defence. The claimant argued that in a pre-arranged studio interview with a known participant it would be possible to lay down ground rules in advance, or intervene or moderate what was said by the interviewee.

The BBC argued that the sub-section referred to effective control over the maker of the statement rather than over the statement made by him or its transmission. It argued that the issue was not whether the BBC could have taken steps to achieve effective control, but whether in fact such control existed at the time of the broadcast.

4–019 The judge held that section 1(3)(d) was addressing the relationship between the broadcaster and the individual who made the allegedly defamatory statement; and that the word "control" in this context connoted the "power of the broadcaster in relation to that individual as regards his conduct during the interview, in particular to direct or determine what is and what is not said by that individual". The judge went on to say that qualifying "control" by use of the word "effective" was intended to do no more than indicate that the power of control must be real and not theoretical or illusory.

The judge decided that the relevant question was the control in fact possessed by the BBC at the time of the interview, not what the BBC could have done to acquire control. So the possibility of laying down ground rules was not relevant to the issue of effective control.[21] The judge decided that there was sufficient evidence of effective control by ability to direct the interview so as to avoid provoking the interviewee and to intervene when he embarked on his attack on MORI and if necessary cut him off, for this question to be considered by the jury.

4–020 The judge also commented that one situation where effective control might be said to exist would be where the maker of the statement was the employee of the broadcaster, so that the broadcaster could stipulate what might or might not be said and impose sanctions which would have the effect of conferring control over the employee; and that there would be other situations where, by virtue of a contractual relationship or perhaps by means of volunteer consent on the part of the interviewee, it could be said that the broadcaster had or had available to him the means of obtaining effective control over the maker of the allegedly defamatory statement.

It is notable that the words "effective control" are also used in section 1(3)(e), in connection with the relationship between the operator of or provider of access to a communications system and a person by whom the statement is transmitted, or made available by means of the system. The extent to which the *MORI* analysis would be relevant to a case falling within section 1(3)(e) would depend upon the particular facts of the case.

4.3.4 Publication at common law and the 1996 Act

4–021 The meaning of "publisher" for the purposes of section 1 of the Act is confined to that section. It is very different from the normal meaning of publisher (*i.e.* one who publishes) in defamation, and does not affect the normal meaning of "publish" or "publication" either in the Act or for other defamation purposes (section 17(1)).

It therefore remains necessary to show that a defendant has published the offending statement in the common law sense before proceeding to consider the question of whether he is a primary or secondary publisher within the meaning of the Act.[22]

However, notwithstanding the explicit preservation of the common law meaning of "publish", it may yet be influenced in practice by the terms of the Act. For in making the innocent dissemination defence available to, for instance, a person involved only in "operating or providing any equipment, system or service by means of which the statement is retrieved, copied, distributed or made available in electronic form" (section 1(3)(c)) the Act contemplates that all such activities would have constituted publication at common law.   **4–022**

That is debatable. Liability at common law did not extend to those who merely facilitated publication.[23] Although the boundary between participation and facilitation was by no means easy to draw, the categories of secondary disseminators under the Act would appear to include some who arguably were mere facilitators at common law. It remains to be seen whether a mere facilitator whose activities fall within one of the categories of section 1(3) can successfully dispose of the case by arguing that that he did not publish the defamatory statement, or whether he will be required to establish a defence under section 1.

4.3.5 Authors, editors and publishers under the 1996 Act

It can be seen that there are three ways in which someone can be held strictly liable for a defamatory statement—if he is the author, editor or publisher. This immediately highlights one respect in which the Act requires careful analysis—the distinction between editor and publisher. Under the Act the risk attached to exercising editorial control, or more accurately of assuming editorial responsibility, is of being found to be an editor, not a publisher. Conversely the definition of publisher appears to have nothing to do with whether editorial control is exercised, so that someone who falls within the definition of "publisher" may be held liable whether or not he assumes editorial responsibility. Thus a commercial publisher who hosts a discussion forum may be in a different position from someone whose business is not commercial publishing. As noted above, in *Godfrey v. Demon Internet Ltd*, the judge held that the defendant, an Internet Service Provider which hosted newsgroups, was "clearly" not a publisher within the meaning of sections 1(2) and 1(3) and could "incontrovertibly" avail itself of section 1(1)(a).   **4–023**

Authors versus subordinate disseminators
The scope of the explanatory subsections which define the categories of subordinate disseminators is not easy to discern. In particular, it is unclear how the subsections "explain" each of the primary definitions. It does not seem possible that they operate on each primary definition in the same way. For example, it seems tolerably clear that an author can never fall within any of the subsections. Someone who originates the defamatory statement can surely never "only" be involved in any of the activities described in the subsections. The act of originating the statement must of itself disentitle the author from the protection of the subsections. Any other result would be absurd.   **4–024**

Publishers versus subordinate disseminators

4–025 However, the same does not appear to apply to a publisher. "Issuing" material is on its face a wide concept, apt to cover much of the activity contemplated in the explanatory subsections. So unless "issue" is intended to have a very restricted meaning, it would seem that a person whose business is in the wide sense issuing material to the public may yet be able to qualify as a subordinate disseminator if he "only", for instance, provides a service by means of which a defamatory statement is made available. This is different from the case of the author, where the act of origination in the primary definition must be taken to preclude subordinate disseminator status. However, the questions of how narrow is the residual definition of commercial publisher, and what activities would disqualify a potential commercial publisher from being held to be "only" carrying on the activities in the subsections, and their relationship to the activities described in the primary definition, are obscure.

Editors versus subordinate disseminators

4–026 The case of the editor appears to work differently again. The definition of "editor" describes a status—someone who has assumed editorial or equivalent responsibility. It is not dependent on an act of editing. Yet the explanatory subsections describe acts, not a status. How do the subsections relate to the primary definition, and how can one discern whether someone has assumed editorial responsibility? The relationship may simply be that assumption of editorial responsibility is not to be inferred from only carrying on the activities described in the subsections. That leaves at large, to be answered without any real assistance from the Act, the question of what activities may result in actual or inferred assumption of editorial responsibility.

   The consequence appears to be that, whatever may have been the position before the Act, activities from which assumption of editorial responsibility may be inferred are now to be avoided if subordinate disseminator status under the Act is to be preserved. Of course if a person has assumed that responsibility (*e.g.* by undertaking a contractual obligation to edit), failing to discharge it will not permit him to claim subordinate disseminator status.

4–027 As to what activities could result in an inference of editor status, some assistance may now be gained from *Market Opinion and Research International Limited and another v. BBC.*[24] In this case Gray J. ruled that to use a time delay device in a live broadcast so as to enable the producer to cut out swear words or, if he thought quickly enough, a libellous comment would not render the broadcaster an "editor" within the meaning of section 1(1)(a). He said:

> "I consider that the function of an editor is to adapt, fashion and organise information so as to enable it to be communicated to the public in a journalistically acceptable or desirable fashion. An equivalent function is a function closely allied to an editorial function in the sense which I have described. The person who presses the button of the delay mechanism in order to cut out the profanity or libel is not, in my judgment, exercising an editorial function in the sense I have described. It is the function akin to that of a lawyer vetting material prior to publication. I do not consider that lawyers performing that task are exercising an editorial function."

That may be contrasted with the U.S. case of *Stratton Oakmont v. Prodigy,*[25] in which the screening of offensive words from messages posted to discussion forums was held to involve editorial control and render Prodigy a primary publisher. However, the apparent contrast is illusory. In that case there were journalistic reasons for screening offensive words since Prodigy made a selling point of the fact that it was family-oriented and controlled the contents of its bulletin boards. In an article quoted in the judgment Prodigy stated: "We make no apology for pursuing a value system that reflects the culture of the millions of American families we aspire to serve. Certainly no responsible newspaper does less when it chooses the type of advertising it publishes, the letters it prints, the degree of nudity and unsupported gossip its editors tolerate." The judge commented that Prodigy had made a conscious choice to gain the benefits of editorial control and that "presumably Prodigy's decision to regulate the content of its bulletin boards was in part influenced by its desire to attract a market perceived to exist consisting of users seeking a 'family-oriented' computer service.[26]"

Such removal of profanity for journalistic, as opposed to legal, reasons would fall within Gray J.'s definition of the function of an editor.

4.3.6 Which Internet players can claim subordinate disseminator status?

We listed above some examples of the different varieties of relationship between disseminator and content. Which of these could claim "subordinate disseminator" status under the 1996 Act?   **4–028**

The Usenet host
The first example was the Usenet host. As discussed above, that was considered in *Godfrey v. Demon Internet Ltd*. Demon was found to have subordinate disseminator status in relation to its hosting of newsgroups.   **4–029**

The Web journal discussion forum
The second example was the proprietor of a Web journal who included a "letters to the editor" feature on the journal's Web site, in which on-line readers were free to post "letters" directly to a forum on the Web site. Other readers could reply in like manner.   **4–030**

The proprietor would have to overcome a number of serious obstacles to take advantage of a defence. The first is that the proprietor of such a journal is quite likely to be a "commercial publisher" within the ordinary meaning of section 1(2), namely a person whose business is issuing material to the public, or a section of the public, who issues material containing the statement in the course of that business. There is, however, some ambiguity in the phrase "issues material containing the statement". This fails to recognise that (as discussed above) much material on the Internet, especially the contents of discussion forums, is "unwrapped". It makes little sense to speak of material containing the statement, since it is extremely difficult to ascertain where any item of material begins and ends in a seamless, dynamically changing, linked environment.

The proprietor could seek to argue that the discussion forum on the Website was of a different nature from the material in the journal issued by him and should be treated separately from it, so that the statement was not contained in that material. The material within which the statement was contained could be argued to be the remainder of the message posted by the third party to the discussion forum. It could also be open to argument whether the proprietor of the journal had "issued" the offending posting at all.   **4–031**

The proprietor would also have to argue that he was not an "editor" within the meaning of the Act. Clearly he (or his employed editor) would be an editor in relation to the main content of the journal. Would that necessarily extend to the content of the discussion forum included in the journal? Or would he be able to argue that, in relation to the discussion forum alone, he undertook no function of adapting, fashioning and organising the information to enable it to be communicated to the public in a journalistically acceptable or desirable fashion?[27]

4–032   As to the explanatory categories of section 1(3), if necessary he would probably have to bring himself within section 1(3)(c), arguing that he was only providing a service by means of which the statement was made available in electronic form. In concept, if separation from the edited parts of the journal can be established, the provision of the Website discussion forum is little different (volume of messages apart) from the hosting of newsgroups considered in *Godfrey v. Demon Internet Ltd*.

A proprietor of a website discussion forum seeking to rely on an innocent dissemination defence would no doubt seek to draw comfort from the statements of Owen J. in *Totalise plc v. The Motley Fool and Another*[28] regarding the responsibility, for the purpose of section 10 of the Contempt of Court Act 1981, of the defendants in that case for discussion fora on their websites (see Chapter 6). However, while the judge's comments may be helpful in showing that no editorial responsibility was assumed, they do not address the question of being a publisher.

The academic mailing list

4–033   The third example was of an academic who collated interesting postings from a Usenet newsgroup and periodically e-mailed them to subscribers to an electronic mailing list. It is difficult to see how the academic could avoid being categorised as an editor. He performs the traditional editorial functions of selection and collation and has clear responsibility for the decision to publish the selected postings by e-mailing them on to his mailing list subscribers.

The Internet access and Web hosting ISP

4–034   This example was of an Internet service provider who provided Internet access and free Web hosting facilities to its customers. In relation to Internet access, the ISP would stand some chance of arguing that, as its activities were entirely passive, at common law it did not publish the material transmitted across its facilities in response to its customers' commands and requests (see the discussion above of *Godfrey v. Demon Internet Ltd*). If it did not succeed in that, it would almost certainly fall within the scope of section 1(3)(c). Its Web hosting activities would also do so. However, as the operator of a communications system it would also potentially fall within section 1(3)(e), which carries the further condition that it had no effective control over the person who transmitted or made the statement available by means of the system. On the face of it, if section 1(3)(c) applies that should be the end of the matter. Could, however, it be argued that if section 1(3)(e) is applicable, the person should not be able to escape the "effective control" condition by relying on section 1(3)(c)? The interrelationship of these explanatory subsections is obscure.

4–035   Section 1(3)(e) does contain a potential trap, in that an ISP will have contracts in place with its Internet access and Web hosting customers. If the defamatory statement for which it is sought to make the ISP liable was generated by one of its customers, then there may be a question whether the contractual arrangements give the ISP "effective control" over the customer.[29]

In the case of Web hosting, the questions of whether in the factual circumstances the ISP took reasonable care and did not know or have reason to believe that what it did caused or contributed to the publication of a defamatory statement are likely to be far more contentious than in the case of a statement merely transmitted across its network.

The managed virtual network

In this example, a telecommunications operator agreed to provide and manage a virtual   **4–036**
network to enable a group of companies to operate an intranet. All the group's e-mail
traffic and requests for documents flow over the network.

   The telecommunications operator is in an excellent position to take advantage of
section 1(3)(c) and (e). The "effective control" condition of section 1(3)(e) should be less of
a concern, as it is difficult to conceive of a contractual arrangement that would give the
telecommunications company "effective control" over all the staff of the group of
companies using the network.

The Web design company

In this example a Web design company receives text from its customer, codes the text   **4–037**
using HTML and Java, and passes the finished product by e-mail to another company
which will host the Web site. At common law the Web design company is probably
participating in the publication on the Web site. Because of its direct involvement with
the text its activity is more akin to a printer than to, say, a designer who may not have
been a publisher at common law.[30] On the plain reading of "author, editor, or publisher"
as defined by section 1(2) of the Act, the Web designer appears to have a good argument
that he is none of those (assuming that he resisted the temptation to improve the text
while coding it). Unfortunately none of the explanatory subsections read directly on to
his activity, and if necessary he may have to argue by analogy from section 1(3)(a) "in
printing, producing, distributing or selling printed material containing the statement".

The search engine

Last, let us consider the position of search engines.[31] Search engines set out to index the   **4–038**
Web. They do this by sending out automated "crawlers" which are pre-programmed to
seek out Web sites and index their contents on a mammoth full-text database. It should be
noted that (other than page headings and short extracts) the database does not contain the
actual contents of the Web pages, but only a list of words and pointers to their location on
the Web.

   A user enters search words and the search engine will respond by displaying a page of
links, page headings and short extracts. The search engine is certainly publishing, at
common law, the page headings and short extracts. It is more debatable whether, for each
link, it is publishing the target page or site (see discussion of linking, section 4.4.2 below).
Assuming that it is, can the search engine rely on the subordinate disseminator
exceptions?

   The first hurdle it has to overcome is to demonstrate that it is not a commercial
publisher within the definition of section 1(2). The trouble is that there is no wholly
analogous off-line equivalent to the search engine. However, given that the pure search
engine will be providing access only to third party material with which it has no direct
connection,[32] it should have reasonable arguments that it is not a commercial publisher.
Is it an editor? The search engine undoubtedly selects the material that it indexes, if only
to the extent that the search algorithm instructs the crawler to seek out Web sites
according to certain rules. It also has careful programming in place to determine the
order in which "hits" are displayed to the user. However, all this is done automatically
by software. Does this amount to editorial responsibility for the decision to publish,
especially when the search criteria are keyed in by the user?

4–039   The Act appears to envisage that someone may be an editor even if they have only partial responsibility for the decision to publish. Otherwise the factors to be taken into account in assessing "reasonable care" would make little sense. On the other hand, can a purely automated process amount to editorial responsibility?[33]

Perhaps the most powerful argument in favour of the search engine is that it is doing no more than putting a sophisticated tool in the hand of the user to enable the user to locate sites; and that as such it is no different from a library transposed onto the Internet, with a more sophisticated card index; and that it therefore either falls squarely within the provisions of section 1(3)(c), or should benefit from subordinate disseminator status by virtue of the analogy provisions.

4.3.7 Defamation Act 1996—standard of care

4–040   As mentioned above, even if a person is able to show that he is not an author, publisher or editor within the meaning of the Act, to escape liability for a defamatory statement he has to show that he took reasonable care in relation to its publication and that he did not know, and had no reason to believe, that what he did caused or contributed to the publication of a defamatory statement.[34]

Notice and take-down

4–041   In *Godfrey v. Demon Internet Ltd* the court, having found (as discussed above) that Demon Internet had published the newsgroup posting in question and was not a publisher within the meaning of section 1(2) and (3) of the 1996 Act, considered whether it satisfied these conditions.

The factual background was that Demon carried the Usenet newsgroup "soc.culture.thai" and stored postings within the "soc" hierarchy for about a fortnight. On January 13, 1997 someone unknown made a posting in the USA on the soc.culture.thai newsgroup. The posting was "squalid, obscene and defamatory of the Plaintiff". It purported to come from the plaintiff and invited replies to the plaintiff's e-mail address. The posting was in fact a forgery. The posting was replicated from the originating American ISP through the newsgroup system to Demon's news server.

4–042   On January 17, 1997 Dr Godfrey sent a fax letter to the managing director of Demon, informing him that the posting was a forgery and requesting Demon to remove the posting from its Usenet news server. Demon admitted that the posting was not removed, but stayed on the server until it expired on about January 27, 1997. There was no dispute that Demon could have obliterated the posting from its news server after receiving Dr Godfrey's request. Dr Godfrey claimed libel damages for the period after January 17, 1997.

The judge held that because after January 17, 1997 Demon knew of the defamatory posting but chose not to remove it that posed an "insuperable difficulty" for their defence. The judge concluded that Demon's defence under section 1 of the Act was "hopeless" and struck it out.

It should be noted that the test of knowledge is whether the defendant can establish that he did not know and had no reason to believe that what he did contributed to the publication of a *defamatory* statement—not an actionable statement. This means that if the defendant takes the view that the defamatory statement can be justified, that will not assist him in establishing an innocent dissemination defence. The practical consequence of this is that once a defendant has had the existence of a defamatory statement on his system drawn to his attention (for instance by the potential claimant, as in *Godfrey v. Demon Internet*), he will no longer be able to rely on section 1 of the 1996 Act even if he makes inquiries of the author and has good grounds to believe that a defence of justification, fair comment or privilege would succeed.

Whether this "notice and take-down" regime draws the right balance between the   **4–043**
interests of potentially libelled claimants and freedom of speech may be open to question. The Lord Chancellor, during the debate on the Bill, took the view that the formulation in the Act reflected the common law. He said that to give an innocent dissemination defence to an intermediary because he formed the view that some other defence might be available would be to "create an entirely new defence".[35]

In *Goldsmith v. Sperrings Ltd*[36] Bridge L.J. adopted a formulation of the common law defence similar to that of the Act. On the other hand Lord Denning M.R., in a dissenting judgment, referred to "a libel on the plaintiff which could not be justified or excused". If this formulation is correct, the possible survival of the common law defence of innocent dissemination may be significant. Lord Denning's judgment also contains a trenchant criticism of the consequences for freedom of speech of visiting too stringent a defamation liability regime on distributors.[37] It could be applied with little modification to the consequences of strict "notice and take-down" regimes on the Internet.

Since the coming into force on October 2, 2000 of the Human Rights Act 1998 these   **4–044**
issues have assumed greater significance than previously. A case complaining about the defamation "notice and take-down" regime had already, prior to the 1998 Act, been brought against the United Kingdom Government in the European Court of Human Rights, by the editor of a magazine whose website was taken down by an ISP.[38] As regards the statutory provisions of the Defamation Act 1996, the courts are bound under the Human Rights Act to read and give effect to them as far as possible in a manner compatible with the Convention rights[39] or, if that is not possible, the court may make a declaration of non-compatibility.[40] If the common law defence survives, then the obligation on the courts to act themselves in a manner compatible with Convention rights[41] would require the courts to consider again the questions discussed by Lord Denning and, if necessary for Convention compliance, to reformulate the common law defence so as to make actionability the touchstone of the defence.

It should also be noted that the "notice and takedown" provisions of the Electronic Commerce Directive concerning the liability of hosting intermediaries[42] refer to knowledge of "illegal" activity or information. This may require the current defamation legislation to be amended.

Previous conduct or character

The requirement to have regard to the previous conduct or character or the author, editor   **4–045**
or publisher raises the question of whether the defendant is required to take positive steps to make some investigation of the antecedents of, for instance, subscribers to an on-line or Internet access service, or of those to whom Web space is offered. This places service providers and Web hosts in the difficult position of trying to avoid activities which would disqualify them from secondary disseminator status, but at the same time do enough to be held to satisfy the requirement to take reasonable care.

The emphasis on the previous conduct or character of the author may have particular implications for a Usenet host, who may be able to make a distinction between receiving individual messages from its direct subscribers and receiving a feed containing a stream of messages collated from the rest of the Internet.

In the Demon case the offending posting was made in the USA and sent to Demon via   **4–046** the updating Usenet feed. The *Netcom* copyright case (see Chapter 2) also contains a good description of a typical arrangement. The defendant subscribed to a bulletin board service (BBS), which in turn connected to an Internet access provider (Netcom). When the defendant posted an article to the alt.religion.scientology newsgroup the message was held initially on the BBS's version of the newsgroup (where other subscribers to the BBS could read it), then copied on to Netcom, who also stored it and forwarded it. The BBS kept messages for three days, Netcom for 11 days. So the BBS received and made available a message received direct from its subscriber, whereas Netcom received a general feed of all articles posted to that BBS.

The standard of care could effectively be more onerous in relation to the Usenet host's direct subscribers than in relation to other contributors to newsgroups.

4–047   Before the Defamation Act 1996 there were a number of cases dealing with the liability of traditional distributors of printed matter. There was at least one example of a distributor or other subordinate disseminator being held liable having failed to establish that it was not negligent. In *Vizetelly v. Mudie's Select Library Ltd*[43] the proprietor of a circulating library was held liable for a book that he lent out containing a libel. Following litigation, the publishers had placed notices in the trade press asking for the book to be withdrawn. Although the proprietors took the trade papers, they were not checked for notices. The Court of Appeal found that the proprietors admitted that they ran their business on the basis that it was cheaper to run the risk of an occasional libel suit than to employ someone to read the books for libel. The proprietors' contentions that the number of books circulated was so great that it was impossible in the ordinary course of their business to read them did not avail them.

4–048   The question remains whether the positive obligation to take reasonable care in relation to publication of a defamatory statement can be discharged by an ISP who takes no positive steps to make any checks on content that it carries or hosts. In this regard, it is arguable that the wording of the Act places a more onerous burden on the defendant than did the common law defence, since the Act places a positive burden on the defendant. Even in *Vizetelly* notices had been issued of which the defendant ought to have been aware.

The question could be asked, for instance, whether an ISP should make any random checks on content (to be required to check everything would be wholly unreasonable in view of the volumes of messages and websites carried by most ISPs). In other contexts, traditional magazine distributors have been found to have satisfied a due diligence requirement where they had traded over a long period of time with a reputable publisher and made no checks themselves (see *e.g. London Borough of Harrow v. W H Smith Trading Ltd*, discussed in Chapter 5). However, while that is helpful in establishing that there is no rule of law that some steps must always be taken in order to satisfy a due diligence requirement, that leaves unanswered the question of whether any positive steps need to be taken where the ISP is receiving content direct from the public, as opposed to from a reputable publisher.

4.4 What constitutes publication?

4–049   The essence of publication is communication of the defamatory statement to someone other than the person defamed. This superficially simple statement has, however, to be considered in conjunction with issues such as burden of proof and intention to publish. In the context of the Internet, this raises several issues: first, whether an e-mail is published to anyone other than the recipient of the e-mail; secondly, whether on the World Wide Web there can be liability for linking to other sites containing defamatory material. The third question of in what circumstances the content of a foreign site will be taken to have been published within the English jurisdiction or, if not published here, may yet be actionable here, is dealt with in Chapter 6.

4.4.1 E-mail

There is no liability for a defamatory statement sent only to the defamed person. So at first sight an e-mail sent only to the defamed person ought not to found any liability. However, Internet e-mails pass through intermediate routers on the way to their destination and are capable of being read by technicians at those intermediate sites. Could this constitute publication to a third party?   **4–050**

Two different situations need to be considered: first, where it is proved that a third party did in fact read the e-mail; and secondly, where the court is being asked to infer publication without actual proof that someone read it.

If a third party does read the e-mail, the court will have to consider whether the defendant intended, or ought to have foreseen, that the e-mail would or could be read by someone other than the intended recipient. If, for instance, the defendant knows that the plaintiff is in the habit of letting his assistants open his e-mails, the defendant will be liable for publication to the assistant who opens it. On the other hand, if it is opened by someone at an intermediate router, much may depend on whether the defendant knew that this was possible, whether it was proper for the person at that intermediary to do so and other factual circumstances. A plaintiff would most probably make great play of the much-publicised insecurity of Internet e-mail. If the e-mail were encrypted before transmission and some third party managed to decrypt and read it, the defendant would have a strong case that he neither intended nor ought to have foreseen that publication.

The second situation is where there is no proof that anyone other than the recipient read the e-mail, and the plaintiff instead asks the court to infer from the facts that some third person read it. So, for instance, if a libel is written on the back of a postcard that will be evidence of publication, the words being visible to anyone through whose hands it passes. The same applies to a telegram, as the contents will have been communicated to the clerks who transmit it. But the presumption will not be made in the case of an unsealed envelope sent through the post, as there is no presumption that the post office staff will have opened it.[44] It is submitted that an unencrypted e-mail is more analogous to the unsealed note than to a postcard so that the inference of publication ought not to be drawn; and that the inference will certainly not be drawn in the case of an encrypted e-mail. However, if an unencrypted e-mail is in fact read by a third party the sender may find himself liable for that publication as described above.   **4–051**

4.4.2 Liability for linked content

A Web site can provide access to a collection of journals and periodicals without any of the content being physically on the site at all. A Web page has a series of links, which when clicked will take the user to the linked material. These links may be "internal", leading to material held on the same site, or "external", leading to material held on someone else's site held elsewhere on the Internet. So a site can be created consisting of   **4–052** nothing but external links to other sites. To the user it will look superficially identical to a site on which the same materials are held internally on that site.

What is the status and liability of such a site, with regard to defamatory material contained on one of the linked sites? Should the liability be any different from someone who holds the materials themselves? There is old authority[45] that drawing attention to an existing defamatory statement can amount to publishing it. In that case someone sat in a chair pointing out to passers-by a defamatory sign erected over the road. The author of the sign was unknown, but the person pointing it out was found thereby to have published it. That would seem to suggest that providing a link to another site can amount to publishing material contained on it.[46] Much may depend on the facts. For instance, was the link to the site as a whole, or to a particular article on it?

4–053   Whether the person providing the link could rely on the innocent dissemination defence of the Defamation Act 1996 must be a matter of speculation. The activity does not obviously fall within any of the explanatory categories of section 1(3). It would be necessary to rely on the plain words of section 1(3) to argue that the person creating a link is neither an author, an editor, nor a commercial publisher, reinforced if necessary by reliance on the "analogy" provision of section 1(3). If this hurdle is overcome, greater difficulty may be encountered in discharging the standard of care requirements. In the case of a direct link to a defamatory article it is difficult see how a person could establish reasonable care without proving that they read the offending page before linking to it. In that event (unless the fact that it was defamatory was not apparent from the text) how could they establish that they did not know and had no reason to believe that what they did contributed to the publication of a defamatory statement? The situation may be less clear in the case of a link to a Web site containing defamatory text elsewhere within it.

Although the Electronic Commerce Directive does not address the question of linking liability, Art 21 of the Directive requires the European Commission before July 17, 2003 to submit a report on the application of the Directive, which is required (among other things) to analyse the need for proposals concerning the liability of providers of hyperlinks.[47]

4.5 Some U.S. comparisons

4–054   In the field of defamation analogies with U.S. law are dangerous: "...I refer to [the American authorities] but only shortly because I found them only of marginal assistance because of the different approach to defamation across the Atlantic" (Morland J., in *Godfrey v. Demon Internet Ltd*). However, the earliest on-line defamation judgments were delivered in the U.S. and commanded considerable attention worldwide. Those and some later decisions are of interest as examples of how another jurisdiction has approached the problem of determining on-line liability of intermediaries.

The two early U.S. cases were *Cubby Inc v. CompuServe Inc.*[48] and *Stratton Oakmont v. Prodigy Inc.*.[49] These cases concerned on-line discussion forums of the traditional pre-Internet type, provided by CompuServe and Prodigy respectively. The main difference from an Internet newsgroup is that rather than being replicated around publicly available hosts on the Internet, a Prodigy or CompuServe forum of that era was held only on the provider's computer and was accessible only by subscribers to the service.

4–055   In *Cubby*, CompuServe agreed with a third party publisher to provide, as part of CompuServe's Journalism Forum, a magazine called *Rumorville USA*. The contract stated that the publisher would have responsibility for *Rumorville*'s contents. The magazine was produced regularly by the third party publisher, loaded direct into the Journalism Forum and made available to those CompuServe subscribers who had made arrangements with *Rumorville*'s publishers. CompuServe had another contract with a company whose job it was to manage the Journalism Forum in accordance with CompuServe's editorial and technical standards and conventions of style. The manager had the ability under the contract to edit, delete and control the contents of the Forum. On the evidence CompuServe had no opportunity to review the contents of *Rumorville* before the publishers placed it on the forum.

Cubby alleged that *Rumorville* contained a defamatory statement and sued Compu-Serve, claiming that it was a publisher. CompuServe maintained that it was a distributor and was innocent.

The court held that CompuServe was indeed a distributor in this case and subject to the same standard of liability as a traditional public library, bookstore or newsstand. The judge described it as an "electronic, for-profit library that carries a vast number of publications". He emphasised that although CompuServe could decide not to carry a publication, once it had decided to carry the publication it would have little or no editorial control over its contents. He also laid some emphasis on the management of the forum by a company unrelated to CompuServe.

The facts of the case were closely analogous to hard copy publication and distribution, involving as they did the uploading of a pre-edited third party magazine to CompuServe's system. There was no consideration in the case of the position regarding posting of individual messages to a discussion forum.   **4–056**

The question of discussion forums came before the courts in the second U.S. case, *Stratton Oakmont v. Prodigy Inc.* This time the complaint was about a message posted to a discussion forum, hosted by Prodigy. The plaintiff sued Prodigy. On a preliminary point the court held that Prodigy was liable as a primary publisher, as it had exercised some editorial control over the content of postings. It had, for instance, screened postings for offensive material and also held itself out as controlling the content of its bulletin boards. Prodigy, like CompuServe, contracted out management of the forum to a third party, but that was held not to prevent liability arising.

Since then, in *Lunney v. Prodigy Services Company*[50] Prodigy have been held not liable in defamation for the contents of an e-mail and two bulletin board messages sent using its system. The court found that Prodigy did not publish the messages. The court put forward four reasons for disagreeing with the first Prodigy case: (1) insofar as the current case concerned e-mail, the rationale of the original case would not apply to that since Prodigy clearly could not screen all the e-mail sent by its subscribers; (2) on the evidence Prodigy abandoned in 1994 the efforts at editorial control which formed the factual basis of the earlier case; (3) the decision in *Anderson v. New York Telephone Co.*[51] stated that a telephone company was to be considered a publisher only of those messages in whose transmission it actually participated. It would not matter if Prodigy exercised power to exclude vulgarities from certain messages, if there was no proof that it exercised such control in connection with transmission of the messages complained of by the plaintiff; (4) Even a telephone company which participated in the transmission of a libellous message could not be held liable unless it knew it was libellous.   **4–057**

Bracken J.P. held that Prodigy did not publish the statement and that even if it could be considered a publisher of the statement it attracted qualified privilege in the absence of proof that Prodigy knew such a statement would be false. Bracken J.P. also criticised the policy implications of the earlier *Prodigy* case: **4–058**

"...in *Stratton Oakmont* Prodigy was punished for allegedly performing in an inadequate way the very conduct (exercise of editorial control) which, initially, it had no legal duty to perform at all. The rule of law announced in *Stratton Oakmont* discourages the very conduct which the plaintiff in *Stratton Oakmont* argued should be encouraged."

In the *Demon Internet* case Morland J. observed that, unlike in the *Lunney* case, in English law Prodigy would clearly have been the publisher of the e-mail message.

It should also be noted that section 230 of the Communications Decency Act now provides that no provider or user of an interactive computer service shall be held liable on account of "any action voluntarily taken in good faith to restrict access to or availability of material that the provider or user considers to be obscene ... or otherwise objectionable" or on account of "any action taken to enable or make available to information content providers or others the technical means to restrict access to [such material]". It also provides that "No provider or user of an interactive computer service shall be treated as the publisher or speaker of any information provided by another information content provider". This was applied in *Zeran v. America Online, Inc.*[52] so as to render the defendant immune from suit.

---

1.   *Cubby Inc v CompuServe Inc*, 776 F Supp 135 (SDNY 1991) and *Stratton Oakmont v Prodigy Inc.*, 1995 NY Misc LEXIS 229. See section 4.5 for an account of these cases.
2.   *Godfrey v. Demon Internet Ltd* [1999] 4 All E.R. 342.
3.   On-Line in Print, June 1996.
4.   The first reported U.K. settlement of a defamation claim concerning company internal e-mails was the Asda case in 1995 (*The Lawyer*, April 25, 1995). This concerned a policeman who was refused service at an Asda store as a result of having being identified in an e-mail circulated to stores. The case was settled with an apology and undisclosed damages. In 1997 a defamation claim brought by Western Provident Association against Norwich Union Insurance Company concerning an internal Norwich Union e-mail was settled on payment of £450,000 damages by Norwich Union. In 1999 a defamation case brought by Exoteric Gas Solutions and its owner Mr Andrew Duffield against British Gas was settled when the plaintiffs accepted a payment into court of £101,000. The case concerned an internal e-mail circulated by a British Gas area manager after Mr Duffield left British Gas to set up EGS (*Legal Week*, July 1, 1999). The question of liability for internal e-mails and the Norwich Union case are discussed further in Chapter 5.
5.   European Parliament and Council Directive 2000/31 O.J. L178 on certain legal aspects of information society services, in particular electronic commerce, in the Internal Market (Directive on electronic commerce). See also, as regards certain acts in relation to copyright, "Proposal for a European Parliament and Council Directive on the harmonisation of certain aspects of copyright and related rights in the Information Society"; modified Commission proposal COM (99) 0250. See Chapter 5 for full discussion of these provisions for liability of intermediaries.
6.   Jurisdiction questions are discussed in Chapter 6.
7.   For a detailed exposition of the law of defamation generally, see *Gatley on Libel and Slander* (9th edition, Sweet & Maxwell, 1997.)
8.   Under the Defamation Act 1996 there is now greater scope for the trial of defamation actions by a judge alone.
9.   The relevant provisions of the Defamation Act 1996 apply to causes of action which arose on or after September 4, 1996.
10. *Gatley*, para. 6.15. Even so, "participate" may have a broad meaning. In *Marchant v. Ford* [1936] 2 All E.R. 1510 the Court of Appeal refused to strike out a pleading that the printer of the book jacket containing the "blurb" for a book had published the book. The Court of Appeal held that the matter should be left for evidence at the trial. See the main text as to whether the provisions of s. 1 of the Defamation Act 1996 may influence the common law meaning of "publish".
11. See above, n. 2.
12. As is the case in U.S. law (*Anderson v. New York Telephone Co.* 1974 35 N.Y. 2d 746). But see section 4.5 as to the dangers of comparisons with U.S. caselaw. See also the discussion below regarding s. 1(3) of the Defamation Act 1996 and its possible influence on the common law meaning of "publish".
13. Main text, section 4.5.
14. *Gatley*, para. 6.8.

15. The Consultation Paper "Reforming Defamation Law and Procedure" (Lord Chancellor's Department, July 1995) stated (S.2.6) that the new defence was to "replace and modernise innocent dissemination". In moving the Second Reading of the Bill in the House of Lords the Lord Chancellor stated that Clause 1 was a "new statutory defence which will supersede the common law defence of innocent dissemination" *Hansard*, H.L. March 8, 1996 col. 577. The Parliamentary Secretary, Lord Chancellor's Department made an identical statement when moving the Second Reading of the Bill in the House of Commons *Hansard*, H.C. May 21, 1996 col. 129. However, in Commons Committee the Parliamentary Secretary used slightly different words when moving amendments to Clause 1 of the Bill: "a new statutory defence to defamation proceedings that will *effectively* supersede the common law defence of innocent dissemination" (emphasis added) *Hansard* H.C. Standing Committee A June 6, 1996 col. 4.

16. The Faulks Committee in 1975 recommended that the ambit of the innocent dissemination defence be extended to printers.

17. The potential significance of the disappearance of the wrapping function is illustrated by the *Lunney v. Prodigy* case (main text, section 4.5), in which the court's third reason for disagreeing with the earlier *Prodigy* decision relied upon treating each message transmitted across its system as being separate and distinct from the rest.

18. See, for instance, the Response of CompuServe, Europe Online and Microsoft to the Lord Chancellors' Department on the July 1995 Consultation Paper: "Technology permits on-line services to edit or delete content when problems are pointed out to the service provider, but the sheer volume of works, services and communication prevents this being done in advance".

19. See, for instance, on the question of negligence, *Weldon v. 'The Times' Book Co Ltd* (1912) 28 T.L.R.143 "It was quite impossible that distributing agents such as the respondents should be expected to read every book they had. There were some books as to which there might be a duty on the respondents or other distributing agents to examine them carefully because of their titles or the recognised propensity of their authors to scatter libels abroad. Beyond that the matter could not go." (Cozens-Hardy, M.R.). But volume and lack of time to inspect are not exonerating if no care is taken. See *Sun Life Assurance Company of Canada v. W.H. Smith and Son Ltd* (1934) 150 L.T.R. 211, C.A. "...by the system they have adopted, Messrs. W.H. Smith & Son Limited have made it next to impossible that they should exercise any care whatever in seeing whether posters they put up for reward for themselves contain defamatory statements against some other person ... It is not sufficient for the defendants to say that it is inconvenient for them and difficult for them, having regard to their large business, to make any other arrangements than the arrangements which they have in fact made." (Greer L.J.).

20. Transcript of reasons for ruling given during trial, June 17, 1999.

21. Although it was relevant to the issue of reasonable care under s. 1(1)(b).

22. *Godfrey v. Demon Internet Limited* (n. 2 above).

23. n. 10 above.

24. n. 20 above.

25. n. 1 above.

26. Prodigy abandoned editorial control in 1994—see *Lunney v. Prodigy* (main text, section 4.5). The policy implications of the earlier *Prodigy* decision also were criticised in *Lunney* (see main text, section 4.5). Similar policy concerns may lie behind Gray J.'s formulation of the editorial function in *MORI v. BBC*.

27. See *MORI v. BBC*, n. 20 above.

28. [2001] E.M.L.R. 29.

29. See *MORI v. BBC*, above.

30. And see *Marchant v. Ford*, n. 9 above.

31. Note that Article 21 of the Electronic Commerce Directive (2000/31) requires a re-examination of the Directive 2000/31 [2000] O.J. L178/1 before July 17, 2003, encompassing the liability position of search engines.

32. This may exclude "portals", which seek to combine search engines with direct content.

33. Note that in the U.S. case of *Lunney v. Prodigy* (main text, section 4.5) the court held that "intelligent editorial control involves the use of judgment, and no computer program has such a capacity".

34. Defamation Act 1996 s. 1(1)(b) and (c).

35. *Hansard* H.L. April 2, 1996 col. 214.

36. [1977] 2 All E.R. 566.

37. At page 573.

38. *Morris v. United Kingdom*.

39. Human Rights Act 1998, s. 3(1).

40. Human Rights Act 1998, s. 4(2).

41. Human Rights Act 1998, s. 6(1) and (3).

42. Art. 16.

43. [1900] 2 QB 170.

44. *Huth v. Huth* [1915] 3 KB 32.

45. *Hird v. Wood* [1894] 38 SJ 234.

46. In Germany a Web site owner has been held liable in defamation for providing a link to third party sites containing defamatory statements about the plaintiff, notwithstanding a disclaimer stating that

responsibility for linked third party statements would lie only with the respective authors. The defendant's claim that he was only providing a "market of opinions" failed. [1998] C.T.L.R. 7 N-113.

47.   The report is also required to address the liability of the providers of location tool services, "notice and take down" procedures and the attribution of liability following the taking down of content, as well as the need for additional conditions for the exemption of liability under Articles 12 and 13 (mere conduits and caching) and the possibility of applying internal market principles to unsolicited e-mail.

48.   n. 1 above.

49.   n. 1 above.

50.   250 A.D. 2d 230. Upheld on appeal to the Supreme Court of New York, 94 N.Y. 2d 242.

51.   n. 12 above.

52.   1997 129 F3d 327

5

Content Liability and Protection

5.1 Introduction

The content available on the Web and other Internet sources ranges from pure **5–001** entertainment to information that verges on professional advice. Tax sites, offering tips and tax calculation facilities, are one example of the latter. Medical and health sites have proliferated. Some NHS patients are to be offered consultations with psychotherapists in an online chatroom.[1] It is easy to envisage sites providing legal advice, do-it-yourself hints and all manner of content on which the user may rely.[2] If the information were inaccurate and the user suffered harm, could the content provider (or the host) be liable? Can anything be done to minimise liability?

Negligence is the main legal basis on which liability for incorrect information on web sites could accrue. The more remote possibility of strict liability under the Consumer Protection Act 1987 is also discussed.

We also address the increasingly important topic of the liability of employers for use by their employees of e-mail and the Internet. This includes the development of staff policies to reduce and manage the risk of liability and the ability of employers and other network operators to access and make use of electronic communications on their networks, both for the purposes of their businesses and to police the use of their networks.

5.2 Incorrect information – negligence liability

5.2.1 General principles of negligence liability

The prerequisite for negligence liability is that the person accused owed a duty of care to **5–002** the person harmed to take reasonable care to avoid the harm that occurred. The mere fact that a person has suffered harm as a result of another person's actions or omissions does not mean that a duty of care existed so as to found liability.

There are two main strands of negligence liability, which to an extent coalesce when considering liability for on-line information. The first originates from liability for defective products. In the leading case of *Donoghue v. Stevenson*[3] the House of Lords for the first time imposed direct liability to the end-user on the manufacturer of defective products causing physical injury. The liability arises directly from acts or omissions such as one-off manufacturing defects in products, design defects, or incorrect labelling on hazardous materials.[4] The class of persons to whom the duty of care is owed is very wide; in effect to all those who could foreseeably be damaged by a defect in the product. The liability principles apply equally to personal injury and physical damage to property. However, the courts have not been willing to allow a claimant to recover pure economic loss, ie financial loss where the product defect did not cause any physical damage to property or persons. Nor can the claimant recover for the loss of the defective product itself.

5–003   The second strand of liability concerns information and advice. Although the courts have been prepared to impose a wide duty of care in the case of product liability, the position is very different in the case of incorrect information. Where a person has suffered damage as a result of relying upon incorrect information, the courts have (unlike in a product liability case) been prepared to allow recovery for pure economic loss where it would be fair, just and reasonable to do so. But that is balanced by a drastic reduction in the class of persons to whom the duty of care is owed. The courts have been extremely unwilling to impose a duty of care to the world at large in respect of reliance on information. Liability has tended to be imposed only in respect of a small class of known persons with a sufficiently close relationship to the giver of the information that the duty of care should apply. This type of liability was established in the leading case of *Hedley Byrne & Co Ltd v. Heller & Partners Ltd*.[5] While the formulation of the test for determining whether a duty of care exists has tended to fluctuate, most recently it has been stated in terms harking back to the *Hedley Byrne* case, namely whether the provider of the information has assumed responsibility for it to the plaintiff.[6]

5.2.2 Liability for incorrect information

Duty of care

5–004   Other than cases of close proximity (such as in a professional relationship), there have been no English cases dealing directly with incorrect information causing physical injury or damage. Where there is sufficient proximity and it is fair, just and reasonable to do impose a duty of care, a duty of care will be owed.[7] Recovery for economic loss is permitted if there is a sufficiently close relationship, so it would be surprising if recovery for physical damage or personal injury was not permitted. The difficult and uncertain question is whether in the case of physical damage the class of persons to whom the duty of care is owed is wider than for economic loss, and if so how much wider. Could, for instance, the duty of care extend to anyone who reads a Web page and suffers physical injury as a result?

Interactivity

5–005   The question is not unique to on-line information. It applies to books and newspapers. But the potential for liability is exacerbated by two things. First, the scope for interactivity on an electronic site allows information to be provided that responds closely to a request made by the user. Such information could be provided by an expert system sitting behind the Web page analysing requests. This begins to look more like personal advice than does the plain information available from a passive book. It could thus lead to liability.

For instance in *De La Bere v. Pearson Ltd*.[8] a case decided early last century, a newspaper advertised that its City editor would answer inquiries from readers of the paper desiring financial advice. The paper published a reader's question asking for the name of a good stockbroker, together with a reply recommending someone who the editor ought to have known, if he had made proper inquiries, was an undischarged bankrupt. The reader dealt with the stockbroker and lost his money. The case was brought in contract, the consideration for the contract being either the publication of the reader's question or the addressing of the inquiry. The newspaper was found liable. That was described by Lord Devlin in *Hedley Byrne* as a "just result". Nowadays, given the development in negligence liability since *Pearson*, it would probably be unnecessary to force the facts into the straightjacket of contract theory.

Mass advice

The second exacerbating factor is that the lower cost of providing information **5–006**
electronically permits wider and readier dissemination of the information. The result is that it becomes economic to provide, electronically, the sort of information and quasi-advice that has previously had to be custom-made and delivered personally by professional advisers. This may parallel the developments in the market for goods which preceded the imposition of manufacturers' liability for defective goods in *Donoghue v. Stevenson* in 1932.

It is possible to glean some pointers to these liability issues from more recent decided cases, although these are all *obiter dicta* in cases not directed specifically to the question. Lord Oliver in *Caparo v. Dickman*,[9] a case concerning reliance on audited company accounts, commented that:

> "...reliance upon a careless statement may give rise to direct physical injury which may be caused either to the person who acts on the faith of the statement or to a third person. One only has to consider, for instance, the chemist's assistant who mislabels a dangerous medicine, a medical man who gives negligent telephone advice to a parent with regard to the treatment of a sick child, or an architect who negligently instructs a bricklayer to remove the keystone of an archway ... In such cases it is not easy to divorce foreseeability simpliciter and the proximity which flows from the virtual inevitability of damage if the advice is followed."

If the doctor is liable, why not the publisher of a Web site that provides information in **5–007**
response to a description of the symptoms? Is the greater degree of anonymity sufficient to take the case beyond the bounds of a duty of care? But if the reader in *De La Bere* could sue for his financial loss, why not the user of a Web site who suffered physical injury?

In *Candler v. Crane, Christmas & Co*,[10] another case concerning liability for accounts, Lord Denning commented that:

> "...a scientist or expert (including a marine hydrographer) is not liable to his readers for careless statements in his published works. He publishes his work simply for the purpose of giving information, and not with any particular transaction in mind at all. But when a scientist or an expert makes an investigation and report for the very purpose of a particular transaction, then, in my opinion, he is under a duty of care in respect of that transaction."

This suggests that there is no liability for mere information made available to the world at large. However, the question has never been decided in an English court and remains open.

Physical damage and economic loss

5–008   There has been a number of cases in other countries in which the question of liability for books and charts has been litigated. Courts in different countries have reached different conclusions. In the USA the publishers of aeronautical charts have been held liable under U.S. product liability laws, whereas the publishers of an encyclopaedia of mushrooms were held not liable. In France, on the other hand, a publisher of a book on edible plants is reported to have been held liable for injury caused by eating hemlock instead of wild carrot.[11]

Given the uncertainty over liability for physical damage caused by incorrect information, the possibility of liability for pure financial loss must be remote for information made generally available (as opposed to advice given in response to a request). There have been many cases concerning financial loss suffered as a result of reliance on audited accounts, profit forecasts and similar information. The courts have consistently restricted liability to a narrow class of persons. The courts have resisted imposing liability for pure economic loss "in an indeterminate amount for an indeterminate time to an indeterminate class".[12] In the present state of English law it is most unlikely that liability would be incurred for pure economic loss caused by general information made available for free on a Web site.

5–009   One sure prediction, however, is that at least some of today's personal, custom-tailored, individually provided professional advice services will be tomorrow's branded, mass-provided interactive information services. That trend can only increase the pressure to widen the scope of liability for economic loss caused by incorrect information. The courts are currently set against this. But only a few years before *Donoghue v. Stevenson* imposed product liability on manufacturers, judges were insistent that such liability should not be contemplated. In *Mullen v. Barr*[13] Lord Anderson said:

> "In a case like the present, where the goods of the defenders are widely distributed throughout Scotland, it would seem little short of outrageous to make them responsible to members of the public for the condition of the contents of every bottle which issue from their works. It is obvious that, if such responsibility attached to the defenders, they might be called upon to meet claims of damages which they could not possibly investigate or answer."

The imposition of liability on manufacturers was preceded by the advent of mass-marketed, branded, advertised consumer products. These created an economic link between the consumer and the manufacturer, which was eventually recognised and reflected in the *Donoghue v. Stevenson* decision. A move from personal advice to mass-marketed quasi-advice could presage a similar change in liability for the provision of information services.

5–010   To the extent that quasi-advice services are provided to known, individual, paying users, liability to those users is likely under present law and will also most likely be governed by express contracts. However, information provision on the World Wide Web may not always follow that commercial model. Many sites are free to the user and paid for by advertising and sponsorship. Even those sites that do charge the user tend to have a substantial amount of free information available. In this situation it is less easy to hold the user to contractual terms; and the steps necessary to do so may be regarded from a marketing point of view as creating too great a deterrent to users. Even if there is a paying user, the possibility of liability to others who may use the information but who are not in a contractual relationship with the content provider, friends and family members for instance, has to be considered.

5.3 Incorrect information – strict liability

Part I of the Consumer Protection Act 1987 implemented the EC Directive on Product Liability.[14] It established a regime, parallel with negligence liability, for liability for defective products irrespective of whether there was fault on the part of the manufacturer. It is unlikely that any liability would accrue under the Act for "information defects" such as incorrect information contained on a Web site. On the other hand, it is more arguable that program files do fall within the Act as being products within the meaning of the Act. However, this is not at all clear and the question remains a matter of debate.[15] The Act applies only to defects causing death or personal injury; or physical damage to non-business property exceeding £275 (which could include damage to data on the recipient's disk.[16]) **5–011**

Section 7 of the Act prohibits limitation or exclusion of liability under the Act to a person, or to a dependant or relative of such a person, who has suffered damage caused wholly or partly by a defect in a product.

5.4 Viruses

In addition to damage caused by human beings relying on incorrect information, electronic communication gives rise to the possibility of damage to data as the result of receiving maliciously written computer programs, or viruses. There are many varieties of virus, some verging on the playful, many capable of causing serious damage to the functioning of computer systems. Originally viruses existed only within executable program files. The prevailing wisdom was that data files, such as word processed documents, were safe. Now, however, the sophistication of macro languages incorporated in word processor and other document production software is such that even ordinary documents are capable of containing viruses. These macro viruses can be especially lethal when distributed as attachments to e-mail.[17] **5–012**

The authors and originators of viruses may be subject to criminal liability. Virus authors have been successfully prosecuted under the Computer Misuse Act 1990.[18] Our concern here is with the possible civil liability of those who unintentionally disseminate viruses.

Potential liability may arise in three ways: negligence, strict liability under the rule in *Rylands v. Fletcher* and trespass.

5.4.1 Negligence liability for virus dissemination

Duty of care and physical damage
As discussed above, for negligence it is generally easier to establish the existence of a duty of care owed to the world at large where the case involves the foreseeable risk of physical damage or personal injury. It is strongly arguable that a malicious virus causes foreseeable physical damage to any computer affected by it. In *R v. Whiteley*,[19] a prosecution of a hacker under the Criminal Damage Act 1971, the prosecution had to establish that the defendant had caused damage to tangible property. The Court of Appeal found that this requirement was satisfied. The defendant's argument that his activities had affected only the intangible information contained in the disk, and not the disk itself, failed. Lord Lane C.J. said: **5–013**

"It seems to us that the contention contains a basic fallacy. What the Act requires to be proved is that tangible property has been damaged, not necessarily that the damage itself should be tangible. There can be no doubt that the magnetic particles upon the metal disks were a part of the disks and if the appellant was proved to have intentionally and without lawful excuse altered the particles in such a way as to cause an impairment of the value or usefulness of the disks to the owner, there would be damage within the meaning of Section 1. The fact that the alteration could only be perceived by operating the computer did not make the alterations any the less real, or the damage, if the alteration amounted to damage, any the less within the ambit of the Act."

The finding that a requirement of "damage to tangible property" was satisfied, suggests that in the context of negligence a requirement of physical damage would also be satisfied. This would provide a foundation on which to claim for consequential economic loss. Pure economic loss would remain irrecoverable.[20]

Foreseeability of physical damage

5–014 As to foreseeability, since the very purpose of a virus is to spread and to cause such physical damage, the element of foreseeability appears to be satisfied. The question of whether it is "fair, just and reasonable" to impose a duty of care on all classes of persons (including, for instance, private individuals), would require careful consideration by the courts.

Standard of care

5–015 A difficult question with negligence liability for distribution of a virus is that of the standard of care to be expected of the defendant. Is everyone who handles electronic files expected to take precautions by virus-checking files and e-mails before passing them on? Or must they do so only when, for instance, they knew or should have known that there was, or that there was a real risk of, a virus being present? Does the same standard apply to everyone? Or should software publishers, IT professionals, business people and private individuals (assuming a duty of care to have been imposed) be held to different standards of care? These questions remain to be answered.

5.4.2 *Rylands v Fletcher* and virus dissemination

General

5–016 The rule in *Rylands v. Fletcher*,[20a] now regarded as a variety of the law of nuisance applicable to an isolated escape,[21] imposes strict liability for foreseeable damage on someone who brings onto his land an inherently dangerous thing which subsequently escapes to some other place not under his control and which causes damage. While there appears to be no reason in principle why recovery should not extend to economic loss consequent upon the physical damage, so long as the relevant type of damage is foreseeable, pure economic loss would be regarded as too remote.[22]

Accumulation of dangerous material

5–017 The rule primarily imposes liability on someone who accumulates dangerous material on his land. The manufacturer of anti-virus software or the university computer science department maintaining a collection of computer viruses would constitute precise analogies with traditional categories of persons subject to the rule. However, most people do not set out to maintain collections of computer viruses. Their systems become infected by accident and they pass on the viruses by accident or neglect.

Third party acts

The rule recognises that where the dangerous thing has been brought onto the land, or the escape has occurred, through the unforeseeable act of a third party, then the defendant is not liable. However he may become liable if he was himself negligent. So in the case of fire, a person is not liable to a neighbour whose house is destroyed by fire that escapes from his own property if the fire on his own property was started by a third party.[23] However, if the person negligently fails to prevent the spread of the fire, he then becomes liable.[24] This reasoning suggests that even if a person's computer systems become infected with a virus due to the act of some third party, he may become liable for the onward transmission of the virus if, through the exercise of reasonable care, he could have prevented its further spread.

5–018

Natural use of land

Although there is considerable uncertainty about the extent of the exception, the rule in *Rylands v. Fletcher* does not apply if the use of the land in question is a "natural use", which in *Rickards v. Lothian*[25] the Privy Council interpreted as meaning that the rule only came into play if there were "some special use bringing with it increased danger to others, and must not merely be an ordinary use of the land or such a use as is proper for the general benefit of the community". It may be that since the House of Lords has held in *Cambridge Water Co. v. Eastern Counties Leather plc*[26] that foreseeability of harm of the relevant type is a necessary ingredient of liability in damages under *Rylands v. Fletcher*, the natural use exception may be easier to control in the future[27] and so become less important.

5–019

5.4.3 Liability in trespass for virus dissemination

The tort of trespass to goods may in some circumstances be prayed in aid by someone whose property has been damaged by a computer virus. Trespass to goods is an unlawful disturbance of the possession of goods by seizure or removal, or by a direct act causing damage to the goods.[28] The logic of the decision in *R v. Whiteley*, discussed above, suggests that virus damage to the data on a computer disk would constitute damage to goods for the purposes of trespass. The tort of trespass certainly includes intentional conduct (such as that of a person who deliberately releases a virus into the wild) and may include negligent conduct.[29] However, no liability will attach if the conduct of the defendant involved no fault.

5–020

5.5 Restricting liability

5.5.1 Unilateral notices and contractual terms

Disclaiming or restricting liability for Internet content usually takes the form of preventing a liability-inducing situation arising or disclaiming or restricting liability that may exist, and restricting the territories at which the content is aimed. These are

5–021

done either by means of unilateral notices or as part of a broader attempt to bind the user to contractual terms. The latter is often achieved by requiring the user to signify acceptance of a set of terms and conditions by clicking on a button. These are known as "Web-wrap" or "click-wrap" contracts, by analogy with software shrink-wrap licences, and are discussed in Chapter 10. Here we discuss unilateral disclaimer notices.

The unilateral notice approach may be appropriate on a free site where the only likely liability is tortious.[30] But a unilateral notice can do no more than restrict pre-existing liability. If the site owner wishes the user to assume obligations to the owner (such as by indemnifying the owner for liabilities that could occur through the user's use of the site), then the owner must create a contract with the user. Even on free sites many owners seek to bind their users to lengthy contracts governing their use of the site. These have to be implemented with especial care. It is all too common to find a carefully (and no doubt expensively) drafted site use contract, complete with indemnity and exclusion clauses rendered in capital letters to draw them to the attention of the reader, hidden behind inconspicuous, anodyne or even misleading buttons and links.[31] Such practices are likely to achieve little other than to provide the legal profession with the pleasure of conducting modern day re-enactments of the Victorian ticket cases.[32] While the site user may fairly expect that a purchase made from a site will be governed by some terms and conditions, many users would be surprised to find that the site owner was purporting to govern their use of the site itself under a detailed set of contractual terms and conditions including, for instance, indemnities on the part of the user.

5–022   By their very nature, contractual site use terms have to be incorporated at the entry point or home page of the site. Insofar as they purport to govern the provision of an "information society service" (e.g. the use of a commercial site) under the E.U. Electronic Commerce Directive, the question could arise of compliance with the contractual transparency requirements of Article 10 of the Directive when that is implemented in the United Kingdom (as to which, see Chapter 10). However, since those requirements are predicated on the placing of an "order" by the recipient of the service, their potential application to general site use contracts must be doubtful.

Unilateral notices must also be properly drawn to the attention of the relevant person if they are to be effective.

5–023   Both unilateral notices and contracts are subject to consumer protection legislation, which affects the degree to which liability can be excluded and may prohibit some types of exclusion. This causes great difficulties. Each jurisdiction has its own consumer protection legislation, and exclusions that are lawful in one jurisdiction may be unlawful in another.[33] A Web site owner may well have no reliable indication of the country from which a particular user is accessing the site, or of the residence or domicile of the user.[34] There are great difficulties in drafting disclaimers of worldwide validity. Software publishers have resorted to printing booklets of sets of licences tailored for each jurisdiction. A similar approach on a Web site would require an elaborate screen with questions designed to ascertain the country from which the user was accessing the site (or the domicile or residence of the user, as appropriate) and displaying the appropriate disclaimer. The practical problem with this approach, apart from the obvious expense, is that it may deter users. But anything less risks being ineffective.

One approach that may be an acceptable compromise is to divide the site into free and restricted access sections. The free access section includes the opening screen and any other sections with risk-free content. The restricted access sections are gated with a contract acceptance screen, the user answering whatever questions are required to ascertain the relevant jurisdiction and to serve up an appropriate form of contract.

5.5.2 Preventing liability arising

Disclaimers

It will be seen from the discussion above that on the currently ascendant theory of   **5–024**
negligence liability, one question that may determine the existence of a duty of care is
whether the information provider assumed responsibility to the person who relied upon
the information. Many disclaimers are aimed at preventing the inference being drawn
that the content provider has assumed responsibility. Thus a typical disclaimer may state
that the contents of the site are for general information only, that nothing on the site
constitutes professional advice, that the reader should take advice from a suitable
qualified professional in relation to any specific problem and that the site owner takes no
responsibility for any loss caused as a result of reading the content of the site. The bank
reference in *Hedley Byrne* itself was given with a disclaimer of responsibility. The House
of Lords held that this prevented a duty of care arising. It was at pains to state that this
was not a case of seeking to contract out of a pre-existing duty. The disclaimer was part of
the material from which one deduces whether a duty of care was assumed. However, a
Web site disclaimer is unlikely to be read in isolation from the content of the site. If the
overall assessment of the site content leads to the conclusion that the owner has in fact
assumed responsibility to the user, then the disclaimer may not defeat that. Nowadays,
the need to take into account the effect of any disclaimer when considering whether a
duty of care exists also leads to consideration of the Unfair Contract Terms Act 1977 as an
integral part of the exercise.[35] The effect of such consumer protection legislation is
considered in more detail below.

Boundary markers

Another aspect of preventing liability arising is the use of "boundary markers". As noted   **5–025**
in Chapter 1, one effect of the World Wide Web is to blur the boundaries between
documents. It is very easy for a user to slip from one site to another without realising that
the identity of the site proprietor has changed. The problem occurs acutely with online
shopping malls. If a site owner provides space on his own advertised site to other
companies, it is very easy for the user to become unclear whether he is dealing with the
site owner or the tenant. The site owner may not even hold any of the tenant's materials
on his site, if all he provides is a Web link to the tenant's own site held on some other
host. The site owner will wish to make clear that he is not responsible for the content of
the tenants, and will wish to make clear to the user when he is moving from the site
owner's content to the tenant's content. Similar problems can occur when a site owner
acts an introducer to third party suppliers. The transition from dealing with the site
owner to dealing with the third party has to be made clear to avoid confusion over who
the user is contracting with.

Similar considerations will apply if a Web site contains links to wholly unconnected   **5–026**
third party sites. It is increasingly common practice to warn users by means of a suitably
placed notice or buffer page that linked third party sites are not the responsibility of the
site owner. The potential effectiveness of such a disclaimer should always be reviewed by
reference to the type of liability being considered. A disclaimer making clear that the
proprietor assumes no responsibility for third party linked material may be effective in
relation to negligence liability based on a theory of assumption of responsibility.
However, it is unlikely to be directly effective in relation to, for instance, defamation
liability where liability accrues through the act of publication. On the other hand, if for
any purpose the site owner's degree of responsibility for content depends on whether the

site owner has (say) assumed editorial responsibility for the material, then a disclaimer could be useful evidence about that. If drawing attention to the defamatory statement by linking to it amounts to publication of the target material by the creator of the link,[36] it is difficult to see how any disclaimer or responsibility could affect that.

5.5.3 Territory statements

5–027 A territory statement specifies that the site may be accessed from, or that the goods or services advertised are available only in, certain jurisdictions. Territory statements have to date been of most relevance if there is a risk that the content of the site or the services advertised are illegal in certain jurisdictions (examples of this range from pornography to financial services). Territory statements are likely to assume greater importance with increasing acceptance in a variety of areas of the principle that the mere availability of a web site in a country is insufficient to trigger that country's jurisdiction, and that jurisdiction should be triggered only if the site is targeted or directed at that country. This principle is emerging in a number of different areas. Examples include the so-called *Zippo* continuum in US inter-state jurisdiction cases,[37] the increasingly unified international approach to financial services regulation,[38] recent English caselaw on cross-border use of trademarks,[39] a report from the World Intellectual Property Organisation Standing Committee on Trade Marks, Industrial Designs and Geographical Origins,[40] and Article 15 of the pending "Brussels Regulation" on Jurisdiction and Enforcement of Judgments.[41] Cases asserting national laws on a 'mere availability' basis may not stand the test of time,[42] although it will be many years (if ever) before a wholly settled approach is achieved. The Tobacco Advertising and Promotion Bill, intended to prohibit tobacco advertising in the United Kingdom, would provide that it is not an offence for a person who does not carry on business in the United Kingdom to publish a tobacco advertisement "by means of a web site which is accessed in the United Kingdom".

5–028 The efficacy of a territory statement is unlikely to be considered in isolation from other aspects of the site. Its efficacy may vary, depending on the nature of the risk that is sought to be guarded against. In some cases a mere statement, with no attempt to discover the country from which the user is attempting to access the site, may be of little use. However, for potential negligence liability a statement making clear (assuming it to be the case) that the information is relevant only to certain countries excluding England could well influence a determination as to whether any responsibility was assumed in respect of users in England.

5.5.4 Consumer protection legislation

5–029 Consumer protection legislation is highly relevant to Web site disclaimers. The owner of a freely accessible site faces a dilemma. In general, the kind of information most likely to give rise to liability (*e.g.* information which, if incorrect, could cause personal injury), is precisely that in respect of which legislation is most likely to prohibit, or render ineffective, disclaimers of liability. The kinds of information for which disclaimers of liability are possible are those for which as the law currently stands liability is very unlikely: typically information which, if incorrect, is likely to cause pure economic loss.

The distinction between contractual disclaimers and unilateral disclaimers by notice is important in the context of consumer protection. Both are covered by the Unfair Contract

Terms Act 1977. The United Kingdom has also implemented the EC Unfair Contract Terms Directive 1993[43] by means of the Unfair Terms in Consumer Contracts Regulations 1994[44] which came into force on July 1, 1995. These Regulations, which supplement the 1977 Act, apply only to terms in consumer contracts. Unilateral notices restricting tortious liability are still covered only by the 1977 Act.

The effect of the 1977 Act and of the Regulations on Web site contracts is dealt with in Chapter 10. Here the discussion will be restricted to unilateral notices. A notice under the 1977 Act includes an announcement, whether or not in writing, and any other communication or pretended communication (section 14).

5–030

Section 2(1) of the 1977 Act provides that a person cannot by reference to a notice exclude or restrict liability for death or personal injury arising from negligence. Notices which exclude or restrict liability for negligence other than death or personal injury are valid only if reasonable.

These provisions apply to business liability, in other words breach of obligations or duties arising from things done or to be done by a person in the course of a business (whether his own business or another's). The requirement of reasonableness in respect of a non-contractual notice is (under section 11(3) of the 1977 Act) that it should be fair and reasonable to allow reliance on it, having regard to all the circumstances obtaining when the liability arose or (but for the notice) would have arisen. The burden of showing that a notice is reasonable is upon the person seeking to rely upon it.

The 1977 Act applies to notices which exclude or restrict the relevant obligation or duty (section 13(1)). This is especially relevant to notices designed to prevent a duty of care arising. In *Smith v. Eric S Bush*[45] the House of Lords held that such a disclaimer was caught by the 1977 Act where a surveyor retained by a lender attempted to disclaim liability to the borrower who relied upon the survey.

5–031

The medical advice Web site

NetMed is a fully interactive Web site, driven by a database of medical information. It is provided as a free attraction by a newspaper. Users can key in symptoms and after a few seconds a suggested diagnosis appears, with possible home treatments.

The proprietors are acutely aware of the liability implications of this site. It is more than a general information system, as it provides tailored responses to specific queries. They wish to disclaim liability for actions taken in reliance upon the information provided. However, they are advised that excluding liability for death or personal injury is prohibited by the Unfair Contract Terms Act 1977 and (insofar as relevant) the Consumer Protection Act 1987. They speak to their insurers.

In *McCullagh v. Lane Fox and Partners Ltd*[46] the Court of Appeal held that a disclaimer of responsibility in a set of estate agents' particulars was effective to prevent a duty of care to the purchaser arising as regards the description of the area of the garden of the property. The form of the disclaimer was "none of the statements contained in these particulars as to this property are to be relied upon as statements of representations of fact". The court also found that the exclusion of liability was reasonable under the 1977 Act.

In *First National Bank plc. v. Loxleys (a firm)*[47] the Court of Appeal held that the existence of a duty of care could not be decided as a discrete point separately from whether it was fair and reasonable under the 1977 Act to allow the defendants to rely upon a disclaimer, since it was at least possible that the existence of a duty of care would be held to depend at least partly on the effect of the disclaimer.

5.6 Protecting content

5–032 Content owners are often concerned about the ease with which content on the Internet can be downloaded and copied. The least that a content owner can do to ease these concerns is to ensure that suitable copyright notices, warnings against copying and express licences are prominently displayed on the Web site. It is insufficient simply to state, for instance, that all content is copyright and all rights are reserved. The reason why this is not good enough is that the very act of viewing the Web page involves transmitting a copy of the page to the user's computer and holding a copy of it in memory. Thus a blanket prohibition on copying is nonsense. There is clearly some implied licence to copy for the purposes of viewing the page. Once the existence of the implied licence is admitted, then there is room for debate about its scope. It is far better to avoid that debate by placing express limited permissions on the Web page, sufficient to enable the user to view the page and do whatever else the content owner is prepared to permit. Matters to be addressed might include: is temporary or permanent storage on the user's local hard disk permissible? For instance, most Web browsers "cache" (*i.e.* store) pages on the local hard disk to speed up access to a site. Is that to be permitted? It is hardly practicable not to permit that, when many users may not even realise that the Web browser is caching pages on their disks or know how to prevent it happening. Can users send e-mail extracts to others? If so, under what conditions? Can corporate users copy any content on to their intranets? If the site owner wishes to assert any control over linking to the site, especially "deep-linking" to sub-pages, then that should be included in the notice.

A fuller discussion of copyright issues is contained in Chapter 2.

5.7 Liability of on-line intermediaries

5–033 The liability of on-line intermediaries such as access providers, network providers and hosts has to date had to be considered individually for each tort or criminal offence. The substantive components of the relevant wrong have had to be assessed, together with any other relevant principles such as vicarious liability, joint tortfeasorship and so on. The result of this has been that the potential liability of on-line intermediaries has been complex to assess, and may vary as between different wrongs in a rather arbitrary fashion, depending on how the substantive components of the wrong read onto the activities of the on-line intermediary.

5.7.1 Electronic Commerce Directive

5–034 For a wide range of torts and crimes this piecemeal approach will change when the United Kingdom implements the E.U. Electronic Commerce Directive. This must be done before January 17, 2002. Articles 12–15 of the Directive establish a single set of threshold requirements for the liability of certain on-line intermediaries in respect of a broad range of wrongs. The relevant intermediaries are "conduits" (which equate broadly to network and access providers), "hosts" (storage) and "caches" (those who create temporary caches of material to make for more efficient operation of the network).

Information society services

The scope of the Directive is set out in Article 1, which in Articles 1(1) and (2) sets out the **5–035** general objective of contributing to the proper functioning of the internal market by ensuring the free movement of information society services between Member States including, to the extent necessary to achieve that objective, approximating certain national provisions on (*inter alia*) liability of intermediaries.

An "Information society service" is, by virtue of Article 2(a), a service within the meaning of the E.U. "Transparency Directive".[48] Recital 17 summarises the definition: "any service normally provided for a remuneration, at a distance, by means of electronic equipment for the processing (including digital compression) and storage of data, and at the individual request of a recipient of the service". The Recital goes on to state that those services referred to in the indicative list of Annex V to the Transparency Directive that do not imply data processing and storage are not covered by the definition.

Recital 18 goes on to provide examples of economic activities that do and do not fall **5–036** within the definition. Some of these are as follows.

Activities falling within the definition:

- selling goods on-line

- insofar as they represent an economic activity:

- offering on-line information or commercial communications

- providing tools allowing for search, access and retrieval of data

- transmission of information via a communication network

- providing access to a communication network

- hosting information provided by a recipient of the service

- video-on-demand

- provision of commercial communications by electronic mail

Activities not falling within the definition:

- delivery of goods as such

- provision of services off-line

- television and radio broadcasting (because they are not provided at individual request)

- use of electronic mail or equivalent individual communications by natural persons acting outside their trade, profession or business including their use for conclusion of contracts between such persons

- the contractual relationship between an employee and his employer

- statutory auditing of company accounts

- medical advice requiring the physical examination of a patient

So, for instance, a solicitor giving advice at the request of a client through a web site or e-mail would be likely to fall within the provisions of the Directive. However, if the solicitor were to confirm the advice by letter, that confirmatory advice would fall outside the Directive.

Article 1(4) states that the Directive does not establish additional rules on private international law nor does it deal with the jurisdiction of courts.

Exclusions from the scope of the Directive

5–037   Certain areas are by Article 1(5) excluded entirely from the scope of the Directive, so that the liability of intermediaries provisions will not apply to these areas. The exclusions are:

(a)   the field of taxation;

(b)   questions relating to information society services covered by Directives 95/46 and 97/66 (Data Protection Directive and the Telecommunications Data Protection Directive);

(c)   questions relating to agreements or practices governed by cartel law;

(d)   the following activities of information society services:

—   the activities of notaries or equivalent professions to the extent that they involve a direct and specific connection with the exercise of public authority,

—   the representation of a client and defence of his interests before the courts,

—   gambling activities which involve wagering a stake with monetary value in games of chance, including lotteries and betting transactions.

Article 1(6) provides that the Directive does not "affect measures taken at Community or national level, in the respect of Community law, in order to promote cultural and linguistic diversity and to ensure the defence of pluralism". The effect of this provision is obscure. Presumably the use of the word "affect" rather than "apply to" means that this provision is not intended to be a complete exclusion of the Directive.

Recital (58) states that the Directive should not apply to services supplied by service providers established in a third country.

Mere conduits

5–038   Article 12 addresses the liability of "mere conduits", which should be contrasted particularly with hosting liability addressed in Article 14. Article 12(1) provides that:

"1. Where an information society service is provided that consists of the transmission in a communication network of information provided by a recipient of the service, or the provision of access to a communication network, Member States shall ensure that the service provider is not liable for the information transmitted, on condition that the provider:

(a)   does not initiate the transmission;

(b)   does not select the receiver of the transmission; and

(c)   does not select or modify the information contained in the transmission."

The typical telecommunications network provider will fall within this provision as regards its transmission services. If the same company also provides hosting services, those will fall under Article 14 notwithstanding that the company providing them is at first blush a traditional telecommunications company.

Article 12(2) goes on to state: **5–039**

> "2. The acts of transmission and of provision of access referred to in paragraph 1 include the automatic, intermediate and transient storage of the information transmitted in so far as this takes place for the sole purpose of carrying out the transmission in the communication network, and provided that the information is not stored for any period longer than is reasonably necessary for the transmission."

The purpose of this provision is to make clear that a mere conduit can still take advantage of Article 12 even though the transmission involves automatic, intermediate and transient storage of the information. The use of the word "transient" may be contrasted with the use of the word "temporary" in Article 13 concerning caching. "Transient" storage would presumably cover the storage of data in RAM as it travelled through a switch, or buffering of data to relieve transmission bottlenecks. However the point at which storage ceases to be transient is not clear, save that it is governed by the requirement that the storage be no longer than reasonably necessary for the transmission.

Article 11(3) provides: **5–040**

> '3. This Article shall not affect the possibility for a court or administrative authority, in accordance with Member States' legal systems, of requiring the service provider to terminate or prevent an infringement.'

Exposure to an injunction would therefore, under Article 11(3), be assessed by reference to the underlying national law regarding an intermediary's possible liability for the tort or crime in question. If, some reason, an intermediary falls outside the protection of the Directive it would (if the national implementation is structured in this way) still be necessary to examine the underlying national law to ascertain whether the intermediary had done an act that attracted the relevant civil or criminal liability.

Hosting

Article 14 addresses hosting liability. It provides: **5–041**

> "1. Where an information society service is provided that consists of the storage of information provided by a recipient of the service, Member States shall ensure that the service provider is not liable for the information stored at the request of a recipient of the service, on condition that:
>
> (a) the provider does not have actual knowledge of illegal activity or information and, as regards claims for damages, is not aware of facts or circumstances from which the illegal activity or information is apparent; or
>
> (b) the provider, upon obtaining such knowledge or awareness, acts expeditiously to remove or to disable access to the information.
>
> 2. Paragraph 1 shall not apply when the recipient of the service is acting under the authority or the control of the provider.

3. This Article shall not affect the possibility for a court or administrative authority, in accordance with Member States' legal systems, of requiring the service provider to terminate or prevent an infringement, nor does it affect the possibility for Member States of establishing procedures governing the removal or disabling of access to information."

5–042   This Article, by contrast with the mere conduit provisions, provides a "notice and takedown" regime for immunity from liability for damages (the service provider remains vulnerable to an injunction). The reference to "illegal" information is unfortunate, since it could be taken to connote only criminal liability.[49] However, the references to damages would be inappropriate if that were intended. The intent of the Directive appears to be to provide immunity from both civil and criminal liability. Unlike conduits or caching intermediaries, the reservation of infringement termination rights against hosts extends to procedures governing the removal or disabling of access to information.

Caching

5–043   Article 13 addresses liability for caching. It provides:

"1. Where an information society service is provided that consists of the transmission in a communication network of information provided by a recipient of the service, Member States shall ensure that the service provider is not liable for the automatic, intermediate and temporary storage of that information, performed for the sole purpose of making more efficient the information's onward transmission to other recipients of the service upon their request, on condition that:

(a)   the provider does not modify the information;
(b)   the provider complies with conditions on access to the information;
(c)   the provider complies with rules regarding the updating of the information, specified in a manner widely recognised and used by industry;
(d)   the provider does not interfere with the lawful use of technology, widely recognised and used by industry, to obtain data on the use of the information; and
(e)   the provider acts expeditiously to remove or to disable access to the information it has stored upon obtaining actual knowledge of the fact that the information at the initial source of the transmission has been removed from the network, or access to it has been disabled, or that a court or an administrative authority has ordered such removal or disablement.

2. This Article shall not affect the possibility for a court or administrative authority, in accordance with Member States' legal systems, of requiring the service provider to terminate or prevent an infringement."

5–044   It may be noted that the wording of this provision differs from that of the conduit and hosting provisions, in that the exemption is from liability for the defined act of "automatic, intermediate and temporary storage" of the information, rather than (in the case of the other two provisions) liability for the information generally. That could mean that the exemption in this case is only from liability that could attach to that act (such as copyright infringement), rather than liability attaching to the onward transmission of the information or its receipt by the ultimate recipient.

The reference to rules regarding updating information refers to the fact that caching of information may result in the recipient, without his knowledge, receiving out of date information. In time-critical cases such as stock prices this could be seriously misleading. The reference to technology used to obtain data on the use of the information recognises that web sites rely on usage data to justify advertising rates. If a user "hits" a cache instead of the source site, then the site may not capture the hit and will underestimate the usage.

The reservation of infringement termination rights against a caching intermediary is in identical terms to that in respect of conduits.

No obligation to monitor

Article 15 of the Directive prohibits Member States from imposing a general obligation on **5–045** intermediaries to monitor the information which they transmit or store, or a general obligation actively to seek facts or circumstances indicating illegal activity.

5.7.2 Beyond the Electronic Commerce Directive

The question of on-line intermediary liability regularly comes to public attention in the **5–046** context of particular issues of topical interest. Examples during the course of 2000/2001 include Internet advertising by overseas adoption agencies, the Tobacco Advertising and Promotion Bill and the application of the Bulger injunction to Internet service providers. So long as these fall within the scope of the Directive, then a degree of uniformity will be brought to these issues. However, the Directive does not provide a complete protective mantle. In particular, as we have seen, the Directive does not affect the grant of injunctions. Nor does it specify the terms in which injunctions may be granted. Indeed it specifically permits national courts to require an intermediary to "terminate or prevent" an infringement. Taken at face value, this could allow an injunction to be cast in wide terms, so that an intermediary could be at risk of breaching of an injunction in circumstances in which it would otherwise gain the protection of the Directive. However, as we shall see when we examine the Bulger injunction, there has been some recognition by English courts of the special position of Internet service providers.

Internet adoption advertising

The question of liability of Internet service providers under the Adoption Act 1976 arose **5–047** in the context of the publicity surrounding the "Internet twins" case. The only role of the Internet in the case was enabling the putative United Kingdom adopters to identify a U.S. adoption broker. Subsequently, the Department of Health wrote to United Kingdom ISPs suggesting that they faced criminal prosecution if they knew that they had material on their servers that contravened section 58(1) of the 1976 Act, but failed to remove it.[50] Although this letter caused concern in the ISP community, the stance of the Department (albeit based on the provisions of the 1976 Act) appears to have been in line with the hosting liability provisions of the Electronic Commerce Directive.

Tobacco advertising

Consternation was caused among ISPs at the beginning of 2001 by the Tobacco **5–048** Advertising and Promotion Bill, intended to prohibit tobacco advertising. Withdrawn before the General Election, it was reintroduced in July 2001 in the same form. The Bill contains broad definitions of publication and distribution, extending to publishing by any electronic means including the Internet, and (in the case of distribution) transmitting in electronic form, participating in doing so and providing the means of transmission.

An Internet service provider would have a defence to an electronic publication offence that he was unaware that what he published was, or contained, a tobacco advertisement. This (insofar as publishing equates to hosting) is a poor approximation to the hosting liability provision of the Directive. Placing the burden of proof of lack of knowledge on the defendant may perhaps be inconsistent with the Directive (the Directive is silent on burden of proof). The glaring omission is that there is no defence of having removed the material once the ISP gained the requisite knowledge.

5–049   As to distribution, an electronic distributor would have a defence that he was unaware that what he distributed or caused to be distributed was, or contained, a tobacco advertisement; or that having become aware of it, he was not able to prevent its further distribution. Since the definition of distributor would clearly encompass a conduit within the meaning of the Directive, this defence would not provide a conduit with the protection required under the Directive.

The Bulger injunction

5–050   *Venables and another v. News Group Newspapers Ltd v. Others*[51] Butler-Sloss P. granted an injunction restraining the publication of information that would reveal the identity or whereabouts of the claimants. In 1993 the claimants had been convicted (when both were aged 11) of the murder in February that year of a two year old boy, James Bulger. The claimants had spent their minority in detention and, having reached age 18, were likely to be considered for release during 2001.

The injunction granted by the judge was extremely unusual, in that it was an injunction against the world at large, not merely against the newspapers who were defendants to the proceedings. As originally granted on January 8, 2001, the injunction (so far as relevant for these purposes) restrained:

'1. . . . the Defendants and any person with notice of this order (whether themselves or by their servants or agents or otherwise howsoever or in the case of a company whether by its directors or officers servants or agents or otherwise howsoever) from:

(1)   publishing or causing to be published in any newspaper or broadcasting in any sound or television broadcast or by means of any cable or satellite programme service or public computer network: [the prohibited material] . . .''

5–051   The Order also provided for service on:

(a)   such newspapers and sound or television broadcasting or cable or satellite programme services and public computer networks as [the First and Second Claimants' Solicitors] may think fit, in each case by facsimile transmission or pre-paid first class post addressed to the Editor in the case of a newspaper, or Senior News Editor in the case of a broadcasting or cable or satellite programme service, or person responsible for any public computer network in the case of that network; . . .''

There was a clear possibility that an Internet Service Provider could be in breach of this order if a third party posted material to its servers, even though the ISP did not know it was there. While contempt of court requires both *actus reus* and *mens rea*,[52] so that it may be doubted whether an ISP could in fact have been in contempt for an act that it did not know it had done, clearly the wording of the injunction would create considerable unease in an ISP served with a copy of it.

Thus plc, the proprietors of the ISP Demon Internet, applied to court in July 2001 for a variation of the injunction to allay these concerns. The injunction was varied by consent, by insertion of the following proviso to paragraph 1(1):   **5–052**

"in relation to any internet service provider ("ISP"), its employees and agents:

(a)   an ISP shall not be in breach of this injunction unless it, or any of its employees or agents:
  i.   knew that the material had been placed on its servers or could be accessed via its service; or
  ii. knew that the material was likely to be placed on its servers, or was likely to be accessed via its service; and in either case
  iii. failed to take all reasonable steps to prevent the publication;

(b)   an employee or agent of an ISP shall not be in breach of this injunction unless he or it:
  i.   knew that the material had been placed on its servers or could be accessed via its service; or
  ii. knew that the material was likely to be placed on its servers or was likely to be accessed via its service; and in either case
  iii. failed to take all reasonable steps to prevent the publication and to induce the ISP to prevent the publication;

(c)   an ISP, employee or agent shall be considered to know anything which he or it would have known if he or it had taken reasonable steps to find out;

(d)   "taking all reasonable steps to prevent the publication" includes the taking of all reasonable steps to remove the material from the ISP's servers or to block access to the material."

The service provisions were also amended to permit service on a public computer network by e-mail.

The amended order bears certain similarities to the hosting liability provisions of Article 14 of the Directive, especially the combination of knowledge and failure to take reasonable steps to prevent publication. The knowledge standard as defined—"anything which he or it would have known if he or it had taken reasonable steps to find out" – is perhaps more onerous than that in the Directive, which requires lack of actual knowledge or, for damages, lack of awareness of "facts or circumstances from which the illegal activity or information is apparent". Other comparisons could be made with the deemed knowledge standard for secondary infringement of copyright "knows or has reason to believe",[53] or with the defence under section 2(5) of the Obscene Publications Act 1959 "no reasonable cause to suspect".   **5–053**

As a matter of general English law, knowledge includes the state of mind of someone who deliberately shuts his eyes to the obvious or refrains from inquiry because he suspects the truth but does not want to have the suspicion confirmed.[54] That, however, is different from mere neglect to carry out reasonable inquiries. A negligence or due diligence standard invites the question whether it requires positive steps to be taken to discharge the duty, or whether in the particular factual circumstances it can be reasonable to take no positive steps.

5–054   So, for instance, in *London Borough of Harrow v. W H Smith Trading Ltd*,[55] a case under the Video Recordings Act 1984, the Divisional Court held that the Crown Court was entitled to acquit the respondent newsagents of a charge of supplying an unclassified video recording in the form of a computer game covermounted on a computer magazine. The Act provided a defence that the commission of the offence was die to the act or default of a person other than the accused; and that the accused "took all reasonable precautions and exercised due diligence to avoid the commission of the offence by any person under his control". The magazine was supplied by a reputable publisher with whom the respondents had dealt for 20 years, which carried out its own checks. The Divisional Court found that the only question was whether the respondents should have made some checks. As to that, the court found: "Checking on a random basis would not in itself provide any significant protection for the respondent. And checking every item would be unrealistic. ... Random checking was a step which the court could properly conclude was not required in relation to this publisher."

5–055   This, as with all such cases, was a decision on its facts. It still leaves unanswered the question whether, if a negligence or due diligence standard is applied to an ISP which receives content direct from members of the public (as opposed to a distributor receiving magazines from a reputable publisher), that may require the ISP to take any positive steps in relation to any of that content. This is similar to the conundrum faced by ISPs in relation to establishing the innocent dissemination defence under the Defamation Act 1996 (see Chapter 4).

It is noteworthy that the Bulger Order addresses both removal from the ISP's own servers and blocking access from others (including, presumably, where the material could be accessed in this country from an overseas web site). These provisions reflect the hosting and access provision roles respectively of the ISP.

5.8 Employer liability, e-mail and Internet access policies

5.8.1 Electronic communication risks

5–056   The civil and criminal liability of employers for the acts of their employees on electronic networks raises increasingly complex issues. The starting point is to consider in what circumstances an employer can be liable for illegal or unlawful acts of its employees when sending or circulating e-mails and attachments, or when downloading material from the Internet and storing it on the employer's network, or indeed when using voicemail.[56]

The element common to all these technologies, and which distinguishes them from corridor chat or the ordinary telephone, is that they are self-recording. The act of communicating automatically creates and leaves behind electronic footprints as the message is stored and forwarded around the system. All these technologies create electronic documents that may have be to be produced subsequently if a disclosure obligation arises in, for instance, litigation.

5–057   Consequential issues arise from the steps that employers may wish to take to minimise their risk of liability or to ensure that they can discipline offending employees. We have to consider whether employers are free to monitor and read their employees' communications made using the employer's network. The introduction on October 24, 2000 of provisions of the Regulation of Investigatory Powers Act 2000 rendering operators of private networks (including employers) potentially liable to civil action for intercepting communications on their own networks is especially significant, as is the increasing emphasis on human rights, including a possible right of privacy, following the introduction on October 2, 2000 of the Human Rights Act 1998.

An important aspect of content liability is that attaching to e-mail messages, both those sent via the Internet and internal e-mails. Postings to Usenet newsgroups, which are in effect e-mails published to the world at large, are also potentially high-risk. Much of the relevant defamation litigation to date has concerned postings to Usenet newsgroups or to analogous on-line discussion forums. However, the largest United Kingdom e-mail defamation damages paid to date (£450,000) arose from the circulation of e-mails internally within an organisation.[57] The *Netcom* copyright infringement decision[58] concerned Usenet postings. The informal and uninhibited nature of e-mail and Usenet newsgroups encourages unguarded comment which can and does attract lawsuits. Incoming material is also high risk. Some Usenet newsgroups are very likely to contain illegal or infringing material which an employer will not wish to find stored on its systems.

It is also possible for employees to bind the company to contracts by means of e-mail. **5–058** Here we look generally at employer liability: how an employer may be liable for the legal incidents of e-mail sent by its employees using the company e-mail system, and of other employee Internet activities, and what the employer can do to minimise the liability.

The criteria for the existence of direct tort and criminal liability differ in respect of each type of liability (copyright, defamation, confidentiality, liability for virus damage etc). Reference should be made to the relevant discussions elsewhere in this book. A summary of some typical activities and corresponding statutory definitions and rules of law that may read onto such activities is contained in Table 5.1.

The potential risks have led many companies to enforce e-mail, voicemail and Internet **5–059** use policies. Following the introduction of the Telecommunications (Lawful Business Practice) (Interception of Communications) Regulations 2000, made under section 4(2) of the Regulation of Investigatory Powers Act 2000 (hereafter the "RIP Act Lawful Business Practice Regulations"), the desirability of having such a policy is even greater since it may enhance the company's ability lawfully to access communications on its network. This has two benefits: first, the avoidance of civil or criminal liability in connection with unlawful access; second, the ability to resist an argument in a court or tribunal that the evidence was unlawfully obtained and should excluded from consideration. Although there is no rule of law that unlawfully obtained evidence should be excluded, with the advent of the Human Rights Act 1998 the court should consider whether admitting the evidence will affect the fairness of the trial.[59]

The wise company will also educate its staff to understand that sending an e-mail is not (as they may think) akin to using the telephone, but is tantamount to sending written company correspondence. Like a letter or memo, e-mail can be produced in court as evidence and may to be disclosed to opponents in litigation during disclosure of documents. An e-mail is also extremely difficult to delete from a system.[60]

5.8.2 Liability for acts of employees

Vicarious liability

The principle on which an employer may be held liable for a civil wrong committed by **5–060** one of its employees is simply stated, but not easily applied. The employer is vicariously liable for a wrongful act committed by an employee in the course of his employment.

Activity	Consequence	Typical classes of liability-inducing act	Examples of applicable legislation
Downloading from Web sites, newsgroups, ftp sites etc; incoming e-mail	Data stored on company's servers. Programs may execute on company's system	Possession (indecent photograph) Copying, storage	Criminal Justice Act 1988 Copyright Designs & Patents Act 1988
Internal e-mails	Information (both body text and attachments) circulated within company	Copying, storage Publication, receipt Transmission Possession (indecent photograph)	Copyright Designs & Patents Act 1988 Defamation, harassment/ discrimination Obscene Publications Act 1959 (as amended) Criminal Justice Act 1988
Outgoing e-mail	The e-mail may conclude a contract, may be relied upon by the recipient, may damage data on the recipient's system if it contains a virus, or may trigger any liability founded upon communication of information to the recipient	Offer/acceptance Assuming responsibility for advice Publication Transmission Causing damage Unauthorised modification of contents of a computer	Contract Negligent misstatement Defamation (*cf.* passing off, trade mark infringement) Obscene Publications Act 1959 (as amended) Negligence, trespass Computer Misuse Act 1990
Uploading to web site discussion forums, newsgroups, mailing lists	Information made available to world-wide audience.	Publication Transmission Issuing copies to the public, distribution, copying	Defamation Obscene Publications Act 1959 (as amended) Copyright Designs & Patents Act 1988

Table 5.1

Until recently the test was whether the act was of a type which the employee was employed to carry out. If so, the employer was liable even if the act was done in an unauthorised way. But if the act was not one of a type which the employee was employed to carry out, then the employer was not liable. However, the House of Lords has now re-stated this test. In *Lister and Others v. Hesley Hall Ltd*[61] their Lordships held that the test is whether the tort is so closely connected with the employment that it would be fair and just to hold the employer vicariously liable. This test is more flexible, and probably broader, than the old one. It enables an employer to be held liable for acts done, as in the *Lister* case itself, "in the time and on the premises of the defendants" while the employee had also been busy carrying out his duties. The tort (in this case sexual abuse of pupils by the warden of a school boarding house) had been "inextricably interwoven" with the carrying out by the warden of his duties. This new approach perhaps increases the chance of an employer being held vicariously liable for infringing or defamatory employee personal e-mails sent on the employer's network and in its time. Even under the old test, merely prohibiting the sending of infringing or defamatory e-mails would not have relieved an employer of liability if the e-mail was otherwise sent in the course of its business.

Criminal liability
A corporate employer's potential liability for its employees' criminal acts is more limited than that for civil wrongs. This may be so if the employer authorised the act or turned a blind eye to it. Or a company may be vicariously liable on the clear words or construction of a statute.[62] Or if any necessary acts and mental state were those of individuals who represent the controlling mind and will of the company and therefore can be identified with it, the company can be liable for criminal acts of the individuals.[63]   **5–061**

Personal e-mail
Difficult questions may arise with personal e-mail. Many companies routinely tolerate a certain level of personal telephone calls, but would be very surprised if an employee were to use company headed paper for personal letters. Should a company tolerate or prohibit personal e-mail? If a company explicitly permits its system to be used for personal e-mail (even with appropriate disclaimers attached to the messages), then a claimant might try to argue (especially under the new, more flexible *Lister* test) that that brings it within the realm of vicarious liability. A prohibition honoured only in the breach could afford the claimant a similar opportunity.   **5–062**

Direct liability
A claimant seeking to make the employer liable for personal e-mail could also rely upon other forms of liability specific to certain rights, such as participating in the publication of a defamatory statement or authorising copyright infringement. For defamation, in particular, there are several bases on which a claimant could seek to hold the employer liable: **5–063**

1. Vicarious liability for the act of the employee in publishing the e-mail by sending it to a recipient.

2. As a publisher in its own right through participating in the employee's act of publication by providing the computer system by means of which the publication took place.

3.   As a publisher in its own right through participating, by providing the computer system, in any further acts of publication in which the e-mail is further disseminated, or by means of which other users see the e-mail.

As to the basis of holding an employer directly liable for defamation in its own right as a publisher, and the possible availability of the "innocent dissemination" defence, in defamation law anyone who participates in the first or main publication of a defamatory statement is liable for the defamation. In the traditional commercial publishing context this applies not only to the author, the editor and the publisher, but also to the printer and the distributor. Although subordinate disseminators such as printers, distributors and Internet service providers have an "innocence" defence available to them under section 1 of the Defamation Act 1996, they have prima facie participated in the publication and so will be liable if they cannot make out the innocence defence.

5–064   The publication of an employee's e-mail, using the employer's e-mail system, undoubtedly takes place on and by means of the employer's network. The question then is whether the employer is thereby to be regarded as having participated in the publication, or having merely facilitated it. If the former, then the employer would be regarded as having published the e-mail and be prima facie liable. If the latter, the employer would not be liable. This approach would apply to employees' personal e-mails us much as business e-mails, since it is irrelevant to the question of publication whether an e-mail was sent in the course of employment. The argument for employer liability on this basis is untested, although in one Canadian case[64] a printing company was held liable for a defamatory newssheet printed on its presses by some of its employees. The court found that the company's manager knew about and made no effort to stop the printing of the newssheet. See also the discussion in Chapter 4 regarding whether the pre-Defamation Act 1996 distinction between participation and facilitation has been modified as a result of the innocent dissemination provisions of the 1996 Act. If the employer were found to have published the e-mail, then it would be strictly liable for the defamation unless it can establish both that it is within the categories of those entitled to rely on the innocent dissemination defence and that it conformed to the necessary standard of care and other conditions laid down in the Act (see Chapter 4).

An employer may also find that, even if it escapes vicarious liability for an act of harassment carried out by an employee, it may still, as a consequence of failing to control the type of material in circulation in its office, including electronic material, become vulnerable to direct liability for sexual harassment.[65]

5–065   As regards contracts, the increasing availability of access to the Internet from employees' computers raises issues relating to the ability of those employees to bind their employer to contracts. Whereas contracts entered into in writing are likely to be subject to management procedures such as a review process and to formal signing off, such procedures may be circumvented in respect of contracts formed by e-mail or in response to a Web page. An employee may bind his employer in accordance with the general principles of agency. Of course, if the employee has actual authority to act in such a way, the Internet raises no particular issues as regards agency. The real concern must be as to whether the granting of the right to an employee to send and receive Internet e-mails and respond to Web pages confers ostensible authority to contract. The test is whether the employee is being held out by the employer as having that authority.

Common sense would suggest that the mere granting of access to the Internet does not confer ostensible authority to bind an employer. However, this must depend on the circumstances of each case. It would seem prudent for employers to review internal procedures and guidelines as to who is permitted access and for what purposes, to avoid the problem arising, and to ensure that the risks of creating a contract in this way are understood by all employees having access to the Internet.

5.8.3 Employment Tribunal decisions

Some examples of industrial tribunal claims that have involved the use and misuse of electronic communications and reliance on e-mail and Internet access policies are as follows.[66]

5–066

In deciding whether unauthorised access to any computer system constitutes grounds for dismissal a Tribunal will look closely at the circumstances of the particular case.

Unauthorised access

In *Denco Limited v. Joinson*,[67] Mr Joinson's password only gave him access to a particular part of the data held on his employer's computer system. He gained access to other more sensitive data by learning another password from his daughter who also worked for the same company. He was summarily dismissed. He had no improper motive. He had simply been "playing around with the system". Although at first instance his summary dismissal was considered unfair, on appeal the EAT overturned that decision ruling that if an employee deliberately uses an unauthorised password to enter a computer known to contain information to which he is not entitled, this in itself constitutes gross misconduct.[68]

5–067

By contrast, in the case of *BT v. Rodrigues*,[69] Mr Rodrigues was summarily dismissed for having obtained unauthorised access to computer data but his dismissal was found to have been unfair. He wanted access for legitimate work related purposes and although he had not been authorised to use the computer to access the information he had acquired, he would have been entitled to that information if he had asked for it over the telephone.

In both cases the Tribunal stressed that employers should make it abundantly clear to employees in disciplinary codes or other company literature that computer misuse would automatically result in summary dismissal so that employees should be aware of the seriousness of their actions.

5–068

Pornography

Using Internet facilities at work to access pornographic material may not necessarily justify dismissal on grounds of gross misconduct. Much will depend on the circumstances. In the case of *Parr v. Derwentside District Council* decided in 1998, the local authority employer did not accept the employee's claim that he had accessed a pornographic website by mistake when it could be established that he had accessed the site for a considerable period and had then re-visited it. In view of the fact that the employer was a local authority with standards to uphold, the Tribunal was satisfied that the dismissal was fair.

However, other employers may find it harder to convince a Tribunal. In the case of *Dunn v. IBM United Kingdom Limited*, also decided in 1998, the employee was summarily dismissed for gross misconduct. He admitted that he had accessed pornography via the Internet and made print-outs of downloaded pictures. However, the Tribunal found that his dismissal was not fair because he had admitted the offences without appreciating that the consequence would be his dismissal and the Tribunal did not feel that any disciplinary procedure had been properly applied. In these circumstances summary

5–069

dismissal was inappropriate but the Applicant's compensation was reduced by 50 per cent to take account of the fact that he had contributed by his behaviour to his own dismissal.

Harassment

5–070   Employees who access or transmit pornography while at work may use it to harass unlawfully their colleagues in the workplace. Their employers may be liable for their unlawful actions.

In the case of *Morse v. Future Reality Limited*, decided in 1996, the female Applicant was required to share an office with several men who spent a considerable amount of their time poring over sexually explicit or obscene images downloaded from the Internet facilities available to them at work. She accepted that these activities were not directed at her personally, but they did cause her to feel uncomfortable. Eventually she resigned and made a claim against her employers of sex discrimination on the grounds of harassment citing the pictures, bad language and general atmosphere of obscenity in the office as the basis of her complaint. The Tribunal held that her claim was well founded. No-one had taken any action to prevent the behaviour complained of. She was awarded three months' lost earnings and £750 for injury to feelings.

5.8.4 Electronic communication policies

5–071   An e-mail and Internet policy should extend to incoming messages and other forms of Internet access using the employer's facilities. The issue here is protection of the employer's business systems from viruses or other similar damaging incomers, and seeking to prevent liability for illegal, infringing or other damaging material downloaded and stored on the company's system. If employees (or some of them) have full Internet access, the policy will need to go wider than just e-mail, and extend to all forms of Internet access including reading Web pages and downloading files on to the employer's system.

In theory it can be useful to draw a distinction between executable and non-executable files. A non-executable (text) file ought to be harmless, whereas an executable (or program) file can potentially harbour a virus. Unfortunately, the distinction is now not so clear. Word processed documents often contain macros capable of operating as viruses. Program files can be converted to text for transmission as e-mail attachments and converted back to executable form on receipt. Java and ActiveX, programming languages increasingly used to animate and drive Web pages, require the recipient to download mini-programs to his computer, in addition to the page text.

5–072   So an e-mail and Internet access policy will need to address a variety of issues. Which employees can send e-mail on behalf of the company? What materials (if any) may be downloaded from outside the company network? What procedures should be adopted to quarantine and check such materials before allowing them onto the company network? Is personal e-mail permitted, and if so what signature file should be appended to indicate that? What signature tags should be appended to indicate the sending company and the position of the individual sender? Are postings to Usenet newsgroups permitted?

A formal e-mail and Internet access policy should be promulgated to staff and other system users and made part of the employee handbook and preferably incorporated in the contracts of employment.[70] The seriousness of non-compliance should be emphasised and the sanctions made explicit. The reasons for the policy and the risks to the company of non-compliance should be communicated clearly to employees. If the employer wishes be able to do anything that would constitute interception of a communication on its network, then if it wishes to take advantage of the RIP Act Lawful Business Practice Regulations it must (among other things) make all reasonable efforts to inform all persons who may use the telecommunications system in question that communications transmitted by means of the system may be intercepted.

5.9 Employer access to workplace communications

The ability of an employer to gain access to and utilise the contents of employee electronic communications is now affected by up to three separate pieces of legislation. These are the Regulation of Investigatory Powers Act 2000, the Data Protection Act 1998 and the Human Rights Act 1998. Each of these came into force during the course of 2000.[71]   **5–073**

5.9.1 Regulation of Investigatory Powers Act 2000

The Regulation of Investigatory Powers Act introduces a new statutory regime, replacing   **5–074**
the Interception of Communications Act 1985, governing the interception of telephone and electronic communications. Sections 1(1) and 1(2) of the Act create criminal offences of intercepting communications on public and private telecommunications systems respectively. By Section 1(6) of the Act interception on a private telecommunication system is excluded from criminal liability if it is carried out by a person with a right to control the operation or the use of the system, or by someone with the express or implied consent of such a person to make the interception. However, such a person making such an interception may still be subject to civil liability under Section 1(3). Under Section 1(3) any interception of a communication in the United Kingdom by, or with the express or implied consent, of a person having the right to control the operation or use of a private telecommunication system is actionable if it is without lawful authority. The tort is actionable at the suit of the sender, recipient or intended recipient of the communication.

"Private telecommunication system" is defined in Section 2(1) as meaning: **5–075**

> "any telecommunication system which, without itself being a public telecommu-
> nication system, is a system in relation to which the following conditions are
> satisfied—
>
> (a)   it is attached, directly or indirectly and whether or not for the purposes of the
>   communication in question, to a public telecommunication system; and
> (b)   there is apparatus comprised in the system which is both located in the United
>   Kingdom and used (with or without other apparatus) for making the
>   attachment to the public telecommunication system"

"Public telecommunication system" means:

> "Any such parts of a telecommunication system by means of which any public
> telecommunications service is provided as are located in the United Kingdom"

"Public telecommunications service" means:

"Any telecommunications service which is offered or provided to, or to a substantial section of, the public in any one or more parts of the United Kingdom."

"Telecommunications service" means:

"Any service that consists in the provision of access to, and of facilities for making use of, any telecommunication system (whether or not one provided by the person providing the service)"

"Telecommunications system" means:

"Any system (including the apparatus comprised within it) which exists (whether wholly or partly in the United Kingdom or elsewhere) for the purpose of facilitating the transmission of communications by any means involving the use of electrical or electro-magnetic energy"

Since "private telecommunication system" includes only systems attached directly or indirectly to a public telecommunication system, any private network not so attached is excluded from the scope of the Act, since it is neither a private nor a public telecommunication system as defined. However, this is unlikely to exclude more than a small minority of physically isolated networks.

5–076   "Private telecommunication system" is likely to catch any private network on which, for instance, it is possible to send or receive Internet e-mail, even by means of a dial-up connection. This will include most office networks. Since an employer will be a person with the right to control the operation or use of its own network, these provisions have clear potential to affect the ability of employers to read e-mails and other communications in their own systems.

The Explanatory Notes to the Act (paragraph 27) state that "an office network, linked to a public telecommunication system by a private exchange, is to be treated as a private system. ... An entirely self-standing system, on the other hand, such as a secure office intranet, does not fall within the definition". The reference to a secure office intranet is puzzling. Most intranets, while located behind secure firewalls to prevent unauthorised access from the outside world, are nevertheless connected to the outside world and permit traffic to flow between the intranet and the public network beyond the firewall. According to the definition in the Act it would seem that a secure intranet would only fall outside the definition of "private telecommunication system" if it were completely physically isolated from the public network.

5–077   The distinction between "private" and "public" telecommunication systems was also commented on by the Home Office Minister during the House of Commons Committee debate. He stated:

"...on the matter of public-private systems and domestic systems, I am advised, and we believe, that domestic systems are unequivocally private systems. The end of the public system is the network termination point, which is usually the white BT box just inside the front door of a house. Any extensions after that, whether to the PC or anything else, are part of the householder's private system."[72]

Unfortunately, while this explanation is certainly in accordance with established telecommunications regulatory distinctions between public and private networks, it does not fully reflect the definition in the Act. One of the determining factors under the Act is whether any public telecommunications service is provided by means of any part of the system. A telecommunications service includes provision of "access to" a telecommunications system. If offered or provided to a substantial section of the public it becomes a public telecommunications service. So if someone in a household were to host a website or a collection of MP3 files on a domestic PC, or store webcam pictures, and make them available to the public through the domestic telephone line[73] that would appear on the face of it to constitute offering the public access to the system consisting of the domestic PC. If apparatus used for the provision of hosting services (as opposed to mere transmission) is to be regarded as apparatus for the purpose of "facilitating" the transmission of communications within the definition of "telecommunications system", that would render the parts of the domestic system used for that purpose a public telecommunications system for the purposes of the Act.

Interception in the course of transmission

To fall within the civil liability provisions of section 1(3) the interception must either be in the course of transmission by the private telecommunications system or by a public telecommunication system to or from the private system. These definitions have their genesis in the subject-matter of the old Interception of Communications Act 1985, which mainly concerned real-time tapping of communications such as telephone conversations. The Regulation of Investigatory Powers Act, somewhat ill-advisedly in the light of the anomalies thereby created, ventures beyond real-time interception into some aspects of storage.   **5–078**

The general definition of interception under section 2(2) is that

"a person intercepts a communication in the course of its transmission by means of a telecommunication system if, and only if he:

(a)   so modifies or interferes with the system, or its operation,
(b)   so monitors transmissions made by means of the system, or
(c)   so monitors transmissions made by wireless telegraphy to or from apparatus comprised in the system,

so as to make some or all of the contents of the communication available, while being transmitted, to a person other than the sender or intended recipient of the communication"

Under section 2(6) references to the modification of a telecommunication system include references to the attachment of any apparatus to, or any other modification or interference with (a) any part of the system; or (b) any wireless telegraphy apparatus used for the making of transmissions to or from apparatus comprised in the system.

As regards storage, the times when a communication is being transmitted are extended by section 2(7) to include any time when the system is used for storing the communication in a manner that enables the intended recipient to collect it or otherwise have access to it. So an incoming pending e-mail stored in a mailbox would be covered. Curiously, to access a copy of an outgoing e-mail stored in a mailbox appears unlikely to constitute interception, since as a separate archive copy it probably does not form part of the actual communication in the course of transmission and it is not covered by the Section 1(7) extended meaning of "while being transmitted", which deals only with storage for access by intended recipients of communications. A further issue that may   **5–079** require resolution by the courts is at what point in time (if at all) an incoming e-mail ceases to be covered by the extended definition of section 2(7). For instance, once the intended recipient has accessed the e-mail is it no longer within section 2(7)? Or does section 2(7) continue to bite until, for instance, the communication has been deleted from the mailbox?[74]

When is the purpose of an interception to be determined?

5–080   Under Section 2(8) the cases in which any contents of a communication are to be taken to be made available to a person while being transmitted shall include any case in which any of the contents of the communication, while being transmitted, are diverted or recorded so as to be available to a person subsequently.

The Department of Trade and Industry, in its Response to Consultation[75] on the RIP Act Lawful Business Practice Regulations, appears to suggest that the determining factor is the purpose for which the recording is made at the time it is made. So, the DTI suggests, if a consumer were to record a telephone call with a business for his own use, that would not amount to interception under the Act (presumably because the recording would not be "so as to be available to a person [other than the sender or intended recipient][76] subsequently"). But, says the DTI, nothing in the Act[77] would prevent the consumer from choosing subsequently to make use of the recording in, for instance, court proceedings.

Can the recipient be guilty of interception?

5–081   This interpretation also suggests that the intended recipient of a communication can be liable for intercepting that communication, for instance by recording it so as to make it available to some other person. This appears to be consistent with the wording of Section 2(2), which places no obvious limitation on the class of person who may be found to have intercepted a communication. It differs, however, from Article 5 of the Telecommunications Data Protection Directive, which these provisions of the Act purport to implement. Article 5 requires Member States to prohibit interception or surveillance of communications "by others than users", without the consent of the users concerned. The Directive therefore places no obligation on Member States to prohibit interception by a user in any circumstances. Unlike the Act, it draws no distinction based on the purpose for which the user intercepts the communication. The Directive is discussed further below.

If it is correct that the intended recipient of a communication is among those who may be regarded as intercepting the communication, the consequences for users of voicemail and e-mail verge on the bizarre and are certainly arbitrary.

5–082   It would presumably not constitute an interception for the user to forward an incoming e-mail to a colleague after reading it, either because the user having collected the e-mail it is no longer caught by Section 2(7),[78] or because no modification or interference with the system, or monitoring of transmissions, is involved. Section 2(8) extends the cases in which a communication is taken to be made available to a person while being transmitted to include any case in which any of the contents of the communication, while being transmitted, are diverted or recorded so as to be available to a person subsequently. This could read well onto forwarding copies of e-mails to a colleague. However, it does not override the time requirement of Section 2(7), nor on the face of it detract from the requirement that there be a modification or interference with the system, or monitoring of transmissions made by the system, "so as" to have the consequences described. "Monitor" is not defined in the Act. While its meaning is well understood for real-time communications such as telephone calls, it is inapt to describe activities such as forwarding an e-mail, or even gaining access to an e-mail box of stored communications.

However, what is the position if the user programs his e-mail system automatically to **5–083** forward incoming e-mails from a particular sender to the same colleague? The extended Section 2(7) time bar does not drop until, at the earliest (if at all) the intended recipient has collected his e-mails. The programming of the e-mail facility could, more plausibly than the manual forwarding in the first example, be regarded as a modification or interference with the system or its operation. Alternatively, the colleague to whom the e-mails are forwarded could more plausibly be regarded as "monitoring" transmissions made by means of the system, even if he took no part in the decision or the steps necessary to forward the e-mails to himself.

Lastly what if the user, instead of setting up an auto-forward system, configures his e-mail software so as to grant access privileges to his colleague, or provides his colleague with a password to gain access? Again, could this be regarded as a modification or interference with the system or its operation? And would the colleague granted access privileges be regarded as monitoring?

If these examples, or any of them, do constitute interception under the Act then if the **5–084** Act applies to those acts when done by users it has consequences that were certainly not alluded to by its government promoters. The Act would, for no discernible policy reason, restrict the ordinary, everyday use of e-mail by users themselves. If, on the other hand, at least the second and third examples (auto-forward and granting access privileges) do not constitute interception under the Act (whether done by users or third parties), then the Act would be unlikely to achieve its presumed intent. Since the system operator has complete control over system privileges and configuration, it would be a simple matter to set up auto-forwards, or to grant widespread e-mail access privileges. Even if some distinction could validly be made between acts of the intended recipient and of the network operator,[79] so that only when carried out by the user do the acts not amount to interception, it would still be a relatively simple matter[80] for the network operator to require any user of the system to permit other system users to have access privileges to their e-mail box, if necessary constituting the employer the agent of the user for the purpose of configuring the system on behalf of the user to achieve that.

Yet if such steps are effective, the practical impact of the Act on e-mail and other self-storing, non-real-time, communications would become minimal and the RIP Act Lawful Business Practice Regulations would be largely superfluous.

Ephemeral versus self-recording communications

Generally, the very concept of "interception" has implications that differ significantly as **5–085** between ephemeral real-time communications such as telephone calls, and e-mail or voicemail. In the first case, the act of interception creates a record where none would have existed but for the interception. To the extent that any party to the telephone call has a legitimate expectation of privacy in relation to it, the covert creation of a record of the call would raise understandable concerns as to whether that expectation had been respected.[81] In the case of e-mail and voicemail, however, the very sending of the communication creates a record of it. The position is far more akin to a person who sends a letter, and thereby places a record of the communication in the hands of the recipient organisation. The act of "interception" in this case bites not on the creation of a record where none would otherwise have existed, but on gaining access to or creating further copies of a record that has already been placed in the hands of the recipient organisation by the sender. Any legitimate expectation of privacy in this case is likely to be far weaker than in the case of recording a telephone call. This distinction has been recognised in some U.S. cases on the interception of e-mail.[82]

Much of the difficulty encountered in this area, such as the public controversy during the Department of Trade and Industry consultation on the RIP Act Lawful Business Practice Regulations, can be traced back to the legislature treating these two different things (ephemeral and self-recording communications) as being the same and attempting to create one set of rules to fit both.

Who is a recipient?

5–086   Another example of this kind of difficulty stems from the fact that the Act does not define "sender", "recipient" or "intended recipient". In the case of a telephone call, it makes reasonable sense to assume that under the Act the recipient or intended recipient of the communication is the individual person who participates in the call, and not any organisation by whom that person is employed, or to whom the telephone apparatus belongs. But if "recipient" or "intended recipient" under the Act always refers to an individual recipient, that creates severe difficulties in the case of e-mail since there are common cases in which no intended individual recipient is identifiable. By analogy with the post the sender (whose intent can be the only relevant intent for the purpose of ascertaining the "intended recipient") often intends to place the communication in the hands of the recipient organisation, even if it be marked for the attention of an individual within the organisation. And what of the common case where someone sends an e-mail to "info@companyname.com", or "support@companyname.com"? That will be routed to some e-mail box or e-mail management system within the organisation, to which one or more individuals within the organisation will have access. But no individual intended recipient of the e-mail is identifiable.[83] If the Act does not embrace the concept of an organisational intended recipient, what is the status of such an e-mail? Since an integral part of the definition of "interception" under section 2(2) is that there be an intended recipient, if no individual intended recipient can be identified does the e-mail fall outside the scope of these provisions altogether? Or could the intended recipient(s) be regarded not as the organisation, but as all individuals within the organisation? If the sender of the e-mail receives a reply from an individual within the organisation, and sends a further e-mail to that individual (either to "namedindividual@companyname.com", or still to "info@companyname.com" but addressed to the individual within the body of the e-mail), does the further e-mail fall within the Act because there is now an identifiable intended recipient?

5–087   If, on the other hand, the Act does embrace the concept of a recipient organisation, then much of the protection against interception afforded by section 1(3) of the Act may fall away. That is because, as discussed above, it is easy to argue that the true intended recipient of most electronic communications sent to a business organisation (even those addressed to an individual mailbox) is in fact, as with business post, the organisation and not an individual within it. If that is so, then an organisation would fall foul of the interception provisions only if the interception were such as to make the communication available to someone outside the organisation.

Article 5 of the Telecommunications Data Protection Directive

5–088   Since these provisions purport to implement Article 5 of the E.U. Telecommunications Data Protection Directive,[84] some clue as the intent of the legislature may perhaps be gleaned from the Directive. However, Article 5 of the Directive arguably did not actually require any legislation to be implemented for communications on private networks.[85] Even if that is wrong, the Act clearly applies to a broader category of communications than those that fall within the scope of Article 5 of the Directive.

Article 5(1) of the Telecommunications Data Protection Directive, which had to be **5–089** implemented by Member States by October 24, 2000, requires Member States to:

> "1. ... ensure via national regulations the confidentiality of communications by means of a public telecommunications network and publicly available telecommunications services. In particular they shall prohibit listening, tapping, storage or other kinds of interception or surveillance of communications, by others than users, without the consent of the users concerned, except when legally authorised, in accordance with Article 14(1)."

Article 5(2) provides: **5–090**

> "2. Paragraph 1 shall not affect any legally authorised recording of communications in the course of lawful business practice for the purpose of providing evidence of a commercial transaction or of any other business communication."

"User" is defined in Article 2 as: **5–091**

> "Any natural person using a publicly available telecommunications service, for private or business purposes, without necessarily having subscribed to this service".

The first sentence of Article 5(1) of the Directive is a general obligation, making no reference to users. The second sentence, however, is clearly concerned with natural, not legal, persons. To the extent that the Act is to be regarded as implementing the Directive, this may suggest that "sender", "recipient" and "intended recipient" are intended to refer to natural persons.

The Department of Trade and Industry has taken the view that Article 5 of the **5–092** Directive applies to any communications on a private telecommunication system that travel on a public telecommunication system before or after travelling on the private system.[86] The government also justified these provisions of the Act by reference to the Directive during the passage of the Bill through Parliament.[87] This interpretation is not obvious from the terms of Article 5(1), which refer explicitly to public telecommunications networks and publicly available telecommunications services. It may be argued that the DTI interpretation is implicit in Article 5(2), since there could be no circumstances in which the activities described in Article 5(2) could be legitimately be exercised in relation to communications while on a public telecommunications network or while being conveyed by means of a publicly available telecommunications service. However, this does not stand up to scrutiny. For instance, a financial services company might wish to record telephone calls for compliance purposes. If it were to do that on its own network, on the private side of the public network termination point, then Article 5(1) would not apply. If it decided, instead, to employ the public network operator to record its calls at the public exchange, as part of a managed service provided by the public network operator, then without Article 5(2) that would be a breach of the prohibition in Article 5(1). Thus Article 5(2) has a perfectly sensible purpose without the need to extend the ambit of Article 5(1) beyond its apparent scope to communications on private networks. It is, therefore, open to serious question whether there was ever any obligation to enact section 1(3) at all in order to give effect to the Directive.

It may also be noted that, in its implementation, section 1(3) is not restricted to communications on a private telecommunications system that have also travelled or will travel on a public telecommunications system. It applies to all communications on a private telecommunications system. So even on the DTI's own interpretation of the Directive section 1(3) applies to a broader class of communications than would be required by the Directive.

5–093   A further difference between the Directive and the Act is that Article 5 does not, on its face, require Member States to secure the confidentiality of stored communications. If on its true interpretation the obligation does extend to stored communications,[88] Article 5 makes no distinction (unlike the Act) between stored copies of outgoing communications and stored incoming communications.

The significance of this comparison with the Directive is twofold. First, the degree to which the Act actually implements the Directive may be relevant to any attempt to construe provisions of the Act by reference to the Directive. Second, when we come to discuss the Lawful Business Practice Regulations we will see that the Regulations include a saving on the authority conferred by the Regulations by reference to the Directive. Since the relevance of the Directive to section 1(3) is at most only partial, and (as we have suggested) it may be wholly irrelevant, the reference to the Directive in the Regulations may be of little or no significance.

5–094   Finally, it should be noted that there is no need to extend the scope of Article 5 to communications on private networks, since such communications are covered by the Data Protection Directive. This is reflected in Recital (11) of the Telecommunications Data Protection Directive, which states:

"for all matters concerning protection of fundamental rights and freedoms, which are not specifically covered by this Directive, including the obligations on the controller and the rights of individuals, Directive 95/46/EC [the Data Protection Directive] applies; whereas Directive 95/46/EC applies to non-publicly available telecommunications services;"

Lawful authority

5–095   Interception is not actionable under section 1(3) of the Act if it has lawful authority. Interception has lawful authority (so far as likely to be relevant for the purposes of this discussion) in three situations. First, under section 3(1) of the Act it is authorised if the interception has, or the person intercepting has reasonable grounds for believing it has, the consent of both the sender and the intended recipient of the communication.

The usefulness of this exception differs significantly depending on the nature of the communication. For a real-time communication that requires the active participation of all concerned to initiate the connection (*e.g.* a telephone call), it is at least feasible to obtain the prior consent of all concerned to record the call. However, that is not the case for communications (such as e-mail and, to a lesser extent, voicemail) which are sent unilaterally to publicly available addresses and stored until such time as the recipient decides to access his mailbox. In the case of Internet e-mail, at least, it is literally impossible to comply with a requirement of prior consent.

5–096   Secondly, interception has lawful authority under section 3(3) of the Act if it is conduct by or on behalf of a person who provides a telecommunications service and it takes place for purposes connected with the provision or operation of that service or with the enforcement, in relation to that service, of any enactment relating to the use of telecommunications services. Since this section applies to all telecommunications services, not just public telecommunication services, operators of private telecommunications systems ought to be able to take advantage of it.

Thirdly interception has lawful authority if it is authorised by regulations made by the Secretary of State under section 4(2). The Secretary of State may make regulations authorising conduct that appears to him to be a legitimate practice reasonably required for the purpose, in connection with the carrying on of any business, of monitoring or keeping a record of (a) communications by means of which transactions are entered into in the course of that business; or (b) other communications relating to that business or taking place in the course of its being carried on.

5.9.2 The RIP Act Lawful Business Practice Regulations

The Telecommunications (Lawful Business Practice) (Interception of Communications) Regulations made under sections 4(2) and 78(5) of the Act came into force at the same time as section 1(3) of the Act, on October 24, 2000. Some assistance in understanding the intent of the Regulations may be gained from the Notes for Business published by the Department of Trade and Industry as Annex C to the Response to Consultation, which also included the final version of the Regulations. The final version of the Regulations differs significantly from the draft Regulations on which the DTI consulted in August 2000. The Response to Consultation makes clear that there was a distinct policy change between the draft and final Regulations. **5–097**

Paragraph 3(1) of the Regulations sets out various categories of conduct that are authorised for the purposes of section 1(5)(a) of the Act. That section provides that conduct is authorised for the purposes of Section 1 if (*inter alia*) it is authorised under Section 4 of the Act. It also provides that authorised conduct shall be taken to be lawful for all other purposes.

General preconditions to lawful interception

Paragraph 3(2) of the Regulations sets out certain general preconditions that must be satisfied before any of the categories of conduct under paragraph 3(1) are authorised. The first of these is under paragraph 3(2)(a), that "the interception in question is effected solely for the purpose of monitoring or (where appropriate) keeping a record of communications relevant to the system controller's business". **5–098**

"Business", "system controller" and "relevant to the system controller's business" are defined in paragraph 2 of the Regulations.

References to a business "include references to activities of a government department, of any public authority or of any person or office holder on whom functions are conferred by or under any enactment".

"System controller" "means, in relation to a particular telecommunication system, a person with the right to control its operation or use".

A reference to a communication as "relevant to a business" is a reference to:

"(i) a communication—
    (aa) by means of which a transaction is entered into in the course of that business, or
    (bb) which otherwise relates to that business, or
(ii) a communication which otherwise takes place in the course of the carrying on of that business."

The restriction of the authorisation to monitoring or (where appropriate) keeping a record of communications relevant to the system controller's business derives from the restrictions on the power to make Regulations contained in section 4(2) of the Act itself.

5–099   The second general precondition, under paragraph 3(2)(b) of the Regulations, is that the telecommunication system in question is provided wholly or partly in connection with the system controller's business. This reflects a restriction on the power to make Regulations contained in section 4(3) of the Act.

The third general precondition is that "the system controller has made all reasonable efforts to inform every person who may use the telecommunication system in question that communications transmitted by means thereof may be intercepted". This is a potentially far-reaching provision. It suggests that if it can be demonstrated that the system controller has failed to make all reasonable efforts to inform one user of the system, or one small category of users of the system, then the system controller's conduct is unauthorised in respect of all users, even those whom the system controller did inform. So it will be important for the system controller to be able to demonstrate, if called upon to do so, its procedures for discharging this obligation, and that such procedures cover all classes of users.

5–100   Users of the system extend wider than merely employees. They will include contract staff, secondees, temporary staff, extranet users (which could include customers and suppliers) and so on. The Regulations do not define "use" of the system. On a broad interpretation it might be thought that third parties who telephone or e-mail in to the system, or leave a voicemail, are using the system. The DTI Notes for Business state: "The persons who use a system are the people who make direct use of it. Someone who calls from outside, or who receives a call outside, using another system is not a user of the system on which the interception is made." It is to be hoped that the courts adopt this sensible interpretation, which reflects the policy change between the draft and final Regulations noted at paragraph 30 of the Response to Consultation. If not, then what is required to satisfy the "reasonable efforts" test in relation to external users will be judged in the light of what is practicable. This could require warnings to be incorporated in outgoing e-mails and proximate to website feedback facilities. If (as will often be the case) it is not possible to issue a warning to the external sender of an incoming e-mail before the e-mail is received, then it is difficult to see what "reasonable efforts" could be required of the system controller, at least in the case of interception that takes place upon receipt.

5–101   As to the time period over which the system controller needs to inform users of the system that interception may take place, clearly the precondition needs to have been satisfied prior to the particular interception whose legality is under scrutiny. Even though the Regulations contain no provision suggesting that a warning, once given, can expire, it would nonetheless be prudent to repeat it. Also, it could be argued that if a new network or e-mail system is installed, or sufficiently major changes made to an existing one, then previous warnings are ineffective since they no longer relate to "the telecommunication system in question".

The Regulations do not state that the information to users should specify any particular kinds of interception that may take place. However, as we have seen "interception" within the meaning of the Act is a concept much broader than the ordinary understanding of the word. So if the information is to be capable of being understood by users, it may need to identify the telecommunication systems in question, illustrate the types of communications involved and explain what is meant by "interception". Also, the information will need to be prepared with the provisions of the Data Protection Act

1998 and any relevant Codes of Practice made under it[89] in mind. These may necessitate more detailed descriptions of the circumstances in which interception may take place.

Authorised categories of conduct

Subject to satisfying the three general preconditions (and any specific preconditions noted below), the categories of conduct authorised under paragraph 3(1) of the Regulations are[90]:

5–102

(1) interception effected by or with the express or implied consent of the system controller for the purpose of monitoring or keeping a record of communications in order to establish the existence of facts (paragraph 3(1)(a)(i)(aa))

(2) interception effected by or with the express or implied consent of the system controller for the purpose of monitoring or keeping a record of communications in order to ascertain compliance with regulatory or self-regulatory practices or procedures which are applicable to the system controller in the carrying on of his business or applicable to another person in the carrying on of his business where that business is supervised by the system controller in respect of those practices or procedures (paragraph 3(1)(a)(i)(bb))

"Regulatory or self-regulatory practices or procedures" means "practices or procedures:

   (i) compliance with which is required or recommended by, under or by virtue of—

      (aa) any provision of the law of a member state or other state within the European Economic Area, or

      (bb) any standard or code of practice published by or on behalf of a body established in a member state or other state within the European Economic Area which includes among its objectives the publication of standards or codes of practices for the conduct of business, or

   (ii) which are otherwise applied for the purpose of ensuring compliance with anything so required or recommended' (para 2(c))

(3) interception effected by or with the express or implied consent of the system controller for the purpose of monitoring or keeping a record of communications in order to ascertain or demonstrate the standards which are achieved or ought to be achieved by persons using the system in the course of their duties (paragraph 3(1)(a)(i)(cc))

Conduct falling within items (1) to (3) above is authorised only to the extent that Article 5 of the Telecommunications Data Protections Directive so permits (paragraph 3(3)). We have discussed above the extent, if any, to which Article 5 of the Directive applies to communications on private networks.

(4) interception effected by or with the express or implied consent of the system controller for the purpose of monitoring or keeping a record of communications in the interests of national security, so long as the person by or on whose behalf whom the interception is effected is a person specified in section 6(2)(a) to (i) of the Act (paragraphs 3(1)(a)(ii) and 3(2)(d)(i)). The persons so specified include the Director-General of the Security Service, the Chief of the Secret Intelligence Service, the Director of GCHQ, the Director General of the National Criminal Intelligence Service, the Commissioner of Police of the Metropolis, the

Commissioners of Customs and Excise and the Chief of Defence Intelligence.

(5)   interception effected by or with the express or implied consent of the system controller for the purpose of monitoring or keeping a record of communications for the purpose of preventing or detecting crime (paragraph 3(1)(a)(iii)).

(6)   interception effected by or with the express or implied consent of the system controller for the purpose of monitoring or keeping a record of communications for the purpose of investigating or detecting the unauthorised use of the system controller's or any other telecommunication system (paragraph 3(1)(a)(iv))

(7)   interception effected by or with the express or implied consent of the system controller for the purpose of monitoring or keeping a record of communications where that is undertaken in order to secure or as an inherent part of the effective operation of the system (including any monitoring or keeping of a record which would be authorised by section 3(3) of the Act if the conditions in paragraphs (a) and (b) thereof were satisfied)

(8)   interception effected by or with the express or implied consent of the system controller for the purpose of monitoring communications for the purpose of determining whether they are communications relevant to the system controller's business which fall within regulation 2(b)(i) (*i.e.* a communication by means of which a transaction is entered into in the course of that business, or which otherwise relates to that business, but not (due to the exclusion of regulation 2(b)(ii)) a communication which otherwise takes place in the course of the carrying on of that business). For conduct to be authorised under this provision the communication must be one which is intended to be received (whether or not it has been actually received) by a person using the telecommunication system in question (paragraph 3(2)(d)(ii)).

This provision is thought to be aimed at the difficulties that could otherwise be encountered by an employer who wished to access an employee's e-mail box, perhaps during the employee's absence from the office, to check for business correspondence. This is the example give by the DTI in their Notes for Business. The use of the word "monitoring" to describe such activity is inapt. However, that derives from the equally inapt use of the same wording in the enabling provision of the Act. 'Monitoring' is undefined in both the Act and the Regulations.

This provision is limited to interception for the purpose of monitoring, and not for the purpose of keeping a record. Does it prevent an employer who accesses an employee's e-mail box and reads a business communication for the permitted purpose, from creating a new record by printing it out or forwarding it to another e-mail box? This arguably involves two acts of interception: the accessing of the e-mail box (an interception under the ordinary definition of interception in section 2(2) of the Act as extended to stored communications by section 2(7)); and the forwarding or printing (which arguably constitutes interception under the extended definition of section 2(8), which includes any case in which any of the contents of the communication are diverted or recorded so as to be available to a person subsequently). It could perhaps be argued that printing out the e-mail did not constitute recording it under section 2(8). It is difficult to see how forwarding it would not constitute "diverting" it, unless the diverted communication must be prevented by the diversion from reaching the intended recipient. As to whether forwarding constitutes "recording", that could depend on whether the technology used caused a new copy of the e-mail to be made, or simply resulted in another person gaining access to an existing copy in a central e-mail database. The Act contains no definition of "diverted" or "recorded". Nor do the Explanatory Notes to the Act make any comment on section 2(8).

So long as the purpose for which the interception is carried out is permitted by the Regulation, then conduct consisting of the interception is authorised and there is no actionable interception under the Act (since it is not without lawful authority). So it could be argued that so long as the purpose remains a permitted purpose throughout the two acts of interception involved in accessing an e-mail box and printing out or forwarding the e-mail, all the conduct is authorised.

On the other hand, it could powerfully be argued that once the employer has accessed the e-mail box and read the business e-mail, then at that point he will have ascertained whether the e-mail relates to the business or not. Having done so, any further act of interception involved in forwarding or printing the e-mail cannot be for that purpose and can only be for the purpose of keeping a record, which is specifically excluded from the permitted purposes for which conduct is authorised under this paragraph.

A result that would prevent the employer from printing or forwarding an e-mail which, by definition, relates to his business would be absurd. It may be that having justified the initial access under this paragraph, the making of a record could then be justified under one of the other provisions of the Regulations.

(9)   interception effected by or with the express or implied consent of the system controller for the purpose of monitoring communications made to a confidential voice-telephony counselling or support service which is free of charge (other than the cost, if any, of making a telephone call) and operated in such a way that users may remain anonymous if they so choose (paragraph 3(1)(c)).

5.9.3 The Data Protection Act 1998

For a full discussion of the Data Protection Act the reader is referred to Chapter 7. Here, it **5–103** is sufficient to note that even if the interception is lawful under the Regulation of Investigatory Powers Act, the use that can be made of personal data to which the system controller gains access is constrained by the Data Protection Act. In particular, the First Data Protection Principle requires that personal data shall be processed fairly and lawfully. Although compliance with the RIP Act Lawful Business Practice Regulations can ensure that personal data is accessed lawfully, it does not guarantee that the data has been processed fairly.

Draft Code of Practice on The Use of Personal Data in Employer/employee Relationships.
The Data Protection Commissioner in October 2000 issued for consultation a draft Code **5–104** of Practice under section 51(3)(b) of the Data Protection Act 1998 on The Use of Personal Data in Employer/employee Relationships. This was published before the final form of the RIP Act Lawful Business Practice Regulations was known. Since the Regulations were altered significantly compared with the public consultation draft, the relevant sections of the draft DPC Code of Practice may also require substantial revision.

Some of the major themes of the draft Code of Practice are: **5–105**

- Monitoring can be categorised as Performance Monitoring, directed at the quantity and quality of an employee's work output, and Behavioural Monitoring, aimed at checking an employee's conformity with the employer's rules and standards of conduct. Behavioural monitoring includes surveillance by CCTV and e-mail interception.

- Monitoring should be designed so as to operate in such a way that it does not intrude unnecessarily on employees' privacy and autonomy. This is intended to mean respect not only for an employee's right not to have information about his/her private life or behaviour widely known, but also a right to expect a degree of trust from his/her employer and be given reasonable freedom to determine his/her actions without constantly being watched or asked to explain.

- Any intrusion on an employee's privacy or autonomy should be in proportion to the benefits of the monitoring to a reasonable employer.

- Any monitoring should be targeted on those areas where it is actually necessary and proportionate to achieving the business purpose. Monitoring of all staff to address a risk posed only by a few would not be justified.

- All staff subject to monitoring should be made aware of the fact that it is taking place and the purpose for which personal information is collected other than in certain exceptional circumstances set out in the Code.

- Personal information collected through monitoring should not be used for purposes other than those for which the monitoring was introduced and the staff told about unless the information reveals criminal activity or gross misconduct.

- Covert Performance Monitoring is difficult to see how it could ever be justified.

- Covert Behavioural Monitoring can only be justified in limited circumstances. The Code suggests standards to be complied with in those circumstances.

- Information obtained through covert monitoring should only be used for prevention or detection of the criminal activity or the apprehension or prosecution of offenders to which it was directed. Other information collected during the course of the monitoring should be disregarded unless the information reveals criminal activity or gross misconduct.

5–106   In relation to monitoring of communications, some key points in the draft Code are:

- Ensure that employees are not, for instance by lack of consistency between formal policy and actual practice, led into false expectations that their communications are private.

- Be realistic in the assessment of risks used to justify monitoring. The risk may not justify routine, as opposed to targeted, monitoring.

- Unless such monitoring would be ineffective and the circumstances justify the additional intrusion, limit monitoring to traffic data rather than the contents of communications, undertake spot checks and audit rather than continuous monitoring, use automated monitoring as far as possible and target monitoring on areas of highest risk.

- To the extent that monitoring of content may be justified, remind staff that the telephone and email should not be used to communicate sensitive personal details.

In relation to monitoring of e-mail, some key points in the draft Code are: **5–107**

- Do not monitor the content of e-mail messages unless it is clear that the business purpose for which the monitoring is undertaken cannot be achieved by the use of a record of e-mail traffic.

- Only consider the monitoring of content if neither a record of traffic nor a record of both traffic and subject achieves the business purpose. In assessing whether monitoring of content is justified take account of the privacy of those sending e-mails as well as the privacy and autonomy of those receiving them. Wherever possible restrict the monitoring of e-mails sent to specific employees to those that the employee has received and chosen to retain rather than delete. Do not open e-mails that are clearly personal.

- If monitoring the content of incoming e-mails is justified on the basis of detecting viruses use an automated process. Only use information obtained for the purpose of virus detection. Virus detection does not justify reading the content of incoming e-mails.

- If it is necessary to check the e-mails of employees in their absence ensure they are aware this will happen. The purpose of such monitoring is to ensure the business responds properly to its customers and other contacts. Only use the information for this purpose unless it reveals criminal offences or gross misconduct. Do not open e-mails that are clearly personal.

- Provide a means by which employees can effectively expunge from the system e-mails they receive or send.

In relation to monitoring of Internet access, some key points in the draft Code are: **5–108**

- Monitoring should be a proportionate response to the risk faced by the employer

- Do not monitor sites visited or content viewed unless the business purpose for which monitoring is undertaken cannot be achieved simply by recording time spent accessing the Internet.

- As far as possible enforce an Internet access policy by technical means to restrict access rather than by monitoring behaviour.

- Information obtained from monitoring should be disregarded unless it discloses a significant risk to the employer.

- In using the results of monitoring take account of the ease with which websites can be visited unwittingly through unintended responses of search engines, unclear hypertext links, misleading banner advertising or miskeying.

- Ensure, as far as possible, that if employees are allowed to access the Internet for personal reasons no record is kept in the system of sites visited or content viewed. To the extent that this is not technically possible, ensure employees are aware of what is retained and for how long.

5–109 Whether these principles will be retained in the Code in its final form remains to be seen. The draft Code has encountered significant criticism, not least due to its underlying assumption that any attempt by an employer to access and use its own electronic business communications and records that include personal data constitutes "monitoring" of its employees and so has to be strictly justified.

5.9.4 The Human Rights Act 1998

Public v. private employers

5–110 The ability of employers to access and make use of employee communications on their networks may be affected by the Human Rights Act 1998, which incorporated the European Convention on Human Rights into UK domestic law. The Act came into force in England and Wales on October 2, 2000. The Act directly affects the activities of public bodies (including "any person certain of whose functions are of a public nature"),[91] for whom the Act renders it unlawful to act in a way incompatible with Convention rights.[92] It also requires that, so far as it is possible to do so, primary legislation and subordinate legislation must be read and given effect in a way which is compatible with Convention rights. Whether the Act will affect the activities of private bodies depends on the extent to which the Act creates a positive obligation on the State to secure the relevant Convention rights as between private individuals, as opposed to creating rights only as against the State. This is a difficult and controversial topic, which in due course will have to be resolved by the courts.[93] The Lord Chancellor in the Third Reading of the Bill in the House of Lords stated:

> "We have not provided for the Convention rights to be directly justiciable in actions between private individuals. We have sought to protect the human rights of individuals against the abuse of power by the state, broadly defined, rather than to protect them against each other."[94]

5–111 However, this does still leave open the possibility that rights as between private individuals may indirectly have been created, in circumstances where the State is held to have abused its power by failing to protect one individual against another. Whether such a positive obligation is placed on the State depends very much on the particular circumstances, the particular Convention right under consideration and the effect of the mode of incorporation of the Convention into domestic law adopted in the 1998 Act.

For instance, when considering Article 8 of the Convention, which secures (subject to various possible derogations by a public authority) the right to respect for private and family life, home and correspondence, in particular cases the European Court of Human Rights has sometimes found for a positive obligation to secure rights under Article 8,[95] and sometimes against.[96] As yet there has been no decision in which establishes conclusively that Article 8 creates a positive obligation on a State to secure a right of privacy as between private individuals, although Butler-Sloss P. in *Venables and Another v. News Group Newspapers and Others*[96a] took the view that it did so.[97] The reference in Article 8(2) to the circumstances in which interference with Article 8 rights by a "public authority" is justified is difficult to understand if the rights apply between private individuals, although if that were a complete objection then no Article 8 right could ever create a positive duty to secure a horizontal obligation. Article 8(2) on the face of it provides no circumstances in which a private individual would be justified in interfering with another individual's privacy right, even though a public authority may be justified in doing so "for the protection of the rights and freedoms of others". Resort would have to be had to a tortuous argument that, the Article 8 right having been established as being in play as against another private individual, the court as a public authority would be justified in interfering with it (by derogating from it) only in the circumstances set out in Article 8(2).

Whether the specific obligation placed on the courts under the Human Rights Act 1998 **5–112** to act in a way compatible with Convention rights will reinforce arguments for the imposition of positive horizontal rights remains to be seen. Even allowing for the fact that under the 1998 Act "act" includes "failure to act", there would appear to be an element of circularity in the suggestion that the argument is reinforced. For if on the true construction of the Convention the Convention right under consideration does not create a positive obligation on the State to secure the right as between private individuals in the circumstances under consideration, how can the court be acting in a way incompatible with the supposed Convention right by failing to secure the right in question?

Even if the Act does not create a positive obligation on the State to secure Article 8 rights between individuals, there is still room for the development of the existing common law and of implied contractual rights (such as an implied duty of trust and confidence between employer and employee) to be influenced by the Convention rights, in much the same way that without implementing a horizontal Convention right as such, the Court of Appeal in *Douglas v. Hello!*[97a] took account of Article 8 in extending the existing tort of breach of confidence to embrace a fully-fledged privacy right. Whether that would also occur in the context of the workplace is a matter of speculation.

Reasonable expectation of privacy

The decision of the European Court of Human Rights in *Halford v. United Kingdom*[98] **5–113** establishes that communications (in that case telephone calls) made by an employee from business premises (in that case the Merseyside Police Authority, obviously a public authority) may be covered by the right of respect for private life under Article 8 of the Convention. Article 8(1) provides that "everyone has the right to respect for his private and family life, his home and his correspondence". Article 8(2) provides that there shall be no interference by a public authority with the exercise of this right except in accordance with the law in certain specified circumstances.

One of the factors that the court took into account when deciding that Ms Halford, who was bringing a sex discrimination case against her employers, had a reasonable expectation of privacy for her telephone calls was that she had not been warned that her telephone calls made using the internal telephone system were liable to be intercepted. Indeed, this was reinforced by the facts that a particular telephone in her office was designated for personal calls and she had received a positive assurance that she could use her office telephones for the purposes of her industrial tribunal case. The court found that no domestic law provided protection against interference by a public authority on a private network, so that any interference by a public authority could not be "in accordance with the law".[99]

Displacing an expectation of privacy

The questions that *Halford* leaves unanswered are first, whether the default position (if **5–114** nothing is said) is that the employee has a reasonable expectation of privacy for any, and if so which, communications using the employer's equipment. If not, what conditions have to exist for such an expectation to arise? Secondly, if the conditions are such that a reasonable expectation of privacy would otherwise arise, can an employer displace any such reasonable expectation of privacy that might arise simply by so informing the employee, or are there situations in which the privacy right is so fundamental that it cannot be displaced?

This is a controversial topic. *Halford* appears to imply a two stage process so that in the workplace context (at least as regards employee communications), one has first to ask whether the privacy right is in play at all, since it only arises if there is a reasonable expectation of privacy; and only then go on to consider whether interference is justified under Article 8(2).

5–115   That may suggest that if the employer takes sufficient steps to displace a reasonable expectation of privacy in respect of communications, Article 8 simply does not come into play. However, the court in *Halford* was silent on what steps would be required to displace the privacy expectation. It is possible in the wider employment situation to envisage circumstances in which the employer would be unable to displace a reasonable expectation of privacy (*e.g.* CCTV monitoring of lavatories) by giving warnings. If that could apply in some circumstances to communications, then the employer might not have total freedom to set a "no privacy" rule. However, it is not at all obvious in what, if any, circumstances use of the employer's system for communications could give rise to any such non-displaceable expectation of privacy.

The issue is most likely to arise where an employer permits use of its computer system for personal e-mails, but explicitly states that they will not be regarded as private. If employees know the rules (and especially if they have the use of alternative means of communication for personal matters, such as an office telephone), then it would seem quite arguable that an employer should be able to displace any reasonable expectation of privacy.[100]

5–116   Because of concerns about the ability of an employer to displace a reasonable expectation of privacy, some have argued for recognition of a broader concept of autonomy, which cannot be displaced by the employer.[101] While from a broad human rights perspective it may be appropriate to view privacy as derived from notions of personal autonomy,[102] that does not of itself justify a separate legal concept of non-displaceable employee autonomy, especially if that concept were to amount to a purported right not to be supervised by the employer.

This issue is of most concern to public sector employers who are directly subject to the 1998 Act. As we have discussed, the question whether private sector employers are subject to these Convention rights has not been resolved.

Compatibility of Regulations and draft Code with the 1998 Act

5–117   It has been suggested[103] that the RIP Act Lawful Business Practice Regulations may not be compatible with the Human Rights Act, due to a failure to secure sufficient respect for the employee's right of privacy. As we have seen, at least as far as private sector employers are concerned that begs the question whether the Convention secures any such right of privacy, even a qualified right of privacy, as against the employer in the first place. Another, less publicised, human rights aspect of the Regulations is that they have the potential directly to interfere with the employer's ability to access its own business correspondence. Since Article 8 of the Convention secures the right to respect for correspondence,[104] regulations that went too far in restricting a business's access to its own correspondence could infringe that right.[105] Unlike in the case of the employee's right of privacy, there would be no need to show that the Convention imposes a positive obligation on the State to Secure the Convention right. The argument would be the far simpler one that the regulations constituted a direct infringement by the State on the business's Convention right. Similar, there would be potential for direct interference with the employer's Article 10 rights (freedom to impart and receive information) and possibly the First Protocol Article 1 right (Protection of property).

Similar considerations will apply to the draft Data Protection Code of Practice on The Use of Personal Data in Employer/employee Relationships, discussed above. The Data Protection Commissioner is clearly required to act in a way that is not incompatible with Convention rights. But the question whether that requires the Commissioner to seek to secure positive rights of privacy as between private individuals has not been determined. However, since the Code will seek to place restrictions on employers there is the potential, if the Code is too restrictive, for it to infringe Convention rights of the employers.

5–118

---

1. *The Independent*, May 14, 2001.
2. The automation and electronic delivery of advice services formerly the preserve of professional advisers can give rise to regulatory problems. In Texas the publishers of a software product, "Quicken Family Lawyer", were held to have contravened a Texas statute prohibiting the unauthorised practice of law (*Unauthorized Practice of Law Committee v. Parsons Technology, Inc*, 1999 U.S. Dist. LEXIS 813; on appeal, injunction vacated after amendment of the statute in question, 179 F.3d 956). In the United Kingdom, the sale of a software product generating buy, sell or hold signals in relation to specified traded stock options was held to constitute not mere software retailing, but the giving of investment advice. Authorisation under the Financial Services Act 1986 was therefore required (*Re Market Wizard Systems (UK) Ltd* [1998] 2 B.C.L.C. 282).
3. [1932] A.C. 562.
4. *e.g. Vacwell Engineering Co. Ltd v. BDH Chemicals Ltd* [1971] 1 Q.B. 111.
5. [1964] A.C. 465.
6. *Henderson v. Merrett Syndicates Ltd* [1994] 3 All E.R. 506, H.L.; and see *First National Commercial Bank plc v. Loxleys (a Firm)* [1996] E.G.C.S. 174.
7. For an example of a case in which it was held not fair, just and reasonable to impose a duty of care notwithstanding the reasonable foreseeability of physical damage, see *Marc Rich & Co. v. Bishop Rock Marine* [1995] 3 All E.R. 307.
8. [1908] 1 K.B. 280.
9. [1990] 2 A.C. 605.
10. [1951] 2 K.B. 164.
11. See Section 7 of the *Encyclopedia of Information Technology Law* (Sweet & Maxwell) for further details.
12. *Caparo Industries plc v. Dickman & Others* [1990] 2 A.C. 605, at p.621 per Lord Bridge.
13. [1929] S.C. 461.
14. Directive 85/374 [1985] O.J. L210/29.
15. See Section 7 of the *Encyclopedia of Information Technology Law* for a detailed discussion.
16. This conclusion is based on the logic of the decision in *R v. Whiteley* [1993] F.S.R. 168, a case concerning criminal liability of a computer hacker under the Criminal Damage Act 1971. Although such liability is now governed exclusively by the Computer Misuse Act 1990, the reasons employed to support the finding of liability remain relevant to questions of civil liability concerning damage to property.
17. The first demonstration that macro viruses could be written was the Concept virus for Microsoft Word documents. Since then macro viruses such as the Melissa and Ethan e-mail viruses have been distributed.
18. "Prosecutions under the Computer Misuse Act 1990", R. Battock, *Computers and Law* Feb/March 1996.
19. [1993] F.S.R. 168, CA. Although the application of the Criminal Damage Act 1971 to hacking has now been largely excluded by 3(6) of the Computer Misuse Act 1990 the principle established in *R v. Whiteley* may still be applied by analogy to civil liability.
20. For a case in which recovery of pure economic loss was denied following the release of a real life virus into the wild, see *Weller v. Foot & Mouth Disease Research Institute* [1966] 1 Q.B. 569.
20a. (1866) L.R.I.Ex. 265.
21. *Cambridge Water Co. v. Eastern Counties Leather plc* [1994] A.C. 264.
22. *Cattle v. Stockton Waterworks* (1875) 10 L.R. 453 QB.
23. *Turberville v. Stampe* (1697) 1 Ld.Raym. 264.
24. *Job Edwards Ltd v. Birmingham Navigations* [1924] 1 K.B. 341.
25. [1913] A.C. 263, per Lord Moulton at page 280.

26. n. 21 above.
27. *ibid.*, per Lord Goff, at page 309.
28. Halsbury's Laws of England, Vol 45(2) 4th ed. (Reissue) 1999 para. 659.
29. *ibid.*, para 660.
30. The boundary between tort and contract may be different in other jurisdictions such as the USA.
31. It is not unknown to find such contracts lurking behind links marked "copyright" or "privacy notice".
32. The series of Victorian cases concerning the legal effect of seeking to incorporate, typically, railway company general terms and conditions by reference on the back of a ticket.
33. Such national laws will often have the status of mandatory rules and be enforceable notwithstanding attempts to exclude their effect by choice of law and jurisdiction clauses. See Chapters 6 and (for choice of law in contract) 10.
34. In the case brought against Yahoo! in France for permitting French users to participate in auctions of Nazi memorabilia on its US Yahoo.com auction site, a 3-person technical panel appointed by the French court concluded that Yahoo! would be able to exclude reliably 90% of French users by a combination of technical means based on identifying the location of users' IP addresses and obtaining declarations of residence from users in the case of ambiguous IP addresses. An English translation of the judgment of November 20, 2000 is available on www.gigalaw.com.
35. *First National Commercial Bank plc v. Loxleys (a Firm)* (n. 6 above).
36. See Chapter 4, section 4.4.2.
37. See Chapter 6.
38. See the International Organisation of Securities Commissions (IOSCO) reports "Securities Activity on the Internet" (Sept. 1998) and "Report on Securities Activity on the Internet II" (June 2001) at (www.iosco.org/docs-public/1998-internet_security.html) and previous guidance from the U.S. Securities and Exchange Commission and the United Kingdom Securities and Investments Board (as it then was).
39. *800 FLOWERS Trade Mark, Euromarket Designs Inc. v. Peters and Another*, discussed in Chapter 6.
40. Protection of Industrial Property Rights in Relation to the Use of Signs on the Internet (www.wipo.org/sct/en/documents/session_5/pdf/sct5_2.pdf).
41. See Chapter 6.
42. For a contrary view, see "Yahoo! brought to earth", *Financial Times*, November 27, 2000.
43. Directive 93/13 [1993] O.J. L95/29.
44. S.I. 1994 No. 3159, S.I. 1999 No. 2083, S.I. 2001 No. 1186.
45. [1990] 1 A.C. 831.
46. [1996] 18 E.G. 104, CA.
47. Note 6 above.
48. Directive 98/34 as amended by Directive 98/48 [1998] L37/35.
49. And see Chapter 4 as to the interpretation of "illegal" in the context of defamation liability.
50. *Financial Times*, January 23, 2001.
51. [2001] 1 All E.R. 908.
52. *A-G v. Punch Ltd and Another* [2001] 2 All E.R. 655 CA.
53. Copyright, Designs and Patents Act 1988, section 23.
54. *Westminster City Council v. Croyalgrange Ltd and Another* [1986] 2 All E.R. 353, at page 359 HL.
55. [2001] E.W.H.C. Admin 469, June 19, 2001.
56. For an example of a voicemail incident, see M. Hart, Corporate Liability for Employee Use of the Internet and E-mail, C.L.S.R. Vol. 14 No.4, 1998, p.223.
57. The Norwich Union case (see Chapter 4).
58. See Chapter 2.
59. See, for instance, *R v. Khan* [1997] A.C. 558 and *Khan v. United Kingdom* EctH.R. 12.05.2000 No 35394/97; also *R v. P* [2001] 2 W.L.R. 463 and *R v. Wright and Another* June 14, 2001 CA.
60. For some vivid examples of e-mails disclosed on discovery, see "Big Brother is Watching" Computer Litigation Journal, Peter C. Spiel, July 1999. The effective use of disclosed e-mails in the Microsoft anti-trust litigation gave rise to the idiom "self-toasting". See also M. Hart, *op.cit.* on the surprise of Oliver North, testified to in the Iran-Contra hearings, that hitting the delete button did not erase the message from the system.
61. [2001] 2 All E.R. 769.
62. See *e.g. Alphacell Ltd v. Woodward* [1972] 2 All E.R. 475, *National Rivers Authority v. Alfred McAlpine Homes East Ltd* [1994] 4 All E.R. 286.
63. The "identification principle" was enunciated by Lord Reid in *Tesco Supermarkets Ltd v. Nattrass* [1972] A.C. 153 at p. 170.
64. *Lobay v. Workers and Farmers Publishing Co.* [1939] 2 D.L.R. 272
65. See, for instance, as regards racial harassment, *Tower Boot Co. Ltd v. Jones* [1997] 2 Al E.R. 406. The case was decided before the House of Lords decision in *Lister*.
66. All the cases mentioned are reported in IDS Brief 637, May 1999 (Incomes Data Services) (also available at www.incomesdata.co.uk/brief/ecases.htm).
67. [1991] I.C.R. 172
68. On the authority of *R v. Bow Street Stipendiary Magistrates ex p. Government of the United States of America*

[20001 2 A.C. 216 such conduct also constitutes a criminal offence under the Computer Misuse Act 1990, since an offence is committed if an employee who is authorised to work on some accounts accesses other accounts to which she has access, but to which that authority did not extend.

69.   [1998] Masons C.L.R. Rep. 93.

70.   If the contents of the policy are not properly communicated, then the employer may not be able to justify taking disciplinary action on the basis of it, for instance in employment tribunal unfair dismissal proceedings.

71.   The relevant part of the Regulation of Investigatory Powers Act 2000 came into force on October 24, 2000, the Human Rights Act 1998 (for England and Wales) on October 2, 2000 and the Data Protection Act 1998 on March 1, 2000. For a comprehensive and balanced discussion of employee privacy issues generally, see *Employee Privacy in the Workplace* (Incomes Data Services Employment Law Supplement) May 2001.

72.   *Hansard* March 16, 2000, standing Committee F, House of Commons, Charles Clarke MP (Minister of State for the Home Office).

73.   This is an increasingly likely possibility with the advent of "always-on" telecommunication services to the home such as ADSL. Unlike traditional "dial-up" telephone services these provide a permanent connection from the home apparatus to the public telecommunication network.

74.   Similar issues have arisen under U.S. statutes. See G.Y. Porter, "Electronic Communication Tests Boundaries of Privacy Statutes", E.C.L.R. Vol. 6 No. 23, p.602; and "Voice Mail Message May Be 'Intercepted' Even If Already Heard by Intended Recipient", E.C.L.R. Vol. 6 No. 22, p.575.

75.   www.dti.gov.uk/cii/regulatory/telecomms/telecommsregulations/lawful_business_practice_response.shtml.

76.   The words in square brackets derive from the main definition of interception in Section 2(2).

77.   If personal data were involved, then subsequent use for a different purpose might be constrained under the Data Protection Act 1998.

78.   However, it is not at all clear whether s. 2(7) does cease to have effect when the user has collected the e-mail. It could readily be construed to have effect until such time a the user has deleted the message from the system

79.   For instance, by reading the words "other than the sender or intended recipient of the communication" into s. 2(2) after the word "person" in the second line.

80.   At least it is simple with new users. The position with existing users may be more difficult.

81.   In the case of telephone calls privacy concerns were long recognised by the restrictions on recording telephone calls contained in the Privacy of Messages condition in the Telecommunications Services Class Licence and the Self-Provision Class Licence issued under the Telecommunications Act 1984. The specific restrictions were removed from both Licences on April 9, 2001 following the implementation of the Regulation of Investigatory Powers Act 2000 and the Lawful Business Practice Regulations made under it. Each Licence contains a general obligation on the Licensee to take all reasonable steps to safeguard the privacy and confidentiality of any Message conveyed for a consideration by means of Applicable Systems and of any information acquired by the Licensee in relation to such conveyance.

82.   *Washington v. Townsend*, Washington Court of Appeals, April 5, 2001 (World Internet Law Report, May 2001, p.22; E.C.L.R. Vol. 6 No. 16 p.416).

83.   It could be argued that the recipients are those individuals who have access to the relevant e-mail box. However, s. 2(2), defining "interception", requires that the content be made available to "a person other than the sender or intended recipient". The only relevant intent can be that of the sender. In the scenario under discussion the sender has no intent to send the e-mail to any specific individual, so even if it were possible to identify individual recipients it is difficult to see how any of them could be "intended" recipients.

84.   Directive 97/66 [1997] O.J. L24/1 concerning the processing of personal data and the protection of privacy in the telecommunications sector.

85.   The Dutch implementation of the Directive adopts the interpretation that it does not apply to communications on private networks. The proposed new Directive concerning the processing of personal data and the protection of privacy in the electronic communications sector retains the emphasis on public telecommunications services and networks.

86.   See e.g. paragraph 6 of the DTI Public Consultation Exercise (August 1–25, 2000) on the draft Lawful Business Practice Regulations: "The requirement also extends to communications on private networks (*e.g.* office telephone networks or email systems) which will also travel or have also travelled on a public network."

87.   See *e.g. Hansard* March 16, 2000, Standing Committee F, House of Commons, Charles Clarke MP (Minister of State for the Home Office).

88.   There are general statements in, for instance, Articles 1 and 3 of the Directive stating that the Directive is concerned with the "processing of personal data", an expression that is apt to cover storage. However, Article 5 does not include this wording and indeed, notwithstanding the general words referred to, is not limited to personal data.

89.   The Data Protection Commissioner in October 2000 issued for consultation a draft Code of Practice on the Use of Personal Data in Employer/Employee relationships, containing detailed provisions on telephone and e-mail monitoring, discussed below in the main text.

90. At the cost of some repetition, we have set out each category of authorised conduct *in extenso*. Some of the categories require consideration of double or treble purposes, which can more easily be understood by setting out the full text of each category of authorised conduct.

91. Human Rights Act 1998, s. 6(3)(b). Note, however, that under s. 6(5) "in relation to a particular act, a person is not a public authority by virtue only of subsection (3)(b) if the nature of the act is private". This still leaves open the possibility that in the case of a clearly public body whose public body status is not dependent on the operation of subsection (3)(b), private acts of the body are subject to the Convention.

92. *ibid.* s. 6(1).

93. M. Hunt, "The 'Horizontal Effect' of the Human Rights Act" [1998] Aut. P.L. 423; Buxton L.J. (writing extra-judicially) "The Human Rights Act and Private Law" [2000] 116 L.Q.R. 48; H.W.R. Wade." Horizons of Horizontality, [2000] 116 L.Q.R. 217; and see *Douglas v. Hello!*, C.A. [2001] 2 All E.R. 289.

94. *Hansard*, House of Lords, February 5 1998 column 840.

95. See *e.g. Marckx v. Belgium* (1979–80) 2 E.H.R.R. 330, *Airey v. Ireland* (1979–80) 2 E.H.R.R. 305, *X and Y v. Netherlands* (1986) 8 E.H.R.R. 235.

96. See *e.g. Johnston v. Ireland* (1987) 9 E.H.R.R. 203.

96a. [2001] 1 All E.R. 908.

97. The point was discussed, but not decided, in *Douglas v. Hello!*. Butler-Sloss P. in *Venables and Thompson v. News Group Newspapers Ltd and Others* expressed the view that it did so, but the authorities cited for the view do not appear to go as far as suggested in the judgment.

97a. [2001] 2 All E.R. 289, CA.

98. [1997] I.R.L.R. 471.

99. At the time of the case the only legislation governing interception was the Interception of Communications Act 1985, which did not extend to communications on private telecommunications networks. The introduction of the Regulation of Investigatory Powers Act 2000 was at least partly motivated by the need, especially with the introduction of the Human Rights Act 1998, to put all interception on a legal footing.

100. For a contrary view, see JUSTICE's Response to the Government Consultation Paper "Interception of Communications in the United Kingdom".

101. Michael Ford *Surveillance and Privacy at Work*, (Institute of Employment Rights), 1998 p.16–17. The concept of employee autonomy as something separate and different from privacy has been endorsed in the Information Commissioner's draft Code of Practice on the use of Personal Data in the Employer/Employee Relationship. This is extremely controversial and would seem to conflict with the employer's right to supervise its employees.

102. *Douglas v. Hello!* (above) per Sedley L.J. at paragraph 126.

103. *Financial Times*, October 4, 2000.

104. The case of *Niemitz v. Germany* (1992) 16 E.H.R.R. 97 in the ECtHR establishes that this extends to business correspondence

105. Whatever the merits of the debate over whether companies can enjoy a right of privacy under Article 8 (see *R v. Broadcasting Standards Commission ex p. British Broadcasting Corporation* C.A, [2000] 3 All E.R. 989), it should not be forgotten that many employers are individuals and partnerships.

6

Enforcement and Jurisdiction

6.1 Enforcement in England

While knowing one's substantive rights when trading on the Internet is important, the practical question then arises of how they can be enforced. The owner of rights will want to be able to stop others infringing them. Someone venturing on to the Internet will need to know if other rights owners can enforce their rights against him if he were to infringe, however inadvertently. Practitioners have had to address some fundamental issues anew for the purposes of rights enforcement on the Internet, such as who can be sued and where the infringing act is committed.

6–001

The clash of national jurisdictions in the cross-border world of the Internet has given rise to much debate about the appropriate regime for deciding Internet disputes and the possible need for an international convention. Those possibilities for the future are discussed in Chapter 12. In this chapter we address practical questions of enforcement and jurisdiction under the law as it exists today, looking at jurisdiction first from the point of view of England and Wales and then internationally.

Examples of intellectual property rights owners asserting their rights have become common. A number of unlicensed Web sites containing images of works of MC Escher were closed down after receiving lawyers' letters. Some media rights owners have pursued "fan" Web sites which used copyright material without permission, in some cases coming to agreements with the fan sites to enable them to continue either independently or under the control of the rights owner. The controversial pursuit of remedies by the Church of Scientology made pioneering waves in several countries (see for instance the *Netcom*[1] and *XS 4ALL*[2] cases in the USA and The Netherlands respectively). There have been numerous disputes over ownership of domain names.[3] More recently there has been a rash of U.S. litigation over on-line music, with the cases against MP3.com and Napster, and a goodly number of "deep-linking" cases in Europe, often based on database right. All this is part of the maturing process of the Internet, as an increasing number of intrepid litigants create the building blocks of the future law of the Internet.

6–002

The growth of the Internet has given rise to concerns over the enforceability of intellectual property and other rights in cyberspace. English courts have shown themselves remarkably adept at devising new remedies to maintain the potency of the law. The *Anton Piller* order, the *Mareva* injunction, the world-wide *Mareva* injunction, the

6–003

Norwich Pharmacal order, the "*ne exeat regno*" injunction and the class injunction were all fashioned by English courts who were not prepared to see the law rendered powerless to assist rights owners against rogues. There is every reason to think that the courts will rise to the challenge of dealing with infringers who lurk in the dark corners of the Internet.

6.1.1 Identifying the defendant

6–004 The first challenge is to identify the infringer. This may not be easy. Someone e-mailing infringing material or posting to a Usenet newsgroup may do so from behind an anonymous remailer, which offers the service of stripping identifying material from e-mails and passing them on. Even if that does not happen, the person with the account may be using a false e-mail identity, and even masquerading behind a false IP address (a technique known as spoofing). Although a genuine IP address would in many cases enable the sending computer to be identified, it might only show that the sender was a subscriber to a particular commercial Internet access provider.

In the case of infringing material held on a more permanent Internet resource, such as a Web page, or ftp site, it may be difficult to identify the person responsible for putting material onto the resource. The claimant will usually be able to identify the apparent source of the posting to a Usenet newsgroup; and should, with a little technical knowledge, be able to identify the apparent owner of the host on which a Web site is held. But that may be a university or commercial host. The identity and whereabouts of the individual or company responsible for the content may not be apparent.

6–005 English law should be well able to help with this problem. In the case of material infringing copyright held on a third party host, it is possible that the host is itself committing infringing acts by storing the material on its computer and by making copies when users access it. As explained in Chapter 2, even transient copies are considered to be copies for the purposes of United Kingdom copyright law. The host would therefore be a legitimate defendant to copyright infringement proceedings unless the English courts choose to follow the reasoning in the *Netcom* case where a host was held not to have directly infringed in those circumstances. For defamation, even though an Internet service provider may have an innocent dissemination defence available to it, it has nevertheless published the materials that it carries and so is a potential defendant.

It has been long established that English courts are, by way of "advance disclosure", able to order infringers to disclose information to enable the rights owner to track back up the chain to the source of the infringing material. There would, therefore, seem to be no reason why the university or commercial host should not be required to disclose the identity of the person who put the infringing or defamatory material on their host computer. On its true analysis we suggest that *Totalise v. The Motley Fool*, discussed below, is such a case.

6.1.2 Identifying the wrongdoer—*Norwich Pharmacal* orders

6–006 Even if the host were not committing an infringing act itself, if it were sufficiently mixed up in the commission of the tort and is within the jurisdiction of the court, the court has discretion to grant a disclosure order under its *Norwich Pharmacal* jurisdiction. In the case of *Norwich Pharmacal Co v. Customs and Excise Commissioners*,[4] the House of Lords held that such an order could be made against a third party who was mixed up in the commission of a tort, but otherwise innocent. The difference from being a normal defendant would be that the claim would be for disclosure only (not damages or an injunction) and the claimant would normally have to pay the legal costs of the host. A *Norwich Pharmacal* order should be available not only to ascertain the identity of the person who placed infringing material on a host, but also to disclose the identity of the holder of an e-mail account used to disseminate infringing matter.

The *Norwich Pharmacal* order has mainly been used in intellectual property cases. However, there is no reason why it should not be used in connection with other torts, such as defamation, or indeed breach of contract.[5] In the case of defamation it has been held that an order cannot be made against someone who has no connection with the publication.[6] Some hosts could be potentially liable for defamation in their own right, although many may be able to claim the protection of the Defamation Act 1996.[7]

In *P v. T Ltd*[8] Scott V.—C. held that the court could order discovery against a party so as to assist the plaintiff in bringing proceedings for malicious falsehood or libel against a third party, even where without that information the plaintiff could not determine whether it in fact had a cause of action against the third party. In this case a senior employee of a company had been dismissed after a third party had made allegations against him, the nature of which the company refuse to disclose. The company also refused to disclose the identity of the informant. It was known in the industry that the plaintiff had been dismissed for impropriety, which he was unable to explain. He applied successfully for an order that the company disclose the identity of the informant and the nature of the allegations and that he be at liberty to use the information in proceedings against the informant for libel or malicious falsehood.

In a defamation case that went to a full trial, *Takenaka (United Kingdom) Ltd and another v. Frankl*[9] the Defendant steadfastly denied that he was the author of the defamatory e-mails in question. The Claimants obtained disclosure orders against various Internet service providers in the course of identifying the defendant to enable it to commence proceedings.

In *Totalise plc v. The Motley Fool and Another*[10] the defendants were the proprietors of websites which contained discussion forums. An anonymous contributor who went under the pseudonym Z Dust had made numerous postings about the claimant, which the claimant asserted were defamatory. The claimant applied for disclosure of the identity of Z Dust or of any material in the defendants' possession which could lead to the identification of Z Dust. The first defendant had refused disclosure in correspondence, relying on the Data Protection Act 1998, but neither consented to nor opposed the disclosure application, stating that it was under an obligation to protect the privacy of the information of which disclosure was sought. The second defendants also resisted disclosure, based on the Data Protection Act and its privacy policy incorporated in its customer terms and conditions.

The application proceeded on the basis that the court was exercising its *Norwich Pharmacal* jurisdiction. However, it is far from clear that this was in fact a true *Norwich Pharmacal* case. These defendants had clearly published the postings concerned[11] and, subject to an innocent dissemination defence, would have been liable for any defamation in their own right. Further, in the case of operators of a discussion forum on a web site it is far less clear than in the case of an Internet service provider that they would have been able to rely on the innocent dissemination defence at all (see discussion of this point in Chapter 4). Lastly, on the facts the first defendant had allowed Z Dust back onto the forum after initially revoking his access following the claimant's complaint—a situation that could have prevented the first defendant from successfully relying on the innocent

6–007

6–008

dissemination defence in respect of subsequent postings before revoking Z Dust's access for a second time. For all these reasons it appears from the facts set out in the judgment that the defendants could have been made defendants to substantive proceedings.

For the arguments under the Data Protection Act, see the discussion of this case in Chapter 7.

6–009   The first defendant sought to argue that section 10 of the Contempt of Court Act 1981was relevant to the exercise of discretion. That, subject to exceptions for the interests of justice, national security or the prevention of disorder or crime, prohibits a court from requiring a person to disclose "the source of information contained in a publication for which he is responsible". The court found that this section had no application in this case:

> "It is concerned with the protection of a journalist's sources and is directed at resolving the tension that may arise between the public interest in a free press and in enabling justice to be attained by a party seeking to enforce or protect its legal rights. The journalist is responsible at law for the material which he publishes. The defendants take no such responsibility. They exercise no editorial control. They take no responsibility for what is posted on their discussion boards. ... [quotes second defendant's disclaimer] ... The defendants simply provide a facility by means of which the public at large is able publicly to communicate its views. In my judgment, they are not responsible for the publication of such material within the meaning of the section. But if I am wrong as to that, then, for the reasons which I will subsequently set out, I am satisfied that disclosure is necessary in the interests of justice."

6–010   In exercising his discretion, the judge stated:

> "I am mindful of the fact that both defendants have a policy of confidentiality with regard to personal information relating to those using its web sites and do not wish to deviate from that policy. But the claimant argues that it simply wants the author of the Z Dust postings to take responsibility for his actions, and that, when balancing the interests of the parties, the respect for and protection of the privacy of those who chose to air their views in the most public of fora must take second place to the obligation imposed upon those who become involved in the tortious acts of others to assist the party injured by those acts.
>
> I have no hesitation in finding that the balance weighs heavily in favour of granting the relief sought. To find otherwise would be to give the clearest indication to those who wish to defame that they can do so with impunity behind the screen of anonymity made possible by the use of websites on the Internet."

6–011   If the judge's conclusions regarding the responsibility of the defendants for their discussion fora for the purposes of section 10 of the Contempt of Court Act 1981 were to be translated into defamation liability, that would still not necessarily mean that the defendants could take advantage of the innocent dissemination defence. Certainly they would not be regarded as having assumed editorial responsibility, but that still leaves the difficult question of whether or not they would be a publisher within the special meaning of Section 1 of the Defamation Act 1996.

When it came to costs, the judge departed from the usual *Norwich Pharmacal* order that the party seeking disclosure should bear the costs of a blameless defendant. He found that the situation was very different from the classic *Norwich Pharmacal* situation and that there was

> "considerable force in [the claimant's] argument that those who operate websites containing discussion boards do so at their own risk. If it transpires that those boards are used for defamatory purposes by individuals hiding behind the cloak of anonymity then in justice a claimant seeking to establish the identity of the individuals making such defamatory contents ought to be entitled to their costs."

The judge held that both defendants ought to have acceded to the claimant's requests and ordered the defendants to pay the claimant's costs.

6.1.3 Transient nature of Internet evidence

Infringing material often stays in one place on the Internet only for very short periods. Usenet hosts may retain postings only for a matter of days before deleting them. Sites may spring up, close down and pop up again elsewhere extremely rapidly. Even the content of Web sites is increasingly dynamic and may change rapidly. This undoubtedly poses challenges for rights holders and their lawyers, who must move fast if the evidence is not to disappear. However, it should not be forgotten that once the person who is perpetrating a wrong within the jurisdiction has been identified, it should be possible to obtain an injunction against that person. Because the injunction restrains the defendant personally from doing infringing acts, the effect of the injunction would not merely extend to the site that formed the basis of the complaint, but (subject to any questions of territorial jurisdiction) would also affect other sites on which the defendant thereafter placed the infringing material.

6–012

In July 1997 the Norwich Union insurance company made an agreed payment of £450,000 to the Western Provident Association in settlement of defamation proceedings brought by WPA against Norwich Union. The proceedings were based on a statement made in an internal Norwich Union e-mail. WPA obtained an *ex parte* injunction requiring Norwich Union to preserve and deliver up a copy of the e-mail. WPA also obtained an order that the company secretary of Norwich Union interrogate its salesforce as to whether they had repeated the defamatory statement to potential customers. The company secretary was then required to produce an affidavit setting out the results of his inquiries.

In the *Takenaka* case referred to above, a court-appointed expert conducted a detailed forensic examination of the computer, ultimately delivering an opinion that the e-mails had been sent by the Defendant. The court accepted this opinion and liability was established.

6–013

It should also borne in mind that Internet service providers typically retain traffic data for relatively short periods. So, if it is desired to require an ISP to disclose (say) the identity of the customer who was allocated a particular IP address at a particular time, timely steps will have to be taken if the data is not to be lost.

6.1.4 Transportability of sites

The ability of sites to reappear, perhaps out of the jurisdiction, but equally available as if they were located in the jurisdiction, poses real problems for rights owners. If a rights

6–014

owner has an injunction against an infringer, can he do anything to deny people access to the infringing site if it reappears out of the jurisdiction?

One possible approach would be to seek to have the infringing site's domain name and IP address removed from domain name servers and routing tables respectively. If notice of the injunction were to be given to the operator of a domain name server, the operator would be bound not knowingly to assist in or permit the commission of a breach of the injunction. In the case at least of a wholly pirate site, it may be that the operator could be required to prevent access being granted to the site by removing the name from the domain name server. The same could be required of owners of routing tables as regards the IP address of the site.

6–015   The possibility of doing this is speculative. Operators of domain name servers and routers could have serious points to make about their ability to filter the defendant's site. The defendant might retaliate by rapidly changing the IP address of his site, or by asking others to mirror his content on other sites. None the less, the courts are concerned to ensure that their orders are effective and might be willing to contemplate requiring operators to take such steps. The effectiveness of the *Mareva* (asset freezing) injunction has been greatly assisted by the ability to give notice of the injunction to banks thought to hold relevant accounts of the defendant. The interests of the bank are preserved by a requirement that the claimant pay the reasonable costs of the bank in complying with the order. A similar approach may be possible to ensure that injunctions against infringing Internet site operators are effective while the interests of access providers are preserved.

In the Bulger case, broad injunctions preserving confidentiality were granted against public computer networks, as well as against newspapers, broadcasters, cable and satellite companies. However, the injunction was amended subsequently to recognise that ISPs should not be held in contempt of court for material placed on their servers or accessible via their services without their knowledge (see Chapter 5 for the detailed terms of the injunction).

However, the Bulger injunction concerned broad categories of content, not an identified web site. That is different from the position where the identity and location of a particular web site is known. In that case there may well be scope for holding an ISP to a tighter standard of liability once notice of the injunction is given.

6–016   In *Marks & Spencer plc v. Cottrell*,[12] a an application to commit the perpetrator of fake web sites for contempt of court, Lightman J. commented (*obiter*):

> "I am told that one of the problems that exist today for companies like Marks & Spencer faced with persons of the like of Mr Cottrell is that orders such as those that have been made in this case prohibiting an individual from using a particular domain name can be evaded by adopting a minuscule variation upon it. The domain name providers will comply with a court order prohibiting the use of a particular name but because all questions of registration and domain name and monitoring are computer driven, no scope at the moment is available to prevent colourable imitations of the names though they are prohibited from being used. I do not think it can or should safely be assumed by domain name providers, that they have no responsibility to monitor whether court orders prohibiting use, not merely of particular names, but of colourable imitations are being broken by registrations made with names that fall foul of the prohibition. That is not a matter that I need go into now but it does seem to me far from clear that they can abdicate responsibility in respect of names which they permit it is registered on their sites. But that is a matter which requires very careful consideration on another occasion."

6.1.5 Mirror sites

A common tactic among defendants threatened with proceedings, especially where **6–017** freedom of speech issues arise, is to issue a call for help to the Internet community by requesting others to mirror (i.e. copy) the site. This tactic is designed to nullify the effect of local legal proceedings by multiplying the site across numerous jurisdictions. This undoubtedly creates practical problems for claimants, who are then faced with the task of trying to put the genie back in the bottle by pursuing defendants, many of whom may regard themselves as performing a public service by mirroring the original threatened site, around the world. The prospective claimant may, if the circumstances warrant, wish to consider moving for an injunction without notice, sufficiently broadly worded to put the defendant in contempt of court if it requests others to mirror the site or if it creates hypertext links to mirror sites.

The difficulties that can be encountered in pursuing web site infringement cases with a **6–018** freedom of speech element are well illustrated by the Nottinghamshire County Council ''JET Report'' case in 1997. The JET Report was a report by a Joint Enquiry Team into the Broxtowe case, one of the first instances of a United Kingdom social services department forming a view that 'satanic abuse' may have occurred. Three journalists published the report on a web site. Nottinghamshire County Council asserted copyright in the report and obtained an *ex parte* injunction restraining the reproduction of and other specified dealings with the JET Report.[13] The report appeared on various mirror sites around the world. The council wrote letters before action to a number of them objecting to both copying of the report and the inclusion of any hypertext links to it. This drew caustic responses from some of the mirror sites. Ultimately the council accepted that it could not effectively prevent the availability of the report and dropped the action.

With the advent of the Human Rights Act 1998, in rare cases the Article 10 right of freedom of expression may come into conflict with the protection afforded by the Copyright, Designs and Patents Act 1988. In such cases a court may decline in its discretion to grant an injunction (either interim or final), leaving the claimant to its remedies of damages or an account of profits. In other rare cases the defendant may be able to rely on a substantive public interest defence wider than the specific defences provided in the Copyright Designs and Patents Act 1988, so that the copyright work may be published by the defendant without sanction. In any event, the implications of the Human Rights will always be considered where the discretionary relief of an injunction is sought.[14]

6.2 Jurisdiction—when can the claimant bring proceedings in England?

6.2.1 Background

It was inevitable, with the advent of cheap cross-border communication for all, that **6–019** sooner or later questions of jurisdiction and applicable law would bubble to the surface of the cauldron of legal and policy issues raised by the Internet. They have done so now. Jurisdiction and applicable law have been at the heart of many recent Internet-related policy debates. These are some of them.

Domain names
The protracted discussions about the ICANN dispute resolution procedures for global **6–020**

top level domain names encompassed some heavily debated jurisdictional and choice of law issues. The solution arrived at for jurisdiction was that a complainant using the ICANN Uniform Disputes Resolution Procedure (UDRP) is required to agree to submit, for the purpose of a challenge to a Panel decision, to at least one of the jurisdictions of the principal office of the Registrar who registered the domain name, or the domain holder's address as shown in the Registrar's WHOIS database at the time of the filing of the Complaint.[15] For applicable law the Panel shall decide a complaint on the basis of "...any rules and principles of law that it deems applicable".[16]

Consumer contracts

6–021   Various provisions of the 1968 Brussels Convention on Jurisdiction and Enforcement of Judgments in Civil and Commercial Matters[17] and of the 1980 Rome Convention on the Law Applicable to Contractual Obligations[18] create a regime under which a consumer may invoke the protection of the courts of his domicile and the mandatory rules of his country of habitual residence, by way of exception to the otherwise applicable rules governing jurisdiction and choice of law. So in the Brussels and Rome Conventions there is an existing framework that favours, for consumers, the country of destination.

The appropriateness of these existing rules has been put in question by the advent of cheap cross-border on-line trade, where by default a web site is available throughout the world. The web site proprietor who wishes to trade only with certain jurisdictions must take positive steps to prevent transactions occurring with customers in other jurisdictions. This is the reverse of the position that obtained when the Brussels and Rome Conventions were written, when trade was domestic by default and a supplier would generally have to take positive steps to market overseas.

6–022   The Brussels Convention is due to be superseded[19] in March 2002 by a Council Regulation on Jurisdiction and the Recognition and Enforcement of Judgments in Civil and Commercial Matters,[20] commonly known as the Brussels Regulation. The original Commission proposal,[21] which would clearly have reinforced the existing consumer protection carveouts in the on-line context, sparked vigorous lobbying.

Trade bodies argued that any revisions should reflect the new country of origin philosophy which underlies, to an extent, the Treaty of Rome and the Electronic Commerce Directive; and that consumers will be harmed through suffering restricted choice if e-commerce providers are inhibited from providing their services across borders. Consumer organisations argued that consumers should not forfeit their existing legal protections when contracting electronically. The final form of the Regulation represents something of a compromise on this issue, substantially retaining the principle of the consumer carveouts but leaving considerable uncertainty as to when a web trader will fall within their provisions. This is discussed in more detail below. The outcome may be viewed by some as a precedent for future revisions to the 1980 Rome Convention.

Regulated industries

6–023   Suppliers in licensed and highly regulated industries such as financial services and pharmaceuticals must typically comply with a detailed domestic compliance regime. Once such suppliers go online, the question arises whether the mere global availability, by default, of the web site, is sufficient to trigger the compliance regimes of other jurisdictions. National regulators have tended towards evolving solutions which recognise that mere availability should not be sufficient to trigger a country's compliance regime, thus permitting peaceful co-existence of websites established under a variety of domestic regimes.

Hague Convention

The advent of e-commerce has had an impact on the proposed Hague Convention on **6–024**
International Jurisdiction and Foreign Judgments in Civil and Commercial Matters. A
special Round Table was convened in Geneva in September 1999 to discuss electronic
commerce and private international law, resulting in recommendations that could
eventually result in a significantly modified draft Convention.

Mere availability

At the heart of many jurisdiction debates is the question whether the jurisdiction of the **6–025**
courts of a country can be invoked by the "mere availability" of a web site in that
country, or whether more (such as targeting of the site to that country) is required. This
regularly gives rise to controversy, the most recent example being the case brought in
France against Yahoo! Inc over the availability of Nazi memorabilia on yahoo.com
auction sites (discussed in Chapter 12).

In this summary of English jurisdictional rules especial attention is paid to those rules
that could be used to found jurisdiction against a "merely available" web site, notably
Article 5(3) of the Brussels Convention and the tort-related provisions of CPR Rule 6.20.

6.2.2 Jurisdiction—Defendant domiciled within a Brussels Convention Contracting State

The Brussels Convention applies generally to civil and commercial matters.[22] However it **6–026**
does not extend to revenue, customs or administrative matters, nor to a variety of
specifically excluded subject-matter.

The general rule

The general rule under Article 2 of the Brussels Convention is that a Defendant domiciled **6–027**
within a Contracting State shall be sued in the Courts of that State.

The general rule concerning defendants domiciled in Contracting States is subject to a
number of exceptions provided for by the Convention, the most relevant of which for
Internet and e-commerce are described below. There is also an unresolved question
whether the general rule requires an English court to assume jurisdiction where an
English domiciled defendant is sued in England by a claimant domiciled outside a
Convention State, or whether the court retains discretion on grounds of *forum non
conveniens* to grant a stay of such proceedings in favour of a non-Convention forum. This
question was ventilated in the House of Lords case of *Lubbe et al. v. Cape plc.*[23] The
question did not require decision in that case since no stay was in fact granted, but Lord
Bingham commented that the answer to the question was by no means clear and that he
would have thought it necessary to seek a ruling from the European Court of Justice.

The most relevant cases in which a Defendant domiciled within a Contracting State
may be sued in the court of another Contracting State are as follows.

Jurisdiction agreements

Article 17 provides that if the parties, one or more of whom is domiciled in a Contracting **6–028**
State, have agreed that a court or the courts of a Contracting State are to have jurisdiction
to settle any disputes which have arisen or may arise in connection with a particular legal
relationship, that court or those courts shall have exclusive jurisdiction.

Such an agreement is required to be either:

(a)   in writing or evidenced in writing, or

(b)   in a form which accords with practices which the parties have established between themselves, or

(c)   in international trade or commerce, in a form which accords with a usage of which the parties are or ought to have been aware and which in such trade or commerce is widely known to, and regularly observed by, parties to contracts of the type involved in the particular trade or commerce concerned.

6–029   "Writing" is not defined in the Convention. The Brussels Regulation uses the same wording as the Convention, but goes on state that "Any communication by electronic means which can provide a durable record of the agreement" shall be deemed to be in writing.[24] The draft Hague Convention on Jurisdiction and Foreign Judgments in Civil and Commercial Matters proposes that a jurisdiction agreement should be valid as to form if it is entered into in writing or "by any other means of communication which renders information accessible so as to be usable for subsequent reference". This formulation is drawn from the UNCITRAL Model Law on Electronic Commerce 1996.

The substantive provision of Article 17 does not apply to consumer contract proceedings,[25] for which jurisdiction is determined by Articles 13–15. However the requirements of form laid down by Article 17 are thought to apply to the limited jurisdiction agreements that Article 15 does permit for consumer disputes, even though not expressly stated to do so.[26]

Registered rights

6–030   Article 16 of the Convention provides in certain cases for exclusive jurisdiction to vested in designated Member State courts, regardless of domicile. For proceedings concerned with the validity of patents, trade marks, designs or other similar rights required to be deposited or registered, the courts of the Contracting State in which the deposit or registration has been applied for, or has taken place, or is under an international convention deemed to have taken place, shall have exclusive jurisdiction. The English courts have taken the view that in patent proceedings where questions of validity and infringement both arose, since the infringement claim could not be determined without also determining validity, a claim for infringement of a United Kingdom patent came within the exclusive jurisdiction of the English court.[27]

However, the general domicile rule under Article 2 of the Convention can apply to some intellectual property rights. In *Pearce v. Ove Arup Partnership*[28] it was accepted that under the terms of Article 2 the court was required to accept jurisdiction in a case where an English company domiciled in England was sued for infringement of a Dutch copyright.[29]

An agreement conferring jurisdiction has no legal force if the courts whose jurisdiction it purports to exclude have exclusive jurisdiction by virtue of Article 16.[30]

Contract

6–031   Article 5(1) provides that in matters relating to contract, a person domiciled in a Contracting State may be sued in another Contracting State in the courts for the place of performance of the obligation in question. Ascertaining the place of performance of the obligation requires consideration of issues outside the scope of this text. It may sometimes be necessary to ascertain the law applicable to the contract before the place of performance of the obligation can be ascertained.[31] The Brussels Regulation will introduce some general rules for ascertaining the place of performance.[32]

Tort

Article 5(3) provides that in matters relating to tort, delict or quasi-delict,[33] a person **6–032**
domiciled in a Contracting State may be sued in another Contracting State in the courts
for the place where the harmful event occurred.[34] The scope of Article 5(3) is especially
relevant to the possibility of being exposed to tort litigation in a Contracting State in
which a web site is "merely available".

There has always been a trickle of cross-border tort cases: waste released into the Rhine
in France damaging crops in the Netherlands;[35] a defamatory newspaper article
published in the France finding its way into England;[36] assurances given by telephone
from Switzerland to London,[37] are just some. But the true cross-border tort, in which the
activities comprising the chain of constituent events cross national boundaries, has
tended to be the exceptional case.

However the Internet is set to propel the cross-border tort, founded on simultaneous **6–033**
multi-jurisdiction activity, into the mainstream. The effect of Article 5(3) could be to open
up forum-shopping as never before, particularly in the case of those torts which, in the
context of transmitted information, may be characterised as "receipt-oriented". If the
receipt of information through the mere availability of the web site were enough to satisfy
Article 5(3), then the potential claimant would have a choice, in respect of receipt-
oriented torts, of litigating in any Member State constrained only by the *Shevill*
restrictions on the damage that can be recovered in an Article 5(3) case. This result would
be contrary to the scheme of the Convention, in which Article 5(3) is intended to be a
limited exception from the basic rule that a defendant is to be sued in the courts of his
domicile.[38]

The torts that we characterise as "receipt-oriented" are those in which it is potentially
easy for the court to hold that at least the damage, and perhaps all the components of the
tort, have occurred in the country of receipt of information transmitted from outside the
jurisdiction. This lays the ground for the court to assume jurisdiction. These torts may, to
a greater or lesser extent, include trade mark infringement, passing off, defamation,
misrepresentation, negligent misstatement and possibly some aspects of copyright.[39]

U.S. courts in inter-state Internet cases have used "purposeful availment of the **6–034**
jurisdiction" principles derived from the U.S. Constitution requirement of 'minimum
contacts', so that the mere availability of a Web site, with nothing more, does not found
jurisdiction. Where the Brussels/Lugano Convention applies, however, the court is not
permitted to have regard to such considerations. Where the claimant claims jurisdiction
under Article 5(3), then if a harmful event has occurred within the jurisdiction and the
matter relates to a tort, delict or quasi-delict, the court *must* assume jurisdiction.[40] In the
case of receipt-oriented torts, it may be relatively easy to show that a harmful event has
occurred within the jurisdiction. However, that will be tempered in England by
consideration of the requirement to show a good arguable case that the matter comes
within Article 5(3), and the components required to establish an English tort.

The claimant must demonstrate a good arguable case that the terms of Article 5 are
satisfied.[41] He must also establish that there is a serious issue to be tried on the merits.[42]
This raises the territorial question whether the availability of the foreign web site in
England and Wales constitutes a substantive tort in this jurisdiction.[43] This, for some torts
at least, allows the court to consider whether a web site is directed to or targeted at this
jurisdiction, even though Article 5(3) of the Convention does not explicitly refer to this as
a relevant factor. However, since this is a question of the substantive components of the

tort in question, not a broad rule of jurisdiction, the relevance of targeting has to be considered individually for each tort.

6–035   The question where the harmful event occurs for the purpose of Article 5(3) has been elaborated by several decisions of the European Court of Justice.

The phrase "harmful event" can include both the event giving rise to the damage and the damage itself.[44] So where a French company discharged pollutants into the Rhine in France, which flowed downstream and damaged the claimant's crops in the Netherlands, the damage occurred in the Netherlands and the claimant could sue there.[45] However, the place where the "damage" occurs covers only "the place where the event giving rise to the damage, and entailing tortious, delictual or quasi-delictual liability, directly produced its harmful effects upon the person who is the immediate victim of the event".[46] So a different place where indirect victims suffer consequential loss as a result of the harm initially suffered by direct victims is not a place where damage has occurred within Article 5(3).

6–036   The *Dumez* case also emphasised that the place where the initial damage manifests itself is usually closely related to the other components of the liability and that in most cases the domicile of the indirect victim is not so related.[47]

In *Shevill v. Presse Alliance SA*,[48] the court also held that the criteria for assessing whether the event in question is harmful and the evidence required of the existence and extent of the harm alleged are governed by the substantive law determined by the national conflict of laws rules of the court seised, provided that the effectiveness of the Convention was not thereby impaired.

In view of this we will consider both the substantive components of the tort and the existence of a harmful event on a tort by tort basis. The validity of this tort by tort approach is reinforced by the *obiter* comments of Buxton L.J. in the Court of Appeal decision in *800-FLOWERS Trade Mark*,[49] discussed below under "trade marks and passing off"

6–037   *Defamation*   For defamation, the requirement to prove that the action is founded on a tort will be determined according to English common law principles, unaffected by the Private International Law (Miscellaneous Provisions) Act 1995 (which excludes defamation from its scope). If the tort is found to have been committed in this country (which is likely in traditional defamation cases, since they will usually be founded on evidence of actual publication by circulation of physical copies in this jurisdiction[50]), then only English law is relevant. In ascertaining this the court will apply the test of where in substance the cause of action arose. If the tort has in substance been committed abroad, then the rules of double actionability will be applied to determine whether an actionable tort has been committed.[51] The requirement to prove that damage has been sustained in the jurisdiction will normally be easy in libel, given the presumption of damage from publication of a defamatory statement.[52]

The question of liability in England and Wales for defamatory content on merely available foreign Internet sites raises more difficult questions.[53]

6–038   As a preliminary, it should be noted that in the case of Usenet newsgroups the question of publication of an article posted to a newsgroup will tend to be relatively simple. The very nature and purpose of the Usenet system is to enable messages to be disseminated to sites around the world for public consumption. In those circumstances it would be very difficult for the author to suggest that he did not intend publication to the world at large, including England. A court might well be prepared to infer publication in England without proof that anyone within the jurisdiction actually read the posting. If someone at the instigation of the claimant were to read the posting in order to provide evidence of actual publication for the purpose of legal proceedings, that ought to be sufficient to support the assertion that a tort has been committed within the jurisdiction.

A similar analysis can be applied to foreign Internet sites. The material may be held on a database in one country. The content provider may be a company registered in a second country and the computer holding the database be owned by a company registered in a third country. None of these factors, however, really address the key component of defamation, which is not keeping the defamatory statement but communicating it to a third party. Material placed on the Internet, such as on a public Web site, is prima facie available for viewing anywhere in the world. In the absence of any contrary factual circumstances someone who puts up a Web site would, on existing principles, be taken to know that it can and will be read in England and to authorise that publication.[54] In English law the cause of action in libel arises when the words come to the attention of the reader.

That is the position with foreign newspapers and with foreign broadcasts. Even if only   **6–039** a few copies of a foreign newspaper are distributed in England, each will constitute a publication in England and the publisher of the newspaper will normally be taken to have authorised it, thereby committing a tort within the jurisdiction. A radio broadcast is published where it is received.[55] A letter from abroad opened and read in England is published within the jurisdiction.[56] In the *Jenner* case McRuer CJHC said:

> "Radio broadcasts are made for the purpose of being heard. The programme here in question was put on the air for advertising purposes. It is to be presumed that those who broadcast over a radio network in the English language intend that the messages they broadcast will be heard by large numbers of those who receive radio messages in the English language ... The "ears" of the recipients of a foreign broadcast are the receiving sets within the jurisdiction and such a set is not dissimilar in law to a hearing device such as may be used by one whose hearing is impaired or the glasses that one with defective vision puts on so that he may read.

> I cannot see what difference it makes whether the person is made to understand by means of the written word, sound-waves or ether-waves insofar as the matter of proof of publication is concerned. The tort consists in making a third person understand actionable defamatory matter."

Although in defamation publication is sufficient to found liability, the effect on   **6–040** jurisdiction of mere availability on the Internet has not yet been examined by the English courts. In *Berezovsky v. Michaels*,[57] a non-Brussels Convention libel case in which the House of Lords decided by a 3–2 majority not to stay libel proceedings brought by Russian businessmen against a U.S. magazine with a small circulation in England, the magazine was stated also to be available on the Internet within the English jurisdiction. However their Lordships were able to come to a conclusion without reference to this aspect. Lord Steyn commented:

> " In their statements of claim the plaintiffs relied on the fact that the Forbes article is also available to be read on-line on the Internet within the jurisdiction. The Court of Appeal referred to this aspect only in passing. During the course of interesting arguments it became clear that there is not the necessary evidence before the House to consider this important issue satisfactorily. Having come to a clear conclusion

without reference to the availability of the article on the Internet it is unnecessary to discuss it in this case." (p. 996 h–j)

In his dissenting speech Lord Hoffmann stated:

"...But that does not mean that we should always put ourselves forward as the most appropriate forum in which any foreign publisher who has distributed copies in this country, or whose publications have been downloaded here from the internet, can be required to answer the complaint of any public figure with an international reputation, however little the dispute has to do with England."

6–041   These questions were addressed in detail for the first time in the Australian case of *Gutnick v. Dow Jones & Co. Inc.*,[58] decided in August 2001. The case concerned an article in the online version of *Barrons* magazine, alleged to be defamatory of a resident of the State of Victoria. The magazine was provided by means of a password access, subscription web site. The web site was operated from the USA, where the servers were located and maintained. It was admitted that the article had been downloaded by subscribers in the State of Victoria.

The court (Hedigan J.) considered the questions of what constituted publication and where publication took place; and who was responsible for the publication, the subscriber or the web site proprietor? The court also considered the broader policy implications of country of origin versus country of receipt rules, for which see Chapter 12.

6–042   As to what constituted publication, the defendant argued that publication took place not on reception by the user but on delivery, which in this case equated to the "uplift" (*i.e.* transmission) of the article upon receipt of a request from the user's browser. It therefore followed, argued the defendant, that publication took place in the USA, where the servers were located, and that there was no publication in Australia.

The court held, following *Jenner v. Sun Oil* and other authorities, that publication took place at the time and in the place where it was made manifest in a form capable of being comprehended by a third party. It rejected the argument that publication took place on delivery as being contrary to centuries of authority. The defendants sought to distinguish *Godfrey v. Demon Internet Ltd*,[59] in which Morland J. had held that transmission of a defamatory posting from the storage of a Usenet news server constituted a publication of that posting to any subscriber who accessed the news group, whenever one of its subscribers accessed the newsgroup and saw that posting. The defendants contended that this case was of no assistance because it involved Usenet, not the Internet. The judge rejected that, noting Morland J.'s reference to seeing the posting defamatory of the plaintiff and holding that that was equivalent to downloading in this case.

Even if he was wrong as to publication occurring on downloading, the judge rejected the defendant's contention that it was possible to separate uplift from download. In the court's view these were indivisible, the reception by the user taking place to all intents and purposes simultaneously with the transmission by the Web server. Therefore if delivery was the correct test, publication took place in both the USA and Victoria at the same time. However the judge decided the case on the basis that publication took place on downloading.

6–043   As to who was responsible for, or caused, the publication, the defendant argued that the Web was a "pull" rather than a "push" technology, so that the article was only sent into Australia in response to a request by the user, the defendant's Web servers being effectively passive. The user was in effect 'self-publishing=' and the defendant did not cause the publication.

The court rejected this argument. The defendant sought to contrast information obtained by the user's own deliberate actions, by clicking to request the defendant's Web server to provide access to the relevant document, with persons listening to a radio or seeing and hearing a television broadcast. However, the judge stated that appreciation of the contrast between push and pull technologies could not dominate the question of publication for the law of defamation:

> "It would be otherwise just as relevant to say that a radio station has not done anything to facilitate the broadcast in the publishing sense because the listener turns the selection control to that station."

The judge also rejected, on the basis that this was a subscription site, the defendant's   **6–044**
contention that the process of extracting the particular article from the Dow Jones Web server involved requests for actions by persons "over whom Dow Jones has no control". The judge commented:

> "This is by no means wholly accurate as Dow Jones has programmed its computers ... to decline requests e.g. for Barrons in the absence of a provided password and also to decline even with a password if the requestor is delinquent in the payment of his or her outstanding account at that time.".

The plaintiff argued that publication to persons in Victoria who read it was the intended natural and probable consequence of what the defendants had done and that the defendant was therefore liable for the publications that occurred in Victoria; and that

> "it was entirely foreseeable and to be expected that the article about the plaintiff, a prominent Victorian resident, would be published in Victoria and that in publishing the article the defendant was author, editor, printer, publisher and librarian".

The judge agreed:

> "It is also absolutely clear that Dow Jones intended that only those subscribers in various States of Australia who met their requirements would be able to access them, and they intended that they should".

The court also rejected an application by the defendant to stay the proceedings on grounds of *forum non conveniens*.

Although the court's determination of place of publication would apply equally to a   **6–045**
free Web site as to the subscription site considered in this case, the determination that the defendant caused the publication in Victoria was heavily reliant on the fact that this was a subscription Web site. It leaves open the question whether, and if so in what circumstances, the proprietor of a free Web site would be taken to have intended publication in all countries in which it is capable of being received. As we have stated earlier in this discussion, existing law provides a strong basis on which to hold that worldwide publication is the natural and probable consequence of putting up a Web site and thus that the Web site proprietor caused the publication.

However, should the courts wish to develop a restriction of liability based on, for instance, directing and targeting, causation would provide a suitable framework within which to do so. Directing and targeting would become an aspect of causation of the publication in law (as opposed to causation in fact, which is the province of scientific and technical analysis). Indeed, the reliance of the court in *Gutnick* on the subscription nature of the site and on the ability of the defendant to control who received the service, and the court's explicit disavowal of making any findings applicable to the freely available public Web, could provide a starting point for the development, in defamation law, of a directing and targeting test in the context of causation.

6–046   It should also be noted that the defendant in the *Gutnick* case was the proprietor of the Web site in question. If the defendant were, say, an Internet Service provider who hosted a third party's Web site, then additional questions concerning the liability of intermediaries would have to be considered when considering whether the defendant could be haled into the overseas jurisdiction, including the jurisdiction's own domestic laws on the liability of intermediaries. In this context it may be observed that the logic of the finding of Usenet publication by an ISP in *Godfrey v. Demon Internet Ltd* is not constrained by territorial boundaries, although since Demon made its newsgroups available to its own customers the case implicitly concerned a subscription service which may not (as regards the ISP) be analogous to a freely available Web site. In the *Gutnick* case there was considerable discussion of analogies based on publication by libraries. These were not found helpful by the judge, and in the case of an ISP are likely to be irrelevant if the jurisdiction has specifically legislated for the liability of electronic intermediaries.

6–047   As to the place of the harmful event, in *Shevill v. Presse Alliance SA*,[60] a defamation case, the Court stated that damage is caused in the places where the publication is distributed, when the victim is known in those places. The court also stated that the place where the event giving rise to the damage occurred is the place where the publisher is established, since that is the place where the harmful event originated and from which the libel was issued and put into circulation. The Court held that a claimant could therefore sue either in the country of publication, pursuant to Article 5(3) of the Brussels Convention, or in the country in which the defendant publisher was established. However, if the claimant chose to sue in the country of publication it could recover damages only in respect of the publication in that country. Otherwise, it could recover for all the Convention countries.

The court also held that the criteria for assessing whether the event in question is harmful and the evidence required of the existence and extent of the harm alleged are governed by the substantive law determined by the national conflict of laws rules of the court seised, provided that the effectiveness of the Convention was not thereby impaired. When the case returned to the House of Lords it was held that the English law presumption of harm to the plaintiff from publication of a defamatory statement was sufficient to constitute a harmful event for the purpose of Article 5(3), without specific proof of damage.[61]

6–048   *Trade Marks and passing off*   In *Mecklermedia*,[62] a passing off case, the plaintiffs (successfully defending an application by the defendants to strike out the proceedings, or to set aside or stay the proceedings on jurisdiction grounds) established that there was a serious question to be tried that they owned goodwill in England in the mark "Internet World" at least for trade shows. The defendants, based in Germany, had organised their own "Internet World" trade shows in Germany and Austria. They had created English language promotional material and sent it out to people including some who appeared in the plaintiff's Internet World trade show catalogue in London. They also established a German Web site under the domain name "www.internet-world.de".

Jacob J. found a serious issue to be tried as to whether what the defendants were doing would mislead the interested public in England and held that the court was entitled to infer damage to the plaintiff's goodwill. The judge commented:

> "To do acts here which lead to damage of goodwill by misleading the public here is plainly passing off. To do those same acts from abroad will not avoid liability."

The judge went on to find that for the purposes of Article 5(3) the harm was to the plaintiff's goodwill in England, so that a harmful event had occurred in England. He concluded, deciding that the proceedings should continue in England: **6–049**

> "...when an enterprise wants to use a mark or word throughout the world (and that may include an Internet address or domain name) it must take into account that in some places, if not others, there may be confusion. Here it is clear DC knew that Mecklermedia used the name "Internet World" and I do not think it is surprising that it is met with actions in places where confusion is considered likely."[63]

By contrast with defamation, which requires only publication, trade mark infringement requires the claimant to show a good arguable case that there has been use of the registered mark. The significance of this point in cross-border Internet cases has most recently been considered by Jacob J. in *Euromarket Designs Ltd v. Peters Ltd*.[64] Commenting on the Irish defendants' advertisement for their local Dublin shop in a magazine which also circulated in England, he said: **6–050**

> "19. ... The right question, I think, is to ask whether a reasonable trader would regard the use concerned as 'in the course of trade in relation to goods' within the Member State concerned. Thus if a trader from state X is trying to sell goods or services *into* state Y, most people would regard that as having a sufficient link with state Y to be 'in the course of trade' there. But if the trader is merely carrying on business in X, and an advertisement of his slips over the border into Y, no businessman would regard that fact as meaning that he was trading in Y. This would especially be so if the advertisement were for a local business such as a shop or a local service rather than for goods. I think this conclusion follows from the fact that the Directive is concerned with what *national* law is to be, that it is a law governing what traders cannot do, and that it is unlikely that the Directive would set out to create conflict within the internal market. So I think Mr Miller is right. One needs to ask whether the defendant has any trade here, customers buying goods or services for consumption here. It was that sort of concept I had in mind in *800 FLOWERS Trade Mark*.[65]
>
> 20. On the facts here, I think the advertisement in *Homes & Gardens* is not an infringing use. I recognise that my view is provisional, this being only an application for summary judgment. Ultimately the question of the extent to which national trade mark law is permitted to impinge on trade within other countries may have to be considered by the European Court of Justice."

The judge then went on to consider the defendants' Irish web site: **6–051**

> "22. Now a person who visited that site would see 'ie'. That would be so, either in the original address of the web site, 'crateandbarrel-ie.com', or the current form,

'crateandbarrel.ie'. The reference to four floors is plainly a reference to a shop. So what would the visitor understand? Fairly obviously that this is advertising a shop and its wares. If he knew 'ie' meant Ireland, he would know the shop was in Ireland. Otherwise he would not. There is no reason why anyone in this country should regard the site as directed at him. So far as one can tell, no one has.

23. Now almost any search on the net almost always throws up a host of irrelevant 'hits.' You expect a lot of irrelevant sites. Moreover you expect a lot of those sites to be foreign. Of course you can go direct to a desired site. To do that, however, you must type in the exact address. Obviously that must be known in advance. Thus in this case you could get to the defendants' site either by deliberately going there using the address, or by a search. You could use 'Crate' and 'Barrel' linked Booleanly. One could even use just one of these words, though the result then would throw up many more irrelevant results.

24. Whether one gets there by a search or by direct use of the address, is it rational to say that the defendants are using the words 'Crate & Barrel' in the United Kingdom in the course of trade in goods? If it is, it must follow that the defendants' are using the words in every other country of the world. Miss Vitoria says that the Internet is accessible to the whole world. So it follows that any user will regard any web site as being 'for him' absent a reason to doubt the same. She accepted that my Bootle fishmonger example in *800-Flowers* is that sort of case but no more. I think it is not as simple as that. In *800-Flowers* I rejected the suggestion that the web site owner should be regarded as putting a tentacle onto the user's screen. Mr Miller here used another analogy. He said using the internet was more like the user focusing a super-telescope into the site concerned; he asked me to imagine such a telescope set up on the Welsh hills overlooking the Irish Sea. I think Mr Miller's analogy is apt in this case. Via the web you can look into the defendants' shop in Dublin. Indeed the very language of the internet conveys the idea of the user *going to* the site—'visit' is the word. Other cases would be different—a well-known example, for instance, is Amazon.com. Based in the U.S. it has actively gone out to seek world-wide trade, not just by use of the name on the Internet but by advertising its business here, and offering and operating a real service of supply of books to this country. These defendants have done none of that.''

Thus it can be seen that the hurdle that a claimant has to surmount to prove use of a trade mark in a cross-border context is significantly higher than that for defamation. Since to found jurisdiction the claimant must establish a good arguable case that a tort has been committed, the vulnerability of a ''merely available'' foreign web site to English jurisdiction is likely to be much less for trade mark infringement than for defamation.

6–052   This conclusion is reinforced by the *obiter* comments of Buxton L.J. in the Court of Appeal decision in *800 FLOWERS Trade Mark*,[66] in which he addressed trade mark use for both registrability and infringement purposes:

"136. The implications of internet use for issues of jurisdiction are clearly wide-ranging, and will need to be worked out with care in both domestic and private international law. ... I do venture to suggest that the essence of the problem is to fit the factual circumstances of internet use into the substantive rules of law applying to the many and very different legal issues that the internet affects. It is therefore unlikely, and it is nowhere suggested, that there will be one uniform rule, specific to the internet, that can be applied in all cases of internet use. That consideration is of importance in our present case, because it was a significant part of the applicant's submissions that, for instance, 'publication' of statements in a particular jurisdiction by downloading from the internet according to the rules of law of defamation or of misrepresentation was of at least strong analogical relevance to whether a trade mark downloaded from the internet had been 'used' in the jurisdiction to which it was downloaded; and, even more directly, that when A placed a mark on the internet that was downloaded by B, the same criteria should apply in determining whether A thereby used the mark as determine whether A thereby infringed the same mark in the jurisdiction where B was located.

137. I would wish to approach these arguments, and particularly the last of them, with caution. There is something inherently unrealistic in saying that that A 'uses' his mark in the United Kingdom when all that he does is to place the mark on the internet, from a location outside the United Kingdom, and simply wait in the hope that someone from the United Kingdom will download it and thereby create use on the part of A. By contrast, I can see that it might be more easily arguable that if A places on the internet a mark that is confusingly similar to a mark protected in another jurisdiction, he may do so at his peril that someone from that other jurisdiction may download it; though that approach conjured up in argument before us the potentially disturbing prospect that a shop in Arizona or Brazil that happens to bear the same name as a trademarked store in England or Australia will have to act with caution in answering telephone calls from those latter jurisdictions.

138. However that may be, the very idea of 'use' within a certain area would seem to require some active step in that area on the part of the user that goes beyond providing facilities that enable others to bring the mark into the area. Of course, if persons in the United Kingdom seek the mark on the internet in response to direct encouragement or advertisement by the owner of the mark, the position may be different; but in such a case the advertisement or encouragement in itself is likely to suffice to establish the necessary use. Those considerations are in my view borne out by the observations of this court in *Reuter v. Mulhens* [1954] Ch 50. The envelopes on the outside of which the allegedly infringing mark was placed as advertising matter were sent by post into the United Kingdom by the defendants. It is trite law that the Post Office is the agent of the sender of the letter to carry it, and thus it was the defendants who were to be taken to have delivered the letter to the recipients and to have displayed the mark to them within this jurisdiction. No such simple analysis is available to establish use by the applicant within this jurisdiction if he confines himself to the internet."

Although the distinction drawn between trade mark use for purposes of registrability and that for infringement may suggest a lower standard for infringement, both the comments of Buxton L.J. and the decision of Jacob J. in *Euromarket* (which was not referred to by the Court of Appeal in *800-FLOWERS*) show that mere availability of a mark on the Internet is unlikely to amount to use within the United Kingdom for infringement purposes.

In *V&S Vin & Sprit Aktiebolag AB v. Absolut Beach Pty Ltd* (May 15, 2001) the claimant relied on the availability of an Australian Web site in the United Kingdom bearing the mark complained of; willingness to accept orders placed via the Web site; and (the judge commented probably most importantly) the circulation in the United Kingdom by the defendant of its brochure in response to orders from the Web site. Pumfrey J. found that there was, just, a good arguable case of trade mark infringement sufficient to found jurisdiction.

6–053   *Negligent misstatement*   As to actionability, Section 11(1)) of the Private International Law (Miscellaneous Provisions) Act 1995[67] lays down the general rule that the applicable law is the law of the country in which the events constituting the tort in question occur. For many receipt-oriented torts this will be sufficient to dispose of the question of actionability.[68]

If a court were to consider that in a case of negligent misstatement on a foreign Web site elements of the events occur in different countries, then under section 11(2)(c) the general rule is that the applicable law is the law of the country in which the most significant element or elements of those events occurred. This has similarities to the "substance" test. However, under section 12 in both cases the general rule can be displaced by factors connecting the tort with another country, including factors such as those relating to the parties, to any events which constitute the tort in question or to any of the circumstances or consequences of those events. If it is substantially more appropriate for the applicable law to be the law of the other country, the general rule is displaced.

Once the applicable law is determined, the question of whether the allegations amount to a tort, delict or quasi-delict can be answered.

As to the place of the harmful event, there has been no ECJ case directly on the point of the application of Article 5(3) to cases of negligent misstatement. One English case has, however, considered the point in the light of the ECJ decisions. In *Domicrest Ltd v. Swiss Bank Corporation*,[69] the statement originated in Switzerland and was relied upon in England. Rix J. held that in the case of negligent misstatement the place where the harmful event giving rise to the damage occurred was where the misstatement originated, not the place where it was relied upon. On the particular facts of the case he held that although the statement was relied on in England, the damage was suffered in Italy and Switzerland, so that on no basis did the harmful event occur in England and the court had no jurisdiction under Article 5(3).

6–054   *Copyright*   So far as copyright is concerned, a variety of acts will constitute infringement and these are set out in detail in Chapter 2. Since it is clear under the current United Kingdom copyright law that even a transient copy of a copyright work in a computer can amount to an infringement if unauthorised, in theory if an unauthorised copy of a copyright work is routed on the Internet via a server in the United Kingdom there will be an infringement of copyright in the United Kingdom giving the copyright owner the right to sue for infringement the person causing that copy to be made.

6–055   *Patents*   In the case of a patent it is an infringement to make, dispose of, offer to dispose of, use, keep or import a patented product in a country where the relevant patent subsists. In the case of the Internet one is most likely talking about a technique of some sort such as a compression technique and it will depend on the particular nature of the patented item as to where infringement might occur. There are certainly going to be a number of situations where someone accessing some part of the Internet where such a technique is used will technically be infringing the patent for the technique providing such a patent is registered in the country from which that person is accessing the relevant part of the Internet.

Breach of confidence   Claims for breach of confidence, while certainly non-contractual, are an exercise of the court's equitable jurisdiction and do not arise in tort.[70] The question whether they are within Article 5(3) is unresolved.[71] In *Kitechnology BV v. Unicor GmbH Plastmaschinen*,[72] an English breach of confidence case, it was held at first instance that the damage to the owner of the right was a damage in his ability to exploit it wherever he wished and in particular in the country where he was based and therefore where he might well most wish to exploit it. The plaintiff was therefore able to maintain proceedings in England under Article 5(3), even though the breach of confidence was alleged to have occurred in Germany. That conclusion was overturned on appeal. In the absence of any evidence that that the defendants had publicised the information in England or elsewhere, or that they had exploited it otherwise than in Germany, there was no damage directly caused to the plaintiff in England and therefore no harmful event in England. If the plaintiff's argument was correct, the plaintiff would be able to establish jurisdiction in any country in which it was entitled to protect the confidentiality of the information, regardless of whether the defendants' alleged activities had any effect on their commertcial interests there. That would be a major derogation from the general rule stated in Article 2.

6–056

The Brussels Regulation   The Regulation will make no changes of substance to this aspect of the Convention.

6–057

Consumer contracts

Articles 13–15 of the Convention determine jurisdiction in proceedings concerning a contract concluded by a person for a purpose which can be regarded as being outside his trade or profession ("the consumer"), in the following cases:[73]

6–058

1.   A contract for the sale of goods on instalment credit terms.

2.   A contract for a loan repayable by instalments, or for any other form of credit, made to finance the sale of goods.

3.   Any other contract for the supply of goods or a contract for the supply of services, and:

      (a)   in the State of the consumer's domicile the conclusion of the contract was preceded by a specific invitation addressed to him or by advertising; and
      (b)   the consumer took in that State the steps necessary for the conclusion of the contract

Article 14 provides that a consumer may bring proceedings against the other party to a contract either in the courts of the Contracting State in which that party is domiciled or in the courts of the Contracting State in which the consumer is domiciled.

Article 15 restricts the cases in which the terms of Articles 13–15 may be departed from by agreement. In particular, Article 15 has the effect that the consumer cannot, by means of a provision in the contract under dispute, be deprived of the right under Article 14 to sue in his home court.

6–059

The Brussels Regulation will, for e-commerce websites, amend these provisions. The new Article 15 provides that the general test for determining whether a consumer can bring proceedings in the courts of the place where the consumer is domiciled is whether:

"the contract has been concluded with a person who pursues commercial or professional activities in the Member State of the consumer's domicile or, by any means, directs such activities to that Member State or to several countries including that Member State, and the contract falls within the scope of such activities".

The Regulation in its original proposed form contained a Recital (13) stating that: "...electronic commerce in goods or services by a means accessible in another Member State constitutes an activity directed to that State."

6–060   The United Kingdom government opposed the inclusion of that recital. In the debate on the Second Reading of the Electronic Communications Bill on November 29, 1999 the Minister introducing the Bill stated:[74]

"The Brussels convention has existed for 31 years and, in that time, almost no consumer has used it to sue for breach of contract. None the less, the Commission sought to extend its provisions to electronic commerce by providing in a draft recital that any web site that could be accessed from another member state would thereby qualify as advertising directed at consumers in that member state and could activate the convention's provisions. That, of course, misses the point that, on the internet, any web site is, by definition, accessible from anywhere else. I am pleased to be able to tell the House that there is growing agreement among member states with our view that the new recital should be dropped."

6–061   Recital 13 was indeed dropped. However, that left the term "directs" in Article 15 wholly undefined. An attempt has been made to remedy this to some extent by the minuting of a joint Council and Commission statement in relation to the Regulation.[75] The relevant part of the statement reads:

"...for Article 15(1)(c) to be applicable it is not sufficient for an undertaking to target its activities at the Member State of the consumer's residence, or at a number of Member States including that Member State; a contract must also be concluded within the framework of its activities. This provision relates to a number of marketing methods, including contracts concluded at a distance through the Internet.

In this context, the Council and Commission stress that the mere fact that an Internet site is accessible is not sufficient for Article 15 to be applicable, although a factor will be that this Internet site solicits the conclusion of distance contracts and that a contract has actually been concluded at a distance, by whatever means. In this respect, the language or currency which a web site uses does not constitute a relevant factor."

6–062   The OECD Consumer Protection Guidelines for E-Commerce adopted on December 8, 1999[76] recognise that existing approaches to jurisdiction may have to be reconsidered. They state:

"Business-to-consumer cross-border transactions, whether carried out electronically or otherwise, are subject to the existing framework on applicable law and jurisdiction. Electronic commerce poses challenges to this existing framework. Therefore, consideration should be given to whether the existing framework for applicable law and jurisdiction should be modified, or applied differently, to ensure effective and transparent consumer protection in the context of the continued growth of electronic commerce. In considering whether to modify the existing framework, governments should seek to ensure that the framework provides fairness to consumers and business, facilitates electronic commerce, results in consumers having a level of protection not less than that afforded in other forms of commerce, and provides consumers with meaningful access to fair and timely dispute resolution and redress without undue cost or burden."

In parallel with the discussion about appropriate law and jurisdiction in business to consumer disputes there is a growing realisation that most consumer disputes are of such low value that traditional court proceedings, especially in a cross-border environment, are likely to be too burdensome to consumers. There is, therefore, considerable discussion as to whether suppliers and/or suppliers' organisations can be encouraged, or should be required, to provide inexpensive cross-border dispute resolution mechanisms, perhaps conducted on-line.

There is a growing degree of overlap between questions of jurisdiction and dispute resolution mechanisms. For instance, a submission by Professor Catherine Kessedjian, then Deputy Secretary General of the Hague Conference on Private International Law, at the Geneva Round Table on Electronic Commerce and Private International Law in September 1999, proposed what might be termed a "conditional country of origin" regime. This would allow a site which obtained certification (*e.g.* under a scheme promoted by the International Chamber of Commerce or other such organisations) to take advantage of a country of origin regime by providing for the application of the law of the country of origin of the site proprietor, and for the courts of that country where a case could not be solved by the dispute resolution mechanism part of the certification. The certification process would include "minimum substantive rules and protection of the consumer including warranties, and fair and easy dispute resolution mechanism which could possibly be free of charge to the consumer".

6–063

Debates about linking on-line consumer dispute resolution to jurisdiction have also took place in the context of the proposed Brussels Regulation. The European Parliament's amendment to achieve this was rejected by the Commission. However, in the Council and Commission joint statement annexed to the Regulation they stressed the importance of alternative methods of dispute settlement and that the purpose of the Regulation, especially Articles 15 and 17, was not to prohibit the parties from making use of these.

6.2.3 Jurisdiction—Defendant not domiciled within a Brussels Convention Contracting State

Jurisdiction over non-domiciliaries by virtue of the Brussels Convention
The main provisions of Article 17 concerning jurisdiction agreements apply where one or more of the parties to the jurisdiction agreement are domiciled in a Contracting State.[77] A jurisdiction agreement is therefore capable,[78] by virtue of the Convention, of conferring jurisdiction on the court of a Contracting State where the defendant is domiciled in a non-Contracting State.[79] Otherwise under Article 4 of the Brussels Convention, if the Defendant is not domiciled within a Contracting State the jurisdiction of the courts of each Contracting State shall be determined by the national law of that State. This is subject only to Article 16 of the Convention, which provides in certain cases (such as

6–064

proceedings concerned with the validity of patents, trade marks, designs or other similar rights required to be deposited or registered) for exclusive jurisdiction to vested in designated Contracting State courts, regardless of domicile.

Cases outside the Brussels Convention

6–065   In a case not within the scope of Article 1 of the Brussels Convention, or in which Article 4 delegates the question of jurisdiction to national law, the substantive rules of English common law and the procedure of the Civil Procedure Rules will apply.

In such cases the English court will prima facie be competent if:

1.   The defendant is served within the jurisdiction;[80] or

2.   The defendant has submitted to the jurisdiction of the English court; or

3.   The defendant has been served with English proceedings out of the English jurisdiction pursuant to permission granted under Rule 6.21 of the Civil Procedure Rules.

Each of these cases is subject to the possibility of the defendant applying to stay the proceedings on grounds of *forum non conveniens*[81] and in the case of service out of the English jurisdiction also to apply to dispute jurisdiction and to set aside the permission to serve out of the jurisdiction.[82]

6–066   An application for permission to serve the proceedings outside the jurisdiction is made without notice to the intended defendant.[83] The claimant must show that it has a good arguable case that the court has jurisdiction under one of the categories set out in the CPR Rule 6.20;[84] and that there is a serious issue to be tried on the merits of the claim.[85] It must also demonstrate that England is clearly the appropriate forum in which to try the case for the interests of all the parties and for the ends of justice.[86]

The court therefore retains a discretion whether or not to grant leave. So in a libel case, for instance, even if there is a publication within the jurisdiction, the court may yet in its discretion refuse leave to serve a defendant out of the jurisdiction. In *Kroch v. Rossell*,[87] leave was refused on the ground that there was no question of substance in England. Only a small quantity of foreign newspapers had circulated here, the plaintiff was a foreigner and there was no evidence that he had a reputation or associations here.[88]

The *Spiliada* principles will apply to the determination whether the England is the most appropriate forum. However, it is not inconsistent with those principles to apply a prima facie assumption that the jurisdiction where in substance the tort is committed is the appropriate forum, or at least to treat that as a weighty factor.[89]

6–067   The categories in CPR Rule 6.20 within which a claimant has to bring his claim that are most relevant to the Internet and e-commerce are:

- A claim is made for a remedy against a person domiciled within the jurisdiction (Rule 6.20(1)).

- A claim is made for an injunction ordering the defendant to do or refrain from doing an act within the jurisdiction (Rule 6.20(2)). For the court to grant leave on this basis the injunction must be a genuine part of the substantive relief sought[90] and there must be a reasonable prospect of the injunction being granted at trial.[91]

- A claim is made in respect of a contract where the contract: (a) was made within the jurisdiction; (b) was made by or through an agent trading or residing within the jurisdiction; (c) is governed by English law; or (d) contains a term to the effect that the court shall have jurisdiction to determine any claim in respect of the contract (Rule 6(5)).

The question whether a contract was made in the jurisdiction will be determined by consideration of the point at which the contract was concluded, in particular whether it was concluded upon the sending (the "postal rule") or the receipt or deemed receipt (the "telex rule")[92] of the acceptance. Although it is tempting to assume that all Internet transactions are instantaneous and so analogous to telex, the reality is that there is a variety of different types of Internet communications, and that some (*e.g.* Internet e-mail, especially using dial-up accounts) is by no means instantaneous. While these differences may in some cases go more to the time of receipt, rather than to the question whether acceptance is effective at the place of sending or receipt, the application of these rules is still by no means fully worked out.

6–068

- A claim is made in respect of a breach of a contract committed within the jurisdiction (Rule 6(6)); or a claim is made for a declaration that no contract exists where, if the contract were found to exist, it would comply with the conditions set out in Rule 6(5) (Rule 6(7)).

- The claim is made against a person on whom the claim form has been or will be served and (a) there is between the claimant and that person a real issue which it is reasonable for the court to try and (b) the claimant wishes to serve the claim form on another person who is a necessary or proper party to that claim (Rule 6.20(3)) In this case the claimant must state in written evidence the grounds on which the witness believes that there is a real issue which it is reasonable for the court to try (Rule 6.21(1)(c)).

- The claim is made in tort where (a) the damage was sustained within the jurisdiction; or (b) the damage sustained resulted from an act committed within the jurisdiction (Rule 6.20(8)). This head is similar to Article 5(3) of the Brussels Convention discussed above. However, the scope is restricted to tort alone, according to its English law meaning.

As with cases under Article 5(3) of the Brussels Convention, the claimant will have to show that he has a good arguable case that an actionable tort has been committed. The question of actionability has to be determined according to the relevant English law principles[93] and requires the court to consider substantively the tort alleged to have been committed.

- The whole subject matter of a claim relates to property located within the jurisdiction (Rule 6.20(10). This head is wider than the corresponding provision of the previous Rules of the Supreme Court, which related only to land. It could have application in, for instance, a dispute about rights to a *.uk* domain name registered at Nominet.

6.2.4 Extra-territorial injunctions

Traditionally under English law it has not been easy to obtain an injunction restraining a

6–069

particular act both in the United Kingdom and in countries outside it. This was because of an old rule called the "double actionability" test. However, there is now a statute (the Private International Law (Miscellaneous Provisions) Act 1995) which as from May 1, 1996 has done away with this test for most types of action and make it much easier for an English court to grant what is known as extra-territorial relief, both in the form of a final as well as an interlocutory injunction. At least in the E.U. by virtue of the Brussels Convention such relief would be easily enforceable in the countries covered by any such English court injunction. The enforceability of any such relief outside the E.U. will depend largely on the treaties between the United Kingdom and the relevant countries. In general the United Kingdom has a large number of such mutual enforcement treaties with other countries in the world with the notable exception of the U.S. Accordingly, a United Kingdom court may well be persuaded to exercise such extra-territorial jurisdiction in instances of some types of intellectual property rights infringement brought before it concerning activities on the Internet in order to ensure that the will of the court is not defeated.

6.3 "Country of origin" rules

6.3.1 Background

6–070   We discuss in Chapter 12 a variety of possible policy approaches to the problem of whether a web-site proprietor, due to the fact that his web site is by its very nature available in any country with Internet facilities, is potentially subject to the laws of all those countries.

We have also discussed above the development in the United Kingdom in some areas of law, on a piecemeal basis, of rules suggesting that only if a web site is in some sense directed at the United Kingdom should it be subject to United Kingdom laws.

Within the European Community an attempt has been made, in the Electronic Commerce Directive, to provide for a broader 'country of origin' rule. A pure country of origin rule would provide that a web site proprietor would only be required to comply with the laws of the state in which it is established, thus protecting web site proprietors established in a country within the European Union from the laws of other European Union countries even if they direct their activities to those countries.

6–071   We discuss in Chapter 12 the political reasons why a pure country of origin rule is unlikely ever to be adopted. The Electronic Commerce Directive does indeed contain a number of exceptions and derogations. We discuss here the scope of the country of origin provisions of the Directive and the exceptions and derogations from it.

The Directive does not purport to alter international jurisdiction or applicable law rules. However, it can affect the ability of a Member State to enforce the domestic laws that would apply as a consequence of those rules, if to enforce those domestic laws would amount to a prohibited restriction on the freedom to receive "information society services" from another Member State.

6.3.2 The Electronic Commerce Directive

6–072   The Directive has been promoted primarily by the old Commission Directorate DGXV and now the Internal Market Directorate, which have been responsible for Single Market initiatives. The focus of the draft Directive is on removing obstacles to cross-border electronic commerce within the Community and on implementing, as far as possible, a regime of control of cross-border services by country of origin and concomitant mutual recognition of Member State national laws.

Information Society Services

The Directive applies to "Information Society Services". These are defined as services **6–073** within the meaning of Article 1(2) of the "Transparency Directive"[94] (Article 2(a)). The full definition in the Transparency Directive is set out below. However, there appear to be some qualifications to this definition as a result of the recitals to the Electronic Commerce Directive. The Transparency Directive definition is:

> "'service', any Information Society service, that is to say, any service normally provided for remuneration, at a distance, by electronic means and at the individual request of a recipient of services.
> For the purposes of this definition:
>
> > 'at a distance' means that the service is provided without the parties being simultaneously present,
> > 'by electronic means' means that the service is sent initially and received at its destination by means of electronic equipment for the processing (including digital compression) and storage of data, and entirely transmitted, conveyed and received by wire, by radio, by optical means or by other electromagnetic means,
> > 'at the individual request of a recipient of services' means that the service is provided through the transmission of data on individual request.
>
> An indicative list of services not covered by this definition is set out in Annex V. This Directive shall not apply to:
>
> > radio broadcasting services,
> > television broadcasting services covered by point (a) of Article 1 of Directive 89/552/EEC."

Annex V of the Transparency Directive provides: **6–074**

> "ANNEX V
> Indicative list of services not covered by the second subparagraph of point 2 of Article 1
> 1. Services not provided 'at a distance'
> – Services provided in the physical presence of the provider and the recipient, even if they involve the use of electronic devices
>
> (a)   medical examinations or treatment at a doctor's surgery using electronic equipment where the patient is physically present;
> (b)   consultation of an electronic catalogue in a shop with the customer on site;
> (c)   plane ticket reservation at a travel agency in the physical presence of the customer by means of a network of computers;
> (d)   electronic games made available in a video-arcade where the customer is physically present.

2. Services not provided "by electronic means"
– Services having material content even though provided via electronic devices:

(a)   automatic cash or ticket dispensing machines (banknotes, rail tickets);
(b)   access to road networks, car parks, etc., charging for use, even if there are electronic devices at the entrance/exit controlling access and/or ensuring correct payment is made,

– Off-line services: distribution of CD roms or software on diskettes,
– Services which are not provided via electronic processing/inventory systems:

(a)   voice telephony services;
(b)   telefax/telex services;
(c)   services provided via voice telephony or fax;
(d)   telephone/telefax consultation of a doctor;
(e)   telephone/telefax consultation of a lawyer;
(f)   telephone/telefax direct marketing.

3. Services not supplied "at the individual request of a recipient of services"
– Services provided by transmitting data without individual demand for simultaneous reception by an unlimited number of individual receivers (point to multipoint transmission):

(a)   television broadcasting services (including near-video on-demand services), covered by point (a) of Article 1 of Directive 89/552/EEC[95];
(b)   radio broadcasting services;
(c)   (televised) teletext."

6–075   The effect of the indicative list of excluded services in Annex V may be modified by Recital 17 of the Electronic Commerce Directive, which states:

"The definition of information society services already exists in Community law in Directive 98/34/EC[96] of the European Parliament and of the Council of 22 June 1998 laying down a procedure for the provision of information in the field of technical standards and regulations and of rules on information society services and in Directive 98/84/EC[97] of the European Parliament and of the Council of 20 November 1998 on the legal protection of services based on, or consisting of, conditional access; this definition covers any service normally provided for remuneration, at a distance, by means of electronic equipment for the processing (including digital compression) and storage of data, and at the individual request of a recipient of a service; those services referred to in the indicative list in Annex V to Directive 98/34/EC which do not imply data processing and storage are not covered by this definition."

This appears to restrict the Annex V exclusions to those in the Annex V indicative list which do not imply data processing (including digital compression) and storage. So although fax is on the Annex V list, it does utilise digital compression techniques and so according to the recital ought to be included in the definition. This approach does create considerable uncertainties.

6–076   A further indication (or confusion) of the scope of the definition is provided by Recital (18) of the Electronic Commerce Directive. This provides a list of services that do and do not constitute information society services. Those that do include selling goods on-line; insofar as they represent an economic activity, services which are not remunerated by those who receive them, such as those offering on-line information or commercial communications, search tools; transmission of information via a communication network, providing access to a communication network, hosting information provided by a recipient of the service; by contrast, video-on-demand or the provision of commercial communications by electronic mail.

Those that do not constitute information society services are stated to include the delivery of goods as such or the provision of services off-line; television broadcasting within the meaning of Directive 89/552[98] and radio broadcasting, because they are not provided at individual request; the use of electronic mail or equivalent individual communications for instance by natural persons acting outside their trade, business or profession including their use for the conclusion of contracts between such persons; the contractual relationship between an employee and his employer; activities which by their very nature cannot be carried out at a distance and by electronic means, such as the statutory auditing of company accounts or medical advice requiring the physical examination of a patient.   **6–077**

The reference to e-mail as included is obscure. It is unclear how, notwithstanding the terms of the recital, the sending of e-mail can be characterised as a service normally provided at individual request as required by the main definition.

Place of establishment
The Directive defines the place of establishment of an information society service provider ("ISSP"). This is important for the principle of country of origin control, since a Member State is required to ensure that the information society services provided by a service provider established on its territory comply with the national provisions applicable in the Member State in question which fall within the coordinated field.   **6–078**

Art 2 provides that an "established service provider" is:

"a service provider who effectively pursues an economic activity using a fixed establishment for an indefinite period. The presence and use of the technical means and technologies required to provide the service do not, in themselves, constitute an establishment of the provider;"

This is further elucidated in Recital (19), which states: **6–079**

"The place at which a service provider is established should be determined in conformity with the case-law of the Court of Justice according to which the concept of establishment involves the actual pursuit of an economic activity through a fixed establishment for an indefinite period; this requirement is also fulfilled where a company is constituted for a given period; the place of establishment of a company providing services via an Internet web site is not the place at which the technology supporting its web site is located or the place at which its web site is accessible but the place where it pursues its economic activity; in cases where a provider has several places of establishment it is important to determine from which place of establishment the service concerned is provided; in cases where it is difficult to determine from which of several places of establishment a given service is provided, this is the place where the provider has the centre of his activities relating to this particular service."

The "country of origin" principle comes to the fore in the statement that the place of establishment is not where the web site is accessible. Although the recital also states that a service provider is not established where the technology supporting its web site is located, in cases of difficulty where the centre of activities relating to the particular service has to be ascertained it is difficult to resist the conclusion that the location of the technology supporting the web site will often be at least one factor to be considered.

Mutual recognition

6–080   The Directive lays down a regime of mutual recognition of Member State national laws and control by Member State of origin and for exclusions and derogations from the Directive and from the country of origin principle. Mutual recognition of the legal regimes of other Member States is achieved in Article 3.2, which states the general principle that Member States may not, for reasons falling within the coordinated field, restrict the freedom to provide information society services from another Member State.

The country of origin provisions reflect the general principles of free movement of goods, freedom of establishment and freedom to provide and receive services under the Treaty of Rome and the specific responsibility of DGXV and now the Internal Market Directorate of the Commission to promote the Single Market.

Treaty of Rome

6–081   The Treaty of Rome contains provisions designed to ensure the free flow of goods and, most relevantly for the purpose of this Directive, services, between Member States.

Articles 28 to 30 (old 30 to 36[99]) of the Treaty of Rome prohibit quantitative restrictions on the free movement of goods between Member States. Article 28 (old 30) states:

> "Quantitative restrictions on imports and all measures having equivalent effect shall be prohibited between Member States."

Article 30 (old 36) states:

> "the provisions of Articles 28 and 29 shall not include prohibitions or restrictions on imports, exports or goods in transit justified on grounds of public morality, public policy or public security; the protection of health and life of humans, animals or plants; the protection of national treasures possessing artistic, historic or archaeological value; or the protection of industrial and commercial property. Such prohibitions or restrictions shall not, however, constitute a means of arbitrary discrimination or a disguised restriction on trade between Member States."

6–082   As to freedom of services, Article 49 (old 59) states:

> "Within the framework of the provisions set out below, restrictions on freedom to provide services within the Community shall be prohibited in respect of nationals of Member States who are established in a State of the Community other than that of the person for whom the services are intended..."

Under Article 50 (old 60) services are within the meaning of the Treaty where they are:

> "normally provided for remuneration, insofar as they are not governed by the provisions relating to freedom of movement for goods, capital and persons."

"Services" is defined in particular to include:

"a) activities of an industrial character; a) activities of a commercial character; c) activities of craftsmen; d) activities of the professions."

Under Article 55 (old 66) the provisions of Articles 45 to 48 (old 55 to 58) apply. In particular, Article 46 (old 56) provides **6–083**

"1. The provisions of this Chapter and measures taken in pursuance thereof shall not prejudice the applicability of provisions laid down by law, regulation or administrative action providing for special treatment for foreign nationals on ground of public policy, public security or public health."

Thus it can been seen that under the Treaty itself the country of origin/mutual recognition regime applied by Articles 28 (old 30) and 49 (old 59) is qualified by a number of exceptions which permit the destination Member State to restrict goods and services received from the Member State of origin.

Further, Article 153 (old 129A) places a specific obligation on the Community in relation to consumer protection: **6–084**

"In order to promote the interests of consumers and to ensure a high level of consumer protection, the Community shall contribute to protecting the health, safety and economic interests of consumers, as well as to promoting their right to information, education and to organise themselves in order to safeguard their interests."

The Article specifies that consumer protection requirements shall be taken into account in defining and implementing other community policies and activities; and that measures adopted by the Council under Article 153(4) (old 129a(4)) shall not prevent any Member State from maintaining or introducing more stringent protective measures, albeit that such measures must be compatible with the Treaty.

The Directive as advertised

In promoting the proposed Electronic Commerce Directive, most emphasis was placed on the principle of country of origin control, for instance: **6–085**

"The proposal builds upon the tried and tested Single Market principles of free movement and freedom of establishment, and would ensure that providers of information society services based within the EU can provide their services throughout the EU if they comply with the law in their country of origin"[100]

"[in the proposed electronic commerce directive] commercial communications emanating from a service provider established in the European Community would be subject to country of origin control. This means that the service provider will have to comply with the rules of the country in which he is established and will benefit from the free provision of services throughout the Community.' ... 'The expectation that consumers are adequately protected by the legislation of the country of origin of the service provider reflects the high level of integration among Member States of the European Community"[101]

The Directive in reality

6–086   However, if a potential ISSP were to believe that once the Directive is implemented he only has to worry about the laws of his home Member State, he would almost certainly be mistaken. Although in principle a country of origin regime properly so called could achieve the ideal that an ISSP would have to have regard only to the laws of the Member State in which it is established, the reality is that the Electronic Commerce Directive does not achieve that. This is hardly surprising when, as we have seen, exceptions from country of origin control are built into the very fabric of the Treaty of Rome. Politically, proposals for a true country of origin regime are always bound to encounter formidable obstacles.[102] Now that the Directive has been adopted, statements are emerging from the Commission that recognise the significance of the Directive's derogations from the country of origin principle.[103]

The broad principle of country of origin control is set out in Article 3 of the Directive. Article 3.1 states:

> "Each Member State shall ensure that the information society services provided by a service provider established on its territory comply with the national provisions applicable in the Member State in question which fall within the co-ordinated field."

Thus a Member State must ensure that its laws apply to an ISSP established within its territory, even if the ISSP has so arranged matters that the services are delivered from a location outside the Member State's territory. The location of the Web server, or the ability to access a site from within a Member State, do not determine the place of establishment.

6–087   The co-ordinated field of the Directive concerns "requirements with which the service provider has to comply in respect of:

- the taking up of the activity of an information society service, such as requirements concerning qualifications, authorisation or notification,

- the pursuit of the activity of an information society service, such as requirements concerning the behaviour of the service provider, requirements regarding the quality or content of the service including those applicable to advertising and contracts, or requirements concerning the liability of the service provider;"

The coordinated field is stated not to cover requirements such as:

- requirements applicable to goods as such,

- requirements applicable to the delivery of goods,

- requirements applicable to services not provided by electronic means.

So although the co-ordinated field includes what may be thought of as regulatory requirements with which a service provider has to comply, it potentially goes much wider than that, for instance extending to general content laws (insofar as they apply to services delivered by electronic means).

6–088   Article 3.2 states:

> "Member States may not, for reasons falling within the co-ordinated field, restrict

the freedom to provide information society services from another Member State."

This reflects the primary mutual recognition provisions of the Treaty of Rome as regards freedom of services (Article 49 (old 59)).

The elevation of consumer protection to a primary objective of the Community under the Treaty of Rome may increase the potential for conflict between country of origin control and the traditional approaches to consumer protection involving preserving the mandatory rules of the consumer's country of habitual residence and exemplified in the Brussels and Rome Conventions (see above).

Exclusions and Derogations

The Directive contains both exclusions from the complete scope of the Directive and derogations from the country of origin principle. The Commission, in its Explanatory Memorandum, justified the exclusions from the complete scope of application of the Directive on various grounds including undesirable clashes with areas covered by other Directives (*e.g.* data protection), or that work is in progress under other initiatives (*e.g.* taxation), or that "it is not possible to guarantee the freedom to provide services between Member States given the lack of mutual recognition or sufficient harmonisation to guarantee an equivalent level of protection of general interest objectives".[104]   **6–089**

As to derogation from the country of origin principle, the Commission put forward three reasons for derogating in specific areas from the country of origin principle:

1).   It is *impossible to apply the principle of mutual recognition* as set out in the case law of the Court of Justice concerning the principles of freedom of movement enshrined in the Treaty, or

2).   It is an area where mutual recognition cannot be achieved and there is *insufficient harmonisation* to guarantee an equivalent level of protection between member states,

3).   There are *provisions laid down by existing Directives which are clearly incompatible* with Article 3 because they explicitly require supervision in the country of destination."[105]

In addition to the exceptions and derogations specifically provided for, Article 3 of the Directive preserves the right, subject to a series of conditions relating to the characteristics of measures and the conduct of the Member State taking them, for Member States to take country of destination measures against Information Society Services emanating from other Member States. It also provides for an emergency procedure and for a supervision and veto procedure by the Commission. The Commission stated:[106]   **6–090**

"It goes without saying that the Commission's approach in this context will be flexible, and, in particular, will seek to avoid cases of disguised or disproportionate restrictions to the free movement of the relevant services. Having said this, the Commission will fully account for the Member States' need to enforce laws seeking to protection fundamental societal interests. It would, for example, be out of the question for the Commission to prevent a Member State from applying a law which would forbid the arrival of racist messages."

The Directive provides the following derogations from the country of origin principle:[107]   **6–091**

- Copyright, neighbouring rights, rights referred to in Directive 87/54/EEC[108] (legal protection of topographies of semi-conductor products) and Directive 96/9/EC[109] (legal protection of databases) as well as industrial property rights.

- The emission of electronic money by institutions in respect of which Member States have applied one of the derogations provided for in Article 8(1) of Directive 2000/46/EC[110] (Directive on the taking up, pursuit of and prudential supervision of the business of electronic money institutions).

- Article 44(2) of Directive 85/611/EC[111] (co-ordination of laws, regulations and administrative provisions relating to undertaking for collective investment in transferable securities).

- Article 30 and Title IV of Directive 92/49/EEC (direct insurance other than life insurance), Title IV of Directive 92/96/EEC (direct life insurance), Articles 7 and 8 of Directive 88/357/EEC (direct insurance other than life assurance) and Article 4 of Directive 90/619/EEC (direct life insurance).

- The freedom of the parties to choose the law applicable to their contract

- Contractual obligations concerning consumer contracts.

- Formal validity of contracts creating or transferring rights in real estate where such contracts are subject to mandatory formal requirements of the law of the Member State where the real estate is located

- The permissibility of unsolicited commercial communications by electronic mail.

6–092 Apart from these specific derogations from the country of origin principle, Article 3.4 of the Directive also lays down that Member States may take measures to derogate from Article 3.2 in respect of a given information society service if the following conditions are fulfilled:

   (a)   The measures shall be:

       (i)   Necessary for one of the following reasons:
           – public policy, in particular the prevention, investigation, detection and prosecution of criminal offences, including the protection of minors and the fight against any incitement to hatred on grounds of race, sex, religion or nationality, and violations of human dignity concerning individual persons,
           – the protection of public health,
           – public security, including the safeguarding of national security and defence,
           – the protection of consumers, including investors;
      (ii)   Taken against a given information society service which prejudices the objectives referred to in point (i) or which presents a serious and grave risk of prejudice to those objectives,
    (iii)   Proportionate to those objectives.

These bases of derogation mirror and (in the case of public policy) amplify the derogations from country of origin for freedom of services set out in Article 46 (old 56) of the Treaty of Rome, with the addition of consumer protection.

6–093 Article 3.4(b) of the Directive provides that prior to taking the measures in question, and without prejudice to court proceedings, including preliminary proceedings and acts carried out in the framework of a criminal investigation, the Member State must have asked the Member State with country of origin control to take measures and the latter either did not take measures or they were inadequate; and also notified the Commission and the Member State in which the service provider is established of the intention to take such measures. The Member State may in the case of urgency, take measures without complying with those conditions so long as it notifies them in the shortest possible time afterwards to the Commission and the Member State in which the service provider is established, indicating the reasons for which the Member State considers that there is urgency.

The Commission under Article 3.6 shall, without prejudice to the Member State's possibility of proceedings with the measures in question, examine the compatibility of the notified measures with Community law in the shortest possible time. Where the Commission comes to the conclusion that the measure is incompatible with Community law, the Commission shall ask the Member State in question to refrain from taking any proposed measures or urgently to put an end to the measures in question. This formulation of the Commission's powers is significantly weaker than the Commission original proposal, which required Member States to cease or refrain from measures in the event of a Commission negative decision.

The derogation provisions potentially provide scope for Member States to seek to justify existing restrictions against a "given" service on one of the grounds set out in Article 3.4,[112] or to put in place new restrictions under the urgency procedure and then to fight a lengthy political campaign seeking to justify the measures taken. It is unclear whether a "given" service can extend to a designated type of service, or means a particular service emanating from a particular provider. They may also provide scope for complex debates in the domestic courts over the justifiability of domestic laws when applied to services emanating from providers established in other Member States. **6–094**

Given that the Treaty of Rome itself does not provide for pure country of origin control it is, perhaps, hardly surprising that the Directive is laden with exceptions and derogations.

Practical effect of the Directive

The practical effect of the derogations may usefully be considered in the light of the Commission's own survey of the key areas giving rise to legal costs associated with electronic commerce.[113] The Commission's survey showed that 64 per cent of those who had undertaken a legal analysis of the regulatory situation had evaluated legal aspects other than those in their own country. 57 per cent believed it was essential to evaluate how the activity would be treated in other Member States. **6–095**

The key areas giving rise to legal costs were, in descending order of significance: copyright, general requirements on advertising, contracts, promotional offers, unfair competition, consumer protection and liability regimes.

It is instructive to assess the affect of the country of origin provisions of the Directive on each of the main topics identified by the Commission's survey: **6–096**

As to copyright, the country of origin provisions will have no effect thanks to the derogation from the country of origin principle under Article 3.3 and the Annex. Other aspects of the Directive, especially the liability of intermediaries provisions, will apply to copyright.

As to advertising, in principle the Directive could have considerable effect. However, the Article 3.4(a) derogations, particularly public policy and consumer protection, may give Member States scope to seek to defend advertising restrictions. Further, any advertising-related trade mark issues would appear to be derogated from the country of origin principle by virtue of the derogation for industrial property rights. Similar remarks could be made about unfair competition laws.

As to contracts, the effect of the country of origin provisions on the need to obtain legal advice on contracts will not be great. On the positive side, Article 9 of the Directive will in many cases require Member States to remove obstacles of form to on-line contract formation. The Directive also creates uniform requirements as to placing of orders and receipt of acknowledgments and information to be provided to the recipient service.[114] These will apply to all contracts within the scope of the Directive, including consumer contracts.

6–097   Notwithstanding these harmonised rules, the derogations for Member States to exercise country of destination control, particularly for the purposes of consumer protection, and the derogation for contractual obligations concerning consumer contracts, will mean that an ISSP cannot assume that his contract terms will comply with the law in all destination Member States.[115]

In principle, promotional offers should be protected by the country of origin provisions of the Directive, particularly as Article 6 of the Directive lays down harmonised minimum requirements for commercial communications, including promotional offers, competitions and games. However, again Member States may seek to rely on the consumer protection derogation to justify measures against a given service.

6–098   As to differing liability regimes,[116] these could only be the subject of the country of origin principles of the Directive if a Member State's liability provisions could be characterised as a restriction on the freedom to provide Information Society services in that State. Since "requirements concerning the liability of the service provider" are stated to be within the coordinated field of the Directive, that could be found to be so. Of course, laws regarding the liability of information society intermediaries are harmonised by the Directive, but that does not affect the position of non-intermediary ISSPs.

There are numerous other areas about which ISSPs might consider taking advice in destination Member States: eg. defamation, privacy laws, obscenity, language laws and many others. Some of these, such as language laws, ought in principle to be among the strongest candidates for country of origin control (although see Recital (63) discussed below).

The Directive, private international law and jurisdiction

6–099   However, uncertain boundaries between the Directive and the Brussels and Rome Conventions on jurisdiction and choice of law respectively may cause problems. Article 1.4 of the Directive states: "This Directive does not establish additional rules on private international law nor does it deal with the jurisdiction of Courts." Similarly Recital (23) states: "This Directive neither aims to establish additional rules on private international law relating to conflicts of law nor does it deal with the jurisdiction of Courts; provisions of the applicable law designated by rules of private international law must not restrict the freedom to provide information society services as established in this Directive."

The interaction between the Directive and private international law is not easy to predict. If, for instance, French law provides that a consumer contract is invalid if it is not in French, the Rome Convention would entitle a consumer habitually resident in France to take advantage of a French "mandatory rule" to that effect, if the conclusion of the contract was preceded by a specific invitation to the consumer or by advertising. But if the Electronic Commerce Directive means anything, such a law should be regarded as a restriction on the freedom to provide services from another Member State and thus, unless it can be justified under one of the derogations from Article 3, contrary to the Directive. If the Rome Convention takes precedence, or if a language law can be justified under one of the derogations (such as for contractual obligations in consumer contracts), it becomes difficult to see what is left of the 'country of origin' principle that is supposed to underlie the Directive. Interestingly, in its Communication on E-Commerce and Financial Services issued in February 2001, the Commission makes the following comment on the interaction between the Rome Convention and the Directive:

> "The effect of the derogation in the field of contract law is to allow Member States other than the other than the State in which a service provider is established to apply rules which restrict the freedom to provide information society services, subject to compatibility of such measures with Article 49 of the EC Treaty."

Further, if national sensitivities are to be given weight under the public policy derogations, then it has to be questioned to what extent the Directive would provide protection against incidents such as the action taken by the German authorities against a left wing magazine hosted on a web site in Holland, which the German authorities regarded as contravening German laws against encouraging terrorism.[117] The recitals to the Directive contain language which might provide some comfort to a Member State seeking to place a wide interpretation on, for instance, the public policy derogation. Recital (63) states:

6–100

> "The adoption of this Directive will not prevent the Member States from taking into account the various social, societal and cultural implications which are inherent in the advent of the information society; *in particular it should not hinder measures which Member States might adopt in conformity with Community law to achieve social, cultural and democratic goals taking into account their linguistic diversity, national and regional specificities as well as their cultural heritage,* and to ensure and maintain public access to the widest possible range of information society services; in any case, the development of the information society is to ensure that Community citizens can have access to the cultural European heritage provided in the digital environment." (emphasis added).

Whilst the Directive may reduce the areas in which those risks exist and in which cross-border advice needs to be taken, it is unlikely to eliminate either the risk or the need. At worst it will simply replace one uncertainty (the nature of the laws of the destination Member State) with another (the justifiability of the destination Member State laws under the derogations from the Directive). At best, if the political will to embrace the Single Market in cyberspace is present among the Member States, it could establish a bridgehead for a true European single market in the on-line world, taking advantage of the de facto destruction of national frontiers pioneered by the Internet to transcend the traditional national boundaries of the off-line world.

6–101

The Directive is due to be implemented before January 17, 2002. It is not as yet apparent what approach the United Kingdom government proposes to take to the implementation of the country of origin aspects of the Directive.

6.4 Australia

6.4.1 Misuse of Registered and Unregistered Trade Marks

Available causes of action

6–102   A range of alternatives are open to an owner of a registered or unregistered trade mark which is used by an unauthorised user on a web site. They are:

- trade mark infringement;

- the consumer protection provisions of the *Trade Practices Act* 1974 and equivalent State and Territory fair trading legislation; and

- the common law passing off.

The availability of trade mark infringement will generally be limited to a situation where the trade mark is used on the web site to sell or advertise goods or services. The *Trade Practices Act* 1974 has a broader application applying even where there are no goods or services being promoted or sold.

Trade mark infringement

6–103   The *Trade Marks Act* 1995 offers protection to the owner of a registered trade mark against use of the trade mark as a trade mark in relation to goods and/or services in respect of which the mark has been registered or closely related goods and/or services. For marks which are "well known" in Australia, use even in relation to unrelated goods or services may be infringing use.

   The application of the *Trade Marks Act* 1995 is geographically limited to Australia and certain Australian territories. Accordingly, it will need to be shown that the infringing use of the trade mark took place within Australia. The offer for sale of goods or services on a web site can be perceived as falling within one of three levels of accessibility to Australian consumers.

- At its highest, the goods or services can be offered specifically to Australian consumers. Provided the other requirements were met, this would be a clear case of trade mark infringement.

- Where the goods or services are generally offered to the world at large without any specific targeting of Australian consumers, trade mark infringement is arguable.

- In a situation where the goods are not able to be purchased by Australian consumers (such as where the site contains a disclaimer), the situation is unclear. At present, a *laissez faire* attitude has been taken by trade mark owners towards use in this manner, with trade mark infringement not being pursued vigourously. However, this does not necessarily mean that there has been no trade mark infringement.

6–104   In order to have standing to sue for trade mark infringement, the person must be either a "registered owner" or an "authorised user" of the trade mark. An "authorised user" is defined under the *Trade Marks Act* 1995 as a person who "uses the trade mark in relation to goods or services under the control of the owner of the trade mark". Control may include quality control and financial control. However, the rights of an "authorised user" to sue for infringement (as set out in section 26) arise only if the registered owner refuses or neglects to bring infringement proceedings and are, in any event, subject to any agreement between the registered owner and the authorised user.

Consumer protection provisions of the Trade Practices Act 1974

Unauthorised use of a trade mark may also constitute a breach of the consumer **6–105** protection provisions of the *Trade Practice Act* 1974. The application of the federal legislation is generally limited to corporations engaging in "trade or commerce". There are State and Territory based Fair Trading Acts which apply equivalent provisions to the conduct of individuals.

Section 52 of the *Trade Practices Act* 1974 prohibits misleading or deceptive conduct in trade or commerce or conduct in trade or commerce which is likely to mislead or deceive by a corporation.

Section 53 prohibits the making of false or misleading representations by a corporation in trade or commerce in connection with the supply or possible supply of goods or services or in connection with the promotion by any means of the supply or use of goods or services. Among the types of representations prohibited are those which represent that the corporation has a sponsorship, approval or affiliation it does not have. A misuse of a trade mark on a web site or as a domain name can constitute this type of misrepresentation.

Passing off

Passing off involves the misrepresentation by one person that their goods, services or **6–106** business are those of another or have some association or connection with them.

To successfully establish passing off, three elements must be satisfied. First, it will be necessary for a plaintiff to show that it has a *reputation* in Australia. So where a defendant has made a misrepresentation on a web site which is accessible in Australia, but the plaintiff has no reputation here, the cause of action will be of no avail. Secondly, the defendant must have made a *misrepresentation* to the public which leads the public or is likely to lead the public to believe that the goods or services offered by it are those of the plaintiff or that the defendant or its business is the plaintiff or has a licence or other connection with the plaintiff. This may occur through the use of the plaintiff's trade marks (whether registered or unregistered) or name on the site or as a domain name or even the appropriation of the "look and feel" of the plaintiff's web site. Thirdly, the plaintiff must have suffered *damage* as a result.

There is almost total overlap between passing off and sections 52 and 53 of the *Trade* **6–107** *Practices Act* 1974 (and equivalent the provisions of the State and Territory Fair Trading Acts). Every case of passing off will constitute misleading and deceptive conduct or a false and misleading representation, with an exception perhaps where the misrepresentation is not in trade or commerce. Furthermore, as damage is required to be made out in a passing off action, but not in an action under the *Trade Practices Act* 1974, passing off is used infrequently.

Both the *Trade Practices Act* 1974 and passing off also have the benefit of protecting unregistered trade marks.

Disclaimers

A disclaimer on a web site may be effective to negate a breach of section 52 of the *Trade* **6–108** *Practices Act* 1974 or passing off, where the disclaimer negates any misleading effect that the use of a trade mark may otherwise have had.

However, under the *Trade Marks Act* 1995, where the infringement alleged is in relation to the use of the mark in relation to the goods or services in respect of which the mark is registered, such a disclaimer will be ineffective. On the other hand, where the infringement alleged is in relation to goods of the same description as the registered goods, services closely related to the registered goods, services of the same description as the registered services or goods closely related to the registered services, a disclaimer may be effective if the defendant can show that using the sign as it did is not likely to deceive or cause confusion.

6.4.2 Copyright

6–109   The *Copyright Act* 1968 protects original literary, artistic, dramatic or musical works. It also protects original sound recordings, films, television and sound broadcasts or published editions of a work. Owners of copyright have a number of exclusive rights in relation to the copyright material, including the right to reproduce, publish, perform, adapt and in some cases enter into a commercial rental agreement. To have standing to sue for copyright infringement, the plaintiff must be either the owner of the copyright or an exclusive licensee of at least some of the rights comprised in the copyright.

Copyright may be infringed by the copying of a person's entire web site, by the reproduction of portions of text from a web site where this amounts to a substantial part of the work, or use of an image from another site. Copyright in a logo may be infringed by unauthorised use of the logo on a web site. Sound and video files available on web sites may infringe copyright. Equally, placement of portions of works, sound recordings, films and broadcasts may also constitute copyright infringement. Printing a web site or saving it to disk may constitute infringement if there is no express or implied licence to do so.

6–110   The *Copyright Act* 1968 has recently been amended in order to make the Act more relevant to, amongst other things, the online environment. These amendments came into effect on March 4, 2001.

Of most relevance to the Internet is the new "right to communicate to the public", a technology neutral right which replaces the technology specific, and somewhat outdated, right to broadcast and the right to transmit to subscribers of a diffusion service.

"Communicate" is defined as "to make available online or electronically transmit (whether over a path, or a combination of paths, provided by a material substance or otherwise) a work or subject matter".

Temporary copies

6–111   An issue which has caused concern in the past is the issue of temporary copies made in the process of ordinary usage of the Internet and whether that constitutes copyright infringement. The recent amendments take this into account through the creation of an explicit exception to what would otherwise be an infringement of copyright in a work for "making a temporary reproduction of the work or adaptation as part of the technical process of making or receiving a communication". Accordingly, the downloading of a web page onto an Internet user's machine which occurs when the web page is viewed, does not constitute infringement of the copyright subsisting in the web page. An interesting issue is the caching of web pages onto a proxy server in order to save bandwith and facilitate faster downloading times. It is unclear whether the exception covers this situation. Some commentators have argued that as the process facilitates the efficient functioning of the Internet, this sort of caching should also be permitted.

Removal or tampering with electronic rights management information
Provisions offering protection against intentional removal or tampering with "electronic   **6–112**
rights management information" in copyright works have been enacted. "Electronic rights management information" is defined in the Act as "information attached to, or embodied in, a copy of a work or other subject-matter that identifies the work or subject-matter, and its author or copyright owner; or identifies or indicates some or all of the terms and conditions on which the work or subject-matter may be used, or indicates the use of the work or subject-matter is subject to terms or conditions; or any numbers or codes that represent such information in electronic form". For example, on a web site containing an article written by an academic, there is often a hyperlink to a copyright notice at the bottom of a which contains the author's name, the year it was written and a statement permitting the user to print one copy of the web page for private use. If the author permitted an electronic journal to reproduce the article, but it did so without the hyperlinked notice, that would be a breach of these provisions. Equally, any attempt to remove a "digital watermark" from copyright material would also be a breach of these provisions.

Further amendments relating to moral rights have also been enacted. These comprise the right to attribution or authorship, the right not to have authorship falsely attributed and the right of integrity of authorship.

Jurisdiction
The definition of the term "to the public", where used in relation to the new right to   **6–113**
communicate, was also inserted by the recent amendments to the *Copyright Act* 1968 to encompass the public "within or outside Australia". This clarifies some of the issues which have arisen in relation to jurisdiction.

6.4.3 Defamation

Defamation law in Australia
Defamation in Australia is governed by the separate laws of each State and Territory.   **6–114**
Differences apply across the States in terms of the tests to be made out and the defences which may be argued. In Victoria, New South Wales, South Australia, the Australian Capital Territory and the Northern Territory defamation law is based on the common law as modified by legislation. In Queensland and Tasmania the law of civil defamation has been codified.

Despite differences across States, in general the plaintiff must be able to show that:

- the plaintiff was the subject matter of the material complained of;

- the published material was "defamatory" of the plaintiff; and

- the material complained of was "published", that is communicated to a person other than the plaintiff.

In the common law jurisdictions, for material to be "defamatory" of a person, it must   **6–115**
either directly, or by implication, tend, in the eyes of ordinary reasonable people, to injure

the reputation of that person according to one of the following tests:

- subjecting the person to "hatred, ridicule or contempt";

- causing others to "shun or avoid" the person; or

- "lower the plaintiff in the estimation of right-thinking members of society".

In the jurisdictions where the law of defamation has been codified, "defamatory matter" is exhaustively defined.

Jurisdiction

6–116   An important element of defamation is that the defamatory imputation be "published" within the jurisdiction. In the context of the Internet, no case has yet conclusively settled the issue in Australia as to whether "publication" occurs at the location of the server, where the information is uploaded, or whether it occurs wherever in the world it is accessed or downloaded. Based on existing case law relating to television broadcasts, it appears that publication occurs where the information is received. This is one of the issues which is central to the Victorian Supreme Court case of *Joseph Gutnick v. Dow Jones and Company Incorporated* (see paras 6–041 and 12–053).

Enforcement

6–117   One difficulty for a plaintiff in a defamation case is the prospect of obtaining an injunction to have the material removed from the web site. The single judge decision of the New South Wales Supreme Court, *Macquarie University v. Berg*[118] has suggested that on the basis that it is technologically not possible to prevent access to information on a web site in a particular geographical location, the effect of granting an injunction would be to impose the law of New South Wales on other places around the world, which would be an unjustified imposition on the right to freedom of speech. This decision has been criticised by some commentators.

6.4.4 Misleading information/False representations—Trade Practices Act 1974/State Fair Trading Acts

6–118   The consumer protection provisions of the *Trade Practices Act* 1974 and the State Fair Trading Acts, referred to in relation to trade marks above, cover not only a scenario involving the misuse of trade marks, but all misleading and deceptive conduct.

Elements of the Action

6–119   In order to establish a breach of section 52, the key elements which need to be shown are that:

- there was conduct engaged in by a corporation in trade or commerce; and

- that conduct misled or deceived the public or was likely to do so.

Section 53 is a specific provision, the breach of which would also contravene section 52. However, whilst a breach of section 52 attracts civil liability, criminal liability may attach to a breach of section 53.

Section 53 prohibits, among other things, a corporation from "falsely representing that   **6–120**
goods are of a particular standard, quality, value, grade, composition, style or model or
have had a particular history..." in trade or commerce in connection with the supply or
goods or services.

Anyone can bring an action under the *Trade Practices Act* 1974 consumer protection
provisions as there are no standing requirements. This is because the provisions are
directed at maintaining a standard of conduct rather than enforcing a particular right the
plaintiff has acquired. Accordingly, a person may bring an action even if they were not
the particular consumer misled or deceived.

Each State Fair Trading Act has equivalents to sections 52 and 53 and each has the same
absence of standing requirements.

Jurisdiction

Where the web site is located or operated by a corporation somewhere other than in   **6–121**
Australia, if it can be shown that members of the Australian public were deceived or
misled, action could be taken against the web site operator as the *Trade Practices Act* 1974
is defined broadly enough to encompass trade between Australia and places outside
Australia and trade by foreign corporations. Section 6 of the Act extends the meaning of
"trade or commerce" to include trade or commerce between Australia and places outside
Australia. Despite this extraterritorial effect, they may, of course, be serious practical
difficulties in enforcing judgments in such circumstances.

It is possible that a foreigner who was deceived or misled could take action against an
Australian–based web site as there is no limitation on the parties who are entitled to take
action under the consumer protection legislation.

If the web site is operated by an individual or an unincorporated association or other   **6–122**
body that does not fall under the Commonwealth *Trade Practices Act* 1974, the equivalent
State Fair Trading Acts will apply. These Acts also make some provision for
extraterritoriality. For example, the Victorian *Fair Trading Act* 1999 will apply where
the conduct occurred outside Victoria if the supplier is a body corporate whose principal
place of business is in Victoria, or a person who is ordinarily resident in Victoria. It also
applies where either the supplier or the consumer enters into the agreement in Victoria,
or the goods or services are proposed to be supplied in Victoria. However, for the
relevant State Act to apply, some nexus with the relevant State must be shown.

6.4.5 Liability of Internet Service Providers for infringing content

Amendments were made to the *Broadcasting Services Act* 1992, taking effect on January 1,   **6–123**
2000. The amendments established a system for regulating Internet content. The system
does not have an automatic blanket application to *all* Internet content, rather it is a
mechanism for regulating content that has already been classified or for classifying and
regulating content when a complaint is made about it. The Australian Broadcasting
Authority (ABA) has responsibility for overseeing the system.

A person may lodge a complaint with the Australian Broadcasting Authority about
"prohibited content" or "potential prohibited content".

"Prohibited content" in Australia is either material that has been classified RC   **6–124**
(Refused Classification) or X by the Classification Board, or material that is rated R and
access to it has not been restricted by a restricted access system. "Prohibited content"
outside Australia is material which has been classified RC or X by the Classification

Board. The Classification Board is the entity responsible for classifying publications, films and computer games in Australia.

"Potential prohibited content" is content which has not yet been classified by the Board but there is a substantial likelihood that it would be prohibited content if it were to be classified.

6–125   If the content is hosted in Australia and is "prohibited content", the Authority can issue a "take down notice" to an Internet content host which must be complied with by 6 p.m. the next day.

If the content is hosted in Australia and is "potential prohibited content" the Board will be directed to classify the content and an interim "take down notice" will be issued.

If the content is hosted outside Australia, the Authority can require that access to that material be restricted by ISPs in Australia by means of appropriate filtering technologies.

One of the amendments, clause 91 of Schedule 5 to 7 the Act, provides immunity to Internet Services Providers or Internet Content Hosts where they have no knowledge of the content. It has been suggested that the broad drafting of this provision can conceivably cover defamatory content and content that infringes copyright.

6.4.6 Cybercrimes

6–126   Criminal sanctions for conduct relating to the Internet have been proposed in the form of the Cybercrimes Bill which is currently being considered by Parliament. It seeks to introduce a range of offences to the federal *Criminal Code Act* 1995. Among the "serious computer offences" are:

- unauthorised access, modification or impairment with intent to commit a serious offence;

- unauthorised modification of data to cause impairment; and

- unauthorised impairment of electronic communication.

6–127   Other computer offences include:

- unauthorised access to, or modification of, restricted data;

- unauthorised impairment of data held on a computer disk, etc;

- possession or control of data with intent to commit a computer offence; and

- producing supplying or obtaining data with intent to commit a computer offence.

6–128   An example of conduct which would constitute unauthorised access, modification or impairment with intent to commit a serious offence is hacking into password protected data in a bank in order to facilitate the theft of large sums of money. Bombarding a Web site with large volumes of email so that it is prevented from functioning could constitute breach of the prohibition of unauthorised impairment of electronic communication. The spreading of a virus by email that deletes or otherwise modifies data impairing the operation of a business would breach the prohibition on the unauthorised modification of data to cause impairment.

6.5 Belgium

6.5.1 Jurisdiction applicable to foreign web sites

In cases where illegal content emanating from a foreign web is accessible in Belgium, **6–129** Belgian legislation and case law favours giving the national courts competence to examine illegal practices on the Internet that originate abroad. Before analysing in greater detail the Belgian law as regards defamation, liability for content, infringement of copyright and trademarks, the Belgian penal and civil law as regards jurisdiction over foreign web sites will be examined below.

Jurisdiction in criminal matters
In criminal matters, "Belgian law applies to offences committed in the territory of **6–130** Belgium, by Belgians or foreigners" (Article 3, Penal Code). Consequently it is important to determine whether the offence was committed within the territory of Belgium. In Belgium, as well as in France, judges interpret the principle of territoriality rather loosely and sanction the theory of extra-territorial jurisdiction ("ubiquity"). According to this theory, "the Belgian judge is competent if one of the constitutive elements of the offence occurs in Belgium".[119] Given the international nature of the Internet, any person exhibiting content on the Internet that would be deemed illegal under Belgian criminal law may be prosecuted and judged in Belgium in accordance with Belgian law.[120]

Jurisdiction in civil and commercial matters
In civil and commercial matters, the national court must apply the Brussels Convention of **6–131** September 27, 1968 on jurisdiction and enforcement of judgements in civil and commercial matters. This Convention will be soon replaced by the Council Regulation (E.C.) No 44/2001 of December 22, 2000 on jurisdiction and the recognition and enforcement of judgements in civil and commercial matters,[121] which will enter into force on March 1, 2002.

The Convention establishes rules to determine which national court is competent as regards the Contracting States.[122] Since the Brussels Convention has not been ratified by all states, general private international law will apply in some cases. Consequently, the following two situations may arise:

(a) *The defendant is resident in a State that is a signatory of the Brussels Convention.* **6–132**
The Brussels Convention and similar conventions apply when the *defendant* is resident in a State that ratified one of the conventions. Thus it is necessary at an early stage to know the place of residence of the defendant. The Brussels Convention provides that the national court in the state where the defendant is resident has jurisdiction for all civil and commercial matters. Consequently, the residence rule prevails over the nationality rule or any other criterion.

The Convention provides, however, for exceptions, particularly as regards tortious and quasi-tortious matters. Thus the defendant can be sued before *"the court of the place where the harmful event occurred"* (Article 5, 3° of the Convention of Brussels). Even if the web site is located, for example, in Spain, the place where the damage occurred would be, according to the European Court of Justice, *"the place where the harmful event giving rise to the damage occurred"* or *"the place where the damage occurred"*.[123]

In a case relating to the press, the European Court of Justice in the *Shevill* judgment[124] sets out the following principle as regards a compensation claim in a case concerning defamation through the press. The Court states that the plaintiff has the choice between, on the one hand, seizing the court of the defendant's place of residence to request compensation for the entirety of the damage, or, on the other hand, seizing the courts of the different places where the incriminating press article was published. In the latter hypotheses the plaintiff can only, however, request compensation for the damage suffered in the State where the court has been seized.

This interpretation could, in our opinion, be applicable to the Internet. The plaintiff can thus sue the person responsible for damaging Internet content broadcast in Belgium before a Belgian court even though this person resides abroad, but will only be able to ask for a partial compensation, namely for the damage suffered in Belgium.

The Convention also enables the surfer, who is the consumer, to bring an action before either the courts of the State of his usual residence or the state where his co-contractor has his residence. However, the latter can only act against the consumer in the place of this usual residence.[125]

6–133 (b) *The defendant does not have his residence in a Contracting State of the Brussels Convention*

If the defendant does not have his residence in the territory of a Contracting State,[126] private international law will determine which courts have jurisdiction over the case. Under Belgian law, this is set out in the Belgian judicial code. If the defendant is not resident in a Contracting State of the Brussels Convention, he may be summoned before the Belgian courts, *"if the obligation upon which the request is based, has originated in Belgium,[127] has been or will have to be executed in Belgium"* (Article 635, 3° of judicial code). In this case, the plaintiff will, however, first of all have to evaluate whether a breach of the Belgian law has been committed. The request may be founded for example on tort or on the Belgian Trade Practices Act.

Finally, if the different basis indicated by the judicial code are not sufficient to determine the competence of Belgian courts, the plaintiff may bring his case to the court of the place where he himself has his place of domicile or residence.[128] This possibility can be useful, particularly when it is not possible to determine where the broadcaster of illegal content on the Internet is situated. The provision applies in the absence of contractual provisions and is, however, additional and subject to the principle of reciprocity. Thus, if the plaintiff summons the foreign defendant in Belgium, the defendant can by virtue of this principle of reciprocity, refuse the competence of the Belgian courts provided this right is, in his country, also applicable to foreigners. The default of the defendant amounts automatically to a challenge to the jurisdiction of the court.[129]

6.5.2 Which law will a Belgian court apply?

6–134 Any individual who encounters Internet content that he finds offensive may bring an action before the Belgian civil courts. If the Belgian court finds that it has jurisdiction, it will apply Belgian international private law.

According to the theories on the applicable law, it is possible to apply:

(a)   the law of the place where the act causing the injury occured (*lex loci delicti commissi*)

(b)   the law of the place where the damage occurs;

(c)   the law of the place with which the damage has the closest links or the law of the place that is the supposed destination of the act.

(a)   Application of the law of the place where the act causing the injury occurred

According to this theory, the judge should choose the law of the country of origin of the Internet site. This theory has been followed by the Belgian Supreme Court in its Bologne ruling of 1957[130] and confirmed by case law afterwards[131] but it has been severely criticised by academic opinion. Whilst the theory is defensible as regards situations where few countries are concerned, it is difficult to apply it to the Internet since it would favour *forum shopping*. A cybermarketing company could set up in an "informational heaven" such as Cabo Verde, for example, and would thus escape the restrictive regulations of countries where the Internet users it wishes to reach have their residence. Consequently, applying the law of the place where the content is put on the Internet could negate the sovereignty of countries.

6–135

(b)   Application of the law of the place where the damage occurs

In order to adequately protect the plaintiff, another solution would be to apply the law of the country where the damage occurs. If the law of the place where the damage occurred applied, Belgian law could be applied to all disputes between an American advertiser and a Belgian Internet user, for example. This solution is supported by academic opinion in Belgium: "*Belgian law will be applicable in all cases of extra-contractual liability which has its source in information broadcast on the Internet and found on the Internet in Belgium by any random user*".[132] However, if this solution were strictly applied it could lead to several different problems. First of all, the advertiser or the cybermarketing company broadcasting on the Internet would have to comply with different legal systems world-wide, which in practice would prove impossible. In any case, the advertiser would not be able to tell the country of residence of every person that visited his Internet site. In addition, legal systems are not uniform and judges could take contradictory decisions even within the same country. Since, according to this theory, every court and tribunal would be theoretically competent to hear the action, the risk of divergent solutions would be quite high. Moreover, the universal effect of the enforcement of a court judgement against an Internet site (for example, closure of a site or changing a site), would allow one country to impose its ethical standards on all the others.

6–136

(c)   Application of the target-market *law*

The "target-market" law theory has been embraced by Belgian academic opinion and some U.S. case law.[133] According to this theory, if an Internet site targets a particular country, then the law of that country should apply to the content of that site.[134] As regards Internet sites, the market is determined according to elements composing the site: presentation, language, content, payment system, etc. This allows the courts to take into account the real effect on the person accessing the site. Several Belgian academic authors support this theory: Prioux supports the application of the law of the place with which the

6–137

situation has *the closest links*.[135] Van Houtte distinguishes the *primary* market from the *secondary* market.[136] The primary market is the one to which the message is expressly destined while the secondary market is the market affected by a *spill over* effect. The solution of the application of the target-market law was followed by some Belgian courts in fields related to the one in which we are interested. For example, a Belgian company that applied for an injunction against advertising published in an American periodical had its case dismissed for the following reason: *"the fact that theoretically the magazine was accessible to Belgian subscribers does not consequently mean that the information that was received in Belgium was published with a view to presenting a product or service to the Belgian public"*.[137]

Like Professor Corbet,[138] we are of the opinion that the criteria of the market law offers the most flexibility. However, the Belgian legislation continues to apply the theory according to which the judge applies the law of the place where the offensive content was put on the Internet.[139]

6–138   In some cases, other laws involving compulsory legal standards apply independently from the principles mentioned in the preceding paragraphs. The Brussels Court of Appeal has decided, in its ruling of May 12, 1953, that the Belgian legal provisions regarding competition, Article 3, paragraph 1 of the Civil Code, are binding on all who live on the territory without distinction of nationality. Are the dispositions contained in the Belgian Trade Practices Act regarding consumers equally obligatory? We may think that the Belgian Trade Practices Act will be applied as soon as the damage, even partially, has occurred in Belgium. The Brussels Court of Appeal has confirmed this principle by its decision, in the Tractebel Case, that:

> *"the Trade Practices Act as a compulsory legal rule is applicable to all facts falling under its territorial field of application, that is, all unfair commercial practices occurring on Belgian territory. If a commercial practice is composed of a chain of facts of which part is situated abroad but which ends in Belgium, where moreover the damage is caused, the Belgian judge is competent and the Belgian law will be applied"*.[140]

6–139   Rejecting on the one hand the exception of incompetence raised by the defendant who had the domain name tractebel.com registered in the United States, and on the other hand the argument stipulating that the Belgian law could not be applied to facts committed in the United States, the judge has in fact ruled that:

> *"the Internet knows no boundaries, meaning that such commercial practice is not limited to the United States but has an influence in the whole world, Belgium included, where the network is accessible and where the practice finalises"*.

Since the Trade Practices Act protects the consumer, we may suppose that the judges will apply it in Belgium.

6.5.3 Criminal responsibility: defamation and slander

6–140   The theory of extra-territorial jurisdiction mentioned above allows the judge to examine the illegal content on a foreign site in so far as the content is accessible in Belgium.

Regarding defamation and slander, Article 443 of the Criminal Code of the Belgian law must be applied.

This article states that:

> *"he who in this case, has spitefully attributed to a person a fact that is of a nature to infringe the honour of that person or to expose that person to public spite, and whereof the legal evidence has not been reported, is guilty of slander when the law admits the proof of this fact, and of defamation if the law refutes the evidence".*

Article 444 of the same code demands that the sayings, in order to be considered slander or defamation, must have been spread in a public way, such as *"by means of writings, images or posters, distributed or sold, put up for sale or exposed to the public eye"*.

However, it appears clearly that the contents diffused by Internet on a web site or in a chat room are exposed to the public eye, except when an access code to this site or chat room is foreseen. This is valid for images but also for writings, article 444, paragraph 5, does not require that they must be printed.   **6–141**

This reasoning is confirmed by the lower criminal court of Brussels which, in its ruling of December 22, 1999, states that *"texts appearing in chat rooms on the Internet meet the conditions of publicity required by the law".*[141] Indeed, even these chat rooms are non-public places, *"it suffices to meet the condition of publicity that [the writings] can be read".*[142]

The sending of slanderous or defamatory contents by electronic mail may also be prosecuted, based on Article 444, paragraph 6, that includes in the public nature of remarks *"writings that remain unpublicised but are addressed or communicated to several persons"*.

6.5.4 Content Liability

In circumstances where there is no contractual relationship between the person responsible for the content of an Internet site and the person suffering the damage because of that site, an individual may be held liable for harmful content under tort law. A tort action may be instituted by relying on Articles 1382 and following of the Belgian Civil Code.   **6–142**

In order to succeed in a tort action, three separate elements must be proven by the plaintiff: first, that a negligent act has been committed, second, the plaintiff has suffered damage, and, third, that there is a causal link between the negligence and the damage suffered by the plaintiff. If these three elements are proven, then the plaintiff can claim compensation for the damages suffered. As a rule, all injury, however small, must be compensated.[143] The causal link exists when it can be established that the damage that occurred would not have happened if the negligent act had not been committed.

To this day, no Belgian court has upheld an action founded on tort concerning Article 1382 and following of the civil code after diffusion of the content over the Internet.   **6–143**

However, an injunction under the Belgian Fair Trade Practices Act has already been brought against an Internet Services Provider (ISP). The latter had omitted to suppress the hyperlinks that could be found on subscriber sites that allowed surfers to end up on sites containing illegal MP3 files. The President of the Brussels Commercial Court condemned the ISP under Article 93 of the Belgian Fair Trade Practices Act which prohibits all *"acts contrary to honest use in commercial matter"* (IFPI/Skynet case).[144]

The Brussels Court of Appeal overturned the decision of the President of the Brussels Commercial Court.[145] Inspired by the Article 14.1 of the European Directive on Electronic   **6–144**

Commerce,[146] the Court of Appeal decided that the following procedure should be followed by hosting providers in case of illicit content on the internet:

(1)   the complainant must notify the illicit content to the hosting provider and give some elements proving that the content is illicit;

(2)   the hosting provider has three working days to prove that the litigious element is not illicit, otherwise he must suspend the access to it;

(3)   the complainant must guarantee and hold harmless the hosting provider in case where the litigious element, having been removed, has been declared licit.

According to this procedure, the Court decided that the ISP had not committed any negligence.

6.5.5 Copyright infringement

6–145   In the *Central Station* case,[147] the Lower Court of Brussels gave the first Belgian decision regarding copyright and the Internet and stated that copyright law applies to the Internet.

International legal provisions protecting copyright, and, in particular, the Belgian Copyright Act of June 30, 1994 as regards copyright and related rights,[148] apply indisputably to the Internet. Several French decisions have already confirmed this interpretation.[149]

The Belgian legislation provides that *"Only the author of a work (...) has the right to reproduce it or to allow its reproduction, in whatever form or manner"* (Article 1, paragraph 1, line 1). Consequently, it is clear that the electronic manipulation that allows the transfer a file to a server constitutes a reproduction. The reproduction is carried out as soon as the work is duplicated. The intermediate storing, solely executed for archival storage or possible future re-use, pertains irrefutably to the right of reproduction since there exists a material fixation of the work and that this fixation renders public communication possible.[150]

6–146   Moreover, Belgian law states that *"only an author of a work (...) has the right to communicate it to the public by any means whatsoever"* (Article 1, paragraph 1, line 4). The case law confirms that the access to a work put on a site *"goes as far as the one reserved to, for example, members of a concert audience"*, and that *"the purpose of the Internet is precisely the communication of information to the public. (...) Thus there is no reason to exclude from the applications [of the law] broadcasting through telematics"*.[151]

Consequently, the person who puts a protected work at the disposal of the public on his site as well as the person who consults this work, makes a reproduction of the work in the sense of the Belgian Copyright Act of June 30, 1994.

Finally we have to determine the notion of private use[152]: in the case of private use the person responsible for the reproduction will be exempt from asking for an authorisation from the owner of copyright or related rights.

6.5.6 Trademark law

6–147   Trademarks are protected in Belgium if they have been registered with the Benelux Trademark Office (the single trademark office for Belgium, the Netherlands and

Luxembourg) in accordance with the Benelux Trademark Act.[153]

Article 13.A.1.d. of this Act prohibits *"all commercial use of a trademark or similar sign for any other purpose beside distinguishing the products, if it would take undue advantage of the distinctive character or the reputation of the trademark or if it would prove detrimental to this trademark"*. According to the case law of the Benelux Court, *"commercial use of a trademark occurs if its use intends to procure an economical advantage"*.[154] Thus the notion of "commercial use" is particularly extensive. Consequently, the Benelux Trademark Act will apply if it can be proven that the unauthorised use of a Benelux trademark on the Internet was aimed at gaining an economic benefit.

6.6 Canada

6.6.1 Jurisdiction

Introduction

Usually, for a matter to be actionable in Canada, the cause of action must arise in Canada. Where the cause of action depends upon the breach of a statute, that statutory breach must have occurred in Canada. Where a cause of action is founded in tort, a sufficient nexus to Canada will have to be established before a Canadian court will assume jurisdiction. Additionally, an order or injunction is normally granted only where the court is satisfied that it could be enforced.   **6–148**

If the Canadian court can assume jurisdiction over a case, then it must do so, unless there is a more convenient forum for the action.

Rules exist within each of the superior courts of the provinces of Canada as well as the Federal Court of Canada providing certain procedural steps for the plaintiff to follow to serve foreign defendants (service *ex juris*).

Accessing a web site from within Canada necessarily involves the display of the contents of the site in Canada. Depending upon the tort, this fact could place the infringing action in Canada and bring it within the jurisdiction of a Canadian court.   **6–149**

A Canadian or provincial action would only be stayed if a proceeding in another court or jurisdiction was more comprehensive (*i.e.* it included the cause of action in the jurisdiction in question as well as additional causes of action). If another action was pending in a jurisdiction outside of Canada relating to the same facts or circumstances, because the foreign court could not have jurisdiction over breach of a Canadian statute or the occurrence of a tort in Canada, a related Canadian action would likely not be stayed by the existence of such foreign proceedings.

Cases such as *Tele-Direct (Publications) Inc. v. Klimchuk, Canadian Kennel Club* and *Canada Post v. Sunview Management Group* (discussed above) all suggest that Canadian courts will not hesitate to assume jurisdiction over Internet actors when there is a real and substantial connection between the activity and Canada.   **6–150**

6.6.2 Defamation

Defamation is a tort at common law. In order to support a defamation action a plaintiff must show that the offending statement was published, that it referred to the plaintiff and that the statement was false and had the effect of discrediting the plaintiff.   **6–151**

Publication merely requires that the offending statement be made known to people other than the author of the statement. This component would seem to be satisfied when the defamatory statement is made available on a web site and the site is accessed by others who then read the statement.

Once publication is established, the contents of the statement are presumed by the court to be false, published maliciously, and it is further presumed that the plaintiff suffered damages.

The defendant may counter each presumption by contending that the statement consists of true facts, and by showing that, in speaking the truth, the defendant was not motivated by malice. Further, the defendant may be in a position to invoke parliamentary or some other privilege. However, it is far more likely in the context of the Internet that an embattled defendant would invoke the defence of innocent dissemination.

6–152   The defence of innocent dissemination will be made out if the following three components are shown:

(1)   the defendant was innocent of any knowledge of the defamatory nature of the work disseminated by him;

(2)   nothing in the work or the circumstances under which it came into his possession should have suggested its defamatory content; and

(3)   the defendant was not negligent in failing to note the defamatory nature of the contents of the work.

In *Southam Inc. v. George Chelekis et al.*,[155] the court applied the same rules to defamatory material distributed by electronic means as have been applied to other types of publications. Canadian law on defamation will apply equally to publications on the Internet. An appeal from this decision to the British Columbia Court of Appeal[156] was dismissed and the Supreme Court of Canada refused leave to appeal without reasons.[157]

6–153   Even if a foreign court can be persuaded to take jurisdiction over an online dispute, its decision won't necessarily be enforced. The highest Canadian court to decide issues relating to the enforcement of a foreign judgment involving jurisdiction on the Internet was the British Columbia Court of Appeal. In *Braintech, Inc. v. John C. Kostiuk*,[158] the British Columbia Court of Appeal refused to recognize the default judgment of a Texas court. Kostiuk was alleged to have made defamatory statements by posting them to a bulletin board. Braintech sued in Texas and relied on the service provisions of Texas law that provide that service can be effected on a non-resident by serving the Secretary of State (who is then statutorily obligated to effect service on the named party). The court found that the principle of comity did not extend to the recognition of the order in the circumstances. The Canadian court found that the Texas court did not have personal jurisdiction over Kostiuk because the three-pronged test for determining whether assuming jurisdiction over the defendant was not satisfied. Adopting the reasoning in *Zippo*, the British Columbia Court of Appeal found that:

> "In these circumstances the complainant must offer better proof that the defendant has entered Texas than the mere possibility that someone in that jurisdiction might have reached out to cyberspace to bring the defamatory material to a screen in Texas. There is no allegation or evidence Kostiuk had a commercial purpose that utilized the highway provided by Internet to enter any particular jurisdiction. A person who posts fair comment on a bulletin board could be haled before the courts of each of those countries where access to this bulletin could be obtained.

It would create a crippling effect on freedom of expression if, in every jurisdiction the world over in which access to Internet could be achieved."

Application for leave to appeal from this decision to the Supreme Court of Canada was dismissed without reasons.[159]

Conversely, *in Kitakufe v. Oloya*,[160] (*"Kitakufe"*), the Ontario motions judge decided that an Ontario plaintiff could sue for defamation in Ontario based on material published in an Ugandan newspaper and republished on the Internet. Although it is likely that the Court was persuaded that Ontario was the proper forum to hear the action on the basis that the plaintiff and the defendant were both Ontario residents, the case is nevertheless important because of the way it has subsequently been interpreted. In *Gutnick v. Dow Jones & Co. Inc.*,[161] (*"Gutnick"*) the Supreme Court of Victoria cited the *Kitakufe* decision as a "case [in] which a superior court assumed jurisdiction over a defamation suit on the basis of access to the Website and its reception (that is, downloading) in Ontario, Canada." (*Gutnick* at para. 47) It would seem that the Australian court has given the *Kitakufe* decision a very broad interpretation.

6-154

6.6.3 Inaccurate information

In Canada, compensation for detrimental reliance on inaccurate information will result in situations where (i) a duty of care based on a "special relationship?" between the representor and the representee is established; (ii) the representation in question is shown to be untrue, inaccurate or misleading; (iii) the representor has acted negligently in making the said representation; (iv) the representee has relied, in a reasonable manner, on the negligent representation; and (v) the reliance has been detrimental in the sense that damages were incurred by the representee.[162]

6-155

There is a duty to exercise such reasonable care as circumstances require to ensure that representations made are accurate and not misleading.[163] In all cases, reliance must be *reasonable*. Liability will not arise in situations where the defendant has warned the plaintiff that it is not assuming any obligation with respect to the information given.[164]

6.6.4 Copyright

The reproduction of a copyrighted work "in any material form"[165] constitutes the making of a copy, which, if not authorised, would be copyright infringement. The copying of a copyrighted work into the central processing unit (CPU) of a computer constitutes copying.[166]

6-156

Because browsing a web page requires the downloading of a copy of that page onto the browser's CPU and screen, a copy is necessarily brought into Canada. There is probably an implied licence to download and store in random access memory (RAM), a copy of a work from a web page (assuming the owner of the web page has the right to permit such use). However, subsequent commercial distribution of the material by the recipient would be an infringement by offering to sell, selling, distributing, exhibiting and/or importing the work.[167] Knowledge of infringement is a prerequisite to collecting damages; registration of the copyright deems such knowledge to be present.[168]

Where material was not permitted to be posted on a web page, and the web page owner allowed Canadians to download copies of it into Canada, the web page owner

6-157

may be liable for authorising infringement,[169] communicating the work to the public by telecommunications[170] or performing the work in public or authorising someone else to do so.[171]

It is an infringement under Canadian copyright law to "authorise" another to make a copy of a copyrighted work. Including a notice on a web site that prohibits browsing from other countries may protect the web site owner from "authorising" the unauthorised copying of the web page into Canada. The person or persons who downloaded the web page would still be liable for infringement in Canada.

6.6.5 Trade marks

6–158   In order for there to be trade mark infringement in Canada, there would have to be "use" of the trade mark in Canada. As discussed above, the *Tele-Direct (Publications) Inc. v. Klimchuk* decision suggests that a web site will be deemed to be using a trade mark in Canada if that site purposely targets Canadian customers.

One possible interpretation is for the court to consider the "imported" web page to be a "ware" (such as a publication, e-zine or electronic book) and the trade mark was marked on the web page and the web page was provided to the Canadian browser "in the normal course of trade", then there would be actionable use of the trade mark in Canada. The term "in the normal course of trade" normally relates to commercial transactions and not to giving away the ware.[172] Merely advertising wares on a Web site in the USA does not constitute "use" of a trade mark in Canada.[173]

Merely advertising a service which is provided outside of Canada does not constitute trade mark use in Canada.[174] If a service is provided to Canadians from the foreign country through the web page utilising the trade mark, then the trade mark is being used in Canada for that service. For example, Saks Fifth Avenue maintained a Canadian trade mark registration for "retail department store services" by providing catalogue shopping services to Canadians from its U.S. stores without ever operating a store in Canada.[175]

6.7 Finland

6.7.1 Defamation

6–159   Defamatory statements are criminalised in the Finnish Penal Code. An Internet user may conduct such a crime through distribution of an offending statement publicly. There is no liability for a defamatory statement transmitted only to the defamed person. However, due to the nature of the Internet the threshold for regarding a message public must be considered rather low.

The liability for defamatory statements lies primarily with the author of the statement. Internet service providers and bulletin board service providers are not liable through mandatory provision as is the case with publishers and broadcasters. It is possible that certain services provided over the Internet could be regarded as very similar to publishing and, for example, the publisher has a strict liability together with the author.

Only individuals are subject to criminal sanctions under the Penal Code. Consequently, corporations and organisations are not liable for defamatory statements. However, the members of the board or the managing director may be subject to criminal sanctions on behalf of the corporation they represent. Accordingly, a corporation may not be subject to defamation as defined by the Penal Code, only individuals. As the Internet to an increasing degree is a format for commercial dealings and advertising, statements that are of a defamatory nature and may harm the business activities of a corporation can be dealt with under the provisions of the Act on Unfair Business Practices. Injunctions against activities contrary to the Act on Unfair Business Practices can be granted by the Market Court and significant wilful conduct contrary to the Act on Unfair Business Practices is also criminalised.

The penalty for defamation is a fine or maximum two years of imprisonment. **6–160**
Compensation to the defamed party may also be awarded by the court.

The Finnish Penal Code is applicable when an unlawful act has been conducted in Finland. With regard to the Internet this would mean that if a defamatory message is received in Finland, the defamatory act has also been conducted in Finland. There does not exist court practice in this respect. If an overseas Web site can be accessed from Finland a Finnish court will most likely consider itself competent. The problematic issues will in many cases be to find the defendant and to serve a summons upon such defendant. Unless multilateral or bilateral agreements on assistance between relevant authorities between Finland and the state of the defendant exist, the criminal act may remain unsanctioned. Consequently, the responsibility of an Internet service provider in Finland will be a critical issue which has not yet been tested in defamation lawsuits.

With regard to corporate liability for statements that may be harmful to a business **6–161**
entity, parallels could be drawn between satellite broadcasting and Internet transmissions. The Market Court has held that the Finnish subsidiary of a foreign company was liable for satellite TV advertising made by the parent company as the Market Court considered that the Finnish subsidiary profited from such marketing when the satellite broadcasting transmission was received in Finland. In the same manner the Market Court could consider itself competent to handle a lawsuit based upon presentation of harmful statements through the Internet made by a foreign commercial entity if such entity has a subsidiary or distributor in Finland profiting from the statement.

It is more problematic if individuals distribute harmful information concerning a commercial entity in Finland. The current Finnish laws have not properly taken into account such situations.

As a whole, defamatory statements on the Internet and liability for the different Internet service providers has not been properly addressed in current Finnish laws, which leaves room for interpretations and uncertainty. The lack of precedent cases also leaves room for interpretations.

6.7.2 Content liability

The content made available on a Web site may be of various types, including advertising, **6–162**
facts about the Web site owner and professional advice. The general principle of Finnish law is that the Web site owner is responsible for the information on the Web site administered by such company. Also, in such situation where the Internet users have been entitled to store information on a company's Web site, the company remains responsible therefore and has an obligation to supervise the Web site on a constant basis. The main principle under Finnish law is, consequently, that the company administering its Web site is held liable, for example, for copyright infringement or trade mark infringement if such infringement occurs on the Web site. If the negligence of the Web site owner is considered minor, the compensation awarded to the infringed party can be

adjusted and in cases of no negligence, the compensation can be adjusted to nil.

If someone has relied upon incorrect information on the Web site, the owner of the Web site is primarily liable to compensate the harm suffered from relying upon such information. Especially with regard to consumer products and services, special attention must be paid as the Consumer Protection Act and the Product Safety Act provide for strict liability with regard to marketing and product information that may be harmful to the consumer. Here again the problematic issue might be to identify the providers of the incorrect information and establish court jurisdiction in Finland.

6.7.3 Copyright infringement

6–163   According to the Finnish Copyright Act, copyright protection subsists in a wide variety of works, whether they are literary or artistic, fictional or descriptive representations in writing or in speech, or whether they be musical, dramatic or cinematographic works, works of fine art, architecture, artistic handicraft, industrial art or works expressed in some other manner. Maps and other descriptive drawings or graphically or three-dimensionally executed works, as well as software, are considered literary works. Rules governing rights such as the rights of performing artists, producers of records, as well as radio and television organisations, are also encompassed in the Copyright Act.

Copyright protection originates automatically through the performance of the author. If the product of creativity fulfils a certain level of originality, the work is protected automatically without any registration.

6–164   It is nevertheless usual and also in the Internet recommended to emphasise the subsistence of copyright in a work by placing an appropriate copyright notice and the year of publishing on it. The author of a work may be one or several individuals. According to the Finnish copyright system, a legal entity, a computer or an animal cannot be considered as an author. Thus, a legal entity's copyright is always derived from an individual. If a work is created by two or more authors whose contributions do not constitute independent works, the copyright shall belong to the authors jointly. However, each of them separately may initiate an infringement action.

With regard to software programs and associated works that have been created within the scope of ordinary duties in an employment situation, it is expressly stipulated in the Copyright Act that the copyright of such programs and works pass automatically to the employer, unless otherwise agreed. Copyright protection now in most cases subsists until the end of the 70th year after the year in which the author died or, in the case of several authors, after the year after the last surviving author died. However, different treatment with regard to different types of work create some problems with regard, for example, to Web sites that may constitute of a combination of text, film, photographs and sound. Under the Copyright Act, the rights of an author have been divided into moral and economic rights. Economic rights may freely be assigned or licensed to a third party.

6–165   For copyright to be infringed, a work or a substantial part of it, must have been made available to the public, imported for distribution or copied without authorisation. Wilful production of a copy of a work or making a work available to the public in violation of a protected work is a criminal offence, as is the importation of an unauthorised copy of a work for distribution to the public, provided that the infringer has committed the infringement for gain. The penalty for such an offence is a fine or a maximum of two years' imprisonment. The author will receive fair compensation for any unauthorised use and, if such use is wilful or results from negligence, the infringer shall, in addition, pay damages for any other loss.

According to case law, piracy is generally considered to be a criminal offence. As the maximum penalty is two years' imprisonment, there are fair possibilities for a copyright owner to enforce confiscation, seizure or other interim measures as well as customs support. In criminal proceedings, confiscation and seizure can be obtained at an early stage of the proceedings, whereas interim measures are usually more difficult to obtain in civil proceedings.

If a Web site without proper authorisation contains a copy of someone else's original **6–166** work this would generally be considered copyright infringement. Copying of a work protected by copyright is, however, permitted for personal use. If the copy is made for a company it would generally be regarded as non-personal use and subject to sanctions under the Copyright Act. Making copyright protected work available to the public also constitutes copyright infringement and consequently, if an individual would use copyright protected material on his Web site, this would be regarded as making the work available to the public and would thus constitute copyright infringement.

From the Internet user's point of view the question of whether mere viewing of a copyright protected work is acceptable under Finnish copyright law is somewhat unclear. The Copyright Act entitles anyone to make a copy of a copyright protected work for personal use. However, copying of a software program is prohibited also for personal use. It is unclear whether mere viewing on the screen would constitute copyright infringement. When the copyright protected work is transmitted it will for a certain period of time be stored in the RAM of the user's computer. The reproduction prohibited in the Copyright Act would, generally, require a certain amount of consistence which the storage in the RAM during viewing does not fulfil. However, this traditional interpretation may be subject to counterargumentation.

Finland, as from 1996, became a member of the European Union and the development of copyright protection in the information society within the E.U. should therefore be taken into account also with regard to Finland.

6.7.4 Trade mark infringement

Trade mark rights in Finland can be obtained through registration and/or establishment. **6–167** Registration that covers Finland is possible to obtain through a national registration, through registration of an EU trade mark or through the Madrid Protocol. It may be noted that unregistered international trade marks more rapidly than previously may become established in Finland through advertising in, for example, satellite broadcasts and on the Internet.

There is no established court practice with regard to trade mark infringement through the Internet, but the general perception is that if commercial use of a trade mark is accessible through the Internet in Finland this will constitute trade mark infringement in Finland. In practice this means that the infringer may be subject to injunction and payment of compensation for trade mark infringement even if the use would be legal in other countries. Here, again one of the difficulties might be that the defendant is difficult to identify and serve a summons upon.

6.8 France

6.8.1 Introduction

6–168   France is far from suffering from an absence of laws likely to apply to the Internet. As with other countries, the main problem lies in enforcing these laws.

Although the questions of governing law and jurisdiction have been discussed in decisions rendered by French courts since the creation of the Internet, this question is still largely in debate.

6.8.2 Governing law and jurisdiction for foreign websites

Civil grounds

6–169   In determining the applicable governing law and jurisdiction under French civil law, a distinction must be made between (i) tortious matters and (ii) contractual situations.

(i) Tortious matters

6–170   Under French international private law in matters of tort, the governing law is the law of the place where the tort was committed *(lex loci delicti)*.

However, it is often difficult to determine the territory in which the tort took place, and opinions diverge.

French legal doctrine and case law are divided between three theories, which advocate jurisdiction of:

—   the law of the country of issue (foreign law);

—   the law of the country of receipt (French law);

—   the law of the country to which the website is directed or targeted ("country of destination") (foreign or French law).

E.U. authorities adopted the principle of the country of issue in the European Directive on Satellites of September 27, 1993. With respect to the Internet, a systematic application of this principle would be dangerous, as it could result in significant abuse and the creation of "informational havens" where the most dangerous information could be diffused in complete impunity and where copyright or other claims would be completely ignored.

6–171   On the other hand, the drawback of attributing jurisdiction to the law of the country of receipt is that any website could be subject to the laws of all countries worldwide.

After comparing to these two theories, the theory advocating the attribution of jurisdiction to the country of destination seems to be the most appropriate to the Internet. Nevertheless, this theory requires determining some criteria, which is not easy to do.

In French case law, courts have applied the theory of reception (Faurrisson,[176] Payline,[177] St. Tropez,[178] Nart,[179] Yahoo! cases[180]). According to this theory, if the service available on the Internet could be received on the French territory and the damage occurs in France, consequently, French law applies.

As far as the determination of the competent court is concerned several courts may be appointed according to various legal theories and the European Conventions of Lugano and Brussels as well as applicable international conventions, such as the court where the offence took place or the court where the act causing the damage took place. In France, when a court declares that French law is the governing law, generally, by way of consequence, it also acknowledges that French courts have jurisdiction (see above cases).

(ii) Contractual situations

In a contractual situation, the question of applicable governing law and jurisdiction is easier to resolve, as the parties (in this case, the overseas site and the French user) may have already determined the governing law in the contract binding them, or, if the contract does not designate such law, international conventions may apply, such as the Rome, Brussels or Hague Conventions. **6–172**

Criminal offences

Article 113-2 of the New Criminal Code provides that: **6–173**

> "French criminal law applies to infractions committed on the territory of the French Republic. The infraction is deemed to have been committed on the territory of the Republic if one of its constitutive elements took place on this territory".

Article 113-7 of the same Code provides that: **6–174**

> "French criminal law applies to any crime as well as any offence punishable by imprisonment, committed by a French person or by a foreigner outside the territory of the Republic when the victim is a French citizen at the time of the offence".

Therefore, French Criminal law applies when a link to a French element is easy to prove. In fact, irrespective of the "pull" and "push" debate if the information in dispute is accessible in France, the law would apply.

However, to be found liable for a criminal offence, the physical and intentional aspects of the offence must be proven. The far from simple problem of enforcing the decision rendered against a foreign website nevertheless remains (see below Yahoo! cases).

In conclusion, the general position is that French law is applicable and French courts are competent whenever a website on which potentially illegal or damaging content is displayed can be accessed from a computer situated in France. This applies to both tortious and criminal matters.

6.8.3 Defamation

Any information that is defamatory or denigrating or infringes on a person's image or private life or is promoting crimes, offences or suicide, is punishable both on civil and criminal grounds. **6–175**

The sole accessibility in France of such information through the Internet constitutes a publication under French law, even through it is not displayed by French sites.

The *BNP Banexi v. Mr Yves Rocher*[181] decision is one of the first court decisions concerning the defamation on the Internet. In this matter, Mr Rocher was ordered to remove some defamatory information from its website. Since this decision, other cases have been rendered, but to our knowledge, there is no court decision in France concerning a foreign defamation.

6.8.4 Copyright

6–176   The French Intellectual Property Code defines infringements as any reproduction, representation or broadcast, by any means whatsoever, of a creative work in violation of copyright as defined and regulated by the law.

In the well known case, *Brel-Sardou*,[182] the court held that the defaulting party infringed on a work covered by copyright (in this case, the words and extracts of songs by Jacques Brel and Michel Sardou) because such works had been, without authorisation from the artists, digitised and made available to the public on a webpage on the website of a school in Paris.

This decision is important in that it officially recognises (for the first time) that making information available to the public on a webpage is considered a publication of such information

6.8.5 Trademarks

6–177   In France, the holder of a registered trademark has a right of ownership over such trademark for certain designated products and services.

Accordingly, the reproduction, use, imitation or appropriation of a trademark as well as its use for products that are identical or similar to the products or services designated in the registration constitutes an infringement of both civil and criminal law. The appropriation of a domain name in violation of an existing trademark right or the unauthorised use of a third party's trademark reproduced on a website may constitute trademarks infringements.[183] In France, courts have acknowledged their own jurisdiction even if the reproduction of the trademark was carried out by a non-French citizen or resident, provided that it was made on a website.[184] Even if the foreign party is not the holder of a trademark, French courts have jurisdiction to assess the conflict and order a preliminary injunction.[185]

6.8.6 Content liability

6–178   Website content may also be considered an offence when it adversely affects the rights and interests of others. The question to be addressed in this situation concerns who are the defaulting parties (*i.e.* users, access providers, operators, content providers or hosts). There are few contracts relating to the Internet that are concluded between users and content providers; for those that do exist, the content provider is contractually bound to provide website content. On the other hand, contracts between users and access or host providers, which are more common, relate to the access to the Internet or the content host, and not the content of the information released. Consequently, under civil law, individuals are most often held liable for the website content on tortious rather than contractual grounds.

Three elements must be proven for a third party to be held liable for a tort: a wrongful act, harm suffered, and a causal link between these two elements.

On a criminal level, French law provides that the mere fact of transporting, releasing or making available the means to release information that is violent, pornographic or adversely affects human dignity, constitutes a criminal offence.

However, case law concerning Minitel shows that French courts have never found a network provider guilty of such offence.

Concerning unlawful foreign content providers, French courts generally acknowledge   **6–179**
their own competence in applying French law. For example, French courts have
jurisdiction to condemn a website with racist content (Faurisson case).

The question is more delicate for intermediary service providers.

In general, French case law acknowledges the possibility to condemn host providers on
the grounds of Article 1382 or 1383 of the French Civil Code if they do not remove the
illicit content after they have been informed of it (Lacoste and Multimania cases[186]).

The Yahoo! case illustrated the possibility to condemn a foreign provider in France. The
case involved the host provider of a racist and negationist website, Geocities, offered on
Yahoo!'s site, and the sale of Nazi items by its auction service. In a preliminary order,
dated May 22, 2000, the court acknowledged its jurisdiction, considering that Yahoo's
services were accessible in France. The court consequently ordered Yahoo! to prevent
French people from accessing its unlawful service.

The law of August 1, 2000, modifying the law of September 30, 1986, relating to   **6–180**
freedom of communication, provided in Article 43-8, for the principle of non-liability of
the host providers unless they fail to remove illicit content after being ordered to do so by
a court.

Civil and criminal laws in France contain all necessary provisions to regulate or, if
necessary, sanction violations. French case law shows that the courts have applied French
law to cases involving the Internet. Nevertheless, concerning technical intermediaries, the
application of French law is still in debate, and we are awaiting the future Law on
Information Society to resolve these kinds of issues (expected for the end of 2001).

6.9 Germany

6.9.1 Jurisdiction

According to German procedural law international jurisdiction lies with the court   **6–181**
competent for the place where the offence was committed. Therefore, German courts are
competent if the infringement was committed in Germany or produces at least effects in
Germany. In the online field it has to be checked at which places the Website operator
"appears" or in which area the company is active according to its economic objectives. In
the absence of a relation to the German market because the business activity of the
Website operator is not directed to Germany, the use of a domain name does not lead to a
trademark infringement in Germany. The purely technically conditioned worldwide
availability of each Website is, under German law, consequently no reason for the
jurisdiction of a German court.

The jurisdiction of German courts is not restricted either to the content of Websites   **6–182**
operated under the Top Level Domain ".de' or to Website contents in German. The
opinion held in court decisions is that the content of a Website can also represent an
infringement in Germany if the Website is operated under the Top Lebel Domain ".com"
or another Top Level Domain. The location of the server is irrelevant in this connection. It
was expressly held in court decisions that also Websites in English are basically
appropriate to address the German market since English is the prevailing language on the
Internet and is, therefore, also understood by a relevant German public without any
problems. The reference to a Website according to which the offer is valid, "worldwide"
was interpreted by a German court in that it held that the content of the Website is also

meant for the German public. In a case decided by the regional court of Frankfurt a German company referred on its homepage by a link to the homepage of its U.S. sister company to the advertisements published on the homepage of the latter. The homepage of the U.S. company showed advertisements admissible in the USA but anticompetitive by German legal standards. In this case the court affirmed a violation of fair competition under German law of the German company by the reference to the homepage of the U.S. sister company.

6.9.2 Defamation

6–183   In the case of a Web site accessible in Germany and containing a defamatory statement, the defamation is completed in Germany if this Web site is accessedby users in Germany and the infringement is committed in Germany. If the elements constitute an offence, the German prosecuting authorities would also be competent for offender's acts that produce an effect on German territory although committed with the help of the Web site accessed from a foreign country. The requirements are met if the data stored in the Internet are accessible in Germany and liable to prosecution under German law. A defamation is then also completed under German civil law so that the victim can bring an action before a German court for an injunction and payment of damages. It remains, of course, to be seen how judgments against a Web site owner situated abroad can be enforced.

6.9.3 Incorrect information

6–184   Claims can also be maintained against the Web site provider under German law and before German courts if harm is caused in Germany by the publication of incorrect information on a Web site. Of course, the harm suffered must be in causal relation under German law to the information accessed on the Internet. These requirements would only be complied with in exceptional cases.

6.9.4 Copyright

6–185   An online use of copyright protected works is not subject to any special German legal regulations other than those which apply to any other kind of use. German copyright protection is also valid on the Internet. This is an agreed fact even though the wording of the pertinent provisions of the Copyright Act do not really fit online use, which leads to discussions of whether it is rather a question of the appearance of a work or the publication of a work within the meaning of the law. Works which exist off the Internet and were created before being accessible on the Internet do not lose their copyright protection in that they are digitized and available on the Internet. The same applies to texts, graphics, musical works, films as well as to computer programs and data banks.

Copyright protected types of works can be created in the form of homepages or other Websites. The few court decisions on this subject-matter are not uniform. The Düsseldorf Court of Appeals has decided that the individual Websites and the arrangement of the data and the data on which they are based are neither protected as data bank works within the meaning of the Copyright Act nor a form of expression of a computer program within the meaning of the Copyright Act. On the other part, courts held the opinion that a list of a great number of Internet addresses in the form of a link collection as data bank is protectable according to the Copyright Act.

6.9.5 Trade marks

The use of a trading name or a sign available on a Web site in Germany, provided by a company located in another country and identical with or confusingly similar to a trading name or sign protected in Germany will normally represent a trade mark infringement under German law. In this case, too, German law is applicable and German courts have jurisdiction because the infringement was committed in Germany. A court will consequently sustain a trade mark infringement if the normal requirements such as identity or similarity of the goods and the opposing marks are met.

6–186

6.10 Hong Kong

6.10.1 Jurisdiction

Introduction
As Hong Kong is a common law territory, traditional *criminal* jurisdiction is generally (but not always) dependent upon the criminal act having been carried out at least in part within the geographical boundaries of the territory, and enforcement requires the presence of the individual in the territory or the individual being susceptible to extradition.[187] A person generally becomes subject to the *civil* jurisdiction of the territory's courts if the person is present in the territory (even fleetingly) and can be served with or notified of "originating process" such as a writ regardless of whether the transaction in question has anything to do with the territory. However, in both criminal and civil matters the court's traditional jurisdictional reach has been extended by statute.

6–187

Criminal Jurisdiction
Any person using the Internet in Hong Kong to commit a criminal act will be liable to criminal prosecution. For example, sending an intimidating or blackmailing message by email from a PC in Hong Kong renders the sender liable to prosecution for criminal intimidation[188–189] or blackmail.[190] In a 1998 case[191] an individual (who happened to be a foreigner) in Hong Kong loaded paedophile pornography images onto a web server in Hong Kong and was duly prosecuted for an offence contrary to Control of Obscene and Indecent Articles Ordinance.[192]

6–188

In another 1998 case[193] the court looked in some detail at how loading pictures onto a web server constituted "publishing" under the Ordinance in view of the fact that the Ordinance was enacted in 1987 before the Internet was contemplated. It was expressly held that the "publication" was complete when the appellant uploaded the files to the web server and his actions thereby constituted "publishing". It was further held that as the images could be seen on screen during downloading they were also "shown and projected" within the meaning of another section of the Ordinance. The finding on uploading may have jurisdictional consequences. The court also held that once the files were uploaded they were available on the Internet to either users: there was no requirement that "*publication*" be "*in public*". A similar case occurred in 2000.[194]

In another 2000 case[195] the defendants had used Back Orifice software to access the

6–189

computers in question through the Internet. The first two defendants were convicted of misuse of computer offences under the Crimes Ordinance[196] (similar to the U.K. offences) and the Organised and Serious Crimes Ordinance[197] as well as criminal damage contrary to the Crimes Ordinance.[198] A third defendant was found guilty of the criminal offence of making infringing copies of copyright works for sale or hire contrary to the Copyright Ordinance.[199]

(The judgments in foregoing reported cases other than *HKSAR v. Cheung Kam Keung* are appeals against sentence.)

6–190　　The HKSAR Government enacted the Criminal Jurisdiction Ordinance[200] in December 1994 to address jurisdictional problems associated with international fraud. The Ordinance extends the court's jurisdiction over certain dishonesty and fraud offences as follows:

- where any part of the offence or of the results required to be proved take place in Hong Kong the offence is triable in Hong Kong;

- an attempt to commit a Hong Kong offence will be triable whether or not the attempt was made in Hong Kong;

- an attempt or incitement in Hong Kong to commit an offence elsewhere is an offence in Hong Kong;

- a conspiracy wherever made to commit an offence in Hong Kong is a Hong Kong offence, whether or not anything in furtherance of the conspiracy is done in Hong Kong; and

- a conspiracy in Hong Kong to do elsewhere something that if done in Hong Kong would be an offence in Hong Kong, is an offence in Hong Kong.

6–191　　The Ordinance only applies to certain offences but the Chief Executive (who replaced the Governor) may extend the list by Order. Of the various offences created by the Computer Crimes Ordinance the Criminal Jurisdiction Ordinance only covers *"false accounting done through a computer"*.

In a September 2000 Consultation Paper the HKSAR Government's Working Group on Computer Related Crimes recommended extending the application of the Ordinance urgently.

Civil Jurisdiction

6–192　　Generally a person who commits a civil wrong in Hong Kong using the Internet will be liable to be sued here on being served with local process here, either personally or under the rules permitting postal service within the territory. Certain substantive wrongs are considered below.

As regards procedure, as in many common law territories, in Hong Kong the general rules on civil jurisdiction by way of personal or postal service have been extended by so-called "long arm" legislation. Under the extended procedural rules Hong Kong process may in certain cases be served on a defendant outside the territory if the transaction in question had certain points of connection with Hong Kong. Once a defendant to an action resident abroad has been served outside the territory with process from the court, the defendant must decide whether to participate in the proceedings, or ignore them and face the risk of a default judgment.

6–193　　In Hong Kong Order 11 of the Rules of the High Court [201] enables persons resident or incorporated outside Hong Kong to be sued in Hong Kong and served with Hong Kong process at their foreign place of residence or business where, amongst other things, they have made contracts in Hong Kong, have committed breaches of contract in Hong Kong or have committed torts in Hong Kong or torts the resulting damage from which is suffered within Hong Kong or the case concerns Hong Kong real property.

In the most cases involving Order 11 the key question for the court in deciding whether to grant leave to "serve out" will be whether the case in question falls factually within any of the limbs of Order 11(1), and there is an important subsidiary question in each case of service out as to whether it is a "proper" case for service out. This depends on the convenience of the parties and other *forum non conveniens* considerations

There is at present in Hong Kong and the Commonwealth a dearth of case law relating to e-commerce and jurisdictional issues.

The Hong Kong Electronic Transactions Ordinance[202] ("ETO") provides answers to some of the questions that will inevitably arise in service out cases involving e-commerce. Section 17 confirms, in case anyone doubted it, that electronic records (which term includes emails or messages sent between web servers and PCs) may be used to conclude contracts. Section 18 provides guidance as to the *attribution* of electronic records and section 19 deals with the *timing* and *place* of dispatch and receipt of electronic records. **6–194**

Tort—The basic rule is that a tort (which includes infringement of intellectual property rights) is considered to have been effected in the place where the relevant acts took place. **6–195**

In the case of misrepresentation, deceit or negligent misstatement that will probably be the place where the statement comes to the attention of the addressee. So where a Hong Kong party is in negotiations with, or is being advised by, a non–Hong Kong resident, and a misstatement is made to the Hong Kong party, the location of the tort constituted by the misstatement will probably be Hong Kong. In the case of defamation, the tort occurs in the place of publication.

Contract—The basic rule at common law is that a contract is made when and where the acceptance of an offer is received by the offeror. This rule can be applied easily enough to contracts concluded by instantaneous means of communication. For non instantaneous means of communication the rule has historically been subject to the common law exception known as the "postal acceptance rule" under which when an offer is accepted by post, the contract thereby concluded is deemed to have been made when, and therefore where, the acceptance is put in the post which is logically before the offeror will in fact receive it. **6–196**

There are as yet no reported Hong Kong cases on whether or how the postal acceptance exception applies to email or interaction through a web site. Some recent U.K. texts treat email as an instantaneous form of communication,[203] although the difficulties with email are acknowledged.

Section 19 of the ETO provides that an electronic message is regarded having been sent at the place of business of the originator and to have been received at that place of business of the addressee with which the underlying transaction is related, or if the addressee has no place of business then where the addressee ordinarily resides. **6–197**

Apart from that, the ETO is silent on when and where contracts concluded over the Internet or otherwise using electronic messages will be regarded as having been made. The general contract rules on these questions will therefore apply.

It seems that by focusing on individual messages themselves, rather than *exchanges* of messages, the drafters of the ETO deliberately avoided providing new substantive contract law rules or clarifying how existing ones apply, and intentionally left open the question of whether the postal acceptance exception will apply to exchanges of Internet communications.

The only provision that touches on contract law is section 17(c) that states expressly that section 17 does not affect any rule of law to the effect that an offeror may prescribe the method of accepting an offer.

6–198   This approach contrasts with other legislative measures dealing with contracts formed electronically. For example, the U.S. Uniform Computer Information Transactions Act of 1999 provides in section 203(4) that a contract formed by exchange of email is formed when the acceptance is received. That clearly excludes the postal acceptance exception.

It was said in *Brinkibon v. Stalag Stahl*,[204] a well known U.K. case dealing with telexes, recently followed in *Eastern Power Limited v. Azienda Communate Energia and Ambiente*[205] as regards faxes, there can be no general rule applicable to all instantaneous or "virtually" instantaneous communications, and the questions of whether and when a contact is concluded by such means will depend on all the circumstances, including the interacting parties' intentions.

6–199   It may be that as between two parties dealing on a "B2B" basis and using "always on" email systems the postal acceptance exception will not apply, but the exception may apply in the "B2C" situation where it is likely that the consumer is using dial-up or other non instantaneous email access. It seems unlikely that the postal acceptance exception would apply to a contract concluded via interaction on a web site where an order is acknowledged immediately as the communication is sufficiently instantaneous. On the other hand, if a transaction on a web site requires a delayed confirmation email sent by the operator to the customer before the contract is concluded the exception may apply.

If matters are left uncertain by poorly drafted terms of business on an e-commerce web site, then where an email or web site contract is entered into by a Hong Kong resident with a non–resident web site operator, the contract is probably made in Hong Kong when the Hong Kong resident receives the web site operator's acceptance of the resident's order.

6–200   The Hong Kong resident may therefore be able to sue the other party for subsequent breaches in Hong Kong by relying on the combined effects of section 19(4) and 19(5)(b) of the ETO and Order 11, Rule 1(i)(d)(i) of the RHC.

In the perhaps unlikely event of the postal acceptance exception applying, the contract would be made abroad when and where the operator dispatched its acceptance of an order.

Conversely, a Hong Kong web site operator may find that it enters into contracts abroad, and is therefore liable to be sued abroad, when sending acceptances to customers abroad.

A Proper Case For Service Out or Prosecution?
6–201   As stated above, where a Hong Kong plaintiff sues a foreign party in Hong Kong alleging that certain web site content or functionality has constituted a civil wrong against that plaintiff or an infringement of that plaintiff's rights in Hong Kong, the plaintiff will, as well as having to show that the case falls within the one of the categories of cases for service out, need to satisfy the court that the case is a "proper" one for service out.

Where the alleged wrong is, for example, a breach of local Hong Kong trade or advertising laws, infringement of a trade mark or passing off by use of the plaintiff's trade get up, the foreign defendant may well say in its defence that even if what the plaintiff says is correct it is only incidental to its activities and the defendant has not intentionally "directed" any of its activities towards Hong Kong such that the defendant should attract the jurisdiction of the Hong Kong courts.

In the U.S. many states have long-arm statues that permit service out of local process in all cases where that is constitutionally permissible. U.S. federal constitutional case law holds that it is constitutional for a state to exercise long-arm jurisdiction over out-of-state defendants who have engaged in "minimum contacts" with the state. There is now a substantial body of U.S. constitutional case law on what type of activities meet this test.

6–202

It is clear that merely establishing a web site that is only viewable in a state because web sites are viewable anywhere will not constitute deliberate engaging in minimum contacts with the state or its residents so as to justify the exercise of long-arm jurisdiction by that state.

It is likely that in the emerging case law of the various Commonwealth jurisdictions and Hong Kong a similar test will evolve focusing on whether the defendant has "directed" any of its activities, including those on the Internet, to the jurisdiction in question.

In the case of defamation, where web content has defamed a Hong Kong plaintiff, the defendant is likely to have little success in arguing that while the content was viewable in Hong Kong the defendant had not deliberately directed the content at Hong Kong.

In the case of trade mark infringement, the plaintiff will have to demonstrate that the foreign defendant had used the plaintiff's Hong Kong trade mark or something similar in "the course of trade" in Hong Kong. To do this the plaintiff will have to show a "sufficient link"[206] with Hong Kong. Merely establishing a web site abroad aimed primarily at other markets without any intent to use a trade mark similar to an established Hong Kong trade mark amongst Hong Kong clientele would not probably amount to a sufficient link for the plaintiff to overcome the service out discretionary hurdle.

6–203

Similarly in the criminal sphere, putting aside the issue of whether as a practical matter the intended defendant is amenable to the Hong Kong criminal process by visiting here or by being liable to extradition, where web content amounts to a Hong Kong criminal offence the Hong Kong authorities are unlikely to mount a prosecution unless there is some intentional act on the part of the defendant to "direct" the web site in some way to the Hong Kong community.

A New Convention?

A Special Commission of the Hague Conference on Private International Law has been convened with the task of producing a Convention on International Jurisdiction and Enforcement and Recognition of Judgments in Civil and Commercial Matters. A representative of the Hong Kong SAR Government is taking part as a member of the Chinese delegation. If a Convention is produced it is likely that the Hong Kong SAR Government would give serious consideration to implementing it by way of local enacting legislation.

6–204

Any convention produced is likely to be influenced by the existing Brussels and Lugano Conventions force in certain European countries.

Constitutional Considerations

In the United States and increasingly in the United Kingdom, the exercise of the so called long-arm jurisdictional powers is subject to constitutional challenge on the ground that such exercise (or the power itself) is a breach of the defendant's human rights or is a failure of "due process" guaranteed by some embedded law.

6–205

Foreign case law on these issues is unlikely to be relevant in Hong Kong. It has not yet been suggested by a non resident sued in Hong Kong, at least in any reported case, that the Criminal Jurisdiction Ordinance or Order 11 is unconstitutional under the Basic Law[207] or contrary to the Hong Kong Bill of Rights.[208]

6.10.2 Defamation

6–206   The essence of defamation is the publication of a statement that tends to lower the plaintiff in the estimation of right thinking members of society generally or cause the plaintiff to be shunned or avoided. Under the law relating to defamation in Hong Kong (English common law and the Defamation Ordinance[209]), any person who participates in the publication of a defamatory statement is liable for the defamation.

However, there is a possible defence for a web site operator under section 8 of the Defamation Ordinance. This provides that where a presumptive case of publication by the act of any other person by his authority is established against a defendant, the defendant may prove that the publication was made without his authority, consent or knowledge *and* that the publication did not arise from want of due care or caution on his part.

6–207   The case law of defamation provides one of the few examples, if not the only example, of consideration of Internet jurisdiction as such by a Hong Kong court. In *Investasia Limited v. Kodansha Co. Limited*[210] the plaintiff commenced proceedings against the defendants for two libellous articles in Japanese written by the first defendant and published by the second defendant. The plaintiffs alleged that one article that was posted on the Internet and another that was published in a magazine distributed in several jurisdictions, including 157 copies in Hong Kong, were defamatory of them.

The court granted leave to serve a Hong Kong writ on the defendants in Japan under Order 11 on the basis that the claim was founded on libel and damage was sustained within Hong Kong. The defendants applied to set aside the writ. The plaintiffs filed evidence showing they had substantial connections with Hong Kong and that they had suffered damage to their reputations in Hong Kong by reason of the publications.

6–208   The evidence was that Mr Wada, the second plaintiff, who had a "controlling hand" in the first plaintiff, had kept a residence in Hong Kong since 1994, was a Japanese national, had had investments in Hong Kong since 1994, was a facilitator whose business depended on the trust his clients could place in him, had built a good reputation in Hong Kong, had the right relationships with financial institutions in Hong Kong, spent four to six months a year in Hong Kong and had no residence elsewhere and that the first plaintiff had bank accounts in Hong Kong and a liaison office in Hong Kong.

The judge refused to set aside the writ. He held that if a plaintiff has a reputation in Hong Kong, as the plaintiffs in this case had, it was not right to tell him or her to go elsewhere to vindicate that reputation because the place to vindicate a damaged Hong Kong reputation is in Hong Kong. Where the circulation of a foreign publication gives rise to a tort in Hong Kong it would be necessary to consider the scale of publication in Hong Kong and elsewhere in deciding whether or not Hong Kong was the natural forum for the resolution of the dispute. The court considered that 157 magazines containing sensational material was sufficient to sustain a complaint within Hong Kong.

A similar decision was reached in the Australian case of *Gutnick v. Dow Jones & Co. Inc.*[211]

6–209   The *Investasia* decision followed *Berezovsky v. Forbes Inc* in the English Court of

Appeal.[212] That case subsequently proceeded to the House of Lords in England[213] and also involved a publication in a magazine and on the Internet and evidence of low circulation in the jurisdiction where the plaintiff wished to proceed and little or no evidence of how many times if at all the Internet version of the publication had been accessed. The Hong Kong and English courts reached the same conclusion. In *Gutnick* downloading in Australia from the defendant's U.S. Internet site was admitted. *Gutnick* followed *Berezovsky* in the House of Lords.

6.10.3 Liability for Erroneous or Misleading Content

There have been no reported cases to date in Hong Kong relating to reliance on incorrect information placed on a web site causing loss or damage. It is unlikely that the Hong Kong courts would have difficulty in treating such information as published in Hong Kong; however, they would retain a discretion whether or not to accept jurisdiction on the grounds discussed above.   **6–210**

Of particular relevance would be whether there was a good arguable case on the merits. In this regard, the court would consider the proximity of the relationship between the plaintiff and the party which placed the information on the web site and whether, following the line of cases beginning with *Hedley Byrne v. Heller*, the plaintiff came within the limited class of persons entitled to rely on the information.

6.10.4 Copyright

As mentioned above, Hong Kong's copyright law (contained in the Copyright Ordinance)[214] is founded principally on the U.K. Copyright, Designs and Patents Act 1988. It is, among other things, an infringement of a copyright work to copy it, which includes storing the work by electronic means in any medium.   **6–211**

However, making transient copies of the work (such as would be made temporarily in a computer's RAM) for the purpose of viewing and listening to a copyright work is not an infringement.

Section 26 of the Copyright Ordinance makes it an infringing act to make available copies of works to the public by wire or wireless means such as the Internet where no permission of the copyright owner has been obtained.   **6–212**

In Hong Kong, copyright infringement can be a criminal offence, as well as lead to civil liability.

There has been an Internet-related case in Hong Kong concerning allegations of copyright infringement. *Action Asia*, a Hong Kong published magazine, claimed that its copyright in a number of articles had been infringed by a California-based diver who posted extracts from *Action Asia's* articles on his home page.   **6–213**

The alleged infringement was only discovered by *Action Asia's* editorial staff because, while "surfing" the Internet for interesting Web sites, they discovered their own material on Mr Taylor's site. *Action Asia* offered Mr Taylor a solution whereby he could, on terms, continue to use the offending material, but he declined the offer. *Action Asia* issued proceedings against Mr Taylor and named Mr Taylor's Internet service provider, Best Internet Communications, as a co-defendant. The case against Best Internet was settled three months after proceedings were issued. Thereafter, *Action Asia* did not pursue Mr Taylor personally, since he removed the offending content from his home page.

6.10.5 Trade marks

6–214   A web site operated from outside Hong Kong that displays a mark identical or substantially similar to a trade mark or service mark registered in Hong Kong could be susceptible to a claim for infringement if such web site offers goods or services in a class for which the mark has been registered and it can be said that the Hong Kong trade mark has been used in Hong Kong without permission.

The English case of *Euromarket Designs Inc. v. Peters*[215] is likely to be followed in Hong Kong as the relevant provisions of the Hong Kong Trade Marks Ordinance[216] are similar to the provisions considered by the English court in that case.

6.10.6 Online Gambling

6–215   The current law on all forms of gambling, gaming and bookmaking is contained in the Gambling Ordinance.[217] This has been more or less in its present form since 1977 and its provisions therefore long predate the Internet.

There is a number of separate offences under the Ordinance. These include:

— **bookmaking** any person who ... holds out in any manner that he solicits, receives, negotiates or settles bets by way of trade or business; or ... in any capacity assists, either directly or indirectly, another person in bookmaking;

— **betting with a bookmaker** any person who bets with a bookmaker ...;

— **promoting lotteries** any person who ... promotes, organises, conducts or manages, or otherwise has control of, an unlawful lottery ... in any capacity assists, either directly or indirectly, in the promotion, organisation, conduct, management or other control of an unlawful lottery ...;

— **publicising lotteries** any person who in any manner ... provides or publishes, or causes to be provided or published, expressly or otherwise ... any tip, hint or forecast relating to the result of an unlawful lottery; or ... any announcement of the result of an unlawful lottery ...; and

— **gambling** in a place other than a licensed gambling establishment.

6–216   The Ordinance clearly applies to onshore web based gambling services and promotional activities and onshore web gambling punters just as it does to offline gambling and promotional activities. However, the Ordinance raises significant jurisdictional problems as regards (a) Hong Kong punters betting on offshore gambling web sites, and more importantly (b), offshore and Hong Kong based operators and promoters of offshore gambling web sites.

Oddly the Ordinance does not include specific offences of *promoting* bookmaking activities or *promoting* betting with a bookmaker. In those circumstances, any prosecution that is undertaken in relation to the promotion in Hong Kong of an offshore gambling web site (assuming it did not constitute a "*lottery*") would have to be based on the provisions of the bookmaking offence, that is assisting in soliciting or actually soliciting bets by way of trade or business or on assisting in the operation of unlawful gambling.

6–217   A prosecution under those provisions may face difficulties in that the promotion in Hong Kong of gambling on an offshore web site may not in itself to amount to assisting in the management or the operation of the site or assisting in the solicitation, etc. of bets.

Accordingly, it is likely that, for example, the owner of a billboard hired to display an advertisement to promote an offshore gambling web site would be unlikely to commit an assisting offence, as it would not be acting to assist in the management of the web site. However, a local employee in Hong Kong of the corporate gambling operation would be much more likely to be taken to be assisting those who manage the offshore web site. It would be difficult to argue that such an offence has not been committed if an employee were involved in making management decisions regarding matters such as, for example, the *direction* of the promotional activities.

The prospects of a prosecution of the operator or local representative of an offshore web site for "bookmaking" being successful would largely depend on the interpretation which the courts give to the word "solicit". The relevant offence would be engaging in soliciting bets. There are no reported cases which have considered the meaning of "*solicit*" in the context of gambling.

The term "*solicit*" must involve some element of inviting relevant persons to engage in   **6–218**
the activity in question. In order to give rise to the offence an advertisement must either expressly or impliedly invite a person or people to place bets through the web site. An advertisement that invites people simply to visit a web site that does not solely consist of gambling activities would most likely not solicit bets. However, an advertisement that includes some form of encouragement for readers to place bets on the site may fall within a broad definition of "*soliciting*".

The separate offence of holding oneself out (as opposed to another person) as a bookmaker could be committed by a person (including a company) who does not actually solicit a bet, but who nevertheless indicates in his promotional activities that he is in the business of bookmaking, but that is unlikely to be committed by a sole local representative of an offshore operator.

A new Gambling (Amendment) Bill designed specially to overcome the jurisdictional   **6–219**
problems of Internet gambling is at the Committee Stage at the time of writing. This is discussed below. It is difficult to obtain any real guidance from statements made by the Government about promotional activities relating to gambling web sites. Prior to the introduction of the Gambling (Amendment) Bill in November 2000 the Government took a strong line in relation to the promotion of gambling web sites. For example, in February last year, the Home Affairs Bureau asked the police to look into a promotional event in Hong Kong being run by an Antigua based company called Easybets. The president of Easybets was scheduled to give a briefing on Internet gambling and sports betting. However, this briefing was cancelled with the president of Easybets stating that "*Having been advised by the relevant authorities that holding this event could possibly contravene section 7 of the Gambling Ordinance, it was my executive decision to cancel the press conference*".

In contrast, since the introduction of the Gambling (Amendment) Bill, the Government   **6–220**
has taken a much less bullish approach. Recently, the Government stated that it is aware of the following promotional activities being conducted by offshore gambling web sites:

(a)   advertising in the mass media in Hong Kong, including in popular newspapers and sports magazines and on buses, handing out leaflets to the public and sending information to the media to promote their business and attract bets;

(b)   setting up on local websites hypertext links to gambling websites;

(c)   broadcasting on local television or radio stations offshore events (and related betting information) on which they take bets; and

(d)   providing betting information (for example, odds on overseas soccer matches) in the local media to stimulate betting interest.

Now that a bill aimed at overcoming the jurisdictional difficulties with offshore web sites exists the Home Affairs Bureau takes the position that the current law contains loopholes in that it does not cover offshore activities. This should be viewed in the political context of a government pushing for a Bill to be passed as quickly as possible and the opinion of the Home Affairs Bureau will not necessarily be shared by the courts. However, in light of the lack of prosecutions made in respect of the promotional activities referred to above, it does appear unlikely that any prosecutions will be brought under the current law in respect of promotional activities for offshore gambling web sites while the Bill is under consideration, at least where those activities are arranged wholly from overseas.

6–221   The Bill is undergoing revision. One of the key new offences proposed by the Bill is *"promoting or facilitating"* bookmaking. This offence is not committed if the bookmaking takes place wholly outside Hong Kong and both/all of the parties to the transaction are outside Hong Kong. However, it is quite clear that it will be an offence to do acts in Hong Kong to promote bookmaking on web sites based offshore that accept bets from punters located in Hong Kong.

The purpose of the new *"promoting"* offence is to criminalise activities that promote a bookmaker but which fall short of assisting a bookmaker in bookmaking. Accordingly, where an associate or employee may not be regarded as assisting bookmaking or assisting unlawful gambling, he or she might very well be regarded as promoting such activities.

The term *"facilitating"* potentially has very broad implications. The Home Affairs Bureau has indicated that one of the aims of the provision is to prevent punters from using their credit cards to place bets. The argument is that the issuer of the credit card would be facilitating the transaction and would thereby commit an offence if it authorised the transaction. The Home Affairs Bureau also anticipates being able to use Hong Kong's anti-money laundering legislation to prevent local banks from providing banking services to known operators of offshore gambling sites.

6–222   An ISP based in Hong Kong maintaining Internet access for its customers would arguably commit an offence of facilitating bookmaking in the event that any of the ISP's customers places a bet on an offshore web site. The risk to ISPs may be such that they will block access to such web sites.

There are currently no reported Hong Kong cases dealing with Internet gambling.

6.10.7 Reunification

6–223   The handover of Hong Kong's sovereignty to the People's Republic of China (PRC) at midnight on June 30, 1997 and the conversion of the former British Dependant Territory into The Hong Kong Special Administrative Region of the People's Republic of China has been well-documented. Since the handover, the PRC has remained committed to the 'one country, two systems' legal doctrine. Under this doctrine, Hong Kong, except insofar as national security, nationality, defence and certain other matters may be affected, is allowed to continue its former laws and make new laws separately from the rest of the PRC, subject where necessary to the adaptation of pre-handover laws to Hong Kong's new status.

These principles are embodied in Hong Kong's mini constitution, the Basic Law, and have been implemented by way of the Hong Kong Reunification Ordinance[218] and an ongoing series of "Adaption of Laws" Ordinances. None of these has affected substantive commercial or criminal law in any significant way and the great majority of pre-handover legislation modelled closely on U.K. legislation remains in force. The Handover has not affected the laws of Hong Kong insofar as they are relevant to the Internet.

Since the handover the procedural law of England and Wales, on which Hong Kong procedure is very closely based, has undergone a radical change commonly referred to as the "Woolf Reforms". The Hong Kong judiciary and the Law Society of Hong Kong have since set up working parties to review civil procedure in Hong Kong and, amongst other things, consider whether any or all of the Woolf Reforms, or similar initiatives in Singapore, Australia and other commonwealth jurisdictions, should be adopted in Hong Kong. In is unlikely that it will be considered appropriate or politically acceptable for the English reforms to be adopted *en masse* in Hong Kong.

6–224

6.10.8 Conclusions

The Hong Kong courts and those in other Asian commonwealth jurisdictions with similar procedural laws may have considerable jurisdiction over Internet activities in which non residents are involved. Where a Hong Kong resident deals with a non–resident provider of goods or services or publisher, and unlawful acts take place or a dispute arises in relation to the contract formation process or performance, the Hong Kong courts may be willing to exercise jurisdiction if the non resident comes here or is liable to be served under Order 11. Whether any particular case will be a "proper" one to be determined in Hong Kong will depend on all the facts of the case.

6–225

6.11 Israel

6.11.1 Jurisdictional issues relating to foreign Web site proprietors

Civil jurisdiction in Israel is founded upon service on the defendant of a summons.[219] Under the civil procedure rules,[220] service may be effected upon a defendant outside of Israel if the court has granted leave under its discretionary power for service outside the jurisdiction in one or more of the circumstances provided for in rule 500. In a case where the defendant is a foreign Web site proprietor, one or more of the following circumstances are likely to apply:

6–226

(1) *Injunctive relief*: An injunction is sought, in respect of an act performed or about to be performed within Israel.[221]

The court may assume jurisdiction for the purpose of granting a temporary injunction in order to prevent damage from occurring pending final resolution of the dispute in the forum where the action will ultimately be tried.[222] The court must be satisfied that the application, whether for an interim or final injunction, has not been made solely for the purpose of the court acquiring jurisdiction.

The injunction may be sought against either the local ISP, or against others responsible for the material reaching Israel, foremost among whom will be the foreign Web site proprietor. An action for an injunction against the ISP may well be sufficient for the court to assume jurisdiction over the foreign Web site proprietor, against whom damages are claimed, as a joint defendant.

(2) *Tort*: The action is based on an act or omission within Israel.[223]

Following the logic of the former English case law, the Israeli rule is that the court may assume jurisdiction over a foreign defendant only when the act or omission takes place within Israel.[224] The occurrence of the damage within Israel is not sufficient.[225] Therefore, a foreign Web site proprietor will only be subject to the court's jurisdiction when the commission of the alleged tort has a connection to Israel. For instance, the sale of books to Israeli customers is likely to constitute an act within Israel.[226] A negligent misstatement may constitute an omission within Israel.

(3) *Necessary/right party*: The person abroad is a necessary party or the right party in an action duly submitted against another person, on whom a summons was duly served within Israel.[227]

6–227   The plaintiff can apply for leave to serve the foreign Web site proprietor as a necessary party or the right defendant to the proceedings if it can identify and serve a potential defendant in Israel, such as an ISP. The court will not grant leave if it determines that there is no real issue to be tried against the Israeli defendant, or that the proceedings have been brought against the Israeli defendant solely to gain jurisdiction against the foreign Web site proprietor. The rule will be most useful in cases where the plaintiff cannot obtain leave for service under rule 500(6) or 500(7) (such as in an action regarding defective software downloaded from a foreign Web site), or to found a third party action by the local ISP against the foreign Web site proprietor.

Procedure

6–228   The application for leave must be supported by affidavit evidence demonstrating that the plaintiff has good grounds for its action, together with evidence supporting the grounds of the application. Given the *ex parte* nature of the application, the plaintiff is obliged to disclose all relevant facts in his possession to the court.

Connection to the Web site owner

6–229   The likelihood of the court assuming jurisdiction over a foreign Web site owner will depend on the circumstances of the application. The court will refuse leave where the case is outside the spirit of the rule.[228] The mere accessibility of the Web site in Israel is not likely to be sufficient to found jurisdiction where the matters dealt with by the Web site are not relevant to Israeli users.[229]

6.11.2 Forum non conveniens

Discretion to determine whether forum is appropriate

6–230   The court, in exercising its discretion whether or not to grant leave to serve proceedings on a defendant outside the jurisdiction under rule 500, will consider whether, in the circumstances of the case, Israel is the appropriate forum for the case to be heard.[230]

As the application for leave under rule 500 is made ex parte, the foreign defendant upon whom service has been effected is granted two opportunities (motion to cancel, and in the pleadings) to move for a stay of proceedings, by persuading the court that Israel is not the *forum conveniens* for the trial of the matter.

The defendant is bound to raise the issue of *forum non conveniens* at its earliest opportunity. Lack of a case at trial will not lead to the jurisdiction issue being reopened; having been wrongfully joined to the proceedings will not assist either.[231]

There is no case law on the application of the doctrine of *forum non conveniens* to Internet litigation. The circumstances of each case will determine the relevant weight to be given to different factors. The general principles are set out below.

6–231

The Israeli law is very close to the English law,[232] although the courts have at times adopted the public interest aspects of the approach taken by the U.S. courts.[233] The test applied is whether the natural forum for resolution of the dispute is Israel or another jurisdiction.[234] The reasonable expectations of the parties, and the public interest in achieving justice, are the major issues to be considered in determining the natural forum.

The court considers all of the circumstances, and the strength of the connections of each forum to the issues raised by the dispute. The court will also give due weight to the reasonable expectations of the parties.[235] All the relevant facts and causes important to the question must be balanced. These include, *inter alia*, nature of the dispute, relevant law in the fora, *lis alibi pendens*, nexus between each forum and the evidence, location of the parties and witnesses, place where the actionable event occurred, costs, availability of similar defences in each forum, ability to enforce a judgment, and the public interest, which includes matters such as the court's familiarity with the applicable law and the absence of an impartial judicial system in the other forum.[236]

6–232

If the defendant has convinced the court that there is another forum that may be more appropriate than Israel, the burden of proof rests on the plaintiff to show that there are special circumstances why the Israel court should hear the matter.[237]

6.11.3 Defamation

Liability for defamation is based on publication of a defamatory statement. "Publication" is defined as any statement directed to a person other than the injured and which has reached that person,[238] and in the case of written materials, whenever the writing is likely to reach any person other than the injured party.[239] For defamation to be actionable its commencement must occur within Israel.[240] The court acknowledged the reach of the law outside the country, when a defamatory letter sent from Israel to the U.S. was held to fall within the scope of the law. Similarly, the Israeli Supreme Court has ruled that a statement made by an Israeli to the Jordanian government, and its publication in a Jordanian newspaper that was also distributed in Israel, are subject to the statute.[241] This is the basis on which defamatory statements posted on bulletin boards, newsgroups, or publicly available Web sites may well be viewed as intended for publication in Israel (as in the case of the Jordanian newspaper), when such services are provided world-wide.

6–233

Besides the primary liability of the person who places a defamatory statement on a Web site, it is a matter of debate whether, and to what extent, an ISP, Web site proprietor, or newsgroup owner will be liable for defamation. The author, editor and publisher of such services may be subject to primary liability if they are deemed to be media persons for the purposes of the Defamation Law or fall within the definition of a "newspaper" in the Press Ordinance, or alternatively, if a court applies general tort principles to fill any lacunae in the current definitions.[242] Distribution of a defamatory statement may be caused by the actions of the foreign Web site owner, the owner of the host server, the service providers who own the routers, or the access provider in Israel. Providers of such services may also be subject to secondary liability if they are found by the court to be

6–234

"printers", "distributors", or "vendors" of the publication. If so, they may be subject to liability only if they knew or should have known that the publication contained defamatory matter.[243]

There have been only two Internet related defamation suits in Israel, both of them concerning alleged defamatory material published on local Web Sites. One suit was settled. The other suit, *Yitzhak v. Rotter*, is still pending.

6.11.4 Content liability

6–235   Incorrect information which causes damage may be actionable under the Civil Wrongs Ordinance (New Version) 1968, either as negligence or fraud. Section 3 of the statute provides that remedies are available to any person injured by a civil wrong (act or omission) which has been committed in Israel.[244]

Liability for misleading advertisements under the Consumer Protection Law 1981,[245] applies to any advertisement that may mislead a consumer in Israel, regardless of whether it was made in Israel. Any person who originated the advertisement or arranged for its publication may be liable. Distributors may be liable for distributing a misleading advertisement if it is misleading at first glance, or if they knew that it is misleading. Note that misleading advertisements include advertisements that do not appear to be advertising materials at first glance.[246] It is also a tort under the Commercial Torts Law 1999 for a dealer to publish false information about a business, profession, asset or service, including his own, where he knows or should know that the information is incorrect.[247] Distributors of such information may be liable if they knew that the information is false, or if it is obviously false.[248]

6–236   In cases where a computer virus downloaded from a Web site unlawfully affects use of a computer or of computer material, compensation for damage suffered as a result may be recoverable under the Computer Law from the person responsible for causing the damage.[249]

To date, the only judgment that has dealt with incorrect information published on the Internet is *Paradise Mombasa Tours (1997) Limited v. New Soil Technologies Limited*.[250] Following the termination of a business relationship between the parties, the defendant retained outdated descriptions of the plaintiff's business activities on the defendant's Website. The court held that the defendant was unduly intervening with customers' access to the plaintiff's business, and granted an interlocutory injunction under section 4 of the Commercial Torts Law 1999. *Paradise Mombasa* concerned a local Web site, and did not involve reliance on the incorrect information. Where there is reliance in an extra-jursidictional situation, the courts may apply section 2 of the Commercial Torts Law, or the provisions of the Consumer Protection Law and Civil Wrongs Ordinance (New Version) discussed above.

6.11.5 Copyright

6–237   Copyright works are protected in Israel under the Copyright Act[251] and the Copyright Ordinance.[252] There is no legislation that regulates the use of works in modern technology. Consequently, the law in this area is primarily case law, which relies in fair measure on foreign precedents.

Posting an infringing copy of a copyright work on a Web site may constitute copyright infringement under Israeli law on several grounds which are discussed below.

Placing a copy of a work in the RAM may infringe the reproduction rights of the copyright owner.[253] In the absence of direct authority under Israeli case law, it is unclear whether reproduction rights apply to unlicensed copies made during the transmission, or when such copies arrive at their destination. The term "infringing copy" under the Act is broad enough to include copies created outside Israel.[254]

The right to publicly perform the work[255] may also be infringed where the work is delivered by means of a mechanical instrument.[256] Israeli courts interpret this section broadly, as applying to any broadcast or transmission, or distribution of the work by any other means.[257] Re-transmission of television broadcasts by cable companies also constitutes public performance. The court has distinguished between a "viewer", namely a passive transmitter of a broadcast, and a "broadcaster", who plays an active role in distributing the broadcast.[258] ISPs and other service providers may thus be liable for public performance. An individual user, who merely views a copy of an infringing work, may be liable for public performance only if they display the copy in public.

There is no general right of public distribution under Israeli law, except in the case of an unpublished work.[259] In *Eisenman v. Qimron* (Dead Sea Scrolls dispute), the Supreme Court held on appeal that the respondent's right of first publication had been infringed by the distribution within Israel of three copies of an infringing book, each of which had been purchased from one of the United States' based appellants via mail order.[260] Following this decision, where a work is previously unpublished in Israel, a Web site proprietor may be liable in respect of e-commerce sales of an infringing copyright work to customers based in Israel.   **6–238**

Exclusive rental and leasing rights apply only to the distribution of physical media on which visual or audio works are fixed (such as DVDs or CDs).[261]

Posting an infringing copyright work on a Web site may, however, expose the Web site proprietor, or the ISP, to indirect liability for the sale, hiring, or distribution for the purpose of trade, exhibition or importation of a work "which to his knowledge infringes copyright".[262] Another way to establish liability is to show that a service provider allowed the use of a "place of entertainment" for the infringing performance of a work in public, unless there is no reasonable ground for suspecting that the performance would be an infringement of copyright.[263] It is not clear whether the courts will apply this section to virtual spaces such as Web sites. Note, that liability under these sections requires some level of knowledge regarding the infringing nature of the copies made by the system.   **6–239**

ISPs, bulletin boards or news groups may claim the defence of innocent infringer, on the ground that the alleged copying occurred automatically. Under Israeli copyright law an innocent infringer may be exempted from liability to pay damages and the plaintiff will be restricted to injunctive relief. An innocent infringer must establish that he was unaware of the existence of the copyright and had no reasonable ground for suspecting that copyright subsisted in the work.[264] Israeli courts, however, interpret this exemption narrowly.

Jurisdictional and international issues
There is very little case law on conflict of laws and jurisdiction in Israeli copyright law. Although copyright is considered a property right under Israeli law, copyright infringement is a tort. Accordingly, to establish a legal claim under Israeli law it would be necessary for the alleged infringement to take place in Israel.   **6–240**

As noted above, the Supreme Court held in the *Eisenman v. Qimron* appeal that mail order distribution of three books from abroad constituted infringement in Israel. Moreover, because the Supreme Court determined that an infringement had occurred in Israel, it did not overrule the District Court's decision that the defendant was liable for copyright infringement even though that court had determined that the infringements had occurred in the US. The District Court had decided that U.S. copyright law governed the dispute, but applied Israeli law under the doctrine of equivalence, whereby Israeli copyright law and American copyright law are considered equivalent for the purpose of using the law of the jurisdiction where the case is being heard.[265] Both the District Court and the Supreme Court decisions have been subject to considerable academic criticism. Nonetheless, they are highly pertinent to any current discussion regarding the possible outcomes of an Internet copyright dispute.

6.11.6 Trade marks

6–241   Registered trade marks are protected in Israel under the Trademarks Ordinance. The proprietor of a registered trade mark has the exclusive right to use the trade mark "upon, and in every matter relating to, the goods in respect of which it is registered."[266]

Every unauthorised use (excluding parallel importation) in Israel may constitute trade mark infringement. Additionally, the plaintiff in a trademark infringement matter does not have to prove that the defendant intended to cause confusion.[267] For example, a Web site proprietor using a trade name or trademark, in order to either sell or promote its goods or services in Israel, and to the world in general, may be liable to the proprietor of the same or similar trademark or trade name that is registered in Israel with respect to those goods or services.

6–242   The Israel Trademark Ordinance has been amended[268] recently to reflect Israel's obligations under the Agreement on Trade-Related Aspects of Intellectual Property Rights Including Trade in Counterfeit Goods, commonly known as TRIPS.[269] The recent amendment extended the Trademark Ordinance protection in Israel to expressly address infringement of "well-known" or "famous" marks.

The amendment defines infringement of a well-known mark as use of an identical or similar mark in a manner that may be confused with the goods to which the well-known mark refers or with goods of a similar type.[270] The amendment distinguishes between the scope of protection afforded to a well-known mark that is registered in Israel and to those that are not registered in Israel. The owner of a well-known mark that is **not registered** in Israel is entitled to the exclusive right to use the mark in conjunction with goods for which the mark is well known, or goods of the same description. However, the rights afforded the owner of a well-known **registered** mark in Israel now extend to use of the mark in conjunction with non-identical goods, provided that use of the mark by an unauthorized third party is likely to create an association with the goods sold under the well-known registered mark and that the proprietor of the registered mark is likely to be injured as a result of such use.

6–243   Unregistered trade marks, trade names and trade dress are protected under a number of other statutes.[271] These statutes, which provide causes of action for passing off, unjust enrichment and trespass on incorporeal property respectively, may be available even where a Web site proprietor is using the trademark or trade name in connection with different goods or services. However, the existence of confusion or damage to the owner of the unregistered mark, the notoriety of the mark, and a lack of good faith by the alleged infringer, are generally required by the court in order to protect such unregistered marks in these cases. Notwithstanding the foregoing, use of a trademark on a Web site by a genuine trademark owner in another country is likely to be allowed.

In view of the above, it may be inferred that the amendment to the Israel Trademark Ordinance may be used in relation to cyber squatting claims, however there is no case law to date.[272]

6.11.7 Web site notices

Notices specifying territorial limitations
There is no Israeli case law regarding the legal effect of notices purporting to limit liability of the Web site proprietor in one way or another. Under contract law, a notice stating that the site is not intended for reading in Israel may be viewed as an offer attempting to subject the end-user to a contractual relationship. The offer will bind the end-user only upon acceptance. The notice itself may then be treated as an attempted disclaimer.

It is more difficult to establish the validity of a disclaimer in Israel than in most common law countries. As a matter of public policy, contract law severely restricts the validity of disclaimers.[273] Indeed, it is unlikely that use of a notice alone, which does not form part of a contract between the Web site proprietor and a user, will limit the Web site proprietor's liability in any area of law.

6–244

Enforcement of notices through restricted access
A Web site proprietor might combine the use of a notice on its Web site with technical measures to prevent Israeli end-users from accessing the material on the site. On this basis (if at all practical), the Web site proprietor may be able to avoid liability for incorrect information published on the site, both under torts and consumer protection legislation. It can demonstrate that it is taking steps to perform its duty of care towards Israeli end-users. A similar strategy may also assist a Web site proprietor in avoiding liability for trade mark infringement on the ground that it is not trading (or even advertising) under the mark in Israel.[274]

6–245

6.12 Japan

6.12.1 General

In an infringement case involving international elements many legal points have to be considered under the conflicts law of Japan. First, whether or not the Japanese court can hear the case should be considered under the heading of "Judicial jurisdiction". Once the court has decided that it can hear the case, the next problem is "the choice of law". In the intellectual property field, we also have to take into account the nature of intellectual property that the right is protected within the territory of the country where the protection is claimed.

6–246

6.12.2 Judicial jurisdiction

If a harmful event takes place which has some international elements, can the Japanese court hear the case?

6–247

This has to be considered as a problem of "judicial jurisdiction". It is said that state jurisdiction consists of legislative jurisdiction, judicial jurisdiction and enforcement jurisdiction. Usually judicial jurisdiction is called simply "jurisdiction" in Japan. There is no distinction between *in personam, in rem* and *quasi in rem* actions in Japan. Therefore the only question to be considered is whether the Japanese court has jurisdiction over the case or not.

6–248   The leading case on jurisdiction is the *Malaysia Air Lines* case (Supreme Court, Showa56 (1981) October 16 Minshu 35, Vol. 7, p. 1224). In 1977, a Malaysia Air Lines aircraft crashed on the way from Penang to Kuala Lumpur. All the passengers died. The family of one of the victims who was Japanese commenced litigation against Malaysia Air Lines at Nagoya District Court. Malaysia Air Lines had a business branch in Tokyo. However, the passenger bought his ticket for the plane in Malaysia. The Supreme Court said about international judicial jurisdiction:

> "It is reasonable to decide according to fairness to the parties and the ideal of fairness and early resolution of the judicial procedure. Reviewing the articles of domestic jurisdiction, when one of the elements, eg domicile of the defendant (Article 2 of the Civil Procedure Law (CPL)), the place where duty should be done (Article 5 of CPL), the place of the property of the defendant (Article 8 of CPL), the place of the tort (Article 15 of CPL) or the other [sic] which are described regarding the venue exists in Japan, it is reasonable that the defendant should be submitted under the judicial jurisdiction of our country."

In that case, as a branch of the defendant existed in Japan, jurisdiction was found.

6–249   After this judgment, lower courts have shown more flexible solutions. According to some judgments, in some exceptional situations, the court has a discretion to dismiss the case because of lack of jurisdiction. An example is the *Taiwan Ento Air Lines* case (Tokyo District Court, Showa61 (1986) June 20 Hanrei Jiho Vol 1196, 87). The court dismissed the case on the basis that it was an "exceptional situation". The situations which the court mentioned are as follows. Regarding the evidence: "There is no official relationship between Taiwan and our country. We cannot use this evidence by the way of international co-operation".[275] Therefore, "it can be said that it is very difficult for our court to do justice based on the evidence." According to the expert examiner, the Taiwan court had jurisdiction over the case. The plaintiff alleged that he could not afford to proceed in Taiwan. But the court did not accept this assertion.

After this judgment, lower courts have shown more flexible solutions. If the proprietor of a Web site lives in Japan or has a branch in Japan, then Japanese courts will have the jurisdiction over the case which is generally based on "domicile of the defendant". If the proprietor of the Web site has property in Japan, then the Japanese court would admit jurisdiction over the defendant.

6–250   In the case of a harmful event having a connection with Japan, the matter will be considered as a tort case. In a tort case, it is said that if the "place of tort" is in Japan, the Japanese court will have judicial jurisdiction. The "place of tort" is construed to include not only "the place of harmful activity" but also "the place in which the result occurred". However, it is severely disputed whether such "result" should be limited to direct or physical harm or not. The Japanese courts have not made a definite decision about this issue. The majority opinion is that harm is not limited to direct result.

In any event, in cases concerning trade mark and copyright infringement, reliance on content and defamation, where the person is suffering from the harmful activity and lives in Japan, it is likely that that would be recognised as the direct result of the harmful activity. In that case the Japanese court should hear the case filed by such a person generally as long as there is no exceptional circumstance.

6.12.3 Choice of law

General

If the court has judicial jurisdiction, we move into the stage of "choice of law". At this stage, we first have to decide the "nature of the problem". If the problem is recognised as one of procedure, the law of the place of the court is applied. If the problem is a substantive problem, it is governed by the choice of the law provided by the conflicts of laws rules of Japan.   **6–251**

If the problem is recognised as a substantive problem, distinctions should be made between contract, tort, property and so on. For example, if the case is recognised as property, the law of the location of the property is applied. If the problem is recognised as a problem of tort, the law of the "place of the tort" is applied. But there are many disputes about where the "place of the tort" is.

If the problem is recognised as infringement of intellectual property, the territorial nature of intellectual property influences the choice of law. There are some disputes about this. But the majority opinion recognises that there is no need to confront the problem of "choice of law" in the case of intellectual property.

Tort

Questions of defamation and liability for reliance on content would be discussed as problems of tort under the conflicts of laws of Japan.   **6–252**

To the problem of the tort, Horei (law concerning the application of laws in general) is applied. According to article 11, section 1 of Horei, the laws of where the facts of the cause of action occur are applied to the existence and the effect of the tort.

Section 2 of article 11 tries to balance the law of the place of tort and law of the court. According to section 2, when the facts would not be illegal if they happened in Japan, section 1 does not apply to the event. Section 3 of article 11 limits the nature of relief. According to the section, a person who suffers from harmful action can request the nature of relief which is admitted in Japan.

The biggest problem is establishing where the "place of the tort" is. Article 11 uses the words "facts of the cause of action," but it is still ambiguous. There is no definite judgment about this problem. Many scholars have debated this. Opinion about this problem is divided into the following five categories: (a) place of action, (b) place of result, (c) place of right, (d) cumulative application, and (e) balancing approach.   **6–253**

The "balancing approach" is probably the majority opinion about this problem. The point of the approach is to make a distinction between actions which have an unethical nature, *e.g.* battery, traffic accident, defamation etc and events which have a weak unethical nature, *e.g.* public nuisance. In the latter case, the law of the place of result should be applied because the suffering person should be relieved. On the other hand, the place of the action should be applied to actions of an unethical nature.

The damaged person can file a suit in Japan as long as he proves he has suffered substantial damage. Once the court decides there is jurisdiction over the case, the court may apply the law of the place of action.   **6–254**

In a defamation case, it is possible that if the court applied the law of the domicile of the wrongdoer, compensatory damage would be ordered. An injunction against an overseas Web site proprietor would be a problem. In Japan, it is not necessary that the defamatory statement is regarded as being published in Japan to found a tort action.

As for reliance on incorrect information, in Japan content liability rules are little developed. But comments similar to those about defamation can be applied to this problem.

Intellectual property

6–255   When it appears that copyright is infringed by international action, what law is applied? In the majority opinion, the law of the country in which the protection would be claimed is applied (article 5 of the Berne Convention).

However, the extra-territorial application of the Japanese Copyright Law is ambiguous. If Disney video tapes are about to be imported from the USA, the copyright law of Japan is claimed to protect Disney's right and the court will order the injunction of the import. No one doubts that Japanese laws will protect the intellectual property in such a case. However, when the infringing activity occurs abroad but the harm results in Japan, it is difficult to know whether the Japanese Copyright Law applies.

6–256   First, if the copyright law of Japan is applied to the action of the infringer the Copyright Law of Japan admits a right of wire transmission in art 23 which states: "The author shall have the exclusive rights to broadcast and to transmit by wire his work". Therefore the protection of the author's right is clear.

Next, whether the Copyright Law of Japan can be applied or not is unclear. This is a problem of legislative jurisdiction. It is recognised in Japan that temporary loading into RAM or viewing a work on the screen are not infringements of copyright. However, if the question of infringement were to depend on whether the infringement affected the Japanese market, then there could be infringement of Japanese copyright.

6.12.4 Cases

Some cases show that consideration of choice of law can affect judicial jurisdiction.

6–257   A case decided by Tokyo district court on January 28, 1999 concerned jurisdiction over a copyright claim. The plaintiff was a company located in Japan, whose business was to produce movie films and television films. The defendant was a natural person living in Thailand. The plaintiff filed a suit in Tokyo district court on following causes of actions, following which the plaintiff filed a suit in Thailand.

The causes of action were:

(a)   based on copyright

(1)   to request court to declare that the contract was void as regards the defendant being exclusive licensee in the countries other than Japan.

(2)   to request court to declare that the plaintiff was the legitimate holder of the copyright in the work in Thailand.

(3)   to request court to declare that the defendant had no licence in the work.

(b)   based on the unfair competition prevention law

(4)   an injunction against defendant to insist that the plaintiff had the exclusive right in countries other than Japan.

    (c)   Tort

        (5)   compensation damage for 10,000,000 Yen.

The court denied jurisdiction based on the following reasons;   **6–258**

    (1)   The main issue was whether the defendant had the exclusive right or not in countries other than Japan.

    (2)   The plaintiff's legal agent in Hong Kong sent letters from Hong Kong to Hong Kong, Bangkok and the branch offices located in East Asia. The court said that the main activities occurred outside Japan.

    (3)   Even if the work was authored in Japan, the laws of the countries where the work was exploited were disputed. The court could not say that the right is located in Japan.

    (4)   The defendant was a natural person and had no business base in Japan. Therefore, if the court admitted jurisdiction in Japan, it would be a serious burden for the defendant.

Two defamation cases are also of interest. The first was a Tokyo district court case decided on   **6–259** August 28, 1989. The publisher of a magazine filed a suit which requested court to declare that the magazine did not harm the defendant, who was a Japanese living in California. The Japanese court declined jurisdiction because the defendant insisted that the magazine issued in Japan was not itself the tort, but that the distribution in California was a tort.

    The second was a Tokyo district court case decided on September 30, 1992. The plaintiff was a Japanese horse jockey who was successful in Malaysia and Singapore. He filed a suit complaining that newspaper companies had defamed him. The court admitted the defamation and ordered the defendants to pay the damage for 3,000,000 Yen. Whether the compensation damage was limited merely to Japan or not was not disputed in the judgement. The judge found that the plaintiff had a hope to be successful all over the world including Japan, Malaysia and Singapore.

6.12.5 Territory notices

As mentioned above, the contents of Web pages may infringe someone else's right in the   **6–260** other country. In Japan, some people advise that the site should contain a notice that it is intended for specified countries. There is no definite discussion on the effectiveness of the notices. But in intellectual property litigation, not only is the existence of illegality important but the degree of infringement is also important. Such notices may weaken the degree of infringement.

6.13 The Netherlands

6.13.1 Jurisdiction

In the case of a "foreign" Web site (*i.e.* a Web site whose proprietor and host computer   **6–261** are not located in The Netherlands) which can be accessed from The Netherlands, Dutch courts can assume jurisdiction over disputes about the contents of such Web site where the plaintiff or one or more of the defendants is domiciled in The Netherlands or where it could be argued that the unlawful or harmful event was committed in The Netherlands.

Under almost all circumstances, even if the harmful event took place outside The Netherlands, Dutch courts can hear the case, in which case Dutch courts can assume jurisdiction based on the Brussels or Lugano Convention or on Article 126 of the Dutch Code of Civil Procedure.

If one or more of the defendants is domiciled in The Netherlands, jurisdiction of Dutch courts can be based on Article 2 and 6(1) of the Brussels or Lugano Convention and Article 126(1) and (7) of the Dutch Code of Civil Procedure.

If the defendants are not domiciled in The Netherlands and if the Brussels or Lugano Convention is *not* applicable, Dutch courts can still assume jurisdiction if the plaintiff is domiciled in The Netherlands pursuant to Article 126(3) of the Dutch Code of Civil Procedure.

6–262   It should be noted, in this respect, that *forum non conveniens* arguments may generally not be taken into consideration with regard to the jurisdiction question in the Netherlands. More specifically, Dutch courts may generally not refuse to hear a case based on the argument that the case is not sufficiently connected to the Dutch legal sphere, such as where the harmful event took place outside The Netherlands. This implies that Dutch courts have a very limited possibility of retaining discretion whether or not to assume jurisdiction.

If the plaintiff and the defendant are *not* domiciled in The Netherlands and if the Brussels or Lugano Convention *is* applicable, jurisdiction cannot be based on Article 126(3) of the Dutch Code of Civil Procedure. In that case, jurisdiction must be based on the argument that the unlawful or harmful event was committed in The Netherlands.

6–263   In this respect, Dutch courts may rely on the *Fiona Shevill v. Presse Alliance SA*.[276] In this case, which was decided under the Brussels Convention, a libellous newspaper article had been distributed in several different countries where the plaintiff had a reputation. Jurisdiction in this case was based on Article 5(3) of the Brussels Convention, which provides that in matters relating to tort (and infringement of intellectual property rights) the defendant may be sued in the Court for the place where the harmful event, such as the tortious and/or infringing activity, occurred.

The ECJ had provided a choice of forum in its interpretation of Article 5(3) in its judgment in *Bier v. Mines de Potasse d'Alsace*[277] where the ECJ held that the "place where the harmful event occurred" in Article 5(3) was to be interpreted so as to give the plaintiff an option to initiate proceedings *either* at the place where the *damage* is incurred *or* the place where the *harmful event* giving rise to such damage occurred.

6–264   In the case of "international" infringements of intellectual property rights or "international" tortious acts, such as the publication of libellous information on the Internet, this would give the plaintiff a choice between the forum of the place where the infringing or tortious activity took place or the forum where the damage was incurred.

In the *Fiona Shevill v. Presse Alliance SA* Decision, the ECJ gave the following explanation of Article 5(3) of the Brussels Convention:

"(a) The Courts of each Contracting State where the article was distributed could rule on the injury caused *in that State* to the victim's reputation.

(b) Although there are disadvantages to different Courts ruling on various aspects of the same matter, the plaintiff always has the option of bringing his *entire (cross-border) claim* before the Courts of the defendant's domicile."

This is especially relevant to The Netherlands, now that Dutch courts can actually issue far reaching cross-border relief based on the ruling in the landmark decision of the Dutch Supreme Court of November 24, 1989 in *Interlas v. Lincoln*.[278]

After the *Fiona Shevill v. Presse Alliance SA* Decision of the ECJ, it is clear that Dutch courts cannot issue cross-border relief, if their jurisdiction is based on Article 5(3) of the Brussels or Lugano Convention.

It is generally assumed in The Netherlands that the *Fiona Shevill v. Presse Alliance SA* **6–265** Decision of the ECJ is especially relevant for Internet publications. It is argued that the publication of information on a Web site should be considered a publication of libellous information in different jurisdictions, just like the libellous newspaper article in the *Fiona Shevill v. Presse Alliance* case.

In this respect, a defamatory statement on a "foreign" Web site which can be accessed from the Netherlands, may be regarded as having been published in The Netherlands as well. Someone in The Netherlands who relied upon incorrect information on the Web site, and who suffered harm as a result, could therefore successfully claim that the information was also *published* in The Netherlands and that the harmful event took place in The Netherlands also.

This would not be different in the case of a Web site containing notices stating that the **6–266** site is intended for reading only in specified countries outside The Netherlands. The key issue is whether the Web site is accessible from The Netherlands without any special procedures.

If the Web site can be accessed from The Netherlands, then Dutch courts will most likely hold that the harmful event took place in The Netherlands also, notwithstanding any notices on the Web site stating that the site is not intended for reading in The Netherlands.

6.13.2 Applicable law

Copyright

For copyright matters, Article 5.2 of the Berne Convention and Article 47 of the Dutch **6–267** Copyrights Act (Nederlandse Auteurswet 1912) provide that the Dutch Copyrights Act is applicable to infringement matters relating to the publication of copyrighted works in The Netherlands.

As indicated before, Dutch courts will most likely hold that the publication of copyrighted material on the Internet implies that such copyrighted material is *also* published in The Netherlands, and Dutch courts will therefore most likely apply the Dutch Copyrights Act, if the Web site can be accessed from The Netherlands. It should be noted, however, that there is an ongoing debate in The Netherlands as to whether copyrighted material on the Internet is actually "published" in all countries where the copyrighted material can be accessed in the sense of the Berne Convention and Article 47 of the Dutch Copyrights Act.[279]

Tort

With regard to the law of torts, Dutch courts will apply the basic *lex loci delicti* rule, **6–268** implying that Dutch courts apply the law of the country where the tortious act took place.

In its Green Paper on Copyright and Related Rights in the Information Society, the European Commission indicated that on matters relating to the publication of tortious information on the Internet, the law of the "country of origin" must be applied. This point of view has been criticised in The Netherlands. In The Netherlands, it is argued that in Internet matters, the *lex loci delicti* rule should be applied and interpreted broadly. In this respect, it is argued that the tortious act also took place where the tortious information can be accessed on the Internet. This would mean that tortious information originating from outside The Netherlands, which can be accessed from The Netherlands, must be deemed to be a tortious act that took place in The Netherlands *also*, so that Dutch law must be applied.

6–269   This criterion has been applied by the U.S. District Court for the Southern District of New York of June 19, 1996 in *Playboy Enterprises Inc. v. Chuckleberry Publishing Inc. (Playboy/Playmen)*. In this judgment, the District Court held that U.S. law could be applied to tortious information originating from Italy (the use of the trade mark Playmen infringing the registered trade mark rights of Playboy Enterprises Inc), which can be accessed from the U.S.

It should be noted that the Commission issued a Follow Up Communication to the Green Paper on 20 November 1996. This indicated that rather than harmonise the law applicable to transnational acts of exploitation under the one 'country of origin' rule, the Commission is now considering issuing a clarifying Communication addressing applicable law issues and enforcement.

Trade marks

6–270   In trade mark matters, Dutch courts will usually apply the Uniform Benelux Trademarks Act to the use of trade marks on "foreign" Web sites which can be accessed from The Netherlands.

6.13.3 Copyright

6–271   If a Web site contains a copy of someone else's original work, there could be an infringement of copyright in The Netherlands whenever the copyrighted work is viewed on screen or whenever there is a transient copy in the RAM of the users' computer.

It could certainly be argued under the Dutch Copyrights Act (Nederlandse Auteurswet 1912) that any electronic copying such as viewing a copyrighted work on screen or holding a transient copy in the RAM of the user's computer, falls within the reproduction right of the copyright holder.

In this respect, it should be noted that Article 4(A) of the European Software Directive of May 17, 1991 and Articles 5(B) and 7(2)(A) of the European Database Directive of March 11, 1996 specifically refer to "temporary reproduction".

6–272   Moreover, Article 4(A) of the European Software Directive gives a very broad interpretation of the reproduction right, providing that the acts protected under the reproduction right include:

> "the permanent or temporary reproduction of a computer program by any means and in any form, in part or in whole. Insofar as loading, displaying, running, transmission or storage of the computer program necessitates such reproduction, such acts shall be subject to authorisation of the right-holder."

Article 4(A) of the European Software Directive was implemented in The Netherlands on July 19, 1994.

Article 45(I) of the Dutch Copyrights Act now provides that the reproduction of a copyrighted work includes the "loading, displaying, running, transmitting or storing of the computer program, inasmuch as such acts necessitate the reproduction of the copyrighted work".

Article 4(A) of the European Software Directive and Article 45(I) of the Dutch Copyrights Act do not guarantee an exclusive right of loading, displaying or running the protected computer program. These acts are only protected under the reproduction right inasmuch as these acts 'necessitate reproduction'. This leaves a certain latitude to Dutch courts in determining the scope of the notion of 'reproduction'.

Nevertheless, although the Dutch Copyrights Act does not contain a clear and unambiguous provision such as section 17(6) of the U.K. Copyright, Designs and Patents Act, it is generally assumed that holding a transient copy in the RAM of the user's computer constitutes a 'reproduction' of someone else's copyrighted work.

Moreover, viewing a copy of the copyrighted work on screen, such as displaying an electronically delivered document on a user terminal, implies that the document is temporarily stored in the RAM of the user's computer and therefore such screen display may be considered a "reproduction" of the copyrighted work as well.

6–273

It should be noted that the question whether or not screen display amounts to a reproduction of the work displayed, is under severe criticism in The Netherlands. It is argued that qualifying screen display as reproduction would be overstretching the reproduction right and extending the reproduction right to a use right.

Nevertheless, to date Dutch courts will most likely hold that viewing a copyrighted work on screen or holding a transient copy in the RAM of a user's computer constitutes a "reproduction" of the copyrighted work and therefore copyright infringement.

6.13.4 Trade mark/trade name in a Web site

If a Web site contains a trading name which conflicts with a registered trade mark in The Netherlands, such use of this trading name on the Web site would constitute a trade mark infringement under Dutch law, more specifically the Uniform Benelux Trademarks Act.

6–274

In fact, Dutch courts have recently rendered judgments in matters relating to trade mark infringement on the Internet.

In its judgment of June 3, 1996 in *Re Flevonet*,[280] the President of the District Court of Zwolle held that the trade name Flevonet of the defendant infringed the trade name Flevonet of the plaintiff and issued an injunction enjoining the defendant from using the trade name Flevonet, including the use of the trade name Flevonet for the domain name 'Flevonet.nl'.

In its judgment of August 29, 1996 in *Re X LINK/XX LINK*,[281] the President of the District Court of Amsterdam held that the trade name/trade mark XX LINK of the Web presence provider XX LINK IS does not infringe the trade mark rights of the German access provider NTG Netzwerk und Telematik GMBH on the registered Benelux Trademark X LINK, now that the services provided by XX LINK IS and NTG are quite distinct and now that there will therefore be no likelihood of association between the trade mark X LINK and the trading name XX LINK. The judgment has recently been affirmed on appeal.

6–275

In *Ouders van Nu/Ouders Online*,[282] it was held that the Benelux trademark OUDERS ONLINE (Parents Online) registered for an electronic magazine published on the Internet and the domain name Ouders.nl (Parents.nl) did not infringe the Benelux trademark OUDERS VAN NU (Parents of Today) registered for a "traditional" magazine. The reason therefore was that the distinctive character of OUDERS VAN NU was considered to be limited, since it was basically the same as its target group, whereas the additions ''online'' and ''.nl'' sufficiently stressed that the defendants trademark and domain name related to another media. No likelihood of association was therefore established. Decision affirmed on appeal.

6–276   In *Labouchere v. IMG Holland*[283] it was held that IMG Holland's registration and use of the domain names Labouchere.com, SNS Bank.com, Delta Lloyd.com and so on infringed the trademarks and trade names of the corresponding financial institutions. IMG Holland was prevented from using these domain names and ordered to immediately ''re-route'' the infringing domain names to the .nl domain names of the financial institutions. In the mean time, IMG Holland was ordered to arrange for assignment of its .com domain names to the relevant financial institutions.

In first instance of *Passies/Gaos*[284] it was held that the mere registration of the domain name www.passies.com did not amount to the use of an identical or corresponding trademark. On appeal however (Amsterdam Appeal Court December 7, 2000, IER 2001, 10), the Court reversed this aspect of the first instance decision, by stipulating that the mere possibility of use or the possibility to sell the domain name concerned did constitute such use. Since the Court, just like the President, considered that Gaos did have far less interest in the domain name concerned than Passies, the transfer thereof to Passies was ordered.

However, in *Ministers. NL*[285] the Court again held that the mere registration of a domain name does not amount to use of a trademark/trademark infringement.

6.14 New Zealand

6.14.1 Defamation

6–277   Under New Zealand law, defamation occurs upon the publication, to one or more people, of an untrue imputation against the reputation of another. The reputations of trading organisations can also be injured. A body corporate may sue for defamation in New Zealand but, if it is to succeed, it must prove that the publication has caused, or is likely to cause, pecuniary loss.

The legal position in New Zealand concerning defamation on the Internet can be understood by considering the existing law of defamation and how it is likely to be applied, extended or modified to cope with new issues arising from electronic publication. At the time of publication, the Palmerston North District Court is considering New Zealand's first Internet defamation case. Former CEO of Domainz, Patrick O'Brien, was alleged to have been defamed by the ISOCNZ member Alan Brown during a series of emails sent to approximately 170 ISOCNZ members but could also be read on the Internet using any search engine and had been read by O'Brien's friends and colleagues.

It is likely that publication of a statement on the Internet will amount to publication for the purposes of the law of defamation. It has been held in the New Zealand High Court that a statement in the media or otherwise directing readers to a defamatory statement at a particular website might itself amount to publication of the defamation.[286] However, an important issue arises over whether an ISP can be liable for the publication of defamatory material.

6–278   Traditionally, anyone who has had a role in publishing defamatory material may be liable. There are various ways in which material may be published on the Internet and all of the parties who take part in the process of publication of defamatory material on the Internet theoretically face potential liability. In practice, however, there will often be a defence available to those who are only secondarily involved as processors and distributors where they have innocently distributed defamatory material.

Under section 21 of the Defamation Act 1992, the defence of innocent dissemination is available to any person who has published defamatory material solely in the capacity of a processor or distributor, or employee or agent of a processor or distributor. In order to make out the defence, the processor or distributor must have been unaware that the relevant information contained or was likely to contain defamatory material.

In New Zealand, the section 21 defence of innocent dissemination applies only to a "processor" or a "distributor". "Distributor" is not exhaustively defined (it is only defined as including booksellers and librarians). "Processor" is defined in the Act as meaning "a person who prints or reproduces, or plays a role in printing or reproducing, any matter".

In order for a host or owner of a bulletin board or network to be entitled to rely on this defence in New Zealand, it will need to show that it is a "processor" or "distributor" and establish the requisite lack of knowledge and negligence. It is not immediately clear that a host or owner of a bulletin board or network will fall within either of these definitions, although such a defence ought to apply where they have acted merely as an innocent conduit for defamatory material.   **6–279**

A party outside New Zealand may be sued in New Zealand for publication of defamatory material within New Zealand.[287] Likewise, a foreign plaintiff cannot be stopped from suing in New Zealand in relation to a publication occurring abroad, provided that the conduct is actionable both here and in the place where it occurred.[288] However, in order to sue in New Zealand, it is necessary for the plaintiff to show damage to his or her reputation *in* New Zealand. Proceedings issued in New Zealand need to be served on the defendant overseas.

The New Zealand Law Commission, in its report, *Electronic Commerce Part Two, A Basic Legal Framework* recommended that the Defamation Act 1992 be amended to include ISPs in the definition of "distributor" so as to limit the liability of ISPs where they have acted merely as an innocent conduit for defamatory material. These proposed changes have not been implemented at the time of writing.

6.14.2 Content Liability

There is no New Zealand authority to date relating to reliance on incorrect information placed on a Web site causing loss or damage. However, it is likely that New Zealand's consumer protection legislation will apply to activities undertaken through the Internet.   **6–280**

The Fair Trading Act 1996 regulates conduct by persons in trade in New Zealand, including representations made about products or services. The purpose of the Fair Trading Act is, among other things, to protect persons who deal with businesses that engage in deceptive or misleading conduct. The Fair Trading Act prohibits conduct in trade that is, or is likely to be, misleading or deceptive; it also prohibits making various false and misleading representations in trade.

The Fair Trading Act's provisions are capable of extending to activities undertaken overseas through the Internet. Section 3 of the Fair Trading Act states: **6–281**

"[The Fair Trading] Act extends to the engaging in conduct outside New Zealand by any person resident or carrying on business in New Zealand to the extent that such conduct relates to the supply of goods or services, or the granting of interests in land, within New Zealand."

It is not settled whether a person who sells goods or services on the Internet to New Zealanders is "carrying on business in New Zealand". Arguably, however, a person who is not physically present in New Zealand, but who advertises in New Zealand through the Internet and delivers goods and services to New Zealand, does in ordinary usage "carry on business in New Zealand". Misleading information relating to those goods and services could be classified as "conduct relating to the supply of goods or services within New Zealand".[289]

6–282   The Fair Trading Act imposes both criminal and civil liability. It is not possible contractually to exclude the liability that a person may face for breaches of the Fair Trading Act.[290] A New Zealand Court may therefore apply the Fair Trading Act notwithstanding any disclaimers or disclosures incorporated into, or any express choice of foreign law governing, a Web site.

The Consumer Guarantees Act 1993 deems certain guarantees to be given where goods or services are supplied to a consumer and provides rights of redress against suppliers, manufacturers and others in respect of any failure of goods or services to comply with those guarantees.

The Consumer Guarantees Act provides that a consumer is a person who acquires from a supplier goods or services of a kind ordinarily acquired for personal, domestic or household use or consumption. The Consumer Guarantees Act is therefore likely to apply to goods or services supplied through the Internet, unless the particular securities or services are not of a kind ordinarily acquired for personal, domestic or household use or consumption.

6–283   There are limited rights to contract out of the Consumer Guarantees Act. A New Zealand Court is likely to apply the Consumer Guarantees Act notwithstanding any disclaimers incorporated into, or any express choice of foreign law governing, a Web site unless the disclaimers comply with the limited statutory rights to contract out.

It is not settled in New Zealand whether a Web site proprietor owes a duty of care, actionable in negligence if there is a breach, in relation to the provision of inaccurate or misleading information over the Internet. Parties to a contract may agree that, if a duty of care exists between them, the liability of one party to the other may be limited by agreement. In principle, therefore, where the Web site proprietor expressly disclaims liability in the Web site, it should be difficult successfully to sue the proprietor in negligence.

6.14.3 Copyright Infringement

6–284   The Copyright Act 1994 offers protection for original works including literary, dramatic, musical or artistic works; sound recordings; films; broadcasts; and cable programmes. The works are broadly defined, with computer programs included in the definition of literary work. Copyright does not require registration and will effectively exist from the time the work is recorded, whether this is in writing or otherwise.

Once copyright exists, the owner has exclusive right in New Zealand to copy the work, issue copies of the work to the public, broadcast the work or make an adaptation of the work.

Many things, which reside on the Internet, could fall within the types of work protected by copyright. The requirement that they be recorded in writing or otherwise could be met by their residing on the Internet. As a result, pictures, articles and layouts of home pages are likely to be afforded copyright protection as literary or artistic works (provided that they are also original and of some substance).

Material on a website can also be a cable programme service. The definition of cable programme service is essentially a service for transmission of images, sound or other information for reception at two or more places, either simultaneously or at different times, in response to requests by different users.   **6–285**

As a restricted act is an act the owner of copyright has an exclusive right to do in New Zealand, the High Court of New Zealand will only be able to assume jurisdiction if the particular restricted act takes place in New Zealand.

It is unlikely that copyright would reside in an Internet address, since small combinations of words are not generally regarded as literary works. For example, earlier cases have held that titles such as "Opportunity Knocks" are either not substantial enough or not sufficiently original to qualify as a copyright work.[291]

The uploading of the whole or a substantial part of a copyright work on to a Web site in New Zealand will constitute infringement. However the uploading of that work on to a Web site overseas will not, and the High Court is unlikely to hear a claim in that situation.   **6–286**

However if the uploaded work appears on the overseas Web site, and the Web site is accessible by a computer in New Zealand, the High Court would likely assume jurisdiction.

When a person views a website, a copy of what is viewed is downloaded onto the viewer's computer's RAM. Therefore, it is arguable that viewing this material without permission for possible later use breaches the Copyright Act in New Zealand (unless any of the fair dealing exceptions apply). It is, however, equally as arguable that there is an implied licence to make such "copies", as the making of a copy in viewing or holding a transient copy is a necessary part of operating on the Internet. To resolve this dispute, it may be necessary for the industry and legislature to formalise acceptance.

On the other hand, the copying of a New Zealand copyright work by viewing it on, or downloading it from, an overseas computer would be outside the scope of the Copyright Act, and not an infringing act in New Zealand.

The question of copyright infringement becomes complicated in relation to hyper-linking.   **6–287**

If an overseas Web site accessible in New Zealand has a hyper-link to the copyright work on a New Zealand based site, and that link is unwanted by or undesirable to the copyright owner, the copyright owner may have a cause of action in New Zealand.

If the hyper-link involves the inclusion of a "cable programme" (being the work) in a "cable programme service" provided by the hyper-linker, this also may infringe copyright. Infringement may be found if the hyper-linking is "embedded" and shortcuts the copyright owner's home page or results in the "framing" of the copyright owner's web page.

As the law in this area develops, copyright owners may find they will not be able to prevent hyper-linking under the Copyright Act, except the more blatant forms that justify a finding of infringement such as embedded links and framing.   **6–288**

Some hyper-linking simply will not amount to an infringing act in breach of the Copyright Act. Further, it may be held in many situations that third parties have an implied licence to link to another Web site (unless the copyright owner expressly prohibits linking). This may be claimed due to the fact that hyper-linking is arguably an integral part of the Internet and has generally been an accepted commercial practice.

6.14.4 Trade Mark Infringement

6–289   It seems clear that the well established principles relating to infringement embodied in the Trade Marks Act 1953 can be comfortably applied to unauthorised use of marks on the Internet, particularly where that use is to advertise and offer goods for sale or to promote and provide certain services.

Infringing activity will, however, require conduct by the infringing party directed at New Zealand Internet users. In other words, use of an infringing mark on an overseas registered or hosted web site, in relation to a product or service, should be directed towards New Zealanders when they access the site, and be likely to cause harm in New Zealand.

6–290   This was the approach adopted by the High Court in the *New Zealand Post* decision.[292] This case involved the U.S.registered domain name "nzpost.com" and the defendant's web site using that domain name.

The *New Zealand Post* case was an interlocutory decision and an injunction was granted on the basis of there being an arguable case of passing off and breach of the Fair Trading Act, with the balance of convenience favouring the plaintiff. The plaintiff could not claim trade mark infringement, as its NZ POST trade mark was not registered in New Zealand. Further, the defendant later consented to a permanent injunction and transfer of the domain name to the plaintiff, so the substantive issues were not taken to trial.

Under the Trade Marks Act, the owner of a registered trade mark has the exclusive right to use the trade mark in relation to the goods or services for which it is registered. The Act only applies to trade marks registered in New Zealand, so this exclusive right is limited to New Zealand.

The exclusive right shall be deemed to be infringed by use by another person of a "sign" (*i.e.* a trade mark), which is identical or confusingly similar to the trade mark, on or in relation to the goods or services for which the trade mark is registered or "similar" goods or services.

6–291   That use by another person would have to take place in New Zealand for the High Court to hear claims of infringement. This issue of jurisdiction was contemplated by the court in the *New Zealand Post* case.

The court in the *New Zealand Post* case held that it had jurisdiction to hear the passing off and unfair trading claims, as the nature of the medium (the Internet) in which the conduct complained of occurs does not alter the nature of the conduct and can still amount to passing off; that despite the defendant's "nzpost.com" domain name being attached to a U.S. host computer, the conduct was directed at New Zealand (as New Zealanders could access the U.S.-based site); and that there was a real likelihood of confusion occurring resulting in harm to New Zealand Post.

Another case in which jurisdiction was considered was *Hirepool Auckland Limited v. Uren*.[293] Here, the plaintiff was successful in obtaining an interim injunction restraining the defendant from using the word "Hirepool" or the domain name "hirepool.com". The court held that, although it was not clear that the plaintiff had established a reputation in other jurisdictions, the New Zealand market was encompassed in the broader international market and therefore the plaintiff's New Zealand reputation in its name "Hirepool" was relevant. Additionally, the court held that the defendant had not provided sufficient information to establish that "hirepool.com" would be used only outside New Zealand.

Having regard to the decisions in the *New Zealand Post* and *Hirepool* cases (despite them not having been trade mark infringement claims), it appears that a New Zealand court will be willing to assume jurisdiction on the basis that the infringing use is directed at New Zealand computers and their users, and that the New Zealand trade mark owner may be harmed by the use.   **6–292**

In a substantive action for trade mark infringement, the court would have to be satisfied that the mark (whether a domain name or a trade mark used on the web site) is being used "in the course of trade" in relation to the goods or services for which the mark is registered, and that the ability to access the web site and view the trade mark on a computer in New Zealand in fact amounts to use of the mark in the course of trade in New Zealand.

6.15 Singapore

6.15.1 Jurisdiction

Any matter may be brought before the Singapore courts. Whether or not the court would have jurisdiction to hear the matter would be for the parties to present to the court. In any event, the plaintiff must be in a position to serve the writ, summons or motion on the defendant. This is usually possible if the defendant is physically present in Singapore or if the defendant has appointed a local agent to accept service of process. However, in situations where the defendant is located out of jurisdiction, an application would have to be made to the court for service out of jurisdiction. Therefore, even if a Web site is located out of Singapore, legal process could be commenced in Singapore if there are sufficient interests in Singapore to protect.   **6–293**

6.15.2 Defamation

A defamatory statement may either be made verbally or in some other recorded form. Such a statement would be one which lowered the target (*i.e.* the subject of the statement) in the mind of right-thinking members of society. A defamatory statement may either be slanderous or libellous. In the context of Web sites, newsgroup postings or just simple e-mail, the cause of action would most probably be libel because such statements may be considered to have been published in recorded form; that is to say, that the statements have been stored in a computer system somewhere in permanent or quasi-permanent form.   **6–294**

One essential element of the tort of defamation is that the allegedly damaging statement must have been published to a third party. If the statement was merely made to, or made known only to, the plaintiff and no other party, the plaintiff would not have been defamed. In the context of the Internet, the issue is therefore whether a defamatory statement has been published in the jurisdiction where the action is brought or whether publication *per se* of the statement in a manner which could be accessed in any part of the world would be sufficient to found a cause of action.

Given that a Web site could be accessed from any part of the world, action could be brought in Singapore if the plaintiff could show that computer users in Singapore could   **6–295** have access to the statement and that somebody in Singapore had read the damaging statement. Alternatively, the plaintiff could show that users in another country have read the statement and that his esteem among the people in that other country has been lowered; the reason why an action was brought in Singapore and not in the other country being left to be argued during any contest as the Singapore court's jurisdiction to hear the matter and/or when there is a question of conflict of laws (*cf. Philips v. Eyre*). In any event, the plaintiff would have to present evidence to show publication and this would normally be in the form of putting a witness on the stand to prove that the defamatory statement has been so published to the witness by the defendant.

There is no doubt that the defendant may rely on the various defences available, depending on his status (if he was the person who made the statement, or merely the publisher of the statement or had just innocently distributed the statement).

6.15.3 Inaccurate information

6–296   An action of the sort contemplated in this question would only arise if the plaintiff had relied on the information provided by the defendant and acted on such statement to the plaintiff's detriment. This sort of action would normally only result if:

(a)   a contractual relationship between the plaintiff and defendant came about only because the of the false statement made by the defendant to the plaintiff (an action for misrepresentation usually claiming avoidance of a contract as a relief); or

(b)   there is some other relationship between the plaintiff and the defendant which may not amount to a direct contractual relationship but none the less, the plaintiff has suffered some damage as a result of the statement made by the defendant (negligent misstatement variety).

In both cases above, it would be necessary to ascertain the nature of the relationship between the parties. It is also understood that publication would have occurred in Singapore even if the Web site was physically situated outside of Singapore but that the information contained therein was available to the Singapore user.

6–297   In the first type of case, there would be the additional need to determine the law governing the contract which had been made between the parties. If the contract was governed by Singapore law, rescission of the contract by reason of misrepresentation would be available. Otherwise, it falls to be determined whether the governing law of the contract allows for rescission in the first place and specifically, rescission by reason of misrepresentation.

In the second type of case, again, it would be necessary to determine where the tort was committed so that the right law might be applied.

6.15.4 Copyright

6–298   In general, the Singapore Copyright Act provides that it would be an infringement of an author's rights if his work was reproduced without permission. There is no statement in the Copyright Act which requires that the reproduction be in more than transient form.

The Copyright Act provides that:

(a)   software is a type of literary work;

(b)   reproduction of a work shall include references to the storage of that work or adaptation thereof in a computer; and

(c)   the copyright in the work would be infringed if the work was reproduced without the consent of the copyright owner.

In the light of these provisions, the very act of loading a computer program into the computer's RAM would infringe the copyright in the program since the software has been reproduced in the computer's (transient) RAM memory. However, the Copyright Act provides that: **6–299**

> "39(3) Notwithstanding section 31, it is not an infringement for the owner of a copy of a computer program or of a compilation within the meaning of section 7A in an electronic form to make or authorise the making of another copy or adaptation of that computer program or compilation provided that such a new copy or adaptation is created as an essential step in the utilisation of the computer program or compilation in conjunction with a machine and that it is used in no other manner."

This section therefore makes it legal for the owner (perhaps the term licensee might be more accurate in most cases) of a computer program to make a transient copy of the computer program if such transient copy is an essential step in the utilisation of the software (it usually is).

However, if the software itself is an infringing copy, the likelihood of this exception   **6–300** applying is virtually nil since it would not make sense otherwise. Therefore, if the Web site contains infringing software, all further copies of that infringing software would not be legitimate copies.

The Copyright Act has been amended recently to clarify the existing law with regards to the digital age and the Internet.

Briefly, these amendments confirms that incidental copies such as caching do not constitute an infringement of copyright when made for the purpose of allowing a user to view, listen or utilise materials from the Internet. The amendments also protect Network Service Providers from liability from both the copyright proprietor and the web-page owner as long as they remove the allegedly infringing materials from a web page upon receipt of a Statutory Declaration from the copyright proprietor stating that the web page contains materials which infringes his copyright.

Section 139 of the Copyright Act also provides that it shall be an offence to publish or   **6–301** cause to be published in Singapore an advertisement offering to supply in Singapore infringing copies of computer software even if the publication was made from outside of Singapore. Further, for the purposes of that section, supply shall be deemed to have been made if the transmission of the computer program when received and recorded resulted in the creation of a copy of the computer program. Therefore, if a Web site contains such infringing programs and the Web site proprietor knew that the programs contained at the site were infringing software, an offence would have been committed, the only issue being whether the law in Singapore could be effectively enforced against a foreign Web site proprietor who is out of jurisdiction.

It is worth noting that some software houses have in the past proceeded against bulletin board operators in Singapore under this provision when it was found that infringing software was being up/down loaded onto or from the bulletin board. In principle, there is little to distinguish a Web site from a bulletin board in this respect.

6.15.5 Trade marks

6–302   Under the new Trade Marks Act which came into force on January 15, 1999, the following are considered use of a trade mark:

(a)   applying the trade mark to goods or the packaging thereof;

(b)   offering or exposing goods for sale, putting them on the market or stocking them for those purposes under the trade mark, or offering or supplying services under the trade mark.

(c)   importing or exporting goods under the trade mark;

(d)   using the trade mark on an invoice, wine list, catalogue, business letter, business paper, price list or other commercial document; or

(e)   using the trade mark in advertising.

Where the owner of a Web site has offered his goods or services via the Web under a trade mark, such use would be considered use in the trade mark sense. Similarly, advertising on the Web ought not to be treated differently from other forms of advertising since all the ingredients are present, namely, there is a trade mark, by which the goods or services are distinguished from those offered by other traders and that the mark has been used in the course of trade.

6–303   It is therefore thought that an owner of a registered Singapore trade mark may have a cause of action against a trader who utilised a mark that is identical or similar to his registered mark on goods or services for which the mark has been registered when such use is via the World Wide Web.

6.15.6 Territory disclaimers

6–304   It is questionable if such restrictions would be completely effective in shielding the Web site owner from liability. Unless technical measures are put in place to bar any Singapore user from having access to the Web, Singapore users would be able to receive information from that site unimpeded regardless of the (legal) restrictions imposed by the Web site owner. However, if litigation was to ensue, the restrictions might operate to lessen culpability or as mitigating factors.

6.15.7 General

6–305   Thus far, there have been no reported cases in Singapore dealing with issues relating to the Internet. However, in respect of regulation of the Internet, the Singapore Broadcasting Authority (SBA) has promulgated regulations and a code of practice to ensure that salacious and other prohibited content would not be introduced onto the Internet by

Singapore content providers and access to overseas sites with undesirable content may be blocked. In brief, the regulatory structure under the Singapore Broadcasting Authority Act is as follows:

(1)   All Internet access service providers (*i.e.* those which provide access to the Internet to members of the public) are to be registered with the SBA.

(2)   Certain content providers must also be registered with the SBA. Firstly, those which are determined by the SBA to be a political party registered in Singapore providing any programme, or any body of persons engaged in the propagation, promotion or discussion of political or religious issues relating to Singapore, through the Internet. Secondly, if required by SBA in writing, a content provider who is determined by the SBA to be in the business of providing an on-line newspaper for subscription, or an individual providing any programme for the propagation, promotion or discussion of political or religious issues relating to Singapore through the Internet.

(3)   Service providers are obliged to block access to sites which contain materials which are objectionable. While the Authority does not specify the means which must be employed to block access to these sites, the service providers here have used proxy servers to achieve this objective.

(4)   Content providers must ensure that their sites do not contain objectionable material.

(5)   Amongst other things, objectionable material include:

   (a)   pornography;
   (b)   material which incites, promotes or otherwise provokes racial or religious intolerance/strife; and
   (c)   material which incites, promotes or otherwise provokes the commission of offences or disrespect for the law.

(6)   Breaches of the licensing conditions would result in the licence being revoked and/or penalties.

6.16 Sweden

Swedish laws on jurisdiction and choice of law are often very old and based on geographical connection and not adapted to the Internet. However, they are existing law and must therefore be applied.   **6–306**

6.16.1 General Principles of Penal Jurisdiction

Swedish law is naturally applicable in respect of crimes committed in Sweden. According to the Swedish Penal Code a crime is considered to have been committed both where the criminal act *occurred* as well as where the crime was *completed* (*i.e.* where the criminal "effect" occurred). This means for example that if someone in Sweden makes a defamatory statement about someone in France or if a person from England illegally intrudes into a computer in Sweden both situations may be punished in Sweden   **6–307** according to Swedish law. The foregoing also shall apply when it is uncertain where the crime was committed but grounds exist for assuming that it was committed within Sweden. Furthermore the same provision provides that an attempt to commit a crime is committed either where the act of attempt was committed or where the crime would have been completed.

As for crimes committed outside Sweden, the Swedish Penal Code establishes jurisdiction for Swedish courts according to the personality principal which states that Swedish courts have jurisdiction and that Swedish law shall apply if the crime was committed by (i) a Swedish citizen or a foreigner who is domiciled in Sweden, (ii) a foreigner not domiciled in Sweden, but who has become a Swedish citizen or has become domiciled in Sweden after the crime was committed or who is a Danish, Finnish, Icelandic or Norwegian citizen who is present in Sweden, or (iii) any other foreigner who is within Swedish territory and the crime in question is punishable according to Swedish law by imprisonment for more than six months.

6.16.2 General Principles of Civil Jurisdiction

6–308   The main body for establishing jurisdiction in Europe are the Brussels and Lugano Conventions. These Conventions are implemented in Sweden and are therefore applicable if the parties to the conflict are domiciled in the E.U. or the EES.

The general rule of the Conventions is that a defendant shall be sued in the Contracting State where he is domiciled. Special grounds for jurisdiction are applicable alternatively with the general rule. Thus, in matters of tort, delict and quasi-delict it is possible to confer jurisdiction to Swedish courts if the act or harmful event occurred in Sweden or if the matter regards a crime and Swedish courts have assumed jurisdiction over the accused. Furthermore, in contractual matters a person domiciled in a Contracting State may be sued in Sweden if the place of performance of the obligations in question is within Sweden.

6–309   Concerning jurisdiction over civil matters regarding a defendant domiciled in a Non-Contracting State (i.e. outside the EU or the EES) the courts apply by analogy the venue rules of the Swedish Code of Judicial Procedure. For example, the venue rule establishing that a tort claim may be heard in the court of the judicial district within which a tortuous act or injury has occurred (*forum delicti*) will support Swedish jurisdiction over the claim, if there is a Swedish court competent to hear the case under that rule. Such analogous application is based on the premise that if a dispute is so closely connected to the judicial district of a given Swedish court as to render that court competent under existing venue rules, then the dispute is likely to have as sufficiently close connection to Sweden as to justify Swedish jurisdiction in that matter. Venue rules will not however form the basis of jurisdiction where this would cause unreasonable results in cases of an international character. On the other hand, even where the venue rules do not indicate any particular judicial district, the courts have displayed a willingness to find jurisdiction where the case in question has had a sufficiently close and relevant connection to Sweden.

6–310   A legal entity may be sued in Sweden when its board has its permanent seat there. Where a legal entity lacks a permanent seat for its board or where there is no such board, suit may still be brought in Sweden if the legal entity carries out its administration there.

Swedish courts will as a rule hear a case when the defendant appears in the proceedings without raising any objection to jurisdiction. But neither a silent appearance nor an agreement between the parties is necessarily sufficient to establish jurisdiction if the case lacks any connection to Sweden.

6.16.3 Server Location

In Sweden it has been a widespread opinion that the geographical location of a server **6–311** should be of major importance to issues of jurisdiction and choice of law. Today it is quite clear that such an opinion is wrong, which inter alia follows from the above mentioned general principles. Instead it is of importance where certain kinds of actions occur or are completed, where the parties are domiciled or where the place of performance of contractual obligations are carried out. This is not to say that the location of the server is of no interest. Its location may together with other circumstances contribute to establish enough connection to Sweden in order for Swedish courts to assume jurisdiction. However, the location of the server is in itself very seldom decisive and the fact that a server is located in for example the USA does not stop Swedish courts from assuming Swedish jurisdiction and applying Swedish law in relation to any act on the Internet that has a relevant connection to Sweden.

6.16.4 Defamation

If a person makes a defamatory statement regarding another person, the crime is **6–312** completed and thus committed when the statement reaches a third party. As mentioned above, if a crime is completed in Sweden, the Swedish Penal Code would apply and Swedish courts would have jurisdiction. If a defamatory (criminal) statement is made on an overseas website and the statement (crime) is considered to have been committed in Sweden (by reaching a third party), Swedish courts would have jurisdiction. The mere fact that someone posts a defamatory statement on a Web site and that the statement thereafter is read by someone in Sweden is however, not necessarily sufficient to establish Swedish jurisdiction. It normally requires a more obvious connection to Sweden, such as that the perpetrator (sender) has knowledge of the fact that the Web site is directed towards Sweden and that he has an intention to cause the victim harm in Sweden or that the perpetrator and/or the victim are Swedish citizens and/or domiciled in Sweden.

A Swedish Court of Appeal, has sentenced a person for grave defamation when an obscene personal ad in the perpetrator's former girlfriend's name was posted by him on an overseas Bulletin Board System ("BBS"). The ad, which was in English, led to the former girlfriend receiving offensive telephone calls and e-mail messages. The court's decision to assume jurisdiction and apply Swedish law was based on several circumstances such as the fact that the victim as well as the perpetrator were Swedish citizens domiciled in Sweden and that the posting of the ad and the effect thereof took place in Sweden.

6.16.5 Content liability

In content liability matters, Swedish courts may assume jurisdiction based on the above **6–313** mentioned general principles. Since the Internet reflects a very large number of different cultures, values and legal systems a strict application of Swedish general principles of penal and civil jurisdiction would lead to an unreasonable number of cases were Swedish courts should or could interfere. In order for the Swedish legal system to work efficiently and maintain its international reputation it is required that it limits the reach of the Swedish legal system to situations that have a direct connection to Sweden and Swedish interest. This means that the Swedish legal system in general accepts Web sites that are legal according to their "home country", provided that the content of such Web sites is not directly intended for the Swedish market or otherwise directed towards Sweden. By home country is meant the country where the person/entity who has the factual control over the content of the Web page is domiciled. If, however, an overseas Web page is directed towards Sweden its content also need to be in accordance with Swedish law.

6.16.6 Copyright Law generally

6–314 Most countries of some importance to international trade and international relations, including Sweden, have adopted international conventions on copyright regulations, such as the Bern Convention (1886) and the World Convention (1952). This means that copyright legislation in most democratic states is very similar and that foreign copyright protected work often has the same protection as Swedish work. The aforementioned conventions do not directly treat issues on how cross border use of copyright protected work shall be dealt with. Therefore matters dealing with jurisdiction and choice of law have to be dealt with in accordance with the abovementioned general principles. Considering the significant similarities between the major legal systems, choice of law matters are often of minor interest. The same apply to jurisdiction. Therefore it is normally recommended to initiate legal action in the jurisdiction of the defendant in order to avoid any problems with enforcement.

6.16.7 Copyright infringement

6–315 Only the creator of a work may reproduce the work and make it available in public. When someone else makes a copyright protected work available to the public, without the consent of the creator, he violates the exclusive right for the creator which would most certainly qualify as a copyright infringement. Intentional or grossly negligent copyright infringement is penalised and may result in imprisonment for up to two years.

The same copyright laws apply to the Internet as to any other media in society. When a work has been legally published it is normally permissable to make copies of the work for private use. Naturally a person is allowed to surf on the Internet and to view pictures, read text, look at films or listen to music, etc. However, it can not be taken for granted that it is allowed to store the copyright protected work in question on a computer (at least not the server of your employer) or to make a print out copy of the work. Any such use (reproduction) is dependant on (i) the limits of private use and (ii) what it reasonably can be taken for granted that the copyright owner has consented to by making the work available on the Internet. Private use is normally defined as use within close family and a small circle of friends. The exception for private use does not cover computer programs or digital databases. Furthermore, to upload protected work to a BBS or Web site is normally not considered to be private use. It should also be noted that if the person who has made the work available on the Internet does not have the right to do so, then any consents to reproduction are, of course, not valid. In such cases it is probable that even the right to make copies for private use no longer exists if the "original" is reproduced illegally.

6.16.8 Trade Mark Infringement

Trademarks are protected by being registered at the Swedish Patent and Registration Office. To remain in effect, registration must be renewed every ten years. Exclusive right to a certain trademark may also arise from use in manufacture, trade or other business in Sweden. Intentional or gross negligent trademark infringement is penalised and may result in imprisonment up to two years. **6–316**

As is the case with copyright legislation, Swedish trademark legislation is based on international conventions and therefore bears many similarities with trademark legislation in most western countries. It should however be kept in mind that a trademark protected in Sweden—through registration or use—only receives such protection nationally, *i.e.* within Sweden.

Generally Swedish courts would have jurisdiction in a trademark infringement case and Swedish law could be applied if (i) the trademark in question is protected in Sweden and (ii) the infringement is occurring in Sweden. Thus, if someone is displaying a trademark on a overseas Web site and such display could be a possible infringement of a trademark protected in Sweden, the main question would be to decide if the infringement is occurring in Sweden. Facts supporting that the Web site is "used" in or directed at Sweden, and that a possible infringement therefore is occurring in Sweden, could be that it is in Swedish or deals with information, products or advertising of specific interest to people within Sweden or that it states prices in Swedish currency or otherwise makes references that could be considered connected to Sweden. **6–317**

A notice on a Web site stating that the site is not intended to be read in Sweden does not automatically mean that any facts supporting a connection between the site and Sweden are of no importance. In fact, such notice would probably only be of significance if there are no other or only very weak connections to Sweden.

6.17 Switzerland

6.17.1 International jurisdiction of Swiss courts—general comments

Swiss courts generally only have jurisdiction if there is an adequate connection with Switzerland in the facts of the case. A connection of this kind could, for instance, exist if a certain action is performed in Switzerland, or the effect of a particular course of conduct takes place in Switzerland, or effects are identifiable on the Swiss market, or if the habitual residence of the injured party is Switzerland. **6–318**

The criteria according to which jurisdiction is determined in each individual case is governed by the type of subject matter involved in the case. For criminal law, the law of civil torts, the law against unfair competition and in the case of infringements of trademarks and copyrights, similar but not entirely identical principles apply where international jurisdiction is concerned.

However, generally speaking it can be said that the simple fact that the owner of a website and the server on which this is maintained are located in a foreign country does not in itself mean that the jurisdiction of the Swiss courts is excluded.

The fundamental principles for determining international jurisdiction of Swiss courts are regulated by law. This means that the courts do not have the option of refusing the jurisdiction which is determined by legal principles because they are of the opinion that, in a specific individual case, Swiss jurisdiction would not be appropriate. Swiss law does **6–319** not recognise the doctrine of *forum non conveniens*.

However, as the Internet is creating new sets of circumstances and as yet no fixed judicial practice exists for interpreting legal provisions relating to international jurisdiction in connection with the Internet, the courts currently still have a great amount of flexibility in judging whether they should deem the legally defined criteria for international jurisdiction in a specific case to have been fulfilled or not.

6.17.2 Defamation

6–320   Under Swiss law, defamatory statements may be of legal relevance from three points of view. Defamation is a criminal offence. At the same time, defamation is also a civil law offence in relation to which the defamed person may apply for an injunction or enforce claims for redress and compensation. Finally, in the case of defamatory or disparaging statements against business companies, there is also an infringement of the law against unfair competition. Different principles apply in determining the jurisdiction of the Swiss courts in the case of a defamatory website, depending on whether it is judged from the point of view of the criminal law, the law of civil torts or the law against unfair competition.

Criminal law

6–321   The Swiss criminal courts have jurisdiction if the criminal act is committed in Switzerland or if the effect of a criminal act takes place in Switzerland. In the case of websites with defamatory content located on servers in a foreign country, the relevant actions are committed in that foreign country. There is an exception to this, of course, in cases where the content is produced in Switzerland and then loaded onto a server in a foreign country.

Thus, generally speaking, where websites on foreign servers are concerned, it is question of determining whether any effect of a defamatory action took place in Switzerland. The effect of defamatory statements is considered to be the cognisance thereof by the defamed party itself or by a third party. In the case of websites with defamatory content, therefore, Swiss jurisdiction will, in principle, always exist, as websites are accessible all over the world from Switzerland, and note can be taken of their content. However, in the case of websites which are produced in a language which is not usual in Switzerland (*e.g.* Chinese) and which contain defamatory material directed against persons who are completely unknown in Switzerland, however, it cannot be said that any effect has actually taken place in Switzerland. It can therefore be assumed that the Swiss criminal courts would not have jurisdiction in these circumstances.

On the other hand, it is of no help to a website operator to include a notice stating that its website is not directed at Internet users in Switzerland if it contains defamatory material directed against persons who are well known in Switzerland, such as internationally famous politicians, artists, entrepreneurs, etc, even if these individuals are not themselves domiciled in Switzerland.

The law of civil torts

6–322   Defamatory and slanderous statements constitute a violation of the personality of the person concerned and thus a civil tort. In the case of civil torts, even if the violating party is not domiciled in Switzerland and has acted outside Switzerland, international jurisdiction will lie in Switzerland provided that the effect took place in Switzerland.

Thus, the same principles apply as in the case of international jurisdiction in relation to criminal offences.

In Switzerland a defamed person may therefore take action against the operator of a foreign website which contains defamatory material. The action instigated may seek redress (*e.g.* publication of a correction of false statements), an injunction, and the reimbursement of possible losses incurred.

Even if, according to the principles mentioned, it is found that international jurisdiction for a claim exists in Switzerland, the question of whether a Swiss judgment can be enforced abroad needs to be investigated in each case. However, this is a matter for the plaintiff and not for the Swiss courts. The latter may not refuse jurisdiction because they consider the chances of enforcing the judgment against the defaming party abroad to be slight.

Unfair competition

Under Swiss law, disparagement of the good reputation of a company or its products through the dissemination of false, misleading or unnecessarily offending statements constitutes a typical example of unfair competition. The international jurisdiction of Swiss courts in the event of unfair competition is governed by the issue of whether or not an effect on the market in Switzerland can be ascertained. **6–323**

In the case of disparaging comments, an effect on the Swiss market is deemed to exist if the defamed company is active on the Swiss market and offers its services here. This is because in these circumstances the disparagement can affect sales prospects in Switzerland. It is enough that the goods or services provided by the defamed company are imported into Switzerland or provided to customers in Switzerland. The defamed company therefore does not need to have a head office in Switzerland nor any subsidiary of its own.

Provided that the requirement of an effect on the market in Switzerland is fulfilled, it is irrelevant where the defamed statement has been issued or where the defaming party is based. Swiss jurisdiction is thus uncontested even for websites with defamatory content if the operator of the website and the server on which they are maintained are located abroad. **6–324**

In the case of defamatory statements it is also irrelevant whether they originate from a competitor of the defamed party or from a third party. Thus newspapers were, for instance, found guilty of unfair competition because articles published by them contained false or unnecessarily defamatory statements about a company.

6.17.3 Content liability

Under Swiss law, liability for the content of websites is significant from the point of view of both criminal law and the law of civil torts. **6–325**

Websites which contain pornographic or racist material or which depict violence may be subject to prosecution under criminal law. As already mentioned, the Swiss criminal courts have jurisdiction if the criminal act is committed in Switzerland or if the effect of the criminal act takes place in Switzerland.

In the case of pornography, racism and depictions of violence, the offences are not ones which require an identifiable effect. In these cases the criminal circumstances are constituted by the committal of the act which is designated criminal. If this takes place abroad, the Swiss courts will therefore not have jurisdiction. **6–326**

However, the law describes the criminal conduct in very broad terms. In the case of pornography, for instance, the production, import, storage, marketing, recommendation, exhibiting, offering, display, assignment and making available of material or objects of a pornographic nature are all liable to prosecution.

6–327   In the case of websites which are operated by foreign owners on servers located abroad, it can therefore be assumed that the Swiss courts will have jurisdiction if the criminal content is freely available to Internet users in Switzerland. This is because Swiss jurisprudence assumes that an act has taken place in Switzerland if the content concerned has been disseminated or made available in Switzerland by means of telecommunications channels. This certainly applies if the criminal conduct is described in broad terms such as making available, recommending or offering, as is the case for the above-mentioned offences, which are particularly pertinent in connection with the Internet.

In order to avoid criminal liability it is not enough for the website operator to put a notice on the website stating that it is not intended for users in Switzerland. It can only be assumed that the Swiss courts have no jurisdiction if an effective control system is set up which prevents access to the illegal content of a website by users in Switzerland. It is only on websites of this type that the content will not be offered, recommended or made accessible in Switzerland.

6–328   In terms of current legislative developments in Switzerland on illegal Internet content, attention is drawn to a motion presented on December 14, 2000 by Staenderat Pfisterer of the Swiss upper chamber. The main aim of the motion is to adapt Swiss criminal law on the liability of Internet Service Providers for criminal acts committed on the Internet to the current legal framework outside Switzerland, particularly that in the EU. For example Access Providers, who only provide customers with Internet access would be excluded from criminal liability. In addition Hosting Providers, who make storage space available on their servers to customers for website publication or input of other data on the Internet would only have criminal liability if they were aware that one of their customers was distributing illegal content using their infrastructure and took no action against that customer.

If someone relies on the content of a website and suffers loss or damage as a result, for example because he or she follows incorrect medical advice given on the website concerned, this will lie within the jurisdiction of the Swiss courts. As mentioned previously, where civil law offences are concerned, international jurisdiction in Switzerland is contingent upon Switzerland being the location of the action or the location of the effect of the damaging conduct. The effect indisputably occurs in Switzerland if someone suffers loss or damage in Switzerland as a result of incorrect website content.

6.17.4 Copyright infringement

6–329   Where copyright law is concerned, the jurisdiction of Swiss courts is contingent upon either the infringing party being domiciled in Switzerland or the act of infringement taking place in Switzerland.

Where copyright infringements on the Internet are concerned, therefore, websites operated by persons domiciled abroad on servers which are located abroad are of particular interest from a Swiss point of view if Swiss website visitors are offered the possibility of downloading unauthorised copies of protected works. Where these circumstances prevail, it can be assumed that the work concerned is distributed in Switzerland. However, the right of distribution is one which is exclusively reserved for the copyright holder.

The inclusion of a notice stating that the website concerned is not intended for persons   6–330
in Switzerland cannot exclude the jurisdiction of the Swiss courts. The possibility of
downloading by website users in Switzerland must be prevented through an effective
control system. Only when this is guaranteed can the website owner successfully prove
that the works concerned are not distributed in Switzerland.

Work is currently in progress to revise the Swiss copyright law of 1993. The IGE, the
Institute for Intellectual Property in Berne, has already prepared a preliminary draft and
this was sent to interested parties for comment in the summer of 2000. The main aim of
the revision is to implement the so-called WIPO Treaties concluded in December 1996. In
addition this revision of copyright law is likely to include amendments arising from
various parliamentary initiatives such as the introduction of an equipment levy and a
provision establishing a producer copyright. It is currently impossible to predict which of
these provisions will become law and because of a major divergence of interests the
revision process is likely to take some considerable time. It will also be the subject of
intense political debate. However, it should be noted that the current definition of the
exclusive rights of the originator under existing copyright law in Switzerland means that
the use of protected works on the Internet is already largely covered.

6.17.5 Trademark infringement

As is the case with copyright infringements, in the case of trademark infringements, if the   6–331
infringing party is not domiciled in Switzerland, the Swiss courts will have jurisdiction if
an act of infringement takes place in Switzerland. This is only the case if there is some
kind of connection between the act in question and the territory of Switzerland.

The fact that goods or services are offered on a website under a trademark which is
protected in Switzerland is not enough to constitute an infringement of Swiss trademark
law. A further condition is that it must be assumed, on the basis of the actual
circumstances, that the goods or services offered on the website concerned are also
supplied to Switzerland, and thus to customers in Switzerland.

If the operator places a notice on his website stating that his offer is not intended for   6–332
customers in Switzerland, this constitutes an indication that no trademark infringement
will occur in Switzerland. However, if it can be proved that, despite this notice, goods are
supplied to Switzerland, trademark infringement in Switzerland would exist and the
Swiss courts would have jurisdiction. Any website operator wishing to avoid Swiss
jurisdiction must therefore ensure that no goods are in fact delivered to Switzerland and
that no services are supplied to customers in Switzerland.

6.18 USA

6.18.1 U.S. jurisdictional analysis

Determining whether personal jurisdiction exists over foreign defendants when the   6–333
allegedly wrongful acts have all been committed outside the U.S. can be a difficult legal
challenge for U.S. courts.[294] When the alleged acts are purely electronic in nature and the
defendant has no physical presence in the U.S., the challenge is especially formidable.

Although numerous U.S. courts have ruled on whether and when personal jurisdiction exists over parties engaged in Internet activities, relatively few of these cases have involved non-resident international defendants. However, the jurisdictional analysis is virtually the same as that employed to determine whether a court of one U.S. state (*e.g.*, New York) has jurisdiction over a defendant resident in a "foreign" state (such as New Jersey).[295] Thus, U.S. cases involving jurisdiction over non-resident *international* defendants should be examined in the broader context of cases involving jurisdiction over out-of-state U.S. defendants.

6–334   A U.S. court may exercise personal jurisdiction over a non-resident defendant based on either general or specific activities within the forum state. General jurisdiction is premised on defendant's "continuous and systematic" activities in the forum state, and may be established regardless of whether the particular cause of action arises from such forum-related activities.[296] On the other hand, even in the absence of general jurisdiction, specific jurisdiction may be established where plaintiff's cause of action is deemed to arise out of or relate to defendant's activities in the forum state.[297] The threshold for the required contacts under general jurisdiction ("continuous and systematic") is higher than it is for specific jurisdiction ("purposeful availment").

Although it can be challenging for a court to rule on whether a defendant's conduct in the forum state is sufficiently "continuous and systematic" to subject him or her to the general jurisdiction of the court, it is often quite difficult for the court to determine whether a defendant's particular forum-related activities are sufficient to establish "specific" jurisdiction in connection with a particular claim. Indeed, the court is required to engage in a highly fact-intensive analysis of defendant's conduct and different courts reach different results based on seemingly similar facts.

6–335   U.S. courts traditionally apply a two-part test to determine whether to exercise specific personal jurisdiction over a non-resident defendant.[298] First, the court must determine whether the defendant's actions satisfy the forum state's particular "long-arm statute" (*i.e.*, the state's guidelines for determining whether personal jurisdiction may be established in the forum state).[299] Second, the court must determine whether exercising jurisdiction over the defendant violates the Due Process clause of the Fourteenth Amendment of the U.S. Constitution.[300] The Due Process Clause establishes the outer boundary of a state court's power to exercise personal jurisdiction. Thus, even if jurisdiction were proper under a particular state's long-arm statute, jurisdiction could not be established where doing so would violate the Due Process guaranteed by the U.S. Constitution.

The Due Process clause requires that a non-resident defendant have "minimum contacts" with the forum state and that the exercise of jurisdiction over the defendant not offend "traditional notions of fair play and substantial justice."[301] Moreover, as one court put it, "jurisdiction is only appropriate in circumstances where defendant has purposely directed his activities at residents of the forum, resulting in litigation that emanates from alleged injuries arising out of or relating to those activities."[302] Certain activities (in and of themselves) are not sufficient to establish minimum contacts. For example, merely placing a product into the "stream of commerce" without purposefully directing that product towards the forum state is not sufficient to constitute minimum contacts.[303]

6–336   Whether personal jurisdiction exists in any given case involves a highly fact-intensive inquiry by the court.[304] For example, in New York, where the long-arm statute is somewhat more restrictive than the permissible limits under the U.S. Constitution,[305] a court would begin with an analysis of the applicable state jurisdictional law before launching into the constitutional analysis set forth by the leading U.S. Supreme Court cases.[306] On the other hand, in a jurisdiction such as California, where the applicable long-arm statute confers jurisdiction to the full extent of the limits set by the federal Due Process Clause, a court would begin (and end) its jurisdictional analysis with a constitutional review.[307]

6.18.2 Internet jurisdiction analysis

For the last few years, U.S. courts, both state and federal, have been wrestling with the thorny issue of personal jurisdiction in the context of Internet-related activities. In deciding these cases, U.S. courts have been reluctant to view the mere general availability of a web site as a "minimum contact" sufficient to establish specific personal jurisdiction over a non-resident defendant, at least in the absence of other contacts with the forum state. As one U.S. judge opined, conferring jurisdiction on the basis of a web site alone "would be tantamount to a declaration that this Court, and every other court throughout the world, may assert [personal] jurisdiction over all information providers on the global World Wide Web."[308] Another court stated in *dicta* that it had no power to shut down a foreign web site "merely because the site is accessible from within one country in which its product is banned."[309] To do so, reasoned the court, "would have a devastating impact on those who use" the Internet.[310] As the U.S. Court of Appeals for the District of Columbia Circuit commented in rejecting the "mere accessibility" of a web site as a basis for jurisdiction, "[w]e do not believe that the advent of advanced technology, say, as with the Internet, should vitiate long-held and inviolate principles of federal court jurisdiction."[311] This principle has been reiterated by several other U.S. federal courts,[312] including in *Minge v. Cohen*, where the court declined to exercise jurisdiction over a Canadian corporation in a securities case where defendant's only contact with the U.S. was the maintenance of a Canadian web site accessible in the U.S.[313]

6–337

Proceeding from the broad principle stated above, that mere accessibility of a web site within the forum state, without more, is not sufficient to justify the exercise of specific jurisdiction, courts have developed two general lines of analysis in determining whether jurisdiction can be exercised in cases involving Internet activity. The first, a "sliding scale" approach, seeks to classify the "nature and quality" of the commercial activity, if any, that the defendant conducts over the Internet. The second analysis seeks to determine to what extent a defendant's intentional conduct outside the forum state, *e.g.*, the posting of defamatory statements on a web site, is calculated to cause injury to a plaintiff within the forum state, *i.e.* an "effects test." These two approaches have been widely applied by the courts (albeit with disparate and inconsistent results) in Internet-related personal jurisdiction inquiries, and courts often employ both lines of analysis in determining whether specific jurisdiction exists.[314] The two approaches are discussed more fully below.

6–338

The "sliding scale" approach to analysing online contacts is perhaps most formulaically stated in *Zippo Manufacturing Co. v. Zippo Dot Com, Inc.*[315] At one end of the spectrum are strictly "passive" web sites that only display information to users. Absent other contact with the forum state, the mere availability of these sites in the forum would generally not result in the exercise of jurisdiction. At the other end of the spectrum are sites where a defendant "clearly" conducts business over the Internet, *e.g.*, where the "defendant enters into contracts with residents of a foreign jurisdiction that involve the knowing and repeated transmission of computer files over the Internet."[316] A defendant conducting business in a U.S. state via such a site would generally be subject to personal jurisdiction in the courts of that state. In the middle are sites that the *Zippo* court classified as "interactive [w]eb sites where a user can exchange information with the host computer."[317] In order to determine whether the operator of such an interactive site is subject to personal jurisdiction, the *Zippo* court explained that a court must review the "level of interactivity and commercial nature of the exchange of information" on the site.[318]

6–339   Consistent with the general rule stated above, under *Zippo*, merely making a passive web site available, without additional conduct directed toward the forum state by the web site operator, will not generally be sufficient to establish personal jurisdiction over the site operator.[319] For example, in *Virtuality LLC v. Bata Ltd*, a U.S. District Court held in a domain name dispute that a passive web site maintained by a Canadian corporation, on which it neither sold products nor conducted any other commercial activity for profit, did not provide a basis for the exercise of personal jurisdiction in the U.S.[320] In *Dawson v. Pepin*, a U.S. District Court found that the web site of a Canadian resident, which contained an 800 number for U.S. orders and a list of dealers located within the forum state, was nevertheless a passive web site which did not give rise to personal jurisdiction in the forum state.[321]

At the other end of the *Zippo* sliding scale are web sites on which business is conducted. In general, a web site that is sufficiently interactive so as to fall into the *Zippo* category of "clearly conducting business" will be subject to the exercise of jurisdiction. For example, in *Alitalia-Linee Aeree Italiane SpA v. Casinoalitalia.com*,[322] a U.S. District Court found that an Italian company could obtain jurisdiction in Virginia in a domain name dispute over an online gambling enterprise located in the Dominican Republic. The court reasoned that a web site on which interactive casino-like gambling was conducted around the clock engaged in repeated and ongoing business transactions online with Virginia residents, which put it on notice that it could be haled into a court in Virginia.[323] Similarly, in *Quokka Sports, Inc. v. Cup Int'l Ltd*,[324] a U.S. District Court found that a web site which targeted U.S. customers and which permitted customers to fill out online order forms, enter credit card information and complete orders online was sufficiently interactive to support the court's exercise of personal jurisdiction over the web site operator in a domain name dispute.[325]

6–340   Between the "passive" and "doing business" extremes of the *Zippo* sliding scale are cases involving "interactive" web sites, such as those through which a consumer can exchange e-mail messages with the site operator or download information or products. Some courts have held that the mere existence of an interactive site is enough to subject an out-of-state defendant to personal jurisdiction,[326] while other courts require evidence that someone in the forum state actually interacted with the site.[327] For example, in *Ty Inc. v. Clark*, a U.S. District Court declined to exercise personal jurisdiction over a private corporation headquartered in England on the basis of its web site.[328] Although the web site was 'interactive' in that it permitted customers to e-mail questions about products and to receive information about orders, no transactions were conducted on line, and the court found that the defendant company had done nothing to direct its activity particularly to the forum state.[329] Similarly, in *LaSalle National Bank v. Vitro Sociedad Anonima*,[330] a U.S. District Court found that a web site operated by a Mexican corporation, which had "a minimal level of 'interactivity,'" including e-mail buttons to obtain information about the company and access to an online product catalog, was still a passive web site under the "sliding scale" test, and declined to exercise jurisdiction. As in *Ty v. Clark*, the court in *LaSalle* found that there was no showing that the defendant's web site targeted residents of the forum state.[331] In contrast, in *Batzel v. Smith*, a web site operated from the Netherlands by a Netherlands resident provided a sufficient basis for establishing jurisdiction in a defamation action where the operation of the web site was coupled with the defendant's actions in e-mailing newsletters and invitations to view the web site to residents of the forum state.[332]

In sum, cases following the *Zippo* sliding scale analysis are highly fact-sensitive and have led to disparate results. However, as a general proposition, it still appears to be the case that the mere general availability of a web site will not—without other contacts—subject site owners to jurisdiction in every jurisdiction in which the site is available.

6–341

In addition to the "sliding scale" analysis propounded by the *Zippo* court, some U.S. courts have cited the pre-Internet "effects test" set forth by the U.S. Supreme Court in *Calder v. Jones* in support of finding personal jurisdiction based on online activity.[333] Under the "effects test," jurisdiction can be premised on the intentional conduct of the defendants outside the forum state that is calculated to cause injury to the plaintiffs within the forum state. The "effects test" was applied in the context of Internet-related activities in *Panavision Int'l v. Toeppen*,[334] a case involving a non-resident U.S. defendant who registered the plaintiff's trademark as a domain name and then sought to extort money from the plaintiff in return for relinquishing the domain name (*i.e.*, a classic "cybersquatting" case). The court concluded that the non-resident defendant's actions satisfied the "purposeful availment" requirement because the defendant knew that his conduct would have the effect of injuring the plaintiff in the forum state, where the plaintiff corporation had its principal place of business.[335]

Courts will more typically consider or apply the *Calder* "effects test" in cases involving defamation[336] or some other alleged tortious act on the part of the defendant.[337] For example, the use of a plaintiff's trademarks as meta tags on the defendant's web site was treated as a tort under the New York State long-arm statute in *Roberts-Gordon LLC v. Superior Radiant Products LTD*.[338] The court applied the *Calder* effects test in exercising jurisdiction over a Canadian corporation (which was not engaged in a "continuous and systematic course of doing business" in New York), concluding that the harm from the defendant's trademark infringement on its web site was cognizable at the plaintiff's place of business in New York and was sufficient to support a finding that the defendant had "'purposely availed' itself of New York law."

6–342

In another Internet-related application of the effects test, the court in *Yahoo! Inc. v. La Ligue Contre Le Racisme*[339] concluded that jurisdiction could be exercised in California over French civil rights groups for acts committed by them in France, because the effects of their acts were experienced by a corporation in California. The effects justifying the exercise of jurisdiction resulted from an action brought against Yahoo! in a French court by French civil rights groups under French anti-hate laws.[340] The French court ordered Yahoo! to block access by French citizens to auctions of Nazi items and threatened to impose large fines if Yahoo! failed to comply. Although it complied, Yahoo! subsequently initiated a federal court action in the U.S. seeking a declaration that the French court order was not enforceable against Yahoo! in U.S. courts. In refusing to dismiss the action for lack of jurisdiction, the court pointed to the effects that the action had on Yahoo! in California and stated that, while the institution of the action may have been proper under French law, "such an act nonetheless may be 'wrongful' from the standpoint of a court in the United States if its primary purpose or intended effect is to deprive a United States resident of its constitutional rights."[341]

The cases discussed above demonstrate that a foreign Internet entrepreneur, although lacking "continuous and systematic" contacts with any U.S. forum state sufficient to subject him or her to general jurisdiction, may nonetheless be subject to personal jurisdiction in the U.S. based on two broad theories of "specific" personal jurisdiction.

6–343

Under the *Zippo* "sliding scale" analysis, a U.S. court will classify the "nature and quality" of any commercial activity that the defendant conducts over the Internet and place it on a continuum ranging from "passive," where no business is conducted, to "clearly conducting business." The closer the Internet activities are to "clearly conducting business," the more likely that a U.S. court will exercise personal jurisdiction. Courts may also apply the *Cader* "effects test" to determine whether the defendant's intentional conduct was calculated to cause harm to plaintiff within the forum state. Where a defendant "purposefully directs" his activities at the jurisdiction, he may be liable to suit for any injury relating to or arising from those activities. On the other hand, "mere awareness" of the ability of U.S. residents to access a web site will probably not subject a foreign web site owner to personal jurisdiction in the U.S.

Thus, non-U.S. citizens should not conduct their Internet activities with disregard for U.S. laws in the belief that operating outside U.S. borders will allow them to avoid personal jurisdiction. In the substantive areas of intellectual property, commercial relations, fair trade, obscenity, and other tortious or criminal conduct, U.S. courts are likely to subject foreign web site owners to a jurisdictional analysis that is virtually the same as that afforded domestic defendants.

6.18.3 Some additional practitioner notes

6–344   The non-U.S. legal practitioner who seeks to advise foreign clients about the scope of liability for Internet-related activities would do well to heed the cautionary tales established by recent U.S. web site cases in the discrete substantive areas discussed below, as well as to keep abreast of recent U.S. legislative developments which may result in increased risk of liability for non-U.S. web site owners. A sampling of recent legal developments in some of these more substantive areas follows.[342]

Online copyright infringement

6–345   In many cases of online copyright infringement,[343] rights holders seek to hold liable the Internet service provider (ISP), web site operator, or bulletin board service (BBS) operator as well as the individual who uploaded or downloaded infringing material.[344] Title II of The Digital Millennium Copyright Act of 1998 (DMCA), the Online Copyright Infringement Liability Limitation Act (the "Act")[345] clarifies some of these issues by providing certain exemptions to "service providers"[346] from copyright infringement liability in certain circumstances.

Specifically, the Act provides certain exemptions or "safe harbors" from liability for claims of copyright infringement that arise out of the following service provider activities: (1) routing;[347] (2) caching;[348] (3) storage;[349] and (4) linking.[350] According to the Act, these safe harbors are additions to, rather than substitutes for, the defenses that service providers already possess under law.[351] To be eligible for these safe harbors, service providers must meet minimum eligibility criteria, including adopting, reasonably implementing, and informing its subscribers and account holders of its policy providing for the termination of subscribers and account holders who repeatedly display or transmit infringing material.[352] In addition, to benefit from some of the limitations on liability, a service provider must designate an agent to receive notifications of alleged infringement.[353] The designated agent's contact information must be made available through (a) the service provider's service, including the service provider's web site in a location "accessible to the public," and (b) registration of the designated agent's contact information with the Copyright Office.[354]

The DMCA also makes it a crime to "circumvent a technological measure that effectively controls access to" a copyrighted work[355] or to sell or distribute to the public a technology that is designed to do so.[356] This circumvention provision has been the subject of several high-profile cases,[357] including one in which a federal district court enjoined the posting of computer code that circumvents a copy protection scheme,[358] and a criminal case in which a Russian computer programmer was charged with offering for sale a software product allowing users to defeat the copy protection on electronic documents encoded in certain proprietary formats.[359]

6–346

Linking, framing and crawling

Although, as a general proposition, one cannot be held liable for simply linking[360] (or hosting a link) to another web site, the act of linking to another web site may in some circumstances be enjoined or otherwise lead to legal liability in the U.S. For example, a hyperlink may point to a website that incorporates textual or graphical materials protected by copyright and/or trademark law.[361] In addition, hyperlinks may be used improperly to engage in a host of unfair trade practices including passing off and misappropriation of goods and services, as well as false advertising. In one case, a federal district court enjoined a non-resident international defendant from using hyperlinks on its U.S.-oriented web site that directed users to its Italian-oriented web site which contained infringing products. The company had previously been enjoined from advertising infringing products in the U.S.[362]

6–347

Hyperlinks that bypass the home page and advertising of a web site (deep links) in a commercial setting have also been the subject of litigation. In *Ticketmaster v. Tickets.com*, a U.S. District Court judge refused to dismiss an action for multiple claims including tortious interference with business advantage, false advertising, unfair competition, reverse passing off and copyright infringement against Tickets.com for its deep links to information on Ticketmaster's site.[363]

The practice of using frames to incorporate third-party content into web sites (*i.e.*, framing), is also a source of controversy.[364]

"Web crawling" or "spidering," which allows Internet users to search for merchandise or other information across many web sites at once, can also lead to legal liability. In *Register.com v. Verio, Inc.*, a federal judge in New York granted a preliminary injunction against Verio, Inc, a provider of web hosting, high-speed Internet access, and e-commerce products, ruling that Verio cannot use software robots to "crawl" the domain name registrar Register.com's computer system, including the "WHOIS" domain registration database, for mass marketing purposes.[365] Similarly, in *eBay v. Bidder's Edge*, a federal court judge preliminarily enjoined an "auction aggregation" web site from using web crawlers to access eBay's computer systems.[366] The court based its decision on the arcane theory of trespass to chattels, finding that the generation of 80,000 to 100,000 requests to eBay's computers each day was a "load on eBay's computer system [that] would qualify as a substantial impairment of condition or value."

6–348

Defamation

It is not clear to what extent U.S. courts will be satisfied that jurisdiction exists in a defamation case where the only harmful event which occurs in a given forum is the actual damage suffered by a plaintiff.[367] Although a defamatory statement on an overseas web site may well be regarded as having been "published" in the U.S.,[368] a significant jurisdictional issue would still remain as to whether the "publisher" has purposefully

6–349

availed himself of any U.S. forum so as to allow a court to exercise personal jurisdiction over him. Allegations of jurisdictional "minimum contacts" have been found to be sufficient in Internet defamation cases by courts applying the *Calder* "effects" test,[369] although a number of others have held that mere allegations that a plaintiff feels harm in the forum state as a result of defamatory statements made on the Internet are not enough to satisfy the "express aiming" required by *Calder*.[370] However, in *Batzel v. Smith*, a federal district court based a finding of sufficient contacts for the exercise of jurisdiction over an overseas defendant in a defamation case on the basis of both the highly interactive nature of the web site and the defendant's purposeful activities in e-mailing newsletters and invitations to view the web site to residents of the forum state, without analysing the *Calder*-type "effects" in the forum state.[371]

Right of publicity

6–350   The unauthorized commercial use of an individual's name or likeness on a web site can lead to liability under the laws of many U.S. states.[372] For example, in *Cuccioli v. Jekyll & Hyde Neue Metropol Bremen Theater Production GMBH & Co.*,[373] a federal court recognized that the plaintiff actor had a right of publicity in his image used on the cover of a CD recording of the German production of a Broadway musical in which he appeared. However, the court held that the offering for sale of the German language CD on a German language Internet web site, created and maintained in Germany in connection with the German production of the show, did not constitute a use within the state of New York as required by the relevant New York statute.

Misrepresentation

6–351   A foreign web site owner or operator might find itself subject to personal jurisdiction in the United States based on the posting of incorrect or misleading information on an overseas Internet site. Someone in the U.S. who has relied to his detriment upon such information might successfully claim that the information was "published in" or "purposefully directed" at the U.S.

For example, in *Cody v. Ward*,[374] a Connecticut stock market investor alleged that a combination of materially false computerised bulletin board postings, e-mail messages, and telephone calls, all from an out-of-state defendant, led him to purchase securities in a company that was actually in poor financial health. Focusing on the various telephone calls and e-mail messages directed by the California defendant toward the Connecticut plaintiff, the court refused to dismiss the case for want of personal jurisdiction.[375] Similarly, the court in *Fowler v. Broussard* held that it could exercise personal jurisdiction over numerous claims (including misrepresentation) relating to a dispute over the ownership and operations of a corporation, on the basis of the e-mail and telephone communications that the non-resident defendants had with the plaintiff.[376] In another case, a Maryland state court considered the jurisdictional impact of alleged misrepresentations made by e-mail and fax in connection with the sale of a business. The court stated that when a party " 'knowingly sends into a state a false statement, intending that it should there be relied upon to the injury of a resident of that state, he has, for jurisdictional purposes, acted within that state' " and the exercise of jurisdiction is therefore constitutionally permissible.[377]

6.18.4 Disclaimer defence?

A foreign web site operator may not avoid liability in the United States relating to the   **6–352**
content of its web site simply by posting a disclaimer notice on the site. For example, in
Euromarket Designs, Inc. v. Crate & Barrel Ltd,[378] the defendant's web site contained the
disclaimer, "Goods Sold Only in Republic of Ireland" and the Irish defendant asserted
that it was not conducting commerce in the forum state. The court found defendant's
claim unpersuasive in light of the fact that the web site allowed users to select United
States as part of both their shipping and billing addresses, the fields in which users
entered their shipping and billing addresses were organized for a United States-format
address, *i.e.*, city, state, zip code, and there was evidence that the company sold to at least
one person in the forum state through its web site.

To the extent that a unilateral notice limiting geographic access to a foreign site is
accompanied by something more, *e.g.*, a blocking mechanism or a choice of forum
agreement, foreign web site operators may be able to limit their liability.[379] In *Tech Heads,
Inc. v. Desktop Service Center, Inc.*, a federal court found that it could exercise jurisdiction
over a non-resident defendant on the basis of the defendant's "highly interactive"
commercial web site, because it encouraged interactivity and the exchange of information
with users in other states as well as globally.[380] However, the court commented in dicta
that enterprises conducting business over the Internet might be able to limit the
jurisdictions to which they could be subject by adopting "(1) a disclaimer that they will
not sell products or provide services outside a certain geographic area; and (2) an
interactive agreement that includes a choice of venue clause to which a consumer or
client must agree before purchasing any products or receiving any service."[381]

---

1.   Chapter 2.
2.   Chapter 2.
3.   Chapter 3.
4.   [1974] 1 A.C. 133.
5.   *Ashworth Hospital Authority v. MGN Ltd* [2001] 1 All E.R. 991.
6.   *Ricci v. Chow* [1987] 1 W.L.R. 1658.
7.   See Chapter 4.
8.   [1997] 4 All E.R. 200
9.   Unreported, Q.B., Alliott J. October 11, 2000. Upheld on appeal [2001] E.W.C.A. Civ 348.
10. [2001] 4 E.M.L.R. 750.
11. *Godfrey v. Demon Internet Ltd* [2001] Q.B. 201.
12. Ch D, Lightman J., February 26, 2001 (unreported).
13. The terms of the injunction are available at www.users.globalnet.co.uk/#sldlheb/legal1.htm. General
     information about the case can be found at www.cyber-rights.org/jetrep.htm.
14. *Ashdown v. Telegraph Group Ltd* [2001] E.W.C.A. Civ 1142.
15. ICANN UDRP Rules Paras 1 and 3(xiii).
16. ICANN UDRP Rules Para. 15(a).
17. Implemented by the Civil Jurisdiction and Judgments Act 1982.
18. Implemented by the Contracts (Applicable Law) Act 1990.
19. The Regulation applies to all Member States except Denmark, which has decided not to participate in the
     adoption of the Regulation. The Brussels Convention will therefore continue to apply as between Member
     States and Denmark.
20. Council Regulation 44/2001 of December 22, 2000.
21. COM (1999) 0348 dated July 14, 1999.
22. Art 1.
23. July 20, 2000. See also the decision of the Court of Appeal in *Re Harrods (Buenos Aires) Ltd* [1992] Ch.72, the
     correctness of which was put in issue in the *Lubbe* case.
24. Art. 23(2).
25. Art. 17, para. 4.
26. Schlosser Report O.J. C 59, March 5, 1979, at page 120.

27. *Fort Dodge Animal Health Ltd v. Akzo Nobel NV* [1998] F.S.R. 222, C.A.. The Court of Appeal in this case referred the relevant questions to the European Court of Justice. See also *Coin Controls Ltd v. Suzo International (United Kingdom) Ltd* [1997] 3 All E.R. 45.
28. [1999] 1 All E.R. 769, C.A.
29. However the court went on to consider the question of justiciability as a separate matter from jurisdiction. It held that the *Mocambique* rule did not require the court to refuse to entertain the case and that the double actionability rule did not render the case bound to fail. The court declined to refer these questions to the European Court of Justice, holding that these were not questions of interpretation of the Brussels Convention but of the policy underlying the relevant rules of English private international law.
30. Art. 17, para. 4.
31. See, for instance, *Definitely Maybe (Touring) Ltd v. Marek Lieberberg Konzertagentur GmbH* [2001] I.L.Pr. 29 QB.
32. Art. 5(1)(b).
33. This expression has an autonomous Convention meaning and should not be interpreted simply as referring to the national law of one or other Convention State (*Kalfelis v. Schroder* [1988] E.C.R. 5565).
34. The Brussels Regulation adds "or may occur".
35. *Handelswekerij GJ Bier BV and another v. Mines de Potasse D'Alsace S.A.* [1976] E.C.R. 1735 ECJ.
36. *Shevill v. Presse Alliance S.A.* [1995] 2 A.C. 18 ECJ.
37. *Domicrest Ltd v. Swiss Bank Corporation* [1998] 3 All E.R. 577.
38. *Kalfelis v. Bankhaus Schroder, Münchmeyer, Hengst & Co.* [1988] E.C.R. 5565.
39. Those aspects of copyright that involve concepts such as "making available to the public" appear to be receipt-oriented. The aspects of copyright that dwell on the making of the copy are by nature not receipt-oriented, although the tendency of the Internet to create a trail of copies along the information transmission path may result in discrete infringing acts in multiple jurisdictions.
40. Assuming that the Claimant satisfies the requirements to show a good arguable case that the case comes within Art. 5(3) and a serious issue to be tried on the merits, and that factors such as *lis pendens* (Art. 21) are absent.
41. The same standard of proof should apply as under the non-Brussels Convention Rules: *Tesam Distribution Ltd v. Schuh Mode Team GmbH* [1990] I.L.Pr. 149, CA and *Mülnycke A.B. v. Procter & Gamble Ltd* [1992] 1 W.L.R. 1112, CA
42. *ABKCO Music & Records Inc. v. Music Collection International Ltd* [1995] R.P.C. 657, CA This test also parallels the requirement in non-Brussels Convention cases.
43. This assumes that the claimant is unable to demonstrate that the activity amounts to a tort in the defendant's home jurisdiction. This will usually be the case in a typical cross border Internet dispute between companies whose websites are based on businesses conducted domestically in their home jurisdictions. The activity gives rise to complaint only when the business goes on-line and so become visible in other countries..
44. *Handelskwekerij G J Bier BV v. Mines de Potasse d'Alsace SA* [1976] E.C.R. 1735, ECJ.
45. *ibid.*
46. *Dumez France v. Hessische Landesbank* [1990] E.C.R. 49, ECJ.
47. Applied by Jacob J. in *Mecklermedia* (above), holding that in a case of passing off the harmful event occurred in England since the harm was to the plaintiff's goodwill in England and was the effect on the reputation in England. Referring to *Dumez*, he said that he was reinforced in that view by the quoted paragraph. "All the components of the tort take place in England. A trial would require proof of goodwill, misrepresentation and damage in England. It would not matter whether or not what DC were doing in Germany was, so far as German law and facts was concerned, lawful or not".
48. [1995] 2 A.C. 18.
49. [2001] E.W.C.A. Civ. 721.
50. See, for instance, the *Berezovsky* case (below).
51. *Metall & Rohstoff v. Donaldson Inc* [1990] 1 Q.B. 391, CA. The double actionability test prevents an English court having to give effect to stricter foreign defamation laws.
52. See *Shevill*, n. 36 above.
53. See the comments of Lord Steyn in *Berezovsky*, below.
54. *Cf R v. Fellows, R v. Arnold* (1996) October, 3 *The Times*, CA. In this case one of the defendants to charges under the Obscene Publications Act 1959 and the Protection of Children Act 1978 argued that giving certain others password access to his archive of indecent pictures on his employer's computer did not amount to "showing" the pictures as contended by the prosecution. The defendant argued that "showing" is active rather than passive, and that he did nothing more than permit others to have access to his archive. The Court of Appeal accepted, for present purposes, that active conduct on the defendant's part was required. Evans L.J. said: "...it seems to us that there is ample evidence of such conduct on his part. He took whatever steps were necessary not merely to store the data on his computer but also to make it available world-wide to other computers via the Internet. He corresponded by e-mail with those who sought to have access to it and he imposed certain conditions before they were permitted to do so. He gave permission by giving them the password. He did all this with the sole object of allowing others, as well as himself, to view exact reproductions of the photographs stored in his archive."
55. *Jenner v. Sun Oil Co* [1952] 2 D.L.R. 526, an Ontario case.

56. *Bata v. Bata* [1948] W.N. 366.
57. [2000] 2 All E.R. 986, HL. This was not a Brussels Convention case.
58. [2001] V.S.C. 305.
59. [1999] 4 All E.R. 343.
60. [1995] 2 A.C. 18.
61. *Shevill v. Presse Alliance* [1996] 3 All E.R. 929.
62. *Mecklermedia Corp. v. D.C. Congress GmbH* [1998] Ch. 40
63. Contrast this with the same judge's comments in *800-FLOWERS Trade Mark* and *Euromarket* (n. 63 below).
64. Ch.D. December 2, 1999.
65. In *800-FLOWERS Trade Mark* (a registrability case) [2000] F.S.R. 697 Jacob J. had said: "Reliance is also placed on Internet use of 1-800 FLOWERS. This name (with the addition of Inc.) is used for a web site. Mr Hobbs submitted that any use of a trade mark on any web site, wherever the owner of the site was, was potentially a trade mark infringement anywhere in the world because web site use is in an omnipresent cyberspace: that placing a trade mark on a web site was 'putting a tentacle' into the computer user's premises. I questioned this with an example: a fishmonger in Bootle who put his wares and prices on his own web site, for instance for local delivery, can hardly be said to by trying to sell fish to the whole world or even the whole country. And if any web surfer in some other country happens upon that web site he will simply say 'this is not for me' and move on. For trade mark laws to intrude where a web site owner is not intending to address the world but only a local clientele and where anyone seeing the site would so understand him would be absurd. So I think that the mere fact that websites can be accessed anywhere in the world does not mean, for trade mark purposes, that the law should regard them as being used everywhere in the world. It all depends on the circumstances, particularly the intention of the web site owner and what the reader will understand if he accesses the site. In other fields of law, publication on a web site may well amount to a universal publication, but I am not concerned with that." In the Court of Appeal Counsel for the applicants disclaimed this more extreme argument as to use attributed to him, but rather relied on the interactive use of the web-site: that is, the accessing of it by customers in the United Kingdom, and thus the inevitable appearance on screens in the United Kingdom of the mark. (Buxton L.J., paras 134-135). The appeal was dismissed on evidential grounds. The *obiter* comments of Buxton L.J. on the wider conceptual issues are set out in the main text.
66. n. 49 above.
67. The relevant provisions of the Act came into force on May 1, 1996.
68. Thus in *Mecklermedia* the claimant's claim was for the English tort of passing off. There was no discussion of applicable law as such, but Jacob J's analysis in relation to "harmful event" under Art. 5(3) of the Brussels Convention was that all the components of the tort had taken place in England.
69. [1998] 3 All E.R. 577.
70. *Kitechnology BV v. Unicor GmbH Plastmaschinen* [1995] F.S.R. 765 at 777–8 C.A.
71. The point was left undecided in *Kitechnology*. After the subsequent House of Lords decision in *Kleinwort Benson Ltd v. Glasgow City Council* [1999] 1 A.C. 153, commenting on the ECJ decision of *Kalfelis v. Schroder* [1988] E.C.R. 5565 and holding that unjust enrichment claims do not fall within Art. 5(3), the point remains debatable.
72. [1994] I.L.Pr. 559 Ch. D; reversed on appeal [1995] F.S.R. 765 CA
73. Article 13 also contains provisions about branches and agencies within a Contracting State of parties not domiciled in a Contracting State; and also disapplies Articles 13-15 to contracts of transport.
74. Hansard, November 29, 1999, Col 48 (House of Commons).
75. http://register.consilium.eu.int/pdf/en/00/st14/14139en0.pdf
76. Available on the OECD web site at www.oecd.org.
77. Art. 17 para. 2 also provides for the situation where an agreement under Art. 17 conferring jurisdiction on the court or courts of a Contracting State is entered into by parties, none of whom is domiciled in a Contracting State. In that case the courts of other Contracting States shall have no jurisdiction unless the courts chosen under the agreement have declined jurisdiction.
78. A jurisdiction agreement contained in a contract under dispute that did not comply with the formal requirements of Art. 17 could still be relied upon for the purpose of seeking permission to serve proceedings out of the jurisdiction in a case not otherwise governed by the Convention. CPR Rule 6.20(5)d).
79. The significance of jurisdiction being conferred by virtue of the Convention is that in such a case it is unnecessary, since it is a Convention case, to seek the permission of the English court to serve the proceedings outside the jurisdiction, even though service may be in a non-Convention country. See Civil Jurisdiction and Judgments Act 1982 and CPR Rule 6.19(1)(b)(iii).
80. As to which, note that a foreign company may be served in England if it has a branch here either by virtue of the Companies Act or under the CPR. See *Saab v. Saudi American Bank* [1999] 4 All E.R. 321.
81. A defendant may, by submitting to the jurisdiction, also forfeit its right to apply for a stay of exercise of the court's jurisdiction (see e.g. *Ngcobo v. Thor Chemicals* (The Times November 10, 1995))
82. CPR Rule 11 sets out the procedure for applying to dispute the court's jurisdiction to try the claim, or to argue that the court should not exercise any jurisdiction which it may have.
83. The application is made under the provisions of CPR Rules 6.20-6.21
84. CPR Rule 6.21(1)(a) requires the claimant to state in written evidence the grounds on which the application is made and the paragraph(s) of Rule 6.20 relied on.

85. *Seaconsar Far East Ltd v. Bank Markazi* [1993] 4 All E.R. 456, HL. CPR Rule 6.21(1)(b) requires the claimant to state in written evidence that he believes that his claim has a "reasonable prospect of success".
86. *Spiliada Maritime Corp v. Cansulex Ltd* [1986] 3All E.R. 843, HL. CPR Rule 6.21(2A) states that the court will not give permission for service out of the jurisdiction unless "satisfied that England and Wales is the proper place in which to bring the claim".
87. [1937] 1 All E.R. 725, CA.
88. Contrast with *Berezovsky v. Michaels*, above, in which the House of Lords by a 3-2 majority allowed the proceedings to continue in England.
89. *Berezovsky v. Michaels*, above.
90. *Rosler v. Hilbery* [1925] 1 Ch. 250, CA
91. *Watson v. Daily Record* [1907] 1 K.B. 853, CA.
92. *Entores v. Miles Far East Corp.* [1955] 2 Q.B. 327; *Brinkibon Ltd v. Stahag Stahl* [1982] 1 All E.R. 293; and see *Schelde Delta Shipping BV v. Astarte Shipping Ltd (The Pamela)* [1995] 2 Lloyds Rep 249.
93. In most cases now the Private International Law (Miscellaneous Provisions) Act 1995 will apply, since section 9(4) of the Act states that the applicable law (as defined by the Act) shall be used for determining issues including the question whether an actionable tort has occurred. In those cases (*e.g.* defamation) excluded from its application the English common law rules will continue to apply.
94. European Parliament and Council Directive 98/34 [1998] O.J. L204/37 as amended by Directive 98/48 [1998] O.J. L37/35.
95. Directive 89/552 [1989] O.J. L333/5
96. Directive 98/34 [1998] O.J. L204/37
97. Directive 98/84 [199 O.J. L320/54
98. See n. 95 above.
99. By virtue of the Treaty of Amsterdam, which came into force on May 1, 1999, the articles of the Treaty of Rome have been renumbered. This article will use the new numbering with the old numbering in brackets.
100. Commissioner Mario Monti, *Global Electronic Commerce—the Next Phase*.
101. *US Perspectives on Consumer Protection in the Global Electronic Marketplace—Comments by the European Commission, April 21, 1999*.
102. See Chapter 12
103. See, for instance, Commission Communication of February 9, 2001 on E-Commerce and Financial Services: "There are significant derogations in the e-commerce Directive from the internal market approach described above."
104. Explanatory Memorandum, page 32. See also Recitals (11) to (16) of the Directive.
105. Explanatory Memorandum, page 32.
106. Explanatory memorandum, page 33.
107. The Annex to the Directive
108. Directive 87/54 [1987] O.J. L45/43
109. Directive 96/6 [1996] O.J. L2/14
110. Directive 2000/46 [2000] O.J. L275/39
111. Directive 85/611 [1985] O.J. L375/3
112. The effect of the Directive on existing legislation is not spelt out. It is not clear whether Member States can seek to justify existing legislation under the Art. 3.4 derogations, or whether any attempt to enforce existing legislation is a "measure" subject to the notification procedures of Art. 3.4.
113. Explanatory Memorandum, page 9.
114. Arts 9 to 11.
115. There is of course a degree of harmonisation of consumer protection in contract by virtue of, among others, the Distance Selling Directive 97/7 [1997] O.J. L144/19 and the Unfair Contract Terms Directive 93/13 [1993] O.J. L95/29.
116. It is assumed that this refers to issues such as liability for inaccurate content, possibly defamation and so on.
117. The *Radikal* incident (see Chapter 12).
118. [1999] N.S.W.S.C. 526.

Belgium

119. P. Gerard and V. Willems, "Prévention et répression de la criminalité sur Internet", in *Internet face au droit*, Cahier du CRID, N°12, 1997, E. Montero (Ed.), p. 157 and mentioned writs.
120. *cf. supra.*
121. [2001], O.J. L 12/1.
122. Meaning all states of the European Community. The consolidated version of the convention and the protocol as regards the interpretation of this convention by the ECCJ (1971) after the joining of Austria, Sweden and Finland, was published in [1998] O.J. C 27. The convention of Lugano of September 16, 1988 ([1988] O.J. C 189), widening the area of territorial competence, applies to the Member states of the European Association for Free Exchange.
123. Case 21/76 *Bier v. Mines de Potasse d'Alsace* [1976] ECR 1735.
124. CJCE Case 68/93, March 7, 1995, *Rec. CJCE*, I, 415.
125. Articles 13 to 15 of the Convention of Brussels
126. He for example resides in the United States or Japan.

127. Comp. Brussels Convention, Article 5, 1°.
128. Article 638, Juridical Code.
129. Article 636 Juridical Code.
130. Cass., May 17, 1957, Pas., I, 1111; Cass., October 30, 1981, Pas. 1982, I, 306; Cass., April 29, 1996, J.T., 1996, 842.
131. Cass., March 10, 1988, I, 829.
132. D. Fesler, "Responsabilité en cascade ou la reponsabilité aquilienne sur Internet", in *Internet sous le regard du droit*, (ed. J.B. Bruxelles, 1997), p. 88.
133. See also: *Playboy Enterprises Inc. v. Chuckleberry Publishing inc.*, USPQ, 2d, 1746, 1996, WL337276, S.D.N.Y., June 19, 1996.
134. P. Péters, "L'internet et la protection des consommateurs", *Internet sous le regard du droit*, Jeure Barreau de Bruxelles (ed.) 1997 p. 138.
135. R. Prioux, "Questions de droit international privé", in *Les pratiques du commerce, l'information et la protections des consommateurs*, (ULB, 1994), p. 331 *et seq.*
136. H. Van Houtte, "De toepassing van de wet betreffende de handelspraktijken op transnationale gevallen van oneerlijke mededinging", in *Liber Amicorum P. De Vroede* (Kluwer, 1991), p. 1410.
137. Ghent, June 16, 1990, *Commercial Practices*, 1990, p. 70.
138. J. Corbet, "Le droit d'auteur et les réseaux de l'information", in *Internet sous le regard du droit*, (ed. J.B. Bruxelles, 1997), p. 138.
139. Namely Brussels, December 21, 1989, *Ing. Cons.*, 1990, p. 127.
140. See Tractebel case, reference in n. 11.
141. Lower criminal Court of. Brussels, December 22, 1999, unpublished.
142. O. Vandemeulebroeke in *Internet sous le regard du droit*, (ed., J.B. Bruxelles, 1997), p. 221, quoted by the Magistrate's court Brussels, December 22, 1999, unpublished.
143. Cass. March 30, 1994, Pas. 1994, I, 337.
144. Comm. Brussels, November 2, 1999, *A&M, 2000*, 134.
145. Not published, available on the web site *http://www.droit-technologie.org*.
146. Directive 2000/31 of the European Parliament and of the Council of June 8, 2000 on certain legal aspects of information society services, in particular electronic commerce, in the Internal Market, [2000] O.J. L 178/1, Article 14.1 states that:
    "1. Where an information society service is provided that consists of the storage of information provided by a recipient of the service, Member States shall ensure that the service provider is not liable for the information stored at the request of a recipient of the service, on condition that: (a) the provider does not have actual knowledge of illegal activity or information and, as regards claims for damages, is not aware of facts or circumstances from which the illegal activity or information is apparent; or (b) the provider, upon obtaining such knowledge or awareness, acts expeditiously to remove or to disable access to the information."
147. Lower Court of Brussels, October 16, 1996, available on the Internet on *http://www.legalis.net*; confirmed by the Court of Appeal of Brussels (9° chamber) October 28, 1997, *A&M, 1997/4*, p. 383.
148. *Moniteur belge*, July 27, 1994.
149. *cf.* For example: TGI Paris, ref.6138/96, August 14, 1996 JCP Ed G 1996, II, n°22727, note; TGI Paris, ref. May 5, 1997, JCP, 1997, II, 22906, note.
150. J. Folon and R. Bailly, "La musique on line: une nouvelle gestion du droit d'auteur et des droits voisins?", in *Ubiquité*, n°2, May 1999, Revue du D.G.T.I.C., F.U.N.D.P., Namur, p. 67.
151. Trib. Brussels, aforementioned; *cf.* also TGI Paris, August 14, 1996, aforementioned.
152. J. Folas and R. Bailly, *op. cit.*, p. 73.
153. Uniform Benelux Law on trademarks, signed in Brussels on March 19, 1962 (*Moniteur belge*, October, 14 1969), on November 10, 1983 (*Moniteur belge*, October 30, 1986) and December 2, 1992. This provides that Belgium, the Netherlands and Luxembourg have a common trademark regime and register trademarks in a single common trademark office.
154. JCB, July 9, 1984, Case 82/2 and 82/3, *Recueil de jurisprudence de la Cour de Justice Benelux*, 1984, p. 7 and 8.
Canada
155. [1998] B.C.J. No. 848 (BCSC)
156. (2000), 73 B.C.L.R. (3d) 161 (BCCA)
157. ([2000] S.C.C.A. No. 177)
158. (1999) 63 B.C.L.R. (3d) 156 (BCCA)
159. ([1999] S.C.C.A. No. 236)
160. [1998] O.J. No. 2537 (Ont. SCJ)
161. [2001] VSC 305 (August 28, 2001)
162. *Queen v. Cognos Inc.* [1993] 1 S.C.R. 87 at 117.
163. *ibid.*, at 121.
164. *Hedley Byrne Ltd v. Heller* [1963] 2 All E.R. 575; [1964] A.C. 465.
165. Copyright Act, s. 3(1).
166. *Mackintosh Computers Ltd v. Apple Computer Inc. (No. 4)* [1990] 2 S.C.R. 209; 30 C.P.R. (3d) 257 at 261.
167. Copyright Act, s. 27(4).

168. Copyright Act, s. 39.
169. Copyright Act, ss. 3(1) and 27(1).
170. Copyright Act, s. 3(1).
171. Copyright Act, s. 3(1).
172. *Ports International Ltd v. Registrar of Trade Marks* (1983) 79 C.P.R. (2d) 191 (FCTD).
173. *Pro-C Limited v. Computer City, Inc.* (Ont. C.A. per Carthy J.A., Doherty and Moldaver J.J.A. concurring) Docket C34719, September 11, 2001.
174. *Marineland Inc. v. Marine Wonderland & Animal Park Ltd* [1974] 2 F.C. 558 (FCTD).
175. *Saks & Co. v. Registrar of Trade Marks* (1989) 24 C.P.R. (3d) 49 (FCTD).

France
176. Proc. Rep, *UNADIF, FNDIR et autres c/ Robert F.*, TGI Paris, ch. Correctionnelle, 13/11/1998
177. *Sté SG2 c/ Brokat Informations Systeme GmbH (Allemagne), Tribunal de Grande Instance de Nanterre, Ordonnance de référé du 13 octobre 1997.*
178. 21/08/1997, TGI Draguignan, aff. Saint-Tropez c/ Eurovirtuel.
179. *Chambre nationale des Commissaires-priseurs, Chambre de Discipline des Commissaires-priseurs de la Compagnie de Paris / NART SAS (société de droit français), NART Inc. (société de droit américain) et le ministère public, Tribunal de Grande Instance deParis,1ère chbre,1ère sec. Jugement du 3 mai 2000.*
180. *UEJF et Licra c/ Yahoo ! Inc. et Yahoo France*, TGI Paris, Référé, 22/05/2000.
181. *BNP Banexi v. Mr Yves Rocher*, TGI Paris, April 16, 1996
182. *Brel-Sardou, Tribunal de Grande Instance de Paris*, August 14, 1996
183. See Chapter 3 above.
184. 10/13/1997, Référé, TGI Nanterre, aff. Sté SG2 c. Brokat.Informations Systeme GmbH.
185. *1/28/00, Tribunal de commerce de Paris, aff. ALTAVISTA Internet Solutions Limited c/ Monsieur R. P., Sarl Adar Web.*
186. Madame L. / les sociétés Multimania Production, France Cybermedia, SPPI, Esterel, Tribunal de Grande Instance de Nanterre Jugement du 8 décembre 1999.

Hong Kong
187. *Air India v. Wiggers* [1980] 1 W.L.R. 815.
188–189. Section 24, Crimes Ordinance, Chapter 200, Laws of Hong Kong.
190. Section 23, Theft Ordinance, Chapter 210, Laws of Hong Kong.
191. *HKSAR v. H Takeda* [1998] 1 H.K.L.R.D. 931.
192. Section 2, Chapter 390, Laws of Hong Kong
193. *HKSAR v. Cheung Kam Keung* [1998] 2 H.K.C. 156.
194. *HKSAR v. Wong Tat Man* [2000] H.K.E.C. 915.
195. *HKSAR v. Tam Hei Lun* [2000] H.K.E.C. 1178.
196. Section 161, Chapter 200, Laws of Hong Kong
197. Section 25, Chapter 455, Laws of Hong Kong
198. Section 60, Chapter 200, Laws of Hong Kong
199. Section 118, Chapter 528, Laws of Hong Kong
200. Chapter 461, Laws of Hong Kong
201. Under the High Court Ordinance, Chapter 4, Laws of Hong Kong
202. Chapter 553, Laws of Hong Kong
203. See for example Dicey & Morris, *The Conflict of Laws* (13th ed, 2000), p. 319 and *Chitty on Contracts*, (28th ed, 1999), para. 2-048.
204. [1983] 2 A.C. 34.
205. [1999] O.J. 3275, Ontario CA.
206. *Euromarket Designs Inc. v. Peters* [2001] F.S.R. 20.
207. The Basic Law Of The Hong Kong Special Administrative Region Of The People's Republic Of China (Adopted at the third Session of the Seventh National People's Congress on April 4, 1990), reprinted at Chapter 2101, Laws of Hong Kong.
208. Hong Kong Bill of Rights Ordinance, Chapter 383, Laws of Hong Kong.
209. Chapter 21, Laws of Hong Kong.
210. [1999] 3 H.K.C. 515.
211. [2001] V.S.C. 305 (August 28, 2001), Supreme Court of Victoria. This case is discussed further in Chapter 12.
212. [1999] E.M.L.R. 287.
213. [2000] 2 All E.R. 986 (see above, section 6.2.2).
214. Chapter 528, Laws of Hong Kong.
215. [2001] F.S.R. 20 (see above, section 6.2.2).
216. Chapter 43, Laws of Hong Kong.
217. Chapter 148, Laws of Hong Kong.
218. Chapter 2601, Laws of Hong Kong.

Israel
219. Civil Law Procedure Regulations 1984, r. 477.
220. Civil Law Procedure Regulations 1984, r. 500.
221. Civil Law Procedure Regulations 1984, r. 500(6).

222. *Unger v. Paris Israel Movies Ltd*, Supreme Court Reports, Vol. 20(5), p. 6 (1966).
223. Civil Law Procedure Regulations 1984, r. 500(7).
224. *Ephraim Mizrachi v. Nobel's Explosives Co Ltd*, Supreme Court Reports, Vol. 32(2), p. 115 (1977).
225. *ibid.* Followed in *Hoida v. Hindi & The Israel Technion*, Supreme Court Reports, Vol. 44(4), p. 545 (1990).
226. *Eisenman, Shanks v. Kimron*, known as the "The Dead Sea Scrolls Case", Supreme Court Reports, Vol. 54(3), p. 817 (2000). The court held that mail order sales of three copies of a book from the United States to customers in Israel sufficed as evidence of publication of the book in Israel. This recent decision may establish a low threshold for an act to be considered as having occurred within the jurisdiction.
227. Civil Law Procedure Regulations 1984, r. 500(10).
228. *Rad v. Chai*, Supreme Court Reports, Vol. 40(2), p. 141 (1986).
229. Once a connection has been established, the courts may decide to follow the approach taken by the District Court in a purely local dispute, which concerned municipal rates levied on a Tel Aviv artist who sold his works via the Internet. In *City of Tel Aviv (Rates Division) v. Zarfati*, the judge suggested that in certain forms of e-commerce, transactions occur at the user's location, rather than at the location of the Web site's server. *City of Tel Aviv (Rates Division) v. Zarfati*, Tel Aviv District Court Civil File 002527/99, Decision dated July 11, 2000.
230. *Abu Jihalah v. East Jerusalem Electric Company Ltd*, Supreme Court Reports, Vol. 44(1), p. 554 (1993).
231. *Rad v. Chai*, Supreme Court Reports Vol. 40(2) p. 141 (1986) at 147.
232. As enunciated in *Spiliada Maritime Corp v. Consulex Ltd* [1987] A.C. 460.
233. *Shechem Arabic Insurance Company v. Abed Zerikat*, Supreme Court Reports, Vol. 48(3), p. 265 (1994).
234. *Abu Attiah v. Arbitisi*, Supreme Court Reports, Vol. 39(1), p. 365 (1985).
235. The two conditions of the old English test are subsumed into the "expectations of the parties". See *Abu Jihalah v. East Jerusalem Electric Company Ltd* Supreme Court Reports, Vol. 44(1), p. 554 (1993).
236. *ibid.*
237. *ibid* at p. 568.
238. Defamation Law 1965, s. 2(b)(1).
239. *ibid*, s. 2(b)(2).
240. Defamation exists only if the material is published to at least one person other than the injured (Defamation Law 1965, s. 7). As the tort of defamation is subject to s. 3 of the Civil Wrongs Ordinance (New Version) 1968, the commencement of the tort must occur within Israel in order for the defamation to be actionable.
241. *Shaha v. Serderian*, Supreme Court Reports, Vol. 29(4), p. 734 (1985).
242. Defamation Law 1965, s. 11. Press Ordinance, Laws of Palestine, Chapter 116, Vol. B, p. 1191.
243. *ibid.*, s. 12.
244. The wording here is "civil wrong" rather than the "act or omission" of r. 500(7).
245. Consumer Protection Law 1981, s. 7.
246. *ibid.*, s. 7(c).
247. Commercial Torts Law 1999, s. 2(a).
248. *ibid.*, s. 2(b).
249. Computer Law 1995, s. 7.
250. *Paradise Mombasa Tours (1997) Limited v. New Soil Technologies Limited*, Tel Aviv District Court Civil File 001509/01, Decision dated May 8, 2001. For a more detailed discussion of the case, refer to Chapter 3, endnote 218.
251. Copyright Act 1911, which dates from the British mandatory period.
252. Copyright Ordinance 1934, also dating from the British mandatory period, as amended on several occasions by the Israeli Parliament.
253. Copyright Act 1911, s. 1 (2).
254. *ibid.*, s. 35(1). "Infringing copy" means "any copy, including any colourable imitation, made, or imported in contravention of the provisions of this Act".
255. *ibid.*, s. 1 (2).
256. *ibid.*, s. 35(1).
257. See, for instance, *Ernest Bloomers v. The Israeli Chapter of the International Federation of Record Industry*, District Court Reports, Vol. 1982(2), p. 156. The district court of Tel Aviv held that the delivery of radio broadcast to hotel guests' rooms constituted a public performance. The court found that any distribution of a work, by whatever means, constitutes a performance, and that a broadcaster is a performer even if it only transmits and broadcasts the work.
258. See, for instance, *Tele-Event Ltd v. Aruzey Zahav & Co.*, District Court Reports, Vol. 1994(2), p. 328. The court considered the use of a sophisticated technical procedure and of expensive equipment, not regularly used by individual users, to indicate the function of a "broadcaster" rather than a "viewer".
259. Copyright Act 1911, s. 1(2).
260. *Eisenman, Shanks v. Kimron*, Supreme Court Reports, Vol. 54(3), p. 817 (2000).
261. Copyright Ordinance, ss. 3b and 3f (1996 amendment).
262. Copyright Act 1911, s. 2(2):
    "Copyright in a work shall also be deemed to be infringed by any person who:
    (a) sells, or let for hire, or by way of trade exposes or offers for sale or hire, or
    (b) distributes either for the purposes of trade or to such an extent as to affect prejudicially the owner of

the copyright, or
(c) by way of trade exhibits in public, or
(d) imports for sale or hire
any work, which to his knowledge, infringes copyright".

263. *ibid.*, s. 2(3):
"Copyright in a work shall also be deemed to be infringed by any person who for his private profit permits a theatre or other place of entertainment to be used for the performance in public of the work without the consent of the owner of the copyright, unless he was not aware, and had no reasonable ground for suspecting, that the performance would be an infringement of copyright."

264. *ibid.*, s. 8.

265. *Eisenman, Shanks. v. Qimron*, Supreme Court Reports, Vol. 54(3), p. 817 (2000). *Qimron v. Shanks*, District Court Reports, Vol. 1993(3), p. 10, at 21.

266. Trademarks Ordinance (New Version) 1972, s. 46. An exception is made in the case of genuine use by a person of his own name, of the name of his or his predecessor's place of business, or of a genuine description of his goods (s. 47).

267. *Frou Frou Biscuits (Kfar Saba) Ltd v. Froumine & Sons Ltd & Frou-Bisc Ltd*, Supreme Court Reports, Vol. 23(2), p. 43 (1969).

268. Amendment of the Intellectual Property Law (adjustment to the TRIPS provisions)-1999, dated December 21, 1999.

269. Annex 1 C of the Agreement establishing the World Trade Organization (1994).

270. See Trademarks Ordinance (New Version) 1972, ss. 1(3), 1(4), 46A.(a) and 46A.(b).

271. See Commercial Torts Law 1999, s. 1; Unjust Enrichment Law 1981, s. 1; Property Law 1969, s. 17; and Chattels Law 1971, s. 8.

272. *supra.*, Chapter 3, Domain Names.

273. Contracts (General Parts) Law 1967, s. 30 and Standard Terms Contracts Law, ss. 3 and 4(1).

274. See the arguments in *City Central Ltd et al v. Chanel (French Societe Anonyme)* Dinim V'od (District Court), Vol. 26(5), p. 351 (1995).

Japan

275. Owing to the "two China problem" there is no diplomatic relationship between Taiwan and Japan. Therefore Japanese courts cannot use the international co-operation system of collecting evidence through diplomatic channels.

The Netherlands

276. Decision of the ECJ of March 7, 1995 (Case C-68/93)

277. November 1976 (Case 21/76)

278. BIE 1991, 23

279. See Dutch Report International Private Law Aspects, ALAI 5X June 1996, *Copyright* in *Cyberspace*.

280. IER 1997, 9

281. IER 1997, 4

282. (President of the District Court of Amsterdam September 20, 1996, I.E.R. 1996, 44)

283. (President of the District Court of Amsterdam May 15, 1997, I.E.R. 1997, 44)

284. (President of the Distict Court of Utrecht February 24, 2000, I.E.R. 2000, 41)

285. (President of the District Court Utrecht, January 11, 2001)

New Zealand

286. *International Telephone Link Pty Ltd v. IDG Communications Ltd* (unreported, February 20, 1998, High Court, Auckland CP 344/97)

287. *Eyre v. Nationwide News Pty Ltd* [1967] N.Z.L.R. 851.

288. *Cooper v. Independent News Auckland Ltd* (unreported, April 21, 1997, District Court, Auckland NP 552/96).

289. Tokeley, "Shopping on the Net: Legal Protection for Consumers" (1997) 9(1) *Otago Law Review* 51–70, 65.

290. *Smythe v. Bayleys Real Estate Ltd* (1993) 5 T.C.L.R. 454, 472; [1994] A.N.Z. Conv.R. 424, 428–429.

291. *Green v. BCNZ* [1998] 2.N.Z.L.R. 490.

292. See n. 4.

293. unreported, HC, Auckland, CP29/00, Cartwright J., September 11, 2000.

USA

294. See, *e.g.*, *Klinghoffer v. SNC Achille Lauro*, 937 F2d 44 (2d Cir 1991).

295. One need only compare the jurisdictional analysis conducted by the U.S. Supreme Court in *Burger King Corp v. Rudzewicz*, 471 U.S. 462 (1985) (upholding jurisdiction over Michigan franchisee sued in Florida) to that used in *Asahi Metal Industry Co. Ltd v. Superior Court*, 480 U.S. 102 (1987) (reversing grant of jurisdiction over Japanese manufacturer sued in California) to see that the underlying "minimum contacts" and "fair play" analysis is virtually the same for interstate and international disputes.

296. See, *e.g.*, *Helicopteros Nacionales de Colombia SA v. Hall*, 466 U.S. 408 (1984) (Colombian corporation's contacts with Texas, consisting of one trip to Texas by corporation's CEO for purpose of negotiating service contract, acceptance of cheques drawn on Texas bank, and helicopter and equipment purchases from Texas manufacturer, were insufficient to allow Texas court to assert general personal jurisdiction over corporation in wrongful death action which occurred in Peru).

297. *International Shoe Co. v. Washington*, 326 U.S. 310, 316 (1945) (citation omitted).

298. The constitutional and policy framework employed by courts to analyse whether or not it may exercise personal jurisdiction over a defendant is derived from *International Shoe Co. v. Washington*, 326 U.S. 310 (1945) and its progeny: *Burger King Corp v. Rudzewicz*, 471 U.S. 462, 471–78 (1985) (setting forth the two-part Due Process test for analysing defendant's litigation-related connections with the forum, and the fairness of exercising jurisdiction over a nonresident defendant); *Asahi Metal Industry Co. Ltd v. Superior Court*, 480 U.S. 102, 113–16 (1984) (applying multi-factor test to determine fairness and reasonableness of exercising personal jurisdiction over non-resident, foreign defendant); *World-Wide Volkswagen Corp v. Woodson*, 444 U.S. 286, 294 (1980) (suggesting that geographically distant defendants must sometimes be protected from inconvenient litigation).

299. See, *e.g.*, NY CPLR 302 (Consol 2001) (enumerating those categories of contacts, including committing a tortious act within the forum, which suffice to confer jurisdiction); 42 Pa Cons Stat § 5322 (2001).

300. See U.S. Const amend XIV.

301. *International Shoe Co. v. Washington*, 326 U.S. 310, 316 (1945) (citation omitted).

302. *Alitalia-Linee Aeree Italiane SpA v. Casinoalitalia.com*, 128 F Supp 2d 340, 348–49 (ED Va 2001) (citing *Burger King Corp v. Rudzewicz*, 471 U.S. 462 (1985).

303. See, *e.g.*, *Asahi Metal Industry Co. Ltd v. Superior Court*, 480 U.S. 102 (1987) (holding that a Taiwanese company that manufactured and sold its products in Taiwan was not subject to personal jurisdiction in California merely because its products eventually made their way into California through the "stream of commerce").

304. See, *e.g.*, *Burger King*, 471 U.S. at 471–78.

305. See NY CPLR 302(a) (Consol 2001).

306. See 297.

307. See Cal Civ Proc Code § 410.10 (Deering 2001) (providing that California courts "may exercise jurisdiction on any basis not inconsistent with the Constitution of this State or the United States") (enacted 1969).

308. *Hearst Corp v. Goldberger*, 1997 U.S. Dist LEXIS 2065, *55 (SDNY Feb 26, 1997). In *Hearst*, the magistrate judge found that the New Jersey defendant's only contact with the New York forum was via electronic "visits" from New York residents, plus a few e-mail messages sent to New-York based newspapers after commencement of the litigation.

309. *Playboy Enterprises Inc. v. Chuckleberry Publishing Inc.* 939 F. Supp. 1032, 1039 (SDNY 1996) (dicta). Playboy was one of the earliest cases to touch (though not rule directly) upon personal jurisdiction in the Internet age. In Playboy a federal judge in New York found no constitutional or other impediment to exercising personal jurisdiction over an Italian web site owner who had been enjoined by the same court from publishing or distributing its magazine in the US in traditional print form. The court held that it retained personal jurisdiction over the defendant for the purposes of enforcing the existing injunction and that although the existing injunction did not specifically mention the Internet, the injunction would still be applicable to this new media. See also *Jeri-Jo Knitwear v. Club Italia*, 94 F. Supp. 2d 457 (SDNY 2000) (Italian company ordered to remove web site hyperlinks deemed to violate prior injunction against advertising or promoting trademark-infringing apparel in the U.S.).

310. *Playboy*, 939 F. Supp. at 1039–40.

311. *GTE New Media Services Inc. v. Bellsouth Corp*, 199 F3d 1343 (DC Cir 2000).

312. See, *e.g.*, *Remick v. Manfredy*, 238 F3d 248, 259 (3d Cir 2001) ("the mere posting of information or advertisements on an Internet website does not confer nationwide personal jurisdiction"); *Bensusan Restaurant Corp v. King*, 126 F3d 25, 27 (2d Cir 1997) (approving the application of "well-established doctrines of personal jurisdiction law" to an Internet-related case); *ESAB Group Inc. v. Centricut LLC*, 34 F Supp 2d 323, 331 (D SC 1999) ("something more" than a mere Internet presence is required to assert personal jurisdiction); *McDonough v. Fallon McElligot Inc.*, 1996 U.S. Dist LEXIS 15139, *7 (SD Cal August 6, 1996) (merely operating a web site used by forum residents not sufficient to establish jurisdiction). See also the following cases where jurisdiction was found lacking: *Barrett v. Catacombs Press*, 44 F Supp 2d 717 (ED Pa 1999) (defamation action); *Millennium Entertainment v. Millennium Music LP*, 33 F Supp 2d 907 (D Or 1999) (trademark infringement action); *Rannoch Inc. v. Rannoch Corp.* 52 F Supp 2d 681 (ED Va 1999) (defendant's posting of web site satisfied state long-arm statute, but failed constitutional prong of jurisdictional test).

313. *Minge v. Cohen*, 2000 U.S. Dist LEXIS 403 (ED La January 19, 2000) ("maintaining a web site on the Internet ... cannot without more satisfy the 'purposefully availing' element"). See also *Re Magnetic Audiotape Antitrust Litigation*, 2001 U.S. Dist LEXIS 5160 (SDNY Apr 25, 2001) (declining to exercise personal jurisdiction over the Korean parent corporation of a US subsidiary based upon the accessibility of the Korean parent corporation's English language web site).

314. See *e.g.* *Amway Corp v. P&G*, 2000 U.S. Dist LEXIS 372 (WD Mich January 6, 2000) (analysing the defendant's web site under both the *Zippo* and *Calder* tests and finding jurisdiction proper).

315. *Zippo Manufacturing Co. v. Zippo Dot Com Inc.* 952 F Supp 1119 (WD Pa 1997). In *Zippo*, an out-of-state defendant was using the plaintiff's registered trademark 'Zippo' as part of a web site domain name accessible in Pennsylvania. Some 140,000 subscribers around the world—not all of them in Pennsylvania— had registered and paid for Dot Com's Internet news service. In holding that personal jurisdiction over the defendant existed in Pennsylvania, the US District Court for the Western District of Pennsylvania determined that "Dot Com's conducting of electronic commerce with Pennsylvania residents constitutes the purposeful availment of doing business in Pennsylvania."

316. *ibid.*, at 1124.
317. *ibid.*
318. *ibid.*
319. See, *e.g., Harbuck v. Aramco, Inc.* 1999 U.S. Dist LEXIS 16892 (ED Pa October 22, 1999) (holding that subjecting Saudi Arabian defendant to jurisdiction in Pennsylvania for having a "passive" web site would be unreasonable); *Smith v. Hobby Lobby Stores Inc.* 968 F Supp 1356, 1364–1365 (WD Ark 1997) (Hong Kong fireworks manufacturer's advertisement in Internet trade publication constituted insufficient contact for Arkansas court to exercise personal jurisdiction in products liability action, where manufacturer did not contract to sell goods and services to citizens of Arkansas over the Internet).
320. *Virtuality LLC v. Bata Ltd*, 138 F Supp 2d 677 (D Md 2001). The defendant had been the successful complainant in a domain name dispute conducted under the Uniform Domain Name Dispute Resolution Policy, and the plaintiff had filed suit in the U.S. court in order to challenge the decision in the UDRP proceeding, as permitted under the UDRP (see Chapter 3). The court also found that the defendant's consent to the jurisdiction of the court pursuant to the provisions of the UDRP did not constitute consent to the jurisdiction of the court with respect to the other claims asserted by the plaintiff.
321. *Dawson v. Pepin*, 2001 US Dist LEXIS 10074 (WD Mich March 29, 2001).*But see Inset Systems Inc v. Instruction Set, Inc.* 937 F. Supp. 161 (D Conn 1996) (domain name trademark infringement action; jurisdiction established by web site accessible to Connecticut Internet users that solicited U.S. residents generally by providing a toll-free number).
322. *Alitalia-Linee Aeree Italiane SpA v. Casinoalitalia.com*, 128 F. Supp. 2d 340 (ED Va 2001). As the Court noted, "the product is an inherently interactive activity ... and necessarily requires [defendant] to enter into contacts with member, who must purchase 'credits' in order to play individual names." *ibid.* at 350 (citing *Millennium Entertainment Inc. v. Millennium Music LP*, 33 F. Supp. 2d 907, 916 (D Or 1999).
323. See also *U.S. v. Cohen*, No 00-1574 (2d Cir July 31, 2001) (upholding conviction under federal Wire Wager Act for activities involving an online gambling web site located outside the U.S.); *People v. World Interactive Gaming Corp*, 185 Misc 2d 852 (NY Sup Ct 1999) (trial court exercised jurisdiction in criminal prosecution over defendant who maintained gambling web site using servers located outside U.S.).
324. See *Quokka Sports Inc. v. Cup Int'l Ltd*, 99 F. Supp. 2d 1105 (ND Cal 1999) (citing *Zippo* and finding that "this type of interactive commercial activity, aimed at U.S. consumers [is] evidence of purposeful availment").
325. See also *Kollmorgen Corp v. Yaskawa Electric Corp*, 1999 U.S. Dist LEXIS 20572 (WD Va December 13, 1999) (Japanese parent corporation subject to jurisdiction in Virginia based on subsidiary's web site and sales in Virginia from orders taken over the Internet). *cf. Inset Systems, Inc. v. Instruction Set Inc.* 937 F. Supp. 161 (D Conn 1996) (early Internet-related case exercising personal jurisdiction over non-resident defendant based on defendant posting an advertisement including a toll-free 800 number on its web site). But see *Mink v. AAAA Dev LLC*, 190 F3d 333, 336 (5th Cir 1999) ("the presence of an electronic mail access, a printable order form, and a toll-free phone number on a website, without more, is insufficient to establish personal jurisdiction").
326. *3DO Co. v. Poptop Software Inc.* 1998 U.S. Dist LEXIS 21281 (ND Cal October 27, 1998) (exercising personal jurisdiction where non-resident defendants' web site "encourage[d] and facilitate[d]" people in the forum state and elsewhere to download allegedly copyright infringing software).
327. See *e.g., Millennium Entertainment Inc v. Millennium Music LP*, 33 F. Supp. 2d 907, 923 (D Or 1999) ("Until transactions with Oregon residents are consummated through defendants' Web site, defendants cannot reasonably anticipate that they will be brought before this court, simply because they advertise their products through a global medium which provides the capability of engaging in commercial transactions."); *Advanced Software, Inc. v. Datapharm Inc.* 1998 U.S. Dist LEXIS 22091, *12 (CD Cal November 9, 1998) (finding that, absent a showing that anyone in the forum state utilised defendant's web site, "the fact that it has interactive potential is irrelevant").
328. *Ty Inc. v. Clark*, 2000 U.S. Dist LEXIS 383 (ND Ill January 14, 2000) (noting that the defendants "do not clearly do business on their web site, for they do not take orders nor enter into contracts over the web site").
329. *Ty Inc. v. Clark*, 2000 U.S. Dist LEXIS 383 at *9-*11.
330. *LaSalle National Bank v. Vitro Sociedad Anonima*, 85 F. Supp. 2d 857 (ND Ill 2000) (declining to exercise personal jurisdiction over a Mexican corporation).
331. *ibid.*
332. *Batzel v. Smith*, 2001 U.S. Dist LEXIS 8929 (CD Cal June 5, 2001).
333. *Calder v. Jones*, 465 U.S. 783 (1984) (holding that personal jurisdiction over non-resident defendants in a libel case involving a print publication was properly applied where the publication of defendants' libelous statements was calculated to cause injury to plaintiff in the forum state).
334. *Panavision Int'l v. Toeppen*, 141 F3d 1316 (9th Cir 1998).
335. See also *Macconnell v. Schwamm*, 2000 U.S. Dist LEXIS 13850 (SD Cal July 25, 2000). (Court exercised jurisdiction in a domain name dispute where the defendant, a resident of Japan, contacted the plaintiff in the forum state and offered to sell the infringing domain name to the plaintiff. The defendant had registered a domain name that had been previously registered by the plaintiff but lost due to the bankruptcy of the domain name registrar. Although the defendant claimed that he intended to use the domain name to market products in Asia, he contacted the plaintiff and offered to sell the domain name to the plaintiff. The court concluded that the there was no evidence of a legitimate business operation on the

part of the plaintiff, thereby suggesting "the type of tort-like purposeful behavior" involved in *Panavision*.) Compare these decisions with the earlier decision of the Ninth Circuit Court of Appeals in *Cybersell Inc v. Cybersell Inc*, 130 F3d 414 (9th Cir 1997) (considering the *Calder* effects test; declining to exercise jurisdiction in domain name dispute where there was no "express aiming" at the forum state).

336. See discussion of defamation cases infra and see, *e.g. Revell v. Lidov*, 2001 U.S. Dist LEXIS 3133 (ND Tex March 20, 2001) (declining to exercise personal jurisdiction in defamation case); *Lofton v. Turbine Design Inc.* 100 F. Supp. 2d 404 (ND Miss 2000) (same); *Barrett v. Catacombs Press*, 44 F Supp 2d 717 (ED Pa 1999) (same); *EDIAS Software Int'l, LLC v. Basis Int'l Ltd* 947 F Supp. 413 (D Ariz 1996) (holding that jurisdiction was established in defamation case).

337. See, *e.g., Bancroft & Masters Inc. v. Augusta Nat'l Inc.* 223 F3d 1082 (9th Cir 2000) (in a trademark dispute over domain name, defendant's letter to the domain name registrar asking that domain name be put on hold was conduct individually targeting plaintiff, whom defendant knew to be resident of forum state and which had effects felt primarily in forum state); *Intercon Inc. v. Bell Atlantic Internet Solutions Inc.* 205 F3d 1244 (10th Cir 2000) (exercising personal jurisdiction where defendant's transmissions through plaintiff's mail server constituted conduct purposefully directed at the forum state that caused plaintiff's harm); *American Information Corp v. American Infometrics Inc.* 139 F. Supp. 2d 696 (D Md 2001) (use of a service mark as a web site address without evidence of entry into forum state, deliberate targeting of plaintiff, or concentration of harmful effects in forum state, does not satisfy effects test).

338. *Roberts-Gordon LLC v. Superior Radiant Products LTD*, 85 F. Supp. 2d 202 (WD NY 2000).

339. *Yahoo! Inc. v. La Ligue Contre Le Racisme*, 2001 U.S. Dist LEXIS 7565 (ND Cal June 7, 2001).

340. See *Ligue Contre le Racisme et L'Antisemitisme v. Yahoo! Inc.* No RG:00/05308 (TGI Paris, November 20, 2000) available at http://www.juriscom.net/txt/jurisfr/cti/tgiparis20001120.pdf.

341. *ibid.*

342. The foreign practitioner should bear in mind that common and statutory law in any given area is not necessarily uniform from state to state. Particularly in the realm of Internet law, legal standards are evolving at different rates as U.S. courts and state legislatures continue to grapple with the implications of the Internet. Retention of local counsel may be essential to timely addressing a given issue.

343. The three primary theories of copyright infringement—direct infringement, contributory liability and vicarious liability—have been articulated in the context of online activities. For a leading pre-DMCA example see *Religious Technology Center v. Netcom On-Line Communications Services, Inc*, 907 F. Supp. 1361 (ND Cal 1995) (analysing all three theories in relation to the liability of an ISP). See also *Religious Technology Center v. Lerma*, 1996 U.S. Dist. LEXIS 15454 (ED Va October 4, 1996) (direct infringement); *Playboy Enterprises Inc. v. Frena* 839 F. Supp. 1552 (MD Fla 1993) (direct infringement); *Sega Enterprises Ltd v. MAPHIA*, 948 F Supp 923 (ND Cal 1996) (contributory liability); *Sega Enterprises Ltd v. Sabella*, 1996 U.S. Dist. LEXIS 20470 (ND Cal December 18, 1996) (contributory liability); *Playboy Enterprises v. Webbworld Inc.* 991 F Supp 543 (ND Tex 1997) (vicarious liability). For a more complete discussion of copyright issues related to the Internet, see Julian S. Millstein, Jeffrey D. Neuburger, Jeffrey P. Weingart, *Doing Business on the Internet: Forms & Analysis* (Law Journal Press, 1997–2001).

344. See *e.g. A&M Records v. Napster Inc.* 239 F3d 1004 (9th Cir 2001) (upholding the federal district court's issuance of a preliminary injunction directing Napster to prevent infringing music files from being distributed through its online, peer-to-peer music file-sharing system); *UMG Recordings Inc. v. MP3.com Inc.* 92 F. Supp. 2d 349 (SDNY 2000) (holding that defendant infringed plaintiffs' copyrights and denying defendant's "fair use" defense where defendant copied plaintiffs' recordings onto its computer servers and replayed the recordings for its subscribers). In another music piracy case, several record labels filed suit against Aimster, a service allowing users to trade files using America Online's Instant Messenger software, alleging contributory and vicarious copyright infringement and unfair competition. *Zomba Recording Corp v. Deep*, 01-CV-4452 (SDNY filed May 24, 2001) available at http://www.riaa.com/pdf/aimster_complaint.pdf. Prior to the filing of this action, Aimster and its ISP had filed two suits against the Recording Industry Association of America (RIAA) seeking declaratory judgments that their actions did not violate the DMCA. See *Abovepeer Inc. v. RIAA*, 1:01CV632 (NDNY filed April 30, 2001); *Buddyusa Inc. v. RIAA*, 1:01CV631 (NDNY filed April 30, 2001).

345. Online Copyright Infringement Liability Limitation Act (OCILLA), 17 USC § 512 (2001).

346. See 17 USC § 512(k)(1)(defining 'service provider'). OCILLA defines "service provider" in two different ways, depending on the activity in which the entity is engaged. When an entity transmits, routes, or provides connections for third party material within the meaning of the safe harbor in 17 USC § 512(a), a "service provider" is defined as "an entity offering the transmission, routing or providing of connections for digital online communications, between or among points specified by a user, of material of the user's choosing, without modification to the content of the materials as sent or received." OCILLA, N. 219 supra, § 202 (new § 512 (k)(1)(A) (defining the term "service provider" for purposes of the safe harbor in 17 USC 512(a)). This definition is based on the definition of "telecommunications" in the Communications Act of 1934 and, according to the legislative history of the OCILLA, is intended to focus on providers of conduit functionality. H. Rep. No. 105-551, pt. 2, at 63 (1998). The legislative history further provides that "hosting a web site" does not fall within the definition, while the "mere" provision of connectivity to a Web site does. Id. at 63–64. A university Intranet is specifically envisioned as qualifying for the exemption. OCILLA, § 202 (new § 512(e)). For all other online activities addressed in the remaining safe harbor provisions of OCILLA,

in 17 USC §§ 512(b), (c) & (d), the term "service provider" is expanded to include "providers of online services or network access or the providers of facilities therefor." OCILLA § 202 (new § 512(k)(1)(B)). The legislative history states that the definition includes, for example, "providing Internet access, e-mail, chat room and web page hosting services." H. Rep. No. 105-551, pt. 2, at 64 (1998). It is unclear whether the provider of a Web site that does not include such functionality is a "service provider" under this definition. In this regard, the frequent use of the terms "subscriber" and "account holder" suggests that OCILLA may not have been intended to apply generally to all Web sites, but only to those in which a "subscriber" or "account holder" relationship exists.

347. See 17 USC § 512(a).

348. See 17 USC § 512(b).

349. See 17 USC § 512(c).

350. See 17 USC § 512(d).

351. See 17 USC § 512(l).

352. See 17 USC § 512(i).

353. While the DMCA requires that a copyright owner provide notice of alleged infringement to the ISP in a detailed manner, at least one court has held that such notice need not "perfectly" comply with the format described in the act. Rather, in order to take advantage of the DMCA's safe harbor provision, an ISP must remove or disable access to allegedly infringing material upon receiving a notice from the copyright owner that "substantially" complies with the notification requirement. *ALS Scan, Inc. v. RemarQ Communities, Inc,* 239 F3d 619, 625 (4th Cir 2001).

354. On November 3, 1998, the Copyright Office issued Interim Regulations that explain how service providers can properly register a designated agent for purposes of the Act. 37 CFR § 201.38 (2001).

355. 17 USC § 1201(a)(1)(A).

356. 17 USC § 1201(b)(1)(A).

357. See, *e.g., Real Networks Inc. v. Streambox Inc.* 2000 U.S. Dist. LEXIS 1889 (WD Wash January 18, 2000) (holding that plaintiff, a developer of products that enable users to access streaming audio and video content over the Internet, had demonstrated a reasonable likelihood of success on its claims that defendant's software violated the DMCA because at least a part of defendant's product was "primarily, if not exclusively, designed to circumvent the access control and copy protection measures that RealNetworks affords copyright owners").

358. See *Universal City Studios Inc. v. Reimerdes* 82 F. Supp. 2d 211 (SDNY 2000) (preliminary injunction) and 111 F Supp 2d 294 (SDNY 2000) (permanent injunction), *appeal docketed*, No 00-9185 (2d Cir 2000) (enjoining web site from posting or linking to a program capable of circumventing the copy protection of digital versatile disks (DVDs)). See also *DVD Copy Control Assoc. v. McLaughlin* CV-786804 (Super Ct Cal, Santa Clara Cty, January 21, 2000) available at http://www.eff.org/ip/Video/DVDCCA_case/20000120-pi-order.html (enjoining defendants from distributing a program to defeat the copy protection of DVDs and other information regarding the copy protection scheme used on DVDs in an action brought under California state trade secret law).

359. See *U.S. v. Sklyarov* No 5-01-257 (ND Cal filed July 7, 2001) available at http://www.eff.org/IP/DMCA/US_v_Sklyarov/20010707_complaint.html (criminal complaint alleging that a product offered for sale by a Russian company allowing users to defeat the copy protection on electronic documents encoded in certain proprietary formats violates the DMCA).

360. Hyperlinks, also known as links, are points in web documents through which users may "branch" to other bodies of information. Web pages may contain any number of hyperlinks, each of which may point to files or documents on different machines in different locations. The power of linking lies in the fact that the links themselves can be embedded in content, thus allowing users of the web to easily locate information and seamlessly follow relationships between documents. As a general rule, materials published on the web may be viewed by all Internet users unless affirmative steps are taken to limit access. As a result, web sites are widely linked without prior consent from web site owners.

361. See, *e.g., Intellectual Reserve Inc. v. Utah Lighthouse Ministry Inc.* 75 F Supp 2d 1290 (CD Utah 1999) (preliminarily enjoining the defendant from linking to copyright-protected material on third-party web sites); *DVD Copy Control Association Inc. v. McLaughlin* CV-786804 (Super Ct Cal, Santa Clara Cty, January 21, 2000) (enjoining defendants from distributing a program to defeat the copy protection of DVDs and other information regarding the copy protection scheme used on DVDs in an action brought under California state trade secret law); *Universal City Studios Inc. v. Reimerdes* 82 F. Supp. 2d 211 (SDNY 2000) (preliminary injunction) and 111 F. Supp. 2d 294 (SDNY 2000) (permanent injunction), *appeal docketed*, No 00-9185 (2d Cir 2000) (enjoining, under the anticircumvention provision of the Digital Millennium Copyright Act, the posting of source code, as well as linking to the source code, of a computer program that decrypts the copyright protection scheme for DVDs).

362. *Jeri-Jo Knitwear Inc. v. Club Italia Inc.* 94 F. Supp. 2d 457 (SDNY 2000). The defendant, an Italian clothing manufacturer, was accused of violating a prior injunction against "advertising or promoting" apparel bearing the plaintiff's trademark in the U.S. The defendant operated two web sites that were intended to market its non-infringing products to U.S. consumers and another web site, intended for consumers in Italy, where apparel bearing the plaintiff's trademarks was displayed. The two U.S. web sites contained links to the Italian web site. The court found that the presence of these links on the U.S. web sites violated

the injunction, and ordered defendant to immediately "de-link" its Italian site from the others.

363. *Ticketmaster Corp. v. Tickets.com Inc.* 2000 U.S. Dist. LEXIS 4553 (CD Cal March 27, 2000) (denying preliminary injunction) and 2000 U.S. Dist. LEXIS 12987 (August 11, 2000) (denying preliminary injunction), *aff'd*, 2001 U.S. App. LEXIS 1454 (9th Cir January 22, 2001) (summarily affirming denial of preliminary injunction). In its opinion denying in part and granting in part defendant's motion to dismiss the plaintiff's complaint, the court found that "hyperlinking does not itself involve a violation of the Copyright Act ... since no copying is involved," and that there was no deception involved in Tickets's links, comparing them to "using a library's card index to get reference to particular items, albeit faster and more efficiently." 2000 U.S. Dist. LEXIS 4553 at *6 & *9. The court also dismissed Ticketmaster's breach of contract claim, holding that the agreement on Ticketmaster's home page setting forth terms and conditions of use—including no deep linking to its pages and no commercial use of the information—did not create an enforceable contract, and dismissing the claim with leave for Ticketmaster to amend to show that Tickets.com had knowledge of and agreed to those terms. *ibid.* at *8. However, the decision explicitly let stand the claim that Tickets.com's links tortuously interfered with Ticketmaster's business advantage by disrupting income that would have been derived from its home page banner ads. *ibid.* at *11-*12. The court also denied the motion to dismiss several other of Ticketmaster's claims, including false advertising, unfair competition, reverse passing off, and even the copyright infringement claim, on grounds separate from the linking. *ibid.* at *9. The court refused, however, to grant the preliminary relief sought by the plaintiff. 2001 U.S. Dist LEXIS 12987.

364. See *e.g. Hard Rock Café Int'l Inc. v. Morton* 1999 U.S. Dist LEXIS 13760 (SDNY September 9, 1999) (amending prior judgment prohibiting defendant from framing a third party web site). See also *Shetland Times Ltd v. Wills* Scot. Sess. Cas (10/24/96) 1 E.I.P.L.R. 723 (11/1/96) (temporary judgment requiring defendant to remove all links to the pages of the plaintiff's web site). The case settled November 11, 1997. The court's October 1996 Order granting interim interdict in the case is available online at http://www.jmls.edu/cyber/cases/shetld2.html (visited August 6, 2001).

365. *Register.com v. Verio Inc.* 126 F. Supp. 2d 239 (SDNY 2000).

366. *eBay Inc. v. Bidder's Edge Inc.* 100 F. Supp. 2d 1058 (ND Cal 2000). Bidder's Edge both modified its site and appealed the injunction, which specifically barred Bidder's Edge "from using any automated query program, robot, web crawler or other similar device" to access eBay's servers.

367. There is much controversy surrounding federal and state law regarding the elements of defamation and, in particular, relating to on-line defamation. For a more complete discussion of defamation issues related to the Internet, see Julian S. Millstein, Jeffrey D. Neuburger, Jeffrey P. Weingart, *Doing Business on the Internet: Forms and Analysis* (Law Journal Press, 1997–2001).

368. See *American Civil Liberties Union v. Reno*, 929 F Supp 824, 837 (ED Pa 1996) aff'd, 521 US 844 (1997) (characterizing as publishers those who post information on a web site). While not a defamation case, *ACLU v.Reno* has been cited by at least one US court for its definition of what it means to 'publish' via the World Wide Web. See *Hearst Corp v. Goldberger*, 1997 U.S. Dist. LEXIS 2065 (SDNY February 26, 1997).

369. See *EDIAS Software Int'l, LLC v Basis Int'l Ltd*, 947 F. Supp. 413, 420 (D Ariz 1996) (jurisdiction established by New Mexico defendant's posting on web site of allegedly defamatory press release, which had 'effects' in Arizona) and discussion *infra*. See also *Bochan v. La Fontaine*, 68 F. Supp. 2d 692 (ED Va 1999) (jurisdiction established by defendants' using their AOL account to post to Usenet newsgroup). In *Bochan*, the alleged defamatory statement was transmitted to AOL's Usenet server hardware located in Virginia, was temporarily stored on the server, and was then transmitted to other Usenet servers around the world. The court explained that because publication is a required element of defamation and because a "prima facie showing has been made that the use of Usenet server in Virginia was integral to that publication, there is a sufficient act in Virginia" to satisfy the state's long-arm statute.

370. See *Revell v. Lidov*, 2001 U.S. Dist LEXIS 3133 (ND Tex March 20, 2001) (applying effects test in declining to exercise personal jurisdiction in defamation case); *Lofton v. Turbine Design Inc.* 100 F. Supp. 2d 404 (ND Miss 2000) (applying effects test in declining to exercise personal jurisdiction in defamation case); *Bailey v. Turbine Design Inc.* 86 F. Supp. 2d 790 (WD Tenn 2000) (holding that posting of defamatory statements concerning the plaintiff on a passive web site is not sufficient to support jurisdiction in Tennessee, the plaintiff's home state, because the plaintiff "was not attacked as a Tennessee businessman"); *Barrett v. Catacombs Press*, 44 F. Supp. 2d 717 (ED Pa 1999) (holding that the effects test of *Calder* was not satisfied because the defamatory statements were not expressly aimed at Pennsylvania: "If anything, the defamatory statements concern the plaintiff's non-Pennsylvania activities and impugn his professionalism as a nationally-recognised consumer health advocate").

371. *Batzel v. Smith*, 2001 U.S. Dist. LEXIS 8929 (CD Cal June 5, 2001) (holding that the e-mails, the republication of California newspaper articles on the defendant's web site, and a trip to California and sponsorship of the Web site by a California company "demonstrate that the Defendants purposefully availed themselves of numerous opportunities to conduct significant activities in the state).

372. See, *e.g., Gridiron.com, Inc. v. National Football League*, 106 F. Supp. 2d 1309 (SD Fla July 11, 2000) (construing a contract with National Football League players concerning their rights of publicity in connection with an Internet web site); *Suze Randall Photography v. Reactor Inc.* 2000 U.S. Dist. LEXIS 6576 (ND Ill May 12, 2000) (awarding damages under federal copyright law and the Illinois Right of Publicity Statute for posting of photographs on Internet web site).

373. *Cuccioli v. Jekyll & Hyde Neue Metropol Bremen Theater Production GMBH & Co.* 2001 U.S. Dist. LEXIS 8699 (SDNY June 28, 2001).
374. *Cody v. Ward*, 954 F. Supp. 43 (D Conn 1997).
375. The court held that defendant Ward's four telephone calls and 15 e-mail transmissions to Cody rendered Ward liable to suit in Connecticut, where Ward's transmissions contained fraudulent misrepresentations made for the purpose of inducing Cody to buy and hold securities. *Cody*, 954 F. Supp. at 44. Thus, under the "purposeful availment requirement of *Burger King*, the court's exercise of personal jurisdiction over Ward would not violate due process." *ibid.* at 46–47.
376. *Fowler v. Broussard*, 2001 U.S. Dist. LEXIS 573 (ND Tex January 22, 2001).
377. *Christian Book Distributors Inc. v. Great Christian Books Inc.* 137 Md App 367 (Ct App 2001) (upholding the exercise of jurisdiction)(quoting prior Massachusetts opinions, in a case involving the enforcement of a Massachusetts judgment).
378. *Euromarket Designs Inc. v. Crate & Barrel Ltd*, 96 F. Supp. 2d 824 (ND Ill May 16, 2000).
379. *cf. Ligue Contre le Racisme et L'Antisemitisme v. Yahoo! Inc.* No RG:00/05308 (TGI Paris, November 20, 2000) available at http://www.juriscom.net/txt/jurisfr/cti/tgiparis20001120.pdf (ordering a U.S. web site operator to block access by French citizens to auctions of Nazi items).
380. *Tech Heads Inc. v. Desktop Service Center Inc.* 105 F. Supp. 2d 1142 (D Ore July 11, 2000).
381. *ibid.* at 1152.

7

Data Protection

7.1 Why data protection is relevant to the Internet

The use of the Internet for handling information may raise data protection issues in broadly the following areas.

7–001

7.1.1 Publishing personal data

Broadly, publishing personal data concerns publishing any information relating to an identifiable living individual on a Web site. This raises some issues which differ from publication in a hard copy medium:

7–002

- publication on a Web site renders the material, by default, immediately available for transfer to a user in any country in the world. Although publication locally in hard copy may result in the material being taken to another jurisdiction, publication on a Web site may have different consequences regarding, for instance, restrictions on transborder data flows.

- publication on a Web site may, due to its greater reach, be regarded as different in kind from publication in a hard copy medium. For instance, personal data might be volunteered for publication in a small circulation magazine having a defined audience with a common interest. Publishing the same magazine on the Web, even if primarily for the benefit of the same audience, exposes the personal data to a vastly wider readership than that which may have been contemplated by those who submitted personal data for publication. The fact that a Web site is a computerised medium also brings the publication firmly within the scope of data protection legislation.

- publication on a Web site will give rise to issues concerning the security of the computer system driving the Web site and the ease or difficulty with which the system may be hacked and material altered or damaged.

- the Internet has thrown up some novel forms of publication. For instance, Webcams are now common. These are cameras, connected to a Web site, pointed at views of offices, streets, beaches, ski slopes, townscape and landscape views or almost anything. They typically refresh every few minutes, or in some cases deliver live video. Their output can be viewed by anyone visiting the Web site. In some cases the visitor to the Web site can take control of the camera and pan and zoom it.

7.1.2 Holding material on an internal database or computer system with Internet connectivity.

7–003   Most internal corporate computer systems have Internet connectivity, for instance to allow staff to access the Internet or to allow third parties to access parts of the system (*e.g.* members of a closed "extranet" user group accessing their customer or supplier relationship data, or public access to a self-hosted Web site). As soon as Internet connectivity is made available, security concerns will arise from the fact that the internal computer system is now connected to the public network. These concerns will extend both to the protections built in to ensure that unauthorised third parties do not enter the private parts of the system and to whether the data are encrypted so as to be useless to a hacker who does breach the system's defences. Issues will also arise within an international corporation as to cross-border data flows, for instance when customer and supplier staff (or indeed the corporation's own staff) are able to access the system from wherever in the world they may be.

Where personal data are incorporated into material held on an Internet site available for public access or for access by members of a closed user group, different considerations apply. Unless access is restricted to a closed user group and is coupled with encryption and/or a firewall, any person with access to the Internet can visit the site and extract information held on it. Such wide dissemination exposes data subjects to the risk that information relating to them may be acquired by strangers in other countries and used for unregulated purposes which were not in contemplation when the information in question was originally obtained from the data subjects concerned.

7.1.3 Sending information by Internet e-mail.

7–004   This chapter is concerned primarily with the data protection implications of exposing personal data to public access through Web sites, but e-mails incorporating personal data, if addressed to users outside the United Kingdom or if unprotected by encryption, could carry less obvious risks of contravening E.U. or United Kingdom data protection law.

Internet e-mail raises security issues as to whether the information can be intercepted during transmission, or at any of the points at which the e-mail may be stored, and the significance of the country of location of such storage (*e.g.* an English resident who uses a U.S. ISP for his dial-up Internet access, so that his mail is held on a server in the USA). Again, the use of encryption may be relevant to the security concerns. Any Internet transmission, not just e-mail, may be routed through a number of different countries and may potentially be "sniffed" during transmission. E-mail differs in often being stored in mailboxes hosted by intermediaries pending being accessed by the recipient, whereas a Web or file download session is conducted in real time between the server and the user's PC. This also raises issues as to the obligations on intermediaries to comply with data protection principles.

The use of Internet e-mail may occasionally carry unexpected publication conse-   **7–005**
quences. An example is the famous Clare Swire e-mail incident, in which personal data of
a salacious character was forwarded to a small local group of e-mail recipients and within
hours had found its way onto computer screens around the world. When this effect is
achieved intentionally, to promote a product or service, it goes under the name "viral
marketing"; taking its name from the behaviour of e-mail viruses that multiply as they
are forwarded from one address list to the next.

7.1.4 Acquisition of data from a person visiting an Internet resource such as a Web site

It is common for Web site operators, or banner advertisement companies and others, to   **7–006**
acquire data about visitors to Web sites, Such acquisition may be overt, through the
visitor completing a form, or may be invisible to the user (*e.g.* a "cookie" which tracks the
user's path through the site and can be used to personalise the site for the individual
visitor).

All these areas raise questions about the degree to which any activity falls within the
territorial scope of E.U. or United Kingdom data protection legislation. Particular
problems may be encountered in ascertaining where and by whom "processing" is
taking place in a distributed network environment such as the Internet.

The E.U. Directive on the protection of individuals with regard to the processing of   **7–007**
personal data and on the free movement of such data[1] (Directive 95/46) requires Member
States to legislate so that individuals have the right on compelling legitimate grounds to
object to further processing of their personal data.[2] Subject to limited exceptions the
transfer to third countries of personal data is allowed only if the country in question
provides an adequate level of protection. Publishing personal data on the Internet
potentially enables such data to be accessed from and transferred to any country in the
world: once transferred to a country without adequate data protection laws, further
control of the use of such data may become impracticable.

Directive 95/46[3] was required to be implemented in each EEA state, including each of
the E.U. Member States before 24 October 1998. The United Kingdom has enacted the
Data Protection Act 1998 (the "1998 Act"). The 1998 Act received the Royal Assent on July
16, 1998, and was brought into effect on March 1, 2000. It repealed and replaced the 1984
Data Protection Act 1984 (the "1984 Act").

The Data Protection Principles
The 1998 Act includes, in Schedule 1, a set of eight data protection principles. These may   **7–008**
be briefly summarised as follows:

First principle—that personal data shall be processed fairly and lawfully and shall not be
processed unless at least one of the conditions in each of Schedule 2 (all personal data)
and Schedule 3 (sensitive personal data) is met

Second principle—that personal data shall be obtained only for one or more specified and
lawful purposes, and shall not be further processed in any manner incompatible with that
purpose or those purposes

Third principle—that personal data shall be adequate, relevant and not excessive in
relation to the purpose or purposes for which they are processed

Fourth principle—that personal data shall be accurate and, where necessary, kept up to date

Fifth principle—that personal data processed for any purpose or purposes shall not be kept longer than is necessary for that purpose or those purposes

Sixth principle—that personal data shall be processed in accordance with the rights of data subjects under the 1998 Act

Seventh principle—that appropriate technical and organisational measures shall be taken against unauthorised or unlawful processing of personal data and against accidental loss or destruction of, or damage to, personal data

Eighth principle—that personal data shall not be transferred to a country or territory outside the EEA unless that country or territory ensures an adequate level of protection for the rights and freedoms of data subjects in relation to the processing of personal data

These principles are not identical to, but reflect and broadly follow, the 1984 Act's principles. They are considered more fully at 7.9 below. Each of the principles is subject to further interpretation in accordance with the detailed provisions of Schedule 1 Part II of the 1998 Act.

7–009   The Internet is an open environment which exists to publicise information and which encourages browsing. It presents unrivalled opportunities for the widespread dissemination of personal data. The scope for breach, whether through inadvertence or deliberate abuse, of the data protection principles is enormous.

For these reasons, it is important to take data protection considerations into account, and in doing so to consider the provisions of Directive 95/46[4] and the 1998 Act, before allowing any personal data to be transmitted through the Internet, or adding personal data to any Web site or Internet accessible database.

7–010   In April 1997 the Data Protection Registrar (as she then was) issued guidance on registration for Internet users under the 1984 Act. This followed general guidance on data protection and the Internet published in June 1995 as Appendix 6 to the Registrar's Eleventh Annual Report. The Appendix stressed the purpose of the Internet as facilitating the exchange of information, and that protecting information runs counter to its culture: any proposal to use the Internet to provide access to personal data or to communicate personal data from one user to another therefore needed to be regarded with caution. The whole tenor of the Appendix was to warn against the risks to privacy inherent in the use of personal data in a way which allowed access to or from the Internet.

In her Notification Handbook under the 1998 Act the Commissioner points out that data controllers must indicate in their notifications whether personal data are, or are to be, transferred outside the EEA: "transfer" in this context is not defined, but the ordinary meaning of the word is transmission from one place or person to another and this will include posting information on a Web site which can be accessed from overseas. In these circumstances the Commissioner states it is appropriate to indicate that worldwide transfers may be made.

7–011   Copies of the Notification Handbook are available from the Office of the Information Commissioner, Wycliffe House, Water Lane, Wilmslow, Cheshire SK9 5AF. There is a telephone notification service available on 01625-545740, and notification by e-mail may be made to "mail@notification.demon.co.uk". There is an information line on 01625-

545745. The Commissioner's homepage is http://www.dataprotection.gov.uk. General e-mail should be addressed to ''mail@dataprotection.gov.uk?'', but when sending e-mail expecting a postal reply the Commissioner reminds correspondents to give a postal address.

7.2 EU Directive on Data Protection

7.2.1 General

On October 24, 1995 the European Union adopted Directive 95/46[5]. The United Kingdom was required to enact the Directive's provisions not later than October 24, 1998, and did so on July 16, 1998 when the Royal Assent was given to the Data Protection Act 1998 (the ''1998 Act''). The 1998 Act was brought into effect on March 1, 2000, when it repealed the 1984 Act in its entirety.   **7–012**

Compared with the 1984 Act, the Directive provides strengthened remedies for data subjects for breaches of the Directive's requirements, extends controls over the transfer of personal data to third countries (that is to say, countries outside the European Economic Area (the ''EEA'')), and gives data subjects new rights, including the right to object on legitimate grounds to continued processing of their personal data.

The objects of Directive 95/46[6] are stated as being to protect the fundamental rights and freedoms of natural persons, and in particular their right to privacy with respect to the processing of personal data, and to prevent the restriction or prohibition of the free flow of personal data between Member States for privacy reasons (Article 1).

The scope of Directive 95/46[7] is stated to extend to the processing of personal data wholly or partly by automatic means, and to the processing otherwise than by automatic means of personal data which form part of a filing system or are intended to form part of a filing system. These references to filing systems relate to the Directive's extension of the European Community's data protection regime to manual personal data held in structured sets which are accessible according to specific criteria (Article 2(c)). However, the Directive does not apply to the processing of personal data in the course of an activity which falls outside the scope of Community law, and in any case to processing operations concerning public security, defence, State security (including the economic well-being of the State where the processing operation relates to State security matters) and the activities of the State in areas of criminal law, or to processing of personal data by a natural person in the course of a purely personal or household activity. The precise boundaries of Community law are thus difficult to define.   **7–013**

The Directive is concerned primarily with the control of the purposes and methods of processing of personal data, and persons exercising such control, either alone or jointly or in common with others, are described by the Directive as ''controllers''.

7.2.2 Applicable national law

The national law applicable to any processing of personal data in the EEA is to be the law of the Member State where processing is carried out in the context of the activity of an establishment of the controller within the territory of that Member State. Where a controller is established in the territory of several Member States, the controller must take the necessary measures to ensure that each of these establishments complies with the   **7–014** obligations laid down by each of these applicable national laws. Where a controller is not established within any EEA territory, but makes use of equipment situated in a Member State for the purpose of processing personal data otherwise than only for the purposes of transit through EEA territory, the controller must comply with the law of the Member State in which the equipment is situated and must designate a representative established in that territory (Article 4). On a strict reading of the Directive, a controller established outside the EEA resident's hard drive will be making use of that residents equipment and so must comply with the date protection law of that resident's EEA state.

7.2.3 Cross-border data transfers to non-EEA countries

7–015   Directive 95/46 requires Member States to provide that the transfer to a non-EEA country **or** territory ("third country") of personal data which are undergoing processing or which are intended for processing after transfer may take place only if the third country ensures an adequate level of protection. For this purpose, adequacy is to be assessed in the light of all the circumstances surrounding a data transfer operation, with particular consideration to be given to the nature of the data, the country of origin, the country of final destination, and the laws of that country (Article 25).

7–016   Subject to the domestic laws of Member States governing particular cases, transfers to third countries which do not ensure an adequate level of protection may take place only when

- the data subject has given his consent unambiguously to the proposed transfer; or

- the transfer is necessary for the performance of a contract between the data subject and the controller or the implementation of pre-contractual measures taken in response to the data subject's request; or

- the transfer is necessary for the conclusion or performance of a contract concluded in the interest of the data subject between the controller and a third party; or

- the transfer is necessary or legally required on important public interest grounds, or for the establishment, exercise or defence of legal claims; or

- the transfer is necessary in order to protect the vital interests of the data subject; or

- the transfer is made from a register which according to laws or regulations is intended to provide information to the public and which is open to consultation either by the public in general or by any person who can demonstrate legitimate interest, to the extent that the conditions laid down in law for consultation are fulfilled in the particular case (Article 26 (1)).

7.2.4 Application of the Directive to the Internet

7–017   In the context of exposing personal data on a Web site accessible from the Internet without restriction of access to the site, it follows from the above provisions that:

- it is not practicable to distinguish between access to such personal data from EEA Member States and from other countries or territories except by establishing extranets allowing access only to identified controllers established in one or more EEA Member State;

- personal data made accessible from the Internet are potentially at risk of transfer to any country in the world including third countries which do not ensure an adequate level of protection;

- where data subjects have given consent unambiguously to the exposure of their personal data to the Internet, any such transfer, including a transfer to a third country not ensuring an adequate level of protection, will be outside the Directive's prohibition. An approximately drafted, displayed and accepted privacy statement may be the best way of obtaining consent from Web site visitors for the use and further distribution of information relating to them obtained by means of cookies;

- it may be practicable to apply any of the Directive's other Article 26 exceptions listed above, but each such exception requires necessity for its accepted purpose and necessity may be difficult to prove. Taking consent from the data subject seems, therefore, to be preferable except where personal data can be so controlled as to ensure that transfer is restricted either to transfer to a controller established in an EEA Member State or is restricted to circumstances which clearly fit one of the Article 26(1) exceptions.

Where transfers can be restricted and controlled, the following options are available in addition to taking the data subject's unambiguous consent to the proposed transfer: **7–018**

- to restrict transfer to EEA Member States and to third countries which ensure an adequate level of protection;

    Adequacy has been considered by the Working Party established by the Commission under Article 29 of Directive 95/46[8] whose Working Document adopted in July 1998 sets out the Working Party's views on:

    - what constitutes "adequate protection";
    - the role of contractual provisions; and
    - procedural issues and examples.

- to subject transfers to standard contractual clauses authorised by the Member State of the controller of the Web site as offering sufficient safeguards, which are then imposed upon transferee controllers (Article 26(2)):

    — In June 2001 the Commission approved Standard Contractual Clauses ensuring adequate safeguards for personal data transferred from countries within the E.U. to countries outside the European Union: these clauses apply equally to transfers from countries within the EEA.
    — In the case of transfers to recipients in the United States, to ensure that the proposed recipient has signed up to the Safe Harbor principles which have been negotiated between the Department of Commerce and the European Commission, and which have been available for signature since November 1, 2000.

7.3 The 1998 Act's definitions

7–019   The 1998 Act redefines a number of expressions previously defined under the 1984 Act, and in some cases in significantly different terms. In an Internet context, the most important changes are in relation to the definitions of "data", "personal data", "processing", "data controller" and "data processor". There are also significant extensions to the meanings of the terms "obtaining", "recording", "using" and "disclosing" in relation to personal data.

These definitions and extended meanings have the effect of broadening the range of information and information-related activities to which the United Kingdom's data protection regulatory scheme applies, and bring within the ambit of the 1998 Act information made accessible to the Internet which might previously not have been subject to data protection regulation.

7.3.1 "Data"

7–020   "Data" under the 1998 Act means information which:

(a)   is being processed by means of equipment operating automatically in response to instructions given for that purpose,

(b)   is recorded with the intention that it should be processed by means of such equipment,

(c)   is recorded as part of a relevant filing system, as defined by the 1998 Act, or with the intention that it should form part of a relevant filing system, or

(d)   does not fall within paragraph (a), (b) or (c) but forms part of an accessible record as defined by section 68 of 1998 Act (1998 Act, section 1(1)). Broadly, an accessible record is defined by section 68 as a health record, local authority or special school record, local authority housing record or local authority social services record, in each case whether or not processed automatically.

7.3.2 "Personal data"

7–021   "Personal data" under the 1998 Act means data which relate to a living individual who can be identified from those data or from those data and other information which is in the possession of, or is likely to come into the possession of, the data controller, and includes any expression of opinion about the individual and any indication of the intentions of the data controller or any other person in respect of the individual.

This definition is substantially wider than the old definition of "personal data" under the 1984 Act: under the 1998 Act it is not essential that the data subject be immediately identifiable from the data held, or from those data and other information in the possession of the data controller, if other information identifying the data subject is likely to come into the possession of the data controller at some future time. It follows that encrypted or otherwise anonymised data relating to an individual whose identity is hidden by the anonymisation will nevertheless be personal data if there is a likelihood of future identification, or capability of future identification, by the data controller either by decryption or by discovery by or disclosure to the data controller of other identifying information. "Likelihood" in this context is to be distinguished from probability on the one hand, and possibility on the other, and is presumably to be judged from current circumstances and not from hindsight.

It seems clear that more information relating to individuals is within the 1998 Act's definition of personal data than was within the 1984 Act's definition.

The Information Commissioner has issued a guidance note[9] setting out her views on the meaning of 'personal data' under the 1998 Act. This includes discussion of some specific Internet issues. As to e-mail addresses, the Commissioner suggests that many e-mail addresses are personal data, where the e-mail address clearly identifies a particular individual. This might suggest that e-mail addresses that do not identify a particular individual are not personal data. However, that would be too simplistic an approach. It is a question of fact in each case whether data relate to a particular individual. The Commissioner suggests that data can relate to more than one individual and still be personal data about each of them, such as individuals who use the same e-mail address. However, the individual must still be capable of being identified from the data or from other data in the possession of, or likely to come into the possession of, the data controller. The Commissioner's view is that it is sufficient if the data are capable of being processed by the data controller to enable the data controller to distinguish the data subject from any other individual. So an e-mail address that does not clearly identify an individual, but in combination with other data in the possession of the data controller can identify an individual, would be personal data.[10]   **7–022**

The Commissioner also takes the view that information compiled about a particular Web user, even if there is no intention to link it to a name and address or to an e-mail address, is still personal data: "In the context of the on-line world the information that identifies an individual is that which uniquely locates him in that world, by distinguishing him from others." In this context the unique number and other information implanted in a cookie would be personal data. However, an IP address alone, at least in the context of the public Internet, would in most cases be unlikely to be personal data. This is because, as used in the public Internet, an IP address does not uniquely locate a user in the on-line world. Although a computer may be permanently associated with one IP address (a static IP address), many users of the Internet do not have static IP addresses. They may be allocated a different IP address by their ISP each time they dial up to the Internet (a dynamic IP address), or they may access through an anonymiser, or they may access through a corporate network, in which case the IP address visible to the outside world will often (for all users on the network) be that of a network proxy server. Conversely, in a private network that uses static IP addresses the data controller could identify at least the computer associated with the IP address, in which case the IP address could well be regarded as personal data relating to the regular user or users of that computer.   **7–023**

7.3.3 "Processing"

The term "processing" is defined by the 1998 Act in such wide terms, by comparison with the 1984 Act's definition, that it is difficult to imagine any activity in relation to information which is not included, from obtaining to destruction and including retrieval, disclosure, dissemination, alteration and combination. The addition of information to, or the alteration or deletion of information on or from, a Web site will be processing, as will   **7–024** the obtaining of information with a view to its addition to a Web site database or collection of pages.

7.3.4 "Data controller"

7–025   The term "data controller" under the 1998 Act replaces the 1984 Act's "data user", and means a person who, either alone or jointly or in common with other persons, determines the purposes for which and the manner in which any personal data are, or are to be, processed. This definition is subject to an exception where personal data are processed only for statutory purposes, in which case the person on whom the statutory obligation to process is imposed is the data controller for the purposes of the 1998 Act.

The 1984 Act's definition of a "data user" referred to controlling the contents and use of a collection of data, which concept differed from, and may have been somewhat narrower than, determining purposes and manner of processing: members of a group of networked companies may together control purposes and manner without controlling content, and so may be data controllers under the 1998 Act where they may not have been data users under the 1984 Act.

In one respect, a data controller under the 1998 Act is a narrower concept than a data user under the 1984 Act: a person who determines the purposes and manner of processing of data none of which are personal data as defined by the 1998 Act is not a data controller for the purposes of that Act, whereas a person who controlled, or alone or jointly with others controlled, the contents and use of a collection of data none of which were personal data under the 1984 Act was a data user for the purposes of that Act.

7.3.5 "Data processor"

7–026   The 1998 Act's "data processor" is defined in relation to personal data as any person (other than an employee of a data controller who processes the data on behalf of the data controller) (1998 Act Section 1(1)). This definition appears effectively to exclude from the definition of data controller persons who process personal data solely on a data controller's behalf and replaces the 1984 Acts references to computer bureaux.

7.3.6 "Obtaining", "recording", "using" and "disclosing"

7–027   The terms "obtaining" and "recording" in relation to personal data under the 1998 Act include obtaining and recording information to be contained in personal data, and "using" and "disclosing" in relation to personal data include using and disclosing the information contained in personal data (1998 Act Section 1(2)). This appears to extend the concept of processing personal data to include obtaining, recording, using and disclosing information to be contained in, or contained in, or extracted from, personal data even though that information may not itself be personal data having, for example, been anonymised. Whether this extends to anonymised so-called meta-data, or meta-information, deduced from personal data remains to be seen. The first instance decision in *R v. Department of Health ex parte Source Informatics Ltd*[11] suggested that a United Kingdom court may construe confidence, and so the 1998 Act's control over unlawful processing, as extending to personal medical information even after the information has been anonymised, though the first instance finding of a breach of confidence was reversed on appeal.[12]

7.4 The 1998 Act's data protection principles

The 1998 Act replaced the 1984 Act's data protection principles with new principles which are in broadly similar but not identical terms. The main changes relate to the first (fair and lawful obtaining and processing), sixth (rights of data subjects), seventh (appropriate technical and organisational security measures) and eighth (transfers to countries outside the EEA) principles.   **7–028**

7.4.1 First principle (fair and lawful obtaining and processing)

Under the 1984 Act the first principle was the most significant. Much analysis which was applied to this part of the 1984 Act is applicable to the 1998 Act, albeit (as discussed below) the conditions for compliance with the first principle have been substantially elaborated. Processing as defined by the 1998 Act includes obtaining. Fair obtaining of personal information requires that the source of the information be not misled and be made aware of the identity of the data controller acquiring the information and the purposes for which the information is to be used or disclosed.   **7–029**

In the context of Internet use, potential disclosure and redisclosure is unlimited and almost any conceivable use by a third party may result from disclosure. To obtain information from a data subject, in response to a personal enquiry by a known data user for use by that data user in further dealings with the data subject giving the information, could be unfair if, unknown to the data subject providing the information, the data user proposed to make the information available to other third parties. Making information accessible over the Internet, either to the public or to a closed user group, has this effect.

Informing the data subject about non-obvious purposes
Under the 1984 Act the Data Protection Tribunal supported the Registrar's view that personal information was not fairly obtained unless, before the information was obtained, the individual was informed of any non-obvious purpose for which the information was required (*Innovations (Mail Order) Ltd v. Data Protection Registrar*[13]). This principle applies equally to obtaining, as being processing, under the 1998 Act. If the data controller intends to include personal data on a database which will be publicly accessible over the Internet, that fact should be made clear to the data subject to whom the data relate before the data controller obtains the relevant information from the data subject. Alternatively, the data controller should obtain the data subject's express positive consent before making the data publicly accessible over the Internet.   **7–030**

The same principle applies to making personal data accessible to a closed user group, as opposed to making the data publicly accessible, though the consequences may be less serious in the former case. The Commissioner takes the view that disclosure by one company in a group of its customers' names and addresses to another company in the same group may be unfair unless either the intention to disclose was made clear to data subjects before their information was obtained, or data subjects' express consent to disclosure is given before disclosure is made.

Information obtained other from the data subject

7–031   Where information is obtained from a source other than the data subject to which the information relates, consideration should be given to the position of the data subject. The Data Protection Registrar's Guidelines under the 1984 Act gave as an example a marketing company obtaining information from a secretary about his or her boss's lifestyle (Registrar's Guidelines (Fourth Series September 1997), at page 55). The same principle applies to the 1998 Act. Personal data including information obtained from a source which had itself obtained the information for a limited purpose could be unfairly processed if the result of the processing were to make such personal data available over the Internet, either publicly or to a closed user group.

Information obtained from a Web site

7–032   Where information is obtained by an Internet user from a Web site, the user obtaining the information will usually be doing so at the implied invitation of the information provider controlling the site. Since one of the main purposes of such sites is to disseminate information to site visitors, a visitor could hardly be said to be unfairly obtaining any of the information offered. However, if the information offered was of a kind which manifestly should not have been made available without the consent of the relevant data subjects, and was in fact made available without their consent, there may be unfair obtaining, and so unfair processing, of those data by site visitors: alternatively or additionally making the information available may be unfair processing by the data controller controlling the site.

Further conditions under the 1998 Act

7–033   Under the 1998 Act the first principle is elaborated with conditions which must be satisfied in relation to the processing of all personal data (Schedule 2) and further conditions which must additionally be satisfied in relation to the processing of sensitive personal data (Schedule 3). The term 'sensitive personal data' means personal data consisting of information as to:

- the racial or ethnic origin of the data subject;

- his political opinions;

- his religious beliefs or other beliefs of a similar nature;

- whether he is a member of a trade union;

- his physical or mental health of condition;

- his sexual life;

- the commission or alleged commission by him of any offence; or

- any proceedings for any offence committed or alleged to have been committed by him, the disposal of such proceedings or the sentence of any court in such proceedings (1998 Act Section 2).

Information to be provided to the data subject

7–034   A fair processing code is imposed (Schedule 1 Part II paragraphs 1 to 4) to regulate the obtaining of all forms of personal data, and requires that the following information be provided or made readily available to the data subject:

- the identity of the data controller;

- the identity of any representative nominated by the data controller;

- the purposes for which the data are to be processed; and

- any further information which is necessary, having regard to the specific circumstances in which the data are or are to be processed, to enable processing in respect of the data subject to be fair.

So far as is practicable, this information is to be provided to the data subject, or made readily available to him, whether the personal data are obtained either directly from him or from a third party. Where the personal data are obtained otherwise than directly from the data subject the required information is to be provided or to be made available when the data controller first processes the data, or before disclosure of the data to a third party. Where the personal data are obtained from a third party, providing the required information to the data subject is excused where its provision would involve a disproportionate effort, or where the recording or disclosing of the personal data is necessary for compliance by the data controller with a legal obligation other than an obligation imposed by contract.

In the context of personal data published on or made accessible through the Internet,   **7–035**
the following points in relation to the first principle are to be noted:

- the requirement of fair and lawful processing will be contravened if information is obtained in confidence, and then exposed on or made accessible through a Web site in breach of confidence;

- the fairness requirement will be contravened if information is obtained from the data subject for one purpose, and then used for another, non-obvious, purpose. Publication of personal data is likely to be a non-obvious use unless either the intention to publish was made clear to the data subject before the information was obtained from him, or the data subject has given consent to the publication. However, this may not be sufficient to legitimise publication on the Internet. Since personal data published on a Web site is exposed to an unlimited and worldwide audience, publication on the Internet may amount to a separate and non-obvious use even if the intention to publish in a traditional way to a limited audience has been made clear. Thus it may be at the least advisable (and often essential) to draw attention to, or gain consent for, an intended publication on the Internet. This is certainly the view of the Information Commissioner.[14]

- if the information is obtained from a third party source, notification to the third party of the intention to display the information on the Internet would not necessarily be fair to the data subject, from whom express consent to the display may be necessary;

- subject to the exceptions permitted by Schedule 4 to the 1998 Act's eighth principle (transfers to non-EEA countries or territories which do not provide adequate protection), publication of personal data on or through the Internet without the consent of the data subject may be in contravention of the eighth principle as well as being in contravention of the first principle.

Collecting information about Web site users

7–036 If site controllers collect information about their visitors, and do so surreptitiously or make that information available to others or otherwise use that information beyond re-contacting the visitors concerned, fair obtaining notices should be displayed at the site. A fair obtaining notice should state succinctly that the data are being collected, the identity of the controller of the site collecting the information or for whom the collection is being made, and any non-obvious purposes for which the collected information will be used.

If the site is maintained by a host or service provider for the site's controller, that controller will usually be the data controller in relation to the site and the service provider will be a processor for the 1998 Act's purposes. However, the Commissioner recognises that a person may decide the purposes for which personal data are to be processed but delegate to another person responsibility for the way in which those data are to be processed: in such circumstances determination of the purpose for which personal data are to be processed is paramount in deciding whether or not a person is a data controller. If both the service provider and the controller contribute to the control of the purposes and manner in which personal data are processed, each will be a data controller in the 1998 Act's terms.

7–037 In deciding whether any particular processing was fair for the purposes of the 1984 Act's first principle the Data Protection Tribunal has held that first and paramount consideration must be given to the data subject, and that processing must be carried out in accordance with the principles laid down by the 1984 Act (*CCN v. Data Protection Registrar*).[15] The same principle applies to the 1998 Act. It follows that the exposure of any item of personal information on the Internet is at risk of being held to be unfair processing if that item includes information relating to an identifiable individual who provided it for a limited purpose, was not then aware of a risk of its virtually world-wide exposure, and who had not subsequently given express and informed consent to disclosure of the data through the Internet, whether publicly or to a closed user group or by e-mail.

In the context of E.U. Directive 95/46,[16] the Article 29 Working Party has considered these issues. On February 23, 1999 it adopted a working document on the processing of personal data on the Internet and its recommendation 1/99 on invisible and automatic processing of personal data on the Internet performed by software and hardware. The working document criticises the secret collection of personal data and makes recommendations against such practices.

Cookies

7–038 The practice of compiling "cookies" and storing them on a Web browser user's own hard disk involves the automatic collection of information about the user's site visits and searches as they are made. The process is not necessarily apparent to the user. Its main purpose is to enable responses to later requests by the same user to be focused to a profile of the user's interests, but "cookies" may also be used by a site operator to collect information about the user for disclosure to the site operator installing the cookie. This information may then be made available by the site operator to third parties.

7–039 The data protection implications of this practice are of the same kind as the implications of the practice, noted above, of collecting names and addresses of site visitors. Even if the only purpose of installing a cookie on a user's hard disk is to enable improved responses to the user's future requests by the cookie installer, the practice is, at least at present, not an obvious use of personal information and unless drawn to the user's attention may be said to be unfair. A preferred course may be for a fair obtaining notice to be displayed to site visitors, drawing attention to the user's ability to disable cookies in his or her browser preferences.

More sophisticated means of allowing users to interact with Web sites over privacy policies may become available if initiatives such as the World Wide Web Consortium (W3C) P3P (Platform for Privacy Preferences) come to fruition.

7.4.2 Second principle (specified and lawful purposes)

The second principle under the 1998 Act conflates and substantially repeats the 1984 **7–040** Act's second and third principles. It requires that personal data shall be obtained only for one or more specified and lawful purposes, and shall not be further processed in any manner incompatible with that purpose or those purposes.

The data controller may, in particular, specify the purposes for which personal data are obtained either in a notice to the data subject, or in a notification to the Commissioner under the notification provisions of Part III of the Act (Schedule 1, Part II paragraph 5).

In determining whether any disclosure of personal data is compatible with the purposes for which the data were obtained, regard is to be had to the purposes for which the personal data are intended to be processed by any person to whom they are disclosed (Schedule 1 Part II paragraph 6). In the context of disclosure through the Internet without the data subject's consent, the lack of any means of controlling the purposes for which the data may be used by persons to whom they are disclosed is likely to result in contravention of the second principle.

7.4.3 Third, fourth and fifth principles (adequacy, relevance, up-to-dateness and period of retention)

The third, fourth and fifth principles under the 1998 Act repeat the fourth, fifth and sixth **7–041** principles under the 1984 Act without change. For the most part these principles, while important, have not to date had any particular relevance to the Internet. However, data retention is becoming an increasingly contentious issue. The fifth principle provides that personal data processed for any purpose or purposes shall not be kept for longer than is necessary for that purpose or purposes. This principle is highly relevant to the data retention practices of Internet service providers and others involved in the transmission of data through the Internet.

The retention of traffic and billing data by providers of public telecommunications services or public telecommunications networks is specifically addressed by Article 6 of the Telecommunications Data Protection Directive (Directive 97/66). The principle of restricting retention of personal data to that which is necessary for the purpose for which the data were originally processed potentially conflicts with the desire of law enforcement agencies that private sector entities should retain data for long periods. Although the Regulation of Investigatory Powers Act 2000 (Part 1, Chapter II) enables certain government agencies to serve notices requiring disclosure of communications data, there is no corresponding requirement on private entities to retain such data. This is seen by some as a lacuna. Others regard compulsory data retention as a threat to civil liberties and unattractive to business.

This debate is ongoing. The forthcoming Communications Data Protection Directive **7–042** (which will replace the Telecommunications Data Protection Directive) at present appears likely to permit Member States to introduce communications data retention requirements for law enforcement and similar purposes and there is clearly pressure from law enforcement agencies to do so.

7.4.4 Sixth principle (rights of data subjects)

7–043   The sixth principle under the 1998 Act requires that personal data shall be processed in accordance with the rights of data subjects and, by comparison with the seventh principle under the 1984 Act which it replaces, is simplified and broadened. The 1984 Act's seventh principle was more elaborate and was restricted to compliance with the right of subject access.

The 1998 Act's sixth principle goes substantially further and requires compliance with the widened range of data subject rights set out in the 1998 Act. Section 13 of the 1998 Act provides for compensation for a data subject who suffers damage and distress by reason of any contravention by any data controller of any of the requirements of the 1998 Act, so that any contravention of that Act, whether or not a contravention of any of the principles, may ground a claim for compensation. It is not clear whether denial of a claim for compensation under section 13 may be treated as a contravention of the sixth principle as being based on a breach of the data subject right to compensation. If that is the case, denial of a claim to compensation may open the door to an allegation of breach of data subject rights in contravention of the sixth principle, with consequent possibility of a request for assessment and/or issue of an enforcement notice under the 1998 Act.

7–044   In the context of the sixth principle, data subject rights, and publication of personal data on the Internet:

- publication by a data controller of personal data on a Web site without the consent of a data subject exposes the data controller to the obligation to provide subject access information as to the source of the data and a description of the recipients or classes of recipients to whom the data may be disclosed (sections 7(1)(b)(iii) and 7(1)(c)(ii) of the 1998 Act);

- a data subject may exercise the right to prevent processing likely to cause damage or distress by serving a notice on the data controller requiring the data controller to cease processing the data subject's personal data on the Web site on the grounds that the processing is likely to cause substantial damage or substantial distress and that the damage or distress is or would be unwarranted (section 10 of the 1998 Act);

- if the data are alleged to be inaccurate, the data subject may apply to the court for rectification, blocking, erasure or destruction (section 14); and

- the data subject may request the Commissioner for assessment as to whether processing of the data subject's personal data on the Web site has been or is being carried out in compliance with the provisions of the 1998 Act (section 42).

7.4.5 Seventh principle (security)

7–045   The seventh principle requires that appropriate technical and organisational measures shall be taken against unauthorised or unlawful processing of personal data and against accidental loss or destruction of, or damage to, personal data. This replaces and extends the provisions of the 1984 Act's eighth principle which required that appropriate security measures should be taken against unauthorised access to, or alteration, disclosure or destruction of, personal data and against accidental loss or destruction of personal data. In the context of the Internet and its known lack of security, storage of personal data on a database underlying a Web site without either firewall or other protection may be a breach of the seventh principle.

It is suggested in the Information Commissioner's draft Code of Practice for the Use of Personal Data in Employer/Employee Relationships that it is good practice, where an employer accepts job applications electronically (*e.g.* through a Web site), for the employer to provide a secure method of transmission. This is justified by reference to the seventh principle. It would extend the application of the seventh principle beyond the data controller's own IT systems or those of persons acting on his behalf, since the secure method would apply to the transmission over a public network of a message sent by a member of the public to the data controller's system.

Where any processing, including disclosure of personal data on a Web site, is **7–046** undertaken by a data processor on behalf of a data controller, the 1998 Act includes express provisions for compliance with the seventh principle which require that:

- the data controller must choose a data processor providing sufficient guarantees in respect of the technical and organisational security measures governing the processing to be carried out; and

- take reasonable steps to ensure compliance with those measures (1998 Act Schedule 1 Part II para 11).

Additionally, the processing must be carried out under a contract which is made or evidenced in writing and under which the data processor is to act only on instructions from the data controller, and the contract must require the data processor to comply with obligations equivalent to those imposed on a data controller by the seventh principle (Schedule 1 Part II paragraph 12 to the 1998 Act).

Since control of the purposes for which personal data are processed on a Web site is **7–047** usually retained by the person promoting the Web site it is likely that that person will be the data controller in relation to that processing and, even though the processing is undertaken or managed by an ISP, host or other third party, the third party is likely in this context to be a processor only. A written contract between the Web site promoter and the ISP will then be required to comply with the seventh principle.

7.4.6 Eighth principle (transborder data flows)

The eighth principle under the 1998 Act, which had no equivalent in the 1984 Act, **7–048** requires that personal data shall not be transferred to a country or territory outside the EEA unless that country or territory ensures an adequate level of protection for the rights and freedoms of data subjects in relation to the processing of personal data.

An adequate level of protection is one which is adequate in all the circumstances, having regard in particular to:

- the nature of the personal data;

- the country or territory of origin of the information contained in the data;

- the country or territory of final destination of that information;

- the purposes for which and period during which the data are intended to be processed;

- the law in force in the country or territory in question;

- the international obligations of that country or territory;

- any relevant codes of conduct or other rules which are enforceable in that country or territory (whether generally or by arrangement in particular cases); and

- any security measures taken in respect of the data in that country or territory (Schedule 1 Part II paragragh 13 to the 1998 Act).

7–049   This principle is subject to express exceptions in cases where the eighth principle does not apply, namely where:

- the data subject has given his consent to the transfer;

- the transfer is necessary for the performance of a contract between the data subject and the data controller, or for the taking of steps at the request of the data subject with a view to his entering into a contract with the data controller;

- the transfer is necessary for the conclusion of a contract between the data controller and a person other than the data subject which is entered into at the request of the data subject or is in the interest of the data subject, or for the performance of such a contract;

- the transfer is necessary for reasons of substantial public interest; or

- the transfer is necessary for the purpose of or in connection with legal proceedings, obtaining legal advice, or otherwise for establishing, exercising or defending legal rights; or

- the transfer is necessary to protect the vital interests of the data subject; or

- the transfer is part of the personal data on a public register and any conditions subject to which the register is open to inspection are complied with by any person to whom the data are or may be disclosed after the transfer; or

- the transfer is made on terms which are of a kind approved by the Commissioner as ensuring adequate safeguards for the rights and freedoms of data subjects; or

- the transfer has been authorised by the Commissioner as being made in such a manner as to ensure adequate safeguards for the rights and freedoms of data subjects (Schedule 4 to the 1998 Act).

In the context of the exposure of personal data on a Web site accessible from the Internet, it is likely that there will be a contravention of the eighth principle unless the data subject has given his consent to the inclusion on a Web site of personal data relating to him.

7–050   The 1998 Act does not elaborate further on the concept of consent in this context, but Directive 95/46[17] provides that "the data subject's consent" shall mean any freely given and specific and informed indication of his wishes by which the data subject signifies his agreement to personal data relating to him being processed (Article 2(h)).

The Commissioner has not indicated that any approval or authorisation of the kinds referred to in Schedule 4 paras 8 or 9 in relation to transfers to third countries will be given by the Commissioner, though forms of contract have been proposed by the International Chamber of Commerce and the Confederation of British Industry. Pre-empting the need for approval or authorisation by the Commissioner, the Safe Harbor principles agreed between the U.S. Department of Commerce and the E.U. Commission enable transfers of personal data from any EEA State, including the United Kingdom, to be made to a U.S. recipient which has signed up to the Safe Harbor. Standard Contractual Clauses approved by the Commission in June 2001 enable transfers of personal data to be made to date to importers in third countries who have entered into contracts in the approved terms with an EEA data exporter. As with contravention of any other principle, contravention of the eighth principle may trigger claims by the data subject for damage and associated distress (Section 13 of the 1998 Act) and a request to the Commissioner for assessment (Section 42 of the 1998 Act).

7.5 The 1998 Act's exemptions

The 1998 Act provides for a number of exemptions which are of varying scope and effect. **7–051** In relation to the Internet, many of these exemptions are only likely to be relevant to personal data transmitted by e-mail to specified addressees and most of them are unlikely to apply to personal data exposed to the Internet on a Web site: however, for completeness a summarised list of the 1998 Act's exemptions is set out below.

Some of these exemptions are expressed in section 27 to be from:

- the 1998 Act's subject information provisions: these are, broadly, that part of the fair processing code under the first data protection principle (Schedule 1 Part II para 2) which requires information to be provided to the data subject, together with subject access right (sections 7 and 8); and/or in the alternative from:

- the 1998 Act's non-disclosure provisions: these are broadly the first data protection principle, except Schedules 2 and 3 imposing conditions on the processing of all personal data and of sensitive personal data respectively, the second, third, fourth and fifth data protection principles, the right to prevent processing likely to cause damage or distress (Section 10) and the rights to rectification, blocking, erasure and destruction (section 14(1) to (3)).

The subject information provisions may broadly be characterised as provisions of the **7–052** 1998 Act which entitle data subjects to be given information about personal data relating to them, and the non-disclosure provisions may broadly be characterised as provisions of the 1998 Act which protect data subjects in certain circumstances from the adverse consequences of disclosure and certain other processing of personal data relating to them.

The 1998 Act's exemptions have been classified by the Commissioner as primary and miscellaneous respectively: the primary exemptions are set out in Part IV of the 1998 Act, and the miscellaneous exemptions are set out in Schedule 7.

7.5.1 Primary exemptions

7–053   The primary exemptions may be summarised as follows:

National security (section 28)
7–054   Personal data are exempt from:

- the data protection principles;
- Part II (rights of data subjects);
- Part III (notification and registration);
- Part v. (enforcement); and
- Section 55 (unlawful obtaining and sale of personal data)

if the exemption is required for the purpose of safeguarding national security. The exemption is by certificate given by a Minister of the Crown.

In *Norman Baker MP v. Secretary of State for the Home Department* (Information Tribunal, October 1, 2001), the Information Tribunal held that even the wide terms of this provision did not allow the Home Secretary to issue a blanket certificate exempting the Security Service from complying with a subject access request under section 7(1)(a) of the 1988 Act;

Crime and taxation (section 29)
7–055   Personal data processed for the purposes of:

- prevention or detection of crime;
- apprehension or prosecution of offenders; or
- assessment or collection of taxes

are exempt from the subject information provisions (see above) in any case to the extent that the application of those provisions would be likely to prejudice those purposes. The inclusion of the words "in any case", which do not appear in Section 29 (national security), avoid the use of claims to exemption in general terms without consideration of particular facts;

Health, education and social work (section 30)
7–056   The Secretary of State may by order exempt information from the subject information provisions (see above) where the information relates to:

- the physical or mental health of a data subject;
- present or former pupils of a school; or
- social work

Regulatory activity (section 31)
7–057   Personal data processed for certain specified regulatory activities (*e.g.* financial services, charities and health and safety at work) are exempt from the subject information

provisions (see above) in any case to the extent that their application would be likely to compromise the proper discharge of those regulatory functions;

Journalism, literature and art (sections 3 and 32)
Personal data processed for journalistic, artistic or literary purposes (the "special purposes") are exempted from: **7–058**

- the data protection principles, except the seventh (security);

- subject access (sections 7 and 8);

- the right to prevent processing likely to cause damage or distress (section 10);

- rights in relation to automated decision-taking (section 12); and

- certain of the rights to rectification, blocking, erasure or destruction (section 14(1) to (3)).

These special purposes exemptions are only available if the processing is undertaken with a view to publication of journalistic, literary or artistic material and the data controller reasonably believes that, having regard in particular to the special importance of the public interest in freedom of expression, publication will be in the public interest and that, in all the circumstances, compliance with the provision exempted is incompatible with the special purposes.

While directed primarily at protecting the freedom of the media, and in particular the   **7–059**
press, the special purposes exemption is in broad terms and may have a wider effect than is immediately apparent. The terms "journalism", "artistic" and "literary" are not defined, and in the context of the Internet any person may claim to be a journalist or engaged in literary or artistic expression.

There is a requirement (section 32(4)(b)) that, when proceedings are brought against a data controller under certain provisions of the 1998 Act, the court shall stay the proceedings if it appears to the court that any personal data to which the proceedings relate are being processed only for the special purposes and with a view to publication by any person of any journalistic, literary or artistic material which, at the time twenty four hours immediately before the court's consideration, had not previously been published by the data controller. Prior publication by another person is not relevant. There is a separate requirement under section 12 of the Human Rights Act 1998 which applies if a court is considering whether to grant any relief which may affect the rights of freedom of expression under Article 10 of the European Convention on Human Rights, to which the United Kingdom is a party. Apparently aimed at preventing applications to the court to restrain publication on privacy grounds, these provisions may be difficult to apply if publication occurs on or through the Internet.

Research, history and statistics (Section 33)
Personal data processed only for research purposes are, subject to detailed and complex   **7–060**
conditions, exempted from:

- the second principle (processing to be compatible with specified and lawful purposes), to the extent that the processing for research purposes may be said to be incompatible with the purposes for which the personal data were obtained;

- the fifth data protection principle (personal data not to be kept longer than necessary); and

- subject access (section 7);

Information statutorily available to the public (section 34)

7–061 Personal data consisting of such information are exempt from:

- the subject information provisions;

- the fourth data protection principle (accuracy and up-to-dateness);

- certain of the rights to rectification, blocking, erasure or destruction (section 14(1) to (3)); and

- the non-disclosure provisions;

Disclosures required by law or made in connection with legal proceedings (section 35)

7–062 Personal data are exempt from the non-disclosure provisions where the disclosure is required by or under any enactment, by any rule of law or by order of a court (section 35(1)), or where the disclosure is necessary for the purpose of or in connection with any legal proceedings (including prospective legal proceedings) or for the purpose of obtaining legal advice or otherwise for the purposes of establishing, exercising or defending legal rights (section 35(2)).

In *Totalise plc v. The Motley Fool Ltd and Another*[18] Owen J. held that the exemption under section 35(2) was not limited to legal proceedings brought by the data controller or to legal advice obtained by the data controller. So section 35(2) did not restrict the jurisdiction of the court under *Norwich Pharmacal* principles[19] to order the proprietor of a web site discussion board to disclose the identity of someone who had made defamatory postings to the discussion board. The judge also held, when considering the question of the legal costs of the application, that the proprietors of the web site discussion boards ought to have complied with the claimant's requests to identify the author of the postings. It must be implicit in that finding that the Web site proprietors would have been protected by section 35(2) if, in the particular circumstances under consideration, they had disclosed the identity of the author voluntarily, without a court order.

Domestic purposes (Section 36)

7–063 Personal data processed by an individual only for the purposes for that individual's personal, family or household affairs (including recreational purposes) are exempt from the data protection principles and the provisions of Part II (rights of data subjects) and Part III (notification and registration).

7.5.2 Miscellaneous exemptions

7–064 The miscellaneous exemptions are set out in Schedule 7 and in summary comprise:

Confidential references (paragraph 1)

7–065 References given or to be given by a data controller in confidence for the purposes of education, employment or appointment of the data subject, or for the purpose of the provision by the data subject of any service, are exempted from subject access (section 7);

Armed forces (paragraph 2)
Personal data are exempt from the subject information provisions in any case to the **7–066**
extent to which the application of those provisions would be likely to prejudice the
combat effectiveness of any of the armed forces of the Crown;

Judicial appointments and honours (paragraph 3)
Personal data processed for the purposes of assessing any person's suitability for judicial **7–067**
office or the office of Queen's Counsel, or the conferring by the Crown of any honour, are
exempt from the subject information provisions;

Crown employment and Crown or ministerial appointments (paragraph 4)
The Secretary of State may by order exempt from the subject information provisions **7–068**
personal data processed for the purposes of assessing any person's suitability for
employment or appointment by the Crown;

Management forecasts (paragraph 5)
Personal data processed for the purposes of management forecasting or management **7–069**
planning to assist the data controller in the conduct of any business or other activity are
exempt from the subject information provisions in any case to the extent to which the
application of those provisions would be likely to prejudice the conduct of that business
or other activity;

Corporate finance (paragraph 6)
Where personal data are processed for the purposes of or in connection with a corporate **7–070**
finance service the data are exempt from the subject information provisions to the extent
that the data controller reasonably believes that the application of those provisions to the
data could affect the price of a financial instrument, or if the exemption is required for the
purpose of safeguarding an important economic or financial interest of the United
Kingdom;

Negotiations (paragraph 7)
Personal data which consist of records of the intentions of the data controller in relation **7–071**
to any negotiations with the data subject are exempt from the subject information
provisions in any case to the extent to which the application of those provisions would be
likely to prejudice those negotiations;

Examination marks (paragraph 8)
Personal data consisting of marks or other information processed by a data controller for **7–072**
the purpose of determining the results of an academic, professional or other examination
are subject to an exemption from subject access (section 7) under detailed provisions
intended to suspend subject access for a period of time until and after the announcement
of the results of the examination;

Examination scripts (paragraph 9)
Personal data consisting of information recorded by candidates during an examination **7–073**
are exempt from subject access (section 7);

Legal professional privilege (paragraph 10)
Personal data are exempt from the subject information provisions if the data consist of **7–074**

information in respect of which a claim to legal professional privilege or in Scotland to confidentiality as between client and professional legal adviser, could be maintained in legal proceedings

Self-incrimination (paragraph 11)

7–075   A person need not comply with a subject access request to the extent that compliance would, by revealing evidence of the commission of any offence other than an offence under the 1998 Act, expose him to proceedings for that offence, and information disclosed by any person in compliance with a subject access request is not to be admissible against him in proceedings for an offence under the 1998 Act.

7.6 Offences under the 1998 Act

7–076   The following is a summary of offences under the 1998 Act, any of which may relate to processing in connection with the inclusion of personal data on a Web site openly accessible from the Internet or the transmission of personal data by e-mail over the Internet:

- Sections 17 and 21: processing without notification

- Sections 20 and 21: failure to notify changes to registrable particulars

- Section 22: in the case of processing designated by a Secretary of State's order as "assessable processing", undertaking processing of that kind before expiry of the 28 days' period allowed for assessment by the Commissioner, or before expiry of that period and any extension of up to a further 14 days notified by the Commissioner. No assessable processing order has been made to date

- Section 24: failure to comply within 21 days with a written request for relevant particulars which a data controller has elected not to notify to the Commissioner in respect of manual data in relevant filing systems

- Section 47(1): failure to comply with a Commissioner's supervisory notice

- Section 47(2): knowingly or recklessly making a false statement in response to an information notice

- Section 50 and Schedule 9: intentional obstruction of, or failure to give reasonable assistance in, execution of a warrant of entry and inspection granted to the Commissioner by a circuit judge

7.7 Enforcement and remedies under the 1998 Act

7.7.1 Enforcement notices (sections 40 and 41)

7–077   The enforcement notice concept established under the 1984 Act is continued, extended and qualified under the 1998 Act, but the 1984 Act's provisions for de-registration and transfer prohibition notices are not repeated.

The Commissioner may serve an enforcement notice on a data controller if the Commissioner is satisfied that the data controller has contravened or is contravening any of the data protection principles. A person who processes only data none of which are personal is not a data controller as defined by the 1998 Act, and a data controller who contravenes any provision of the 1998 Act but who does not contravene any of the data protection principles may not be served with an enforcement notice. However, it is immaterial for the purposes of issue of an enforcement notice under the 1998 Act that a data controller who contravenes any of the data protection principles is not registered: These provisions represent changes from the 1984 Act.

As under the 1984 Act, in deciding whether to serve an enforcement notice the **7–078** Commissioner is required to consider whether the contravention has caused or is likely to cause any person damage or distress, but it is not necessary for the issue of an enforcement notice that any such damage or distress should in fact have been caused.

An enforcement notice is obliged to require the person on whom the notice is served to take such steps as are specified in the notice for complying with the principle or principles contravened.

The 1998 Act contains additional provisions beyond those contained in the 1984 Act in relation to inaccurate data and the rectification, blocking, erasure or destruction of data containing expressions of opinion based on inaccurate data.

The power to issue enforcement notices under the 1998 Act is substantially restricted in relation to processing for the special purposes (journalism etc.: see 7.5 above). There is power for the Commissioner to cancel or vary an enforcement notice.

7.7.2 Request for assessment (section 42)

Any person who is, or who believes himself to be, directly affected by any processing of **7–079** personal data may request the Commissioner for an assessment as to whether it is likely or unlikely that the processing in question has been or is being carried out in compliance with the 1998 Act. The person making the request need not be a data subject and may, for example, be a competitor of a data controller whose alleged non-compliance directly affects the person making the request. The Commissioner must make the assessment requested, but may determine the manner of its making and is not required to take further action beyond informing the person making the request as to whether the assessment has been made and, to the extent that the Commissioner considers it appropriate, any view formed or action taken as a result of the request.

The provision replaces the right of complaint to the Data Protection Registrar under the 1984 Act: in each case, there was and is an obligation on the Registrar and now the Commissioner, to promote compliance, so that a request for assessment may trigger enforcement action.

7.7.3 Information notices (sections 43 and 44)

The Commissioner is given power under the 1998 Act (sections 43 and 44) to serve a **7–080** notice on a data controller requiring the provision by the data controller of information as specified in the notice. An information notice may be served either:

- following a request for assessment under section 42 (see above); or

- in order to determine compliance by the data controller with any of the data protection principles.

There is a right of appeal from an information notice, and there are urgency provisions.

7–081   An information notice may not require:

- any breach of legal professional privilege; or

- the provision of information which may reveal the commission of offences other than offences under the 1998 Act.

The Commissioner is given power to cancel an information notice.

7–082   The Commissioner's information notice powers in relation to processing for the special purposes (journalism etc: see 7.5 above) are restricted to a limited 'special information notice' (section 44), but the Commissioner is given power to determine that personal data are not being processed only for the special purposes or are not being processed with a view to publication by any person of journalistic, literary or artistic material which has not previously been published by the data controller. Such a determination is subject to a right of appeal, but is not to take effect until the end of the period within which an appeal can be brought and, where an appeal is brought, pending the determination or withdrawal of the appeal.

Failure to comply with an information notice or a special information notice is an offence (Section 47(1)).

7–083   Points to be considered in connection with information notices include the following.

An information notice may only be served on a data controller. The 1998 Act's definition of a data controller, by contrast with the 1984 Act's definition of a data user, is restricted to persons who determine the purposes for which and the manner in which personal data are, or are to be, processed, and so does not extend to processing of data which are not personal data.

Accordingly, an information notice may not be served on:

- a person who processes only data which are not personal data; or

- a person who processes personal data but only does so as a "data processor" as defined by the 1998 Act, who is not otherwise a data controller and who processes personal data only on behalf of data controllers. Except in respect of data controllers, the Commissioner appears to be as powerless under the 1998 Act as the Registrar under the 1984 Act to obtain information, including information as to whether or not a person is a data controller;

7–084   An information notice served pursuant to a request for assessment under section 42 may address any issue relating to compliance with the 1998 Act: by contrast, an information notice served otherwise than in consequence of a request for assessment may only require information for the purpose of determining compliance with the data protection principles. It may not, for example, require information relating to an offence under the Act which does not also involve a contravention of one or more of the principles.

7–085   The widened definitions of "data", "personal data" and "processing" bring a broad range of activities relating to information within the scope of the principles and so within the scope of an information notice. For example, the automatic wholesale recording of visual data in a public place by means of a CCTV system may be within the scope of an information notice if the person responsible for the CCTV system is a data controller in relation to personal data recorded by means of the system. In such a case, the Commissioner may be in a position validly to serve an information notice on the person responsible for the CCTV system if the information so obtained is exposed on a Web site in contravention of the eighth principle.

The growing practice of using Webcams to allow live viewing by Internet users of individuals' activities, often without their consent, is at risk of contravention of the first principle (fair and lawful processing) and of regulatory action by the Commissioner. The use of Webcams may in some circumstances fall within the journalism or art exceptions discussed above. It is noteworthy that although the Commissioner has issued a detailed statutory Code of Practice on the use of CCTV in public places (issued July 2000, and available on the Commissioner's Web site), the document makes no mention of Webcams.

7.7.4 Powers of entry and inspection (section 50 and Schedule 9)

Powers of entry and inspection exercisable under a warrant issued by a circuit judge are provided under the 1998 Act substantially in the form of similar powers given under the 1984 Act (Section 50 and Schedule 9 to the 1998 Act). The new power to issue information notices under the 1998 Act, coupled with the associated offence of failure to comply with an information notice, will make the powers of entry and inspection under the 1998 Act more effective than were the equivalent powers under the 1984 Act.   **7–086**

Under the 1998 Act a judge may issue a warrant even though entry into premises was granted if the occupier then unreasonably refuses to comply with a request by the Commissioner to permit searching, inspection, examination, operation and testing of equipment or inspection or seizure of documents and other materials. This new requirement for compliance with such a request did not appear in the 1984 Act.

A judge may not issue a warrant unless the Commissioner has given seven days' notice in writing to the occupier of the premises demanding access and access and searching has been unreasonably refused, but this provision is not to apply if the judge is satisfied that the case is urgent and that compliance with the notice requirement will defeat the object of the entry.   **7–087**

The powers of entry and seizure conferred by a warrant are not exercisable in respect of personal data:

- exempted by virtue of section 28 (national security); or

- protected by legal professional privilege.

7.7.5 Civil Remedies

Civil remedies under the 1998 Act are substantially extended beyond those available under the 1984 Act.   **7–088**

Subject access (sections 7 and 8)
Subject access under the 1998 Act broadly follows the 1984 Act, but with the following amendments: **7–089**

- the forty day period allowed for response to a subject access request does not start to run until the data controller has received the required fee and any information reasonably requested by the data controller in order to satisfy himself as to the identity of the person making the request and to locate the information sought;

- the data controller must specify the purposes for which the relevant personal data are being processed and to whom they are or may be disclosed;

- information constituting personal data relating to the subject access applicant and required to be supplied must be in permanent form by way of a copy, except where the supply of a copy is not possible or would involve disproportionate effort;

- the data controller must provide any information available as to the source of the data, except where the source is an individual who may be identified and who has not consented to the disclosure; and

- where processing by automatic means is used to evaluate matters relating to the subject access applicant, such as for example his performance at work, his creditworthiness, his reliability or his conduct, and has constituted or is likely to constitute the sole basis for any decision significantly affecting him, the applicant is entitled to be informed of the logic involved in that decision-taking.

Where a subject access request is made to a credit reference agency the request will be deemed to be limited to personal data relevant to the individual's financial standing unless the request shows a contrary intention.

Request for assessment (section 42)

7–090   This remedy has been referred to in 7.7.2 above in relation to enforcement. Any person who is or believes himself to be directly affected by any processing of personal data may request the Commissioner to make an assessment as to whether it is likely or unlikely that the processing has been or is being carried out in compliance with the provisions of the 1998 Act. On receiving such a request the Commissioner is required to make an assessment, and is empowered to serve an information notice requiring any data controller to furnish the Commissioner with such information relating to the request as may be specified in the notice (section 43).

In determining in what manner it is appropriate to make an assessment, the Commissioner is to have regard to:

- the extent to which the request raises a matter of substance;

- any undue delay in making the request; and

- whether or not the person making the request is entitled to make an application for subject access (section 7).

7–091   The Commissioner is required to notify the person making the request whether or not the Commissioner has made an assessment as a result of the request. The Commissioner is also required, to the extent that she considers it appropriate having regard in particular to any exemption from subject access applying in relation to the personal data concerned, to notify the person who made the request of any view formed or action taken as a result of the request.

The request for assessment substantially replaces and extends the right of complaint to the Registrar under section 36 of the 1984 Act, and is reinforced by the information notice provisions of section 43 of the 1998 Act.

Right to prevent processing likely to cause damage or distress (section 10)
An individual is entitled by written notice to a data controller to require the data   **7–092**
controller to cease or not to begin processing personal data relating to that individual
where such processing is causing or is likely to cause unwarranted substantial damage or
substantial distress, either to the data subject or to another individual. This right is subject
to exceptions where the data subject has consented to the processing or where the
processing is necessary:

- for the performance of a contract to which the data subject is a party, or for taking
  steps at the request of the data subject with a view to entering into such contract;

- for compliance with any legal obligation to which the data controller is subject,
  other than an obligation imposed by contract; or

- to protect the vital interests of the data subject.

The data controller has 21 days to respond to the data subject's notice to prevent
processing: the response is to be by written notice to the data subject stating that the data
controller has complied or intends to comply, or alternatively setting out reasons for
regarding the data subject's notice as unjustified.

Where the data subject considers that the data controller has not complied with the   **7–093**
request to prevent processing the data subject can seek a court order, and the court may
order the data controller to take such steps as are necessary to comply with the notice. In
practice, a data subject may be reluctant to incur the expense of applying to a court, and
may look to other remedies by way of complaint to the Commissioner and by request by
assessment under section 42.

The right to prevent processing is required to be exercised by written notice to the data
controller. Failure to give notice would not necessarily deprive a data subject of the right
to claim compensation for unfair processing in contravention of the first principle.

The right to prevent processing may be of particular relevance if defamatory material is
posted on Web sites, such as anonymously on a Web site discussion forum. However, the
journalism exemptions may also be relevant.

Right to prevent processing for direct marketing (section 11)
An individual is entitled by written notice to a data controller to require the data   **7–094**
controller to cease, or not to begin, processing personal data relating to the applicant for
purposes of direct marketing. 'Direct marketing' means the communication (by whatever
means) of any advertising or marketing material which is directed to particular
individuals, and there is a right to apply to the court if a data controller fails to comply
with the data subject's notice. The court may order the data controller to take such steps
to comply with the notice as the court thinks fit: alternatively, the data subject may
request assessment by the Commissioner under Section 42. The use of 'cookies' to collect
personal data for direct marketing purposes may be within the concept of use of personal
data for direct marketing where a "cookie" is used to enable focused direct marketing
material to be directed to a data subject, or for profiling a Web site visitor's preferences.

Rights in relation to automated decision-taking (section 12)
In addition to the extended right of subject access under section 7 in relation to automated   **7–095**
assessment and decision-taking (see above), an individual is entitled by notice in writing
to a data controller to require the data controller to ensure that no decision taken by or on

behalf of the data controller which significantly affects the individual is based solely on processing by automatic means of personal data relating to the individual, where the processing is for the purpose of evaluating matters relating to the individual as, for example, his performance at work, his credit worthiness, his reliability or his conduct.

Where no such notice has effect and a decision which significantly affects an individual is based solely on processing by automatic means of personal data relating to that individual the data controller must, as soon as is practicable, notify the individual that the decision was taken on that basis and the individual is entitled, within 21 days of receiving the notification, by notice in writing to require the data controller to reconsider the decision.

7–096   These provisions have no effect in relation to "exempt decisions". These are defined as decisions taken in the course of steps taken:

- for the purpose of considering whether to enter into a contract with the data subject; or

- with a view to entering into or in the course of performing such a contract; or

- which are authorised or required by or under any enactment; or

- if the effect of the decision is to grant a request of the data subject; or

- if steps have been taken to safeguard the legitimate interests of the data subject, for example by allowing him to make representations.

An individual may apply for relief to the court, but the court's power is limited to ordering the person responsible for the decision to re-consider it or to take a new decision not based solely on automated processing.

7–097   As for the rights to prevent processing under sections 10 and 11, this right must be exercised by written notice to the data controller but failure to give written notice would not necessarily deprive the data subject of the right to claim compensation for unfair processing in contravention of the first principle.

The provision that this right relates only to decisions based solely on automatic processing of personal data will presumably exclude decisions which are in any respect based on any other factors, and the remedy available, namely application to the court, is limited. It may be possible alternatively to apply to the Commissioner for assessment under section 42.

Compensation (section 13)

7–098   An individual who suffers damage by reason of any contravention by a data controller of any of the requirements of the 1998 Act is entitled to compensation from the data controller for that damage, and for associated distress. It is a defence to a claim for compensation to prove that the data controller had taken such care as in all the circumstances was reasonably required to comply with the requirement concerned.

It is not clear to what extent the right to compensation is in addition to other specific remedies available to an individual for particular contraventions of the provisions of the 1998 Act: for example, is an individual entitled to compensation for contravention of the rights in relation to automated decision-taking in addition to the right to apply to the court?

The right to compensation under the 1998 Act is substantially broader than was the right to compensation under the 1984 Act.

Rectification, blocking, erasure and destruction (section 14)

If a court is satisfied on the application of a data subject that personal data of which the applicant is the subject are inaccurate, the court may order the data controller to rectify, block, erase or destroy those data and any other personal data in respect of which he is the data controller, and which contain an expression of opinion which appears to the court to be based on inaccurate data.

7–099

This provision broadly follows, but extends, the right to rectification and erasure contained in section 24 of the 1984 Act. There is a new additional provision that, where the court makes an order and is satisfied that personal data which have been rectified, blocked, erased or destroyed were inaccurate, the court may also, where it considers it reasonably practicable, order the data controller to notify third parties to whom the data have been disclosed of the rectification, blocking, erasure of destruction ordered by the court. In determining whether it is reasonably practicable to require such notification the court is to have regard, in particular, to the number of persons who would have to be notified.

If a Web site were to contain inaccurate personal data which a court were to order to be deleted from the site, it would be open to the court to order the data controller to trace visitors to the site and to inform them of the deletion, to the extent that it was reasonably practicable to do so.

Request for notifiable particulars (section 24)

In order to exercise most of the rights available to him under the 1998 Act a data subject needs to be able to discover which data controllers hold personal data relating to him. The publicly available register of data users and computer bureaux under the 1984 Act did not readily enable a data subject to identify a registered person holding personal data relating to the data subject, and that difficulty continues under the 1998 Act's provisions for access to the register.

7–100

As under the 1984 Act, the Commissioner is required to provide facilities for making the information contained in entries in the register available for inspection by members of the public at all reasonable hours and free of charge, and to supply to any member of the public on payment of a fee, to be prescribed in regulations (currently £2.00), a duly certified copy in writing of the particulars contained in any entry made in the register.

The notification provisions of the 1998 Act broadly restate the registration provisions of the 1984 Act and are expanded and elaborated by detailed notification regulations. Notification does not compulsorily apply to personal data which are not processed automatically, or which are not intended to be so processed, and which are held in relevant filing systems. Accordingly, personal data held in manual files falling within the 1998 Act's definition of a "relevant filing system" need not be notified to the Commissioner. If the data controller elects not to notify such manual files the data controller must, within 21 days of receiving a written request from any person, make certain relevant particulars available to that person in writing free of charge. "Relevant particulars" for this purpose are the particulars which would otherwise have been notifiable had the processing been automatic, and comprise:

7–101

- the data controller's name and address;

- the name and address of any nominated representative of the data controller;

- a description of the personal data being or to be processed by or on behalf of the data controller, and the category or categories of data subject to which they relate;

- a description of the purpose or purposes for which the data are being or are to be processed;

- a description of any recipient or recipients to whom the data controller intends or may wish to disclose the data;

- the names or a description of any countries or territories outside the EEA to which the data controller directly or indirectly transfers or intends or may wish to transfer the data.

In most circumstances, personal data held on Web sites will not be manual data, but manual data held in relevant filing systems may be behind Web site data. Controllers who hold such manual files in support of their Web sites but elect not to notify such files should accordingly be aware of the requirement to provide notifiable particulars on request.

7.8 Transitional provisions (Schedule 8)

7–102 Schedule 8 to the 1998 Act sets out complex transitional relief reflecting the provisions of Article 32(2) of Directive 95/46[20] which requires Member States to ensure that processing already under way on the date that national provisions adopted pursuant to the Directive entered into force is brought into conformity with those provisions within three years of that date. Further relief is permitted by the Directive, by way of derogation, in relation to the processing of data already held in manual filing systems at the date of entry into force of the national provisions adopted in implementation of the Directive, but these provisions are unlikely to affect personal data exposed to, or transmitted by means of, the Internet.

7–103 The 1998 Act's transitional relief is centred round the concept of "eligible automated data". Personal data are "eligible data" at any time if, and to the extent that, they are at that time subject to processing which was already under way immediately before October 24, 1998, and "eligible automated data" means eligible data which are being processed by means of equipment operating automatically or are recorded with the intention that they should be so processed.

During the first transitional period, which expired on October 23, 2001, eligible automated data were not to be regarded as being "processed" unless the processing is by reference to the data subject, and the former payroll and accounts, unincorporated members' clubs and mailing lists, and back-up data exemptions under the 1984 Act are to continue as re-expressed in Schedule 8 of the 1998 Act. Further exemptions were given for eligible automated data which, in effect, continue the regime established under the 1984 for eligible automated data during the currency of the first transitional period until October 23, 2001. More limited transitional relief continues to be available for certain manual records which were in existence at October 23, 1998: this residual relief will expire on October 23, 2007.

7–104 For most practical purposes, personal data processing on or accessible from Web sites, or contained in e-mail sent over the Internet, must as from October 23, 2001 fully conform to the requirements of the 1998 Act, and in particular the eighth principle prohibiting (subject to the exceptions set out in Schedule 4) the transfer of personal data from within the EEA to third countries which do not ensure an adequate level of protection.

In the context of the establishment of new Web sites, new processing and new data controllers, it seems probable that transitional relief will have had little effect. Those who have created Web sites since October 23, 1998, or who have started transmitting personal data over the Internet since that date, are likely to have been subject to the provisions of the 1998 Act as soon as those provisions come into effect and unable to take the benefit of transitional relief, which in any event expired on October 23, 2001. It has therefore been, and continues to be, prudent to structure the use of personal data on Web sites, and their transmission over the Internet, on the basis that compliance with the 1998 Act has been mandatory since March 1, 2001, in order to avoid the risk of contraventions and consequent enforcement action.

7.9 Conclusions

The scope and broad thrust of the 1984 Act are replaced but repeated and extended by the 1998 Act, in particular by new and enlarged definitions of "data", "personal data" and "processing". Subject to the possibility of some processing of personal data on Web sites and over the Internet being processing which was already under way immediately before October 24, 1998, and so subject to transitional relief which continued until expiry of the first transitional period on October 23, 2001, all new processing since March 1, 2000 has been excluded from this transitional relief and has been subject to the provisions of the 1998 Act.   **7–105**

The Data Protection Registrar's lack of power to compel data users to provide information in response to questions has been made good by the information notice provisions of the 1998 Act (see 7.7 above), and by the extended right to obtain a warrant of entry and inspection where admission to premises is permitted by the occupier but the Commissioner is not allowed by the occupier to search, inspect, examine, operate and test equipment and to inspect and seize documents or other material found at the premises (see also 7.7 above).

In the result, the United Kingdom's data protection regime, coupled with the right of privacy introduced under the Human Rights Act 1998, has been broadened and strengthened by comparison with the 1984 Act except only for the new exemptions in favour of journalistic, literary and artistic expression. These are broad, and their full effects have yet to be experienced and assessed. They may be of particular significance for publication through the Internet.   **7–106**

---

1. Directive 95/46 [1995] O.J. L281/31
2. Art. 14(a)
3. See n. 1 above
4. See n. 1 above
5. See n. 1 above
6. See n. 1 above
7. See n. 1 above
8. See n. 1 above
9. Personal Data Definition, Guidance Note, December 14, 2000.
10. See also "E-mail Addresses—are they personal data? An assessment of the potential implications for Web site owners" P. Carey [2000] Ent. L.R. 11 and "Data Protection and E-mail Addresses Revisited; is the DPA Workable?" J. Harrington [2000] Ent. L.R. 141.
11. Queen's Bench Division. Judgment given May 28, 1999, and reviewed on appeal.
12. [2001] 1 All E.R. 788
13. Case DA/92 31/49/1
14. Internet—Protection of Privacy—Data Controllers. Compliance Note (version 4) issued by the Information Commissioner, January 2000.

15. Case DA/90 25/49/9, at para. 52.
16. See n. 1 above
17. See n. 1 above
18. February 19, 2001 (unreported) Q.B.D.
19. See Chapter 6.
20. See n. 1 above

8

Telecommunications and Broadcast Regulation

8.1 Introduction

This Chapter explains how current U.K. and E.C. telecommunications and broadcasting regulation apply to the Internet, and to services provided by means of the Internet. When considering regulation in this context, it is important to ask who is doing what. A telecommunications operator that owns and operates the telecommunications infrastructure which makes up the Internet is performing a different function from an Internet service provider (ISP), that provides Internet access and Web hosting services to its customers across the telecommunications operator's infrastructure, or an Application service provider (ASP) that provides online applications across the Internet to its customers. The way that operators at different parts of the "value chain" are treated under the current regulatory framework depends, whatever labels they may apply to their activities, on the specific functions that they perform.

8–001

Considerable progress has been made in the last year or so towards adapting the telecommunications regulatory framework to the activities of ISPs and ASPs. This has resulted in some curious paradoxes. The Internet has become an open environment through the effectiveness of the self-regulation and non-discrimination in which it has its origins. Despite this, now that it is established as a competitive industry, telecommunications-style regulation is being considered.

Despite the geographical and technical neutrality of the Internet making regulation difficult to apply, a desire to promote convergence has prompted regulators to try to extend existing telecommunications regulatory principles to include the Internet, rather than rolling back telecommunications regulation to avoid it. This may be a short term trend: if current proposals prove unenforceable or appear to constrain rather than promote competition, regulation may be rapidly scaled down, if not eliminated altogether. The regulatory framework which affects the Internet for the time being, is discussed below.

8–002

Although, as we discuss later in this chapter, there may be potential for existing broadcasting regulation to impact on some Internet activities, in practice to date the United Kingdom broadcast regulators have, for the most part, not attempted to assert any regulatory authority over Internet content.

The rapid speed at which the Internet has evolved has demonstrated that established regulations and procedures appear outmoded and in some cases inappropriate. The Internet has been a contributing factor to the increasing breakdown of the distinction between broadcasting and telecommunications. Telecommunications regulation seeks to control the provision and operation of the underlying physical network and access to that network through imposition of service supply obligations on operators with market power, promotion of competition, sophisticated interconnection rules and non-discriminatory tariffing policies. In contrast, broadcast regulation has tended to focus on preventing a concentration of media ownership and the imposition of controls on content, such as requiring a balanced and impartial range of programme content.

8–003   As we explain in this Chapter, technical and commercial convergence between telecommunications and broadcasting service provision is making it increasingly nonsensical to maintain distinct regulatory structures, designed for separate activities with differing aims in mind. The task becomes impossible where a single dynamic new technology is involved. For instance, any regulatory structure which seeks to regulate according to content, *e.g.* distinguishing between voice and data traffic or regulating video graphics as opposed to text, is fraught with problems. The convergence of the broadcasting, telecommunications and I.T. industries has allowed text, data, video, audio and images to be reduced to binary code before transmission to the end-user, often rendering it impossible to know what type of content is being transmitted. This is particularly the case with the Internet where, generally,[1] data is reduced to uniform packets transmitted using the TCP/IP protocol.

Technical and commercial convergence have, in turn, brought about pressure for regulatory convergence, which would replace the existing separate telecommunications and broadcast regulatory structures with a single regulatory framework. In the United Kingdom this has been proposed in the Communications White Paper of December 2000, which is expected to lead to a new Communications Act in early 2004. A paving bill introducing a single regulator, the Office of Communications (OFCOM) is currently before Parliament. This proposal for a single statutory regulator for communications raises the question whether the type of content regulation that has been thought appropriate for broadcast media has any place in relation to interactive content. For instance, much content on the Internet has its roots in print media (which are unregulated) rather than in television (which is heavily regulated). These issues are discussed further in Chapter 12.

8.1.1 Regulatory background

8–004   The telecommunications sector is a regulated industry. In common with water, gas, electricity and rail, telecommunications services were for many years provided by a Government owned utility company with monopoly rights. The UK monopolist, British Telecommunications plc ("BT") was privatised in 1984, by the Telecommunications Act (the "T. Act") to make way for a competitive market. However, BT's historical monopoly gave it market power in practically every services market which other operators might wish to enter. The situation was, and is, complicated by the "networked" nature of the telecommunications industry, which means that BT's competitors are reliant on BT for essential inputs into their services, the most important of which is BT's national and international network infrastructure, particularly its access lines into end-user premises.

A sectoral regulator was appointed to ensure competition and to protect consumers of telecommunications services. In practice, at the time of privatisation, the regulator's job was to impose constraints on BT, so that other operators might offer competing services on something like a level competitive playing field. Until this could happen, the Regulator had to ensure that consumers' rights did not take second place to shareholders interests, through the imposition of retail price controls.

The telecommunications regulator is the Director General of Telecommunications, whose Office of Telecommunications is generally known as "OFTEL". Whereas OFTEL's primary function at the time of privatisation was regulation of BT's retail prices for voice services, technological change and in particular the commercialisation of the Internet, brought about a sea-change in OFTEL's remit. At the beginning of the twenty-first Century, the principal focus of telecommunications regulation is to remove barriers to a flourishing IP and Internet based electronic communications industry. **8–005**

Broadcast regulation has a completely different genesis from telecommunications regulation. Broadcast regulation has historically been justified mainly on the basis of spectrum scarcity—that broadcast airwaves being limited in what they can carry, broadcast programming should be subjected to a degree of control that does not apply to traditional media such as newsprint. Spectrum scarcity does not exist on the Internet. Some may argue that other justifications for broadcast regulation, such as intrusiveness or pervasiveness, can apply to some types of Internet content. However, the Internet has developed fundamentally as a user-selectable medium, in contrast to the programmed, 'push' environments characteristic of traditional broadcasting.

8.2 Telecommunications licensing and regulation

8.2.1 Licensing systems

OFTEL's primary tool for imposing and enforcing telecommunications regulation is a system of licensing. Under the T. Act, any person who "runs" a telecommunications system in the United Kingdom requires a licence to do so.[2] Running a system without a licence currently constitutes a criminal offence.[3] **8–006**

A "telecommunications system" is very widely defined in the T. Act[4] and broadly speaking, means anything that allows communications between separate premises using wires, radio, or light. However, the term "to run" a telecommunications system is not defined at all and has not been tested in the courts. Where all telecoms services and infrastructure are owned, controlled and commercialised by a single, vertically integrated operator such as BT, it is clear who is running the system. However, fragmentation of the value chain, whereby one operator legally owns the network infrastructure in the ground, another owns rights to provide electrification, transmission and switching, another leases wholesale capacity and provides conveyance and routing and yet another has the retail relationship with the end-user who buys the services provided over it, can make it far from clear who is running the system and thus who needs a licence for the purposes of the T. Act.

Informal guidance on who "runs a system" has been provided by the Department of Trade and Industry (DTI), which is responsible for issuing licences on the advice of OFTEL. The DTI considers that the system is "run" by the person who has authority over it, in particular the control over how the system is made up and how and for what purposes it is used. It does not necessarily mean the owner of the system, nor the person with day to day operational control such as a facilities management company. In practice, **8–007** several licences may cover activities on a single network, because individual operators have management control of traffic and routing for their own separate customer sets. The 1984 Act does not require telecommunication *services* to be licensed—the licence is required to run the systems over which services are conveyed. However, it may be a breach of the licence if the Licensee permits services which it is specifically prohibited from providing, to be conveyed over its system. This is an important rule, particularly for Internet content providers.

Application of the licensing rules to Internet Service Providers is discussed below.

8.2.2 Interconnection and access

8–008   Whereas retail service is increasingly open to intense competition, regulation at the network level still underpins relationships between all providers of telecoms networks and services. The Internet has raised a host of new issues, principal amongst which, to date, is unmetered access.

Interconnection is the process by which end-users on one network can be connected to end-users on another network. It is also a way of providing access to services and content which are hosted by a service provider other than the operator which controls access to customers.

8–009   The E.U. Interconnection Directive (97/33) as implemented into U.K. law by Statutory Instrument (S.I. 1997 No. 2931, the Telecommunications (Interconnection) Regulations 1997) and new licence conditions, establishes "a regulatory framework for securing in the Community the interconnection of telecommunications networks and in particular the interoperability of services, and with regard to ensuring provision of universal service in an environment of open and competitive markets. It concerns the harmonisation of conditions for open and efficient interconnection of and access to public telecommunications networks and publicly available telecommunications services".[5]

The Directive imposes obligations to interconnect and provide access amongst network operators. It fixes a considerable degree of responsibility on fixed operators determined to have significant market power (SMP),[6] to allow access to their networks, not to discriminate or show preferential treatment between their own downstream activities and those of other operators, to publish standard terms and conditions for service supply and to offer cost-orientated interconnection and access charges. These operators must also publish separate accounts to prevent anti-competitive cross subsidies. Mobile operators with SMP are subject to a lesser set of obligations.

8–010   The Directive defines who should be granted interconnection rights in general terms, to be interpreted and given practical effect by national regulatory authorities. OFTEL has taken an inclusive approach to granting these rights, extending what was historically known as "Relevant Connectable System" (RCS) status to Internet Service Providers for the first time.

Perhaps most importantly, the Interconnection Directive includes dispute resolution provisions which require OFTEL to resolve disputes between network operators and service providers, according to objective criteria and within defined timescales. Internet Service Providers who are eligible for interconnection rights fall within the class of operators who may bring to OFTEL a dispute with another telecoms operator over interconnection, access, supply of a service, or service terms, conditions or charges, for resolution.

8.2.3 Competition rules

In addition to regulatory obligations in operating licences, general competition law applies to the electronic communications sector. The Competition Act, introduced into U.K. legislation in 2000, adopts established E.U. concepts, such as the prohibitions against abuse of a dominant position and anti-competitive concerted practices. Internet Service Providers, whose activities are frequently dependent on services provided by third party operators with established market power, may need to have recourse to competition remedies. These are dealt with in detail in Chapter 14. **8–011**

8.2.4 Regulation of the Internet and ISPs

The Internet is not, in itself, the subject of telecoms style regulation. This is because, as the platform for a commercial industry, it has grown organically from a situation of commercial parity, rather than out of a monopoly. Service diversification and technological innovation have promoted competition, making regulation unnecessary. Nevertheless, convergence between traditional circuit switched telecoms networks and modern infrastructure which uses Internet Protocol (IP) routing, as well as erosion in the distinction between Internet Service Providers and telecoms service providers means that some telecoms regulation now maps directly onto the Internet industry. It can be both a risk factor and a strategic tool. How telecoms regulation directly affects the Internet and the businesses which provide its constituent networks and services, is discussed in the next section. **8–012**

8.3 Licensing Internet service provision

The U.K. rules for licensing electronic communications operators recognise two main classifications: the distinction between systems and services and the distinction between voice and data. As explained above, it is the running of systems which requires a licence, rather than the provision of services. Thus, as a general rule, Internet access providers which have management control of their own routing and/or switching are usually considered to be running a system which requires a licence. By contrast, Internet content providers who only provide information or applications accessed by end-users but who do not provide access or conveyance services, do not run licensable systems, even though they provide what might be considered a telecommunications service. A company which establishes a page on the World Wide Web will use a host to store the data which makes up the Web page, but neither the host (unless it is also an access provider) nor the Web site owner is necessarily involved in the routing and switching of messages and therefore requires no licence under the T. Act. **8–013**

Providers of voice services, and infrastructure, generally receive closer supervision than pure data service providers. This policy has its origins in E.U. law, which uses regulation to ensure quality and availability in the historical voice services market but which generally treats the newer data services market as competitive. Consequently, E.U. law constrains the use of individual licences for data systems, whilst individual licensing for voice systems is permitted. Application of this policy is not straightforward when packet switching networks which do not distinguish between voice and data packets are the systems in question. How this is accommodated in the United Kingdom is discussed below.

8.3.1 Licensing Internet systems and services

8–014   There are two types of licence (defined in section 7) which may be granted under the T. Act by the Secretary of State. They are the class licence (granted to a particular class of persons) and the individual licence (granted to a particular person).

Since a wide-ranging licence standardisation exercise took place to comply with E.U. harmonisation rules, the main individual licence is the Public Telecommunications Operator (PTO) licence. This permits the broadest range of services to be supplied across owned or leased networks and usually provides the holder with access to "Tele-communications Code Powers" which permit infrastructure development on both public and private land. In addition, the PTO licence authorises the development of international facilities.

Providers of Internet network infrastructure—Tiers 1 to 3 backbone providers, for example, offering international routing and conveyance—will generally have to build or take a long term lease in international cables. Since this qualifies as running a telecommunications system for the purposes of the T. Act and involves the construction or management of international facilities, it will generally require a PTO.

8–015   Where a telecommunications system is geographically limited, in particular where less than 20 facilities installations are linked together, using self-provided links, to form an integrated network, the necessary licence is likely to be the Telecommunications Services Licence (TSL). This is a class licence, which, despite its name, authorises the running of a telecommunications system, but one of a lower order of magnitude than those systems requiring an individual licence. A class licence permits any person or operator which falls within its scope to provide specific telecommunications services without (in the case of the most widely drawn class licences) the need to obtain any additional validation or pay a licence fee. However, where the licensee breaches any of the conditions of the class licence, the Director General of Telecommunications (DGT) may by notice, revoke the licence as it applies to that particular person. Most U.K.–based Internet Service Providers operate their servers and systems under the TSL. The deciding factor in whether an ISP's activities are covered by the TSL or require an individual licence, is often a question of who provides the network infrastructure between the ISP's servers and operational premises. If the ISP leases private circuits which are "run" by a different network operator, then the TSL is likely to be adequate. However, should the ISP build or otherwise own the links between its facilities, and if there are more than 20 sets of premises, then it is likely to require a PTO licence.

The TSL (the most recent version of which was issued on April 9, 2001) permits a licensee to provide telecommunication services of any description by means of the "Applicable Systems", other than International Simple Voice Resale (Voice ISR), certain broadcasting services, mobile radio services, conditional access and access control services. For such purposes, the "Applicable Systems" cover those systems actually run by the licensee itself—for example, a telecommunications switch located in a building.

8.3.2 Voice and Data

8–016   As mentioned earlier, E.U. rules on licensing treat voice and data differently. Voice service providers may be subject to individual licensing procedures, whereas data service providers generally may not, although they may be subject to general authorisations or class licences. The U.K. licensing framework is designed for systems, rather than services, and most systems do not distinguish between voice and data. The U.K. solution is to move to a system of class licensing for most types of system, irrespective of whether it is used for voice or data services. This will remove such awkward anomalies as data systems which technically require a licence in the United Kingdom, and voice services which technically do not, both of which may, if strictly enforced, conflict with E.U. law.

An important exception is International Simple Resale, which may be described as a "hybrid" between running a system and providing a service. It usually involves leasing international infrastructure for the provision of international conveyance to retail customers. It is typically popular with operators providing cheap voice calls through indirect access or carrier pre-selection.

Voice ISR is defined as a service where two-way live speech is conveyed over a public switched telephone network (PSTN), an international private leased circuit (IPLC) and the equivalent of a PSTN in another country or territory.[7] In layman's terms, this effectively means that there must be dial-up access in one country, and dial-out in another country over the public network, with an IPLC being used in between. Data ISR is essentially the same except that it covers all services other than two-way live speech, so it would include graphics, text and recorded sound (*e.g.* voice mail). **8–017**

These distinctions are fundamental when looking at the range of services being provided over the Internet.

The systems run by Internet access providers consisting of routers, switches and private circuits leased from public telecommunications operators can be used to provide Data ISR services between the United Kingdom and all countries in the world under the TSL. The definition of Data ISR is wide enough to cover most types of traffic conveyed over the Internet and for this reason many access providers are able to operate under the TSL. **8–018**

If a company wishes to provide Voice ISR, it must register its activities with the Department of Trade and Industry (DTI) under the ISVR class licence. Following liberalisation of all international telecommunication services in August 1996, ISVR registrations permit the licensee to provide Voice ISR on all international routes subject to a requirement to meet proportionate return of ISR traffic on routes which are not yet deemed to be liberalised (*i.e.* countries which do not yet permit Voice ISR services to be provided by foreign operators to the same extent as in the United Kingdom).[8]

8.3.3 Internet voice telephony services

It is possible, using Internet protocols and packet-switching techniques to provide voice telephony services over the Internet or "VON" (a subset of Voice over IP, or VoIP—see next section). This service is in theory a substitute for traditional circuit switched voice telephony, even though it is a data-based technology. Mass commercialisation may happen when the quality of voice calls over the Internet reaches the standards to which users are now accustomed from traditional circuit switched technology. **8–019**

VON originally only enabled voice messages to be transmitted between personal computers logged on to the Internet. Video-conferencing applications were also developed which enabled voice and visual messages to be transmitted over the Internet. Before flat rate internet access became widespread, Internet voice telephony services were marketed as a means of making international and/or long distance calls for the price of a local telephone call. The caller would typically need a multimedia computer with an Internet connection, a modem capable of transmitting voice and a soundcard allowing the computer to record sounds and play them back. A commercially available software package would allow international calls to be made at local call rates by sending calls from the user's home via the PSTN to the nearest Internet access provider's server. The calls were then routed over private circuits to the country of destination and then via the PSTN to an Internet user in that country.

8–020   The regulatory status of VON was, until recently, unclear. Essentially a data service, using data transmission systems, VON should require no individual licence under E.U. rules. But the strong similarities between circuit switched voice services and VON as a retail service suggest that VON services should be licensed under the ISVR rules as a minimum, since international simple resale may be used by ISPs for international conveyance, but ISVR is excluded from the TSL.

For VON to fall within the definition of ISVR such that an Internet access provider would need to make an ISVR registration in order legally to provide such a service, all the elements of ISVR must be met. This means two-way live speech conveyed over a PSTN, an international private leased circuit (IPLC) and the equivalent of a PSTN in another country or territory.[9] The only element which may not be present is the requirement for two-way live speech (the "voice telephony" component of ISVR), because of the delay which occurs in the conveyance of packets of digitised voice messages.

8–021   The E.U. Commission has taken the view that VON does not qualify as voice telephony unless it meets certain conditions. These were established in 1998 and are based on the definition of voice telephony set out in Directive 90/388, known as the "Services Directive".[10] The necessary conditions are:

- voice telephony is offered commercially as such;
- it is provided for the public;
- it is provided to and from public switched network termination points; and
- it involves direct speech transport and switching of speech in real time, in particular the same level of reliability and speech quality as produced by the PSTN.

Internet service packages which allow voice telephony but are not based on it, are therefore generally outwith the scope of E.U. voice telephony regulation and will not require individual licences. Conversely, Internet service packages which market voice telephony and which, by also satisfying the other conditions in the Commission Notice are effective substitutes for circuit switched voice telephony services, are likely to require a licence. Not only may this have financial implications if a licence fee is payable, but it may also lead to imposition of EU consumer protection obligations.[11]

8.3.4 Voice over IP

8–022   VON should not be confused with voice conveyance using Internet protocol, "voice over IP" or VoIP. This means the conveyance of voice calls as data packets, using Internet Protocol as a routing and transmission technology, frequently over private, point to point networks. VoIP may be used with a broad spectrum of existing technologies, such as ATM or SDH. VON is a subset of VoIP and is limited to conveyance of voice calls over the public Internet.

VoIP is increasingly the technology of choice for the international backbone networks of ISPs who use their own infrastructure to convey PSTN traffic nationally and internationally and to support the public Internet. For regulatory purposes it is generally not distinguished from conveyance networks which use alternative technologies. Thus an operator of a network, which uses IP transport, which originates or terminates calls into and out of the United Kingdom, will generally require a PTO licence which authorises construction and running of international facilities.

VoIP has the potential to fundamentally re-shape the economics of the voice telephony market because packet switching permits much more efficient use of network capacity than circuit switching. E.U. and U.K. regulation are both being addressed to ensure technological neutrality so that operators of systems which defy classification for regulatory purposes do not get an unfair advantage over traditional networks for whom the current rules were designed. An example is where operators with certain licences must contribute to a universal service fund, but operators providing competing services over alternative technologies do not and can reduce retail prices accordingly.

8–023

8.4 Access rights and network services

A minority of Internet service providers control their own network infrastructure. The majority depend on access and conveyance being provided by network operators, with whom they, in many cases, compete, or whose business it is to maximise revenues according to a business model whose economics are inconsistent with how the Internet works. Put simply, broadband infrastructure maximises the potential of the Internet and can make Internet services economically and commercially viable, but traditional narrowband charging approaches to broadband capacity can make its use prohibitively expensive.

8–024

Securing access to third party facilities on commercially viable terms is fundamental to being able to provide Internet services. This section explains how regulation is being used to achieve this.

8.4.1 Interconnection and peering

Networks which carry Internet traffic may require both interconnection and peering. In very simple terms, interconnection is the process of making a physical or logical connection at a geographic boundary between one set of infrastructure and another over which various types of electronic communications traffic may be exchanged. Peering is based on a similar principle but involves technical processes which are exclusive to IP traffic. Peering may take place at the physical interconnection boundary or somewhere else entirely.

8–025

Interconnection
Interconnection is firmly regulated in most liberalised national jurisdictions. Regulators determine the interconnection services which must be offered by the former monopolist, as well as the terms, conditions and charges at which they must be supplied. Pursuant to the Interconnection Directive, referred to earlier, in the United Kingdom, OFTEL has granted rights to interconnect to Internet service providers as long as they fulfil certain criteria. These are:

8–026

(a)   that they are running a system which is correctly licensed for the purposes of the Telecommunications Act; and

(b)   that they are offering "publicly available network services", defined by OFTEL as voice telephony, ISDN, leased lines, basic data transport, *e.g.* IP, telex, or other qualifying services falling into the category of services "consisting only of functions which enable end-users to send, receive, or both, messages to or from one or more end-users, including functions which enable the establishment of a prior connection between such end-users; or, a service which consists only of functions which could not practically be provided to any end-user in identical form by anyone other than the Licensee, because those functions are dependent upon the functions referred to"[12]; and

(c)   that the services which they provide are publicly available, in other words services are not exclusively offered to a closed user group; and

(d)   that they provide the sole means of IP–based inward access to the end-user, which may be physical or logical access.

8–027   Inclusion in OFTEL's "Annex 2 list" allows an ISP to purchase BT's network services at cost. However, because private circuits are not currently considered to be an interconnection product, inclusion in the Annex 2 list does not at present allow ISPs to buy private circuits at cost. Since private circuits make up most of an ISP's system, Annex 2 status is in fact of limited financial value, although it does bring non-financial benefits. For example, it gives an ISP the right to bring a dispute over interconnection before OFTEL,[13] and to require OFTEL to resolve the dispute in accordance with the Interconnection Directive. Annex 2 status also allows the ISP to ask OFTEL to require other Annex 2 operators to provide interconnection services which are not available but which may be reasonably required. OFTEL will usually only consider such requests in relation to operators with significant market power.

Interestingly, a service provider which is not entitled to Annex 2 rights and therefore cannot have or perhaps cannot use interconnection services, may still seek "access" to the network of an operator with significant market power using rights given by the Interconnection Directive. What "access" actually means has not yet been satisfactorily tested through requests for access to OFTEL but may extend to customer information as well as interfaces other than the network termination point to which most ISP servers are connected, or at the C7 signalling interface at which interconnection usually takes place.

Peering and transit

8–028   Every ISP requires access to the public Internet. This is achieved through commercial agreements for either peering or transit. Peering may be defined as a reciprocal business agreement between network operators who are ISPs to accept at no charge all traffic originating from the other's network. Transit, on the other hand, may be defined as a business relationship where one ISP pays another ISP for routing its Internet traffic to and from all destinations. In effect one ISP becomes the customer of the other. Since peering requires no outflow of payments, it is generally considered commercially preferable to paying for transit. At present, ISPs have no legal or regulatory obligations to offer peering to other ISPs, but are likely to do so if the balance of traffic between them is comparable. Peering may be refused to smaller ISPs, forcing them into paying for transit instead. Because the public Internet generally, and peering in particular, are not regulated, an

ISP's licensing status in a particular jurisdiction is not an indicator of the terms on which it may gain access to the public Internet. This said, an ISP which owns it own network facilities which require a major telecommunications licence, is more likely to be the sort of ISP which offers and is offered peering, so that the major operators who are entitled to peering do have telecommunications licences, but it is not the licence which gives rise to the peering rights. The ISPs who use peering rather than transit are a self–selecting group. Larger ISPs may however, take a commercial decision to offer peering to smaller ISPs.

Peering may take place at either public or private "peering points". For public peering amongst ISPs in the United Kingdom there are two public peering points, LINX[14] and MANAP. LINX, which is a non-profit making organisation, is currently the largest and most successful Internet exchange point in Europe. ISPs who meet the criteria in the LINX Memorandum of Understanding, most of which are based on technical systems compatibility, may apply to join, whether U.K. or overseas based.   **8–029**

Some of the most common criteria for any sort of peering arrangement include:

- likely traffic flows
- overall traffic volume
- traffic exchange ratios
- backbone capacity
- geographically equal backbones
- geographic location,
- overall desirability of provider with factors such as capacity, number of web-sites and location being key measures

The alternative to joining a public peering point is to arrange private peering. Major ISPs, such as UUNET and GENUITY, publish their guidelines for ISP's wishing to peer with them. The perceived advantage of using private peering is the opportunity for guaranteed service levels and higher speed connections, through avoiding bottlenecks which are at present still experienced at public exchange points.   **8–030**

The disadvantage, at least for the bigger players, is growing regulatory scrutiny of peering arrangements[15] and the risk of introduction of telecommunications interconnection–style tariff regulation. This could happen as a result of discussion at international level or through a competition complaint, possibly in the E.U. or the United Kingdom.

8.4.2 Access to end-users

It is one thing to secure access to the public Internet, and another to secure access to end–users. Whereas dial-up Internet access has been widely possible for some time, key issues for the Regulator have been the provision of high bandwidth infrastructure and unmetered Internet access for the mass market, both of which are seen as key to promoting widespread retail use of the Internet.   **8–031**

Because BT controls the access lines into the majority of U.K. households, use of high bandwidth infrastructure is still largely dependent on investment by BT. BT offers a range of high bandwidth access products, which all ISPs have rights to purchase.[16] Alternatively, BT is required by Condition 83 of its licence to unbundle individual local   **8–032** loops at the request of Annex 2 operators, who may then co-locate their facilities in BT's local exchanges and install high bandwidth equipment, such as ADSL modems. The terms, conditions and charges for local loop unbundling are regulated by OFTEL.[17]

As for unmetered Internet access, BT is required by OFTEL to offer flat rate Internet access call origination (FRIACO), an unmetered call origination interconnection service, to all Annex 2 operators. This means that operators pay a non-discriminatory, regulated charge to use BT's local access network for Internet access and are not charged on a per minute basis. This makes it economically viable for ISPs to offer unmetered Internet services over BT's network to end customers.[18]

8.5 Broadcasting regulation

8.5.1 Background

8–033   The regulation of broadcasting in the United Kingdom is contained primarily in the Broadcasting Acts 1990 and 1996 (the 1990 Act or the 1996 Act as applicable). The principal aim of the 1996 Act was to put in place the necessary legislative framework for digital terrestrial broadcasting.

In contrast to telecommunications regulation, broadcasting regulation in the United Kingdom as in many other regimes, is concerned with the licensing of services and in particular the content of broadcast material. At first glance, it might seem odd that broadcasting regulation can apply to services provided over the Internet, as mainstream broadcasting normally involves the transmission of programmes for simultaneous reception by a group of persons. In contrast, services over the Internet are generally made available in response to a request by users who dial up a service provider. However, there is some potential for licensing requirements under the 1990 Act to be applied to Internet services as we discuss below. The current position of the broadcasting regulator, the Independent Television Commission, is stated to be: "The ITC's powers under the Broadcasting Act 1990 extend to television programmes on the internet and to advertisements which contain still or moving pictures. We are not seeking to apply these powers at present, although in the area of programmes we are contributing to the self-regulatory system established for the internet through the Internet Watch Foundation."[19] The discussion that follows should be read in the light of that policy statement. In particular any question of the need for licences will be affected by the current policy of the ITC. It may also be noted that applying the 1990 Act's broadcast content rules (such as impartiality, exclusion of the views of the proprietor and so on) to the Internet would most likely result only in the regulator being exposed to public ridicule. These policy issues are discussed further in Chapter 12.

8.5.2 Broadcasting licensing in the United Kingdom

Licensable programme services
8–034   The 1990 Act regulates the television transmission and content of, among other things, "licensable programme services". Section 46(1) defines a "licensable programme service" as:

> "...a service consisting in the provision by any person of relevant programmes with

a view to their being conveyed by means of a telecommunications system —

(a)   for reception in two or more dwelling-houses in the United Kingdom otherwise than for the purpose of being received there by persons who have a business interest in receiving them . . .

[. . .]

whether the telecommunications system is run by the person so providing the programmes or by some other person, and whether the programmes are to be so conveyed as mentioned in paragraph (a) for simultaneous reception or for reception at different times in response to requests made by different users of the service."[20]

Any person who provides such a service without a licence is guilty of a criminal offence and is liable to a fine under section 13 of the 1990 Act.

The term "telecommunications system" is given the same meaning as in the 1984 Act. **8–035** The term "relevant programme" means a television programme other than one consisting wholly or mainly of non-representational images, ie the programme does not consist wholly or mainly of text. Unfortunately, the 1990 Act does not define "television programme". However, it seems clear from the 1990 Act that still or moving pictures are capable of amounting to "relevant programmes", which would require to be licensed. This would have a far reaching impact for Internet content providers if section 46(1) did not also specify that a relevant programme must be a television programme.[21]

The point is best illustrated by considering some different types of Internet services.

A Web site consisting of still pictures or graphics which are not updated does not **8–036** appear to have the characteristics of a television programme and almost certainly does not require a licence under section 46 of the 1990 Act. On the other hand, an estate agency service offered to Internet users, where still pictures of the interior of houses are updated every couple of minutes, begins to look and feel more like a television programme and is not exempted by the non-representational images limb of a licensable programme service. There is little doubt that motion picture services provided over the Internet would be likely to be regarded as licensable programme services within the meaning of section 46 and thus would, if the ITC decided to exercise its powers in relation to the Internet, require to be licensed. Many such services are now available, although because of the length of time it takes to receive moving video images over the typical user's narrowband dial-up Internet connection, they are still at an early stage of take-up. The advent of broadband to home services such as ADSL is likely to make such services more widely used. Netcasting services which provide access over the Internet to live events in the form of sounds and images could amount to licensable programme services.[22]

Certain services are exempted from the need to obtain a licensable programme service **8–037** licence under a provision contained in section 46(2)(c). The exemption applies to a "two-way service", defined as:

"a service of which it is an essential feature that while visual images or sounds . . . are being conveyed by the person providing the service there will or may be sent from each place of reception, by means of the same telecommunications system . . . visual images or sounds (or both) for reception by the person providing the service or other persons receiving it (other than signals sent for the operation or control of the service)."

This exemption applies to videophone and teleconferencing services.

Licences for licensable programme services

8–038 A section 46 licence to provide a licensable programme service can be obtained through a fairly simple process. The applicant must complete an application form providing details of the licensee and the service to be provided. The licence fee is calculated by reference to revenues.

8–039 Where an application is duly made, the ITC may only refuse to grant the licence if it appears to it that the service provided under the licence would not comply with the requirements of section 6(1) of the 1990 Act. Section 6(1) details the general requirements which relate to a licensed service, including:

— that it includes nothing which offends against good taste or decency or is likely to encourage or incite to crime or to lead to disorder or to be offensive to public feeling

— that any news is presented with due accuracy and impartiality

— that due impartiality is preserved on the part of the person providing the service as respects matters of political or industrial controversy or relating to current public policy

— that due responsibility is exercised in respect of religious programmes

— that the views and opinions of the person providing the service on matters of political or industrial controversy or relating to current public policy are excluded from the service.

Certain persons are disqualified from holding licences under the Broadcasting Act 1990. However, the foreign ownership restrictions do not apply in relation to licensable programme service licences. There are restrictions on cross-media holdings, so, for example, a broadcasting or newspaper company which takes a stake in an Internet content provider which offers licensable programme services may not be able to obtain a licence under section 46. These rules are under review, however and may change radically when the new Communications Act is introduced.

ITC Codes

8–040 Broadcasting Act licences generally include obligations to observe the ITC Codes of Conduct, for example the Programme Code which sets out constraints on programming freedom relating to taste and decency, strong language and sexual portrayal, violence, privacy, impartiality, charitable appeals, religious programmes, undue prominence for commercial products, and protection of children. Many of these would in practice be difficult for Internet based content providers to comply with. However, as long as the ITC forbears from exercising its licensing powers for Internet based broadcast entertainment, it has no mechanism for enforcing the Codes and there is no legal requirement for Internet broadcasters to comply with their provisions.

The Programme Code is written with broadcast programming schedules for a single time zone in mind. It includes watershed requirements and rules on advertising breaks. The ITC's Programme Code requires certain types of programme material which are not suitable for children to be scheduled for transmission at particular times. This requires the holders of licences to restrict access to adult material to late evening and night-time slots. However, special rules apply to subscription channels and Pay Per View services. Where the viewer has elected to take a specialist service, it is considered to take a greater share of responsibility for protecting children from the channels content and the watershed is consequently an hour earlier than for generally available channels. Likewise, where security mechanisms such as PIN numbers restrict access to programming, watershed rules may be waived altogether, although other restrictions in the Programme Code are not necessarily affected.

The rules regarding advertising are contained in the ITC's Programme Code and the **8–041** Rules on Amount and Scheduling of Advertising which a licensee is required to comply with. These rules, which generally allow a maximum of nine minutes advertising in any hour and prescribe the minimum time periods between advertisements, are disapplied to home shopping programming and dedicated tele-shopping channels and other similar services which consist purely of advertising. The concept of an advertising break is, in any event, meaningless in the context of most Internet services and indeed any service which is not based around sequential scheduling. Interestingly, although the Internet is not subject to licensing rules, the Web sites of licensed broadcasters are treated as programme related services and are subject to the Programme Code and provisions relating to editorial responsibility, advertising content and promotion which apply to licensed broadcast services. In order not to fall foul of the advertising rules, Internet addresses which appear on screen must be limited to the name of the Licensee or the title of the programme concerned. Conversely, Web sites which are not controlled by the Licensee or which are not directly related to the licensed programme service are considered by the ITC to be commercial products and must comply with the rules on advertising for such products.

Interactive services
The ITC has issued a Guidance Note on interactive channels and services.[23] Its purpose is **8–042** principally to ensure that advertising and editorial content are clearly distinguished in those cases where interactivity is designed to permit cross selling of products or services. for example, where the Licensee provides interactive access to a commercial web site, it must ensure that the viewer is aware of this before any advertising is shown. Such connections are not permitted from services which are prohibited from carrying advertising in the first place, eg programmes for schools. In any event, advertising which is directly accessed from the licensable programme service must comply with the ITC's rules on Advertising Standards an practice. Because, presumably, the ITC does not have powers to enforce these rules on Internet content providers, it places an expectation on Licensees to ensure observation of the rules through commercial arrangements. It is not clear how such an expectation can be enforced or indeed whether it would constitute a breach of the Broadcasting Act licence should compliance not be secured. The ITC distinguishes between Web content which is moderated or selected by a licensed broadcaster and Internet via TV services which provide unrestricted access to the public Internet and the World Wide Web. These latter services simply treat the TV as a PC and are treated as falling outside the scope of the rules on interactive services.

Licensable sound programme services
A very similar provision in section 112 of the 1990 Act regulates "licensable sound **8–043** programme services", which consist of the provision of "sound programmes" delivered by means of a telecommunications system in the same way as a licensable programme service.

Any person who without a licence provides what is generically termed an "independent radio service" (the definition of which includes a licensable sound programme service) is guilty of an offence and is liable for a fine under section 97 of the 1990 Act. There are general requirements relating to these licensed services which are almost identical to those which apply to licensable programme services, the effect of which is that the content of such programmes is regulated by the Radio Authority.

8–044   The term "sound programme" is not defined, but it seems reasonable to assume that a service which consists of text, visual images and sound as part of the service cannot be a sound programme within the meaning of section 112. This is supported by the reference in section 97 to a licensable sound programme service being one of the independent radio services which the 1990 Act seeks to regulate. Radio services do not include text or visual images and are meant to be listened to rather than watched on a screen. In addition, the construction of section 112 when compared with section 46 of the 1990 Act supports the view that programmes consisting purely of sound and not programmes consisting of a mix of sound, text and images require a licensable sound programme licence. In section 46, a "relevant programme" is defined as a television programme but not one consisting wholly or mainly of non-representational images. In section 112 there is no analogous qualification in relation to sound programmes which would be expected if the section was intended to refer to programmes consisting of other than sound. Otherwise, there would be potential for overlap between a licensable programme service and a licensable sound programme service, with two licences being required in the case of a multimedia service. That cannot have been the intention of the draftsman.

It seems unlikely, therefore, that traditional Internet Web sites and other services consisting of audio, text and visual images will qualify as licensable sound programme services, because they do not contain sound without text or visual images, and therefore a licence under section 47 of the 1990 Act would not be required to provide such services.

Internet radio services

8–045   For different reasons, Internet radio services are unlikely to require the provider of such services to obtain a licensable sound programme service licence under section 113 of the 1990 Act. These services typically consist of a Web site which allows the user to access radio stations via the Internet which would normally be accessed by traditional radio apparatus. These radio stations will probably be licensed as national or local sound broadcasting services under the 1990 Act, or they could be foreign radio stations not so licensed. As the provider of the Internet site which allows access to these stations is merely providing access to radio programmes provided by others, he cannot be said to be providing sound programmes and should not need to be licensed under section 113 of the 1990 Act.[24] However, as we explain below, this type of activity might in principle require a licence under section 72 of the 1990 Act (see below). If, on the other hand, specific audio/radio based services which do not merely involve the provision of access to existing radio station programming (whether or not such services are intended to be received simultaneously by two or more persons) become available on the Internet a licence under section 113 of the 1990 Act would in principle almost certainly be needed by the providers of such services. In any event, when examining the licensing position in any particular case, the relationship (if any) of the Web site proprietor to the audio content would have to be carefully considered. It is notable that the policy of the Radio Authority appears to be that Internet radio services do not require to be regulated. Indeed, in its 1998 response to the government Green Paper *Regulating Communications: Approaching Convergence in the Information Age* the Radio Authority stated: "Existing legislation should not be used to introduce the regulation of new, interactive services by the back door. The Broadcasting Acts were never intended to cover such services, and their growth will be better served by self-regulation (under whatever co-ordinating 'umbrella' is appropriate) and by the application of general law than through the uncomfortable enforcement of inappropriate broadcasting-specific legislation".[25]

Local delivery services

The final category of licence granted under the 1990 Act which could potentially be required in order to provide Netcasting or Internet radio services is a local delivery service (LDS) licence under section 72 of the 1990 Act.[26] There are two key differences between a licensable programme service or a licensable sound programme service and a local delivery service (or LDS). The first is the requirement for the LDS service to be provided "for simultaneous reception in two or more dwelling houses in the United Kingdom..." A Netcasting service allows Internet users to access live events over the Internet by means of sound and/or images, and would appear to meet the requirement for simultaneous reception described above, as would an Internet radio service which has the characteristics of a traditional radio service or which involves the provision of access via a Web site to traditional radio broadcast services.

The second key difference is that an LDS consists in the use of a telecommunications system for the delivery of the services described in section 72 of the 1990 Act, unlike licensable programme services and licensable sound programme services which involve the actual provision of programmes.

An LDS licence would only be required if the services being delivered over the Internet (*i.e.* Netcasting or Internet radio services for our purposes) fall within the categories of service listed in section 72(2) of the 1990 Act. These include television and sound broadcasting (*i.e.* radio) services, together with licensable programme services and licensable sound programme services. For the reasons stated above, most types of services currently available on the Internet are unlikely to fall into the category of licensable programme services (with the exception of Netcasting services as noted above which may have the characteristic of television programmes). However, an Internet radio service which consists of a Web site by means of which users can access domestic and foreign radio stations would appear to fall within section 72 of the 1990 Act. This is because the radio programmes which a user can access by means of this service will either amount to "sound broadcast services" (if the radio stations are established and licensed in the United Kingdom) or "licensable sound programme services" (if the radio stations are foreign or are otherwise not licensed as sound broadcast services) and are in each case intended "for simultaneous reception in two or more dwelling-houses in the United Kingdom...".

If the ITC were to determine that an LDS licence was required by persons providing Netcasting or Internet radio services, a national LDS licence could be applied for.

8.6 Future regulation

Although the U.K. regulatory authorities have come a long way in adapting the regulatory framework for telecommunications to the Internet, more fundamental change to the underlying legislation is now in sight.

The European Commission is introducing a series of new Directives which will replace the directives introduced in 1998, keeping in place those measures which continue to be relevant and replacing the rest with new rules based on technological neutrality. The new measures include a Framework Directive which clarifies the responsibilities and powers

8–046

8–047

8–048

of national regulatory authorities and sets out ground rules for identifying significant market power based on competition rules. There will also be an Access and Interconnection Directive which, in certain respects, deals specifically with the Internet and its interdependence with switched networks. In addition, a new Authorisations Directive will impose strict limits on Member State powers to require any type of operator to obtain prior authorisation before offering commercial services, and where this is permitted, general authorisations will become the norm, instead of individual licences. There will also be new rules on data protection and universal service. Crucially, disparity of regulatory treatment between voice telephony and data are likely to disappear and existing telecommunications regulation will, where possible, be extended to broadcasting and ancillary services. The Directives are expected to take effect in the United Kingdom sometime in 2002.

8–049   In the United Kingdom, the Communications White Paper has laid the groundwork for new unified legislation to replace the Telecommunications Act and relevant sections of the Broadcasting Acts. The new Communications Act is expected to be in place early in 2004. The White Paper has already led to an Office of Communications Bill, which will pave the way for a new, single regulator for all electronic communications networks, services and content. This is expected to take effect in 2002.

8.7 Conclusion

8–050   This Chapter has described how current telecommunications and broadcasting regulation applies to the services and infrastructure which make up the Internet.

The approach taken to telecommunications licensing in the United Kingdom is for operators of telecommunications systems to require a licence under the 1984 Act. In most cases, the activities of ISPs are covered by the Telecommunications Services Licence, a class licence for which no application is required. Providers of commercial voice telephony services over the Internet may have to register as a provider of ISVR, if they meet the other criteria established by the European Commission. Many ISPs could benefit from Annex 2 rights to connect their systems to those of network operators, benefiting from cost based conveyance charges including unmetered access to customers, and rights to seek resolution of disputes.

8–051   U.K. broadcasting regulation seeks to regulate the content of different types of broadcast services. Such services can include television programmes other than those consisting wholly or mainly of non-representational images. Despite the lack of a precise definition of what amounts to a "licensable programme service", it appears that some Internet services containing still pictures, and which have the look and feel of a television programme, could in principle require a licence under section 46 of the 1990 Act, although the ITC has to date refrained from exerting authority over Internet content. New legislation within the next two to three years can be expected to introduce the most fundamental reform to the regulation of electronic communications this country has seen since privatisation of the telecommunications industry in 1984.

---

1.   Some specialised protocols do exist within the general Internet protocol structure. For instance, UDP (Uniform Datagram Protocol) can be used instead of TCP (Transmission Control Protocol). Because of its particular characteristics UDP is more suitable for real-time applications such as voice or video. However, that does not mean that the type of content contained within a UDP packet can reliably be deduced from the use of UDP.

2. Licences are granted under section 7 of the 1984 Act.
3. The Government has, in the Communications White Paper, proposed the abolition of criminal sanctions for running a telecoms system without a licence, in favour of a scheme of general authorisations.
4. Section 4(1) of the 1984 Act (as amended) defines a telecommunications system as:
   "...a system for the conveyance, through the agency of electric, magnetic, electro-magnetic, electro-chemical or electro-mechanical energy, of—
   (a) speech, music and other sounds;
   (b) visual images;
   (c) signals serving for the impartation (whether as between persons and persons, things and things or persons and things) of any matter otherwise than in the form of sounds or visual images; or
   (d) signals serving for the actuation or control of machinery or apparatus."
5. Article 1 of the Interconnection Directive.
6. An organisation shall be presumed to have significant market power when it has a share of more than 25 per cent of a particular telecommunications market in the geographical area in a member state within which it is authorised to operate. National regulatory authorities may nevertheless determine that an organisation with a market share of less than 25 in the relevant market has significant market power. They may also determine that an organisation with a market share of more than 25 per cent in the relevant market does not have significant market power. In either case, the determination shall take into account the organisation's ability to influence market conditions; Its turnover relative to the size of the market, its control of the means of access to end-users, its access to financial resources and its experience in providing products and services in the market. Annex 1 of the Directive defines the relevant markets as the fixed public telephone network for voice telephony, the leased lines service, public mobile telephone networks and public mobile telephone services. At present, BT, Kingston Communications in Hull, Vodafone and BTCellnet have SMP status, as determined by OFTEL.
7. A PSTN is in turn defined as being a public telecommunications system by means of which messages are switched incidentally to their conveyance, but does not include the private leased circuit part or parts of such a network.
8. The aim of the proportionate return condition is to prevent Voice ISR being transmitted to countries which have themselves not yet liberalised ISR services. This condition requires the licensee to ensure that the ratio of inward ISR traffic (which potentially bypasses the accounting rate system) to outward Voice ISR and Data ISR traffic carried by the licensee on a particular route does not become greater than the ratio of all inward to outward telecommunications traffic on that route. If the Secretary of State is unable for some reason to specify the ratio of all inward to outward traffic on a particular route, he can require the licensee to secure that the amount of inward and outward ISR traffic is equal. This means that in those countries to which the condition applies, ie the rest of the world outside the European Economic Area, and WTO signatories, the licensee will automatically be in breach of its licence where it is unable to send any ISR traffic to that country or territory.
9. The Internet is essentially made up of switches, routers, IPLCs and national private leased circuits.
10. See Communication from the Commission on the status of voice on the Internet under Community Law and in particular under Directive 90/388 (OJ 98/C 6/04) and Supplement to the Communication by the Commission to the European Parliament and the Council on the status and implementation of Directive 90/388 on competition in the markets for telecommunications services ([2000] O.J. C 369/03)
11. See in particular the Revised Voice Telephony Directive 98/10, implemented in the U.K. by the Telecommunications (Open Network Provision) Voice Telephony Regulations 1998.
12. See "Rights and Obligations to interconnect under the E.C. Interconnection Directive", a statement issued by the Director General of Telecommunications, April 1999
13. For an example of OFTEL's approach to resolving an interconnection dispute affecting the Internet, see http://www.oftel.gov.uk/publications/internet/surf0501.htm
14. LINX's commercial membership terms and conditions are available at www.LINX.net/joining/procedure and www.LINX.net/joining/mou.
15. At the ITU World Telecommunications Standards Assembly (WTSA) held in Autumn 2000, a proposal was considered for regulating exchange of Internet traffic, known as ICAIS, or International Charging Arrangements for Internet Service. The proposal was to replace commercially negotiated peering and transit with a regulated international settlements system similar to the one followed by national incumbent telecommunications operators. Charges would be based on fixed, per minute fees for call termination. The proposal was generally supported in smaller countries with net inflows and resisted in countries with net outflows, such as the United States of America.
16. Currently on offer are such products as Videostream, IPStream and Datastream, details of which are available on BT's website at www.broadband.bt.com
17. For details of local loop unbundling, see http://www.oftel.gov.uk/publications/local_loop/index.htm> and www.btinterconnect.com
18. For details of BT's unmetered Internet access products, see http://www.oftel.gov.uk/publications/internet/index.htm
19. www.itc.org.uk ("Regulating Commercial TV: Internet Issues").
20. Note that the definition specifically envisages a service in which programmes may be received at different

times in response to requests made by different users of the service and thus includes "relevant programmes" delivered by the Internet.

21. Section 2(6) of the 1990 Act provides some guidance as to the meaning of the term "non-representational images". It states that these are "...visual images which are neither still pictures nor comprised within sequences of visual images capable of being seen as moving pictures."

22. The ITC, as a matter of practice, does not use its licensing powers for Internet services, although it has reserved the right to change this position. Instead it expects Internet service providers to observe self–regulation, as developed by organisations such as the Internet Watch Foundation, for details of which see www.iwf.org.uk

23. The full text is available at www.itc.org.uk/word_does/interactive_guidance_statement.doc

24. It should also be noted that section 112(2) of the 1990 Act expressly excludes from the definition of licensable sound programme services 'a service which the programmes are provided for transmission in the course of the provision of a sound broadcasting service...'. The term 'in the course of' is not defined but could have the effect of excluding services which involve merely the provision of access to sound broadcasting services (ie existing radio stations).

25. Radio Authority Response, p. 28–29.

26. Under section 72(1), "local delivery service" means a service provided by any person which:

"(a) consists in the use of a telecommunications system (whether run by that or any other person) for the purpose of the delivery of one or more of the services specified in subsection (2) for simultaneous reception in two or more dwelling-houses in the United Kingdom; and

(b) is of a class or description specified in an order made by the Secretary of State."

The services referred to in subsection (2) include a licensable programme service and a licensable sound programme service.

9

Contracts between Internet Service Providers, Content Owners and Others

9.1 Introduction

This Chapter examines some of the legal issues surrounding three of the most important **9–001** commercial contracts relating to use of the Internet: the contract for the creation of a Web site; the contract for the placing of advertising or sponsorship on a Web site; and the contract for the provision of Internet access. Contracts with and between the providers of Internet access services themselves are considered briefly. Contracts formed in connection with Web sites for the sale or supply of goods and services are dealt with separately in Chapter 10.

In this Chapter the term "site owner" refers to the party on whose behalf a Web site is created or hosted. "User" refers to a person accessing the Web site.

9.2 Contracts for the provision of a Web site

Before goods and services can be marketed or sold, the site owner will need to establish a **9–002** Web site as its shop window to the world. Both the design of the site and its establishment on the Internet are typically contracted out to a third party. This section looks at the legal issues involved.

9.2.1 The contract with the Web site designer

If the site owner intends to use an agency to design its Web site, his first concern is to **9–003** ensure that he selects a designer that understands how the Internet works and the way in which visitors to the Web site are likely to access it. Many issues can arise. For instance, if most of the visitors to the Web site are home users who are dialling up over normal voice telephone lines, large graphics may not download on a timescale which users will find acceptable. Users behind corporate firewalls may be able to download faster, but may have difficulty in accessing streaming audio and video or Java applets if they are barred by the firewall. The Web utilises a limited palette of colours and has limited resolution, both of which place limits on the type of design that is suitable for use on the Web. Usability and ease of navigation are difficult to achieve and, legally, not easy to define. The range of browsers (including different versions of the same browser) with which the site is to be compatible has to be decided. Should the site cater for disabled users? (Blind users typically use text-to-speech converters, which cannot convert text contained in image files).[1] Is the site to include a content management system for the site owner to allow direct updating of the content? If so, what facilities should it provide and to what level of user (business user, I.T. expert etc)? Will the content management system allow the site owner merely to add content, or to create additional instances of existing content types, or to create new content types and sections of the site? What level of skill will be required to use these facilities?

The contract with the design agency will primarily address the question of ownership of the intellectual property rights in the design of the Web site and in any content or code that is specially written or created by the agency. Essentially, this will be a question of copyright and database right.[2] The design agency will be the first owner of the copyright in any works created by its employees under the Copyright, Designs and Patents Act 1988. As noted in Chapter 2, under section 90 of the Act copyright can only be assigned if the assignment is signed by or on behalf of the assignor and in writing.[3] Therefore the site owner will need to ensure that its contract with the design agency includes a current assignment of the future copyright in the designs created by the agency.[4] The site owner should also require contractually binding undertakings from the agency that the design work for the Web site will be undertaken by persons employed by it and that the works produced by those employees will be original works and will not infringe any third party copyright. The contract between the site owner and the design agency should also impose a requirement on the agency to obtain waivers from those employees which undertake the design work of their moral rights in that work since otherwise the site owner will need to credit those employees as the authors of the works if they choose to assert their moral rights.

9–004   As no intellectual property rights will exist in the ideas underlying the design of the Web site (as opposed to the design itself), the site owner will need to place a contractual restriction on the agency designing a similar site for a rival organisation, if it wishes to secure a measure of exclusivity in respect of these ideas. It is beyond the scope of this chapter to consider the possible U.K. or E.U. competition law aspects of such restrictions.

Whilst the intellectual property issues are key to the design contract, the site owner will also want to ensure that the design contract covers the more mundane but nonetheless important issues of the deadline for the creation and delivery of the design and the fee for the design work. Liability for the cost of materials should also be addressed.

9.2.2 The contract for building the Web site

9–005   The contract for building the Web site will be akin in many ways to a software development agreement, being typically divided into phases with milestones for delivery of work product and payment.

Specification and initial design

9–006   From the Web site owner's perspective, the key to a contract for the creation of a Web site is to include a detailed design specification and to provide for acceptance testing of work product before fees are paid to the designer. In many cases the creation of the specification will be the first work undertaken by the designer and, it is only once this is agreed, that the remainder of the contract for the creation of the Web site will come into place.

The specification for the Web site will usually consist of a description of the Web site and/or storyboards for the appearance of various sections of the site and details of how the site will be navigated by users. It will set out the operating system on which the site is to run, and any necessary third party software such as database managers and web servers. It will also set out whether certain sections of the site are to have restricted access. It will specify with which browsers the site must work and whether, for example, the site should work both with and without frames, or whether there should be a text-only version. It may address any number of the issues outlined above. The site owner will wish to build in requirements for minimum response times in use. The designer is likely to resist this, especially if the designer is not also providing the platform on which the site will be hosted. Even if he is, he will be unwilling to be tied down to response times when the site is accessed over the public Internet, which introduces its own delays. The specification may also address security standards, especially if the site holds financial or personal data.

The specification will usually be based around text, graphics and other materials provided by the site owner. The designer will wish to specify the format in which these are to be provided or provide for the costs of conversion into a suitable format.

Creation and testing

The designer will code the text, graphics and other material provided by the site owner, **9–007** and/or create any necessary database(s) and create the Web site. Depending on the timescales and complexity of the site, the contract may subdivide this process into further stages. The contract may allow for periodic inspection of the work by the site owner or for the site owner to monitor progress through the provision of remote access to the work. The site owner should, in any event, ensure that the designer is required to keep him regularly updated of progress and problems in order that he can identify and deal with potential delays that might impact on the launch of his Web site as soon as possible. If there are serious delays to the agreed timetable the site owner will want the right to bring in additional resources to perform particular tasks at the cost of the designer or the right to move the work elsewhere. Whether the designer is being paid on a fixed fee or a time and materials basis, payments should be linked to the achievement of key milestones and thought should be given to using variable payments (that increase or decrease depending on the achievement or otherwise of specified tasks) to provide an incentive to the designer to meet or exceed delivery deadlines.[5]

The site owner will usually conduct acceptance tests on the site once the designer has **9–008** completed his own internal tests. These may be carried out in a variety of ways but typically the designer will create a prototype site on a closed system which the site owner will test as to functionality, compliance with specification and reliability. There may then be further live testing on the Internet but with the site hidden under a dummy name until it is ready to be made public. The site owner will want to ensure that the site runs acceptably fast, that multiple end–users can access the site simultaneously and that the site works with all major browsers. For e–commerce sites, where the number of possible multiple users may be extremely large, the site owner may want to provide for "stress-testing" of the site, to simulate the effect of large numbers of users. Testing of the site's security may also be provided for, at least if the design agency is to perform the hosting function. If the site is to be transferred to a third party host on completion, careful thought will need to be given as to whether testing in the live environment is required, and if so how the agency and the third party host are to co-operate to achieve that. The contract should address how any dispute as to whether an acceptance test has been passed should be resolved.

Ownership of intellectual property rights

9–009   The issue of ownership of the intellectual property rights in the site is another key issue which needs to be addressed and one which is frequently overlooked. Before considering the strict legal position, it is important to understand the parties' commercial needs. The site owner will be concerned about Web site portability: that is, its ability to move the site to another service provider should it wish to do so, with the minimum delay. Given the nature of the Internet, the site owner will not wish to countenance a period during which the site ceases to be available while it is recreated by another provider but instead will wish to take whatever material is necessary from the existing provider to enable a seamless transfer to take place. The designer, however, will not wish to grant rights in its underlying proprietary software to the site owner and still less to see a competitor taking advantage of it.

Static content and code

9–010   It is also important to understand the nature of the components that go to make up a web site. In the early days of the Web, Web sites were almost always constructed as "flat HTML" sites. These were relatively simple sites in which the web pages themselves were stored on the server and uploaded to the user's browser on request. More complex interactivity was typically provided by program scripts stored on the web server. HTML itself is nothing more than a text mark-up language, controlling the format of the pages. It has no facilities to, for instance, change the formatting or content of pages dynamically according to the existence or absence of pre-set criteria. So, for instance, if a site-owner wanted to offer the user a choice of languages by selecting from a list, the program to achieve this would be separate from the web pages and would be stored on the server. The web pages themselves would be duplicated in separate language versions, each stored discretely on the server.

At this time, therefore, there was generally a reasonably clear distinction between programming and content, although even then the HTML code could be relatively complex and look remarkably like a computer program.[6] Nonetheless, it was generally possible to look at a web page in a browser and identify a corresponding HTML file or files stored on the web site server. Both the content and the HTML code were static. This made the task of the contract draftsman, tasked with allocating rights as between the parties, relatively simple.

Dynamic content and code

9–011   Since then things have become much more complicated. A number of changes have taken place which significantly blur the distinction between programming and content. First, the introduction of client-side programming facilities such as Javascript and Dynamic HTML means that some of the programming that previously was executed on the server can now be written into the web pages themselves, so that it is executed by the user's PC when the pages are uploaded.

This means that the uploaded web page, instead of corresponding reasonably well to the page as viewed by the user, may now contain a vast amount of programming and also contain content only some of which is selected for viewing in a particular format by a particular user. The selection of content and format presented to the user is created "on the fly" at the user's PC, in response to the programming built into the web page. However, although the content is dynamic the code that generates the content is still static, embedded in the pages stored on the server.

When allocating rights in content and format, it is necessary to allocate rights in all possible combinations of form and content resulting from the operation of the client-side programming. It is no longer enough (assuming that it might once have been) to define the content by, for instance, annexing a copy of the set of web pages to the contract. The possible permutations and combinations render such an approach unrealistic.

The next level of complexity is brought about by the increasing use of databases to manage web site content. In this case no web pages may be stored on the web server at all,[7] but the components (text, graphic elements, forms, controls etc) are stored separately in the database and combined "on the fly" to generate pages in response to a request from the user's browser. Since the user's browser still needs to receive the pages in HTML (or similar compatible language such as Javascript), the database has to generate the pages in HTML or Javascript code. So whereas in the case of plain Javascript/DHTML the code is static, in the case of database-driven sites not only content, but also the HTML or similar program code itself may be dynamically generated.

9–012

Additionally, sites may contain numerous other types of content: downloadable programs (screensavers and games), downloadable video files, streaming audio and video, real-time animations, and so on.

Allocating intellectual property rights

As regards ownership of copyright, to the extent that the dynamically generated content, format or program code represents a computer-generated work attention needs to be paid to the provisions of the Copyright Act regarding the authorship of such works.[8]

9–013

In practice, there is likely to be little dispute over the material originally provided by the site owner and over the "look and feel" of the site. Clearly the designer does not own the site owner–supplied material and, at least in the case of static HTML, will have little interest in the coded version of that material. If the site owner has agreed that the designer can use proprietary software in the creation of the site, the site owner will have no legitimate claim to the ownership that proprietary software or to the underlying server operating software. The site owner will, however, need to seek a licence to use this proprietary software in order to operate the Web site and will want to put escrow arrangements in place to ensure it has continued access to this software if the designer becomes insolvent. Where the designer has written software or other routines specifically for the site, as noted above, copyright will vest in the designer. The site owner may wish to specify that copyright is assigned to it. If the designer wishes to use that software for other clients—and if the site owner is prepared to agree to this—the site owner may be satisfied with a licence to use that software. Where database design or dynamically generated content and/or code are involved, considerable care will need to be taken to ensure that the contract achieves an appropriate and acceptable division of rights.

Proprietary software

In some cases, the site owner will not wish the designer to use proprietary software in the creation of the Web site as it will not wish to run the risk of losing its licence to use that software in the future through, for example, an inadvertent breach of the terms of the

9–014

licence. The site owner may also wish to ensure that the designer is prevented from using the software for its rivals and (in addition to any competition law issues) may be unhappy about relying on a contractual undertaking from the designer not to do so. In this case the site owner may wish to insist that all software and routines used in the creation of the site are written specifically for it and that the designer assigns the intellectual property rights in that software to the site owner. If the site owner wishes to take this approach he will need to make it clear in the specification for the Web site and will need to have budgeted for the consequential increase in the cost of the creation of the site.

Physical materials

9–015   Ownership of intellectual property rights in a work does not entitle the owner to have physical possession of the work. So although the site owner who owns the copyright/ database right can prevent the web designer or any third party from infringing, that does not entitle him to demand that the designer provides him with a copy of the site materials. The contract should therefore provide for delivery to the site owner of copies of the site (preferably at regular intervals throughout the initial development and, if the designer is hosting the finished site, beyond). It should also provide for the form in which the copies are provided and for provision of any ancillary materials or information required to render the materials usable and understandable. For instance, if the site has been built using a particular web development tool the site owner may need to know what tool was used in order to make proper use of the materials.

Third party software

9–016   Where the Web site runs on third party software (such as operating systems, database management systems or content management systems), careful thought will be required as to the licensing of such software especially if, on completion of development, the site is to be transferred to a third party host, or taken in-house onto the site owner's system. While the agency will have a licence to run such software on its development servers, what is the position for the live and back-up servers? The site owner should require the designer to identify to it at the outset any third party software that it intends to use in the creation of the site so that the site owner can identify whether there are any particularly onerous terms attached to the licence of that software and whether the software has one unique source or whether equivalent software is available from other suppliers.

Domain name

9–017   If a domain name for the Web site is to be registered by the agency, provision should be made for this. It may be necessary to consider carefully who is to be notified to the domain name registry as the administrative contact, since changes (such as re-delegating the domain name to a different server) are made on the instructions of that person. If the agency is named as the contact, then in the event of a dispute, the agency may effectively be able to prevent the site being transferred elsewhere. (As a result of such incidents, the Internet Service Providers Association Code of Conduct now mandates ISPA members to provide, in some circumstances, a degree of protection for their customers in such situations). Similarly, thought should be given as to whom is to be nominated as the billing contact.

9.2.3 The contract for Web site hosting

Once the Web site has been accepted, the role of the agency (if it is to undertake the role) becomes that of host and maintainer. The contract will be similar to other information technology services contracts. Specifically, however, it needs to address two key issues, reflecting the two key roles of the host's server. Firstly, the server is the storage device on which all the information constituting the Web site is kept. Secondly, it connects with the Internet and provides a conduit through which visitors to the Web site access that information. **9–018**

Storage of the Web site data

As regards storage, the contract needs to set out not only how much capacity on the server will initially be made available but also the basis on which this is varied. In particular, the basis of calculating any difference in the charges should be set out. **9–019**

A Web site is not static: the site owner will want to retain its immediacy by regular updates. The contract should set out how updates to the site are to be made, the frequency with which they can be made, the time it will take for the host to implement an update and the cost of doing so. The site owner may want the ability to update its own site remotely by using an editing address and a password.

The contract may also deal with security issues, such as whether the server data is mirrored on another server for safety and whether particular security or encryption protocols are supported. If (as will almost inevitably be the case) the host is processing personal data on behalf of the site owner, the site owner will need to satisfy himself that the host offers the guarantees required by paragraph 11 of Schedule 1 of the Data Protection Act 1998 concerning security, and ensure that the contract is made or evidenced in writing and otherwise complies with the requirements of paragraph 12 of Schedule 1. Since "writing" is not defined in the Act, it should be construed in accordance with the definition in the Interpretation Act 1978. Although it may perhaps be open to doubt whether all varieties of contract in electronic form would necessarily satisfy the requirement that the contract be made in writing,[9] the alternative requirement that it be evidenced in writing would appear to permit a printout of the relevant electronic documents to be adduced in evidence. **9–020**

Access to the site

The capacity (bandwidth) of the host's connection to the rest of the Internet will be of vital importance to both the host and its customers. The host will not want to pay for unused bandwidth; the site owner will not want its site to be unavailable to potential clients due to bandwidth congestion. **9–021**

The contract should specify the obligations of the host to manage peaks and troughs in bandwidth requirement effectively, so as to ensure that the site is reliably available but that this is balanced against the host's concern to avoid carrying excess bandwidth. It is becoming increasingly the case that hosts can buy variable bandwidth on demand. More hosting permutations have become available, such as locating the site owner's servers at a third party server farm with high Internet connectivity, with varying allocations of responsibilities between the site owner and the operator of the server farm.

Other performance indicators and service levels should also be set out in the contract, including the availability of the site (*i.e.* whether and when down time is permitted). Defining "availability" in information technology contracts is notoriously difficult. The parties should aim to tie it specifically to clearly measured criteria and set out how it is to **9–022** be monitored and reported. The contract should also specify what responsibility the host may have to provide alternative or back up server capacity if the main system is down or there is a problem with a particular communications link. These obligations need to reflect the global nature of the Internet marketplace and therefore the time zones which are important to the site owner.

Of course, in specifying service levels the parties need to take into account that quality of access will depend on a number of factors outside the host's control, such as quality of the provider through which each end-user is accessing the site and the level of traffic on the Internet as a whole.

Information and reports

9–023   If a Web site allows for the sending of e-mails or the collecting of other information, the contract with the host should specify how and at what frequency this information is passed to the user. Even for a relatively passive site, the owner will normally require meaningful statistical information about the number of visitors not only to measure the success of the Web site but to provide to potential advertisers and sponsors. For e-commerce and advertising-driven sites, the owner may require extremely detailed information about usage patterns, page impressions and so on. These may need to be capable of being audited by third parties.

Where the site contains forms allowing for the requesting of information or for the sending of contractual messages (see Chapter 10) the user will wish to ensure that the data in forms submitted by potential customers is passed through immediately, that any appropriate automatic response is generated and that appropriate records of the transactions are kept for compliance and evidential purposes.

The contract should contain provisions dealings with ownership of this data and requiring the host to comply with the provisions of the Data Protection Act 1998 if it processes this data on behalf of the site owner.

The host's concerns

9–024   The host will be anxious to avoid liability for any defamatory, infringing or obscene material which may appear on a page on its server. To this end, it will seek to impose an obligation on the site owner to exercise appropriate control over content and to indemnify the ISP should there be a claim. Such an indemnity will usually stand outside any limitations on liability that are agreed in the contract and, since like any indemnity its value will depend on the ability of the indemnifying party to pay up, hosts should consider requiring the site owner to obtain insurance to cover third party claims or do so themselves.

Where the host is hosting material supplied in final form by the site owner or which can be updated by the site owner on-line, the contract should set out guidelines as to taste and decency which must be observed and give the host the right to remove material which it believes could give rise to liability. In relation to pornographic material, there is the risk that, as it is effectively being published to the world at large, including children, it will be held to be obscene. See Chapter 5 for a discussion of the liability of the host in such event. To reduce this risk, the host may insist on a standard warning screen being implemented or the use of an age verification system. In any event, the host will wish to ensure that it is free to remove materials in compliance with a request received from bodies such as the Internet Watch Foundation. (Similarly, where the site owner does not have the ability to update its own site remotely, it will want the right to require the host to promptly remove any material that is discovers to be defamatory, infringing or obscene).

However the host must be careful, from the point of view of defamation liability, not to **9–025** assume too great a degree of control over the content provided by the site owner. If a third party were to argue that the host had assumed editorial responsibility for the purposes of the Defamation Act 1996, then the allocation of responsibilities under the contract would be strong evidence of what responsibilities the host had assumed. On the other hand (as discussed in Chapter 4), it is unlikely that reserving the right to delete unlawful material would be regarded as assuming editorial responsibility.

Sharing of risk

Where the Web site is being used for commercial purposes, the site owner may wish to **9–026** specify financial remedies for failures to provide services, for example if the server goes down or access is impossible to compensate him. The host will wish to exclude liability for lost business, which may in any event be impossible to quantify.

9.3 Sponsorship and advertising agreements

A significant development in the commercialisation of the Internet has been the placing **9–027** of advertising within and commercial sponsorship of Web sites. The advertiser or sponsor pays the owner of the site in return for the display of a logo or other advertising material on that site and, typically, a hypertext link to the Web site of the advertiser or sponsor. A number of specific content based sites exist purely to generate revenue from advertisers and sponsors who are interested in promoting themselves to users of that site who, because they are interested in the subject matter of the site, believe they will also be interested in the advertisers/sponsor's goods or services.

As Web sites, which have e-mail capabilities, offer a cheap way of communicating with individual consumers, site owners and advertisers are increasingly seeking ways to capture and utilise "rich" data from Web site users in obtain the holy grail of advertising—the ability to target advertising at individual users.

If a content provider has a valuable site, such as in relation to a major sporting event, it **9–028** will be concerned to maximise its revenue from advertising and/or site sponsorship. This involves analysing the package or packages of rights which it can most effectively sell. For example, it may sell all the rights to insert graphic logos and hypertext links to one advertiser or it may divide the rights among a number of advertisers. It may distinguish between a "sponsor", who is entitled to a more prominent place on the site, and other advertisers who will receive lesser billing.

On the other hand the advertiser or sponsor will be concerned about how much prominence its brand will have on the Web site and where it sits in the "hierarchy." It may want to ensure that none of its rivals will be permitted to display their branding or advertising on the Web site.

Both parties will want to make the advertising or sponsorship work for them. The site owner will want to ensure that the advertising placed on its site and the sponsors with which it is associated are in keeping with the content and purpose of the site. The advertiser or sponsor will want to ensure that the Web site is a suitable medium to carry its advertising and that it fits with its overall advertising and marketing strategy.

With this in mind, a contract for advertising on a Web site should address the issues discussed below.

9.3.1 The rights being granted in respect of the Web site

9–029   As regards the site itself, is the advertiser to have exclusive or non-exclusive rights? Are there categories of advertising within which the advertiser will have exclusivity, *e.g.* that it will be the only food retailer on the site?

If the site is established in connection with a prestigious event or a high profile product (such as a rock group), is the advertiser to be granted a designation which it can use in other advertising, such as "Official Sponsor of the XYZ Web Page"?

9.3.2 Positioning and size

9–030   The advertiser will wish to specify where on the Web site its advertisement will appear, in what form and at what size relative to other text and graphics. Unlike with a paper based campaign where sizes are constant, this will involve a consideration of the working of the hypertext mark-up language and the operation of the Web browsers (discussed in Chapter 1) which are likely to be used to access the site. The advertiser may want to specify the technical details of how, in particular, its logo is created so as to ensure that it both downloads at an acceptable speed and is attractive. This of course also involves an analysis of the likely market: if the Web site is aimed at students, who may have "free" access, download time may not be so much of an issue. However, students accessing via a mainframe may use different browsers from home users so this will also need to be taken into account.

The advertiser may also want some contractual assurance that the Web page itself will be changed over time to keep up with new versions or releases of relevant browsers or, conversely, that it will remain usable with older versions. Whether this is a concern will depend very much on whether the site and advertising are relatively static or are relevant only for a campaign of short duration, such as in connection with a specific event.

9.3.3 Obligations in relation to promotion of the Web site

9–031   Where the site relates to a campaign by the owner in other media, advertisers may also wish to have assurances about the promotion of the Web site within that campaign, such as by the inclusion of the Web site's URL (Uniform Resource Locator) on posters and other forms of advertising. Conversely, and particularly where there is one major sponsor, the owner may wish to oblige that sponsor to promote the site as part of the sponsor's own advertising.

9.3.4 Hypertext links

9–032   Both parties will have concerns relating to the hypertext links from the advertisement to the advertiser's own Web page. The advertiser will want to ensure that the link is correctly created and that the site owner is obliged to update it correctly should there be a change in the URL of the advertiser's Web site. The advertiser will also no doubt want to ensure that the link can be triggered either from a text message or a graphic.

The owner of the site will want to ensure that the link to the advertiser's Web site will not give rise to any liability to third parties for defamation (see Chapter 4) or otherwise and that the advertiser will advise him promptly of changes: a non-functioning link will detract from the original Web site.

Both parties will want to ensure that they are not linked to or associated with inappropriate material.

9.3.5 Intellectual property

The advertiser will wish to specify the extent of the right of the owner of the Web site to **9–033** use any trade or service marks on the site and to ensure that the owner applies the marks consistently with any standard guidelines. The form of the advertising in general will be of concern to the advertiser and he will wish to have prior approval of relevant copy.

The owner of the site will seek an indemnity in respect of third party claims arising out of the use of the advertiser's marks on the World Wide Web, particularly bearing in mind the global nature of the Internet (see Chapter 3).

9.3.6 Use of information about visitors to the site

Both parties will be interested in information about who visits the site: the owner so as to **9–034** justify its rate card for advertising and the advertiser to judge whether the site is an appropriate place to advertise. Both parties will need to be aware of the distortion of these figures which 'hits' to a cached version of the site will cause.

Where specific information about the identity of particular visitors to the site and those who visit the advertiser's site via the hypertext link is collected, the parties will need to ensure that this is dealt with in compliance with applicable data protection regulations (see Chapter 7).

9.4 Internet access agreements

These are the agreements under which the end-users of the Internet are provided with **9–035** access to the Internet via an ISP.

There will be a distinction between the terms which are offered to a domestic as opposed to a corporate user, reflecting the different methods of access and the importance of the service.

Domestic users
Typically there will be a flat monthly fee for unlimited access (excluding telephone **9–036** charges) and the Internet will be reached by dial-up access. Alternatively, some ISPs offer a combination of a lower fee for a certain number of hours access with a usage charge above that threshold. Some offer non-subscription services, for which the user pays only the network provider's telephone charges (if any—some services provide access through a free telephone number) and any extra charges, for instance for support. Such extra charges may be levied indirectly, for instance by providing telephone support through a premium rate telephone number.

It is unlikely that the contract will contain any specific pledges as to availability or quality of service, although the ISP should bear in mind that any exclusions of liability or attempts to limit its responsibility will be subject to reasonableness criteria (see Chapter

10). The ISP will seek to impose contractual restrictions on the ability of the user to access unlawful information and may spell out guidelines for use designed to minimise the risk that the ISP will carry infringing, defamatory or obscene material.

As regards any software provided by the ISP, the contract should make clear the terms on which it may be used, especially if third party software, such as a browser, is being provided. The ISP may provide that the user must register use of the software directly with the copyright owner.

9–037   ISPs commonly provide a range of services in addition to Internet access: free or chargeable web space, domain name registration and maintenance, chat room and instant messaging facilities, overseas roaming access, and others. The contract will clearly need to address the full range of services of which user may make use. Further, if the ISP software makes any unexpected changes to the user's computer configuration (especially any that may hinder the use of other ISPs), or collects any information about the user or his computer usage, then the contract may need to address these. If the "click-wrap" approach to contract formation is adopted, care may need to be taken to ensure that no potentially contentious system changes or data collection take place before the user has had the opportunity to review and accept the contract terms.[10]

It should not be assumed that ISP contracts can be regarded as mere small print which will lie unnoticed. It only takes one user to notice an unusual or apparently unfair term and to raise the issue on the Internet, for it to snowball into a very public controversy.

Corporate users

9–038   Increasingly, corporate users are demanding service contracts akin to other telecommunications contracts, with statements as to service quality and remedies such as service credits for default. The issue for the ISP in such circumstances is to ensure that it only accepts responsibility for matters within its control. Those ISPs which own substantial infrastructure will be able to offer greater guarantees of service quality than those which are more dependent on third party infrastructure.

As with other IT services contracts, there will be a tension between the ISP's desire to define the service by way of end result and the desire of the user to set out the means by which this result is to be obtained. For example, the ISP may simply wish to state that the service is available for a certain percentage of the time; the user may wish to specify that the ISP safeguards service provision by using mirrored servers or alternative leased lines to an information exchange.

The contract will also need to address issues of the type of material which is accessed using the ISP's system and to require indemnities from the user should the ISP be liable for the transmission of obscene, defamatory or infringing material.

Allocation of resources: anti "spamming" clauses

9–039   With any user, the ISP may wish to prohibit the posting of e-mails to multiple newsgroups for advertising purposes ("spamming") to avoid the danger of the ISP's mail server being clogged up with multiple responses or "flaming". The ISP may also wish to restrict the use of bandwidth–hungry applications such as video-conferencing.

Internet telephony and other specialist traffic

9–040   As explored in Chapter 8, ISPs may fall foul of telecommunications regulation if they carry some types of Internet telephony service without an appropriate licence. The ISP may therefore also wish to prohibit the use of some Internet telephony services over its network. In any event, some ISPs for technical reasons impose restrictions on certain types of traffic, particularly those such as video-conferencing that can cause congestion on their networks.

9.5 Peering agreements

These are the Internet equivalent of telecommunications interconnect agreements and set out the basis on which ISPs exchange traffic. This exchange can be either via direct bilateral links or via traffic exchanges which act as central multilateral clearing houses.

9–041

Initially, these agreements amounted to little more than an informal agreement to exchange traffic without payment. However, the growth in Internet traffic and the increasing investment in infrastructure has led to some similarities with interconnect agreements being introduced. For example, there may be volume-related payments between ISPs and statements as to service quality. It remains to be seen whether peering agreements will continue to grow to resemble interconnect agreements and whether this will lead to users being charged on a time basis.

1. This arose as an issue in relation to the 2000 Sydney Olympics web site. A complaint to the Australian Human Rights and Equal Opportunity Commission under the Disability Discrimination Act 1992 Act that the site did not cater for disabled users in three respects including lack of alternate text was upheld (http://scaleplus.law.gov.au/html/ddadec/0/2000/0/DD000120.htm). The Royal National Institute for the Blind has published guidelines for web design for partially sighted and blind users. See also the W3C Content Accessibility Guidelines at www.w3.org/WAI/Resources/. Section 21(1) of the U.K. Disability Discrimination Act 1995, which applies to providers of services, could be relevant to the provision of websites.
2. As to the subsistence of database right in websites, see discussion in Chapter 2.
3. Note, however, that the definition of "writing" in section 178 of the Act is relatively broad and is apt to cover electronic form. The requirement that the assignment be signed should, by necessary implication, extend to include signatures in electronic form. Such signatures are admissible in evidence by virtue of section 7 of the Electronic Communications Act 2000, if they satisfy the definition of signatures for the purposes of the section. However, since there was no real doubt about the admissibility of signatures in electronic form anyway, it may be that such signatures remain admissible as evidence even if they do not fall within the definition of the section. See further, Chapter 10.
4. Under regulation 23 of the Copyright and Rights in Databases Regulation 1997, section 90 of the 1988 Act is applied to database right as it applies in relation to copyright and copyright works. Although the definition of "writing" in section 178 is not specifically applied, it must be implicit that 'writing' should be construed in the same way when the section is applied to database right.
5. Care must obviously be taken to avoid imposing an illegal penalty on the designer for failure to meet a deadline.
6. See discussion in Chapter 2 regarding whether web pages qualify as computer programs for the purposes of copyright protection.
7. In practice, in order to provide acceptable response times most databases store ("cache") temporary copies of recently or frequently requested pages, rather than generating them from scratch in response to each request.
8. Copyright, Designs and Patents Act 1988, s.9(3). The author is taken to be the person by whom the arrangements necessary for the creation of the work are undertaken.
9. See discussion of requirements of form in Chapter 10.
10. Note the U.S. case of *Williams v. America Online Inc.*, Mass. Super. Ct., No 00-0962, February 8, 2001 (ECLR Vol. 6 No. 10 p.242).

10

Electronic Contracts and Transactions

10.1 Introduction

The increase in interest and investment in the Internet has arisen largely as a result of its increasing commercialisation. The Internet has evolved from an academic and military resource to a global marketplace. The essence of a marketplace is that it is the forum for exchanging goods and services for money or other value. Underpinning such buying and selling are commercial contracts between the parties. This Chapter considers these contracts in the context of the Internet. In so doing, basic principles of contract law will be examined in the light of the types of contracts being formed over the Internet and the means of formation. However, this Chapter is not intended to be a treatise on contract law but to consider the application of that law to contracts made over the Internet. For further detail on the underlying legal principles, the standard texts on the subject should therefore be consulted.

In order to set the scene, the chapter begins with a brief comparison with the principles of law relating to electronic data interchange then a consideration of the types of contracts typically formed over the Internet, the methods by which such contracts are formed and the impact of recent E.U. legislation concerning on-line contracts. The chapter also considers developments in the law applicable to electronic signatures and other aspects of conducting transactions electronically. We also consider the evidential aspects of proving electronic transactions.

10.1.1 Comparison with the law relating to electronic data interchange

Forming on-line contracts by communication between computers was carried out prior to the advent of the Internet. For some time, commercial concerns have been using electronic data interchange (EDI). EDI is the exchange by computers of business information in a standard format. It pre-supposes that both parties to the communication use a standard format and, in most cases, that they have pre-agreed what this format will be. It is often used where companies exchange similar information on a frequent basis and where the process can readily be mechanised. One example of this is "just in time" stocking systems used by supermarkets where the tills automatically record purchases, which updates an inventory system which in turn automatically orders new stock from suppliers. EDI is also much used in the vehicle manufacturing industry and by airlines.

A body of law and regulation has built up around EDI and it has been suggested that useful comparisons can be drawn between contracting over the Internet and EDI. However, there are some vital distinctions between EDI, as defined above, and trading over the Internet (at least in the "b2c" (*i.e.* business to consumer) sector. EDI assumes that the computers involved use a highly structured form of messaging with pre-defined fields and contents: contracting over the Internet usually involves free-form communications. EDI assumes an ongoing relationship and, usually, that the parties have signed an "interchange agreement" setting out the basis of exchange: Internet trading is likely to involve a casual buying of goods or services with little or no prior contract between the parties and no necessity for a continuing relationship. EDI frequently has no direct human involvement as the communicating computers may exchange information automatically: as yet, trading over the Internet usually involves the conscious act of the buyer, at least, in ordering the goods and services. EDI is likely to be carried out over a value added network with guarantees of service quality and certainty as to the identity of the carriers: the Internet cannot as yet provide either. The trading partners in an EDI relationship are likely to be substantial commercial concerns: with the Internet, in a b2c transaction the commercial organisation will be selling to an individual.

10–003   It is therefore suggested that, although many of the legal principles which have been considered in the context of EDI will be common to Internet trading, the application of these principles, the balance of convenience between the parties and the solutions to problems are likely to be different.

Having said that, it should be noted that b2c is only one aspect of Internet trading. B2b (business to business) constitutes a significant element of Internet activity, especially when transactions are measured by value rather than by volume. For b2b, some aspects of existing EDI knowhow may usefully be applied. Indeed, there is a move to promote "Internet EDI" as a trading concept.[1]

10.1.2 Current means of forming contracts in relation to the Internet

10–004   Before considering the application of contract law to contracts formed in relation to the Internet, it may be helpful to put the methods of contract formation in context. Broadly, these divide into two main methods: forming contracts by the exchange of electronic messages and the formation of contracts "off-line", by telephone, facsimile or post. This chapter considers largely only the former method, save where the Internet adds a new factor to the existing law relating to contract formation in the latter ways and where the voice telephony service is over the Internet itself.

Looking more closely at electronic contract formation, this includes the direct exchange of e-mails, an e-mail response via a Web page, incorporation of contract conditions into a Web page, and the exchange of e-mails over a Usenet group. This last method, involving the publication of e-mails in an open forum is least likely to be utilised in commercial practice as it necessarily involves the public disclosure of what may be a bi-partite agreement and because the ethos of these groups largely precludes their use for commercial purposes. It is therefore suggested that the most likely scenarios for the conclusion of contracts over the Internet are via e-mail or in connection with a Web page.

10.1.3 The typical subject matter of contracts currently formed over the Internet

This breaks down into three broad categories: **10–005**

- *Contracts for the sale of physical goods*. Typically, these arise where a Web page is being used in conjunction with more traditional advertising as an alternative shop window, *e.g.* for the sale of alcohol, books or compact disks. Although the contract is formed over the Internet, the performance by the supplier is constituted by the despatch of the goods to the purchaser.

- *Contracts for the supply of digitised products*. These contracts involve the on–line supply of data, such as software, text or multimedia products, often together with the granting of a licence of any copyright material comprised within the products.

- *Contracts for the supply of services and facilities*. This would include on-line banking and other financial services, the giving of professional advice over the Internet and, increasingly, the provision of voice telephony and potentially video-conferencing.

At present the majority of contracts are probably formed between businesses and consumers, rather than between businesses themselves, and certainly high value or high complexity electronic contracts are created using EDI rather than the Internet. As the Internet increases in reliability and security, this distinction is becoming less valid. However, the assumption underlying this chapter is that the majority of contracts created over the Internet at present are of relatively low value between parties which do not have an existing or continuing business relationship.

10.1.4 Content of contracts

As discussed below, there can be a tension between the desire to ensure that all relevant **10–006** contractual terms are incorporated into a contract and the limitations of screen size and the need to use the medium attractively. In respect of contracts to be formed over or in relation to the Internet, the parties will need to consider, as with any contract, the appropriate extent and content of the contractual terms. This section considers additional points to be borne in mind in relation to contracts to be formed electronically and draws together some of the points already made.

- *Contract formation*. The contract terms should state the method and procedure for accepting the offer and the duration of, or conditions relating to, the offer.

- *Delivery*. The method and timing of delivery of the relevant goods should be spelled out and whether these vary depending on method of payment, availability of stock or jurisdiction of the recipient.

- *Risk and insurance*. Where physical goods are to be despatched, the question of risk of damage or loss and the responsibility for insurance should be stated: again, this may vary with jurisdiction.

- *Price, currency and payment*. The contract should state clearly the price (including any applicable taxes and insurance) and the currency and acceptable means of payment. Where payment is to be made by physical means, such as the sending of a money order, the offeror will no doubt wish to have the right to delay delivery until this is received.

- *Subject matter.* This is particularly relevant where there is a grant of rights in digitised material, where the extent of the licence should be clearly spelled out.

- *Geographical limitations.* Where goods or services are available only in certain countries, or advice can only be given in or in respect of certain jurisdictions, this should be stated.

- *Limitations and exclusions of liability.* To the extent permitted by the relevant legal systems, the supplier will wish to limit its liability and to exclude implied terms. See also section 10.2 below.

- *Governing law.* See section 10.3 below.

Some of these points are now, or shortly will be, the subject of specific requirements under the transparency provisions of the Distance Selling Directive and the Electronic Commerce Directive, discussed below.

10.2 Exclusions, limitations and consumer protection measures

10–007   In respect of contracts made within England and Wales, and in particular in respect of contracts made with consumers, the supplier of goods or services will need to take into account the provisions of various relevant legislation. In brief, these include:

The Consumer Credit Act 1974
10–008   This regulates the content of agreements for the provision of credit, sets out various procedures which must be followed to protect consumers and establishes a regime for licensing businesses which provide consumer credit or consumer hire.

The Unfair Contract Terms Act 1977
10–009   Among other things, this prohibits a supplier from excluding or restricting its liability for death or personal injury caused by negligence (section 2); or circumscribes the limitation of liability in respect of certain implied terms in relation to goods or services (sections 3, 6 and 11).

The Consumer Protection Act 1987
10–010   This imposes in certain circumstances strict liability on the manufacturer and other members of the distribution chain of defective goods which cause death or personal injury or loss of or damage to property.

The Unfair Contract Terms Directive 1993 (93/13)
10–011   This applies to standard contracts entered into between the sellers or suppliers of goods or services to consumers. It introduces a general concept of "unfairness" and terms which are found to be unfair will be unenforceable as against the consumer. It was implemented in the United Kingdom by the Unfair Terms in Consumer Contracts Regulations 1994 (the 1994 Regulations), which came into force on July 1, 1995.

The Distance Selling Directive (97/7)

This has been implemented by the Consumer Protection (Distance Selling) Regulations **10–012**
2000 (S.I. 2000 No. 2334), which came into force on October 31, 2000. It and the Electronic
Commerce Directive (2000/31) are discussed in detail below.

10.2.1 The Distance Selling Directive

E.C. Directive 97/7 of the European Parliament and of the Council on the protection of **10–013**
consumers in respect of distance contracts was adopted on May 20, 1997. It has been
implemented in the United Kingdom by the Consumer Protection (Distance Selling)
Regulations 2000 (S.I. 2000 No. 2334), which came into force on October 31, 2000.

The Regulations apply to certain "distance contracts". This means "any contract
concerning goods or services concluded between a supplier and a consumer under an
organised distance sales or service provision scheme run by the supplier who, for the
purpose of the contract, makes exclusive use of one or more means of distance
communication up to and including the moment at which the contract is concluded".

"Means of distance communication" means any means which, without the
simultaneous physical presence of the supplier and the consumer, may be used for the
conclusion of a contract between those parties' An indicative list of such means is
contained in Schedule 1 of the Regulations. Insofar as it may include electronic or similar
communications, the list includes: catalogue; telephone with human intervention;
telephone without human intervention (automatic calling machine, audiotext); radio;
videophone (telephone with screen); videotext (microcomputer and television screen)
with keyboard or touch screen; electronic mail; facsimile machine (fax); television
(teleshopping).

"Supplier" means any person who, in contracts to which the Regulations apply, is
acting in his commercial or professional capacity.

"Consumer" means any natural person who, in contracts to which the Regulations
apply, is acting for purposes which are outside his business (which includes a trade or
profession).

Although not specifically named in the indicative list, sales through web sites are **10–014**
clearly covered by the Regulations. Although the Regulations have their origins in
traditional mail-order and telephone sales transactions, they (and the underlying
Directive) have been drafted so as to include Internet transactions. It may be that
thought rules devised for mail order do not translate well into the interactive Internet
environment.

Certain types of contract are excepted from the Regulations under regulation 5(1).
These are any contract:

(a)   for the sale or other disposition of an interest in land except for a rental
       agreement (the Regulations contain further provisions regarding what constitu-
       tes a rental agreement);

(b)   for the construction of a building where the contract also provides for a sale or
       other disposition of an interest in land on which the building is constructed,
       except for a rental agreement;

(c)   relating to financial services (a non-exhaustive list of which is contained in
       Schedule 2 of the Regulations);

(d)   concluded by means of an automated vending machine or automated commercial premises;

(e)   concluded with a telecommunications operator through the use of a public pay-phone;

(f)   concluded at an auction.

10–015   The bulk of the Regulations (regulations 7 to 20) do not apply to timeshare agreements within the meaning of the Timeshare Act 1992. Similarly, regulations 7 to 19(1) do not apply to:

(a)   contracts for the supply of food, beverages or other goods intended for everyday consumption supplied to the consumer's residence or to his workplace by regular roundsmen; or

(b)   contracts for the provision of accommodation, transport, catering or leisure services, where the supplier undertakes, when the contract is concluded, to provide these services on a specific date or within a specific period.

Regulations 19(2) to (8) and 20 do not apply to a contract for a package within the meaning of the Package Travel, Package Holidays and Package Tours Regulations 1992 which is sold or offered for sale in the territory of the Member States.

There are also exceptions from individual regulations which are noted below.

10–016   The Regulations provide various rights for the benefit of consumers: transparency rights (*i.e.* the right to be provided with information), cancellation rights and rights as to the period within which the contract must be performed. These to an extent interconnect. We shall concentrate in this discussion on aspects of particular relevance to the Internet. Reference may be made to the Regulations for full details of the rights in question, and of associated rights such as cancellation of related credit agreements.

Transparency

10–017   Under regulation 7(1), the supplier must in good time prior to the conclusion of the contract:

(a)   provide to the consumer the following information—

(i)   the identity of the supplier and, where the contract requires payment in advance, the supplier's address;

(ii)   a description of the main characteristics of the goods or services;

(iii)   the price of the goods or services including all taxes;

(iv)   delivery costs where appropriate;

(v)   the arrangements for payment, delivery or performance;

(vi)   the existence of a right of cancellation (except where Regulation 13 excludes the right to cancel);

(vii)   the cost of using the means of distance communication where it is calculated other than at the basic rate;

(viii)   the period for which the offer or the price remains valid; and

(ix)   where appropriate, the minimum duration of the contract, in the case of contracts for the supply of goods or services to be performed permanently or recurrently;

(b)   inform the consumer if he proposes, in the event of the goods or services ordered by the consumer being unavailable, to provide substitute goods or services (as the case may be) of equivalent quality and price; and

(c)   inform the consumer that the cost of returning any such substitute goods to the supplier in the event of cancellation by the consumer would be met by the supplier.

Under regulation 7(2) the supplier must ensure that the information required by paragraph (1) is "provided in a clear and comprehensible manner appropriate to the means of distance communication used, with due regard in particular to the principles of good faith in commercial transactions and the principles governing the protection of those who are unable to give their consent such as minors".

Under regulation 7(3) the supplier must ensure that his commercial purpose is made clear when providing the information required by paragraph (1).

Failure to observe these requirements of regulation 7 does not appear to affect the   **10–018** validity of any contract between the supplier and the consumer (although under regulation 19(7) the ability of the supplier to provide substitute goods or services depends upon the contract providing for this and upon the information about this having been provided under regulation 7). However, regulation 25 provides that a term in a contract to which the Regulations apply is void if and to the extent that it is inconsistent with a provision for the protection of the consumer contained in the Regulations. The provisions may, however, be enforced by injunction by an appropriate enforcement authority under regulations 26 and 27 and, in due course by a private sector consumer protection body designated under the Stop Now Orders (E.C. Directive) Regulations 2001.

Confirmatory and other information
The Regulations further provide, in regulation 8, for the supplier to provide to the   **10–019** consumer in writing, or in "another durable medium which is available and accessible to the consumer", the information referred to in regulation 8(2), either:

(a)   prior to the conclusion of the contract, or

(b)   thereafter, in good time and in any event —

   (i)   during the performance of the contract, in the case of services; and
   (ii)   at the latest at the time of delivery where goods not for delivery to third parties are concerned.

Under regulation 8(2) the information required to be provided by paragraph (1) is —   **10–020**

(a)   the information set out in paragraphs (i) to (vi) of regulation 7(1)(a) (see above);

(b)   information about the conditions and procedures for exercising the right to cancel under Regulation 10, including —

   (i)   where a term of the contract requires (or the supplier intends that it will require) that the consumer shall return the goods to the supplier in the event of cancellation, notification of that requirement; and
   (ii)   information as to whether the consumer or the supplier would be

responsible under these Regulations for the cost of returning any goods to the supplier, or the cost of his recovering them, if the consumer cancels the contract under Regulation 10;

(c)   the geographical address of the place of business of the supplier to which the consumer may address any complaints;

(d)   information about any after-sales services and guarantees; and

(e)   the conditions for exercising any contractual right to cancel the contract, where the contract is of an unspecified duration or a duration exceeding one year.

Under regulation 8(3), prior to the conclusion of a contract for the supply of services, the supplier must inform the consumer in writing or in another durable medium which is available and accessible to the consumer that, unless the parties agree otherwise, he will not be able to cancel the contract under regulation 10 once the performance of the services has begun with his agreement.

10–021   The Regulations do not define what is meant by "in writing or in another durable medium which is available and accessible to the consumer". The question arises whether this requires e-commerce providers to send out information in hard copy (or on another physical medium such as disk), or whether provision of the information by e-mail or on the provider's web site is sufficient. The Directive on which the Regulations are based does not make this clear. The Department of Trade and Industry, consulting on draft Regulations to implement the Directive,[2] stated[3]:

> "We consider that confirmation by electronic mail would meet the definition of confirmation 'in another durable medium available and accessible to [the consumer]', where the order has been made by means of e-mail. We have not however specified this in the Draft Regulations since the Directive is not specific on the point, and only a court can determine the meaning of the wording."

10–022   The argument in favour of the suggestion that provision of information on a web site would satisfy this requirement is that the information is stored, at least, on the hard disk of the web site server, that this is a durable medium and that that medium is available and accessible to the user, albeit at a distance through the Internet. Conceptually, a user opening the document on the web site is no different from the user opening the document on a floppy disk in his possession. Subject to the question of durability, a problem would only appear to arise if the provisions mean that the user must be provided with the durable medium as well as the information contained in it. If so, that would rule out providing the information on a web site. The requirement of accessibility does not mandate this. The requirement that the medium be "available" to the consumer is perhaps more problematic, since if it is not mere surplusage it presumably means something more than "accessible". But if that means that the medium must be "available", that could suggest that the consumer has to have, or have the right to have, possession of a physical medium.

For an e-mail, the question could be whether the fact that when downloaded (should he choose to do so) to the consumer's computer the e-mail ultimately resides on the consumer's own hard disk (or other memory medium, in the case of, *e.g.* PDAs) would satisfy the requirement, since nothing in the Regulations requires the durable medium to be one provided by the supplier.

For e-mail, it should also be noted that a similar formulation is used in regulation 10 **10–023** (below), governing notices sent by a consumer to the supplier. Regulation 10(d) provides for the place of sending of a notice sent by e-mail. This provision would be nonsensical if e-mail did not comply with the underlying requirement for the notice to be in a durable medium. That would suggest (assuming that the meaning is the same in both regulations) that e-mail would satisfy the requirements of regulation 8. However, the Directive itself contains no provisions regarding how the consumer is to give notice, so that regulation 10(d) has no equivalent in the Directive and is of no assistance in construing the meaning of the requirement for a durable medium in the Directive.

Under regulation 9, regulation 8 does not apply to a contract for the supply of services which are performed through the use of a means of distance communication, where those services are supplied on only one occasion and are invoiced by the operator of the means of distance communication. However, the supplier must take all necessary steps to ensure that a consumer who is a party to such a contract is able to obtain the supplier's geographical address and the place of business to which the consumer may address any complaints.

Cancellation right

Regulation 10 provides for the consumer's right to cancel within a certain period. That **10–024** period may be affected by whether the supplier has complied with the information provision requirements of regulation 8. The cancellation period varies depending on whether the contract is for the supply of goods or services. Under regulation 13 certain contracts are excluded, unless the parties have agreed otherwise, from the cancellation provisions. Those are contracts:

(a)   for the supply of services if the supplier has complied with regulation 8(3) (see above) and performance of the contract has begun with the consumer's agreement before the end of the cancellation period applicable under regulation 12;

(b)   for the supply of goods or services the price of which is dependent on fluctuations in the financial market which cannot be controlled by the supplier;

(c)   for the supply of goods made to the consumer's specifications or clearly personalised or which by reason of their nature cannot be returned or are liable to deteriorate or expire rapidly;

(d)   for the supply of audio or video recordings or computer software if they are unsealed by the consumer;

(e)   for the supply of newspapers, periodicals or magazines; or

(f)   for gaming, betting or lottery services.

The consumer's notice to cancel has to be given within the relevant cancellation period **10–025** and comply with the requirements of regulation 10. Under regulation 10(3) a notice of cancellation is a notice in writing or in another durable medium available and accessible to the supplier (or, if the supplier has notified another person to receive cancellation notices, that other person) which, however expressed, indicates the intention of the consumer to cancel the contract. This is a "home-grown" provision which has no equivalent in the Directive. Nor does regulation 10(4), which states circumstances in which a notice of cancellation given by a consumer to a supplier or other person is to be treated as having been properly given. These include the following, of particular relevance to electronic transactions:

—   if the consumer sends it by facsimile to the business facsimile number last known to the consumer (in which case it is to be taken to have been given on the day on which it is sent); or

—   if the consumer sends it by electronic mail, to the business electronic mail address last known to the consumer (in which case it is to be taken to have been given on the day on which it is sent).

The cancellation periods are set out in regulations 11 and 12, for goods and services respectively. The calculation of the cancellation period is complex, and depends on the extent to which and when the supplier has complied with the information provision requirements of regulation 8, in particular regulation 8(2) concerning information about the right to cancel.

Regulation 25(5) provides that the regulations shall apply notwithstanding any contract term which applies or purports to apply the law of a non-Member State if the contract has a close connection with the territory of a Member State.

10.2.2 The Electronic Commerce Directive

10–026   Directive 2000/31 of the European Parliament and Council on "certain legal aspects of information society services, in particular electronic commerce, in the Internal Market (Directive on electronic commerce)" was adopted on June 8, 2000. It has to be implemented in Member States before January 17, 2002. At the time of writing the United Kingdom had not yet done so. The Directive covers a broad range of issues. The "country of origin" aspects of the Directive are discussed in Chapter 6 and the liability of intermediaries provisions in Chapter 5. Here we shall concentrate on the consumer protection aspects of the Directive, in particular the transparency provisions. These overlap with those of the Distance Selling Directive that we have already discussed.

The Directive applies to "information society services". As discussed in Chapter 6, these are defined as services within the meaning of Art 1(2) of a previous Directive, the so-called Transparency Directive.[4] In essence these are any service normally provided for remuneration, at a distance, by means of electronic equipment for the processing (including digital compression) and storage of data, and at the individual request of a recipient. The Transparency Directive provides an indicative list of such services. However, Recital (17) of the Electronic Commerce Directive states that those services contained in the list that do not imply data processing and storage are not covered by the definition. Recital (18) of the Electronic Commerce Directive provides a list of services that do and do not constitute information society services.

10–027   Different aspects of the same transaction may fall within and without the scope of the Directive. So concluding an online contract for the sale of a book may be within the scope of the Directive, but the fulfilment of the contract by delivery of a physical book would not be. If the book were to be downloaded in electronic form from the supplier's web site, however, the whole transaction would fall within the scope of the Directive. Some matters are excluded from the scope of the Directive: taxation, data protection, questions relating to agreements or practices governed by cartel law, certain activities of notaries or equivalent professions, the representation of a client and defence of his interests before the courts and certain gambling activities.

An information society service provider is any natural or legal person providing an information society service. A recipient of an information society service is any natural or legal person who, for professional ends or otherwise, uses an information society service, in particular for the purposes of seeking information or making it accessible.

Recital (58) of the Directive states that the Directive should not apply to services supplied by service providers established in a third country.

Transparency requirements—general

Under Article 5 of the Directive, Member States must ensure that the service provider shall render easily, directly and permanently accessible to the recipients of the service and competent authorities, at least the following information: **10–028**

(a) the name of the service provider;

(b) the geographic address at which the service provider is established;

(c) the details of the service provider, including his electronic mail address, which allow him to be contacted rapidly and communicated with in a direct and effective manner;

(d) where the service provider is registered in a trade or similar public register, the trade register in which the service provider is entered and his registration number, or equivalent means of identification in that register;

(e) where the activity is subject to an authorisation scheme, the particulars of the relevant supervisory authority;

(f) as concerns the regulated professions (as defined in the Directive):

— any professional body or similar institution with which the service provider is registered,
— the professional title and the Member State where it has been granted,
— a reference to the applicable professional rules in the Member State of establishment and the means to access them;

(g) where the service provider undertakes an activity that is subject to VAT, the VAT identification number

Further, under Article 5.2 Member States must at least ensure that, where information society services refer to prices, these are to be indicated clearly and unambiguously and, in particular, must indicate whether they are inclusive of tax and delivery costs. This provision, if it bites on the accuracy of the pricing as well as on its presentation, should be compared with section 39 of the Consumer Protection Act 1987 (misleading price indications). That contains a due diligence defence, which on at least one occasion[5] has saved a vendor from the consequences of a computer error. The provisions of the Directive contain no due diligence defence. **10–029**

Transparency requirements—commercial communications

Article 6 of the Directive contains further transparency provisions for commercial communications. A "commercial communication" is defined in Article 2(f) as any form of **10–030** communication designed to promote, directly or indirectly, the goods, services or image of a company, organisation or person pursuing a commercial, industrial or craft activity or exercising a regulated profession.

Article 2(f) goes on to provide that the following do not in themselves constitute commercial communications:

— information allowing direct access to the activity of the company, organisation or person, in particular a domain name or an electronic-mail address,

— communications relating to the goods, services or image of the company, organisation or person compiled in an independent manner, particularly when this is without financial consideration.

10–031   Under Article 6, Member States must ensure that commercial communications which are part of, or constitute, an information society service comply at least with the following conditions:

(a)   the commercial communication shall be clearly identifiable as such;

(b)   the natural or legal person on whose behalf the commercial communication is made shall be clearly identifiable;

(c)   promotional offers, such as discounts, premiums and gifts, where permitted in the Member State where the service provider is established, shall be clearly identifiable as such, and the conditions which are to be met to qualify for them shall be easily accessible and be presented clearly and unambiguously;

(d)   promotional competitions or games, where permitted in the Member State where the service provider is established, shall be clearly identifiable as such, and the conditions for participation shall be easily accessible and be presented clearly and unambiguously.

Unsolicited commercial communications

10–032   As for unsolicited commercial communications, Article 7 provides that Member States which permit unsolicited commercial communication by electronic mail shall ensure that such commercial communication by a service provider established in their territory shall be identifiable clearly and unambiguously as such as soon as it is received by the recipient. Member States are required to take measures to ensure that service providers undertaking unsolicited commercial communications by electronic mail consult regularly and respect the opt-out registers in which natural persons not wishing to receive such commercial communications can register themselves. These provisions are stated to be without prejudice to the Distance Selling Directive and the Telecommunications Data Protection Directive (97/7 and 97/66 respectively). Article 10 of the Telecommunications Data Protection Directive has not been implemented in the United Kingdom following severe disagreement in the business community about the merits of opt-in versus opt-out for unsolicited electronic commercial communications. The existing Telecommunications Data Protection Directive arguably does not apply to e-mail. However, the proposed Electronic Communications Data Protection Directive[6] would apply to e-mail. The European Commission's initial proposal would allow e-mail for the purpose of direct marketing to natural persons only with their prior consent. Use of personal data for direct marketing purposes is generally subject to the Data Protection Act 1998 (see Chapter 7).

Regulated professions

As for the regulated professions (as defined in Article 2), in addition to the transparency requirements referred to above, under Article 8, Member States are required to ensure that the use of commercial communications which are part of, or constitute, an information society service provided by a member of a regulated profession is permitted subject to compliance with the professional rules regarding, in particular, the independence, dignity and honour of the profession, professional secrecy and fairness towards clients and other members of the profession. Without prejudice to the autonomy of professional bodies and associations, Member States and the Commission must encourage professional associations and bodies to establish codes of conduct at Community level in order to determine the types of information that can be given for the purposes of commercial communication in conformity with such professional rules. When drawing up proposals for Community initiatives which may become necessary to ensure the proper functioning of the Internal Market with regard to such information, the Commission must take due account of codes of conduct applicable at Community level and is required to act in close cooperation with the relevant professional associations and bodies.

10–033

Conclusion of contract—technical and transparency requirements

Article 11 of the Directive lays down certain technical requirements with which the on-line contracting process must comply. Member States are required to ensure, except when otherwise agreed by parties who are not consumers, that in cases where the recipient of the service places his order through technological means, the following principles apply:

10–034

— the service provider has to acknowledge the receipt of the recipient's order without undue delay and by electronic means,

— the order and the acknowledgement of receipt are deemed to be received when the parties to whom they are addressed are able to access them.

Member States must also ensure that, except when otherwise agreed by parties who are not consumers, the service provider makes available to the recipient of the service appropriate, effective and accessible technical means allowing him to identify and correct input errors, prior to the placing of the order.

The first paragraph (first indent) and second paragraph are stated not to apply to contracts concluded exclusively by exchange of electronic mail or by equivalent individual communications.

The twin of this provision is Article 10, which specifies information about the contract formation process to be provided to the user. Member States are required to ensure, except when otherwise agreed by parties who are not consumers, that at least the following information is given by the service provider clearly, comprehensibly and unambiguously and prior to the order being placed by the recipient of the service:

10–035

(a) the different technical steps to follow to conclude the contract;

(b) whether or not the concluded contract will be filed by the service provider and whether it will be accessible;

(c) the technical means for identifying and correcting input errors prior to the placing of the order;

(d) the languages offered for the conclusion of the contract.

Member States are also required to ensure that, except when otherwise agreed by parties who are not consumers, the service provider indicates any relevant codes of conduct to which he subscribes and information on how those codes can be consulted electronically.

10–036   Further, contract terms and general conditions provided to the recipient must be made available in a way that allows him to store and reproduce them.

Similarly to Article 11, these provisions (with the exception of the previous paragraph) do not apply to contracts concluded exclusively by exchange of electronic mail or by equivalent individual communications.

Assuming that a similar approach is adopted as with the Distance Selling Directive, it may be expected that the provisions discussed above will be implemented as regulatory requirements rather than in a manner that might affect existing law as to contract formation. If so, then enforcement would be by way of injunction by either the appropriate authorities or by private sector designated consumer protection bodies pursuant to the Injunctions Directive (which is applied to the Electronic Commerce Directive by Article 18.2 of the Electronic Commerce Directive).

10.3 International contracts

10–037   Clearly, the expectation is that contracts made on the Internet will be as international in nature as the Internet itself. However, this is not something the parties should jump into without their eyes being open to the issues. There may also be differences between those contracts where the parties are commercial entities (rather than one being an individual consumer) negotiating at arm's length over a non-standard form of contract and those which are not.

Applicable law and jurisdiction

10–038   The contract should specify a governing law. If it does not do so there will be even more room than usual to argue over which country's law governs the terms of the contract and its operation. Where no governing law is referred to in a contract, a court in England and Wales will decide on what law should be applied according to the provisions of the Contracts (Applicable Law) Act 1990, which enacts a "proper law of the contract" doctrine. Under the Act the applicable law is that with which the transaction has the closest connection.

However, in consumer contracts, in some circumstances, the applicable law will be that in which he has his habitual residence.[7,8] Those circumstances could certainly cover a consumer in one country responding to an advertisement on a Web site based in another country. If courts in other countries are seized with a dispute under the contract they may apply different rules for deciding what is the governing law, such as the law of the place of contracting or the law of the place of performance.[9]

10–039   When it comes to choosing a governing law the obvious choice will be the law with which the persons preparing the contract are most familiar. However, at the time of specifying a governing law of any contract it is normal to also specify in the courts of which country it is at least preferred that any dispute is dealt with, and it is clearly going to be easier for those courts and the conduct of any dispute if the governing law of the contract is that of the court dealing with the matter. In choosing the preferred such courts (the jurisdiction) some consideration needs to be given to enforceability of the judgment of any such court against the parties. If a person has a place of business in the same country as the court giving the judgment there is no problem but if this is not the case then one has to look to the availability of reciprocal enforcement treaties between the country in which the court is situated and the country in which the person against whom the judgment is given is based. As between countries in the E.U. there is not such a problem with reciprocity of enforcement because of the Treaty between all Member States dealing with this (the Brussels Convention, to be superseded in 2002 by the Brussels Regulation—see discussion in Chapter 6).

Some companies may try to deal with this sort of problem by making it clear that certain products they are offering over the Internet are only available for order on-line from certain countries where they know that they will not experience problems with enforcement and refuse to accept such orders on-line from individuals in other countries.

However, over the Internet there can be real problems in knowing from which **10–040** jurisdiction the purchaser is in fact accessing the site. The seller may be tempted to specify the law of its own country in order to simplify matters and achieve some certainty. However, a choice of law or jurisdiction clause may be affected by consumer protection legislation in the country of the purchaser. For instance the Unfair Contract Terms Regulations 1994 specify that they "shall apply notwithstanding any contract term which applies or purports to apply the law of a non-member state, if the contract has a close connection with the territory of the member states". The Distance Selling Regulations (see above) contain a similar provision. The Contracts (Applicable Law) Act 1990 provides that a choice of law clause shall not, in some circumstances, deprive a consumer of the protection of the mandatory rules of his country of habitual residence. There are similar provisions in the Brussels Convention and the forthcoming Brussels Regulation regarding choice of jurisdiction clauses (see Chapter 6). "Mandatory rules" are those which cannot be derogated from by contract. The European Court of Justice has held that a clause conferring exclusive jurisdiction on the court of a city in which the seller had its principal place of business but the consumer was not domiciled, and which was not individually negotiated, must be regarded as unfair within the meaning of Article 3 of the Unfair Contract Terms Directive insofar as it causes, contrary to the requirement of good faith, a significant imbalance in the parties' rights and obligations arising under the contract, to the detriment of the consumer.[10]

Also, there is a problem when it comes to making contracts with consumers in terms of **10–041** exclusions or limitations of liability and warranties. Different countries have different rules about what is acceptable. One way of attempting to deal with this is the way in which, for example, this issue is dealt with in software licensing, by providing separate country–specific clauses of the contract for individual countries.

We discuss in Chapter 6 the potential application of the "country of origin" rules of the Electronic Commerce Directive, which is to implemented before January 17, 2002.

10.4 Forming electronic contracts

10.4.1 Introduction: the formation of a contract

At its most basic, a contract is an agreement between or among two or more parties which **10–042** the law recognises and which can be enforced in the courts. For simplicity, this Chapter will assume that contracts are being formed between two parties but the principles apply equally to multi-partite agreements. A contract is formed when one party makes an offer which is accepted in unequivocal terms by the other party and that acceptance is communicated to the offeror. In addition, consideration needs to flow between the parties and there has to be the intent to create legal relations. Each of these requirements will be considered in turn in the context of the Internet.

10.4.2 Pre-contractual information

10–043   Although this Chapter is concerned primarily with the exchange of messages to form a contract, there may be other information imparted by either party prior to the contract which may have legal consequences for one or other of them.

Advertising and other regulation

10–044   In the context of goods and services the advertising of which is regulated in other media, the advertiser will need to be aware of the extent to which the relevant regulations or restrictions will apply to Web pages or to goods or services offered via e-mail. The most common restrictions or regulations relate to: the identity or some other feature of the recipient (for example age restrictions on the advertising of alcohol or tobacco); or the information which must be imparted (such as in connection with the advertising of financial services, credit or shares); or the accuracy of that information (such as the provisions of the Trade Descriptions Act 1968). See also the discussion of the transparency requirements of the Distance Selling and Electronic Commerce Directives, above.

Misrepresentation

10–045   Irrespective of their incorporation into the final contract, certain statements of either party made prior to the formation of a contract may constitute representations which, if untrue, can give rise to a right to damages and/or rescission by the party to whom the representation is made. A representation is a statement of fact (and not, generally, opinion) which induces the recipient to enter into the contract concerned.

   Thus, untrue statements made in a Web page or in an e-mail about the quality of goods or services, may amount to misrepresentations. The state of mind of the maker of the statement is relevant to determine the remedy of the recipient of the misrepresentation who has relied on that representation, in entering into a subsequent contract. In outline, if the maker of the misrepresentation has acted fraudulently the recipient will be entitled to damages and/or to rescind the contract. Rescission results in the parties being treated as if the contract had never come into being. If he has been negligent or has made the misrepresentation innocently, the recipient will generally not have an absolute right to either remedy. The common law relating to misrepresentation was clarified and, to some extent, modified by the Misrepresentation Act 1967.

Collateral contracts

10–046   A collateral contract is one which may underpin or supplement another contract. Typically, such a contract is entered into in order to induce one party to enter into the other contract either with the other party to the collateral contract or with a third party. In practice, a court will determine whether a statement made amounts to a representation or whether the elements necessary to constitute a contract are also present and that the representation therefore has contractual effect. If this is the case, it may have the effect of allowing a contract claim to be brought even where the representation has not been incorporated into the main contract.

10.4.3 Offer/invitation to treat

An offer is made when one party offers to do or to supply something on the basis that it will be legally bound by the acceptance of that offer by the offeree. The intention can either be stated or can be apparent from the circumstances. The terms of the offer must be certain: for example, if the subject matter of the offer or the price are not stated there may be too great a degree of uncertainty for the courts to give effect to the contract. There are, however, important qualifications to this principle: for example, section 8(2) of the Sale of Goods Act 1979 gives the court the ability to determine a "reasonable price" and the courts may also imply the terms in certain circumstances. **10–047**

There can also be uncertainty over whether a particular action or statement constitutes an offer or merely an "invitation to treat" which is intended to provoke an offer from another party. Depending on the proper construction of the action or statement, a response by the other party may either constitute acceptance of an offer or the making of an offer which itself may be accepted. The most common example given of an invitation to treat is the display of goods in a shop window or on supermarket shelves. The picking up of the goods by the shopper and their presentation at the checkout amounts to the offer which is accepted by the cashier. By analogy, the description of goods in a Web page advertisement may also be regarded as being an invitation to treat. The analogy is aided by the presentation of some Web pages as "virtual shops" within the Internet version of a shopping mall. However, the test is essentially one of the intention of the person putting the information on the Web page: did he intend to be bound by a response (in which case he has made an offer) or did he intend that he would need to acknowledge the response by word or action, such as despatching the goods (in which case the Web page constitutes an invitation to treat).

The importance of the distinction in the context of the Internet is likely to arise in two circumstances: where the Web page owner has only a limited stock of goods to despatch or where it is prepared only to sell to a limited class of persons. In the former case, it will not wish to find itself in breach of a binding obligation to supply goods where it has underestimated the demand. The fact that, by the very nature of a campaign mounted on the Internet, it will not be able to assess in advance the success of such a campaign makes it unlikely that it will want to make an unqualified offer to supply tangible goods in material form to all applicants or rely on an implied term that the offer lapses with the exhaustion of his stock. In the latter case, the Web page owner may wish to reserve the right not to supply goods or services to certain jurisdictions, to applicants under a certain age or to exercise other forms of discretion, such as requiring payment to be received prior to despatch. In these cases, therefore, the information contained in the Web page or preliminary e-mail will be intended to constitute an invitation to treat and not an offer. **10–048**

The test of the offeror's intention is essentially an objective one, in the absence of express statement or actual knowledge by the recipient that the maker does not intend to be bound. There is unlikely to be any prior dealing between the parties or any interchange agreement, and in the absence of any established recognised market practice as regards offers made via the Internet, there is therefore the risk of uncertainty as to whether a Web page statement or preliminary e-mail should be treated as an offer or not. In this context, the practical approach must be to state expressly the procedure to be followed for a binding contract to come into existence.

10.4.4 Acceptance and communication of acceptance

10–049   The second element for the creation of a contract is that the offer is accepted by the offeree and that the acceptance is communicated to the offeror. The offer must be accepted unequivocally: any suggested variation or qualification of the terms of the offer is likely to constitute a counter-offer. It is unlikely in the context of contracts formed over the Internet that the "battle of the forms" (where the parties exchange incompatible sets of standard terms) will arise. The nature of the methods of contract formation outlined above and the likely classes of offeree suggest that a relatively informal response will be made or that, alternatively, the format of the response to a Web page will be pre-determined by the offeror as part of the implementation of the page itself. Clearly this is something which should be taken into account in the design of the page.

Acceptance need not be express and can be inferred from the conduct of the offeree. However, again in the context of the Internet where the parties' only knowledge of each other is via that medium, it is most likely that some positive action, such as the sending of an e-mail or the filling in of an automated response form, will be the means of acceptance. Electronic acceptance could be relevant where the Web page states that it can or should be used, or where (although this is unlikely in the context of the Web) it is silent or where it is otherwise reasonable for electronic communication to be used. Conceivably, where a Web page provides for the completion of a standard form but does not state that it is mandatory, the sending of a separate e-mail by the offeree could also constitute acceptance, as could the sending of a message via a general feedback hypertext link (even though the recipient of the message may be a separate organisation which maintains the page on behalf of the apparent owner). Conversely, the sending of a response by post or facsimile could also be appropriate.

The key therefore must be for the offeror to state expressly how acceptance should be made and that other methods of communication will not be valid.

10–050   Even where the method of communication of acceptance has been stated, there may still be uncertainty as to when or if that communication is deemed to be effective and to bind the offeror. The time that the contract comes into force and the place where it is formed may be crucial to crystallise its terms, to determine the priority of two parties wishing to accept an offer where there is insufficient stock to satisfy them both and to determine the legal system which will govern certain aspects of the contract.

Where the method of communication is stated to be by telephone or by post, the normal rules will apply. In essence, in respect of a domestic as opposed to an international contract, acceptance by telephone is deemed to happen at the place and at the time it is heard by the offeror. This is logical because instantaneous communication, such as over a working telephone line, is unlikely to lead to any dispute between the offeror and the offeree about whether there has been communication of the acceptance. Similar rules have been held to apply to telex. Conversely, acceptance by post is deemed to be effective when the letter is posted, not when it is received.

10–051   A gloss has recently been put on the established rules regarding the receipt of telexes. The basic rule is that the telex is deemed to be received effectively by the intended recipient at the time of despatch because this is also the time of receipt. However, in the case of *Schelde Delta Shipping BV v. Astarte Shipping Ltd (The Pamela)*,[11] the court took a pragmatic approach to a telex received at nineteen minutes to midnight on a Friday. The court held that receipt was not effective until opening of business on the following Monday morning. Although this still amounted to deeming receipt to occur at that time (whether or not a human being had actually read the telex), the result suggests that the time when the sender could reasonably expect the telex to be read was more important rather than the actual time of receipt. It was clear that during business hours this would still be the time of dispatch. Strictly, the case did not deal with a telex which amounted to the acceptance of an offer to form a contract, but the principle should be equally applicable in such circumstances.

The problem with electronic contracting over the Internet is to determine whether the rule as regards instantaneous communication should apply (so that receipt or deemed receipt by the offeror is the key) or whether the postal rule is the more appropriate analogy (so that despatch of the accepting e-mail or response form is effective). Before considering this, it is important to explore in this context what "receipt", "despatch" and "instantaneous" could mean and whether the offeree will have knowledge either of whether his message has been received or of whether it has been received in the form it was sent.

Receipt of electronic communication

Depending on the means by which the offeror has established its presence on the Internet, there are a number of points at which it could be considered to have "received" an electronic message. If (as is frequently the case) its e-mail capability is operated on the server of a third party service provider, it could be said that an e-mail is received when it arrives on that server. However, it could be argued that it would be fairer to the offeror that receipt should be when the e-mail is received in the local mailbox of the offeror. It could also be argued that actual knowledge either of the e-mail's arrival or even of its content should be the point of communication, ie when the offeror is notified that the e-mail has arrived or reads it. A similar series of arguments could apply to a Web site which is hosted on a remote server: receipt of a response could be deemed to take place on its arrival on the remote server or at the local server of the offeror. **10–052**

There are additional complications. Should it make a difference whether the offeror's system has an open line to a remote server or periodic dial-up access? Should whether data transfer is initiated by the remote or the local server affect the position? Should ownership of the remote server by a third party affect acceptance? What if the remote server is in a different jurisdiction from the local one? **10–053**

These are questions which are difficult to answer, and which in the final analysis are likely to be addressed only by the courts if and when disputes of this nature arise.

Despatch of acceptance

A similar series of arguments can be applied to the offeree, especially (as is likely) when his e-mails are routed via an Internet access provider. Does sending the e-mail from the offeree's system entitle him to assume that the acceptance is effective? The answer is likely to turn to some extent on what the offeree is able, and can reasonably be expected to check. The offeree's system may or may not notify a successful transfer to the access provider or via, for example, a gateway from another protocol (such as X400) to the Internet. The system may or may not confirm that an attachment has been successfully delivered along with the basic e-mail. The offeree may be entitled to have greater confidence in the safe despatch of a pre-formatted response to a Web page rather than a free-form e-mail. **10–054**

Is the Internet instantaneous?

Can one assume that the gap between deemed despatch and deemed receipt is as narrow as possible? This could be the case if neither the offeree nor the offeror uses remote **10–055** servers or intermediaries or because despatch is deemed to take place only at the departure of the message from the offeree's Internet access provider's server and receipt is deemed to be at the remote server of the offeror. It is still the case that there is as yet no guarantee when or if an e-mail will arrive. However, there is no certainty over the route of the e-mail or even that all of the e-mail will take the same route over the packet-switched network.

Therefore if the present Internet cannot be regarded as being analogous to the telephone or telex systems, the rules on instantaneous communication should not apply. However, the alternative postal rule depends on there being a single reliable organisation responsible for the postal service, which it is reasonable for the offeree to trust. This again is not the case with the Internet.

It would seem therefore that neither the rules on instantaneous communication nor postal acceptance can slavishly be applied to the Internet.

Application of the normal rules to the Internet

10–056 It is important to bear in mind that the rules evolved to deal with other forms of communication were intended to meet the need for certainty and the fair allocation of risk, as between offeror and offeree, of a problem in communication. A similar approach should be taken in considering the position with Internet communication.

It is suggested that, in the context of a system primarily used by commercial offerors to elicit acceptance from individuals, the balance of convenience would tend to render most of the questions as to receipt irrelevant. The offeree will not know, or have any means of knowing the answers. Certain of the risks, such as the breakdown of communication between the offeror and the host of a remote server, can be covered in the service contract between those parties. The question ought therefore to be as to when the offeree is entitled to believe that its response has been reliably despatched. The test of this will be a matter of fact but must depend on the information available to the offeree as to the progress of the e-mail. This approach is consistent with that taken in *The Pamela*, discussed above, in which it was the time at which the message could be *expected* to have been read that was the key.

10–057 However, harsh as this may seem to the offeror, there are balancing factors. Given the current status of the Internet, neither party is likely to place absolute reliance on it and both are likely to be aware of the risk that an e-mail will be mis-routed. Where the service to be provided is the delivery of on-line material, the customer will know quickly if there is a problem and will simply request that the offeror resends the material. This may in fact take place automatically. If physical goods are not received, the customer is again likely to query the situation (this should be distinguished from the question of risk in goods which have been despatched, which is a matter for the contract). Where payment is also made electronically, depending on the exact means, the customer is unlikely to lose money if the message to the offeror is not delivered as the offeror will not act, for example, to debit a credit card account.

Minimising the risks of uncertainty

10–058 Given that it is not possible to be certain about the communication of acceptance of an offer over the Internet, the offeror should take steps to avoid the issue becoming a problem. The first question must be to assess, in the light of the continuing development of the Internet, whether it is appropriate to sell particular goods or services over the Internet at all. This will depend on the value of the transactions and the importance of incorporating particular contract terms, such as the extent of a licence or the limitation of liability. The potential offeror must then incorporate terms in its Web page (or preliminary e-mails) as to the acceptable methods of communication; the time of despatch of goods; when the contract is formed and how the offeree should raise queries in the event of problems.

Communication over Internet voice link

A final issue is where the telephone is used to communicate acceptance but the telephone service used is over the Internet itself rather than over the public switched telephone network. It is suggested that, where the service is full duplex (*i.e.* both parties can speak without cutting the other off) and in real-time, the position should not differ from that where a more traditional telephone service is used.

10–059

Electronic agents

The use of electronic agents introduces some uncertainty into the process of contract formation. An electronic agent is software programmed to conclude contracts with other persons or electronic agents according to predetermined criteria. The agent will search for offers that match the criteria and (without any intervention from the person on whose behalf the agent is contracting) conclude the contract. For instance, an electronic agent could be programmed to purchase supplies within a particular range of prices if the proprietor's stocks fall below a set level. It is quite possible that an electronic agent could conclude the contract on each side of the transaction. The lack of human involvement in the contract has led to concerns as to whether there is a true offer and acceptance in this situation.

10–060

It has long been accepted in English law that a contract can be formed without the intervention of a human being at the time of formation of the contract, such as when a driver enters an automatic car park.[12] However, in that case a human being has (by displaying prices and terms and conditions) made a specific offer capable of acceptance by the person who enters the car park. The electronic agent takes the process further, by effectively allowing the agent to negotiate terms within a range of authority programmed into the agent. In principle, there seems to be no reason why English law should not embrace this development and find that a binding contract has been formed.

However, some jurisdictions (not the United Kingdom as yet) have thought it necessary to legislate for the validity of transactions conducted through electronic agents. The Bermuda Electronic Transactions Act 1999, for instance, in implementing provisions concerned with the attribution of messages to a person, refers to the action of a person acting, *inter alia*, through his "electronic agent device" (defined as "a program, or other electronic or automated means configured and enabled by a person that is used to initiate or respond to electronic records or performance in whole or in part without review by an individual". The U.S. Uniform Electronic Transactions Act (a model law) also provides that a contract may be formed by the interaction of electronic agents "even if no individual was aware of or reviewed the electronic agents" actions or the resulting terms and agreements' and between an electronic agent and an individual.

10–061

10.4.5 Revocation and lapsing of offer

An offer can be revoked at any time before it is accepted (or deemed to be accepted) and it can also lapse after a specified time or on a specified event. As with acceptance, communication of revocation is required. In the context of a Web page where the offeree

10–062

is required to respond directly, merely amending the page to end the offer and remove any electronic order form is likely to suffice. Where an offer by e-mail has been sent, revocation may not be effective unless another e-mail is sent (and possibly received) prior to acceptance or revocation is communicated in some other way. Again, it would be prudent, where there is a risk of the offeror being bound by an unwanted contract, to specify in the initial offer how it can be revoked. This may also be the case where there could be a risk of a delay between an alteration to a Web page and its availability to all users, such as where certain access providers cache pages.

As noted above, if there is a risk of the supply of goods not meeting demand, it would also be prudent to have an express statement that the offer is subject to the availability of the goods, rather than to rely on an implied term or the assumption that there is merely an invitation to treat.

10.4.6 Consideration and intention to create legal relations

10–063   The two remaining required elements for the creation of a binding contract are less likely to be problematic in the context of Internet contracts. Consideration (that is the passing of benefit between the parties) is likely to be clear: the offeror offers to supply goods and/or services and the offeree agrees to pay for them. The necessary intention to create a binding contract is likely to be able to be readily inferred from the circumstances.

10.4.7 Incorporation of terms

10–064   The terms of the contract will comprise those expressly agreed by the parties and any which are implied, either by the courts or by the general law (to the extent that they are not successfully excluded). Where there has been an exchange of e-mails which contain the full terms of the agreement and there has been acceptance of an offer incorporating those terms, there is no more likely to be a dispute about those terms than with other forms of contracting (although see section 10.9 below as to the evidencing of those terms).

The most likely issue to arise in the context of the Internet is where a party attempts to incorporate standard terms into a contract formed via a Web page. The basic rule is that, for him to be bound, the other party must have sufficient notice of the terms and that they must be brought to his attention prior to the contract being formed (see section 10.4.4 above). One option is to ensure that no-one can place an order via the Web page until he has signed a separate contract exchanged by post. Another is for the terms and conditions to be set out in full as part of the Web page so that the reader must scroll through them and specifically acknowledge them by clicking a hypertext link to that effect before he can proceed to order the goods or services. Yet another is to have a hypertext link to the terms and conditions so that they can be accessed from the Web page. The simplest option is to refer to standard terms which are not set out on the Internet at all. There are a number of variations on each option.

The appropriateness and adequacy of each of these methods will depend on the importance of the terms themselves, which in turn may depend on the value of the goods or services and whether certain terms must be incorporated to protect the supplier, such as the extent of a copyright licence, or issues of liability or the means of communication of acceptance. It is a general principle also that the more onerous or unusual the terms, the more that must be done to bring them to the attention of the person to be bound by them.

The options above are given in decreasing order of "safety".

One analogy seems to be with the practice adopted in respect of shrinkwrapped **10–065** software. As with Web pages, there are limitations of space and considerations of attractive presentation. With such software, the practice is to state clearly on the packaging that the software is subject to a licence and that by breaking the plastic wrapping the user is bound by the terms of that licence. The user may decline to proceed and return the software unopened and obtain a refund. With a Web page, there is a kind of "click wrapping" if the user cannot proceed without clicking a hypertext link acknowledging acceptance of the terms. It is generally assumed that shrink-wrap licences are efficacious as contracts, but this is not certain.[12a]

However, it should be noted that the analogy is not exact. Shrink-wrapped software is generally sold as a package by a retailer or bundled by a third party hardware manufacturer. There is therefore no direct contact between the copyright owner and the ultimate user. Many copyright owners therefore seek additional acknowledgement of terms by offering an inducement (such as ongoing support) if the licensee completes and returns a guarantee card. In the case of a Web page, there will be direct communication between the parties (unless the Web page is operated by a distributor) and less need for such devices.

One other point to note is that a licence of copyright material must be distinguished **10–066** from a contract. A licence is simply a permission to do something which would otherwise be forbidden: in the case of software, it sets out the basis on which the user can make use of the program. In theory, therefore, all a software licence need do is describe the permitted use of the software. If the user goes beyond what is permitted, this will infringe copyright and the licensor will have a right of action against him. The main concern would be the necessity of setting out clearly the terms of the licence in such a way as to ensure that the user could not claim that he was unaware of the restrictions. This could be done by an on-screen notice without the need for a contract.

However, the breadth of types of material which can be supplied on-line over the Internet would tend to make this a less attractive approach in practice. Even where there is an on-line publication of material which is also available in hard copy, the normal copyright notice may not offer sufficient protection. This is because material supplied in digital form is inherently easier to copy. In addition, unlike with, for example, books, the copyright owner cannot rely on a general understanding of recipients of what is and is not permitted. Taking this with the frequent need to incorporate other terms suggests that most providers of copyright material over the Internet will prefer to rely on a binding contract rather than purely on copyright.

10.4.8 Certainty of identity of parties

There may be certain circumstances where the identity or some other quality of one of the **10–067** contracting parties may be of particular concern. This may be, for example, where certain goods can only be sold to persons over a certain age or cannot legally be sold in certain jurisdictions. The nature of services may also be relevant: an on-line bank will wish to ensure that it minimises the risk of fraud by the impersonation of one of its customers. In such cases, the precautions to be taken will vary but it would be usual to incorporate in any contract a declaration by the other party that he or she meets certain criteria, or to enter into a preliminary written contract accompanied by appropriate evidence of age or other qualification.

10.5 Formalities of contracting

10–068   Under the laws of England and Wales, most contracts can be concluded without formality and need not be in writing. As a matter of practice, all but the simplest contracts of course tend to be evidenced in writing to aid certainty. This is considered further in section 10.10 below.

However, certain contracts do need to be in writing or to be signed in order to be effective, and failure to comply with such requirements may render the contract void or unenforceable or difficult to enforce. The most obvious examples are certain contracts transferring title to land or otherwise falling within section 2 of the Law of Property (Miscellaneous Provisions) Act 1989. Guarantees and certain contracts relating to the giving of credit and contracts effecting the transfer of shares also must be in writing.

10–069   The question of what is "writing" has received some attention. The question is essentially whether writing in electronic or digital form, as opposed to handwritten writing on paper, complies with any relevant requirement of writing under English law. Some statutes, such as the Copyright Designs and Patents Act 1988, contain their own autonomous definitions of writing. So an assignment of copyright complies with the requirements of that Act if it is in writing as defined in that Act: "any form of notation or code, whether by hand or otherwise and regardless of the method by which, all medium in or on which, it is recorded". The Arbitration Act 1996 also contains an autonomous definition of writing: "References in this Part to anything being written or in writing include its being recorded by any means". That definition effectively equates the concept of writing with that of a document.

Many statutes that impose requirements of writing do not contain autonomous definitions. They are likely to be governed by the Interpretation Act 1978. "Writing" under the 1978 Act "includes typing, printing, lithography, photography and other modes of representing or reproducing words in a visible form".[13] This definition includes a requirement for something to be in visible form. By this analysis, writing in digital form (at least when called up on screen) is sufficiently visible to fall within the definition. However, although the courts may be expected to construe the Act so as to take account of technological advances,[14] the requirement of visibility has nonetheless led to academic debate about whether the requirement would in all circumstances be satisfied. Essentially, the debate turns on the question whether the fact that something may be rendered into visible form is sufficient to satisfy a requirement that the thing be *in* writing, when the transaction may take place without anything in fact appearing on a screen or being rendered visible at all. All the examples of writing listed in the Interpretation Act inevitably result in the creation of something which, if it is to be used for communication, is rendered visible (even if the process that leads up to it, such as photography, includes a stage where the material is not visible). The same is not true of electronic communications, using which (for instance through communications between electronic agents) a transaction can be concluded without anything being rendered visible. Take for example, an exchange of voice-mail messages. These are undoubtedly recorded, so that they would fall within a broad definition of "document".[15] However are they "writing" within the meaning of the Interpretation Act, when voicemail is not normally contemplated as being rendered visible? What about voice attachments to e-mails? Examples such as these suggest that although in many cases electronic form will satisfy the Interpretation Act definition of writing, there may be some instances where it does not do so even though the electronic form in question has a sufficient element of recordal to qualify as a document for, for instance, purposes of disclosure in litigation.

Similar arguments in other contexts, such as that computer data were not a **10–070** photograph,[16] have usually failed—at least where to hold otherwise would deprive the statute of its effectiveness. However, the definition of "writing" in the Interpretation Act is presumably there as a form of protection for the unwary, so that the court when considering the mischief of the statute may consider (within the constraints of the wording of the statute) whether the medium that is argued to fall within it offers equivalent protection to those media that undoubtedly do so.[17]

In relation to particular types of contract, and those which may need to be enforced in other jurisdictions with stricter requirements, the parties will need to analyse the specific requirement for "writing", both to ensure that the contract is legally effective and in relation to its use in evidence.

It should also be borne in mind that even if there is no direct statutory requirement of writing, there may be other requirements that render the statute incapable of being complied with electronically. For instance, under the Consumer Credit Act 1974 there is no requirement in the Act that the statutory forms be in writing. However, one of the regulations made under the Act refers to paper. Another example is section 3 of the Unsolicited Goods and Services Act 1971, which refers to a customer's order being placed by means of "an order form or other stationery belonging to the person".

10.6 Electronic signatures

10.6.1 General law on signatures

Validity of electronic signatures
In the absence of a specific statutory requirement, there is no requirement in English law **10–071** for any document to be signed in order to be legally valid or effective. So even for a class of contract required to be in writing or evidenced in writing, that does not require a signature unless the legislation so specifies. However, there are many statutory requirements for signature, usually in combination with one or more other requirements such as that the document be in writing (however defined). While it is very rare (if at all) for a statute to define what amounts to a signature, accompanying requirements may restrict in practice the mode of signature. If a requirement of writing mandates signed paper, that would preclude signature by most (but not necessarily all[18]) forms of electronic signature. If, on the other hand, a writing requirement is broadly defined so as to encompass a document in electronic form, that would suggest that an accompanying signature requirement can be satisfied by signing the document electronically.

English law has traditionally taken a liberal view of what satisfies a legislative requirement for a signature. Indeed, there is no English case in which a signature has been held not to satisfy a legislative requirement for a signature merely because it is not in the correct form. Signatures have been disqualified because they were applied by an agent when the particular statute on its true construction requires a personal signature (*i.e.* one applied by the signatory);[19] or because the name that was alleged to be a signature simply was not a signature,[20] or because the signature was mass-produced and pre-printed on a document, when the particular statute (on its true construction) required a signature to be applied individually to each form.[21] In the few cases in which the form of signature has been in issue, the court has each time permitted the signature to stand.

Jenkins v. Gaisford, Re Jenkins (decd)'s goods[22] concerned both form of signature and **10–072** whether signature by an agent was permitted. Section 9 of the Wills Act 1837 required a will or codicil to be signed at the end by the testator. The testator became infirm and had difficulty writing or signing his name. He had an engraving of his signature made and this was used under his direction by a person acting as his agent, including to sign the codicil in issue. The court held that the codicil was duly executed:

> "It has been decided that a testator sufficiently signs by making his mark, and I think it was rightly contended that the word 'signed' in that section must have the same meaning whether the signature is made by the testator himself, or by some other person in his presence or by his direction, and therefore a mark made by some other person under such circumstances must suffice. Now, whether the mark is made by pen or by some other instrument cannot make any difference, neither can it in reason make a difference that fac-simile of the whole name was impressed on the will instead of a mere mark or X. The mark made by the instrument or stamp used was intended to stand for and represent the signature of the testator. In the case where it was held that sealing was not signing, the seals were not affixed by way of signature."

It can be seen that, insofar as this case related to the form of signature, it placed no restriction on the form of signature but turned on the intent of the signatory.

10–073   *Goodman v. J. Eban Ltd*[23] addressed both form of signature and the mode of its application. A rubber stamp facsimile signature was individually applied and held to comply with the statutory requirement. Evershed M.R. stated:

> "It follows, I think, that the essential requirement of signing is the affixing, either by writing with a pen or pencil or by otherwise impressing on the document one's name or 'signature' so as personally to authenticate the document."

The question whether a rubber stamp consisting of a typed or printed representation, as opposed to a facsimile of the signature, would have sufficed was expressly left open by the majority of the Court of Appeal.[24]

10–074   The most recent case to consider the form of a signature was *Re a debtor (No. 2021 of 1995)*.[25] This concerned a proxy form for a creditors' meeting under section 257 of the Insolvency Act 1986. The proxy form was faxed to the chairman of the meeting. The question was whether the form was signed within the meaning of rule 8.2(3) of the Insolvency Rules 1986, which provided that a proxy form "shall be signed by the principal, or by some person authorised by him". It was common ground in the case that signing "could not be restricted to the narrow concept of marking a substrate manually by direct use of a pen or similar writing instrument. It was conceded that a proxy form could be 'signed' by use ... of a stamp". Similarly, it was conceded that if a form had a signature impressed on it by a printing machine in the way that share dividend cheques frequently are signed by company secretaries[26], the form can be said to be "signed". Laddie J. held that the proxy was signed within the meaning of the rule. In his view the concession as to stamping and printing was correct. After pointing out that even if the rule required direct manual marking of the form the authentication is not perfect, he went on to say:

> "It seems to me that the function of a signature is to indicate, but not necessarily prove, that the document has been considered personally by the creditor and is approved of by him. ... Once it is accepted that the close physical linkage of hand,

pen and paper is not necessary for the form to be signed, it is difficult to see why some forms of non-human agency for impressing the mark on the paper should be acceptable while others are not.

For example, it is possible to instruct a printing machine to print a signature by electronic signal sent over a network or via a modem. Similarly, it is now possible with standard personal computer equipment and readily available popular word processing software to compose, say, a letter on a computer screen, incorporate within it the author's signature which has been scanned into the computer and is stored in electronic form, and to send the whole document including the signature by fax modem to a remote fax. The fax received at the remote station may well be the only hard copy of the document. It seems to me that such a document has been 'signed' by the author.

Finding that the proxy form was signed for the purposes of rule 8.2(3) if it bore upon it some "distinctive or personal marking which has been placed there by, or with the authority of the creditor", Laddie J. also commented: "If it is legitimate to send by post a proxy form signed with a rubber stamp, why should it not be at least as authentic to send the form by fax?"

An Australian decision has assumed that a printed name sent by telex is sufficient.[27] In **10–075** *Clipper Maritime Ltd v. Shirlstar Container Transport Ltd (The "Anemone")*[28] Staughton J. (as he then was) said (*obiter*) in relation to section 4 of the Statute of Frauds 1677: "I reached a provisional conclusion in the course of the argument that the answerback of the sender of a telex would constitute a signature, whilst that of the receiver would not since it only authenticates the document and does not convey approval of the contents." If that was correct, the form of the signatures (telex answerbacks) was of no significance, whereas the purposes for which the two signatures were affixed was significant in relation to the particular statute under consideration, namely a signature requirement in relation to an agreement. Hence the distinction drawn between the effect of the two signatures, each in identical form.

In summary, therefore, the English cases on compliance with statutory requirements for signature place little or no emphasis on the form of the signature as such. The emphasis is on whether the statute requires the personal and individual application of the name, mark or signature to the document and the purpose for which it is applied, not on the form of the name, mark or signature. When we come to consider the implementation of the EU Electronic Signatures Directive, the fact that English law therefore attaches little or no significance to the existence of, in particular, a hand-written signature will assume some importance.

These cases would suggest that under existing English law any electronic signature **10–076** regardless of inherent reliability (such as typing the sender's name at the end of an e-mail), would be capable of satisfying a generally expressed requirement of signature, so long as the requisite intention was present and (if necessary) some extrinsic evidence such as oral testimony could be adduced to identify the person who signed.[29]

However, this broad facilitative approach has been complicated: first, by the provisions of section 7 of the Electronic Communications Act 2000; and second by the need to implement the E.U. Electronic Signatures Directive. These are discussed below.

Allocating risk in the use of electronic signatures

A separate question from whether an electronic signature satisfies a legislative **10–077** requirement for a signature is that of who bears the risk of a forged signature, or one affixed without authority. This is of especial concern with electronic signatures since it is less easy to detect forgery or impersonation than with manuscript signatures where (at least at leisure after the event if not in the heat of the transaction) a forensic handwriting expert can provide expert evidence to the court).

The basic rule regarding ordinary signatures in English law is that a forged signature is a nullity. That, taken in isolation, would tend to place any risk of forgery firmly on the recipient. However, that risk allocation can be modified to suit the surrounding circumstances by application of, for instance, the rules of mistake, estoppel and representation.

10–078   Further, the nature of the underlying risk depends on what is being signed, since the legal significance of a signature may vary widely. Forgery of a signature may render the instrument a nullity. Thus, for a cheque, "...a forged cheque is of course in law not a cheque or negotiable instrument but a mere sham piece of paper".[30] Where the validity of the legal instrument does not depend on it having been signed, then an allegation that a signature is forged is likely to be an evidential matter as to what conclusions can be drawn from the document; for example whether the person who is alleged to have signed it was aware of the contents of the document. In the case of a signed contract, the outcome of a dispute over a signature may be determinative of the question whether a contract was concluded, or was void for mistake or was voidable for fraud—not because the contract is invalid without a signature, but because proof of forgery may demonstrate, if the identity of the opposing party to the contract be material (which in many cases it is not), that there was in fact no offer and acceptance between the apparent parties.[31] There is also a practical risk that a person who did in fact sign a document later repudiates the signature. With handwritten signatures the resolution of this dispute will turn largely on forensic evidence. A commonly expressed concern with electronic signatures is that, since the characteristics of handwritten signatures that underlie traditional forensic examination are lacking, the evidential risk of repudiation (either of the signature, or of the document alleged to have been signed) is correspondingly increased.[32] This has led to the development of technologies that seek to reduce or eliminate the risk of repudiation.[33]

The examples that we have discussed all concern ordinary signatures, where there is no attempt to put in place special procedures to authenticate the signature. Where such procedures are put in place, then even where (such as in the case of negotiable instruments) the forged signature renders the instrument a nullity, application of estoppel and representation rules can result in the risk being shifted away from the recipient. This, as we have mentioned, is of especial significance given the emphasis in the electronic environment in devising digital signatures certified by third parties, intended to offer the recipient (among other things) a guarantee of certainty as to the identity of the signatory and the ability to prevent the signatory denying that the signature was his.

10–079   In England there has been one case concerning reliance on a fraudulently issued digital signature, albeit of a primitive nature. The case, *Standard Bank London Ltd v. The Bank of Tokyo Ltd*[34] concerned a "tested telex", which is a telex authenticated by a secret code known only to the sender and the recipient. The recipient bank relied upon the tested telex received from the sending bank as confirming the authenticity of a documentary letter of credit. The documentary credit was in fact forged and the fraudsters had dishonestly procured the issue of the tested telex by the sending bank.

The court held that the recipient of the tested telex would be able to rely on it unless the recipient was on notice of dishonesty, or of facts that should put it on inquiry as to dishonesty, or if it had been wilfully blind. The sending bank was therefore liable for the loss suffered by the recipient bank. The decision was in the context of evidence that the banking system relies on tested telexes and that they are intended to avoid arguments about authority.

The decision placed the responsibility for keeping keys secure fairly and squarely on   **10–080**
the person using the key to authenticate a message. It absolves the recipient from any duty to enquire into the authenticity of the message unless he is on notice of dishonesty.

That appears to be an efficient economic result in the particular commercial circumstances of the case. It reduces the individual transaction costs, and gives senders an incentive to take security precautions. Whether this allocation of risk would be appropriate in the consumer context, where unsophisticated individuals may use digital signature keys, is perhaps open to debate.

Electronic signature technologies vary widely in their purposes and methodologies.   **10–081**
Some technologies are intended, as with the "tested telex" in the *Standard Bank* case, to allow the sender to offer the recipient in an online environment a higher than normal degree of confidence that the sender is who he claims to be. Other technologies provide an electronic substitute for written signatures in the paper environment, capturing the handwritten signature electronically and storing its characteristics for later comparison if necessary. It does not follow that the legal consequences of using such technologies should always be the same, nor that the legal consequences should depend only (or at all) upon the technology being used. The legal consequences may, as we have seen, depend on a variety of commercial and societal factors, including any contractual relationship with the other parties to the transaction.

The use of a digital signature, especially one verified by a third party certifying authority, to offer reassurance to the recipient is in some ways akin to the use of a cheque guarantee card. The bank (= certifying authority) issues the card (=certificate) to its customer, and by means of the customer's presentation of the card (=certificate) makes a unilateral offer to the payee (=signature recipient) that, on fulfilment of certain conditions, it will honour the cheque (=use of the signature) up to a specified limit. The question arose in *First Sport Ltd v. Barclays Bank plc*[35] whether the bank was bound to honour a cheque where a retailer accepted the cheque from an imposter in possession of a cheque card and where the signature on the cheque, although it corresponded with that on the cheque card, was forged. The Court of Appeal held that the terms of the unilateral contractual offer made by the bank, as reflected in the terms printed on the cheque card, were such that the bank assumed the risk of forgery. The Court of Appeal made clear that the terms could have been written so as to place the risk of theft and forgery on the retailer accepting the cheque and card.

The issuance of a card (which will often function as a cash withdrawal card as well as a   **10–082**
cheque guarantee card) is itself governed by a contract between the bank and the customer, which will seek to allocate risk as between the bank and the customer for unauthorised use of the card and accompanying PIN number.

Thus a certifying authority could in principle govern its relationship with its own customer by contract and could (so long as it could bring the relevant terms to the notice of the person relying on its certificate, and subject to the constraints of consumer protection legislation) specify its degree of liability to third parties relying on the certificate (both in terms of a unilateral contractual offer and also in terms of seeking to limit any liability in tort).

However, as we shall see in the discussion of the E.U. Electronic Signatures Directive, the liability of certain types of certifying authorities to third parties will be provided for by statute when the Directive is implemented in U.K. law.

10.6.2 E.U. Electronic Signatures Directive

10–083 Directive 1999/93 of the European Parliament and Council on a Community Framework for Electronic Signatures[36] was adopted on December 13, 1999. It is due to be implemented in Member States by July 19, 2001.

The Directive addresses a number of topics surrounding electronic signatures, including: the legal effects of ordinary and 'advanced' electronic signatures, certain standard-setting issues, the application of internal market principles to the circulation of signature products and services within the Community, the liability of certain certification service providers, recognition of certain certificates from non-Community countries, and certain data protection issues.

10–084 The Directive defines an electronic signature relatively broadly: "data in electronic form which are attached to or logically associated with other electronic data and which serve as a method of authentication" (Article 2.1). It may be observed, however, that this would not include data in electronic form attached to or associated with non-electronic data.[37] Nor does it include signatures used other than as an authentication method. It does not specify that the signature must be used to authenticate the data to which it is attached or logically associated. So, for instance, would a sample scan of a handwritten signature provided by a customer to a third party for record purposes fall within the definition? It is clearly not an authentication method for the document to which it is attached, but could be used to authenticate other signatures received by the third party in the future. It could also be argued that in some circumstances the purpose of signing a contract is not (or not only) to authenticate the document but to indicate acceptance of its terms.[38] However, it is to be expected that the definition will be broadly interpreted, since the expressed purpose of the Directive is to facilitate the use of electronic signatures and to contribute to their legal recognition (Article 1).

The Directive does not define "electronic". This may give rise to uncertainty as to whether signatures attached to documents whose life-cycle goes through both electronic and paper phases are within the Directive. On the other hand, the wide variety of definitions in other electronic transactions legislation suggests that the task is far from easy and may be better not attempted.

Electronic signatures

10–085 As to electronic signatures, Article 5.2 of the Directive provides that a Member State shall ensure that an electronic signature is not denied legal effectiveness and admissibility solely on the grounds that it is:

— in electronic form, or

— not based upon a qualified certificate, or

— not based upon a qualified certificate issued by an accredited certification-service-provider, or

— not created by a secure-signature-creation device

We discuss below the concepts of qualified certificate, accredited certification-service-provider (CSP) and secure-signature-creation device (SSCD). Suffice it to say that this provision is intended broadly to facilitate the use of electronic signatures, while Article 5.1 permits a special status for advanced signatures created by a SSCD and supported by a qualified certificate.

The United Kingdom has already implemented, in section 7 of the Electronic **10–086**
Communications Act 2000, a provision broadly similar to Art 5.1 concerning electronic
signatures generally. Section 7 provides:

"(1) In any legal proceedings —

    (a) an electronic signature incorporated into or logically associated with a
        particular electronic communication or particular electronic data, and

    (b) the certification by any person of such a signature, shall each be admissible
        in evidence in relation to any question as to the authenticity of the
        communication or data or as to the integrity of the communication or data.

(2) For the purposes of this section an electronic signature is so much of anything
    in electronic form as —

    (a) is incorporated into or otherwise logically associated with any electronic
        communication or electronic data; and

    (b) purports to be so incorporated or associated for the purpose of being
        used in establishing the authenticity of the communication or data, the
        integrity of the communication or data, or both.

(3) For the purposes of this section an electronic signature incorporated into or
    associated with a particular electronic communication or particular electronic
    data is certified by any person if that person (whether before or after the
    making of the communication) has made a statement confirming that —

    (a) the signature,
    (b) a means of producing, communicating or verifying the signature, or
    (c) a procedure applied to the signature,

    is (either alone or in combination with other factors) a valid means of
    establishing the authenticity of the communication or data, the integrity of the
    communication or data, or both."

"Electronic communication" is defined as meaning a communication transmitted **10–087**
(whether from one person to another, from one device to another or from a person to
a device or vice versa):

(a) by means of a telecommunication system (within the meaning of the
    Telecommunications Act 1984); or

(b) by other means but while in an electronic form.

"Communication" includes a communication comprising sounds or images or both and a
communication effecting a payment.
    References to the authenticity of any communication or data are stated to be references
to any one or more of the following—

(i) whether the communication or data comes from a particular person or other
    source;

(ii) whether it is accurately timed and dated;

(iii) whether it is intended to have legal effect;

and references to the integrity of any communication or data are stated to be references to whether there has been any tampering with or other modification of the communication or data.

There is no definition of "electronic".

10–088   It appears to be the view of the government that these provisions meet the obligation to implement Article 5.2 of the Directive.[39] However, section 7 is not a straight transposition of Article 5.2. It is considerably more detailed and on the face of it differs in certain respects from the Directive, for instance:

—   it introduces a definition of authenticity which does not appear in the Directive.

—   it requires that a signature be "incorporated into", rather than "attached to".

—   it omits any reference to "legal effectiveness", restricting itself to admissibility.

—   it places a restriction on the purposes for which the electronic signature is stated to be admissible which does not appear in the Directive.

There are also other provisions (references to integrity, admissibility of certificates) which are not expressly included in the Directive.

10–089   None of this may matter at all if section 7 is regarded as purely permissive and not intended to restrict the admissibility of signatures and certificates under the general evidential rules regarding documentary evidence. Certainly there is nothing in the Act that purports to restrict the admissibility of other electronic signatures and certificates and the Act does not include any express amendments to other evidence legislation. In both civil and criminal proceedings a signature (whether on paper or electronic) would, we suggest, be likely to constitute 'real' evidence (see discussion of evidential issues below) and therefore admissible with appropriate founding testimony. If that is correct, then no further legislative provision was ever required to secure the admissibility of electronic signatures of any nature in English proceedings. It would be most unfortunate if section 7 were to be regarded as having introduced, by implication, a restriction on such admissibility.

Advanced electronic signatures

10–090   The Directive, by Article 5.1, permits Member States to accord a special status to advanced electronic signatures which are based on a qualified certificate and which are created by a secure-signature-creation device. Member States are required to ensure that such signatures (which may perhaps be described as "qualified signatures"[40]) "satisfy the legal requirements of a signature in relation to data in electronic form in the same manner as a handwritten signature satisfies those requirements in relation to paper-based data; and are admissible as evidence in legal proceedings." Notably, the Directive does not require Member States to ensure that only qualified signatures satisfy those requirements. It is therefore open to a Member State to permit ordinary electronic signatures also to satisfy that requirement. That approach would be the closest to the existing English law, which (as we have noted) takes a liberal view of signature requirements in the off-line environment.[41] It is, indeed, doubtful whether under existing English law any legislation is required to implement this aspect of the Directive, since such signatures would be within the broader class of signatures that (as a matter of pure form) are already capable of satisfying English signature requirements. However, the DTI is currently of the view that legislation is required to implement this aspect of the Directive.[42]

We discuss below the requirements for an advanced electronic signature. These are reminiscent of, but not limited to, the use of public key cryptography (see Chapter 12 for a discussion of this), to enable the sender of a message to "sign" it with an encrypted identifier, which the recipient can decrypt using the sender's public key.

An "advanced electronic signature" is an electronic signature that meets the following requirements:

10–091

— it is uniquely linked to the signatory;

— it is capable of identifying the signatory;

— it is created using means that the signatory can maintain under his sole control; and

— it is linked to the data to which it relates in such a manner that any subsequent change of the data is detectable.

A "qualified certificate" means a certificate which meets the requirements laid down in Annex I of the Directive and is provided by a CSP who fulfils the requirements laid down in Annex II of the Directive. A "certificate" means an electronic attestation which links signature-verification data to a person and confirms the identity of that person. "Signature–verification-data" means data, such as codes or public cryptographic keys, which are used for the purpose of verifying an electronic signature.

A SSCD (secure-signature-creation device) means a signature-creation device which meets the requirements laid down in Annex III of the Directive. A signature-creation device means configured software or hardware used to implement the signature-creation data. "Signature–creation data" means unique data, such as codes or private cryptographic keys, which are used by the signatory to create an electronic signature.

10–092

Annexes I, II and III of the Directive contain detailed terms with which the certificate, CSP or signature creation device must comply if they are to qualify as a qualified certificate, CSP for the purpose of issuing a qualified certificate, or SSCD respectively.

These criteria are also of relevance to the supervision and internal market aspects of the Directive. As to supervision, the Directive establishes the general principle that certification services (*i.e.* certificates or other services in relation to electronic signatures) are not to be subject to prior authorisation. So State licensing of providers would be contrary to the Directive. However, Member States may introduce voluntary accreditation schemes aiming at enhanced levels of certification-service provision. The DTI proposes to continue to encourage the private-sector "T-Scheme". Although Part 1 of the Electronic Communications Act 2000 empowers the government to introduce a statutory (but still voluntary) accreditation scheme, the government gave undertakings during the passage of the Bill as to the limited circumstances in which it would consider doing this. The provisions are also subject to a "sunset" clause under which the provisions lapse if they have not been brought into force after five years.[43] The Directive also requires Member States to introduce a system allowing for the supervision of CSPs established on its territory that issue qualified certificates to the public (Article 3.3). The DTI currently proposes to operate *de minimis* supervision by observation, recording and publicity, conducted by the DTI with assistance from T-Scheme. The internal market provisions have the effect that (other than under the public sector exceptions noted below) a Member State cannot impose stricter requirements for valid electronic signatures than are

10–093

represented by an advanced signature based on a qualifying signature and created by a SSCD.

Liability of certain certification service providers

10–094   As to liability, we have discussed above the likely liability position of third parties who verify electronic signatures and issue certificates to persons who rely upon them. This would involve the certificate issuer in strict liability, rather than the negligence standard of a tortious duty to take reasonable care.

The Directive requires Member States to make special provision for the liability of CSPs who issue qualified certificates to the public. Article 6.1 provides that, as a minimum, Member States must ensure that as a minimum by issuing a certificate as a qualified certificate to the public or by guaranteeing such a certificate to the public a certification-service-provider is liable for damage caused to any entity or legal or natural person who reasonably relies on that certificate:

(a)   as regards the accuracy at the time of issuance of all information contained in the qualified certificate and as regards the fact that the certificate contains all the details prescribed for a qualified certificate;

(b)   for assurance that at the time of the issuance of the certificate, the signatory identified in the qualified certificate held the signature-creation data corresponding to the signature-verification data given or identified in the certificate;

(c)   for assurance that the signature-creation data and the signature-verification data can be used in a complementary manner in cases where the certification-service-provider generates them both;

unless the certification-service-provider proves that he has not acted negligently.

10–095   Further, under Article 6.2 as a minimum Member States shall ensure that a certification-service-provider who has issued a certificate as a qualified certificate to the public is liable for damage caused to any entity or legal or natural person who reasonably relies on the certificate for failure to register revocation of the certificate unless the certification-service-provider proves that he has not acted negligently.

Since these liabilities must attach to the CSP regardless of the existence of a duty of care, it appears that legislation will be required to implement them.

Member States must, under Article 6.3, ensure that a certification-service-provider may indicate in a qualified certificate limitations on the use of that certificate (provided that the limitations are recognisable to third parties), and that the certification-service-provider shall not be liable for damage arising from use of a qualified certificate which exceeds the limitations placed on it.

10–096   Similarly, Member States must, under Article 6.4, ensure that a certification-service-provider may indicate in the qualified certificate a limit on the value of transactions for which the certificate can be used, provided that the limit is recognisable to third parties and that the certification-service-provider shall not be liable for damage resulting from this maximum limit being exceeded.

All the provisions of Art 6 regarding liability are stated to be without prejudice to the Unfair Contract Terms Directive.[44]

It should noted that these liability provisions apply only to CSPs who issue qualified certificates within the meaning of the Directive. Since one of the requirements for a qualified certificate is that the certificate should contain an indication that it is issued as a qualified certificate,[45] it appears that a CSP who issues certificates that in all other respects comply with the requirements of the Directive for qualified certificates would avoid the Directive's liability regime if he made no claim in the certificate that it was a qualified certificate.[46]

Data Protection
The Directive places especially strict data protection obligations on certification-service– providers who issue certificates to the public. Unlike the liability provisions of the Directive, these obligations apply to all CSPs who issue certificates to the public, not just to those who issue qualified certificates.

10–097

Under Article 8.2 Member States must ensure that a certification-service-provider which issues certificates to the public may collect personal data only directly from the data subject, or after the explicit consent of the data subject, and only insofar as it is necessary for the purposes of issuing and maintaining the certificate. The data may not be collected or processed for any other purposes without the explicit consent of the data subject.

The requirements for explicit consent are analogous to those under the Data Protection Act 1998 for the processing of sensitive personal data, as to which see Chapter 7.

CSPs must be permitted in a certificate to indicate a pseudonym instead of the signatory's name (Article 8.3).

Third country qualified certificates
Article 7 of the Directive provides for the recognition of qualified certificates issued by non–EU CSPs. Member States must treat them as legally equivalent to certificates issued by an E.U. CSP if:

10–098

— the CSP fulfils the requirements laid down under the Directive and has been accredited under a voluntary accreditation scheme established in a Member State; or

— the certificate is guaranteed by a CSP established within the Community which complies with the Directive's requirements; or

— the certificate or CSP is recognised under a bilateral or multilateral Community agreement.

Public sector
Under Article 3.7, Member States may make the use of electronic signatures in the public sector subject to possible additional requirements. Such requirements must be objective, transparent, proportionate and non-discriminatory and must relate only to the specific characteristics of the application concerned. Such requirements may not constitute an obstacle to cross-border services for citizens. Under Article 11.1(a), the Member State must notify any such additional requirements to the Commission and other Member States. Thus any order made under section 8(4) of the Electronic Communications Act 2000, which enables conditions to be imposed for the use of electronic communications and storage, would (insofar as it affects the use of electronic signatures in the public sector) have to respect these principles.

10–099

Use of signatures in the public sector must also take account of the internal market principle enunciated in Article 4, notably that Member may not restrict the provision of certification-services originating in another Member State in the fields covered by the

Directive; and that Member States must ensure that electronic-signature products which comply with this Directive are permitted to circulate freely in the internal market. Thus, although government may specify the use of advanced electronic signatures for certain transactions with government, it may not specify the use of particular service providers or of service providers based in a particular E.U. country. Even if it wishes to specify additional requirements, again those cannot specify particular service providers. However Recital (6) of the Directive should be noted, since it provides that the Directive does not harmonise the provision of services with respect to the confidentiality of information where they are covered by national provisions concerned with public policy or public security.

Exclusions

10–100   Under Art 1, the Directive is stated not to cover aspects related to the conclusion and validity of contracts or other legal obligations where there are requirements as regards form prescribed by national or Community law, nor does it affect rules and limits, contained in national or Community law, governing the use of documents. Recital (16) also states that the Directive is not intended to affect national law governing private agreements regulating electronic transactions between the parties, such as EDI agreements: "a regulatory framework is not needed for electronic signatures exclusively used within systems, which are based on voluntary agreements under private law between a specified number of participants; the freedom of parties to agree among themselves the terms and conditions under which they accept electronically signed data should be respected to the extent allowed by national law". Further, Recital (17) states that the Directive does not seek to harmonise national rules concerning contract law, particularly the formation and performance of contracts, or other formalities of a non-contractual nature concerning signatures; and that for this reason the provisions concerning the legal effect of electronic signatures should be without prejudice to requirements regarding form laid down in national law with regard to the conclusion of contracts or the rules determining where a contract is concluded.

10.7 Electronic transactions legislation—a discussion

10.7.1 Background

10–101   It has become extremely fashionable to legislate for electronic commerce and electronic transactions. At the time of writing such legislation has been proposed or implemented in, for instance, the United Kingdom, USA, Australia, Bermuda, Guernsey, Hong Kong, Ireland, Jersey, the Isle of Man, and Singapore. Some of this legislation is based, to a greater or lesser degree, on the UNCITRAL Model Law on Electronic Commerce. Much E.U. legislation addresses e-commerce in the broadest sense, some of it (for instance parts of the Electronic Commerce Directive) specifically addressing facilitation of electronic transactions.

10.7.2 Removing obstacles to electronic transactions

10–102   The most compelling reason to legislate for electronic commerce is to reform any existing laws that create obstacles to e-commerce. Such obstacles usually consist of laws laying down requirements of form as preconditions to legal effectiveness. Such laws expressly or impliedly stipulate a particular medium (*e.g.* paper) in which information must be contained. These laws may clearly exclude electronic form, or may create uncertainty as to whether electronic form satisfies the requirements.

A primary objective of electronic commerce legislation is therefore to remove such obstacles and create clarity, certainty and equality of treatment between media. Further, for those areas in which there are no requirements of form in the existing off-line environment, the law should naturally permit similar activities to take place on-line.

It is also important, and may be regarded as an aspect of equality of treatment between media, that while electronic commerce legislation should facilitate electronic transactions it should not require or prescribe their use. This is, however, as we discuss below, easier to state than to achieve.

We also suggest that electronic commerce legislation should create, so far as possible, a **10–103** single medium-neutral legal environment governing paper and non-paper transactions, rather than to create separate parallel regimes for paper and electronic form. As far as possible an electronic commerce actor should not be subjected to a two-stage process of deciding whether his transaction is in paper or electronic form, then complying with the rules that govern that particular form. That is not only unnecessarily burdensome, but is also predicated on an increasingly unmaintainable distinction between paper and electronic form.

For instance, a hard copy may be scanned as a digital image, attached to an e-mail and sent to a mailbox equipped with text-to-voice conversion that enables the recipient to listen to e-mails. The mailbox also forwards the e-mail and attachment via a fax conversion service to a fax machine which stores the incoming fax on disk and prints it out on demand. What starts and finishes as paper goes through a number of different electronic communication stages. Similarly, is there any real difference between sending a fax to a memory-resident fax machine, and sending an e-mail to someone who has his e-mail client set to print out the e-mail? In each case it is almost impossible to say whether the transaction is paper or electronic; and whether a paper record is created depends entirely on how the recipient configures his machine.

10.7.3 Achieving certainty

A second reason for legislating may be to create confidence in the legal environment **10–104** among laypersons and industry. This may involve legislating, even when the majority of lawyers are agreed that the existing legal environment accommodates electronic transactions. The argument in support of the proposition that it is necessary to legislate so as to eliminate even wrongly perceived uncertainties in the legal environment[47] was well expressed, in relation to electronic signatures, by the Minister introducing the Second Reading of the U.K. Electronic Communications Bill:[48]

> "Lawyers argue about whether electronic signatures would be recognised as valid by the courts, but we cannot afford to wait while lawyers argue and the courts decide. Instead, clause 7 will allow businesses and consumers to have confidence in electronic signatures, because it puts beyond doubt that a court can admit evidence of an electronic signature and a certificate in support of that signature not only to establish from whom the communication came, but to establish the date and time at which it was sent and whether it was intended to have legal effect."

10–105   The Chair of the U.S. Uniform Electronic Transactions Act drafting committee also stated:

> "Legal uncertainty about the enforceability and admissibility of electronic communications and records is inefficient, creates barriers to electronic commerce, and imposes unnecessary costs on participants in legitimate electronic commerce."[49]

10.7.4 Traps to be avoided when legislating for electronic commerce

10–106   Generally, electronic commerce legislation may be vulnerable to criticism for various reasons, including:

- it prescribes and requires, rather than facilitates, the use of electronic communications and form;

- it deliberately or inadvertently, and without sufficient justification, sets minimum standards that exclude some categories of electronic information from being legally effective;

- it is explicitly or implicitly biased towards a particular technology or assumed business model;

- it carries unacceptably high risks of unintended and undesirable consequences;

- it creates the potential for unnecessary disputes over compliance with new electronic requirements of form;

- it creates inefficient rules for which it is costly to determine the outcome;

- it seeks to intervene or regulate in inappropriate ways.

10.7.5 Facilitation versus prescription

10–107   Extreme caution should be exercised when proposing legislation that lays down new prescriptive rules for electronic commerce, as opposed to removing obstacles and uncertainties. Since electronic commerce is a nascent and fast-evolving field the risk of unintended and undesirable consequences as a result of implementing new prescriptive rules is very high.

Caution also has to exercised even when attempting to legislate only to facilitate electronic commerce by removing obstacles and uncertainty. When legislating to achieve facilitation it is possible, by laying down minimum standards of, for instance, reliability and permanence with which the relevant records or communications must comply, inadvertently to introduce new electronic requirements of form. Legislatures have sometimes found the temptation to legislate for the reliability of electronic records to be overwhelming. We suggest that this temptation should be resisted.

10–108   The imposition of more restrictive requirements on-line than off-line is generally undesirable. To specify minimum standards of reliability and permanence in order to conclude a contract electronically, or to adduce electronic evidence of it, would be anomalous in jurisdictions such as the United Kingdom which permit the making of oral contracts. Although an oral contract may be regarded colloquially as being "not worth the paper it is written on" (reflecting the inherent unreliability of oral testimony), a court is still able to find that an oral contract has been concluded. A legal system that permits that should logically also permit electronic contracts to be made using informal means, notwithstanding concerns about unreliability and impermanence of some electronic records.

Even where existing law does set minimum standards in the off-line world by legislating for "writing" "signature" and so on there is a risk, when legislating for equivalent minimum standards for electronic communications, of in fact setting higher standards than for paper compliance. In English law, for instance, a pencil cross on a piece of paper can qualify as a signature notwithstanding its impermanence and inherent unreliability. Paper is not an inherently reliable medium. To regard it as inherently reliable when legislating for electronic equivalence can result in the creation of a class of electronic communications outlawed as unreliable, but whose unreliable paper siblings still benefit from being within the law. Legislation such as that of Singapore, whose avowed purpose is "to facilitate electronic communications by means of *reliable* electronic records" (emphasis added),[50] is unlikely to achieve true equivalence between on-line and off-line transactions.

These risks were noted by the Australian Electronic Commerce Expert Group in its Report to the Attorney General:[51] **10–109**

> "There is always the temptation, in dealing with the law as it relates to unfamiliar and new technologies, to set the standards required of a new technology higher than those which currently apply to paper and to overlook the weaknesses that we know to inhere in the familiar"

Such "minimum standards" provisions lead to considerable difficulties of definition. They also run the risk of being over technology-specific, since the standards are inevitably drawn with today's technology and communications structures in mind.

Further, the more restrictive and the more widely applicable are such "minimum standards", the greater the risk that a jurisdiction will re-introduce the injustices associated with widespread legal requirements of form. In the United Kingdom in 1937 the Sixth Interim Report of the Law Revision Committee[52] set out a number of reasons why most of section 4 of the Statute of Frauds 1677 and section 4 of the Sale of Goods Act 1893[53] should be repealed (as they subsequently were in 1954). Amongst the many criticisms noted, the following was especially powerful: **10–110**

> " 'The Act', in the words of Lord Campbell ... 'promotes more frauds than it prevents'. True, it shuts out perjury; but it also and more frequently shuts out the truth. It strikes impartially at the perjurer and at the honest man who has omitted a precaution, sealing the lips of both. Mr Justice FitzJames Stephen ... went so far as to assert that 'in the vast majority of cases its operation is simply to enable a man to break a promise with impunity, because he did not write it down with sufficient formality'."

The temptation to legislate for minimum acceptable standards of electronic form should, we suggest, be tempered by the risk of doing injustice by denying a person his rights through failure to comply with a required form. That risk is compounded in a new environment in which sophisticated technical knowledge may be required on the part of the user to determine what complies with the electronic requirement of form, such as to **10–111** identify an appropriately reliable identification method for an electronic signature (as required by Article 7 of the UNCITRAL Model Electronic Commerce Law).

Electronic commerce legislation, if it is to remove uncertainty, should be clear. The E.U. Distance Selling Directive illustrates the problems that can be caused by lack of clarity in legislating for e-commerce. Article 5 of the Directive specifies information that the consumer must receive by way of confirmation of the transaction. The consumer must receive "written confirmation or confirmation in another durable medium available and accessible to him" of the relevant information. However, as discussed above (section 10.2.1), this is not defined so as to make clear which electronic forms would comply with this. To leave a point of such significance open to serious doubt in legislation promulgated with e-commerce specifically in mind is most undesirable.

10.7.6 The evolution of electronic transactions legislation

10–112   Electronic transactions legislation typically allows and legislates for electronic versions of traditional legal concepts such as contract, document, record, notice, instrument, signature, attestation, sealing and notarisation. Such legislation typically also seeks to translate into the electronic environment traditional legislative requirements of form and process such as writing, record and document retention requirements, requirements to produce documents, service and delivery of documents and aspects of sending and receipt of documents such as time and place of sending and receipt.

Legislation may also address issues such as the liability of electronic intermediaries, the ability to use encryption and more esoteric issues such as the use of electronic agents.

10–113   Early legislation in, for instance, the field of electronic signatures, was highly technology specific. Typically it legislated for the use of digital signatures based on public key encryption. Such legislation was criticised on the basis not only that it sought to enshrine particular, unproven, technologies in legislation, but also that it sought to legislate for particular assumed business models that would not evolve naturally in the marketplace.[54] Such legislation was highly prescriptive, tending to legislate for high levels of reliability and security.[55]

Such legislation was also medium-specific, in that it effectively established separate regimes for electronic and non-electronic transactions. As we have noted above, the increasing convergence of electronic and non-electronic transactions means that the attempt to distinguish between the two is already relatively meaningless.[56]

10–114   Following the criticism of earlier electronic transactions and signature legislation, more recent legislation has tended to be more technology neutral and more facilitative. Thus legislation such as the E.U. Electronic Signatures Directive recognises the legal effectiveness and admissibility in evidence of all forms of electronic signature (including, for instance, typing one's name at the end of an e-mail). Similarly, the UNCITRAL Model Law on Electronic Commerce does not seek to enshrine a particular technology for electronic signatures.

Nonetheless, legislation such as these still tend to lean in favour of enshrining minimum standards. This is reflected in the favourable treatment given in the E.U. Electronic Signatures Directive to "advanced" electronic signatures (which are somewhat akin to the old PKI digital signature model). Article 7 of the UNCITRAL Model Law provides that where the law requires a signature of a person, that requirement is met if (*inter alia*) the method used to identify the person and indicate the person's approval of the information is "as reliable as was appropriate for the purpose for which the message was generated or communicated in the light of the all the circumstances including any relevant agreement". Thus, although not enshrining any particular technology, this provision contemplates a hierarchy of electronic signatures of differing reliability, some of which will not satisfy legal requirements in relation to some types of transaction. The same criticism can be made of the draft UNCITRAL Model Law on Electronic Signatures, which adopts the same terminology. Much of this draft Model Law is also predicated on the existence of business and technology models based on certifying reliable signatures. Since as yet it is not known whether these models will be prove to embody an appropriate balance of cost, benefit and ease of use, the assumption may or may not turn out to be justified.

Some of the most recent legislation takes a further step forward by being wholly technology neutral, more medium neutral and highly facilitative. Legislation of this type contains, for instance, broad electronic signature definitions with no minimum standards. This can be seen in, for instance, the US Uniform Electronic Transactions Act (UETA) and the U.S. Federal "E-SIGN" legislation.[57] The definition of "electronic signature" used in section 7 of the UK Electronic Communications Act 2000 is also broadly facilitative, although slightly more restrictive than that used in the U.S. legislation.

10–115

The differing approaches to electronic commerce legislation are explained not only by evolving views about what such legislation should aim to achieve, but also the variety of legal systems with differing requirements of form in the off-line environment.

Jurisdictions that place great store by formal requirements of notarisation, sealing and so on to validate traditional transactions[58] are likely to be naturally inclined towards replicating such systems in the electronic environment. Those jurisdictions such as the United Kingdom, on the other hand, that traditionally impose few requirements of form in the off-line environment are likely to be more open to the view that electronic transactions legislation should be broadly facilitative and not prescriptive.

10–116

We have noted above that one of the objections to the prescriptive approach is that the imposition of minimum standards creates new electronic requirements of form and that such requirements can be used by the unscrupulous to evade what would otherwise be binding legal obligations. The UNCITRAL Model Law on Electronic Commerce has been influential and certain of its electronic requirements of form have been widely reproduced in legislation. For instance, the U.S. E-SIGN legislation (which on the question of signatures is extremely facilitative) defines "writing" as involving a "electronic record .... in a form which is capable of being retained and accurately reproduced for later reference....". This is similar to the UNCITRAL provision, that where the law requires information to be in writing that requirement is met by a data message if "the information contained therein is accessible so as to be useable for subsequent reference".

However, these type of provisions will inevitably lead to debate, uncertainty and costly court arguments about whether any particular electronic record satisfies the requirement. For instance, a document saved in a common word processing format may appear differently, even using the same word processor software, depending on what fonts are installed on the software and how it is configured. We suggest that formal requirements of this sort are unhelpful. A useful comparison may be drawn with section 178 of the U.K. Copyright Designs and Patents Act, 1988 which defines writing for the purposes of Part 1 of that Act as including "any form of notation or code, whether by hand or otherwise and regardless of the method by which, all medium in or on which, it is recorded".

10–117

We have already mentioned the UNCITRAL Model Law electronic signature provision. Such a provision will inevitably engender immense uncertainty as to the type of signature that is appropriate for a particular type of transaction. It also suffers from the problem that it requires the user to assess the reliability of the proposed type of signature and therefore to be familiar with electronic and digital signature technologies. This is wholly unrealistic. Few IT experts understand these technologies, let alone non-expert users.

10.7.7 Efficient and inefficient rules

10–118   We have referred to some difficulties with technology-specific approaches. There is also danger in creating rules that require technological investigation to determine the outcome of the rule. This investigation is inevitably costly and results in an inefficient rule. A good example of such a rule is the UNCITRAL Model Law provisions regarding time of receipt of an electronic message. For an information system which has not been designated by the recipient, UNCITRAL Article 15 provides that the message is deemed received "when the data message enters an information system of the addressee". Such a rule may be practicable where two large companies with IT departments are communicating electronically with each other on a pre-agreed basis. If necessary, the two companies can keep gateway logs that can be examined to determine when the relevant event occurred. However, a rule such as this is wholly unrealistic for a home PC user. A rule that requires IT experts to be employed to determine (if it can be done at all) the deemed time of receipt of a message is, we suggest, inappropriate, costly and inefficient.

10–119   In the off-line world, rules about service and delivery of documents tend to provide for a presumption of service or delivery after the expiry of a conventional period after, for instance, posting, and do not investigate when the post office actually delivered the item. Such a factual investigation tends to take place only if the alleged recipient wishes to challenge actual receipt, if at all.[58a]

The Australian Electronic Transactions Act 1999 provides for receipt "when the electronic communication comes to the attention of the addressee".[59] Again, conventional rules of service tend to focus on an easily ascertainable event, such as posting or delivery, to establish a presumption of service, and not to enquire except perhaps in the case of a challenge to the presumption when the individual actually became aware of it.

When considering appropriate rules of delivery and receipt for electronic communications, as with off-line provisions both the efficiency of the rule and justice to the recipient have to be taken into account and an appropriate balance achieved.

10–120   A recent example of a conventional rule to determine service of an e-mail notice is contained in regulation 10 of the Consumer Protection (Distance Selling) Regulations 2000. This provides that a cancellation notice given by a consumer is to be treated as properly given if the consumer 'sends it by electronic mail, to the business electronic mail address last known to the consumer (in which case it is to be taken to have been given on the day on which it is sent)'. Here can be seen an attempt to replicate the traditional concept of the last known business address, coupled with an attempt to avoid the need for technical (although not all factual) enquiries. However, it may be commented that the notion of when an e-mail is 'sent' is by no means as simple as may first appear. What if the sender presses the send button, but the e-mail remains in the Outbox for some period until the system is ready to forward it through a gateway to the outside world? What if the sender presses the send button, but sets a time delay? Considerations such as these have led to UNCITRAL-style formulations such as when the message enters or leaves a person's information system. But as we have pointed out, these have their own problems.

It will probably only be with experience of applying early attempts at rules that the appropriate balance can be achieved.

10.7.8 Facilitating without requiring the use of electronic transactions

While the facilitative approach to electronic transactions has been gaining ground, that **10–121** approach is not free of difficulties. The main problem is how to facilitate use of electronic form, while avoiding legislation that compels the use of electronic form or means. In the case of a bilateral transaction, one party's facilitation is the other party's compulsion.

While, as enacted some jurisdictions, it is possible to provide that use of electronic form in bilateral transactions requires the other party's consent, that substantially reduces the utility of the legislation from the point of view of the party who wishes to use electronic form. But the alternative amounts to compelling the other party to use electronic form.

The problem is especially acute where the document or communication has direct legal consequences, such as service of proceedings, statutory notices and so on. Take, for example, the case of a company receiving notices under companies legislation. Should a company be entitled to insist on receiving hard copy notices? If so, does that apply whether or not the company has electronic facilities such as an e-mail address? If it is prepared to accept electronic notices, should it be entitled to specify particular rules and processes for receipt of such notices, including its own rules as to when they will be deemed received?

These questions do raise extremely difficult issues which have only recently been seriously addressed.[60]

There are also often questions about whether facilitation should apply to transactions **10–122** with government in the same way as for transactions between private persons.

These difficulties have led to two widely differing approaches. First there is the "macro" approach of the U.S. E-SIGN legislation, which is to legislate, as an overlay over existing legislation, a broad and wide-ranging facilitation of electronic form and means. This has been done in the knowledge that it may lead to potential anomalies. As the Chair of the Drafting Committee for the U.S. Uniform Electronic Transactions Act Law (UETA) put it:

> "...UETA preserves the requirements concerning the manner of sending, posting, displaying, formatting, etc. contained in other State law. If other State law requires information to be furnished in a conspicuous manner, UETA § 8 states that you can furnish the information electronically, but must do so in a conspicuous manner. If other State law requires the information to appear in purple ink sprinkled with glitter, you can furnish the information electronically only if you can assure that it appear to the recipient in purple sprinkled with glitter.[61]"

The alternative, "micro" approach is that adopted by the United Kingdom in section 8 of the Electronic Communications Act 2000. This provides a rule-making power whereby existing legislation can be amended to provide for electronic form and means on a case by case basis. This allows for the elimination of anomalies and unintended consequences. However, it suffers from the disadvantage of potential institutional inertia, bearing in mind the massive amount of legislation that may have to be amended on a case by case basis.[62]

Typical examples of exclusions from the "macro" approach are areas such as real **10–123** property, wills and testamentary instruments, trusts, negotiable instruments, documents of title and powers of attorney. The E-SIGN legislation carries the exclusions into other fields such as proximity requirements concerning warnings and notices, notices of cancellation or termination of utility services, notice of default, foreclosure, eviction etc in relation to an individual's primary residence, notice of cancellation or termination of health or life assurance, notice of product recall and any document required to accompany transportation or handling of hazardous materials and the like.

The E-SIGN provisions for consumer consent to use of electronic records state that a consumer may consent to the use of an electronic record where a statute requires information to be provided or made available to a consumer in writing. The writing requirement is satisfied if the consumer has affirmatively consented and not withdrawn that consent and, prior to consenting, a clear and conspicuous statement has been provided satisfying a lengthy list of statutory requirements.

10–124   In summary, it is suggested that electronic transactions legislation should be facilitative and technology neutral. It should also be medium neutral, avoiding the creation of new electronic requirements of form and avoiding the temptation to legislate for reliability. However, such legislation has to respect the rights of recipients of electronic records and communications and reconcile the inherent conflict between sender and recipient's rights. Legislation should seek efficient and just solutions to the problems raised by the facilitating electronic form and means. That may require a very different approach to electronic transactions legislation than has been common in many countries to date.

The only legislation so far enacted in the United Kingdom that could be described as electronic transactions legislation is the Electronic Communications Act 2000. Section 7 of this Act, concerning electronic signatures, is discussed above. Section 8 provides power to amend, by Statutory Instrument, existing legislation so as to facilitate the use of electronic form and means. This has been used so far only to a limited extent.

10.8 Evidence—proving the transaction

10–125   As with other contracts, there may be occasions on which the existence and/or terms of a contract formed over the Internet must be established in court. The most likely scenario for this is where there is a dispute as to its terms and whether they have been complied with, or even where a party denies that he was the person who made the contract. Problems of identity are of particular relevance with regard to the Internet, given that the parties are unlikely to have any other form of personal contact.

There are two main considerations in this context: what evidence of the contract will be admissible and what weight will that evidence carry in court?

10.8.1 Which law of evidence?

10–126   The first point to note is that matters of evidence and procedure are generally a matter for the law of the forum in which the case is tried. So if a cross-border contract dispute were heard in an English court, English rules of evidence would apply even if the substantive law of the contract were that of some other jurisdiction. Under the E.C. Convention on the Law Applicable to Contractual Obligations 1980 (the Rome Convention), enacted in the United Kingdom by the Contracts (Applicable Law) Act 1990, the following principles generally apply to cross-border contract disputes tried in England:

- As regards matters of form, a contract is valid if it satisfies the laws of any of the following three countries: the country of the applicable law, or either of the countries in which the parties were when the contract was concluded (Article 9(2)).

- A contract can be proved by a method recognised by the law of the forum or of any of the laws mentioned in art 9 under which the contract is formally valid, provided that such method of proof can be administered by the forum (Article 14(2)).

- The applicable law applies on matters of presumptions of law or burden of proof (Article 14(1)).

The dividing line between form and evidence is not always clear. However, assuming (as is the case) that English requirements of form (such as writing) are relatively few, it might be thought that someone setting up a Web site in England should not be too concerned about the possibility of formal requirements affecting the validity of on-line contracts in countries from which the site can be accessed, so long as the dispute is litigated in England. However, while that may be true of commercial contracts, if the contract is a consumer contract concluded in circumstances in which the applicable law is that of the consumer's habitual residence (as to which see above, previous section), then the formal requirements of that country will apply.[63]   **10–127**

10.8.2 Proving the transaction

On the assumption that the contract has been formed by the exchange of e-mails or the response by the offeree to a Web page, the contract may be recorded in a number of different ways. The offeror may have made an electronic record of the exchange of electronic messages. The offeree may have such a record. Either party may have printed out a hard copy of the exchange. Each party may have a record of part of the exchange.   **10–128**

Problems are likely to arise only where there is a disagreement between the parties to the exchange of messages, either as to their content or their timing, and there is conflicting oral evidence. In such event, the court is likely to be requested to look at the electronic or hard copy records of the transaction to resolve the issue.

Until relatively recently, in civil litigation, the admissibility of electronic records in evidence was bedevilled by technical rules which applied to computer-produced documents, combined with restrictions on hearsay evidence (including documentary evidence). However, the Civil Evidence Act 1995, which came into force on January 31, 1997, abolished the computer evidence rules and introduced a relaxed scheme for admission into evidence of hearsay. It also includes a provision that a document which is shown to form part of the records of a business or public authority may be received in evidence in civil proceedings without further proof. There are provisions for certificates to be provided as to the status of the documents as business records. 'Documents' include electronic documents.   **10–129**

Notwithstanding the relaxation of the rules about admissibility of evidence, the judge is given a wide discretion as the weight he will attach to the evidence before him. It is little use the judge reading the document if he does not believe it. So a party must pay careful attention to ensure that its procedures and record keeping will enable it to satisfy the court as to what occurred when, who the parties were, what the contents of the electronic documents were and so on. Bearing in mind that these matters may have to be proved years after the event, it is sensible either to generate hard copies at the time and keep them safe, or to put in place tamper-proof electronic archiving systems (*e.g.* on CD-ROM) operated by persons who can give evidence to the court of the way in which the information was recorded (to show that it was a true record at the time) and of the way in which it has been preserved since. Issues such as the source and reliability of date and time-stamping and other information contained in the record should be carefully considered.

10–130   Consideration must be given to the subject matter, value and significance of the contract, the likelihood of disputes arising and the purposes for which the evidence will be needed. Until verifiable electronic signatures and other similar technology become widely available, the Internet may remain a relatively risky medium through which to complete contracts. Whether the risk is acceptable will depend on the factors set out above.

We now discuss in more detail the rules of evidence. For completeness we have included criminal, as well as civil, proceedings.

Admissibility and weight of evidence

10–131   If a document is admissible the court is able to look at it. It is not excluded from the court's consideration. There remains, however, the question of the weight that the court will attach to an admissible document. How much reliance will the court place on the document? How useful will the document be? This is nowadays a much more important question than admissibility.[64]

The modern trend of the English courts is to admit the evidence and leave the judge to gauge its weight, rather than become embroiled in technical disputes about whether the judge should look at the document at all. For instance, under the Civil Evidence Act 1995 the general prohibition on admitting hearsay evidence (including hearsay in documentary form) has been abolished. This trend can be expected to apply as much to electronic records as to any other form of documentary evidence. However, an electronic record will be of little use if the judge will not accept it as a reliable guide to what actually happened. Procedures to be adopted in relation to electronic records should be directed as much at maximising the court's confidence in the record as to overcoming any perceived obstacles to admissibility as such.

What are electronic records?

10–132   Electronic records are a form of documentary evidence and, subject to any specific requirements applicable to computer evidence, their evidential status will be assessed as such. The application of the rules of documentary evidence to electronic records is discussed in detail below. At the risk of oversimplifying a complex topic, an electronic record is potentially inadmissible only if:

(1)   It constitutes real evidence and admissible evidence to establish its provenance is not available;[65] or

(2)   The court in question is operating under old legislation such as the Evidence Act 1938 and the electronic record does not satisfy the admissibility requirements of such legislation.[66]

10–133   An electronic record may also be accorded no weight (which is tantamount to being held inadmissible) if (in the absence of special circumstances) it is a copy of another document and the original document is readily available and withheld.[67] A copy may be admissible under section 8 of the Civil Evidence Act 1995 ("CEA") (for civil proceedings) or section 27 Criminal Justice Act 1988 (for criminal proceedings). If it is a copy of a copy and is not admissible by virtue of those statutory provisions, then it may still be a requirement of admissibility that evidence be available to authenticate each copy in the chain, although the modern practice is to approach these matters as a question of weight of evidence, allowing the judge discretion whether to admit evidence and how much weight to place on it rather than laying down absolute prohibitions on admissibility.[68]

Otherwise an electronic record ought to be admissible to the same extent as any other documentary evidence.

Documentary evidence can for present purposes be divided into three categories: hearsay evidence, real evidence and copies. The basis on which each is admissible in evidence may differ.

Hearsay evidence

This is a record that embodies information emanating from a human being—*e.g.* a note made by a scientist recording his observation or opinion. Hearsay is admissible as evidence in criminal proceedings if it falls within an exception to the hearsay rule (see below) and is now generally admissible in civil proceedings. A computer record or output may constitute hearsay evidence, but does not necessarily do so (see below).   **10–134**

Real evidence

Real evidence generally refers to physical objects such as smoking guns or bloody knives. Someone gives evidence that the item was found at the scene, describes how it was preserved for the trial and the item is then admitted in evidence. As extended to documents, real evidence means a non-human statement in a document. For instance, a recording made by an unattended radar scanner or an automatic camera would be real evidence, the trace or film representing an observation made entirely by the machine. There would need to be founding testimony establishing that the trace or film was in fact produced by the machine.[69]   **10–135**

Evidence for this purpose would be, for instance, evidence from someone who was responsible for the machine and could give evidence of the trace or film having been removed, logged and stored, thereby establishing the authenticity of the document.

Some computer records may constitute real evidence, not hearsay. In *R. v. Governor of Brixton Prison ex parte Levin*[70] the House of Lords held that computer printouts recording transfers of funds were not hearsay and therefore were not inadmissible as hearsay. The printouts recorded the transfers themselves, created by the interaction between whoever purported to request the transfers and the computer. The evidential status of the printouts was no different from that of a photocopy of a forged cheque.

Another form of real evidence is a document which contains no relevant assertive statements. An example of this is a disputed contract. The issue may be whether or not the defendant signed it. In that case the document is real evidence on the basis of which a forensic document examiner will give expert evidence. If the dispute is about the interpretation of the contract, the document is real evidence because it evidences the legal obligations entered into, not statements by the author of the document asserting some fact on which someone wants to rely. This applies to documents in electronic form as much as to paper documents. Similarly a signature (whether manuscript or electronic) ought to be regarded as real evidence. However a certificate authenticating a digital   **10–136** signature would be a hearsay record of a statement made by the issuer of the certificate.[71]

The boundary between real evidence and hearsay is sometimes blurred, particularly if the interaction between human being and machine is such that it is not clear whether the document has recorded information observed only by machine—for instance, where a human being is operating the machine.[72]

10–137   *Direct versus hearsay evidence.* Because documents so often constitute hearsay evidence, it is impossible to consider the admission of documentary evidence (including electronic records) without taking into account the rules about hearsay evidence. In civil proceedings the distinction is far less important than it used to be, since hearsay is now generally admissible in civil proceedings. The distinction still retains considerable importance in criminal proceedings.

The courts have always been suspicious of hearsay evidence and have in the past excluded it unless it falls within special exceptions permitting admissibility. Unfortunately the subject of hearsay evidence is complex and confusing, so much so that Lord Reid said in 1964 that it was "difficult to make any general statement about the law of hearsay evidence which is entirely accurate",[73] and went on to comment that even so concise an author as Professor Cross took over 100 closely packed pages to explain hearsay evidence. We shall attempt it in one paragraph.

10–138   The core of a trial is that human witnesses in person tell the court what they themselves *did* and *saw*. That is direct evidence. What the witness *heard* is also direct evidence of events such as bangs, crashes, screams and gunshots. But if Client A says that he heard Trainee Z saying "I saw Lawyer X drunk on the street", that could be either direct evidence or hearsay evidence, depending on what is to be proved. If Lawyer X complains that he was defamed by Trainee Z's statement, then Client A is giving direct evidence that he heard Trainee Z make the statement. If Lawyer X is prosecuted for drunkenness, then Client A would be giving hearsay evidence of what Trainee Z saw. That would be first-hand hearsay (i.e. evidence at one remove). If Trainee Z wrote on a board "I saw Lawyer X drunk in the street", then the board would be first-hand hearsay evidence of what she saw. In a libel action by Lawyer X against Trainee Z the board would be real evidence, not hearsay, because the relevant facts to be proved would be the existence and publication of the statement on the board. But Lawyer X would still have to prove that the inscription on the board originated from Trainee Z.

10–139   *Civil evidence—hearsay.* Under the Civil Evidence Act 1995, hearsay is generally admissible in civil proceedings. This is subject to procedural safeguards—notice has to be given that hearsay evidence will be adduced, and the person whose statement has been tendered as hearsay can be called. Further, guidelines (discussed further below) are given as to the weight a court should place on hearsay statements.

10–140   *Criminal evidence—hearsay.* The rules about documents constituting 'real' evidence are the same in criminal proceedings as in civil proceedings. In fact most of the law concerning this has been made in criminal cases, where the rules as to evidence tend to be more strictly observed than in civil proceedings.

As to hearsay statements in documents, the relevant provisions governing admissibility are in the Criminal Justice Act 1988. They are as follows.

(1)   First-hand hearsay (*i.e.* a statement of a fact of which direct evidence by the author would have been admissible). This is admissible under section 23 of the 1988 Act if the witness is:

- dead
- outside the United Kingdom and it is not reasonably practicable to secure his attendance
- unfit to attend as a witness
- cannot be found

(2) Business records. For the purposes of section 24 of the 1988 Act an admissible business record is a document created or received by a person in the course of a trade, business, profession or other occupation, or as the holder of a paid or unpaid office; and the information contained in the document was supplied by a person (whether or not the maker of the statement) who had, or may reasonably be supposed to have had, personal knowledge of the matters dealt with.

This applies whether the information contained in the document was supplied directly or indirectly but, if it was supplied indirectly, only if each person through whom it was supplied received it in the course of a trade, business, profession or other occupation; or as the holder of a paid or unpaid office.

The judge still retains a discretion not to admit the statement, and in exercising that discretion must have regard to (among other things): the nature and source of the document containing the statement and to whether or not, having regard to its nature and source and to any other circumstances that appear to the court to be relevant, it is likely that the document is authentic. **10–141**

It may be necessary to produce a witness who can testify as the origin of the documents, so as to demonstrate that they fall within the scope of section 24. However, it is open to the court to infer from the documents themselves and the method or route by which they are produced to the court the they fall within the section, although often oral evidence as to their origin may be desirable.[74]

Copies

We have mentioned above the modern approach of the courts to the admissibility of secondary evidence of documents, including copies. The historic rules restricting admissibility of copies (to the small extent, if any, that they are still relevant) are becoming increasingly difficult to apply when the very concept of an "original" document is vanishing in the electronic environment in which temporary and transient copies are common, and a digital copy is a 100 per cent bit for bit reproduction of its predecessor. Even if an "original", can be identified and is relevant, what constitutes an original depends on what is sought to be proved. For the purpose of establishing a hacking offence, an electronic document on the system may be regarded as an original document. But for the purpose of proving the contents of a letter sent from the organisation, the same electronic document is only a copy of the original document sent out. While it is from a technical point of view it is valid to describe one document as a copy of another, for evidential purposes it is conceptually impossible to categorise any document (including an electronic document) as an original or a copy without knowing what is to be proved with it. **10–142**

Civil evidence—Current law

Section 8 of the Civil Evidence Act 1995 provides that where a statement contained in a document is admissible in civil proceedings, it may be proved by production of the document or (whether or not that document is still in existence) by the production of a **10–143** copy of that document authenticated in such manner as the court may approve; and it is immaterial how many removes there are between a copy and an original. In the light of the apparent demise of the best evidence rule as a rule of admissibility, this provision may now be regarded as merely governing the fashion in which copies are to be proved, rather than rendering copies admissible.

Criminal evidence

10–144   Under section 27 of the Criminal Justice Act 1988, where a statement contained in a document is admissible in criminal proceedings, it may be proved by production of the document or (whether or not that document is still in existence) by the production of a copy of that document authenticated in such manner as the court may approve; and it is immaterial how many removes there are between a copy and an original.

Copies of copies

10–145   As noted above, the old rule was that copies of copies were not admissible unless it could be proved by admissible evidence that each copy in the chain was a true copy of the previous one, back to the original. Whether that is still the case in the light of the demise of the best evidence rule and the modern approach to admissibility may be doubtful.

We have noted that in both criminal and civil proceedings there are provisions that where a statement contained in a document is admissible, it may be proved by production of a copy of the document (irrespective of how many removes there are from the original), authenticated in such manner as the court may approve.

10–146   However, neither provision appears necessarily to apply where the document is not being produced for the purpose of evidencing a statement whose truth is asserted. If it is produced merely as evidence that the statement was made or to evidence a legal obligation (*e.g.* a contract) then if the rule against copies of copies survives it could still be relevant. On the other hand, it would appear artificial that a multiple copy may be admitted to prove the truth of a statement made in the document, but not to prove the mere fact that the statement was made.

The rule (if it still exists) against copies of copies becomes extremely difficult to apply when, as is increasingly the case with computer systems and word processors, it is not at all clear what (if anything) constitutes the "original" and the vast majority of electronic documents can be characterised as copies of predecessor documents.

10.8.3 Factors affecting weight of evidence

Statutory provisions

10–147   For criminal proceedings, under Schedule 2 of the Criminal Justice Act 1988, in estimating the weight, if any, to be attached to an admissible hearsay statement regard shall be had to all the circumstances from which any inference can reasonably be drawn as to its accuracy or otherwise.

Under the Civil Evidence Act 1995, the court when estimating the weight to be given to hearsay evidence in civil proceedings shall have regard to any circumstances from which any inference can reasonably be drawn as to the reliability or otherwise of the evidence.

The Act provides a list of particular matters to which the court may have regard. They are:

—   whether it would have been reasonable and practicable for the party by whom the evidence was adduced to have produced the maker of the original statement as a witness;

— whether the original statement was made contemporaneously with the occurrence or existence of the matters stated;

— whether the evidence involves multiple hearsay;

— whether any person involved had any motive to conceal or misrepresent matters;

— whether the original statement was an edited account, or was made in collaboration with another for a particular purpose; and

— whether the circumstances in which the evidence is adduced as hearsay are such as to suggest an attempt to prevent proper evaluation of its weight.

These factors should heavily influence the way in which companies who wish their computer records to carry weight in court and be accepted as authentic design and implement their systems and procedures.

10.8.4 Electronic records procedures

In the quest to allay concerns from industry that their electronic records and document **10–148** images may not stand up in court, the British Standards Institution has produced two relevant publications. One is BS7768:1994, *Recommendations for management of optical disk (WORM) systems for the recording of documents that may be required as evidence*. The other is PD0008:1999, *Code of Practice for Legal Admissibility and Evidential Weight of Information Stored Electronically.*[75]

The purpose of these documents, especially the Code of Practice, is to suggest procedures which will maximise the authenticity, weight and usefulness of information (including source electronic data) stored (in particular) on optical disc.

For electronic records derived from source electronic data, such as records of electronic transactions, the objective of the recording process must be to create a record that can be demonstrated to have captured complete and accurate information about the relevant events at the time the record was created and to have been preserved without alteration since the events took place.

The factor that usually causes most immediate concern with stored electronic records, **10–149** due to the ease with which alterations can be made to an electronic record, is convincing the court that the document has not been tampered with and so is authentic. This is, in principle, easily dealt with by implementing proper procedures. The principle is similar to that of microfilm: put in place procedures which create an audit trail upon which you can rely to show that the original was correctly stored, and that there has been no possibility of tampering with the stored copy. If the court thinks that the stored copy may have been altered, it will attach little or no weight to it (and may decide that it is not admissible at all). So it is crucial that suitable procedures are put in place to satisfy the court that no alteration has taken place. The Code of Practice should assist greatly with this. However, it is not the case that a court will require complete and positive proof of lack of alteration of an electronic document in order to attach weight to it. It will approach the matter pragmatically. Indeed for the vast majority of documents that pass through the courts there is no real challenge to their authenticity.

10–150   Useful as the Code of Practice may be in enhancing the weight to be attached to stored electronic records, it would be a mistake to reverse the process and imagine that it would be desirable to exclude electronic data that did not comply with the Code. This would be wrong in principle, since it would revert to the old practice of creating bars to admissibility rather than leaving the judge to assess weight. It would also be undesirable in practice, since it would impose costs on business and in practice exclude most data stored on home computers. Worst of all, it would constitute a malefactor's charter if incriminating electronic records could be objected to simply because they had not been stored in accordance with the Code.[76]

While assessing the reliability of electronic records undoubtedly presents challenges for the courts,[77] those challenges need to be met in a way that recognises the ubiquity of informally generated and stored electronic data and that, as with informal paper documents, their reliability should be approached as a matter of weight, not admissibility.

---

1.   See for instance Internet Engineering Task Force EDIINT Working Group Internet Draft "Requirements for Inter-operable Internet EDI" (www.ietf.org/internet-drafts/draft-ietf-ediint-req-09.txt).
2.   "Distance Selling Directive—Implementation in the U.K.".
3.   Para 3.9.
4.   Directive 98/34 as amended by Directive 98/48.
5.   *Berkshire County Council v. Olympic Holidays* [1994] Crim L.R. 277, DC.
6.   Proposal for a Directive of the European Parliament and of the Council Concerning the Processing of Personal Data and the Protection of Privacy in the Electronic Communications Sector, COM(2000) 385 final, July 12, 2000.
7.   Contracts (Applicable Law) Act 1990, Sched 1, Art. 5. The Act enacts the E.C. Convention on the Law Applicable to Contractual Obligations 1980 (the Rome Convention).
8.   The circumstances are:
     "1 If in that country the conclusion of the contract was preceded by a specific invitation addressed to him or by advertising, and he had taken in that country all the steps necessary on his part for the conclusion of the contract; or
     2 If the other party or his agent received the consumer's order in that country; or
     3 [omitted]."
     The provisions do not apply to a contract of carriage, or to a contract for the supply of services where the services are to be supplied to the consumer exclusively in a country other than that in which he has his habitual residence. However, they do apply to a contract which, for an inclusive price, provides for a combination of travel and accommodation (Contracts (Applicable Law) Act 1990, Sched 1, Art. 5).
9.   But a country which is a signatory to the Rome Convention, discussed below, will operate the same rule.
10. Case C240/98 *Océano Grupo Editorial SA v. Rocío Murciano Quintero* June 27, 2000, ECJ.
11. [1995] 2 Lloyd's Rep. 249.
12. *Thornton v. Shoe Lane Parking Ltd* [1971] 2 Q.B. 163 Lord Denning M.R.: '...the offer is made when the proprietor of the machine holds it out as being ready to receive the money. The acceptance takes place when the customer puts his money in the slot. ... In the present case the offer was contained in the notice at the entrance giving the charges for garaging. ... The offer was accepted when Mr Thornton drove up to the entrance and, by the movement of his car, turned the light from red to green, and the ticket was thrust at him. The contract was then concluded...' Although Lord Denning distinguished the old "ticket" cases on the basis that the customer could not refuse the ticket once he had put his money in the machine, he did (if he was wrong in that) consider the position if the machine was "a booking clerk in disguise" (pp. 169–170).
12a. Some support for the enforceability of shrink-wrap licences can be gained from the Scottish case *Beta Computers (Europe) Ltd v. Adobe Systems (Europe) Ltd* [1996] F.S.R. 367.
13. Interpretation Act 1978, Sched. 1.
14. For examples see Bennion, *Statutory Interpretation* (3rd ed., Butterworths), p. 696 *et seq.*; and see *Victor Chandler International Ltd v. Customs & Excise Commissioners & Another* [2000] 1 W.L.R. 1296.
15. See *e.g. Derby v. Weldon (No. 9)* [1991] 1 W.L.R. 652; and note the comments of the Vice-Chancellor in *Victor Chandler*: "VCI's computers, Teletext's central editing system and the remote databases, each of which held the relevant information, can be regarded as documents. Each of them possesses the essential characteristic of a document, namely containing recorded information".
16. *R. v. Fellows, R. v. Arnold* [1997] 2 All E.R. 548.
17. As to whether requirements of form in fact achieve the desired protection, and as regards the unreliability of traditional media such as paper, see the discussion in section 10.7.5.

18. The U.S. E-SIGN legislation specifically contemplates the possibility of a non-electronic document being signed electronically.
19. *e.g. Re Prince Blucher ex parte Debtor* [1931] 2 Ch. D. 70.
20. *e.g. Firstpost Homes v. Johnson* [1995] 4 All E.R. 355. The Court of Appeal, interpreting s.2 of the Law of Property (Miscellaneous Provisions) Act 1989, rejected the previous 'generous' interpretations of the Statute of Frauds and s.40 of the Law of Property Act 1925 as inapplicable to the 1989 Act. They held that the printing or typing of the name of an addressee of a letter, when the addressee had printed or typed the document, was not the signature of the addressee. However, this was not on the grounds that the 'signature' was printed or typed, but on the grounds that inserting the name of an addressee of a letter did not amount to signing the document. Peter Gibson L.J. stated: "This decision is of course limited to a case where the party whose signature is said to appear on the contract is only named as the addressee of a letter prepared by him. No doubt other considerations will apply in other circumstances." The decision focused not on the form of the signature, but on the fact that the name was typed as the addressee of the letter, leaving open the possibility that in other circumstances a typed signature would suffice. Although not expressly stated, on the logic of the reasoning the same result would have been reached if the addressee had written out the letter by hand.
21. *R. v. Cowper* [1890] 24 Q.B.D. 533 This case was concerned not with the form of signature, but with the mode of its application. The Divisional Court held that a pre-prepared lithographed version of a solicitor's name did not comply with the particular requirement for signature. The two-judge Court of Appeal disagreed, so the Divisional Court decision stood. Fry L.J., who agreed with the court below, made clear that this was not because the signature was a facsimile, but because of the lack of cognizance of the individual document inherent in a mass-produced pre-prepared facsimile (and see the explanation of the decision in *France v. Dutton* [1891] 2 Q.B. 208). The case did not suggest that the solicitor could not sign by, for instance, inscribing his name in block capitals, or typing his name individually on each form that came before him.
22. (1863) 3 Sw. & Tr. 93, 164 E.R. 1208.
23. [1954] 1 All E.R. 763.
24. Denning L.J. (as he then was), in his dissenting judgment, stated: "Suppose he were to type his name or to use a rubber stamp with his name printed on it in block letters, no-one would then suggest that he had signed the document". However, Evershed M.R. left this question open: "It is unnecessary for the purposes of this case to express any view whether or not the same result would follow if the 'signature' impressed by the stamp was not a fac-simile representation of the solicitor's handwriting, but a mere typed or printed representation of his name or the name of his firm." Romer L.J. agreed with the judgment of Evershed M.R and expressed no view on this point. See also *Brydges v. Dix* (1891) 7 T.L.R. 215, in which (distinguishing *R. v. Cowper*) a printed signature was held sufficient to satisfy the relevant statutory requirement for a signature.
25. [1996] 2 All E.R. 345.
26. As to cheques, see the comments of Professor Goode in *Commercial Law* (2nd ed., Butterworths), p. 582: "The cheque must carry the drawer's signature, but despite doubts that have been expressed [*e.g.* by Denning J. in *Goodman v. J. Eban Ltd*], it would seem that this need not be handwritten and that a stamped facsimile suffices. The same would appear to be true even of a pre-printed facsimile…."
27. *Torrac Investments Pty Ltd v. Australian National Airline Commission* (1985) ANZ Conv. R. 82, cited by the Australian Electronic Commerce Expert Group at para 2.7.32 of their Report to the Attorney General.
28. [1987] 1 Lloyd's Rep. 546.
29. For a similar view of pre-existing U.S. signature law, see "The Verdict on Plaintext Signatures: They're Legal", Benjamin Wright, [1994] 10 C.L.S.R. 311.
30. Kerr J. in *National Westminster Bank Ltd v. Barclays Bank International Ltd* [1975] Q.B. 654 at 656.
31. See *Chitty on Contracts* (28th edition, Sweet & Maxwell) para. 5-045 *et seq.* for a full discussion of the effect of mistaken identity. Of course the party whose signature is established to have been forged could not be bound by the alleged contract. The complexities arise when considering the effect of the forgery on the other party to the contract, or on third parties whose title to goods sold under the contract derives from the fraudster.
32. It should be appreciated that although traditional forensic handwriting examination may be impossible, there is a new and growing body of experts with forensic expertise in the digital environment. However, acquisition and use of such evidence to establish identity is complex and costly. See, for example, *Takenaka (U.K.) Ltd v. Frankl* (Alliott J.) October 11, 2000, QBD (upheld on appeal [2001] EWCA Civ. 348).
33. The converse risk is that, due to the ease of impersonating someone electronically, a person may wrongly be bound to a contract that he or she did not make. For a discussion of the ease with which e-mail addresses can be spoofed, see "I never sent that…", Barry Fox, *New Scientist* March 28, 1998.
34. [1996] 1 C.T.L.R. T-17.
35. [1993] 3 All E.R. 789
36. [2000] O.J. L13/12.
37. Compare the definition in the U.S. E-SIGN legislation, which does include such cross-media signatures.
38. See *Clipper Maritime Ltd v. Shirlstar Container Transport Ltd (The "Anemone")* (main text, above), in which Staughton J. (as he then was) made, albeit *obiter*, precisely this distinction in relation to the sender's and receiver's telex answerback.

39. DTI Consultation on the Directive, March 2001, para. 36.
40. An example of descriptions adopted by some Member States to distinguish signatures that meet all the stated requirements from mere advanced signatures (see DTI Consultation Paper, para. 23 (n. 4)).
41. This contrasts with the position of Member States which have a tradition of requiring written contracts and accord a special status to hand-written signatures. See, for instance, "Digital Signature Legislation in Europe", Vincenzo Sinisi I.B.L. 2000, 28(11), 487–493.
42. DTI Consultation Paper, paras 36–38.
43. Electronic Communications Act 2000, s. 16(4).
44. Council Directive 93/13 of April 5, 1993, implemented in the UK by the Unfair Terms in Consumer Contracts Regulations 1994.
45. Annex I, para. (a).
46. This assumes that the relevant Member State does not, as it is permitted to do under the Directive, apply the same liability scheme to CSPs who issue certificates of any description.
47. A similar situation occurred in the early 1980s regarding the copyright protection of computer programs as literary works. There was no doubt among lawyers expert in the field that computer programs were protected. However, the software industry was not content until the copyright legislation was amended to make this clear.
48. Hansard, November 29, 1999, Col. 46.
49. Professor Patricia Blumfeld Fry, "Impressions on California's Changes to the Uniform Electronic Transactions Act" *Electronic Commerce and Law Report*, December 22, 1999.
50. Electronic Transactions Bill 1998, s. 3.(a).
51. *Electronic Commerce: Building the Legal Framework*, March 31, 1998. See also the comments of Laddie J. in *Re a debtor (No. 2021 of 1995)* [1996] 2 All E.R. 345, at 351b.
52. May 1937, Cmnd 5449.
53. Which laid down *inter alia* a requirement of writing as a condition of the enforceability of contracts for the sale of goods of the value of 10 or upwards.
54. See, for instance, C. Bradford Biddle, "Legislating Market Winners" *World Wide Web Journal* Volume II Issue 3, Summer 1997 (www.w3j.com/7/s3.biddle.wrap.html).
55. The Utah Digital Signature Act 1995 was the first USA state legislation. For surveys of U.S. and international digital and electronic signature legislation from 1997 onwards refer to the Internet Law and Policy Forum Electronic Authentication Working Group (www.ilpf.org/groups/index.htm#authentication)
56. It should be noted, for instance, that the most recent definition of an electronic signature (in the U.S. UETA and E-SIGN legislation), encompasses electronic signature of a non-electronic document. This differs from the definitions in the EU Electronic Signatures Directive and the U.K. Electronic Communications Act 2000, which only encompass electronic signature of an electronic document.
57. Electronic Signatures in Global and National Commerce Act, Pub. L. No. 106–229.
58. See, for instance, the presentations at the Joint Keidanren/Internet Law and Policy Forum Workshop on Electronic Signatures and Authentication held in Tokyo in November 1999, especially those describing the Japanese "Inkan" seal system (www.ilpf.org/events/keidanren/).
58a. See *e.g. Godwin v. Swindon Borough Council* CA, *The Independent*, October 19, 2001.
59. section 14.
60. The U.S. E-SIGN legislation contains the most comprehensive attempt so far to address the issues. In the UK, some of the difficulties involved in facilitating electronic transactions can be seen from the fact that legislation addressing one area alone (communication with shareholders and filing returns at Companies House), the Companies Act 1985 (Electronic Communications) Order 2000, runs to 32 sections and two Schedules.
61. Professor Patricia Blumfeld Fry, "A Preliminary Analysis of Federal and State Electronic Commerce Laws", *Electronic Commerce and Law Report*, Vol. 5 No. 7, July 12, 2000.
62. At the time of writing only the Companies Act 1985 (Electronic Communications) Order 2000 has been made. Others are under consideration, including one permitting electronic conveyancing.
63. Contracts (Applicable Law) Act 1990, Sched. 1, art. 9(5).
64. Although in courts still governed by old legislation, such as magistrates courts (which for some purposes will continue to operate under the Evidence Act 1938), questions of admissibility may still raise difficulties.
65. See *e.g. R. v. Cochrane* [1993] Crim.L.R. 48, CA, for an example of a case in which insufficient evidence of the workings of a building society ATM system was adduced. Compare with *R. v. Shephard* [1993] A.C. 380.
66. See, for instance, *LB Camden v. Hobson, The Independent*, January 28, 1992.
67. This situation is now to be approached as a matter of weight of evidence, rather than admissibility. The old "best evidence" rule has finally expired. *Masquerade Music Ltd and Others v. Springsteen* [2001] 4 E.M.L.R. 654.
68. *ibid.*
69. *Statue of Liberty* [1968] 2 All E.R. 195.
70. [1997] A.C. 741.
71. Note the comment to this effect at paragraph 42 of the Digital Signature Guidelines, July 2000, published by the Judicial Studies Board (www.jsboard.co.uk). Although the Guidelines suggest that in criminal

proceedings the admissibility of the certificate would have to be considered under s.24 Criminal Justice Act 1988, that would only appear to be necessary if the certificate were to be used for a purpose outside the scope of the 'deemed admissibility' provisions of S.7 of the Electronic Communications Act 2000.

72. See the case of *R. v. Pettigrew* (1980) 71 Cr. App. R. 39 for an example of this confusion. The case involved a printout from a Bank of England computer which listed the first and last numbers of a consignment of checked banknotes. The operator of the checking machine entered the first number of the sequence. The computer calculated the last number taking into account any notes rejected and also calculated the numbers of the rejected notes. The court rejected the printout as inadmissible as a business record under the Criminal Evidence Act 1965. It has been suggested that the court could have admitted the record on the basis that it was real evidence (even though the counter was set initially by a human being), the basis of the court's decision having been that the information on the printout contained no human knowledge. That appears to have been the approach of the House of Lords in *R. v. Governor of Brixton Prison ex parte Levin* (above).

73. *Myers v. DPP* [1964] 2 All E.R. 881.

74. *R. v. Foxley* [1995] 2 Cr. App. R. 523.

75. British Standards Institution-DISC, 1999.

76. There may well be room for a code of practice governing the collection and storage of electronic evidence by officials such as the police. However, that is an entirely different matter from excluding evidence because the data were not stored in a particular way in the world outside.

77. See, for instance, *Takenaka (U.K.) Ltd v. Frankl* (above).

11

Payment Mechanisms for Internet Commerce

11.1 The ideal Internet payment mechanism

Surprising though it may seem given the extensive development of the Internet as a commercial medium, it is fair to say that the ideal Internet payment mechanism still does not exist. Such a system would:

11–001

- be capable of remote utilisation using nothing more than transmissions through the Internet, *e.g.* it should not also require the making of a phone call to be carried out off-line;

- be easy to use;

- be available for use by all potential sellers and buyers;

- be costless for both the payer and the recipient or would, at least, have a cost which is very low relative to the size of the underlying transaction it is supporting;

- be capable of being applied equally to substantial payments (such as for the supply of a large piece of software) and to very small ones, such as the few pence that might be charged for access to a particular page of a database (often referred to as "micropayments");

- be safe to use—it should not expose either the payer or the recipient to the risk of loss as a result of fraud;

- be internationally acceptable, enabling purchases to be made from suppliers in any country in the world;

- result in immediate settlement of the payment obligation, *i.e.* there should be no delay before the recipient of the payment knows that it has been made and the goods or services ordered can be supplied; and

- deal with the problem which arises in a remote transaction where the buyer will not pay until it knows the goods have been despatched but the seller is unwilling to despatch until it has received payment.

11–002 There are conflicting views as to whether new payment systems for the Internet should allow the payer and/or the payee to remain anonymous. There are those who argue that such anonymity is critical to the protection of civil liberties. On the other hand, it is suggested that the widespread use of anonymous electronic payment systems will have a disastrous effect on the control of such activities as money-laundering, tax evasion and fraud. This issue is considered briefly at the end of this chapter.

11.2 The reward for successful mechanisms

11–003 An analysis of the existing payment mechanisms for the Internet reveals that there is still some way to go before a system fully evolves which comes close to meeting all the ideal-mechanism criteria. Given the rapidly growing volume of e-commerce, there is no doubt that the rewards to the creators of systems which become widely accepted can be substantial. However, it also seems probable that both retailers and buyers will be averse to using a plethora of different systems, so it may ultimately be a case of a relatively small number of winners taking it all.

Most commentators seem to agree that the inadequacies of payment mechanisms currently available on the Internet are acting as a brake on its commercial development, at least in certain areas. In particular, there are still problems handling micropayments cost-effectively and many potential Internet buyers still have security concerns about disclosing their credit card details on the Internet.

11.3 Adaptation of conventional payment mechanisms for Internet commerce

11–004 The vast majority of small-to-medium size retail transactions in the United Kingdom are settled using one of four payment mechanisms, namely:

- cash;
- cheque;
- electronic funds transfer at point of sale (EFTPOS); and
- credit, charge or debit card.

It is useful to begin by considering the application, or potential application, of these conventional payment mechanisms to the Internet, before going on to consider the Internet-specific mechanisms currently available or being developed. Indeed, in many cases, it will be seen that these latter new mechanisms are actually adaptations of conventional mechanisms in an Internet context.

11.3.1 Cash

11–005 Cash in its conventional form clearly falls at the first hurdle as an Internet payment mechanism. It requires the physical delivery of notes or coins of the required value and currency and is thus ill-suited to situations other than where the buyer and retailer are face to face. However, if that problem could be overcome, it is clear that cash would have a high score in relation to the other ideal mechanism criteria. Accordingly, it is not surprising that considerable effort is being focused on the creation of "electronic cash". In its purest form, such electronic cash is intended to have the principal commercial characteristics of physical cash although it would be represented by electronic impulses rather than tangible notes and coins. The fact that such electronic impulses are capable of being transmitted through the Internet makes a successful electronic cash system a serious contender as a future Internet payment mechanism. Current developments in this regard are considered more fully below.

11.3.2 Cheque

A cheque is essentially an instruction by the drawer of the cheque to his or her bank to make payment of a specified amount to the cheque's payee. Like cash, the conventional cheque requires the physical delivery of the payment instrument to the retailer by the buyer and thus appears poorly suited to payment on the Internet. It also has a further problem. Unless a cheque is supported by a guarantee card, the buyer's bank has no obligation to the retailer to comply with the payment instruction which the cheque contains (and will not do so if, for example, there are insufficient funds in the buyer's account). Accordingly, the retailer will not know whether such a cheque will actually be honoured until it passes through the clearing system. However, cheques have traditionally been a very popular form of payment. They have the significant advantage that they are relatively low-cost for both the retailer and the buyer and can be used by anyone with a bank account to pay anyone else who has a bank account. It is not, therefore, surprising that efforts are being made (particularly in the United States, where cheques are still widely used in ordinary commerce) to develop the concept of an electronic cheque which could, in principle, be transmitted through the Internet. If these efforts are to be successful, they will need to overcome security concerns in relation to the potential for cheque forgery. In the United Kingdom at least, they would also need to overcome the difficulty that the existing law concerning cheque payments, dating back to 1882, is based on the concept of a written instrument actually being presented for payment. **11–006**

11.3.3 EFTPOS

Compared with payment by cash and cheques, EFTPOS (electronic funds transfer at point of sale) payment systems are very much newcomers. It was not until 1987 that the Barclays *Connect* card scheme came into full operation, the *Switch* system (supported originally by Midland Bank, National Westminster Bank and Royal Bank of Scotland) following on in 1988. As in the case of payment by cheque, payment by EFTPOS is essentially effected by the giving of an instruction by the buyer to his or her bank to make payment to the retailer. However, the instruction is given electronically by the swiping of the buyer's card through the relevant EFTPOS terminal. **11–007**

Unlike a cheque, an EFTPOS transaction will generally result in immediate settlement of the payment obligation. For an on-line EFTPOS system, this would occur because the electronic payment instruction would be passed to and accepted by the buyer's bank while he or she was still at the cash desk. For off–line systems, certainty of payment to the retailer can be achieved by virtue of a combination of the automatic honouring of payments up to a limit agreed with the retailer (often referred to as the retailer's "floor limit") and on-line or telephone authorisation for amounts above this level.

11–008   Because the instructions given in an EFTPOS transaction are electronic, in principle they would be capable of being transmitted over the Internet. In fact, as will be seen below, a number of mechanisms currently being developed specifically for payment over the Internet are really adaptations of the EFTPOS principle.

11.3.4 Credit, charge or debit card

11–009   The credit and charge card have, in a relatively short period of time, achieved a very high degree of popularity as payment mechanisms. Systems such as those operated by Visa and Europay/Mastercard (which now also cover certain debit cards) have also achieved a very impressive level of international acceptance.

Where payment in a transaction is made by credit, charge or debit card, that payment is made by the buyer giving an instruction to the issuer of the relevant card to make payment to the retailer on the buyer's behalf. It is a term of the contract between the card issuer and the buyer that the card issuer is entitled to debit the buyer's account with the amount of those payments which it is validly instructed to make. For a credit card, the resulting debit balance on the account will be required to be paid off in accordance with the terms of that contract. For a charge card the balance must be discharged in full by a set date following the statement date. For a debit card, the card issuer will reimburse itself by debiting the bank account against which the card is issued, just as the card-issuing bank does for an EFTPOS transaction.

11–010   The payment instruction can be given in writing or, with on-line systems, by the retailer transmitting the instruction through its terminal at the point of sale (in a similar way to an EFTPOS transaction; indeed, where a debit card instruction is given in this way, the transaction becomes an EFTPOS transaction). It can also be given by the buyer simply submitting details of his or her card number (normally together with the card's expiry date) to the retailer on the basis that the retailer is authorised to transmit this information, together with details of the payment requirement for the relevant transaction, to the buyer's card issuer.

It is this last means of effecting payment on a credit, charge or debit card that enables it to be used for Internet purchases. All that the buyer has to do to effect payment is to arrange for the transmission of his or her credit card number and expiry date to the retailer and payment can then be put into the payment-processing system by the retailer in the ordinary way applicable to non-Internet purchases.

11.4 The present reality

11–011   Even at the time of writing this chapter for the third edition of this book, the use of credit, charge and debit cards is the only widely accepted form of payment on the Internet. This is derived partly from the fact that it is a tried-and-tested conventional mechanism which requires only a minor change in the way in which the debiting instruction is given for effective use on the Internet. But they also have certain other significant advantages as an Internet payment mechanism. These advantages are discussed below.

11.4.1 Card issuer's joint liability with supplier

For credit cards issued in the United Kingdom, an individual (but not a corporate) buyer generally has the benefit of sections 56 and 75 of the Consumer Credit Act 1974 in respect of purchases made using the card—although for section 75 to apply and for section 56 to be available without a specific representation having been made by the merchant, the cash price of the item purchased must fall within the relevant statutory limits (currently a minimum of £100 and a maximum of £30,000) and the amount of credit provided must not be more than £25,000. This means that the credit card issuer will be liable in respect of misrepresentations or breaches of contract by the retailer and is of particular comfort to a buyer purchasing from a retailer of whose commercial standing he or she is unaware. There is some uncertainty as to whether the protection of section 75 also extends to U.K. debit cards (although it clearly does **not** where they are used in EFTPOS situations as there is a specific exemption in the legislation). In relation to purchases from suppliers outside the United Kingdom, there is a debate which is currently unresolved as to whether section 75 was intended to cover transactions where the retailer is overseas. Until December 31, 1996, an informal agreement was in place on this issue between certain card issuers (those who are members of the APACS clearing system) and the Director General of Fair Trading. Under this, the relevant card issuers agreed to treat foreign supply transactions as being covered by the section on an *ex gratia* basis but with the qualification that the liability that they would so accept in respect of such transactions was limited essentially to the price of the goods or service supplied. It was expected that legislation would follow along similar lines but in the end this never materialised. It is believed that card issuers may be continuing to adhere to the informal agreement notwithstanding that it has lapsed. It is also known that the Office of Fair Trading (OFT) remains interested in the resolution of this issue and it is possible that legislation might ultimately be introduced to resolve it or that there will be a court case in which the issue is considered and determined.

11–012

Even for transactions which fall outside the section 75 limits, by opting for payment with a card under one of the international card payment schemes (such as Maestro, Mastercard or Visa), consumers do obtain some practical protection in relation to retailer defaults such as complete non-delivery of a contracted-for supply. This is because these card organisations operate complex dispute resolution systems in relation to purchased goods or services which are not supplied and are able to put considerable pressure on a retailer who is found to be in default. For this reason, card payment effectively helps solve the chicken–and-egg problem which arises where a buyer does not wish to part with payment without certainty of receiving the goods.

11–013

11.4.2 International acceptance

The fact that credit, charge or debit card payment, using one of the internationally recognised systems such as Visa, Maestro or Mastercard, can be made in almost any country in the world makes it particularly well suited to international trading on the Internet. The key to this acceptability is the role of the international card organisation concerned. A retailer in Sydney, Australia who accepts a Visa card payment from a U.K. buyer may not even have heard of the name of the card's issuing bank. However, he/she will be relying on the international card organisation (or, more precisely, the local bank operating the retailer's interface with the relevant card scheme—known as the retailer's

11–014

"merchant acquirer") to effect settlement of duly authorised claims, thus enabling it to accept all card payments made under the umbrella of this organisation.

11.4.3 Immediate settlement and credit period

11–015   A duly authorised payment using a credit card results in the retailer effectively receiving an immediate guarantee of payment from the retailer's merchant acquirer. From the buyer's point of view, it also has the added advantage that it gives the buyer time to pay. A large number of credit card holders utilise this facility simply on a short-term basis (and discharge their balances in full by the stipulated day after which interest is charged) but others use it to provide them with extended credit on a revolving basis.

11.5 Weaknesses in current card payment mechanism

11–016   So the credit/charge/debit card is currently the dominant form of Internet payment, but it is not without its problems as an Internet payment mechanism. The principal problems are:

- security;
- transaction costs;
- limitation of users; and
- privacy.

11.5.1 Security

11–017   Since payment using a credit, charge or debit card over the Internet currently requires the transmission to the retailer of the buyer's credit card number, there is clearly a risk that such transmission will be intercepted, enabling the card number to become known to fraudsters who can use it to make purchases (or cash withdrawals) for their own benefit. In particular, it is suggested that fraudsters have developed programs which scan Internet transmissions looking for any message which contains the tell-tale characteristics of a payment card number. There is sufficient concern on this score to mean that a substantial proportion of Internet users are still not confident in sending credit card information over the Internet.

Part of the solution to this problem is to be found in the adoption of generally accepted encryption protocols for Internet transmissions of sensitive information of this kind, and this has become widespread over the past few years. However, there remains a lack of public confidence in the unbreakability of commercially available encryption methods and it has to be recognised that the potentially vast rewards for breaking encryptions used for financial transactions mean that significant resources may be applied to the task by those with nefarious purposes.

11–018   A further security concern is that the retailer itself (or fraudulent members of the retailer's staff) will make fraudulent use of a credit/debit card number provided over the Internet. Here encryption of the card number to protect it during transmission will not assist (although it is fair to say that this concern is not a new one, since the exact same issue arises whenever a credit card is handed over in a restaurant or shop). Equally serious is the danger that the retailer will store card details which it has received for purchases in a non-secure manner. At the time of writing, at least two major retailers (one U.K. and one U.S.) have recently suffered the embarassment of highly-publicised thefts of card details from insufficiently secure servers.

The large card-issuing companies, Europay, Mastercard and Visa have recognised these problems and have launched a joint initiative called "Secure Electronic Transactions" or "SET" to solve them. The concept is that special software (on the retailer's network and the cardholder's personal computer) enables a buyer's card details to be encrypted at the time of their transmission to the retailer and remain encrypted when transmitted on by the retailer to the relevant card organisation for authorisation and payment. In this way, the card details will never become known even to the retailer. The system uses digital signatures to ensure the integrity of payment messages and also ensures that retailers and cardholders are authenticated to one another by digital "certificates" issued by the relevant card organisation. Widespread implementation of the system has, however, taken a lot longer than expected, in part because of the significant cost to merchants of the required electronic infrastructure.

In this connection, it is worth noting that, once unauthorised card transactions are **11–019** identified, it is generally the case that (and in the United Kingdom, there are various statutory, and industry code of conduct, provisions to ensure that) the loss resulting from those transactions does not fall on the card user (other than, in some cases, where the card user has been grossly negligent at least). Instead, that loss will normally fall on the card issuing bank or on the merchants with whom the fraudulent transactions are made. However, card users understandably remain concerned either because they are unaware of the provisions which would relieve them of liability (or are uncertain that those provisions will work to their advantage without a fight), or because they are concerned that they may not readily identify the fraudulent use of their card if it is effected at a sufficiently low level. There must, after all, be few of us who do not often find one or two items on our credit card statements which we find difficult to trace back to the original transaction.

11.5.2 Transaction costs

By their very nature, credit, charge and debit card payments require central processing. **11–020** In relation to credit cards, the card issuer also bears a bad-debt risk—namely the risk that the buyer will not ultimately discharge the resulting debit balance. This means that a credit/debit card issuer will incur costs in providing the payment system. It is conventional in the United Kingdom that these costs are, in the main, passed on to the retailer by way of transaction commissions. In practice such commissions are levied by reference to the value of the transaction concerned. However, as much of the processing of a particular payment will be (and therefore cost) the same whether the payment is for £100 or 50p, minimum transaction charges are often applied and this can make credit, charge and debit cards uneconomic for small or "micro" payments. Given that many Internet transactions may be of small economic value—*e.g.* music clips, database access payments—this is potentially a significant drawback.

Where a business is likely to have regular dealings with a particular customer, this **11–021** problem can be overcome by the business allowing the customer's account to run up a debit balance until a credit card debit can be put through of a sufficiently large amount to justify the transaction charge involved (although if this approach is adopted some care can be needed to avoid becoming subject to the U.K.'s consumer credit legislation). Alternatively, a credit card can be used to pre-fund a customer account or a subscription basis of charging can be adopted. What neither of these approaches deals with is the situation where a business wants to receive micropayments from a customer who is likely to make only one purchase or whose purchases are likely to be made on such an irregular basis that the opening of a specific customer account would not be practicable.

11.5.3 Limitation of buyers and sellers who can use it

11–022   It is obvious that, in order to use a credit, charge or debit card, a buyer must have had such a card issued to him or her. Although the market penetration of such cards in developed countries is substantial, there is, nonetheless, a vast number of people using the Internet who will not be in this position. A particular problem arises in relation to the uncreditworthy or the young. The issue of a credit card requires that the issuing bank be prepared to take a credit risk on the cardholder, while even a debit card requires that the cardholder must hold a bank account and (at least while some debit card use operates without on-line authorisation as it still does in the United Kingdom) that the relevant bank takes some risk in relation to card use causing unauthorised overdrafts.

Even more significant is the position in relation to retailers. In order to receive payment by means of a credit, charge or debit card, the retailer must join the system operated by the relevant card organisation. For the small retailer this may not prove economic. Furthermore, an individual, such as a hobbyist software writer, might wish to sell products from time to time on the Internet and yet not really be running a business. Obviously such a person would not want to have to become a credit card acceptor simply in order to be able to receive occasional small payments for their work.

11.5.4 Privacy

11–023   Because all transactions using credit, charge or debit cards require central processing, they also involve a complete record being maintained by the card issuer of each of its card user's spending patterns. Useful though this may be for home accounting purposes, many people are concerned that this entails an unacceptable invasion of their privacy and would prefer a payment mechanism where their spending could be entirely anonymous, unrecorded and untraceable.

11.6 Conclusion on present reality

11–024   Credit and debit cards obviously have a head start on the other payment mechanisms which are being, or may in future be, developed for the Internet. But equally they clearly fall short of fulfilling all the criteria for the ideal Internet payment mechanism set out at the beginning of this Chapter. This leaves scope for new payment mechanisms to fill the gap and provides one of the imperatives for the development of the so-called "electronic cash" systems which are considered below.

11.7 Electronic cash: similar names, different concepts

The past decade has seen the emergence, and in some cases the subsequent collapse, of a number of payment mechanisms marketed as "electronic cash"—often with names involving some combination of "e-", or another typically "e-commerce" word, and a money one—*e.g.* "e-cash", "digicash", "cyberbucks", etc. Many initiatives have been limited to the U.S. market, but several European countries can point to schemes under an "electronic cash" banner—*e.g.* Proton. Some of these are marketed specifically for Internet payment. Others, on the other hand, set out to provide a general alternative to physical cash but are suitable for Internet payment because they involve payment using the transmission of electronic impulses which can be passed through the Internet.

11–025

The similarity of the names used for such products masks the fact that their underlying legal and commercial concepts are often very different. There is a spectrum of possibilities, at one end of which are systems which are essentially electronic adaptations of conventional payment mechanisms to Internet situations. The systems at the other end of the spectrum are more radical in concept and, potentially, their effect.

11.7.1 Electronic cash systems operating on EFTPOS principles

At the conventional end of the spectrum are systems which involve the application of EFTPOS or debit/credit card principles to Internet payments. In other words, systems of this type provide a way in which electronic messages sent through the Internet can be used to initiate transfers from and to relatively conventional accounts. Where they diverge from EFTPOS systems is that the entity holding the account is not always a normal bank and they do not require the retailer to possess dedicated hardware. Instead, they use software to provide digital signature and encryption mechanisms for the accurate identification of payers and the security for, and proper authorisation of, payment instructions. Not surprisingly, each system developer claims that their product provides a high level of protection against fraud.

11–026

A typical system of this kind operates along the lines of the structure set out in Figure 11.1, below.

In order to use the system, the buyer deposits funds (or arranges a credit line) with an issuer of electronic value—its participating bank in the example, although the issuer may not always be a bank. In return for this deposit, the buyer receives electronic confirmation that the relevant funds are held on his/her behalf. In order to make a payment, the buyer sends a payment message to the retailer which can be generated using the electronic confirmation it has been given by the value issuer. This payment message will be transmitted using an encryption protocol accepted by all users of the system (although some systems provide security in a different way—*e.g.* a separate confirmation of payment instructions by a follow–up telephone call). The payment message which is received by the retailer is then submitted by it to the buyer's participating bank and operates as an instruction to the buyer's bank to pay the retailer (by credit to the retailer's account with the same or another participating bank) and an authority to debit the buyer's deposited funds or arranged a credit line for this purpose.

11–027

In some systems, there is actually only one value issuer who holds accounts for all persons participating in the scheme, so transfers of value can be effected simply by altering the respective account balances of the payer and payee in the books of the value issuer.

The legal nature of what has occurred is very similar to what occurs when an EFTPOS

11–028

transaction is effected. Most significantly, in this type of system, the only thing which the retailer can do with the "electronic payment message" it receives from the buyer is to pass it to the buyer's bank for settlement. The retailer cannot transfer the message on to third parties to pay for purchases of its own.

A number of systems of this kind have been developed and are growing in acceptance. Where a system of this kind operates with multiple value–issuing/redeeming entities, then there is a need for clearing arrangements between those entities, and both complexity and transaction cost start to rise (although modern straight-through processing techniques may, however, ensure that clearing costs can be lower than they are with, say, the clearance of conventional cheques). Where there is only one value issuer/redeemer, transaction cost can be very low given that all payment processing is handled simply by electronic transfers between accounts held on the one value issuer's server. Clearly, for both situations, a payment can only be made using the system if both the payee and the payer hold accounts with an issuer/redeemer entity in the particular system, and this can be a disadvantage. So the usefulness of the system to an end-user will vary according to how many of the retailers with whom that customer is likely to want to deal participate in the system.

Figure 11.1

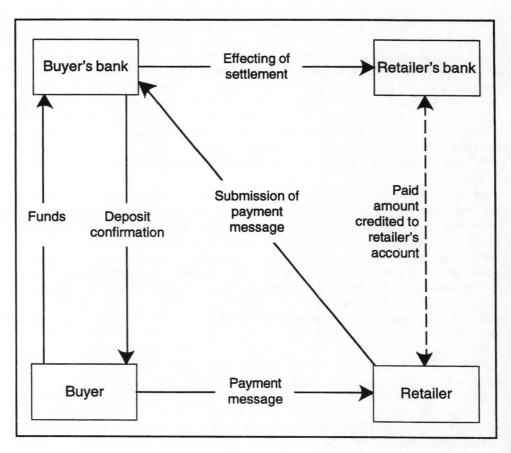

11.7.2 "True" electronic cash

When we think of "cash" in the conventional sense, we think of a note or a coin which can circulate between holders without any need for it to be returned to, and processed by, a bank each time it is used to effect payment. At the other end of the spectrum of systems under the electronic cash banner is the type of system which seeks to replicate this feature of conventional cash. This type of system will therefore be referred to in this chapter as a "true" electronic cash system. **11–029**

The basic concept of a "true" electronic cash scheme is that consumers will buy electronic value from the issuing system. The electronic value so purchased is represented by electronic data held either on a personal computer hard drive or on an integrated circuit or "microchip" on a smart card which consumers can carry around with them.

The most prominent system of this kind is that operated by Mondex. Originally a joint venture between Midland and National Westminster Bank, Mondex is now a wholly-owned subsidiary of MasterCard International. It is ultimately proposing to license its system to approved providers in countries all over the world. Importantly, it attributes considerable importance to the potential for its system to be used for Internet payments.

The operation of a "true" electronic cash system is most easily understood by reference to the Mondex example. Figure 11.2 below depicts, in a simplified form, the operation of the Mondex system in a typical jurisdiction (the model is to be adapted in each jurisdiction to take account of any local regulatory or legal constraints). **11–030**

Our buyer in this example is a customer of Bank A. In anticipation of her making payments using Mondex money, she has been issued with a smart card onto which can be loaded electronic impulses which will be treated by the system as representing monetary value. To load her smart card with money, she goes to a cashpoint at Bank A and inserts her card into the automated teller machine. Her card is loaded with the relevant units and her account is debited immediately with the "purchase price" of the units.

In order to make a purchase with her electronic money, the buyer transfers the necessary value of the electronic impulses on her own card to the retailer's Mondex terminal. However, the retailer need not simply redeem those impulses by cashing them at Bank A (as in an EFTPOS-type system). Instead it can, for example, transfer them to its wholesaler by way of payment for stock (provided, of course, that the wholesaler has its own Mondex facility). In the example represented by Figure 11.2, it is assumed that the wholesaler proceeds to use electronic impulses received by it from the retailer to pay the wages of one of its employees. It is also assumed that it is only when the relevant electronic impulses reach the wholesaler's employee that they are "redeemed" by being transferred to a participating bank in the system. On redemption, the employee's bank credits his account with the value of the electronic impulses surrendered. **11–031**

To complete the picture, above both Bank A and Bank B is a clearing system. Essentially, in order to provide our buyer with the electronic impulses which she loads at the cashpoint, Bank A buys those impulses from a value issuer in the clearing system. When Bank B receives those impulses back from the employee of the wholesaler, it sells them back to the value issuer in the clearing system and thus receives the funds to reimburse it for the credit it has made to the employee's account.

For completeness, it should be mentioned that, in practice, business recipients of impulses are likely to redeem them promptly following receipt (indeed, it is understood that Mondex's system will generally work on the basis that retailers' terminals **11–032** automatically retire value received from consumers as and when received). Doing this will enable them to receive interest on the payments received (or reduce their overdraft). However, the important point to note is that it is not an intrinsic element of the operation of a true electronic cash system that impulses must always be redeemed when received. It is the defining feature of any such system that impulses can circulate and pass through many hands to effect payments before being redeemed.

Figure 11.2

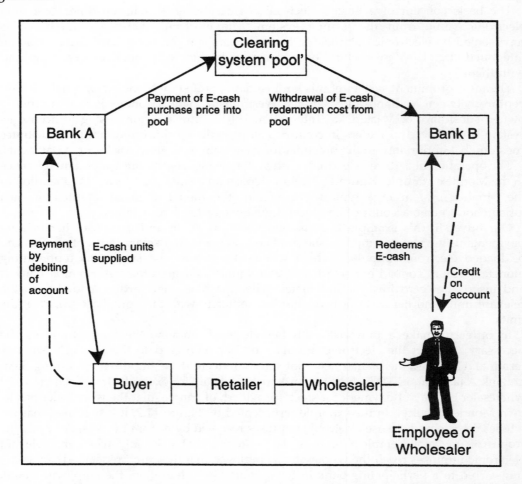

11.7.3 Advantages and disadvantages of true electronic cash as an Internet payment mechanism

11–033   The similarity of true electronic cash to real cash is striking. In particular, it can be transferred instantly and without cost to either the payer or the recipient (although it is likely that standing charges will be made for hardware needed to use the system). Most importantly, once received it can be immediately reused by the recipient to make further payments.

From the point of view of making payments over the Internet, this type of electronic cash has a great deal to commend it. In particular:

- because it consists of electronic impulses, it is, in principle, capable of being transferred over the Internet;

- in principle, it can be used by a very wide range of buyers and sellers, requiring only possession of the necessary smartcard hardware. Because the providers of electronic cash facilities do not take a credit risk on its holders, there should be no creditworthiness barrier to being able to use this form of payment;

- because transfers of it are effectively free from transaction charges, it can be used to make very small payments in a cost-effective way; it also has a significant advantage over real cash in that it can also be used for large payments;

- when transferring it across the Internet, even if there were a risk of it being intercepted and re-routed, at least that risk is limited to the value of the payment sent (there is not, for example, the risk that arises where the disclosure of a credit card number enables multiple fraudulent debits to be made at some stage in the future);

- in principle, it can be issued in any currency and thus be used for making payment in any country in the world; and

- systems can be arranged to ensure that transfers of it leave no "audit trail" of the kind that exists when payments are made through bank accounts or on credit/debit cards (this would satisfy the requirements of those who want their Internet dealings to be confidential, although it also has other implications which are discussed below).

It is, however, not perfect. There remains a risk of the interception of payment messages in Internet transmission and, perhaps more significantly, payment using electronic cash does not offer any protection in respect of goods or services which are inadequate or maybe not supplied at all. It is obvious that it also does not offer the "time-to-pay" feature that a credit card provides.   **11–034**

11.8 Acceptance of true electronic cash systems

It is suggested that there are a number of features that any true electronic cash system will need to possess if it is to gain general acceptance. Features of particular importance are discussed below.   **11–035**

11.8.1 Convertibility

Users of electronic cash will be unwilling to treat it as having value unless it is capable of being converted more-or-less instantly into real cash or a bank account credit with a bank acceptable to the cash's recipient. This means that a recipient will have either to be a participant in the scheme himself or herself or be able to use the services of another participant (*e.g.* his or her own bank) who will redeem electronic cash on his or her behalf.   **11–036**

11.8.2 Good credit backing

11–037   It is clear that electronic cash impulses are only as good as the credit standing of the entities which underwrite their conversion into conventional cash. Thus, for example, electronic cash issued by an unknown bank in a foreign jurisdiction will not be appealing to a retailer in the United Kingdom but Mondex obligations would be likely to be accepted in the United Kingdom without question if underwritten by any of the U.K. clearing banks. To achieve general international acceptance, an electronic cash system will probably need to be underwritten by parties of internationally recognised standing.

11.8.3 Low vulnerability to fraud

11–038   Any provider of an electronic cash product will need to be able to show that its system is sufficiently safe from the risk of counterfeiting and this is considered further below at para. 11.10. Historical experience in the sphere of physical cash has shown that successful counterfeiting of a currency may rapidly destroy the value which is attributed to it in the market place.

11.9 Systems in the middle of the spectrum

11–039   In the middle of the spectrum of electronic cash systems are those which have some but not all of the features of "true" electronic cash. For example, one of the first creators of an e-cash payment system was Digicash system. Their system involved the issue of electronic "coins", but those coins still had to be redeposited with (*i.e.* cleared through) the issuing bank each time that they were spent, at least if any risk of their proving to have been double spent was to be avoided.

The Visa international payment card organisation has also experimented with a number of different forms of what they term "Visa Cash". Some of these involve the loading of pre-paid value onto conventional payment cards. Others, on the other hand, have envisaged the possibility of anonymous disposable cards where the similarity to cash is greater. All current variants, however, seem to involve money being spent only with merchants participating in the Visa scheme with peer-to-peer transfers not being possible (other, perhaps, than by handing over a prepaid disposable card with value loaded on it).

11.10 Fraud involving abuse of credit/charge/debit cards and analogous systems

11–040   Where a payment system operates through the debiting of an account of the buyer on the basis of instructions given by him or her, there is obviously scope for fraud to occur where instructions are fraudulently given or validly given instructions are altered so as to effect payment to an unintended recipient. Where the resulting loss lies in these circumstances will primarily be a matter to be determined in accordance with the terms of the contracts between the relevant parties, *i.e.* the bank or credit card issuer making payment, the payment's intended recipient (*e.g.* the retailer) and the person whose account has been fraudulently drawn upon. Some general principles of English law do, however, remain significant.

11.10.1 The basic principle

On the principle established in the case of *Orr v. Union Bank of Scotland*[1] (as confirmed by **11–041** the more recent case of *Tai Hing Cotton Mills*[2] and the even more recent case of *Price Meats Limited v. Barclays Bank PLC*[3]), it is generally considered that a bank is not entitled to debit a customer's account in respect of a forged cheque, even though the forgery may have been undetectable and there may have been no negligence on the part of the bank. It seems likely that this principle would be applied by analogy to other unauthorised payment instructions given by fraudsters including instructions given under electronic cash systems which work on the basis of EFTPOS principles.

11.10.2 Exceptions to the basic principle

The principle in *Orr* is, however, subject to certain exceptions, in particular: **11–042**

- where the fraudster has apparent authority (*e.g.* from the terms of the bank mandate) to draw a cheque which is in fact drawn outside the scope of his actual authority. This exception could be relevant where, for example, a company allowed an employee authority to operate an electronic payment system on its behalf but the employee overstepped internal limits applicable to him/her, but not imparted to, and accepted by, the system operator; and

- where the relevant forgery has been facilitated by negligence on the part of the customer in the drawing of cheques (see *London Joint Stock Bank v. Macmillan*[4] although note that the *Tai Hing* case established some limitations to this principle).

Again, it is thought likely that these exceptions would be applied by analogy to payment instructions given by electronic means.

11.10.3 Alteration of the basic principle by express contract terms

The principle in *Orr* is capable of variation by the express terms of the contract between a **11–043** bank and its customer, but the scope of U.K. banks and credit card issuers to impose such variations is limited by the "Good Banking" Code of Practice (a voluntary code of conduct drawn up by the British Bankers Association) and the Consumer Credit Act 1974. Furthermore, the effectiveness of any variations which are sought to be imposed may be subject to challenge under the Unfair Contract Terms Act 1977 and (in the case of contracts with consumers), the Unfair Terms in Consumer Contracts Regulations 1999 (S.I. 1999 No. 2083).

11.10.4 Retailer risk where fraudulent payment innocently received

For retailers who accept payment from a fraudster using a stolen card or, in an Internet **11–044** context, stolen card details, the key question will be whether the card issuer is still obliged to honour payment under the transaction as if the card use had been genuine.

The case of *First Sport Ltd v. Barclays Bank plc*[5] (which involved the fraudulent use of a cheque and guarantee card) makes it clear that this will depend on the exact terms of the contract under which the retailer is claiming payment. A critical issue is likely to be whether the retailer has complied with the authentication procedures it is required to perform in relation to card payments of the relevant kind.

11.10.5 Transmission of card numbers through the Internet

11–045 At least until the Secure Electronic Transactions (SET) protocol (or another suitable encryption mechanism) is implemented for all credit card transactions, an interesting legal question may arise where a credit, charge or debit card number is divulged to a fraudster as a result of being passed through the Internet. Most agreements governing the issue of such cards will contain a requirement that the cardholder must safeguard the card number and a question may arise as to whether its unencrypted transmission through the Internet will comply with such requirement. The answer to that question will depend in part on the wording of the particular agreement but where E.C. country "consumers" are concerned, additional protecion is offered by Article 8 of the Distance Selling Directive (Directive 97/7). This requires member states to ensure that appropriate measures exist to allow a consumer (1) to request cancellation of a payment where fraudulent use has been made of his payment card in connection with distance contracts covered by the Directive; and (2) in the event of fraudulent use, to be recredited with the sums paid or have them returned. The Directive is implemented into U.K. law by The Consumer Protection (Distance Selling) Regulations 2000 (S.I. 2000 No. 2334). It is noteworthy that there is no exclusion of this protection simply because the consumer has been negligent.

11.11 Fraud involving true electronic cash

11–046 True electronic cash of the Mondex kind raises some substantially novel legal issues where fraud is concerned. Two crucial civil law questions which it seems will ultimately need to be answered are:

- Where such electronic cash is stolen, can a later innocent recipient get good title to it?

- Where digital money is counterfeited, who will bear the loss?

11.11.1 Stolen electronic cash

11–047 If a car is stolen, then, even after its sale through a chain of entirely innocent purchasers, it remains the property of the original owner (subject to certain limited exceptions). The same is not true of cash. If a thief steals £5 and with it buys a bottle of wine, then the £5 in the cashtill of the wine merchant belongs to the wine merchant, even though the thief had no title to it.

The reason for the distinction is that the £5 note is what is termed a "negotiable instrument" under the Bills of Exchange Act 1882 and, by virtue of that Act, a person acquiring such a note for value and in good faith acquires good title to the instrument irrespective of any defect in the title of the person from whom it was acquired. Can a wine merchant who accepts £5 of stolen Mondex money be sure that he is as safe as he would be accepting a £5 note?

As it is currently drafted, the Bills of Exchange Act is unlikely to assist since it is **11–048** confined to instruments in writing. It is, however, possible for an instrument which does not comply with the Act to acquire negotiable status by "mercantile usage", provided that such usage is "notorious", "certain", "reasonable" and "general". It remains to be seen whether general use of Mondex money would enable it to meet these tests. For electronic cash which fails to meet the requirement of negotiability, the danger to the holder of it is that a defect in title anywhere along the chain of ownership leading to the current holder may leave the current holder out of pocket.

11.11.2 Counterfeit money

It is not surprising that those marketing electronic cash products are insistent that their **11–049** product cannot be counterfeited. In this connection it is interesting to note that one of the driving forces behind the Finnish AVANT electronic purse scheme was a concern that the general availability of sophisticated printing devices was making conventional bank notes too easy to forge—the assumption presumably being that electronic cash is a much harder target.

To be incapable of being counterfeited, the codes used in the creation of electronic cash must be incapable of being broken. Yet, given the huge potential reward for the successful counterfeiter, it is likely that considerable resources may be mobilised to the task. Indeed, it is generally recognised that there is no such thing as a perfectly secure system, and that the key is constantly updating security devices to keep at least one step ahead of the criminal fraternity. If the unthinkable should happen and perfect, or near perfect, counterfeit electronic cash should be created, where would the loss fall?

By analogy with the position in relation to counterfeit conventional cash, it seems likely **11–050** that payment with counterfeit cash would be ineffective. Thus in theory the loss could be forced back down its chain of ownership. However, since earlier holders may be difficult to identify or locate, in most cases the loss is, for practical purposes, likely to fall on the person holding the cash at the time when it is discovered to be a forgery.

One possibility is, however, that counterfeit electronic cash will be undetectable as a forgery while circulating but will be detectable as such when it is sought to be redeemed (for example, because it is only at this point that the existence of multiple units with the same serial number is revealed). In this situation, it will be the party who seeks to redeem forged electronic cash rather than simply transferring it on who will bear the loss.

Another possibility is that, where forged electronic cash is created by the perfect digital **11–051** copying of genuine electronic cash, it may be undetectable even when redeemed. Furthermore, if the only means whereby a forgery can be detected is when the issuing system detects that the same serial number unit is being redeemed twice, then the issuing system may nonetheless have to honour both units—even though one is known to be a forgery—for the simple reason that it is not known which is the genuine one. It is far from clear how this situation would be treated under English law.

If the banks operating an electronic cash system end up honouring counterfeit electronic cash redemptions (either accidentally or because they are legally obliged to do so) then this will be a matter of concern to bank regulators, since the introduction of substantial sums of counterfeit cash into a system could then threaten the ability of the underwriting banks to meet their obligations to their depositors.

11–052   Another risk area which should not be overlooked is the danger that a concern that counterfeit money is in circulation may suddenly and dramatically reduce public confidence in the use of an electronic cash product, meaning that the issuing system is immediately required to redeem the great majority of the units in issue.

11.12 Who can issue electronic cash? The FSMA 2000 and the EMI Directive

11.12.1 Account-based and cash-based systems

11–053   A key regulatory question for any electronic cash system is whether the person who issues value under it, in return for payments in "real money", requires any form of authorisation to perform this role. It has been noted above that there are essentially two types of electronic cash system at present. The first is the type in which "accounts" are held for participants in the system which are credited and debited according to the transfers made between participants (this will be referred to as an "**account-based system**"). The second is the type where electronic value is issued on a non-accounted basis and may circulate between system participants before finally being redeemed (this will be referred to as a "**cash based system**").

11.12.2 The deposit taking restriction

11–054   There has, for some time now, been a debate as to whether either or both types of system require that the value issuer should be authorised to take deposits. Deposit taking activity was previously regulated by the Banking Act 1987 and is now covered (along much the same lines) by the Financial Services and Markets Act 2000 (the "**FSMA**") and the Financial Services and Markets Act 2000 (Regulated Activities) Order 2001 (the "**Regulated Activities Order**"). Section 19 of the FSMA stipulates that no person may carry on a regulated activity in the United Kingdom, or purport to do so, unless he is an authorised or exempt person. Article 5 of the Regulated Activities Order stipulates a form of regulated activity as being the taking of "deposits" in the course of a business where either:

(a)   money received by way of deposit is lent to others; or

(b)   any other activity of the person accepting the deposit is financed wholly, or to a material extent, out of the capital of or interest on money received by way of deposit.

11–055   A "deposit" is defined by Article 5(2) of the Regulated Activities Order as being an amount of money which is paid on terms under which it will be repaid, with or without interest or premium, and either on demand or at a time or in circumstances agreed by or on behalf of the person making the payment and the person receiving it. There is an exclusion from the definition of any amount which is "referable to the provision of property (other than currency) or services or the giving of security"—this exclusion being intended to cover such things as advance payment deposits and rent deposits. There is also an exclusion (in Article 9 of the Regulated Activities Order) for any monies accepted in return for the issue of "debt securities"—an expression which (subject itself to certain exceptions) includes any debentures, loan stock, bonds, certificates of deposit and any other "instrument creating or acknowledging indebtedness".

11.12.3 Deposit taking and account-based systems

The above provisions do appear to raise some issues for a non-bank entity operating an **11–056** account-based electronic cash system in the United Kingdom. Under that system, the entity will be taking money in from the system users and crediting an account for them from which payments can be made. Since the money so taken will normally be repayable to the system users at any time, there seems to be a strong argument that the system operator will, unless authorised, find itself in breach of the FSMA restriction on deposit taking, and thus committing a criminal offence. One possible qualification to this conclusion relates to what the operator does with the float of money which derives from the deposits made by its customers. In particular, that there will only be a breach of the FSMA under Article 5 if that float is either lent to others or any other activity of the business is financed wholly or to a material extent out of the capital of, or interest on, the float. The difficulty with this is that most system operators will look to interest on the float as an important source of income to make their business plan work. Additionally, there is no clear delineation of what "to a material extent" actually means. Finally, it is not clear whether "lent to others" would include placing the relevant monies on deposit with a bank.

For a non-U.K. entity operating overseas but from time to time issuing value to U.K. customers, a critical question will be whether any deposits which it is taking are taken "in the U.K.". This is because the FSMA limits its territorial reach to deposit-taking actually occurring in the United Kingdom. The use of agents in the United Kingdom to accept deposits from U.K. persons can be problematic in this respect.

11.12.4 Deposit taking and cash-based systems

The position of the value issuer under a cash-based system is somewhat less clear. There **11–057** are some commentators who take the view that the issuer of value under a cash-based system is not really taking deposits—*i.e.* they are not accepting sums of money on terms that those sums will be repaid, even if the value issued is redeemable at any time. Instead they argue that what is occurring is a "sale" of the electronic value acquired by the system's customers. It could even be argued that such sales of value can benefit from the exclusion in Article 9 of the Regulated Activities Order for monies accepted in return for the issue of debt securities, on the grounds that the electronic value issued is an electronic form of acknowledgement of indebtedness. However, this might not be a happy argument for an electronic value issuer to run since, although it might save them from the application of the deposit-taking regime, it would place them right in the middle of the FSMA's regime relating to the issue of, and all types of dealing with, investments in the nature of securities. Other commentators observe that, if accepting money from the public on the basis of a promise to repay it constitutes deposit-taking, there is no reason why it should cease to constitute deposit-taking simply because it is accompanied by the issue of electronic tokens which can be used by the customer when they, or an assignee from them, want to demand repayment. Unfortunately, there is no case law authority to resolve this debate but, to a degree, at least, the debate is currently being overtaken by events in the form of the implementation of the Electronic Money Institutions Directive. This is discussed in the following paragraphs.

11.12.5 The Electronic Money Institutions Directive

11–058   The regulatory framework concerning electronic money in the United Kingdom and elsewhere in the E.U. is set to undergo significant change when a recent E.C. Directive is implemented into U.K. law and the national law of the other member states. The directive concerned is Directive 2000/46 on the taking up, pursuit of and prudential supervision of the business of electronic money institutions (the "EMI Directive") which is required to be implemented in the United Kingdom (and all other E.U. member states) by the end of April 2002. The primary purpose of the EMI Directive is to create an authorisation and regulation structure for the issue of electronic money. The idea is that this structure will give non-bank institutions a clear right to be issuers (in place of the previously existing legal uncertainty) but only provided that they meet the necessary authorisation criteria and comply with certain rules in relation to the operation of their business. This Directive needs to be read in conjunction with the parallel Directive 2000/28 which adds electronic money institutions to the definition of "credit insitutions" for certain (but not all) purposes.

11.12.6 What is an EMI and what is "electronic money"

11–059   The EMI Directive introduces a new concept of an "electronic money institution" which is defined as "an undertaking or any other legal person which issues a means of payment in the form of electronic money". The concept of electronic money is defined as "monetary value as represented by a claim on the issuer which is:

  (i)   stored on an electronic device;

  (ii)   issued on receipt of funds of an amount not less in value than the monetary value issued;

  (iii) accepted as means of payment by undertakings other than the issuer."

One of the recitals to the Directive describes electronic money as "a surrogate for coins and notes". Being only a recital, this description does not form part of the definition, but it is instructive. At a first look, this seems to be a wide ranging definition which should catch all the types of scheme currently thought of as electronic cash. However, on a closer look it becomes apparent that value issued under a purely account-based system may not necessarily be caught within the definition of "electronic money". An account-based system does not have to issue monetary tokens so there is in fact no need for any "value" to be "stored on an electronic device". Even the wording of the recital may not help since account based systems are not really "a surrogate for coins or notes", given that they do not involve the free circulation of negotiable instruments; they are rather more of a surrogate for debit card transfers or cheques.

11–060   If the EMI Directive is to have its intended effect of creating a new framework for all types of electronic money, these definitional issues will need to be overcome. For the time being, however, it should be noted by any potential issuer of money planning to rely on the Directive (and so avoid being subject to the more rigorous regime on deposit-taking), that it may be important to structure its product in such a way as to make it fit as closely as possible within the definition of "electronic money". For example, a primarily account based system may be well advised to structure its technical solution so as to ensure that its customers appear to hold "coins" on their hard drive or smartcard rather than just having account balances.

An electronic money institution which is duly authorised to operate in any E.U. member state will have a passport to provide the same product in other member states.

11.12.7 Waivers

The Directive envisages that member states will be allowed to grant waivers from its application to certain types of scheme, provided that they operate only within the national boundaries of the member state concerned. At the time of writing, the FSA has announced that it does intend to implement most of the waivers in the United Kingdom although the exact scope of what will be introduced remains unclear. The waivers envisaged by the Directive are: **11–061**

(a) **Small schemes:** schemes where the total issued value does not normally exceed Euro 5 million and never exceeds Euro 6 million;

(b) **Only same-group acceptors of value:** schemes where the acceptance in payment of the value issued is restricted to persons in the same corporate group as the issuer (schemes where value is accepted in payment only by the issuer itself are outside the scope of the Directive altogether because they do not involve any "money" in the first place; they may, however, still involve deposit taking);

(c) **Limited acceptors of value:** schemes where the acceptance in payment of the value issued is restricted to a limited number of undertakings which can be clearly distinguished by:

(i) their location in the same premises or other limited local area; or

(ii) a close financial or business relationship with the issuer such as a common marketing or distribution scheme.

11.12.8 Supervision of EMIs and requirements for authorisation

If an issuer of electronic value decides to obtain authorisation as an EMI, it should be noted that the EMI Directive imposes a number of restrictions on the initial authorisation of EMIs and the way in which they subsequently carry on business. In particular: **11–062**

(a) **Business restriction:** An EMI cannot carry on any business other than running the relevant scheme and other ancillary business. There is a specific prohibition on the provision of credit.

(b) **Minimum capital:** an EMI must have a minimum of own capital equal to the greater of:

(i)   Euro 1 million; and
(ii)   between 2 and 5 per cent of the amount of its electronic money liabilities
        (see below).

(c)   **Investment of the float:** an EMI is subject to restrictions on what it can do with
      the float of money yielded by selling electronic value. It is limited to highly liquid
      and very safe investments. There are two classes of these, called 0 per cent-
      weighted and 20 per cent-weighted. The 20 per cent-weighted assets are
      generally more risky than those that are 0 per cent-weighted and once more than
      40 per cent of the float is invested in 20 per cent-weighted assets, the own capital
      requirement increases from 2 per cent of electronic money liabilities on a straight
      line basis until it is 5 per cent if all such investment is in 20 per cent weighted
      assets.

(d)   **Supervision:** EMIs will be subject to supervision by the Financial Services
      Authority, but it is intended that the supervision will be with a ''lighter touch''
      than that applied to banks. Such supervision is expected, however, to cover such
      things as the resistance of the value issuer's system to fraud, technological
      collapse and money laundering and its compliance with such things as data
      protection laws. It will undoubtedly also include an element of verification of the
      suitability of persons controlling the EMI to run it (covering both competence and
      integrity issues).

11.12.9 Unauthorised schemes after the EMI Directive

11–063   With the introduction of the EMI Directive throughout the E.U., there will be
considerable pressure for any issuer of electronic money to bring their scheme either
within the new regime or within the deposit-taking authorisation regime (requiring
authorisation as a bank). It is unlikely that regulators will want to countenance the
existence of schemes operating within the E.U. which are argued to fall outside both
schemes of regulation but nonetheless involve the taking of money from members of the
public. It will be interesting to see whether the introduction of the EMI Directive
genuinely opens up the field for competition in the electronic cash domain.

11.14 Should true electronic money offer payment anonymity?

11–064   In the banking world as it stands at the moment, most medium- and large-scale fund
movements will depend on the alteration of entries in the books of trusted third parties,
i.e. banks and credit card companies. As a result, each such transaction will therefore
leave an audit trail. Considerable efforts are necessary to obscure or erase any such trail.
On the other hand, the transfer of electronic value under a true electronic cash system
needs no book entries with third parties and can thus be structured so that no audit trail
is left as the value is moved around. Essentially, an audit trail feature would need to be
built into a true electronic cash scheme rather than being an intrinsic feature of it.
    It is clear that the widespread acceptance of true electronic cash may, therefore, have
considerable significance for those who wish to conceal the movement of funds for
unlawful purposes—and for those who are charged with the duty of trying to control
them. To give just two examples:

- If money requiring laundering could be converted into electronic cash, it might thereafter become extremely difficult if not impossible to trace. It could be moved between jurisdictions in potentially unlimited amounts or in a series of very small amounts at the touch of a button.

- In countries such as the United Kingdom, the fact that the vast majority of payments leave a clear audit trail is a significant obstacle to tax evasion. If the advent of electronic cash means that it becomes possible to make many more payments on a cash basis, it seems likely seriously to undermine the ability of tax authorities to keep track of payments and levy the taxes which ought to be due. Essentially, the black economy could become easier to operate.

System operators such as Mondex are alive to these issues and have incorporated in their system safeguards such as a restriction on the maximum amount that can be held on any card. There are those who argue that such steps are not enough and that more steps must be taken to build safeguards into any true electronic cash system which is allowed to operate in the United Kingdom. The next obvious step is to build into electronic cash systems devices which remove or limit the anonymity that such systems can in principle offer to both payers and payees. This can be done at least in part by ensuring that the devices which hold electronic value identify their owner whenever they effect a payment transaction and that such devices also keep a record of past inward and outward transactions which they have effected, including the identity of the counterparty. The Mondex smart card is issued to an identified account holder and is said to keep a record of the last ten transactions it has effected. It is understood, however, that such cards could be configured to hold records of considerably more transactions than ten and even to download their transaction information each time that they are linked to the issuer's system, *e.g.* when reloaded at an automated teller machine or over the telephone. **11–065**

Criminals have shown themselves to be a resourceful and highly adaptable breed when it comes to new technology and there is every reason to think that they will be quick to find ways to add the abuse of a new payment system to their armoury of criminal devices. Against this background there might at first seem to be irrefutable arguments for minimising the payee/payer anonymity that electronic cash payments can offer to the greatest extent possible. **11–066**

On the other hand, respected commentators have identified significant potential civil liberties risks in such an approach.[6] They start by stressing the obvious but important point that if we cannot pay for anything anonymously, then we cease to be able to buy anything anonymously. From this, they construct a disturbing picture in three stages.

First they point out that with virtually all retailing moving in the direction of automation, retailers are starting to have the ability to create and store away a complete record of all the sales they make, including the name of the buyer. Buyer anonymity is obviously not possible when payment is made using such devices as credit cards. If traditional cash ceases to exist and electronic cash replaces it, buyer anonymity will be impossible unless electronic cash itself offers such a possibility. **11–067**

This in turn gives rise to the possibility that it would, in principle, be possible to construct a complete record of a person's spending by consulting the databases of the retailers with whom he or she has spent money. Although this may sound like a difficult and time consuming task, it is pointed out that "data mining" techniques, together with the linking of all retailer systems through networks such as the Internet, mean that this could actually become a very easy and virtually instantaneous task.

11–068   The final piece of the jigsaw is the fact that access to written information is becoming less hardcopy and more on-line based. So, in the future we may no longer buy a newspaper but instead download articles which we think sound interesting from the newspaper's on-line server. As we will pay-as-we-read, the consumer profiling that "data mining" may permit will be able to extend beyond what we buy to what we are reading, and therefore thinking.

An argument that appropriate data protection legislation can deal with such concerns is not entirely convincing. The consumer may justifiably be concerned that such legislation will contain exceptions that permit access to relevant data by government bodies. They may also be sceptical as to whether such legislation will always be complied with by information gatherers and processors. True protection, it could be said, lies in the information not being collected in the first place rather than its use being restricted once it is in existence.

So what emerges is a conflict between the needs of law enforcement and the protection of the privacy of the individual. It is not a technical issue or one which can be left simply to the regulators of electronic money to resolve: it is an issue which requires a well-informed public debate.

11.15 Conclusion

11–069   The area of payment on the Internet is one of potentially rapid change. It is likely that credit, charge and debit cards will retain their current dominance for some time to come. They have considerable appeal for medium-to-large value purchases made both on and off the Internet. The use of such things as subscription-based charging models or account pre-funding can sometimes be used to circumvent the micropayments problem. However, they cannot easily be made to work for consumer-to-consumer transfers.

True electronic cash is a real threat of competition for the future and would appear particularly well suited to low value payments on the Internet. For international acceptance, it may need to be underwritten by a suitably widely recognised and trusted body or bodies and particularly significant in this respect is the involvement, for example, of Mastercard in acquiring Mondex. On the other hand, where used for only small payments, end-users may be less concerned about the credit standing of their issuer.

11–070   So far as its legal status is concerned, issues such as the effect of the use of electronic cash by a thief do give rise to some thorny problems. It seems possible that legislation will be necessary to give the new cash the same protections as have been afforded for centuries to its physical counterpart. From a regulatory point of view, there are some difficult and highly political questions to be tackled in relation to whether payment anonymity should be permitted.

In the middle of this battleground are symbols which use specially created software and hardware to offer payment solutions along EFTPOS lines. Provided that they achieve sufficient market penetration, these systems are capable of being very cost-effective for low value payments and can also offer value-added services (*e.g.* merchant identification) which true electronic cash systems cannot.

For those setting out to provide alternative cash systems, the current dominance of conventional payment cards is a concern. However, there are needs which they do not fulfil and in these areas we can expect to see alternative models continuing to exist to satisfy end-user demand.

1. [1854] Macq H.L. Cas. 512.
2. [1985] 3 W.L.R. 317, PC.
3. [2000] 2 All E.R. (Comm.) 346.
4. [1918] A.C. 777.
5. [1993] 1 W.L.R. 1229.
6. For an excellent analysis of the arguments on this issue, see A Michael Froomkin's article "Flood Control on the Information Ocean: Living With Anonymity, Digital Cash and Distributed Databases" in the Spring 1996 edition of the University of Pittsburgh *Journal of Law and Commerce*, Vol. 15, Issue 2.

12

Prohibited and Regulated Activities

12.1 Introduction

In this Chapter we examine various fields in which the Internet has presented particular challenges to law enforcement agencies and to the regulators of licensed industries. These encompass traditional media laws such as obscenity and contempt of court, regulated industries such as gambling, pharmaceuticals and financial services, and encryption—a topic that the Internet has thrust into the limelight. We also touch on advertising regulation.

    We start, however, with a policy-oriented discussion of the ways in which governments and others have responded, and may in the future respond, to the cross-border nature of the Internet. This is a companion to Chapter 6, in which we discussed jurisdiction in civil matters. Here we address at a more general policy level the consequences, in particular for freedom of speech, of different rule-making approaches to the cross-border nature of the Internet. This is an area in which legal rules that have worked well in the off-line environment may have completely different consequences in the on–line world and so may require re-examination from first principles.

12–001

12.2 Cross-border content

Now a mainstream communication medium, the Internet has entered the consciousness of governments, non-governmental organisations and law enforcement agencies around the world. Many attempts have been made to enforce national laws against content transmitted internationally across the Internet. The relationship between national laws and the international nature of the Internet has become increasingly strained. As a result, attention has turned to the international legal framework within which communication takes place on the Internet. Discussion of the framework and suggestions for changes to it (including the possibility of an international convention or similar framework to govern use of the Internet) emanate from a variety of constituencies with differing interests and motivations. In this section we look at possible forms of an international convention to govern the flow of content on the Internet. We also examine the types of national laws and regulations which could inspire the content of a convention and the possible implications for freedom of speech on the Internet of such international action.

12–002

12.2.1 Why international action?

12–003   Pressure for an international framework to govern the Internet emanates from a variety of constituencies. These have different, often conflicting, motivations and self-interest so that even if all are agreed on the need for an international framework, that masks fundamental disagreement on what that framework should seek to achieve and what it should contain. Here are five factors that motivate the desire for an international framework.

Uncertainty and cost

12–004   The task of copy-clearing a Web site in every jurisdiction from which it can be accessed is extremely expensive and may, due to the wide variety of national laws, be impossible. If it were simply a matter of complying with the most restrictive standard for each type of potential liability the task could theoretically be achieved, even if the resulting content were so bland as to be commercially useless. But in some areas (especially in highly regulated industries) national regimes are so detailed that there is no lowest denominator of content common to all. Compliance with all regimes is then impossible, and the publisher has to resort to devices of uncertain legal efficacy—territory disclaimers, entry screens and so on—to minimise the risk of civil or criminal sanctions in a country in which he may have no commercial interest. Commercial users of the Internet have a clear interest in action which would reduce the cost and risks of publishing on the Internet. An effective international framework would have the potential to deliver that.

Extra-territorial effect

12–005   Incidents in which national powers have exerted authority over foreign content on the Internet, such as the German CompuServe and *Radikal* cases in 1995 and 1996 respectively and the French Yahoo! case in 2000, have given rise to concern over extra-territoriality as the effects of such actions spill out across the Internet without regard for national borders. Such concern has arisen notwithstanding the oft-repeated belief that national action to prohibit content can never be effective because, as expressed by John Gilmore (a co-founder of the Electronic Frontier Foundation), the Internet interprets censorship as damage and routes around it.

While that belief may to some extent be true of the content itself, it is not true of the human originators, publishers and distributors of the content. These people and companies exist in the real world, not in cyberspace. In practice they (and their directors and employees) may be subject to the criminal laws of the jurisdictions in which they reside or have assets, to which they travel or to which they can be extradited; and may be subject to the civil laws of countries whose judgments can be enforced against their persons and assets. Extra-territoriality is therefore a real concern, at least to those who do not wish to spend their days behind the borders of some content haven from which they cannot be extradited.

12–006   If an international convention could be devised which created rules for cyberspace independent of national regimes, then content on the Internet and its human progenitors could both be insulated from extra-territorial effects. Such a scheme would be attractive to those who regard cyberspace as a domain which ought to be subject only to its own rules. On the other hand, there can be no guarantee that an international convention would take a liberal form. As we discuss below, a convention cannot be value-neutral as to content standards. It must either embody its own content standards or have the effect of preferring some national laws over others. Even a convention that addresses only jurisdiction, purporting to have nothing to say about substantive law, will have different practical consequences for substantive law, depending on how the jurisdiction rules are written.[1] Since, realistically, a formal convention could only emerge from a multilateral inter–governmental process,[2] a convention setting up cyberspace as an independent dominion would not necessarily embody rules and values more liberal than those of many restrictive national regimes who would participate in such discussions.

Fear of a foreign flood

If users of the Internet fear extra-territoriality, governments fear the opposite: that the Internet will render their laws impotent as citizens gain access to material originating outside the jurisdiction which local laws cannot reach. Such concerns arise acutely in matters of culture (especially attitudes to alcohol, gambling, exposure of flesh and protection of language) and political and religious dissent. Much of the pressure for international rules to govern the Internet originates from governments anxious to preserve the efficacy of their local laws. **12–007**

The urge to regulate

Previous forms of new media such as television and radio have been subjected to controls of a fundamentally different type from those applying to old media such as the printing press. It has for many years been regarded as acceptable to require new media to operate under licence from the state, under the immediate control of a regulatory body (such as the Independent Television Commission or the Radio Authority) empowered with a wide degree of discretion to devise detailed codes of practice to achieve general objectives laid out in the relevant legislation. Those objectives have often been highly restrictive, for instance in their requirements of political impartiality.[3] **12–008**

Such a regulatory regime, backed up by the sanction of withdrawal of licence, contrasts with the freedom traditionally accorded to the print media, who can set up and operate without licence[4] and are in the main subject only to general laws applied and interpreted by an independent judiciary.[5]

The licensing and regulatory model has also been used in the telecommunications industry to govern provision of telecommunication services. So widespread have such regulatory schemes become that there is sometimes almost an unspoken assumption that a regulatory scheme is necessary and appropriate for any new medium of communication. Existing new media regulators are frequently involved in the debate about appropriate laws for the Internet, and occasionally their existing areas of authority may touch upon Internet issues. That has certainly occurred in the broadcast area, where the Independent Television Commission has issued guidelines for websites operated by regulated broadcasters,[6] and where the question whether the scope of the Broadcasting Act 1990 could extend to some types of Internet content occasionally causes anxiety.[7] More alarmingly there is a precedent for OFTEL, the telecommunications regulator (whose brief under section 3 of the Telecommunications Act 1984 makes no explicit reference to content carried by telecommunication systems, restricting itself to the "prices charged for, and the quality and variety of, telecommunication services"), involving itself in approving rules about content. This occurred in the area of premium rate telephone services, in which through a telecommunications licence amendment following a Monopolies and Mergers Commission report OFTEL took powers to approve codes of practice for the provision of chatline services. The approved codes of practice (submitted for approval by ICSTIS, the Independent Committee for the supervision of Standards of Telephone Information Services) included relatively restrictive content rules.[8] OFTEL **12–009** justified its involvement in this area as reducing the "impairment of quality of service" associated with chatlines, which had been identified by the MMC as being to the detriment of the public interest.[9] ICSTIS is now lauded by the government as a prime example of "self-regulation".[10]

Certainly the predominance of the regulatory model has subverted the language, so that the concept of content being "regulated" has gained ascendancy, obscuring the distinction between laws and discretionary regulation. The debate about the laws that should govern content on the Internet is usually conducted as a discussion of the appropriate form of "content regulation". The U.K. government has even, in the Communications White Paper of December 2000,[11] referred to general content laws as "tier zero", or "negative" "content regulation". Phrases such as these obscure the important distinction between on the one hand a regulatory regime founded on licensing or similar principles, and on the other the freedom to publish without prior permission from a government body, subject only to general laws adjudicated upon by independent courts and applicable to anyone who chooses to publish.

12–010   Concepts such as co-regulation are similarly of concern when applied to the content field. Co-regulation was defined by the government in "*e-commerce@its.best.uk*" as follows:

> "Government defines the public policy objectives that need to be secured, but tasks industry to design and operate self-regulatory solutions and stands behind industry ready to take statutory action if necessary."[12]

The idea that individual citizens and companies, whipped on by the threat of statutory action, are there to act as the servants of government in achieving its policy objectives is wholly out of place in a discussion of content laws in a liberal society. The distinction between self-regulation and co-regulation can be hard to fathom where self-regulation is backed up with statutory powers, as with the new ICSTIS scheme noted above.

In the USA the Citizens Internet Empowerment Coalition, one of the parties challenging certain sections of the Communications Decency Act (CDA) in Philadelphia,[13] based its challenge on the proposition that "the Internet is newspaper, not TV". The case was considered both at first instance and on appeal by the U.S. Supreme Court. The distinction between newspaper and television was taken up in the judgment of District Judge Dalzell (one of three judgments of the first instance court), who in a section of his judgment dealt with "medium-specific analysis" of the constitutionality of the CDA. He commented that the government's argument relying on the *Pacifica*[14] decision assumed that "what is good for broadcasting is good for the Internet". He pointed out that in *Turner Broadcasting System Inc v. FCC*[15] the Supreme Court declined to adopt the broadcast rationale for the medium of cable television, citing the fundamental technical differences between broadcast and cable transmission. This, said the judge, meant that the justification for the constitutionality of the broadcast rules arose out of scarcity of the medium, not the end product that the viewer watches. Therefore the question had to be addressed whether the government had the power to regulate protected speech at all, not just whether the CDA was a constitutional exercise of that power.

12–011   The judge commented that far from justifying broadcast-style regulation, his examination of the special characteristics of Internet communication led him to conclude that:

> "The Internet deserves the broadest possible protection from government-imposed,

content-based regulation. If 'the First Amendment erects a virtually insurmountable barrier between government and the print media', Tornillo, 418 U.S. at 259 (White J. concurring), even though the print medium fails to achieve the hoped-for diversity in the marketplace of ideas, then that "insurmountable barrier" must also exist for a medium that succeeds in achieving that diversity.'

District Judge Dalzell concluded his judgment thus:

"As the most participatory form of mass speech yet developed, the Internet deserves the highest protection from governmental intrusion ... The absence of governmental regulation of Internet content has unquestionably produced a kind of chaos, but as one of the plaintiffs' experts put it with such resonance at the hearing: 'what achieved success was the very chaos that the Internet is. The strength of the Internet is that chaos'. Just as the strength of the Internet is chaos, so the strength of our liberty depends upon the chaos and cacophony of the unfettered speech the First Amendment protects."

The Supreme Court, holding that the challenged parts of the CDA were unconstitutional, **12–012** also engaged in a medium-specific analysis. The Supreme Court pointed out that the "vast democratic fora" of the Internet had not been subject to the type of government supervision and regulation that had attended the broadcast industry, and that the Internet was not as "invasive" as radio or television. The court also pointed out that 'unlike the conditions that prevailed when Congress first authorised regulation of the broadcast spectrum, the Internet can hardly be considered a 'scarce' expressive commodity." The court went on to state:

"This dynamic, multi-faceted category of communication includes not only traditional print and news services, but also audio, video and still images, as well as interactive, real-time dialogue. Through the use of chat rooms, any person with a phone line can become a town crier with a voice that resonates farther than it could from any soapbox. Through the use of Web pages, mail exploders, and newsgroups, the same individual can become a pamphleteer. As the District Court found, 'the content on the Internet is as diverse as human thought' ... We agree with its conclusion that our cases provide no basis for qualifying the level of First Amendment scrutiny that should be applied to this medium."

The Supreme Court has, at the lowest, put down a marker challenging any assumption that the Internet should be subject to broadcast-style licensing and regulation. The findings raise the question whether the USA would be constitutionally incapable of adhering to an international Internet convention based on licensing and regulation. They are also of more domestic relevance now that the United Kingdom has incorporated the European Convention of Human Rights into its domestic law.

There has been some recognition in the United Kingdom of the fact that Internet is not **12–013** a broadcast medium. In its 1998 report *The Multi-media Revolution*[16] the House of Commons Culture Media and Sport Select Committee remarked:

"The Internet will increasingly become a platform for audio–visual content barely distinguishable from broadcast content. This does not mean it can be subject to regulation comparable to broadcasting. Self-regulation through service providers is in its early stages and should be encouraged. We are far from persuaded that any particular legislative provision for regulation for Internet content (as opposed to legislation to clarify the application of the current general law to the Internet) is viable."

The Committee repeated this position in its Second Report of 2001, *The Communications White Paper*[17]:

"Although the Internet is being used and will be used increasingly as a medium for audio and video material, the Internet is fundamentally different to traditional broadcast media. Whereas there is closely controlled and licensed access to broadcast media, there is no spectrum scarcity on the Internet and no tradition of licensing. The Internet has flourished with a minimum of regulation, partly because the Internet first developed in the United States, a country that provides specific constitutional protection for freedom of speech. We have noted previously that, due to the almost infinite scale and international character of the Internet, content regulation of the traditional kind is not viable for the Internet."[18]

Order and chaos

12–014   The last driver is the natural tendency of, especially, lawyers to want to tidy up chaos and replace it with order. The Internet is undoubtedly chaotic—that is how it grew up—and has minimal centrally imposed authority. When addressing this chaos, there may be a desire to create structures designed to impose order in a top-down fashion. Whether or not that is wise, the tendency exists and can be expected to contribute to calls for an international structure to bring order to the Internet.

While the temptation to try to impose top-down order on the Internet continues to attract some, others are more sanguine about the prospects of succeeding in such an endeavour. Although, as we have noted, the adage that the Internet routes around censorship tends to ignore the fact that laws can be enforced against people and assets, in a very real sense the Internet is able to route around bad laws. A local dispute can, as in the Nottinghamshire County Council (JET Report)[19] and *Radikal*[20] cases suddenly become a worldwide and insoluble problem as Internet sites mirror the content under threat. Even if a conviction or judgment is obtained initially, the resulting outcry (especially over attempts to enforce local laws in ways that have extra-territorial effect in countries in which the content is legal) is often enough to stimulate a change in the law in due course.[21]

12–015   As a matter of probable outcomes, it may be thought that the cause of freedom of speech on the Internet is better served by the current chaos than by any achievable form of international convention. As a matter of pragmatic politics, the potential ignominy of being associated with futile laws may be expected to act as a brake on some of the more ill-considered proposals to legislate for (or against) the Internet. For instance, the House of Commons Culture Media and Sport Select Committee remarked in its 1998 MultiMedia Revolution report:

"The potential of the Internet as an engine of economic growth and social progress is enormous; it would be an act of self-indulgence to purport to jeopardise this unique opportunity by means of a virtually unenforceable law."[22]

Illustrations of the effects of some of the drivers outlined above can be found in the following examples of national enforcement and legislation.

12.2.2 National action—the urge to regulate

Australia
Australia is an example of a country which, in the teeth of controversy,[23] has gone down the discretionary content regulation route. Its legislation[24] is less draconian than, for instance, the Singapore model discussed below, since it does not implement a full licensing model. However the legislation does, as well as putting in place a complex content-rating system, permit the Australian Broadcasting Authority in certain circumstances to impose content standards on Internet service providers and content hosts, backed up by criminal sanctions.

12–016

European Union
The European Commission published, on December 3, 1997, a Green Paper entitled *Convergence of the Telecommunications, Media and Information Technology Sectors, and the Implications for Regulation. Towards an Information Society Approach.*[25] The Green Paper raised a series of wide-ranging questions, largely stemming from the challenge to existing regulatory structures (in the regulated industries of telecommunications and broadcasting) posed by the cutting of traditional ties between content and delivery channels. It could no longer be assumed, for instance, that voice telephony is restricted to the public switched telephone network, or that video is restricted to traditional broadcast and cable channels.

12–017

The Green Paper and speeches by the then Commissioner Martin Bangemann floated the possibility of a European Communications Act and a single regulator, possibly at a European level, which would include content in their scope. Commissioner Bangemann also suggested an International Charter for global communications, in particular the Internet. The proposed content of such a Charter was unclear.

On February 4, 1998, the Commission in its Communication on the Need for Strengthened International Co-ordination[26] suggested that an International Charter would be a "multi-lateral understanding on a method of coordination to remove obstacles for the global electronic marketplace". It would not define the key issues to be solved as such, but contain an "understanding on how a process of strengthened international coordination should be organised, with as wide as possible a participation of the international community." The Commission suggested that a Charter could be agreed by or in the course of 1999. This did not occur.

12–018

In its Proposal for a Directive on a common regulatory framework for electronic communications networks and services,[27] the Commission has now excluded content from the definition of "electronic communications service". The Commission recognises that regulation of content should be separate from regulation of transmission.[28]

Other Community measures, such as the Action Plan on promoting safer use of the Internet,[29] emphasise the development of guidelines at European level for self-regulatory codes of conduct, through building of consensus. It also emphasises the development of hotlines for reporting illegal content and of filtering and rating systems. The Convergence Green Paper saw as a "risk" for the Internal Market the greater possibility for divergent approaches in developing self-regulation, unless co-ordinated to some degree at Community level. The most detailed proposals for the content of codes of conduct are

12–019

contained in the Council Recommendation of September 24, 1998 on the protection of minors and human dignity.[30] This followed the Commission Communication of November 18, 1997 on the follow-up to the Green Paper on the Protection of Minors and Human Dignity in Audiovisual and Information Services.[31] The Recommendation, while purporting to take into account the voluntary nature of self-regulation, distinguishes between legal content which is liable to harm minors by impairing their physical, mental or moral development, and illegal content which is offensive to human dignity. It sets out detailed "indicative guidelines" for national self–regulatory frameworks including the content of codes of conduct. This includes, in relation to both types of content, matters such as information for users, conditions of supply of filtering tools, complaint handling by hotlines and (in the case of illegal content offensive to human dignity) co-operation with police and judicial authorities. For content that may be harmful to minors the guidelines also suggest that codes of practice should address the conditions when protection measures should be put in place, such as a warning page, visual or sound signal; descriptive labeling and/or classification of contents; and systems to check the age of users.

Germany

12–020   The German Multimedia Act of August 1, 1997 provides that "teleservices" falling within it shall not be subject to any licensing requirement. However, the Act may permit Broadcasting Authorities deriving power from the German states to assume broadcast regulatory jurisdiction over a potentially wide range of material.

United Kingdom

12–021   In December 2000 the government issued a White Paper, *A New Future for Communications* (commonly known as the "Communications White Paper"). This primarily addresses the challenges to the regulatory structure in broadcasting and telecommunications brought about by convergence. It proposes the creation of a new statutory regulatory body, the Office of Communications (OFCOM) to replace OFTEL, the ITC, and some other existing regulatory bodies. OFCOM would be responsible for all aspects of regulation, ranging from competition to content.

The impact of the proposal on Internet content is unclear. At various points the White Paper suggests that the appropriate approach for Internet content is self-regulation. However, the White Paper is vague as to whether that means that OFCOM would have no jurisdiction over Internet content, or whether it would have jurisdiction but would be expected to exercise it sparingly. Indeed, at one point (para. 1.3.8) the White Paper alludes to the possibility of OFCOM having statutory back-up powers to intervene in respect of Internet content. The general content standards and factors propounded in the White Paper (including concepts such as consumer protection, generally accepted community standards, unfairness and impartiality) are inappropriate for a medium which (as District Judge Dalzell commented in the U.S. CDA case), "deserves the highest degree of First Amendment protection" and is a haven of both individual speech on an unprecedented scale and of the commercial press.

12–022   It does not take a John Milton to appreciate that to delegate to a statutory agency the discretionary power to devise content rules for the Internet, backed up with statutory powers and ultimately (no doubt) criminal sanctions, would represent a flagrant intrusion into fundamental principles of freedom of expression. The Commons Select Committee on Culture, Media and Sport, in its Second Report of the 1999–2000 Session,[32] criticised the parts of the White Paper that could be interpreted as going beyond the principle that the general law should apply online as offline. It recommended that OFCOM be explicitly excluded by statute from imposing regulatory obligations relating to Internet content and recommended that the government should clarify that it does not envisage any form of co-regulation of the Internet. It remains to be seen whether the government and Parliament will heed this wise advice.

12.2.3 National action—illegality, language, culture, political and religious expression

Governments of some countries, anxious to preserve the cultural identity of their citizenry, legislate for matters such as language. Or they may legislate against content that is especially sensitive, often for historical reasons. Others have simply been prepared to enforce local laws against overseas Internet content, regardless of the consequences for other countries with more liberal laws.

12–023

Governments of other countries have attempted to restrict access to content that they deem politically unacceptable or subversive, or as undermining official cultural values. Generally, details of such actions can be found at the web sites of organisations such as Amnesty International,[33] the Freedom Forum,[34] Reporters sans Frontieres[35] and the Committee to Protect Jounalists.[36]

Some examples follow of all the types of activity mentioned.

Burma (Myanmar)
On September 21, 1996 a Computer Science Development Law was announced. It provided that anyone who wished to import, keep in his possession or utilise a computer for purposes other than teaching or transacting business must obtain prior permission from the Ministry of Communications, Posts and Telegraphs. Further, anyone who wished to set up a computer network or connect a link inside the computer network must also obtain permission. Contraventions were punishable by from seven to fifteen years' imprisonment and a fine. Full details of the legislation are contained in the Amnesty International Country Report for Myanmar, September—December 1996.[37]

12–024

China
China is reputed to have issued more than sixty sets of regulations governing Internet content since 1995.[38] These included in February 1996 a requirement for service providers and users to register with public security departments. In December 1997 the China Ministry of Public Security promulgated new Computer Information Network and Internet Security, Protection and Management Regulations. The regulations provided, among other things, that connecting network units, entry point units and corporations that use computer information networks and the Internet should, within 30 days of opening the network connection, register with a unit designated by the local Public Security organisation.

12–025

Recent activities have including closing down over 2,000 cyber-cafes and various arrests. Visitors to web site chatrooms may be warned that if Chinese nationals break the local content laws within the chatroom the web site proprietor is obliged to report them to the Public Security Bureau.[39]

Cuba
For an account of the Cuban government's attempts to restrict Internet access by Cuban citizens, see *Wired* Magazine, Issue 6.02 February 1998.

12–026

France

12–027   France has well-known legislation, the Loi Toubon, designed to preserve the use of the French language in public places. Two pressure groups, Defence of the French Language and Future of the French language, sued the French branch of a U.S. college, the Georgia Tech Lorraine International School, because its Web site was written only in English. In 1997 the action was dismissed on a technicality.

The French government has been active in lobbying the European Commission to ensure that cultural issues are fully reflected in European multimedia policy. The problem of culturally based content quotas was raised as a potential barrier to the free flow of information in the NIIT Global Electronic Commerce Framework paper.[40] The E.U. Electronic Commerce Directive (Article 1.6) includes language designed to preserve respect for cultural issues: "This Directive does not affect measures taken at Community or national level, in the respect of Community law, in order to promote cultural and linguistic diversity and to ensure the defence of pluralism."

12–028   In 2000 a French court, in the case of *League against Racism and Anti-Semitism and Union of French Jewish Students v. Yahoo! Inc*,[41] assumed jurisdiction over the U.S. company Yahoo! Inc and ordered it to prevent access to Nazi memorabilia offered for sale by individuals on its yahoo.com on-line auction site, contrary to French law. Yahoo! contended that the court had no jurisdiction and that compliance with the order was impossible since it could not reliably exclude access to the site from France.

The French court found that it had jurisdiction on several bases: first, that the mere display of the items offended against French law; second, that although (as Yahoo! argued) some aspects of the auction site could be regarded as aimed at the USA, that was not true of Nazi memorabilia, which would be of interest to anyone (including French people); third, there was obvious harm to the particular plaintiffs; and fourth, that the yahoo.com site was in any event targeting France, since it used geographical IP address filtering to serve up French language banner advertisements to users who appeared to be come from France. This latter factor was doubly damaging to Yahoo!, since the court relied heavily upon it when assessing Yahoo!'s ability to comply with the order by filtering out users coming from France.

12–029   As to compliance, a three man panel of technical experts was empanelled and asked to consider whether it was technically possible for Yahoo! to comply with the order, and if not to what extent could compliance be achieved.

The panel reported that Yahoo! could exclude about 70 per cent of users emanating from France.[42] It could not achieve 100 per cent for three reasons: first, a number of large ISPs (of which AoL was the best-known example) allocated IP addresses to their users from their bank of U.S. addresses, so that a French AoL user would appear to be accessing Yahoo! from Virginia, USA; second, users of multinational corporate networks similarly would often appear to be accessing from a country other than that in which they were located; thirdly, users could readily make use of anonymising services, which hide the IP address of the user and replace it with another one. Indeed one of the empanelled experts, Mr Ben Laurie, in a personal statement[43] after the judgment, commented that the "rather flakey guess at nationality, using IP address or domain name" could be "trivially circumvented".

12–030   The majority of the expert panel (Vinton Cerf dissenting as the feasibility of geographical filtering) suggested that the filtering effectiveness could be increased to about 90 per cent by requiring a statement of nationality (which the court interpreted to mean geographical origin) in cases of ambiguous IP addresses.

The expert panel also examined the question of how Yahoo! should identify the material to which French users were to be denied access, such as filtering on the item descriptions and on users' search keywords.

On compliance, the court decided that geographical localisation was possible and, in dismissing Yahoo!'s objections that this was a crude tool, relied heavily on Yahoo!'s own use of the technique to serve up banner advertisements to users whom it thought came from France, and on the representations that the court assumed Yahoo! must have made to its advertisers about the effectiveness of that service.

The court also suggested that Yahoo! could rely on delivery addresses for items (although it is not clear how that is relevant, when the mere display of items on the auction site was held to violate French law) and identify the language version of the user's browser. Finally, the court found that Yahoo! had not demonstrated that it would consume significant resources to implement geographical filtering. **12–031**

The court also suggested that if Yahoo! were, at little cost, to prohibit the sale of symbols of Nazism on its site that would have the merit of "satisfying a requirement of ethics and morals which are shared by all democratic societies" and that Yahoo! could implement filtering "if only for the sake of elementary public morals". However, that accords no respect to the fact that the USA (Yahoo!'s home country) places a greater moral value on protecting freedom of expression than it does on obliterating the insignia of Nazism. It suggests that the French court regarded French law as embodying a higher morality than different laws elsewhere in the world and was content for the consequences of its ruling to be visited on the citizens of other countries which do not share the same laws.

Germany

The German authorities have taken action to prevent access to a Dutch Web site hosting a copy of a political magazine. In September 1996, German authorities requested German Internet service providers to block access to a Dutch service provider's site in Holland, which hosted copies of a magazine, *Radikal*. The German authorities considered that issue 154 of this magazine contained material justifying a preliminary suspicion of promoting a terrorist organisation and other offences under the German Criminal Code. The German Public Prosecutor General informed the ICTF (Internet Content Task Force, an association of German on-line providers) that German ISPs could be subject to criminal prosecution for aiding and abetting criminal activities if they continued to allow the pages to be called up via their access points and network nodes. **12–032**

After an exchange of correspondence the ICTF agreed to recommend its members to block access to Access for All (XS4ALL), the Dutch service provider which hosted *Radikal* and thousands of other unrelated pages. The proprietor of Access for All publicly expressed his fear that he could be in danger of arrest if he travelled to Germany. It is understood that the issue of the magazine in question has been removed from Access for All by the user, but that the pages have been mirrored (duplicated) on about 50 other sites around the world. The German authorities also unsuccessfully prosecuted the German MP Angela Marquardt over a Web link to the *Radikal* web site. The prosecution were unable to show that the offending material was present on the target site when Ms Marquardt created the link to it.

Germany was also the location for the notorious *CompuServe/Felix Somm* case. Felix Somm was the local CompuServe manager in Germany. A Munich prosecutor charged him in 1997 with offences under German obscenity legislation, arising out of the accessibility via CompuServe's system in Germany of nearly 300 Usenet newsgroups. The newsgroups were hosted by CompuServe in the USA and were not tailored to different **12–033** countries. In December 1995 CompuServe had, in response to the police action in raiding CompuServe's office, decided to suspend, temporarily, access to the newsgroups. The effect of that action was to suspend access to the newsgroups world-wide through CompuServe's Internet news facilities. Mr Somm's subsequent conviction was overturned on appeal.

Saudi Arabia

12–034   The *San Jose Mercury* on November 4, 1997 reported that Saudi Arabia was planning to introduce Internet access in a way which would prevent "objectionable material that goes against the country's religious and moral values" from being accessible. Local ISPs are routed through a government proxy server. However, as in any country with international telephone facilities, government proxy servers can be bypassed (at a price) by dialling up on an international call to a foreign ISP.

Singapore

12–035   The Singapore authorities introduced in July 1996 a licensing scheme for Internet activities,[44] closely based on a broadcast model. The scheme introduced a class licence governing Internet activities and required all Internet service providers to register with the Singapore Broadcasting Authority (SBA). Certain Internet content providers (*i.e.* anyone providing information on the Web, including Web publishers and server administrators) were also required to register, namely:

- political parties registered in Singapore who provide Web pages;

- groups of persons engaged in political or religious discussions related to Singapore on the Web;

- individuals providing Web pages for political or religious purposes and who are notified by the SBA to register; and

- on-line newspapers targeting sales in Singapore through the Internet and which are notified by the SBA to register.

The SBA stresses that registration "serves to reinforce responsible use of the medium and ensure that discussions are conducted in a mature fashion without harmful intent" and that "political and religious organisations are free to conduct discussions provided they guard against breaking the law or disrupting social harmony".

12–036   Under Clause 11 of the Class Licence a licensee is required to use its best efforts to ensure that its service complies with the Code of Practice and is not used for any purpose, and does not contain any programme, that is against the public interest, public order or national harmony, or offends against good taste or decency. Under Clause 14 of the Class Licence a licensee shall remove material included in its service if the SBA informs it that the material is in breach of the conditions in Clause 11.

The Code of Practice sets out various types of prohibited Internet contents, such as:

- "contents which present information or events in such a way as to alarm or mislead all or any of the public";

- "contents which tend to bring the Government of Singapore into hatred or contempt, or which excite disaffection against the Government of Singapore";

- "contents which propagate permissiveness or promiscuity";

- "contents which depict or propagate sexual perversions such as homosexuality, lesbianism, and paedophilia".

The Singapore authorities have also introduced a proxy server system with major ISPs, with the object of preventing access by technical means to blacklisted Web sites, and require re-sellers to connect to those servers.

12.2.4 Responses to national action

Reconciling international co-operation with freedom of expression

What is the appropriate response to inter-jurisdiction problems, especially where foreign   **12–037** content is regarded as criminal in the state receiving the content? In this context inter-jurisdictional rules are not value neutral, since the rules will necessarily favour more or less liberal content regimes. So is international co-operation to result in indiscriminate mutual enforcement of criminal content laws? If so, the result will be multilateral export to liberal countries of the most restrictive domestic content regimes. The opposite solution, that governments agree to respect the domestic laws of more liberal regimes, is unlikely to be acceptable to governments anxious to prevent foreign material reaching their citizens for political, religious or cultural reasons. Papers such as the E.U. paper on Illegal and Harmful Content on the Internet (see below) tend to suggest that common minimum standards can be agreed and enforced only in limited areas, such as child pornography, trafficking in human beings, racial hatred, terrorism and fraud. Even in these areas there is less consensus than might be expected. Two of the most controversial cases of extra-territoriality discussed above (the German *Radikal* incident and the French Yahoo! case) were within these areas (terrorism and racial hatred respectively).

On October 16, 1996 the European Commission published a Communication to the   **12–038** European Parliament and other European Union institutions discussing the question of Illegal and Harmful Content on the Internet.[45] This document, and a subsequent working party report,[46] recognised the difficulties of taking an international approach without compromising freedom of speech. The Communication drew a line between illegal content (for which greater international co-operation was recommended) and content which might be harmful but not illegal (for which voluntary adoption of rating systems was suggested). The communication commented that:

> "Some third countries have introduced wide-ranging legislation to block all direct access to Internet via access providers by introducing a requirement for 'proxy servers' similar to those used by large organisations for security reasons, combined with centralised blacklisting of documents, for reasons which go far beyond the limited category of illegal content as defined in this communication. Such a restrictive regime is inconceivable for Europe as it would severely interfere with the freedom of the individual and its political traditions."

The subsequent working party report suggested that information on the Internet should be allowed the same free flow as paper-based information, and that any restrictions should respect fundamental rights such as freedom of expression and the right to privacy. It says that any international agreement should be in conformity with fundamental rights and European traditions of free expression.

12–039   The paper "A Framework for Global Electronic Commerce"[47] published by the US Information Infrastructure Task Force (NIIT) also touched on the subject. The "Content" section suggested that the U.S. Administration would pursue negotiations to ensure that measures, policies and regulations that limit the ability of content providers to communicate through the Internet are promulgated only when necessary and implemented in a manner that minimises trade distortion. The paper identified five priority areas of concern: foreign content quotas, regulation of advertising, regulation of content, regulation to prevent fraud, and differences in defining "seditious" material.

The difficulties of reconciling international governmental co-operation with freedom of expression have again become apparent with the proposed Cybercrime Convention (discussed in section 12.9.5 below).

Content blocking

12–040   Another possible response, alluded to in the Communication on Illegal and Harmful Content mentioned above, is the retrograde, and technically difficult, solution of governments or other national authorities seeking to impose technical methods of blocking content at their virtual borders (ie at their domestic ISPs). These were attempted by the Singapore authorities under its Class Licence arrangements and by the German government in the *Radikal* case. The outcome of the French Yahoo! court case provided a clear economic incentive for content providers to choose between complying with the international most restrictive common denominator, or incurring the cost of content filtering and blocking on a nation by nation basis.

Rating and filtering

12–041   The last solution is to rely on a rating-enabling system such as PICS (Platform for Internet Content Selection).[48] PICS allows for the voluntary adoption of multiple criteria upon which to select viewable content. It does not specify the content of rating systems, but defines a technical platform upon which content labeling schemes can be built. The labeling schemes can be built and made available by content providers, access providers, hosts, or even independent third parties such as campaigning organisations who wish to label content according to their own sets of values. PICS, while likely to be acceptable in many countries as a way of dealing with a diversity of views as to what constitutes "harmful" content, is perhaps unlikely to satisfy governments nervous that the voluntary nature of PICS-based rating systems would still permit their citizens to choose to access foreign content regarded as illegal domestically. On the other hand, such a system if widely adopted could perhaps make the third option of compulsory content blocking at virtual borders easier for so minded governments to impose. The potential use of PICS and other rating systems by governments for such purposes is controversial and has been recognised as a serious concern by, for instance, INCORE (see below).

In December 1997 the World Wide Web Consortium (W3C) published PICSRules Version 1.1,[49] a W3C Recommendation which defines a language for writing filtering rules which allow or block access to URLs based on PICS labels that describe those URLs. Such filtering rules are known as "profiles". The PICSRules also allow filtering by URL, independently of PICS labeling. A PICSRule profile could rely on the content provider's own rating, or specify the use of one or more third party PICS rating services, and one or more PICS label bureaus to query for labels.

12–042   The U.K. Internet Watch Foundation, on March 3, 1998, published for consultation a paper proposing the development of a rating system using PICS. The paper promoted the idea of one agreed global system of "objective" PICS labels, to be applied by content providers. That reflected a more restrictive view than that inherent in the PICS system itself which permits, indeed encourages, a multiplicity of rating and labeling systems based on the PICS rating-enabling platform, reflecting a potentially infinite range of user preferences about subject matter. The IWF was "not convinced" of the need for dedicated server-based ratings engines. The concept underlying the paper was that one labeling scheme could and should reflect a single view of "U.K. requirements", to be incorporated into an international approach to rating. The IWF recommended that a variety of profiles be prepared, working with other bodies, but based on the one objective labeling system.

The IWF stated that the system should be based on voluntary rating by content providers, but with a concerted effort by government bodies, internet services providers and other interested parties to encourage the rating of content according to an agreed system.

The IWF is the lead agency in a European consortium of organisations (INCORE[50]— **12–043** Internet Content Rating for Europe) intended to work with the European Union and to establish an international working group on content rating. INCORE's work was funded by the European Commission under the Action Plan on promoting safer use of the Internet and resulted in a Final Report completed in April 2000 and published in June 2000.[51] This report identified the main practical difficulty with current rating and filtering systems as being that too much content is unlabeled and hence (assuming that the browser is so set) blocked by the filter. Existing systems were found not to have attained the necessary critical mass of labeled content to be viable. A critical mass of labeled content is necessary for each language block. The report recommended that the European Commission should support the development of at least one first party labeling system suitable for European consumers. The system should be marketed to European content providers so as to encourage larger numbers of content providers with sites most relevant to children to label them. In addition to self-labeling by content providers, users should have the facility to download third party green lists of sites that, even if they are unlabeled and so would otherwise be blocked, the browser would recognise as permissible. In order to facilitate interoperability of labeling systems and also so as to assist in achieving critical mass, an open source vocabulary of defined descriptions of content should be developed. These should be objective and not include value judgments, that being left to consumer preference. The report suggests that the vocabulary could be overseen by a "Labels Board", which would operate as an international standards body to co-ordinate the process of developing the systems and to monitor their interoperability, quality and scalability. In order to minimise freedom of speech risks (such as governments misusing the systems as a censorship tool), the report suggests a number of measures, including that designers of filtering systems should be discouraged from using content definitions that distinguish between legal and illegal content. The control of illegal content should be addressed by other means, especially the use of hotlines and improved law enforcement. That is consistent with the distinction between illegal and harmful content drawn in the Communication on Illegal and Harmful Content on the Internet discussed above.

12.2.5 Differing approaches to an international convention

An international regime relating to the laws governing illegal Internet content could take **12–044** a number of different forms. Two possible types of international Internet convention are:

first, one designed to define the boundaries of national laws in cyberspace and to reduce the scope for jurisdictional conflict. Secondly, one designed to create an Internet-specific regulatory regime. First, some boundary-oriented approaches:

Country of origin

12–045   This solution is to a limited extent embodied in the Treaty of Rome (see discussion of E.U. Electronic Commerce Directive is Chapter 6). The principle of the internal market within Europe demands that Member States should not use national laws to restrict the free flow of goods and services from other Member States. However, this principle is subject to severe qualification in a number of respects, reflecting the political reality that no country will lightly give up its right to enforce its domestic laws against incoming goods and services. Before the Electronic Commerce Directive, the closest to pure "country of origin" was the regime governing satellite broadcasting within Europe.[52] Essentially, broadcast content cannot be restricted in the country of reception if it is legal in the country of establishment of the broadcaster. However, even in such a tightly licensed and regulated area as broadcasting, Member States were still permitted under the terms of the Directive some residual, closely circumscribed, powers to suspend broadcasting if (for instance) there was perceived to be a serious threat to minors. The effect of the Directive on the balance between home and destination country control has come before the ECJ on a number of occasions.

A country of origin solution without derogations for the country of receipt is, in reality, politically feasible only (if at all) if a substantial degree of uniformity ("harmonisation") of national laws is achieved. That raises the difficult question of what minimum content standards would be internationally acceptable. If in the tightly regulated area of broadcasting, in the relatively homogenous zone of Europe, pure country of origin could not be achieved, what chance in the unregulated area of individual and press speech, on a worldwide basis?

12–046   It is difficult to see the more restrictive governments accepting internationally harmonised liberal standards. Having taken the trouble to, for instance, create a licensing regime with the specific objective of preventing access to objectionable material on the Internet, would a restrictive country's government accede easily to the suggestion that it should permit access to any foreign Web site which was legal in its country of origin? The recipient country would almost certainly wish to retain wide residual power to block unacceptable content, negating the point of a country of origin convention. It is predictable that there would be a long list of permissible national derogations from an international country of origin regime.

The converse, a restrictive harmonised standard, would require acceptance by liberal states of restrictions on freedom of expression within their own borders. While multilateral agreement might be possible in a field (such as broadcasting) in which it is traditionally accepted that regulatory content restrictions are justifiable, it is difficult to see how such agreement could be reached in the case of the Internet without sacrificing the high degree of speech protection accorded to non-broadcast speech in liberal democracies, and so far jealously defended on the Internet.

The Electronic Commerce Directive has provided a laboratory for such an attempt within Europe. Unsurprisingly, given the broader scope of the Directive, in its final form it contains many more exceptions and derogations for countries of receipt than does the satellite broadcasting regime. Additionally, the powers granted to the European Commission, in the event of a Member State notifying to the Commission a measure to restrict a given incoming information society service which the Commission decides are incompatible with Community law, are limited to requesting that the Member State refrain from taking or urgently put an end to the measure.[53] These powers were considerably diluted from the Commission's original proposal.

Where is the country of origin?

What would constitute the country of origin in an Internet convention? Some Internet afficionados may say that on the Internet content has no location. However, while content on the Internet may be everywhere it is not nowhere. To the user the storage location of the content is irrelevant. Pages can be switched from a server on one side of the world to the other without affecting the user's browsing experience and without substantially affecting the cost of access. And, of course, that user may access the content from anywhere in the world.

    However, that does not mean that the content is nowhere. While many liabilities on the Internet essentially revolve around the place of reception (*e.g.* publication for purposes of defamation, reliance upon inaccurate information, advertising of financial services), others depend upon storage (copying of copyright works, possession of obscene materials and so on). To an Internet service provider faced with a visit from the local police carrying a warrant to seize his hard disks, the idea that content is "nowhere" on the Internet may seem a little far-fetched. It is true that, at least in theory, the service provider could site its servers out of the jurisdiction and continue to provide its service. However, in practice that would not be a trivial or cost-free decision. Location still matters.

    Nor is it beyond the wit of legislators to devise a rule to define country of origin of content. Within the European Community the Electronic Commerce Directive has adopted the concept, well known in European Community law, of place of establishment of the service provider. The outcome of this rule, where virtual enterprises split their operations among different locations and instantaneously switch among servers located in different countries, may be unpredictable. However that has not deterred the legislators from adopting it.

12–047

12–048

Country of receipt

A country of receipt regime would be similar to many aspects of the current situation where, notwithstanding movement in some areas towards a "targeting" or "directed to" test, there is still serious vulnerability to the laws of other jurisdictions. However, a true country of receipt regime would imply greater international co-operation between governments leading to enforcement by prosecution across borders. This regime would seem to imply the wholesale import of restrictive standards, reinforcing the notion of an international "most conservative common denominator" system.

12–049

Competing national laws

A third alternative is continuance of the status quo in which national laws compete on the basis of existing applicable law and jurisdiction rules. These can produce a variety of outcomes. Governments in countries of receipt may try to put up barriers and enforce content blocking at their virtual borders. As we have seen, national courts from time to time make orders (as in the French Yahoo! case) that have the practical effect of requiring the service provider either to ensure that its personnel and assets never venture out of its home country, or to remove the content completely and deny it to users worldwide, or to attempt some form of geographic filtering, blocking and verification.[54]

12–050

Directing and targeting

12–051 A more enlightened approach is to adopt a mid-way position that a web site is not to be regarded, through its mere availability in the country of receipt, as susceptible to that country's jurisdiction or as infringing its laws. However, if it targets that country or directs activities towards it, then it is so susceptible. As discussed in Chapter 6, in some areas there is significant movement towards such a test. For the test to be meaningful it would require acceptance that a site is not to be taken as directed at a country simply because it does not take positive steps to block access to the site from that country. If positive steps were required, then it would effectively be a country of receipt test. The cost of maintaining a matrix of all countries' content rules and taking positive steps to filter access for each country could well be so great[55] that in practice providers would take the least cost route of adopting the most restrictive common content denominator across the board on their sites.

12–052 A true "directed at" test would require governments to accept that when their citizens go on-line and access sites that are not targeted at their home country, they are effectively travelling out of the country.[56] It would also mean that, for instance, the court in the French Yahoo! case could not have found that the mere display of Nazi memorabilia was sufficient to violate French law, without some element of targeting or direction at France. Nor would it have been open to it to find jurisdiction, as it did, on the basis that because Nazi memorabilia were of interest to all, the areas containing those items were directed at all countries simultaneously including France. However, it might still have been be possible for a court to find that Yahoo!'s serving up of French banner advertisements to French IP addresses would satisfy a "directed at" test. While it is doubtful whether the use of a particular language alone ought to suffice,[57] this was not a mere use of language. It was a serious attempt to serve up French language advertisements to users coming to the site from French territory.

A true "directed at" test would also mean that an English court could not, as we have suggested in Chapter 4 is the likely result if current law is applied to Internet publication, assume libel jurisdiction over a foreign website based on mere publication. The meaning of publication would have to be restricted to connote an element of targeting.

12–053 In the context of libel the contrasting policy arguments for country of receipt and country of origin were extensively canvassed in the Australian case of *Gutnick v. Dow Jones & Co. Inc,*[58] decided in August 2001. The court rejected the policy argument that liability for cyberspace defamation should be determined by the jurisdiction of the Website. The defendant had argued that applying a country of download (*i.e.* receipt) approach to the Internet would result in a serious "chilling effect" on free speech and would have the likely effect of diminishing the amount of information made available on the Internet. The judge said:

> "The defendant's argument really is that liability for cyber-space defamation must be determined by the jurisdiction of the Website. It was virtually admitted that the reason for this is the claimed policy of the law to assist free speech, apparently including defamatory free speech...
>
> To say that the country where the article is written, edited and uploaded and where the publisher does its business, must be the forum is an invitation to entrench the United States, the primary home of much of Internet publishing, as the forum. The applicant's argument that it would be unfair for the publisher to have to litigate in the multitude of jurisdictions in which its statements are downloaded and read, must be balanced against the world-wide inconvenience caused to litigants, from

Outer Mongolia to the Outer Barcoo, frequently not of notable means, who would at enormous expense and inconvenience have to embark upon the formidable task of suing in the USA, with its different fee and costs structures and where the libel laws are, in many respects, tilted in favour of defendants, or, if you will, in favour of the constitutional free speech concepts and rights developed in the USA which originated in the liberal construction by the courts of the First Amendment."

The judge also said:

"...I am also of the view that [the conclusion that publication took place in Victoria and that the defendant caused it] is a correct and just law, and that the arguments advanced against it are primarily policy-driven, by which I mean policies which are in the interests of the defendant and, in a less business-centric vein, perhaps, by a belief in the superiority of the United States concept of the freedom of speech over the management of freedom of speech in other places and lands."

Although the judge's adverse reaction to suggestions that, for the sake of freedom of speech on the Internet, the court should forgo jurisdiction in favour of the USA was understandable in this case, if the policy issues were to be debated in the context of a freely available rather than a subscription Website the arguments against country of receipt could not be so easily dismissed. As we have discussed above, in an environment in which the Website proprietor cannot restrict availability on a country by country basis, or would find it uneconomic to do so, the practical effect of a country of receipt rule is to give extra-territorial effect to the law of the most restrictive country of receipt: a result which is every bit as undesirable, or more so, than Hedigan J. considered the international entrenchment of U.S. freedom of speech rules to be. **12–054**

The court's detailed findings on the law are discussed in Chapter 6. The proceedings concerned an article about a Victoria resident published by the defendant on its U.S. subscription website and downloaded in the State of Victoria. The court held that it had jurisdiction. In summary, the article was held to be published in Victoria since it was there that it was made manifest in a form capable of being comprehended by the reader. Arguments that publication took place on delivery by serving up the article from the web server, not when it was received by the user, were rejected.

Arguments that the user of the site, not the defendant, caused the publication by requesting the article by means of his Web browser, were also rejected. It should be observed, however, that this was a subscription website, requiring payment and password access. The court relied on this fact in suggesting that the defendant had the ability to control whether users from Victoria could receive the article, and therefore could choose to restrict its dissemination on the Internet. The case is not therefore authority for the proposition that the proprietor of a freely available Website would be responsible for publication that took place anywhere that it was received. That question was not addressed. It could be argued that it would be paradoxical if a Website owner who made the contents of his site freely available without restriction were in a better position than one who assumed a degree of control by restricting access and accepting subscriptions. However, such a distinction could be justified in the context of a directing or targeting test. There could perhaps be scope for developing such a test within the framework of causation at law. **12–055**

The court also rejected an application by the defendant to stay the proceedings on grounds of *forum non conveniens*.

International regimes

12–056 An alternative to boundary-oriented approaches is to create an international regulatory regime, based not on arbitrating among existing national laws, but on creating a new supra-national code, possibly enforced by an internationally accepted body. Such a regime would particularly lend itself to being based on the broadcast, premium rate telephone services or advertising regulation models. It would be most likely to find acceptance if there were consensus among governments that the Internet should be a restricted form of communication. However, it is difficult to see how such an international regulatory regime could be consistent with, for instance, the approach to Internet content protection promulgated by District Judge Dalzell in *ACLU v. Reno*.

The American Bar Association, in its report on jurisdiction in cyberspace,[59] suggests the formation of a Global Online Standards Commission, which would seek to achieve global consensus on matters of jurisdiction in the on-line environment. While not explicitly setting content standards, jurisdiction rules do (as we noted at the outset) have consequences for substantive laws in a cross-border environment.

A market in virtual legal regimes?

12–057 Another possibility is international, but may require no international convention. It is based on the premise that the Internet transcends national boundaries and creates a new domain, cyberspace, which is effectively independent of national laws. The consequence is that the diverse proprietors of multiple networks can set different content and behaviour rules within their virtual boundaries, so that a market in quasi-legal regimes arises which is independent of national boundaries.[60] This solution, while attractive, would probably be regarded as deeply subversive by many governments.

12.3 Gambling

12–058 Gambling is potentially an attractive service to offer on the Internet. The type of service offered will determine the regulatory regime applicable. By way of example, a cable TV station may wish to offer broadcasts which, among the possible programming, will offer an interactive gambling facility. In order to play, viewers will have to make a wager on the telephone or through a pay-per-view chart. In the US such a set-up must comply with the Federal Communications Commission (FCC) rules against broadcasting games of "chance" and the service provider must offer programmes that the regulators consider are based on "skill". Similarly in the United Kingdom, betting, gaming and lotteries are governed by rules under the Betting, Gaming and Lotteries Act 1963 (the 1963 Act), Gaming Act 1968 (the 1968 Act), Lotteries and Amusements Act 1976 (the 1976 Act) and the Betting and Gaming Duties Act 1981. It is important to note that betting by those under 18 is a criminal offence.

The regulatory regime in England is complex and there are, for instance, difficulties in distinguishing between pool betting (governed by the 1963 Act) and lotteries (governed by the 1976 Act). These difficulties can be highlighted by the fact that the word "lottery" is not defined by statute. Instead, one must look to case law to establish what is meant by this term.

12–059 This has set a three-fold test to establish whether or not a lottery has been established. Firstly, there must be the distribution of prizes. Second, such distribution should be dependent upon "chance". Any competition in which genuine skill or effort is involved is not a lottery, even though the skill or effort involved may be small, as it would still remove the pure element of chance which is central to the idea of a lottery. However, there is the danger that where a competition is won in which success does not depend to a substantial degree on the exercise of skill, it may be a prize competition and, consequently, unlawful under section 14 of the 1976 Act. Third, there should also be some actual contribution made by the participants in return for their obtaining a chance to win. For example, a "contribution" could well be the additional charge that may be levied on participants by those operating the "lottery", such as a charge to access the relevant Web site. In any event, if a particular scheme *does* amount to a lottery it would be unlawful under section 1 of the 1976 Act unless it fell within one of the excepted classes. We will do no more here than illustrate some of the offences which can be committed in relation to gambling.

It is an offence under section 2 of the 1976 Act, in connection with any lottery promoted **12–060** or proposed to be promoted either in Great Britain or elsewhere to (among other things):

- offer for sale or distribution any tickets or chances in the lottery;

- print, publish, distribute or have in one's possession for the purpose of publication or distribution;
    — any advertisement of the lottery,
    — any list of prizewinners or winning tickets in the lottery,
    — any such matter descriptive of the drawing or intended drawing of the lottery as is calculated to act as an inducement to persons to participate in that lottery or in other lotteries,

- bring, or invite any person to send, into Great Britain for the purpose of sale or distribution any ticket in, or advertisement of, the lottery;

- send or attempt to send out of Great Britain any money or valuable thing received in respect of the sale or distribution, or any document recording the sale or distribution, or the identity of the holder, of any ticket or chance in the lottery;

- use any premises, or cause or knowingly permit any premises to be used, for purposes connected with the promotion or conduct of the lottery;

- cause, procure or attempt to procure any person to do any of the above.

A "ticket" includes any document evidencing the claim of a person to participate in the chances of a lottery. "Distribute" includes distribution to persons or places within or outside Great Britain. "Printing" includes writing and other modes of reproducing words in a visible form.

There are some defences, including one designed to protect those who print tickets and **12–061** advertisements for foreign lotteries which are not promoted in Great Britain. It should be noted that the offences are wide enough to cover electronic media. It is clear that advertising foreign lotteries in Great Britain is illegal.

In relation to bookmaking, the Court of Appeal in *Victor Chandler International v Customs and Excise Commissioners and another*[61] held that if an overseas bookmaker placed advertisements on Teletext, that would amount to circulating or distributing an advertisement or other document in the United Kingdom for the purposes of section 9(1)(b) of the Betting and Gaming Duties Act 1981. The provision, which was for the protection of the revenue and to protect domestic bookmakers from unfair offshore competition, should be given an 'always speaking' construction to take account of technological developments since the provision was first enacted in the Finance Act 1952.

The Gambling Commission, in its *Gambling Review Report* of July 2001, has surveyed the existing state of legislation in relation to on-line betting and gaming and has made recommendations for the future. The Commission takes a realistic view of the cross-border nature of the Internet, restricting its recommendations to proposals for regulating British on-line services, so that the punter has a choice between using a regulated British service and taking the risk of using an unlicensed overseas service. The commission states (para. 30.18)

> "We cannot hope to regulate all those [overseas] sites, but what we can do is regulate those based in Great Britain, so that the punter has the choice of gambling in a regulated environment or taking a chance with an overseas operator (who may, of course, be regulated in another jurisdiction)."

12–062   The Commission goes on to suggest (para. 30.21) that it should not be an offence for punters in Britain to use unlicensed sites, but that they would do so at their own risk. The Commission also suggests that the existing ban on advertising unlicensed overseas sites in Britain should continue, and that a licensed operator should at a minimum be registered as a British company, locate its server in Great Britain and use a U.K. web address for its gambling site. Only sites licensed by the Gambling Commission should be permitted to advertise in Great Britain.

The Commission comments that it would not expect a hyperlink to be regarded as advertising. This refers to a current practice of many U.K. licensed bookmakers of including hypertext links to overseas sites within a U.K. site. However, the Commission suggests that should it become clear that a licensed site was diverting much of its business to an unregulated offshore site, the Commission should have the power to take enforcement action.

The Commission acknowledges (para. 12.3) comments made by the Gaming Board for Great Britain in its submissions to the review, that gambling legislation impinges on on-line gambling in ways that were unintended when the legislation was written and are erratic.

12.4 Pornography and sexual offences

12–063   A great deal of concern has from time to time been expressed in the press and elsewhere about the spread of computer pornography, in particular, how it is readily available to children and young teenagers. Access by children to "top shelf" magazines and adult films and videos can be controlled by parents and by newsagents and cinemas. However, parents may not be aware of what can be accessed from their own home, and are likely to be less computer literate than their offspring. This concern, together with pressure from government and the police, led during 1996 first to the adoption of a Code of Practice by the Internet Service Providers Association[62] (ISPA—an organisation representing a number of UK service providers), then to the formation of the Internet Watch Foundation,[63] a more widely supported independent body which acts as a focus for the identification and removal of illegal material from U.K. ISPs' servers and encourages the classification of legal material in the Internet.

12.4.1 Obscenity

The U.K. Obscene Publications Act 1959 covers material which has the effect such as to **12–064** tend to deprave and corrupt. There has been a great deal of case law on what constitutes obscenity. A major factor in determining whether accused material is obscene is whether it would, taken as a whole, tend to deprave and corrupt the type of persons who may get hold of the material. Children are regarded as particularly at risk. Whereas conventional printed "hard" pornography can only be obtained in general under very controlled circumstances, electronic pornography on the Internet can be accessed by anybody with the right equipment. The prosecution should have no problem in convincing a jury that much of the "adult" material on the Internet is obscene in those circumstances.

Criminal liability for obscenity is an area in which it is especially important to bear in mind the differing activities which persons involved in providing Internet services undertake. There are two main routes to liability: having an obscene article (*e.g.* of a disk containing obscene material) for publication for gain; and publication. An "article" means any description of article containing or embodying matter to be read or looked at or both, any sound record, and any film or other record of a picture or pictures (section 1(2)). The 1959 Act was amended by the Criminal Justice and Public Order Act 1994 (the 1994 Act) to include the transmission of electronically stored data.

Publication
A person "publishes" an article who distributes, circulates, sells, lets on hire, gives, or **12–065** lends it, or who offers it for sale or for letting on hire (section 1(3)(a)); or in the case of an article containing or embodying matter to be looked at or a record, shows, plays or projects it, or, where the matter is data stored electronically, transmits that data (section 1(3)(b)). A person also publishes an article to the extent that any matter recorded on it is included by him in a programme included in a programme service (as to which see below)(section 1(4)).

It is an open question whether "shows" requires active conduct on the part of the defendant. In *R. v. Fellows, R. v. Arnold*[64] (see above) one of the defendants to charges under both the Obscene Publications Act 1959 and the Protection of Children Act 1978 (see below) argued that giving certain others password access to his archive of indecent pictures on his employer's computer did not amount to "showing" the pictures as contended by the prosecution. The defendant argued that "distributes" and "shows" were active rather than passive, and that he did nothing more than permit others to have access to his archive.

As to "shows", the Court of Appeal accepted, for the purposes of the case, that active **12–066** conduct on the defendant's part was required. Even so Evans L.J. said:

> "…it seems to us that there is ample evidence of such conduct on his part. He took whatever steps were necessary not merely to store the data on his computer but also to make it available world-wide to other computers via the Internet. He corresponded by e-mail with those who sought to have access to it and he imposed certain conditions before they were permitted to do so. He gave permission by giving them the password. He did all this with the sole object of allowing others, as well as himself, to view exact reproductions of the photographs stored in his archive."

The court expressed no view on whether the conduct amounted to distribution.

An offence is committed under section 2(1) of the 1959 Act if the defendant publishes an obscene article, even if not for gain. The amendment to the meaning of "publishes" introduced by the 1994 Act means that the Internet service provider may in principle be prosecuted for transmitting material hosted by a third party and made available across the Internet without the service provider's consent (but see the defences discussed below).

There is no requirement under the Obscene Publications Act that the defendant must have actually have had an intent to deprave or corrupt.

12–067 As to cases with an overseas element, in *R. v. Waddon*[65] His Honour Judge Hardy ruled that where the defendant uploaded obscene materials from England to a web server in America, and an English police constable accessed that website from England and downloaded the material here, the defendant had published the materials in England for the purposes of the 1959 Act notwithstanding the intermediate elements that took place outside the jurisdiction. He said:

> "I have no difficulty in finding in this case that an act of publication took place when the data was transmitted by the defendant or his agent to the service provider and that the publication was in effect still taking place when PC Ysart acting on instructions originating from the defendant received the data into his computer. Since both the sending and the receiving took place within the jurisdiction, in my view, it matters not, that the transmission in between times may have left the jurisdiction."

If the defendant has stored the material himself and he can be proved to have transmitted it to others, then prosecution for publication will be a clear option. A physical disk can be seized and presented to the court as evidence of what was published. Thus, subject to the defences available to him (which are discussed below), an Internet service provider may be potentially at risk of committing publication offences in respect of material contained on its own disks, such as Usenet newsgroups and material on Web sites which it hosts. However, proving the elements of a transmission-based offences in relation to material not stored by the defendant, although possible in principle, may be potentially more difficult, especially given the requirement to prove that what was transmitted originated from an article, in other words that the original matter was electronically stored.

Broadcasting and programme services

12–068 Another route to liability for transmitting obscene material across the Internet may be provided by the Broadcasting Act 1990. The 1990 Act made amendments to the 1959 Act designed to apply its obscenity provisions to recorded and live "programme services". A programme service under section 201 of the 1990 Act includes "…any other service which consists in the sending, by means of a telecommunication system, of sounds or visual images or both … for reception at two or more places in the United Kingdom (whether they are so sent for simultaneous reception or at different times in response to requests made by different users of the service)". This does not apply, *inter alia*, to a local delivery service or a two-way service, each as defined under the 1990 Act. The provisions would appear to apply to activities on the Internet. Section 1(4) of the 1959 Act, as amended, provides that a person publishes an article to the extent that any matter recorded on it is included by him in a programme included in a programme service. A programme includes any item included in that service. Section 1(5) contains provisions applying the Act to live as well as recorded material.

Under Schedule 15, para. 4 of the Broadcasting Act 1990, proceedings for offences **12–069** under section 2 of the Obscene Publications Act 1959—either for publishing an obscene article or for having an obscene article for gain—shall not be instituted without the consent of the Director of Public Prosecutions in cases where the relevant publication, or the only other publication which followed from the relevant publication, took place in the course of the inclusion of a programme in a programme service. This would appear to mean, given the wide definition of "programme service", that the consent of the DPP is required to institute a prosecution under the Act in respect of material on the Internet where the content of the "service" consists of sounds or visual images or both.

Possession

An offence is also committed if the defendant has an obscene article for publication for **12–070** gain (whether gain for himself or gain for another). A person is deemed to have an article for publication for gain if with a view to such publication he has the article in his ownership, possession or control. References to publication for gain apply to any publication with a view to gain, whether the gain is to accrue by way of consideration for the publication or in any other way. These provisions provide the basis for an argument that a commercial Internet service provider who acts a host, by providing in return for a subscription fee access to (among other things) materials which it stores on its disks, has the disks for publication for gain. An ISP who acts merely as a "pass through" or "conduit" access provider and who does not host anything itself ought to be in a strong position as regards these possession-based provisions of the Act.

In relation to possession offences, the provisions of Sched 15, para. 3 of the Broadcasting Act 1990 should also be noted. These provide that where a person has an obscene article in his ownership, possession or control with a view to the matter recorded on it being included in a relevant programme, the article shall be taken to be an obscene article had or kept by that person for publication for gain.

Defences and ISPs

It is a defence to both the publication and possession based offences for the defendant to **12–071** prove both that he had not examined the article and that he had no reasonable cause to suspect that it was of such a nature that its publication, or his having it (as appropriate) would constitute an offence under the Obscene Publications Act. For inclusion in a programme, the defendant must show that he did not know and had no reason to suspect that the programme would include matter rendering him liable to be convicted.

As both elements of these defences must be proved, it is not enough for an Internet service provider to simply shut its eyes to material which it stores or transmits; it must have no reasonable cause to suspect. Clearly an ISP could be liable in respect of material on a Web site which it hosts for a customer, if it was aware of facts which should have put it on inquiry as to the nature of the material on the Web site. The potential liability of ISPs for obscene material posted to Usenet newsgroups hosted by them is controversial. In legal terms the question must turn around whether the explicit names and notoriety of certain newsgroups is sufficient to put a Usenet host on notice of the nature of the materials likely to be posted to the newsgroups which it hosts. In July 2001 the Internet Watch Foundation resolved upon a new policy of furnishing ISPs with regular information about the number of illegal items identified in newsgroups, which ISPs could use to inform their policies on carrying newsgroups. It also suggested that this would be an appropriate time for ISPs to review their policies in the light of the new information that would be available to them from IWF on a regular basis. The IWF stated that there was a growing recognition that the majority of illegal content in newsgroups is concentrated in a small but changing selection of groups.

12–072   There is also potential liability for publishing obscene material not hosted by the ISP. In this case the prosecuting authority would have a far more difficult task in resisting the ISP's innocence defence. However, it is possible to imagine situations in which an ISP could be liable, for instance where it provides a known publisher of obscene materials with a leased line link to the Internet by which the publisher makes its self-hosted Web site available to the public.

12.4.2 Child pornography

12–073   There are distinct offences relating to child pornography. The Protection of Children Act 1978 (as amended by the 1994 Act) makes it an offence to take, make, permit to be taken (section 1(1)(a)); distribute or show (section 1(1)(b)); or possess with a view to their being distributed or shown (by the defendant or others)(section 1(1)(c)); any indecent photograph or indecent pseudo-photograph of a child. Section 1(1)(d) creates an offence in relation to the publication of advertisements.

The 1994 Act amended the definition of photograph in section 7 of the 1978 Act to include "data stored on computer disk or by other electronic means which is capable of conversion into a photograph." References to an indecent photograph include a copy of an indecent photograph. The term "pseudo–photograph" was introduced by the 1994 Act. "Pseudo–photograph" means an image, whether made by computer-graphics or otherwise, which can be resolved into an image which appears to be a photograph. Further, if the impression conveyed by the pseudo-photograph is one which is difficult to classify as either an adult or a child, but the predominant impression is that the person shown is a child, then it shall be treated as such. This is intended to cover computer-generated and manipulated images.

12–074   Both a person and a company may be charged with an offence under this Act. The material covered by the 1978 Act must be "indecent", which is different from obscene. Indecency occurs at a lower threshold than obscenity, particularly where children are involved. Most people would consider indecent photographs of children which imitated the widely accepted "Page 3" photographs of adult women. There are two potential defences to offences under section 1(1)(b) and (c) (there is no defence under section 1(1)(a) or (d)). The first defence is similar to that under the 1959 Act—that the defendant did not see the image and had no knowledge or suspicion that it was indecent. It is also a defence that there was a legitimate reason for possessing or distributing the image.

The Criminal Justice Act 1988 s.160 also covers the area of child pornography, providing a summary offence of possession of an indecent photo of a child. The 1994 Act has amended the Act in a similar way to the amendments to the Protection of Children Act. The defences under the 1978 Act are available. A further possible defence is that the image was not requested and was not kept for an unreasonable length of time after receipt.

"Making" and downloading

12–075   We have referred above to the meaning of "show" in both the 1959 Act and the 1978 Act. The meaning of "makes" under the 1978 Act and "possession" under the 1988 Act have also been judicially considered in relation to the Internet.

In *R. v. Bowden*[66] the Court of Appeal considered the meaning of "makes" under the

1978 Act. The defendant had taken his computer hard drive for repair, and while examining the computer the repairer found indecent material on the hard drive. The defendant had downloaded images from the Internet and either printed them out himself or stored them on his hard disk. The images were all for his own use. The Court of Appeal held that "make" applied not only to original photographs but (by virtue of section 7) also to copies of photographs and to data stored on computer disk. The court accepted the submissions of counsel for the Crown, that:

> "A person who either downloads images on to disc or who prints them off is making them. The Act is not only concerned with the original creation of images, but also their proliferation. Photographs or pseudo-photographs found on the Internet may have originated from outside the United Kingdom; to download or print within the jurisdiction is to create new material which hitherto may not have existed therein".

This point was considered again in *Atkins v. DPP*,[67] in which argued that the application **12–076** of "making" to acts of copying and storage, as opposed to an act of creation, could lead to injustice since the Act provided no defence to offences under section 1(1)(a). People engaged in innocent activity (such as making copies for the purpose of collecting of evidence) could be caught by an absolute offence. However, although the force of the argument was recognised (and the interpretation to include copies described as "problematic"), the court concluded that it was bound by *Bowden* and should not regard it as wrongly decided. The defendant should have been convicted by the magistrate in respect of images downloaded and stored in a directory on his computer hard drive.

Cache copies
Atkins also decided a point that was not in issue in *Bowden*, namely whether "making" **12–077** under the 1978 Act extended to copies made unknowingly.[68] Some of the images found on the defendant's computer were stored in the cache created automatically by the defendant's Internet browser. The magistrate had stated that he could not be sure that the defendant knew of the operation of the cache, "knew in other words that the computer would automatically retain upon its hard disk information sent to it at the user's request." The Divisional Court held that "making" did not extend to unintentional copying.

The defendant in *Atkins* was also charged with possession under the 1988 Act, in relation to the cache copies. The question arose whether knowledge (in the sense of knowledge of the existence and effect of the cache, as opposed to knowledge of its contents[69]) was an element of possession. The Divisional Court held that it was, so that in this case the defendant could not be convicted.

Screen images
It was common ground in *Atkins* that the defendant would have had no defence (subject **12–078** to the prosecution being able to establish that the offence had occurred within the time limit for prosecution) to a prosecution under the 1988 Act for possession based on the "transient downloading of the image onto the screen". As a technical statement this is inaccurate, conflating two entirely distinct events: the temporary storage of a copy of the image in the computer's volatile memory (RAM); and the transient appearance of the image on the computer screen as a result of cathode rays energising the phosphor dots on the screen.

It has been argued, in relation to copyright, that the image displayed on the screen is not a copy because it is not stored, by contrast with the RAM copy which, while admittedly transient, is stored.[70] On the other hand, it was held in *Bookmakers' Afternoon Greyhound Racing Services v Wilf Gilbert (Staffordshire) Ltd*,[71] a case under the now superseded Copyright Act 1956, that a screen display did amount to reproduction in a material form.

If a distinction were to be drawn between the RAM copy and the screen display, it could lead to a conundrum: the image displayed in screen is so evanescent as not to amount either to a copy or to stored data under the definitions of indecent photograph in section 7 of the 1988 Act; yet the copy held in RAM, while probably "stored" within the meaning of the section 7 definitions, may not be known to the user to exist and so is subject to the same objection as the browser cache copies. The firmness of the common ground in *Atkins* may be questionable.

12–079   In any event, whether one is considering browser cache copies or (even more so) transient RAM copies, it does seem curious that the commission of an offence should depend on the degree of technical knowledge that the user happens to possess of the inner workings of the computer and its software.

Whether viewing on screen would also amount to "making" under the 1978 Act was not specifically discussed in either *Atkins* or *Bowden*. Would creating the temporary copy in RAM, or creating the transient image on the computer screen, amount to "making" as well as (apparently) possession? If it does, that would create the situation described in *Atkins* as a "striking oddity", that the same self-same set of facts would involve the commission of two quite distinct offences, no additional proof being required for the more serious offence of "making" under the 1978 Act.

12–080   We have seen that "making" under the 1978 Act includes the intentional making of a copy. If the screen image is a copy, then in the case of ordinary websites it is perfectly clear to the user (since he is viewing it) that he is creating that copy, so lack of knowledge cannot be an issue. An offence has been committed. If the screen image is not a copy, and the question turns around the making of the RAM copy, then again the offence would seem to turn on the technical knowledge of the user. In some cases, notably sites which deliberately hide their graphical content by using zero height and width images, it is possible for an image to be automatically stored in the browser cache without ever being displayed on screen. In this way an innocent user can visit what appears to be an innocuous website, yet end up with a browser cache full of illegal images.[72] In this situation the lack of knowledge either that he had visited a site containing illegal material, or that it had been downloaded to the cache, ought to give the innocent user a good answer to a prosecution. However, there may also be concern that this would also enable guilty parties to escape prosecution through the difficulty in proving that the guilty party knew that he was visiting an illegal site. Of course, once the user copies the material from the cache to a permanent directory (which would have to be done in order to prevent the copies expiring from the cache) then, as was the case in *Atkins*, the requisite knowledge becomes relatively easy to prove in respect of the manually created permanent copies.

12–081   In *Atkins* it was pointed out in argument that before the amendments to the 1978 Act introduced by the 1994 Act, the absolute offence under section 1(1)(a) applied only to the taking of indecent photographs of children, an activity involving the direct exploitation of children in their actual presence for which there could be no defence. Parliament could not, it was argued, have intended when inserting "making" and "pseudo-photographs" into section 1(1)(a), to extend the offence beyond such acts of primary creation. Less morally culpable acts in section 1(1)(b)and(c), it was pointed out, such as distribution, showing, or possession with a view to distribution or showing, were provided with a defence.

These arguments did not hold sway. Yet the consequence of holding that "making" extends to copies would appear to be that the mere act of personal viewing could also amount to "making", a result which does not fit at all into the hierarchy of offences created in section 1; offends against the principle expressed in *Atkins* that the same facts should not amount to two distinct offences of different seriousness; may render the commission of the offence dependent on the degree of technical computer knowledge possessed by the user; and creates a gulf between the criminal consequences of merely viewing a hard copy photograph and merely viewing an image on a computer screen.

Linking

In January 1998 a student pleaded guilty at Preston Crown Court to offences under the **12–082** 1959 Act and the 1978 Act. He had been charged with publishing obscene articles on the Internet contrary to the 1959 Act and with making indecent photographs of children contrary to the 1978 Act. He created a U.K. based Web site for the purpose of providing links to other Web sites, including a Web site of his own hosted in the USA, which contained what the police described as "extreme adult pornography". A search of his home also found "extreme child pornography" downloaded from the Internet. As the prosecution was not contested, the case sets no legal precedent. However, the police commented that "any attempt by a person in this country to escape prosecution by lodging material elsewhere will fail".

Clearly the case involved more activities by the defendant than simply creating hypertext Web links to overseas pornography sites. However, it does raise the question whether creating a link to material, the publication of which is illegal under the 1959 Act or the 1978 Act, is an offence.

The prosecution would have to establish, under the 1959 Act, that the person **12–083** responsible for creating the Web link thereby published the obscene article in one of the following ways (omitting those of no apparent relevance):

- Showed, played or projected it; or

- Where the matter embodied in the article was data stored electronically, transmitted the data; or

- Included the matter in a programme included in a programme service.

Under the 1978 Act the prosecution would have to establish that the defendant did one of the following acts in relation to an indecent photograph or pseudo-photograph of a child:

- Distributed or showed it; or

- Published or caused to be published an advertisement likely to be understood as conveying that the advertiser distributed or showed indecent photographs of a child, or intended to do so

Under section 1(2) of the 1978 Act, a person is to be regarded as 'distributing' if he parts with possession to, or exposes or offers for acquisition to, another person.

A number of difficult issues arise in relation to Web links.   **12–084**

If the link is to a site on which the offending material is available, but not displayed on the top level, does that constitute an offence? If so, how many links removed does the material have to be before no offence is committed? Or is an offence only committed (if at all) if clicking on the link causes the offending material to be displayed on the user's screen?

Does providing a hypertext link constitute "showing"? On the basis of *R. v. Fellows*, the fact that a defendant does not "push" the material to the user's screen does not appear to be determinative. If providing a link is "showing", would providing the URL of the material without coding it as an active hypertext link also amount to "showing"? If so, that is tantamount to finding that merely to publish information about where obscene material may be found is an offence.

Can the person who includes a link to another site be said to transmit the data from that site for the purposes of section 1(3)(b) of the 1959 Act? This seems far-fetched. No transmission occurs until the user executes the link. The data is then transmitted from the target site, not that of the defendant. At the most the defendant provides the user with means to cause the target site to transmit the data to the user (see also the discussion of copyright infringement by Web linking, section 2.5.3). If the target site is also operated by the defendant, then the defendant's position is likely to be more difficult. Even if the defendant's own target site is abroad, at least part of the transmission path to an English user will be through the English jurisdiction (but note comments on *R. v. Waddon* above).

12–085 Does providing a link to obscene material amount to including the matter in a programme included in a programme service under section 1(4) of the 1959 Act? A "programme" includes an advertisement and, in relation to any service, any item included in that service. The Act (unlike the Copyright, Designs and Patents Act 1988 in relation to cable programme services—see main text, section 2.6.3) provides no guidance as to the meaning of "include". On a broad construction of the word, a court might be prepared to find that linked material was "included" in the service. However, that still suffers from the difficulty of distinguishing sensibly, in the context of the Web, between including the material itself and including information about where to find the material.

How are the requirements for a conviction affected by the possibility that the content on the target site may change, or that the precise matter regarded as illegal may not have been present when the link was created? It is notable that the German prosecution of Angela Marquardt over a Web link to the *Radikal* Web site (see section 12.2.3) failed on this point. The prosecution were unable to show that the offending material was present on the target site when Ms Marquardt created the link to it.

Could a link in some circumstances be regarded as an "advertisement" under section 1(1)(d) of the 1978 Act? Or if a Web page creator links to material which is itself clearly an advertisement, could the person creating the link be regarded as 'causing' the advertisement to be published? Does the fact that the user has to execute the link break any chain of causation?

12.4.3 On-line harassment and offensive electronic communications

12–086 The Telecommunications Act 1984 provides that it is a summary offence to send any message by telephone originating in the United Kingdom, which is grossly offensive or of an indecent, obscene or menacing character; or to send by those means, for the purpose of causing annoyance, inconvenience or needless anxiety to another, a message that he knows to be false or persistently makes use for that purpose of a public telecommunication system. This extends to data transmitted by a telephone line and therefore catches the use of the Internet. It does not apply to anything done in the course of providing a programme service (within the meaning of the Broadcasting Act 1990). The ambit of the Act is to catch the originator of the material rather than the person distributing it. Therefore, it is unlikely that the Internet service provider will be caught by this provision in the Act but the originator of the material will be caught.

From May 1, 2001 the Malicious Communications Act 1988 was extended to include electronic communications.[73] It is therefore a summary offence, under section 1(1) of the Act, for a person to send (a) a letter, electronic communication or article of any description which conveys a message which is indecent or grossly offensive; a threat; or information which is false and known or believed to be false by the sender; or (b) any other article or electronic communication which is, in whole or in part, of an indecent or grossly offensive nature, if the purpose, or one of the purposes, of the person in sending it is that it should cause distress or anxiety to the recipient or to any other person to whom he intends that it or its contents or nature should be communicated. An electronic communication is defined as "any oral or other communication by means of a telecommunication system (within the meaning of the Telecommunications Act 1984 (c12); and any communication (however sent) that is in electronic form". There is a specific defence to the offence concerning threats.

The Protection from Harassment Act 1997, although enacted to deal with stalkers, applies to a much broader category of conduct. It is capable of applying to on-line harassment. Section 1 provides that a person must not pursue a course of conduct which amounts to harassment of another and which he knows or ought to know amounts to harassment of the other. A course of conduct must involve conduct on at least two occasions (section 7(3). A person ought to know, if a reasonable person in possession of the same information would think the course of conduct amounted to harassment of the other. There are various defences. A breach of the prohibition on harassment is both a summary offence and may also be the subject of civil proceedings by an actual or apprehended victim of harassment for damages (including for anxiety and financial loss) and an injunction. There is also a more serious offence of putting people in fear of violence. A course of conduct consisting of sending two letters four and a half months apart was capable of amounting to harassment,[74] as were two articles published in a newspaper.[75]

12–087

12.4.4 Public display of indecent matter

Section 1(1) of the Indecent Displays (Control) Act 1981 makes a person guilty of an offence if he publicly displays indecent matter. Those caught are the person making the display, and any person causing or permitting the display. The prime aim of the Act is to control displays in places which people can physically enter. Under section 1(2) matter displayed in or so as to be visible from any public place is deemed to be publicly displayed; this would include for example, Internet terminals in public libraries, "cyber-cafes", etc. Section 1(3) makes it clear that payment of a fee to access a place to view the material where the fee includes payment for the display has the effect of making that place not a public place for the purposes of section 1(2), so long as persons under 18 are barred. However, the general provisions of section 1(1) (which could possibly apply directly to the provider of a Web site accessible to the public, as opposed to a person locating the screen in public premises), contains no such qualifications. Once again, bodies corporate may face liability as well as individuals. Nothing in the Act applies to a

12–088

television programme service within the meaning of the Broadcasting Act 1990.

12.4.5 Sex tourism

12–089   The Sexual Offences (Conspiracy and Incitement) Act 1996 became law on October 1, 1996. The Act is directed mainly at child sex tourism, and aims to make triable in England and Wales acts of conspiracy and incitement to commit certain sexual offences abroad. Section 2(3) of the Act provides that any act of incitement by means of a message (however communicated) is to be treated as done in England and Wales if the message is sent or received in England and Wales. That would clearly apply to Internet e-mails. It should also cover advertising on Web sites, whose contents can easily be characterised as messages received by the viewer of the site.

12.4.6 Cross-border content standards

12–090   Public concern about Internet pornography in the United States caused the Congress to pass, by an overwhelming majority, the Communications Decency Act 1996. Aspects of the legislation were strongly opposed by Internet providers and civil liberties groups, and some parts of it were declared unconstitutional by Philadelphia and New York courts in the light of the First Amendment and subsequently by the U.S. Supreme Court.

Because of the First Amendment, the USA has probably the world's most highly developed case law on what constitutes obscenity. One factor that must be considered in determining whether something amounts to obscenity and therefore unprotected speech is local community standards. What might be considered utterly shocking and depraved in rural Arkansas may be merely titillating in Los Angeles. This sensible test has been undermined by a recent successful prosecution for obscenity in Tennessee of a bulletin board operator based in California, for material that very likely would not have been considered obscene by a California jury. The possibility of being prosecuted in a jurisdiction with very strict standards (such as Saudi Arabia) for material which would probably not offend in its place of origin must be a great concern to the major service providers. The decision of CompuServe in December 1995 to suspend, temporarily, access to about 200 Usenet newsgroups in response to action by a German prosecutor is a good example of this. CompuServe stated that it was investigating ways in which it could restrict user access to selected newsgroups by geographical location. In the meantime the effect of the action was to suspend access to the newsgroups world-wide through CompuServe's Internet news facilities. For further discussion of these cross-border issues see section 12.2 above.

12.4.7 Chat rooms

12–091   Following the 2001 election a Task Force on Child Protection on the Internet has made recommendations to the Home Secretary for a new criminal offence relating to a meeting with a child with intent to commit a sex offence; and for a new civil order to protect children from an adult making contact with them for a harmful or unlawful sexual purpose, which would include contact through email or Internet chat rooms.

12.5 Contempt of court

The term "contempt of court" covers a wide range of conduct which in some way **12–092** interferes with the administration of justice. The types of conduct relevant to the Internet are those that relate to publishing matter which could prejudice the fair trial of a civil or criminal case and those concerning breach of a court injunction. The law of contempt of court has been developed through the common law since early times, although most of the types of contempt applicable to Internet activities are now covered by the Contempt of Court Act 1981. There are two types of contempt, civil and criminal. Civil contempt concerns disobedience to court orders such as injunctions. That is of little direct relevance to the Internet, although as we shall see a third party who seeks to undermine the effects of an injunction pending trial, for instance by publishing injuncted material, may find that he is accused of criminal contempt.

12.5.1 Criminal contempt

The 1981 Act makes it an offence of strict liability to publish to the public at large or any **12–093** section of the public, while proceedings are active, anything which "creates a substantial risk that the course of justice in the proceedings in question will be seriously impeded or prejudiced." "Strict liability" means that it is an offence even if the person making the publication did not intend to interfere in the course of justice. "Publication" is defined to include any speech, writing, broadcast or "other communication in whatever form", so Usenet newsgroup messages and publications through Web sites would be covered. Other contempts of court remain governed by the common law rules.

A publication relating to a case will only be an offence if it occurs while the proceedings are *sub judice*. At common law this certainly covered the period from the commencement of the proceedings, which would include the arrest in a criminal case, to their final determination. However, anyone knowing or having good reason to believe that proceedings are imminent when they publish matter likely to prejudice a fair trial is also liable to be charged with contempt. Because of the uncertainty caused by the common law rules, the 1981 Act sought to define more exactly the commencement and ending of the period in which the proceedings are "active", within which the strict liability rule would apply. It is possible that publications outside this period which would otherwise come under the 1981 Act could be common law contempt.

Charges of contempt are nowadays more often brought with respect to criminal than to **12–094** civil proceedings. This is because it is felt that jurors are more likely to be prejudiced than a judge, and almost all civil trials in this country are tried by a judge alone. Publications which have been held to be in contempt of court fall into a number of categories. A common cause for contempt is that the publication prejudges the merits of the case, in particular assuming that the accused in a criminal trial is guilty of the crime charged. There have been few modern cases of an express imputation of guilt, but a tacit assumption can be just as prejudicial. For example, immediately after Peter Sutcliffe was arrested, almost every newspaper reported the fact under headlines referring to the Yorkshire Ripper, clearly implying that he was guilty of the series of horrific murders of women. Even without any assumption of guilt, emotive or disparaging remarks may carry a serious risk or prejudice, in particular when they amount to guilt by association. For example, one newspaper insinuated that the man who broke into Buckingham Palace and was found in the Queen's bedroom was linked to the Queen's personal police officer who had just resigned after the revelation that he had had a homosexual affair with a male prostitute.

It is also a contempt to publish matter which is likely to be inadmissible in evidence at the trial. For example, the prejudicial nature of previous convictions is recognised by the law which provides that they may only be put in evidence under certain circumstances; publishing them so that they become known to the jury where those circumstances have not occurred would be a contempt. The same is true of confessions, admissions and improperly obtained evidence. The publication of a photograph may also be prejudicial, for example where identification will be an issue at trial.

12–095   The trial of Rose West raised serious concerns about the publication of interviews with witnesses, particularly when the witnesses had been paid large sums of money for those interviews. This could be contempt if the interview were published before that witness gave evidence, or if the payment caused the witness to "embellish" their evidence at the trial. It could also be contempt to attempt to prevent a witness from testifying by subjecting them to abuse or threats.

Although most judicial proceedings take place in public, where they do not it may be a contempt to publish an account of those proceedings. For example, in this country jury deliberations are kept secret, so disclosing jury deliberations is contempt under the 1981 Act. That Act also made it an offence to record legal proceedings without the consent of the court and to publish any recording of legal proceedings. It is a serious contempt to publish an account of proceedings which are closed to the public for the protection of one of the parties, usually a child or a mental patient, or to protect commercially valuable confidential information, or where there is an issue of national security. There are also occasions where it is a contempt to publish matters relating to proceedings held in open court, such as most details of committal proceedings in the magistrates' court unless the reporting restrictions are lifted. There are specific legislative provisions prohibiting the publication of information identifying children involved in proceedings or rape victims. A court also has power to order that reports of the proceedings be postponed where a contemporaneous report poses a serious risk of prejudice. It is notorious that transcripts of the Rose West committal hearing were available on the Internet notwithstanding that reporting restrictions in England were not lifted.

12–096   The 1981 Act provides three specified defences to the strict liability offence, which had developed as common law defences. It is a defence that the publisher, acting with all due care, did not know and had no reason to know that proceedings were active, and the distributor of such publication will not be liable if, again having taken reasonable care, he did not know and had no reason to suspect that the material contains matter giving rise to the offence. The other statutory defences are that the publication was a fair and accurate report of the proceedings where there was no reporting restriction in effect, and that it was part of a discussion in good faith of matters of general public interest and any prejudice was merely incidental to the discussion. The balancing of the right of free speech and a free press against the right to a fair trial is never an easy one.

At common law a superior court could commit a person found guilty of criminal contempt to prison for a fixed but unlimited period, or could impose a fine of unlimited amount. Lower courts only have power to punish contempts which are acts committed in the court itself. For contempts under the 1981 Act, the penalties available to a superior court are committal to prison for a fixed term not exceeding two years or an unlimited fine, inferior courts may imprison for up to one month and fine up to £1,000.

12.5.2 International aspects of contempt

The international nature of the Internet poses challenges to the system of protecting **12–097**
judicial proceedings. A foreign national could publish prejudicial matter, or could attend
a hearing subject to reporting restrictions and publish a report on his return home. The
Spycatcher case showed the difficulties even without the Internet; although publication
was banned in the United Kingdom, the book was on sale in the United States and it was
not difficult for individuals to obtain copies. In these circumstances, the authorities could
seek to proceed against any UK-based Internet service provider through whose service
the contempt is published. The law relating to the liability of parties to an offending
publication in the print medium is well established, that relating to broadcast media less
so. As in the case of liability for defamation (discussed in Chapter 4), courts faced with an
Internet service provider will probably look for an analogy with established categories.
The defence of innocent publication is likely to be of importance, although the proviso
that all reasonable care must have been taken may cause difficulties. When the Electronic
Commerce Directive is implemented, the liability of Internet service providers for
damages will be restricted by the terms of the Directive (see Chapter 5).

12.5.3 Third parties and injunctions

Civil contempt concerns breach of a court order. The situation with which we are **12–098**
particularly concerned is where a court grants an injunction against a person and
someone else does an act which would breach the injunction if it had been granted
against him. So if a court grants an interim injunction against a national newspaper
restraining publication of certain material pending trial and the grant of the injunction is
widely publicised, is it a contempt of court for someone else to publish the material, for
instance if an individual were to post it on a website?

    This question has received some attention from the courts. Where an interim or final
injunction has been granted, a third party who aids and abets the defendant in a breach of
the injunction is guilty of contempt.[76] Where an interim injunction has been granted, a
third party who with knowledge of the purpose for which it was made acts so as to defeat
that purpose is in contempt of court, not because he is in breach of the injunction (an
injunction made *in personam* does not bind a third party) but because by so doing he
knowingly impedes and interferes with the administration of justice (*i.e.* the ongoing
proceedings and future trial).[77] Where a third party, of his own volition, does an act that
he knows will defeat the purpose of a final injunction it appears that he may not be guilty
of contempt, because even though by so doing he interferes with the ends of justice, to
hold him in contempt would offend against the principle that an injunction does not bind
a third party.[78]

    A different situation may arise where an injunction is granted against the whole world. **12–099**
The jurisdiction to do so is extremely limited, for instance in wardship proceedings.[79] An
example current at the time of writing is the case of the murder by two ten year old boys
of the two year old child James Bulger. The case caused widespread public revulsion.
When the time came for the boys' release from detention at age 18, the question arose
whether they should be able to preserve the confidentiality of the new identities with
which they would be provided on their release and other information about themselves.
In *Venables and Another v News Group Newspapers Ltd*[80] the judge, consciously departing
from authority of 200 years' standing that "you cannot have an injunction except against

a party to the suit",[81] granted injunctions *contra mundem* (against the world) restraining publication in various media of various information about the claimants. The subsequent amendment of the injunction at the behest of an Internet service provider is discussed in Chapter 5. The judge did make the following observations about the enforceability of the order in relation to the Internet:

> "I am, of course, aware that injunctions may not be fully effective to protect the claimants from acts committed outside England and Wales resulting in information about them being placed on the Internet. The injunctions can, however, prevent wider circulation of that information through the newspapers or television and radio. To that end, therefore, I would be disposed to add, in relation to information in the public domain, a further proviso, suitably limited, which would protect the special quality of the new identity, appearance and address of the claimants or information leading to that identification, even after that information had entered the public domain to the extent that it had been published on the Internet or elsewhere such as outside the U.K."

The order provided an exception in the injunction for information in the public domain at the time of the original order of January 8, 2001, but provided that that should not permit publication of certain of the material merely on the ground that material had at any time been published on the Internet and/or outside England and Wales.

12.6 Financial services

12–100   This section has been written on the assumption that the Financial Services and Markets Act 2000 comes fully into force on the currently anticipated date of December 1, 2001.

12.6.1 Regulated activities and financial promotion

12–101   Some of the most innovative and sophisticated sites on the World Wide Web are those that provide financial information and services. In many ways financial services are an ideal product for Internet commerce. In particular, effective selling of them requires the provision of large volumes of tailored financial information (an easy task for a smart web site) and fulfilment of orders does not require any physical product delivery. However, the provision of financial services is highly regulated in many jurisdictions, the United Kingdom being no exception.

12.6.2. Two key areas of concern

12–102   There are two key areas of concern in the context of financial services provided through the Internet:

   (a)   anyone developing a new Internet-based product in the United Kingdom must ensure that no element of the product involves the unlawful carrying on of regulated financial services activity in the United Kingdom. If it fails to do this and a breach of U.K. financial services law is committed then, in addition to criminal sanctions, the product provider may find that all customer contracts are unenforceable[82]; and

(b) anyone providing a financial services product from outside the United Kingdom will want to ensure that it does not, through a Web site available in the United Kingdom, either contract with, or market its products to, persons in the United Kingdom in breach of U.K. financial services law. If it does so, once again, in addition to potential criminal sanctions, any contracts with U.K. customers may be void.[82]

For duly authorised persons providing financial services in the United Kingdom, there are additional issues related to ensuring that the provision of their services in a virtual manner complies not only with applicable financial services law but also with the various financial service code of conduct and other regulatory requirements which cover them. Consideration of these latter issues is, however, outside the scope of this Chapter.

12.6.3. The Financial Services and Markets Act 2000

A defining issue for both of the above key areas of concern is the exact scope of U.K. financial services regulation. The main source of such regulation is the Financial Services and Markets Act 2000 (the "**FSMA**") and the various detailed rules and regulations created under it. This replaces, with effect from midnight November 30, 2001, the previous scheme of regulation under the Financial Services Act 1986. The approach of the FSMA in relation to the conduct of financial service business is to create a general prohibition on the carrying on of "regulated activities" in the United Kingdom by way of business, other than by persons who are duly authorised to carry them on. It does, however, provide for exclusions from that general prohibition which may be available in certain cases.

12–103

12.6.4 The General Prohibition

Under section 19 of the FSMA, no person may carry on a regulated activity in the United Kingdom, or purport to do so, unless such person is an "authorised person" or an "exempt person" (this is referred to in the FSMA, and will be referred to in this chapter, as the "**General Prohibition**"). It is an offence punishable by up to two years imprisonment, a fine or both to breach this prohibition. However, it is a defence to establish that a person took all reasonable precautions and exercised all reasonable diligence to avoid the commission of the offence (see section 25 of the FSMA).

12–104

Authorisation can be obtained in the United Kingdom by applying to the Financial Services Authority (the statutory regulator under the FSMA) for authorisation to carry out the particular intended regulated activity or activities. The applicant will need to be able to satisfy the Financial Services Authority of its suitability for authorisation with regard to such things as its business plan and procedures, compliance systems, expertise, capital adequacy and controlling persons (in particular, their fitness to be involved in regulated business etc.). Authorisation also involves compliance with a rigorous ongoing supervision regime which will include complying with "Conduct of Business Rules" promulgated by the Financial Services Authority (different rules applying to different regulated activities).

12–105   Under what is known as the "Investment Services Directive", a firm authorised to carry on investment business in another EEA Member State can, subject to certain formalities, carry on the same business in the United Kingdom without requiring a separate U.K. authorisation. It will, however, generally have to comply with U.K. Conduct of Business Rules in relation to its activities here.

12.6.5. Regulated Activities

12–106   An activity is a regulated activity for the purposes of the FSMA if it is (a) specified as such in any statutory instrument made under that Act and (b) carried on by way of business.[83] At the time of writing, there is one such statutory instrument which is The Financial Services and Markets Act 2000 (Regulated Activities) Order 2001 (S.I. 2001 No.544) (the "**Regulated Activities Order**"). The approach of using statutory instruments to define the scope of regulated activity was adopted (rather than setting out all classes of regulated activity in the FSMA itself) to facilitate the easy and rapid addition of new classes of regulated activity by U.K. regulators.

A non-exhaustive list of the activities classified as regulated activities by the Regulated Activities Order includes:

- activities relating to "investments", including: dealing in (i.e. buying/selling) investments as principal or as agent (although many dealings as principal are excluded); arranging deals in investments; managing investments; safeguarding and administering investments; providing advice on the purchase, sale and exercise of rights under investments; sending dematerialised instructions; establishing, operating or winding up collective investment schemes; and agreeing to carry on any of these activities. The definition of "investments" is widely cast to include virtually all types of security (whether debt or equity) as well as rights derived from securities or, indeed, derivative rights in respect of assets which are not themselves securities or investments;

- taking "deposits", defined as sums of money accepted on terms that they will be repaid (with or without interest);

- effecting and carrying out contracts of insurance;

- operating or winding up a stakeholder pension scheme;

- certain activities relating to the Lloyd's insurance market;

- providing funeral plan contracts; and

- lending under, or administering, regulated mortgage contracts—essentially mortgages on property which is to be used (or a substantial part of which is to be used) for domestic purposes by the borrower.

12–107   If an internet service proposed to be offered includes any activity within the above list, it is necessary for the person providing the service to consider whether an authorisation is needed or whether an exclusion is available. Similarly an overseas financial service provider who may be intending to undertake any of the above activities with a customer base which may include people in the United Kingdom will need to consider its regulatory position carefully and what, if any, of its activities with those customers will actually be carried on in the United Kingdom.

12.6.6 Exclusions

An activity which would otherwise be a regulated activity can be carried on by a person who is not authorised provided that such person's conduct of that activity falls within one of the exclusions allowed by the FSMA. Such exclusions as exist at the time of writing are set out in the Regulated Activities Order. Once again, the approach of including exclusions in a statutory order simplifies the addition of new exclusions where considered necessary by U.K. regulators and this is an important element of flexibility built into the U.K. legislation. Different activities have different exclusions. So, for example there is an exclusion from the regulated activity of "insurance" for breakdown insurance which satisfies certain conditions. Similarly, an exclusion from the activity of "deposit taking" exists for "deposits" taken by companies issuing commercial paper on certain terms. There is a wide range of exclusions for various activities related to dealings with, and arrangements concerning, securities. For example, one key exclusion permits a person who is not FSMA–authorised to deal in securities for its own account in most circumstances, provided that such person is not generally holding itself out to the public as being willing to buy or sell the relevant type of investments. A detailed analysis of the various exclusions available is beyond the scope of this book. However, there are two types of exclusion which are of particular interest in the context of the key areas of concern mentioned in earlier in this chapter and these are discussed in the succeeding paragraphs.

12–108

12.6.7 Financial Information Web Sites

Good independent financial advice is a much sought after commodity. Furthermore, with the growing (one may even say, bewildering) diversity of investment options now available, well-informed and unbiased advice becomes ever more important for the ordinary investing member of the public. The need for such advice is something which is addressed in the United Kingdom by "independent financial advisers" or "IFAs" as they are commonly known. To be permitted to give the investment advice they provide, IFAs are required to be authorised under the FSMA.

12–109

Newspapers have, right from their beginnings, used the provision of financial information and advice as a way of selling more copies and most U.K. papers have a section concerning personal money matters and/or a "tipster" section where the likely future movement of key stock prices is considered. Furthermore, in more recent times, many specialist journals have been created with a focus on investing (*e.g. Investors Chronicle* to name but one).

The provision of financial advice of a general kind and which is not related to particular investments (*e.g.* "technology stocks look strong at present") is not a regulated activity, however, newspapers and specialist journals will often provide advice in relation to particular investments which, on the face it, is a type of advice which should only be provided by a person duly authorised under the FSMA. The U.K. regulatory position has, however, always sought to draw a distinction between persons providing such advice as a profession on the one hand and, on the other, newspapers or journals

12–110

providing it for the general entertainment of their readership without an overlay of professional responsibility or professed specialist knowledge or expertise. This distinction is continued under the FSMA by the provision of an exclusion from the regulated activity of providing investment advice if the advice (1) is contained in a newspaper, journal, magazine, or other periodical publication, or (2) is given by way of a service comprising regularly updated news or information. The second limb is an important new addition to the regulatory framework, because it extends an exclusion previously only appearing to be available to forms of real world publication (*e.g.* newspapers, journals etc. which could be expected to have a physical form) to their virtual world equivalent, such as investment information web sites.

However, there is an important limitation to this exclusion. In order to benefit from it, the principal purpose of the relevant publication or service, taken as a whole and including any advertisements or other promotional material contained in it, must be neither (1) to provide investment advice related to particular securities nor (2) to lead or enable persons to buy, sell or subscribe for securities or contractually based investments.[84]

12–111   For a web site which sets out to provide financial information and is published by persons who are not authorised to provide financial advice in the United Kingdom, this exclusion is very useful. But it is clear that there is a dividing line between an essentially "journalistic" site where some investment advice is incidental to the main purpose of the site and a site which has, as its main purpose, providing investment advice. Whether a site crosses this line may not always be easy to determine and it should be noted that the publication has to be looked at as a whole, including any advertisements, etc. on it. An area of concern might, for example, be a site which contained certain pages of advice related to buying or selling particular shares and, on each relevant page, also set out an advertisement for a share dealing service.

12.6.8 Overseas Financial Service Providers

12–112   In certain areas, the way in which the Internet opens up possibility of cross–border contracting is a significant benefit. In the field of financial services, however, it can raise some difficult issues. In particular, a financial services provider which is not authorised to provide financial services in the United Kingdom but contracts with U.K. persons through its web site may commit a criminal offence in the United Kingdom and may also find that the contracts it has made are unenforceable. There are, however, two key potential sources of comfort for an overseas financial services provider in this respect:

    (a)   The General Prohibition only applies to regulated activity which is carried on "in the U.K.". So, if the activities of an overseas financial service provider, although conducted with U.K. persons, do not involve the conduct of regulated activity "in the U.K.", then there will be no breach of the General Prohibition. However, the usefulness of this geographic delimitation of the General Prohibition to an overseas financial services provider is restricted by the difficulty that exists in determining what "in the U.K." actually means. In traditional tests of whether a business is being carried on in the United Kingdom, a key issue has always been the degree of physical presence maintained by the business in the UK. For overseas persons who do have such a physical presence, it should be noted that section 418 stipulates that activity carried on from any establishment in the

United Kingdom will be deemed to be carried on "in the U.K.". For persons without a physical establishment in the United Kingdom, the position is less clear. In an Internet world, it would seem illogical to focus only on a bricks-and-mortar test and it may be expected that, in future, the English courts will adopt a more purposive approach—looking at such factors as the degree to which a business is actively soliciting, and contracting with, customers in the United Kingdom.

(b)   There are certain additional exclusions provided by the Regulated Activities Order which are available to persons who, although they may be carrying on regulated activities in the United Kingdom, do not carry on such activities from a permanent place of business in the United Kingdom (any such person being defined as an "overseas person"). There are, in particular, exclusions for overseas persons dealing in securities (as agent or principal), arranging deals in securities and providing advice in relation to securities. However, an important point to note is that, for a number of these exclusions to apply to dealings between the overseas person and persons in the United Kingdom, those contracts must not have derived from any form of promotional approach from the overseas person which has breached the UK law on financial promotions described below.

12.6.9 Financial Promotions Restriction

The FSMA (like the Financial Services Act 1986 before it) does not only restrict the carrying on of regulated activity in the United Kingdom. It also restricts the issue of promotional material inviting or seeking to induce members of the public to enter into agreements relating to certain types of investments. The restriction (the "**Financial Promotion Restriction**") is set out in section 21 of the FSMA and creates an offence for any person who, in the course of business,[85] communicates an invitation or inducement to engage in investment activity unless that person is either an authorised person or the content of the communication is approved by an authorised person. The detail of the Financial Promotion Restriction is set out in a statutory instrument called The Financial Services and Markets Act 2000 (Financial Promotion) Order 2001 (S.I. 2001 No. 1335) (the "**Financial Promotion Order**"). **12–113**

There are two important points to note in relation to the Financial Promotion Restriction:

(a)   The words "invitation" and "inducement" are not defined but are likely to be construed broadly. It is clear that they can include material disseminated through a web site, and can also include communications by e-mail.

(b)   An invitation or inducement to enter into investment activity can constitute an offence even if, were that investment activity actually to be entered into by the issuer of the invitation or inducement, there would be no "regulated activity" by virtue of the existence of an exclusion applying. So, a business which advertises to sell shares it holds in another company without procuring the approval of the advertisement by an authorised person will be committing an offence even though the actual sale of those shares may not constitute regulated activity on the part of that business because it would be a "dealing as principal".

12–114   The Financial Promotion Restriction will create problems for any person who seeks to advertise an investment scheme through the Internet or even by e-mail communications to a selected potential investor base. However, the Financial Promotion Order does contain some exemptions which may be available in certain cases of this kind—for example, where the target audience on the investment promotion consists of investment professionals or sophisticated high net worth individuals. There are also other exclusions available under the order and different types of advertised product have different exemptions. For some exemptions a distinction is drawn between real time (*e.g.* personal meetings and telephone calls) and non-real time communications (including e-mails) and between solicited (initiated by the customer or expressly invited by them) and unsolicited communications.

12.6.10 The Financial Promotion Restriction and Overseas Financial Service Providers

12–115   The Financial Promotion Restriction also needs to be borne in mind by overseas financial service providers. Because the restriction operates independently from the General Prohibition, it is possible for such a financial service provider to breach the Financial Promotion Restriction even though it is not actually carrying on any regulated activity in the United Kingdom. Importantly, it should be noted that, by virtue of section 30 of the FSMA, a contract which is entered into with a person in the United Kingdom may be rendered unenforceable if entry into that contract was induced by a promotion issued in breach of the Financial Promotion Restriction (although the English courts have a discretion to permit enforcement of the contract if this is considered just and equitable in all the circumstances). The effect of a breach can therefore be draconian.

This raises an issue for overseas financial service providers who advertise their services or products on their web sites. It is currently difficult for any such provider to impose an effective barrier on access to its site to people located in the United Kingdom. Accordingly, their web sites and promotional material on them will be available in the United Kingdom and thus potentially breach the Financial Promotion Restriction. However, recognising that this may sometimes be an unfair result, Article 12 of the Financial Promotion Order Restriction stipulates that, with certain exceptions,[86] the Financial Promotion Restriction will not apply to any communication which is "directed (whether from inside or outside the United Kingdom) only at persons outside the U.K." (Article 12(1)(b)).

12–116   The Financial Promotion Order sets out the conditions to be met for a communication to be regarded as "directed only at persons outside the U.K." (Article 12(4)). These conditions are:

- the communication is accompanied by an indication that it is directed only at persons outside the U.K.;

- the communication is accompanied by an indication that it must not be acted upon by persons in the U.K.;

- the communication is not referred to in, or directly accessible from, any other communication which is made to a person, or directed at persons, in the U.K. by or on behalf of the same person;

- there are in place proper systems and procedures to prevent recipients in the

U.K. (other than those to whom the communication might otherwise have lawfully been made) engaging in the investment activity to which the communication relates with the person directing the communication, a close relative of his or a member of the same group; and

- the communication is included in a website, newspaper journal, magazine or periodical publication which is principally accessed in or intended for a market outside the U.K. or a radio or television broadcast or teletext service transmitted principally for reception outside the U.K.

12.6.11 Exclusion from Financial Promotion Restriction for hosts and access providers

Because the Financial Promotion Restriction renders it an offence to "communicate" an invitation or inducement to engage in investment activity, on the face of things it could pose a problem for web site hosts or access providers who may be said to be "communicating" infringing material on web sites for which they act as a host or provide access services. However, Article 18 of the Financial Promotion Order provides an exemption for persons whose role in any restricted communication is that of a "mere conduit". A person acts as a mere conduit for a communication if: **12–117**

- that person communicates it in the course of business carried on by him, the principal purpose of which is transmitting or receiving material provided to him by others;
- the content of the communication is wholly devised by another person; and
- the nature of the service provided by that person in relation to the communication is such that the person does not select, modify or otherwise exercise control over its content prior to its transmission or receipt.

However, it is important to note that a person does not select, modify or otherwise exercise control over the content of a communication merely by removing or having the power to remove material: **12–118**

- which is, or is alleged to be, illegal, defamatory or in breach of copyright;
- in response to a request to a body which is empowered by or under any enactment to make such a request; or
- when otherwise required to do so by law.

12.7 Pharmaceuticals

The specific issues which face the pharmaceutical industry so far as the Internet is concerned are the restrictions on advertising of pharmaceutical products and data protection. Data protection is dealt with elsewhere in detail in Chapter 7, but it is worth noting that in addition to the greater protection afforded to health data under the Data Protection Directive, a number of jurisdictions have further specific restrictions concerning the use and dissemination of health related data.   **12–119**

The advertising of pharmaceutical products is regulated in many countries. However, the nature and extent of the regulation varies enormously. New Zealand and the United States permit direct to consumer advertising of prescription only products. In the European Union, the advertising of medicinal products is governed by Council Directive 92/28 which prohibits the advertising to the general public of prescription only medicines or medicinal products containing psychotropic or narcotic substances. The advertising of medicines available "over the counter" is permitted by the Directive, subject to restrictions on the mentioning of certain types of indications.

12–120   The bare framework set out in the Directive is fleshed out by the various self regulatory codes which the pharmaceutical industry follow, which include the IFPMA[87] code, the EFPIA[88] code and the ABPI[89] code. The codes attempt to deal with the problems faced by the Internet. Detailed information which may be legally provided to the consumers in one country can be accessed by a consumer in another country where such promotion would be contrary to the law or codes of practice of that country. The ABPI code of practice governs websites which are operated by U.K. companies or by their affiliates where information concerning the use or availability of a product in the United Kingdom is mentioned. The ABPI code provides that open access sites must not include promotional material relating to prescription only medicines, but the summary of product characteristics, patient information leaflet and European public assessment report relating to medicinal products can be published. Sites which are restricted to members of the medical profession can contain promotional material, although the Medicines Control Agency has advised that each page should be labeled "intended for health professionals".

There are proposals to amend Directive 92/28 to permit Member States, on an initial five year trial basis, to allow the dissemination to the public of products authorised for the treatment of AIDS, asthma and chronic broncopulmonary disease and diabetes, which again would be subject to self-regulatory codes.

12–121   In addition to the restrictions on advertising, the rules relating to the sale of pharmaceuticals vary between countries. Germany, for example, has a law prohibiting mail-order pharmacies. The German pharmacists' trade association has brought proceedings against a Dutch online pharmacy which was supplying medicines into Germany. The association were granted injunctions preventing the pharmacy from selling medicines over the Internet. However, apparently German customers are continuing to collect the products themselves from the Netherlands or to receive them by courier. The injunction is being challenged on the basis of restriction of the free movement of goods and a reference to the ECJ may be made.[90]

12.8 Advertising on the Internet

12–122   Advertising is generally regulated in the United Kingdom by voluntary codes, although there are a large number of statutes which may affect advertising. In particular, there are a number of offences relating to misleading advertising. Some sectors, such as advertising of cigarettes, alcoholic drinks, medicines and financial products and services, are subject to more stringent regulation.

The main voluntary code in the United Kingdom is the British Codes of Advertising Practice (the Codes). The Codes are drawn up by the Committee of Advertising Practice, which includes representatives of the advertising, sales promotion and media businesses. Compliance is monitored by the Advertising Standards Authority (ASA), an independent body. The Codes set out the rules for what is acceptable in advertisements, sales promotions and direct marketing. There are some special rules in addition to the general Advertising Code, for example for alcohol, advertising directed at children, motoring, environmental claims, health and beauty products and slimming, and there is a special Cigarette Code. The Codes cover advertising in all non–broadcast media. Broadcast commercials are the responsibility of the Radio Authority and the Independent Television Commission.

ASA has focused on U.K.-originated Web sites, but if it is faced with a foreign site it may be able to refer the complaint to an equivalent regulatory body in the foreign jurisdiction, for instance, via the European Advertising Standards Alliance. The ASA's remit for the Internet includes advertisements in paid-for space, such as banner and pop-up advertisements, on-line sales promotion and commercial e-mails. It does not extend to general product information on home pages.

In general, advertising regulations impose stricter standards for justification of claims **12–123** than are required by the general law, such as defamation, for editorial content. The combination of advertising and broadcasting standards has especial potential to be restrictive. During the debate on proposed revisions to the Television without Frontiers Directive, one of the European Parliament's proposed amendments to the Directive was that advertising should not be offensive to "religious, *philosophical* or political beliefs" (amendment italicised).

On the Internet, problems may arise with the distinction between advertising/promotional material and editorial on Web sites, especially given the seamless linking of pages on the Web which renders it difficult to separate the two. This could result in the inadvertent extension of advertising content restrictions to editorial content.

In one case ASA upheld a complaint against a cinema advertising campaign run by Friends of the Earth (FoE). FoE placed the same material on its campaigning Web site. ASA felt powerless in practice to pursue the matter because FoE was hosting the site on its own server, so that there was no media owner to turn to. If ASA had pursued the matter, the question could well have arisen whether the material on the Web site was still advertising or promotional material at all, or whether it was in fact editorial material.

Such an issue arose in a case in Ireland under regulations equivalent to the U.K. **12–124** Control of Misleading Advertisements Regulations 1988.[91] A trade union representing the plaintiff's workforce placed an advertisement in the national press seeking to justify strike action by the union's members over Christmas pay. The Irish Supreme Court held that the trade union's advertisement had nothing to do with the promotion of a supply of goods or services, and so was not "advertising" within the meaning of the Directive from which the regulations were derived.

If an advertisement breaks the Code's rules, ASA will ask the advertiser to withdraw or amend it.[92] Other sanctions include adverse publicity, the refusal of further space, removal of trade incentives and finally legal proceedings via a referral from ASA to the Office of Fair Trading (OFT) under the Control of Misleading Advertisements Regulations 1988. OFT has the power to obtain an injunction against advertisers to prevent them from repeating the same or similar claims in future advertisements.

Certain professional or trade bodies may control advertising by their members. For example, advertising by solicitors is governed by the Solicitors' Publicity Code promulgated by the Law Society.

Advertising may also be unlawful because the advertisement is in breach of other legal **12–125** rules, such as being defamatory or infringing another's copyright or trade mark, matters that are dealt with elsewhere in this book.

In the United Kingdom there are also various statutory regulations which if breached can amount to a criminal offence with penalties such as fines and even imprisonment attached. For example, there are the various offences of applying a false trade description to goods under the Trade Descriptions Act 1986. And there are particular offences relating to unfair pricing such as very specific rules about advertising prices in a sale. While the authorities in the United Kingdom have not yet used any of these provisions against traders on the Internet, there is no reason to believe that they will not do so, particularly in view of the fine imposed by the U.S. Department of Transportation on Virgin Atlantic for misleading pricing. In that instance Virgin Atlantic violated the department's regulations by failing to disclose the full price of flights advertised on the Virgin Web site when it advertised a fare for flights between Newark in New Jersey and London which was not in fact available.

Junk e-mail

12–126   Blatant commercial exploitation in traditional areas of the Internet such as Usenet and e-mail was originally resented by Internet users because it was only recently that the Internet had been used for commercial purposes. In the early days two U.S. attorneys famously used the Internet to advertise their services in connection with U.S. immigration to every newsgroup. This was a breach of the unwritten rules of Internet etiquette, but the attorneys refused to apologise. Internet users retaliated by clogging the attorneys' electronic mailbox with enormously long messages, which caused their service provider's system to become unusable, so the provider terminated service to the offenders.

Although the use of much of the Internet for commercial purposes is now accepted, junk e-mail and spam continue to be regarded as something that needs to be controlled. It has provoked series of lawsuits in the USA, in which ISPs have successfully invoked trespass laws against spammers.[93] This is reminiscent of the reportedly successful use of trespass laws in England against junk faxes.[94]

12–127   Specific legislation, actual and proposed, on unsolicited e-mail is in disarray. The Telecommunications Data Protection Directive permitted Member States to adopt either an opt-in or an opt-out policy. The Department of Trade and Industry encountered widely differing views on the merits of these and chose to defer any steps to implement Article 12 of the Directive.[95] It was in any event doubtful whether that aspect of the Directive applied to e-mail. The Electronic Commerce Directive also contained provisions about unsolicited commercial communications, but other than encouraging the use of opt-out registers left the matter to national law. The Communications Data Protection Directive, still under negotiation, currently requires opt-in for unsolicited e-mail. Meanwhile, the use of personal data for electronic mailing purposes is in any event subject to the constraints of the Data Protection Act 1998 (see Chapter 7).

12.9 Encryption

12.9.1 Introduction

12–128   Encryption has emerged as one of the potential cornerstones of e-commerce, for a variety of uses. The most widely known use is to enable secure, confidential communications between businesses and their customers, but encryption technologies are also used in several other ways, primarily relating to:

— the use of digital signatures to establish the identities of the parties to a transaction, and provide evidence of intention to contract;

— watermarking documents to aid in the enforcement of intellectual property rights (such as the copyright in materials published on or broadcast over the Internet);
Encryption is not the only mechanism available to perform these functions[96] but for historical reasons has been the subject of more controversy than the potentially competing alternatives. Encryption technology was historically the province of the security services, with the result that governments, in particular the United States, viewed its release into civil society with deep suspicion. The result is that development of the law in this area was initially premised on conflicting agendas—business utility versus government anxiety—and the discussions as to where the law should intervene are only now beginning to address encryption as an essential element in e-commerce, the appropriate legal framework for which should be viewed from a primarily civilian perspective.

This is still a relatively new area in terms of commercial solutions. Many of the products in use are either tailor-made for particular client applications, or at a very basic level.[97] Solutions proposed today could well be superseded in a few years or even months by alternatives not yet on the drawing board. Thus, legislation ought to be framed as broadly as possible, in an attempt not to incorporate any unnecessary assumptions as to the technical nature, function or usage of materials. However, for the moment at least, areas of uncertainty as to the legal status of particular encryption transactions and services persist. **12–129**

12.9.2 Technical background

Terminology
"Cryptography" is the art of writing messages in such ways that they cannot be read by third parties; it was developed in order to ensure the confidentiality of the message. The process of transforming a readable "plaintext" message into an unreadable form or "cipher" is encryption. Hundreds of different codes and enciphering techniques have been developed over the centuries.[98] However, the methods of code-breaking ("cryptanalysis" or "decryption"), such as frequency analysis of the appearances of given letters, are well known and tend to be painstaking but mechanical, making them ideally suited for computer attack. Thus, the subtlest encryption techniques developed before the advent of computers, cracking which required enormous skill and patience over many weeks of study, can now be done by an average PC in a matter of hours. **12–130**

Cryptographic systems
There are two common forms of cryptography which are in widespread use: private key encryption and public key encryption, otherwise known as symmetric and asymmetric key encryption. In both of these, a complex cryptographic algorithm is applied to the plaintext to produce the cryptogram. The algorithm in each case calculates the transposition of each letter of the plaintext based upon a number which is called the key. **12–131**

In private key encryption,[99] both parties use the same key—the system is symmetric from either side. The disadvantages of this are that it is necessary for both sides to know and agree the key in advance, and to keep it completely secret thereafter. Thus, there is a need for a "key exchange mechanism" before the encrypted transmissions can start, and two possible attack points for any third party trying to obtain the key. The risk of loss of key secrecy can be reduced by using the keys only for one exchange of messages, or "session", but the obvious disadvantage is the need constantly to generate new keys even for communications between the same two parties.

12–132   Public key encryption[100] does away with both of these disadvantages. Instead, in public key systems, each party has two keys: a public key, which can harmlessly be published to the world at large, and a private key, which must be kept to oneself at all costs. There is no need for one party to any exchange to know the other's private key. Further, the private key cannot (if the key is sufficiently long) feasibly be deduced from the public key. Instead, they can each use the other's public key to encrypt the message; the message will then only be decryptable by someone holding the right private key. Public key systems are therefore in theory stronger than private key systems; the downside is that they are also considerably heavier in terms of computing power needed.

In practice the security of any encryption system depends upon the length of the key used. The "key" is just a number, expressed in binary form. Any encryption problem can therefore be attacked by trying to guess the key, known as the "brute force" attack. A key one 'bit' long must be either 0 or 1, so it can take no more than two attempts to guess. It will take a fast PC or two quite a number of hours to run through all of the possibilities for a 40 bit key, but is not impossible. The DES (Data Encryption Standard) private key system is generally used with a 56 bit key—enough to tie up a serious amount of computing power for some time but not beyond the reach of any reasonably sized business or very determined hacker.[101]

Key administration infrastructure

12–133   Correct handling of keys is clearly a vital aspect of any cryptographic system. Apart from the initial function of generating keys, there must also be means for:

(1)   establishing or verifying the "real world" identity of a particular keyholder, which in commercial terms is likely to be through certification by a neutral party ("certification authority");

(2)   enabling distribution (by publication or secure exchange, depending on the cryptographic system being utilised) of keys to those who need and are entitled to have them;

(3)   revocation and deletion of keys whose security is suspected to have been compromised by any means, and letting those who need to know with certainty of the revocation. In the absence of such systems, the uncertainty and potential incompleteness of changes (some people still using old keys, contractors not sure exactly when a key was revoked) may be a substantial handicap to electronic commerce. Further,

(4)   the multitude of keys any one user will need must also be safely stored and indexed for use as required.

(5)   In some contexts, it may be necessary to incorporate some system to facilitate retrieval of data without recourse to the key. Most discussion has centred on governments' desire to be able to read communications intercepted in the course of criminal intelligence gathering, but it could be necessary in the private context too: the key management system may break down,[102] or it may be suspected that communications are taking place either between unauthorised persons or for unauthorised purposes. The principal solutions proposed are key escrow[103] and

key recovery,[104] but there may be security issues associated with both of these solutions.[105] There has also been controversy over the terms on which police or government should be allowed to obtain access: in particular, whether this should require a warrant to be obtained from the courts, or merely some administrative procedure to be carried out.

A considerable administrative infrastructure is likely to arise, to provide Trusted Third   **12–134**
Party[106] ("TTP") services associated with transactions using encryption, at least to support digital signatures. Some service providers are already operating commercially and with substantial success on an unregulated basis, notably VeriSign in the USA. Various other organisations are emerging to offer similar services, either commercially or on an industry basis—for example, banking and insurance TTP schemes are in the process of being established. Some governments have considered that regulation is required to promote user trust in the certificates and notices given by these third parties. In Singapore, for instance a licensing and approval scheme has been implemented. In Europe, the Electronic Signatures Directive prohibits Member States from implementing prior authorisation schemes for the provision of certification services in relation to electronic signatures. The Directive permits the establishment of voluntary accreditation schemes for certification service providers. In the United Kingdom, Part I of the Electronic Communications Act 2000 provides for the establishment of a statutory, but voluntary, register of approved providers of cryptography support services. The government has stated that it does not intend to implement these provisions if the private sector T-Scheme is successful. If the provisions are not implemented within five years of commencement they will lapse.

Digital signatures
Probably the most common application of cryptography in connection with Internet   **12–135**
transactions, after simple encryption of messages, is the production of digital signatures. These require the use of public key cryptography but are widely promoted as the most effective and workable means of establishing the level of trust required between parties to business transactions.

A digital signature is calculated by taking the message to be signed and applying to it a "Message Digest" or "hash" function. This calculates a data string, analogous to a fingerprint of the message. No two messages will produce the same short string. The sender then encrypts this data string with his or her private key. The resulting data string is the digital signature.

A digital signature can identify with certainty the originator of the message, since it can only be decrypted with that person's public key. A digital signature can also assure the integrity of either a communication or of stored data, and establish the time of creation of a message or document.[107] Further, there should be no issue as to people using copies of other people's signatures by the "cut and paste" method—unless they wish to retransmit the identical message, the signature is incorrect.

A digital signature does not, as such, make any contribution to the confidentiality of   **12–136**
the message: the message itself may be transmitted in plaintext, with only the message digest encrypted to give the signature. For complete confidence, the sender can have two private keys, one to be used to produce the signature and another to encrypt the plaintext. Technical means exist[108] to signal when keys are being used for functions other than the one for which they were generated. However, where users have more than one key each, it will be important for the sake of certainty in transactions to ensure that each

person has only one key per function—that they must use Key A if they are producing a signature which signals "adopting the writing", Key B if they are encrypting for confidentiality and so on. Otherwise, the possibility arises of a contracting party repudiating their signature on the basis that the individual who signed was not authorised to sign for that purpose but did so anyway using an inappropriate key. This will clearly require an unambiguous means of ensuring that the keys being used are those appropriate to the function. Use of a separate key for digital signature purposes is also advisable in the light of the key disclosure provisions of the Regulation of Investigatory Powers Act 2000, discussed below.

12.9.3 The Legal Environment

12–137 Legislation relating to encryption technology falls into three distinct areas: that governing dealings in encryption goods, such as software packages; that concerning services associated with cryptographic functions, such as certification of keys for digital signatures; and that concerning the circumstances in which state agencies can require the delivery up of encryption keys.

Legislation relating to the former stems principally from the international level and derives from the potential for encryption devices or methods to be used for military, terrorist or criminal as readily as for commercial purposes: they are categorised as "dual use" goods. As a result they fall within the classes of goods subjected to export controls by many countries.

12–138 Legislation relating to the latter is aimed more at pursuing government policy objectives to ensure secure transactions over the Internet and to build up confidence in those, among both businesses and consumers. Governments are increasingly of the view that they need to encourage Internet users to be confident in passing confidential information such as credit card numbers: and to encourage technology designed to ensure that Internet users are passing the information to the entity they think they are; that it will not be open to detection in the course of the transaction; that the transaction will be legally binding and enforceable. The extent to which it is appropriate for governments to pursue such policy objectives through legislation, when the technology and business models are in embryonic states, is a matter of great controversy. While there has been a flurry of legislative activity at European as well as national levels, the initial tendency to establish strict regulatory schemes has now largely ebbed away. The situation may well continue to change rapidly over the next few years while the various schemes which emerge are thoroughly tried and tested.

12.9.4 Dealings in encryption products

International level

12–139 The major international instrument is the Wassenaar Arrangement, which came into force on November 1, 1996.[109] The Arrangement is the successor to the old COCOM, the Coordinating Committee for Multilateral Exports Control; 33 states are party to it. It aims to promote transparency and responsibility with respect to transfers of potentially military technologies, and to enhance co–operation to prevent the acquisition of armaments and sensitive dual-use goods for military end-uses by regions or states which are causing the Participating States concern. The Arrangement applies to both conventional arms and dual-use goods. The provisions of this Arrangement are reflected in the export controls imposed by the European Union (discussed below) and the various other signatories.

The Arrangement was amended in December 1998 to loosen the controls in respect of private key encryption software which uses a key length of less than 64 bits and is generally available to the public through "over the counter" or equivalent channels, as long as the cryptographic function cannot easily be changed by the user. This is likely to include most commercial private key encryption products already in circulation, many of which use keys of this sort of length or less. In addition, cryptographic products designed solely for authentication or digital signatures and products for the protection of copyright-protected data are excluded from the control scheme. The European and relevant national regimes are likely to be amended in the near future to follow suit.

In a more peripheral fashion the two Copyright Treaties which the World Intellectual **12–140** Property Organisation adopted in December 1996 also affect encryption products. Among other matters, they aim to restrict dealings in and use of devices for circumventing copy-protection devices (including encryption methods). This is an attempt to reinforce the effectiveness of copy protection and the integrity of rights management information incorporated in any digitised copyright work. These Treaties have so far been ratified by only twenty four of the signatories and will not come into effect for some time. The EU Copyright in the Information Society Directive, discussed in Chapter 2, implements the WIPO treaties and it is expected that the E.U. Member States will ratify the treaties once this Directive has been implemented.

European Union

A new Regulation (1334/2000) governing the Community-wide regime for the control of **12–141** export of dual-use goods was adopted by the European Council of Ministers on June 22, 2000 and came into force on September 28, 2000. This Regulation was passed to update the Community regime to conform with the revised Wassenaar Arrangement. It extended the meaning of "export" to include the transmission of software or technology by electronic media, fax or telephone to a destination outside the Community.

The Dual-Use list in the Regulation agrees broadly with the agreed Dual-Use list from the Wassenaar Arrangement, as it is intended to do. Cryptographic products, including software, are included in Annex IV of the related E.C. Council Decision 94/942/CFSP[110] and thus (subject to some stated exceptions not relevant to use of encryption by Internet users) in principle require a licence for export from the European Union. No licences are required for movement of cryptographic goods within the Union.

The only other piece of European legislation with relevance to encryption products is the European Commission's Conditional Access Directive.[111] This takes pains to point out that it is not directly concerned with the legal status of encryption technology as such. Rather, it aims to provide a framework for the use of encryption as a mechanism whereby services which depend for their remuneration on limiting access should be able to be certain of achieving effective limitation—that is, ensuring that access to their services is conditional upon meeting the subscription conditions. This is the foundation for providers of on-line services such as digital radio services or video on demand to broadcast commercially over the Internet.

The Directive, which was meant to have been implemented by Member States by May **12–142** 2000, requires Member States to prohibit the commercial sale, installation or use of "illicit devices", that is equipment or software designed or adapted to give access to a protected service in an intelligible form without the authorisation of the service provider.[112] It does not include any express regulation of encrypting mechanisms or devices except to ban Member States from restricting free movement of conditional access devices.[113]

The European Commission's explanatory notes accompanying the adopted Directive hinted that this Directive may form the model for a broader international instrument on the control of illicit devices, but there has been no further indication of any intention to proceed further.

National

12–143   The U.K. Dual-Use Items (Export Control) Regulations 2000 (S.I. 2000 No. 2620)("the U.K. Regulations") came into force on September 28, 2000. They implement certain aspects of the E.C. Council Regulation discussed above and govern the procedures for obtaining export licences for encryption products and software from the United Kingdom.

Annex 1 of the Regulations contains the General Software Note which gives a general exception in respect of software generally available without restriction at retail points and through mail order, etc, or otherwise "in the public domain" (by which is meant publicly available, rather than that the term of copyright has expired). However, the significant changes from the 1996 Regulations which they replace are that the U.K. Regulations now apply to exports of items, including software and technology, in both tangible and intangible form as newly controlled under the E.C. Regulation. They also include a requirement for detailed information to be retained about encryption products which are exported to other Member States, including: descriptions of all relevant encryption algorithms and key management schemes, and descriptions of how they are used by the item (for example, which algorithm is used for authentication, which for confidentiality and which for key exchange); and details (for example, source code) of how they are implemented (for example, how keys are generated and distributed; how key length is governed and how the algorithm and keys are called by the software); details of any measures taken to preclude user modification of the encryption algorithm, key management scheme or key length; and details of programming interfaces that can be used to gain access to the cryptographic functionality of the item.

This represents a significant tightening up from the previous regime, under which it was possible to put software on a Website to be uploaded by users abroad, without necessarily falling foul of them.[114] Although unfortunate the change is not surprising since this loophole contrasted strongly with the highly restrictive approach taken in the USA when Phil Zimmerman originally put PGP onto the Internet.

12–144   Other specific technologies are also excepted by Annex 1: certain personalised smart cards; equipment for radio broadcasting or pay-TV which includes decryption technology for audio/ video or management functions; mobile telephones for civil use; decryption functions to allow the execution of copy-protected software, as long as these are not accessible to the user.

Although the Regulations have been updated to reflect the changes to the Wassenaar Arrangement in December 1998 they remain Byzantine,[115] and it would be prudent to check with the DTI before exporting or uploading any encrypting technology.

Other Wassenaar signatory states will have more or less equivalent restrictions on export for encryption software.

12.9.5 Cryptography services/service providers

International

No legally binding instruments have yet been signed on this issue at the international   **12–145**
level, and there are no proposals for any to be introduced.

On the non-binding level, the most important document is the recommended
cryptography policy Guidelines issued on March 27, 1997 by the OECD (Organisation
for Economic Co-operation and Development).[116] This was under prompting from the
USA, which in 1997 raised the status of its representative to this forum to that of
Ambassador, possibly in part to emphasise the seriousness with which it views the issue
of widespread availability of strong encryption.[117]

The Guidelines envisage that governments will require lawful access to plaintext or to   **12–146**
the cryptographic keys for encrypted data. They nevertheless require that the policies
implementing such access should respect to the greatest extent possible the other
principles set out in the guidelines. These are: trustworthiness of cryptographic methods;
availability to users of a choice of methods; market-driven development; international
and national standards for cryptographic methods; respect for privacy; and clear
allocation of liability. The factors the Guidelines propose should be taken into account
are: the benefits for public safety, law enforcement and national security; the risks of
misuse; the additional expense of the necessary supporting infrastructure; the prospects
of technical failure; and other costs. They also lay down that access should only be given
where there is a legal right to possession of the plaintext, and that it must only be used for
lawful purposes. The access process should also be recorded, to enable judicial review if
necessary.

European Union

A draft Council of Europe Convention on Cybercrime[118] has been finalised and is due to   **12–147**
be considered by the Committee of Ministers in September 2001. It is intended to address
problems of substantive and procedural criminal law connected with information
technology, including the following subjects:

— criminal computer misuse laws; including unauthorised access to computers,
   illegal interception of communications, intentional damage to computer data,
   intentional serious hindering of the functioning of a computer system, and
   misuse of devices (including software) designed or adapted primarily for
   committing any of the aforesaid.

— computer-related offences such as computer-related forgery and computer-
   related fraud,

— computer-related offences in relation to child pornography (there are significant
   opt-outs for pseudo-photographs and other aspects of these offences)

— copyright and related offences; copyright and related rights (but not moral
   rights) infringement when undertaken wilfully, on a commercial scale and by
   means of a computer system;

— measures to enable authorities to order the expeditious preservation of specified
   computer data, including traffic data, for up to 90 days to enable the authorities
   to seek disclosure; and to ensure that sufficient traffic data is disclosed to enable
   the service providers and the path through which the communication was

transmitted to be identified; production orders; search and seizure of stored computer data; real-time collection of traffic data from service providers; interception of content data from service providers in relation to serious offences;

— jurisdiction over criminal offences; international co-operation; extradition principles; mutual assistance and provision of spontaneous information.

12–148 The Convention, during its drafting process, drew considerable fire on privacy and civil liberties grounds.

The criminal provisions relating to accessing of computer systems and transmitted data, in each case where the access or interception is "without right", are likely to include any measure requiring the breaking of any form of encryption in order to obtain access. It remains to be seen whether the Convention will be approved by the Committee of Ministers and, if so, whether it will be ratified.

National—The Regulation of Investigatory Powers Act 2000 and access to encrypted material

12–149 The government's requirement for access to encrypted material was originally mooted as part of the proposed Secure Electronic Communications Bill, which became the Electronic Communications Act 2000. The topic was the subject of controversy throughout the consultations leading up to the Bill. A key escrow scheme, as originally proposed, was dropped after stiff opposition from industry, civil liberties groups and the European Commission. The arrangements that replaced it were eventually enacted as Part III of the Regulation of Investigatory Powers Act 2000 (the "RIP Act"). This is not yet in force, at the time of writing.

Under Part III of the RIP Act, various government agencies will be empowered, if certain threshold conditions are satisfied, to issue disclosure notices requiring the production of the encryption key[119] which will enable them to unlock encrypted material which they have lawfully obtained (for example, under a search warrant). The recipient of the notice can in most cases comply with the notice providing a copy of the plaintext and so avoid giving up the key.[120] If a "section 51 direction" has been issued, he must disclose the key. If he is not in possession of the protected information, or needs another key to obtain access to it or put it into intelligible form, then he must also disclose the key. There is also a requirement to disclose information that would facilitate obtaining or discovery of a key or putting the information into intelligible form. Section 50 also sets out the circumstances in which disclosure of one of several keys is sufficient. Knowing failure to comply with the disclosure notice would be a criminal offence. Two defences are provided: one, not having the key; and the other, that it was not reasonably practicable to produce the key in the time allowed but the key was disclosed as soon as reasonably practicable thereafter. A further offence of "tipping off" is introduced: if the notice requires its existence to be kept secret, failure to do so would be an offence. No disclosure can be required of any key intended, and in fact, used for the purpose only of generating electronic signatures (section 49(9)). For that reason it is important to ensure that signatures used for that purpose are used for that purpose alone.

12.10 Computer misuse

12.10.1 The Computer Misuse Act 1990

12–150 The Computer Misuse Act 1990 ("the 1990 Act") was introduced in the United Kingdom to create specific offences in relation to unauthorised access to computer systems. Although aimed mainly at the activities of traditional computer hackers, the Act has caught a wider class of activities, such as the release of viruses.[121] The Act created three separate offences.[122]

Unauthorised access to computer material
A person is guilty of an offence under section 1 of the Act if he causes a computer to perform any function with intent to secure access to any program or data held in any computer, the access he intends to secure is unauthorised and he knows at the time when he causes the computer to perform the function that that is the case. The section specifically provides that the intent of the person need not be directed at any particular program or data, a program or data of any particular kind or a program or data held in any particular computer. This renders the Act peculiarly suitable for use against activities carried out across networks.   **12–151**

Under section 17(5) a person's access is unauthorised if: the person is not himself entitled to control access of the kind in question to the program or data; and he does not have consent to access by him of the kind in question to the program or data from any person who is so entitled.

A person secures access to any program or data held in a computer if by causing the computer to perform any function he: **12–152**

(a)   alters or erases the program or data;

(b)   copies or moves it to any storage medium other than that in which it is held or to a different location in the storage medium in which it is held;

(c)   uses it; or

(d)   has it output from the computer in which it is held (whether by having it displayed or in any other manner).

An offence under this section is punishable by imprisonment of up to six months or a fine of up to £5,000 or both.

Unauthorised access with intent to commit or facilitate commission of further offences
This is, in essence, an aggravated version of the offence under section 1. Under section 2 a person is guilty of an offence if he commits an offence under section 1 with intent to commit one of certain further specified offences, or to facilitate the commission of such an offence by himself or any other person. An offence under this section is punishable on summary conviction by the same penalties as under section 1, or on indictment by imprisonment for a term not exceeding five years, or to a fine (unlimited) or to both.   **12–153**

Unauthorised modification of computer material
Under section 3 a person is guilty of an offence if he does any act which causes an unauthorised modification of the contents of any computer and at the time when he does the act he has "the requisite intent and the requisite knowledge". The requisite intent is an intent to cause a modification of the content of any computer and by so doing: **12–154**

(a)   to impair the operation of any computer;

(b)   to prevent or hinder access to any program or data held in the computer; or

(c)   to impair the operation of any such program or the reliability of any such data.

The requisite knowledge is knowledge that any modification he intends to cause is unauthorised. The section provides that intent need not be directed to any particular computer, any particular program or data or a program or data of any particular kind or any particular modification or modification of any particular kind.

12–155   Under section 17(7) a modification of the contents of any computer takes place if, by the operation of any function of the computer concerned or any other computer, any program or data held in the computer concerned is altered or erased; or any program or data is added to its contents.

Under section 17(8) such modification is unauthorised if: the person whose act causes it is not himself entitled to determine whether the modification should be made; and he does not have consent to the modification from any person who is so entitled.

The penalties for an offence under section 3 are the same as under section 2.

12.10.2 E-mail viruses and the 1990 Act

12–156   The Act clearly applies to those who release damaging viruses into the wild, even though the person doing so does not have an intent to damage a particular computer.

Some e-mail may not be specifically intended to destroy data or prevent programs from operating, but simply use e-mail directories to propagate themselves around e-mail systems. There could still be the possibility of a conviction. Notwithstanding that e-mail systems are intended to receive e–mails, nonetheless under section 1 the use of the recipient's e-mail program to cause the incoming e-mail virus to propagate onwards by means of the e–mail system is arguably access of an unauthorised nature and would therefore be liable to prosecution under section 1.

Unauthorised access

12–157   However, the nature of unauthorised access can cause difficulties. In *DPP v. Bignall*[123] two police officers, who were authorised to do so for their work, used the Police National Computer System to obtain information for their personal purposes. The Divisional Court, on appeal, reasoned that the Defendants did have authorised access to the system and so could not be in violation of section 1 of the 1990 Act, notwithstanding that the purpose for which they accessed the system was not a purpose for which they were given access to the system.

Could it be argued, in the case of an e-mail virus, that if the virus makes use only of those aspects of the receiving system which are intended to be available to and used by incoming e-mails, in a way contemplated by the receiving system, so that that access is authorised no offence committed? For that argument to succeed would require that access to the particular data was authorised, that the kind of access secured was authorised and that the authorisation existed in the sense of express or implied permission, not the mere technical ability to access the data in question. It would be a question of fact in each case whether the virus made use of and accessed parts of the receiving system beyond those to which access was authorised to incoming e–mails, or whether the access was of a kind not authorised.

12–158   This approach derives from the House of Lords decision of *R. v. Bow Street Stipendiary Magistrate, ex parte Government of the United States of America*,[124] in which *Bignell* was considered. The House of Lords held (when considering a case involving unauthorised access by an employee) that the pertinent question is whether access to the data in question was authorised; whether the kind of access secured to that data was authorised; and that the question of authorisation was a question of entitlement to control access in the sense of having the right to authorise or forbid access—not the physical ability to operate or manipulate the computer. The actual decision in *Bignell* was considered to be probably right, since the defendants were authorised to access the particular data in question, but the broader statements in *Bignell* as to the purpose and interpretation of the 1990 Act were disapproved.

Unauthorised modification

As regards section 3, the question is firstly whether an e-mail virus has caused an   **12–159** unauthorised modification of the contents of any computer. Although the receiving system is open for receipt of e-mails and modifications to the contents of that computer as the result of such access are inevitable, there could still be an argument that by going beyond the intended use of the receiving e-mail system the actual modification made would be regarded as unauthorised. There is, as noted above, a further requirement that there should be intent to impair the operation of any computer, to prevent or hinder access to any program or data held in a computer or to impair the operation of any such program or the reliability of any such data. It would be a question of fact in each case as to the state of mind of the person charged and the actual effect of the modifications of the content of the receiving computer. However, "impair" is a broad concept and in many cases it could be possible to bring the effect of the virus within that provision.

12.10.3 Access to websites and the 1990 Act

Questions may arise as to when, if at all, accessing a website could be an offence under   **12–160** the Act. Clearly, accessing a publicly available website could not be an offence in itself, since there is an implied authorisation for the public to visit the website.

Denial of service attacks

However a difficult question arises where the access is abused. Is, for instance, a denial of   **12–161** service attack an offence? Such an attack consists of sending massive quantities of otherwise normal messages or page requests to an Internet host. The server is overloaded, cannot deal with legitimate requests and effectively becomes unavailable. If the access could be regarded as unauthorised, there would seem to be a section 1 offence and possibly (given the effect on the server) a section 3 offence. As to whether the access was unauthorised, the *Bow Street* decision discusses the provisions of section 17(5) (see above). "[Section 17(5)] makes clear that the authority must relate not simply to the data or program but also to the kind of access secured". An example is given that "Authority to view data may not extend to authority to copy or alter that data." If the kind of access secured could be interpreted to import an implied restriction on the authority to visit a website that it be used only for viewing and other reasonable purposes, then that could provide a basis for an argument that the kind of access was unauthorised. However, it could be argued that this really concerns the purpose of the access, not the kind of access, and that where the access simply consists of a large quantity of otherwise normal accesses, that is a question of degree not one of kind.

Websites generally

12–162   There could be a variety of other situations in which access to a website becomes unauthorised: for instance, if part of the website is restricted to persons who are qualified by age, occupation, or some other criteria and someone gains access by making untrue statements; or if someone has been banned from a discussion forum and re-enters it under an alias. These would seem to fall pretty clearly within the parameters of a section 1 offence, certainly on the basis of the *Bow Street* criteria for unauthorised access, but not a section 3 offence.

The example given in *Bow Street* concerning a distinction between viewing and copying data raises the surprising possibility that someone who downloads material from a website in contravention of a copyright licence that only permits viewing on screen, may commit an offence under the 1990 Act. Their Lordships may not have fully considered the fact that, in the electronic environment, viewing necessarily involves copying.

---

1.   This has been apparent in the negotiations over the proposed Hague Convention on International Jurisdiction and Foreign Judgments in Civil and Commercial Matters (www.hcch.net). For cross-border information torts, an "effects" based jurisdiction rule makes it very easy for a court to take jurisdiction and then to apply its home law to the conduct complained about. If the jurisdiction rule is more limited, then the court may have to decline jurisdiction and will not get the opportunity to apply its home law. If a jurisdiction rules allows a consumer to sue in his home country then, then the court will have the opportunity to apply the mandatory rules (*e.g.* consumer protection laws) of the home country. So even pure jurisdiction rules have consequences for the substantive law applied to Internet content. See also the Report of the American Bar Association Jurisdiction in Cyberspace Project (www.abanet.org/buslaw/cyber).

2.   See, however, the ABA Jurisdiction Project recommendation that a "multinational Global Online Standards Commission ("GOSC") should be empanelled to study jurisdiction issues and develop uniform principles and global protocol standards by a specific sunset date, working in conjunction with other international bodies considering similar issues" (Report, para. 1.4).

3.   For instance, if the requirements of political impartiality under the Broadcasting Act 1990 were to be applied to the Internet, Web versions of print newspapers would have to be rewritten to remove the political partisanship characteristic of the print press. A partisan editorial line would be impermissible. See also *R. v. Radio Authority, ex p Bull* [1997] E.M.L.R. 201 in which the Court of Appeal upheld a decision by the Radio Authority to prohibit radio advertising by Amnesty International (British Section) on the ground that the organisation's objects were wholly or mainly of a political nature, contrary to s. 92(2)(a) of the Broadcasting Act 1990.

4.   John Milton's famous *Areopagitica* (1644) was a criticism of Cromwell's practice of licensing books and periodicals: "Truth and understanding are not such wares as to be monopolised and traded in by tickets and statutes and standards. We must not think to make a staple commodity of all the knowledge in the land, to mark and licence it like our broadcloth and our woolpacks." In contrast, the licensing of broadcast media has flourished without serious opposition

5.   Recent years have seen an increase in the importance of self-regulatory bodies such as the Press Complaints Commission, in response to heavy criticism of some activities of the print press, especially in the area of privacy. For the first time, with the enactment of section 12(4) of the Human Rights Act, linkage has been established between private codes of practice and statutory rules.

6.   ITC Programme Code, section 8.

7.   See Chapter 8. The ITC claims that its powers under the Broadcasting Act 1990 extend to television programmes on the Internet and to advertisements which contain still or moving pictures (see www.itc.org.uk/regulating/internet_reg/index.htm), but that it is "not seeking to apply these powers at present".

8.   Chatline Services Code of Practice recognised by Director-General of Telecommunications December 7, 1989, para. 2.3.2 (recognition was subsequently withdrawn in 1992). OFTEL now intends to bring most of ICTSIS's codes of practice under OFTEL's jurisdiction, so that ICSTIS's codes have to be recognised by OFTEL and affording OFTEL a last-resort power to intervene. This proposal had the potential to impact on some Internet services where charges are paid through the customer's telephone bill, although OFTEL and ICSTIS have disclaimed any intention to regulate the Internet in this regard (Statement by Director-General of Telecommunications, 24 July 2001). See also J. Edwards and A. Sylvester,"A Law by Any Other Name—ICSTIS" [1997] 4 C.T.L.R. 157.

9.   Statement from the Director General of Telecommunications July 27, 1989.

10. Communications White Paper, p. 83. The White Paper describes the proposal to bring all of ICSTIS's codes

of practice under the jurisdiction of OFTEL as "licence changes to help make ICSTIS even more effective".

11. *A new future for Communications* (Cm. 5010) December 12, 2000.
12. *e-commerce@its.best.uk*, para. 5.6.
13. *ACLU v. Reno*, 929 F. Supp. 824 (DC EPa 1996).
14. *FCC v. Pacifica Foundation*, 438 U.S. 726 (1978).
15. 114 S. Ct 2445 (1994).
16. Session 1997-98, Fourth Report, May 6, 1998.
17. Session 2000-01, Second Report, March 15, 2001.
18. Para. 112.
19. See Chapter 6.
20. Discussed below, under Germany.
21. For instance, in the German prosecution of Felix Somm over the CompuServe newsgroups in 1995, not only was the initial conviction reversed on appeal, but new legislation (the German Multimedia Act) had by then been introduced which gave online service providers a measure of protection in respect of third party content that they carried.
22. Para. 114.
23. For a collection of critical articles see www.libertus.net/liberty/oppress.html.
24. The Broadcasting Services Amendment (Online Services) Act 1999.
25. www.ispo.cec.be/convergencegp/.
26. COM(98)50, www.ispo.cec.be/eif/policy/com9850en.html.
27. COM(2000) 393, July 12, 2000.
28. The definition of "electronic communications service" in Art. 2(b) excludes "services providing, or exercising editorial control over, content transmitted using electronic communications networks and services". Recital (7) states that it is "necessary to separate the regulation of transmission from the regulation of content".
29. Decision No. 276/1999 of the European Parliament and of the Council of January 25, 1999 adopting a multiannual Community action plan on promoting safer use of the Internet by combating illegal and harmful content on global networks ([1999] O.J. L33/1).
30. Council Recommendation of September 24, 1998 on the development of the competitiveness of the European audiovisual and information services industry by promoting national frameworks aimed at achieving a comparable and effective level of protection of minors and human dignity (No. 98/560, [1998] O.J. L270/48).
31. COM (97) 5, http://europa.eu.int/en/comm/dg10/avpolicy/new_srv/comlv-en.htm.
32. Second Report, paras 112 to 118, "The limits of Internet regulation".
33. www.amnesty.org.
34. www.freedomforum.org.
35. www.rsf.fr.
36. www.cpj.org.
37. www.amnesty.org/ailib/aipub/1997/ASA/31600197.htm.
38. Human Rights Watch Backgrounder "Freedom of Expression and the Internet in China" (www.hrw.org/backgrounder/asia/china-bck-0701.htm)
39. See *e.g.* http://javachat.sohu.com/english/chat.php3.
40. See below, n. 11.
41. English translations of the decision of November 20, 2000 are available on www.gigalaw.com/library/france-yahoo-2000-11-20.html. The decisions of 20 November 2000 and May 22, 2000, together with the expert reports, are available in French on www.legalis.net/cgi-iddn/french/affiche-jnet.cgi?droite=internet_illicites.htm.
42. The panel report occasionally seems to use French nationality and French location interchangeably. In context, the panel must be taken to be referring to French location, at least in the case of IP address filtering.
43. Ben Laurie, *An Expert's Apology*, November 21, 2000; www.apache-ssl.org/apology.html.
44. The scheme can be found at http://www.sba.gov.sg.
45. COM (96) 487.
46. Welcomed by the Telecommunications Council on November 28, 1996.
47. www.iitf.nist.gov/eleccomm/ecomm.htm.
48. For a description of PICS see www.w3.org/pub/WWW/PICS/.
49. www.w3.org/TR/REC-PICSRules.
50. www.incore.org.
51. www.incore.org/final_report.htm.
52. The Television without Frontiers Directive (89/552, amended by Directive 97/36).
53. Electronic Commerce Directive, Art. 3.6.
54. Another example is a decision of the Italian Corte de Cassazione on December 27, 2000, assuming criminal jurisdiction in a libel case over non-Italians who made postings about an Italian citizen to a website located outside Italy. Libel is a criminal offence in Italy. The court held that the effects of the postings were perceived inside Italy and that was sufficient to assume jurisdiction. *World Internet Law Report* May 1, 2001 p. 16.

55. See Ben Laurie, *An Expert's Apology* (n. 43 above).
56. *cf.* the remarks of Jacob J. in the *Crate & Barrel* case discussed in Chapter 6: "Indeed the very language of the internet conveys the idea of the user going to the site—'visit' is the word".
57. See, for instance, the Joint Statement of the Council and Commission annexed to the Brussels Jurisdiction Regulation, concerning the interpretation of "directs" : "...the mere fact that an Internet site is accessible is not sufficient for Article 15 to be applicable.... In this respect the language or currency which a website uses does not constitute a relevant factor." However, different inferences could in principle be drawn from the use of English and, say, Icelandic.
58. [2001] V.S.C. 305.
59. n. 1 above.
60. David G Post, "Anarchy, State, and the Internet: An Essay on Law-Making in Cyberspace," 1995 *J. Online L.* art. 3 (www.law.cornell.edu/jol/post.html).
61. [2000] 2 All E.R. 315.
62. ISPA can be found at www.ispa.org.uk.
63. The Internet Watch Foundation can be found at www.internetwatch.org.uk.
64. [1997] 2 All E.R. 548, CA.
65. [1999] Masons C.L.R., 396.
66. [2000] 2 All E.R. 418, CA.
67. [2000] 2 All E.R. 425, QBD, Divisional Court.
68. See also Angus Hamilton, "Caught Looking" and "Caught Looking Revisited" *Computers and Law*, August/September and October/November 1998.
69. Ignorance of the indecent nature of the contents of the cache would fall to be considered under the defence provided by s. 160(2)(b) of the 1988 Act.
70. Laddie Prescott and Vitoria, *Modern Law of Copyright*, 3rd ed., (2000), para. 14.12.
71. [1994] F.S.R. 723.
72. See Clive Grace, "Unseen, obscene and dangerous," *The Guardian* November 18, 1999.
73. Criminal Justice and Police Act 2001, s. 43.
74. *Baron v. Crown Prosecution Service* June 13, 2000 (DC, unreported).
75. *Thomas v. News Group Newspapers Ltd* July 25, 2001, CA, TLR.
76. *Attorney-General v. Punch Ltd* [2001] 2 All E.R. 655 (cases discussed by Lord Phillips M.R. at paragraphs 56 to 88).
77. *ibid.* at paras 87–88.
78. *ibid.* at paras 85–86 (but it can be seen from the difficulty expressed by Lord Phillips (para. 87) in analysing previous caselaw, especially the speeches of the House of Lords in *Att.-Gen. v. Times Newspapers* [1991] 2 All E.R. 398 ("*Spycatcher*") that the position is not wholly clear.
79. *X County Council v. A* [1985] 1 All E.R. 53 (the Mary Bell case).
80. [2001] 1 All E.R. 908.
81. *Iveson v. Harris* (1802) 7 Ves. 251, 32 E.R. 102, *per* Lord Eldon.
82. See section 26 of the FSMA
83. See the Financial Services and Markets Act 2000 (Regulated Activities) Order 2001
84. For exact definition of these expressions see Article 3 of the Regulated Activities Order.
85. Note, this does not have to be a business which constitutes "regulated activity"
86. Note that this exclusion will not apply to an "unsolicited real time communication" (*e.g.* a personal visit or telephone call not initiated or specifically requested by the customer) unless it is made from a place outside the U.K. and it is made for the purposes of a business which is carried on outside the U.K. (which is also not carried on in the U.K.) (Article 12(2))
87. The International Federation of Pharmaceutical Manufacturers Associations (www.ifpma.org).
88. The European Federation of Pharmaceutical Industries and Associations (www.efpia.org).
89. The Association of the British Pharmaceutical Industry (www.abpi.org).
90. www.time.com/time/europe/biz/printout/0,9869,101418,00.html; *Lawyer International* Issue 97, July/August 2001.
91. *Dunnes Stores Ltd v Mandate* [1996] 2 C.M.L.R. 120.
92. Under the U.K. Internet Service Providers Association Code of Practice, members of the Association must comply with the Codes of Practice supervised by ASA (cl. 2.1.2).
93. See discussion of "spidering" in Chapter 2. It is also reported that Intel succeeded in obtaining a trespass injunction in the USA against an ex-employee who had mass e-mailed 30,000 messages to Intel employees at their company e-mail addresses. *Computer Litigation Journal* July 1999, 3.
94. See "Junk faxes" 90/24 *L.S. Gaz.*, June 23, 1993, 9; "Faxamatosis: fresh outbreak" *New Law Journal* February 26, 1993, 278.
95. See, for instance, "Online sales rules postponed to settle dispute" *Financial Times* June 7, 2000.
96. For example, Virtual Private Networks using controlled Internet pathways offer confidence about the identity of correspondents since only authorised parties are able to communicate through them.
97. Arthur Andersen's February 1998 report showed that the majority of commercial and public users of cryptography have a limited experience; informed opinion was principally to be found amongst the financial institutions and government departments, although the health and "high-tech" sectors were also

using encryption to a greater or lesser extent.

98. A thorough discussion of the evolution of cryptography is given in David Kahn's book *The Codebreakers* (Simon & Schuster, 1996 revised ed.).

99. For example, using the Data Encryption Standard (DES) of the United States, the International Data Encryption Algorithm (IDEA) from Switzerland, algorithms RC4 and RC5, and so on. DES has been the most commonly used private key algorithm for some time, but the search is underway to produce a replacement, tentatively known as AES—Advanced Encryption System.

100. The best known public key algorithm is the RSA (Rivest, Shamir, Adelman) now licensed by RSA Data Security in the United States. The PGP (Pretty Good Privacy) encryption software, developed and released onto the Internet by Phil Zimmerman, uses the RSA algorithm.

101. Pragmatically, it should be remembered that in reality there are very few problems which warrant the dedication of unlimited time and resources to solve.

102. If an employee who was able to generate keys, or the sole holder of a particular key, leaves without disclosing one, for example.

103. A system under which legitimate users of encryption will deposit a copy of their private key with an escrow agent. This may be an external "trusted third party", where communication between companies or other organisations is concerned, or within an organisation it may be an additional function of the system administrator in respect of keys for use with corporate data or communications. The Electronic Communications Act 2000, s. 14, prohibits the use of powers under the Act to impose key escrow requirements.

104. In this scenario the TTP, a "Key Recovery Centre", has a public key of its own. Compliant encryption users would, in every message sent, include a copy of their own private key, encrypted with the Centre's public key so that only the Centre would be in a position to decrypt it. As long as the Centre has at least one message from each party to the exchange they will have access to all of the relevant keys. Alternatively, the data needed to "recover" the key is included, encrypted, in either a header or appendix to each message. Different agencies would have to be invoked to get access to the different parts of the data. Further, some of the data may be left over to be cryptanalysed, to discourage casual requests for access and reduce the prospect of collusion amongst the recovery agencies.

105. The disadvantages of key escrow arrangements are
    — the increased vulnerability of having keys held in a single place;
    — the increased number of communication paths required for dealings with the archived key;
    — the inherent distrust of consumers and users generally for any potential imposed third party;
    — users' loss of control over key management; and
    — the high entry cost of setting up such an arrangement in the first place.
    In either version of key recovery, no communication with any third party is required in the preparatory stage and no third party holds a key, so reducing the vulnerability of the system compared with a key escrow. The remaining disadvantages still apply.

106. The term TTP is used for a service provider which carries out functions other than simple certification of identities: keeping directories, effecting and notifying users of changes such as revocation of keys (for example, where their security was believed to have been compromised), time-stamping electronic documents and so on.

107. Any alteration to the contents of the message or stored data will produce a new fingerprint. Thus, all the recipient has to do is decrypt the signature and calculate the fingerprint of the message/ data as received/ retrieved. If it matches the fingerprint originally calculated by the sender/ archivist, the message/ data has not been altered. If it does not match, there has been tampering—although it will not be possible to tell what kind.

108. Albeit subject to reservations as to their security.

109. Text available at http://www.wassenaar.org; the relevant sections are the General Software Note and related materials.

110. as amended by E.C. Council Decisions 96/613/CFSP, 99/54/CFSP and 99/193/CFSP.

111. Published in the Official Journal at [1998] O.J. L320/54.

112. Definition in Article 1; prohibition in Article 3.

113. Article 2.

114. The DTI confirmed this in at least one case, in relation to software using the Blowfish algorithm, although clearly not wishing to encourage the practice of intangible technology transfer .

115. For a detailed discussion of the U.K. export regime, see Conor Ward's article "Regulation of the Use of Cryptography and Cryptographic Systems in the United Kingdom: the Policy and the Practice" [1997] 3 C.L.T.R. 3, 105.

116. Available at http://www.oecd.org/dsti/iccp/crypto_e.html.

117. Although since then even the U.S. has taken a slightly more relaxed stance in that in the course of 2000 it successively abandoned the export controls on mass market cryptographic commodities and software with a key length of up to 64 bits, subject to a prior review on a product-by-product basis unless the proposed export is to the E.U. or certain other designated destinations. Finance specific, 56-bit non-mass market products with a key length between 512 and 1024 bits, network-based applications and other products which are functionally equivalent to retail products are also exempt.

118. Http://conventions.coe.int/treaty/EN/projets/FinalCybercrime.htm.
119. "Key" is in fact defined far more widely than an encryption key. "Protected information" is information that requires a key for access or to render it intelligible. A "key" is any "key, code, password, algorithm or other data".
120. These are to a limited extent equivalent, in that possession of the plaintext would enable a cryptanalyst to deduce the encryption algorithm and key; but this would still require some effort, and it may be that the security services will not in general have the resources to devote to this degree of cross-checking the information with which they have been provided.
121. For a survey of prosecutions under the 1990 Act, see R Battcock, "Prosecutions under the Computer Misuse Act 1990", *Computers and Law* Vol. 6 issue 6, February/March 1996.
122. The Act (s. 3(6)) also abolished, in cases where there is no impairment of the physical condition of the computer, the previously available possibility of obtaining a conviction for hacking under the Criminal Damage Act 1971. In *R. v. Whiteley* [1993] F.S.R. 168 the Court of Appeal upheld a conviction of a hacker under this Act. In order to obtain a conviction the prosecution had to demonstrate that the defendant caused damage to tangible property. The Court of Appeal held that it was sufficient that the particles on the hard disk were altered in such a way as to cause an impairment of the value or usefulness of the disk to the owner.
123. (1998) Crim. L.R. 53.
124. [1999] 4 All E.R. 2.

13

Tax

13.1 Introduction

A general comment that seems to pervade all legal analysis of the Internet is that the law has not kept pace with the technological developments. This is as true in tax as in any other legal field. What this means is that, whilst there are some areas in which the existing tax rules work sensibly in relation to business conducted over the Internet, in others there are problems. Most of these problems arise from the truly global nature of the Internet and the ease with which e-commerce transactions cross borders. It is further complicated by the Internet's intangible nature and the flexibility and superficial anonymity it affords users and transactions, all of which make cross-border supplies less transparent and businesses potentially invisible to the tax authorities.

13–001

Just as regulation of the technological development of the Internet features on policy agendas at the highest political levels internationally, so too does the taxation of e-commerce. Work in formulating tax policy has been approached on the basis that it is in all interests that taxation does not create a barrier to the growth of e-commerce while, at the same time, each nation's tax base is appropriately secured (in order that public services be adequately funded), a fair sharing of the tax base from e-commerce between countries is maintained and any double taxation or unintentional non taxation is avoided. Through the OECD (Organisation for Economic Co-operation and Development—the primary forum for co-operation in matters of international taxation) and the European Union ("E.U.") there is a particular emphasis of ensuring global solutions intended to lead to a fiscal climate where e-commerce can flourish with a minimum of burden.

This Chapter will examine the major tax issues which are of most significance to e-commerce, namely value added tax (VAT), customs duties and particular direct tax issues such as withholding tax and taxable presence. It will also cover emerging Internet tax policy in the United Kingdom and elsewhere. The chapter will address these issues principally from a U.K. tax perspective (although the issues are common to all jurisdictions) and will centre on the four main types of person around whom e-commerce revolves: the user, the ISP, the content provider and the telecommunications company.

13–002

13.2 Emerging tax policy—an overview

13–003   Tax issues related to e-commerce are currently the subject of international discussion and collaboration through the OECD, the E.U. and the World Customs Organisation ("WCO"). The United Kingdom, along with both E.U. and OECD member and non-member countries, have been contributing to the on-going work. Input into the collaboration has been received from all levels of the international community—governments, the various taxing authorities, tax professionals and the business community itself.

As of the date of publication, there are still no answers to some of the questions discussed below. Nevertheless, a consensus is emerging.

In a Communication in April 1997,[1] the E.U. Commission stressed the need to ensure that tax obligations in relation to e-commerce were clear, transparent, predictable and, so that there was no extra burden on e-commerce as opposed to more traditional forms of commerce, neutral. Furthermore, the importance of implementing tax rules which did not create market distortions was also emphasised. In the Joint E.U.-U.S. Statement on Electronic Commerce of December 5, 1997, it was also accepted that the taxation of e-commerce should be "clear, consistent, neutral and non-discriminatory".

13–004   The subsequent Commission Communication of June 1998[2] expanded upon the principles laid down in the 1997 Communication and set out the following key guidelines for the way forward:

(i)   Efforts should be concentrated on adapting existing taxes, and in particular VAT, to the developments of e-commerce: no new or additional taxes should be considered;

(ii)   A supply of digitised products via an electronic network should be treated for VAT purposes as a supply of services;

(iii)   Services, whether supplied by e-commerce or otherwise, which are supplied for consumption within the E.U. should be taxed within the E.U. (whatever their origin) and services supplied for consumption outside the E.U. should not be subject to E.U. VAT, although VAT on related costs or "inputs" should be eligible for deduction;

(iv)   The VAT regime should ensure that taxation is enforceable on supplies of services received within the E.U. via e-commerce by both businesses *and* private individuals.

13–005   This Communication had been prepared in anticipation of the OECD Ministerial Conference on Electronic Commerce which took place in Ottawa in October 1998. The Taxation Framework Conditions published by the OECD Committee on Fiscal Affairs pursuant to the Ottawa conference addressed four areas: tax treaties, consumption taxes, tax administration and taxpayer service. The key conclusions mirrored those reached independently by the E.U. and U.S. It was stated that the taxation principles that guide governments in relation to conventional commerce should also guide them in relation to e-commerce. These principles were the principles of neutrality, efficiency, certainty and simplicity, effectiveness and fairness, and flexibility. Thus, the consequences of taxation should be the same for transactions in goods and services regardless of the mode of commerce used, whether they are purchased from within or from outside the E.U. and whether delivery is effected on-line or off–line, so that no particular form of commerce is advantaged or disadvantaged. Compliance costs for taxpayers and administrative costs for tax authorities should be minimised as far as possible. The rules should be clear and simple to understand so that the taxpayer can anticipate in advance the tax consequences of a transaction. Furthermore, the rules should not result in double or unintentional non-taxation but in the right amount of tax being paid at the right time and in the right country. They should minimise the potential for evasion and avoidance and be flexible and dynamic enough to keep pace with technological and commercial developments. The Committee believed, at that stage of development of Internet commerce, that existing taxation measures could implement these principles. However, new or modified measures were not precluded provided that they assisted in the application of existing principles and were not intended to impose a discriminatory tax treatment of e-commerce or resulted in an unfair distortion of competition which would result from a de facto double taxation or non-taxation of e-commerce *vis-à-vis* fully taxed traditional commerce. The Framework Conditions also established an ambitious timetable to study and decide upon the various implementation options identified in the paper. Key elements of the work programme (which are currently ongoing) include how payments for digitised products should be characterised under tax treaties, in what circumstances a web site may constitute a permanent establishment giving rise to tax jurisdiction in the country where the server on which it is hosted is located and, in relation to consumption taxes such as VAT, obtaining a consensus on defining place of supply and on internationally compatible definitions of services and intangible property.

Also in October 1998, the U.K. Inland Revenue and HM Customs and Excise published a joint paper on U.K. tax policy[3] regarding e-commerce. Not surprisingly, the paper was almost identical in content to that of the OECD Framework Conditions. At about the same time legislation was passed in the USA[4] which imposed a three year moratorium (until October 2001) on new taxes on Internet access fees and prohibited "multiple and discriminatory" taxes on e-commerce at either the state or the federal level. It did not, however, prevent a tax authority from imposing a previously existing tax on e-commerce transactions provided that the tax was equally applicable to e-commerce companies and traditional companies. This legislation also created a Congressionally appointed commission, whose remit it is to determine how e-commerce should be taxed, if at all.

13–006

So it can be seen the present consensus is that there are to be no new taxes. Rather, the existing tax structure should be made to work using the guiding principles of neutrality, certainty and transparency, effectiveness and efficiency. As will be seen from the commentary which follows, existing taxes are sufficiently robust to be able to accommodate certain forms of e-commerce (for example, the "e-mail" order of goods which are then delivered by traditional means) but not others, where work is still necessary both at the domestic and international level to agree upon the tools needed to put policy in place.

13.3 VAT

The application of VAT to the supply of goods and services via the Internet will be considered first because correct application of VAT presents the biggest practical problem for businesses operating over the Internet, as well as for the tax authorities themselves.

13–007

The importance to governments of the correct VAT treatment of e-commerce must be appreciated. It (and other consumption taxes) are an increasingly important means of raising tax revenues worldwide. Over the last 25 years the proportion of OECD country tax revenue from consumption taxes has increased by about four per cent points of GDP, while the outturn from personal income tax has fallen. Perhaps more tellingly, a VAT (or GST) is now in place in every OECD member state except the U.S. In the E.U., VAT rates currently vary between 15 per cent and 25 per cent, with eight of the 14 member states having rates of over 20 per cent. It accounts for nearly a fifth of member states' tax receipts and, as an own resource, for 44 per cent of the Community budget.

13.3.1 Summary of United Kingdom VAT law

13–008   VAT is a creature of the E.U. and its primary legislative basis is the Sixth Council Directive (77/388) which has been the subject of substantial amendment since its promulgation in 1977. The Directive has been implemented by local legislation in each member state. In the United Kingdom, the current legislation is mainly to be found in the Value Added Tax Act 1994 and the various orders and regulations made thereunder.

VAT is intended eventually to be fully harmonised within the E.U. If full harmonisation is achieved, VAT will apply across the boundaries of each E.U. member state in a way that it does not at present. Under the current system, each member state charges VAT at its own rates under its own local legislation and special rules have to apply to cross-border supplies within the E.U. Under a fully harmonised system, transactions within the E.U. should be treated in the same way as transactions are currently treated if made within the boundaries of a member state: the "international" element only arising where the transaction involves services supplied to or by a person outside the E.U., or goods are imported from or exported to a jurisdiction outside the E.U. If full harmonisation ever is achieved, some of the difficulties which arise at present within the E.U. should be simplified.

13.3.2 Basic elements of VAT

13–009   The essential elements of U.K. VAT are relatively straightforward and may be summarised in the following propositions:

U.K. VAT is generally chargeable in three situations:

(i)   on a supply of goods and services made in the United Kingdom;

(ii)   on the acquisition in the U.K. of goods from another E.U. member state; and

(iii)   on the importation of goods into the U.K. from outside the E.U.

Supplies of goods and services in the United Kingdom

13–010   For the charge to U.K. VAT under (i) above to apply, each of four elements must be satisfied:

(i)   there must be a supply of goods or services;

(ii)   this must be made in the United Kingdom;

(iii)   it must be made by a taxable person in the course or furtherance of a business carried on by him; and

(iv)   the supply must be a taxable supply.

We consider each of these requirements in turn.

In essence, anything "done for a consideration" will be a supply of either goods or services, unless specifically excluded. One example of an excluded supply is the transfer of the assets of a business as part of the transfer of the business as a going concern. Certain types of supply are expressly defined as supplies of goods or services (so that, for example, a lease of an asset is generally a supply of services while the lease of land for more than 21 years is a supply of goods). While a "supply of goods" is not defined on a general basis in the U.K. legislation, a supply of services is anything "done for a consideration" which is not a supply of goods.

The complex "place of supply" rules determine in which member state, if any, a supply of goods or services should be taxed. The result is that U.K. VAT is only chargeable where the place of supply under these rules is the United Kingdom. U.K. VAT is not chargeable if the place of supply is outside the United Kingdom, even if made by a taxable person. If the place of supply is another member state of the E.U., that member state has the jurisdiction to charge its local equivalent of VAT on the supply. If the place of supply is outside the E.U., no member state has the jurisdiction to charge VAT on the supply although value added or sales tax may be chargeable outside the E.U.   **13–011**

These place of supply rules differ fundamentally in approach in relation to supplies of goods and supplies of services. For goods, the rules essentially look to where the goods are "delivered" or made available to the customer. For services, the crucial question is normally where the *supplier* "belongs". The supplier's place of "belonging" has a particular meaning for VAT purposes and is broadly the place where it has its business establishment or, if it has more than one business establishment, that which is most directly concerned with the supply of services in question.

Schedule 5 services

However, there are special place of supply rules for certain types of services, in particular those services which are listed in Article 9.2(e) of the Sixth Directive, as implemented in the United Kingdom by Schedule 5 of the Value Added Tax Act 1994 ("Schedule 5 services"—see Table 13.1 below). Schedule 5 services (which are of particular relevance to the Internet) include advertising services, data processing and the provision of information, banking, financial and insurance services, and telecommunication services. For these services, (other than Table 13.1, item 9) the place of supply will be the place where the *customer* "belongs" if the customer either: **13–012**

(a)   belongs outside the E.U. (irrespective of whether the customer carries on business or is a private individual); or

(b)   belongs in a different member state to that of the provider, is registered for VAT in that member state and it receives the supply in its business capacity.

Again, the place where the customer "belongs" has a particular meaning for VAT purposes. In all other cases involving a supply of a Schedule 5 service (for example, where the customer is a private individual who does not use the service for business purposes), the general rule for determining the place of supply of services applies and the place of supply will be where the supplier "belongs".   **13–013**

Table 13.1: Schedule 5 Services

Sched. 5, paragraph	Services included
1.	transfers and assignments of copyright, patents, licences, trademarks and similar rights
2.	advertising services
3.	services of consultants, engineers, consultancy, bureaux, lawyers, accountants and other similar services; data processing and provision of information (but not any services relating to land)
4.	acceptance of any obligation to refrain from pursuing or exercising any business activity or any rights within (1) above
5.	banking, financial and insurance services (including reinsurance but not provision of safe deposit facilities)
6.	supply of staff
7.	letting on hire of goods other than a means of transport
7A.	telecommunication services
8.	services rendered by one person to another in procuring for the other any of the services listed above
9.	any service not within (1)–(7) and (8) above when supplied to a U.K. taxable person (*i.e.* a customer who is registered for VAT in the U.K.)

A "taxable person" is essentially a person who makes taxable supplies in the United Kingdom in the course or furtherance of a business carried on by him and the aggregate value of the supplies that have been made by him in the previous 12 months, or are expected to be made in the forthcoming 12 months, exceeds the prevailing registration limit.[5] Businesses may also register voluntarily for VAT. For U.K. VAT purposes, registration therefore determines whether a person is a taxable person.

A "taxable supply" is a supply of goods and services which is of such a kind as to be chargeable to U.K. VAT at 17.5 per cent (the current standard rate), 5 per cent (the current reduced rate) or nil (that is to say, 0 per cent or the zero rate). An example of a supply of goods chargeable at the reduced rate is the supply of fuel for domestic use, and of a zero rated supply is the sale of children's clothing and footwear.

13–014 It should also be noted that there are two other categories of supply which are important for VAT purposes: exempt supplies where no VAT is chargeable and input tax recovery is not possible (for example certain financial services) and "outside the scope" supplies whereby a supply is treated as not involving a supply of goods or services, or as otherwise outside the scope of VAT, with the result that VAT is not chargeable. An example of an "outside the scope" supply is the supply of certain international services.

The difference between zero rated and exempt supplies is that "input VAT" is recoverable in relation to zero rated supplies but not for exempt supplies, for which recoverability is "blocked" (see section 13.3.4 below). Importantly, the zero rate applies to certain types of supply (such as books), the export of goods outside the E.U. or the export of goods to another member state where the purchaser is registered for VAT purposes in that member state.

Acquisitions of goods from other member states in the United Kingdom
As mentioned above, a charge to U.K. VAT also arises on the acquisition in the United **13–015** Kingdom of goods from a supplier in another E.U. member state. There are special rules relating to "distance selling" of goods into the United Kingdom by persons registered for VAT in another E.U. member state. Broadly speaking, the distance selling rules cover sales to "non-taxable" U.K. customers where the E.U. supplier's aggregate supplies exceed the prevailing special registration limit applicable to distance selling.[6] A "non-taxable" customer will usually be a private individual, but may also be a public body, charity or any business whose supplies do not exceed the current VAT registration threshold or whose activities are totally exempt. The effect of the distance selling rules is that the customer pays U.K. VAT rather than VAT in the supplier's home state. These rules operate in reverse for supplies of goods made by U.K. suppliers to non–taxable customers in other member states, although registration limits vary between the member states.[7]

Imports into the United Kingdom from third countries
A charge to U.K. VAT also arises on the importation of goods into the United Kingdom **13–016** from countries outside the E.U. ("third countries"). Such a supply of goods is chargeable to U.K. VAT at the standard rate as if it were a duty of customs. This treatment applies if the goods have never previously be exported to the third country from one of the E.U. member states and is irrespective of whether the customer is a business or private individual and whether or not the customer is registered for U.K. VAT.

There are anti-avoidance provisions which are designed to prevent 'partially exempt traders' (see paragraph 13.3.4 below) from buying services from outside the United Kingdom (which if the services had been provided by a U.K. supplier would have involved a VAT cost). These provisions are known as the "reverse charge" and apply to Schedule 5 services. Where the reverse charge applies, the *recipient* of the services (rather than the supplier of the services) is required to account for VAT at the rate applicable in the member state in which he belongs to the relevant tax authority. It also gives the right to input tax deduction in respect of purchases related to taxable outputs. The effect of the reverse charge in the United Kingdom is to treat Schedule 5 services brought in from outside the United Kingdom in the same way as services that are actually supplied in the United Kingdom if the recipient of the services is VAT registered. It is important to note, however, that the reverse charge has no effect on persons acting in a private capacity.

13.3.3 Exports

As stated in 13.3.2 above, U.K. VAT is not chargeable if a supply is treated as made **13–017** outside the United Kingdom. This is the case even if the supply is made by a U.K. taxable person. However, not all exports of goods and services from an E.U. member state escape VAT.

Generally speaking, the export of goods to private customers in other E.U. member states attracts VAT in the member state of the exporter, except where the exporter is required to register locally for VAT under the so-called "distance selling" rules described above (in which case local VAT will be chargeable instead). The export of goods outside the E.U. will not attract VAT in any member state.

Exports of certain services outside the E.U. will escape VAT (both U.K. and E.U. VAT). **13–018** These include the "Schedule 5 services" referred to above (which mirror the rules on the importation of such services). As outlined above, exports of most types of Schedule 5 services from one member state of the E.U. to another are chargeable to VAT in the member state where the recipient of the services belongs where the recipient is registered for VAT purposes in that other member state and receives the services for the purposes of its business. Exports of Schedule 5 services to E.U. private customers continue to attract VAT in the member state of the supplier. Exports of Schedule 5 services to recipients belonging in third countries do not attract U.K. (or E.U.) VAT. There are, however, further special rules relating to the supply of telecommunication services, for which see below.

13.3.4 "Input" and "Output" VAT

13–019 The "cost" of VAT is intended to be borne by the end-user but the tax is collected at different stages in the production process (or "chain of supply"). A VAT registered person who only makes taxable supplies is able to offset the VAT it pays on supplies received by it ("input tax") against the VAT it charges to its customers on supplies made by it ("output tax"). It pays to HM Customs & Excise (generally on a monthly or quarterly basis) the difference between its output & input tax (or receives a repayment where input tax exceeds output tax). Where a VAT–registered person makes both taxable and non-taxable supplies (*i.e.* supplies which are exempt from or outside the scope of VAT), only a proportion of his input tax will be able to be offset or "recoverable" against output tax. This is because input tax is generally only recoverable to the extent attributable to taxable supples. In particular, the recovery of input tax attributable to exempt supplies is blocked (the principle being that the irrecoverability of input tax should be built into the price for the supply). Businesses which make taxable and exempt supplies are generally referred to as "partially exempt traders", typical examples of which are banks and insurance companies. The recovery of input tax attributable to outside the scope supplies varies. Suffice in this context to say that recovery is not blocked in the case of exports of services that would be taxable if made in the United Kingdom.

13.3.5 VAT implications of e-commerce

13–020 For E.U. VAT purposes, anything "done for a consideration" will be a supply of either goods or services and therefore within the VAT regime, unless specifically excluded. This means that where the use of the Internet is free, VAT issues will not be relevant because no consideration is given. But, where payment or another form of consideration is given for a supply made over the Internet, VAT will be an issue.

Without a doubt, the opportunities that the Internet offers to businesses of all sizes cannot be underestimated. Importantly, suppliers of goods and/or services over the Internet no longer need a physical presence in the country of their customers. From the very brief outline of the current system of VAT that operates in the United Kingdom and European Union (as given above), it will be apparent that the place of supply rules for *services* offer scope for tax planning by locating the supplier's business establishment in a tax friendly environment outside the E.U. If the place of supply rules for such services are based on the place where the supplier belongs, then VAT in the E.U. can easily be avoided. As mentioned above, there are provisions in the legislation designed to prevent such devices, such as the reverse charge procedure (in relation to Schedule 5 services) and the use and enjoyment principle (as applied to the supply of telecommunication services, for which see below). But the question remains as to how effective these provisions are, how effectively they can be policed by the relevant taxing authorities and whether (particularly in light of the non-harmonisation of VAT within the E.U.) any distortion of competition, or double taxation or unintentional non-taxation, is avoided. All these issues are further complicated by the fact that users of the Internet can be afforded a certain degree of anonymity (in terms of identity, location and/or transactions) and the Internet itself has no respect for national borders.

These points can be brought out more clearly by looking in more detail at the relevance **13–021** of VAT to business conducted over the Internet falling within the following five broad categories of transaction:

(i)   supplies of physical goods to both business and private customers;

(ii)   business to business supplies of services and digitised products;

(iii)   business to private customer supplies of services and digitised products;

(iv)   supplies of telecommunication services;

(v)   supplies of "packages" containing a variety of Internet related elements.

Supplies of physical goods to both business and private customers
An example of the kind of transaction contemplated here is where the Internet user visits **13–022** a web site and uses the Internet as a means of communication in order to conclude a contract for home delivery of goods with payment, *e.g.* by way of credit card. The goods so ordered are delivered to the user by traditional means such as the post or datapost.

There is little difference between this type of Internet transaction and a conventional mail order sale and, generally speaking, the existing VAT rules are readily applicable to such a situation. From a U.K. perspective, the transaction will either be a "supply" of goods made in the United Kingdom, an "acquisition" of goods in the U.K. from another member state of the E.U. or the "import" of goods into the U.K. from a territory outside the E.U. with the following consequences (just as if the customer had purchased the goods from a shop or via mail order):

(i)   If the supplier of the goods and the customer are both in the United Kingdom, the supplier must charge U.K. VAT at the standard rate on the supply (unless the supply is an exempt or zero rated supply for U.K. VAT purposes, such as the supply of books) and account to HM Customs and Excise for the VAT so charged.

(ii)   Goods ordered via the Internet and supplied by a U.K. supplier to "private customers" in another E.U. member state (in effect, all customers who are not registered for VAT in the member state in which they belong) will generally attract U.K. VAT at the standard rate, unless the supplier is required to register locally for VAT under the distance selling rules (as outlined in paragraph 13–015). If this is the case, the supplier will be required to register, charge and account for VAT in the customer's member state at the rate applicable in that state.

(iii)   Goods ordered via the Internet and supplied by a U.K. supplier to a VAT–registered customer in another E.U. member state who receives the supply for the purposes of a business carried on by him will be zero rated in the United Kingdom (or in E.U. terms "exempt with input tax recovery") and will attract VAT at the rate applicable in the customer's member state.

(iv)   Exports of goods ordered via the Internet by a U.K. supplier to customers in third countries will generally be zero-rated and may be subject to any relevant sales (or use, turnover or consumption) tax in the third country.

(v)   Acquisitions of goods by a U.K. customer from a supplier based in another E.U. member state will attract either VAT in the member state of the supplier or U.K. VAT, depending upon the circumstances. Generally speaking, if the customer is VAT registered, he will be required to pay and account for U.K. VAT on the supply whereas, if the customer is a private customer, VAT will be chargeable and accountable in the supplier's member state.

(vi)   Imports of goods into the United Kingdom from third countries will attract U.K. import VAT.

13–023   U.K. import VAT is the liability of the importer and is applied as though it is a duty of customs. The importer may be the supplier or the customer. If the title in the goods passes to the U.K. customer prior to importation, it is the customer who will be the importer for VAT purposes. The value of the goods for U.K. import VAT purposes will be their customs value plus, if not already included in the price, all incidental expenses such as commission, packing, transport and insurance costs, and any customs and/or excise duty or levy payable upon importation into the United Kingdom.

There are, however, a number of reliefs in the United Kingdom from the charge to import VAT. Most relevant to the import of goods into the United Kingdom ordered via the Internet, is that no U.K. VAT is charged on the import of goods (other than alcoholic beverages, tobacco products, perfumes or toilet waters) not exceeding £18 in value or small occasional non-commercial consignments less than £36 in value consigned by one private individual to another.

13–024   In the simplest of cases, and assuming that the goods will be sent by post to the United Kingdom and that the value of the goods does not exceed £2000, the VAT (and duty) payable is paid by the purchaser to the U.K. Post Office when the parcel is delivered. This treatment may, however, change if, for example, the third country supplier has an agent in the United Kingdom which imports the goods and then uses such stocks to satisfy orders placed with the third country supplier.

The most significant problem in relation to the supply of goods through e-commerce is that faced by the taxing authorities in ensuring that VAT is properly charged and collected where appropriate, especially where it is a supplier in a third country making a supply to a recipient in the E.U. The application of customs duties to such supplies of goods also has its problems (see section 13.4 below).

13–025   A further point to note is that there can be differences between the VAT treatment of a conventional sale of goods and its equivalent transaction on or via the Internet. This can be of relevance to the rate of VAT charged and there may be additional issues (for example, related to the place of supply) if the equivalent transaction is a supply of *services* (and not "goods"). Two U.K. cases illustrate this point. One involved an "e-meal" facility which involved the ordering of sandwiches, confectionary and drinks from a catering company by electronic mail.[8] The catering company would deliver the food ordered to the client's premises. HM Customs and Excise argued that the treatment of this arrangement differed from a conventional cold food takeaway shop and that the service was standard rated (as a supply of catering services) rather than zero-rated (as a supply of food). This argument was, however, rejected by the court who viewed the arrangement as no different from a telephone ordering service (which could be zero-rated). However, in *Forexia (U.K.) Ltd.*,[9] the London VAT and Duties Tribunal upheld a decision of the Commissioners of Customs and Excise that the publication and distribution of a regular news communicated to most customers by fax, electronic mail or by accessing their web site was a supply of services (namely the provision of information) which was standard rated when supplied in the United Kingdom. In contrast, a supply of a book or other written material (such as a brochure, pamphlet or newspaper) is treated as a supply of goods which, if supplied in the United Kingdom, is zero-rated. The Tribunal reached its decision with the "greatest reluctance". Amongst the reasons given for this reluctance was the fact that such a decision clearly offended against the principle of neutrality (between e-commerce and traditional commerce) and produced distortion of competition.

The VAT treatment of computer software is another example where there is a difference between e-commerce transactions and their conventional equivalent. Software downloaded via the Internet is always treated as a supply of services.

In contrast, the United Kingdom VAT treatment on the importation of tangible software from a country outside the EC depends on whether, at the time of importation, the software is "normalised" (off the shelf) or "specific" (custom made or bespoke). If the software is "normalised" software, it will be regarded as an importation of goods (made up of the carrier medium) and services (the data and/or the instructions). Where the goods and services are not identified separately, the whole importation may be treated as an importation of goods which means that U.K. VAT at 17.5 per cent must be paid on the goods at the time of importation or under duty deferment arrangements. If, however, the customer is registered for VAT in the United Kingdom, and the value of the goods and services are separately identified, the client may pay VAT on importation only on the cost or value of the carrier medium and VAT on the supply of the service element may be accounted for by the customer under the reverse charge procedure. If the software is bespoke software, the importation of such an item is also made up of an importation of goods (the carrier medium) and a supply of services (the data and/or the instructions). However, to simplify import procedures, the carrier medium is treated as an accessory to the data and the importation is treated as a supply of services to the customer. No import VAT is therefore charged on the carrier medium at importation. However, if the customer is registered for VAT in the United Kingdom, he may be required to account for VAT at 17.5 per cent on the licence fee under the reverse charge procedure. **13–026**

Business to business supplies of on-line services and digitised products
A diverse range of services is now available over the Internet. Examples include advertising services, translation services, educational and training services, the ability to make travel and ticketing reservations and on-line banking services. **13–027**

Application of the existing VAT rules to such supplies does not, generally speaking, cause many problems: the VAT treatment of supplies of services which are simply delivered via the Internet is determined by the actual nature of the services, rather than their means of delivery (that is to say, the fact that a service is delivered via the Internet has no effect on its treatment for VAT purposes). It is therefore necessary to determine the precise nature of the service provided in order to decide the appropriate place of supply rule and thereby the E.U. member state (if any) which has the jurisdiction to levy VAT.

The reverse charge mechanism (see above, Imports into the United Kingdom from Third Countries) exists to ensure that local suppliers are not unfairly disadvantaged (as compared with non-local suppliers), that VAT is accounted for and that the non-local supplier is not required to register for VAT in the customers home state.

13–028   Thus, a site owner deriving income from advertisements held on its web page is making a supply of advertising services to the advertiser. Advertising services are a Schedule 5 service and the place of supply (and therefore the place where VAT is chargeable and by whom it should be accounted for to the relevant tax authorities) will be determined by applying the special place of supply rules which relate to Schedule 5 services and which have been outlined above.

However, if the service is not within one of the categories in items 1 to 8 of Schedule 5 (see Table 13.1) the general place of supply rule will apply with the result that the place of supply is where the supplier is located. Such services will include, for example, subscriptions to broadcasting services and Internet related services such as web site design and web site hosting. This means that a non-E.U. supplier will not be required to charge VAT when it supplies these particular services to E.U. customers.

13–029   E.U. operators, however, may be required to charge VAT at the applicable rate in their member state on supplies made to customers based outside the EU and customers established in another member state. Customers based outside the EU and customers registered for VAT in another member state will then need to claim this VAT back under the unwieldy terms of the eighth or thirteenth Directives. This has the potential to distort competition and place E.U. service providers at a competitive disadvantage to non-E.U. suppliers.

Furthermore, as was the case with supplies of goods using the Internet, there can be differences between the VAT treatment of a conventional supply of services and its equivalent transaction on or via the Internet. For example, the supply of conventional translation services and educational and training services are generally treated for VAT purposes as supplied where the service is performed. However, where these services are supplied over the Internet, U.K. Customs and Excise state in their internal guidance manuals that the service cannot be treated as supplied where performed since the supply will not involve physical performance. Rather, where the service consists of supplying educational material over the Internet, the nature of the supply may more properly be characterised as the provision of information (which is a Schedule 5 service). Where tutorial support is provided over the Internet, the service may be one of consultancy (again a Schedule 5 service). Likewise, translation services supplied over the Internet do not involve physical performance but may be consultancy services within Schedule 5. Thus, the place of supply rules in relation to Schedule 5 services (given above) will apply in relation to supplies of these services over the Internet (and not the rules relating to services supplied where physically performed) to determine where VAT is chargeable and by whom it should be accounted for to the relevant tax authorities.

13–030   With respect to the VAT treatment of a supply of digitised products, both the E.U. and the OECD have concluded that, in order to provide certainty, such a supply is not to be treated as a supply of goods but of services. This means that, in the United Kingdom (and presumably the rest of the E.U.) the VAT place of supply rules in relation to the supply of services (and not goods) will determine which member state (if any) has the jurisdiction to charge VAT. ("Digitised products" mean those forms of intangible property (computer software, information, music, video) that are able to be accessed and down loaded via the Internet directly from the content provider. They are not tangible products when received initially by Internet users. A tangible product may be created thereafter (by downloading onto a CD) but this is a matter of choice.)

Invariably, the supply of a digitised product will involve the provision of information services and/or the grant or transfer of intellectual property rights. For VAT purposes, both types of service are Schedule 5 services and, as such, the place of supply will be the place where the customer "belongs" if the customer either belongs outside the E.U. (irrespective of whether the service is used for business or non-business purposes) or it belongs in another member state to that of the content provider, it is registered for VAT in that member state and it receives the supply in its business capacity (in which case it will account for local VAT under the applicable reverse charge procedure). In all other cases, the general rule will apply and the place of supply will therefore be where the content provider "belongs".

The above, however, raise a number of practical problems for most Internet based businesses if they are to apply and collect VAT correctly. Apart from determining the precise nature of the service they are providing over the Internet, they will need to be able to determine whether the customer is a taxable person and where that customer belongs. For some industries, such as on-line banking, this will not raise new issues. However, banks are in a unique position in that they will know and have to hand details information on their customer base. Additionally, electronic delivery of banking services does not generally alter the character of the service provided.   **13–031**

A further problem, especially for the VAT authorities, is VAT collection, particularly where Schedule 5 services are supplied to business customers who belong in a different member state to that in which the supplier of the service belongs. In this situation, collection of VAT relies on the business customer voluntarily accounting for VAT in his own member state under the reverse charge procedure. The question begs asking as to how truly efficient this mechanism is for collecting VAT. At present, it seems the Commission is satisfied that the reverse charge procedure is an effective mechanism for the taxation of business to business transactions. The OECD has, however, recommended that the use of the reverse charge mechanism (and any self assessment or other equivalent mechanisms) be examined in the longer term.

Business to private customer supplies of on-line services and digitised products
The vast majority of business currently conducted over the Internet comprises the two categories of transactions already discussed: supply of physical goods to business and private customers; and business to business supplies of on-line services and digitised products. However, it is this third category of transaction—supplies of services and intangible property to individuals in their private capacity—that offers the greatest opportunities to small and medium sized businesses and is recognised by most taxing authorities as the greatest test to effective tax administration. This is especially the case where the supply crosses frontiers.   **13–032**

Across the whole of the E.U. the most important difference from a VAT point of view between e-commerce transactions involving private customers rather than business customers is that the reverse charge procedure does not apply in relation to services supplied to E.U. customers by suppliers outside the E.U.

In general no VAT is currently chargeable in relation to such transactions (the reverse charge procedure only applying to taxable persons). The volume of business to private consumer transactions in services over the Internet is still relatively low (along with the revenue involved) but the volume and value of these sales is likely to increase rapidly as technological developments facilitate transfer of data such as software, music and video at high speeds. If the level of this type of e-commerce increases to a level which is   **13–033** economically significant, and the current situation is not remedied (that is to say, such transactions continue not to be subject to VAT), E.U. operators may find themselves at a double competitive disadvantage to non-E.U. operators. They will be required to charge VAT on supplies to E.U. private customers and may, if the member state also subjects such transactions to VAT at the place of origin, also be required to charge VAT on all the services they supply to non-E.U. private customers. In contrast, a non-E.U. supplier is not required to charge VAT on supplies to either E.U. or non-E.U. private customers. This situation clearly offends against the principle of neutrality. Both the E.U. and the OECD have stated that it may be necessary, in conjunction with the business community, to design mechanisms to tax such supplies.

13–034   By way of example, where a U.K.–based content provider supplies computer software to an individual in his private capacity via the Internet which the individual down loads:

   (i) If the customer belongs in the United Kingdom or in any other member state of the E.U., the place of supply will be the U.K. This means that the content provider must charge VAT at the standard rate of 17.5 per cent, and account for the VAT to HM Customs and Excise.

   (ii) If the customer belongs in a third country, the place of supply will be outside the United Kingdom, and will thus be outside the scope of the charge to U.K. VAT.

Some member states (such as France, Italy and Denmark) utilise the "use and benefit" provisions in Article 9(3) of the Sixth Directive to bring supplies made over the Internet by operators based in their home territories to private customers belonging in third countries within the charge to local VAT. The United Kingdom has so far declined to do this except in relation to supplies of telecommunication services (see below), probably because it would be very difficult to enforce the rule.

13–035   Contrast the treatment where a U.S.-based content provider supplies computer software to an individual in his private capacity via the Internet which is down loaded:

   (i) If the customer belongs in the United Kingdom (or any other member state of the E.U. which does not utilise the "use and benefit" provisions in Article 9(3) of the Sixth Directive), the place of supply will be the United States and the supply thus outside the scope of U.K. (or E.U.) VAT.

   (ii) If the customer belongs in a third country, the place of supply will be outside the E.U., and thus outside the scope of the charge to E.U. VAT.

   (iii) In the United States sales/use tax position, generally speaking, state or federal sales or use taxes are not applied to software supplied outside the U.S., whether delivered by traditional means in tangible form or electronically.

Again, the correct application of U.K. (and E.U.) VAT requires that the content provider be able to satisfy itself where the customer belongs and that the customer is down loading the product for his own personal or private use. There is an inherent difficulty involved in identifying the customer in Internet based transactions, particularly where the customer is a private consumer. The difficulty of associating on-line activities with physically defined locations will mean that there will be problems for content providers in applying VAT correctly and for the authorities in policing the application of VAT. It is certainly an area where international co-operation is needed to lay down rules which determine the circumstances in which supplies are held to be consumed (and thereby chargeable to VAT) in a jurisdiction and an efficient mechanism needed to collect the tax. The reverse charge procedure seems hardly practical where the customer is a private individual and there can be no doubt that serious problems of control and enforcement would arise if VAT was required to be collected from private individuals in this way.

Supplies of telecommunication services

For VAT purposes, telecommunication services are defined as services relating to the transmission, emission or reception of signals, writing, images and sounds or information of any nature by wire, radio, optical or other electromagnetic systems, including the related transfer or assignment of the right to use such capacity for such transmission, emission or reception and the provision of access to global information networks.[10] This definition draws on definitions already adopted at international level and will include international telephone call routing and termination services, as well as basic Internet access.   **13–036**

Under the current U.K. VAT regime, telecommunication services are a Schedule 5 service for which the place of supply is determined according to the special rules already discussed. However, as distinct from other Schedule 5 services, the place of supply of telecommunication services as determined under these rules is subject to the application of the "use and enjoyment principle". The U.K. "use and enjoyment principle" implements the "use and benefit" provisions in Article 9(3) of the Sixth Directive and applies to telecommunication services supplied on or after March 18, 1998. The purpose of the principle is to correct instances of distortion which still remain as a result of only considering where the supplier and the customer belong. Basically, the use and enjoyment provisions are applied under U.K. law in one of two situations, with the following VAT consequences:

(a)   where telecommunication services would otherwise be treated as supplied in the United Kingdom, they will not be treated as supplied in the U.K. (and VAT will not therefore be charged) to the extent that the effective use and enjoyment of the services takes place outside the E.U.;

(b)   where telecommunication services would otherwise be treated as supplied in a place outside the E.U., they shall be treated as supplied in the United Kingdom (and VAT will therefore be charged) to the extent that the effective use and enjoyment of the services takes place in the U.K.

Thus, effective use and enjoyment is only a consideration when telecommunication services made by a U.K. provider are consumed outside the E.U. or telecommunication services made by a non-E.U. provider are consumed in the United Kingdom. It would be distortive for telecommunication services that are actually consumed outside the E.U. to be subject to U.K. VAT, or for there to be no charge to VAT where these services are consumed in the United Kingdom.

All member states are obliged to implement the Sixth Directive "use and benefit" provisions where telecommunication services are otherwise treated as supplied outside the E.U., or where such services are supplied by persons established outside the E.U. to private persons established in the E.U.[11] There is, however, no such requirement to implement the principle where the services are otherwise treated as supplied in the E.U. but used and enjoyed outside the E.U. It is understood that the United Kingdom is in the   **13–037** minority in treating telecommunication services which are supplied by United Kingdom providers, but used outside the E.U., as outside the scope of U.K. VAT.

The term "effective use and enjoyment" is not defined in the U.K. legislation. However, the U.K. HM Customs and Excise's published guidance on its application states that effective use and enjoyment takes place where the customer actually consumes the telecommunication services and that, in practice, this will be where the services are physically used, irrespective of place of contract, payment or beneficial interest.

13–038   In practice, where only part of a supply is consumed in the United Kingdom, the extent of use and enjoyment will in most cases be difficult to quantify. HM Customs and Excise has said that, in these cases, it will adopt a pragmatic approach in order to reach a mutually agreeable solution with the supplier. Invariably, the approach adopted will have as its basis factual data available, such as measured usage, internal company management records showing intercompany recharges, or percentage business transactions at the specific location.

Table 13.2 below provides a convenient summary of the place of supply rules in relation to telecommunication services as they are applied in the United Kingdom and the implications of the use and enjoyment principle.

Table 13.2:   Place of supply and VAT treatment of telecommunications services

Supplier belongs	Customer belongs	U.K. VAT position
In the U.K.	in another E.U. member state and receives the services for non-business purposes, or in the U.K. (irrespective of whether or not the services are received for business purposes)	services are supplied in the U.K. and the supplier must charge and account for U.K. VAT on the supply (subject to the registration threshold)
In the U.K.	in another E.U. member state and receives the services for business purposes	services are supplied in the other member state; U.K. VAT is not chargeable; however, the customer must charge and account for VAT in the member state where he belongs
In the U.K.	outside the E.U.	services are supplied outside the E.U. and are outside the scope of U.K. (and E.U.) VAT
In another E.U. member state, or outside the E.U.	in the U.K. and receives the services for business purposes	services are supplied in the U.K. and the customer must account for U.K. VAT under the reverse charge procedure (subject to the registration threshold); use and enjoyment provisions may apply with the result that services used outside the E.U. are outside the scope of U.K. (and E.U.) VAT

In another E.U. member state	in the U.K. and receives the services for non-business purposes	services are supplied in the supplier's member state; the supply is therefore outside the scope of U.K. VAT but the supplier must account for VAT in his member state
In another E.U. member state	in another member state (which is not the U.K.)	the place of supply will be outside the U.K. (but not the EU) and therefore outside the scope of the charge to U.K. VAT (but not E.U. VAT)
In another E.U. member state, or outside the E.U.	outside the E.U.	services are supplied outside the E.U. and are outside the scope of U.K. (and E.U.) VAT; use and enjoyment provisions, however, may apply with the result that services used in the U.K. are supplied in the U.K. and the supplier must charge and account for U.K. VAT (subject to the registration threshold)
Outside the E.U.	in the U.K. (or another E.U. member state) and receives the services for non-business purposes	services are supplied in the supplier's country and are outside the scope of U.K. (and E.U.) VAT; use and enjoyment provisions may, however, apply with the result that services used in the U.K. are supplied in the U.K. and the supplier must charge and account for U.K. VAT (subject to the registration threshold)
Outside the E.U.	in another member state and receives the services for business purposes	services are supplied in the other member state and are outside the scope of U.K. VAT (but not E.U. VAT)

Packages containing a variety of Internet related elements
The provision of Internet "packages" by service providers is a complicated area. If the **13–039** package extends only to basic Internet access (although it may include, for example, software, some information and customer support facilities), the package of services will fall within the rules relating to telecommunications services discussed above. However, the treatment of Internet packages comprising a variety of related elements, and not just mere access, is less straightforward. Typically such packages present the user, on log-in, with a specially developed and regulated environment rather than just delivering the user directly into the Internet or World Wide Web. They may include, in addition to access to specially prepared information pages (*e.g.* news, weather, stock market or travel reports), access to on-line shopping facilities, web space to create a web site and games fora.

Where such a package is provided for a single inclusive price, HM Customs and Excise **13–040** has issued guidance to the effect that it will treat the package as a single composite supply for U.K. VAT purposes which falls within Schedule 5, but not within the special rules for telecommunications services. It is understood that, since the publication of this view in 1997, some overseas businesses have included, for a flat fee, the telecommunications element previously supplied by a telecommunications provider direct to the consumer. No VAT is being accounted for on these supplies and this causes a distortion of competition with U.K. businesses. It is understood that Customs is considering the withdrawal and replacement of this guidance.

Where a package is not to be treated as a single composite supply of Schedule 5 services, the VAT treatment of each service supplied has to be looked at separately, some of which will be classified as telecommunications services and some as Schedule 5 (but not telecommunication) services. For example, basic Internet access, electronic mail addresses and chat-line facilities will fall within the definition of telecommunications services. Information pages and the like will fall within Schedule 5, para. 3 as the provision of information.

13–041   Broadly, this means that ISPs based in the United Kingdom supplying these packages should charge U.K. VAT on all sales to customers belonging in the U.K. and also to customers who belong in other member states who do not receive the package for business purposes. They will not be required to charge U.K. VAT on supplies to business customers in other member states but must satisfy themselves that the supply is made for business purposes and retain sufficient evidence to support this decision.

ISPs supplying such packages who are not established in the United Kingdom or are established outside the EU are not required to charge United Kingdom VAT on their sales to U.K. customers. However, they will usually charge their own local VAT (or sales tax) on such supplies.

Where a United Kingdom business who is registered for U.K. VAT purchases such an Internet package from a non-U.K. ISP, those services are chargeable to U.K. VAT under the reverse charge procedure and this VAT must be declared on their VAT returns in the usual way.

Invoicing and returns

13–042   The E.U. system of VAT is invoice-based, by which it is meant that a VAT–registered supplier must issue a valid VAT invoice for all taxable supplies of goods and services it makes and it must, in order to be able to claim input tax, be in receipt of such a valid VAT invoice in respect of supplies received.

In the United Kingdom, electronic invoicing by U.K. VAT registered businesses is permitted. Subject to certain conditions, a U.K. supplier is treated as providing his customer with a valid VAT invoice if all the information required for a conventional invoice is recorded in a computer and transmitted by electronic means directly to his customer's computer, without the delivery of hard copy. Invoices received in this way are acceptable as evidence for input tax deduction, subject to normal rules. The conditions are that the supplier must give HM Customs & Excise at least one month's notice in writing of his intention to provide electronic invoices and he must comply with any regulations or with such requirements as Customs & Excise may impose in his particular case. No regulations have been made to date. Conditions will, however, be imposed when the supplier applies to Customs & Excise to provide or receive VAT invoices by these means. Conditions generally include requiring the business to make a trial run of the computer system (giving HM Customs and Excise the opportunity to observe the trial run and inspect the results thereof) and to compile summary control documents detailing particular information for every computer file of VAT invoices held. Failure to comply will result in the need for VAT invoices to be issued to customers in the conventional way.

In other E.U. member states, electronic invoicing may not be so easy. It is understood, **13–043** for example, that Luxembourg does not allow electronic invoicing in any form and that non-E.U. businesses supplying to French customers will find it almost impossible in practice to obtain official authorisation to send invoices by e-mail.

The Internet based form for electronic VAT returns are interactive with guidance, help messages and in-built validation of data. Discounts have been offered to businesses which have filed VAT returns filed over the Internet. HM Customs & Excise is also working with software developers to incorporate Internet filing applications for VAT into business accounting software.

The future

The Commission and the OECD recognise that the VAT rules currently in force do not **13–044** meet the objectives of taxing those services supplied for consumption within the E.U., while not taxing those supplied for consumption outside the E.U. The Commission and the United Kingdom are also aware of the complexity of the existing regime and the very real practical difficulties it poses for businesses involved in international transactions, both in terms of the lack of certainty in applying the rules and the potential for commercial distortion.

The EU and the OECD's work programmes are both progressing along the same lines: a clear definition for place of consumption and effective tax collection mechanisms that do not impose undue burdens on business. The OECD published a draft report from its Working Party on Consumption Taxes to its Committee on Fiscal Affairs in February 2001. The Working Party has considered five methods of collection consumption taxes in the case of e-commerce transactions: the reverse charge system for supplies between businesses, remote registration for non-E.U. vendors, tax at source and redistribution (between tax authorities), collection by third parties, and technology based facilitated withholding mechanisms. The report considers the reverse charge and remote registration options to be useful. However taxation at source and subsequent transfer and collection by third parties are seen as involving unfeasible complications. The development of technology based/facilitated options is seen as a medium to long term solution to the problem, and is currently the subject of ongoing research.

The draft report contained draft guidelines on the place of consumption for the **13–045** purposes of consumption taxation of cross-border services and intangible property, and recommended approaches to the practical application of those guidelines. The guidelines recognise the place of consumption as the place of taxation, in the case of business to business transactions located in the place where the recipient has located its business presence and, in the case of business to consumer transactions, located by reference to the consumer's "usual jurisdiction of residence" (although it recognises that further work is required on finding an appropriate means to verify the latter). This approach is consistent with a number of proposals which have been put forward by the E.U. Commission. The latter's proposals include changing the rules so that electronically delivered services will be subject to VAT in the place in which they are consumed (on the same basis as the OECD's draft report). The emerging international view is that this will be the country where the business customer is established or the private consumer has his or her permanent address or is usually resident. This would simplify decision making for suppliers, most of whom routinely collect such information for marketing purposes. In cases where consumption occurs in a different country an additional rule, to overcome avoidance opportunities, would operate to ensure that VAT accrued where consumption actually took place. Consequently, it is proposed that the reverse charge procedure be retained as the basis for taxing cross-border business to business transactions but imposing registration obligations on third country operators in the member state of consumption for supplies to final consumers (that is, anyone not registered for VAT). With regard to the latter, the preferred option (although a number of others are being considered) is that non-E.U. operators would register in a single member state and account to a single tax administration. How this would be achieved, however, is not discussed. Although it is proposed that legislative measures should be put forward at the earliest possible date, the process of turning such provisions into law usually takes at least two to three years.

13–046   Correct operation of such a system will depend upon there being a dependable mechanism in place whereby a supplier is able to distinguish between VAT registered businesses and private customers and is able to obtain confirmation that his customer holds a valid VAT registration number. The electronic record of the transaction will need to contain sufficient evidence to prove that the recipient is established in the country identified as the place where consumption takes place. The Commission have made it clear that the responsibility for developing tax compatible operating systems, which include the ability to compute and collect VAT on the basis of the customer's location, lies with business and those involved in the development of the operational systems which enable e-commerce to function. By doing so, tax collection on international sales may be automated, removing the need for registering overseas suppliers. The Commission's paper also makes it clear to businesses and their advisers that VAT can and will be applied. It warns : "Any long term business strategy which assumes that on-line sales can be made into the Community without regard to E.U. VAT would be most injudicious".

The E.U. has also recognised that, subject to uniform E.U. conditions, fiscal administration should provide for operators conducting business over or via the Internet to discharge their fiscal obligations by means of electronic VAT invoices, declarations and accounting. As paperless electronic invoicing will be a characteristic of e-commerce, it needs to be authorised for VAT purposes for transactions within the E.U. and a framework of co-operation between the E.U. and other countries established to ensure that conditions, equivalent to those provided in the E.U., are also created for international electronic invoicing. A comprehensive study of all invoicing requirements has been undertaken and the E.U. is now in the process of introducing a directive on electronic invoicing in order to harmonise practice throughout its history.

13.4 Customs duties

13–047   Customs duties are, like VAT, a creature of the E.U. Customs duties are payable on the importation of goods (but not services) into the E.U. at the point of entry of the goods into the E.U. Duties are charged at rates specified in the Combined Customs Tariff which incorporates special rates agreed by treaty with other jurisdictions with goods originating from such jurisdictions.

As customs duties only apply to goods, the main implications for the Internet are concerned with computer software (whether in the form of "packages" produced by access providers to enable users to access the Internet, or software down loaded via the Internet) and tangible goods ordered electronically over the Internet but delivered by traditional means. In relation to the latter, the only real issue for customs is the anticipated increase in small packages brought about by customers using the Internet to buy from abroad.

13.4.1 Computer software

The United Kingdom subscribes to the WTO's declaration on Global Electronic **13–048**
Commerce in which it was stated that it was necessary to distinguish goods ordered
electronically, but delivered by traditional means, and direct on-line delivery of digitised
products. The former were to continue to attract customs duties at the appropriate rate of
duty, while the latter were to constitute a supply of services and, as such, were to be free
of import duties. No additional import duties were to be introduced relating to electronic
transmissions.

Thus, the extent to which software constitutes goods is assessed by reference to the
same considerations which apply to VAT. Software packages provided by access
providers which are imported into the United Kingdom are likely to attract duty (subject
to any exemptions such as importation from an EFTA nation). Customs duties will not be
chargeable on down loaded software, including audio and visual material.

13.4.2 Goods ordered electronically but delivered by traditional means

As with VAT, the customs treatment of goods imported into the United Kingdom via **13–049**
traditional means pursuant to a contract concluded over the Internet is no different from
a similar transaction effected outside the Internet. In general, therefore, the purchaser of
the goods will be the "importer" for customs purposes and, as such, liable to pay duty on
the goods imported.

The opportunity for cross-border trade, especially between businesses and private
consumers, is greatly increased by the Internet. The United Kingdom is seeing an ever–
increasing use of the Internet as a method of ordering goods and this has been parallelled
by an increase in the number of small packages imported from outside the E.U. As a
result, the United Kingdom has recently introduced new simplified import procedures to
speed the importation of consignments from third countries. HM Customs and Excise has
also said that it will continue to monitor and review the revenue and commercial
implications of the *de minimis* limit, presumably in order to assess and minimise any
distortion of competition that may result against local suppliers as well as reduce the
burdens of compliance.

It should also be borne in mind that the E.U. is a customs union so that the E.U. **13–050**
member states have no customs duty barriers between them but all have a common
customs duty tariff against goods arriving from outside the E.U. As a result, goods which
are free from customs duty in one part of the E.U., because they originate there or because
any duty on them has already been paid, are free to circulate within the rest of the E.U.
without any liability to pay further customs charges when they move from one member
stated to another. The E.U.'s common external tariff ensures that goods imported from
non-E.U. countries are subject to the same customs duties wherever they enter the E.U.
Overall, these arrangements prevent distortion of competition since a private consumer
cannot "shop around" the EU for the lowest rate of duty.

13.5 Direct Taxes

The issue for income and corporation taxes is how to apply the direct tax rules to **13–051**
international e-commerce bearing in mind that, typically, such rules were not designed to

cope with e-commerce. The rules currently causing e-commerce businesses the most concern are those relating to:

(i)   withholding tax and the characterisation of income;

(ii)   where Internet traders are taxed on their profits (*i.e.* "taxable presence" issues); and

(iii)   quantification of business profits, including transfer pricing.

13.6 Characterisation of income and withholding taxes

13.6.1 U.K. law

13–052   In the United Kingdom, withholding taxes are only applicable to particular types of income: there is no general obligation to withhold tax at source from payments made to non-U.K. residents. Of most relevance in the context of the Internet is that tax (at the basic rate of income tax[12]) must be withheld from payments of royalties or sums paid periodically in respect of a copyright by a U.K. resident to a non-U.K. resident.

In the United Kingdom, computer software is protected by copyright under the Copyright, Designs and Patents Act 1988 and this treatment flows through for tax purposes. Therefore, the U.K. withholding tax machinery will apply where a copyright owner, not resident in the U.K. for tax purposes, is paid royalties and/or licence fees by a U.K. resident for the use of computer software.

13–053   Excluded from the U.K. withholding obligation are royalties paid in respect of cinematograph films or video recordings and their soundtracks, provided that the soundtrack is not exploited separately. Double tax treaties also generally exempt film and video royalties, sometimes more expansively than the basic U.K. rules. If excluded under the terms of a double tax treaty, royalties and fees may be paid gross if an appropriate direction is obtained in advance from the U.K. Inland Revenue. Alternatively, the tax can be reclaimed from the Inland Revenue. Note that the withholding obligation is not generally excluded if the licensor has a permanent establishment in the United Kingdom (see section 13.7 below).

13.6.2 The problem

13–054   As discussed above, certain products may be transmitted electronically rather than in physical form. Examples already given include written material (such as books, newspapers, and reference material) and computer software. Further examples include audio and visual material such as music, video and photographs. The Internet is also likely to become the principal music and film market of the future, where "goods" (music CDs, video tapes, stereos, compact disc players) are replaced with "services" bought directly through the Internet on a "pay per performance basis".

The Internet customer may have to pay a fee before being allowed to sample or view the product and will, in any event, usually have to pay a fee before being able to down load the product. He may be allowed to modify the down loaded product or incorporate it into other products which he develops himself, either for his own use or to sell to others. The issue which arises is whether payments to sample and/or down load such items for these various purposes are, in whole or in part, payments for the right to use a copyright (that is to say, they are a "royalty" which may be subject to withholding tax) or are payments for the purchase of goods and services not involving the use of copyright (and therefore not subject to withholding tax). Practical problems arise for businesses supplying digitised products via the Internet because the rules which distinguish between such payments were developed in relation to physical products.

13.6.3 Current position

The OECD is looking at this problem and the United Kingdom is participating in the   **13–055**
discussions. Specifically, the OECD is in the process of updating the Commentary to the Model Tax Convention in order to clarify how the concepts of intangible property, royalties and services used in the Convention apply to e-commerce and, in particular, to digitised products obtained from the Internet.

For the present, in relation to computer software at least, the OECD takes the view that withholding taxes should only apply in relation to the commercial exploitation of software, rather than its personal use. The U.K. Inland Revenue subscribes to this approach. This means that where a content provider supplies software via the Internet to a customer for the customer's personal use, the provider and customer do not need concern themselves with the need to withhold U.K. tax from any payment(s) made. Such an approach avoids the significant problems of enforcement which would otherwise arise.

However, the question remains as to whether the U.K. withholding tax machinery   **13–056**
applies to music, film and video provided via the Internet. Strictly speaking, neither the general exclusion from withholding obligations which applies to royalties paid in respect of cinematograph films or video recordings, nor any double tax treaty provision, may apply. However, withholding tax questions should not arise for home-users if they only pay a one-off fee "per performance", since the payment in that case is unlikely to be in the nature of a royalty and nor would any sum be paid periodically. The main withholding tax issues are likely to arise in relation to the commercial arrangements entered into by content providers, especially if the payment of royalties becomes more of a feature. However, if withholding was to apply, and the market developed as envisaged, it is very difficult to see how the Inland Revenue could enforce the withholding obligations.

13.7 Taxable presence issues

One important tax question related to the Internet, which perhaps reflects most obviously   **13–057**
the tension between advances in technology and current tax rules, arises from the fact that an e-commerce business can provide goods or services to Internet users located in a country without necessarily having any significant physical presence in that country. This raises the question of the extent, if any, to which the provider is taxable on its income in that country and the treatment of any such tax liability in its home territory. This question is receiving considerable attention from the OECD and the United Kingdom.

13.7.1 U.K. law

13–058   The United Kingdom, like most other jurisdictions, determines "taxability" by reference to the concepts of residency, the source of the income and, where a double tax treaty is applicable, "permanent establishment". Each concept evolved in relation to traditional forms of commerce and is based largely on requirements related to physical presence.

A company will be treated as resident in the United Kingdom for tax purposes if it is either incorporated in the U.K. or the central management and control of the company is based in the U.K. Such a company is subject to U.K. corporation tax on its worldwide income and gains. A non-U.K. resident company trading in the U.K. is chargeable to U.K. corporation tax on the trading income and capital gains (arising both within and outside the U.K.) attributable to any branch or agency which the company has in the U.K. or, if it is not operating through a branch or agency, to U.K. income tax on the profits and gains which arise through the exercise of its trade in the U.K. This means that, as well as taxing a genuine branch operation, the U.K. may also tax trading operations conducted through a third party selling agent.

13–059   This basic position is modified where a trader is resident in a country with which the United Kingdom has concluded a double tax treaty. Due to the extent of the U.K. double treaty network, this will normally be the case. Although the terms of the United Kingdom's double tax treaties vary, the general position on trading income is that a non-resident is only taxable on such of that income as is attributable to a "permanent establishment" of the trader in the United Kingdom. A "permanent establishment" is normally defined, subject to specific inclusion and exclusion, as a "fixed place of business through which the business of the [non-resident] is carried on". This definition is based on the OECD Model Treaty. Third party agents do not generally constitute permanent establishments of their principals but dependent agents with habitual authority to conclude contracts on behalf of their principal do.

The OECD has produced a commentary on the Model Treaty which is binding in U.K. law. The commentary contains a discussion of the "fixed place of business" concept from which it is clear that some form of permanent physical presence is required to constitute a permanent establishment, normally including personnel but which can, in appropriate cases, be constituted by the mere presence of equipment (for example, in the context of a vending machine business). Fixed places of business are, however, generally excluded from constituting permanent establishments where the activities carried out there are of a preparatory or auxiliary nature to the non-resident's business, for example advertising or the storage of stocks of goods (where this is the only activity carried out).

13.7.2 Applying the rules to e-commerce

13–060   It is not yet clear as to what constitutes a permanent establishment in the context of e–commerce. Where a non-resident trader has no physical presence in the United Kingdom at all, it is difficult to see how a permanent establishment could be constituted. It also seems unlikely that traders hosting a web page on a server in another jurisdiction, in order to sell their own products or services, can be treated as having set up a permanent establishment. More debatable, however, is the position where, for example, an ISP has leased lines from a U.K. telephone company or is selling the use of its server. With respect to the former, whether a permanent establishment is constituted may depend on the terms of the lease (for example, whether only capacity or an identifiable network is being leased). As regards the latter, it may depend upon the scope and functionality of the server and the extent of the supporting human resources.

In January 2001 the OECD published the outcome of discussions on the concept of permanent establishment in the context of e-commerce. It has stated that there is a broad agreement that:

- a website cannot, of itself, constitute a permanent establishment;

- a website hosting arrangement typically does not constitute a permanent establishment for the enterprise which trades through that medium;

- an ISP will not, except in very unusual circumstances, be a dependent agent of another business such as to constitute a permanent establishment of that business;

- a place where computer equipment, such as a server, may constitute a permanent establishment of a business. However for this proposition to apply it is required that the functions performed at that place be significant as well as an essential or core part of the business activity of the enterprise.

The OECD is continuing its review of the appropriateness of the permanent establishment concept for the long term as a requirement for taxing the profits of a non-resident.

With regard to the fourth point above, the Inland Revenue have published guidance stating that the United Kingdom holds the view that in no circumstances will servers, of themselves or together with websites, constitute permanent establishments in the U.K. for the purposes of enterprises engaged in e-commerce. The Revenue have expressed the view that, although the permanent establishment concept may become less appropriate as the threshold for taxation in the long term, it is a long standing concept and one which is widely supported. In light of this and the fact that no clearly better alternative has emerged, it considers there is at present no compelling reason to depart from it. **13–061**

13.8 Quantifying business profits and transfer pricing

From the preceding discussion, it can be appreciated that a company conducting business over the Internet such as an ISP will need to consider the difficult question of whether it has sufficient presence in a country to constitute a permanent establishment there. If it does, the separate but related question arises of what part of the total profits of the company are to be properly attributed to the permanent establishment (over which the country in which the permanent establishment exists will have primary taxing rights). **13–062**

Moreover, where related or "associated" enterprises resident in different countries each have some participation in e-commerce transactions, a further separate but related issue which may also require consideration is "transfer pricing". Transfer pricing is the term used to describe the process whereby prices are set by associated enterprises in respect of, *inter alia*, sales or transfers of goods and the provision of services, including finance, between them. Obviously, the "transfer prices" will affect more than one tax jurisdiction and if both jurisdictions do not agree on the appropriate transfer prices (and thus the share of taxing rights), there is the risk of double taxation or of less than single taxation. An example of where this issue may arise is where connected companies are involved in, say, web site hosting outside the United Kingdom and on-the-ground activities (for example, web site design) in the United Kingdom.

13–063   The U.K. transfer pricing rules were amended in 1998 to bring them into line with the international consensus reached by the OECD as reflected in the OECD's 1995 transfer pricing guidance.[13] By these rules an "arm's length principle" is to be used to determine transfer prices for tax purposes. This states that the transfer prices for dealings between associated enterprises is to be those which would have been agreed between them, for comparable transactions in comparable circumstances, had they been independent entities acting at arm's length. The present international consensus appears to be that e-commerce poses no new fundamental problems for transfer pricing. However, governments recognise that some of the factors relevant to its application may be more difficult to take into account (for example, finding comparable transactions between independents by reference to which the principle can be applied) and that, as e-commerce opens up cross-border trade, transfer pricing issues may occur more frequently for a much wider range of companies, including small and medium sized enterprises. E-commerce also gives rise to increasing integration and co-operation in trading activities and this will inevitably add to the complexities of transfer pricing, both for business and the tax administrations.

As yet, little or no guidance has been forthcoming on either of these issues. They are, however, the subject of consideration by the OECD, to which the United Kingdom is contributing. In particular, the OECD work programme includes a review of how the rules in double tax treaties for the attribution of profits to permanent establishments should be applied to e-commerce as well as ensuring that the 1995 Transfer Pricing Guidelines can be supplemented or changed as necessary to reflect developments in e-commerce. In relation to the former, it is considering whether the same considerations that underlie application of the arm's length principle to transfer pricing between associated enterprises can be adopted in addressing the process of attribution. No timetable has yet been published as to when it is expected that such guidance may be issued.

13.9 Other points

13–064   We have highlighted briefly three direct tax issues (withholding tax, taxable presence and quantification of business profits) that are of relevance to the Internet. Clearly, this only deals with some of the many tax issues that may be relevant to a business which has trading operations in the United Kingdom or is contemplating whether to set up trading operations in the United Kingdom. For example, if significant development expenditure is to be incurred by, for example, a content provider, it will need to investigate the extent to which tax relief is available (for example, under the capital allowance legislation or the special regimes applicable to films, discs and tapes—although this is another area where legislative change is imminent in the United Kingdom). For a multinational, such considerations may be relevant factors in determining whether to site trading operations in the United Kingdom or in a more favourable jurisdiction.

Other existing taxes may also be affected by the progress of e-commerce. For example, it may be that as the applications of the Internet develop the existing U.K. stamp duty regime may become obsolete if the Internet becomes a medium through which commercial transactions are effected. Stamp duty at present applies only to documents (rather than transactions), although in the case of shares and other securities stamp duty reserve tax catches transactions not covered by stamp duty. It may be that as the number of dealings in shares over the Internet increases and if, for example, land can be transferred and registered through the Internet, stamp duty reserve tax will be extended while stamp duty itself becomes of less relevance.

Advances in technology are also facilitating the provision of betting and gaming services electronically. There are six betting, gaming and lottery duties in the United Kingdom and the U.K. government perceives that e-commerce poses risks to them if, for example, the major bookmakers were to transfer all their credit betting facilities offshore (the United Kingdom has the largest and most highly developed bookmaking industry in Europe). It is taking this risk to public revenue seriously and, as a first step, is to reinforce the present advertising ban on offshore bookmakers to prevent them targeting U.K. clients and diverting U.K. betting revenue abroad. It is also exploring other options to protect the revenue from such duties and is seeking to raise the issues internationally. **13–065**

As a final point, the Internet provides many new opportunities for improving taxpayer service and the OECD, in its Taxation Framework Conditions, identified a number of options as to how it saw this could be achieved. In the United Kingdom, the Inland Revenue and HM Customs and Excise are actively taking advantage of Internet technology as a means of communication, information processing and tax collection. Legislation in the Finance Act 1999 allows HM Customs and Excise and the Inland Revenue to develop new electronic services which taxpayers can use as an alternative to paper communication. The Inland Revenue have stated that they intend, by 2008, taxpayers to be able to conduct all their dealings with Government departments electronically. At present, both departments host web sites which contain a wealth of valuable information for taxpayers and which are updated regularly. Facilities for direct bank to bank payment and repayment of tax are also being used. Both departments are making it possible for forms and returns to be filed via the Internet. The 2000/2001 tax year saw the launch of the Inland Revenue's Internet filing service for Self Assessment for individuals. During 2001 services are being introduced in order that employers, agents and payroll intermediaries can submit PAYE forms and returns over the Internet. In order to encourage Internet filing the Inland Revenue are offering certain discounts if PAYE returns are filed over the Internet and payments are made electronically. **13–066**

---

1. Communication from the Commission to The European Parliament, the Council, the Economic and Social Committee and the Committee of the Regions: A European Initiative in Electronic Commerce, COM (1997) 157.
2. Communication from the Commission to the Council, The European Parliament and the Economic and Social Committee : Electronic Commerce and Indirect Taxation, COM (1998) 374 final.
3. *Electronic Commerce: U.K. Policy on Taxation Issues* OECD Conference in Ottawa, Canada, October 8–9: News Release 25/98 dated October 6, 1998. This paper enlarged on the tax issues identified in the paper entitled "Net Benefit: The Electronic Commerce Agenda for the U.K." published by the U.K. Department of Trade and Industry on the same date.
4. Internet Tax Freedom Act.
5. In the U.K. this is £54,000 for the tax year 2001/2002.
6. In the U.K. this is £70,000 for the tax year 2001/2002.
7. Each member state has the option of applying a distance selling threshold of either 35,000 ECU (about £25,000) or 100,000 ECU (about £71,000) per calendar year which is set in its own currency. The U.K., Austria, France, Germany, Luxembourg and the Netherlands have adopted a threshold of 100,000 ECU while Belgium, Denmark, Finland, Greece, Ireland, Italy, Portugal, Spain and Sweden have adopted the 35,000 ECU threshold.
8. *Emphasis Limited* [1995] V.A.T.D.R. 419 (13759).
9. VAT and Duties Tribunal Decision No. 16041, April 22, 1999.
10. New indent added to Art. 9(2)(e) of the Sixth Directive by Art. 1 of Council Directive 99/59; see [1999] O.J. L162/64.

11. The former is required under the terms of the derogation and the latter by Art. 2 of Council Directive 99/59; see [1999] O.J. L162/64.
12. Currently set at 20 per cent for the tax year 2001/2002.
13. *Transfer Pricing Guidelines for Multinational Enterprises and Tax Administrations* (OECD July 1995).

14

Competition Law and the Internet

This Chapter looks at the application of E.C. and U.K. Competition law to the Internet **14–001**
and e-commerce.

In terms of E.C. Competition law, this means analysis of:

- The E.C. Merger Regulation

- The application of the rules on restrictive agreements under Article 81 of the E.C.
Treaty.

- The application of the rules on abuse of dominance under Article 82 of the E.C.
Treaty.

The section on U.K. Competition law at the end of the Chapter looks at U.K. merger
provisions, and the provisions of the Competition Act 1998, which contains rules
prohibiting restrictive agreements and the abuse of market dominance which mirror
those applying under Article 81 and Article 82 of the E.C. Treaty.

This chapter does not examine the rules on restrictive agreements (Article 53) or abuse
of dominance (Article 54) contained in the European Economic Area Agreement. Those
rules mirror Article 81 and 82 of the EC treaty, and the territory that they affect covers the
States of the European Economic Area ("EEA") which include the 15 European Union
States, in addition to Norway, Iceland and Liechtenstein. Nor does it cover any other
national competition rules other than those of the United Kingdom.

14.1 Relevant Markets

Before looking at the substance of these rules, it is useful to look at the question of what **14–002**
are the relevant markets for competition purposes. Such an exercise is essential for nearly
all application of the competition rules. Defining relevant markets is fundamental to the
analysis applied under the rules on abuse of a dominant market position, and the E.C.
rules on Merger Control. The market power of the parties to an agreement may also
determine whether the agreement is seen by the European Commission as having a
sufficiently appreciable effect to come within the rules on restrictive agreements. There
are market share thresholds for the application of the E.C. Block Exemptions under

Article 81, as will be seen below. In addition, market shares may be relevant in deciding whether an agreement can obtain exemption under Article 81(3).

In this section, we look at some of the markets which have been defined by the European Commission, mostly in Merger Cases, but occasionally under Article 81.

14.1.1 Access Markets

Access Infrastructure

14–003   The communications infrastructure "access" market, may potentially comprise all types of infrastructure that can be used for the provision of a given service. For instance, in *Nortel/Norweb*,[1] the Commission recognised that electricity networks using "Digital Power Line" technology could provide an alternative to existing traditional local telecommunications access loop, commenting that[2]:

> "in assessing the possible market dominance by the joint venture it should be taken into account that in enabling the existing electricity distribution network to act as a local loop, DPL technology provides an alternative to the existing traditional local telecommunications access loop and that there are still several other alternative solutions available. The findings of the Commission also suggest that the alternative access technologies mentioned above such as fast modem, cable modem, ADSL, HDSL and wireless should provide strong alternatives to DPL technology."

In that case, the Commission did not have to decide, however, whether DPL technology was in the same market as these other forms of access.

14–004   There are of course a number of other access technologies for Internet that exist or are in the process of being developed including ADSL (asymmetric digital subscriber line), HDSL (hierarchical digital subscriber line) on existing copper telephone wire, cable modems which allow the use of a cable TV network as the access loop, and wireless broadband technologies via satellite or stationary ground stations.

In its draft guidelines on market analysis and calculation of market power under the proposed new telecoms regime[3] the Commission comments that

> "whether the market for network infrastructures should be divided into as many separate submarkets as there are existing categories of network infrastructure, depends clearly on the degree of substitutability among such (alternative) networks and should be decided on a case- by-case basis. This exercise should be carried out in relation to the class of users to which access to the network is provided. A distinction should, therefore, be made between provision of infrastructure to other operators (wholesale level) and provision to end users (retail level). At the retail level, a further segmentation may take place between business and residential customers."

14–005   The Commission considers that at the retail level, when the service to be provided concerns only end users subscribed to a particular network, access to the termination points of that network may well constitute the relevant product market. This will not be the case if it can be established that the same services may be offered to the same class of consumers by means of alternative, easily accessible competing networks. For example, in its Communication on unbundling the local loop, the Commission stated that although alternatives to the PSTN for providing high speed communications services to residential consumers exist (fibre optic networks, wireless local loops or upgradable TV networks), none of these alternatives may be considered as a substitute to the fixed local loop infrastructure." This was because "[f]iber optics are currently competitive only on upstream transmission markets whereas wireless local loops which are still to be deployed will target mainly professionals and individuals with particular communications needs. With the exception of certain national markets, existing cable TV networks need costly upgrades to support two ways broadband communications, and, compared with xDLS technologies, they do not offer a guaranteed bandwidth since customers share the same cable channel." However, "future innovative and technological changes may, however, justify different conclusions."[4]

In the eventually unsuccessful *Telia/Telenor*[5] merger, the Commission found that there was a market for "connection to the local loop" for new entrants:

> "Before he or she can access any higher level telephone services, a subscriber has to be physically connected to the PSTN, which is usually done by allocating him or her a twisted copper pair to his nearest local exchange. There is accordingly a demand on the part of subscribers and telecom entrants for connection to the local loop".

The Market for Top Level or Universal Internet Connectivity/Wholesale ISP Services
In *Worldcom/MCI*[6] and subsequently in *MCI Worldcom/Sprint*[7] the Commission described **14–006** a vertical hierarchical view of the provision of "Internet connectivity". Internet service providers must offer their customers universal connectivity on the Internet, and must be able to deliver traffic from their customers to other ISPs, networks either through direct connection or via intermediate connection. One option is a bilateral peering agreement where an agreement is reached with another ISP to reciprocally terminate traffic from each other, traditionally on a no-charge basis, but not including traffic coming from other ISPs through peering agreements. Another option for an ISP is to enter into a "transit" agreement, and to pay another ISP to acquire the right for its' traffic to be treated as traffic from that other ISP which can then be transferred across that ISP's peering interfaces for delivery on other networks, under the other party's peering agreements, or through its transit agreements. Such transit traffic spends much of its time ascending or descending through successive hierarchies, linked to one another by such vertical customer/provider relationships, with a horizontal movement across a peering interface usually only happening once on the journey. The "top level" networks or ISPs are the only organisations capable of delivering complete Internet connectivity entirely on their own account, and this connectivity is referred to as "top level" or "universal" connectivity. Top level ISPs deliver their traffic, and that of their dependent "transit" customer ISPs through peering arrangements with other ISPs, and do not have to rely on any paid interconnection such as transit. "Secondary peering" ISPs may be able to deliver some of their own peering-based connectivity, but have to supplement it through bought "transit" agreements. Resellers operate totally on the basis of transit agreements, and can only supply resold connectivity, although depending on who they bought it from, it might be a combination of first and second tier connectivity.

For an ISP to have a peering agreement with a top level ISP is dependent on factors influencing traffic flows such as the number of customers and websites hosted, capacity of the ISP network, and geography, as well as historical legacy.

The products offered by the top-level networks were differentiated in that the **14–007** connectivity is supplied entirely by peering arrangements between these top level ISPs. Neither secondary peering ISPs or resellers are able to constrain the behaviour of these top-level networks, and preventing them from acting independently. If the top level networks increased the price of their Internet connectivity by five per cent, the cost base of the resellers would be increased by this amount, and this would have to be passed on to the customer. Secondary peering ISPs could not avoid continuing to buy some transit from the top-level networks, and therefore, according to the Commission, they would not be capable of providing an adequate service in response to the price increases. The ISPs outside of the top level group could still provide a competitive constraint, to the extent that that they were able to use their peering arrangements with the top-level networks to avoid the increase in transit charges. However, if faced with such a challenge to their price increase strategy, the top-level networks could react by charging for all Internet interconnection, whether described as peering or transit. In that event, the unequal bargaining power of the secondary peering ISPs would not permit them to offer an effective competitive response. The Commission therefore defined a market for "top level" or "universal" Internet connectivity, comprised of top level, or first tier, providers rather than a market which included all ISPs with backbone capacity. In *MCI Worldcom/ Sprint*, decided two years later, the parties argued that structure of the market had changed, due to new techniques, including controlled content distribution, mirroring, caching and multihoming, but the Commission was not convinced and persisted with basically the same view of the market definition.

14–008   In the eventually unsuccussful *Telia/Telenor*[8] merger the Commission discussed the market in Wholesale ISP services, stating:

> "Wholesale ISP services comprise the resale of transit in Internet terms, which involves an obligation by the offering ISP to provide connectivity to the whole of the Internet to its customer ISP. This market is global. The information supplied by the parties show that neither of the merging parties would have fitted the definition of a top level network as applied in Commission Decision 1999/287 (WorldCom/MCI) and they are in part resellers of transit obtained from such networks. Moreover, as will be described below in the Internet section of the competitive assessment Telenor's business as an Internet transit providers is marginal; Telia is stronger at a European level, but still small on a global basis."

Consumer Internet Access
Internet dial-up access distinguished from dedicated access (narrow band access)

14–009   In the *Telia/Telenor*[9] merger decision, the Commission identified a demand for the supply of Internet access services, and distinguished between dial-up and dedicated access. These were considered to be two separate product markets, on the basis that dial-up access is targeted at residential and small and medium sized businesses, whereas dedicated access was requested mainly by large corporate customers. In *BT/ESAT*[10] it emerged in the course of the market investigation that within dial-up access it could be possible to distinguish between residential and business (large companies) dial-up access, the latter being provided on the basis of more sophisticated dial-up mechanisms. However, the Commission has so far found it unnecessary to establish whether residential and business dial-up constitute two separate relevant product markets.

Broad-band Internet access

14–010   In the course of its inquiry in *AOL/Time Warner*[11], the Commission found evidence of the existence of a developing demand for the provision of residential broad-band Internet access. This was considered to include high-speed Internet access delivering greater audio and visual functionality than dial-up (narrow-band) access, including streaming video and audio, video e-mail, interactive advertising and video conferencing, none of which can be delivered effectively over traditional narrow-band lines.

The Commission noted that Broadband access was not yet widely available in Europe and is generally more expensive than dial-up access. It discussed Digital Subscriber Line (DSL) access and cable modems as being broad-band alternatives. However, for the purposes of the assessment in that case, it was not necessary to conclude whether there existed a separate broadband Internet access market, or whether DSL, cable and other forms of fast Internet access belong to the same relevant product market, since the conclusion was reached that the transaction did not give rise to the creation of a dominant position in this area.

14.2.1 Internet/E-commerce-specific markets

Internet Browsers
The Commission started a competition investigation against Microsoft in respect of the terms under which Microsoft made available its Internet Explorer browser to European Internet service providers. However, the case was settled informally, and there is no indication as to whether the Commission considered that browsers could constitute a relevant market, or on what basis the Commission was putting its case (see below). **14–011**

Search Engines
As regards other software needed to access the web, the Commission looked at search engines in the *WSI Webseek* case which involved a joint venture between Deutsche Telekom, Springer, Holzbank and Infoseek to provide search and navigation services for German-speaking Internet users.[12] The Commission concluded that since the search engine would be offered free of charge to Internet users, the services provided could not constitute a relevant market in themselves. On the other hand, the Internet advertising market, the paid-for content market and the Internet access market did represent relevant markets. **14–012**

Web-sites, Portals and Gateways
It is implicit in the early market definitions which had been accepted by the Commission that the provision of portals or gateways cannot be regarded as a market as such if they are accessible without any subscription or charge, although to the extent that such portals or gateways earn money from advertising, the Internet advertising market will be a relevant market. This was confirmed in the case of *Telia/Telenor/Schibsted*[13] where the parties were intending to provide gateway services, through which users could have access to a range of services including financial information, games, business and financial information, shopping, travel and ticket sales. Revenues would be generated by advertising, commission on transactions generated and subscriptions to other services accessed through the gateway. The Commission considered that gateway services could not constitute a market in themselves. The Commission in this case considered that the service was essentially a kind of web-site hosting several different services or groups of services some or all of which would be provided by third parties. They were generally financed through advertising rather than subscription income and most were supplied **14–013**

free of charge to subscribers by ISP's as part of the access package. The Commission did not consider that such gateway services constituted a market in themselves, but considered that the relevant markets were those for Internet advertising and paid-for content.

In the "Vizzavi"[14] joint venture between Vodafone, Vivendi and Canal+ and in Vivendi/Canal+/Seagram[15] the Commission, however, identified developing national markets for TV-based Internet portals and developing national and pan-European markets for horizontal portals offering WAP based Internet access.

Internet Advertising

14–014   The Commission has in a number of cases considered that Internet advertising was a relevant market. Implicit within this definition is the suggestion that Internet advertising is a market on its own, which is not part of a broader advertising market based on different media (in a similar way to that in which the Commission has recognised that there are separate markets in TV advertising). Nor has the Commission considered whether there might be any further breakdown of Internet advertising into separate markets. However, the U.K. case of *NMTV v. Jobserve*[16] considered below, which involved a site which acted as a notice board for recruitment agencies to advertise job vacancies, which was considered by recruiting agencies to be a site which they would need to use in order to obtain access to responses from good quality IT personnel, could point the direction to a much narrower market definition in certain circumstances (although that case has not come to a final judgment at the time of writing).

Web-site production and related services

14–015   There may be a separate market for the production of web-sites. The parties to the *Telia/Telenor/Schibsted*[17] joint venture considered that production demands design and computer skills, which implied that the service constituted a separate market. The Commission did not have to decide the issue in this case, but suggested that web site production might be sufficiently technical and specialised to justify a separate market definition.

14.1.3 B2C Products and Services Sold over the Internet

14–016   A fundamental question in the definition of e-commerce markets is whether online sales of a particular product or service are to be considered to be in the same market as offline sales. Are traditional and the online distribution channels merely two different channels of distribution in the same market, or do the distribution channels define different markets?

Where sales of traditional goods or services are concerned, the European Commission may often[18] consider the following questions as being relevant to this issue:

- does the online sale of the product have characteristics different from the offline sale (availability of offline goods, range of goods available, product search, product delivery)

- is it possible to price discriminate between offline and online users of the good (bearing in mind that price discrimination here is being used for market definition, non indication of anti-competitive activity)

The Commission has had to consider this point in a number of cases:

Online sales/distant sales of books
In a number of cases involving Bertelsmann, relating to the establishment of joint   **14–017**
ventures for the sale of books online,[19] the Commission has had to consider whether the
relevant market was that for all retail sales of books, or a smaller market for "distant
sales" of books (including book clubs, mail order as well as Internet), or whether the
online sales of books through the Internet could be considered as a market in itself. The
Commission never had to resolve this question, since in the cases it had to consider, there
were no competitive concerns under the Merger Regulation on any of the plausible
market definitions. However, it did seem to shift from considering that a market for all
retail books could be the relevant market,[20] to considering that it is at least as narrow as
"distant sales", and possibly as narrow as Internet sales.[21]

Online Travel Agencies
In *T-Online/TUI/C&N Touristic*,[22] which involved the creation of a joint venture to   **14–018**
establish an online travel agency, offering package tours, last minute trips, and flights, the
Commission's preliminary investigation identified online travel agency services as a
product market in its own right, distinct from traditional "bricks and mortar" travel
agencies. It found that both demand- and supply-side elements supported such a
conclusion: online-consumers can search and book trips any time, i.e. including outside
regular shopping hours, and without leaving their home while, on the other hand, online
suppliers face lower distribution costs. The Commission had concerns that because of the
strength of the parent companies, the joint venture might achieve such a strong position
in online travel that it could progressively foreclose this still emerging market. The
merger was eventually abandoned.

Online Music
The above cases relate to situations in which traditional goods or services are distributed   **14–019**
through the Internet, but where they could be distributed through channels other than
the Internet. Another situation which has distinguished by the European Commission, is
where there are online sales which have no exact offline equivalents, such as where the
Internet itself is the delivery mechanism for the services.
    In the *AOL/Time Warner*[23] merger, the Commission concluded that there was a market
for online music, which it described as a form of narrow-band content, distinguishing this
from a separate market for broadband content. The Commission included within this
description both downloadable music files, as well as audio streaming services.
    In respect of downloadable music, the parties to the did not consider that
downloadable music constituted a separate market, but were of the opinion that it
formed part of the larger market for recorded music. They claimed that downloadable
music was substitutable for music distributed on physical carriers.
    The Commission commented that there were a number of significant differences which   **14–020**
make downloadable music an entirely different business model, and a separate market:

> "For example, from the demand side, consumers can access or buy and receive
> music immediately (instead of e-commerce, where they have to wait for the CD that
> they have ordered) from any computer with Internet access, without having to visit
> a store, no matter the time and the location. They can download individual tracks,
> instead of buying the entire album or a single, and create customised compilations.

They also need, beside the hardware, special software to play the music that they have downloaded. From the supply side, the structure of on-line distribution of downloadable music is completely different from the physical distribution of music (both in bricks and mortar shops and in e-commerce). Music downloading does not involve manufacturing, warehousing, physical sales and distribution. These differences make downloads and physical CDs two completely separate product markets. In addition, downloads and CDs have different pricing structures and the price and volume of CDs have not decreased as a result of the offering of music downloads. In the present case, the parties have provided no empirical evidence showing that the pricing of music distributed on physical carriers is restrained by the pricing of downloading or that the pricing of physical CDs has gone down as a result of the offering of music downloads. It is, therefore, concluded that there is an emergent, but separate, market for downloadable music."

14–021   The Commission did not fully discuss the implications of the fact that the vast majority of music currently downloaded from the Internet is downloaded for free, in terms of its effect on market definition. In respect of audio streaming services, however, it noted that:

"streaming is at present generally given free of charge and is financed out of Internet advertising revenues. However, it can reasonably be expected that users will be charged for streaming in the near future. It can be mentioned in this context that following its licensing agreement with Time Warner and Bertelsmann, the Internet music company MP3 has announced plans to launch a subscription music service over the Internet that is a system based on subscription fees to be paid by users for lockers."

The Commission concluded that there was an emerging market for on-line music delivery. For the purpose of its assessment in that case, though, it was unnecessary to decide whether music downloads and streaming constituted one or two separate product markets as the transaction would in any event lead to the creation of a dominant position as originally proposed.

In *Vivendi/Canal+/Seagram*[24] the Commission had to consider the further question as to whether there was a separate, emerging market for online music delivery to mobile telephone customers. It concluded that this would be premature, since it was not possible to receive downloadable or streaming music over a standard GSM telephone, during the first phase of the service under GPRS the service was likely to be poor, and consumer demand was unclear. Ultimately, however, it was unnecessary to decide the issue.

Online Medical Services
14–022   A joint venture by Bertelsmann, Burda and Springer, to be called The Health Online Service ("HOS"), was intended to provide a closed online medical service for professional users only.[25] This was to include offers for office management, office equipment and help with billing systems for doctors and pharmacists. In addition it would offer articles especially produced for HOS. The service would mainly be financed by user fees, but there would also be some subject-specific advertisement. The parties suggested that there was a special market for closed medical online services for professional users, and the Commission agreed with that market distinction. It pointed out that from the users point of view other sources of information like specialist journals

or conferences were not a sufficient alternative to the complete offer of an online service.

This can be contrasted with another case, decided on the same day, September 15, 1997, involving a joint venture between two of the same parties, Bertelsmann and Burda.[26] The joint venture service, Lifeline, was to offer consumer-orientated online health, beauty, food and fitness information called Bodyline, Fitnessline, Foodline, Psycholine and Beautyline. The service was at no charge to consumers, and was financed by advertising. The Commission considered that the relevant market was that for Internet advertising. More significantly, however, the Commission refused to decide if health care information distributed at no charge could be a relevant market in itself.

Online Computer Games

In another case, the Commission had to consider games played online. The case involved a joint venture between Bertelsmann and Viag, which would offer online games, the possibility for players to be linked up with each other in playing computer games, and editorial content. The service would initially be provided for free, but later on charges would be introduced.[27] The Commission stated clearly that games playing provided for free could not be a relevant market. However, paid-for online games services could be taken into account in defining the relevant market. The parties suggested that the relevant market was for offline and online electronic games, on the basis that the borderline between the two was not clear, and online games were often offered in conjunction with CD-ROM games. The Commission pointed out that in previous decisions, it had defined the relevant market as that for paid-for content in general. However, it considered that it did not have to resolve the issue as to whether the market was one of games, or whether the relevant market was the broader market for paid-for Internet content in this case.

14–023

Broadband content

The Commission defined a market for paid-for content in *Telia/Telenor/Schibsted*.[28] In the course of its investigation in *AOL/Time Warner*[29] it found evidence of the existence of an emerging demand for the one-stop integrated supply of broadband content via the Internet. This demand was for bundled audio/video content (such as film plus sporting contests plus pop music concerts) via the Internet and as such appeared to be separate from the demand for films and TV programmes supplied through more traditional distribution channels (such as pay-per-view, video on demand or DVD/video rental). The different broadband contents would not be substitutes, according to the Commission, but complementary goods. An ISP able to offer such a range of content could be compared to a supermarket offering a wide range of complementary products in a single place.

14–024

Audio Player Software

In the *AOL/Time Warner*[30] case, the Commission also considered that there was a separate market for player software such as Realplayer, Winamp, Quicktime and MusicMatch Jukebox.

The Commission noted that most of these software products are normally given free over the Internet; but that for some others there was a price to pay. It suggested that Music Match Jukebox was one of the players for which there was a price to pay (although in fact at the time it was only a higher functionality version of MusicMatch which had to be paid for). Once again, the decision did not deal with the impact on market definition that most of these players were given away for free. It concluded that there was already a market for the supply of player software. This could be seen as a contrast to earlier cases,

14–025

in which the Commission suggested, in areas where the majority of the services are given away for free, that there may be a future market for such services, even if one does not exist at the time of the decision.

14.1.4 B2B Markets

14–026   The Commission has considered a number of B2B exchanges under both the E.C. Merger Regulation and Article 81.

The Commission considers that it might appear that in many cases, the question as to whether e-commerce creates an additional sales channel would be less pertinent than for B2C distribution, because in industrial supply arrangements, customers are often served directly by the suppliers, or there are mixed forms of vertical delivery chains where bigger customers are served directly and smaller customers via wholesalers.[31]

The question will therefore be whether electronic market places compete with normal bilateral sales or whether they constitute a separate, narrower product market. The former may be more likely if the parties used electronic market places only as an additional sales channel, the latter if the exchange offered additional services which clearly differentiated it from other sales forms. This issue was discussed by the European Commission in a case involving the *MyAircraft* exchange,[32] a B2B exchange for aerospace parts and services and supply chain management services. The Commission considered whether the exchange was part of the wider market for airline equipment or whether it constituted part of a narrower market for exchanges, such as that for exchanges involving aircraft equipment.

14–027   The parties suggested that the relevant market was the market for aerospace parts and services and that e-commerce should be considered as one segment among the many means by which companies transact business. This was on the basis that customers, including airlines and service providers remained free to decide how they wanted to conduct business with UTC, Honeywell or other suppliers, through MyAircraft, e-mail, fax, telephone, etc. The parties explained that MyAircraft.com would increase the efficiency of communications between aerospace industry participants without changing the way transactions are conducted in the aerospace industry and without having an impact on the definition of underlying markets of aerospace parts and services. The Commission undertook a market investigation which revealed that third parties in general considered B2B exchanges as one among many methods by which they transact business.[33] Some of these third parties seemed to believe that it would not be relevant to distinguish between the general sector of e-commerce and the sub-segment of B2B e-commerce. In any case, third parties considered it premature to draw distinctions between B2B e-commerce in different industry segments.

The services offered by MyAircraft.com to its customers included supply chain management tools and e-procurement. To a large extent these services formed an integrated part of the services offered by MyAircraft.com in order to enable customers of the site to use MyAircraft.com. as a purchasing or selling tool. However, some elements of the supply chain management service might, according to the Commission, have seemed to go beyond what was normally required by a user of MyAircraft.com in order to use the site to do business. This applied in particular to the inventory planning tools and forecasting tools. However, the market investigation revealed that a majority of third parties considered that these services were distinct components that might be offered separately or in combination but third parties did not at the time consider that they formed a distinct market.

The Commission considered that the results of the investigation suggested that the B2B **14–028** market place formed part of a wider market. However, in the MyAircraft case itself, the Commission did not have to decide the question. The precise relevant market definition could be left open since irrespective of the market definition chosen, the proposed concentration did not give rise to the creation or strengthening of a dominant position.

In fact, in none of the B2B cases which have been considered by the European Commission under the E.C. Merger Regulation have resulted in a decision giving a precise definition of the relevant market. On the other hand, the cases demonstrate the variety of different ways of looking at B2B markets, through the submissions made by the parties as to what the relevant market was:

In *Chemplorer*[34] the market place was to fulfil the needs of the chemical and **14–029** pharmaceutical industry, in the procurement of technical and administrative goods and services (known as MRO goods), as well as packaging materials. The parties submitted that the relevant market was the market for the operation of electronic marketplaces for bringing together supply and demand for MRO products, packaging materials, and related services. They had not therefore limited the market to the chemical or pharmaceutical industry, which was the target of the exchange. Whether or not the market should be defined more narrowly as solely applying in the chemical and pharmaceutical sector, or whether it included further participants, such as traditional suppliers or distributors of MRO products could be left open in this case.

In *ec4ec*[35] (e-commerce for engineered components) the market place related to plant **14–030** and machine construction and was initially set to cover the US and European markets. The parties proposed that the relevant market in which the exchange would be active would be IT services for e-commerce. They did not suggest any narrower definition relating to the products being traded. The parties considered that the various markets for plant construction and the production of components were neither upstream, down-stream or neighbouring markets to the market for IT services for e-commerce, since the electronic market place was only a means of communication which connected the individual market participants.

Emaro[36] concerned a business-to-business ("B2B") trading platform, which would **14–031** provide an IT infrastructure via which third parties would be able to carry out e-commerce transactions in the office equipment sector.

According to the view of the parties, the joint venture created a platform in the market for IT services for B2B e-commerce. The relevant market would thereby include all such products and services which enable undertakings to electronically procure products and to enable other undertakings to distribute products.

Date[37] involved a B2B marketplace for procurement of "non-strategic" office supplies, **14–032** *i.e.* stationary equipment and consumables such as pencils, pens, paper, hardware, cell phones, office accessories and flowers. After a start-up period, Date would also provide supplementary services such as payment, financing and shipment. None of the parent companies were active in the same activities as Date.

The notifying parties stated that the relevant product market was the procurement media or the procurement channels for "non-strategic" products such as stationary equipment and consumables to the corporate market. For the purpose of this notification the parties submitted that the relevant geographical market was Norway and that the notified concentration could be assessed on this basis. However, it was not necessary for the Commission to resolve the question in this case.

It is interesting to contrast the European Commission discussions on relevant markets **14–033** in B2B cases with the discussions of the U.S. Federal Trade Commission ("FTC"). An FTC Staff Paper[38] was published in November 2000. In addition to discussing the possible competitive concerns in the markets for goods traded on B2Bs, it also discussed the emerging competition for the provision of B2B services. The staff report points out that just as competition issues can arise in connection with other business-support activities, such as commercial telephone service or commercial Internet access, competition in the market for marketplaces raises its own set of antitrust concerns. In this respect, it suggested that the "market for market places" was not intended to suggest that the relevant antitrust market was necessarily limited to B2B e-marketplaces. In theory, more traditional alternatives, such as EDI connections, could remain competitive restraints.[39]

14.1.4 Geographic market

14–034   For infrastructure access markets, the geographic market will in many cases continue to be national. For Internet dial-up access, the geographic market was considered to be essentially national, based on the need for a local loop service. In *Telia/Telenor*[40] the Commission concluded that this characteristic limits the extent to which existing markets could be wider than national.

For B2C markets, the Internet enables customers to search much more widely for goods and services, and therefore will tend to broaden geographic markets. The markets may still be limited by whether or not services can be provided at a distance, and the costs and time taken for the transport of goods, as well as cross-border payments and exchange rates. The need to physically deliver traditional products even when bought online may therefore be a significant constraining factor to geographic market definition. Where these factors do not limit markets, then it may still be expected that other issues, such as language, or access through particular national gateways may tend to limit the geographic scope of the search for goods.

14–035   In the BOL cases referred to above concerning the formation of joint ventures to supply books on line in various countries, the issue was ultimately left open. In some of these cases the parties suggested that the market was national, or broader, encompassing for example the "Spanish speaking world" or the "Italian speaking world", and the issue never had to be decided. In one of the very early cases, *Bertelsmann/Havas/BOL*[41] the parties submitted that the geographic market for the publishing and the retail sales might be national, but that for Internet sales it was world-wide. The sales by Internet have a wider scope than traditional book club or mail order sales because of the international accessibility of the Internet. The Commission considered, "on the one hand, that for the reason given by the parties, the market may indeed be wider than France. On the other hand, the first experiences shows that sales in France represent the large majority (70 to 80 per cent) of total sales via the Internet, which would indicate the existence of a national market. The decision suggests that even the market for online sales of books is national".

The Commission has also pointed out[42] that in the case of *BOL Nordic*[43] sales were done via national subsidiaries necessary both for purchasing and for distribution because the on-line sales needed a national logistic system of storage and next-day delivery. Even for books written in English the geographical market seems to remain national, because there is as yet only limited trade between countries. This may be due to longer terms of delivery and higher costs for the consumer in relation to cross-border payments and exchange rates. The need to physically deliver traditional products even when bought online may therefore be a significant constraining factor to geographic market definition.

As the European Commission comments,[44] the above considerations of transport costs and similar factors should be irrelevant "where purely electronic products or services are being provided (given that, under current charging arrangements, use of the Internet is not distance-sensitive). More generally, however, concern over cross border trade, consumer protection and complaints mechanisms may dissuade consumers from trading cross border, leaving market definitions national. The relative strengths of these concerns compared to the fundamentally international nature of the Internet will require careful analysis in each case." **14–036**

When looking at the definition of relevant geographic market, for b2b exchanges, the relevant question is likely to be the question whether the geographic market will be widened as geographic location becomes less important for the interaction between buyers and sellers. It is to be expected that such a widening of the geographic market will be brought about by many B2B electronic market places. In many instances, such as the MyAircraft case, however, this question may be largely irrelevant, as even the "traditional" market is likely to be worldwide.[45]

14.1.6 Characteristics of Internet and E-commerce markets

Low marginal production costs
Like many new economy industries, a large number of e-commerce businesses are characterised by low marginal production costs. Once the initial investment is made, which can in some cases be substantial, it is cheap to create additional units. Electronic distribution of software, for example, can be done at low cost, and it doesn't cost much to add a new subscriber to the AOL network. Production may therefore exhibit increasing returns. This may result in more concentrated markets. **14–037**

"Soft durable goods"
Many e-commerce undertakings produce "soft durable goods". This is particularly true of downloaded software, games and content such as music. The services of these goods can be enjoyed for a long period of time, since they can be used and reused without limit. In practice however, the useful lifetime of these products may be more limited. **14–038**

Competition races and leapfrogging
In many areas of e-commerce, competition may consist of a series of races. Initially, firms invest heavily to develop a product that creates a new category, such as AOL Instant Messenger or the Napster MP3 search engine. Winners obtain very significant market shares initially, but that may be no guarantee of continued success. Subsequently, other firms may invest heavily and develop new innovations which leapfrog the leader's technology. The information economy is sometimes described as being a sector of "fragile monopolies" where today's top seller is at constant risk of being displaced by a new entrant with superior technology or other advantages. **14–039**

Dynamic competition
Markets may therefore be in a state of dynamic competition, where, in contrast to static competition which takes place in the market, with each participant trying to produce goods within that improved features at lower costs within that market, competition takes place for the market, each participant trying to come with significantly new innovations and technology which will displace the old market. Fragile monopolists may only be able **14–040**

to retain their position if they continue to be ahead of the game in innovation. First mover advantages, scale economies in production and/or network effects may ensure that for a time there is a single leading firm with a large share of the market. Many firms may invest and fail. Successful innovators may seek to charge high prices to compensate for their significant investment and high risk, although such high prices may not be sustainable in the long term.

Network effects

14–041 Many new economy industries are active in markets which exhibit network effects. Their products and services will be more valuable to each user if more people use them. For example, an instant chat service is more valuable the more users are subscribed to it.

Tippy markets

14–042 A slightly different effect, which may or may not be connected with network effects, is the notion of "tippy" markets. This notion relates to the fact that, once an undertaking achieves more than a certain critical mass in terms of absolute or comparative market power, or ownership of key assets, or number of users, then there may be factors in the market which will tend to further increase the market power of that undertaking, to the exclusion of, or at the expense of, other market participants. An example can be seen in the *MCI/Worldcom*[46] case, where the Commission suggested that while the system of top level interconnectivity was at the time in a state of some equilibrium, once one network became overly powerful, it cold prevent potential competitors from assuming the status of top-level networks by making sure that the prices at which it supplied transit were high enough to prevent the new entrant from building sufficient market share, or preventing competitors from granting a new entrant peering rights by exercising the threat of disconnection or degradation against them. The merger might well create a snowball effect, making the combined entity better placed than any of its competitors to capture future growth though new customers, because of the attractions for any new customer of direct interconnection with the largest network, and the lack of attractiveness of competitors offerings due to the threat of disconnection or degradation of peering.

14.2 The E.C. Merger Regulation

14–043 The E.C. Merger Regulation[47] (hereafter the "Merger Regulation") applies to "concentrations", which have a "community dimension", meaning that certain turnover thresholds described below are satisfied. A concentration arises where (i) two or more previously independent undertakings merge, or (ii) one or more undertakings acquire, whether by purchase of securities or assets, contract or other means, direct or indirect, control of the whole or parts of another.[48] An undertaking controls another if, as a matter of fact or law, it has the ability to exercise a decisive influence over it. This covers most forms of merger or acquisition. It also covers many joint ventures.

While the possible application of the Merger Regulation to mergers and acquisitions is something which may be easily understandable, it is likely to strike the future shareholders in many e-commerce joint ventures, such as joint venture establishing a B2B exchange/site as strange that the possible application of the E.C. Merger Regulation needs to be considered. A joint venture to form a start-up Internet venture might not appear to be a merger in the normal meaning of the word. However, the E.C. Merger Regulation can also apply to joint ventures between separate companies, even where they involve "start-up" or "greenfield" operations, including the formation of Internet portals or other web-site operations.

The E.C. Merger Regulation will apply to a joint venture if all of the following are fulfilled: **14–044**

- the parents acquire "joint control" over the joint venture;

- the joint venture is "full function";

- the parents satisfy the turnover thresholds applying under the EC Merger Regulation.

These elements are explained in more detail below.

14.2.1 The Thresholds

A concentration will have a community dimension where the turnovers of the undertakings concerned meet the threshold tests set out in the Merger Regulation. The Merger Regulation contains two, alternative, threshold tests, which are referred to here as the first tier test and the second tier test, although these descriptions are neither used in the Regulation, nor are they terms of art. A concentration meeting either the first tier test or the second tier test will fall under the Merger Regulation.   **14–045**

First Tier Test
A concentration will have a community dimension under the first tier test (and the Merger Regulation will therefore apply) if and only if all of the following three thresholds are satisfied for the preceding financial year[49]:   **14–046**

- the combined aggregate worldwide turnover of all the undertakings concerned is more than €5 billion;

- the turnover within the European Community ("Community-wide turnover") of each of at least two of the undertakings concerned separately is more than €250 million; and

- it is not the case that each of the undertakings concerned achieve more than two thirds of their individual Community-wide turnovers in one and the same Member State.

As to the meaning of the "undertakings concerned", for acquisitions, this means roughly the acquirer group plus the part of the target being acquired, for joint ventures this means roughly the groups of the parent companies which have joint control over the joint venture, as well as the joint venture company itself, if it already exists.

Second Tier Test
A merger will be regarded as having a community dimension under the second tier test if and only if all of the following five thresholds are satisfied for the preceding financial year[50]:   **14–047**

(i)   the combined aggregate worldwide turnover of all the undertakings concerned is more than €2.5 billion, and

(ii)   the turnover within the European Community ("Community-wide turnover") of each of at least two of the undertakings concerned separately is more than €100 million, and

(iii)   within each of at least three Member States, the combined national turnover of all of the undertakings concerned is more than €100 million, and

(iv)   within each of at least three Member States for which condition (iii) above is satisfied, the national turnover of each of at least two of the undertakings concerned is more than €25 million, and

(v)   it is not the case that each the undertakings concerned achieves more than two thirds of their individual Community-wide turnovers in the same Member State.

14.2.2 Control and Joint Control

14–048   Individual control will arise where ownership or other rights, contracts or other means, having regard to the elements of fact or law involved, confer the possibility of exercising decisive influence on another undertaking.[51]

Joint control exists when two or more undertakings have the possibility of exercising decisive influence over a joint venture. This normally means the power to block actions which determine the strategic commercial behaviour of an undertaking. The essential feature of joint control is the possibility of deadlock arising from the power of two or more parent companies to veto proposed strategic decisions, which effectively requires them to reach a common understanding in determining the commercial policy of the joint venture.[52]

The most basic example of joint control is where there are two participants with equal voting rights in the joint venture, such as where they both hold 50 per cent of the shares in the company and the shares have the same voting rights attached, or where they each have the power to appoint 50 per cent of the board with no provision for a casting vote. In this situation, each participant exercises decisive influence over the joint venture, as the consent of both is required for any decisions to be taken.[53]

14–049   However, there are also many other situations in which minority shareholders may be deemed to be in joint control. Normally, it is sufficient for a finding of joint control that there are unanimity requirements or negative veto rights for two or more individual parent shareholders over one or more of the following[54]:

- the appointment of senior management;
- major investments;
- the business plan;
- other market-specific rights; and
- the budget.

In the *MyAircraft*[55] decision involving a B2B exchange notified under the E.C. Merger Regulation, each of the shareholders was able to veto strategic decisions of MyAircraft.com relating to the annual business plan, acquisitions, and hiring and terminating the CEO's contract. This was sufficient to give joint control.

Where such veto rights or unanimity requirements are only given for a short period, of **14–050**
say less than three years, there may nevertheless be an absence of joint control.[56]

Even without veto rights, or unanimity requirements, it is still possible that there could in some circumstances be joint control, where decisive influence is acquired by some other means. The legal means to ensure the joint exercise of voting rights could include the formation of a holding company, to which the minority shareholders transfer their rights, or a legally binding agreement by which they undertake to act in the same way. Very exceptionally, even in the absence of such veto rights or unanimity requirements for minority shareholders, de facto joint control may be found to exist where there are strong common interests between the minority shareholders so that one would not act against the interests of the other. However, normally joint control will not exist where there is a possibility of changing coalitions between minority shareholders.

14.2.3 Full Function

A joint venture will only fall under the Merger Regulation if it is "full function", that is to **14–051**
say it is capable of "performing on a lasting basis all the functions of an autonomous economc entity".[57] The question here is really whether the joint venture business could stand on its own in the long run, in the same way as other businesses performing the same function.

In respect of portals or other sites these may not only be providing these products or services against payment, but may also charge for participation, as well as charging for advertising in one form or another, and for individual transactions. It must be remembered that there are many web-sites which have operated in the market on the basis that they are providing information, and basing their business model on making money out of advertising, with little likelihood of making a profit in the short, or even medium term. The degree to which the joint venture depends on finance from the parents on an ongoing basis could be relevant in showing that it is not full function, but may not ultimately be conclusive.

In the *MyAircraft* case, the Commission considered that the joint venture was full-function because it would have its own premises and its own staff and its own sales and marketing force, as well as initial cash contributions from the parents, who would also provide the necessary software.

14.3 Notification Requirement Under the Merger Regulation

If the EC Merger Regulation applies, then the transaction including any shareholders' **14–052**
agreement and other agreements which are essential to the transaction have to be notified on the basis of "Form CO" no more than one week after the conclusion of the agreement.

Notification is obligatory under the E.C. Merger Regulation and fines can be imposed for failure to notify within the one week period.[58] Normally, however, provided that contact has been established with the Merger Task Force within the seven day period, this period may be extended. Such a request must be made within the seven day period however. On the other hand, implementing the agreement without notifying can make the parties subject to potential fines of up to 10 per cent of aggregate turnover.[59]

The EC Commission normally has to clear the merger within one month of a valid **14–053** notification,[60] and the joint venture cannot be implemented until a clearance had been given.

If the Commission has serious doubts about the merger or joint venture then it may decide to initiate an in-depth investigation which could last a further four months.[61]

14.3.1 Assessment by the E.C. Commission

14–054 The substantive test under the E.C. Merger Regulation is whether or not it the merger or joint venture creates or strengthens a dominant position as a result of which effective competition would be significantly impeded.[62] Where the parties are competitors in markets related to the joint venture, the Commission also have to consider whether the joint venture may result in co-ordinated or collusive behaviour in those markets.

Nearly all e-commerce mergers or joint ventures which have fallen under the Merger Regulation have been cleared, as they have not been found to raise concerns in respect of the creation or strengthening of a dominant position. The following section contains examples, however, of some of the cases which have raised issues.

14.3.2 Decisions in Merger Cases Relating to E-commerce and the Internet

Strengthening of dominance in the local loop

14–055 In the eventually abandoned *Telia/Telenor* merger, the Commission found that the proposed operation would strengthen the dominant position already enjoyed by the two incumbent operators in their respective domestic market for the provision of local loop infrastructure in each country.

In order to obtain clearance, the parties gave a commitment that they would unbundle the local loop:

> "that they would allow competitors access to their respective local access networks in order to provide any technically feasible services on non-discriminatory terms. The undertaking will enable competitors to establish a sole customer relationship with telecommunications customers."

This commitment to provide unbundled local loop access was to take effect within three months from the date of the Commission's decision.

Dominance in Top Level Internet Connectivity

14–056 In the *MCI/Worldcom* case, the Commission had to assess whether the merger would result in the formation of a dominant position in the market for top level Internet connectivity. As regards their combined market shares, the parties originally submitted that they did not have more than 20 per cent of the backbone market, based on the premise that any ISP with its own cable facilities was a backbone provider. However, the Commission had difficulty in accepting this definition, which made no distinction between a small locally based ISP with local clients, and the large multinational top level networks. No convincing existing measure for the Commission's purposes was available, so the Commission developed a measure of the top level network market based on the notion that any top level network would necessarily have to peer, at minimum, with all of the top four ISPs (at the time—Worldcom, MCI, Sprint, GTE/BBN), which were capable of supplying universal interconnectivity without recourse to transit. On this basis there was little doubt that the combined entity would hold over 50 per cent of the market, however widely defined, and would be significantly larger than the nearest competitor, Sprint.

The Commission considered that a network of such absolute and relative size would be created that the combined entity would achieve market dominance, and would be able to pursue various strategies to reinforce its market position. It could control market entry by denial of new peering requests, foreclosure or the threat of foreclosure. It could raise rivals costs and decrease the quality of their service offerings, and the threat of such actions could give the combined entity the opportunity to dictate to whom its competitors could grant transit or peering, and on what terms. Further, the combined entity could degrade the offering of competitors by deciding not to upgrade capacity. The originally proposed combined entity's chances of implementing such a strategy might well be improved by picking off customers and competitors one by one. As it grew larger, it could change the nature of its interconnection arrangements with competitors, or threaten to do so, oblige them to pay for access to its network, either paid peering or transit, whilst offering no payment in reverse, and influencing their cost position by charging prices which made their prices less competitive. Once it had obtained dominance, the less likely the new entity was to be challenged, since the more it grew, the less need it would have to interconnect with competitors and the more need they would have to interconnect with it. The larger it became, the greater its ability to control the costs of new entrants, by denying the opportunity to peer. The Commission suggested that once one network became overly powerful, it cold prevent potential competitors from assuming the status of top-level networks by making sure that the prices at which it supplied transit were high enough to prevent the new entrant from building sufficient market share, or by preventing competitors from granting a new entrant peering rights though exercise of the threat of disconnection or degradation against them. The merger might well create a snowball effect, making the combined entity better placed than any of its competitors to capture future growth though new customers, because of the attractions for any new customer of direct interconnection with the largest network, and the lack of attractiveness of competitors offerings due to the threat of disconnection or degradation of peering.

In order to allow the Merger to go ahead, the parties were therefore forced to agree to divest MCI's Internet business as a whole, including its wholesale dedicated access, retail dedicated access business, consumer and business dial-up businesses, web hosting, broadcast network services and managed firewall services. This included all the equipment, routers, services, switches etc., wholesale and retail customer contracts, so far as possible, peering arrangements, including those with Worldcom (which Worldcom would not terminate for at least 5 years), and all necessary employees. MCI would also provide basic transmission and international leased capacity for the contracts being transferred.

Dominance in Online Music and Player Software
In AOL/Time Warner, the Commission was concerned that the possible combination of AOL with the Time Warner music catalogue, bearing in mind an existing relationship between AOL and Bertelsmann, which also had a strong music catalogue, could give the combined entity a dominant position in the market for online music, and that the combined entity would become dominant in the market for music player software. The Commission looked at whether the new entity would be able to play a gatekeeper role

14–057

14–058

and dictate the technical standards for online music distribution over the Internet, and also whether AOL would be able to impose Winamp, its software based music player, as the dominant software player.

AOL and Bertelsmann had been partners since the beginning of the commercialisation of the Internet. In 1995 they established the 50:50 joint venture AOL Europe, which permitted AOL's expansion in Europe. In addition, AOL and Bertelsmann, together with Vivendi, had a joint venture in France. In March 2000 AOL and Bertelsmann entered into a joint promotion, distribution and sales agreement. Bertelsmann and Time Warner each had 10 to 20 per cent of the music publishing rights for mechanical and performance rights in the EEA, giving a combined 30 to 40 per cent share of rights.

14–059   The deal was only cleared after the parties put in place a mechanism whereby Bertelsmann would progressively exit from AOL Europe and AOL CompuServe France, and AOL would forego certain rights under its marketing agreement with Bertelsmann. In particular, AOL would not exercise its rights to reformat Bertelsmann music content to make it compatible with AOL's music player in a manner which would promote or favour a format which was not available by licence to third parties on reasonable commercial terms. Further, AOL would not enforce any provision in the marketing agreement which prohibited Bertelsmann from promoting third party ISPs.

Online Travel Agency Services

14–060   In *T-Online/TUI/C&N Touristic*[63] the Commission was concerned that the venture, which was to be an online travel agency, would have privileged access to the content of TUI and Neckermann, the leading tour operators in Germany, as well as to T-Online's very large Internet customer base. Competing online agents had submitted that they depended on TUI and Neckermann's product offer and brands and they feared that the new company would end up dominating the online segment. They were also concerned about potential discriminatory measures with regard to access to essential content. To address these concerns, TUI and Neckermann offered to conclude supply contracts with any other online agents. But according to the Commission, a number of conditions were attached to this general commitment which would have provided numerous opportunities for circumvention and *de facto* discrimination. The Commission therefore concluded that the commitments offered did not fully and clearly remove the competition concerns and decided to enter into an in-depth ("Second-phase") inquiry. The venture was eventually abandoned after no satisfactory solution could be found.

Dominance in Portals

14–061   In the "Vizzavi"[64] joint venture between Vodafone, Vivendi and Canal+, the Commission was only able to clear the joint venture under the E.C. Merger Regulation after the parties gave commitments regarding access to the mobile telephone and TV portals which would be created.

Vizzavi was to develop, market, maintain and provide a branded multi-access Internet portal throughout Europe, providing customers with a seamless environment for web-based interactive services, across a variety of platforms, such as fixed and mobile telephony networks, PCs and palm-tops, as well as television sets. The Commission's investigation concluded that the joint venture would have led to competitive concerns in the developing national markets for TV-based Internet portals and developing national and pan-European markets for mobile phone based Internet portals.

14–062   In order to address these competitive concerns identified by the Commission, the parties provided undertakings to ensure that the default portal could be changed, should the consumer so wish. The undertakings would allow consumers to access third party portals, to change the default portal themselves, or to authorise a third party portal operator to change the default setting for them.

In *Vivendi/Canal+/Seagram*,[65] the Commission was concerned about the effect on the emerging pan-European market for portals and the emerging market for online music due to the acquisition of Universal's music libraries. Vivendi eventually gave a commitment to give non-discriminatory access to third parties regarding terms and conditions. The commitment provided for an arbitration procedure in case of a dispute concerning the access conditions. The commitment was limited to five years, with a possibility for review after three years.

Ancillary Restrictions

A clearance under the E.C. Merger Regulation, can also cover "ancillary restrictions"   **14–063** which are directly related to and necessary for the implementation of the concentration.

For example in the *MyAircraft.com*[66] decision the following clauses were found necessary to ensure that the joint venture was established on a solid base, but were only cleared under the Merger Regulation for certain limited periods:

- restrictions on the parties from engaging in activities relating to competing Internet platforms in the aerospace sector;

- the requirement not to use the services of any competitor Internet platform for the purchase and sale of the relevant product and services for a certain period from the formation date;

- the requirement not to make any of their consulting resources or services available to competing Internet platforms for a certain period from the formation of the joint venture;

- the requirement not to promote any competitor Internet platform for a certain period from the formation date;

- the restriction on acquiring an equity interest in any competitor platform for a certain period after they have reduced their shareholding below x per cent;

- an obligation on the site provider for a certain period from the formation date, not to sell or license to a competitor or certain identified businesses, any of the software to be made available to the Internet platform.

14.4 Application of Article 81 of the E.C. Treaty

14.4.1 The Scope of Article 81

Article 81(1) of the E.C. Treaty prohibits agreements between undertakings, decisions by   **14–064** associations of undertakings and concerted practices that, to an appreciable extent, affect trade between Member States and have as their object or effect the prevention, restriction or distortion of competition within the E.U. As a result, in determining whether Article 81(1) applies it is necessary to consider whether there is:

(i)   an agreement or concerted practice exists between undertakings;

(ii)   which prevents, distorts or restricts competition within the E.U.;

(iii) which affects trade between Member States; and

(iv) which has an appreciable effect.

Agreements and concerted practices

14–065   Most forms of co-ordination or agreements between undertakings are covered by the terms "agreement" and "concerted practice". There is no requirement that a legally binding contract exist between the parties, or that there be any agreement in writing; a so-called 'gentlemen's agreement' is sufficient.[67] Similarly, several separate contracts may be found, together, to form a single agreement.[68] It is sufficient to constitute a "concerted practice" that undertakings co-ordinate their behaviour in a way that "knowingly substitutes practical co-operation between them for the risks of competition".[69]

Between undertakings

14–066   The term "undertaking" is defined broadly and covers virtually any entity, regardless of its legal status, engaged in economic or commercial activity.[70] Limited companies, partnerships and individuals may all be undertakings. State-owned companies will also be covered by the term if they engage in commercial or economic activity.[71] The fact that an entity is non-profit making will not prevent it being an undertaking.[72]

   To be caught by Article 81(1), an agreement or concerted practice must exist between at least two undertakings. A parent company and its wholly controlled subsidiaries are usually considered to form a "single economic entity" and, as a result, are treated as a single undertaking for this purpose.[73] Consequently, many inter-group transactions will fall outside Article 81(1).

Effect on trade between Member States

14–067   Again, the concept of effect on trade between Member States is broad. It is sufficient that an agreement "may have an influence direct or indirect, actual or potential, on the pattern of trade between Member States, such as might prejudice the aim of a single market."[74] In practice, an effect on trade will generally be found where an agreement includes terms which relate to imports or exports, extends to more than one Member State or covers the whole of the territory of a single Member State (since this may have the effect of partitioning that state from the rest of the E.C. market).[75] For these purposes, most if not all economic activity will qualify as "trade". Since e-commerce and Internet agreements are usually at least national, if not worldwide, this test will very often be satisfied.

Preventing, restricting or distorting competition in the E.U.

14–068   In principle, any agreement that may lead to reduced competition between the parties or restrict the ability of third parties to compete may be caught by Article 81(1), and there is no particular significance in the distinction between "preventing", "restricting" and "distorting" competition. Particular types of agreements and clauses which may amount to restrictions of competition are described below. It should be pointed out, in respect of the relationship of Article 81 to joint ventures, that Article 81 can apply to the formation of a joint venture or other collaboration which does not fall under the Merger Regulation because it lacks the necessary elements of being "full function" or of the parties having joint control. In addition, even if a joint venture does fall under the Merger Regulation,

Article 81 may still apply to other existing or future agreements that relate to the joint venture which have not been cleared under the Merger Regulation.

Among the factors that will be considered in determining whether an agreement leads to a restriction of competition, the most important is likely to be the size of the parties combined share of the relevant market (the concept of "relevant market" is discussed below in the section dealing with Article 82).

Appreciable effect

The European Court of Justice has established that an agreement will not be caught by   **14–069**
Article 81(1) if it has no appreciable effect.[76] The scope of this exception has never been precisely defined by the Court. The European Commission has, however, issued a notice identifying several categories of agreement to which, in its view, Article 81(1) will not apply by reason of their limited impact. This notice states that:

(i)   agreements between parties that compete or have equivalent activities in separate geographic markets ("horizontal agreements") will not be considered appreciable where the parties have a combined market share of five per cent or less on the relevant market[77],

(ii)   agreements between parties that operate at different levels in the chain of supply or demand ("vertical agreements") will not be considered appreciable where the parties have a combined market share of 10 per cent or less on the relevant market[78]; and

(iii)   agreements (whether horizontal or vertical) in which all the parties are small and medium-sized enterprises ("SMEs") will not be considered appreciable. To qualify as an SME, an undertaking must belong to a group that has less than 250 employees and either an annual turnover not exceeding € 40 million or an annual balance-sheet total not exceeding € 27 million. For these purposes, an undertaking's group includes all undertakings linked by a holding, in capital or voting rights, of 25 per cent or more.[79]

However, the Commission states that, even if they are below the market share   **14–070**
thresholds above, agreements that fix prices, limit production or sales, confer territorial protection or share markets or sources of supply may be considered to have an appreciable impact and therefore to be caught by Article 81(1).[80] In addition, agreements falling within the SME threshold may, nonetheless, fall within Article 81(1) where they significantly impede competition in a substantial part of the relevant market.[81] Further, neither the market share nor the SME thresholds will exclude the application of Article 81 where competition in the relevant market is restricted as a result of the cumulative effect of parallel networks of similar agreements between different undertakings.[82]

Agreements that do not have an appreciable effect on competition when entered into may nonetheless subsequently be caught by Article 81(1) if changes in the size or market positions of the parties (or other factors) bring them outside the scope of the exception. For this reason, and because proper identification of the relevant market may be complex (see below), care should be taken by undertakings seeking to rely on the appreciable effect exception.

It should be noted that the European Commission has published the draft of a new notice on agreements whose effect on competition are *de minimis*.[83] This is intended to replace the existing notice of 1997.

14–071   In the draft notice, the market share thresholds for there to be no appreciable effect are higher than those contained in the existing notice. Where the parties are actual or potential competitors, there will not normally be an appreciable effect on competition where the aggregate market share of the parties does not exceed 10 per cent on any relevant markets (up from five per cent in the previous notice). On the other hand, where the parties are not competitors, a 15 per cent threshold applies (up from 10 per cent previous notice). In cases where it is difficult to say whether or not the parties are competitors, the 10 per cent threshold is the relevant one. Where competition is restricted by parallel networks of agreements, established by several suppliers or distributors, the market share threshold for any particular agreement is five per cent. Agreements which do not exceed this limit are not taken to contribute significantly to any cumulative foreclosure effect. Agreements will also be seen as having an inappreciable effect where any of these thresholds are exceeded by no more than one per cent during two successive calendar years.

As in the previous notice, the market share thresholds do not apply in the case where agreements contain certain types of restrictive clause. Apparently, there is no lower market share threshold for there to be an effect on competition where agreements contain such "hardcore" clauses, although Article 81 may in some circumstances not apply where the effect on trade is insignificant. For Horizontal agreements, between those operating at the same level of the production or distribution chain, the hardcore clauses include price fixing, limitation of output or sales and the allocation of markets or customers. For vertical agreements between undertakings operating at a different level of the production or distribution chain for the purposes of the agreement the forbidden clauses are the hard-core restrictions set out in the vertical agreements block exemption described below. These include:

- minimum or fixed resale pricing restrictions on the buyer

- restriction of the territory into which, or customers to whom, the buyer can sell the contract goods or services except:

  - a restriction of active sales into the exclusive territory or an exclusive customer group reserved to the supplier or another buyer

  - restriction of sales to end users by a buyer operating at the wholesale level of trade

  - restriction of sales to unauthorised distributors by the members of a selective distribution system

  - restriction of a buyer's ability to sell components supplied for incorporation to customers who would use them to manufacture the same type of goods as those produced by the supplier

- restriction of active or passive sales to end users by members of a selective distribution system operating at the retail level of trade

- restriction of cross supplies between distributors within a selective distribution system

- restriction agreed between a supplier of components and a buyer who incorporates those components, which limits the supplier's ability to sell the components as spare parts to end users or to repairers or other service providers not entrusted by the buyer with the repair or servicing of its goods exemption (see below for fuller analysis of all of these clauses)

The draft notice suggests that the quite separate exception for agreements between **14–072**
Small- and Medium-sized enterprises as defined in Recommendation 96/280 also
continues to apply, such agreements being "rarely capable of affecting trade between
Member States". Small and medium-sized enterprises are those which have fewer than
250 employees and either a turnover not exceeding 40 million or an annual balance-sheet
total not exceeding 27 million, and which are not owned as to more than 25 per cent of
there share capital or voting rights by one undertaking on jointly by several undertakings
falling outside of the definition of an SME.

14.4.2 The Effect of Falling Within Article 81(1)

Several consequences may follow if an agreement falls within Article 81(1), unless the **14–073**
agreement is notified to the E.C. Commission and receives an exemption under Article
81(3). First, under Article 81(2), the anti-competitive aspects of an agreement that falls
within Article 81(1) are void and will not be enforced by national courts in the E.U. This
may, depending on the relevant national legal provisions, result in the whole of the
agreement becoming unenforceable. Nor will E.U. courts enforce judgements of foreign
courts based on aspects of an agreement which are contrary to Article 81(1). Second, the
Commission has powers to impose fines of up to 10 per cent of turnover on undertakings
involved in a breach of Article 81(1).[84] Fines are, however, typically imposed only in the
most serious cases. Third, the Commission may, by decision, order infringing
undertakings to take such action as is necessary to terminate the infringement.[85] Finally,
it should be possible for third parties injured as a result of a breach of Article 81(1) to sue
the offending undertakings for damages, although the circumstances under which such a
remedy is available are governed by the relevant national law. Under English law, it has
been confirmed that such damages are, in principle, available.[86]

14.4.3 Exemption from Article 81(1)

Exemption from Article 81(1) may be obtained under Article 81(3). Two routes are **14–074**
available to undertakings wishing to obtain an Article 81(3) exemption: (i) compliance
with one of the Commission's so-called "block exemption" regulations, in which case the
exemption is automatic, and (ii) individual exemption, which requires a notification to
the European Commission.
   Complying with a block exemption regulation ensures immunity from fines, legal
enforceability of the agreement and protection from damages actions under Article 81. In
the case of individual notification, it is the act of notification itself which ensures
immunity from fines. However, it is the subsequent exemption which ensures that an
agreement is legally enforceable and that the parties are protected from damages actions.

14.4.4 Individual exemption

If no block exemption applies, an agreement that risks falling within Article 81(1) may be **14–075**
notified to the Commission for an individual exemption.[87] To qualify for exemption, an
agreement must improve production or distribution or promote technical or economic
progress, while allowing consumers a fair share of the resulting benefit, and, at the same

time, must not impose restrictions that are not indispensable to these objectives or eliminate competition in respect of a substantial portion of the relevant products.[88]

There is no obligation to notify agreements falling within Article 81(1) and no time limit for doing so. The downside is that in the respect of the time during which the agreement is not notified, the parties are exposed to the risks outlined above and that any clearance ultimately obtained from the Commission may only be backdated to the date of notification (with the exception of vertical agreements — see below). Notification must be made on the correct form, Form A/B, which requires a substantial amount of information to be supplied, including information about the notified agreement, the parties to it and the markets affected by it.[89] As a result, notification can be costly and time consuming. Also, there is no time limit within which the Commission must reach a decision on a notified agreement. However, notification gives the parties immunity from fines, pending a formal decision by the Commission, so that a notified agreement may be implemented meanwhile with this protection.[90]

14–076   It is also possible to apply to the Commission for a formal declaration that an agreement falls outside the scope of Article 81(1), a so-called "negative clearance". Where such an application is made, it is usually combined with a request for an individual exemption, since an application for negative clearance alone gives no immunity from fines.[91]

In practice, most notifications are dealt with by way of an administrative "comfort letter" rather than a formal commission decision of exemption or negative clearance.

14.4.5 Block exemption regulations

14–077   The European Commission has enacted block exemption regulations in relation to various categories of agreement.

Existing block exemption regulations include the Technology Transfer Block Exemption[92] and the Vertical Agreements Block Exemption.[93] These two block exemptions will be analysed in some detail in the following sections.

Another block exemption, the research and development block exemption[94] which applies to joint research and/or development agreements, may also be relevant in some cases, but is not discussed in this chapter.

14.4.6 The Technology Transfer Block Exemption

14–078   The Technology Transfer Block Exemption applies to patent licences, know-how licences, and combined patent and know-how licences. It also covers patent and know-how licences which include terms relating to additional intellectual property rights to the extent that such rights are licensed together with patents or know-how and subject to similar (or more limited) restrictions of competition.

Know-how is defined for the purposes of the block exemption as "a body of technical information that is secret, substantial and identified".[95] This means that, for a know-how license to come within the block exemption it must cover know-how that is:

   (i)   technical, rather commercial or marketing information (*e.g.* not customer lists or market surveys);

(ii)   secret, in the sense of not generally known or easily accessible, so that part of its value consists in the lead time which the licensee gains when it is communicated to him (this may require that it is confidential and supplied under an obligation of confidentiality)[96];

(iii)   substantial, in the sense that it includes information which can reasonably be expected at the date of the agreement to be capable of improving the competitive position of the licensee, for example by helping him enter a new market, or giving him an advantage in competition with others who do not have access to comparable information[97]; and

(iv)   identified, in that the know-how must be described or recorded, either in the licence or at the time, or shortly after know-how is transferred, in a way which makes it possible to verify the fulfilment of the previous two criteria above.

A further limitation is that the Block Exemption only applies where the licensee is actually manufacturing a product under the licence, or having it manufactured on his account, or is providing the licensed service or having it provided on his account.[98] It does not apply to pure sales licences.[99]

Unfortunately, the block exemption only applies to licensing agreements relating to   **14–079**
patents and/or know-how, and only applies to provisions in licences of other intellectual property such as copyright and trade marks if the provisions relating to the exploitation of those other rights are ancillary. This means that those provisions would only be covered to the extent that they are contained in a licence of patent or know-how rights, and do not contain restrictions other than those which are already attached to the patent or know-how, and exempted under the block exemption. In addition, these licences must contribute to the licensed technology protected by the patent and/or know-how. Further, it should be noted that, as discussed below, the technology transfer block exemption does not apply to pure sales licences.

This unfortunately means that the block exemption will not directly apply to many licensing arrangements relating to e-commerce and the Internet, because many of these agreements relate to copyright and neighbouring rights, software rights and database rights and trademarks, which are not ancillary to patent and know-how licences, and/or may involve sales licences. Nevertheless, the technology transfer block exemption may well be a good guide to the types of restrictions which will be permitted or prohibited in licensing arrangements related to the new economy.

Structure of the Block Exemption
Apart from the principal exemptions described in Article 1 of the Block Exemption (see below) the following is the structure of the Block Exemption:

White list
Article 2 of the Block Exemption contains a list of those clauses which will not generally   **14–080**
be found to come within Article 81 (1), but which are exempted in case they do as a result of the circumstances of any particular agreement. The clauses listed are exempted under the block exemption even if they are not accompanied by any of the principal provisions exempted under Article 1. The block exemption also applies where licences contain clauses of the type listed but with a more limited scope.

Black list

14–081   Article 3 of the block exemption contains a black list of clauses whose presence in any agreement excludes the application of the block exemption.

Grey list

14–082   A variety of clauses may be contrary to Article 81(1), but may neither be exempted as principle exemptions, or under the white list, nor mentioned in the black list as specifically excluding the application of the block exemption. Agreements containing such clauses which fall within the scope of the block exemption and which are not contained in a type of agreement which is excluded from the application of the block exemption may benefit from the opposition procedure described in Article 4 of the block exemption. In effect, such agreements will have to be individually notified to the Commission, but will benefit from the fact that if the Commission has not indicated its opposition within four months, then the agreement is deemed to comply with the block exemption. By the nature of these clauses, there is no "grey list" as such.

Scope and Inclusions

14–083   The block exemption only applies to agreements "between two parties".[100] The concept of an agreement under Article 81 is not necessarily limited to one contract, and a number of different contracts or licences may be deemed to form part of one agreement. On the other hand, where several companies within a group, which constitute a single economic entity for the purposes of Article 81, are all parties to an agreement, they should be treated as one party for the purposes of the block exemption.

There is also a good argument that "connected undertakings" as defined in the block exemption[101] should also be seen as a single undertaking for the purpose of the counting of heads, even where there might be some question as to whether the single economic entity doctrine applies. "Connected undertakings" are basically undertakings in a relationship defined by ownership of more than half of the capital or business assets, having the power to exercise more than half the voting rights; to appoint more than half the members of the supervisory board, board of directors, or other representative body; or to manage the affairs of the undertaking.

The block exemption applies to patent licences, know-how licences, and mixed patent and know-how licences, as well as patent and/or know-how licences containing ancillary provisions relating to intellectual property rights other than patents,[102] such as trade marks or copyright.

14–084   The following are deemed to be "patents" for these purposes: patent applications, utility models, and applications for registration of utility models, *certificats d'utilite' and certificats d'addition* under French law, and applications for such *certificats*, semiconductor topography rights, supplementary protection certificates and plant breeder's certificates.[103]

Know-how is defined for the purposes of the block exemption as "a body of technical information that is secret, substantial and identified.[104] The information must be technical, rather than commercial or marketing information. It must be secret, in the sense that the know-how package as a body or in the configuration of its components is not generally known or easily accessible, so that part of its value consists in the lead time which the licensee gains when it is communicated to him.[105] The know-how must also be substantial, in the sense that it includes information which can reasonably be expected at the date of the agreement to be capable or improving the competitive position of the licensee, for example by helping him enter a new market, or giving him an advantage in competition with others who do not have access to comparable information.[106] Lastly, the know-how must be identified, in that it must be described or recorded, either in the licence or at the time, or shortly after know-how is transferred, in a way which makes it possible to verify the fulfilment of the previous two criteria above.[107]

Ancillary provisions are ones relating to the exploitation of intellectual property rights other than patents, and which contain no obligations other than those also attached to the licensed know-how or patents and exempted under the block exemption.[108] This means that licences relating to trade marks, copyright, and other intellectual property rights can come within the block exemption to the extent that such rights are licensed together with patents or know-how and are subject to similar or more limited restrictions of competition. **14–085**

The block exemption also applies to agreements where the licensor is not the holder or the know-how or the patentee, but is authorised by the holder or the patentee to grant a licence.[109] Further, assignments of patents and/or know-how come within the scope of the block exemption where the risk remains with the assignor, in particular where the sum payable in consideration of the assignment is dependent on the turnover obtained by the assignee in respect of products made using the know-how or the patents, the quantity of such products manufactured or the number of operations carried out using the know-how or the patents.[110] A licensing agreement in which the rights or obligations of the licensor or the licensee are assumed by undertakings connected with them can also benefit from the block exemption.[111]

Exclusions

Certain types of patent and know-how licence are specifically excluded from the application of the Block Exemption: **14–086**

Pure Sales Licences

The Block Exemption only applies where the licensee is actually manufacturing a product under the licence, or having it manufactured on his account, or is providing the licensed service or having it provided on his account.[112] It does not apply to pure sales licences.[113] **14–087**

Licences of other intellectual property rights which are not ancillary

The block exemption does not apply where the licence contains provisions relating to the exploitation of intellectual property rights other than patents which contain restrictive obligations other than, or more restrictive than, those also attached to the licensed know-how or patents.[114] **14–088**

Patent or know-how pools

The application of the block exemption is excluded in relation to agreements between members of a patent or know-how pool which relate to the pooled technologies, unless the parties are not subject to any territorial restrictions in the EEA with regard to the manufacture, use, or putting on the market of the licensed products or with regard to the use of the licensed or pooled technologies.[115] **14–089**

Joint ventures between competitors

The block exemption does not apply to licensing agreements between competitors which hold interests in a joint venture, or between one of them and the joint venture, if the licensing agreements relate to the activities of the joint venture.[116] How-ever, the block exemption may still apply to agreements whereby a parent undertaking grants the joint **14–090** venture a licence, provided that the combined market shares of the parties do not exceed 20 per cent in the case of a licence limited to production, or 10 per cent in the case of a licence which also covers distribution. The block exemption continues to apply provided that these limits are not exceeded by more than one tenth in any two consecutive financial years. Where that limit is exceeded, block exemption continues to apply for a period of six months from the end of the year in which the limit was exceeded.

Reciprocal agreements or cross-licences between competitors

14–091   The block exemption will not apply to agreements under which one party grants the other a patent and/or know-how licence and in exchange the other party, even in separate agreements or through connected undertakings, grants the first party a patent, trade mark, or know–how licence or exclusive sales rights, in relation to the products covered by those agreements.[117] Such reciprocal agreements may come within the block exemption, however, where the parties are not subject to any territorial restriction within the EEA.

Sole and exclusive licence terms

14–092   The grant of a sole or exclusive licence will often be contrary to Article 81 (1), but a sole and exclusive licence is exempted under the principle exemptions contained in Article I of the block exemption for specific periods.[118] The block exemption permits a restriction on the licensor exploiting patent and/or know–how rights by directly selling or manufacturing or granting other licences in the territory of the licensee for the period of the licensed patents or, in the case of know-how, for 10 years from the first marketing of a product within the EEA by a licensee.

However, the 10-year period only applies so long as the know-how remains secret and substantial and has been identified. In the case of a combined patent and know-how block exemption, the permissible period is whichever of the above two alternatives gives the longer period. However, in that case the longer period based on the patent only applies in Member States in which a "necessary" patent continues to be valid. Getting the period of the sole and exclusive nature of the licence is vital, because the block exemption specifically excludes under the black list the possibility of its applying to agreements under which the duration of the relevant clauses is for longer periods.[119] Consequently, for a know-how and patent licence in which the licensee's territory covers several Member States, the sole or exclusive nature of the licence must expire at the end of the 10-year period in respect of those countries in which there ceases to be a valid necessary patent.

Territorial Restrictions on the Licensee

14–093   Restrictions on the licensee exploiting the licensed technology outside of its territory within the EEA-whether by manufacturing, using the licensed product or process, or selling in the territory of other licensees or of the licensor-will be contrary to Article 81(l), but are exempted for specific time periods under the principle exemptions contained in Article 1.[120] In this respect, a distinction is made between restrictions on sale, manufacture, or use in the "territory of the licensor" defined as those territories in which no other licensees have been appointed,[121] and restrictions on such exploitation in territories of other licensees.

The exemption relating to a restriction on sales, manufacture, or use in territories in which no other licensees have been appointed applies for the full periods suggested above in respect of sole and exclusive licences, except that in the case of reliance on patent rights, the exemption is "only to the extent that and for as long as the licensed product is protected by parallel patents" in the territory of the licensee and the licensor. On the other hand, where other licensees have been appointed, a restriction on the licensee selling the licensed product in the territories of such other licensees in response to unsolicited requests (a restriction on "passive sales") can only be exempted for a period of five years from the date when the licensed product is first put on the market within the common market by a licensee.[122]

This five-year period only applies to the extent that, and for as long as, in these **14–094** territories, the product is protected by parallel patents (where reliance is being placed on patent rights) or the know-how remains secret and substantial and has been identified (where reliance is being placed on know-how). Again, it is vital that the duration of any restriction on sales or manufacturing or use by the licensee outside of its territory is carefully defined so as not to exceed the duration limits set out in the block exemption, since exceeding them in any respect will cause the loss of the block exemption under the black list. This definition of the duration of the restrictions also has to take into account the fact that other licences may be granted after the grant of the licence under consideration and in respect of which the application of the block exemption is being sought.

Obligation to use licensor's trade mark or get up
Another of the principal exemptions contained in Article 1 applies to an obligation on the **14–095** licensee to use only the licensor's trade mark or get up to distinguish the licensed product during the term of the agreement, provided the licensee is not prevented from identifying himself as the manufacturer of the licensed products.[123]

Own use licence
The last of the principal exemptions relates to own use licences. The licensee can be **14–096** obliged to limit his production of the licensed product to the quantities he requires in manufacturing his own products and to sell the licensed product only as an integral part of or a re-placement part for his own products or otherwise in connection with the sale of his own products.[124] The exemption only applies, however, if the quantity of those own products are freely determined by the licensee.

14.4.7 Technology Transfer Block Exemption—Other Specific Clauses

While the main exemptions have been discussed separately above, the following section **14–097** analyses the white-listed, black-listed and grey-listed clauses together, in respect of specific types of clause.

Quality specifications and tying in of goods or services
Requiring the licensee to accept quality specifications or further licences or to purchase **14–098** goods or services will not normally be contrary to Article 81 (1) where such an obligation is necessary for a technically satisfactory exploitation of the licensed technology or to ensure conformity with quality standards respected by the licensor and other licensees.[125] Where neither of these justifications applies, it is possible to notify an agreement containing quality specifications or tying provisions of the type just mentioned under the opposition procedure.[126]

Improvements and new applications

14–099   Requiring the licensee to assign back rights to improvements or new applications of the licensed technology is contrary to Article 81 and will cause the loss of the block exemption under the black list.[127] On the other hand, a requirement to license back rights relating to improvements or new applications, as opposed to assigning them, will not usually be restrictive contrary to Article 81, and is exempted under the white list provided that: (i) in the case where improvements are severable from the licensed technology, the licence is non-exclusive; and (ii) the licensor is obliged to license its own improvements either exclusively or non-exclusively to the licensee.[128]

A licence which requires an exclusive licence back of severable improvements, or which requires the licensee to license back improvements or new applications but does not require the licensor to license its improvements, could in theory be notified for an exemption under the opposition procedure.

Confidentiality of know-how

14–100   The licensee may be obliged not to divulge the know-how communicated by the licensor, even after the agreement has expired. Such a clause will not generally be considered restrictive of competition, and is exempted under the white list in the case where it does become restrictive.[129]

Restriction on sub-licensing or assignment

14–101   An obligation on the licensee not to grant sub-licences or assign the licence is not generally restrictive of competition, and is exempted under the white list in the case where it does become restrictive.[130]

It is not clear whether a clause which permitted sub-licensing but only with the consent of the licensor, or one which allowed sublicensing but not to competing companies, would also be exempted on the basis that the white list also applies to clauses of the type listed, but of more limited scope. It should also be noted that the block exemption does not indicate the position with respect to a restriction on assignment by the licensor.

Post-term use ban

14–102   The licensee may be prohibited from exploiting the know-how or the patents after the termination of the agreement as long as the know-how is still secret or the patents are still in force. Such a clause is white-listed.[131]

Most favoured licensee clause

14–103   The licensor can be required to grant the licensee any more favourable terms that the licensor may grant to another undertaking after the agreement is entered, under the white list.[132]

Non-competition clauses

14–104   A requirement on one party not to compete with the other or with connected undertakings within the EEA in respect of research and development, production, use, or distribution of competing products will cause the loss of the block exemption pursuant to the black list.[133] On the other hand the licensor may impose an obligation on the licensee to use its best endeavours to manufacture and market the licensed product,[134] and to produce minimum quantities.[135] The licensor may also reserve the right to terminate the licensee's exclusivity and stop licensing improvements to it, where the licensee enters into competition in any of the ways just mentioned, and the licensee may also be required to prove that the licensed know-how is not being used for the production of products and the provision of services other than those licensed.[136] All of these possibilities are exempted under the white list in the case where they constitute restrictions of competition.

Export and parallel import restraints

The benefit of the block exemption will be lost where either party is required, without any objectively justified reason, to refuse to meet orders from users or resellers in their respective territories within the EEA.[137]   **14–105**

The same applies where either party is required to make it difficult for users or resellers to obtain the products form other resellers within the EEA, and in particular to exercise intellectual property rights or take measures so as to prevent users or resellers form obtaining outside, or from putting on the market in the licensed territory, products which have been lawfully put on the market within the EEA by the licensor or with his consent.[138] The block exemption will also not apply if the parties engage in any of the behaviour just mentioned as a result of a concerted practice between themselves. In fact, parallel import restrictions are not only black-listed under the block exemption, but will also give rise to a serious risk of fines.

Field of use and customer restrictions

The licensee can be obliged to limit its exploitation of the licensed technology to one or more technical fields of application, or one or more product markets, which will not generally be seen as restrictive of competition, and is in any case exempted under the white list.[139] On the other hand, where the parties were already competing manufacturers before the grant of the licence and one of them is restricted, within the same technical field of use or within the same product market, as to the customers they may serve, then the application of the block exemption is specifically excluded under the black list.[140] This applies whether the customer restriction is in the form of a prohibition from supplying certain classes of user, employing certain forms of distribution, or using certain forms of packaging with the aim of sharing customers.   **14–106**

There are two situations where customer restrictions are automatically exempted under the block exemption. Where the licensee has been appointed so that a customer could have a second source of supply within the licensed territory, the licensee may be restricted to supplying only a limited quantity of the licensed product to that particular customer. The customer may himself assume these second source supply obligations, in which case he may be subject to the same restrictions. This second source exception will normally not be restrictive of competition but is exempted under the white list in any case.[141]

A second situation is the principal exemption described above for the requirement on the licensee to use the trade mark or get up of the licensor. Where the parties were not competing manufacturers before the grant of the licence, and none of the other exemptions applies, then a customer restriction within a particular field of use or product market might still be contrary to Article 81, but the agreement may be notified to the Commission under the opposition procedure.   **14–107**

Quantity restrictions

The block exemption blacklists any clause whereby the quantity of the licensed products that one party may manufacture or sell, or the number of operations exploiting the licensed technology which may be carried out, are subject to limitations.[142] There are a   **14–108** number of situations where quantity restrictions are exempted automatically under the block exemption, however. One is the second-sourcing restriction described above. Another is the exemption for own use licences described above in relation to the principal exemptions. This is an exception in that the quantity that can be sold by the licensee is limited by the requirement to sell only as a component part of the licensee's own product, but the exemption only applies so long as the quantities of the licensee's own product of which the licensed products are forming a part are not restricted. A requirement to produce a minimum quantity of the licensed product or to carry out a minimum number of operations exploiting the licensed technology will not normally be restrictive of competition, but is exempted under the white list in case it is restrictive.[143]

Construction of facilities for third parties and site licences

14–109   The licensee may be prevented from using the licensor's technology to construct facilities for third parties, a term which is exempted under the white list.[144] The white list does not explicitly refer to licences which restrict the licensee to operating at a particular site. However, the block exemption explains that a licence granted for specific production facilities where the licensee is allowed to increase the capacity of the facilities or to set up further facilities for its own use on normal commercial terms will not be seen as a quantity restriction. Where a site licence did not allow an increase in capacity, it might therefore be seen as a blacklisted quantity restriction.[145]

Price restrictions

14–110   The block exemption cannot apply where one party is restricted in the determination of prices, components of prices, or discounts for the licensed products.[146] Such a pricing restriction is not only blacklisted under the block exemption, but in many cases could give rise to a serious risk of fines being imposed.

Royalties

14–111   The requirement to pay a minimum royalty will not generally be restrictive of competition and is in any case exempted under the white list.[147] In addition, an obligation to continue to pay royalties until the end of the agreement in the amounts, for the periods, and according to the methods freely determined by the parties in the event of the know-how becoming publicly known other than by the action of the licensor is exempted, as is a requirement to pay royalties for a period going beyond the duration of the licensed patents, in order to facilitate payments.[148] On the other hand, the block exemption makes it clear that the setting of royalty rates in order to achieve one of the black-listed restrictions will result in the block exemption ceasing to apply.[149]

A further question is the degree to which royalties can be charged on the basis of products which are not covered by the licensed know-how, or patents. For example, in a pure patent licence is it permissible for royalty calculations to include amounts related to manufacture and sales in countries in which there never were any applicable patents, or in respect of products for which there is no patent protection anywhere? There does seem to be a risk that such a royalty basis would constitute a restriction which was not exempted under the block exemption, and which would therefore cause the loss of the automatic exemption, but this is not entirely clear.

No-Challenge clauses

14–112   The block exemption treats no-challenge clauses differently, according to whether they simply enable the licensor to terminate the agreement or if there is an enforceable clause preventing a challenge. If the licensor reserves the right to terminate the agreement if the licensee contests the secret or substantial nature of the licensed patents within the EEA, or challenges the validity of licensed patents belonging to the licensor or undertakings connected with him, then this will normally not be considered restrictive of competition, and will be exempted in case for some reason it is restrictive.[150] The same applies where the licensor reserves the right to terminate a patent licence if the licensee claims that the patent is not necessary.[151] On the other hand, if the licence applies a blanket prohibition on the licensee contesting the secrecy or substantiality of the licensed know-how, or the validity of patents licensed within the EEA, then the agreement will no longer have automatic exemption under the block exemption, although it may be notified for an exemption under the opposition procedure.[152]

Marking obligations
An obligation on the licensee to mark the licensed product with an indication of the   **14–113**
licensor's name or of the licensed patent is white-listed.[153]

Assistance in enforcement
An obligation on the licensee to inform the licensor of any misappropriation of the know-   **14–114**
how or of infringements of the licensed patents, or an obligation on the licensee to take legal action or assist the licensor to take legal action against such misappropriation or infringements, will not generally be restrictive of competition and is in any case exempted under the white list.

14.4.8 The Vertical Agreements Block Exemption

The vertical agreements block exemption[154] has been applicable since June 1, 2000. It   **14–115**
replaced three existing block exemptions: the exclusive distribution, exclusive purchasing and franchising block exemptions. The new approach was not only intended to unify the provisions relating to vertical agreements contained in these block exemptions, but also to widen the scope of the block exemption further, and respond to some of the criticisms of the previous block exemptions.

The Commission also published a set of explanatory guidelines,[155] which not only explain the interpretation of the block exemption, but also give a competition analysis of vertical agreements which fall outside of the block exemption because they are above the market share thresholds.

Meaning of "vertical agreements"
Vertical agreements are defined in the Block Exemption as agreements or concerted   **14–116**
practices "between two or more undertakings each of which operates, for the purposes of the agreement, at different level of the production or distribution chain, and relating to the conditions under which parties may purchase, sell or resell certain goods or services".[156]

There are a number of points to notice about this definition. Firstly, the block exemption can apply to agreements between more than two parties. This is an advance on the previous block exemptions, which only applied where there were no more than two parties to the agreement. On the other hand, for the purposes of this block exemption, each of the parties to the agreement must operate at a different level of the production or distribution chain. So, for example, an agreement between a manufacturer, a wholesaler and a retailer could come under the block exemption, but not one which included the manufacturer and more than one wholesaler, or more than one retailer.

14–117   The definition also indicates that the parties need only operate at a different level of the market "for the purposes of the agreement". So the fact that two parties actually operate at the same level of the market for other purposes—for example they manufacture competing products—would not exclude them automatically from the block exemption, provided that for the purposes of the relevant agreement they were acting at different levels of the market—for example as manufacturer for one party, and as distributor for another party. That is not to say that all agreements between competitors come within the block exemption, however (see below). The definition is deliberately broad enough to include intermediate sales, where one party to the agreement is buying products to be used as an input into a production process. It also applies to the purchase, sale or resale of services.

This is in contrast with the previous block exemptions (or at least the exclusive distribution and exclusive purchasing block exemptions) which applied only to the resale of goods, and did not apply to the sale of services, or to any transaction where the goods purchased by the distributor were to undergo any substantial change in their nature which would amount to more than "resale".

Exclusion of agreements between competing companies

14–118   The Block Exemption will not apply to vertical agreements between actual or potential competitors, even if they operate at different levels of the production/distribution chain for the purposes of the agreement, unless the agreement is non-reciprocal and either:

(i)   the buyer's annual turnover does not exceed €100 million; or

(ii)   the buyer is a distributor and does not manufacture goods or services that compete with the contract goods or services.

(iii)   the supplier is a provider of services at several different levels of trade, while the buyer does not provide competing services at the level of trade where it purchases the contract services.

14–119   Competing undertakings are undertakings that are actual or potential suppliers of the contract goods or services or goods or services that are substitutes for the contract goods or services.[157] A potential supplier is an undertaking that does not actually produce a the goods or services supplied by the supplier competing product but could and would be likely to do so in the absence of the agreement in response to a small and permanent increase in relative prices. This applies where the undertaking would be able and to undertake the necessary additional investments and supply the market within one year.[158] This assessment has to be based on realistic grounds; the mere theoretical possibility of entering a market is not sufficient.

The exceptional circumstances where agreements between competitors may come under the block exemption are intended to cover (i) situations in which the buyer is a relatively small undertaking and (ii) situations in which the supplier distributes the contract goods directly to certain customers or territories as well as appointing distributors. In other words, if a supplier competes with its distributor by selling the contract goods to end users itself, the block exemption is not excluded provided the distributor does not operate at the level at which it purchased the goods or services (*e.g.* if he is a competing manufacturer).

Exclusion of Intellectual Property Agreements and Agreements coming under other Block exemptions

As regards intellectual property agreements and licences, the Block Exemption states[159]   **14–120**
that:

> "the exemption ... shall apply to vertical agreements containing provisions which relate to the assignment to the buyer or use by the buyer of intellectual property rights, provided that those provisions do not constitute the primary object of such agreements and are directly related to the use, sale or resale of goods or services by the buyer or its customers."

The Guidelines suggest[160] that the Block Exemption Regulation applies to vertical   **14–121**
agreements containing IPR provisions when five conditions are fulfilled:

(1)   The IPR provisions must be part of a vertical agreement, *i.e.* an agreement with conditions under which the parties may purchase, sell or resell certain goods or services

This means that agreements where one party provides another with a master copy and licenses the other to produce and distribute copies will not come under the block exemption, nor will trade mark licensing agreements for the purpose of merchandising, sponsorship contracts or copyright licenses such as broadcasting contracts concerning the right to record and/or broadcast (or presumably webcast) an event.

(2)   The IPRs must be assigned to, or for use by, the buyer;

Consequently, the block exemption does not apply to agreements where IPRs are provided by the buyer to the supplier. This means in particular that subcontracting involving the transfer of know-how to a subcontractor to enable the subcontractor to manufacture products does not fall within the scope of application of the Block Exemption. However, vertical agreements under which the buyer provides only specifications to the supplier which describe the goods or services to be supplied are exempted.

(3)   The IPR provisions must not constitute the primary object of the agreement;

According to the guidelines, this means that the primary object of the agreement must not be the assignment or licensing of intellectual property rights but the purchase or distribution of goods or services and the IPR provisions must serve the implementation of that vertical agreement.

(4)   The IPR provisions must be directly related to the use, sale or resale of goods or services by the buyer or his customers.

According to the guidelines, the goods or services for use or resale are usually supplied by the licensor but may also be purchased by the licensee from a third party supplier. The IPR provisions will normally concern the marketing of goods or services. This is for instance the case in a franchise agreement where the franchisor sells to the franchisee goods for resale and in addition licenses the franchisee to use its trade mark and know-how to market the goods. In the case of franchising where marketing forms the object of the exploitation of the IPRs, the goods or services are distributed by the master franchisee or the franchisees.

(5)   The IPR provisions, in relation to the contract goods or services, must not contain

restrictions of competition having the same object or effect as vertical restraints which are not exempted under the Block Exemption Regulation

This means that they cannot include any of the forbidden hardcore restrictions (see below) or the various non-compete provisions excluded from the block exemption.

14–122 The block exemption further states that it "does not apply to vertical agreements the subject matter of which is regulated by other block exemption regulations".[161] The guidelines explain in this respect that the block exemption does not apply to vertical agreements "covered by" the technology transfer block exemption, the research and development block exemption or the specialisation block exemption.

It may be that as a result of this, any agreement which includes a licence of patent rights or technical know-how and which allows manufacturing using these rights may not come within the scope of the block exemption, because it comes within the technology transfer block exemption. However, this may have some unintended consequences. Giving the purchaser of any products or services any technical information concerning its manufacture of a further product could mean loosing the benefit of the block exemption, as might even an implied patent licence.

Trade Marks

14–123 In respect of trade marks, the guidelines[162] comment that a trade mark licence to a distributor may be related to the distribution of the licensor's products in a particular territory. If it is an exclusive licence, the agreement amounts to exclusive distribution.

Copyright and Software

14–124 The guidelines[163] indicate that agreements under which hard copies of software are supplied for resale and where the reseller does not acquire a licence to any rights over the software but only has the right to resell the hard copies are to be regarded as agreements for the supply of goods for resale for the purposes of the block exemption. Under this form of distribution, the licence of the software only takes place between the copyright owner and the user of software. This may take the form of a shrink-wrap licence, *i.e.* a set of conditions included in the package of the hard copy which the end user is deemed to accept by opening the package. Buyers of hardware incorporating software protected by copyright may be obliged by the copyright holder not to infringe the copyright, for example not to make copies and resell the software or not to make copies and use the software in combination with other hardware, and these restrictions will be covered by the block exemption regulation.

It is a pity that the guidelines devote such little discussion to copyright, related rights, database rights and trade marks when it was intended that the regime should extent to new forms of distribution of goods or services. It would be doubly sad if agreements containing provisions relating to such rights were to be mostly excluded from the block exemption, as appears to be the case.

The Market Share Cap

14–125 The Block Exemption is subject to a 30 per cent market share threshold, above which the block exemption no longer applies.[164] The relevant market share is that of the supplier, except in the case of exclusive supply arrangements where the relevant market share is that of the buyer. An "exclusive supply obligation" is defined as "any direct or indirect obligation causing the supplier to sell the goods or services specified in the agreement only to one buyer inside the Community for the purposes of a specific use or for resale."[165]

Market shares should then be calculated on the basis of the sales value of the contract goods or services for the proceeding calendar year.[166] If value figures are not available, estimates based on market data, including data on sales volume, may be used.

After the market share breaks through the 30 per cent barrier the exemption can continue to apply for a period of two years so long as the market share is less than 35 per cent.[167] Once the market share breaks through the 35 per cent barrier the exemption can only apply for a further period of one year. These two extensions cannot be combined, so that the exemption can only continue to apply for a maximum of two years if the market share threshold is exceeded.[168]

Calculating the market share

The usual rules of market definition under E.C. competition law must be applied, in addition to which, the guidelines deal with certain specific issues. The relevant product market comprises goods and services which are regarded by the supplier as interchangeable. The relevant geographic market is the area in which the undertakings concerned are involved in the supply and demand of relevant goods or services, in which the conditions of competition are sufficiently homogenous.   **14–126**

In calculating the market share in the supplier's market, the market share is the market share of the supplier in the market in which it sells to buyers. This market depends first on substitutability from the buyer's perspective. Where the supplier's product is used as an input to produce other products and is not generally recognisable in the final product, the product market is normally defined by the direct buyer's preferences, since customers will normally not have a strong preference concerning the inputs used by the buyers. However, in the case of distribution of final products, what are substitutes for the direct buyer will normally be influenced or determined by the preferences of the final consumers when it purchases final goods. In a case where there are three parties, the market share cap must be satisfied for each supplier. For example, where there is a manufacturer, wholesaler and retailer, the market share cap must be satisfied for both the manufacturer and the supplier.

In the case of exclusive supply, the market share of the buyer is its share of all purchases on the market in which it purchases the goods and services.   **14–127**

The problem with the market share cap, as with all market share tests is that, especially in relation to intermediate markets, market share data may often be unavailable or unreliable, creating uncertainty in the application of the exemption.

Hardcore Restrictions

The block exemption contains a list of "hardcore" restrictions that, if included in an agreement, will prevent the block exemption from applying:[169]   **14–128**

(i)   restrictions on the buyer's ability to determine its sale price, with the exception of recommended resale prices and maximum resale price obligations (provided that these do not act amount to fixed or minimum resale prices as a result of pressure or incentives);

(ii)   a restriction of the territory into which, or the customers to whom, the buyer may sell the contract goods or services apart from:

— a restriction on active sale to territories or customer groups that the supplier has exclusively reserved to itself or allocated exclusively to another buyer;

— restrictions on sales to end users by wholesalers;

— restrictions on resale to unauthorised distributors by members of a selective distribution network;

— a restriction of the buyer's ability to sell components, supplied for the purposes of incorporation, to customers who would use them to manufacture the same type of goods as those produced by the supplier;

(iii) the restriction of active or passive sales to end users by members of a selective distribution system operating at the retail level of trade, without prejudice to the possibility of prohibiting a member of the system from operating out of an unauthorised place of establishment;

(iv) restrictions on cross-supplies between members of a selective distribution system;

(v) restrictions preventing a buyer of spare parts that uses them for resale and incorporation from selling them to independent repairers or service providers.

The restrictions in the hardcore list are clearly now the central guidance as to what clauses may be permitted in vertical agreements, and merit close examination.

Resale Prices

14–129   Resale price maintenance is the first of the hardcore list.[170] There can be no restriction on the buyer's ability to freely determine its resale prices, with the exception of the possibility of recommended resale prices and maximum resale price obligations. However, these recommended and maximum prices must not act amount to fixed or minimum resale prices as a result of pressure or incentives. The guidelines[171] make it clear that it is not only direct resale price maintenance, but also indirect price maintenance which is forbidden. Thus, the fixing of distribution margin, or maximum level of discount the distributor can grant, or making the grant of rebates or reimbursement of promotional costs by the supplier subject to the observance of a given price level, linking the prescribed resale price to the resale prices of competitors, threats, intimidation, warnings, penalties, delay or suspension of deliveries or contract terminations in relation to observance of a given price level. A number of activities are described in the guidelines as measures which can make direct or indirect means of price fixing more effective, but are not blacklisted in themselves. These include monitoring systems, requirements on retailers to report other retailers who deviate from the standard price, printing a recommended relate price on the product or the supplier obliging the buyer to apply a most-favoured-customer clause. On the other hand, if they are used to make recommended prices or maximum prices function as fixed or minimum resale prices, then the recommended price or maximum price may be blacklisted.[172]

Restrictions on territories or customers to whom the buyer can sell

14–130   Restrictions on the territories into which the buyer can sell, or the customers to whom he can sell are blacklisted[173] with certain exceptions.

Before turning to the exceptions, it is important to note that in is not just a straight contractual ban on selling in particular territories or customers which is aimed at, but anything which brings about market partitioning by territory or by customer.[174] That would include the obligation to refer orders from customers to other distributors, for example. It would also include refusal or reduction of bonuses or discounts, refusal to supply, reduction of supplied volumes or limitation of supplied volumes to the demand within the allocated territory or customer group, threat of contract termination or profit pass-over obligations. Not providing a Community-wide guarantee service which enables all distributors are required to provide guarantee services, and are reimbursed by the supplier, even where the product was sold by other distributors into the territory. These measures are more likely to be viewed as a restriction of the buyers ability to sell to such territories or customers where they are combined with monitoring systems such as the use of differentiated labels or serial numbers. However, a prohibition imposed on all distributors from selling to certain end users is not a hardcore restriction if there is an objective justification related to the product, such as a ban on selling dangerous substances to certain customers for reasons of health or safety. Obligations relating to the display of the supplier's brand name are also not classified as hardcore.[175]

The first exception to the hardcore prohibition on sales restrictions concerns restrictions on active sales by the buyer. The distinction in E.C. competition law between active and passive sales is a well established one. Active sales are those in which customers are approached by active marketing and promotions, such as advertising, in media or other promotions specifically targeted at a particular customer group or territory, as well as direct mail or visits, or establishing a warehouse or distribution outlet in another distributor's territory. Passive sales, on the other hand, are sales to customers who have made an unsolicited request for a good or service. In this case, it would also be a restriction on passive sales if distributors were prevented, not from selling, but from delivering the goods or services to such customers.[176] The distinction is significant because the general principle in the past has been that in distribution arrangements, while there might be a ban on active sales, a ban on passive sales into another territory, such as would be implied by a complete ban on exports into that other territory by the distributor, was not permitted and raised a high risk of fines. The new rules are slightly different however, in that only certain restrictions on active sales are allowed. **14–131**

Only restrictions on active sales by direct buyers to territories or customer groups that the supplier has exclusively reserved to itself or allocated exclusively to another buyer are permitted.[177] A territory or customer group will be taken to be exclusively allocated when the supplier agrees to sell his product only to one distributor for distribution within a particular territory or to a particular customer group and that exclusive distributor is protected against active selling into his territory or to his customer group by the supplier and all the other buyers of the supplier inside the community. The allocation of exclusive territories and customer groups can be combined, so that an exclusive distributor can be appointed for a customer group within a particular territory. On the other hand, it is only a restriction on active sales to such exclusive territories or customer groups which is permitted. A restriction on passive sales to such exclusive groups or territories will never be permitted.[178]

It should be noted that the restrictions on active resale permitted under this vertical agreements block exemption are more limited than those permitted under the previous block exemptions, where, for example the exclusive distribution block exemption allowed a prohibition on active resale outside an exclusive contract territory of the distributor, whether or not the other territories were exclusively reserved to another distributor or to the supplier.

Application to sales via the Internet
According to the guidelines,[179] resale of goods and services via the Internet is generally not considered to be a form of active sales, but a form of passive sales. The fact that the **14–132**

Internet site may be accessed by customers in other territories results from the fact that the web is accessible from everywhere. If a customer from a territory outside of the buyer's visits the web site, resulting in a sale, that is considered passive selling, and that is the case whatever the language or languages which may be used on the web site. On the other hand actions specifically targeted at customers outside of the territory, such the use of banner advertising or links to pages of providers specifically available to other exclusive territories or customer groups could be considered to be active sales to those other territories or customer groups, as could unsolicited e-mails sent to individual customers or customer groups, or use of a ccTLD, such as the use of .de where the distributors is only appointed to the territory of France in the offline world. On the other hand, the restrictions which may be possible on meta-tagging in this new scheme of things is not entirely clear. The same rules apply to sales by catalogue.

At the same time, the guidelines makes it clear that[180] the supplier may require quality standards for the use of the Internet site to resell his goods, just as it may impose quality standards for a shop or for advertising and promotion in general. The guidelines suggest that this may be relevant in particular for selective distribution. This could include, presumably, online equivalents of the type of conditions regarding quality of presentation and service that are applied to the offline goods, such as the amount of space required to present the product and the quality of presentation of the goods. It might also include the obligation to have sufficient staff available to give advice online, which is the equivalent of that supplied during office hours offline, as well as quality service levels for response which match those offline, and requirements relating to the use of help desk and customer service provision. Provisions might also be included regarding payment and currency. Standards and requirements relating to advertising might also be required to match those provided offline. Similarly, the equivalent of non-compete provisions might be imposed to prevent sales of competitor products through the site, or perhaps even mention of competitors names, or any links to any sites which sell competitor products.

However, any set of restrictions which have the overall effect of making it commercially impossible for distributors to advertise or sell goods online and which cannot be properly justified, or which are disproportionate, may be treated as a blanket ban.

14–133   In general the guidelines make it clear that a blanket ban on sales via the Internet will be considered by the Commission to deprive an agreement of the benefit of the Block Exemption, and if it is treated in the same way as restrictions on passive sales have been treated in the past, such a restriction could give rise to a high risk of fines. An outright ban on Internet sales would only be permissible where there is an objective justification. In a previous unpublished version of the guidelines, the Commission indicated that health and safety reasons could justify such a ban. Whatever the case, the supplier cannot reserve to itself sales and/or advertising over the Internet.

This does not mean that the supplier is forced to allow all buyers to resell goods over the Internet. In a selective distribution system, the supplier can choose only to sell goods to those distributors who have physical sales locations, and to require that no sales be made to distributors who are not appointed to the network. This could also imply limiting the amount of product which can be purchased by end-users in some instances.

The impact of the treatment of Internet advertising and sales on distribution is considered below, together with the recent case law of the Commission implementing this policy.

Other exceptions to the hardcore prohibition on customer restrictions
Apart from the possibility of restrictions on active sales by the buyer to other exclusive **14–134**
territories or customers, there are three other exceptions to the hardcore exclusion of
restrictions on the territories or customers to which the buyer can sell.[181] A buyer who is a
wholesaler can be prevented from selling to end users, members of a selective
distribution network can be restricted from selling to unauthorised distributors, in
markets where such a system is operated, and there can be a restriction on a buyer's
ability to sell components, supplied for the purposes of incorporation, to customers who
would use them to manufacture the same type of goods as those produced by the
supplier. In the latter case, the term "component" includes any intermediate goods and
term "incorporation" refers to the use of any input to produce goods.

Restrictions on sales to end-users by selective distributors
Restriction of active or passive sales to end users by members of a selective distribution **14–135**
system operating at the retail level of trade is also a hardcore restriction.[182] The guidelines
explain[183] that not only does this mean that dealers in a selective distribution system
cannot be restricted in the users to whom they can sell, but it also means that there can be
no restriction on selling to purchasing agents acting on behalf of end-users. Selective
distributors must also be free to advertise and sell using the Internet. According to the
guidelines, selective distribution may be combined with exclusive distribution, provided
that active and passive selling is not restricted anywhere. The supplier may therefore
commit itself to supplying only one dealer, or a limited number of dealers in a certain
territory.
    The restriction on sales to end users by selective distributors is expressed to be without
prejudice to the possibility of prohibiting a member of the system from operating out of
an unauthorised place of establishment. This means that it is permitted under the block
exemption to impose a location clause on a selective distributor, preventing them from
running their businesses from any location other than that specified, or opening a new
outlet.[184]

Restriction on cross-supplies between appointed distributors
Cross supplies between appointed distributors in within a selective distribution network **14–136**
cannot be restricted under the hardcore list.[185] There must be no direct or indirect
restriction on passive or active sales to other selective distributors, operating at the same
or at a different level of trade. One consequence is that selective distribution cannot be
combined with vertical restraints aimed forcing distributors to purchase the contract
products exclusively from a given source, for instance exclusive purchasing. Another is
that there cannot be a restriction on appointed wholesalers selling to appointed
retailers.[186]

Restrictions relating to the supply of spare parts
The final hardcore restriction is:

> "the restriction agreed between a supplier of components and a buyer who **14–137**
> incorporates those components, which limits the supplier to selling the components
> as spare parts to end-users or to repairers or other service providers not entrusted
> by the buyer with the repair or servicing of its goods."[187]

The guidelines make it clear[188] that the intention is that end-users, independent repairers and service providers should not be prevented from obtaining spare parts directly from the manufacturer of these spare parts. An agreement between a manufacturer of spare parts and a buyer who incorporates these parts into his own products (OEM) may not, directly or indirectly, prevent or restrict sales by the manufacturer of these spare parts to end users, independent repairers or service providers. Indirect restrictions would include restrictions on the supply of technical information and special equipment which are necessary for the use of spare parts by users, independent repairers or service providers. On the other hand, it is permissible to restrict the supply of spare parts to the repairers or service providers entrusted by the OEM with the repair or servicing of his own goods, and for the OEM to require his own repair and service network to buy the spare parts from it.

Other provisions not exempted

14–138   Apart from the hardcore list of prohibited restrictions, there are is also an exclusion for certain types of non-competition provisions that are not allowed under the block exemption. However, by contrast with the prohibited hardcore restrictions, whose inclusion will exclude the whole agreement from the application of the exemption, the presence of any of these non-competition restrictions in the agreement only means that those specific clauses are not exempted and are therefore invalid. It does not prevent the block exemption from applying to the remainder of the agreement, according to the guidelines.[189] These provisions include[190]:

- any "non-compete obligation" as defined by the block exemption

- post term restrictions on competition and

- restrictions on a selective distributor selling specific competitor brands

These will now be analysed in more detail.

Non-competes during the term of the agreement

14–139   A non-compete obligation is defined as:

> "any direct or indirect obligation causing the buyer not to manufacture, purchase, sell or resell goods or services which compete with the contract goods or services, or any direct or indirect obligation on the buyer to purchase from the supplier or from another undertaking designated by the supplier more than 80 per cent of the buyer's total purchases of the contract goods or services and their substitutes on the relevant market, calculated on the basis of the value of its purchases in the preceding calendar year"[191]

Such restrictions are not covered by the block exemption if they are indefinite or exceed five years.[192] A non-compete obligation which is tacitly renewable beyond a period of five years is not allowed,[193] so a provision which provides for continuation of any kind of non-compete arrangement unless one of the parties gives notice of their objection more than a certain period before the end of the term would not comply. This does not prevent a non-compete clause of this nature from being renewed after the five year period, so long as the parties expressly consent to the extension, *i.e.* expressly re-negotiate or agree to it. The extension would have to conform to the five year limit, however, in order to benefit from the block exemption. There should also not be any barrier, such as loan arrangements, which hinders the ability of the buyer to effectively terminate at the end of the five year period. The five- year limit does not apply, however, where the goods or services are resold by the buyer from premises and land owned by the supplier or leased by the supplier from third parties not connected with the buyer. In these cases the non-compete may be of the same duration as the occupancy of the premises by the buyer.

Post-term restrictions

Any post term restriction which, directly or indirectly requires the buyer not to manufacture, purchase, sell or resell goods or services, is not covered by the block exemption[194] unless it: **14–140**

- relates to goods or services which compete with the contract goods or services, and

- is limited to the premises and land from which the buyer has operated during the contract period, and

- is indispensable to protect know-how transferred by the supplier to the buyer, and

- the duration of such non-compete obligation is limited to a period of one year after termination of the agreement.

The know-how needs to include information which is indispensable the buyer for the use, sale or resale of the contact goods or services.

Restriction on a selective distributor selling specific brands

The third condition which is not covered by the block exemption is any direct or indirect obligation causing the members of a selective distribution system not to sell the brands of particular competing suppliers.[195] This would allow the selective distributor to be restricted from selling all competitors brands but not a restriction only on selling the brands of certain competitors. The thinking behind this provision was the concern to avoid a situation where a number of suppliers using the same selective distribution outlets prevent one specific competitor or certain specific competitors from using these outlets to distribute their products.[196]   **14–141**

14.4.9 The implications of Article 81 for the distribution of goods and services through the Internet

The fact that no distributor or purchaser (apart from perhaps unauthorised dealers in the case of selective distribution) can be prevented from making sales of goods or services via the Internet under Article 81 (see above) and that the supplier or manufacturer cannot reserve sales by Internet to itself has a considerable impact on the distribution of goods and services in the E.C., and in many cases has ramifications on the distribution strategy worldwide. It would be extremely inadvisable to ignore these rules on the basis that the agreement has no appreciable effect (see above) and would not come within Article 81. It would be inadvisable not only because the market share thresholds of five or 10 per cent are an ongoing condition which require to be satisfied throughout the course of the agreement, but because a restriction on sales and advertising through the Internet, since it   **14–142** is deemed a restriction of passive sales, may cause the agreement not to fall within the de minimis exception for agreements which only have an inappreciable effect. Further, the draft new *de minimis* test which has been proposed (see above) makes it clear that for an agreement to be deemed inappreciable, it could not contain any of the hardcore restrictions set out in the vertical agreements block exemption.

14–143   The Commission is clearly serious about this point. As it states in the Competition Report for the year 2000[197]:

> "…moves by manufacturers to protect their traditional distribution channels from the pro-competitive effects of electronic commerce will be challenged. In this context it can be mentioned that in December the Commission opened formal proceedings against B&W Loudspeakers Ltd as, among other things, this company prohibits its authorised dealers from engaging in distance selling—including sales over the Internet—without objective reasons. Such behaviour prevents the benefits of electronic commerce from being fully achieved. The Commission is investigating similar cases in the area of consumer electronics and its position can be expected to be clarified in the course of 2001."

14–144   In the case of the Yves Saint Laurent[198] distribution system approved in May 2001, the Commission seems to have convinced Yves Saint Laurent that it had to allow distributors to distribute its luxury perfumes via the Internet. The Commission commented, with respect to this point:

> "In … [the vertical agreements] guidelines the Commission stressed the importance of the Internet for the competitiveness of the European economy and encouraged widespread use of this modern means of communication and marketing. In particular it believes that a ban on Internet sales, even in a selective distribution system, is a restraint on sales to consumers which could not be covered by the 1999 regulation
>   The YSLP system satisfies the exemption conditions set by this regulation. YSLP has applied selection criteria authorising approved retailers already operating a physical sales point to sell via the Internet as well."

14–145   This point, as well as the new structure of the vertical agreements block exemption, especially its rules limiting the circumstances in which distributors, dealers and others can be restricted from making active sales into other territories outside of their own, or to other customers, and those concerning selective distribution and non-competes means that it is now necessary for suppliers and manufacturers to think about their whole strategy before entering the market, and proceeding in a piecemeal basis in the E.U./EEA could result in major problems.

It should be noted that in general the block exemption itself is not only important for those transactions which fall within it, but may also be a guide to similar resale-type arrangements which do not fall within its scope.

14.4.10 Application of Article 81 to IPR licences other than patent and know-how licences

14–146   It was commented above that the technology transfer block exemption will not directly apply to many licensing arrangements relating to e-commerce and the Internet, because many of these agreements involve licences of copyright and neighbouring rights, software rights and database rights and trademarks, which are not ancillary to patent and know-how licences, and/or may involve sales licences. It was also suggested that the technology transfer block exemption might well be a good guide to the types of restrictions which will be permitted or prohibited in licensing arrangements related to the new economy. This could particularly apply to those arrangements which involve more than just resale of the licensed product, software, database or content, since as was seen above, the technology transfer block exemption does not apply to pure sales licences, and tends to relate more to manufacturing or the use of processes.

On the other hand, it was also noted above that the vertical agreements block exemption only applies to intellectual property licences to the buyer, where these are not the primary objective of the agreement, but support other provisions relating to the supply of goods and services. The guidelines only concede that sales of packaged software can come under the block exemption. The result is to leave many of the agreements which are so fundamental to the new economy in an unfortunate position of legal uncertainty. They may well contain restrictions which fall under Article 81, but there is no block exemption applying to them, and there are no guidelines as to which regime they should follow: that of the technology transfer block exemption or that of the vertical agreements block exemption.

The Commission has in the past had a tendency to treat copyright licences in particular   **14–147** in a similar way to patent licences, albeit applying particular considerations which relate specifically to copyright in some instances. Nevertheless, it is not clear that many new economy licenses, especially those which are similar to resale agreements, would be analysed in the same way as technology transfer agreements. Another factor which must be remembered is that whereas in the past a distinction could be made between rules for vertical agreements relating to pure resale, under the exclusive distribution and exclusive purchasing block exemptions, and rules which related to activities involving manufacturing, or at any rate, more than resale under the technology transfer block exemption, this distinction can no longer be made. The vertical agreements block exemption now applies to industrial supply and other manufacturing agreements for goods, and arrangements for services which involve more than just resale of those services. A previous distinction might have been drawn between development or value added services agreements relating to software, which should follow the technology transfer agreements, where they involve some value being added to what was supplied under the license, before the result is sold by the licensee, and those which are more similar to resale, which might have followed the exclusive distribution or exclusive purchasing block exemptions. However, that distinction may no longer be a good one.

The distinction as to whether the technology transfer block exemption or the vertical agreements rules should be followed is crucial also, since they differ fundamentally on some very crucial points. The technology block exemption allows complete bans on active sales outside the territory, and the licensee can be prohibited from even passive sales into the territory of the licensor or other licensees, although in the latter case, only for five years from the first marketing of the licensed product in the EEA. On the other hand, under the vertical agreements block exemption, no restriction on passive sales outside of the distributors' territory is possible, and restrictions on active sales are only permissible in respect of the exclusive territories or customer groups of others. Under the technology transfer block exemption, no restrictions on competition by either party are permitted (whether in terms of R&D, production use or distribution of competing products), whereas under the vertical agreements block exemption, non-compete obligations can be permitted on the buyer for up to five years. The list of differences is longer, and careful comparison of the two regimes is necessary in any particular case.

14–148   The case law relating to copyright and related rights does not resolve this issue either, although it may provide a useful point of departure in certain situations. In respect of film performance rights, the European Court of justice has indicated that the grant of exclusive rights to show a film in a particular territory may not in itself restrict competition,[199] although the Court in that case also suggested that an exclusive licence might infringe Article 81(1) where it created artificial and unjustifiable barriers and restricted competition. In a case involving film purchases by German television stations,[200] involving exclusive licences to broadcast a large number or films in the MGM/UA film library for a period of 15 years, the Commission found that Article 81 did apply to the exclusivity, and the licensee was obliged to carve out licences which had to be granted in respect of its films to other broadcasting organisations, before the Commission would give an exemption under Article 81(3). The Commission has also in a number of cases held that a ban on exports of goods produced under copyright licence, such as books, cassettes, tape recordings and records, was contrary to Article 81 and not permissible. It has also found that terms prohibiting the licensee from challenging the validity of copyright are not permissible, that terms requiring the payment of royalties on products which are not protected by the licensed copyright are not permitted. In the light of the changes in approach which has taken place under the technology transfer block exemption and the vertical agreements block exemption, many of these points will have to be reexamined.

In any specific case, legal advice should clearly be sought as to the Application of Article 81, Article 81(3) and Article 82 (see below).

Licences to end users

14–149   Licences to end-users may in some cases fall within the application of Article 81, although the lack of guidance from the European Commission or the European Court of Justice in respect of end-user copyright licences in general means that the rules in this area are to a great extent a matter of conjecture. Limitations restricting the use of copyright material, or a database to a particular physical site, or to a particular computer platform or CPU will arguably fall outside of Article 81 in many cases, as would other restrictions designed to control the number of users of the subject matter of the copyright or database rights. However, Article 81 might well apply to a restriction which merely limited the use to a particular manufacturer's hardware platform. (if, for example, the licensor was thereby attempting to tie the use of his own hardware, without an objective justification). Restrictions on copying or sub-licensing may also arguably fall outside of the scope of Article 81 in many cases. On the other hand, a restriction on the use of competing products, or on the user himself competing with the licensor is likely to fall within the application of Article 81, and it may be very difficult to justify under Article 81(3).

Contract for development

14–150   A company may hire a developer to develop copyright material or software on its behalf. It may want to require that the developer assign to it all the rights in the material or grant it an exclusive licence, to oblige the developer not to develop similar material for competing companies, or to require the developer not to start competing in the market itself. Clauses attempting to achieve these objectives could potentially fall under Article 81, and legal advice should be sought.

14.4.11 Particular cases which have been considered under Article 81

Internet Registry agreements[201]
The European Commission has investigated the area of Internet domain name registries   **14–151**
under the competition rules.

Until the beginning of October 1998, the system for generic Top Level Domains
(gTLDs) such as .com, .net, and .org was operated by the Internet Assigned Numbers
Authority (IANA) and Network Solutions Inc. (NSI), the latter under contract from the
U.S. Government, acting as the only registry and registrar of .com, .net and .org worldwide. The registry functions relate to the operation (*e.g.* administration, maintenance and
up-dating) of the database into which registrants details as well as the second-level
domains details are registered. The registrar function relates to the registration in the
relevant database and allocation of second-level domain names to registrants, as well as
all related marketing, billing and other related activities.

ICANN (Internet Corporation for Assigned Names and Numbers) a private not-for-
profit corporation was incorporated in the US on October 1, 1998 to administer policy for
the Internet Name and Address System and succeed IANA. In addition, the gTLD MoU
and related agreements foresaw a further substantial modification of the domain name
system.

The Commission appeared to consider that a system for allocating domain names that   **14–152**
would be used by companies in the EEA/E.U. was capable of affecting competition in the
E.U., founding jurisdiction under the E.U./EEA competition rules. It apparently also
considered that the agreement by non-governmental organisations to reform the system
could fall within Article 81 of the E.C. Treaty. Its concerns with the gTLD MoU and
associated agreements related to the establishment of the governance system for domain
name allocation and those relating to the mechanisms for allocating domain names and
resolution of disputes.

In particular, the participants in the domain name system should be a fair
representation of interested parties, and membership of all relevant bodies should be
based on objective, transparent and non-discriminatory criteria, a requirement which
continues to apply to all consideration of this area. In addition, the operation of the
system in practice should not be anticompetitive. Even if competition could not be
introduced at every level of the DNS (Domain Name System), it should exist to the
maximum extent possible. The Commission was concerned that there should be
safeguards to prevent Registrars acting, solely or jointly, in an anticompetitive manner.
Artificial limits on Registrars, such as, for example, giving one Registrar allocation rights
in respect of a particular gTLD, or limiting the number of Registrars without justification,
might have been difficult to justify under Article 81.

Under the progressive liberalisation proposed, NSI was required in an initial phase   **14–153**
establish a test bed supporting actual registrations in .com, .net, and .org with five
registrars to be accredited by ICANN ("Test Bed Registrars") in accordance with
ICANN's published accreditation guidelines. Later, an unlimited number of competing
registrars could be accredited by ICANN ("Accredited Registrars").

To implement this system and allow for competing registrars, NSI was (directly or
indirectly) to develop a protocol and associated software supporting a system permitting
multiple registrars to provide registration services for the registry of the existing gTLDs.
This was then licensed by NSI to registrars under a standard licensing agreement, the
initial version of which was only intended to be valid for the test bed period. These
agreements enabled the new registrars to register second-level domain names within the

registry of Top-Level Domain Names managed by NSI such as .com, .org and .net. The Competition directorate received a number of informal complaints about the test bed standard licensing arrangements, and opened an informal investigation. It identified a number of clauses in that standard NSI standard registrar licensing agreement that might have raised anti-competitive concerns.

In particular, DG Competition looked into the question of whether the licensing agreements fell within the scope of Article 81(1) of the E.C. Treaty and of Article 53 of the European Economic Area (EEA) Agreement. It also examined whether certain provisions in the agreements or related actions taken by NSI might also constitute an abuse of NSI's dominant position under Article 82 E.C. Treaty and Article 54 of the EEA Agreement.

14–154   In informed the U.S. governmental authorities who were supervising the liberalisation process of concerns related to:

- the lack of safeguards to prevent NSI registry from discriminating against competing registrars in favour of NSI acting as a registrar;

- the fact that NSI as a registrar was not subject to the conditions and obligations set out in ICANN accreditation agreements and NSI-Registrar Licensing agreements, since NSI was not required to go through the accreditation procedure by ICANN as a registrar. DG Competition believed that NSI should be required to get accreditation from ICANN and be subject at least to the same obligations as competing registrars which arose from those accreditation rules;

- certain requirements to enter the market, *e.g.* a performance bond of USD 100,000, which could constitute barriers to market entry; and

- the domain name portability rules and NSI's related policy, which DG Competition believed could act as strong deterrents for TLD holders to transfer their TLD to another competing registrar.

These issues were subsequently resolved to the Competition DG's satisfaction, and the Commission Closed its investigation in the matter.[202]

14–155   However, the Commission continues to be active in a wide range of matters relating to the development of Internet organisation and management and the domain name system.[203]

It has indicated that it will closely follow developments in this area, to ascertain whether agreements and business registration practices fall under the E.U. competition rules contained in Article 81 and 82 and, where necessary, will take appropriate action under the E.C. Treaty.

In terms of Article 82, the Commission has previously received a number of complaints against ccTLD registry bodies in some Member States, alleging violation of Article 82, and addressed formal requests for information to some to the ccTLD registry bodies.[204]

Microsoft Internet Explorer Agreements with ISPs[205]

14–156   In March 1997 DG Competition opened an investigation into the agreements between Microsoft and European ISPs. Under these agreements, Microsoft promoted the ISPs by including them in a list of available services pre-installed on new Personal Computers which used Windows operating system. Microsoft also licensed its Internet Explorer software to ISPs who made it available to their subscribers. In return the ISP paid Microsoft a fee for every subscriber gained via this feature and promoted Internet

Explorer products. ISPs could further be granted a license to customise Microsoft's Internet Explorer software in accordance with specific instructions and use the Internet Explorer logo in conjunction with its use and distribution of the licensed software.

During this inquiry, DG Competition advised Microsoft to re-examine the agreements in the light of E.U. competition rules to ensure that they did not contain restrictions that might have the effect of illegally foreclosing the market for Internet browser software from Microsoft's competitors and of illegally promoting the use of Microsoft's proprietary technology on the Internet.

It appears that the Commission objected to clauses to the effect that: **14–157**

- the ISPs' failure to attain minimum distribution volumes or percentages of Internet Explorer browser technology would result in termination of their agreements; and

- ISPs were not allowed to promote and advertise competing browser software.

Microsoft then modified the agreements so that the failure to attain minimum volumes or percentages would not result in the termination of the agreement, and ISPs were not prevented from promoting or advertising competing software. It then notified the agreements under Article 81(1). It then formally notified the agreements to the Commission. The Commission indicated that the agreements were not contrary to Article 81 by means of an informal comfort letter.

The *comfort letter* only covered the agreements between Microsoft and ISPs. The Commission did not therefore given any ruling on the global behaviour of Microsoft concerning a possible abuse of dominant position, and the case was different in scope and substance from the court case currently pending in the US. However, the Commission stressed that it could reopen its investigation into Microsoft's ISP agreements if there were any future change in the factual or legal situation affecting any essential aspect of these agreements.

14.4.12 Concerns in B2B Marketplaces

Article 81 can apply to B2B websites for a number of reasons: **14–158**

- *The mere fact of establishing a joint venture*: even without any of the other effects below, the mere joining together of actual or potential competitors may restrict competition if it results in them doing together an activity which they might have otherwise done separately, and which is a parameter of competition between them;

- *Cartel behaviour*: the arrangement may result in express or tacit price fixing, or fixing of output, even if not intended by the parties;

- *Sharing of information*: the arrangement may result in a sharing of confidential information;

- *Foreclosure of competitors*: the arrangement may exclude competitors of those who are participating in a web site from obtaining the benefits of the site, leading to market foreclosure;

- *Exclusion of existing intermediaries*: the arrangement may exclude existing intermediaries in the market for a finished product or service related to the site;

- *Portal exclusivity and exclusion of competing portals*: requiring that participants in the site may not participate in competing web-sites may result in the exclusion of competing web sites from the market, or at least a competitive disadvantage to those web-sites;

- *Restricting cross-border trade*: if the arrangements restrict the possibility for purchases from other states in a way which may limit cross-border trade, this is likely to be considered a significant restriction of competition;

- *Joint sales*: in some cases, where the portal involves parties joining together to jointly sell their products or services, this may have an anti-competitive effect on the market;

- *Joint purchasing*: in some cases, where the portal involves parties joining together to purchase products or services, this may have an anti-competitive effect on the market.

Simple reduction of competition

14–159   In some cases, the fact that competitors join together to enter into an activity, (*i.e.* the formation of a joint venture) can in itself be seen as a restriction of actual or potential competition, if the parties could have entered into the market and performed the activity independently. Because they have joined together to carry out an activity together which they could have carried out separately, there has been a reduction of competition.

Cartel behaviour

14–160   B2B exchanges offer increased risk of a cartel to fix prices or quantities, share markets limit production, or jointly boycott either certain sellers or buyers, activities which are hardly ever exemptable, and often result in significant fines. The parties to a B2B exchange or cooperative B2B site are usually not intending to engage in this type of activity, but care must be taken to avoid the possibility of apparently engaging in such activities. Avoiding the antitrust risks often needs careful thought, and rules, procedures and contractual provisions may have to be put in place.

Exchange of confidential information

14–161   The exchange of commercially sensitive business information may be contrary to Article 81, and is usually regarded as a serious infringement which can lead to significant fines being imposed on the parties. It is clear that the use of participation in a joint venture as a deliberate method for the parties to exchange commercially sensitive information in a manner which would otherwise infringe the competition rules is unacceptable. However, parties must in any case take care about the information which they exchange in the course of their formation of the portal, and the information that they exchange as part of their ongoing participation. The information which it is risky to discuss could concern prices, output, underlying costs or business strategies or investment plans of the relevant businesses.

14–162   There is no set list of information that cannot be exchanged without infringing the competition rules, and specific advice must be obtained which relates to the particular exchange, rather than general advice. However, the following principles may offer some guidance:

- The sharing of sensitive and detailed information in an oligopolistic market (one where there are only a few suppliers) may in itself be a restriction of competition;

- Exchange of data which would normally be considered a business secret or commercially sensitive between companies may well be anti-competitive;

- Exchange of data on prices or sales of individual firms stands a high risk of being considered anti-competitive;

- The sharing of aggregate information which does not allow the identification of particular prices charged by particular firms or particular quantities sold by particular firms is not generally problematic;

- The publication of historical data is generally less important;

- Collection of sensitive data should not be performed by a market participant;

- The publication of data which is objectively vital to the achievement of the benefits of the exchange will in many cases be justified, even it could have an effect on competition.

Ultimately, the risks from sharing confidential information can only be assessed by: **14–163**

- looking at the individual portal and its functioning;

- assessing what market information may be produced which would not otherwise be available;

- assessing which information must be exchanged for the portal to function properly;

- identifying information which is commercially sensitive, which doesn't need to be exchanged;

- looking at methods of quarantining the information/making Chinese walls/ firewalls to prevent the transfer of business sensitive information.

The need to guard against the sharing of confidential information may require competition compliance rules and procedures, the insertion of clauses in employment and other contracts, as well as technical measures and organisational procedures to prevent confidential information from leaking from the portal.

In one case, *Volbroker*,[206] the parents provided the following assurances to the   **14–164**
European Commission to avoid the exchange of commercially sensitive confidential information with parent companies:

- None of the platform's staff or management would have any contractual or other obligation towards any of the parents and vice versa;

- The staff and management would be in a geographically distinct location from that of the parents;

- The representatives of the Parents on the platform's Board of Directors would not have access to commercially sensitive information relating to each other or to third parties;

- The Parents would not have access to the information technology and communication systems of the platform;

- The Parents would also ensure that the staff and management of all the parties understand and appreciate the importance of maintaining the confidentiality of sensitive commercial information and that sanctions for breach are spelled out.

Such stringent requirements may not be necessary in every case, and are dependent on the specifics of each market. The case is cited only to show that information sharing may be a significant concern. This issue needs to be considered carefully in each case. However, the adoption of these "Volbroker conditions" may be required in a number of cases. In any case the adoption of a competition compliance programme will very often be necessary, and in many cases, adherence to strict rules concerning the conduct of meetings will often be required.

Foreclosure of competitors by restricting their participation as users of the portal

14–165   In some circumstances, it may be contrary to the competition rules to refuse a competitor access to the portal. This could be the case, for example, where the refusal to allow access to the portal would amount to an agreement between the parents to boycott the relevant party.
  This may be contrary to the competition rules if:

- There is not a sufficient number of other portals offering a similar kind of function to the relevant portal;

- Another portal offering a similar function could not be easily established;

- There are strong network effects, which lead to the fact that the joint venture portal tending to attract increasing numbers of participants and making it increasingly difficult for other portals to establish;

- Not participating in the portal would lead to the excluded party having a serious competitive disadvantage, which might eliminate it from a market for any of the goods or services sold through the exchange.

14–166   It is undoubtedly easier from a competition perspective to apply open; non-discriminatory access to all interested buyers or sellers who fall within the class of those for whom a B2B marketplace is intended. Otherwise it may be necessary to show that the above factors do not apply. On the other hand, that does not necessarily mean that other competitors must be allowed to participate as founding parties, or that they must be allowed to participate on exactly the same terms as the founding parties. Founding parties are sometimes fully justified in giving a financial incentive to those who are willing to join from the outset, and might, in order to keep the establishment of the joint venture manageable, want to restrict the number of initial parents.
  On the other hand, it may be less possible to exclude competitors from accessing the site as suppliers of data to the site as external users where the above bullet-point factors apply. It is also possible that the parents could be deemed to be entering into an infringing boycott agreement by not making access open to competitors on fair and reasonable terms.
  It may also be justified, and in some cases necessary, to apply objective criteria to membership of the site, so that only parties that meet those criteria are accepted as

participant on the suppliers' or buyers side. The necessity may result from the fact that a B2B marketplace will often only be aimed at transactions in certain types of goods or services, or particular types of seller, purchaser or market segment. In addition, however, objectively justified requirements relating to such matters as creditworthiness or ability to meet the rules and requirements of participating in the exchange should be unproblematic. Other criteria which may be objectively justifiable may depend on the specific nature of the exchange.

Exclusion of intermediaries

In some circumstances, it may be a restriction of competition to prevent intermediaries, **14–167** who perform a function similar to that of the portal functions, from accessing the portal (and/or the services provided over the portal).

In the *Volbroker* case, the Commission received complaints from a number of "voice broker" sellers who acted as intermediaries, and occasionally as principals, in the sale of foreign currency options, which they did by dealing over the telephone. The voice brokers complained that the exchange, set up by six major market-makers in the industry (Deutsche Bank, UBS, Goldman Sachs, Citibank, JP Morgan and NatWest), excluded them from participation. The Commission required that the voice brokers, when acting as principal, should be permitted access to the market place, as a condition of issuing a comfort letter under Article 81.

In some cases, where such intermediaries are able to perform their function by being a member of a web-site, it may be restrictive of competition to exclude them. In other cases, the formation of a portal which may replace existing intermediary functions will simply be part of the inevitable march of progress, and may not be objected to.

Portal exclusivity and foreclosure of competing portals

It may be restrictive of competition contrary to Article 81 to prohibit the founders of the **14–168** portal or others from participating in competing portals.

This goes both for those participating as potential suppliers, and for potential purchasers. It is not a universal rule, however, and like the other factors considered here, will depend on the assessment of each individual case. As was seen above in relation to the *MyAircraft* case, in certain circumstances, it will not always be viewed as anti-competitive under the E.U. merger regulation to require the founder members not to become actively involved in participating in another site, at least for a certain period. That is especially true where there are a number of other competing portals already in the market, and the restriction on the founders sponsoring competing sites is necessary to allow the portal to become established. That analysis also holds good under Article 81.

On the other hand, in many cases there may be less justification for restricting founders or users from using a competing web site, and this could be viewed as a restriction of competition.

That may be particularly true where there are network effects or externalities, or the **14–169** market is "tippy". This could arise in the case where, once a portal has more than a certain number of members or users, all other vendors or purchasers are going to want to use that portal, and another portal will not be a good substitute. In such a situation, it may become increasingly difficult for other portals to establish themselves whether that is a problem or not will depend on the particular facts of each case.

Restrictions on cross-border trade

Restrictions on cross-border trade are some of the most serious infringements of E.C. **14–170** competition law, which can often result in a fine. Such restrictions may be found to exist where, for example, there is an attempt to segment national markets, by providing separate portals for each national market, and providing that only purchasers established in the relevant jurisdiction, or who will take delivery within that jurisdiction, may become users of the portal services or otherwise have access to the site.

Specific B2B marketplaces under Article 81: Covisint
The first major B2B exchange to be looked at under Article 81 rather than under the Merger Regulation was Covisint, an electronic marketplace joint venture between, DaimlerChrysler, Ford General Motors, Nissan, Peugeot Citroen and Renault.[207] The joint venture was intended to provide the automotive industry with procurement, collaborative product development and supply chain management tools, primarily to serve the procurement needs of major carmakers and suppliers. Many major component suppliers had indicated that they would use the exchange. Covisint did not constitute a merger under the E.U. Merger Regulation, since the companies that created the exchange did not exercise joint or sole control over the new company, and hence it fell to be considered under Article 81.[208]

The Commission noted that such B2B marketplaces potentially have a major impact on the way that companies in certain industries do business, and are in general expected to have pro-competitive effects. They should create more transparency, thereby helping to link more operators and to integrate markets, and they may also create market efficiencies by reducing search and information costs and improving inventory management, leading ultimately to lower prices for the end consumer.

In certain circumstances, however, the Commission considered that the "negative effects on competition may outweigh market efficiencies. This may in particular be the case where there is discrimination against certain classes of users leading to foreclosure, where it is possible for users to exchange or have access to market-sensitive information, or where buyers or sellers club together to 'bundle' their purchases or sales in a way liable to fall within the scope of Article 81(1) of the Treaty."

The Commission concluded that in this case there were adequate provisions to eliminate the potential competition concerns, and "[i]n particular, the agreements show that Covisint is open to all firms in the industry on a non-discriminatory basis, is based on open standards, allows both shareholders and other users to participate in other B2B exchanges, does not allow joint purchasing between car manufacturers or for automotive-specific products, and provides for adequate data protection, including firewalls and security rules."

The European Commission consequently sent the parties a comfort letter indicating that the joint venture would meet the requirements for obtaining a negative clearance under Article 81(1).

14.4.13 Standardisation Agreements

14–171   The approach under Article 81 of the E.C. Treaty to standardisation agreements is relevant to e-commerce in a number of ways, not only in terms of high level of Internet standards development, governance and management, and the domain name system, but also in terms of more specific standardisation agreements between e-commerce undertakings. This includes standardisation of catalogues and processes which takes place within B2B business sites and agreements between B2B exchanges concerning the adoption of standards. This section discusses the treatment of standards under Article 81, examining the past case law, and concludes with the guidance given in the horizontal agreements guidelines.

Effects of Standards under E.C. law

From a competition perspective, the mere ownership or establishment of a standard may   **14–172**
potentially affect competition on two levels: first, it may restrict competition between the parties establishing or using the standard, and second, it may foreclose competition from third parties who wish to have access to the standard.

The foreclosure effect of a standard will depend, in particular, on the following factors:

(i)   the extent to which access to the standard is necessary for participation in the market;

(iii) whether third parties have access to the standard and the standards setting procedure (if any); and

(iv) the conditions attached to such access, in particular, whether access is granted on unreasonable or discriminatory terms.

The extent to which access to a standard is necessary for market participation will in   **14–173**
turn depend on a range of factors, including:

(i)   the competitive importance of the benefits accruing from access to the standard or the standard setting procedure: this will depend on the market context and, as in the case of a compulsory *de jure* standard, may include the ability to compete in the market at all;

(ii) the availability of alternative standards: in the case of standards permitting interoperability this will be determined by the market share of the parties using the standard; and

(iii) whether there are barriers to establishing a competing standard.

A standard's effects on competition between the parties with access to it will depend,   **14–174**
first, on whether the parties are actual or potential competitors. If not, the standard can have no restrictive effect on competition between them. If the parties are actual or potential competitors, the standard may reduce the ability of parties using the standard to compete by reducing product diversity and reducing the scope and incentive for innovation. The extent of these restrictive effects will in general depend on:

(i)   the market shares of the parties;

(ii) whether the parties agree to use the standard exclusively;

(iii) whether the parties agree to share innovations relating to the standard; and

(iv) the depth of the standard.[209]

In addition, the market power associated with ownership of a standard may enable the owner to impose additional anti-competitive terms and conditions, for example tying, on licensees of the standard.

14–175   While seeking to limit these anti-competitive effect that may flow from standardisation, competition law must also take account of the potential advantages of standardisation. In the European Union context, these may include the elimination of barriers to trade between Member States. In addition, standardisation may permit private firms to capture the benefits of network effects in marketing, rationalisation of productions, economies of scale, R&D efficiencies and others, while at the same time offering consumers benefits in terms of the interoperability and substitutability of products and know product qualities. Where a standard actually or potentially offers such advantages, these must be set off against any potentially anti-competitive effects.

Multilateral and Unilateral Standards

14–176   The scope of Article 81(1) may mean that it applies differently to those standards that are jointly owned or jointly established (multilateral standards) and those that are owned and established by a single firm (unilateral standards). Although, in principle, the issues raised by multilateral and unilateral standards are the same.

The ownership and often the development of a multilateral standard will be subject to agreements and/or arrangements between undertakings to which Article 81(1) may apply if their effect is exclusive. The Commission has applied Article 81 to require the parties to such agreements to grant access both to the standard itself (as well as any intellectual property included in it) and membership of bodies charged with establishing or developing the standard.[210]

14–177   In the case of unilateral standards, the scope for Article 81(1) to apply is more limited. The ownership and development of unilateral marks is not, by definition, subject to any agreement or arrangement between undertakings. However, the situation changes once the standard has been licensed, since at that point there is an agreement on which Article 81(1) may bite.[211] It is clear that the Commission will apply Article 81(1) to terms in the licence of a standard that create obstacles to competition.

The Foreclosure Effects of Standards and Standardisation

14–178   Of the two levels of competitive effects a standard may have, the foreclosure effect will depend on the extent to which access to the standard is necessary for participation in the market, the whether third parties are allowed access to the standard, and whether such access is allowed on fair and reasonable terms. The treatment of these issues under Article 81 may be illustrated by the contrast between another two cases: *IGR Stereo Television* and *X/Open Group*.[212]

The first case, *IGR Stereo Television*, concerned the acquisition, in 1981, of two patents for the production of stereo television sets by IRG, a body whose members included all German TV manufacturers. Following the acquisition, IRG's membership passed a resolution not to licence the patents to non-members until 1983, and at that time to licence them only for the production of a limited numbers of sets. This effectively excluded non-German manufacturers of television sets from the market at a time when stereo television was being launched, since it seems that these patents covered a de facto standard for stereo television that could not be duplicated or invented around.[213] Following a complaint from a Finnish manufacturer, Salora, the Commission intervened and persuaded IGR to agree to grant licences for the patents free of all restrictions and on reasonable terms to all other manufactures in the Community.

14–179   The second, *X/Open Group*, concerned a collaboration between a number of major computer manufacturers. The objective of the collaboration was to develop an open industry standard for a "stable but evolving common application environment" ("CAE") based on AT&T's UNIX operating system. The purpose of the CAE was that programs written in conformity with it would be capable of running on computers using the current version of UNIX, regardless of the identity of the computer manufacturer. The group intended to establish the CAE initially by selecting existing interfaces, and to proceed in due time to the standardisation of selected interfaces by appropriate national and international standards organisations. In order to achieve this, group members agreed to exchange technical and market information.

Membership of the group was however restricted. Applications for membership would be considered only from major manufacturers in the European information technology industry or others with "special attributes" that would significantly contribute to the achievement of the group's objectives. Major manufacturers were understood to be those with revenues from information technology in excess of U.S.$ 500 million. In addition, applicants would have to obtain the approval of more than half of the existing membership in a vote in order to become members.

The Commission found that in the context of the relevant market membership of the **14–180** group would confer an appreciable competitive advantage. Members would be able to influence the results of the work of the group and would acquire the know-how and technical understanding relating to these results. In addition, members would obtain important advantages of lead time in implementation of the standards due to early knowledge of the final definitions and, potentially, of the direction in which work was going. This advantage in lead time would directly affect the market entry possibilities of those not members of the group. Consequently, the Commission took the view that the restrictions on membership of the group infringed Article 81(1). In particular, the Commission noted that the ability to admit members with special attributes and the requirement for a majority vote of existing members meant that the restrictions on membership were potentially discriminatory.

However, the Commission concluded that the group arrangements fulfilled the conditions for exemption under Article 81(3). Opening membership of the group to all would create practical and logistical difficulties so that, it was reasonable impose restrictions that would limit the membership to a manageable size. In addition, the requirement that new members be approved by majority vote could be justified, as this would enable members to prevent the admission of companies that might have an adverse effect on the co-operation and the achievement of the group's objectives. It was appropriate for members of the group to decide on this issues as they were in the best position to assess it. Moreover, the aim of the group was to publish its work as widely and as quickly as possible, something that the Commission considered to be an "essential element" in allowing exemption. Nonetheless, as a condition of exemption, the Commission required that the group submit an annual report to the Commission on cases where membership was refused and changes in membership, in order to ensure that the conditions for membership were not being applied in an unreasonable manner.

A number of factors in relation to the two cases should be noted. First, as regards the **14–181** need for access to the standard, in *IGR Stereo Television*, it seems that access to the standard was absolutely necessary for supply of stereo television sets to the German market. In *X/Open Group* restrictions on participation in the standard setting group were found to fall within Article 81(1) on the grounds that, in the relevant market, membership constituted an appreciable competitive advantage and that the market entry possibilities of non-members would be affected as a result.[214] Second, as regards the possibility of third party access, in *X/Open Group*, the Commission considered the fact that the standards adopted by the group would be open and available to all as an essential element in its decision to grant exemption. Similarly, in *IGR Stereo Television*, IGR was obliged to agree to licence its patent rights to all E.C. manufacturers. It is also noteworthy that, although the standard was to be open and widely published, restrictions on membership of the standard setting group in *X/Open Group* were found sufficiently important to infringe Article 81(1). Finally, as regards the terms of which access is granted, while in *X/Open Group* restrictions on access to the standards setting group were acceptable only to the extent that they were not implemented in an unreasonable manner, and the Commission expressed particular concern that the restrictions were potentially discriminatory.[215]

Restrictions on Competition Between Users of a Standard

14–182 In addition to foreclosure effects, a standard may also give rise to restrictions on competition between the parties with access to the standard. The importance of these effects will depend on the market share of the parties, whether they agree to use the standard exclusively, whether the parties agree to share future innovations relating to the standard, and the depth of the standard. The treatment of these issues Article 81 is well illustrated by three cases, *Video Cassette Recorders*, *Philips/Matsushita—D2B*, and *ETSI Interim IPR Policy*.[216]

14–183   *Video Cassette Recorders* concerned the terms on which Philips licensed the patents covering its VCR standard for video recorders. At the time of the decision, Philips owned the more successful one of only two video system standards available in Europe. Philips licensed its patents to other manufactures on condition that they manufacture and distribute only video cassette recorders and cassettes observing detailed technical specifications describing the VCR system. No changes could be made to these standards without the consent of all Philips and all other licensees. In addition, the licences provided that Philips and the licensee were obliged to grant each other royalty-free cross-licences in respect of patented innovations, where necessary to ensure compatibility and that such cross-licences should extend to all other licensees of the VDR standard. Any party terminating a licence agreement forfeited its right under such cross-licences, while the remain parties retained theirs. The Commission found that the obligation on licensees to use exclusively the VCR standard and the cross-licensing provisions fell within Article 81(1).[217] The Commission considered these restrictions "particularly marked" in light of Philips pre-eminent market position: together with its largest competitor, Sony, it accounted for more than 70 per cent of video recorder sales in the E.U. Further, the Commission took the view that the licences could not benefit from exemption under Article 81(3), although it recognised that the licences would create interoperability benefits. In its view, the exclusivity requirements could not benefit from exemption as they "led to the exclusion of other, perhaps better, systems", and interoperability benefits could have been achieved through the much less restrictive requirement that licensees observe the VCR standards when manufacturing VCR equipment.

14–184   *Philips/Matsushita—D2B* concerned the establishment of a joint venture by Philips and Matsushita to develop a standard that would allowing Televisions, VCRs, CDs and other consumer electronics products of different brands to operate together using a common remote control. Philips and Matsushita agreed to pool their patents covering the D2B system, which had originally been established by Philips but which they had developed together, in the joint venture, which would be controlled by Philips. Licences would be granted to any manufacturer adopting the DB2 standard for ten years, extendable by another the years. Licensees would be required to enter into a mutual worldwide non-assertion clause, with the effect that neither the licensor nor the licensee would be able to seek royalties for the use of further patents covering the system for the duration of the licence. The Commission found that the D2B joint venture arrangements could fall within Article 81(1), but would in any event qualify for exemption pursuant to Article 81(3). The arrangements contributed to technical progress and were not excessive, and competition in the market would remain effective as a number of alternative systems were available.

ETSI Interim IPR Policy concerned the interim IPR policy adopted by ETSI in March **14–185** 1993. ETSI is a private, non-profit association under French law that was formally recognised as a European standard institute for the telecommunications sector by the EC in 1992. As such, it is charged with establishing common European standards in the telecommunications sector that have an important role under EC law.[218] According to ETSI's statutes its membership comprised five groups: (i) national standards organisations and administrations, (ii) public network operators, (iii) manufacturers, (iv) users, and (v) private service providers. The interim IPR policy that required its members to sign an IPR undertaking. Broadly, the IPR policy foresaw a system in which members would agree, in advance, to licence any of their intellectual property rights ("IPRs") deemed "essential" to an ETSI standard, unless they notified ETSI that they did not wish to do so within six months from the relevant draft standard appearing on ETSI's work program. This system was referred to as "licensing by default". The IPR undertaking set forth conditions under which licences of such IPRs had to be offered to ETSI members. These included: (i) that only monetary consideration could be demanded in return for such a licence, and (ii) that IPR holders should notify a maximum royalty rate to the Director of ETSI. The CBEMA, a trade organisation for computer and business equipment manufacturers, some of which were ETSI members who would be require to sign the IPR undertaking, submitted a complaint to the Commission claiming that these aspects of ETSI's interim policy infringed Article 81(1).

Although the Commission reached no formal decision on the complaint, it set out its preliminary views on it in a letter to ETSI of February 21, 1994. The Commission took the view that the "licence by default" system amounted to a "mutual renunciation of the ability to gain a competitive advantage through technical efforts" and therefore restricted innovation. Nonetheless, it considered that such a systems could be legitimate under competition rules where IPR holders were given a genuine opportunity to withhold a licence. However, due to the amount of information supplied to members by ETSI regarding standards in development, arguably no such genuine opportunity existed within the framework of ETSI's interim IPR policy. The Commission was also of the view that the prohibition on the holders of IPRs included in ETSI standards' requiring non-monitory compensation for licences of those IPRs acted as a restriction on the ability of the IPR holder to negotiate cross-licences and as such fell under Article 81(1). Although, it considered that the restriction could potentially qualify for exemption under Article 81(3). The Commission, however, regarded the provisions concerning the notification of a maximum royalty rate to be prima facie legitimate. As a result of the Commission's intervention, ETSI's interim IPR policy was amended to replace the "licence by default" system with a system whereby holders of essential IPRs would be requested to give an undertaking in writing of their preparedness to grant irrevocable licences on fair, reasonable and non-discriminatory terms. The provisions as to non-monetary consideration and maximum royalty rates were also removed.

A number of factors in relation to these three cases are worthy of note. First, the **14–186** importance attached to the pre-eminence of Philips' market share in the Commission's decision not to grant exemption in *Video Cassette Recorders* should be contrasted with its reliance on the fact in *Philips/Matsushita—D2B* that competition in the market would remain effective due to the available alternative systems. Second, the fact that the exclusivity requirement in relation to the VCR standard in *Video Cassette Recorders* was considered to fall within Article 81(1) and not to merit exemption under Article 81(3). Third, the Commission's preliminary view in *ETSI Interim IPR Policy* that the cross-licensing by default system it involved restricted innovation but might be compatible with competition rules. This is reflected in the Commission's view that the bilateral non-enforcement requirement to be imposed on licensees in *Philips/Matsushita—D2B* was found to fulfil the requirements for exemption. Although, the multilateral cross-licensing arrangement in relation to innovations in *Video Cassette Recorders* was found to infringe Article 81(1) and not to merit exemption, this may be explained by the harsh conditions imposed on termination. Finally, the Commission's refusal in *Video Cassette Recorders* to grant exemption to restrictions that went beyond those necessary to achieve the interoperability benefits offered by the standardisation is worth of note in that it supports the conclusion that multilateral standards that are unnecessarily deep may infringe Article 81(1) and would not qualify for exemption under Article 81(3).[219]

Conditions Attached to Licences

14–187 Certain cases suggest that Article 81(1) may be infringed by clauses in the licence of a standard other those on cross-licensing and exclusivity discussed above. One example arose from a second complaint against IGR, this one concerning the level of royalties charged by IGR for access to the stereo television patents.[220] The Commission again intervened, finding that the royalties constituted a "private tax" on other European television manufacturers, which, in view of the level of royalties could have an appreciable effect on competition contrary to Article 81(1). As a result to the Commission's intervention, IGR agreed to lower its royalty rate considerably.

A second example is provided by the agreements the Commission reached with the suppliers of video games consoles *Nintendo* and *Sega* regarding the terms under which they license their intellectual property rights to games developers.[221] The Commission required the deletion of licence clauses that:

(i)   limited the number of games licensees could release;

(ii) required prior approval from the console supplier for all games before release, regardless of whether the game was sold under a trade mark belonging to the console supplier; and

(iii) required the licensee to have games manufactured by the console supplier or an authorised manufacturer.

14–188 *Nintendo* and *Sega* were allowed to continue to require prior approval if a licensee wished to attach one of their trademarks and to require limited pre-release testing (bug checking, compatibility testing and to ensure compliance with programming conventions) by an independent tester. Although the press releases issued by the Commission does not specify the reasons why it considered the above term objectionable, it seems reasonable to speculate that it considered the requirements that only limited numbers of games be produced and of prior approval as restrictions on licensees ability to compete with the supplier's own video games and that its considered the requirement as to the manufacture of games to be an unjustified tie.

Discussion of Standards setting in the Horizontal Agreements Guidelines

The most recent discussion of the attitude towards standards under Article 81 is **14–189**
contained in the Guidelines on horizontal co-operation agreements.[222]

This suggests that where participation in standard setting is unrestricted and transparent, standardisation agreements which set no obligation to comply with the standard or which are part of a wider agreement to ensure compatibility of products, do not restrict competition. Further, there may be no "appreciable" restriction of competition in agreements that standardise aspects such as minor product characteristics, which have an insignificant effect on the main factors affecting competition.[223]

On the other hand, an agreement whereby a group of manufacturers set a standard and put pressure on third parties not to market products that did not comply with the standard almost always fall under Article 81.

Standardisation agreements may be caught by Article 81 if they grant the parties joint control over production and/or innovation, thereby restricting their ability to compete on product characteristics, while affecting third parties like suppliers or purchasers of the standardised products.

The existence of a restriction of competition in standardisation agreements depends on **14–190**
the extent to which parties remain free to develop alternative standards or products that do not comply with the standard. Those that entrust certain bodies with the exclusive right to test compliance with the standard go beyond the primary objective of defining the standard and may also restrict competition.

Standards that are not accessible to third parties may discriminate or foreclose third parties or segment markets according to their geographic scope of application. The assessment as to whether they restrict competition may depend on the extent to which such barriers are likely to be overcome.

As to the likelihood of an exemption being granted under Article 81(3), this depends on the satisfaction of the criteria of exemption, which requires a demonstration that there are economic benefits, that the restriction is indispensable to the achievement of those benefits, and that there is no elimination of competition. As regards the demonstration of economic benefits, the necessary information to apply the standard must be available to those wishing to enter the market, and an appreciable proportion of the industry must be involved in the setting of the standard in a transparent manner. For these purposes, standards should not limit innovation. This will depend primarily on the lifetime of the associated products, in connection with the market development stage. The parties may also have to provide evidence that collective standardisation is efficiency enhancing for the consumer when a new standard may trigger unduly rapid obsolescence of existing products, without objective additional benefits.

As to the requirement of indispensability, the guidelines suggest that where only one **14–191**
technological solution must be chosen, the standard must be set on a non-discriminatory bases. Standards should ideally be technologically neutral or "[i]n any event, it must be justifiable why one standard is chosen over another." All competitors in the market affected by the standard should have the possibility of being involved in the discussions. Consequently, participation in standard setting should be open to all, unless the parties demonstrate important inefficiencies in such participation, or unless recognised procedures are foreseen for the collective representation of interests. Agreement should cover no more than is required to ensure their aims. For example, it may be difficult to justify why an agreement for a standard in and industry where only one competitor offers an alternative should oblige the parties to the agreement to boycott the alternative.

To avoid the elimination of competition, the Commission suggests that access to the standard must be possible for third parties on fair, reasonable and non-discriminatory terms.

14.5 Abuse of dominance and Article 82 of the E.C. Treaty

14–192   Article 82 prohibits any abuse by one or more undertakings of a dominant position with the E.U. or a substantial part of it that affects trade between Member States. To determine whether an abuse contrary to Article 82 has occurred, it is, therefore, necessary to consider whether an undertaking:

(i)   holds a dominant position in a substantial part of the E.U.;

(ii)   has abused that dominant position; and

(iii)   has, as a result, affected trade between Member States.

The Commission may impose fines on undertakings in breach of Article 82 of up to 10 per cent of their turnover.[224] In addition, it may, by decision, order infringing undertakings to take such action as is necessary to terminate the infringement.[225] Damages or injunctions may also be available to third parties harmed as a result of an infringement of Article 82.

14.5.1 Dominance

14–193   The European Court of Justice has defined dominance as: "a position of economic strength enjoyed by an undertaking which enables it to hinder the maintenance of effective competition on the relevant market by allowing it to behave to an appreciable extent independently of its competitors and customers and ultimately of consumers".[226]
           To determine whether an undertaking holds a dominant position, it is first necessary to identify the relevant market. This has two aspects: (i) the relevant product market and (ii) the relevant geographic market.

The relevant product market

14–194   The relevant product market will include "all those products and/or services which are regarded as interchangeable or substitutable by the consumer, by reason of the products' characteristics, their prices and their intended use."[227] Non-substitutable products may also come within the relevant product market definition if their producers are able to switch to manufacturing substitutable products in the short term without significant additional costs or risk.[228] To date, the Commission's practice has tended to be to define product markets narrowly, restricting the definition to the relevant products and close substitutes.
           In its communication on the definition of relevant markets, the Commission adopts a test which starts by examining the projects directly affected by the agreement, and adding in substitutable products. The Commission suggests that products are sufficiently substitutable to be included within the relevant product market if sufficient customers would switch to them in response to a small but significant non-transitory increase in price of between five and 10 per cent in the price of the affected products to make such a price rise unprofitable (the so-called SSNIP test).[229] While this test often proves difficult to

apply in terms of obtaining empirical data, it can in fact often provide a useful measure even in terms of hypothetical examination of the market or the future market.

The approach of E.C. antitrust law in focusing on demand side substitutability in **14–195** market analysis has been criticised in that it is said to be unresponsive to new economies such as the Internet and e-commerce, where the main competitive constraint comes from new, superior products, whose time of introduction, or existence, is uncertain, and where some of the most significant potential competition may come from those who are not present in the market at the time of the analysis. Nevertheless, the analysis of future markets, even in conventional competition analysis, often has to look at future markets and innovations. Such market analysis can never be precise, because of the impossibility of predicting the future in innovative markets, but on the other hand it may be the best analysis available. The criticism could also be that of engaging in too much prediction of the future by the competition authorities in some instances.

The relevant geographic market

The relevant geographic market has been defined as: "the area in which the undertakings **14–196** concerned are involved in the supply and demand of products or services, in which the conditions of competition are sufficiently homogeneous and which can be distinguished from neighbouring areas because the conditions of competition are appreciably different in those areas".[230] As with the relevant product market, the Commission suggests that an area should be included within the relevant geographic market if sufficient customers would switch their purchases to it in response to a small permanent rise of between five and 10 per cent in the price in the affected area to make such a price rise unprofitable

Whether an area constitutes a substantial part of the E.U. market is a question of fact dependent on the economic significance of an area as well as its geographic scope. Consequently, the ports have been found to be substantial parts of the E.U. due to their importance for shipping,[231] and it seems that an area as small as Luxembourg (which represents less than 0.25 per cent of the population of the E.U.) may qualify.[232]

Measuring economic strength on the relevant market

A firm will usually be regarded as having sufficient economic strength to be regarded as **14–197** dominant where it controls a large share of the relevant market for a significant period, at least provided that other relevant factors point in the same direction. For example, the Court of Justice has found that a market share in excess of 84 per cent held for three years was proof of dominance.[233] Similarly, a market share of around 50 per cent held for around three years was sufficient, in the absence of counter indications, to raise a presumption of dominance.[234] Conversely, it is unlikely that an undertaking controlling less than 25 per cent of the relevant market would be considered dominant.[235] Dominance may typically be found at levels above 40 per cent.

However, an undertaking's static market share is not the only factor which determines dominance, and a high market share may not be conclusive of dominance where there are other factors which negate it, a point which is particularly significant in e-commerce and new economy areas. Other relevant factors include: the market shares of the other undertakings in the market, the evolution of market shares over time, control of key technology and other barriers exist to market entry.

The analysis under E.C. antitrust law is criticised for being inappropriate for the new **14–198** economy industries where one entry typically has a large market share, where competition is often for the market as a whole, and large market shares are under permanent threat from innovating competitors and they are only able to retain their position if they continue to innovate. However, E.C. antitrust law has never focused solely on static analysis, and particularly in the new economy areas, looks at evolution of market shares over time and all possible factors which could influence market strength in future. In addition, in many cases there are clearly so many indicators of increasing market power giving an ability to quash or hijack innovation from other competitors in the market, that clear indications of dominance are provided.

It is often said that a better indicator of market power in this situation is that of contestability. If the market is contestable, a firm with high market share does not enjoy a position of dominance because potential entry imposes an effective competitive constraint. Contestability analysis often seems to result in the same type of analysis as is engaged in under the more traditional analysis of dominance.

The notion of an Essential Facility

14–199 A doctrine is currently developing under Article 82 in relation to "essential facilities" without access to which competitors cannot provide services to their customers in a related market. Those who control essential facilities are under special obligations and may be required to grant access to those facilities even if they would not be required to do so if they were merely dominant on the conventional assessment suggested above. In addition, they may be required to grant access on terms which are no less favourable than those they grant to themselves as participants in a related market. An early case concerned a port authority which was operating a ferry service from the port, and which, in its capacity as port authority, was allegedly applying sailing schedules that disadvantaged other ferry operators.[236] The Commission reasoned that a dominant undertaking which both owns or controls and uses an essential facility and which refuses access to that facility or grants access to competitors on terms less favourable than it applies to its own services (thereby placing them at a competitive disadvantage) infringes Article 82 unless it has an objective justification for its actions. In another case concerning a port controller, the Commission decided that this principle would apply even if the dominant undertaking did not operate a ferry company and so was not active in the relevant market.[237] A refusal of the right to use the port without a valid reason could be an abuse even where the port controller had no economic interest in any of the ferry operators using the port.

14–200 The doctrine would be of little interest however if it applied only to ports and it is developing on a more general level. Some decisions which were taken before the doctrine was expressly formulated by the Commission are now being recast as applications of the principal. One example of a case which is claimed to have been an application of the principle is the London European-Sabena case.[238] In that case, the Commission decided that the Belgian national airline, Sabena, had infringed Article 81 by refusing to grant another airline, London European, access to its computerised reservation system which would allow its flight schedules and fares to be quoted and reservations to be made.

Clearly the essential facilities doctrine could have important consequences, especially in relation to possible obligations to grant rights to content. However, the doctrine is still in the process of being developed, and many aspects of it are still unclear. In one case, the Commission defined an essential facility as "a facility or infrastructure which is essential for reaching customers and/or enabling competitors to carry on their business, and which cannot be replicated by any reasonable means".[239] However, a much more detailed consideration of this question will be necessary before the issue is fully clarified. The issue is in practice very much intertwined with consideration of compulsory licensing, and will be considered further below.

Joint or Collective Dominance
The European Court of Justice has in a number of cases[240] confirmed that the expression "one or more undertakings" in Article 82 of the Treaty implies that a dominant position may be held by two or more economic entities legally independent of each other. That only applies, however where from an economic point of view they present themselves or act together on a particular market as a collective entity *vis-à-vis* their competitors, their trading partners and consumers on a particular market.[241] Establishing the existence of such a collective entity requires examination of whether there are economic links or factors which give rise to a connection between the undertakings concerned, which enable them to act together independently of their competitors, their customers and consumers. This could result from an agreement, decision or concerted practice between them. It may flow from the nature and terms of an agreement, from the way in which it is implemented and, consequently, from the links or factors which give rise to a connection between undertakings which result from it. The Court has stated that the existence of an agreement or of other links in law is not indispensable, and a finding of a collective dominant position under Article 82 may be based on other connecting factors and on an assessment of the structure of the market in question. However, under Article 82 the ECJ has not yet gone so far as to explicitly follow its pronouncements in the assessment of collective dominance under Regulation 4064/94, which suggest that the existence of a "tightly oligopolistic" market structure could in itself found a finding of collective dominance.[242]

14.5.2 Abuse

The following sections list forms of behaviour and contractual requirements which may be considered to be abusive. **14–201**

Obtaining exclusive rights to content
In certain circumstances, an operator which is dominant in the market for certain content which formed a market in itself might be committing an abuse if it acquired such a degree of exclusivity regarding the content of such that competitors were excluded from the market. Considerations of this type may well have been behind the *Nielsen* case.[243] This concerned retail tracking services (also know as sales or market tracking services), which involve information on product sales, prices, and other market information being obtained electronically from retailers and aggregated, with the aggregated information then being supplied to manufacturers of the relevant products and others. AC Nielsen Company is the worlds leading provider of these services. The second largest provider, IRI, complained to the Commission that the terms of Nielsen's contracts with retailers were preventing it from entering the market. The Commission issued a statement of objections alleging infringement of Article 82. The case never resulted in a formal decision, but was resolved by Nielsen giving undertakings to the Commission, one of which was that in relation to the purchase of data from retailers, Nielsen would not to conclude exclusive contracts or contracts including any restriction on the retailers freedom to supply data to any retail tracking services provider. **14–202**

Excessive pricing
A dominant company which charges prices which are unfairly high in comparison to the "economic value" of the products or services being supplied may be committing an **14–203**

abuse. Whether or not this is the case may be assessed by examining prices for comparable goods or services or the costs production of the relevant goods or services,[244] or even in some circumstances comparing prices in different geographic markets in the absence of other data.[245] However, there are considerable difficulties in determining when a price is so high that it constitutes an abuse, with the result that Article 82 has been applied in respect of excessive prices only in very few cases. On the other hand, it may be that where excessive prices relate to an essential facility (see above) the Commission will be more keen to take action. The case of *ITT/Belgacom* may suggest that prices for access to an essential facility cannot exceed cost plus a reasonable rate of return.[246] The case concerned the prices charged by Belgacom, the incumbent Belgian telecoms operator, to ITT Promedia N.V., a provider of alternative telephone directories, for lists of its telephone subscribers and other data (which the Commission may well have seen as an essential facility). ITT complained that the prices were excessive and discriminatory. The Commission closed its case after Belgacom agreed to reduce such prices to a level that would cover its costs in collecting, compiling and providing such data plus a reasonable profit margin. The new price constituted a reduction of 90 per cent over that originally charged by Belgacom. In other informally settled cases in the telecoms sector, the Commission has determined that interconnection prices set at 100 per cent above those on comparable markets could be regarded as excessive.[247]

In new economy markets where there is often competition for the market, it is sometimes suggested that very significant profits are justified for those who manage to win the market, since they compensate for the risk undertaken by the winner, and offset the losses suffered by the many losers. However, it is not clear that profits need compensate for the losses suffered by the losers in order to create an efficient market. Consequently, a conventional analysis, which takes into account the cost of developing the product over its lifetime in an analysis of whether or not the price is excessive does not appear to be an unjustified approach.

Predatory Pricing

14–204   Predatory pricing, meaning pricing below cost aimed at eliminating a competitor may be abusive contrary to Article 82. The European Court of Justice has held that pricing below average variable cost is an automatic abuse under Article 81 and that pricing below average total cost may be abusive if it forms part of a plan to eliminate a competitor.[248] It has been suggested that this test (which is related to the economic analysis applied by Areeda and Turner[249]) of predatory pricing is inappropriate in the analysis of new economy sectors. In particular, it is suggested that much competition in new economy markets which involve scale economies and network effects will involve firms which engage in significant loss making activities in the early stages of the market, often going beyond merely promotional activities, in order to acquire the whole market for their goods. On the above test, such behaviour, designed to exclude competitors from the market, might be classed as predatory.

However, it is claimed that such loss-making activities in the new economy may not require intervention, because competition takes place in a different form, that of constant innovation, and intervention is likely to slow the innovation race. While this argument might be justified in some circumstances where the market has not been established, and the low pricing is a necessity in order to establish the market, this argument may mean that these factors should also be taken into consideration in the assessment of abusive behaviour. However, where the market is clearly established or there is no necessity for the low pricing in the market, the existing predatory pricing test may continue to be a valid one.

Discriminatory Pricing

Discriminatory pricing may be condemned as an abuse. Article 82 itself lists "applying   **14–205**
dissimilar conditions to equivalent transactions with other trading parties, thereby
placing them at a competitive disadvantage" as an example of abuse.[250] Does this mean
that companies in a dominant position cannot charge different prices for a product in
different countries? One practice which has been condemned is where a dominant
company charges distributors different prices for particular goods delivered to the same
place, according to the country where the distributor is intending to resell them.[251] On the
other hand, where the discrimination is less artificial, and there some objective
justification for the difference in price, a price difference may in many cases be
permitted. Where discriminatory pricing cannot be justified and has a significant effect on
the purchaser's ability to compete in a neighbouring or downstream market on which it
competes with the dominant firm, it may however be objectionable.

E-commerce has characteristics that might be expected to facilitate price discrimination, both in the B2C and the B2B areas. As the U.K. Office of Fair Trading commented in
its paper to the OECD round table on Competition Issues In Electronic Commerce[252]:

> "The direct one-to-one nature of many transactions may enable the seller to more
> easily price to each individual customer at that customer's maximum willingness to
> pay. The growing use of auctions and exchanges within online marketplaces allows
> the seller to extract the maximum price offered for a good, without setting a firm
> price. Third-degree price discrimination may be facilitated by the use of 'cookies'
> alongside detailed customer databases, which enable companies to tailor their
> offerings to different categories of customers. The possibility of price discrimination
> offered by e-commerce might result in smaller or more segmented relevant markets.
> Although price discrimination can be efficient and beneficial for welfare, it may also
> both distort competition and facilitate excessive pricing. On-line companies are
> more easily able to gather and even share sensitive information about customers
> and their shopping habits. Nevertheless, this should only concern competition
> authorities when there is market power. Market solutions, such as the ability for
> individuals to conduct searches, will constrain this behaviour. There is a strong
> probability that it will be harder to apply competition law on price discrimination to
> e-commerce. Market segmentation may make the analysis harder, but the main
> problem is likely to be effective monitoring and market intelligence, and where it
> facilitates (*e.g.*) excessive pricing, allocating costs objectively."

There are already reports of particular sites attempting to price discriminate in this
way, and the reaction of the competition authorities is unclear, at least where it relates to
discriminatory pricing to end users by dominant companies where the pricing is not
excessive.

Tying

A typical form of abusive tie-in or tying occurs where, as a condition of purchasing one   **14–206**
product or service in which an undertaking is dominant, a buyer is forced to purchase
another product or service which it could otherwise have bought from a competing
supplier, or which it could have self-provided.[253] However, this is not the only form of
tying behaviour that may be considered abusive. If a dominant company gives a
reduction in price when products or services are purchased together, compared with the
price of purchasing them separately, then that may also be abusive, especially where it

forecloses the market because competitors which offer the products or services separately are unable to compete. On the other hand, if the difference in price reflects a reduction in the costs of supplying the bundled package, then it should be permitted. This is illustrated by a case involving *Digital* which did not reach the stage of a formal decision, and which was resolved by Digital giving undertakings to the Commission.[254] Digital, which was alleged to be dominant in the supply of software and hardware maintenance services for its products offered a combined package of software maintenance services and hardware maintenance services at a price lower than the combined prices for software and hardware maintenance services if purchased separately. To avoid action by the Commission under Article 82, Digital had to undertake that the discount in respect of software services which were bundled would not be greater than 10 per cent compared with the price for purchasing software maintenance services and hardware maintenance services separately. A greater discount would have made it uneconomic for competitors to offer hardware maintenance services alone. The Commission commented that the 10 per cent discount "allows cost savings and other benefits to be passed on to system users while ensuring the maintenance of effective competition in the supply of hardware services".

Exclusive purchasing requirements and loyalty bonuses

14–207   An obligation imposed by a dominant firm on its customers or distributors requiring them to purchase all or a percentage of their requirements from the dominant firm may be an abuse of a dominant position because it has a foreclosure effect on other suppliers. Pricing practices such as loyalty or fidelity discounts or rebates where a rebate or discount is conditional on a customer purchasing all or a proportion of its requirements from the undertaking offering the discount may also be abusive for the same reason. Even discounts or rebates which are based on the purchase of fixed amounts may be contrary to Article 82, where those fixed amounts are in fact calculated for each customer to cover all or a substantial amount of that customer's requirements.

Refusal to supply and refusal to licence

14–208   Refusals to supply, in particular refusals to continue supplies to existing customers, may be abusive. For example, it has been held to be abusive for an undertaking which has previously supplied raw materials to a producer of finished goods to refuse to supply the raw materials to that customer because it wishes to break into the market for finished goods itself.[255] A refusal to supply an existing distributor because it starts to sell the products of a competitor, or starts to compete by itself providing competing products or services could also be an abuse.[256] While refusal to supply a new customer may not in many cases be an abuse, there are some cases where refusal to supply a new customer has been held to be one. These cases are difficult to categorise, but factors involved have included the fact of having a legal monopoly over the service refused, as well as essential facilities considerations.

14–209   A special case of a refusal to supply is a refusal to licence, an issue which will be of considerable relevance to holders of intellectual property rights in e-commerce. In certain circumstances, a refusal to grant a licence of intellectual property rights may be abusive. In the *Magill* case, which involved copyright material, the Court of Justice held that, in exceptional circumstances, the owner of intellectual property rights may be obliged by Article 81 to grant licenses to third parties.[257] *Magill* concerned a refusal by a number of television broadcasters in the United Kingdom and Ireland to license weekly programme schedules said to be covered by copyright to Magill for inclusion in a weekly television listings magazine. The following were some elements which the Court identified as exceptional in that case:

(i)   the requested material concerned basic information concerning channel, day, time and title of the programme; and each of the broadcasters was the only possible source of information on its programming schedule. As a result the refusal to license was preventing the emergence of a new product, namely a comprehensive television guide, for which there was ''specific, constant and regular'' potential demand;

(iii) by their conduct, their conduct, the broadcasters reserved to themselves the market for weekly television guides;

(iv) there was no justification for such a refusal either in the activity of television broadcasting or in that of publishing television programmes.

The scope of *Magill* judgement has now been interpreted in later cases.

Tiercé Ladbroke[258] concerned the broadcasting of sound and pictures of French horse races, the rights to which were controlled by the French horse racing companies, or ''sociétés de courses''. Ladbroke wanted a right to broadcast the French races in its booking shops in Belgium, but the French horse racing companies refused. The Court in this case found that there was no obligation to licence. The Magill case could not be relied on because in contrast to Magill, in this case the applicant was not only present in but had the largest share of the main betting market in Belgium, on which the product in question would be offered to consumers, while the French horse racing companies where not present on the market. In the absence of exploitation by those companies of their intellectual property rights in Belgium, their refusal to supply could not be regarded as involving any restriction of competition. Even if the absence of the horse racing companies was not a decisive factor, the refusal to supply could not be contrary to Article 81, unless it concerned a product or service which was either essential for the exercise of the activity in question in that there was no real or potential substitute, or it concerned a new product whose introduction might be prevented, despite specific, constant and regular demand on the part of consumers. Sound and pictures were not necessary for taking bets, as shown by the Ladbrokes significant position in Belgium for taking bets on French races. Further, broadcasting was not indispensable, because it took place after bets were placed, and therefore did not prevent bookmakers from pursuing their business.

14–210

Oscar Bronner[259] was a newspaper publisher which wanted to have its newspapers distributed through Mediaprint's national home delivery system, the only national home delivery network in Austria, and claimed that it was an abuse of Mediaprint's dominant position for it to refuse such access. The Court of Justice considered the question of whether such a refusal would amount to an abuse, on the ground that it deprived a competitor of a means of distribution judged essential for the sale of the newspaper. It determined that Magill could not be relied upon, even if the Magill principle on the exercise of an intellectual property right were applicable to the exercise of any property right whatever. In particular, unlike the situation in Magill, the refusal of the service would not eliminate all competition in the daily newspaper market. First, there were other methods of distributing papers, such as by post, through shops and kiosks. Further, there were no technical, legal or even economic obstacles capable of making it impossible, or even unreasonably difficult, for any other publisher of daily newspapers to establish, alone or in cooperation with other publishers, its own daily nationwide home-delivery

14–211

scheme. In order to demonstrate that the creation of such a system was not a realistic potential alternative and that access to the existing system was indispensable, it was not enough to argue that it was not viable by reason of the small circulation of the daily newspaper or newspapers to be distributed. It would be necessary to show that it was not economically viable to create a second home-delivery scheme for the distribution of daily newspapers with a circulation comparable to that of the daily newspapers distributed by the existing scheme.

14–212   In *Micro Leader Business*,[260] Micro Leader Business had complained to the European Commission about Microsoft's policy which prevented it importing into France for resale, French language Microsoft software which was originally marketed in Canada. The EC rule on the exhaustion of copyright for computer software, as enshrined in Article 4(c) of Directive 91/250 on the legal protection of computer programs provided that the first sale of a copy of a computer program in the E.U. would exhaust the distribution right to elsewhere in the E.U., but that did not apply where the first sale was in Canada, because of which, Microsoft retained its right to rely on its copyright to prevent distribution in France of such products. The Commission rejected Micro Leader's complaint, on the basis that the prohibition on importation into Europe fell within the legal enforcement of its copyright, and that no evidence had been provided of the wrongful exercise of that right. The Commission had suggested that evidence of such wrongful exercise might be constituted by Microsoft charging lower prices on the Canadian market than on the European market for equivalent transactions, if European prices were, in addition, excessive. The court held that the factual evidence put forward by the applicant constituted, at the very least, an indication that, for equivalent transactions, there Microsoft applied lower prices on the Canadian market than on the Community market, and that the Community prices were excessive. It annulled the rejection of Micro Leader's complaint, forcing the Commission to reconsider it. The significant point about this is that, although not a clear ruling on the point, the tenor of the Court's ruling suggested that there might be an argument on the basis of the Magill case that a compulsory licence might be imposed, or copyright might not be relied on where there was a difference in price between France and Canada, the difference in price put the import in competition with the French product because of its significantly lower price, and the price of the French products was excessive.

14–213   In the *IMS German Brick Structure* "interim measures" decision, IMS Health (IMS), the world leader in data collection on pharmaceutical sales and prescriptions, was required to licence its copyright "1860 brick structure", which segments Germany into 1,860 sales areas or "bricks".[261] Each brick contains at least four pharmacies German data protection law prohibits the provision of sales information for individual pharmacies. The Commission considered that IMS's refusal to grant a licence for the use of the structure, which had become a national standard in the German pharmaceutical industry, constituted a prima facie abuse of a dominant position.

Regional sales reports were an essential tool for the pharmaceutical industry which uses them to create sales territories, develop incentive schemes for their sales force and to know about their products' market shares and trends in sales over time.

The complainants in the case, NDC Germany and AzyX Geopharma, the subsidiaries of respectively an American and a Belgian firm, initially attempted to sell their regional sales data in a structure other than the "1860 brick structure". However, discussions with potential customers showed that data presented in another structure was not marketable, because of the pre-eminent position of the 1860 structure within the industry.

14–214   Inquiries made to around 110 German pharmaceutical companies showed that the sector was very strongly economically dependent on the 1860 structure and that it would not be viable for them to switch to data provided in another structure, partly because the pharmaceutical industry itself contributed to devising the 1860 brick structure to meet its particular requirements. IMS's rivals were unlikely to come up with and sell an alternative structure without infringing IMS' copyright.

The Commission considered therefore, that: (a) the 1860 structure was indispensable for NDC and AzyX to carry on their business, inasmuch as there was no actual or potential substitute for it, (b) IMS's refusal to licence could not be justified objectively and is likely to foreclose the market to potential new entrants and eliminate all prospect of competition in Germany.

IMS was required to grant a licence to its current competitors on non-discriminatory, commercially reasonable terms. The royalties to be paid to IMS were to be agreed by IMS and the party requesting a licence, or in case of disagreement, would be determined by independent experts on the basis of transparent and objective criteria.

14.5.3 Cases Specifically Related to E-commerce

Obligation to disclose interface information and the IBM System/370 case
Long before the issue of compulsory licences and essential facilities came into the centre stage of European Competition law, the European Commission in 1980 alleged in a Statement of objections against IBM[262] that IBM had abused its dominant position in the supply of central processing units and basic software for IBM System/370 type mainframe computers, by amongst other matters, failing to supply other manufacturers in sufficient time with the interface information needed to permit competitive products to be used with System/370 computers. A settlement was reached with the Commission, whereby IBM gave extensive undertakings. It agreed to disclose sufficient interface information to allow competing companies in the E.U. to sell hardware and software products of their own design which could interoperate with IBM System/370. Specifically, it agreed to make all System/370 hardware interface information and all information relating to the System/370 CPUs and software products available within 120 of the date of the announcement of the product concerned in the E.U. or at the date of the general availability of the product, if earlier.[263] For the interface between System/370 software products and competitors' software, IBM undertook to disclose the relevant interface information available as soon as the interface was reasonably stable but no later than general availability.[264] Any company which could provide satisfactory evidence that it was doing business in the E.U. and was developing and manufacturing products of the relevant type was entitled to the relevant information. IBM reserved a right to charge a reasonable royalty to cover its costs and for the supply of proprietary information protected by any right enforceable at law. The undertaking was terminated in 1995.

14–215

Microsoft Server and Windows 2000 cases
At the time of writing, the European Commission had issued a statement of objections to Microsoft, alleging that Microsoft had abused its dominant position in the market for personal computer operating systems by using illegal practices to extend its dominant position in the market for personal computer operating systems into the market for low-end server operating systems. A statement of objections is a formal step in European antitrust proceedings prior to the final decision by the Commission, and which does not prejudge the final outcome.

14–216

The Commission suggested that Microsoft could have an overwhelmingly dominant position in the market for personal computer (PC) operating systems and also had a very significant market share in the market for low-end server operating systems.

14–217   The Commission believed that Microsoft may have withheld from vendors of alternative server software key interoperability information that they need to enable their products to talk with Microsoft's dominant PC and server software products. Microsoft may have done this through a combination of refusing to reveal the relevant technical information, and by engaging in a policy of discriminatory and selective disclosure on the basis of a "friend-enemy" scheme. Mario Monti, the Competition Commissioner, was quoted as saying that "Effective protection of copyrights and patents is most important for technological progress. However, we will not tolerate the extension of existing dominance into adjacent markets through the leveraging of market power by anti-competitive means and under the pretext of copyright protection." This aspect of the statement of objections followed complaints by Sun Microsystems relating to refusals to supply interface information in respect of Windows 95, 98, NT 4.0 and all subsequent updates, as well as complaints in respect of Windows 2000.

Furthermore, the Commission believed that Microsoft may have reinforced this strategy of extending its dominance from the PC to the server through the operation of an abusive licensing policy for Windows 2000. Under the Microsoft scheme, if customers choose not to use an all-inclusive Microsoft scenario for PCs and servers, but decided to use competing server products, they were forced to bear a double cost. The effect of this policy may be to artificially drive customers towards Microsoft server products.

A further aspect of the statement of objections related to allegations that Microsoft had illegally tied its Media Player product with its dominant Windows operating system.[265]

14–218   According to the press release[266]:

> "Microsoft's ties its Media Player to its ubiquitous Windows operating system, a channel of distribution which is not available to competing vendors of media players. Microsoft may thereby deprive PC manufacturers and final users of a free choice over which products they want to have on their PCs, especially as there are no ready technical means to remove or uninstall the Media Player product. Competing products may therefore be *a priori* set at a disadvantage which is not related to their price or quality. The result is a weakening of effective competition in the market, a reduction of consumer choice, and less innovation."

Mario Monti, the Commissioner responsible for competition, is quoted as saying:

> "...The Commission ... wants to see undistorted competition in the market for media players. These products will not only revolutionise the way people listen to music or watch videos but will also play an important role with a view to making Internet content and electronic commerce more attractive. The Commission is determined to ensure that the Internet remains a competitive marketplace to the benefit of innovation and consumers alike."[267]

14.6 U.K. Competition Law

14–219   This section looks at the application of U.K. competition law to e-commerce. It comments only on the merger provisions of the Fair Trading Act 1973 and the Competition Act 1998. It does not address the monopoly provisions of the Fair Trading Act 1973.

14.6.1 U.K. Merger Law

The U.K. law relating to mergers in the United Kingdom is contained in the merger provisions of the Fair Trading Act 1973 ("FTA"). Under the FTA a "merger situation qualifying for investigation" arises if: **14–220**

- two or more enterprises, of which at least one is carried out in the United Kingdom, cease to be distinct and either

- as a result, in the United Kingdom at least 25 per cent of goods or services of any description are supplied by or to the same person or the persons by whom the relevant enterprises are carried on; or

- the gross value of the assets taken over, worldwide, exceeds £70 million.

Two enterprises cease to be distinct where one of them ceases to carry on business as a result of an agreement between them or they come under common control. Some joint ventures may come under the merger provisions on this basis.

As regards the requirement that at least one of the enterprises ceasing to be distinct must be carried on in the United Kingdom, this condition will probably be fulfilled where one of two foreign businesses which are being merged have a subsidiary or branch in the United Kingdom.

There is no obligation to notify mergers which qualify for investigation. The reason notification is often made is that it results in deadlines (discussed below) within which the relevant authorities (the Secretary of State for Trade and Industry, acting on the recommendation of the Director General of Fair Trading, who heads the U.K. competition authority which is called the Office of Fair Trading) must either clear the merger, or refer it for a fuller investigation by the Competition Commission. On the other hand, in the absence of notification, a merger may be referred to the Competition Commission up to four months from the date of the completion, or if later, 4 months from the date at which the Director General or the Minister became aware of material facts relating to the merger. **14–221**

The market share test is satisfied only if:

- both of the enterprises ceasing to be distinct either supply or purchase goods or services of a particular description in the United Kingdom, so that their combination increases a market share of goods or services supplied or purchased; and

- the resulting market share of goods or services purchased or sold is greater than 25 per cent.

In other words, if there is no market share overlap before the enterprises cease to be distinct, then the merger will not qualify for investigation, even if the combined market share is above 25 per cent. **14–222**

There are no fines for failure to notify, because as stated above, notification is entirely voluntary. The remedy under the Act is that if a merger is found contrary to the public interest, the Competition Commission may make recommendations to the Secretary of State for Trade and Industry, who may then make an order requiring the parties to modify the arrangement in order to prevent any adverse effects which have been specified by the Competition Commission, and this may include divestiture. The Competition Commission referral process is lengthy, and is used in only a very small minority of cases. On the other hand, of the cases which are referred to the Competition Commission a large number tend to be found to be contrary to the public interest.

14.6.2 The U.K. Competition Act 1998

14–223 The U.K. Competition Act 1998 (the "Act") entered into force on March 1, 2000. It introduced two prohibitions into U.K. law:

(i)   a prohibition on agreements that restrict competition in the United Kingdom (section 2 of the Act, the "**Chapter I prohibition**"); and

(ii) a prohibition of the abuse of a dominant market position in the United Kingdom (section 18 of the Act, the "**Chapter II prohibition**").

The Act repealed much of the existing U.K. competition legislation, including the Restrictive Trade Practices Acts 1976 and 1977, the Resale Prices Act 1976 and the provisions of the Competition Act 1980 concerning anti-competitive practices. The Fair Trading Act 1973, which covers mergers and monopoly situations, remains in force.

14–224   One objective of the 1998 Act was to bring U.K. competition law more closely into line with E.U. competition law. To this end, the Chapter I and Chapter II prohibitions are closely modelled on, respectively, Articles 81 and 82 of the E.C. Treaty. In addition, section 60 of the 1998 Act requires that questions arising in relation to the Chapter I and Chapter II prohibitions are, as far as possible and taking into account relevant differences, dealt with in a manner consistent with the treatment of corresponding questions under E.U. law. In particular, U.K. courts and the Director General of Fair Trading (the "Director General") are required to determine such questions with a view to securing that there is no inconsistency between, on the one hand, the principles they apply and the decisions they reach under the 1998 Act and, on the other hand, the principles laid down by the E.C. Treaty and the E.C. Court of Justice in determining corresponding questions under E.U. competition law. U.K. courts and the Director General must also "have regard" to relevant statements and decision of the European Commission.

14.6.3 The 1998 Act—The Chapter I Prohibition

14–225 The Chapter I prohibition is contained in section 2(1) of the 1998 Act and applies to "agreements between undertakings, decisions by associations of undertakings or concerted practices" that:

* have the object or effect of preventing, restricting or distorting competition within the U.K.,

* may affect trade within the United Kingdom and are implemented in the United

Kingdom.

Agreements Between Undertakings, Decisions Of Trade Associations And Concerted Practices
Most forms of competitive co-ordination between undertakings are potentially caught by   **14–226**
the Chapter I prohibition. The term "agreement" covers agreements that are not legally
binding and, conversely, several separate binding contracts may be found to form a
single agreement. The term "concerted practice" covers all co-ordinated behaviour
between undertakings that "knowingly substitutes practical co-operation between them
for the risks of competition".

   To be caught by the Chapter I prohibition, an agreement or concerted practice must be
"between undertakings". A parent company and its wholly controlled subsidiaries are
considered to form a "single economic entity" and, as a result, are treated as a single
undertaking for this purpose. Consequently, many inter-group transactions will fall
outside the Chapter I prohibition.

The Meaning Of "Undertaking"
The term "undertaking" will be interpreted broadly to cover virtually any entity engaged   **14–227**
in economic or commercial activity, regardless of its legal status. Limited companies,
partnerships and individuals may all be undertakings. State-owned companies will also
be covered if they engage in commercial or economic activity. The fact that an entity is
non-profit making will not prevent it being an undertaking.

Object or effect of preventing, restricting or distorting competition in the United Kingdom
In principle, any agreement that may lead to reduced competition between the parties or   **14–228**
restricts the ability of third parties to compete may potentially be caught by the Chapter I
prohibition. There is no particular significance in the distinction between preventing,
restricting and distorting competition.

Restriction of competition and implementation in the United Kingdom
An agreement may fall within the Chapter I prohibition if it has the object or effect of   **14–229**
restricting competition in the United Kingdom and is, or is intended to be implemented
in the United Kingdom.[268] The latter requirement is a jurisdictional test which reflects the
EC case law under Article 81.[269] An agreement which affects competition in the United
Kingdom and is implemented in the United Kingdom[270] will fall under U.K. law, and if it
also meets the E.C. requirement of having a potential effect on trade between Member
States, it may also fall under Article 81. Article 81 is only infringed where there is an effect
on trade between E.U. Member States. An agreement which has no effect on trade
between Member States for the purposes of Article 81 may nevertheless fall under the
Chapter I prohibition if it affects trade in the United Kingdom

Appreciable Effect
The Chapter I prohibition will not apply to agreements whose effect on trade or   **14–230**
competition is not appreciable. This requirement does not appear in the text of the
prohibition, but is imported from E.U. competition law by the section 60 requirement for
consistent interpretation.

   The Director General has indicated that in general, agreements will generally have no
appreciable effect where the combined market share of the undertakings concerned is less
than 25 per cent. However, even where the 25 per cent threshold is not met an agreement
may be considered to have appreciable effects if it:

(i)   directly or indirectly fixes prices or shares markets;

(ii)   imposes minimum resale prices; or

(iii) is one of a network of similar agreements which have a cumulative effect on the market in question.

In calculating the market shares of the undertakings concerned, the Director General will take into account the market shares of their parents, subsidiaries and affiliates.

14.6.4 The 1998 Act—the Effect of Falling Within the Chapter I Prohibition

14–231   Section 2(4) of the 1998 Act provides that agreements caught by the Chapter I prohibition are void and may not be enforced in U.K. courts. Such voidness will not necessarily extend to the whole agreement but will be limited to the restrictive aspects of the agreement provided they are severable from the rest of the agreement under the normal rules of contract law. In addition to voidness under section 2(4), agreements caught by the Chapter I prohibition may attract enforcement action including fines and directions to terminate. The Chapter I prohibition is also intended to be directly enforceable in the United Kingdom courts, by private parties, by actions for an injunction or damages (see section 14.6.10 below).

Agreements may escape these consequences of falling within the Chapter I prohibition if they fall within one of a wide range of exclusions or benefit from an exemption (see sections 3.7 and 3.8 below).

14.6.5 The 1998 Act—Exclusions From The Chapter I Prohibition

Excluded agreements

14–232   The following categories of agreement are excluded from the Chapter I prohibition:

Vertical agreements

14–233   Unlike the position under Article 81, where vertical agreements are only exempted where they comply with the conditions contained in the vertical agreements block exemption,[271] vertical agreements are wholly excluded from the Chapter I prohibition.[272] The U.K. provision consciously matches the definition of vertical agreements contained in the E.U. block exemption.

There are two major exceptions to the exclusion for vertical agreements. Agreements which directly or indirectly restrict the ability of the buyer to set the sale price of goods or services are not covered by the exclusion, although agreements setting maximum sale prices or recommended sale prices may be covered. Further, like the block exemption, the exclusion does not apply to intellectual property agreements, defined in a similar manner. On the other hand, the exclusion of IP agreements may apply to software agreements, even where the E.C. Block exemption does not. The U.K. Guidelines[273] indicate that "an agreement under which a licence is given to, for example, a software buyer to reproduce that software in order to sell it on may benefit from the exclusion." The E.C. Guidelines only indicate that they apply to resales of packaged software.

Mergers

Mergers as defined under U.K. Merger law (the merger provisions of the Fair Trading Act **14–234**
1973) are excluded from the scope of the Chapter I prohibition[274] as are agreements
giving rise to a concentration falling within the E.C. Merger Regulation.[275]

14.6.6 The 1998 Act—Exemption From the Chapter I Prohibition

The 1998 Act gives the Director General powers to exempt agreements from the Chapter I **14–235**
prohibition where they satisfy certain exemption criteria. The relevant criteria mirror
those under Article 81(3) of the E.C. Treaty. Three categories of exemption are provided
for:

Parallel exemption if an E.C. Exemption Applies

Agreements that benefit from an exemption granted under E.U. competition law **14–236**
(pursuant to Article 81(3) of the E.C. Treaty) are automatically exempt from the Chapter I
prohibition.[276] This applies whether the E.U. exemption was granted on an individual
basis or under one of the E.U. block exemptions. In the 1998 Act, such automatic
exemptions are referred to as "parallel exemptions". Parallel exemption is also granted to
agreements that meet the conditions for exemption under one of the E.U. block
exemptions but do not affect trade between Member States. In certain circumstances, the
Director General may vary or cancel a parallel exemption or impose conditions.

U.K. Block exemptions

The Director General the power to adopt block exemptions granting automatic **14–237**
exemption, without the need for notification, to agreements that fall within the terms
of the block exemption.[277]

Notification for an individual exemption

As in E.C. law, individual notifications may also be made, but under the Competition Act **14–238**
they may be made either for a decision or for guidance. In order to obtain an individual
exemption decision under the U.K. Act an agreement must be notified to the Director
General on Form N. It must also be shown to satisfy the exemption criteria, *i.e.*, to

(i)   contribute to improving production or distribution, or to promoting technical or
       economic progress;

(ii)   allow consumers a fair share of the resulting benefits;

(iii) not impose any unnecessary restrictions; and

(iv)   not afford the possibility of eliminating competition in respect of a substantial
       part of the products in question.

Individual exemptions may have effect retroactively and from a date earlier than the
date of notification. As under E.U. law, once notified an agreement acquires immunity
from penalties under the Chapter 1 prohibition for the period until a formal decision is
reached. A fee of £13,000 is charged in relation to notifications for a decision on
exemption.

Notification for Guidance

14–239   As an alternative to notification for a decision on exemption, an agreement may be notified to the Director General for "guidance" as to its compatibility with the Chapter I prohibition. Such guidance may include whether it might qualify for individual, block or parallel exemption.

If guidance is given to the effect that an agreement is compatible with the Chapter I prohibition, the Director General may not take further action in relation to the relevant agreement unless:

(i)   a complaint is received from a third party;

(ii)   a material change circumstances occurs;

(iii) he suspects that false or misleading information may have been supplied in the initial notification; or

(iv)   a request for formal exemption is made.

As with notification for a decision, notification for guidance gives immunity from penalties under the Chapter 1 prohibition with effect from the date of notification. A fee of £5,000 is charged in relation to notifications for guidance.

14.6.7 The Chapter II prohibition

14–240   The Chapter II prohibition is contained in section 18(1) of the 1998 Act, which provides that:

> "any conduct on the part of one or more undertakings which amounts to the abuse of a dominant position in a market is prohibited if it may affect trade within the United Kingdom".

For these purposes, a dominant position is defined as "a dominant position within the United Kingdom" and the United Kingdom is defined as "the United Kingdom or any part of it".

It follows that conduct will be caught by the Chapter II prohibition where it:

(i)   is carried out by an undertaking holding a dominant position within the United Kingdom;

(ii)   constitutes an abuse of that dominant position; and

(iii) affects trade in the United Kingdom.

Dominant Position

14–241   The European Court of Justice has defined a dominant position for the purposes of Article 82 of the E.C. Treaty as:

> "a position of economic strength enjoyed by an undertaking which enables it to prevent effective competition being maintained on the relevant market by affording it the power to behave to an appreciable extent independently of its competitors and

customers, and ultimately of consumers".

Pursuant to section 60, this definition will apply in relation to the Chapter II prohibition. The definition involves two key concepts:

(i)   the relevant market; and

(ii)   a position of economic strength on that market sufficient to allow an appreciable degree of independence from competitive pressures.

It follows that identification of a dominant position is a two stage process. First, it is necessary to identify the relevant market. Second, it is necessary to assess the position of the relevant undertaking on that market.

Relevant market
In order to identify the relevant market it is necessary to examine two issues: **14–242**

(i)   the range of products that compete with those of the relevant undertaking, referred to as the "relevant product market"; and

(ii)   the geographic extent of the market for such products, referred to as the "relevant geographic market".

As to these, see the discussion above in relation to E.U. competition law.

The assessment of dominance
An undertaking may be considered dominant if it has a position of strength on the   **14–243**
relevant market sufficient to allow it to act independently of competitive pressures to a significant degree. The guidelines on the Chapter II prohibition issued by the Director General identify three potential sources of competitive constraints:

(i)   existing competitors;

(ii)   potential competitors; and

(iii) other constraints.

An important indicator of the strength of existing competitors on the relevant market is market share. Although, according to the guidance notes issued by the Director General, market share is not on its own determinative of the issue of dominance.

If an undertaking controls a very high proportion of a relevant market for a significant time, this may indicate that the undertaking holds a dominant position. The European Court has held that, in the absence of evidence to the contrary, dominance can be presumed if an undertaking has a market share persistently above 50 per cent. The Director considers that an undertaking is unlikely to be considered individually dominant if its market share is below 40 per cent, although dominance could be established below that figure if other relevant factors (such as the weak position of competitors in the market) provided strong evidence of dominance.

The other main issue in assessing the strength of an undertaking's market position is   **14–244**
the potential for new competition to arise as a result of new undertakings entering the market. The importance of such potential competitors is dependent on whether there are

barriers that prevent new entry to the relevant market. The Director General's guidance notes identify three categories of entry barrier:

(i)   absolute advantages—these include access to regulatory licences or permits; access to an essential facility, *i.e.*, an asset or facility that is indispensable in order to compete on the market and is impossible or extremely difficult to reproduce; or access to key technology that is protected by intellectual property rights;

(ii)   strategic or "first mover" advantages—these generally arise where new entrants face significant sunk costs if they wish to enter a market, *i.e.*, costs that must be incurred to enter, but cannot be recovered on exit from the market. If an undertaking will face vigorous competition from existing market participants, the fact that it will face significant sunk cost that it may not be able to recover may deter entry;

(iii) exclusionary behaviour—an undertaking may build up a reputation for predatory behaviour toward new entrants, which may deter entry. Alternatively, an undertaking may conclude contracts that tie-up outlets or distributors, making entry more costly and difficult.

Consideration will also be given to other factors that might constrain an undertakings ability to act independently on a market. According to the Director General, the principle example is strong buyer power, *i.e.*, the ability of large and powerful customers to constrain an undertaking's behaviour by threatening to terminate their purchases, in particular by switching to alternative suppliers.

Abuse

14–245   In general, abuse falls into one of two categories:

(i)   behaviour that reduces competition or restricts its development; and

(ii)   behaviour that exploits customers or suppliers.

For a full discussion of abusive behaviour, see the sections above on E.U. competition law. The following discussion notes in particular the guidelines issued by the Director General.

Excessively high prices

14–246   Excessively high prices are the classic example of an abuse that exploits customers. Under Article 82, the European Court of Justice has held that prices may be excessive where they have no reasonable relation to the "economic value" of the relevant product and indicated that this may be assessed by examining prices for comparable products or the cost of supplying the relevant products. In his guidelines on the Chapter II prohibition, the Director General indicates that the essential issue is whether the prices are above those that could exist in a competitive market. The guidelines go on to state that where a dominant undertaking's profits significantly and consistently exceed its cost of capital this may indicate excessive prices.

Price discrimination

14–247   Price discrimination arises where different conditions (in particular different prices) are applied in equivalent transactions. Two basic forms exist. First, where different prices are demanded from customers in similar positions in relation to similar products. Second, where similar prices are charged despite the fact that the cost supplying certain customers is much less than that of supplying others. In his guidelines, the Director General indicates that price discrimination raises complex economic issues and does not constitute an automatic abuse.

Predatory pricing
Under Article 82, the European Court of Justice has held that below cost pricing aimed at **14–248** eliminating a competitor may qualify as an abuse, with pricing below variable cost being considered an automatic abuse and pricing below average total cost an abusive if it can be shown to form part of a plan to eliminate a competitor. In his guidelines on the Chapter II prohibition, the Director General has indicated that his approach will be similar.

Vertical restraints
Vertical restraints are restrictions imposed between undertakings operating at different **14–249** levels of the production and distribution chain. As discussed, vertical restraints are to be excluded from the Chapter I prohibition (see section 14.6.6 above). However, where they are imposed by a dominant undertaking they may potentially constitute abuses contrary to the Chapter II prohibition. Relevant restraints may include: resale price maintenance, exclusive and selective distribution, exclusive purchasing, tie-in sales, bundling, loyalty discounts, and minimum purchase obligations. In assessing whether a vertical restraint constitutes an abuse, the Director General has indicated that he will examine whether it has efficiency benefits that outweigh its potentially anti-competitive effects.

Refusal to supply
The Director General's guidelines identify two situations in which a refusal to supply **14–250** might constitute an abuse: first, where a dominant undertaking refuses to supply an existing customer without an objective justification; and second, where a dominant undertaking controls an "essential facility", *i.e.* a facility to which access is necessary in order to supply certain goods or services and which is either impossible or extremely difficult to duplicate for physical, geographic or legal reasons.

Notification
Behaviour that potentially infringes the Chapter II prohibition may be notified to the **14–251** Director General. Two forms of notification are possible: (i) notification for guidance, which has the same effect as guidance in relation to the Chapter I prohibition (see Section 14.6.7 above) and (ii) notification for a formal decision as to the legality of the behaviour.

There is, however, no provision for exempting abusive behaviour from the Chapter II prohibition and notification does not give immunity from fines. Fees of £5,000 are charged in relation to notification for guidance and £13,000 in relation to notification for a decision.

14.6.8 Enforcement Agencies And Responsibilities

The Director General and the OFT and other Industry Regulators
Primary responsibility for enforcing the 1998 Act rests with the Director General of Fair **14–252** Trading and, through him, the OFT. The Director General has powers to investigate

potential infringements of the 1998 Act, to determine whether an infringement has occurred and, in such case, direct that the infringement be brought to an end and to impose penalties.

The Director General is also charged with producing a range of guidelines on the application of the 1998 Act and with issuing guidance and granting exemptions in response to notifications made under the Act. The guidelines and a large amount of information about the Competition Act and its application can be found on the OFT web site.[278]

Regulators in regulated industries such as telecommunications, water, electricity, gas and the railways are able to exercise the same powers as the Director General in the sectors within their responsibility. In contrast with the situation prior to the 1998 Act, it is intended that these powers will be used and that regulators will take the leading role in enforcing competition rules in their sectors. This would include carrying out investigations, dealing with notifications (although a copy of all notifications must be sent to the Director General), dealing with complaints from third parties and imposing penalties.

The Competition Commission

14–253 Pursuant to the 1998 Act, the previous Monopolies and Mergers Commission was renamed the "Competition Commission". Appeals from decisions of the Director General and Industry Regulators under the 1998 Act lies to an appeals' tribunal within the Competition Commission, the Competition Commission Appeals Tribunal (CCAT).

On appeal, the Competition Commission has powers to conduct a complete re-examination of the factual and legal basis of the original decision. Decisions of the Competition Commission may in turn be appealed to the Court of Appeal, but only on points of law and the levels of penalties.

Powers Of Investigation

14–254 Under the 1998 Act, the Director General (and industry regulators) enjoy much wider powers of investigation than under previous U.K. competition law statutes. First, it is considerably easier for the Director General to initiate investigations, as he needs only "reasonable grounds for suspecting" that an infringement has occurred.

The Director General's principal powers of investigation will be:

(i)   to order the production of relevant documents (excluding privileged communications) or the provision of information; and

(ii) to authorise on-site inspections of premises.

14–255 In the case of inspections of premises occupied by a person suspected of infringing the 1998 Act, no notice need be give of the inspection, leaving open the possibility of "dawn raids" of the type conducted by officials of the E.C. Commission. In the course of an inspection, officials may require:

(i)   that documents be produced;

(ii) that the location of documents be disclosed; and

(iii) that an explanation of documents be given.

In general, inspections may only be carried out with the consent of the occupier. However, the Director General may apply for a warrant permitting his officers to enter and search premises without consent where they have previously been refused permission to conduct an inspection, where the Director General reasonably suspects that requested documents have not been produced, or where the Director General reasonably suspects that documents might be destroyed to conceal evidence.

Deliberate failure to produce documents requested by the Director General, obstructing his offices in the course of an inspection and deliberately providing false or misleading information all constitute criminal offences that may be punished by fines and, in certain cases, imprisonment.

Interim Measures

The Director General has powers to order interim measures before completing an investigation if he has a reasonable suspicion that an infringement has occurred and considers it necessary to take urgent action to prevent serious irreparable damage to any person or to protect the public interest. **14–256**

Fines And Directions To Terminate

If, following an investigation, the Director General determines that an infringement has taken place he may give directions that appropriate action be taken to terminate the infringement, and impose fines on undertakings involved. **14–257**

Directions may be enforced by the Director General in the courts where the relevant undertakings fail to comply. Failure to comply with a court order enforcing a direction will constitute contempt of court and may result in fines or imprisonment.

Fines may of up to a maximum of 10 per cent of the U.K. turnover of infringing undertaking may be imposed for each year of the infringement. The Director General has published guidelines setting out a five-stage process for setting fines, as follows:

(i) First, a percentage rate based on the seriousness of the infringement will be applied to the turnover of the undertaking. The most serious infringements will include price-fixing, market sharing and other cartel activities, as well as abuses of dominance that are likely to have a significant impact on the competitive process;

(ii) Second, the basic amount will be increased to take into account the duration of the infringement by multiplying it by a number equal to or less than the number of years for which the infringement took place;

(iii) Third, the amount will be adjusted to take account of policy objective, such as deterrent effect on third parties, the need to prevent the undertakings profiting from an infringement and the size of the market on which the abuse took place;

(iv) Fourth, the amount will be further adjusted to take account of aggravating or mitigating factors relating to the undertaking's behaviour. These may include whether the undertaking played a leading role in a joint infringement, whether there may have been genuine doubt as to whether certain behaviour was infringing and whether the undertaking had implemented an adequate compliance programme;

(v) Finally, the fine will be adjusted to ensure that it does not exceed the ceiling of 10 per cent of turnover.

14–258   In addition, the Director General will impose reduced fines on cartel "whistleblowers". Whistleblowers may even obtain complete immunity from fines if they are the first to bring a cartel to the attention of the OFT and the OFT has not already given notice of its intention to adopt an infringement decision in relation to the cartel. Effective co-operation after that stage may also result in reduced fines.

14.6.9 Small agreements and conduct of minor importance

14–259   Undertakings of a size below certain thresholds will be immune from financial penalties unless they are involved in price fixing. The immunity can be withdrawn in certain circumstances and does not prevent third parties from making a claim for damages. The relevant turnover thresholds and details of how to calculate turnover are set out in the Competition Act 1998 (Small Agreements and Conduct of Minor Significance) Regulations 2000.[279] The thresholds are:

- **Chapter I**: the worldwide turnover of the parties to the agreement must not exceed £20 million;

- **Chapter II**: the worldwide turnover of the person whose conduct it is must not exceed £50 million.

14.6.10 Enforcement by Private Parties

14–260   The 1998 Act gives no express right of action to parties injured as a result of an infringement of the Chapter I and II prohibitions. During the passage of the Act through the Houses of Parliament, Government representatives stated several times that the Government's intention was that, pursuant to section 60, private parties would have an right to sue for damages for breach of the 1998 Act equivalent to that existing in relation to Articles 81 and 82 of the E.C. Treaty. The Act also provides that the United Kingdom courts are required to follow the principles of E.C. law in respect of "the civil liability of an undertaking for harm caused by its infringement of Community law", meaning that the principles relating to the right to damages will develop in line with E.C. law.

14.6.11 Transitional Provisions

14–261   Most agreements entered into before March 1, 2000, when the 1998 Act entered into force, were automatically exempt from the Chapter I prohibition for a one-year transitional period. Exceptions include:

- agreements that were referred to the Restrictive Practices Court before the entry into force of the 1998 Act and are found not to operate contrary to the public interest benefit from a five-year period of transitional exemption;

- agreements that before the entry into force of the 1998 Act fell within the scope of an exemption under section 14 of the Resale Prices Act also benefit from a five-year period of transitional exemption;

- void agreements under the RTPA or Resale Prices Act, which will do benefit from any transitional period; and

- agreements made during the three months prior to March 1, 2000 that were notifiable under the RTPA but were not notified before that date, will not benefit from any transitional period.

Pre-existing agreements that were notified under the RTPA but were not referred to the Restrictive Practices Court pursuant to section 21(2) as their effects were not significant are excluded from the Chapter I prohibition for their duration. Transitional immunity (and the exclusion for section 21(2) agreements) may be withdrawn by the Director General on an individual basis. No transitional periods apply in relation to abuse of dominance contrary to the Chapter II prohibition.

14.6.12 Cases related to E-commerce under the 1998 Competition Act

In *Network Multimedia Television Ltd v. Jobserve Ltd*,[280] the High Court considered in a **14–262** decision relating to an interlocutory injunction, that there was a serious issue to be tried as to whether Jobserve had abused its dominant position in the market for online advertising of IT vacancies contrary to the Chapter II prohibition. The company, an Internet job board, accepted postings for vacancies from recruitment agencies in the IT sector, amongst other sectors. Network Multimedia Television ("NMTV") were starting a competing service, ATSCOjobs.com, but Jobserve had made it clear to IT recruitment agencies that if they placed vacancies on the NMTV site their business would not be accepted by Jobserve. NMTV produced evidence that in that case a large amount of their business would disappear, because recruiters felt that they needed to use Jobserve, because of the large number of quality candidates that used the site. The Court considered that there was a serious issue to be tried both in respect of Jobserve's dominance in the relevant service market, and as to whether its behaviour constituted an abuse.

In its decision in *BT Surf Together and BT Talk & Surf Together pricing packages*,[281] the **14–263** Director General of Telecommunications investigated under the Competition Act 1998 the pricing of two new tariff packages for residential customers that BT introduced on December 1, 2000, BT Surf Together and BT Talk & Surf Together. The Director was concerned that the 'Surf' element of the packages (offering off-peak Internet access calls on an unmetered basis) was being provided below cost and that BT was funding the shortfall from profits on local and national residential voice calls in which it appears to the Director that BT is dominant, or wholesale call origination in which BT is dominant. Such behaviour could be an attempt to leverage market power horizontally (from residential voice calls) and/or vertically (from wholesale call origination) into either retail Internet access or wholesale termination of calls to Internet Service Providers. The Director suspected that this could have materially anti-competitive effects.

In the decision, the Director concluded that there was a retail market for retail Internet **14–264** access which was a national U.K. market, and that there was a wholesale market for call origination on fixed networks, which might or might not be divided into residential and business markets (it was unnecessary to decide), and which was also national. The Director concluded that BT was dominant in the market for wholesale call origination on fixed telecommunications networks in the United Kingdom. BT was also found to be dominant in the markets for local and national retail voice calls by residential customers on fixed telecommunications networks in the United Kingdom.

The Director concluded, however, that it was not proven that, at the current prices, BT was pricing or would price "Surf" below cost in the new packages. Furthermore, the Director considered it unlikely that, even if the price were below cost, a material anti–competitive effect would result on the current prices, because of the presence of competing, sustainable 24/7 retail Internet access packages. Consequently, the Director did not consider that BT's pricing of the packages constituted an infringement of section 18 of the Act.

1. Case No IV/M.1113, *Nortel/Norweb*.
2. *ibid*., Point 29.
3. Working Document on Draft Guidelines on market analysis and the calculation of significant market power under Article 14 of the proposed Directive on a common regulatory framework for electronic communications networks and services, March 28, 2001 COM (2001) 175 para. 59.
4. See Working Document cited at n.3 above, para. 60. See also Case No IV/JV.11, *@Home Benelux B.V.*
5. Case COMP/M.1439, *TELIA/TELENOR*, October 13, 1999 at point 76.
6. Case IV/M.1069, *Worldcom/MCI*, July 8, 1998.
7. Case COMP/M-1741, *MCL Worldcom/Sprint*
8. Case COMP/M.1439, *TELIA/TELENOR*, October 13, 1999.
9. *ibid*.
10. Case COMP/M 1838, *BT/ESAT*.
11. Case COMP/M.1845, *AOL/Time Warner* October 11, 2000.
12. Case IV/JV.8, *WSI Webseek*, September 15, 1998.
13. Case IV/JV.1, *Telia/Telenor/Schibsted* May 27, 1998.
14. Case COMP/JV.48, *Vodafone/Vivendi/Canal+*, see IP 00/821.
15. Case COMP/M.2050, *Vivendi/Canal+/Seagram*.
16. Chancery Division Judgment HC 0005478 of April 5, 2001.
17. Case IV/JV.1, *Telia/Telenor/Schibsted* May 27, 1998.
18. Commission contribution to OECD round table, "Competition issues in Electronic commerce", DAFFE/CLP(2000)32.
19. Case IV/M1459, *Bertelsmann/Havas/BOL*, May 6, 1999; Case JV 24, *Bertelsmann/Planeta/BOL Spain*, December 3, 1999; Case JV 45, *Bertelsmann/Kooperativa Förbundet/BOL Nordic*, May 12, 2000; Case COMP/JV.51, *Bertelsmann/Mondadori/BOL Italia*, September 1, 2000.
20. Case IV/M1459, *Bertelsmann/Havas/BOL*, May 6, 1999.
21. Case COMP/JV.51, *Bertelsmann/Mondadori/BOL Italia*, September 1, 2000.
22. Case COMP/M.2149, *T-Online/TUI/C&N Touristic* see IP/01/1670.
23. Case COMP/M.1845, *AOL/Time Warner* October 11, 2000.
24. See n. 15 above.
25. Case IV/M.972, *Bertelsmann/Burda/Springer—HOS MM*, September 15, 1997.
26. Case IV/M.973, *Bertelsmann/Burda—HOS Lifeline* September 15, 1997.
27. Case IV/JV.16, *Bertelsmann/Viag/Gamechannel*, May 5, 1999.
28. See n. 13 above.
29. See n. 11 above.
30. See n. 11 above.
31. See Competition Issues in Electronic Commerce, OECD Roundtable on Competition, DAFFE/CLP(2000)32, contribution from the European Commission, p.117.
32. Case M 1969, *UTC/Honeyewell/i2/MyAircraft.com*, August 4, 2000.
33. See n.31 above.
34. Case COMP/M.2096, *Bayer/Deutsche Telekom/Infraserv/JV*, October 6, 2000.
35. See Case COMP/M.2172, *BABCOCK BORSIG/MG TECHNOLOGIES/SAP MARKETS/ec4ec*, November 7, 2000; Case COMP/M.2270, *BABCOCK BORSIG/MG TECHNOLOGIES/SAP MARKETS/DEUTSCHE BANK/VA TECH/ec4ec*, January 22, 2001.
36. Case COMP/M.2027, *DEUTSCHE BANK/SAP/JV*, July 13, 2000.
37. Case COMP/M.2374, *Telenor/ErgoGroup/DNB/Accenture*.
38. *Entering the 21st Century: Competition Policy in the world of B2B electronic marketplaces*, a report by the Federal Trade Commission Staff, October 2000, Part 3, Antitrust Analysis of B2Bs, pp. 22-24.
39. See n.38 above.
40. Case COMP/M 1439, *Telia/Telenor*, October 13, 1999.
41. Case IV/M1459, *Bertelsmann/Havas/BOL*, May 6, 1999.

42. Competition Issues in Electronic Commerce, OECD Roundtable on Competition, DAFFE/CLP(2000)32, contribution from the European Commission, p. 123

43. Case COMP/JV.45, *BERTELSMANN/KOOPERATIVA FÖRBUNDET/BOL NORDIC.*

44. Competition Issues in Electronic Commerce, OECD Roundtable on Competition, DAFFE/CLP(2000)32, contribution from the European Commission, p. 123

45. Competition Issues in Electronic Commerce, OECD Roundtable on Competition, DAFFE/CLP(2000)32, contribution from the European Commission, p. 117

46. See n.6 above.

47. Council Regulation No. 4064/89 of December 21, 1989 on the control of concentrations between undertakings, as amended by Council Regulation 1310/97 of June 30, 1997.

48. Merger Regulation Article 3(1).

49. Merger Regulation Article 1(2).

50. Merger Regulation Article 1(3).

51. Merger Regulation Article 3(3).

52. Commission notice on the concept of concentration under Council Regulation 4064/89, para. 8.

53. *ibid.*, para. 30.

54. *ibid.*, paras 21-38.

55. Case COMP/M.1969, *UTC/HONEYWELL/i2/MY AIRCRAFT.COM.*, August 4, 2000.

56. *ibid.*, para. 38.

57. Merger Regulation Article 3(2).

58. *ibid.*, Article 14(1).

59. *ibid.*, Article 14(2).

60. *ibid.*, Article 10(1).

61. *ibid.*, Article 10(2).

62. *ibid.*, Articles 2(2) - 2(3).

63. Case COMP/M.2149, *T-Online/TUI/C&N Touristic* see IP/01/1670.

64. Case COMP/JV.48, *Vodafone/Vivendi/Canal+*, see IP 00/821.

65. See n. 15 above.

66. See n. 55 above.

67. Cases 209/78 etc. *Van Landewyck v. Commission* [1980] E.C.R. 3125, paras. 85–91.

68. *BP Kemi*, [1979] O.J. L 286/32.

69. Case 48/69 *ICI Ltd v. Commission* [1972] E.C.R. 619, at para. 64.

70. See, *e.g.*, *EEC Competition Rules—Guide for Small and Medium Sized Enterprises*, (1983) European Documentation, at p. 17.

71. Case 153/73, *Sacchi* [1974] E.C.R. 409; *Aluminium Imports from Eastern Europe*, [1985] O.J. L 92/1, at 37.

72. *GVL*, [1981] O.J. L 370/49.

73. Case C-73/95, *Viho Europe v. Commission*, judgment of October 24, 1996.

74. Case 36/84, *Remia v. Commission* [1985] E.C.R. 2545, para. 22.

75. Case 8/72, *Cementhandelaren v. Commission* [1972] E.C.R. 977.

76. See, *e.g.*, Cases 19 & 20/74, *Völk v. Vervaecke* [1975] E.C.R. 499.

77. Commission notice on agreements of minor importance which do not fall within the meaning of Article 85(1) of the EC Treaty, [1997] O.J. C 372/13, at para. 9.

78. *ibid.*

79. *ibid.*, at para. 19; and the Annex to the Commission recommendation 96/280, [1996] O.J. L 107/4.

80. Commission notice on agreements of minor importance which do not fall within the meaning of Article 85(1) of the E.C. Treaty, [1997] O.J. C 372/13, at para. 11.

81. *ibid.*, at para. 20.

82. *ibid.*, at paras. 18 and 20.

83. [2001] O.J. C149/18

84. Article 15(2), Regulation 17/62, [1962] Spec. ed. 87 O.J.

85. Article 3, Regulation 17/62, *supra*.

86. *Plessey v. GEC and Siemens* [1990] E.C.C. 384, *Cutsforth v. Mansfield Inns* [1986] 1 C.M.L.R. 764, *Lloyds v. Clementson* [1995] C.L.C. 117, *MTV Europe v. BMG Records* [1997] Eu L.R. 100.

87. It should be noted that, in most cases, the Commission will close its file with regard to a notified agreement following the issuance of an administrative ''comfort letter'' without granting a formal negative clearance or exemption.

88. Article 81(3) of the E.C. Treaty.

89. Commission Regulation No. 3385/94 [1994] O.J. L 377/31.

90. Regulation 17/62, Article 15(5)(a).

91. *John Deere*, [1985] O.J. L35/58.

92. Commission Regulation No. 240/96 of January 31, 1996 on the application of Article 85(3) of the Treaty to certain categories of technology transfer agreements [1996] O.J. L 31/2.

93. Commission Regulation No. 2790/99 of December 22, 1999 on the application of Article 81(3) to categories of vestical agreements and concerted practices [1999] O.J. L336/21.

94. Commission Regulation No. 2659/2000 on the application of Article 81(3) of the Treaty to categories of

research and development agreements, [2000] O.J. l304/7.

95. The Technology Transfer Block Exemption, Article 10(1).
96. *ibid.*, Article 10 (2).
97. *ibid.*, Article 10 (3).
98. *ibid.*, Recital 8.
99. *ibid.*, Article 5(1)(5).
100. *ibid.*, Article 1(1).
101. *ibid.*, Article 10(14).
102. *ibid.*, Article 1(1).
103. *ibid.*, Article 8(1).
104. *ibid,*, Article 10(1).
105. *ibid.*, Article 10(2).
106. *ibid.*, Article 10(3).
107. *ibid.*, Article 10(4).
108. *ibid.*, Article 10(15).
109. *ibid.*, Article 6(1).
110. *ibid.*, Article 6(2).
111. *ibid.*, Article 6(3).
112. *ibid.*, Recital 8.
113. *ibid.*, Article 5(1)(5).
114. *ibid.*, Article 5(1)(4).
115. *ibid.*, Article 5(1)(1).
116. *ibid.*, Article 5(1)(2).
117. *ibid.*, Article 5(1)(3).
118. *ibid.*, Article 1 (1)(1) and 1(1)(2).
119. *ibid.*, Article 3(7).
120. *ibid.*, Article 1(1)(3) to 1(1)(6) and Article 1(2), 1(3) and 1(4).
121. *ibid.*, Article 10(12).
122. *ibid.*, Article 1(2), 1(3) and 1(4).
123. *ibid.*, Article 1(1)(7).
124. *ibid.*, Article 1(1)(8).
125. *ibid.*, Article 2(1)(5).
126. *ibid.*, Article 4(2)(a).
127. *ibid.*, Article3(6).
128. *ibid.*, Article 2(1)(4).
129. *ibid.*, Article 2(1)(1).
130. *ibid.*, Article 2(1)(2).
131. *ibid.*, Article 2(1)(3).
132. *ibid.*, Article 2(1)(10).
133. *ibid.*, Article 3(2).
134. *ibid.*, Article 2(1)(17).
135. *ibid.*, Article 2(1)(9).
136. *ibid.*, Article2(1)(18).
137. *ibid.*, Article3(3).
138. *ibid.*, Article 3(3).
139. *ibid.*, Article 2(1)(8).
140. *ibid.*, Article 3(4).
141. *ibid.*, Article 2(1)(13).
142. *ibid.*, Article 3(5).
143. *ibid.*, Article 2(1)(9).
144. *ibid.*, Article 2(1)(12).
145. See Article 2(12) and Recital 24.
146. *ibid.*, Article 3(1).
147. *ibid.*, Article 2(1)(9).
148. *ibid.*, Article 2(1)(7).
149. *ibid.*, Recital 21.
150. *ibid.*, Article 2(1)(15).
151. *ibid.*, Article 2(1)(16).
152. *ibid.*, Article 4(2)(b).
153. *ibid.*, Article 2(1)(11).
154. Commission Regulation (E.C.) 2790/1999 of December 22, 1999 on the application of Article 81(3) of the Treaty to categories of vertical agreements and concerted practices [1999] O.J. L 336/21, hereafter the "block exemption"
155. Guidelines on Vertical Restraints [2000] O.J. C 291/1. References to paragraph numbers in the Guidelines are referred to below by the letter "G" before the relevant paragraph number.

156. Article 2(1).
157. Article 1(a).
158. G 26.
159. Article 2(3). Recital 3 states in this respect that the agreements falling within the block exemption "include certain ancillary agreements on the assignment or use of intellectual property rights."
160. G 30.
161. Article 2(5).
162. G 38.
163. G 40.
164. Article 3(1).
165. Article 1(c).
166. Article 9(2)(a).
167. Article 9(2)(c).
168. Article 9(2)(d).
169. Article 4.
170. Article 4(a).
171. G 47.
172. G 47.
173. Article 4(b).
174. G 49.
175. G 49.
176. G 50.
177. Article 4(b) first indent.
178. G 50.
179. G 51.
180. G 51.
181. Article 4(b), second, third and fourth indents.
182. Article 4(c).
183. G 53.
184. G 54.
185. Article 4(d).
186. G 56.
187. Article 4(e).
188. G 56.
189. G 57.
190. Article 5.
191. Article 1(b).
192. Article 5(a).
193. Article 5(a).
194. Article 5(b).
195. Article 5 (c).
196. G 61.
197. XXXth Report on competition policy 2000 (Published in conjunction with the General Report on the Activities of the European Union—2000) SEC(2001) 694 final. at point 215.
198. Commission approves selective distribution system for Yves Saint Laurent perfume IP/01/713 Brussels, May 17, 2001.
199. *Coditel SA v. Cine Vog Films SA* [1982] E.C.R. 3381.
200. Commission Decision 89/536 [1989] O.J. L 284/36.
201. "Commission investigation of Internet Registry agreements under E.U. competition rules" IP/99/596 Brussels, July 29, 1999.
202. U.S. Internet Governance dispute resolved to E.U.'s satisfaction see EuroInfoTech Number 0202, October 7, 1999.
203. See, *e.g.* Communication from the Commission to the Council and the European Parliament on The Organisation and Management of the Internet International and European Policy Issues 1998–2000 of April 7, 2000 COM(2000)202 and other documents which can be found at http://europa.eu.int/information_society/topics/telecoms/Internet/organisation/index_en.htm]
204. See section 8.2, p. 21, Communication from the Commission to the Council and the European Parliament on The Organisation and Management of the Internet International and European Policy Issues 1998–2000 of April 7, 2000 COM(2000)202 which can be found at http://europa.eu.int/information_society/topics/telecoms/Internet/organisation/index_en.htm
205. "Commission clears Microsoft's agreements with European Internet Service Providers," IP/99/317 Brussels, May 10, 1999.
206. "Commission approves the Volbroker.com electronic brokerage joint venture between six major banks." IP/00/896 Brussels, July 31, 2000.
207. Commission press release IP/01/1155 of July 31, 2001

208. The German competition authority, the Bundeskartellamt, had already examined the joint venture, however, since it had constituted a merger under German law, due to a provision which deemed control to arise where any party acquired more than 25% of the shares in any company.

209. If full design specifications are standardised as opposed to mere functional specifications, product differentiation and further improvements may be foreclosed.

210. See, *IGR Stereo Television*, 1981 Competition Report, point 96, pp. 63 to 64 (access to the standard) and *X/Open Group*, [1987] O.J. L 35/36 (access to the standards setting group).

211. Indeed, it may be arguable that, at least where the licence imposes cross-licensing obligations that extend not only to the standard owner but also to other licensees, that the standard has become multilateral as a result of the licence, see, *Video Cassette Recorders*.

212. *supra*, n. 2.

213. J. Temple Lang, "European Community Anti-trust Law: Innovation markets and Technology Industries", *Proceedings and Papers of the 23rd Annual Fordham Law Institute*, 519, at 573.

214. See also, *Philips/Matsushita B D2B*, [1991] O.J. C 220/2, (discussed further below) where one of the factors on which the Commission considered relevant to its finding that the D2B arrangements were capable of exemption under Article 81(3) was the availability of alternative standards.

215. Note also that in its letter to ETSI in the case *ETSI Interim IPR Policy*, [1995] O.J. C 76/5 (discussed further below), while rejecting on the facts of the case the allegation of a complainant that ETSI's policy of licensing intellectual property rights included in standards discriminated against persons that were not signatories to ETSI's IPR undertaking, the Commission stated that such discrimination could give rise to action under competition rules. The Commission's case law with regard to collective refusals to deal may also be relevant in this regard, see, *e.g.*, the cases discussed in Bellamy & Child, *European Community Law of Competition*, (4th ed. and 1st supplement), paras. 4-083 *et seq*.

216. *Video Cassette Recorders*, [1978] O.J. L 47/42, *Philips/Matsushita—D2B*, [1991] O.J. C 220/2, and *ETSI Interim IPR Policy*, [1991] O.J. C 76/5.

217. As regards the provision on cross licensing, the Commission objected in particular (i) to the fact that the cross-licences were not simply bilateral (between Philips and the licensee) but extended to all licenses creating a "horizontal network of licences" and to the termination provisions.

218. See, Maurits Dolmans, Restrictions on Innovation: An E.U. Antitrust Approach, *ABA Antitrust L.J.*, Vol. 66, 455, at 478.

219. The conclusion that specifications or depth of standardisation going beyond what is necessary to achieve the objectives of the standard may violate Article 81(1) and may not qualify for exemption is also supported by the Commission's position in *Philips/Matsushita DCC*, which concerned agreements between Philips and five other companies in relation to the development and exploitation of the digital compact cassette (ADCC) system. Under the agreements, the participants pooled their patents relating to DCC systems and Philips was granted the exclusive right to licence the relevant patents on their behalf. Philips was to grant ten year licences to third parties on a non-discriminatory, non-exclusive basis. Licences would be subject to a requirement to incorporate a specified piracy protection system in all DCC equipment. The Commission found that the patent pooling and standardisation of specifications resulting from the requirement to include the anti-piracy system could fall within Article 81(1), but that overall, the arrangements would in any event merit exemption under Article 81(3). A second complaint was brought against ETSI by DVSI which concerned, *inter alia*, an allegation that an ETSI standard had involved a level of specification that was unnecessary, however the Commission rejected the complaint. The complaint is discussed in the article by Maurits Dolmans cited above, at 481 *et seq*.

220. *IGR*, 1984 Competition Report, point 92, p. 77.

221. Commission Press Releases IP/97/676 and IP/97/757. See also *Sony*, Commission Press Release, IP/98/1069.

222. Guidelines on the applicability of Article 81 of the E.C. Treaty to Horizontal Cooperation Agreements, [2001] O.J. C 3/2, paras 159 to 175.

223. Guidelines on the applicability of Article 81 of the E.C. Treaty to horizontal Cooperation Agreements, paras 163–164.

224. Article 15(2), Regulation 17/62, [1962] O.J. Spec. Ed. 87.

225. Article 3, Regulation 17/62, *supra*.

226. Case 322/81, *Michelin v. Commission* [1983] E.C.R. 3461 at 3503.

227. Commission Notice on the definition of relevant market for the purposes of Community competition law, [1997] O.J. C 372/5, at para. 7.

228. *ibid.*, para 20.

229. Commission Notice on the definition of relevant market for the purposes of Community competition law, [1997] O.J. C 372/5 para. 17.

230. *ibid.*, para. 8; see also Case 27/76, *United Brands v. Commission* [1978] E.C.R. 207.

231. Case—179/90, *Port of Genoa* [1991] I E.C.R. 5889 and *Sealink/B & I* [1992] 5 C.M.L.R. 255.

232. Advocate General Warner in Case 77/77 *BP v. Commission* [1978] E.C.R. 1513.

233. Case 85/76, *Hoffman-La Roche v. Commission* [1979] E.C.R. 461.

234. C-62/86, *AKZO v. Commission* [1991] I E.C.R. 3359.

235. See Recital 15 to Regulation 4064/89, the "Merger Regulation", [1990] O.J. L257/13, amended by

Regulation 1310/97, [1997] O.J. L180/1.

236. *Sea Containers v. Stena Sealink*, [1994] O.J. L 15/8.
237. *Irish Continental Group v. CCI Morlaix* [1995] 5 C.M.L.R. 177.
238. *London European—Sabena*, [1988] O.J. L 317/47.
239. See the *Notice on the application of the competition rules to access agreements in the telecoms sector* at point 68.
240. *Societa Italiana Vetro SpA v. Commission* [1992] E.C.R. II-1405; *Almelo v. Energiebedijf Ijsselmij* [1994] E.C.R. I-1477; Case C-96/94 *Centro Servizi Spediporto v. Spedizioni Marittima del Golfo* [1995] ECR I-2883, paras 32 and 33; Joined Cases C-140/94, C-141/94 and C-142/94 *DIP and Others v. Comune di Bassano del Grappa* [1995] ECR I-3257, para. 26; Case C-70/95 *Sodemare and Others v. Regione Lombardia* [1997] ECR I-3395, paras 45 and 46; SIV, para. 358; Cases T-24-26 and 28/93 *Compagnie Maritime Belge Transports, SA*, October 8, [1996] E.C.R. II-1201, para. 62.
241. Cases T-24-26 and 28/93 *Compagnie Maritime Belge Transports, SA and others v. Commission* [1996] E.C.R. II-1201, appeal dismissed Cases C-395 & 396/96P [2000] ECR I 1365 para. 36.
242. In Gencor (Case T-102/96, March 25 [1999] 4 C.M.L.R. 971) the "there is no reason whatsoever in legal or economic terms to exclude from the notion of economic links the relationship of interdependence existing between the parties to a tight oligopoly within which, in a market with the appropriate characteristics, in particular in terms of market concentration, transparency and product homogeneity, those parties are in a position to anticipate one another's behaviour and are therefore strongly encouraged to align their conduct in the market, in particular in such a way as to maximise their joint profits by restricting production with a view to increasing prices."
243. See Commission press release IP/96/1117.
244. Case 27/76, *United Brands v. Commission* [1978] E.C.R. 207, at para. 251 *et seq.* (cost of production); Case 226/84 *British Leyland v. Commission* [1986] E.C.R. 3263 (comparisons with equivalent transactions).
245. Case 30/87, *Corinne Bodson v. Pompes Funebres des Regions Liberees SA* [1998] E.C.R. 2479.
246. *ITT/Belgacom*, Commission Press Release IP/97/292.
247. See press releases IP/96/975 of 4.11.96 and IP/98/430 of 13.5.98.
248. Case C-62/86, *AKZO v. Commission* [1991] ECR I-3359.
249. Philip Areeda and Donald Turner, "Predatory prices and related practices under section 2 of the Sherman Act", Harvard Law Review, Volume 88, No. 4. February 1975, pp 697–773.
250. Article 82(c) of the E.C. Treaty.
251. Case 27/76, *United Brands v. Commission* [1978] E.C.R. 207.
252. OECD round table, CIEC DAFFE/CLP(2000)32, January 23, 2001, p. 101
253. Case C-53/92, P. *Hilti v. Commission* [1944] E.C.R. I-667.
254. See Commission press release IP/97/868.
255. Cases 6 & 7/73, *Commercial Solvents v. Commission* [1974] E.C.R. 223.
256. Case 27/76, *United Brands Co v. Commission* [1978] E.C.R. 207, *BBI/Boosey and Hawkes* [1987] O.J. L 286/36.
257. Cases C-241/91 P and C-242/91, *RTE and ITP v. Commission* [1995] E.C.R. I-743.
258. Case T-504/93, *Tiercé Ladbroke v. Commission*, judgment of June 12, 1997.
259. Case C-7/97, *Oscar Bronner GmbH & Co. KG v. Mediaprint Zeitungs- und Zeitschriftenverlag GmbH & Co. KG, Mediaprint Zeitungsvertriebsgesellschaft mbH & Co. KG, Mediaprint Anzeigengesellschaft mbH & Co. KG*, judgment of May 28, 1998
260. Case T-198/98, *Micro Leader Business v. Commission*, judgment of December 16, 1999
261. Commission imposes interim measures on IMS HEALTH in Germany Commission Press Release IP/01/941, July 3, 2001.
262. See Fin Lomholt, "The 1984 IBM Undertaking, Commission's monitoring and practical effects," *Competition Policy Newsletter*, 1998 Number 3, p. 7
263. *ibid.*, p. 8.
264. *ibid.*, p. 8.
265. IP/01/1232 Brussels, August 30, 2001.
266. *ibid.*
267. *ibid.*
268. Section 2(3) of the 1998 Act provides that the Chapter I prohibition applies only if "the agreement, decision or practice is, or is intended to be, implemented in the United Kingdom."
269. See above.
270. Section 2 also includes a requirement that there be an effect on trade in the United Kingdom, but this appears to be superfluous in the light of the requirements for an effect on competition in the United Kingdom and implementation in the United Kingdom.
271. See above.
272. Competition Act 1998 (Land and Vertical Agreements) Exclusion order 2000 (S.I. 2000 No. 310).
273. Office of Fair Trading Guideline on Vertical Agreements and Restraints OFT 419
274. Schedule 1, para. 1(1) of the 1998 Act
275. Schedule 1, para. 6 of the 1998 Act
276. Section 10 of the 1998 Competition Act
277. Section 6 of the 1998 Competition Act
278. www.oft.gov.uk/html/comp-act/technical_guidelines/index.html#guidelines

279. S.I. 2000 No. 262.
280. Chancery Division Judgment HC 0005478 of April 5, 2001
281. www.oft.gov.uk/html/comp-act/case_register/bt.pdf

Technical Glossary

ActiveX	See **Java**
Access provider	A person who provides others with access to the Internet.
Address, IP	See **IP address**
ADSL	Asymmetric Digital Subscriber Line. A method of compressing data to provide a high **bandwidth** connection in one direction on ordinary copper telephone lines. The fact that there is only low bandwidth in the opposite direction is not a hindrance if that is used for user commands and requests.
Appropriate Use Policy	Some non-commercial or government-funded networks connected to the Internet prohibit some types of traffic across their networks. The rules of such a network are its Appropriate Use Policy.
Bandwidth	A term used to describe the capacity of a communications link.
Broadband	High **bandwidth** connection, typically based on optical fibre infrastructure, suitable for transmitting video and other such high volume data.
Cache	An electronic store of data copied from elsewhere; also the function of providing a cache. Caches come in many forms. They may be large scale, more or less permanent collections of, typically, Web pages. These reduce demands on network communications capacity by providing access to the data locally. Or they may be smaller, ever changing, collections of data maintained for similar reasons and changing in response to user demand. On the smallest scale a **Web browser** may cache pages and graphics on the hard disk of the user's personal computer in order to speed up access to **Web sites**.
CGI	Common Gateway Interface. A program standard that enables **HTTP** requests to be executed by internal programs such as databases, and the results to be passed back to the external user.

Client	The client, in the context of the Internet, is the user's computer (or strictly speaking, the browser or similar software on the user's computer). The client complements the **server**, with which it communicates. Web designers may make design decisions as to whether processing takes place at the client or the **server**. *cf.* **DHTML**.
Conduit	A term increasingly used to describe the function of providing telecommunications links. A conduit should be contrasted, in particular, with the function of a **host**.
DHTML	Dynamic **HTML**. Use of DHTML allows changes to appear on a Web page, for instance in response to a mouse movement over a menu, processed entirely within the user's computer. This **client**-side approach, rather than processing the changes on the **server**, means that the changes occur without the need for the server to deliver a new page. DHTML is commonly implemented using a language such as **JavaScript**, in combination with ordinary **HTML** and features such as Cascading Style Sheets.
Digital signature	A type of **electronic signature** utilising technology designed to ensure that the user of the signature and the document intended to be signed can reliably and uniquely be identified.
Domain name	A name (*e.g.* twobirds.com) allocated to an entity with an address on a network. On the Internet a domain name corresponds to an entity with an **IP address**.
Download	The act of retrieving data from a remote site across a communications link to the user's computer. Download is sometimes used to mean retrieving data to the computer's RAM, and sometimes to mean retrieving the data and storing it on the computer's hard disk.
DNS	Domain Name Server. A computer which maintains a list of **domain names** and corresponding **IP addresses**. On receipt of a request from another computer it will deliver the **IP address** corresponding to the requested domain name if it has an authoritative list for that domain name. Otherwise it will refer to the request elsewhere in the DNS system until a computer is found which can give an authoritative response.
EDI	Electronic Data Interchange. A generic description applied to systems whereby parties create legal and technical arrangements governing the exchange of electronic data between them. The data is typically structured rather than free form. EDI arrangements are appropriate where parties have a continuing relationship with each other.
Electronic signature	A signature in electronic form.
Extranet	An **intranet** to which selected outsiders, such as customers or suppliers, are allowed access.

Firewall	A device situated at the entry to a computer network, designed to prevent unauthorised data entering the network.
Ftp	File transfer protocol. The most common means of transmitting a file (which could be a program or data file) across the Internet.
GII	Global Information Infrastructure. A term formerly used by American politicians to describe their vision of a world-wide **information superhighway**.
Host	In the context of the Internet, a host is a computer which stores information in more than transient form and makes it available across the Internet. The stored data may vary from **Usenet newsgroups**, to **Web sites**, to **domain name** databases, to **ftp** resources and many other types. "Host" is often also used to mean the person who owns and operates the computer and who thus carries out the host function. A host should be contrasted, in particular, with a **conduit**.
HTML	HyperText Markup Language. A system of additions to plain text which act as instructions to **Web browsers** or other HTML-compliant programs. The **browser** acting on the instructions will convert the marked up text into formatted pages including **hypertext** links.
HTTP	HyperText Transmission Protocol. The Internet protocol which enables the transmission of an **HTML** document across the Internet.
Hypertext	A hypertext document includes highlighted text which, when clicked upon with a mouse, causes the user to jump to another place in the same document, to another document on the same computer, or (if **HTML** is used on a network with **HTTP**-compliant computers), to a document on another computer altogether. On the Internet hypertext links can exist between documents on computers anywhere in the world.
IANA	The Internet Assigned Numbers Authority (now part of **ICANN**).
ICANN	The Internet Corporation for Assigned Names and Numbers. The body now charged with responsibility for co-ordinating policy on Internet domain name and number allocation.
Information Superhighway	A term formerly used, mainly by politicians, to describe their vision of a pervasive, probably **broadband**, data network. See also **GII**.
Internet Service Provider	An Internet Service Provider is a generic term which covers a wide variety of persons providing services relating to the Internet. At a minimum an **ISP** will be an **access provider**. It will provide **DNS** services and will probably host **newsgroups** and provide Web hosting services. It may own or lease

its own physical network infrastructure, or it may simply connect up to the network of a larger **ISP**. It may provide Web design services. Some ISPs, especially those which originated as proprietary on-line services, may source and publicise their own content, making it available as Web pages, as e-mail services or as content "pushed" across the network to the subscriber's Web browser or other Internet device.

Intranet
An internal network based on Internet protocols. An intranet may be geographically dispersed, for instance across different members of a group of companies, but still be insulated by **firewalls** from the outside world.

IP address
The address of an device on a **TCP/IP** network understood by other computers on the network. The address takes the form 194.72.244.100, where each component of the IP address is a number below 256. On the Internet the authority for allocating IP addresses is **IANA**, the Internet Assigned Numbers Authority.

ISDN
Integrated Services Digital Network. A telephony standard designed to deliver medium **bandwidth** digital voice and data. After a slow start, ISDN become more popular for Internet connections where more than the capacity of a dial-up modem connection is required but the expense of a leased line connection cannot be justified. It is now likely to be overtaken by **ADSL** for domestic connections.

ISP
Internet Service Provider

Java
A programming language originating from Sun Microsystems designed to be usable across many different types of computer and operating system. Many **Web sites** now employ small programs ("applets") written in Java, which are downloaded to the user's computer when he accesses the site. These applets may perform functions such as animating parts of the **Web site**, or providing more sophisticated user interfaces than can readily be built using **HTML**. Another technology capable of performing similar functions on Windows-based systems is ActiveX from Microsoft.

JavaScript
A language in which a Web page can be written and which a Web browser will interpret to display the page. It is a sophisticated alternative to **HTML**, but which unlike **Java** does not require the user's computer to download a separate program from the **Web site**.

Listserver
A **mailing list**

Mailing list
An e-mail based equivalent of a **newsgroup**, in which contributions are sent by e-mail to a central list manager, which forwards them to all subscribers to the mailing list.

Metatag	A keyword within the META section of a Web page. Although not visible to the user in normal use, metatags may be viewed with a browser in "Source" mode.
Mirror site	A site providing a duplicate of the original site, or part of it. Software companies who provide programs for users to download often arrange for mirror sites around the world, both to reduce the demand on the original site and to reduce the strain on network **bandwidth**. A person whose site is being blocked by the authorities may sometimes respond by asking other sites to mirror the content.
Newsgroup	A public discussion forum on the Internet, named according to its intended content (*e.g.* "alt.uk.legal"). Access to newsgroups was originally provided by special news software, but typically the necessary facilities are now included in Web browsers. Although newsgroups represent only one type of content on the Internet (**Web sites** and **ftp** resources are others), they have attracted disproportionate publicity. This is because of the explicit names of and notoriety of type of content posted to some newsgroups.
Peering agreement	An agreement between two or more access providers under which they will exchange Internet traffic across a connection between their networks. Peering agreements differ from conventional telephony interconnect or transit agreements, which charge for network access on a metered traffic basis. A true peering agreement is on a free exchange basis.
POP	Point of Presence. A point at which a user can connect to an **ISP**'s network and thereby gain access to the Internet.
Post	Send a public message ("article") to a **newsgroup**.
Public key encryption	A cryptographic technique that relies on asymmetric mathematical algorithms. So while one cryptographic key (the public key) can easily be derived from the other (the private key), the reverse cannot be achieved without unfeasibly large amounts of computing power (so long as the key is sufficiently long). Used to create **digital signatures**.
Router	A specially designed computer which examines incoming **TCP/IP** data packets for destination information and relays the packets to the next appropriate router on the way to the destination. If the link to the next most appropriate router is unavailable, the router will choose another link. This ability was originally a fundamental part of the design of the Internet, which was built to withstand damage to components of the network. The same ability now makes it very difficult to isolate parts of the network and gave rise to John Gilmore's aphorism "the Internet treats censorship as damage and routes around it".

Search engine	A **Web site** that indexes other **Web sites** and allows users to search their contents. A search engine typically creates a full text index of other **Web sites** and also presents a short contextual abstract of the target page.
Server	Strictly, a server is a piece of software which delivers data from the computer on which it resides across the network in response to requests from elsewhere. Thus a **Web** server delivers **Web** pages, a **domain name** server delivers **IP addresses** in response to **domain name** requests, and so on. The term server is often used to denote the computer itself as well as the software.
Spider	A program that visits **Web sites** in sequence according to a pre-determined algorithm, collecting information from the sites. Search engines employ spiders to index **Web sites**. Also known as **Web crawlers**.
TCP	Transmission Control Protocol. See **TCP/IP**.
TCP/IP	Transmission Control Protocol/Internet Protocol. The set of standards that govern how computers communicate with each other across the Internet. The Internet Protocol is the lower-level aspect of TCP/IP, setting out how devices on a network recognise each other by means of an **IP address** and communicate and route using data packets. TCP governs how data messages are broken up into IP packets and reassembled and verified at the destination. Although TCP is used to control most messaging across an IP network, alternatives such as **UDP** can also be used.
UDP	**User Datagram Protocol**.
User Datagram Protocol	An alternative messaging protocol to **TCP**. Because UDP, unlike TCP, does not contain its own verification mechanism it is faster than TCP and thus more suited to the transmission of real-time messages.
Usenet	Usenet is a method of distributing postings to **newsgroups**. It does not in fact require the Internet in order to function. Usenet was originally a method of distributing news from one computer to another, whereby each computer periodically dialled up another in the Usenet chain and updated its own **newsgroups** from that computer. The computers did not have to use Internet protocols when communicating with each other. Usenet is now mostly distributed by transmissions from computer to computer across the Internet, so that that Usenet is now generally perceived to be part of the Internet.
URL	Uniform Resource Locator. The address of a **Web site** *e.g.* "http://www.twobirds.com", or of a page within a **Web site**.
Web	See **World Wide Web**

Web browser	**Client** software used to access and read Web pages. The best known browsers are Netscape and Internet Explorer.
Web crawler	See **Spider**.
Web site	A cohesive collection of Web pages, usually maintained by or on behalf one entity (e.g. an individual or a company), stored on a **host**.
World Wide Web	The Web is the global collection of **hypertext** linked **HTML** pages linked which a user equipped with a Web browser can view and browse.

Index

Abuse of dominant position (E.C. law)
  abuse
    discriminatory pricing, 14–205
    excessive pricing, 14–203
    exclusive purchasing, 14–207
    exclusive rights to content, 14–202
    introduction, 14–201
    loyalty bonus, 14–207
    predatory pricing, 14–204
    refusal to supply, 14–208—14–214
    tying, 14–206
  Commission decisions, 14–215—14–218
  dominance
    essential facility, 14–199—14–200
    geographic market, 14–196
    introduction, 14–193
    measuring economic strength, 14–197—14–198
    product market, 14–194—14–195
  introduction, 14–192
Abuse of dominant position (U.K. law)
  abuse
    discriminatory pricing, 14–247
    excessive prices, 14–246
    generally, 14–245
    notification, 14–251
    predatory pricing, 14–248
    refusal to supply, 14–250
    vertical restraints, 14–249
  dominant position
    assessment, 14–243—14–244
    generally, 14–241
    relevant market, 14–242
  introduction, 14–240
Academic mailing list
  defamation, and, 4–033
Acceptance of offers
  delay before receipt, 10–055
  despatch of acceptance, 10–054
  electronic agents, 10–060—10–061
  generally, 10–049—10–051
  minimising risks, 10–058
  normal rules, 10–056—10–057
  receipt of electronic communication, 10–052—10–053
  voice link communication, 10–059

Access agreements
  allocation of resources, 9–039
  anti-spamming clause, 9–039
  corporate users, 9–038
  domestic users, 9–036—9–037
  introduction, 9–035
  telephony services, 9–040
Access providers
  defamation, and, 4–008
  generally, 1–022—1–024
Access rights
  end-users, to, 8–031—8–032
  generally, 8–024
  interconnection, 8–025—8–027
  introduction, 8–008—8–010
  peering, 8–028—8–030
Access to workplace communications
  Data Protection Act
    draft Code of Practice, 5–104—5–109
    generally, 5–103
    human rights, and, 5–117—5–118
  Human Rights Act
    data protection Code of Practice, 5–117—5–118
    displacing expectation of privacy, 5–114—5–116
    Lawful Business Practice Regulations, 5–117—5–118
    public bodies, 5–110—5–112
    reasonable expectation of privacy, 5–113
  introduction, 5–073
  Lawful Business Practice Regulations
    authorised conduct, 5–102
    generally, 5–097
    human rights, and, 5–117—5–118
    preconditions to interception, 5–098—5–101
  Regulation of Investigatory Powers Act
    definitions, 5–075—5–077
    e-mail, 5–085
    ephemeral communications, 5–085
    generally, 5–074
    interception in course of transmission, 5–078—5–079
    lawful authority, 5–095—5–096
    purpose of interception, 5–080
    recipient's position, 5–081—5–084

Access to workplace communications—*contd*
  Regulation of Investigatory Powers Act—*contd*
    recipients, 5–086—5–087
    voicemail, 5–085
  Telecommunications Data Protection Directive, 5–088—5–094
Adaptation
  copyright infringement, and, 2–071
Administrators
  generally, 1–020—1–021
Adoption advertising
  content liability, and, 5–047
ADSL
  broadband networks, and, 1–028
  meaning, 1–010
Advanced electronic signatures
  generally, 10–090—10–093
Advertising
  competition law, and, 14–014
  content liability, and
    adoption, 5–047
    tobacco, 5–048—5–049
  contracts
    generally, 9–027—9–028
    hypertext links, 9–032
    nature of rights, 9–029
    ownership of IPR, 9–033
    positioning, 9–030
    promotion obligations, 9–031
    size, 9–030
    visitor information, 9–034
  electronic contracts, and, 10–044
  regulation of activities, and
    generally, 12–122—12–125
    junk e-mail, 12–126—12–127
American Registry for Internet Numbers
  background, 1–021
Anti-competitive practices (E.C. law)
  block exemptions
    introduction, 14–077
    technology transfer, 14–078—14–114
    vertical agreements, 14–115—14–141
  Commission decisions
    B2B exchanges, 14–158—14–170
    Internet Registry agreements, 14–151—14–157
  effect, 14–073
  exemptions
    block, 14–077—14–141
    individual, 14–075—14–076
    introduction, 14–074
  IPR licences
    development contracts, 14–150
    end-users, 14–149
    generally, 14–146—14–148
  meaning
    agreements, 14–065
    appreciable effect, 14–069—14–072
    between undertakings, 14–066
    concerted practices, 14–065
    effect on trade, 14–067
    introduction, 14–064
    prevents, restricts or distorts competition, 14–068
  online distribution, 14–142—14–145
  standardisation agreements
    conditions in licences, 14–187—14–188

Anti-competitive practices (E.C. law)—*contd*
  standardisation agreements—*contd*
    effects, 14–172—14–175
    foreclosure effects, 14–178—14–181
    Guidelines, 14–189—14–191
    introduction, 14–171
    multilateral standards, 14–176—14–177
    restrictions between users, 14–182—14–186
    unilateral standards, 14–176—14–177
  technology transfer exemption
    exclusions, 14–086—14–091
    introduction, 14–078—14–079
    licence terms, 14–092
    own use licence, 14–096
    scope, 14–083—14–085
    specific clauses, 14–097—14–114
    structure, 14–080—14–082
    territorial restrictions, 14–093—14–094
    use of trade mark, 14–095
  vertical agreements exemption
    copyright, 14–124
    exclusion, 14–118—14–122
    "hardcore" restrictions, 14–128—14–137
    introduction, 14–115
    market share, 14–125—14–127
    meaning, 14–116—14–117
    non-competition restrictions, 14–138—14–141
    trade marks, 14–123
Anti-competitive practices (U.K. law)
  effect, 14–231
  exclusions
    introduction, 14–232
    mergers, 14–234
    vertical agreements, 14–233
  exemption
    block, 14–237
    introduction, 14–235
    parallel, 14–236
  meaning
    agreements, 14–226
    appreciable effect, 14–230
    concerted practices, 14–226
    introduction, 14–225
    prevents, restricts or distorts competition, 14–228
    restriction of competition, 14–229
    undertakings, 14–227
  notification requirements
    exemption, for, 14–238
    guidance, for, 14–239
  vertical agreements, 14–233
Anti-spamming clauses
  access agreements, and, 9–039
Anton Piller order
  enforcement of IPR, and, 6–003
APNIC
  IP addresses, and, 1–021
Applicable law
  evidence of transaction, and, 10–126—10–127
  foreign rules
    Belgium, 6–134—6–139
    France, 6–168—6–174
    Japan, 6–251—6–259
    Netherlands, 6–267—6–273
  generally, 10–038—10–041

Application service providers
  telecommunications regulation, and, 8–001
Appropriate Use Policies
  meaning, 1–007
ARIN
  IP addresses, and, 1–021
Armed forces
  data protection, and, 7–066
Art exhibitions
  copyright, and, 2–032
  data protection, and, 7–058—7–054
Artistic works
  copyright, and, 2–042
ASPs
  telecommunications regulation, and, 8–001
Asymmetric Digital Subscriber Line
  broadband networks, and, 1–028
  meaning, 1–010
Audio player software
  Commission decisions, 14–058—14–059
  generally, 14–025
Australia
  content liability, 6–123—6–125
  copyright, 6–109—6–113
  defamation, 6–114—6–117
  disclaimers, 6–108
  domain names
    administrators, 3–085
    disputes, 3–089—3–091
    passing off , 3–090
    registration, 3–086—3–088
  false representations, 6–118—6–122
  misleading information, 6–118—6–122
  passing off, 6–106—6–107
  trade marks, 6–102—6–105
  unauthorised access, 6–126—6–128
  unauthorised modification, 6–126—6–128
  regulation activities, 12–016
Authorisation
  copyright, and, 2–059—2–060
Authors
  defamation, and, 4–023—4–024
Authorship
  copyright, and, 2–045
Automated decision-taking
  data protection, and, 7–095—7–097

Bandwidth
  meaning, 1–010
  website hosting contracts, and, 9–021
Belgium
  applicable law, 6–134—6–139
  content liability, 6–142—6–144
  copyright, 6–145—6–146
  defamation, 6–140—6–141
  domain names
    administrators, 3–092
    disputes, 3–095—3–099
    registration, 3–093—3–094
  governing law, 6–134—6–139
  jurisdiction, 6–129—6–133
  trade marks, 6–147
Black list
  technology transfer exemption, and, 14–081

Block exemptions
  introduction, 14–077
  technology transfer
    exclusions, 14–086—14–091
    introduction, 14–078—14–079
    licence terms, 14–092
    own use licence, 14–096
    scope, 14–083—14–085
    specific clauses, 14–097—14–114
    structure, 14–080—14–082
    territorial restrictions, 14–093—14–094
    use of trade mark, 14–095
  vertical agreements
    copyright, 14–124
    exclusion, 14–118—14–122
    "hardcore" restrictions, 14–128—14–137
    introduction, 14–115
    market share, 14–125—14–127
    meaning, 14–116—14–117
    non-competition restrictions, 14–138—14–141
    trade marks, 14–123
Books
  competition law, and, 14–017
Boundary markers
  content liability, and, 5–025—5–026
Branding
  trade marks, and, 3–006—3–007
Broadband networks
  competition law, and
    access, 14–010
    content, 14–024
  Internet, and, 1–028—1–030
Broadcasting
  copyright infringement, and, 2–068—2–070
  regulation
    and see below
    background, 8–033
    conclusion, 8–050—8–051
    future issues, 8–048—8–049
    licensing, 8–034—8–047
Broadcasting regulation
  background, 8–033
  conclusion, 8–050—8–051
  future issues, 8–048—8–049
  Internet radio services, 8–045
  licensable programme services
    generally, 8–034—8–037
    interactive services, 8–042
    ITC Codes, 8–040—8–041
    licences, 8–038—8–039
  licensable sound programme services, 8–043—8–044
  local delivery services, 8–046—8–047
Broadcasts
  copyright, and, 2–042
Browsers
  competition law, and, 14–011
Brussels Convention state, defendant domiciled in
  confidential information, 6–056
  consumer contracts, 6–0587—6–063
  contract, 6–031
  copyright, 6–054
  defamation, 6–037—6–047
  general rule, 6–027
  introduction, 6–026

Brussels Convention state, defendant domiciled in—
  contd
    IPR, 6–030
    jurisdiction agreements, 6–028—6–029
    negligent misstatement, 6–053
    patents, 6–055
    passing off, 6–048—6–052
    tort, 6–032—6–036
    trade marks, 6–048—6–052
B2B
  meaning, 1–014
B2B exchanges
  characteristics, 14–037—14–042
  Commission decisions, 14–158—14–170
  generally, 14–026—14–033
B2C
  meaning, 1–014
B2C on-line sales
  audio player software, 14–025
  books, 14–017
  broadband content, 14–024
  characteristics, 14–037—14–042
  computer games, 14–023
  introduction, 14–016
  medical services, 14–022
  music, 14–019—14–021
  travel agencies, 14–018
Building the site, contracts for
  creation, 9–007
  initial design, 9–006
  introduction, 9–005
  ownership of IPR
    allocation of rights, 9–013
    domain name, 9–017
    dynamic content and code, 9–011—9–012
    introduction, 9–009
    physical materials, 9–015
    proprietary software, 9–014
    static content and code, 9–010
    third party software, 9–016
  specification, 9–006
  testing, 9–008
Burma
  regulation of activities, and, 12–024
Business method patents
  Europe, 2–159—2–161
  U.S., 2–141—2–145
Business profits
  taxation, and, 13–062—13–063
Business-to-business
  meaning, 1–014
Business-to-consumer
  meaning, 1–014

Cable programme service
  copyright infringement, and, 2–068—2–070
  linking, and, 2–078—2–079
Cable programmes
  copyright, and, 2–042
Caches
  content liability, and, 5–043—5–044
  liability for third party material, and, 2–111—
    2–113
Canada
  copyright, 6–156—6–157

Canada—*contd*
  domain names
    administrators, 3–102
    disputes, 3–107—3–118
    registration, 3–102—3–106
  jurisdiction, 6–148—6–154
  misleading information, 6–155
  trade marks, 6–158
Cancellation right
  Distance Selling Directive, and, 10–024—10–025
Caricatures
  copyright, and, 2–033
Cash
  payment mechanisms, and, 11–005
ccTLDs
  domain names, and, 3–021
Certification-service providers
  advanced signatures, 10–093
  data protection, 10–097
  introduction, 10–085
  liability, 10–094—10–096
  qualified certificates, 10–091
Charge cards
  abuse
    alteration of basic principle, 11–043
    basic principle, 11–041
    exceptions to basic principle, 11–042
    introduction, 11–040
    retailer risk, 11–044
    transmission over Internet, 11–045
  advantages
    card issuer/supplier liability, 11–012—11–013
    international acceptance, 11–014
    introduction, 11–011
    settlement period, 11–015
  disadvantages
    costs, 11–020—11–021
    introduction, 11–016
    market penetration, 11–022
    privacy, 11–023
    security, 11–017—11–019
    transaction costs, 11–020—11–021
  generally, 11–009—11–010
Chat rooms
  pornography, and, 12–091
Cheque
  payment mechanisms, and, 11–006
Child pornography
  cache copies, 12–077
  downloading, 12–075—12–076
  introduction, 12–073—12–074
  linking, 12–082—12–085
  making, 12–075—12–076
  screen images, 12–078—12–081
China
  regulation of activities, and, 12–025
Class injunction
  enforcement of IPR, and, 6–003
Collateral contracts
  electronic contracts, and, 10–046
Communication policies
  generally, 5–071—5–072
  introduction, 5–059
Communication to the public, right of
  copyright, and, 2–015

Compensation
  data protection, and, 7–098
Competition Commission
  fines, 14–257—14–258
  generally, 14–253
  interim measures, 14–256
  investigatory powers, 14–254—14–255
Competition law
  E.C. law
    and see below
      abuse of dominant position, 14–192—14–218
      anti-competitive practices, 14–064—14–191
      Merger Regulation, 14–043—14–063
      relevant markets, 14–002—14–042
    introduction, 14–001
    telecommunications regulation, and, 8–011
  U.K. law
    and see below
      Competition Act, 14–223—14–264
      Fair Trading Act, 14–220—14–222
      introduction, 14–219
Competition law (E.C. law)
  abuse of dominant position (Art. 82)
    and see Abuse of dominant position
    abuse, 14–201—14–214
    Commission decisions, 14–215—14–218
    dominance, 14–193—14–200
    introduction, 14–192
  access markets
    advertising, 14–014
    broadband access, 14–010
    browsers, 14–011
    consumer access, 14–009—14–015
    gateways, 14–013
    infrastructure, 14–003—14–005
    internet connectivity services, 14–006—14–008
    narrow-band access, 14–009
    portals, 14–013
    search engines, 14–012
    website production, 14–015
    websites, 14–013
  advertising, 14–014
  anti-competitive practices (Art. 81)
    and see Anti-competitive practices
    Commission decisions, 14–151—14–170
    effect, 14–073
    exemptions, 14–074—14–141
    introduction, 14–064—14–072
    IPR licences, 14–146—14–150
    online distribution, 14–142—14–145
    standardisation agreements, 14–171—14–191
  audio player software
    Commission decisions, 14–058—14–059
    generally, 14–025
  books, 14–017
  broadband
    access, 14–010
    content, 14–024
  browsers, 14–011
  B2B markets
    characteristics, 14–037—14–042
    generally, 14–026—14–033
  B2C on-line sales
    audio player software, 14–025
    books, 14–017

Competition law (E.C. law)—*contd*
  B2C on-line sales—*contd*
    broadband content, 14–024
    characteristics, 14–037—14–042
    computer games, 14–023
    introduction, 14–016
    medical services, 14–022
    music, 14–019—14–021
    travel agencies, 14–018
  characteristics of markets
    durability, 14–038
    dynamic competition, 14–040
    leapfrogging, 14–039
    low production costs, 14–037
    network effects, 14–041
    "tippy" markets, 14–042
  computer games, 14–023
  gateways, 14–013
  geographic market, 14–034—14–036
  internet connectivity services
    Commission decisions, 14–056—14–057
    generally, 14–006—14–008
  medical services, 14–022
  Merger Regulation
    assessment by Commission, 14–054
    decisions by Commission, 14–055—14–063
    full function, 14–051
    introduction, 14–043—14–044
    joint control, 14–048—14–050
    notification requirements, 14–052—14–053
    thresholds, 14–045—14–047
  music
    Commission decisions, 14–058—14–059
    generally, 14–019—14–021
  portals
    Commission decisions, 14–061—14–062
    generally, 14–013
  relevant markets
    access markets, 14–003—14–015
    B2B markets, 14–026—14–033
    B2C products and services, 14–016—14–025
    characteristics, 14–037—14–042
    geographic market, 14–034—14–036
    introduction, 14–002
  search engines, 14–012
  "tippy" markets, 14–042
  travel agencies
    Commission decisions, 14–060
    generally, 14–018
  website production, 14–015
  websites, 14–013
Competition law (U.K. law)
  abuse of dominant position
    abuse, 14–245—14–2561
    dominant position, 14–241—14–244
    introduction, 14–240
  anti-competitive practices
    effect, 14–231
    exclusions, 14–232—14–233
    exemption, 14–234—14–239
    introduction, 14–225—14–230
  Competition Act
    abuse of dominant position, 14–240—14–251
    anti-competitive practices, 14–225—14–239
    decisions, 14–262—14–264

Competition law (U.K. law)—*contd*
  Competition Act—*contd*
    enforcement agencies, 14–252—14–258
    introduction, 14–223—14–224
    small agreements, 14–259
    third party enforcement, 14–260
    transitional provisions, 14–261
  conduct of minor importance, 14–259
  enforcement agencies
    Competition Commission, 14–253
    directions to terminate, 14–257
    Director General of Fair Trading, 14–252
    fines, 14–257—14–258
    interim measures, 14–256
    investigatory powers, 14–254—14–255
    Office of Fair Trading, 14–252
  Fair Trading Act, 14–220—14–222
  introduction, 14–219
  mergers, 14–220—14–222
  small agreements, 14–259
Compilations
  copyright, and, 2–042
Computer games
  competition law, and, 14–023
Computer misuse
  access to computer material, 12–151—12–152
  intent to commit offences, 12–153
  introduction, 12–150
  modification of computer material, 12–154—12–155
Computer programs
  copyright, and, 2–042
Conduct of minor importance
  competition law, and, 14–259
Confidential information
  generally, 2–119
  industrial espionage, 2–131—2–132
  jurisdiction, and, 6–056
  misuse on Internet, 2–134—2–137
  obligation of confidence
    contract, under, 2–123
    duration, 2–128
    employment contract, under, 2–124—2–125
    equity, in, 2–127
    generally, 2–122
    meaning, 2–121
    professional relationships, from, 2–126
  protectable information, 2–120
  remedies, 2–129—2–130
  theft, 2–131—2–132
  transmission by Internet, 2–133
Confidential references
  data protection, and, 7–064
Consideration
  electronic contracts, and, 10–063
Consumer contracts
  jurisdiction, and, 6–021—6–022, 6–058—6–063
Contempt of court
  criminal proceedings, 12–093—12–096
  international aspects, 12–097
  introduction, 12–092
  third party actions, 12–098—12–099
Content blocking
  generally, 12–040
Content liability
  boundary markers, 5–025—5–026

Content liability—*contd*
  contractual terms, 5–021—5–023
  disclaimers, 5–024
  Electronic Commerce Directive
    caching, 5–043—5–044
    exclusions, 5–037
    hosting, 5–041—5–042
    information society services, 5–035—5–036
    introduction, 5–034
    mere conduits, 5–038—5–040
    monitoring, 5–045
  employers, and
    access to workplace communications, 5–073—5–117
    criminal liability, 5–062
    direct liability, 5–063—5–065
    introduction, 5–056—5–059
    personal e-mail, 5–062
    policies, 5–071—5–072
    tribunal decisions, 5–066—5–070
    vicarious liability, 5–061
  foreign rules
    Australia, 6–123—6–125
    Belgium, 6–142—6–144
    Finland, 6–162
    France, 6–178—6–180
    Israel, 6–235—6–236
    New Zealand, 6–280—6–283
    Sweden, 6–313
    Switzerland, 6–325—6–328
  future issues
    adoption advertising, 5–047
    identity of convicts, 5–050—5–055
    introduction, 5–046
    tobacco advertising, 5–048—5–049
  incorrect information
    negligence, 5–002—5–010
    strict liability, 5–011
    viruses, 5–012
  introduction, 5–001
  negligence
    duty of care, 5–004
    economic loss, 5–008—5–010
    general principles, 5–002—5–003
    interactivity, 5–005
    mass advice, 5–006—5–007
    physical damage, 5–008—5–010
    viruses, 5–013—5–015
  on-line intermediaries, of
    Electronic Commerce Directive, 5–034—5–045
    future issues, 5–046—5–052
    introduction, 5–033
  product liability, 5–011
  restrictions on
    boundary markers, 5–025—5–026
    consumer protection legislation, 5–029—5–031
    contractual terms, 5–021—5–023
    disclaimers, 5–024
    territory statements, 5–027—5–028
    unilateral notices, 5–021—5–023
  territory statements, 5–027—5–028
  unilateral notices, 5–021—5–023
  viruses
    introduction, 5–012
    negligence, 5–013—5–015

Content liability—*contd*
  viruses—*contd*
    Rylands v. Fletcher, 5–016—5–019
    trespass, 5–020
Content, protection of
  generally, 5–032
Content providers
  generally, 1–011—1–015
Contracts
  access to Internet, for
    allocation of resources, 9–039
    anti-spamming clause, 9–039
    corporate users, 9–038
    domestic users, 9–036—9–037
    introduction, 9–035
    telephony services, 9–040
  advertising, for
    generally, 9–027—9–028
    hypertext links, 9–032
    nature of rights, 9–029
    ownership of IPR, 9–033
    positioning, 9–030
    promotion obligations, 9–031
    size, 9–030
    visitor information, 9–034
  building the site, for
    creation, 9–007
    initial design, 9–006
    introduction, 9–005
    ownership of IPR, 9–009—9–017
    specification, 9–006
    testing, 9–008
  creation of website, for
    building the site, 9–005—9–017
    hosting the site, 9–018—9–026
    introduction, 9–002
    site designer, 9–003—9–004
  electronic
    and see Electronic contracts
    content, 10–006
    Distance Selling Directive, 10–013—10–025
    Electronic Commerce Directive, 10–026—10–036
    electronic signatures, 10–071—10–100
    evidence, 10–125—10–150
    exclusions, 10–007—10–012
    formalities, 10–068—10–070
    formation, 10–042—10–067
    international issues, 10–037—10–041
    introduction, 10–001—10–005
    limitations, 10–007—10–012
    transactions legislation, 10–101—10–125
  hosting the site, for
    access to site, 9–021—9–022
    introduction, 9–018
    limitation of liability, 9–024—9–025
    reports and information, 9–023
    risk sharing, 9–026
    storage of data, 9–019—9–020
  introduction, 9–001
  jurisdiction, and, 6–031
  peering, for, 9–041
  site designer, with, 9–003—9–004
  sponsorship, for
    generally, 9–027—9–028

Contracts—*contd*
  sponsorship, for—*contd*
    hypertext links, 9–032
    nature of rights, 9–029
    ownership of IPR, 9–033
    positioning, 9–030
    promotion obligations, 9–031
    size, 9–030
    visitor information, 9–034
Contractual terms
  content liability, and, 5–021—5–023
Cookies
  data protection, and, 7–006, 7–038—7–039
Copies as evidence
  civil proceedings, 10–143
  copies of, 10–145—10–146
  criminal proceedings, 10–144
  generally, 10–142
Copying
  copyright infringement, and, 2–064
Copying for private use
  copyright, and, 2–019
Copy-protection
  generally, 2–038
  infringement, 2–057
Copyright
  authorisation, 2–059—2–060
  authorship, 2–045
  Copyright Designs and Patents Act 1988
    infringement, 2–041—2–062
    restricted acts, 2–063—2–072
  database right
    generally, 2–048—2–049
    infringement, 2–055—2–096
    William Hill case, 2–050—2–054
  dematerialisation, 2–006
  development, 2–041
  digitisation, 2–002—2–007
  duration, 2–046
  electronic publishing, and, 2–116—2–118
  exclusive rights, 2–058
  foreign rules
    Australia, 6–109—6–113
    Belgium, 6–145—6–146
    Canada, 6–156—6–157
    Finland, 6–163—6–166
    France, 6–176
    Germany, 6–186
    Hong Kong, 6–211—6–213
    Israel, 6–237—6–240
    New Zealand, 6–284—6–288
    Singapore, 6–298—6–301
    Sweden, 6–314—6–315
    Switzerland, 6–329—6–330
    USA, 6–344—6–346
  framing, 2–091—2–092
  generally, 2–002—2–007
  Information Society Directive
    background, 2–010—2–012
    communication to public right, 2–015
    copy-protection measures, 2–038
    distribution right, 2–016
    exceptions, 2–017—2–037
    generally, 2–013
    reproduction right, 2–014

Copyright—*contd*
  infringement
    copy-protection, 2–057
    electronic media, 2–062
    introduction, 2–055—2–056
    primary, 2–058—2–060
    remedies, 2–114—2–115
    restricted acts, 2–063—2–072
    secondary, 2–061
  Internet-related issues
    framing, 2–091—2–092
    peer to peer, 2–095—2–096
    search engines, 2–093—2–094
    spidering, 2–089—2–090
    web linking, 2–073—2–088
  jurisdiction, and, 6–054
  legislative provision
    Copyright Designs and Patents Act 1988,
      2–041—2–072
    Digital Millennium Copyright Act, 2–039—2–040
    Information Society Directive, 2–010—2–038
    WIPO Treaties, 2–008—2–009
  liability for third party material
    caches, 2–111—2–113
    Digital Millennium Copyright Act, 2–104
    Dutch case law, 2–103
    Electronic Commerce Directive, 2–098
    introduction, 2–097
    linking, 2–107—2–110
    mirrors, 2–111—2–113
    U.K. case law, 2–105—2–106
    U.S. case law, 2–099—2–103
  meaning, 2–041—2–046
  moral rights, 2–047
  morphing, 2–007
  ownership, 2–045
  peer to peer, 2–095—2–096
  primary infringement
    authorisation, 2–059—2–060
    exclusive rights, 2–058
    restricted acts, 2–063—2–071
  protected works, 2–042—2–044
  restricted acts
    adaptation, 2–071
    broadcasting, 2–068—2–070
    cable programme service, 2–068—2–070
    copying, 2–064
    introduction, 2–063
    issue of copies, 2–065—2–066
    performance, 2–067
  search engines, 2–093—2–094
  secondary infringement
    generally, 2–061
    restricted acts, 2–072
  spidering, 2–089—2–090
  vertical agreements exemption, and, 14–124
  web linking
    copying, 2–080—2–081
    inclusion in cable programme service, 2–078—2–079
    infringement, 2–077
Copyright Designs and Patents Act 1988
  infringement, 2–041—2–062
  restricted acts, 2–063—2–072
Corporate finance
  data protection, and, 7–070

country code top level domains
  domain names, and, 3–021
"Country of origin" rules
  background, 6–070—6–071
  Electronic Commerce Directive
    derogations, 6–089—6–094
    effect, 6–095—6–098
    exclusions, 6–089—6–094
    introduction, 6–072—6–073
    jurisdiction, and, 6–099—6–101
    mutual recognition, 6–080
    place of establishment, 6–078—6–079
    practical issues, 6–085—6–088
    transparency, 6–074—6–077
  Treaty of Rome, 6–081—6–084
Credit cards
  abuse
    alteration of basic principle, 11–043
    basic principle, 11–041
    exceptions to basic principle, 11–042
    introduction, 11–040
    retailer risk, 11–044
    transmission over Internet, 11–045
  advantages
    card issuer/supplier liability, 11–012—11–013
    international acceptance, 11–014
    introduction, 11–011
    settlement period, 11–015
  disadvantages
    costs, 11–020—11–021
    introduction, 11–016
    market penetration, 11–022
    privacy, 11–023
    security, 11–017—11–019
    transaction costs, 11–020—11–021
  generally, 11–009—11–010
Crime
  data protection, and, 7–055
Criminal liability
  workplace communications, and, 5–062
Criticism and review
  copyright, and, 2–026
Cross-border content
  international Convention, 12–044—12–057
  international framework, 12–003—12–015
  introduction, 12–002
  national action, 12–016—12–043
  standards, 12–090
Cross-border dataflow
  data protection, and, 7–007
Cross-supplies
  vertical agreements exemption, and, 14–136
Crown employment
  data protection, and, 7–068
Cybersquatting
  Australia, 3–090
  generally, 3–014
  USA, 3–227—3–229
Cryptography
  administration infrastructure, 12–133—12–134
  dealings, 12–139—12–144
  digital signatures, 12–135—12–136
  introduction, 12–128—12–129
  legal issues, 12–137—12–138
  service providers, 12–145—12–149

Cryptography—*contd*
    systems, 12–131—12–132
    terminology, 12–130
Cuba
    regulation of activities, and, 12–026
Cultural, linguistic and religious identity
    Burma, 12–024
    China, 12–025
    Cuba, 12–026
    France, 12–027—12–031
    Germany, 12–032—12–033
    introduction, 12–023
    Saudi Arabia, 12–034
    Singapore, 12–035—12–036
Current events, reporting of
    copyright, and, 2–025
Customer restrictions
    technology transfer exemption, and, 14–106
    vertical agreements exemption, and, 14–134
Customs duties
    generally, 13–047
    on-line software, 13–048
    physically delivered goods, 13–049—13–050

Data protection
    accuracy of data, 7–041—7–042
    adequacy of data, 7–041—7–042
    armed forces, 7–066
    art, 7–058—7–054
    automated decision-taking, 7–095—7–097
    blocking of data, 7–099
    compensation, 7–098
    confidential references, 7–064
    cookies, 7–038—7–039
    corporate finance, 7–070
    crime, 7–055
    cross-border dataflow, 7–007
    Crown employment, 7–068
    Data Protection Act
        background, 7–007
        conclusions, 7–105—7–106
        definitions, 7–019—7–027
        enforcement, 7–077—7–101
        exemptions, 7–051—7–075
        introduction, 7–008—7–010
        offences, 7–076
        principles, 7–028—7–050
        remedies, 7–077—7–101
        transitional provisions, 7–102—7–104
        workplace communications, 5–103—5–118
    Data Protection Directive
        applicable law, 7–014
        application to Internet, 7–017—7–018
        cross-border dataflow, 7–015—7–016
        generally, 7–012
        introduction, 7–007
        scope, 7–013
    data subject's rights, 7–043—7–044
    definitions
        data, 7–020
        data controller, 7–025
        data processor, 7–026
        disclosing, 7–027
        introduction, 7–019
        obtaining, 7–027

Data protection—*contd*
    definitions—*contd*
        personal data, 7–021—7–023
        processing, 7–024
        recording, 7–027
        using, 7–027
    destruction of data, 7–099
    education, 7–056
    enforcement
        enforcement notices, 7–077—7–078
        entry powers, 7–086—7–087
        information notices, 7–080—7–085
        inspection powers, 7–086—7–087
        request for assessment, 7–079
    enforcement notices, 7–077—7–078
    entry powers, 7–086—7–087
    erasure of data, 7–099
    examination marks, 7–072
    examination scripts, 7–073
    exemptions
        introduction, 7–051—7–052
        miscellaneous, 7–064—7–075
        primary, 7–053—7–063
    fair and lawful obtaining and processing
        collection from website users, 7–036—7–037
        cookies, 7–038—7–039
        further conditions, 7–033
        information on website, 7–032
        information to be provided to data subject, 7–034
        introduction, 7–029
        non-obvious purposes, 7–030
        third party sources, 7–031
    health, 7–056
    holding on internal database, 7–003
    honours, 7–067
    information notices, 7–080—7–085
    inspection powers, 7–086—7–087
    journalism, 7–058—7–054
    judicial appointments, 7–067
    legal professional privilege, 7–074
    literature, 7–058—7–054
    management forecasts, 7–069
    ministerial appointments, 7–068
    national security, 7–054
    negotiations, 7–071
    notice to prevent processing
        cause damage or distress, likely to, 7–092—7–093
        direct marketing, for, 7–094
    principles
        accuracy, 7–041—7–042
        adequacy, 7–041—7–042
        data subject's rights, 7–043—7–044
        fair and lawful obtaining and processing, 7–029—7–039
        generally, 7–028
        introduction, 7–008—7–009
        relevance, 7–041—7–042
        retention period, 7–041—7–042
        security, 7–045—7–047
        specified and lawful purposes, 7–040
        transborder data flows, 7–048—7–050
        up-to-date, 7–041—7–042
    publication of personal data, 7–002
    public domain information, 7–061
    rectification, 7–099

Data protection—*contd*
  registration for Internet users, 7–010
  regulatory activity, 7–057
  relevance of data, 7–041—7–042
  remedies
    automated decision-taking, 7–095—7–097
    blocking, 7–099
    compensation, 7–098
    destruction, 7–099
    erasure, 7–099
    introduction, 7–088
    notice to prevent processing, 7–092—7–094
    rectification, 7–099
    request for assessment, 7–090—7–091
    request for notifiable particulars, 7–100—7–101
    subject access, 7–089
  request for assessment
    enforcement, and, 7–079
    remedies, and, 7–090—7–091
  request for notifiable particulars, 7–100—7–101
  research, 7–060
  retention period, 7–041—7–042
  security of data, 7–045—7–047
  self-incrimination, 7–075
  social work, 7–056
  specified and lawful purposes, 7–040
  statistics, 7–060
  subject access, 7–089
  taxation, 7–055
  transborder data flows, 7–048—7–050
  transmission by e-mail, 7–004—7–005
  up-to-date data, 7–041—7–042
  website use tracking, 7–006
  workplace communications
    draft Code of Practice, 5–104—5–109
    generally, 5–103
    human rights, and, 5–117—5–118
Data Protection Act
  and see above
  background, 7–007
  conclusions, 7–105—7–106
  definitions, 7–019—7–027
  enforcement, 7–077—7–101
  exemptions, 7–051—7–075
  introduction, 7–008—7–010
  offences, 7–076
  principles, 7–028—7–050
  remedies, 7–077—7–101
  transitional provisions, 7–102—7–104
  workplace communications, 5–103—5–118
Database right
  generally, 2–048—2–049
  infringement
    copy-protection, 2–057
    electronic media, 2–062
    introduction, 2–055—2–056
    primary, 2–058—2–060
    remedies, 2–114—2–115
    restricted acts, 2–063—2–072
    secondary, 2–06
  web linking
    generally, 2–082
    infringement, 2–085—2–088
    websites, 2–083—2–084
  William Hill case, 2–050—2–054

Databases
  copyright, and, 2–042
Debit cards
  abuse
    alteration of basic principle, 11–043
    basic principle, 11–041
    exceptions to basic principle, 11–042
    introduction, 11–040
    retailer risk, 11–044
    transmission over Internet, 11–045
  advantages
    card issuer/supplier liability, 11–012—11–013
    international acceptance, 11–014
    introduction, 11–011
    settlement period, 11–015
  disadvantages
    costs, 11–020—11–021
    introduction, 11–016
    market penetration, 11–022
    privacy, 11–023
    security, 11–017—11–019
    transaction costs, 11–020—11–021
  generally, 11–009—11–010
Deep linking
  generally, 2–075
Defamation
  foreign rules
    Australia, 6–114—6–117
    Belgium, 6–140—6–141
    Finland, 6–159—6–161
    France, 6–175
    Germany, 6–183
    Hong Kong, 6–206—6–209
    Israel, 6–233—6–234
    New Zealand, 6–277—6–279
    Singapore, 6–294—6–295
    Sweden, 6–312
    Switzerland, 6–320—6–324
    USA, 6–349
  generally, 4–003—4–004
  introduction, 4–001—4–002
  jurisdiction, and, 6–037—6–047
  nature of publication
    e-mail, 4–050—4–051
    introduction, 4–049
    linked content, 4–052—4–053
  primary disseminators
    common law, at, 4–008
    statute, under, 4–021—4–022
  publication at common law
    generally, 4–005—4–007
    primary dissemination, 4–009—4–010
    primary disseminators, 4–008
    subordinate dissemination, 4–009—4–010
    subordinate disseminators, 4–008
    variety of relationships, 4–011—4–012
  publication under statute
    authors, 4–023—4–024
    editors, 4–026—4–027
    generally, 4–021—4–022
    publishers, 4–025
    subordinate disseminators, 4–013—4–020
  standard of care
    introduction, 4–040
    notice and take-down, 4–041—4–044

Defamation—*contd*
  standard of care—*contd*
    previous conduct, 4–045—4–048
  subordinate disseminators
    academic mailing list, 4–033
    authors, and, 4–023—4–024
    common law defence, 4–008
    editors, and, 4–026—4–027
    managed virtual network, 4–036
    publishers, and, 4–025
    search engines, 4–038—4–039
    statutory defence, 4–013—4–015
    Usenet host, 4–029
    web design company, 4–037
    web hosting ISP, 4–034—4–035
    web journal discussion forum, 4–030—4–032
  U.S. case law, 4–054—4–058
Defective goods
  content liability, and, 5–011
  electronic contracts, and, 10–010
Dematerialisation
  copyright, and, 2–006
Demonstration of equipment
  copyright, and, 2–034
"Digicash"
  payment mechanisms, and, 11–039
Digital Millennium Copyright Act
  generally, 2–039—2–040
  liability for third party material, and, 2–104
Digital signatures
  regulated activities, and, 12–135—12–136
Digitisation
  copyright, and, 2–002—2–007
Direct liability
  workplace communications, and, 5–063—5–065
Director General of Fair Trading
  directions to terminate, 14–257
  generally, 14–252
  fines, 14–257—14–258
  interim measures, 14–256
  investigatory powers, 14–254—14–255
Disabled people
  copyright, and, 2–024
Disclaimers
  Australia, 6–108
  generally, 5–024
  USA, 6–352
Discriminatory pricing
  E.C. law, 14–205
  U.K. law, 14–247
Display of indecent matter
  regulated activities, and, 12–088
Distance Selling Directive
  cancellation right, 10–024—10–025
  confirmatory information, 10–019—10–023
  definitions, 10–013
  exempt agreements, 10–014—10–015
  implementation, 10–012
  introduction, 10–013
  transparency, 10–016—10–018
Distribution right
  copyright, and, 2–016
Distributors' defence
  defamation, and, 4–008

Domain name server (DNS)
  access providers, and, 1–023
  administrators, and, 1–021
  hosts, and, 1–018
Domain names
  administration of system
    ccTLDs, 3–021
    gTLDs, 3–022—3–025
    historical overview, 3–018—3–020
    .uk domain space, 3–026—3–027
  administrators
    Australia, 3–085
    Belgium, 3–092
    Canada, 3–102
    Finland, 3–119
    France, 3–126
    Germany, 3–132
    Hong Kong, 3–142
    Israel, 3–151
    Japan, 3–165
    Netherlands, 3–180
    New Zealand, 3–188
    Singapore, 3–195
    Sweden, 3–199
    Switzerland, 3–206
    USA, 3–221
  corporate protection policies, 3–074—3–077
  dispute resolution policies
    Australia, 3–089
    background, 3–068
    Germany, 3–134
    Japan, 3–169
    ICANN, 3–069—3–072
    Netherlands, 3–184
    Nominent, 3–073
  disputes
    Australia, 3–089—3–091
    Belgium, 3–095—3–099
    Canada, 3–107—3–118
    Finland, 3–121—3–125
    France, 3–129—3–131
    Germany, 3–134—3–141
    Hong Kong, 3–146—3–150
    introduction, 3–047
    Israel, 3–154—3–164
    Japan, 3–169—3–179
    jurisdiction, and, 6–020
    Netherlands, 3–184—3–187
    New Zealand, 3–192—3–194
    Registry policies, 3–068—3–073
    Singapore, 3–197—3–198
    Sweden, 3–204—3–205
    Switzerland, 3–210—3–218
    U.K. case law, 3–048—3–067
    USA, 3–222—3–241
  function
    generally, 3–028—3–030
    passing off, 3–037—3–038
    statutory provisions, 3–031—3–036
  future issues, 3–045—3–046
  introduction, 3–015
  jurisdiction, and, 6–020
  meaning, 3–016—3–017
  non-U.K. names
    Australia, 3–085—3–091

Domain names—*contd*
  non-U.K. names—*contd*
    Belgium, 3–092—3–101
    Canada, 3–102—3–118
    Finland, 3–119—3–125
    France, 3–126—3–131
    Germany, 3–132—3–141
    Hong Kong, 3–142—3–150
    Israel, 3–151—3–164
    Japan, 3–165—3–179
    Netherlands, 3–180—3–187
    New Zealand, 3–188—3–194
    Singapore, 3–195—3–198
    Sweden, 3–199—3–205
    Switzerland, 3–206—3–218
    USA, 3–219—3–241
  overseas registrations, 3–039
  passing off
    Australia, 3–090
    generally, 3–037—3–038
    Israel, 3–159
  registration
    Australia, 3–086—3–088
    Belgium, 3–093—3–094
    Canada, 3–102—3–106
    Finland, 3–119—3–120
    France, 3–127—3–128
    Germany, 3–132—3–133
    Hong Kong, 3–142—3–145
    Israel, 3–151—3–153
    Japan, 3–165—3–168
    Netherlands, 3–180—3–183
    New Zealand, 3–188—3–191
    Singapore, 3–195—3–196
    Sweden, 3–200—3–203
    Switzerland, 3–207—3–209
    USA, 3–221
  scrutiny of applications, 3–040—3–044
  website building contract, and, 9–017
Dramatic works
  copyright, and, 2–042
Dynamic content and code
  website building contract, and, 9–011—9–012

EDI
  electronic contracts, and, 10–002—10–003
Editors
  defamation, and, 4–026—4–027
Education
  data protection, and, 7–056
EFTPOS
  electronic cash, and, 11–026—11–028
  generally, 11–007—11–008
Electronic agents
  electronic contracts, and, 10–060—10–061
Electronic cash
  abuse
    counterfeit money, 11–049—11–052
    introduction, 11–046
    theft, 11–047—11–048
  authorisation of issuers
    and see Electronic money institutions
    account-based systems, 11–053, 11–056
    cash-based systems, 11–053, 11–057
    deposit-taking, 11–054—11–057

Electronic cash—*contd*
  authorisation of issuers—*contd*
    E.U. Directive, 11–058—11–063
    introduction, 11–053
  EFTPOS, and, 11–026—11–028
  introduction, 11–025
  mid-spectrum systems, 11–039
  "true" systems
    acceptance, 11–035—11–038
    advantages, 11–033—11–034
    convertibility, 11–036
    credit backing, 11–037
    disadvantages, 11–033—11–034
    generally, 11–029—11–032
    vulnerability to fraud, 11–038
Electronic Commerce Directive
  content liability
    caching, 5–043—5–044
    exclusions, 5–037
    hosting, 5–041—5–042
    information society services, 5–035—5–036
    introduction, 5–034
    mere conduits, 5–038—5–040
    monitoring, 5–045
  "country of origin" rules
    derogations, 6–089—6–094
    effect, 6–095—6–098
    exclusions, 6–089—6–094
    introduction, 6–072—6–073
    jurisdiction, and, 6–099—6–101
    mutual recognition, 6–080
    place of establishment, 6–078—6–079
    practical issues, 6–085—6–088
    transparency, 6–074—6–077
  electronic signatures
    commercial communications, 10–030—10–031
    conclusion of contract, 10–034—10–036
    introduction, 10–026—10–027
    regulated professions, 10–033
    technical requirements, 10–034—10–036
    transparency, 10–028—10–029
    unsolicited communications, 10–032
  hosts, 1–018
  liability for third party material, 2–098
  liability of online intermediaries, 4–002
Electronic communication policies
  generally, 5–071—5–072
  introduction, 5–059
Electronic contracts
  acceptance
    delay before receipt, 10–055
    despatch of acceptance, 10–054
    electronic agents, 10–060—10–061
    generally, 10–049—10–051
    minimising risks, 10–058
    normal rules, 10–056—10–057
    receipt of electronic communication, 10–052—10–053
    voice link communication, 10–059
  applicable law, 10–038—10–041
  certification-service providers
    advanced signatures, 10–093
    data protection, 10–097
    introduction, 10–085
    liability, 10–094—10–096
    qualified certificates, 10–091

Electronic contracts—*contd*
  consideration, 10–063
  content, 10–006
  defective goods, 10–010
  Distance Selling Directive
    cancellation right, 10–024—10–025
    confirmatory information, 10–019—10–023
    definitions, 10–013
    exempt agreements, 10–014—10–015
    implementation, 10–012
    introduction, 10–013
    transparency, 10–016—10–018
  EDI, and, 10–002—10–003
  electronic agents, 10–060—10–061
  Electronic Commerce Directive
    commercial communications, 10–030—10–031
    conclusion of contract, 10–034—10–036
    introduction, 10–026—10–027
    regulated professions, 10–033
    technical requirements, 10–034—10–036
    transparency, 10–028—10–029
    unsolicited communications, 10–032
  electronic signatures
    allocation of risk, 10–077—10–082
    background, 10–071—10–075
    definitions, 10–084—10–088
    E.U. Directive, 10–083—10–100
    generally, 10–076
  Electronic Signatures Directive
    advanced signatures, 10–090—10–093
    certification-service providers, 10–094—10–096
    definitions, 10–084—10–088
    excluded contracts, 10–100
    generally, 10–085
    implementation, 10–086
    introduction, 10–083
    public sector use, 10–099
    qualified certificates, 10–091
    signature-creation device, 10–092
    third country qualified certificates, 10–098
  evidence of transaction
    admissibility of, 10–131
    applicable law, 10–126—10–127
    electronic records, 10–132—10–133
    hearsay evidence, 10–134, 10–137—10–146
    introduction, 10–125
    physical evidence, 10–135—10–136
    proof of, 10–128—10–130
    real evidence, 10–135—10–136
    storage guidelines, 10–148—10–150
    weight of, 10–131, 10–147
  exclusions, 10–007—10–012
  formalities, 10–068—10–070
  formation
    acceptance, 10–049—10–061
    consideration, 10–063
    identity of parties, 10–067
    incorporation of terms, 10–064—10–066
    intention to create legal relations, 10–063
    introduction, 10–042
    invitation to treat, 10–047—10–048
    lapse of offer, 10–062
    offer, 10–047—10–048
    pre-contractual information, 10–043—10–046
    revocation, 10–062

Electronic contracts—*contd*
  governing law, 10–038—10–041
  identity of parties, 10–067
  incorporation of terms, 10–064—10–066
  intention to create legal relations, 10–063
  international issues
    applicable law, 10–038—10–041
    introduction, 10–037
  introduction, 10–001—10–005
  invitation to treat, 10–047—10–048
  lapse of offer, 10–062
  legislation
    background, 10–101
    certainty, 10–104—10–105
    compulsion, 10–121—10–124
    efficiency of rules, 10–118—10–120
    evolution of, 10–112—10–117
    facilitative approach, 10–107—10–111
    removal of obstacles, 10–102—10–103
    traps to be avoided, 10–106
  limitations, 10–007—10–012
  offer
    generally, 10–047—10–048
    lapse, 10–062
    revocation, 10–062
  pre-contractual information
    advertising, 10–044
    collateral contracts, 10–046
    introduction, 10–043
    misrepresentation, 10–045
  revocation, 10–062
  signatures
    electronic, 10–076—10–101
    generally, 10–071—10–075
  subject-matter, 10–005
  unfair terms
    E.C. Directive, 10–011
    generally, 10–009
  written form, 10–068—10–070
Electronic data interchange
  electronic contracts, and, 10–002—10–003
Electronic mail
  data protection, and, 7–004—7–005
  defamation, and, 4–050—4–051
  meaning, 1–002—1–003
  viruses
    generally, 12–156
    unauthorised access, 12–157
    unauthorised modification, 12–158
  workplace communications, and, 5–062
Electronic media
  infringement, 2–062
Electronic money institutions
  account-based systems
    deposit-taking, and, 11–056
    generally, 11–053
  cash-based systems
    deposit-taking, and, 11–057
    generally, 11–053
  deposit-taking
    account-based systems, 11–056
    cash-based systems, 11–057
    generally, 11–054—11–055
  E.U. Directive
    authorisation, 11–062

Electronic money institutions—*contd*
  E.U. Directive—*contd*
    definitions, 11–059—11–060
    introduction, 11–058
    supervision, 11–062
    unauthorised schemes, 11–063
    waivers, 11–061
  introduction, 11–053
Electronic publishing
  copyright, and, 2–116—2–118
Electronic signatures
  advanced signatures, 10–090—10–093
  allocation of risk, 10–077—10–082
  background, 10–071—10–075
  certification-service providers
    advanced signatures, 10–093
    data protection, 10–097
    introduction, 10–085
    liability, 10–094—10–096
    qualified certificates, 10–091
  definitions, 10–084—10–088
  E.U. Directive
    advanced signatures, 10–090—10–093
    certification-service providers, 10–094—10–096
    definitions, 10–084—10–088
    excluded contracts, 10–100
    generally, 10–085
    implementation, 10–086
    introduction, 10–083
    public sector use, 10–099
    qualified certificates, 10–091
    signature-creation device, 10–092
    third country qualified certificates, 10–098
  generally, 10–076
  qualified certificates
    generally, 10–091
    third country, 10–098
  signature-creation device, 10–092
Employer liability
  access to workplace communications, and
    Data Protection Act, 5–103—5–109
    Human Rights Act, 5–110—5–118
    introduction, 5–073
    Lawful Business Practice Regulations, 5–097—5–102
    Regulation of Investigatory Powers Act, 5–074—5–096
  communication policies
    generally, 5–071—5–072
    introduction, 5–059
  criminal liability, 5–062
  direct liability, 5–063—5–065
  introduction, 5–056—5–059
  personal e-mail, 5–062
  tribunal decisions
    harassment, 5–070
    introduction, 5–066
    pornography, 5–068—5–069
    unauthorised access, 5–067
  vicarious liability, 5–061
Employment contract
  confidential information, and, 2–124—2–125
Encryption
  administration infrastructure, 12–133—12–134
  dealings, 12–139—12–144

Encryption—*contd*
  digital signatures, 12–135—12–136
  introduction, 12–128—12–129
  legal issues, 12–137—12–138
  service providers, 12–145—12–149
  systems, 12–131—12–132
  terminology, 12–130
Enforcement notices
  data protection, and, 7–077—7–078
Enforcement of IPR
  "country of origin" rules
    background, 6–070—6–071
    Electronic Commerce Directive, 6–072—6–101
  extra-territorial inunctions, 6–069
  identification of defendant, 6–004—6–005
  identification of wrongdoer, 6–006—6–011
  introduction, 6–001—6–003
  jurisdiction
    and see Jurisdiction
    background, 6–019—6–025
    defendant domiciled in Brussels Convention state, 6–026—6–063
    defendant not domiciled in Brussels Convention state, 6–064—6–068
  mirror sites, 6–017—6–018
  transient evidence, 6–012—6–013
  transportability of sites, 6–014—6–016
Entry, powers of
  data protection, and, 7–086—7–087
Ephemeral fixation
  copyright, and, 2–021
Evidence of electronic transactions
  admissibility of, 10–131
  applicable law, 10–126—10–127
  copies
    civil proceedings, 10–143
    copies of, 10–145—10–146
    criminal proceedings, 10–144
    generally, 10–142
  electronic records, 10–132—10–133
  hearsay evidence
    civil proceedings, 10–139
    copies, 10–142—10–146
    criminal proceedings, 10–140—10–141
    generally, 10–137—10–138
    introduction, 10–134
  introduction, 10–125
  physical evidence, 10–135—10–136
  proof of, 10–128—10–130
  real evidence, 10–135—10–136
  storage guidelines, 10–148—10–150
  weight of
    factors affecting, 10–147
    generally, 10–131
Examination marks
  data protection, and, 7–072
Examination scripts
  data protection, and, 7–073
Excessive pricing
  E.C. law, 14–203
  U.K. law, 14–246
Exclusive licence
  technology transfer exemption, and, 14–092
Exclusive purchasing
  abuse of dominant position, and, 14–207

Exclusive rights
    abuse of dominant position, and, 14–202
    copyright, and, 2–058
Extranets
    data protection, and, 7–003
Extra-territorial injunctions
    enforcement of IPR, and, 6–069

False attribution
    moral rights, and, 2–047
False representations
    Australia, 6–118—6–122
Field of use restrictions
    technology transfer exemption, and, 14–106—14–
        107
File transfer protocol (Ftp)
    meaning, 1–003
    use, 1–012
Films
    copyright, and, 2–042
Filtering
    regulated activities, and, 12–041—12–043
Financial services
    exclusions, 12–108
    general prohibition, 12–104—12–105
    generally, 12–101
    information websites, 12–109—12–111
    introduction, 12–100
    overseas providers, 12–112
    problem areas, 12–102
    promotional restrictions, 12–113—12–118
    regulated activities, 12–106—12–107
    statutory basis, 12–103
Finland
    content liability, 6–162
    copyright, 6–163—6–166
    defamation, 6–159—6–161
    domain names
        administrators, 3–119
        disputes, 3–121—3–125
        registration, 3–119—3–120
    trade marks, 6–167
Frames
    meaning, 1–013
Framing
    generally, 2–091—2–092
    USA, 6–347—6–348
France
    applicable law, 6–168—6–174
    content liability, 6–178—6–180
    copyright, 6–176
    defamation, 6–175
    domain names
        administrators, 3–126
        disputes, 3–129—3–131
        registration, 3–132—3–133
    governing law, 6–168—6–174
    jurisdiction, 6–168—6–174
    regulation of activities, 12–027—12–031
    trade marks, 6–177
Fraud
    charge, credit and debit cards
        alteration of basic principle, 11–043
        basic principle, 11–041
        exceptions to basic principle, 11–042

Fraud—contd
    charge, credit and debit cards—contd
        introduction, 11–040
        retailer risk, 11–044
        transmission over Internet, 11–045
    electronic cash
        counterfeit money, 11–049—11–052
        introduction, 11–046
        theft, 11–047—11–048
Ftp
    meaning, 1–003
    use, 1–012

Gambling, regulation of
    generally, 12–058—12–062
    Hong Kong, 6–215—6–222
Gateways
    competition law, and, 14–013
generic top level domains
    domain names, and, 3–022—3–025
Germany
    copyright, 6–186
    defamation, 6–183
    domain names
        administrators, 3–132
        disputes, 3–134—3–141
        registration, 3–132—3–133
    jurisdiction, 6–181—6–182
    misleading information, 6–184
    protection of cultural identity, 12–032—12–033
    regulation of activities, 12–020
    trade marks, 6–186
Governing law
    foreign rules
        Belgium, 6–134—6–139
        France, 6–168—6–174
        Japan, 6–251—6–259
    generally, 10–038—10–041
Grey list
    technology transfer exemption, and, 14–082
gTLDs
    domain names, and, 3–022—3–025

Hague Convention
    jurisdiction, and, 6–024
Harassment
    regulated activities, and, 12–086—12–087
    workplace communications, and, 5–070
Health
    data protection, and, 7–056
Hearsay evidence
    civil proceedings, 10–139
    copies
        civil proceedings, 10–143
        copies of, 10–145—10–146
        criminal proceedings, 10–144
        generally, 10–142
    criminal proceedings, 10–140—10–141
    generally, 10–137—10–138
    introduction, 10–134
Hong Kong
    copyright, 6–211—6–213
    defamation, 6–206—6–209
    domain names
        administrators, 3–142

Hong Kong—*contd*
  domain names—*contd*
    disputes, 3–146—3–150
    registration, 3–142—3–145
    gambling, 6–215—6–222
    jurisdiction, 6–187—6–205
    misleading information, 6–210
    trade marks, 6–214
Honours
  data protection, and, 7–067
Hospitals
  copyright, and, 2–022
Hosting contracts
  access to site, 9–021—9–022
  introduction, 9–018
  limitation of liability, 9–024—9–025
  reports and information, 9–023
  risk sharing, 9–026
  storage of data, 9–019—9–020
Hosts
  content liability, and, 5–041—5–042
  generally, 1–016—1–019
  meaning, 1–006
HTML
  meaning, 1–013
HTTP
  meaning, 1–013
Human Rights Act
  data protection Code of Practice, 5–117—5–118
  displacing expectation of privacy, 5–114—5–116
  Lawful Business Practice Regulations, 5–117—5–118
  public bodies, 5–110—5–112
  reasonable expectation of privacy, 5–113
Hypertext link
  advertising contracts, and, 9–032
  meaning, 1–013
  sponsorship contracts, and, 9–032

IANA
  background, 1–021
  domain names, and, 3–018—3–020
ICANN
  background, 1–021
  domain names, and, 3–018—3–020
Identity of parties
  electronic contracts, and, 10–067
Inaccurate information
  Australia, 6–118—6–122
  Canada, 6–155
  Germany, 6–184
  Hong Kong, 6–210
  Singapore, 6–296—6–297
Incidental inclusion
  copyright, and, 2–031
Incorrect information
  negligence
    duty of care, 5–004
    economic loss, 5–008—5–010
    general principles, 5–002—5–003
    interactivity, 5–005
    mass advice, 5–006—5–007
    physical damage, 5–008—5–010
  strict liability, 5–011
  viruses, 5–012

Incorporation of terms
  electronic contracts, and, 10–064—10–066
Industrial espionage
  confidential information, and, 2–131—2–132
Information notices
  data protection, and, 7–080—7–085
Information Society Directive
  background, 2–010—2–012
  communication to public right, 2–015
  copy-protection measures, 2–038
  distribution right, 2–016
  exceptions, 2–017—2–037
  generally, 2–013
  reproduction right, 2–014
Information society services
  content liability, and, 5–035—5–036
Inline linking
  generally, 2–076
Innocence
  defamation, and, 4–008
Inspection, powers of
  data protection, and, 7–086—7–087
Integrated Services Digital Network
  meaning, 1–010
Integrity rights
  moral rights, and, 2–047
Intellectual property rights (IPR)
  anti-competitive practices, and
    development contracts, 14–150
    end-users, 14–149
    generally, 14–146—14–148
  confidential information
    and see Confidential information
    generally, 2–119
    misuse on Internet, 2–134—2–137
    obligation, 2–121—2–128
    protectable information, 2–120
    remedies, 2–129—2–130
    theft, 2–131—2–132
    transmission by Internet, 2–133
  copyright
    and see Copyright
    database right, 2–048—2–054
    electronic publishing, and, 2–116—2–118
    generally, 2–002—2–007
    infringement, 2–055—2–096
    liability for third party material, 2–097—2–115
    meaning, 2–041—2–046
    moral rights, 2–047
    legislative provision, 2–008—2–040
  enforcement of
    and see Enforcement of IPR
    "country of origin" rules, 6–070—6–101
    identification of defendant, 6–004—6–005
    identification of wrongdoer, 6–006—6–011
    introduction, 6–001—6–003
    jurisdiction, 6–019—6–069
    mirror sites, 6–017—6–018
    overseas laws, 6–102—6–352
    transient evidence, 6–012—6–013
    transportability of sites, 6–014—6–016
  introduction, 2–001
  jurisdiction, and
    copyright, 6–054
    generally, 6–030

Intellectual property rights (IPR)—*contd*
  jurisdiction, and—*contd*
    patents, 6–055
    trade marks, 6–048—6–052
  overseas laws
    Australia, 6–102—6–128
    Belgium, 6–129—6–147
    Canada, 6–148—6–158
    Finland, 6–159—6–167
    France, 6–168—6–180
    Germany, 6–181—6–186
    Hong Kong, 6–187—6–225
    Israel, 6–226—6–245
    Japan, 6–246—6–260
    Netherlands, 6–261—6–276
    New Zealand, 6–277—6–292
    Singapore, 6–293—6–305
    Sweden, 6–306—6–317
    Switzerland, 6–318—6–332
    USA, 6–333—6–352
  patents
    and see Patents
    business methods, 2–141—2–145, 2–159—2–161
    generally, 2–138—2–140
    infringement, 2–162—2–166
    prior art, 2–146—2–148
    software, 2–149—2–158
  trade marks
    and see Trade marks
    domain names, 3–015—3–077
    introduction, 3–001—3–009
    keyword sales, 3–083
    metatags, 3–078—3–081
    non-U.K. domain names, 3–085—3–241
    problem areas, 3–010—3–014
    wordstuffing, 3–082
  website building contracts, and
    allocation of rights, 9–013
    domain name, 9–017
    dynamic content and code, 9–011—9–012
    introduction, 9–009
    physical materials, 9–015
    proprietary software, 9–014
    static content and code, 9–010
    third party software, 9–016
Intention to create legal relations
  electronic contracts, and, 10–063
Interactive services
  broadcasting regulation, and, 8–042
Interception of communications
  definitions, 5–075—5–077
  e-mail, 5–085
  ephemeral communications, 5–085
  generally, 5–074
  in course of transmission, 5–078—5–079
  lawful authority, 5–095—5–096
  purpose, 5–080
  recipient's position, 5–081—5–084
  recipients, 5–086—5–087
  voicemail, 5–085
Interconnection
  competition law, and
    Commission decisions, 14–056—14–057
    generally, 14–006—14–008

Interconnection—*contd*
  generally, 8–025—8–027
  introduction, 8–008—8–010
Interconnection Directive
  telecommunications, and, 8–009—8–010
International Simple Resale
  telecommunications, and, 8–016—8–018
Internet
  access providers, 1–022—1–024
  administrators, 1–020—1–021
  broadband networks, and, 1–028—1–030
  concept, 1–005
  content providers, 1–011—1–015
  hosts, 1–016—1–019
  infrastructure, 1–006—1–010
  meaning, 1–001—1–004
  navigation providers, 1–025—1–026
  network providers, 1–007—1–010
  transaction facilitators, 1–027
Internet Assigned Numbers Authority
  background, 1–021
  domain names, and, 3–018—3–020
Internet Corporation for Assigned Names and Numbers
  background, 1–021
  domain names, and, 3–018—3–020
Internet radio services
  broadcasting regulation, and, 8–045
Internet Registry agreements
  Commission decisions, 14–151—14–157
Internet Relay Chat (IRC)
  defamation, and, 4–003
  meaning, 1–004
Internet service providers (ISPs)
  defamation, and, 4–011
  generally, 1–022—1–024
  telecommunications regulation, and
    generally, 8–013
    introduction, 8–012
Internet service provision
  access rights and network services
    end-users, to, 8–031—8–032
    generally, 8–024
    interconnection, 8–025—8–027
    introduction, 8–008—8–010
    peering, 8–028—8–030
  generally, 8–013
  introduction, 8–012
  systems and services, 8–014—8–015
  voice and data systems, 8–016—8–018
  voice over IP, 8–022—8–023
  voice telephony services, 8–019—8–021
Internet Society
  administrators, and, 1–020
Intranet
  meaning, 1–001
Invitation to treat
  electronic contracts, and, 10–047—10–048
IP addresses
  administrators, and, 1–021
  hosts, and, 1–019
IPLC
  telecommunications, and, 8–017
IRC
  meaning, 1–004

ISDN
  meaning, 1–010
ISPs
  defamation, and, 4–011
  generally, 1–022—1–024
  telecommunications regulation, and
    generally, 8–013
    introduction, 8–012
Israel
  content liability, 6–235—6–236
  copyright, 6–237—6–240
  defamation, 6–233—6–234
  domain names
    administrators, 3–151
    disputes, 3–154—3–164
    passing off, 3–159
    registration, 3–151—3–153
  jurisdiction, 6–226—6–232
  territory notices, 6–244—6–245
  trade marks, 6–241—6–245
Issue of copies
  copyright infringement, and, 2–065—2–066
ITC Code
  broadcasting regulation, and, 8–040—8–041

JANET
  meaning, 1–010
Japan
  applicable law, 6–251—6–259
  domain names
    administrators, 3–165
    disputes, 3–169—3–179
    registration, 3–165—3–168
  governing law, 6–251—6–259
  jurisdiction, 6–246—6–250
  territory notices, 6–260
Joint ventures between competitors
  technology transfer exemption, and, 14–090
Journalism
  data protection, and, 7–058—7–054
Judicial appointments
  data protection, and, 7–067
Junk e-mail
  regulated activities, and, 12–126—12–127
Jurisdiction
  background, 6–019—6–025
  Brussels Convention state, defendant domiciled in
    confidential information, 6–056
    consumer contracts, 6–0587—6–063
    contract, 6–031
    copyright, 6–054
    defamation, 6–037—6–047
    general rule, 6–027
    introduction, 6–026
    IPR, 6–030
    jurisdiction agreements, 6–028—6–029
    negligent misstatement, 6–053
    passing off, 6–048—6–052
    patents, 6–055
    tort, 6–032—6–036
    trade marks, 6–048—6–052
  Brussels Convention state, defendant not domiciled in, 6–064—6–068
  consumer contracts, 6–021—6–022
  domain name disputes, 6–020

Jurisdiction—contd
  foreign rules
    Belgium, 6–129—6–133
    Canada, 6–148—6–154
    France, 6–168—6–174
    Germany, 6–181—6–182
    Hong Kong, 6–187—6–205
    Israel, 6–226—6–232
    Japan, 6–246—6–250
    Netherlands, 6–261—6–266
    Singapore, 6–293
    Sweden, 6–306—6–311
    Switzerland, 6–318—6–319
    USA, 6–333—6–343
  Hague Convention, 6–024
  mere availability of website, 6–025
  regulated activities, 6–023

Keyword sales
  trade marks, and, 3–083
Know-how confidentiality
  technology transfer exemption, and, 14–100
Know-how pools
  technology transfer exemption, and, 14–089

Lapse of offer
  electronic contracts, and, 10–062
Lawful Business Practice Regulations
  authorised conduct, 5–102
  generally, 5–097
  human rights, and, 5–117—5–118
  preconditions to interception, 5–098—5–101
Legal professional privilege
  data protection, and, 7–074
Liability for third party material
  caches, 2–111—2–113
  Digital Millennium Copyright Act, 2–104
  Dutch case law, 2–103
  Electronic Commerce Directive, 2–098
  introduction, 2–097
  linking, 2–107—2–110
  mirrors, 2–111—2–113
  U.K. case law, 2–105—2–106
  U.S. case law, 2–099—2–103
Libraries
  copyright, and, 2–020
Licensable programme services
  generally, 8–034—8–037
  interactive services, 8–042
  ITC Codes, 8–040—8–041
  licences, 8–038—8–039
Licensable sound programme services
  generally, 8–043—8–044
Linking
  copyright, and
    copying, 2–080—2–081
    inclusion in cable programme service, 2–078—2–079
    infringement, 2–077
  database right, and
    generally, 2–082
    infringement, 2–085—2–088
    websites, 2–083—2–084
  deep linking, 2–075
  inline linking, 2–076

Linking—*contd*
    introduction, 2–073
    liability for third party material, and, 2–107—2–110
    technical aspects, 2–074
    USA, 6–347—6–348
Literature
    data protection, and, 7–058—7–054
Literary works
    copyright, and, 2–042
Live broadcasts
    defamation, and, 4–017—4–020
Local delivery services
    broadcasting regulation, and, 8–046—8–047
Loyalty bonus
    abuse of dominant position, and, 14–207

Managed virtual network
    defamation, and, 4–036
Management forecasts
    data protection, and, 7–069
Mareva injunction
    enforcement of IPR, and, 6–003
Market share
    vertical agreements exemption, and, 14–125—14–127
Marking obligations
    technology transfer exemption, and, 14–113
Medical services
    competition law, and, 14–022
Mergers
    E.C. Regulation
        assessment by Commission, 14–054
        decisions by Commission, 14–055—14–063
        full function, 14–051
        introduction, 14–043—14–044
        joint control, 14–048—14–050
        notification requirements, 14–052—14–053
        thresholds, 14–045—14–047
    U.K. law, 14–220—14–222
Metatags
    generally, 3–078—3–081
    USA, 3–238—3–241
Ministerial appointments
    data protection, and, 7–068
Mirror sites
    enforcement of IPR, and, 6–017—6–018
    liability for third party material, and, 2–111—2–113
Misleading information
    Australia, 6–118—6–122
    Canada, 6–155
    Germany, 6–184
    Hong Kong, 6–210
    Singapore, 6–296—6–297
Misrepresentation
    electronic contracts, and, 10–045
    USA, 6–351
Misuse
    confidential information, and, 2–134—2–137
Monitoring
    content liability, and, 5–045
Moral rights
    copyright, and, 2–047
Morphing
    copyright, and, 2–007
Most favoured licensee
    technology transfer exemption, and, 14–103

Multilateral traffic exchange centres
    meaning, 1–007
Music
    competition law, and, 14–045—14–047
Musical works
    copyright, and, 2–042

National security
    data protection, and, 7–054
Navigation providers
    generally, 1–025—1–026
Negligence
    duty of care, 5–004
    economic loss, 5–008—5–010
    general principles, 5–002—5–003
    interactivity, 5–005
    mass advice, 5–006—5–007
    physical damage, 5–008—5–010
    viruses, and
        duty of care, 5–013
        foreseeability, 5–014
        physical damage, 5–013—5–014
        standard of care, 5–015
Negligent misstatement
    jurisdiction, and, 6–053
Ne exeat regno injunction
    enforcement of IPR, and, 6–003
Negotiations
    data protection, and, 7–071
Netherlands
    applicable law, 6–267—6–273
    domain names
        administrators, 3–180
        disputes, 3–184—3–187
        registration, 3–180—3–183
    jurisdiction, 6–261—6–266
    trade marks, 6–274—6–276
Network providers
    generally, 1–007—1–010
New Zealand
    content liability, 6–280—6–283
    copyright, 6–284—6–288
    defamation, 6–277—6–279
    domain names
        administrators, 3–188
        disputes, 3–192—3–194
        registration, 3–188—3–191
    trade marks, 6–289—6–292
No-challenge clauses
    technology transfer exemption, and, 14–112
Non-competition clauses
    technology transfer exemption, and, 14–104
    vertical agreements exemption, and, 14–139
Norwich Pharmacal order
    background, 6–003
    generally, 6–004—6–005
Notice to prevent processing
    cause damage or distress, likely to, 7–092—7–093
    direct marketing, for, 7–094

Obscenity
    broadcasting, 12–068—12–069
    defences, 12–071—12–072
    introduction, 12–064
    possession, 12–070
    publication, 12–065—12–067

OFCOM
  telecommunications regulation, and, 8–003
Offensive communications
  regulated activities, and, 12–086—12–087
Offer
  acceptance
    delay before receipt, 10–055
    despatch of acceptance, 10–054
    electronic agents, 10–060—10–061
    generally, 10–049—10–051
    minimising risks, 10–058
    normal rules, 10–056—10–057
    receipt of electronic communication, 10–052—10–053
    voice link communication, 10–059
  generally, 10–047—10–048
  lapse, 10–062
  revocation, 10–062
Office of Fair Trading
  directions to terminate, 14–257
  fines, 14–257—14–258
  generally, 14–252
  interim measures, 14–256
  investigatory powers, 14–254—14–255
Official celebrations
  copyright, and, 2–029
OFTEL
  telecommunications regulation, and, 8–005
On-line databases
  copyright, and, 2–042
On-line research
  copyright, and, 2–036
Own use licences
  technology transfer exemption, and, 14–096
Ownership
  copyright, and, 2–045

Parallel imports
  technology transfer exemption, and, 14–105
Passing off
  foreign rules
    Australia, 3–090, 6–106—6–107
    Israel, 3–159
    generally, 3–037—3–038
  jurisdiction, and, 6–048—6–052
Patent pools
  technology transfer exemption, and, 14–089
Patents
  business methods
    Europe, 2–159—2–161
    U.S., 2–141—2–145
  generally, 2–138—2–140
  infringement
    infringing acts, 2–162—2–163
    jurisdiction, 2–166
    liability, 2–164—2–165
  jurisdiction, and, 6–055
  prior art, 2–146—2–148
  software
    Europe, 2–149—2–155
    U.S., 2–156—2–158
Paternity rights
  moral rights, and, 2–047
Payment mechanisms
  cash, 11–005

Payment mechanisms—contd
  charge card
    abuse, 11–040—11–04
    advantages, 11–011—11–015
    disadvantages, 11–016—11–023
    generally 11–009—11–010
  cheque, 11–006
  conventional systems
    cash, 11–005
    charge card, 11–009—11–024
    cheque, 11–006
    conclusion, 11–025
    credit card, 11–009—11–024
    debit card, 11–009—11–024
    EFTPOS, 11–007—11–008
    introduction, 11–004
  characteristics, 11–001—11–002
  conclusion, 11–069
  credit card
    abuse, 11–040—11–04
    advantages, 11–011—11–015
    disadvantages, 11–016—11–023
    generally 11–009—11–010
  debit card
    abuse, 11–040—11–045
    advantages, 11–011—11–015
    disadvantages, 11–016—11–023
    generally, 11–009—11–010
  "Digicash" system, 11–039
  EFTPOS
    electronic cash, and, 11–026—11–028
    generally, 11–007—11–008
  electronic cash
    abuse, 11–046—11–052
    acceptance, 11–035—11–038
    advantages, 11–033—11–034
    audit trails, 11–064—11–068
    convertibility, 11–036
    credit backing, 11–037
    disadvantages, 11–033—11–034
    EFTPOS principles, on, 11–026—11–028
    introduction, 11–025
    issuer authorisation, 11–053—11–063
    mid-spectrum systems, 11–039
    "true" systems, 11–029—11–038
    vulnerability to fraud, 11–038
  potential rewards, 11–003
  "Visa cash" system, 11–039
Peering agreements
  generally, 9–041
  meaning, 1–007—1–009
  telecommunications regulation, and, 8–028—8–030
Peer to peer
  copyright, and, 2–095—2–096
Performance
  copyright infringement, and, 2–067
Personal data
  data protection, and, 7–002
Offensive communications
  regulated activities, and, 12–086—12–087
Pharmaceuticals
  regulated activities, and, 12–119—12–121
Pipes
  meaning, 1–006

Photocopying
  copyright, and, 2–018
Photographs
  moral rights, and, 2–047
Points of presence (POP)
  generally, 1–022
Political speeches
  copyright, and, 2–028
Pornography
  chat rooms, 12–091
  child pornography
    cache copies, 12–077
    downloading, 12–075—12–076
    introduction, 12–073—12–074
    linking, 12–082—12–085
    making, 12–075—12–076
    screen images, 12–078—12–081
  cross-border content standards, 12–090
  display of indecent matter, 12–088
  harassment, 12–086—12–087
  introduction, 12–063
  obscenity
    broadcasting, 12–068—12–069
    defences, 12–071—12–072
    introduction, 12–064
    possession, 12–070
    publication, 12–065—12–067
  offensive communications, 12–086—12–087
  public indecency, 12–088
  sex tourism, 12–089
Portals
  competition law, and
    Commission decisions, 14–061—14–062
    generally, 14–013
  generally, 1–026
Post-term restrictions
  technology transfer exemption, and, 14–102
  vertical agreements exemption, and, 14–140
Pre-contractual information
  advertising, 10–044
  collateral contracts, 10–046
  introduction, 10–043
  misrepresentation, 10–045
Predatory pricing
  E.C. law, 14–204
  U.K. law, 14–248
Price restrictions
  technology transfer exemption, and, 14–110
Prior art
  patents, and, 2–146—2–148
Prisoners, identity of
  content liability, and, 5–050—5–055
Prisons
  copyright, and, 2–022
Private use
  copyright, and, 2–019
Product liability
  content liability, and, 5–011
Prohibited and regulated activities
  advertising
    generally, 12–122—12–125
    junk e-mail, 12–126—12–127
  Australia, 12–016
  Burma, 12–024
  chat rooms, 12–091

Prohibited and regulated activities—contd
  child pornography
    cache copies, 12–077
    downloading, 12–075—12–076
    introduction, 12–073—12–074
    linking, 12–082—12–085
    making, 12–075—12–076
    screen images, 12–078—12–081
  China, 12–025
  computer misuse
    access to computer material, 12–151—12–152
    intent to commit offences, 12–153
    introduction, 12–150
    modification of computer material, 12–154—12–155
  contempt of court
    criminal proceedings, 12–093—12–096
    international aspects, 12–097
    introduction, 12–092
    third party actions, 12–098—12–099
  content blocking, 12–040
  cost of copy-clearance, 12–004
  cross-border content
    international Convention, 12–044—12–057
    international framework, 12–003—12–015
    introduction, 12–002
    national action, 12–016—12–043
    standards, 12–090
  cryptography
    administration infrastructure, 12–133—12–134
    dealings, 12–139—12–144
    digital signatures, 12–135—12–136
    introduction, 12–128—12–129
    legal issues, 12–137—12–138
    service providers, 12–145—12–149
    systems, 12–131—12–132
    terminology, 12–130
  Cuba, 12–026
  cultural, linguistic and religious identity
    Burma, 12–024
    China, 12–025
    Cuba, 12–026
    France, 12–027—12–031
    Germany, 12–032—12–033
    introduction, 12–023
    Saudi Arabia, 12–034
    Singapore, 12–035—12–036
  display of indecent matter, 12–088
  e-mail viruses
    generally, 12–156
    unauthorised access, 12–157
    unauthorised modification, 12–158
  encryption
    administration infrastructure, 12–133—12–134
    dealings, 12–139—12–144
    digital signatures, 12–135—12–136
    introduction, 12–128—12–129
    legal issues, 12–137—12–138
    service providers, 12–145—12–149
    systems, 12–131—12–132
    terminology, 12–130
  E.U., 12–017—12–019
  financial services
    exclusions, 12–108
    general prohibition, 12–104—12–105

Prohibited and regulated activities—*contd*
  financial services—*contd*
    generally, 12–101
    information websites, 12–109—12–111
    introduction, 12–100
    overseas providers, 12–112
    problem areas, 12–102
    promotional restrictions, 12–113—12–118
    regulated activities, 12–106—12–107
    statutory basis, 12–103
  France, 12–027—12–031
  filtering, 12–041—12–043
  gambling, 12–058—12–062
  Germany
    generally, 12–020
    protection of cultural identity, 12–032—12–033
  harassment, 12–086—12–087
  international Convention
    competing laws, 12–050
    country of origin, 12–045—12–048
    country of receipt, 12–049
    directing, 12–051—12–055
    introduction, 12–044
    targeting, 12–051—12–055
  introduction, 12–001
  junk e-mail, 12–126—12–127
  jurisdiction, and, 6–023
  national action
    Australia, 12–016
    content blocking, 12–040
    E.U., 12–017—12–019
    filtering, 12–041—12–043
    Germany, 12–020
    protection of cultural identity, 12–023—12–036
    rating, 12–041—12–043
    responses to, 12–037—12–043
    U.K., 12–021—12–022
  obscenity
    broadcasting, 12–068—12–069
    defences, 12–071—12–072
    introduction, 12–064
    possession, 12–070
    publication, 12–065—12–067
  offensive communications, 12–086—12–087
  pharmaceuticals, 12–119—12–121
  pornography
    chat rooms, 12–091
    child pornography, 12–073—12–085
    cross-border content standards, 12–090
    display of indecent matter, 12–088
    harassment, 12–086—12–087
    introduction, 12–063
    obscenity, 12–064—12–072
    offensive communications, 12–086—12–087
    public indecency, 12–088
    sex tourism, 12–089
  public indecency, 12–088
  rating, 12–041—12–043
  Saudi Arabia, 12–034
  sex tourism, 12–089
  sexual offences
    chat rooms, 12–091
    child pornography, 12–073—12–085
    cross-border content standards, 12–090
    display of indecent matter, 12–088

Prohibited and regulated activities—*contd*
  sexual offences—*contd*
    harassment, 12–086—12–087
    introduction, 12–063
    obscenity, 12–064—12–072
    offensive communications, 12–086—12–087
    public indecency, 12–088
    sex tourism, 12–089
  Singapore, 12–035—12–036
  U.K., 12–021—12–022
  unauthorised access
    computer material, to, 12–151—12–152
    intent to commit offences, with, 12–153
    viruses, 12–157
  unauthorised modification
    computer material, of, 12–154—12–155
    viruses, 12–158
  viruses
    generally, 12–156
    unauthorised access, 12–157
    unauthorised modification, 12–158
  website access
    denial of service attacks, 12–161
    generally, 12–162
    introduction, 12–160
Proprietary software
  website building contract, and, 9–014
PSTN
  telecommunications, and, 8–017
PTO licence
  telecommunications, and, 8–014
Public domain, information in
  data protection, and, 7–061
Public indecency
  regulated activities, and, 12–088
Public interest
  copyright, and, 2–027
Publication
  common law, at
    generally, 4–005—4–007
    primary dissemination, 4–009—4–010
    primary disseminators, 4–008
    subordinate dissemination, 4–009—4–010
    subordinate disseminators, 4–008
    variety of relationships, 4–011—4–012
  statute, under
    authors, 4–023—4–024
    editors, 4–026—4–027
    generally, 4–021—4–022
    publishers, 4–025
    subordinate disseminators, 4–013—4–020
Publishers
  defamation, and, 4–025
Pure sales licences
  technology transfer exemption, and, 14–087

Quality specifications
  technology transfer exemption, and, 14–099
Quantity restrictions
  technology transfer exemption, and, 14–108

Rating
  regulated activities, and, 12–041—12–043
Reciprocal agreements
  technology transfer exemption, and, 14–091

Reconstruction of buildings
    copyright, and, 2–035
Refusal to supply
    E.C. law, 14–208—14–214
    U.K. law, 14–250
Regulated and prohibited activities
    advertising
        generally, 12–122—12–125
        junk e-mail, 12–126—12–127
    Australia, 12–016
    Burma, 12–024
    chat rooms, 12–091
    child pornography
        cache copies, 12–077
        downloading, 12–075—12–076
        introduction, 12–073—12–074
        linking, 12–082—12–085
        making, 12–075—12–076
        screen images, 12–078—12–081
    China, 12–025
    computer misuse
        access to computer material, 12–151—12–152
        intent to commit offences, 12–153
        introduction, 12–150
        modification of computer material, 12–154—12–155
    contempt of court
        criminal proceedings, 12–093—12–096
        international aspects, 12–097
        introduction, 12–092
        third party actions, 12–098—12–099
    content blocking, 12–040
    cost of copy-clearance, 12–004
    cross-border content
        international Convention, 12–044—12–057
        international framework, 12–003—12–015
        introduction, 12–002
        national action, 12–016—12–043
        standards, 12–090
    cryptography
        administration infrastructure, 12–133—12–134
        dealings, 12–139—12–144
        digital signatures, 12–135—12–136
        introduction, 12–128—12–129
        legal issues, 12–137—12–138
        service providers, 12–145—12–149
        systems, 12–131—12–132
        terminology, 12–130
    Cuba, 12–026
    cultural, linguistic and religious identity
        Burma, 12–024
        China, 12–025
        Cuba, 12–026
        France, 12–027—12–031
        Germany, 12–032—12–033
        introduction, 12–023
        Saudi Arabia, 12–034
        Singapore, 12–035—12–036
    display of indecent matter, 12–088
    e-mail viruses
        generally, 12–156
        unauthorised access, 12–157
        unauthorised modification, 12–158
    encryption
        administration infrastructure, 12–133—12–134

Regulated and prohibited activities—contd
    encryption—contd
        dealings, 12–139—12–144
        digital signatures, 12–135—12–136
        introduction, 12–128—12–129
        legal issues, 12–137—12–138
        service providers, 12–145—12–149
        systems, 12–131—12–132
        terminology, 12–130
    E.U., 12–017—12–019
    financial services
        exclusions, 12–108
        general prohibition, 12–104—12–105
        generally, 12–101
        information websites, 12–109—12–111
        introduction, 12–100
        overseas providers, 12–112
        problem areas, 12–102
        promotional restrictions, 12–113—12–118
        regulated activities, 12–106—12–107
        statutory basis, 12–103
    France, 12–027—12–031
    filtering, 12–041—12–043
    gambling, 12–058—12–062
    Germany
        generally, 12–020
        protection of cultural identity, 12–032—12–033
    harassment, 12–086—12–087
    international Convention
        competing laws, 12–050
        country of origin, 12–045—12–048
        country of receipt, 12–049
        directing, 12–051—12–055
        introduction, 12–044
        targeting, 12–051—12–055
    introduction, 12–001
    junk e-mail, 12–126—12–127
    jurisdiction, and, 6–023
    national action
        Australia, 12–016
        content blocking, 12–040
        E.U., 12–017—12–019
        filtering, 12–041—12–043
        Germany, 12–020
        protection of cultural identity, 12–023—12–036
        rating, 12–041—12–043
        responses to, 12–037—12–043
        U.K., 12–021—12–022
    obscenity
        broadcasting, 12–068—12–069
        defences, 12–071—12–072
        introduction, 12–064
        possession, 12–070
        publication, 12–065—12–067
    offensive communications, 12–086—12–087
    pharmaceuticals, 12–119—12–121
    pornography
        chat rooms, 12–091
        child pornography, 12–073—12–085
        cross-border content standards, 12–090
        display of indecent matter, 12–088
        harassment, 12–086—12–087
        introduction, 12–063
        obscenity, 12–064—12–072
        offensive communications, 12–086—12–087

Regulated and prohibited activities—*contd*
  pornography—*contd*
    public indecency, 12–088
    sex tourism, 12–089
  public indecency, 12–088
  rating, 12–041—12–043
  Saudi Arabia, 12–034
  sex tourism, 12–089
  sexual offences
    chat rooms, 12–091
    child pornography, 12–073—12–085
    cross-border content standards, 12–090
    display of indecent matter, 12–088
    harassment, 12–086—12–087
    introduction, 12–063
    obscenity, 12–064—12–072
    offensive communications, 12–086—12–087
    public indecency, 12–088
    sex tourism, 12–089
  Singapore, 12–035—12–036
  U.K., 12–021—12–022
  unauthorised access
    computer material, to, 12–151—12–152
    intent to commit offences, with, 12–153
    viruses, 12–157
  unauthorised modification
    computer material, of, 12–154—12–155
    viruses, 12–158
  viruses
    generally, 12–156
    unauthorised access, 12–157
    unauthorised modification, 12–158
  website access
    denial of service attacks, 12–161
    generally, 12–162
    introduction, 12–160
Regulation of Investigatory Powers Act
  definitions, 5–075—5–077
  e-mail, 5–085
  ephemeral communications, 5–085
  generally, 5–074
  interception in course of transmission, 5–078—5–079
  lawful authority, 5–095—5–096
  purpose of interception, 5–080
  recipient's position, 5–081—5–084
  recipients, 5–086—5–087
  Telecommunications Data Protection Directive, and, 5–088—5–094
  voicemail, 5–085
Regulatory activity
  data protection, and, 7–057
Religious celebrations
  copyright, and, 2–029
Repair of equipment
  copyright, and, 2–034
Reporting current events
  copyright, and, 2–025
Reproduction right
  copyright, and, 2–014
Request for assessment
  enforcement, and, 7–079
  remedies, and, 7–090—7–091
Request for notifiable particulars
  data protection, and, 7–100—7–101

Resale prices
  vertical agreements exemption, and, 14–129
Research
  data protection, and, 7–060
Restricted acts
  adaptation, 2–071
  broadcasting, 2–068—2–070
  cable programme service, 2–068—2–070
  copying, 2–064
  introduction, 2–063
  issue of copies, 2–065—2–066
  performance, 2–067
Revocation of offer
  electronic contracts, and, 10–062
RIPE
  IP addresses, and, 1–021
Routers
  IP addresses, and, 1–019
  meaning, 1–006
Royalties
  technology transfer exemption, and, 14–111
Rylands v. Fletcher, rule in
  accumulation of dangerous material, 5–017
  generally, 5–016
  natural use, 5–019
  third party acts, 5–018

Saudi Arabia
  regulation of activities, and, 12–034
Scientific research
  copyright, and, 2–023
Sculptures in public places
  copyright, and, 2–030
Search engines
  competition law, and, 14–012
  copyright, and, 2–093—2–094
  defamation, and, 4–038—4–039
  generally, 1–026
Secondary infringement
  generally, 2–061
  restricted acts, 2–072
Secure electronic transactions
  payment mechanisms, and, 11–045
Secure-signature-creation device
  electronic signatures, and, 10–092
Self-incrimination
  data protection, and, 7–075
Service attacks, denial of
  regulated activities, and, 12–161
SET
  payment mechanisms, and, 11–045
Sex tourism
  regulated activities, and, 12–089
Sexual offences
  chat rooms, 12–091
  child pornography
    cache copies, 12–077
    downloading, 12–075—12–076
    introduction, 12–073—12–074
    linking, 12–082—12–085
    making, 12–075—12–076
    screen images, 12–078—12–081
  cross-border content standards, 12–090
  display of indecent matter, 12–088
  harassment, 12–086—12–087

Sexual offences—*contd*
  introduction, 12–063
  obscenity
      broadcasting, 12–068—12–069
      defences, 12–071—12–072
      introduction, 12–064
      possession, 12–070
      publication, 12–065—12–067
    offensive communications, 12–086—12–087
    public indecency, 12–088
    sex tourism, 12–089
Signature of contracts
  electronic
      and see Electronic signatures
      generally, 10–076—10–101
    generally, 10–071—10–075
Singapore
  copyright, 6–298—6–301
  defamation, 6–294—6–295
  domain names
      administrators, 3–195
      disputes, 3–197—3–198
      registration, 3–195—3–196
    jurisdiction, 6–293
    misleading information, 6–296—6–297
    regulated activities, 12–035—12–036
    territory notices, 6–304
    trade marks, 6–302—6–303
Site designer
  contracts, 9–003—9–004
Site hosting contracts
  access to site, 9–021—9–022
  introduction, 9–018
  limitation of liability, 9–024—9–025
  reports and information, 9–023
  risk sharing, 9–026
  storage of data, 9–019—9–020
Small agreements
  competition law, and, 14–259
Social work
  data protection, and, 7–056
Software
  vertical agreements exemption, and, 14–124
  website building contract, and
      proprietary, 9–014
      third party, 9–016
Software patentability
  Europe, 2–149—2–155
  U.S., 2–156—2–158
Sole licence
  technology transfer exemption, and, 14–092
Sound recordings
  copyright, and, 2–042
Spam
  access agreements, and, 9–039
Spare parts
  vertical agreements exemption, and, 14–137
Specifications
  website building contracts, and, 9–009—9–017
Spidering
  generally, 2–089—2–090
  USA, 6–347—6–348
Split marks
  trademarks, and, 3–012—3–013

Sponsorship contracts
  generally, 9–027—9–028
  hypertext links, 9–032
  nature of rights, 9–029
  ownership of IPR, 9–033
  positioning, 9–030
  promotion obligations, 9–031
  size, 9–030
  visitor information, 9–034
SSCD
  electronic signatures, and, 10–092
Standardisation agreements
  conditions in licences, 14–187—14–188
  effects, 14–172—14–175
  foreclosure effects, 14–178—14–181
  Guidelines, 14–189—14–191
  introduction, 14–171
  multilateral standards, 14–176—14–177
  restrictions between users, 14–182—14–186
  unilateral standards, 14–176—14–177
Static content and code
  website building contract, and, 9–010
Statistics
  data protection, and, 7–060
Sub-licensing restrictions
  technology transfer exemption, and, 14–101
Sweden
  content liability, 6–313
  copyright, 6–314—6–315
  defamation, 6–312
  domain names
      administrators, 3–199
      disputes, 3–204—3–205
      registration, 3–200—3–203
    jurisdiction, 6–306—6–311
    trade marks, 6–316—6–317
Switches
  IP addresses, and, 1–019
  meaning, 1–006
Switzerland
  content liability, 6–325—6–328
  copyright, 6–329—6–330
  defamation, 6–320—6–324
  domain names
      administrators, 3–206
      disputes, 3–210—3–218
      registration, 3–207—3–209
    jurisdiction, 6–318—6–319
    trade marks, 6–331—6–332

Taxable presence
  application to e-commerce, 13–060—13–061
  generally, 13–058—13–059
  introduction, 13–057
Taxation
  business profits, 13–062—13–063
  customs duties
      generally, 13–047
      on-line software, 13–048
      physically delivered goods, 13–049—13–050
    data protection, and, 7–055
    direct taxes
      introduction, 13–051
      quantifying business profits, 13–062—13–063
      taxable presence, 13–057—13–061

Taxation—*contd*
  direct taxes—*contd*
    transfer pricing, 13–062—13–063
    withholding tax, 13–052—13–056
  introduction, 13–001—13–002
  other issues, 13–064—13–066
  policy overview, 13–003—13–006
  taxable presence
    application to e-commerce, 13–060—13–061
    generally, 13–058—13–059
    introduction, 13–057
  transfer pricing, 13–062—13–063
  VAT
    application to e-commerce, 13–020—13–046
    elements, 13–009—13–016
    exports, 13–017—13–018
    input tax, 13–019
    introduction, 13–007
    output tax, 13–019
    summary, 13–008
  withholding tax
    current position, 13–055—13–056
    generally, 13–052—13–053
    problems, 13–054
TCP/IP
  generally, 1–001
Teaching
  copyright, and, 2–023
Technology transfer exemption
  exclusions, 14–086—14–091
  introduction, 14–078—14–079
  licence terms, 14–092
  own use licence, 14–096
  scope, 14–083—14–085
  specific clauses, 14–097—14–114
  structure, 14–080—14–082
  territorial restrictions, 14–093—14–094
  use of trade mark, 14–095
Telecommunications Data Protection Directive
  workplace communications, and, 5–088—5–094
Telecommunications regulation
  access rights
    end-users, to, 8–031—8–032
    generally, 8–024
    interconnection, 8–025—8–027
    introduction, 8–008—8–010
    peering, 8–028—8–030
  background, 8–004—8–005
  competition, 8–011
  introduction, 8–001—8–003
  interconnection, 8–008—8–010
  internet service provision
    access rights and network services, 8–024—8–032
    generally, 8–013
    introduction, 8–012
    systems and services, 8–014—8–015
    voice and data systems, 8–016—8–018
    voice over IP, 8–022—8–023
    voice telephony services, 8–019—8–021
  ISPs
    generally, 8–013
    introduction, 8–012
  licensing
    access, 8–008—8–010

Telecommunications regulation—*contd*
  licensing—*contd*
    interconnection, 8–008—8–010
    internet service provision, 8–012—8–032
    telecommunications system operators, 8–006—8–007
  operator licensing, 8–006—8–007
Telephony services
  access agreements, and, 9–040
  telecommunications regulation, and, 8–019—8–021
Territorial restrictions
  technology transfer exemption, and, 14–093—14–094
  vertical agreements exemption, and, 14–130—14–131
Territory statements
  foreign rules
    Israel, 6–244—6–245
    Japan, 6–260
    Singapore, 6–304
  generally, 5–027—5–028
Theft
  confidential information, and, 2–131—2–132
3G networks
  broadband networks, and, 1–028
"Tippy" markets
  competition law, and, 14–042
Tobacco advertising
  content liability, and, 5–048—5–049
Trade marks
  branding, 3–006—3–007
  cybersquatting, 3–014
  domain names
    and see Domain names
    administration of system, 3–018—3–027
    corporate protection policies, 3–074—3–077
    disputes, 3–047—3–073
    function, 3–028—3–039
    future issues, 3–045—3–046
    introduction, 3–015
    meaning, 3–016—3–017
    non-U.K. names, 3–085—3–241
    scrutiny of applications, 3–040—3–044
  foreign rules
    Australia, 6–102—6–105
    Belgium, 6–147
    Canada, 6–158
    Finland, 6–167
    France, 6–177
    Germany, 6–186
    Hong Kong, 6–214
    Israel, 6–241—6–245
    Netherlands, 6–274—6–276
    New Zealand, 6–289—6–292
    Singapore, 6–302—6–303
    Sweden, 6–316—6–317
    Switzerland, 6–331—6–332
  genuine disputes, 3–010—3–013
  introduction, 3–001—3–005
  jurisdiction, and, 6–048—6–052
  keyword sales, 3–083
  metatags, 3–078—3–081
  non-U.K. domain names, 3–085—3–241
  problem areas
    cybersquatting, 3–014
    genuine disputes, 3–010—3–013

Trade marks—*contd*
 proper use, 3–008—3–009
 split marks, 3–012—3–013
 wordstuffing, 3–082
 vertical agreements exemption, and, 14–123
Transaction facilitators
 generally, 1–027
Transfer pricing
 generally, 13–062—13–063
Transient copies
 copyright, and, 2–005
Transmission Control Protocol/Internet Protocol
 and see TCP/IP
 generally, 1–001
Transparency
 Distance Selling Directive, and, 10–016—10–018
 Electronic Commerce Directive, and, 10–028—10–029
Transportability of sites
 enforcement of IPR, and, 6–014—6–016
Travel agencies
 Commission decisions, 14–060
 generally, 14–018
Treaty of Rome
 "country of origin" rules, 6–081—6–084
Trespass
 viruses, and, 5–020
TSL licence
 telecommunications, and, 8–015
Tying
 abuse of dominant position, and, 14–206
 technology transfer exemption, and, 14–098
Typographical arrangements of published editions
 copyright, and, 2–042

Umbrella sites
 generally, 1–025—1–026
Unauthorised access
 Australia, 6–126—6–128
 computer material, to, 12–151—12–152
 intent to commit offences, with, 12–153
 viruses, 12–157
 workplace communications, and, 5–067
Unauthorised modification
 Australia, 6–126—6–128
 computer material, of, 12–154—12–155
 viruses, 12–158
Unfair contract terms
 E.C. Directive, 10–011
 generally, 10–009
Uniform Resource Locator
 meaning, 1–013
Unilateral notices
 content liability, and, 5–021—5–023
URL
 meaning, 1–013
USA
 copyright, 6–344—6–346
 defamation, 6–349
 disclaimers, 6–352
 domain names
  administrators, 3–221
  disputes, 3–222—3–241
  registration, 3–221
 framing 6–347—6–348

USA—*contd*
 jurisdiction, 6–333—6–343
 linking, 6–347—6–348
 misrepresentation, 6–351
 spidering 6–347—6–348
Usenet newsgroups
 defamation, and 4–029
 hosts, and, 1–016—1–017
 meaning, 1–004

Value added tax (VAT)
 application to e-commerce
  introduction, 13–020—13–021
  mixed packages, 13–039—13–041
  on-line services, 13–027—13–035
  physical goods, 13–022—13–026
  telecommunication services, 13–036—13–038
 B2B supplies
  on-line services, 13–027—13–031
  physical goods, 13–022—13–026
  telecommunication services, 13–036—13–038
 B2C supplies
  on-line services, 13–032—13–035
  physical goods, 13–022—13–026
  telecommunication services, 13–036—13–038
 elements
  exports, 13–017—13–018
  imports, 13–015—13–016
  input tax, 13–019
  introduction, 13–009
  output tax, 13–019
  supply of goods and services, 13–010—13–014
 exports, 13–017—13–018
 future issues, 13–044—13–046
 imports
  member states, from, 13–015
  third countries, from, 13–016
 input tax, 13–019
 introduction, 13–007
 invoicing, 13–042—13–043
 mixed packages, 13–039—13–041
 output tax, 13–019
 policy overview, 13–003—13–006
 returns, 13–042—13–043
 summary, 13–008
 supply of goods and services
  generally, 13–010—13–011
  Schedule 5 services, 13–012—13–014
 telecommunication services, 13–036—13–038
Vertical agreements exemption
 copyright, 14–124
 exclusion, 14–118—14–122
 "hardcore" restrictions, 14–128—14–137
 introduction, 14–115
 market share, 14–125—14–127
 meaning, 14–116—14–117
 non-competition restrictions, 14–138—14–141
 trade marks, 14–123
Vicarious liability
 workplace communications, and, 5–061
Video-conferencing
 defamation, and, 4–003
Video recordings
 copyright, and, 2–042

Viral marketing
  data protection, and, 7–005
Viruses, liability for
  introduction, 5–012
  negligence
    duty of care, 5–013
    foreseeability, 5–014
    physical damage, 5–013—5–014
    standard of care, 5–015
  prohibited activities, and
    generally, 12–156
    unauthorised access, 12–157
    unauthorised modification, 12–158
  Rylands v. Fletcher, rule in
    accumulation of dangerous material, 5–017
    generally, 5–016
    natural use, 5–019
    third party acts, 5–018
  trespass, 5–020
"Visa cash"
  payment mechanisms, and, 11–039
Voice and data systems
  telecommunications regulation, and, 8–016—8–018
Voice over IP
  telecommunications regulation, and, 8–022—8–023
Voice telephony services
  access agreements, and, 9–040
  telecommunications regulation, and, 8–019—8–021
Voicemail
  workplace communications, and, 5–085
VoIP
  telecommunications regulation, and, 8–022—8–023
VON
  telecommunications regulation, and, 8–019—8–021

Web design company
  defamation, and, 4–037
Web hosting ISP
  defamation, and, 4–034—4–035
Web journal discussion forum
  defamation, and, 4–030—4–032
Web linking
  copyright, and
    copying, 2–080—2–081
    inclusion in cable programme service, 2–078—2–079
    infringement, 2–077
  database right, and
    generally, 2–082
    infringement, 2–085—2–088
    websites, 2–083—2–084
  deep linking, 2–075
  inline linking, 2–076
  introduction, 2–073
  technical aspects, 2–074
Webcams
  data protection, and, 7–002
Website access
  denial of service attacks, 12–161
  generally, 12–162
  introduction, 12–160
Website building, contracts for
  competition law, and, 14–015
  creation, 9–007
  initial design, 9–006

Website building, contracts for—*contd*
  introduction, 9–005
  ownership of IPR
    allocation of rights, 9–013
    domain name, 9–017
    dynamic content and code, 9–011—9–012
    introduction, 9–009
    physical materials, 9–015
    proprietary software, 9–014
    static content and code, 9–010
    third party software, 9–016
  specification, 9–006
  testing, 9–008
Website hosting, contracts for
  access to site, 9–021—9–022
  introduction, 9–018
  limitation of liability, 9–024—9–025
  reports and information, 9–023
  risk sharing, 9–026
  storage of data, 9–019—9–020
Website use, tracking of
  data protection, and, 7–006
White list
  technology transfer exemption, and, 14–080
WIPO Treaties
  copyright, and, 2–008—2–009
Withholding tax
  current position, 13–055—13–056
  generally, 13–052—13–053
  problems, 13–054
Wordstuffing
  trade marks, and, 3–082
Workplace communications, access to
  Data Protection Act
    draft Code of Practice, 5–104—5–109
    generally, 5–103
    human rights, and, 5–117—5–118
  Human Rights Act
    data protection Code of Practice, 5–117—5–118
    displacing expectation of privacy, 5–114—5–116
    Lawful Business Practice Regulations, 5–117—5–118
    public bodies, 5–110—5–112
    reasonable expectation of privacy, 5–113
  introduction, 5–073
  Lawful Business Practice Regulations
    authorised conduct, 5–102
    generally, 5–097
    human rights, and, 5–117—5–118
    preconditions to interception, 5–098—5–101
  Regulation of Investigatory Powers Act
    definitions, 5–075—5–077
    e-mail, 5–085
    ephemeral communications, 5–085
    generally, 5–074
    interception in course of transmission, 5–078—5–079
    lawful authority, 5–095—5–096
    purpose of interception, 5–080
    recipient's position, 5–081—5–084
    recipients, 5–086—5–087
    voicemail, 5–085
  Telecommunications Data Protection Directive, 5–088—5–094

Workplace communications, liability for
    communication policies
        generally, 5–071—5–072
        introduction, 5–059
    criminal liability, 5–062
    direct liability, 5–063—5–065
    introduction, 5–056—5–059
    personal e-mail, 5–062
    tribunal decisions
        harassment, 5–070
        introduction, 5–066

Workplace communications, liability for—*contd*
    tribunal decisions—*contd*
        pornography, 5–068—5–069
        unauthorised access, 5–067
    vicarious liability, 5–061
World Wide Web (www)
    meaning, 1–004
    use, 1–013—1–015
W3C
    administrators, and, 1–021